Lecture Notes in Computer Science 14602

The series Lecture Notes in Computer Science (LNCS), including its subseries Lecture Notes in Artificial Intelligence (LNAI) and Lecture Notes in Bioinformatics (LNBI), has established itself as a medium for the publication of new developments in computer science and information technology research, teaching, and education.

LNCS enjoys close cooperation with the computer science R & D community, the series counts many renowned academics among its volume editors and paper authors, and collaborates with prestigious societies. Its mission is to serve this international community by providing an invaluable service, mainly focused on the publication of conference and workshop proceedings and postproceedings. LNCS commenced publication in 1973.

Qiang Tang · Vanessa Teague
Editors

Public-Key Cryptography – PKC 2024

27th IACR International Conference on Practice and Theory of Public-Key Cryptography Sydney, NSW, Australia, April 15–17, 2024 Proceedings, Part II

Springer

Editors
Qiang Tang
The University of Sydney
Sydney, NSW, Australia

Vanessa Teague
The Australian National University
Acton, ACT, Australia

ISSN 0302-9743 ISSN 1611-3349 (electronic)
Lecture Notes in Computer Science
ISBN 978-3-031-57721-5 ISBN 978-3-031-57722-2 (eBook)
https://doi.org/10.1007/978-3-031-57722-2

This Springer imprint is published by the registered company Springer Nature Switzerland AG
The registered company address is: Gewerbestrasse 11, 6330 Cham, Switzerland

Paper in this product is recyclable.

Preface

The 27th International Conference on Practice and Theory of Public-Key Cryptography (PKC 2024) was held in Sydney, Australia, on April 15–17, 2024. It was sponsored by the International Association for Cryptologic Research (IACR) and is the main IACR-sponsored conference with an explicit focus on public-key cryptography. PKC 2024 authors represented 24 different countries, bringing a vibrant international community of cryptography researchers to Australia.

The conference received 176 submissions, reviewed by the Program Committee of 68 cryptography experts (including four area chairs) working with 183 external reviewers. The reviewing process took two months and selected 54 papers to appear in PKC 2024. Papers were reviewed in the usual double-blind fashion with an average of just over three reviews per paper. Program committee members and general chairs were limited to 3 submissions (4 if all with students), and their submissions were scrutinized more closely. The two program chairs were not allowed to submit papers. PKC 2024 was the first major cryptography conferences to accept SoK papers.

PKC 2024 welcomed Nadia Heninger (University of California, San Diego) and Aggelos Kiayias (University of Edinburgh) as the invited speakers. The Program Committee also selected two best papers: *An algorithm for efficient detection of (N, N)-splittings and its application to the isogeny problem in dimension 2* by Maria Corte-Real Santos, Craig Costello and Sam Frengley, and *Quantum CCA-Secure PKE, Revisited* by Navid Alamati and Varun Maram.

The award committee (Masayuki Abe, Alexandra Boldyreva, Qiang Tang, Vanessa Teague, Moti Yung) also chose the PKC Test of Time Award for 2024.

PKC is a remarkable undertaking, possible only through the hard work and significant contributions of many people. We would like to express our sincere gratitude to all the authors, as well as to the Program Committee and external reviewers, session chairs and presenters. Special thanks to the area chairs: Steven Galbraith, Giuseppe Persiano, Kazue Sako and Vassilis Zikas. Their specialist knowledge and good judgement were critical for making good decisions.

Additionally, we would like to thank Willy Susilo, Fuchun Guo and the team at the University of Wollongong for making the general arrangements such a success. Also, as always, Kay McKelly and Kevin McCurley provided invaluable support for all things technical behind the scenes.

All of this happens against a backdrop in which even some democratic governments are working to undermine encrypted communications in the name of "safety." In Australia, exporting a new encryption algorithm without a permit can be punished with years in jail. Open, scientific, internationally collaborative research in cryptography is more important than ever.

We hope you enjoyed the conference and the warm welcome of Sydney.

April 2024

Qiang Tang
Vanessa Teague

Organization

General Chairs

Fuchun Guo — University of Wollongong, Australia
Willy Susilo — University of Wollongong, Australia

Program Committee Chairs

Qiang Tang — The University of Sydney, Australia
Vanessa Teague — Democracy Developers Ltd., The Australian National University and Thinking Cybersecurity Pty. Ltd., Australia

Steering Committee

Masayuki Abe — NTT, Japan
Alexandra Boldyreva — Georgia Tech, USA
Jung Hee Cheon — Seoul National University, South Korea
Yvo Desmedt — University of Texas at Dallas, USA
Goichiro Hanaoka — National Institute of Advanced Industrial Science and Technology, Japan
Tibor Jager — University of Wuppertal, Germany
Aggelos Kiayias — University of Edinburgh, UK
Vladimir Kolesnikov — Georgia Tech, USA
Tanja Lange — Eindhoven University of Technology, The Netherlands
Jiaxin Pan — NTNU, Norway & University of Kassel, Germany
David Pointcheval — École Normale Supérieure Paris, France
Qiang Tang — The University of Sydney, Australia
Vanessa Teague — Democracy Developers Ltd., The Australian National University and Thinking Cybersecurity Pty. Ltd., Australia
Moti Yung (Secretary) — Google Inc. & Columbia University, USA
Yuliang Zheng (Chair) — University of Alabama at Birmingham, USA

Area Chairs

Steven Galbraith	The University of Auckland, Aotearoa-New Zealand *Post-quantum cryptography, quantum cryptography, Math & Attacks*
Giuseppe Persiano	University of Salerno, Italy and Google, USA *Theoretical Foundations & Advanced Primitives*
Kazue Sako	Waseda University, Japan *Applied Cryptography, SNARKs & Verifiable Computation*
Vassilis Zikas	Purdue University, USA *Multiparty computation & consensus*

Program Committee

Divesh Aggarwal	National University of Singapore, Singapore
Christian Badertscher	Input Output Global, Switzerland
Foteini Baldimtsi	George Mason University, USA
Sofia Celi	Brave, Portugal
Suvradip Chakraborty	Visa Research, USA
Long Chen	Chinese Academy of Sciences, China
Yilei Chen	Tsinghua University, China
Rongmao Chen	National University of Defense Technology, China
Jung Hee Cheon	Seoul National University, Republic of Korea
Amy Corman	RMIT University, Australia
Luca De Feo	IBM Research Europe, Switzerland
Yi Deng	Chinese Academy of Sciences, China
Xiong Fan	Rutgers University, USA
Hanwen Feng	The University of Sydney, Australia
Rishab Goyal	University of Wisconsin-Madison, USA
Debayan Gupta	Ashoka University, India
Thomas Haines	The Australian National University, Australia
Goichiro Hanaoka	AIST, Japan
Cheng Hong	Ant Research, China
Tibor Jager	University of Wuppertal, Germany
Zhengzhong Jin	MIT, USA
Dmitry Khovratovich	Ethereum Foundation, Luxembourg
Fuyuki Kitagawa	NTT Social Informatics Laboratories, Japan

Chelsea Komlo	University of Waterloo, Canada
Markus Krausz	Ruhr University Bochum, Germany
Péter Kutas	University of Birmingham, UK and Eötvös Loránd University, Hungary
Tanja Lange	Eindhoven University of Technology, The Netherlands
Feng-Hao Liu	Washington State University, USA
Chen-da Liu-Zhang	HSLU and Web3 Foundation, Switzerland
Julian Loss	CISPA Helmholtz Center for Information Security, Germany
Mohammad Mahmoody	University of Virginia, USA
Daniel Masny	Meta, USA
Pratyay Mukherjee	Supra Research, India
Khoa Nguyen	University of Wollongong, Australia
Miyako Ohkubo	NICT, Japan
Omkant Pandey	Stony Brook University, USA
Krzysztof Pietrzak	IST Austria, Austria
David Pointcheval	ENS, Paris, France
Amin Sakzad	Monash University, Australia
Rebecca Schwerdt	Karlsruhe Institute of Technology, Germany
abhi shelat	Northeastern University, USA
Mark Simkin	Ethereum Foundation, Denmark
Yifan Song	Tsinghua University, China
Yongsoo Song	Seoul National University, Republic of Korea
Fang Song	Portland State University, USA
Shravan Srinivasan	Lagrange Labs, USA
Ron Steinfeld	Monash University, Australia
Sri Aravinda Krishnan Thyagarajan	NTT Research, USA and The University of Sydney, Australia
Prashant Nalini Vasudevan	National University of Singapore, Singapore
Daniele Venturi	Sapienza University of Rome, Italy
Xiaoyun Wang	Tsinghua University, China
Huaxiong Wang	Nanyang Technological University, Singapore
Benjamin Wesolowski	CNRS and ENS de Lyon, France
Jiayu Xu	Oregon State University, USA
Rupeng Yang	University of Wollongong, Australia
Kevin Yeo	Google and Columbia University, USA
Yu Yu	Shanghai Jiao Tong University, China
Thomas Zacharias	University of Glasgow, UK
Cong Zhang	Zhejiang University, China
Zhenfeng Zhang	Chinese Academy of Sciences, China
Bingsheng Zhang	Zhejiang University, China

Jiaheng Zhang National University of Singapore, Singapore
Dominique Schroeder Friedrich-Alexander University of Erlangen-Nürnberg, Germany
Wessel van Woerden University of Bordeaux, France

Additional Reviewers

Aydin Abadi
Behzad Abdolmaleki
Masayuki Abe
Miguel Ambrona
Arathi Arakala
Sven Argo
Benedikt Auerbach
Renas Bacho
Weihao Bai
Shi Bai
Fabio Banfi
Andrea Basso
Fabrice Benhamouda
Olivier Bernard
Daniel J. Bernstein
Siddhartha Bhoi
Alex Bienstock
Katharina Boudgoust
Charles Bouillaguet
Pedro Branco
Fabian Buschkowski
Rohit Chatterjee
Binyi Chen
Hyeongmin Choe
Arka Rai Choudhuri
Hao Chung
Michele Ciampi
Valerio Cini
Alexandru Cojocaru
Pierrick Dartois
Poulami Das
Koen de Boer
Paola de Perthuis
Benne de Weger
Giovanni Deligios
Lalita Devadas
Jesus Diaz
Jelle Don
Léo Ducas
Pranjal Dutta
Keita Emura
Daniel Escudero
Muhammed F. Esgin
Thomas Espitau
Prastudy Fauzi
Danilo Francati
Daniele Friolo
Yao Jiang Galteland
Gayathri Garimella
Riddhi Ghosal
Aarushi Goel
Lenaick Gouriou
Anna Guinet
Hui Guo
Kyoohyung Han
Lucjan Hanzlik
Charlotte Hoffmann
Alex Hoover
Yao-Ching Hsieh
David Hu
Zhicong Huang
Andreas Hülsing
Nikai Jagganath
Aayush Jain
Xiaoyu Ji
Haodong Jiang
Haohao Jiang
Ioanna Karantaidou
Sabyasachi Karati
Handan Kilinc Alper
Suhri Kim
Dongwoo Kim
Seongkwang Kim
Sungwook Kim

Miran Kim
Kamil Kluczniak
Anders Konrig
Swastik Kopparty
Alexis Korb
Abhiram Kothapalli
Elisabeth Krahmer
Sabrina Kunzweiler
Kaoru Kurosawa
Qiqi Lai
Georg Land
Changmin Lee
Yun Li
Yanan Li
Xiao Liang
Yao-Ting Lin
Qipeng Liu
Zeyu Liu
Weiran Liu
Fengrun Liu
Wen-jie Lu
Varun Madathil
Lorenzo Magliocco
Monosij Maitra
Easwar Mangipudi
Elisaweta Masserova
Takahiro Matsuda
Daniel McVicker
Simon-Philipp Merz
Ruiqi Mi
Peihan Miao
Arash Mirzaei
Anuja Modi
Johannes Mono
Ethan Mook
Kirill Morozov
Marta Mularczyk
Ky Nguyen
Ryo Nishimaki
Alice Pellet-Mary
Nikhil Pappu
Jeongeun Park
Guillermo Pascual Perez
Alain Passelegue
Rutvik Patel
Sihang Pu
Ludo Pulles
Octavio Pérez Kempner
Wei Qi
Tian Qiu
Wenjie Qu
Willy Quach
Ahmadreza Rahimi
Omar Renawi
Mahshid Riahinia
Jan Richter-Brockmann
Guilherme Rito
Damien Robert
Maxime Roméas
Lawrence Roy
Luigi Russo
Sagnik Saha
Yusuke Sakai
Robert Schaedlich
Sven Schäge
Jacob Schuldt
Mahdi Sedaghat
Sruthi Sekar
Joon Young Seo
Jun Jie Sim
Yongha Son
Bruno Sterner
Atsushi Takayasu
Gang Tang
Guofeng Tang
Yuhao Tang
Khai Hanh Tang
Stefano Tessaro
Junichi Tomida
Monika Trimoska
Yiannis Tselekounis
Akhil Vanukuri
Benedikt Wagner
Hendrik Waldner
Han Wang
Yuchen Wang
Li-Ping Wang
Zhedong Wang
Yi Wang
Jiabo Wang

Charlotte Weitkämper
Chenkai Weng
Jie Xu
Anshu Yadav
Aayush Yadav
Shota Yamada
Takashi Yamakawa
Dan Yamamoto
Zhaomin Yang
Yusuke Yoshida
Zuoxia Yu
Shang Zehua
Xinyu Zhang
Liangfeng Zhang
Raymond K. Zhao
Hong-Sheng Zhou
Tanping Zhou
Zidi Zhuang

Contents – Part II

Commitments

Updatable, Aggregatable, Succinct Mercurial Vector Commitment from Lattice

Hongxiao Wang[1], Siu-Ming Yiu[1](✉), Yanmin Zhao[1], and Zoe L. Jiang[2]

[1] The University of Hong Kong, Hong Kong, China
{hxwang,smyiu,ymzhao}@cs.hku.hk
[2] Harbin Institute of Technology, Shenzhen, China
zoeljiang@hit.edu.cn

Abstract. Vector commitments (VC) and their variants attract a lot of attention due to their wide range of usage in applications such as blockchain and accumulator. Mercurial vector commitment (MVC), as one of the important variants of VC, is the core technique for building more complicated cryptographic applications, such as the zero-knowledge set (ZKS) and zero-knowledge elementary database (ZK-EDB). However, to the best of our knowledge, the only post-quantum MVC construction is trivially implied by a generic framework proposed by Catalano and Fiore (PKC '13) with lattice-based components which causes *large* auxiliary information and *cannot satisfy* any additional advanced properties, that is, updatable and aggregatable.

A major difficulty in constructing a *non-black-box* lattice-based MVC is that it is not trivial to construct a lattice-based VC that satisfies a critical property called "mercurial hiding". In this paper, we identify some specific features of a new falsifiable family of basis-augmented SIS assumption (BASIS) proposed by Wee and Wu (EUROCRYPT '23) that can be utilized to construct the mercurial vector commitment from lattice *satisfying* updatability and aggregatability with *smaller* auxiliary information. We *first* extend stateless update and differential update to the mercurial vector commitment and define a *new* property, named updatable mercurial hiding. Then, we show how to modify our constructions to obtain the updatable mercurial vector commitment that satisfies these properties. To aggregate the openings, our constructions perfectly inherit the ability to aggregate in the BASIS assumption, which can break the limitation of *weak* binding in the current aggregatable MVCs. In the end, we show that our constructions can be used to build the various kinds of lattice-based ZKS and ZK-EDB directly within the existing framework.

Keywords: Vector commitment · Mercurial commitment · Lattice · Zero-knowledge elementary database

1 Introduction

Vector commitment (VC) [8,20] allows the committer to commit a vector of messages and later opens the commitment at one or multiple specific indices. In

Q. Tang and V. Teague (Eds.): PKC 2024, LNCS 14602, pp. 3–35, 2024.
https://doi.org/10.1007/978-3-031-57722-2_1

general, a VC should have these properties: *succinct*, *binding*, and *hiding*. The *succinct* property means that the sizes of the commitment and the opening are *polylogarithmic* with the dimension of the vector. The *binding* property requires that one cannot open the commitment at the same index to different values. The *hiding* property means that no one can learn the committed vector from the commitment until it is revealed. There are many variants of VC proposed, for example, *updatable* VC [8,25,26,28] supports the committer to update the message inside the commitment and provide the update information for the verifier to update the corresponding commitment and opening. The functional VC [3,19,28] allows opening the commitment to a function of the committed data. Subvector commitment (SVC) [14,16], also named *aggregatable* VC [28] supports the committers to aggregate the openings to different indices as one opening.

Furthermore, one of the most important variants of VC is the mercurial vector commitment (MVC) [8,20] which introduces the *mercurial* property. The MVC allows the committer to generate a *hard* commitment of the input vector messages or a *soft* commitment of nothing. The *hard* commitment can be both *hard* and *soft* opened only to the unique value at each index, while the *soft* commitment can only be *soft* opened to *any* value. Furthermore, *mercurial hiding* requires that others cannot distinguish between the *soft* commitment and *hard* commitment with their associated openings. There are also many variants of MVC, such as the *updatable* MVC [8] and the *aggregatable* MVC [17]. The *updatable* MVC supports updating for both *hard* and *soft* commitment. The main difference between *updatable* MVC and *updatable* VC is that the old openings (even to the soft commitment) can be updated to the new openings to the new hard commitment via the update information; The *aggregatable* MVC allows the committer to aggregate *hard* and *soft* openings. The existing *aggregatable* MVC [17] is constructed in the Algebraic Group Model (AGM) model conceptually similar to the *weak* binding [14] which requires that the adversary is unable to generate the commitment without input the message and is only suitable for applications with external protocol constraints or consensus mechanisms, e.g. blockchain. This means that the existing *aggregatable* MVC *does not suffice* to build a secure zero-knowledge elementary database (ZK-EDB) straightforwardly.

Applications of MVC: MVC leads to many cryptography applications such as (l-ary) zero-knowledge set (ZKS) and zero-knowledge elementary database (ZK-EDB) [8,9,20] in which both utilize the soft commitment to denote non-existent elements and the soft openings to prove non-membership. The *updatable* MVCs enable to build the *updatable* ZKS and ZK-EDB [8,21] and the *aggregatable* MVCs can be used to construct ZKS and ZK-EDB with *batch verification* [17]. Unfortunately, to our best known, there is still a huge gap in (l-ary) ZKS or ZK-EDB between supporting updatability and batch verification and resisting the quantum computer attack.

Overall, the existing mercurial vector commitments satisfying advanced properties, i.e. *updatable* and *aggregatable* [8,17,20] are constructed from Diffie-Hellman (DH) assumptions and RSA assumptions which cannot resist the attack of *quantum* computers. Although there exists a generic construction [8] of MVC which trivially implies the lattice-based MVC with the existing lattice-based components [18,25,28], it leads to *large* auxiliary information and *cannot support* such advanced properties, due to its black-box framework.

To solve these problems, informally, we consider that the main challenge of constructing non-black-box lattice-based vector commitments satisfying "mercurial hiding", i.e., MVC, lies in two aspects: (1) how to construct lattice-based vector commitments that satisfy *hiding*; (2) how to add indistinguishable redundant items into the commitments that support generating valid and indistinguishable (with the hard openings) openings, i.e., soft openings *without* trapdoors and messages. To address this, we find that the VC based on the BASIS assumption proposed by Wee and Wu [28] supports hiding the commitment. Thus, we focus on solving the former challenge based on their constructions.

We refer to Table 1 for a summary of the current state of the art.

Table 1. Comparison to current works on MVC. For each scheme, we report the size of the public parameters pp, the size of commitment C, the size of the auxiliary information aux, and the size of opening π as a function of the security parameter λ and the length l of the input vector. Constants and non-dominant terms are omitted and poly$(\cdot)$ represents some arbitrary polynomial. We also indicate the *assumption* (**AS**) of each scheme based on and whether the scheme can support *update* (**UD**) and *aggregate* (**AG**).

Scheme	AS	UD	AG	$\lvert\mathsf{pp}\rvert$	$\lvert C\rvert$	$\lvert\mathsf{aux}\rvert$	$\lvert\pi\rvert$
[8]	RSA	✓	✗	$O(\lambda l)$	$O(\lambda)$	$O(\lambda l)$	$O(\lambda)$
[17]	l-DHE	✗[a]	✓	$O(\lambda l)$	$O(\lambda)$	$O(\lambda l)$	$O(\lambda)$
[18] + [28][b]	SIS	✗	✗	$l^2\mathsf{poly}(\lambda, \log l)$	$O(\lambda^2 \cdot \mathcal{H})$[c]	$O(\lambda^2 l \cdot \mathcal{H})$	$O(\lambda^2 \cdot \mathcal{H})$
Cons. A.1[d]	SIS	✓	✗	$l^2\mathsf{poly}(\lambda, \log l)$	$O(\lambda^2 \cdot \mathcal{H})$	$O(\lambda^2 l \cdot \mathcal{H})$	$O(\lambda^2 \cdot \mathcal{H})$
Cons. 3.1	BASIS	✓	✓	$l^2\mathsf{poly}(\lambda, \log l)$	$O(\lambda^2 \cdot \mathcal{H})$	$O((\lambda^2 + \lambda l) \cdot \mathcal{H})$	$O(\lambda^2 \cdot \mathcal{H})$

[a] Although it allows the committer to update the hard commitment, the soft commitment cannot update to a hard commitment.
[b] A lattice-based MVC can be trivially built by lattice-based components (e.g. [18] and [28]) in the generic framework [8].
[c] To simplify, we denote $\mathcal{H} = \log^2 \lambda + \log^2 l$.
[d] The succinct version of Construction A.1 described in the full version of this paper [27] is used to compare.

1.1 Our Contributions

In this paper, we construct a lattice-based mercurial vector commitment satisfying updatability and aggregatability based on the BASIS assumption. Although the structured version of the BASIS assumption (denoted $\mathsf{BASIS}_{\mathsf{struct}}$) is not a standard lattice-based assumption, it is a *falsifiable* assumption [24,28]. Following the existing framework, our constructions can be used to directly build the lattice-based ZKS and ZK-EDB which support updating and batch verification. We summarize the main contributions of our work in the following.

- **Succinct mercurial vector commitment:** We provide two constructions of the non-black-box lattice-based mercurial vector commitment. One is based on the standard Short Integer Solution (SIS) and satisfies updatability. The other is based on $\mathsf{BASIS}_{\mathsf{struct}}$ assumption and supports updating and aggregating which its auxiliary information has been *greatly reduced* by a level compared to the other standard SIS-based constructions. As an additional contribution, we also revisit the lattice-based mercurial commitment and transform it into transparent setup in the full version of this paper.
- **Updatable mercurial vector commitment:** We generalize the definition of updatable MVC [8] and *first* introduce stateless update and differentially update from the VC [25,28] to MVC. Then, we *first* extend the stronger properties for updatable MVC, named updatable mercurial hiding and updatable hiding. Last, we provide two constructions of differentially updatable MVC respectively based on SIS and $\mathsf{BASIS}_{\mathsf{struct}}$ that satisfy updatable mercurial hiding and can be extended to updatable hiding.
- **Aggregatable mercurial vector commitment:** We propose the *first* construction of aggregatable mercurial vector commitment which can break the limitation of the AGM model and *weak* binding. It is also the *first* construction from lattice. We divide the mercurial binding into the same-set binding and different-set binding. Like [28], our construction supports aggregating the openings to the *bounded* message and achieves the same set binding and different set weak binding.
- **Application for ZKS (ZK-EDB):** We show the applications of our constructions at a high level. Our construction of succinct MVC is the standard one that can be used to build the lattice-based l-ary ZKS (ZK-EDB) straightly in the generic framework [20] and even the partially succinct MVC can also be directly used to build the ZKS (ZK-EDB). Following the framework [8,17,21], our updatable MVC and aggregatable MVC can be utilized to build the updatable ZKS (ZK-EDB) with batch verification.

1.2 Technique Overview

In this section, we provide a general overview of our technique for extending the vector commitment based on the BASIS assumption to mercurial vector commitment from lattices as well as the family of BASIS assumption. In the following description, we denote $D_{\mathbb{Z}^m}$ be the discrete Gaussian distribution over $\mathbb{Z}^m$ and $\mathbf{x} = \mathbf{A}^{-1}(\mathbf{t}) \in \mathbb{Z}_q^m$ as a random vector distributed over the discrete Gaussian conditioned on $\mathbf{Ax} = \mathbf{t}$ for the matrix $\mathbf{A} \in \mathbb{Z}_q^{n\times m}$ and the target vector $\mathbf{t} \in \mathbb{Z}_q^n$. Let $\mathbf{e}_1 = [1, 0, ..., 0]^\mathsf{T} \in \mathbb{Z}_q^n$ be the first standard basis vector. By Theorem 2.5, if there exists a short matrix $\mathbf{R}$ satisfying $\mathbf{AR} = \mathbf{G}$ where $\mathbf{G} = \mathbf{I}_n \otimes \mathbf{g}^\mathsf{T}$ is the gadget matrix and $\mathbf{g}^\mathsf{T} = [1, 2, ..., 2^{\lfloor \log q \rfloor}]$, the matrix $\mathbf{R}$ is the gadget trapdoor for $\mathbf{A}$ and can be used to efficiently sample $\mathbf{x} \leftarrow \mathbf{A}^{-1}(\mathbf{t})$ by the algorithm $\mathsf{SampPre}(\mathbf{A}, \mathbf{R}, \mathbf{t}, s)$ with some Gaussian width s.

A General Framework. We begin by describing a general framework of vector commitments based on the BASIS assumption [28].

- Setup: The public parameters pp including a collection of l matrices $\mathbf{A}_1, ..., \mathbf{A}_l \in \mathbb{Z}_q^{n\times m}$ and a trapdoor $\mathbf{T} = \mathbf{B}_l^{-1}(\mathbf{G}_l)$ for $\mathbf{B}_l$ as follows.

$$\mathbf{B}_l = \begin{bmatrix} \mathbf{A}_1 & & & -\mathbf{G} \\ & \ddots & & \vdots \\ & & \mathbf{A}_l & -\mathbf{G} \end{bmatrix}, \qquad \mathbf{T} = \begin{bmatrix} \mathbf{T}_1 \\ \vdots \\ \mathbf{T}_l \\ \mathbf{T}_\mathbf{G} \end{bmatrix}$$

- Commit: The commitment to a vector $\mathbf{x} = (x_1, ..., x_l) \in \mathbb{Z}_q^l$ is the vector $\mathbf{c} = \mathbf{G}\hat{\mathbf{c}}$ where

$$[\mathbf{v}_1, ..., \mathbf{v}_l, \hat{\mathbf{c}}]^\mathsf{T} \leftarrow \mathsf{SampPre}(\mathbf{B}_l, \mathbf{T}, -\mathbf{x} \otimes \mathbf{e}_1, s_1)$$

  which $\mathbf{e}_1 = [1, 0..., 0]^\mathsf{T}$ is the first standard basis vector and the auxiliary information is $\mathsf{aux} = (\mathbf{v}_1, ..., \mathbf{v}_l)$.
- Open: An opening to index $i \in [\ell]$ is $\mathbf{v}_i$ from $\mathsf{aux} = (\mathbf{v}_1, ..., \mathbf{v}_l)$.
- Verify: A valid opening to index $i \in [\ell]$ and message x_i need satisfy the following condition

$$\|\mathbf{v}_i\| \le \beta, \qquad \mathbf{c} = \mathbf{A}_i\mathbf{v}_i + x_i\mathbf{e}_1$$

For correctness, by the $\mathsf{SampPre}$ in Theorem 2.5, we have

$$\begin{bmatrix} -x_1\mathbf{e}_1 \\ \vdots \\ -x_l\mathbf{e}_1 \end{bmatrix} = \begin{bmatrix} \mathbf{A}_1 & & & -\mathbf{G} \\ & \ddots & & \vdots \\ & & \mathbf{A}_l & -\mathbf{G} \end{bmatrix} \cdot \begin{bmatrix} \mathbf{v}_1 \\ \vdots \\ \mathbf{v}_l \\ \hat{\mathbf{c}} \end{bmatrix}$$

For binding, Denote $\underline{\mathbf{A}_i}$ as $\mathbf{A}_i$ with the first row removed. The BASIS assumption is that it is hard to find a short vector $\mathbf{z}$ where $\underline{\mathbf{A}_i}\mathbf{z} = \mathbf{0}$ for any $i \in [\ell]$ even give the related matrix $\mathbf{B}_l$ and its trapdoor $\mathbf{T} = \mathbf{B}_l^{-1}(\mathbf{G}_l)$. Therefore, if the BASIS assumption holds, for all $i \in [\ell]$, there is no adversary can generate a commitment $\mathbf{c}$ with two openings $\mathbf{v}_i$, $\mathbf{v}_i'$ to *different* message x_i, x_i' $(x_i \neq x_i')$.

For *private openings*, by the Lemma 2.4, the commitment $\mathbf{c}$ is statistically close to uniform over $\mathbb{Z}_q^n$ and for each $i \in [\ell]$, the opening $\mathbf{v}_i$ is statistically close to $\mathbf{A}_i^{-1}(\mathbf{c} - x_i\mathbf{e}_1)$.

We observe the following *features* for the above constructions:

- The property of private openings implies that there exists a *simulating* algorithm that can generate the *fake* commitment $\mathbf{c}'$ without any message and *fake* openings $\mathbf{v}_i'$ only with x_i and the trapdoor of $\mathbf{A}_i$. The *fake* commitment and openings are valid and the distribution of them is statistically close to the *real* ones.

– If we extend $\mathbf{B}_l$ to $\mathbf{B}_l'$, the trapdoor $\mathbf{T}'$ of $\mathbf{B}_l'$ can also be extended from the trapdoor $\mathbf{T}$ of $\mathbf{B}_l$ as follows,

$$\mathbf{B}_l' = \begin{bmatrix} [\mathbf{A}_1|\mathbf{D}_1] & & & -\mathbf{G} \\ & \ddots & & \vdots \\ & & [\mathbf{A}_l|\mathbf{D}_l] & -\mathbf{G} \end{bmatrix}, \quad \mathbf{T}' = \begin{bmatrix} \mathbf{T}_1 \\ \hline \mathbf{0} \\ \vdots \\ \mathbf{T}_l \\ \hline \mathbf{0} \\ \mathbf{T}_\mathbf{G} \end{bmatrix}$$

The validity of the trapdoor $\mathbf{T}'$ is guaranteed by $|\mathbf{T}'| = |\mathbf{T}|$ and $\mathbf{B}_l'\mathbf{T}' = \mathbf{G}$ (by Theorem 2.5).
Therefore, if we use $[\mathbf{A}_i|\mathbf{D}_i]$, $\mathbf{B}_l'$, $\mathbf{T}'$ to *replace* $\mathbf{A}_i$, $\mathbf{B}_l$, $\mathbf{T}$ in the above construction, the properties of correctness, binding, private openings still hold under the BASIS assumption.

Our Approach. We adopt the strategy of *replacing* as mentioned before to construct the main part of mercurial vector commitment and keep the condition of $\mathbf{c} = [\mathbf{A}_i|\mathbf{D}_i]\mathbf{v}_i + x_i\mathbf{e}_1$ in the verification phase.

We provide two algorithms to generate statistically indistinguishable $\mathbf{D}_i$ in the commitment $(\mathbf{c}, \mathbf{D} = (\mathbf{D}_1, ..., \mathbf{D}_l))$ for each $i \in [\ell]$: one is $\mathbf{D}_i = \mathbf{A}_i\mathbf{R}_i$, and the other is $\mathbf{D}_i = \mathbf{G} - \mathbf{A}_i\mathbf{R}_i'$ which $\mathbf{R}_i$ and $\mathbf{R}_i'$ are randomly sampled over $\{0,1\}^{m\times m'}$ (indistinguishability is guaranteed by Lemma 2.3). When $\mathbf{D}_i = \mathbf{G} - \mathbf{A}_i\mathbf{R}_i'$, $\mathbf{R}_i'$ is the trapdoor for $[\mathbf{A}_i|\mathbf{D}_i]$ and a valid $\mathbf{v}_i$ can be sampled from $\mathsf{SampPre}([\mathbf{A}_i|\mathbf{D}_i], \mathbf{R}_i', \mathbf{c} - x_i\mathbf{e}_1, s)$ which is also statistically close to $[\mathbf{A}_i|\mathbf{D}_i]^{-1}(\mathbf{c} - x_i\mathbf{e}_1)$ (by Theorem 2.5). Therefore, we need an additional check for $\mathbf{D}_i = \mathbf{A}_i\mathbf{R}_i$ to differ between soft commitments and hard commitments in the hard verification and take $\mathbf{R}_i$ as the additional part in the hard opening.

The correctness and (mercurial) binding still hold after the above operations and we extend the private openings to the mercurial hiding by the following statistically close distributions for each $i \in [\ell]$:

$$\{(\mathbf{G}\hat{\mathbf{c}}, \mathbf{v}_i) : [\mathbf{v}_1, ..., \mathbf{v}_l, \hat{\mathbf{c}}]^\mathsf{T} \leftarrow \mathsf{SampPre}(\mathbf{B}_l', \mathbf{T}', -\mathbf{x} \otimes \mathbf{e}_1, s)\}$$

$$\{(\mathbf{G}\hat{\mathbf{c}}, \mathbf{v}_i) : \hat{\mathbf{c}} \leftarrow D_{\mathbb{Z}^{m'}}, \mathbf{v}_i \leftarrow [\mathbf{A}_i|\mathbf{D}_i]^{-1}(\mathbf{G}\hat{\mathbf{c}} - x_i\mathbf{e}_1)\}$$

$$\{(\mathbf{G}\hat{\mathbf{c}}, \mathbf{v}_i) : \hat{\mathbf{c}} \leftarrow D_{\mathbb{Z}^{m'}}, \mathbf{v}_i \leftarrow \mathsf{SampPre}([\mathbf{A}_i|\mathbf{D}_i], \mathbf{R}_i', \mathbf{G}\hat{\mathbf{c}} - x_i\mathbf{e}_1, s)\}$$

Following the two instantiations of BASIS assumption, we provide two constructions of our lattice-based mercurial vector commitment.

– If $\mathbf{A}_1, ..., \mathbf{A}_l$ are independently sampled, the above construction is based on the $\mathsf{BASIS}_{\mathsf{rand}}$ which can be reduced to standard SIS assumption. Therefore, $\mathbf{D}_1, ..., \mathbf{D}_l$ are independent with each other and the size of $\mathbf{D} = (\mathbf{D}_1, ..., \mathbf{D}_l)$ is linear with the dimension of $\mathbf{x}$. It leads that the construction of mercurial vector commitment is partially succinct. But it can be transformed into succinct by a standard vector commitment. The formal description and analysis are shown in the full version of this paper.

- If $\mathbf{A}_1, ..., \mathbf{A}_l$ are structured by $\mathbf{A}_i = \mathbf{W}_i\mathbf{A}$ where $\mathbf{W}_i \in \mathbb{Z}_q^{n\times n}$ is a random invertible matrix for each $i \in [\ell]$ and $\mathbf{A} \in \mathbb{Z}_q^{n\times m}$ is sampled randomly. This construction is based on the $\mathsf{BASIS_{struct}}$ assumption. And we set $\mathbf{D}_i = \mathbf{W}_i\hat{\mathbf{D}}$ where $\hat{\mathbf{D}} = \mathbf{AR}$ or $\hat{\mathbf{D}} = \mathbf{G} - \mathbf{AR}$ and $\mathbf{R}$ is randomly sampled over $\{0,1\}^{m\times m'}$. Thus, with the public matrix $\mathbf{W}_i$ for each $i \in [\ell]$, $\mathbf{D} = (\mathbf{D}_1, ..., \mathbf{D}_l)$ can be represented by $\hat{\mathbf{D}}$ whose size does not depend on the dimension of $\mathbf{x}$. It leads to this construction of mercurial vector commitment being fully succinct. We provide the full details in Sect. 3.

Updatable MVC. We extend stateless update and differential update in vector commitment [25,28] to mercurial vector commitment. In the vector commitment based on BASIS assumption, to update the message $\mathbf{x}$ in the commitment $\mathbf{c}$ and the associated openings $\mathbf{v}_i$ to $\mathbf{x}'$, we can first construct the target vector $\mathbf{u} = -\bar{\mathbf{x}} \otimes \mathbf{e}_1$ where $\bar{\mathbf{x}} = \mathbf{x}' - \mathbf{x} = (x_1' - x_1, ..., x_l' - x_l)$ is the difference between the updated messages and old message, then compute the commitment $\bar{\mathbf{c}}$ and the openings $\bar{\mathbf{v}}_i$ of $\bar{\mathbf{x}}$. and send the update information $U_i = \{\bar{\mathbf{c}}, \bar{\mathbf{v}}_i\}$ for users holding old commitment $\mathbf{c}$ and old opening $\mathbf{v}_i$ to update. Both $\mathbf{v}_i$ and $\bar{\mathbf{v}}_i$ are valid that satisfying

$$\mathbf{c} = \mathbf{A}_i\mathbf{v}_i + x_i\mathbf{e}_1, \qquad \bar{\mathbf{c}} = \mathbf{A}_i\bar{\mathbf{v}}_i + \bar{x}_i\mathbf{e}_1$$

By the linear homomorphism of BASIS assumption, $\mathbf{c}' = \mathbf{c} + \bar{\mathbf{c}}$ is the commitment to $\mathbf{x}' = \bar{\mathbf{x}} + \mathbf{x}$ with short opening $\mathbf{v}_i' = \bar{\mathbf{v}}_i + \mathbf{v}_i$.

However, in the mercurial vector commitment, to update the soft commitment i.e. add the message to a hard commitment, we have to sample a new $\mathbf{D}'$ in the updated commitment which leads to a different target vector $\bar{\mathbf{u}} = (\bar{\mathbf{u}}_1, ..., \bar{\mathbf{u}}_l)^\mathsf{T}$ as follows:

$$\bar{\mathbf{u}}_i = -\bar{x}_i\mathbf{e}_1 + (\mathbf{D}_i - \mathbf{D}_i')\mathbf{v}_{i,2}$$

where $\mathbf{v}_{i,2}$ is phased from the old opening $\mathbf{v}_i = [\mathbf{v}_{i,1}|\mathbf{v}_{i,2}]^\mathsf{T}$.

Thanks to the indistinguishability between $\mathbf{D}_i'$ and $\mathbf{D}_i$ for each $i \in [\ell]$, our contributions of updatable mercurial vector commitment achieve a stronger property, named updatable mercurial hiding which was proposed by Catalano et al. [8] in mercurial commitment, and we extend this property to mercurial vector commitment. Informally speaking, the property requires that even given the old commitment $(\mathbf{c}, \mathbf{D})$ with its opening $\mathbf{v}_i$, the updated commitment $(\mathbf{c}', \mathbf{D}')$ with it opening $\mathbf{v}_i'$, and the update information $U_i = \{\bar{\mathbf{c}}, \mathbf{D}', \bar{\mathbf{v}}_i\}$, the adversary still cannot learn the type of old commitment. To prove this property, we define and provide the additional *simulating* update algorithms for the fake commitment and openings. The technique of update can be applied in both SIS-based MVC and $\mathsf{BASIS_{struct}}$-based MVC. We provide the full details of them in the full version of this work, and Sect. 3.1 respectively, and an extension to support updatable hiding in the full version of this paper.

Aggregatable MVC. To beak the limitation of the existing constructions only supports mercurial *weak* binding which the adversary has to use the Hard_com algorithm (input some messages, possibly adversarially chosen) to generate the commitment rather than chosen arbitrarily during the attack. For the (mercurial) vector commitment based on $\mathsf{BASIS}_{\mathsf{struct}}$ assumption, there exists an aggregate algorithm for the *bounded* message $\mathbf{x} \in \mathbb{Z}_p^l$, in which each entity of the target vector $\mathbf{u}$ is replaced from $-\mathbf{W}_i x_i \mathbf{e}_1$ to $-\mathbf{W}_i x_i \mathbf{u}_i$ where $\mathbf{u}_i$ is randomly sampled over $\mathbb{Z}_q^n$. For any set $S \subseteq [\ell]$, we have

$$\sum_{i \in S} \mathbf{W}_i^{-1} \mathbf{c} = \mathbf{A} \sum_{i \in S} \mathbf{v}_i + \sum_{i \in S} x_i \mathbf{u}_i$$

Therefore, $\hat{\mathbf{v}} = \sum_{i \in S} \mathbf{v}_i$ is the aggregated opening to all the indices in S. The security and the correctness are guaranteed by the leftover hash lemma and min-entropy. We show a detailed construction in Sect. 3.2 and a full analysis in the full version of this work.

1.3 Related Work

The first mercurial commitment based on the DH assumption was proposed by Chase et al. [9]. Then, Catalano et al. [7] presented trapdoor mercurial commitments (TMC) based on a one-way function with higher efficiency but weaker assumption. Later Libert et al. [18] proposed the first lattice-based mercurial commitment that supports the commitment to a single message $x \in \{0,1\}^l$. Libert and Yung [20] proposed the concept of MVC and gave two constructions on it based on l-DHE (Diffie-Hellman Exponent) assumption and RSA assumption, respectively, which support commit on a l-length vector with compact proofs for both hard opening and soft opening.

Subsequently, Catalano et al. [8] provided a generic construction for MVC with a standard MC and a standard VC. Briefly speaking, to make a mercurial vector commitment to a vector $\mathbf{x} = (x_1, .., x_l)$, it first uses the standard MC to make the mercurial commitment $(\mathbf{c}_i, \mathbf{D}_i)$ of x_i for each $i \in [\ell]$ and then uses the standard VC to make the vector commitment C of $((\mathbf{c}_1, \mathbf{D}_1), ..., (\mathbf{c}_l, \mathbf{D}_l))$ and put all the mercurial commitments into the auxiliary information. During the phase of opening and verification, the vector commitment must be opened to the mercurial commitment $(\mathbf{c}_i, \mathbf{D}_i)$ on the index i then the mercurial commitment to x_i and finally verify both openings. The drawbacks of the generic construction are that (1) the size of the auxiliary information is large; (2) it is hard to extend other advanced properties into their framework.

The concept of VC was first proposed by Catalano and Fiore in [8]. They provided two different constructions of VC based on computational DH (CDH) assumptions and RSA assumptions. They also introduced many applications of VC and MVC, such as verifiable databases, zero-knowledge elementary databases, and universal dynamic accumulators. Subsequently, Lai and Malavolta [16] first proposed the primitive of SVC and presented two constructions under variants of the root assumption and the CDH assumption. Following their work [14,20], Li et al. [17] proposed the first definitions and constructions of MSVC based on the assumption l -DHE in the AGM model and Random Oracle (ROM). They introduced a hash function to aggregate the openings to the subvector. We can find that the above non-black-box constructions of MVCs are almost based on the l -DHE assumption and the RSA assumption.

Recently, a lot of work [1,3–6,12,25,28] has been done on lattice-based VC, which is regarded as the most possible candidate for the post-quantum cryptography primitive. Therefore, with the lattice-based MC [18] and VC (e.g. [28]), the black-box lattice-based MVC can be built trivially. Among them, Wee and Wu [28] proposed a variant of the SIS assumption, named BASIS assumption to build the lattice-based VC. Compared to standard SIS-based VC, their constructions support more advanced properties, e.g., updatable, aggregatable, and functional opening. Our work is mainly based on their assumptions.

2 Preliminaries

2.1 Notation

Let $\lambda \in \mathbb{N}$ denote the security parameter. For a positive integer l, denote the set $(1, ..., l)$ by $[\ell]$. For a positive integer q, we denote $\mathbb{Z}_q$ as the integers modulo q. We use bold uppercase letters to denote matrices like $\mathbf{A}$ and bold lowercase letters to denote vectors like $\mathbf{x}$. We use non-boldface letters to refer to the components: $\mathbf{x} = (x_1, ..., x_l)$ and $\mathbf{x}[S] := (x_i, i \in S)$ to be the subvector of $\mathbf{x}$ indexed by S. $\|\mathbf{x}\|$ is denoted as the infinity norm of the vector $\mathbf{x}$. When $\mathbf{X}$ is a matrix, $\|\mathbf{X}\| := \max_{i,j} |X_{i,j}|$. For matrices $\mathbf{A}_1, ..., \mathbf{A}_l \in \mathbb{Z}_q^{n \times m}$, let $\mathsf{diag}(\mathbf{A}_1, ..., \mathbf{A}_l) \in \mathbb{Z}_q^{nl \times ml}$ be the block diagonal matrix with blocks $\mathbf{A}_1, ..., \mathbf{A}_l$ along the main diagonal (and $\mathbf{0}$ elsewhere). We denote $\mathsf{poly}(\lambda)$ as a fixed function that is $O(\lambda^c)$ for some $c \in \mathbb{N}$ and $\mathsf{negl}(\lambda)$ as a function that is $o(\lambda^{-c})$ for all $c \in \mathbb{N}$.

2.2 Lattice Preliminaries

Lattice. Let $\mathbf{B} \in \mathbb{R}^{n \times n}$ be a full-rank matrix over $\mathbb{R}$. Then the n-dimensional lattice $\mathcal{L}$ generated by $\mathbf{B}$ is $\mathcal{L} = \mathcal{L}(\mathbf{B}) = \{\mathbf{Bz} : \mathbf{z} \in \mathbb{Z}^n\}$. If $\mathbf{A} \in \mathbb{Z}_q^{n \times m}$ for integers n, m, q, we define $\mathcal{L}^{\perp}(\mathbf{A}) = \{\mathbf{x} \in \mathbb{Z}_q^m : \mathbf{Ax} = \mathbf{0} \mod q\}$.

Definition 2.1 (SIS Assumption [2]). Let λ be a security parameter, and n, m, q, β be lattice parameters. The short integer solution assumption $\mathsf{SIS}_{n,m,q,\beta}$ holds if for all efficient adversaries $\mathcal{A}$,

$$\Pr\left[\mathbf{Ax} = \mathbf{0} \wedge 0 < \|\mathbf{x}\| \leq \beta \;\middle|\; \begin{array}{c} \mathbf{A} \xleftarrow{\$} \mathbb{Z}_q^{n \times m}; \\ \mathbf{x} \leftarrow \mathcal{A}(1^\lambda, \mathbf{A}) \end{array}\right] = \mathsf{negl}(\lambda)$$

Discrete Gaussian over Lattice. For integer $m \in \mathbb{N}$, let $D_{\mathbb{Z}^m,s}$ be the discrete Gaussian distribution over $\mathbb{Z}^m$ with width parameter $s \in \mathbb{R}^+$. For a matrix $\mathbf{A} \in \mathbb{Z}_q^{n \times l}$ and a vector $\mathbf{v} \in \mathbb{Z}_q^n$, we donate $\mathbf{A}_s^{-1}(\mathbf{v})$ as the random variable $\mathbf{x} \leftarrow D_{\mathbb{Z}^m,s}$ conditioned on $\mathbf{Ax} = \mathbf{v} \mod q$. We extend $\mathbf{A}_s^{-1}$ to matrices by applying $\mathbf{A}_s^{-1}$ to each column of the input.

Lemma 2.2 (Gaussian Tail Bound [13]**).** *A sample from a discrete Gaussian with parameter s is at most $s\sqrt{m}$ away from its center with overwhelming probability,*

$$\Pr[||\mathbf{r}|| > s\sqrt{m} | \mathbf{r} \leftarrow D_{\mathbb{Z}^m,s}] \leq 2^{-m}$$

Lemma 2.3 (Leftover Hash Lemma [15]**).** *Let n, m, q be lattice parameters and suppose $m \geq 2n \log q$. Then, the statistical distance between the following distributions is at most 2^{-n}:*

$$\{(\mathbf{A}, \mathbf{Ar}) : \mathbf{A} \xleftarrow{\$} \mathbb{Z}_q^{n\times m}, \mathbf{r} \xleftarrow{\$} \{0,1\}^m\} \approx \{(\mathbf{A}, \mathbf{u}) : \mathbf{A} \xleftarrow{\$} \mathbb{Z}_q^{n\times m}, \mathbf{u} \xleftarrow{\$} \mathbb{Z}_q^n\}$$

When sampling a matrix $\mathbf{R} = [\mathbf{r}_1|...|\mathbf{r}_{m'}] \in \mathbb{Z}^{m\times m'}$ where $\mathbf{r}_i \xleftarrow{\$} \{0,1\}^m$ for all $i \in [m']$, we will use the notation $\mathbf{R} \xleftarrow{\$} \{0,1\}^{m\times m'}$.

Lemma 2.4 (Discrete Gaussian Preimages [28]**).** *Let n, q be lattice parameters and take $m \geq 2n \log q$. Take matrices $\mathbf{A} \in \mathbb{Z}_q^{n\times m}$ and $\mathbf{B} \in \mathbb{Z}_q^{n\times l}$ where $l = \mathsf{poly}(n \log q)$. Let $\mathbf{C} = [\mathbf{A}|\mathbf{B}]$. Then for all target vectors $\mathbf{t} \in \mathbb{Z}_q^n$ and all width parameters for $s \geq \log m$, the distribution of $\{\mathbf{v} : \mathbf{v} \leftarrow \mathbf{C}_s^{-1}(\mathbf{t})\}$ is statistically close to the distribution $\{[\mathbf{v}_1|\mathbf{v}_2]^\mathsf{T} : \mathbf{v}_2 \leftarrow D_{\mathbb{Z}^l,s}, \mathbf{v}_1 \leftarrow \mathbf{A}_s^{-1}(\mathbf{t} - \mathbf{B}\mathbf{v}_2)\}$.*

Trapdoor. Our constructions will use the gadget trapdoors introduced in [23] and adapted in [28]. For any positive integer k, let $\mathbf{I}_k$ denote the identity matrix of order k. Let n be a positive integer, $q \in \mathsf{poly}(n)$ be a modulus, and $m' = n(\lceil \log q \rceil + 1)$. Define the gadget matrix $\mathbf{G} = \mathbf{I}_n \otimes (1, 2, ..., 2^{\lceil \log q \rceil}) \in \mathbb{Z}_q^{n\times m'}$.

Theorem 2.5 (Gadget Trapdoor [23,28]**).** *Let n, m, q, m' be lattice parameters. Then there exist efficient algorithms (*$\mathsf{TrapGen}$, $\mathsf{SampPre}$*) with the following syntax:*

- $(\mathbf{A}, \mathbf{R}) \leftarrow \mathsf{TrapGen}(n, m, q)$*: On input the lattice dimension n, the modulus q, and the number of samples m, the trapdoor-generation algorithm outputs a matrix $\mathbf{A} \in \mathbb{Z}_q^{n\times m}$ together with a trapdoor $\mathbf{R} \in \mathbb{Z}_q^{m\times m'}$.*
- $\mathbf{u} \leftarrow \mathsf{SampPre}(\mathbf{A}, \mathbf{R}, \mathbf{v}, s)$*: On input a matrix $\mathbf{A} \in \mathbb{Z}_q^{n\times m}$, a trapdoor $\mathbf{R} \in \mathbb{Z}_q^{m\times m'}$, a target vector $\mathbf{v} \in \mathbb{Z}_q^n$, and a Gaussian width parameter s, the preimage sampling algorithm outputs a vector $\mathbf{u} \in \mathbb{Z}_q^m$ satisfying $\mathbf{Au} = \mathbf{v}$.*

Moreover, for all $m \geq O(n \log q)$, the above algorithms satisfy the following properties:

- Trapdoor distribution*: The matrix $\mathbf{A}$ output by* $\mathsf{TrapGen}(n, q, m)$ *is statistically close to uniform over $\mathbb{Z}_q^{n\times m}$. Moreover, $\mathbf{AR} = \mathbf{G}$ and $||\mathbf{R}|| = 1$.*
- Preimage distribution*: Suppose $\mathbf{R}$ is a gadget trapdoor for $\mathbf{A} \in \mathbb{Z}_q^{n\times m}$ (i.e., $\mathbf{AR} = \mathbf{G}$). Then, for all $s \geq \sqrt{mm'}||\mathbf{R}||\omega(\sqrt{\log n})$, and all target vectors $\mathbf{v} \in \mathbb{Z}_q^n$, the distribution of $\mathbf{u} \leftarrow \mathsf{SampPre}(\mathbf{A}, \mathbf{R}, \mathbf{v}, s)$ is statistically close to $\mathbf{A}_s^{-1}(\mathbf{v})$.*

Remark 2.6. *More generally, the above properties hold if $\mathbf{AR} = \mathbf{HG}$ for some invertible matrix $\mathbf{H} \in \mathbb{Z}_q^{n\times n}$. In this case, we refer to $\mathbf{H}$ as the tag.*

Remark 2.7. *In the other situation, for* $m = \bar{m} + m'$ *and some* $\bar{m} > m'$. *A trapdoor for matrix* $\mathbf{A} \in \mathbb{Z}_q^{n \times m}$ *can be a matrix* $\mathbf{R} \in \mathbb{Z}^{\bar{m} \times m'}$ *such that* $\mathbf{A}[\mathbf{R}|\mathbf{I}_{m'}]^{\mathsf{T}} = \mathbf{G}$ *and* $\|\mathbf{R}\| = 1$. *In particular, if* $\mathbf{A} = [\bar{\mathbf{A}}|\mathbf{G} - \bar{\mathbf{A}} \cdot \mathbf{R}]$, *where* $\bar{\mathbf{A}} \in \mathbb{Z}_q^{n \times \bar{m}}$, *then* $\mathbf{R}$ *is a trapdoor for* $\mathbf{A}$.

2.3 BASIS Assumption

Definition 2.8 (BASIS Assumption [28]). Let λ be a security parameter and n, m, q, β be lattice parameters. Let s be a Gaussian width parameter. Let Samp be an efficient sampling algorithm that takes a security parameter λ and a matrix $\mathbf{A} \in \mathbb{Z}_q^{n \times m}$ as input and outputs a matrix $\mathbf{B} \in \mathbb{Z}_q^{n' \times m'}$ along with auxiliary information aux. We say that the basis-augmented SIS (BASIS) assumption holds with respect to Samp if for all efficient adversaries $\mathcal{A}$,

$$\Pr\left[\mathbf{A}\mathbf{x} = \mathbf{0} \wedge 0 < \|\mathbf{x}\| \leq \beta \;\middle|\; \begin{array}{c} \mathbf{A} \xleftarrow{\$} \mathbb{Z}_q^{n \times m}; \\ (\mathbf{B}, \mathsf{aux}) \leftarrow \mathsf{Samp}(1^\lambda, \mathbf{A}), \mathbf{T} \leftarrow \mathbf{B}_s^{-1}(\mathbf{G}'_n); \\ \mathbf{x} \leftarrow \mathcal{A}(1^\lambda, \mathbf{A}, \mathbf{B}, \mathbf{T}, \mathsf{aux}) \end{array}\right] = \mathsf{negl}(\lambda)$$

In other words, it requires that SIS assumption is hard with respect to $\mathbf{A}$ even given a trapdoor $\mathbf{T}$ for the related matrix $\mathbf{B}$.

Instantiation 2.9 (BASIS$_{\mathsf{rand}}$ Assumption [28]). Let λ be a security parameter and n, m, q, β be lattice parameters. Let s be a Gaussian width parameter and l be a dimension. The BASIS assumption with random matrices (BASIS$_{\mathsf{rand}}$) is that: the sampling algorithm $\mathsf{Samp}(\lambda, \mathbf{A})$ samples $i^* \xleftarrow{\$} [\ell]$, $\mathbf{A}_i \xleftarrow{\$} \mathbb{Z}_q^{(n+1) \times m}$ for all $i \in [\ell]/i^*$, $\mathbf{a} \xleftarrow{\$} \mathbb{Z}_q^m$, sets $\mathbf{A}_{i^*} \leftarrow \begin{bmatrix} \mathbf{a}^{\mathsf{T}} \\ \mathbf{A} \end{bmatrix}$, and outputs

$$\mathbf{B}_l = \left[\begin{array}{ccc|c} \mathbf{A}_1 & & & -\mathbf{G}_{n+1} \\ & \ddots & & \vdots \\ & & \mathbf{A}_l & -\mathbf{G}_{n+1} \end{array}\right], \qquad \mathsf{aux} = i^*$$

Instantiation 2.10 (BASIS$_{\mathsf{struct}}$ Assumption [28]). The parameters are the same as BASIS$_{\mathsf{rand}}$. The BASIS assumption with structured matrices (BASIS$_{\mathsf{struct}}$) is that: the sampling algorithm $\mathsf{Samp}(\lambda, \mathbf{A})$ samples $\mathbf{W}_i \xleftarrow{\$} \mathbb{Z}_q^{n \times n}$ for all $i \in [\ell]$ and outputs

$$\mathbf{B}_l = \left[\begin{array}{ccc|c} \mathbf{W}_1\mathbf{A} & & & -\mathbf{G}_n \\ & \ddots & & \vdots \\ & & \mathbf{W}_l\mathbf{A} & -\mathbf{G}_n \end{array}\right], \qquad \mathsf{aux} = (\mathbf{W}_1, ..., \mathbf{W}_l)$$

Remark 2.11 (Hardness and Parameter Choices of BASIS [28]). The BASIS$_{\mathsf{rand}}$ assumption can be reduced to the standard SIS assumption and the BASIS$_{\mathsf{struct}}$ assumption is conceptually similar to k-R-ISIS assumption [3] in which some instances are as hard as standard SIS. While BASIS$_{\mathsf{struct}}$ assumption offers more structure and potentially more power to the adversary, it is believed to provide a similar level of security as the standard SIS assumption because there are no known concrete attacks specifically targeting the structured nature of $\mathsf{BASIS}_{\mathsf{struct}}$, and no faster combinatorial attacks on $\mathsf{BASIS}_{\mathsf{struct}}$ compared to standard SIS have been discovered. However, for now, there is not an analogous reduction for the $\mathsf{BASIS}_{\mathsf{struct}}$ assumption or k-R-ISIS assumption to standard lattice assumption.

Following [28], to further support the security claims of $\mathsf{BASIS}_{\mathsf{struct}}$, its parameter choices can be the *same* as $\mathsf{BASIS}_{\mathsf{rand}}$ which means the quality of the basis *decreases* with the dimension. It is conjectured that its security is comparable with the hardness of SIS with a noise-bound polynomially scaling with the dimension of the vector that is similar to the q-type assumptions over groups [11].

2.4 Mercurial Vector Commitment

We provide the definition of (trapdoor) mercurial vector commitment.

Definition 2.12 (Mercurial Vector Commitment [20]**).** A succinct (trapdoor) mercurial vector commitment over message space $\mathcal{M}$ comprises the following algorithms:

- $\{\mathsf{pp}, tk\} \leftarrow \mathsf{Setup}(1^\lambda, 1^l)$: Input a security parameter λ and the dimension of vector l, and it outputs the public parameter pp and a trapdoor key tk optionally.
- $\{(\mathbf{c}, \mathbf{D}), \mathsf{aux}\} \leftarrow \mathsf{Hard\_com}(\mathsf{pp}, \mathbf{x})$: Input the public parameter pp and a vector message $\mathbf{x} \in \mathcal{M}^l$, and it outputs a hard commitment $(\mathbf{c}, \mathbf{D})$ and auxiliary information aux.
- $\pi_i \leftarrow \mathsf{Hard\_open}(\mathsf{pp}, x_i, i, \mathsf{aux})$: Input the public parameter pp, the message x_i, the index i, and the auxiliary information aux, and it outputs a hard opening π_i to prove that x_i is committed at the index i in the hard commitment.
- $0/1 \leftarrow \mathsf{Hard\_verify}(\mathsf{pp}, x_i, i, (\mathbf{c}, \mathbf{D}), \pi_i)$: Input the public parameter pp, the message x_i, the index i, commitment $(\mathbf{c}, \mathbf{D})$, and the hard opening π_i, and it outputs 0 or 1 to indicate whether π_i is a valid hard opening.
- $\{(\mathbf{c}, \mathbf{D}), \mathsf{aux}\} \leftarrow \mathsf{Soft\_com}(\mathsf{pp})$: Input the public parameter pp, and it outputs a soft commitment $(\mathbf{c}, \mathbf{D})$ that is not bound to any vector message, and the corresponding auxiliary information aux.
- $\tau_i \leftarrow \mathsf{Soft\_open}(\mathsf{pp}, \mathsf{flag}, x, i, \mathsf{aux})$: Input the public parameter pp, the $\mathsf{flag} \in \{\mathsf{hard}, \mathsf{soft}\}$ which indicates that the soft opening τ_i is for hard commitment or soft commitment, the message x, the index i and the auxiliary information aux, it outputs the soft opening τ_i. If $\mathsf{flag} = \mathsf{hard}$ and $x \neq x_i$ at the index i, the algorithm aborts and outputs $\perp$.
- $0/1 \leftarrow \mathsf{Soft\_verify}(\mathsf{pp}, x, i, (\mathbf{c}, \mathbf{D}), \tau_i)$: Input the public parameter pp, the commitment pair $(\mathbf{c}, \mathbf{D})$, the message x, the index i, and soft opening τ_i, it outputs 0 or 1 to indicate whether τ_i is a valid soft opening.
- $\{(\mathbf{c}, \mathbf{D}), \mathsf{aux}\} \leftarrow \mathsf{Fake\_com}(\mathsf{pp}, tk)$: Input the public parameter pp and trapdoor key tk, it outputs the *fake commitment* pair $(\mathbf{c}, \mathbf{D})$ and its corresponding auxiliary information aux.

- $\pi \leftarrow \mathsf{Equiv\_Hopen}(\mathsf{pp}, tk, x_i, i, \mathsf{aux})$: Input the public parameter pp and trapdoor key tk, the message x_i, the index i, and the auxiliary information aux, it outputs the *hard equivocation* π.
- $\tau \leftarrow \mathsf{Equiv\_Sopen}(\mathsf{pp}, tk, x_i, i, \mathsf{aux})$: Input the public parameter pp and trapdoor key tk, the message x_i, the index i, and the auxiliary information aux, it outputs the *soft equivocation* τ.

Remark 2.13 (Proper MVC [18]). Including all currently known constructions, the soft opening of a hard commitment is a proper part of the hard opening to the same message. Therefore, Soft_verify performs a proper subset of the tests done by Hard_verify. Such mercurial (vector) commitments are called *proper* mercurial (vector) commitments.

Correctness. The correctness of a trapdoor mercurial vector commitment is as follows. Specifically, for all security parameters λ, all vector message $\mathbf{x} \in \mathcal{M}^l$, and the public parameters $\mathsf{pp} \leftarrow \mathsf{Setup}(1^\lambda, 1^l)$, the following conditions must hold with an overwhelming probability.

- For a hard commitment $\{(\mathbf{c}, \mathbf{D}), \mathsf{aux}\} \leftarrow \mathsf{Hard\_com}(\mathsf{pp}, \mathbf{x})$, a hard opening $\pi_i \leftarrow \mathsf{Hard\_open}(\mathsf{pp}, x_i, i, \mathsf{aux})$ and a soft opening $\tau_i \leftarrow \mathsf{Soft\_open}(\mathsf{pp}, \mathsf{hard}, x_i, i, \mathsf{aux})$ for the hard commitment, there must have $\mathsf{Hard\_verify}(\mathsf{pp}, x_i, i, (\mathbf{c}, \mathbf{D}), \pi_i) = 1$ and $\mathsf{Soft\_verify}(\mathsf{pp}, x, i, (\mathbf{c}, \mathbf{D}), \tau_i) = 1$.
- For a soft commitment $\{(\mathbf{c}, \mathbf{D}), \mathsf{aux}\} \leftarrow \mathsf{Soft\_com}(\mathsf{pp})$, a soft opening $\tau_i \leftarrow \mathsf{Soft\_open}(\mathsf{pp}, \mathsf{soft}, x, i, \mathsf{aux})$ for the soft commitment, there must have $\mathsf{Soft\_verify}\ (\mathsf{pp}, x, i, (\mathbf{c}, \mathbf{D}), \tau_i) = 1$.
- For a fake commitment $\{(\mathbf{c}, \mathbf{D}), \mathsf{aux}\} \leftarrow \mathsf{Fake\_com}\ (\mathsf{pp}, tk)$, where tk is the trapdoor key for the scheme, a hard equivocation $\pi \leftarrow \mathsf{Equiv\_Hopen}\ (\mathsf{pp}, tk, x_i, i, \mathsf{aux})$ and a soft equivocation $\tau \leftarrow \mathsf{Equiv\_Sopen}(\mathsf{pp}, tk, x_i, i, \mathsf{aux})$ for the fake commitment, there must have $\mathsf{Hard\_verify}(\mathsf{pp}, x_i, i, (\mathbf{c}, \mathbf{D}), \pi) = 1$ and $\mathsf{Soft\_verify}(\mathsf{pp}, x, i, (\mathbf{c}, \mathbf{D}), \tau) = 1$.

Mercurial Binding. For a *proper* mercurial vector commitment, given the public parameter pp, for any adversary $\mathcal{A}$ outputs a commitment $(\mathbf{c}, \mathbf{D})$, an index $i \in [\ell]$ and the openings to some values (x, π), (x', π') (or (x, τ), (x', π')), the following probability should be $\mathsf{negl}(\lambda)$.

$$\Pr\left[\begin{array}{c|c} \mathsf{Hard\_verify}(\mathsf{pp}, x_i, i, (\mathbf{c}, \mathbf{D}), \pi_i) = 1 & \mathsf{pp} \leftarrow \mathsf{Setup}(1^\lambda, 1^l); \\ \wedge\ x_i \neq x_i' \wedge & \{(\mathbf{c}, \mathbf{D}), i, (x_i, \pi_i), (x_i', \pi_i')\} \leftarrow \mathcal{A}(1^\lambda, 1^l, \mathsf{pp}) \\ \mathsf{Soft\_verify}(\mathsf{pp}, x_i', i, (\mathbf{c}, \mathbf{D}), \pi_i') = 1 & \end{array}\right]$$

Mercurial Hiding. Given the public parameter pp, for any $\mathbf{x}$, and an index i, no efficient adversary can distinguish between hard commitment with its soft opening $\{\mathbf{x}, \mathsf{Hard\_com}(\mathsf{pp}, \mathbf{x}), \mathsf{Soft\_open}(\mathsf{pp}, \mathsf{Hard}, x, i, \mathsf{aux})\}$ and soft commitment with its soft opening $\{\mathbf{x}, \mathsf{Soft\_com}(\mathsf{pp}), \mathsf{Soft\_open}(\mathsf{pp}, \mathsf{Soft}, x, i, \mathsf{aux})\}$. Generally, use an equivocation game to prove.

Equivocation Game. There are three related conditions for equivocation games that have to be satisfied by mercurial commitments. Each is defined by a pair of games, one *real* and one *ideal*. Given the public parameter pp and the trapdoor tk, no adversary $\mathcal{A}$ can distinguish between them.

- Hcom_Hopen Equivocation: $\mathcal{A}$ picks a vector $\mathbf{x} = (x_1, ..., x_l)$ and an index $i \in [\ell]$. In the real game, $\mathcal{A}$ will receive $(\mathbf{c}, \mathbf{D}) \leftarrow \mathsf{Hard\_com}(\mathsf{pp}, \mathbf{x})$ and $\pi_i \leftarrow \mathsf{Hard\_open}\ (\mathsf{pp}, x_i, i, \mathsf{aux})$. While in the ideal game, $\mathcal{A}$ will obtain $(\mathbf{c}, \mathbf{D}) \leftarrow \mathsf{Fake\_com}(\mathsf{pp}, tk)$, $\pi_i \leftarrow \mathsf{Equiv\_Hopen}(\mathsf{pp}, tk, x_i, i, \mathsf{aux})$.
- Hcom_Sopen Equivocation: $\mathcal{A}$ picks a vector $\mathbf{x} = (x_1, ..., x_l)$ and an index $i \in [\ell]$. In the real game, $\mathcal{A}$ will receive $(\mathbf{c}, \mathbf{D}) \leftarrow \mathsf{Hard\_com}(\mathsf{pp}, \mathbf{x})$ and $\tau_i \leftarrow \mathsf{Soft\_open}\ (\mathsf{pp}, \mathsf{hard}, x_i, i, \mathsf{aux})$. While in the ideal game, $\mathcal{A}$ will obtain $(\mathbf{c}, \mathbf{D}) \leftarrow \mathsf{Fake\_com}(\mathsf{pp},\ tk)$, $\tau_i \leftarrow \mathsf{Equiv\_Sopen}(\mathsf{pp}, tk, x_i, i, \mathsf{aux})$.
- Scom_Sopen Equivocation: In the real game, $\mathcal{A}$ will get $(\mathbf{c}, \mathbf{D}) \leftarrow \mathsf{Soft\_com}(\mathsf{pp})$ and choose x_i for some index $i \in [\ell]$, finally receive $\tau_i \leftarrow \mathsf{Soft\_open}\ (\mathsf{pp}, \mathsf{soft}, x_i, i, \mathsf{aux})$. While in the ideal game, $\mathcal{A}$ first obtains $(\mathbf{c}, \mathbf{D}) \leftarrow \mathsf{Fake\_com}(\mathsf{pp}, tk)$, then chooses x_i for some index $i \in [\ell]$, finally receives $\tau_i \leftarrow \mathsf{Equiv\_Sopen}(\mathsf{pp}, tk, x_i, i, \mathsf{aux})$.

Succinctness. A mercurial vector commitment is succinct if there exists a universal polynomial $\mathsf{poly}(\cdot)$ such that for all $\lambda \in \mathbb{N}$, $|(\mathbf{c}, \mathbf{D})| = \mathsf{poly}(\lambda, \log l)$, and $|\pi_i| = \mathsf{poly}(\lambda, \log l)$ for all $i \in [\ell]$.

3 Succinct Mercurial Vector Commitments Based on BASIS

In this section, we show how to construct a non-black-box succinct mercurial vector commitment based on $\mathsf{BASIS_{struct}}$ assumption. Then we describe the variants of our constructions that satisfy updatability and aggregatability.

Construction 3.1 (MVC Based on $\mathsf{BASIS_{struct}}$). Let λ be a security parameter and $n = n(\lambda)$, $m = m(\lambda)$, $q = q(\lambda)$ be lattice parameters. Let $m' = n(\lceil \log q \rceil + 1)$, and $\beta = \beta(\lambda)$ be the bound. Let $s_0 = s_0(\lambda)$, $s_1 = s_1(\lambda)$ be Gaussian width parameters. Let l be the vector dimension. The detailed construction is shown as follows.

- $\{\mathsf{pp}, tk\} \leftarrow \mathsf{Setup}(1^\lambda, 1^l)$: Input a security parameter λ and a vector dimension l, it first obtains $(\mathbf{A}, \mathbf{R}) \leftarrow \mathsf{TrapGen}(1^n, q, m)$. Then for each $i \in [\ell]$, it samples an invertible matrix $\mathbf{W}_i \xleftarrow{\$} \mathbb{Z}_q^{n \times n}$. Next, it completes $\mathbf{R}_i = \mathbf{R}\mathbf{G}^{-1}(\mathbf{W}_i^{-1}\mathbf{G}) \in \mathbb{Z}_q^{m \times m'}$ for each $i \in [\ell]$ and constructs $\mathbf{B}_l \in \mathbb{Z}_q^{nl \times (lm+m')}$ and $\tilde{\mathbf{R}} \in \mathbb{Z}_q^{(lm+m') \times lm'}$ as follows:

$$\mathbf{B}_l = \left[\begin{array}{ccc|c} \mathbf{W}_1\mathbf{A} & & & -\mathbf{G} \\ & \ddots & & \vdots \\ & & \mathbf{W}_l\mathbf{A} & -\mathbf{G} \end{array}\right], \qquad \tilde{\mathbf{R}} = \left[\frac{\mathsf{diag}(\mathbf{R}_1, ..., \mathbf{R}_l)}{\mathbf{0}^{m' \times lm'}}\right] \tag{3.1}$$

After that, it samples $\mathbf{T} \leftarrow \mathsf{SampPre}(\mathbf{B}_l, \tilde{\mathbf{R}}, \mathbf{G}_{nl}, s_0)$. It outputs the public parameters $\mathsf{pp} = \{\mathbf{A}, \mathbf{W}_1, ..., \mathbf{W}_l, \mathbf{T}\}$ and the trapdoor key $tk = \tilde{\mathbf{R}}$ optionally.

- $\{(\mathbf{c}, \mathbf{D}), \mathsf{aux}\} \leftarrow \mathsf{Hard\_com}(\mathsf{pp}, \mathbf{x})$: Input the public parameter pp and a message $\mathbf{x} \in \mathbb{Z}_q^l$, it first phases $\mathbf{T}$ as $(\mathbf{T}_1, ..., \mathbf{T}_l, \mathbf{T_G})^\top$ where $\mathbf{T}_i \in \mathbb{Z}_q^{m \times m'l}$ for each $i \in [\ell]$ and $\mathbf{T_G} \in \mathbb{Z}_q^{m' \times m'l}$, then samples $\hat{\mathbf{R}} \xleftarrow{\$} \{0,1\}^{m \times m'}$ and constructs $\mathbf{B}'_l \in \mathbb{Z}_q^{nl \times (l(m+m')+m')}$, $\mathbf{T}' \in \mathbb{Z}_q^{(l(m+m')+m') \times m'l}$ as follows,

$$\mathbf{B}'_l = \left[\begin{array}{ccc|c} [\mathbf{W}_1\mathbf{A}|\mathbf{W}_1\mathbf{A}\hat{\mathbf{R}}] & & & -\mathbf{G} \\ & \ddots & & \vdots \\ & & [\mathbf{W}_l\mathbf{A}|\mathbf{W}_l\mathbf{A}\hat{\mathbf{R}}] & -\mathbf{G} \end{array}\right], \quad \mathbf{T}' = \begin{bmatrix} \mathbf{T}_1 \\ \hline \mathbf{0}^{m' \times m'l} \\ \vdots \\ \mathbf{T}_l \\ \hline \mathbf{0}^{m' \times m'l} \\ \mathbf{T_G} \end{bmatrix}$$

Next, it constructs the target vector $\mathbf{u}$ and uses $\mathbf{T}'$ to sample the preimage as follows,

$$\mathbf{u} = \begin{bmatrix} -x_1\mathbf{W}_1\mathbf{e}_1 \\ \vdots \\ -x_l\mathbf{W}_l\mathbf{e}_1 \end{bmatrix}, \quad \begin{bmatrix} \mathbf{v}_1 \\ \vdots \\ \mathbf{v}_l \\ \hat{\mathbf{c}} \end{bmatrix} \leftarrow \mathsf{SampPre}(\mathbf{B}'_l, \mathbf{T}', \mathbf{u}, s_1) \tag{3.2}$$

where $\mathbf{e}_1 = [1, 0, ..., 0]^\top \in \mathbb{Z}_q^n$ is the first standard basis vector. Last, it computes $\mathbf{c} = \mathbf{G}\hat{\mathbf{c}} \in \mathbb{Z}_q^n$, $\mathbf{D} = \mathbf{A}\hat{\mathbf{R}} \in \mathbb{Z}_q^{n \times m'}$. It outputs the hard commitment $(\mathbf{c}, \mathbf{D})$ and the auxiliary information $\mathsf{aux} = \{\mathbf{x}, \mathbf{v}_1, ..., \mathbf{v}_l, \hat{\mathbf{R}}\}$.
- $\pi_i \leftarrow \mathsf{Hard\_open}(\mathsf{pp}, x_i, i, \mathsf{aux})$: Input the public parameter pp, the message x_i, the index i, and the auxiliary information $\mathsf{aux} = \{\mathbf{x}, \mathbf{v}_1, ..., \mathbf{v}_l, \hat{\mathbf{R}}\}$. It outputs the hard opening $\pi_i = \{\mathbf{v}_i, \hat{\mathbf{R}}\}$.
- $0/1 \leftarrow \mathsf{Hard\_verify}(\mathsf{pp}, x_i, i, (\mathbf{c}, \mathbf{D}), \pi_i)$: Input the public parameter pp, the message x_i, the index i, the hard commitment $(\mathbf{c}, \mathbf{D})$, and the hard opening π_i, check if the following conditions hold to verify the opening.

$$\|\mathbf{v}_i\| \leq \beta, \qquad \mathbf{W}_i^{-1}\mathbf{c} = [\mathbf{A}|\mathbf{D}]\mathbf{v}_i + x_i\mathbf{e}_1 \tag{3.3}$$

$$\|\hat{\mathbf{R}}\| \leq 1, \qquad \mathbf{D} = \mathbf{A}\hat{\mathbf{R}} \tag{3.4}$$

If they all hold, it outputs 1; Otherwise, it outputs 0.
- $\{(\mathbf{c}, \mathbf{D}), \mathsf{aux}\} \leftarrow \mathsf{Soft\_com}(\mathsf{pp})$: Input the public parameter pp, it first samples $\hat{\mathbf{c}} \leftarrow D_{\mathbb{Z}^{m'}, s_1}$ and $\hat{\mathbf{R}} \xleftarrow{\$} \{0,1\}^{m \times m'}$, then computes $\mathbf{c} = \mathbf{G}\hat{\mathbf{c}}$ and $\mathbf{D} = \mathbf{G} - \mathbf{A}\hat{\mathbf{R}}$. It outputs the soft commitment $(\mathbf{c}, \mathbf{D})$ and $\mathsf{aux} = \{\mathbf{c}, \hat{\mathbf{R}}\}$.
- $\tau_i \leftarrow \mathsf{Soft\_open}(\mathsf{pp}, \mathsf{flag}, x, i, \mathsf{aux})$: Input the public parameter pp, the $\mathsf{flag} \in \{\mathsf{hard}, \mathsf{soft}\}$ which indicates that the soft opening τ_i is for hard commitment or soft commitment, the message x, the index i and the auxiliary information aux.

If $\mathsf{flag} = \mathsf{hard}$ and x equals x_i in aux, then it outputs $\mathbf{v}_i$ in aux; Otherwise, it outputs $\perp$.
If $\mathsf{flag} = \mathsf{soft}$, it uses trapdoor $\hat{\mathbf{R}}$ with tag $\mathbf{W}_i$ to sample the preimage as follows,

$$\mathbf{v}_i \leftarrow \mathsf{SampPre}([\mathbf{W}_i\mathbf{A}|\mathbf{W}_i\mathbf{G} - \mathbf{W}_i\mathbf{A}\hat{\mathbf{R}}], \hat{\mathbf{R}}, \mathbf{c} - x_i\mathbf{W}_i\mathbf{e}_1, s_1)$$

and outputs the soft opening $\tau_i = \mathbf{v}_i$.
- $0/1 \leftarrow \mathsf{Soft\_verify}(\mathsf{pp}, x, i, (\mathbf{c}, \mathbf{D}), \tau_i)$: Input the public parameter pp, the commitment pair $(\mathbf{c}, \mathbf{D})$, the message x, the index i, and soft opening τ_i, check if Eq. 3.3 holds. If it holds, it outputs 1; Otherwise, it outputs 0.
- $\{(\mathbf{c}, \mathbf{D}), \mathsf{aux}\} \leftarrow \mathsf{Fake\_com}(\mathsf{pp}, tk)$: Input the public parameter pp and trapdoor key tk. It first samples $\hat{\mathbf{c}} \leftarrow D_{\mathbb{Z}^{m'}, s_1}$, $\hat{\mathbf{R}} \overset{\$}{\leftarrow} \{0,1\}^{m \times m'}$ and then computes $\mathbf{c} = \mathbf{G}\hat{\mathbf{c}}$, $\mathbf{D} = \mathbf{A}\hat{\mathbf{R}}$. It generates the fake commitment pair $(\mathbf{c}, \mathbf{D})$ and the auxiliary information $\mathsf{aux} = \{\mathbf{c}, \hat{\mathbf{R}}\}$.
- $\pi \leftarrow \mathsf{Equiv\_Hopen}(\mathsf{pp}, tk, x, i, \mathsf{aux})$: Input the public parameter pp and trapdoor key tk, the message x_i, the index i, and the auxiliary information aux, it uses $\mathbf{R}_i$ from tk to sample the preimage as follows,

$$\mathbf{v} \leftarrow \mathsf{SampPre}([\mathbf{W}_i\mathbf{A}|\mathbf{W}_i\mathbf{A}\hat{\mathbf{R}}], \mathbf{R}_i, \mathbf{c} - x_i\mathbf{W}_i\mathbf{e}_1, s_1) \tag{3.5}$$

It generates the equivocation hard opening $\pi = \{\mathbf{v}, \hat{\mathbf{R}}\}$.
- $\tau \leftarrow \mathsf{Equiv\_Sopen}(\mathsf{pp}, tk, x_i, i, \mathsf{aux})$: Input the public parameter pp and trapdoor key tk, the message x_i, the index i, and the auxiliary information aux, it computes the Eq. 3.5 to obtain $\mathbf{v}$. It generates the equivocation soft opening $\tau = \mathbf{v}$.

Theorem 3.2 (Correctness). *For $n = \lambda$, $m = O(n \log q)$, $s_0 = O(lm^2 \log(ln))$, $s_1 = O(l^{3/2}m^{3/2} \log(nl) \cdot s_0)$, and $\beta = \sqrt{l(m+m')+m'} \cdot s_1$, then the Construction 3.1 is correct.*

Proof. Suppose polynomial $l = l(\lambda)$, $m \geq m' = O(n \log q)$, for all $\mathbf{x} \in \mathbb{Z}_q^l$ and index $i \in [\ell]$. Let $\{\mathsf{pp}, tk\} \leftarrow \mathsf{Setup}(1^\lambda, 1^l)$ where $\mathsf{pp} = \{\mathbf{A}, \mathbf{W}_1, ..., \mathbf{W}_l, \mathbf{T}\}$. Let $\{(\mathbf{c}, \mathbf{D}), \mathsf{aux}\} \leftarrow \mathsf{Hard\_com}(\mathsf{pp}, \mathbf{x})$ and $\pi_i \leftarrow \mathsf{Hard\_open}(\mathsf{pp}, x_i, i, \mathsf{aux})$. Let $\{(\mathbf{c}, \mathbf{D}), \mathsf{aux}\} \leftarrow \mathsf{Soft\_com}(\mathsf{pp})$ and $\tau_i \leftarrow \mathsf{Soft\_open}(\mathsf{pp}, \mathsf{flag}, x, i, \mathsf{aux})$. Let $\{(\mathbf{c}, \mathbf{D}), \mathsf{aux}\} \leftarrow \mathsf{Fake\_com}(\mathsf{pp}, tk)$, $\pi_i \leftarrow \mathsf{Equiv\_Hopen}(\mathsf{pp}, tk, x, i, \mathsf{aux})$, and $\tau_i \leftarrow \mathsf{Equiv\_Sopen}$ $(\mathsf{pp}, tk, x_i, i, \mathsf{aux})$. Consider $\mathsf{Hard\_verify}(\mathsf{pp}, x_i, i, (\mathbf{c}, \mathbf{D}), \pi_i)$ and $\mathsf{Soft\_verify}(\mathsf{pp}, x, i, (\mathbf{c}, \mathbf{D}), \tau_i)$:

Following the same parameters and constructions of $\mathbf{B}_l$ and $\tilde{\mathbf{R}}$ in $\mathsf{BASIS}_{\mathsf{struct}}$, we have $\|\mathbf{T}\| \leq \sqrt{lm+m'} \cdot s_0$.

By the construction and Lemma 2.2, $\|\mathbf{T}'\| = \|\mathbf{T}\| \leq \sqrt{lm+m'} \cdot s_0$, $\|\hat{\mathbf{R}}\| = 1$ and $\|\mathbf{R}_i\| = 1$. Suppose $s_1 \geq \sqrt{(l(m+m')+m')lm'}\|\mathbf{T}'\| \cdot \omega(\sqrt{\log(nl)}) = O(l^{3/2}m^{3/2}\log(nl) \cdot s_0)$ (opening to hard commitment), $s_1 \geq \sqrt{(m+m')m'}\|\hat{\mathbf{R}}\| \cdot \omega(\sqrt{\log(n)}) = O(m\log(n))$ (opening to soft commitment), and $s_1 \geq \sqrt{(m+m')m'}$ $\|\mathbf{R}_i\| \cdot \omega(\sqrt{\log(n)}) = O(m\log(n))$ (opening to fake commitment). Then, by Theorem 2.5 and Remark 2.6, if the opening $\mathbf{v}_i$ is generated by $\mathsf{Hard\_open}$, $\mathsf{Soft\_open}$ or $\mathsf{Equiv\_Hopen}$, it should satisfy $\mathbf{W}_i^{-1}\mathbf{c} = [\mathbf{A}|\mathbf{D}]\mathbf{v}_i + x_i\mathbf{e}_1$ and $\|\mathbf{v}_i\| \leq \sqrt{l(m+m')+m'} \cdot s_1 \leq \beta$ so the verification algorithm accepts with overwhelming probability. □

Theorem 3.3 (Mercurial Binding). *For any polynomial $l = l(\lambda)$, $n = \lambda$, $m = O(n\log q)$, and $s_0 = O(lm^2\log(nl))$. Under the $\mathsf{BASIS_{struct}}$ assumption with parameters $(n-1, m, q, 2(m+m')\beta, s_0, l)$, Construction 3.1 satisfies mercurial binding.*

Proof. Since our construction is a *proper* mercurial vector commitment in which the hard opening contains its corresponding soft opening as a proper subset. Thus, we only need to consider the hard-soft case. We now define a sequence of hybrid experiments:

- Hyb_0: This is the real mercurial binding experiment:
  - The challenger starts by sampling $(\mathbf{A}, \mathbf{R}) \leftarrow \mathsf{TrapGen}(1^n, q, m)$ $\mathbf{W}_i \xleftarrow{\$} \mathbb{Z}_q^{n\times n}$ for each $i \in [\ell]$. Then it constructs $\tilde{\mathbf{R}}$ and $\mathbf{B}_l$ following the Eq. 3.1. It samples $\mathbf{T} \leftarrow \mathsf{SampPre}(\mathbf{B}_l, \tilde{\mathbf{R}}, \mathbf{G}_{nl}, s_0)$. Last, the challenger sends the public parameters $\mathsf{pp} = \{\mathbf{A}, \mathbf{W}_1, ..., \mathbf{W}_l, \mathbf{T}\}$ to the adversary $\mathcal{A}$.
  - The adversary $\mathcal{A}$ outputs a hard commitment pair $(\mathbf{c}, \mathbf{D})$, an index $i \in [\ell]$ and openings $(x, \mathbf{v}, \hat{\mathbf{R}})$, $(x', \mathbf{v}')$.
  - The output of the experiment is 1 if $x \neq x'$ and satisfy the following conditions:

$$\begin{aligned} \|\mathbf{v}\|, \|\mathbf{v}'\| \leq \beta, \qquad \|\hat{\mathbf{R}}\| \leq 1, \qquad \mathbf{A}\hat{\mathbf{R}} = \mathbf{D} \\ \mathbf{W}_i^{-1}\mathbf{c} = [\mathbf{A}|\mathbf{D}]\mathbf{v} + x\mathbf{e}_1, \qquad \mathbf{W}_i^{-1}\mathbf{c} = [\mathbf{A}|\mathbf{D}]\mathbf{v}' + x'\mathbf{e}_1 \end{aligned} \tag{3.6}$$

- Hyb_1: Same as Hyb_0 except the challenger samples $\mathbf{T} \leftarrow (\mathbf{B}_l)_{s_0}^{-1}(\mathbf{G}_{nl})$ without using the trapdoor $\tilde{\mathbf{R}}$ so the public parameters pp is sampled independently of $\mathbf{R}$.
- Hyb_2: Same as Hyb_1 except the challenger samples $\mathbf{A} \xleftarrow{\$} \mathbb{Z}_q^{n\times m}$.

For an adversary $\mathcal{A}$, we write $\mathsf{Hyb}_i(\mathcal{A})$ to denote the output distribution of execution of experiment Hyb_i with adversary $\mathcal{A}$. We omit the proof of $\mathsf{Hyb}_0(\mathcal{A}) \approx \mathsf{Hyb}_1(\mathcal{A}) \approx \mathsf{Hyb}_2(\mathcal{A})$ because they are given in [28] and same as ours. We now analyze the last step.

Lemma 3.4. *Under the $\mathsf{BASIS_{struct}}$ assumption with parameters $(n-1, m, q, 2(m+m')\beta, s_0, l)$, for all efficient adversary $\mathcal{A}$,* $\Pr[\mathsf{Hyb}_2(\mathcal{A}) = 1] = \mathsf{negl}(\lambda)$.

Proof. Suppose there exists an adversary $\mathcal{A}$ where $\Pr[\mathsf{Hyb}_2(\mathcal{A}) = 1] = \epsilon$ for some non-negligible ϵ. And an algorithm $\mathcal{B}$ will use $\mathcal{A}$ to break the $\mathsf{BASIS_{struct}}$ assumption.

$\mathcal{B}$ first receives the challenge $\mathbf{A} \in \mathbb{Z}_q^{(n-1)\times m}$, $\mathbf{B}_l \in \mathbb{Z}_q^{nl\times(lm+m')}$, $\mathbf{T} \in \mathbb{Z}_q^{(lm+m')\times lm'}$ and $\mathsf{aux} = (\mathbf{W}_1, ..., \mathbf{W}_l)$, then generate the public parameters $\mathsf{pp} = \{\mathbf{A}, \mathbf{W}_1, ..., \mathbf{W}_l, \mathbf{T}\}$ and send it to $\mathcal{A}$. The adversary $\mathcal{A}$ can output a hard commitment $(\mathbf{c}, \mathbf{D})$, a hard opening $(x, \mathbf{v}, \hat{\mathbf{R}})$ and its corresponding soft opening $(x', \mathbf{v}')$ for $x \neq x'$ on some index $i \in [\ell]$, satisfying the Eq. 3.6. Thus, $\|\mathbf{v} - \mathbf{v}'\| \leq 2\beta$ and $[\mathbf{A}|\mathbf{D}](\mathbf{v} - \mathbf{v}') = (x' - x)\mathbf{e}_1$. Since $x \neq x'$, so that $\mathbf{v} - \mathbf{v}' \neq \mathbf{0}$ and we have

$$\begin{bmatrix} \mathbf{a}^\mathsf{T} \\ \mathbf{A} \end{bmatrix} [\mathbf{I}_m|\hat{\mathbf{R}}](\mathbf{v} - \mathbf{v}') = \begin{bmatrix} x' - x \\ \mathbf{0}^{n-1} \end{bmatrix}$$

Let $\mathbf{z} = [\mathbf{I}_m|\hat{\mathbf{R}}](\mathbf{v} - \mathbf{v}')$, since $\mathbf{Az} = \mathbf{0}$ and $\|\mathbf{z}\| \leq 2(m + m')\beta$, $\mathbf{z}$ is a valid solution for $\mathcal{B}$ to break the $\mathsf{BASIS}_{\mathsf{struct}}$ assumption with non-negligible probability. □

By the lemmas in [28] and Lemma 3.4, we can conclude that for all efficient adversaries $\mathcal{A}$, $\Pr[\mathsf{Hyb}_0(\mathcal{A}) = 1] \leq \mathsf{negl}(\lambda)$. Thus, mercurial binding holds. □

Theorem 3.5 (Mercurial Hiding). *For $n = \lambda$, $m = O(n \log q)$, q is prime, $s_0 = O(lm^2 \log(ln))$, $s_1 = O(l^{3/2}m^{3/2} \log(nl) \cdot s_0)$, then Construction 3.1 satisfies statistical Hcom_Hopen Equivocation, Hcom_Sopen Equivocation, and Scom_Sopen Equivocation.*

Proof. The Challenger first sets up the scheme and obtains the public parameter $\mathrm{pp} = \{\mathbf{A}, \mathbf{W}_1, ..., \mathbf{W}_l, \mathbf{T}\}$ via the real protocol, and $tk = \tilde{\mathbf{R}}$ is the trapdoor. Then we prove the mercurial hiding of our proposed construction from the following aspects.

For Hcom_Hopen Equivocation. Firstly, $\mathbf{D}$ and $\mathbf{R}$ are generated in the same way in fake and hard commitments. Then, by Theorem 2.5, the distribution of $\{\mathbf{v}_1, ..., \mathbf{v}_l, \hat{\mathbf{c}}\}$ from $\mathsf{SampPre}(\mathbf{B}_l', \mathbf{T}', \mathbf{u}, s_1)$ is statistically close to the distribution $(\mathbf{B}_l')_{s_1}^{-1}(\mathbf{u})$ which the target vector $\mathbf{u}$ is the same as Eq. 3.2.

Let $\bar{\mathbf{A}} = \mathsf{diag}([\mathbf{W}_1\mathbf{A}|\mathbf{W}_1\mathbf{D}], ..., [\mathbf{W}_l\mathbf{A}|\mathbf{W}_l\mathbf{D}])$, then $\mathbf{B}_l' = [\bar{\mathbf{A}}| - 1^l \otimes \mathbf{G}]$. Since $s_1 \geq \log(l(m + m'))$, by Lemma 2.4, the distribution of $\{\mathbf{v}_1, ..., \mathbf{v}_l, \hat{\mathbf{c}}\} \leftarrow (\mathbf{B}_l')_{s_1}^{-1}(\mathbf{u})$ is statistically close to the distribution

$$\left\{\hat{\mathbf{c}} \leftarrow D_{\mathbb{Z}^{m'}, s_1}, \{\mathbf{v}_1, ..., \mathbf{v}_l\} \leftarrow \bar{\mathbf{A}}_{s_1}^{-1}\left(\mathbf{u} + (1^l \otimes \mathbf{G}\hat{\mathbf{c}})\right)\right\}$$

where $\hat{\mathbf{c}}$ is generated in the same way as fake commitment and each $\mathbf{v}_i$ is distributed to $([\mathbf{W}_i\mathbf{A}|\mathbf{W}_i\mathbf{D}])_{s_1}^{-1}(-x_i\mathbf{W}_i\mathbf{e}_1 + \mathbf{G}\hat{\mathbf{c}})$.

Then extend the trapdoor $\mathbf{R}_i$ to $\mathbf{R}_i'$ by filling in some $\mathbf{0}$. By Theorem 2.5, the distribution of $\mathbf{v}_i \leftarrow ([\mathbf{W}_i\mathbf{A}|\mathbf{W}_i\mathbf{D}])_{s_1}^{-1}(-x_i\mathbf{W}_i\mathbf{e}_1 + \mathbf{G}\hat{\mathbf{c}})$ is statistically close to the distribution of $\mathbf{v}_i \leftarrow \mathsf{SampPre}([\mathbf{W}_i\mathbf{A}|\mathbf{W}_i\mathbf{D}], \mathbf{R}_i', -x_i\mathbf{W}_i\mathbf{e}_1 + \mathbf{G}\hat{\mathbf{c}}, s_1)$ in the hard equivocation (since $s_1 \geq \sqrt{(m + m')m'}\|\mathbf{R}_i'\| \cdot \omega(\sqrt{n}) = O(m \log n)$). This leads to fake commitments and hard equivocation having exactly the same distribution as hard commitments and their corresponding hard openings.

For Hcom_Sopen Equivocation. Follow the same arguments as Hcom_Hopen Equivocation.

For Scom_Sopen Equivocation. We note that $\hat{\mathbf{c}}$ are generated in the same way for both fake and soft commitments. By Lemma 2.3, the distributions of $\mathbf{D}$ in fake commitment and $\mathbf{D}'$ in soft commitments are

$$\left\{\mathbf{D} = \mathbf{A}\hat{\mathbf{R}}|\hat{\mathbf{R}} \xleftarrow{\$} \{0,1\}^{m \times m'}\right\}, \qquad \left\{\mathbf{D}' = \mathbf{G} - \mathbf{A}\hat{\mathbf{R}}'|\hat{\mathbf{R}}' \xleftarrow{\$} \{0,1\}^{m \times m'}\right\}$$

both statistically close to uniform over $\mathbb{Z}_q^{n\times m'}$. Thus, the adversary's view remains statistically the same if we generate $\mathbf{D}$ in fake commitments from $\mathsf{Soft\_com}$ instead of $\mathsf{Fake\_com}$ in the ideal experiment. Moreover, by Theorem 2.5, the distribution of the soft opening $\mathbf{v}_i \leftarrow \mathsf{SampPre}([\mathbf{W}_i\mathbf{A}|\mathbf{W}_i\mathbf{D}'], \hat{\mathbf{R}}', -x_i\mathbf{W}_i\mathbf{e}_1 + \mathbf{G}\hat{\mathbf{c}}, s_1)$ and the distribution of the soft equivocation $\mathbf{v}_i \leftarrow \mathsf{SampPre}([\mathbf{W}_i\mathbf{A}|\mathbf{W}_i\mathbf{D}'], \mathbf{R}_i, -x_i\mathbf{W}_i\mathbf{e}_1 + \mathbf{G}\hat{\mathbf{c}}, s_1)$ are both statistically close to $([\mathbf{W}_i\mathbf{A}|\mathbf{W}_i\mathbf{D}'])_{s_1}^{-1}(-x_i\mathbf{W}_i\mathbf{e}_1 + \mathbf{G}\hat{\mathbf{c}})$. This leads to fake commitments and soft equivocation having exactly the same distribution as soft commitments and their corresponding soft openings. □

Remark 3.6 (Succinctness). In Construction 3.1, for $n = \lambda$, $m = O(n\log q)$, $m' = n(\lceil\log q\rceil + 1) \leq m$, Gaussian parameters $s_0 = O(lm^2\log(nl))$, $s_1 = O(l^{3/2}m^{3/2}\log(nl)\cdot s_0) = O(l^{5/2}m^{7/2}\log^2(nl))$, bound $\beta = \sqrt{l(m+m')+m'}\cdot s_1 = O(l^3n^4\log^2(nl)\log^4 q)$, lattice modulus $q = \beta\cdot\mathsf{poly}(n)$ and $\log q = O(\log\lambda + \log l)$. We have the following parameter sizes:

- Commitment size: A commitment to a vector $\mathbf{x} \in \mathbb{Z}_q^l$ is $(\mathbf{c}, \mathbf{D}) \in \mathbb{Z}_q^n \times \mathbb{Z}_q^{n\times m'}$ where
$$|\mathbf{c}| = O(n\log q) = O(\lambda\cdot(\log\lambda + \log l))$$
$$|\mathbf{D}| = O(nm'\log q) = O(\lambda^2\cdot(\log^2\lambda + \log^2 l))$$
- Opening size: A (hard) opening is $(\mathbf{v}, \hat{\mathbf{R}}) \in \mathbb{Z}_q^{m+m'} \times \mathbb{Z}_q^{m\times m'}$ where
$$|\mathbf{v}| = O((m+m')\log\beta) = O(\lambda\cdot(\log^2\lambda + \log^2 l))$$
$$|\hat{\mathbf{R}}| = O(mm') = O(\lambda^2\cdot(\log^2\lambda + \log^2 l))$$
- Public parameters size: The public parameters are $\mathsf{pp} = \{\mathbf{A}, \mathbf{W}_1, ..., \mathbf{W}_l, \mathbf{T}\}$ where $\mathbf{A} \in \mathbb{Z}_q^{n\times m}$, $\mathbf{W}_i \in \mathbb{Z}_q^{n\times n}$, $\mathbf{T} \in \mathbb{Z}_q^{(lm+m')\times lm'}$ and $|\mathsf{pp}| = l^2\cdot\mathsf{poly}(\lambda, \log l)$.
- Auxiliary information size: An auxiliary information for (hard) commitment is $\mathsf{aux} = \{\mathbf{x}, \mathbf{v}_1, ..., \mathbf{v}_l, \hat{\mathbf{R}}\}$ and $|\mathsf{aux}| = O((\lambda^2 + \lambda l)(\log^2\lambda + \log^2 l))$.

Therefore, Construction 3.1 is a succinct mercurial vector commitment.

3.1 Updatable Mercurial Vector Commitments

In this section, we describe a variant of Construction 3.1 that supports differential update and satisfies updatable mercurial hiding. The concepts of stateless update and differential update are proposed in the vector commitment [25,28] and we *first* extend them to the mercurial vector commitment.

The definition of updatable mercurial vector commitment was proposed by Catalano et al. [8] and we extend their definition to update both hard and soft commitment to all (multiple) indices. Specifically, the original definition of updatable mercurial commitment [21] requires updating both types of commitment to the hard (updated) commitment. But Catalano's definition and constructions only support updating the commitment on a single index which may break the integrity and consistency of the soft commitment, e.g. it should update the soft commitment to the whole vector for one time instead of one index by one. If some index of the soft commitment fails to update, this commitment cannot be interpreted as either a hard commitment or a soft commitment.

As an additional contribution, there exists a stronger property of updatable mercurial commitment first proposed by Catalano et al. [8], named updatable mercurial hiding and updatable hiding. We *first* formalize them in the mercurial vector commitment and show how our construction achieves updatable mercurial hiding and its extension to achieve updatable hiding.

Definition 3.7 (Updatable Mercurial Vector Commitment). An updatable mercurial vector commitment is defined as a mercurial vector commitment in Definition 2.12 with the following algorithms:

- $\{(\mathbf{c}', \mathbf{D}'), \mathsf{aux}', \mathsf{st}\} \leftarrow \mathsf{Update\_com}(\mathsf{pp}, \mathsf{flag}, (\mathbf{c}, \mathbf{D}), \mathsf{aux}, \mathbf{x}, \mathbf{x}')$: This algorithm is run by the committer who produced $(\mathbf{c}, \mathbf{D})$ (and holds aux and flag). It takes old message $\mathbf{x}$, new message $\mathbf{x}'$ as input and outputs an updated commitment $(\mathbf{c}', \mathbf{D}')$, an updated auxiliary information aux' and an statement st. Regardless of the type of $(\mathbf{c}, \mathbf{D})$, the updated commitment $(\mathbf{c}', \mathbf{D}')$ is always a *hard commitment.*
- $U_i \leftarrow \mathsf{Update\_open}(\mathsf{pp}, \mathsf{st}, i)$: This algorithm is run by the committer who holds a statement st. Given the index i, it outputs the update information for the user who holds the opening of index i.
- $\{(\mathbf{c}', \mathbf{D}'), \pi_i'\} \leftarrow \mathsf{User\_update}(\mathsf{pp}, (\mathbf{c}, \mathbf{D}), i, \pi_i, U_i)$: This algorithm is run by the users who hold the old commitment $(\mathbf{c}, \mathbf{D})$ and the old opening π_i at index i. Given the update information U_i, it outputs the updated commitment $(\mathbf{c}', \mathbf{D}')$ and the updated opening π_i which will be valid w.r.t $(\mathbf{c}', \mathbf{D}')$ and x_i'. The updated opening π_i' will be of the *same type* of π_i.

The correctness of the updatable mercurial vector commitment is described above. The mercurial binding is defined as usual, namely for any efficient adversary it is computationally infeasible to open a commitment (even an updated one) to two different messages at the same index. The mercurial hiding of the updatable mercurial vector commitment needs not only to satisfy the old commitment but also the updated one, namely even the adversary can see the update information[1,2].

To achieve *global update*, i.e. each user can directly update their holding commitments and openings with the update information, the committer can broadcast all update information $\{U_i\}_{i\in[\ell]}$.

Remark 3.8 (Stateless Updatable MVC). If $\mathsf{Update\_com}$ can be implemented via $\mathsf{Update\_com}(\mathsf{pp}, (\mathbf{c}, \mathbf{D}), \mathsf{aux}, \{x_i, x_i'\}_{i\in[d]})$, the MVC is stateless updatable. Assuming that aux does not consist of vector $\mathbf{x}$, with the same outputs of

[1] We observe that the user can learn the type of the updated commitment which may relax the zero-knowledge property in ZK-EDB. This issue has been fully discussed in [8,21] and this paper will not follow it.

[2] Note that since an updated commitment is always a hard commitment, we are interested only in $\mathsf{Hcom\_Hopen\ Equivocation}$ and $\mathsf{Hcom\_Sopen\ Equivocation}$ for the updated commitment.

the original algorithm and the only difference is the inputs only involve the old and new i-th entries x_i, x_i' of the vector $\mathbf{x}$ instead of all entries of $\mathbf{x}$.

Remark 3.9 (Differentially Updatable MVC). If $\mathsf{Update\_com}$ can be implemented via $\mathsf{Update\_com}(\mathsf{pp}, (\mathbf{c}, \mathbf{D}), \mathsf{aux}, \bar{\mathbf{x}})$, the MVC is differentially updatable. Assuming that aux does not consist of vector $\mathbf{x}$, with the same outputs of the original algorithm and the only difference is the inputs only involve the difference between old and new vector $\bar{\mathbf{x}} = \mathbf{x}' - \mathbf{x}$ instead of all entries of $\mathbf{x}$.

There also exist *more powerful* security properties for the updatable mercurial commitment, named updatable mercurial hiding and updatable hiding introduced by Catalano et al. [8]. Informally, their aims are to guarantee that the message of the old commitment is still hidden even with the update information, i.e. Updatable mercurial hiding requires after the update, the type of *old* commitment is hidden; Updatable hiding says that the adversary cannot extract any information from both the *old* commitment and the updated commitment even given the update information. Although these properties can not make the updatable ZK-EDB more secure[3], Catalano et al. still think they are an important property for the updatable mercurial commitment. We start by showing the definition of updatable mercurial hiding:

Definition 3.10 (Updatable Mercurial Hiding). Given the public parameter pp, for any $\mathbf{x}$ and $\mathbf{x}'$, and an index i, no PPT adversary can distinguish between hard commitment with its soft commitment and soft commitment with its soft commitment even after the commitment is updated and given the updated commitment and update information. We first define the additional equivocation algorithms for updating:

- $\{(\mathbf{c}', \mathbf{D}'), \mathsf{st}\} \leftarrow \mathsf{Equiv\_Ucom}(\mathsf{pp}, tk, (\mathbf{c}, \mathbf{D}))$: This algorithm is run by the challenger who holds trapdoor key tk and produces $(\mathbf{c}, \mathbf{D})$ and aux. It outputs a *fake updated commitment* $(\mathbf{c}', \mathbf{D}')$, and a statement st.
- $\{U_i, \mathsf{aux}'\} \leftarrow \mathsf{Equiv\_Uopen}(\mathsf{pp}, tk, (\mathbf{c}, \mathbf{D}), i, x_i', \mathsf{aux}, \mathsf{st})$: This algorithm is run by the challenger who holds trapdoor key tk. It takes the old commitment $(\mathbf{c}, \mathbf{D})$, the index i, the updated message x_i', the auxiliary information aux, and the statement st as input and outputs the *fake update information* U_i and the updated auxiliary information aux'.

Then, we slightly modify the *equivocation games* for updatable mercurial vector commitment and omit $\mathsf{Hcom\_Sopen}$ to simply.

- $\mathsf{Hcom\_Hopen}$ Equivocation: $\mathcal{A}$ picks a vector $\mathbf{x} = (x_1, ..., x_l)$ and an index $i \in [\ell]$. In the real game, $\mathcal{A}$ will receive the hard commitment $\mathbf{c}, \mathbf{D} = \mathsf{Hard\_com}(\mathsf{pp}, \mathbf{x})$ and the hard opening $\pi_i = \mathsf{Hard\_open}\ (\mathsf{pp}, x_i, i, \mathsf{aux})$, then $\mathcal{A}$ picks a vector $\mathbf{x}'$ to update. And $\mathcal{A}$ will receive the updated commitment $(\mathbf{c}', \mathbf{D}') = \mathsf{Update\_com}(\mathsf{pp}, \mathsf{hard}, (\mathbf{c}, \mathbf{D}), \mathsf{aux}, \mathbf{x}, \mathbf{x}')$, update information

[3] For the structure of building the updatable ZK-EDB [21], the committed messages are the commitments itself.

$U_i = \mathsf{Update\_open}(\mathsf{pp}, \mathsf{st}, i)$ and obtain the updated opening $\pi'_i = \mathsf{User\_update}$ $(\mathsf{pp}, (\mathbf{c}, \mathbf{D}), i, \pi_i, U_i)$. While in the ideal game, $\mathcal{A}$ will obtain the fake commitment $(\mathbf{c}, \mathbf{D}) = \mathsf{Fake\_com}(\mathsf{pp}, tk)$ and the hard equivocation $\pi_i = \mathsf{Equiv\_Hopen}$ $(\mathsf{pp}, tk, x_i, i, \mathsf{aux})$, then $\mathcal{A}$ picks a vector $\mathbf{x}'$ to update, then $\mathcal{A}$ will receive the fake updated commitment $(\mathbf{c}', \mathbf{D}') = \mathsf{Equiv\_Ucom}(\mathsf{pp}, (\mathbf{c}, \mathbf{D}), tk)$ and fake update information $U_i = \mathsf{Equiv\_Uopen}(\mathsf{pp}, tk, (\mathbf{c}, \mathbf{D}), i, x'_i, \mathsf{aux}, \mathsf{st})$ and obtain the updated opening $\pi'_i = \mathsf{User\_update}(\mathsf{pp}, (\mathbf{c}, \mathbf{D}), i, \pi_i, U_i)$.
- Scom_Sopen Equivocation: In the real game, $\mathcal{A}$ will get the soft commitment $(\mathbf{c}, \mathbf{D}) = \mathsf{Soft\_com}(\mathsf{pp})$ and choose x_i for some index $i \in [\ell]$, then receive the soft opening $\pi_i = \mathsf{Soft\_open}$ $(\mathsf{pp}, \mathsf{soft}, x_i, i, \mathsf{aux})$. After that $\mathcal{A}$ picks a vector $\mathbf{x}'$ to update, then $\mathcal{A}$ will receive the updated commitment $(\mathbf{c}', \mathbf{D}') = \mathsf{Update\_com}(\mathsf{pp}, \mathsf{hard}, (\mathbf{c}, \mathbf{D}), \mathsf{aux}, \mathbf{x}, \mathbf{x}')$, update information $U_i = \mathsf{Update\_open}(\mathsf{pp}, \mathsf{st}, i)$ and obtain the updated opening $\pi'_i =$ $\mathsf{User\_update}$ $(\mathsf{pp}, (\mathbf{c}, \mathbf{D}), i, \pi_i, U_i)$. While in the ideal game, $\mathcal{A}$ first obtains $(\mathbf{c}, \mathbf{D}) = \mathsf{Fake\_com}$ (pp, tk), and chooses x_i for some index $i \in [\ell]$, then receives $\pi_i = \mathsf{Equiv\_Sopen}$ $(\mathsf{pp}, tk, x_i, i, \mathsf{aux})$. After that, $\mathcal{A}$ picks a vector $\mathbf{x}'$ to update, then $\mathcal{A}$ will receive the fake updated commitment $(\mathbf{c}', \mathbf{D}') = \mathsf{Equiv\_Ucom}(\mathsf{pp}, (\mathbf{c}, \mathbf{D}), tk)$ and fake update information $U_i =$ $\mathsf{Equiv\_Uopen}(\mathsf{pp}, tk, (\mathbf{c}, \mathbf{D}), i, x'_i, \mathsf{aux}, \mathsf{st})$ and obtain the updated opening $\pi'_i =$ $\mathsf{User\_update}(\mathsf{pp}, (\mathbf{c}, \mathbf{D}), i, \pi_i, U_i)$.

We show how to construct a differentially updatable mercurial vector commitment from Construction 3.1 which satisfies updatable mercurial hiding.

Construction 3.11 (Differentially Updatable MVC Based on $\mathsf{BASIS_{struct}}$). Let λ be a security parameter and $n = n(\lambda)$, $m = m(\lambda)$, and $q = q(\lambda)$ be lattice parameters. Let $m' = n(\lceil \log q \rceil + 1)$, and $\beta = \beta(\lambda)$ be the bound. Let $s_0 = s_0(\lambda)$, $s_1 = s_1(\lambda)$ be Gaussian width parameters. Let l be the vector dimension. Let $\bar{\mathbf{x}} = \mathbf{x}' - \mathbf{x}$ which $\mathbf{x}'$ is the update vector and $\mathbf{x}$ is the old vector. We only present Update_com, Update_open algorithms below, and the other algorithms are the same in Construction 3.1.

- $\{(\mathbf{c}', \mathbf{D}'), \mathsf{aux}', \mathsf{st}\} \leftarrow \mathsf{Update\_com}(\mathsf{pp}, \mathsf{flag}, (\mathbf{c}, \mathbf{D}), \mathsf{aux}, \bar{\mathbf{x}})$: Input the public parameters $\mathsf{pp} = \{\mathbf{A}, \mathbf{W}_1, ..., \mathbf{W}_l, \mathbf{T}\}$, if $\mathsf{flag} = \mathsf{hard}$ that implies $(\mathbf{c}, \mathbf{D})$ is a hard commitment which $\mathbf{c} = \mathbf{G}\hat{\mathbf{c}}$ and $\mathbf{D} = \mathbf{A}\hat{\mathbf{R}}$, the auxiliary information $\mathsf{aux} = (\{\mathbf{v}_i\}_{i \in [\ell]}, \hat{\mathbf{R}})$, $\bar{\mathbf{x}} = \mathbf{x}' - \mathbf{x} = (\bar{x}_1, ..., \bar{x}_l) \in \mathbb{Z}_q^l$;
  If $\mathsf{flag} = \mathsf{soft}$ and $(\mathbf{c}, \mathbf{D})$ is a soft commitment which $\mathbf{c} = \mathbf{G}\hat{\mathbf{c}}$ and $\mathbf{D} = \mathbf{G} - \mathbf{A}\hat{\mathbf{R}}$. And the auxiliary information $\mathsf{aux} = \{\mathbf{c}, \hat{\mathbf{R}}, \{x_i, \mathbf{v}_i\}_{i \in S}\}$ means that the soft commitment $(\mathbf{c}, \mathbf{D})$ has been opened to some message x_i at some indices $i \in S$ ($|S|$ can be 0 which means the commitment have not been opened). Let $\bar{x}_i = x'_i - x_i$ for $i \in S$ and $\bar{x}_i = x'_i - x_i$ where $x_i \xleftarrow{\$} \mathbb{Z}_q$ for $i \in [\ell]/S$. Then, it samples other $\mathbf{v}_i$ for $i \in [\ell]/S$ via $\mathsf{SampPre}([\mathbf{W}_i\mathbf{A}|\mathbf{W}_i\mathbf{G} - \mathbf{W}_i\mathbf{A}\hat{\mathbf{R}}], \hat{\mathbf{R}}, \mathbf{c} - x_i\mathbf{W}_i\mathbf{e}_1, s_1)$.
  For both situation, it samples $\hat{\mathbf{R}}' \xleftarrow{\$} \{0,1\}^{m \times m'}$, phases $\mathbf{v}_i = [\mathbf{v}_{i,1} \in \mathbb{Z}_q^m | \mathbf{v}_{i,2} \in \mathbb{Z}_q^{m'}]^\mathsf{T}$ for $i \in [\ell]$ and constructs the target vector $\bar{\mathbf{u}} \in \mathbb{Z}_q^{nl}$, $\bar{\mathbf{B}}'_l \in \mathbb{Z}_q^{nl \times (l(m+m')+m')}$, $\mathbf{T}' \in \mathbb{Z}_q^{(l(m+m')+m') \times m'l}$ as follows,

$$\bar{\mathbf{u}} = \begin{bmatrix} -\bar{x}_1\mathbf{W}_1\mathbf{e}_1 + \mathbf{W}_1\mathbf{D}\cdot\mathbf{v}_{1,2} - \mathbf{W}_1\mathbf{A}\hat{\mathbf{R}}'\cdot\mathbf{v}_{1,2} \\ \vdots \\ -\bar{x}_l\mathbf{W}_l\mathbf{e}_l + \mathbf{W}_l\mathbf{D}\cdot\mathbf{v}_{l,2} - \mathbf{W}_l\mathbf{A}\hat{\mathbf{R}}'\cdot\mathbf{v}_{l,2} \end{bmatrix} \tag{3.7}$$

$$\bar{\mathbf{B}}_l' = \left[\begin{array}{ccc|c} [\mathbf{W}_1\mathbf{A}_1|\mathbf{W}_1\mathbf{A}_1\hat{\mathbf{R}}'] & & & -\mathbf{G} \\ & \ddots & & \vdots \\ & & [\mathbf{W}_l\mathbf{A}_l|\mathbf{W}_l\mathbf{A}_l\hat{\mathbf{R}}'] & -\mathbf{G} \end{array}\right], \quad \mathbf{T}' = \begin{bmatrix} \frac{\mathbf{T}_1}{\mathbf{0}^{m'\times m'l}} \\ \vdots \\ \frac{\mathbf{T}_l}{\mathbf{0}^{m'\times m'l}} \\ \mathbf{T}_{\mathbf{G}} \end{bmatrix} \tag{3.8}$$

then, uses $\mathbf{T}'$ to sample the preimage as $[\bar{\mathbf{v}}_1, ..., \bar{\mathbf{v}}_l, \bar{\hat{\mathbf{c}}}]^\mathsf{T} \leftarrow \mathsf{SampPre}(\bar{\mathbf{B}}_l', \mathbf{T}', \bar{\mathbf{u}}, s_1)$. Last, it computes $\bar{\mathbf{c}} = \mathbf{G}\bar{\hat{\mathbf{c}}}$, $\mathbf{c}' = \mathbf{c} + \bar{\mathbf{c}}$, $\mathbf{D}' = \mathbf{A}\hat{\mathbf{R}}'$ and $\mathbf{v}_i' = \mathbf{v}_i + \bar{\mathbf{v}}_i$ for all $i \in [\ell]$. It outputs the updated hard commitment $(\mathbf{c}', \mathbf{D}')$, the updated auxiliary information (*updated opening*) $\mathsf{aux}' = (\{\mathbf{v}_i'\}_{i\in[\ell]}, \hat{\mathbf{R}}')$ and the statement $\mathsf{st} = \{\{\bar{\mathbf{v}}_i\}_{i\in[\ell]}, \hat{\mathbf{R}}', \bar{\mathbf{c}}, \mathbf{D}'\}$.

- $U_i \leftarrow \mathsf{Update\_open}(\mathsf{st}, i)$: Input the statement $\mathsf{st} = \{\{\bar{\mathbf{v}}_i\}_{i\in[\ell]}, \hat{\mathbf{R}}', \bar{\mathbf{c}}, \mathbf{D}'\}$ and index $i \in [\ell]$, it outputs $U_i = \{\bar{\mathbf{c}}, \hat{\mathbf{R}}', \bar{\mathbf{v}}_i, \mathbf{D}'\}$.
- $\{\pi_i', (\mathbf{c}', \mathbf{D}')\} \leftarrow \mathsf{User\_update}(\mathsf{pp}, (\mathbf{c}, \mathbf{D}), \pi_i, i, U_i)$: Input the public parameters $\mathsf{pp} = \{\mathbf{A}, \mathbf{W}_1, ..., \mathbf{W}_l, \mathbf{T}\}$, the old commitment $(\mathbf{c}, \mathbf{D})$, the opening π_i, the index $i \in [\ell]$, and the update information $U_i = \{\bar{\mathbf{v}}_i, \hat{\mathbf{R}}', \bar{\mathbf{c}}, \mathbf{D}'\}$. It computes $\mathbf{c}' = \mathbf{c} + \bar{\mathbf{c}}$, and $\mathbf{v}_i' = \mathbf{v}_i + \bar{\mathbf{v}}_i$. Last it outputs the updated commitment $(\mathbf{c}', \mathbf{D}')$ and the updated hard opening $\pi' = \{\mathbf{v}_i', \hat{\mathbf{R}}'\}$ if π is a hard opening or the updated soft opening $\pi' = \mathbf{v}_i'$ if π is a soft opening.
- $\{(\mathbf{c}', \mathbf{D}'), \mathsf{st}\} \leftarrow \mathsf{Equiv\_Ucom}(\mathsf{pp}, tk, (\mathbf{c}, \mathbf{D}))$: Input the public parameters $\mathsf{pp} = \{\mathbf{A}, \mathbf{W}_1, ..., \mathbf{W}_l, \mathbf{T}\}$ and trapdoor key tk, and the old commitment $(\mathbf{c}, \mathbf{D})$, it first samples $\bar{\hat{\mathbf{c}}} \leftarrow D_{\mathbb{Z}^{m'}, s_1}$, $\hat{\mathbf{R}}_i' \xleftarrow{\$} \{0,1\}^{m\times m'}$, then computes $\bar{\mathbf{c}} = \mathbf{G}\bar{\hat{\mathbf{c}}}$, $\mathbf{c}' = \mathbf{c} + \bar{\mathbf{c}}$ and $\mathbf{D}' = \mathbf{A}\hat{\mathbf{R}}'$. Finally, it outputs the *fake updated commitment* $(\mathbf{c}', \mathbf{D}')$ and the statement $\mathsf{st} = \{\bar{\mathbf{c}}, \mathbf{c}', \mathbf{D}', \hat{\mathbf{R}}'\}$.
- $\{U_i, \mathsf{aux}'\} \leftarrow \mathsf{Equiv\_Uopen}(\mathsf{pp}, tk, i, x_i', \mathsf{aux}, \mathsf{st})$: Input the public parameters $\mathsf{pp} = \{\mathbf{A}_1, ..., \mathbf{A}_l, \mathbf{T}\}$, the trapdoor key tk, the index i, the updated message x_i', the old commitment $(\mathbf{c}, \mathbf{D})$, the auxiliary information $\mathsf{aux} = \{\mathbf{c}, \hat{\mathbf{R}}, \{x_j, \mathbf{v}_j\}_{j\in S}\}$ which the fake commitment has been opened to some message x_j at some indexes $j \in S$ $(0 \le |S| \le l)$, and the statement $\mathsf{st} = \{\bar{\mathbf{c}}, \mathbf{c}', \mathbf{D}', \hat{\mathbf{R}}'\}$. If $i \in [\ell]/S$, it first samples $\mathbf{v}_i \leftarrow D_{\mathbb{Z}^{m+m'}, s_1}$ and then constructs the target vector as

$$\mathbf{u}_i = \mathbf{W}_i\mathbf{c}' - x_i'\mathbf{W}_i\mathbf{e}_1 - [\mathbf{W}_i\mathbf{A}_i|\mathbf{W}_i\mathbf{A}_i\hat{\mathbf{R}}']\mathbf{v}_i$$

and then phases $\mathbf{R}_i$ from tk to sample the preimage as $\bar{\mathbf{v}}_i = \mathsf{SampPre}([\mathbf{W}_i\mathbf{A}_i|\mathbf{W}_i\mathbf{A}_i\mathbf{R}'], \mathbf{R}_i, \mathbf{u}_i, s_1)$. Next, it computes $\mathbf{v}_i' = \bar{\mathbf{v}}_i + \mathbf{v}_i$. Finally, it outputs the update information $U_i = \{\bar{\mathbf{c}}, \hat{\mathbf{R}}', \bar{\mathbf{v}}_i, \mathbf{D}'\}$ and the updated auxiliary information $\mathsf{aux}' = \{\mathbf{v}_i', \hat{\mathbf{R}}'\}$.

Theorem 3.12 (Correctness). *For* $n = \lambda$, $m = O(n \log q)$, $s_0 = O(lm^2 \log(ln))$, $s_1 = O(l^{3/2} m^{3/2} \log(nl) \cdot s_0)$, *and* $\beta = \sqrt{l(m+m') + m'} \cdot s_1$, *then Construction 3.11 is correct.*

Proof. We only show the correctness of $\mathsf{Update\_com}$, $\mathsf{Update\_open}$ and $\mathsf{User\_update}$. Suppose polynomial $l = l(\lambda)$, $\mathbf{x} \in \mathbb{Z}_q^l$, $m \geq m' = O(n \log q)$, for all $\mathbf{x} \in \mathbb{Z}_q^l$ and index $i \in [\ell]$. Let $\{\mathsf{pp}, tk\} \leftarrow \mathsf{Setup}(1^\lambda, 1^l)$ where $\mathsf{pp} = \{\mathbf{A}, \mathbf{W}_1, ..., \mathbf{W}_l, \mathbf{T}\}$. Let $\{(\mathbf{c}, \mathbf{D}), \mathsf{aux}\} \leftarrow \mathsf{Hard\_com}(\mathsf{pp}, \mathbf{x})$ and $\pi_i \leftarrow \mathsf{Hard\_open}(\mathsf{pp}, x_i, i, \mathsf{aux})$. Let $\{(\mathbf{c}, \mathbf{D}), \mathsf{aux}\} \leftarrow \mathsf{Soft\_com}(\mathsf{pp})$ and $\tau_i \leftarrow \mathsf{Soft\_open}(\mathsf{pp}, \mathsf{flag}, x, i, \mathsf{aux})$. Let $\{(\mathbf{c}, \mathbf{D}), \ \mathsf{aux}\} \leftarrow \mathsf{Fake\_com}(\mathsf{pp}, tk)$, $\pi_i \leftarrow \mathsf{Equiv\_Hopen}(\mathsf{pp}, tk, x, i, \mathsf{aux})$, and $\tau_i \leftarrow \mathsf{Equiv\_Sopen}$ $(\mathsf{pp}, tk, x_i, i, \mathsf{aux})$. Let $\{(\mathbf{c}', \mathbf{D}'), \mathsf{aux}', \mathsf{st}\} \leftarrow \mathsf{Update\_com}(\mathsf{pp}, \mathsf{flag}, (\mathbf{c}, \mathbf{D}), \mathsf{aux}, \bar{\mathbf{x}})$ and $U_i \leftarrow \mathsf{Update\_open}(\mathsf{st}, i)$. Let $\{(\mathbf{c}', \mathbf{D}'), \mathsf{st}\} \leftarrow \mathsf{Equiv\_Ucom}(\mathsf{pp}, tk, (\mathbf{c}, \mathbf{D}))$ and $\{U_i, \mathsf{aux}'\} \leftarrow \mathsf{Equiv\_Uopen}(\mathsf{pp}, tk, i, x_i', \mathsf{aux}, \mathsf{st})$. Let $\{\pi_i', (\mathbf{c}', \mathbf{D}')\} \leftarrow \mathsf{User\_update}$ $(\mathsf{pp}, (\mathbf{c}, \mathbf{D}), \pi_i, i, U_i)$. Consider $\mathsf{Hard\_verify}(\mathsf{pp}, x_i, i, (\mathbf{c}', \mathbf{D}'), \pi_i')$:

By Theorem 3.2, for old commitment $(\mathbf{c} = \mathbf{G}\hat{\mathbf{c}}, \mathbf{D})$, for all $i \in [\ell]$, we phase $\mathbf{v}_i = [\mathbf{v}_{i,1} | \mathbf{v}_{i,2}]^\mathsf{T}$ and have

$$\mathbf{W}_i^{-1}\mathbf{G}\hat{\mathbf{c}} - x_i \mathbf{e}_1 = \mathbf{A}\mathbf{v}_{i,1} + \mathbf{D} \cdot \mathbf{v}_{i,2}, \qquad \|\mathbf{v}_i\| \leq \beta \tag{3.9}$$

Suppose $s_1 \geq \sqrt{(l(m+m') + m')lm'} \|\mathbf{T}'\| \cdot \omega(\sqrt{\log(nl)})$, by Theorem 2.5 and invertible matrix $\mathbf{W}_i$, we have

$$\mathbf{W}_i^{-1}\mathbf{G}\bar{\hat{\mathbf{c}}} - \bar{x}_i \mathbf{e}_1 + \mathbf{D} \cdot \mathbf{v}_{i,2} - \mathbf{A}\hat{\mathbf{R}}' \cdot \mathbf{v}_{i,2} = [\mathbf{A} | \mathbf{A}\hat{\mathbf{R}}'] \bar{\mathbf{v}}_i, \quad \|\bar{\mathbf{v}}_i\| \leq \beta \tag{3.10}$$

For $\mathbf{G}\hat{\mathbf{c}}' = \mathbf{G}(\bar{\hat{\mathbf{c}}} + \hat{\mathbf{c}})$, $x_i' = \bar{x}_i + x_i$, $\mathbf{v}_i' = \bar{\mathbf{v}}_i + \mathbf{v}_i$, we add Eq. 3.9 and Eq. 3.10 as

$$\mathbf{W}_i^{-1}\mathbf{G}\hat{\mathbf{c}}' - x_i' \mathbf{e}_1 = \mathbf{A}\mathbf{v}_{i,1} + \mathbf{A}\hat{\mathbf{R}}' \cdot \mathbf{v}_{i,2} + [\mathbf{A} | \mathbf{A}\hat{\mathbf{R}}'] \bar{\mathbf{v}}_i = [\mathbf{A} | \mathbf{A}\hat{\mathbf{R}}'] \mathbf{v}_i'$$

where $\|\mathbf{v}_i'\| \leq 2\beta$. Therefore the verification will accept the update hard commitment and its hard (soft) opening if we set the norm bound on the opening to $k\beta$, which can support up to k updates. Besides, similar to [28], we can set the norm bound and the modulus to be super-polynomial to support an arbitrary polynomial number of updates. □

Theorem 3.13 (Mercurial Binding). *For any polynomial* $l = l(\lambda)$, $n = \lambda$, $m = O(n \log q)$, q *is prime and* $s_0 = O(lm^2 \log(nl))$, $s_1 = O(l^{3/2} m^{3/2} \log(nl) \cdot s_0)$. *Under the* $\mathsf{BASIS_{struct}}$ *assumption with parameters* $(n-1, m, q, 2k(m+m')\beta, s_0, l)$, *the Construction 3.11 is mercurial binding.*

Proof (Sketch). We briefly show that the updated commitment and opening satisfy mercurial binding. The proof of the mercurial binding is basically the same as Theorem 3.3. Namely, given the public parameter pp, if the adversary $\mathcal{A}$ can generate a hard (updated) commitment $(\mathbf{c}, \mathbf{D})$ and two valid (updated) openings $(\mathbf{v}_i, x_i, \hat{\mathbf{R}})$, $(\mathbf{v}_i', x_i')$ at same index i to different message which $x_i \neq x_i'$. Then there exist an algorithm $\mathcal{B}$ can use $\|[\mathbf{I}_m | \hat{\mathbf{R}}](\mathbf{v} - \mathbf{v}')\| \leq 2k(m+m')\beta$ as a solution to break the $\mathsf{BASIS_{struct}}$. □

Theorem 3.14 (Updatable Mercurial Hiding). *For $n = \lambda$, $m = O(n \log q)$, q is prime, $s_0 = O(lm^2 \log(ln))$, $s_1 = O(l^{3/2} m^{3/2} \log(nl) \cdot s_0)$, then Construction 3.11 satisfies statistical Hcom_Hopen Equivocation, Hcom_Sopen Equivocation, and Scom_Sopen Equivocation.*

Proof. The Challenger first sets up the scheme and obtains the public parameter $\mathsf{pp} = \{\mathbf{A}, \mathbf{W}_1, ..., \mathbf{W}_l, \mathbf{T}\}$ via the real protocol, and $tk = \tilde{\mathbf{R}} = \mathsf{diag}(\mathbf{R}_1, ..., \mathbf{R}_l)$ is the trapdoor key. Then we prove the updatable mercurial hiding of the construction from the following aspects.

For Hcom_Hopen Equivocation. For any message vector $\mathbf{x}$ and $\mathbf{x}'$, we show that the distribution of fake commitments, hard equivocations, updated fake commitments, and update information is statistically close to that of hard commitments, hard openings, updated commitments, and update information.

Firstly, by Theorem 3.5, we can know that the distribution of fake commitments and hard equivocations is statistically close to the distribution of hard commitments $(\mathbf{c}, \mathbf{D})$ and hard openings $\mathbf{v}$. Then, note that $\hat{\mathbf{R}}$ and $\mathbf{D}$ are generated in the same way in both updated commitments and fake updated commitments. By Theorem 2.5, the distribution of the rest of the update information and updated hard commitment $\{\bar{\mathbf{v}}_1, ..., \bar{\mathbf{v}}_l, \bar{\mathbf{c}}\}$ from $\mathsf{SampPre}$ $(\bar{\mathbf{B}}_l', \mathbf{T}', \bar{\mathbf{u}}, s_1)$ in Eq. 3.7 is statistically close to the distribution $(\bar{\mathbf{B}}_l')_{s_1}^{-1}(\bar{\mathbf{u}})$.

Let $\bar{\mathbf{A}} = \mathsf{diag}([\mathbf{W}_1\mathbf{A}_1|\mathbf{W}_1\mathbf{D}'], ..., [\mathbf{W}_l\mathbf{A}|\mathbf{W}_l\mathbf{D}'])$, then $\bar{\mathbf{B}}_l' = [\bar{\mathbf{A}}| - 1^l \otimes \mathbf{G}]$. Since $s_1 \geq \log(l(m+m'))$, by Lemma 2.4, the distribution of $\{\bar{\mathbf{v}}_1, ..., \bar{\mathbf{v}}_l, \bar{\mathbf{c}}\} \leftarrow (\bar{\mathbf{B}}_l')_{s_1}^{-1}(\mathbf{u})$ is statistically close to the distribution

$$\left\{\bar{\mathbf{c}} \leftarrow D_{\mathbb{Z}^{m'}, s_1}, \{\bar{\mathbf{v}}_1, ..., \bar{\mathbf{v}}_l\} \leftarrow \bar{\mathbf{A}}_{s_1}^{-1}\left(\bar{\mathbf{u}} + 1^l \otimes \mathbf{G}\bar{\mathbf{c}}\right)\right\}$$

which $\bar{\mathbf{c}}$ is the same as fake updated commitment.

Since $\bar{\mathbf{A}} = \mathsf{diag}([\mathbf{W}_1\mathbf{A}_1|\mathbf{W}_1\mathbf{D}'], ..., [\mathbf{W}_l\mathbf{A}|\mathbf{W}_l\mathbf{D}'])$, this leads to that each $\bar{\mathbf{v}}_i$ is distributed to $([\mathbf{A}_i|\mathbf{D}_i'])_{s_1}^{-1}(\bar{\mathbf{u}}_i + \mathbf{G}\bar{\mathbf{c}})$. For $\bar{\mathbf{u}}_i$ is the same in Eq. 3.7, $\mathbf{c}' = \mathbf{G}\hat{\mathbf{c}} + \mathbf{G}\bar{\mathbf{c}}$ and Eq. 3.9 holds in the hard commitment, we have $\mathbf{u}_i$ in fake updated commitment

$$\bar{\mathbf{u}}_i + \mathbf{G}\bar{\mathbf{c}} = \mathbf{u}_i = \mathbf{c}' - x_i'\mathbf{e}_1 - [\mathbf{A}_i|\mathbf{A}_i\hat{\mathbf{R}}_i']\mathbf{v}_i$$

And thanks to Theorem 2.5, the distribution of $([\mathbf{A}_i|\mathbf{D}_i'])_{s_1}^{-1}(\bar{\mathbf{u}}_i + \mathbf{G}\bar{\mathbf{c}})$ is statistically close to the distribution of $\bar{\mathbf{v}}_i \leftarrow \mathsf{SampPre}([\mathbf{A}_i|\mathbf{D}_i'], \mathbf{R}_i, \mathbf{u}_i, s_1)$ in the fake updated information. This leads to fake updated commitments and fake update information having exactly the same distribution as updated commitments and update information.

For Hcom_Sopen Equivocation. Follow the same arguments as Hcom_ Hopen Equivocation.

For Scom_Sopen Equivocation. For any message vector $\mathbf{x}$ and $\mathbf{x}'$, we show that the distribution of fake commitments, soft equivocations, updated fake commitments, and update information is statistically close to that of soft commitments, soft openings, updated commitments, and update information.

The proof is nearly identical to that of the proof of Hcom_Hopen Equivocation. By Theorem 3.5, we can know that the distribution of fake commitments and soft equivocations is statistically close to the distribution of soft commitments $(\mathbf{c}, \mathbf{D})$ and soft openings $\mathbf{v}$. After that, the steps of updating for the soft commitment are the same as the hard commitment. Therefore, the distribution of fake updated commitments and fake update information is statistically close to the distribution of updated commitments and update information. □

Remark 3.15 (Succinctness). In Construction 3.11, if we choose the same parameters in Remark 3.6, after k times update, the sizes of the updated commitment $|(\mathbf{c}', \mathbf{D}')|$ and the updated opening $|\mathbf{v}_i'|$ is $\log k$ times that of the old commitment $|(\mathbf{c}, \mathbf{D})|$ and openings $|\mathbf{v}_i|$ in Remark 3.6. The size of the update information $|U_i| = |(\bar{\mathbf{c}}, \hat{\mathbf{R}}', \bar{\mathbf{v}}_i, \mathbf{D}')|$ is the same as the sum between the size of the old commitment $|(\mathbf{c}, \mathbf{D})|$ and openings $|(\mathbf{v}_i, \hat{\mathbf{R}})|$ in Remark 3.6. Therefore, the Construction 3.11 is a succinct updatable mercurial vector commitment.

Borrowing the idea of [8], we show how to use a standard vector commitment (supporting hiding) to construct an updatable mercurial vector commitment that supports updatable hiding in the full version of this work.

3.2 Aggregatable Mercurial Vector Commitment

In this section, we provide a variant of Construction 3.1 that supports aggregating. The existing aggregatable mercurial vector commitment [17] is a pairing-based construction in the AGM model and the ROM model, which restricts the ability of the adversary to perform only the algebraic operation for the group elements, and cannot generate one, so the only way for the adversary to generate the commitment is to run the Hard_com algorithm with some message. The restriction in AGM is similar to the notation of *weak* binding introduced by Gorbunov et al. [14].

Construction 3.1 perfectly inherits the property of aggregatable in $\mathsf{BASIS}_{\mathsf{struct}}$ that supports the aggregation of the openings to the *bounded* message and satisfies the same-set binding, which can *break* the limitation of AGM (*weak* binding) and ROM in the existing construction [17]. Additionally, like [28], our construction supports different-set weak binding as well.

We start by defining the notion of aggregatable mercurial vector commitment, and leave the proof part in the full version of this paper.

Definition 3.16 (Aggregatable MVC). An aggregatable mercurial vector commitment is a standard mercurial vector commitment in Definition 2.12 with the additional algorithms as follows:

- $\hat{\Pi} \leftarrow \mathsf{Aggregate}(\mathsf{pp}, \mathsf{flag}, (\mathbf{c}, \mathbf{D}), S, \{x_i, \pi_i\}_{i \in S})$: Input the public parameter pp, the flag flag, the commitment $(\mathbf{c}, \mathbf{D})$, the index set S, the message x_i and the opening π_i for $i \in S$. It outputs the aggregated opening $\hat{\Pi}$.

- $0/1 \leftarrow \mathsf{Aggre\_verify}(\mathsf{pp}, \mathsf{flag}, (\mathbf{c}, \mathbf{D}), S, \{x_i\}_{i \in S}, \hat{\Pi})$: Input the public parameter pp, the flag flag, the commitment $(\mathbf{c}, \mathbf{D})$, the index set S and the message x_i for $i \in S$ and the aggregated opening $\hat{\Pi}$. It outputs 0/1 to indicate whether $\hat{\Pi}$ is valid or not.

The correctness is that for an honestly generated aggregated opening from Aggregate, Aggre_verify should be accepted with overwhelming probability. The succinctness is that for all $\lambda \in \mathbb{N}$, the size of aggregated opening $|\hat{\Pi}| = \mathsf{poly}(\lambda, \log l)$. The mercurial hiding is that no adversary can distinguish between the aggregated hard opening and the aggregated soft opening. The definition of binding is described in the full version of this work.

Construction 3.17 (Aggregatable MVC based on $\mathsf{BASIS}_{\mathsf{struct}}$). Let λ be a security parameter and $n = n(\lambda)$, $m = m(\lambda)$, $q = q(\lambda)$ be lattice parameters. Let $m' = n(\lceil \log q \rceil + 1)$, and $\beta = \beta(\lambda)$ be the bound. Let $s_0 = s_0(\lambda)$, $s_1 = s_1(\lambda)$ be Gaussian width parameters. Let l be the vector dimension. Let $\mathcal{M} = \mathbb{Z}_p$ be the message space. The detailed construction is shown below.

- $\{\mathsf{pp}, tk\} \leftarrow \mathsf{Setup}(1^\lambda, 1^l)$: Input a security parameter λ and the input length l, it first runs the $\{\mathsf{pp}, tk\} \leftarrow \mathsf{Setup}(1^\lambda, 1^l)$ in Construction 3.1. For each $i \in [\ell]$, it randomly samples a target vector $\mathbf{u}_i \xleftarrow{\$} \mathbb{Z}_q^n$ and then add all $\{\mathbf{u}_i\}_{i \in [\ell]}$ to pp. It outputs $\mathsf{pp} = \{\mathbf{A}, \{\mathbf{W}_i\}_{i \in [\ell]}, \{\mathbf{u}_i\}_{i \in [\ell]}, \mathbf{T}\}$ and a trapdoor key $tk = \tilde{\mathbf{R}}$ optionally.
- $\{(\mathbf{c}, \mathbf{D}), \mathsf{aux}\} \leftarrow \mathsf{Hard\_com}(\mathsf{pp}, \mathbf{x})$: Input the public parameter pp and a vector $\mathbf{x} \in \mathbb{Z}_p^l$, it constructs $\mathbf{B}_l'$ and $\mathbf{T}'$ like Hard_com in Construction 3.1. Next it constructs the target vector $\hat{\mathbf{u}}$ and uses $\mathbf{T}'$ to sample the preimage as follows,

$$\hat{\mathbf{u}} = \begin{bmatrix} -x_1 \mathbf{W}_1 \mathbf{u}_1 \\ \vdots \\ -x_l \mathbf{W}_l \mathbf{u}_l \end{bmatrix}, \quad \begin{bmatrix} \mathbf{v}_1 \\ \vdots \\ \mathbf{v}_l \\ \hat{\mathbf{c}} \end{bmatrix} \leftarrow \mathsf{SampPre}\left(\mathbf{B}_l', \mathbf{T}', \hat{\mathbf{u}}, s_1\right) \tag{3.11}$$

  Last, it computes $\mathbf{c} = \mathbf{G}\hat{\mathbf{c}} \in \mathbb{Z}_q^n$, $\mathbf{D} = \mathbf{A}\hat{\mathbf{R}} \in \mathbb{Z}_q^{n \times m'}$. It outputs the hard commitment $(\mathbf{c}, \mathbf{D})$ and the auxiliary information $\mathsf{aux} = \{\mathbf{v}_1, ..., \mathbf{v}_l, \hat{\mathbf{R}}\}$.
- $\pi_i \leftarrow \mathsf{Hard\_open}(\mathsf{pp}, x_i, i, \mathsf{aux})$: Same as the Construction 3.1, it generates the hard opening $\pi_i = \{\mathbf{v}_i, \hat{\mathbf{R}}\}$.
- $0/1 \leftarrow \mathsf{Hard\_verify}(\mathsf{pp}, x_i, i, (\mathbf{c}, \mathbf{D}), \pi_i)$: Input the public parameter pp, the message x_i, the index i, the commitment pair $(\mathbf{c}, \mathbf{D})$, and the hard opening π_i, check if the following conditions hold to verify the opening.

$$\|\mathbf{v}_i\| \leq \beta, \qquad \mathbf{W}_i^{-1}\mathbf{c} = [\mathbf{A}|\mathbf{D}]\mathbf{v}_i + x_i \mathbf{u}_i \tag{3.12}$$

$$\|\hat{\mathbf{R}}\| \leq 1, \qquad \mathbf{D} = \mathbf{A}\hat{\mathbf{R}} \tag{3.13}$$

  If they all hold, it outputs 1; Otherwise, it outputs 0.
- $\{(\mathbf{c}, \mathbf{D}), \mathsf{aux}\} \leftarrow \mathsf{Soft\_com}(\mathsf{pp})$: Same as the Construction 3.1, it outputs the soft commitment $(\mathbf{c}, \mathbf{D})$ and $\mathsf{aux} = \{\mathbf{c}, \hat{\mathbf{R}}\}$.

- $\tau_i \leftarrow \mathsf{Soft\_open}(\mathsf{pp}, \mathsf{flag}, x, i, \mathsf{aux})$: Input the public parameter pp, the $\mathsf{flag} \in \{\mathsf{hard}, \mathsf{soft}\}$ which indicates that the soft opening τ_i is for hard commitment or soft commitment, the message x, the index i and the auxiliary information aux.
  If $\mathsf{flag} = \mathsf{hard}$ and x equals x_i in aux, then it outputs $\mathbf{v}_i$ in aux; Otherwise, it outputs $\perp$.
  And if $\mathsf{flag} = \mathsf{soft}$, it uses $\hat{\mathbf{R}}$ with tag $\mathbf{W}_i$ to sample the preimage as follows,
  $$\mathbf{v}_i \leftarrow \mathsf{SampPre}([\mathbf{W}_i\mathbf{A}|\mathbf{W}_i\mathbf{G} - \mathbf{W}_i\mathbf{A}\hat{\mathbf{R}}], \hat{\mathbf{R}}, \mathbf{c} - x_i\mathbf{W}_i\mathbf{u}_i, s_1)$$
  and outputs the soft opening $\tau_i = \mathbf{v}_i$.
- $0/1 \leftarrow \mathsf{Soft\_verify}(\mathsf{pp}, x, i, (\mathbf{c}, \mathbf{D}), \tau_i)$: Input the public parameter pp, the commitment pair $(\mathbf{c}, \mathbf{D})$, the vector x, the index i, and soft opening τ_i, check if Eq. 3.12 holds. If it holds, it outputs 1; Otherwise, it outputs 0.
- $\hat{\Pi} \leftarrow \mathsf{Aggregate}(\mathsf{pp}, \mathsf{flag}, (\mathbf{c}, \mathbf{D}), S, \{x_i, \pi_i\}_{i\in S})$: Input the public parameter pp, the flag flag, the commitment $(\mathbf{c}, \mathbf{D})$, the index set S, and the message x_i and the opening π_i for $i \in S$. It computes
  $$\hat{\mathbf{v}} = \sum_{i\in S} \mathbf{v}_i$$
  where $\mathbf{v}_i$ is phased from π_i for $i \in S$. If $\mathsf{flag} = \mathsf{hard}$, it outputs the aggregated opening $\hat{\Pi} = \{\hat{\mathbf{v}}, \hat{\mathbf{R}}\}$ which $\hat{\mathbf{R}}$ is phase from π_i for $i \in S$; If $\mathsf{flag} = \mathsf{soft}$, it outputs the aggregated opening $\hat{\Pi} = \hat{\mathbf{v}}$
- $0/1 \leftarrow \mathsf{Aggre\_verify}(\mathsf{pp}, \mathsf{flag}, (\mathbf{c}, \mathbf{D}), S, \{x_i\}_{i\in S}, \hat{\Pi})$: Input the public parameter pp, the flag flag, the commitment $(\mathbf{c}, \mathbf{D})$, the index set S, and the message x_i for $i \in S$ and the aggregated opening $\hat{\Pi}$. It first checks
  $$\|\hat{\mathbf{v}}\| \le |S|\beta, \qquad \sum_{i\in S} \mathbf{W}_i^{-1}\mathbf{c} = [\mathbf{A}|\mathbf{D}]\hat{\mathbf{v}} + \sum_{i\in S} x_i\mathbf{u}_i$$
  If $\mathsf{flag} = \mathsf{hard}$, it also needs to check Eq. 3.4. If they hold, it outputs 1; Otherwise, it outputs 0.
- $\{(\mathbf{c}, \mathbf{D}), \mathsf{aux}\} \leftarrow \mathsf{Fake\_com}(\mathsf{pp}, tk)$: Same as the Construction 3.1, it generates the fake commitment pair $(\mathbf{c}, \mathbf{D})$ and the auxiliary information $\mathsf{aux} = \{\mathbf{c}, \hat{\mathbf{R}}\}$.
- $\pi \leftarrow \mathsf{Equiv\_Hopen}(\mathsf{pp}, tk, x, i, \mathsf{aux})$: Input the public parameter pp and trapdoor key tk, the message x_i, the index i, and the auxiliary information aux, it uses $\mathbf{R}_i$ in tk to sample the preimage as follows,
  $$\mathbf{v} \leftarrow \mathsf{SampPre}([\mathbf{W}_i\mathbf{A}|\mathbf{W}_i\mathbf{A}\hat{\mathbf{R}}], \mathbf{R}_i, \mathbf{c} - x_i\mathbf{W}_i\mathbf{u}_i, s_1) \tag{3.14}$$
  It generates the equivocation hard opening $\pi = (\mathbf{v}, \hat{\mathbf{R}})$.
- $\tau \leftarrow \mathsf{Equiv\_Sopen}(\mathsf{pp}, tk, x_i, i, \mathsf{aux})$: Input the public parameter pp and trapdoor key tk, the message x_i, the index i, and the auxiliary information aux, it computes the Eq. 3.14 to obtain $\mathbf{v}$. It generates the equivocation soft opening $\tau = \mathbf{v}$.

4 Application: Lattice-Based ZK-EDB

In this section, we show the application of our constructions.

The main application of mercurial commitment is to build the ZKS and ZK-EDB. ZKS was first proposed by Micali [22] and was first built by the mercurial commitment in a structure of binary tree [9] which supports proving the membership of an element x for a set S without leaking any information (knowledge) of the set after committing the set. In ZK-EDB, the data is extended to key-value pairs (x, v) which users can query the key in the elementary database D. If the queried key x belongs to the database D, the committer will return the proof and the corresponding value v where $v = D(x)$; Otherwise, return the proof and $\perp$. Briefly speaking, to commit to a set (database), the structure of ZK-EDB or ZKS is similar to the Merkle tree with commitment instead of the hash value in each node. The proof of the membership consists of the openings of each node in the path from the leaf node of the element to the root node. Thanks to the mercurial property, the subtrees without any elements can be pruned so the size of the tree can be greatly reduced.

l-ary mercurial commitment (mercurial vector commitment) was proposed [10,20] and can be utilized to build the ZK-EDB or ZKS in a l-ary tree in order to reduce the height of the trees as well as the size of the proof. Liskov and Moses [21] proposed the updatable mercurial commitment to build an *updatable* ZK-EDB that supports the owner (committer) changing the element in the ZK-EDB and the users (verifiers) updating their holding commitments and the associated proofs. And Catalano et al. [8] extended the updatable mercurial commitment to updatable l-ary mercurial commitment. Besides, Li et al. [17] proposed the mercurial subvector commitment (aggregatable mercurial vector commitment), which supports the aggregation of openings that can be utilized to construct the ZK-EDB with *batch verification*. This allows users to verify the aggregated proof once, instead of having to verify multiple proofs of the same commitment.

However, the above constructions are mainly based on the l-DHE assumption and RSA assumption which cannot resist the quantum computer attack. The only lattice-based mercurial commitment proposed by Libert [18] can be built ZK-EDB in a binary tree but cannot support building l-ary, updatable, or aggregatable ZK-EDB.

Following their framework in [8,17,20,21], we'll show how to build the lattice-based l-ary ZK-EDB (ZKS) and its variants, including updatable and batch verification via our proposed MVC at a high level.

In the general case, there are three phases in the ZK-EDB or ZKS: the committing phase, the opening phase, and the verification phase. In the committing phase, the committer will build an l-ary tree and return the root of the tree as the commitment of the database. As we mentioned above, building the tree, or to say the committing phase is made more efficient by pruning subtrees in which all the leaves corresponding to the keys are not in the database. Only the roots of the pruned subtrees are kept in the tree with a soft commitment. For the key x in the database D which $D(x) \neq \perp$, each corresponding leaf contains a hard commitment of the hash value of $D(x)$, and other internal nodes in the tree will contain a hard commitment of its l children (with corresponding hash value); In the opening phase, to prove some key x in the database which $D(x) = v \neq \perp$, the committer generates a proof of membership including all the hard openings for the commitments belonging to the nodes in the path from the root to the leaf x at the corresponding position opening in each commitment. To prove some key x not in the database, i.e. $D(x) = \perp$, the committer first generates the subtree which x lies and is pruned before, and then generates a proof of non-membership including all the soft openings for the commitment belonging to the nodes in the path from the root to the leaf x; In the verification phase, the users will check all the commitments and associated openings of the path from the leaf x to the root. If $D(x) = v \neq \perp$, they run the hard verification algorithm; otherwise, they run the soft verification algorithm.

To update a ZK-EDB, there are two additional phases: the updating ZK-EDB phase and the user updating phase. In the updating ZK-EDB phase, the ZK-EDB owner (committer) is allowed to change the value $D(x)$ of the elements and outputs the updated commitment with some update information for users. During this phase, the owner first needs to update the commitment in the leaf x and then update the commitments in all the nodes of the path from the leaf x to the root. The updated database commitment is the updated commitment of the root, while the update information of ZK-EDB contains the update information for all the nodes involved in the update. In the user updating phase, the users can use the update information from the owner to update their commitments and the associated proofs. In particular, if users hold a proof for the key $x' \neq x$, the updated proof for x' should also be valid.

For batch verification, if the users query multiple keys at one time, the owners (committer) can aggregate the openings for the same commitment in the node and generate the aggregated proof during the opening phase. So, the users only need to check the aggregated proof during the verification phase.

Overall, our constructions of MVC can be used to build the lattice-based ZK-EDB which enables the ZK-EDB owner to commit, open, and update, and allows the users to query, and batch verify without leaking any knowledge except the query result at a post-quantum level.

Acknowledgements. This work is supported by National Natural Science Foundation of China (No. 62202023, No. 62272131), HKU-SCF FinTech Academy, Shenzhen-Hong Kong-Macao Science and Technology Plan Project (Category C Project: SGDX20210823103537030), Theme-based Research Scheme of RGC, Hong Kong (T35-710/20-R), and Shenzhen Science and Technology Major Project (No. KJZD20230923114908017). We would like to thank the anonymous reviewers for their constructive and informative feedback on this work.

References

1. Agrawal, S., Kirshanova, E., Stehlé, D., Yadav, A.: Can round-optimal lattice-based blind signatures be practical? IACR Cryptol. ePrint Arch. **2021**, 1565 (2021)

2. Ajtai, M.: Generating hard instances of lattice problems. In: Proceedings of the Twenty-Eighth Annual ACM Symposium on Theory of Computing, pp. 99–108 (1996)
3. Albrecht, M.R., Cini, V., Lai, R.W., Malavolta, G., Thyagarajan, S.A.: Lattice-based SNARKs: publicly verifiable, preprocessing, and recursively composable. In: Dodis, Y., Shrimpton, T. (eds.) Advances in Cryptology–CRYPTO 2022: 42nd Annual International Cryptology Conference, CRYPTO 2022, Santa Barbara, CA, USA, 15–18 August 2022, Proceedings, Part II, pp. 102–132. Springer, Cham (2022). https://doi.org/10.1007/978-3-031-15979-4_4
4. Albrecht, M.R., Fenzi, G., Lapiha, O., Nguyen, N.K.: SLAP: succinct lattice-based polynomial commitments from standard assumptions. Cryptology ePrint Archive (2023)
5. Balbás, D., Catalano, D., Fiore, D., Lai, R.W.: Chainable functional commitments for unbounded-depth circuits. In: Rothblum, G., Wee, H. (eds.) Theory of Cryptography Conference, TCC 2023. LNCS, vol. 14371, pp. 363–393. Springer, Cham (2023). https://doi.org/10.1007/978-3-031-48621-0_13
6. de Castro, L., Peikert, C.: Functional commitments for all functions, with transparent setup and from SIS. In: Hazay, C., Stam, M. (eds.) Advances in Cryptology–EUROCRYPT 2023: 42nd Annual International Conference on the Theory and Applications of Cryptographic Techniques, Lyon, France, 23–27 April 2023, Proceedings, Part III, vol. 14006, pp. 287–320. Springer, Cham (2023). https://doi.org/10.1007/978-3-031-30620-4_10
7. Catalano, D., Dodis, Y., Visconti, I.: Mercurial commitments: minimal assumptions and efficient constructions. In: Halevi, S., Rabin, T. (eds.) Theory of Cryptography: Third Theory of Cryptography Conference, TCC 2006, New York, NY, USA, 4–7 March 2006, Proceedings 3, vol. 3876, pp. 120–144. Springer, Cham (2006). https://doi.org/10.1007/11681878_7
8. Catalano, D., Fiore, D.: Vector commitments and their applications. In: Kurosawa, K., Hanaoka, G. (eds.) Public-Key Cryptography–PKC 2013: 16th International Conference on Practice and Theory in Public-Key Cryptography, Nara, Japan, 26 February–1 March 2013, Proceedings 16, vol. 7778, pp. 55–72. Springer, Cham (2013). https://doi.org/10.1007/978-3-642-36362-7_5
9. Chase, M., Healy, A., Lysyanskaya, A., Malkin, T., Reyzin, L.: Mercurial commitments with applications to zero-knowledge sets. In: Cramer, R. (ed.) EUROCRYPT 2005. LNCS, vol. 3494, pp. 422–439. Springer, Heidelberg (2005). https://doi.org/10.1007/11426639_25
10. Chase, M., Healy, A., Lysyanskaya, A., Malkin, T., Reyzin, L.: Mercurial commitments with applications to zero-knowledge sets. J. Cryptol. **26**, 251–279 (2013)
11. Cheon, J.H.: Security analysis of the strong Diffie-Hellman problem. In: Vaudenay, S. (ed.) EUROCRYPT 2006. LNCS, vol. 4004, pp. 1–11. Springer, Heidelberg (2006). https://doi.org/10.1007/11761679_1
12. Fisch, B., Liu, Z., Vesely, P.: Orbweaver: succinct linear functional commitments from lattices. In: Handschuh, H., Lysyanskaya, A. (eds.) Advances in Cryptology – CRYPTO 2023. CRYPTO 2023. LNCS, vol. 14082, pp. 106–131. Springer, Cham (2023). https://doi.org/10.1007/978-3-031-38545-2_4
13. Gentry, C., Peikert, C., Vaikuntanathan, V.: Trapdoors for hard lattices and new cryptographic constructions. In: Proceedings of the Fortieth Annual ACM Symposium on Theory of Computing, pp. 197–206 (2008)
14. Gorbunov, S., Reyzin, L., Wee, H., Zhang, Z.: Pointproofs: aggregating proofs for multiple vector commitments. In: Proceedings of the 2020 ACM SIGSAC Conference on Computer and Communications Security, pp. 2007–2023 (2020)

15. Håstad, J., Impagliazzo, R., Levin, L.A., Luby, M.: A pseudorandom generator from any one-way function. SIAM J. Comput. **28**(4), 1364–1396 (1999)
16. Lai, R.W., Malavolta, G.: Subvector commitments with application to succinct arguments. In: Boldyreva, A., Micciancio, D. (eds.) Advances in Cryptology–CRYPTO 2019: 39th Annual International Cryptology Conference, Santa Barbara, CA, USA, 18–22 August 2019, Proceedings, Part I 39, vol. 11692, pp. 530–560. Springer, Cham (2019). https://doi.org/10.1007/978-3-030-26948-7_19
17. Li, Y., Susilo, W., Yang, G., Phuong, T.V.X., Yu, Y., Liu, D.: Concise mercurial subvector commitments: definitions and constructions. In: Baek, J., Ruj, S. (eds.) Information Security and Privacy: 26th Australasian Conference, ACISP 2021, Virtual Event, 1–3 December 2021, Proceedings 26, vol. 13083, pp. 353–371. Springer, Cham (2021). https://doi.org/10.1007/978-3-030-90567-5_18
18. Libert, B., Nguyen, K., Tan, B.H.M., Wang, H.: Zero-knowledge elementary databases with more expressive queries. In: Lin, D., Sako, K. (eds.) Public-Key Cryptography – PKC 2019. PKC 2019. LNCS, vol. 11442, pp. 255–285. Springer, Cham (2019). https://doi.org/10.1007/978-3-030-17253-4_9
19. Libert, B., Ramanna, S.C., et al.: Functional commitment schemes: from polynomial commitments to pairing-based accumulators from simple assumptions. In: 43rd International Colloquium on Automata, Languages and Programming (ICALP 2016) (2016)
20. Libert, B., Yung, M.: Concise mercurial vector commitments and independent zero-knowledge sets with short proofs. In: Micciancio, D. (eds.) Theory of Cryptography: 7th Theory of Cryptography Conference, TCC 2010, Zurich, Switzerland, 9–11 February 2010, Proceedings 7, vol. 5978, pp. 499–517. Springer, Cham (2010). https://doi.org/10.1007/978-3-642-11799-2_30
21. Liskov, M.: Updatable zero-knowledge databases. In: Roy, B. (eds.) Advances in Cryptology-ASIACRYPT 2005: 11th International Conference on the Theory and Application of Cryptology and Information Security, Chennai, India, 4–8 December 2005, Proceedings 11, vol. 3788, pp. 174–198. Springer, Cham (2005). https://doi.org/10.1007/11593447_10
22. Micali, S., Rabin, M., Kilian, J.: Zero-knowledge sets. In: 44th Annual IEEE Symposium on Foundations of Computer Science, 2003. Proceedings, pp. 80–91. IEEE (2003)
23. Micciancio, D., Peikert, C.: Trapdoors for lattices: simpler, tighter, faster, smaller. In: Pointcheval, D., Johansson, T. (eds.) EUROCRYPT 2012. LNCS, vol. 7237, pp. 700–718. Springer, Heidelberg (2012). https://doi.org/10.1007/978-3-642-29011-4_41
24. Naor, M.: On cryptographic assumptions and challenges. In: Boneh, D. (ed.) CRYPTO 2003. LNCS, vol. 2729, pp. 96–109. Springer, Heidelberg (2003). https://doi.org/10.1007/978-3-540-45146-4_6
25. Peikert, C., Pepin, Z., Sharp, C.: Vector and functional commitments from lattices. In: Nissim, K., Waters, B. (eds.) TCC 2021. LNCS, vol. 13044, pp. 480–511. Springer, Cham (2021). https://doi.org/10.1007/978-3-030-90456-2_16
26. Tas, E.N., Boneh, D.: Vector commitments with efficient updates. arXiv preprint arXiv:2307.04085 (2023)
27. Wang, H., Yiu, S.M., Zhao, Y., Jiang, Z.L.: Updatable, aggregatable, succinct mercurial vector commitment from lattice. Cryptology ePrint Archive (2024)

28. Wee, H., Wu, D.J.: Succinct vector, polynomial, and functional commitments from lattices. In: Hazay, C., Stam, M. (eds.) Advances in Cryptology–EUROCRYPT 2023: 42nd Annual International Conference on the Theory and Applications of Cryptographic Techniques, Lyon, France, 23–27 April 2023, Proceedings, Part III, pp. 385–416. Springer, Cham (2023). https://doi.org/10.1007/978-3-031-30620-4_13

Vector Commitments with Proofs of Smallness: Short Range Proofs and More

Benoît Libert(✉)

Zama, Paris, France
benoit.libert@zama.ai

Abstract. Vector commitment schemes are compressing commitments to vectors that make it possible to succinctly open a commitment for individual vector positions without revealing anything about other positions. We describe vector commitments enabling constant-size proofs that the committed vector is small (i.e., binary, ternary, or of small norm). As a special case, we obtain range proofs featuring the shortest proof length in the literature with only 3 group elements per proof. As another application, we obtain short pairing-based NIZK arguments for lattice-related statements. In particular, we obtain short proofs (comprised of 3 group elements) showing the validity of ring LWE ciphertexts and public keys. Our constructions are proven simulation-extractable in the algebraic group model and the random oracle model.

Keywords: Vector commitments · range proofs · ring LWE ciphertexts

1 Introduction

Vector commitments (VCs) [22,66] allow a user to commit to a vector $\boldsymbol{m} \in D^n$ over some domain D by generating a short commitment. Later, the committer can succinctly open individual entries of $\boldsymbol{m}$. Here, "succinctly" means that the partial opening information (called "proof") should have constant size, no matter how large the committed vector is. As in standard commitments, a vector commitment scheme should satisfy two security properties: (i) The *binding* property, which ensures that no efficient adversary can open a commitment to two different values at the same position $i \in [n]$; (ii) The *hiding* property, which guarantees that revealing a subset of components does not reveal any information about messages at remaining positions.

Vector commitments found a number of applications in the context of zero-knowledge databases [66], verifiable data streaming [62], authenticated dictionaries [80], de-centralized storage [20], succinct arguments [6,63], cryptocurrencies [79] and blockchain transactions [6,50].

In this paper, we consider the problem of extending vector commitments with optimally short proofs that the committed vector $\boldsymbol{m}$ has small entries. A straightforward solution is to generically use a general-purpose succinct non-interactive argument (SNARK) for all NP languages [72]. While the SNARKs of

Q. Tang and V. Teague (Eds.): PKC 2024, LNCS 14602, pp. 36–67, 2024.
https://doi.org/10.1007/978-3-031-57722-2_2

[45,53,55] would give constant-size proofs, they would require to represent the statement as an arithmetic circuit. Then, the latter would have to compute the opening algorithm (including exponentiations in a group) of the commitment scheme, which would result in a complex circuit. In turn, this would require a large structured common reference string (CRS) and make the proof generation very expensive since, in pairing-based SNARKs with very short proofs [42,45,55], the CRS size grows linearly with the number of multiplication gates in the arithmetic circuit. Inevitably, the computational cost of the prover grows (at least) linearly with the circuit size as well. In this paper, we aim at proving smallness more efficiently than by generically using a SNARK for all NP statements.

1.1 Our Contributions

We revisit the vector commitment scheme of Libert and Yung [66] and propose a technique allowing to argue the smallness of committed vectors without changing the scheme. Using a very small number of group elements (typically 2 or 3), we can prove that a committed vector is binary, ternary or that it has small infinity norm. By slightly increasing the proof length, we can also prove that a committed vector has small Euclidean norm or a small Hamming weight.

As a key building block, we describe a technique of generating a short proof that a committed $\boldsymbol{m}$ has binary entries using only two group elements. This argument of binarity is proven knowledge-sound in the combined algebraic group model (AGM) [40] and random oracle model. In addition, the scheme retains the useful properties of the original vector commitment [66]. In particular, its CRS size remains linear in the dimension n of committed vectors and it remains possible to succinctly open the commitment for individual vector positions. As in [65], it is also possible to prove that a committed (binary) $\boldsymbol{m} \in \mathbb{Z}_p$ satisfies a linear equation $\langle \boldsymbol{m}, \boldsymbol{t} \rangle = x$ for a public $\boldsymbol{t} \in \mathbb{Z}_p^n$ and a public $x \in \mathbb{Z}_p$. Finally, it retains the aggregation properties [50,65] that make it possible to generate a constant-size proof for a sub-vector opening.

As a first application of our arguments of binarity, we obtain a new construction of range proof featuring very short proofs. Regardless of the range magnitude, each proof consists of only 3 group elements, which matches the proof size of Groth's SNARK [55] and improves upon the short range proof due to Boneh *et al.* [9]. The construction extends to simultaneously prove possibly distinct ranges for the individual entries of a vector $\boldsymbol{x} = (x_1, \ldots, x_m)$ without affecting the proof size. As a special case, it implies very short proofs that a committed $\boldsymbol{x} \in \mathbb{Z}^n$ has small infinity norm.

As a second main application, we provide short pairing-based non-interactive zero-knowledge (NIZK) arguments for many natural statements appearing in lattice-based cryptography. Specifically, we can argue knowledge of small-norm elements $s_1, \ldots, s_n$ of a cyclotomic ring $R = \mathbb{Z}[X]/(X^d + 1)$ that satisfy a linear relation $\sum_{i=1}^{M} \boldsymbol{a}_i \cdot s_i = \boldsymbol{t}$, for public vectors of ring elements $\boldsymbol{a}_1, \ldots, \boldsymbol{a}_M, \boldsymbol{t} \in R_q^N$, where $R_q = R/(qR)$. Using only 3 group elements, we can prove the validity of a ring LWE (RLWE) ciphertext [69], an RLWE public key, or even FHE ciphertexts [14,27]. We can also prove that a committed vector is a solution to an instance of the subset sum problem, which is useful for all the applications considered in [38]. For the specific task of proving the validity of a ciphertext in the Lyubashevsky-Peikert-Regev cryptosystem [69], we provide efficiency comparisons with Groth's SNARK [55], which is the state-of-the art construction featuring the same proof size. We estimate that the size of the common reference string is reduced by a factor 2. While slower on the verifier's side, our scheme decreases the number of exponentiations at the prover by a factor 4. The reason is that, on the prover and verifier sides, the number of exponentiations only depends on the length of the witness and not on the size of the arithmetic circuit describing the relation. We also provide a variant where the verifier computes a constant number of exponentiations. Our constructions thus provide more balanced tradeoffs than SNARKs between the complexities of the prover and the verifier. As such, they can be useful in cloud or blockchain applications where it is desirable to minimize the overhead of the client even at the cost of increasing the workload of the server. For example, in FHE-based private smart contracts [32,77] (which explicitly require ZK proofs of input awareness), a resource-constrained client has to prove the validity of its input FHE ciphertexts before sending them to a computationally powerful server performing homomorphic operations.

As another advantage over SNARKs enabling similarly short proofs, our constructions can be used to prove other relations about encrypted data (like equalities or inequalities between plaintexts) without any change in the CRS and without a relation-dependent pre-processing phase.

Our NIZK arguments of range membership and ciphertext validity can be proven simulation-extractable in the algebraic group model [40] and the random oracle model (recall that all such succinct arguments have to rely on an idealized model [46]). Simulation-extractability guarantees knowledge-soundness even when the adversary can observe proofs generated by honest parties. It thus provides non-malleability [36] guarantees against a malicious prover attempting to create a proof of its own by mauling honestly generated proofs. As pointed out in, e.g., [43,44], it is an important security property in all applications where succinct arguments are easily observable in the wild. For example, if a malleable range proof is used to demonstrate the validity of confidential transactions (as in the use case of [16]), it may fail to ensure transaction independence.

Fortunately, we can prove simulation-extractability without increasing the proof length while even the random-oracle-optimized variants [4,13] of Groth's SNARK have longer proofs. For the optimal proof length, existing SNARKs either provide a relaxed flavor of simulation-extractability [3] or they are significantly more demanding [56] than [55] in terms of CRS size and proving time.

1.2 Technical Overview

In asymmetric pairings $e : \mathbb{G} \times \hat{\mathbb{G}} \rightarrow \mathbb{G}_T$, the scheme of [66] uses a CRS containing group elements $(g, \{g_i = g^{(\alpha^i)}\}_{i \in [2n] \setminus \{n+1\}})$ and $(\hat{g}, \{\hat{g}_i = \hat{g}^{(\alpha^i)}\}_{i=1}^{n})$. The sender commits to $\boldsymbol{m} = (m_1, \ldots, m_n) \in \mathbb{Z}_p^n$ by choosing $\gamma \xleftarrow{R} \mathbb{Z}_p$ and computing

$$C = g^{\gamma} \cdot \prod_{j=1}^{n} g_j^{m_j} = g^{\gamma + \sum_{j=1}^{n} m_i \cdot \alpha^j} .$$

To open a position $i \in [n]$ of $\boldsymbol{m}$, the committer reveals a proof

$$\pi_i = g_{n+1-i}^{\gamma} \cdot \prod_{j=1, j \neq i}^{n} g_{n+1-i+j}^{m_j} = \left(C / g^{m_i \cdot \alpha^i}\right)^{\alpha^{n+1-i}}$$

which is verified by checking that $e(C, \hat{g}_{n+1-i}) = e(\pi_i, \hat{g}) \cdot e(g_1, \hat{g}_n)^{m_i}$.

To aggregate multiple proofs, PointProofs [50] uses the observation [65] that the commitment of [66] allows proving that a committed $\boldsymbol{m} \in \mathbb{Z}_p^n$ satisfies an inner product relation $\langle \boldsymbol{m}, \boldsymbol{t} \rangle = x$ for public $\boldsymbol{t} = (t_1, \ldots, t_n) \in \mathbb{Z}_p^n$ and $x \in \mathbb{Z}_p$. By raising the verification equation to the power $t_i \in \mathbb{Z}_p$ and taking the product over all $i \in [n]$, we obtain

$$e\big(C, \prod_{i=1}^{n} \hat{g}_{n+1-i}^{t_i}\big) = e\big(\prod_{i=1}^{n} \pi_i^{t_i}, \hat{g}\big) \cdot e(g_1, \hat{g}_n)^{\sum_{i=1}^{n} m_i \cdot t_i} . \tag{1}$$

PointProofs [50] aggregates proofs $\{\pi_i\}_{i \in S}$ for a sub-vector $S \subseteq [n]$ by deriving aggregation coefficients $\{t_i\}_{i \in S}$ from a random oracle and defining the aggregated proof as the product $\pi_S = \prod_{i \in S} \pi_i^{t_i}$. Verification then proceeds by testing the equality $e(C, \hat{g}_{n+1-i})^{\sum_{i \in S} t_i} = e(\pi_S, \hat{g}) \cdot e(g_1, \hat{g}_n)^{\sum_{i \in S} m_i \cdot t_i}$. In the following, we further exploit the aggregation properties of PointProofs.

Proving Binarity. Let a commitment $\hat{C} = \hat{g}^{\gamma} \cdot \prod_{i=1}^{n} \hat{g}_i^{x_i}$ to $\boldsymbol{x} \in \{0,1\}^n$.[1] Using its proof aggregation properties, we prove that, for each $i \in [n]$, we have $x_i \cdot (x_i - 1) = 0$. To this end, we use a similar batching technique to BulletProofs [16] and show that $\sum_{i=1}^{n} y_i \cdot x_i \cdot (x_i - 1) = 0$, where $\boldsymbol{y} = (y_1, \ldots, y_n) \in \mathbb{Z}_p^n$ is a vector of random aggregation coefficients obtained by hashing $\boldsymbol{y} = H(\hat{C})$ using a random oracle $H : \{0,1\}^* \to \mathbb{Z}_p^n$. As long as $\boldsymbol{y} \in \mathbb{Z}_p^n$ is chosen uniformly *after* $\{x_i\}_{i=1}^{n}$, the probability to have $\sum_{i=1}^{n} y_i \cdot x_i \cdot (x_i - 1) = 0$ is only $1/p$ if there exists $i \in [n]$ such that $x_i \notin \{0,1\}$.

In order to prove the statement using a constant number of group elements, we first choose $\gamma_y \stackrel{R}{\leftarrow} \mathbb{Z}_p$ and generate an auxiliary commitment

$$C_y = g^{\gamma_y} \cdot \prod_{j=1}^{n} g_{n+1-j}^{y_j \cdot x_j}, \tag{2}$$

to the Hadamard product $\boldsymbol{y} \circ \boldsymbol{x} = (y_1 \cdot x_1, \ldots, y_n \cdot x_n)$ (in the reversed order). Then, we proceed in two steps.

[1] For our applications, we will assume that the commitment is in $\hat{\mathbb{G}}$ rather than $\mathbb{G}$ in order for the proof of knowledge-soundness to work out.

In a first step, our prover has to demonstrate that it really computed C_y as a commitment to $(y_n \cdot x_n, \ldots, y_1 \cdot x_1)$. Since the commitment (2) satisfies

$$e(C_y, \hat{g}_i) = e\big(g_i^{\gamma_y} \cdot \prod_{j=1, j \neq i}^{n} g_{n+1-j+i}^{y_j \cdot x_j}, \hat{g}\big) \cdot e(g_1, \hat{g}_n)^{y_i \cdot x_i} \qquad \forall i \in [n] \tag{3}$$

and the initial commitment $\hat{C} = \hat{g}^{\gamma} \cdot \prod_{j=1}^{n} \hat{g}_j^{x_j}$ satisfies

$$e(g_{n+1-i}, \hat{C}) = e\big(g_{n+1-i}^{\gamma} \cdot \prod_{j=1, j \neq i}^{n} g_{n+1-i+j}^{x_j}, \hat{g}\big) \cdot e(g_1, \hat{g}_n)^{x_i} \qquad \forall i \in [n], \tag{4}$$

we can choose random exponents $\boldsymbol{t} = (t_1, \ldots, t_n) \xleftarrow{R} \mathbb{Z}_p^n$ and use them to raise (4) to the power $t_i \cdot y_i$ and (3) to the power t_i, respectively. If we then take the products over all indices $i \in [n]$ and divide them, we find that

$$\pi_{eq} = \frac{\prod_{i=1}^{n} \Big(g_{n+1-i}^{\gamma} \cdot \prod_{j \in [n] \setminus \{i\}} g_{n+1-i+j}^{x_j}\Big)^{t_i \cdot y_i}}{\prod_{i=1}^{n} \Big(g_i^{\gamma_y} \cdot \prod_{j \in [n] \setminus \{i\}} g_{n+1-j+i}^{y_j \cdot x_j}\Big)^{t_i}}.$$

satisfies

$$\frac{e(\prod_{i=1}^{n} g_{n+1-i}^{t_i \cdot y_i}, \hat{C})}{e(C_y, \prod_{i=1}^{n} \hat{g}_i^{t_i})} = e(\pi_{eq}, \hat{g}), \tag{5}$$

The reason why π_{eq} is a convincing proof that the prover computed C_y as a commitment to $(y_n \cdot x_n, \ldots, y_1 \cdot x_1)$ is the following. Suppose that C_y is a commitment $C_y = g^{\gamma_y} \cdot \prod_{j=1}^{n} g_{n+1-j}^{z_{n+1-j}}$ to some $(z_1, \ldots, z_n)$. Then, (3) becomes

$$e(C_y, \hat{g}_i) = e\big(\pi_{z,i}, \hat{g}\big) \cdot e(g_1, \hat{g}_n)^{z_{n+1-i}} \qquad \forall i \in [n], \tag{6}$$

where $\pi_{z,i} = \prod_{j=1, j \neq i}^{n} g_{n+1-j+i}^{z_{n+1-j}}$ is the proof that a prover can compute to open the $(n+1-i)$-th position of C_y. Now, if we raise (6) to the power t_i and divide it from (4) raised to the power $t_i \cdot y_i$, we obtain

$$\frac{e(\prod_{i=1}^{n} g_{n+1-i}^{t_i \cdot y_i}, \hat{C})}{e(C_y, \prod_{i=1}^{n} \hat{g}_i^{t_i})} = e\Big(\prod_{i=1}^{n} \big(\pi_{x,i}^{y_i} / \pi_{z,i}\big)^{t_i}, \hat{g}\Big) \cdot e(g_1, \hat{g}_n)^{\sum_{i=1}^{n} t_i \cdot (y_i \cdot x_i - z_{n+1-i})},$$

where $\pi_{x,i} = \prod_{j \in [n] \setminus \{i\}} g_{n+1-i+j}^{x_j}$ is the computable proof that allows opening the i-th position of $\hat{C}$ in (4). If $\boldsymbol{t}$ is chosen uniformly after $(z_1, \ldots, z_n)$, $(y_1, \ldots, y_n)$ and $(x_1, \ldots, x_n)$, then the probability to have $\sum_{i=1}^{n} t_i \cdot (y_i \cdot x_i - z_{n+1-i}) = 0$ is $1/p$ if there exists $i \in [n]$ such that $z_{n+1-i} \neq y_i \cdot x_i$. In the construction, we derive $\boldsymbol{t} = (t_1, \ldots, t_n) = H(\boldsymbol{y}, \hat{C}, C_y) \in \mathbb{Z}_p^n$ from a random oracle to make sure that $\boldsymbol{t}$ is computed after $\boldsymbol{y}$, $(x_1, \ldots, x_n)$ and $(z_1, \ldots, z_n)$.

The proof π_{eq} of the first step implies that $C_y \cdot \prod_{j=1}^{n} g_{n+1-j}^{-y_j}$ is a commitment to the vector $(y_n \cdot (x_n - 1), \ldots, y_1 \cdot (x_1 - 1))$, where $(x_1, \ldots, x_n)$ is the vector committed in $\hat{C}$. In a second step, we prove that $(y_n \cdot (x_n - 1), \ldots, y_1 \cdot (x_1 - 1))$

is orthogonal to $(x_n, \ldots, x_1)$: i.e., $\sum_{i=1}^{n} y_i \cdot x_i \cdot (x_i - 1) = 0$. From (1), it can be shown that such a proof is computable as

$$\pi_y = (C_y \cdot \prod_{j=1}^{n} g_{n+1-j}^{-y_j})^{\gamma} \cdot \prod_{i=1}^{n} \Big(g_i^{\gamma_y} \cdot \prod_{j \in [n] \setminus \{i\}} g_{n+1-j+i}^{y_j \cdot (x_j - 1)} \Big)^{x_i}$$

and satisfies

$$e\big(C_y \cdot \prod_{j=1}^{n} g_{n+1-j}^{-y_j}, \hat{C}\big) = e(\pi_y, \hat{g}) \cdot e(g_1, \hat{g}_n)^{\sum_{i=1}^{n} y_i \cdot x_i \cdot (x_i - 1)} = e(\pi_y, \hat{g}) \tag{7}$$

In order to minimize the proof size, we will exploit the linearity of verification equations (5) and (7) to aggregate π_{eq} and π_y into a single group element $\pi = \pi_{eq}^{\delta_{eq}} \cdot \pi_y^{\delta_y}$ using random aggregation coefficients $(\delta_{eq}, \delta_y) \in \mathbb{Z}_p^2$.

Eventually, the proof $\boldsymbol{\pi} = (C_y, \pi) \in \mathbb{G}^2$ that $\hat{C}$ commits to a binary vector consists of the commitment C_y to $(y_n \cdot x_n, \ldots, y_1 \cdot x_1)$ and $\pi \in \mathbb{G}$.

Proving Range Membership. To obtain a constant-size range proof, we use the fact that the commitment scheme of [66] is also an inner product functional commitment. The prover has a Pedersen commitment [74] $\hat{V} = \hat{g}^r \cdot \hat{g}_1^x$ in the group $\hat{\mathbb{G}}$. In order to prove the statement $x \in [0, 2^\ell - 1]$, the prover considers the bit representation $(x_1, \ldots, x_\ell) \in \{0,1\}^\ell$ of x and computes a commitment $\hat{C} = \hat{g}^{\gamma} \cdot \prod_{j=1}^{\ell} g_j^{x_j}$, for a random $\gamma \in \mathbb{Z}_p$. Using the aggregation properties of the commitment, it will prove that the committed $\boldsymbol{x} = (x_1, \ldots, x_\ell \mid \mathbf{0}^{n-\ell}) \in \mathbb{Z}_p^n$ satisfies: (i) $\sum_{i=1}^{\ell} x_i \cdot 2^{i-1} = x$; (ii) $x_i \in \{0,1\}$ for each $i \in [n]$.

In order to prove (i), the prover can adapt (1) and generate a short proof $\prod_{i=1}^{n} \pi_i^{2^{i-1}} \in \mathbb{G}$ such that

$$e\big(\prod_{i=1}^{\ell} g_{n+1-i}^{2^{i-1}}, \hat{C}\big) = e\big(\prod_{i=1}^{\ell} \pi_i^{2^{i-1}}, \hat{g}\big) \cdot e(g_1, \hat{g}_n)^{\sum_{i=1}^{\ell} x_i \cdot 2^{i-1}} \tag{8}$$

and show that the exponent above $e(g_1, \hat{g}_n)$ in (8) is equal to the committed x in $\hat{V} = \hat{g}^r \cdot \hat{g}_1^x$. Since $\hat{V}$ satisfies $e(g_n, \hat{V}) = e(g_1, \hat{g}_n)^x \cdot e(g_n^r, \hat{g})$, the prover can actually compute $\pi_x = \prod_{i=1}^{\ell} \pi_i^{2^{i-1}} / g_n^r$ such that

$$\frac{e\big(\prod_{i=1}^{\ell} g_{n+1-i}^{2^{i-1}}, \hat{C}\big)}{e(g_n, \hat{V})} = e\big(\pi_x, \hat{g}\big) \ . \tag{9}$$

Proving (ii) is addressed as explained earlier. Note that we do not need to prove that the $n - \ell$ last positions of $\boldsymbol{x}$ are zeroes since the inner product in the right-hand-side member of (8) only involves the first ℓ positions of $\boldsymbol{x}$.

In order to minimize the proof size, we will exploit the linearity of verification equations (9), (5) and (7) to aggregate π_x, π_{eq} and π_y into a single group element. In order to ensure knowledge soundness in the algebraic group model, we also need to aggregate a proof element π_v showing that $\hat{V}$ is a commitment to a vector of the form $(x, 0, \ldots, 0)$. The entire proof $\boldsymbol{\pi} = (\hat{C}, C_y, \pi) \in \hat{\mathbb{G}} \times \mathbb{G}^2$ eventually consists of the commitment $\hat{C}$ to the bits of x, the auxiliary commitment C_y to $(y_n \cdot x_n, \ldots, y_1 \cdot x_1)$ and the aggregated proof $\pi \in \mathbb{G}$.

Batching Range Proofs. The above technique extends to prove multiple range membership statements at once about the entries of a committed vector. For a commitment $\hat{V} = \hat{g}^r \cdot \prod_{k=1}^m \hat{g}_k^{x_k}$, the prover will convince the verifier that $x_k \in [0, 2^\ell - 1]$ for each $k \in [m]$ using only 3 group elements (we assume for now that the same range is proven for each x_k but distinct ranges can be handled).

To this end, we can use the same aggregation technique as BulletProofs [16, Section 4.3] and compute $\hat{C}$ as a commitment to a vector of dimension $n = \bar{\ell} \cdot m$ (where $\bar{\ell}$ is an upper bound for ℓ) obtained by appending the binary expansions of all $\{x_k\}_{k=1}^m$. Then, we can use a single group element to prove that, for each $k \in [m]$, the k-th sub-vector $\boldsymbol{x}_k = (x_{k,1}, \ldots, x_{k,\ell}, 0, \ldots, 0)$ hidden by the commitment $\hat{C}$ is a binary vector satisfying $x_k = \sum_{i=1}^{\ell} x_{k,i} \cdot 2^{i-1}$.

Proving Relations in Lattices. Here, we build on an approach considered by del Pino, Lyubashevsky and Seiler [35] to prove lattice-related statements assuming the hardness of computing discrete logarithms. The difference that we replace the BulletProofs component [16] by our more compact proof that a committed vector is binary. We also exploit the fact that the underlying vector commitment [66] allows proving inner-product relations as in (1).

Let the polynomial rings $R = \mathbb{Z}[X]/(\Phi)$, for some cyclotomic polynomial Φ of degree d, and $R_q = R/(qR)$. As in [35], we aim at proving the existence of small-norm ring elements $\boldsymbol{s} = (s_1, \ldots, s_M) \in R^M$ such that $\sum_{i=1}^M \boldsymbol{a}_i \cdot s_i = \boldsymbol{t} \bmod (q, \Phi)$, for public $\boldsymbol{t} \in R_q^N$ and $\boldsymbol{a}_1, \ldots, \boldsymbol{a}_M \in R_q^N$. To this end, we proceed as in [35] and re-write the relation as the following equality over $\mathbb{Z}[X]/(\Phi)$

$$\sum_{i=1}^{M} \boldsymbol{a}_i \cdot s_i = \boldsymbol{t} + \boldsymbol{r} \cdot q \bmod (\Phi) \ , \tag{10}$$

where $\boldsymbol{r} \in R^N$ is a vector of polynomials of degree $\leq d-1$ and the components of $\{\boldsymbol{a}_i\}_{i=1}^M$ and $\boldsymbol{t}$ are interpreted as polynomials with integer coefficients in $\{-\lfloor q/2 \rfloor, \ldots, \lfloor q/2 \rfloor - 1\}$. If $\|s_i\|_\infty \leq B_i$ for each $i \in [M]$, $\boldsymbol{r}$ contains polynomials with coefficients of magnitude $\|\boldsymbol{r}\|_\infty \leq dM \cdot \max_{i \in [M]}(B_i)/2$.

If we denote by $\phi : R \to \mathbb{Z}^d$ the coefficient embedding that maps $s_i = \sum_{j=1}^d s_{i,j} \cdot X^{j-1}$ to its coefficient vector $\phi(s_i) = (s_{i,1}, \ldots, s_{i,d}) \in \mathbb{Z}^d$, we can re-write (10) as a matrix-vector product over $\mathbb{Z}$

$$[\mathbf{A}_1 \mid \ldots \mid \mathbf{A}_M \mid \ -q \cdot \mathbf{I}_{Nd}\ ] \cdot \underbrace{[\phi(s_1) \mid \ldots \mid \phi(s_M) \mid \phi(\boldsymbol{r})]^\top}_{\triangleq\, \boldsymbol{x}} = \phi(\boldsymbol{t}) \tag{11}$$

for structured matrices $\mathbf{A}_1, \ldots, \mathbf{A}_M \in \mathbb{Z}_q^{Nd \times d}$ interpreted as integer matrices over $\{-\lfloor q/2 \rfloor, \ldots, \lfloor q/2 \rfloor\}$. In order to prove (11), the prover can commit to the vector $\boldsymbol{x} \in \mathbb{Z}^{Md+Nd}$ using a vector commitment. Then, it can generate short proof that $\|\phi(s_i)\|_\infty \leq B_i$ for each $i \in [M]$ and $\|\phi(\boldsymbol{r})\|_\infty \leq dM \cdot \max_{i\in[M]}(B_i)/2$. Finally, it can prove that (11) holds over $\mathbb{Z}_p$, where p is the order of pairing-friendly groups. If $p > 2Mqd\max_i(B_i)$, this ensures that (11) also holds over the integers. In order to optimize the proof size, we commit to the binary decomposition of $(\phi(s_1), \ldots, \phi(s_M), \phi(\boldsymbol{r}))$ and prove a relation that implies (11).

In order to minimize the number of exponentiations, we apply the Schwartz-Zippel lemma in a different way than [35]: Instead of proving (10) by considering evaluations of degree-$2d$ polynomials,[2] we compress (11) by left-multiplying both members with a random vector $\boldsymbol{\theta} \in \mathbb{Z}_p^{Nd}$, which allows processing all the rows of (11) using a short proof for a single inner product relation.

Just like [35], our protocol does not preserve soundness against quantum adversaries. However, both protocols still provide viable solutions in applications that only need to guarantee soundness at the moment of the protocol execution (i.e., today and assuming that the adversary is not quantum). In particular, they do not affect the post-quantum security of the encryption scheme as their zero-knowledge property does not rely on any assumption.

Achieving Simulation-Extractability. In our security proofs, one of the main difficulties is to properly simulate proofs for adversarially-chosen statements while remaining able to extract a witness (or break some assumption) from a proof generated by the adversary. As noticed in, e.g. [43], the simulator cannot use the trapdoor $\alpha \in \mathbb{Z}_p$ of the CRS since it would be incompatible with a reduction from a q-type assumption in the AGM.

To address this problem, we build a trapdoor-less simulator [43] that can simulate proofs for adversarially-chosen statements by programming the random oracles and without using α. To do this, we exploit the fact that our range proofs and our proof of valid RLWE encryption are obtained by aggregating various sub-proofs satisfying verifications of the form (5), (7) or (8). In each simulated proof $\boldsymbol{\pi} = (\hat{C}, C_y, \pi)$, we compute $\hat{C}$ and C_y as commitments to vectors which are programmed (as functions of previously chosen aggregation coefficients) in such a way that the unique corresponding valid proof π is computable without knowing the missing element $g^{(\alpha^{n+1})}$ of the CRS. At the same time, we can argue that the adversary cannot fake a proof using the simulator's strategy. We show that, with overwhelming probability, it can only come up with a proof π whose representation depends on $g^{(\alpha^{n+1})}$ if knowledge extraction fails.

1.3 Related Work

Vector commitments with logarithmic-size proofs are known since the Merkle-tree-based construction [71]. In the last decade, several number-theoretic realizations were put forth and offered useful advantages such as additive homomorphism, very short proofs [66], stateless updatability [22], or sub-vector openings

[2] More precisely, [35] proceeds by proving a relation $\sum_{i=1}^{M} \boldsymbol{a}_i \cdot s_i - \boldsymbol{r}_1 \cdot q - \boldsymbol{r}_2 \cdot \Phi = \boldsymbol{t}$ over $\mathbb{Z}[X]$, where $\boldsymbol{r}_1$ and $\boldsymbol{r}_2$ contain polynomials of degree $2(d-1)$ and $d-2$, respectively.

[6,63,79]. The first candidate with constant-size proofs was proposed by Libert and Yung [66] under a q-type assumption. Constructions based on the standard Diffie-Hellman assumption (in pairing-friendly groups) and the RSA assumption appeared in the work of Catalano and Fiore [22]. Lattice-based schemes were suggested by Peikert *et al.* [75]. While more versatile than their hash-based counterparts, algebraic VCs also seem to require more fancy mathematical tools. Indeed, Catalano *et al.* [23] recently proved negative results on the possibility of discrete-log-based vector commitments without pairings.

Polynomial and Functional Commitments. Polynomial commitments [60] allow one to commit to a polynomial and subsequently prove evaluations of this polynomial on specific inputs via a short proof (i.e., of length sub-linear in the degree of the committed polynomial). Succinct polynomial commitments were used in a number of SNARKs realizations (see, e.g., [8,17,42,70]). As shown in, e.g. [19, Section 3.1], polynomial commitments imply vector commitments.

Functional commitments (FC) for inner products [58,65] generalize both vector commitments and polynomial commitments by allowing the sender to commit to a vector $\boldsymbol{m}$ and succinctly prove linear functions of the committed vector. The first flavor of inner product functional commitment was considered in the interactive setting [58] while non-interactive solutions with constant-size proofs are enabled by SNARKs. Libert, Ramanna and Yung [65] generalized the vector commitment of [66] into a non-interactive inner product FC in the standard model while preserving its short proof size. Constructions with short public parameters in hidden-order groups were put forth in [2,28]. Lai and Malavolta [63] proposed the notion of linear map commitments that allows a prover to reveal a linear map evaluation, instead of just an inner product. At the expense of losing the homomorphic property, Lipmaa and Pavlyk [68] provided an FC candidate for sparse polynomials. Boneh *et al.* [10] considered the dual notion of function-hiding FC schemes (where the committer commits to a function instead of a message) for arithmetic circuits, which generalizes vector commitments and other flavors of commitments.

Among lattice-based realizations, Gorbunov *et al.* [51] implicitly described non-succinct functional commitments for bounded-depth circuits. Peikert *et al.* [75] proposed a succinct realization while relying on an online trusted authority to generate proofs. Albrecht *et al.* obtained [1] a construction for constant-degree polynomials over the integers as a building block for lattice-based SNARKs. Succinct FC candidates for circuits recently appeared in the work of Wee and Wu [81]. Independently, de Casto and Peikert [34] proposed a lattice-based function-hiding FC for circuits, but without fully succinct evaluation proofs.

Vector commitments with succinct proofs of smallness can be seen as a special case of functional commitments for Boolean predicates, where the smallness bound is hard-wired in the circuit. However, functional commitments for general circuits [34,81] seem ill-suited to our purposes since we aim at computationally efficient schemes with very short proofs. Indeed, the function-hiding FC scheme proposed by de Castro and Peikert [34] does not provide succinct openings (i.e., the opening size grows with the input length). While succinct, the construction of Wee and Wu [81] would not compete with ours in terms of proof length and CRS size (which is quadratic in the dimension of committed vectors in [81]). Moreover, in our application to NIZK arguments, the scheme of [81] would require the use of ad hoc knowledge assumptions in lattices for lack of a well-defined lattice analogue of the algebraic group model. Balbás *et al.* [5] suggested an alternative realization of FC for arithmetic circuits. However, its proof length grows at least linearly with the depth of the arithmetic circuit, which would translate into much longer proofs than ours.

In an earlier work, Catalano, Fiore and Tucker [24] proposed additively homomorphic FCs for constant-degree polynomials and monotone span programs. While their construction for polynomials and the Lipmaa-Pavlyk construction [68] are both amenable to proving smallness statements, they would be less efficient than our constructions, as discussed in the full version of the paper. Moreover, their more complex CRS structure would make it harder to prove knowledge-soundness in our setting, where the evaluation-binding property considered in [24,68] would not suffice.

AGGREGATION AND SUB-VECTOR OPENINGS. On several occasions, we rely on sub-vector openings and proof aggregation in the vector commitment of [66].

The notion of sub-vector openings was independently introduced and realized by Lai and Malavolta [63] and by Boneh, Bünz and Fisch [6]. It allows a sender to generate a short proof π_S that opens a sub-vector $\boldsymbol{m}_S$ of $\boldsymbol{m}$, for a subset $S \subseteq [n]$. Sub-vector openings are implied by the proof aggregation property considered in [6,20,50,78–80], which allows anyone (and not only the committer) to aggregate n individual proofs $\{\pi_i\}_{i \in S}$ for a committed sub-vector $\boldsymbol{m}_S$ into a constant-size proof π_S. Boneh, Bünz and Fisch [6] and Tomescu *et al.* [79] realized same-commitment aggregation in hidden-order groups and under q-type assumptions in pairing-friendly groups, respectively. Campanelli *et al.* [20] introduced incrementally aggregatable vector commitments, which allow different sub-vector openings to be merged into a shorter opening for the union of their sub-vectors. Moreover, aggregated proofs support further aggregation.

By leveraging the linearity properties of the vector commitment from [66], Gorbunov *et al.* [50] obtained a VC scheme enabling cross-commitment aggregation, which is useful in blockchain applications. The same-commitment variant of their aggregation method is obtained by introducing a random oracle in the inner product functional commitment of [65]. Our technique of proving that a committed vector is a reversed Hadamard product of another committed vector $\boldsymbol{x}$ and a public vector $\boldsymbol{y}$ is inspired by the randomized aggregation technique of PointProofs [50]. The difference is that, while [50] uses proof aggregation to succinctly prove sub-vector openings, we use it to prove linear relations between related positions in distinct committed vectors.

Using aggregation techniques, Campanelli *et al.* [21] described a compiler building linear map commitments from inner product functional commitments.

By instantiating vector commitments from polynomial commitments, Boneh *et al.* [7,8] obtained an alternative VC system supporting cross-commitment aggregation. Hyperproofs *et al.* [78] is yet another VC scheme allowing cross-commitment aggregation with the additional feature that all proofs can be updated in sub-linear time when the vector changes.

Other Proofs of Binarity. Prior works on pairing-based commitments [47,48] considered the problem of constructing constant-size proofs that a committed string is binary. However, these techniques apply to variants of Groth-Sahai commitments [57] that are *not* succinct vector commitments: i.e., either the commitment or partial openings (or both) do not have constant size. The first candidate [48] was designed for perfectly-binding commitments, where the commitment is longer than the committed message. The case of perfectly hiding (compressing) commitments was considered in [47, Section 4.2] but the underlying commitments do not natively support constant-size partial openings. As briefly alluded to in [47, Section 4.2.1], it is actually possible to build a succinct vector commitment to bitstrings on top of the perfectly hiding commitments from [47, Chapter 4]. However, the resulting construction has several limitations: (i) The CRS has quadratic size in the dimension of committed vectors (like the Diffie-Hellman-based vector commitment of [22]); (ii) It does not seem to support constant-size proofs that the committed $\boldsymbol{m} \in \mathbb{Z}_p^n$ satisfies inner product relations $\langle \boldsymbol{m}, \boldsymbol{t} \rangle = x$ for public $\boldsymbol{t} \in \mathbb{Z}_p^n$ and $x \in \mathbb{Z}_p$; (iii) Proofs are somewhat long and contain more than 20 group elements (according to Table 4.1 in [47]).

Das *et al.* [33] recently proposed another constant-size argument showing that a committed vector is binary. While their construction can be modified to build an alternative range proof to ours, it would result in longer proofs.

Range Proofs. Range proofs were introduced by Brickell *et al.* [15] and investigated in a large body of work [12,18,25,26,31,49,54,67] since then.

A standard approach [15,16,18,49,54] consists in breaking integers into bits and committing to these bits using homomorphic commitments. When it comes to proving membership of a range $[0, 2^\ell - 1]$, the resulting proofs generally contain $O(\ell)$ group elements (and thus $O(\lambda \cdot \ell)$ bits, where λ is the security parameter) although somewhat shorter proofs [18,49,54] are achievable using pairings. Using a clever recursive folding technique, Bulletproofs [16] decreased the communication complexity to $O(\log \ell)$ group elements (i.e., $O(\lambda \cdot \log \ell)$ bits) in general discrete-logarithm-hard groups without a bilinear map.

Another approach [12,31,52,67] relies on integer commitments in hidden-order groups, by decomposing positive integers as a sum of squares. The sum-of-squares method was transposed [29,30] to groups of (sufficiently large) public prime order. It was also adapted to class groups and lattices. For some parameters in the standard discrete logarithm setting, the constructions of [29,30] were shown to compare favorably with BulletProofs.

For some applications where the proof size is the primary concern (e.g., confidential transactions in the blockchain [16]), it may be desirable to have even shorter proofs than [16,29,30], even at the expense of losing the transparent setup property. Using polynomial commitments, Boneh *et al.* [9] suggested another range proof inspired by SNARK arithmetization techniques [42]. Their construction can be realized from a variety of polynomial commitments [17,60, 64]. In instantiations from pairing-based polynomial commitments [60,65], it provides the smallest communication cost to date, with proofs as short as 3 group elements and 3 scalars. In our range proof construction, we further decrease the proof length to that of the shortest known SNARKs [55]. A detailed comparison with [9] is given in Sect. 4.4.

DISCRETE-LOG-BASED PROOFS FOR LATTICE RELATIONS. The use of specialized pairing-based arguments to prove lattice relations was considered to prove the correct evaluation of FHE ciphertexts [39]. However, the modulus of the leveled FHE scheme had to match the group order of the pairing. This limitation does not appear in the del Pino *et al.* approach [35] nor in our construction. We note that the motivation of [39] was different since, in their setting, the prover was the server while the verifier was a computationally constrained client. Here, we consider use cases like [77] where the prover is the client (generating the proof on its browser using a single thread) and the verifier runs on a computationally powerful machine that can afford the use of multiple threads.

In applications to private FHE-based private smart contracts [77], the protocol of [35] was actually preferred to SNARKs in order to obtain faster prover. Our system can offer a similarly fast prover with the benefit of shorter proofs.

1.4 Organization

We first present our argument of binarity in Sect. 3. Our constant-size range proof is described in Sect. 4. Its batched multi-range extension is detailed in the full version of the paper. Due to space limitation, our NIZK argument for ring LWE ciphertexts is deferred to the full version of the paper.

2 Background and Definitions

2.1 Hardness Assumptions

Let groups $(\mathbb{G}, \hat{\mathbb{G}}, \mathbb{G}_T)$ of prime order p with a bilinear map $e : \mathbb{G} \times \hat{\mathbb{G}} \rightarrow \mathbb{G}_T$. We rely on the hardness of computing a discrete logarithm $\alpha \in \mathbb{Z}_p$ given $\{g^{\alpha^i}\}_{i \in [2n]}$ and $\{\hat{g}^{\alpha^i}\}_{i \in [n]}$. This assumption is similar to the n-discrete logarithm assumption considered in, e.g. [40], except that powers α^i are given in the exponents in both groups $\mathbb{G}$ and $\hat{\mathbb{G}}$.

Definition 1 ([40]). *Let $(\mathbb{G}, \hat{\mathbb{G}}, \mathbb{G}_T)$ be asymmetric bilinear groups of prime order p. For integers m, n, the (m, n)-***Discrete Logarithm** *((m, n)-DLOG) problem is, given $(g, g^{\alpha}, g^{(\alpha^2)}, \ldots, g^{(\alpha^m)}, \hat{g}, \hat{g}^{\alpha}, \ldots, \hat{g}^{(\alpha^n)})$, where $\alpha \stackrel{R}{\leftarrow} \mathbb{Z}_p$, $g \stackrel{R}{\leftarrow} \mathbb{G}$, $\hat{g} \stackrel{R}{\leftarrow} \hat{\mathbb{G}}$, to compute $\alpha \in \mathbb{Z}_p$.*

2.2 Non-interactive Arguments

Let $\{\mathcal{R}_\lambda\}_\lambda$ a family of NP relations. A NIZK argument for $\{\mathcal{R}_\lambda\}_\lambda$ consists of algorithms $\Pi = (\mathsf{CRS\text{-}Gen}, \mathsf{Prove}, \mathsf{Verify})$ with the following specifications. On input of a security parameter $\lambda \in \mathbb{N}$ and, optionally, language-dependent parameters lpp, algorithm $\mathsf{CRS\text{-}Gen}$ generates a common reference string pp and a simulation trapdoor τ. We allow pp to parameterize the proven relation (when it specifies the public parameters of a commitment scheme), which then becomes $\mathcal{R}_{\mathsf{pp}} \in \{\mathcal{R}_\lambda\}_\lambda$. Algorithm Prove takes as input the common reference string pp, a statement x and a witness w and outputs a proof π when $(x, w) \in \mathcal{R}_{\mathsf{pp}}$. Verify takes in pp, a statement x and a proof π and returns 0 or 1. Correctness requires that, for any $\mathcal{R} \in \{\mathcal{R}_\lambda\}_\lambda$ and any $(x, w) \in \mathcal{R}_{\mathsf{pp}}$, honestly generated proofs are always (or at least with overwhelming probability) accepted by the verifier.

NIZK arguments should satisfy two security properties. The *zero-knowledge* property requires that proofs leak no information about the witness. *Knowledge-soundness* property requires that there exists an extractor that can compute a witness whenever the adversary generates a valid proof. The extractor has access to the adversary's internal state, including its random coins. Let the universal relation $\mathcal{R}^*$ for $\{\mathcal{R}_\lambda\}_\lambda$ that inputs $(\mathcal{R}_{\mathsf{pp}}, x, w)$ and outputs 1 iff $\mathcal{R}_{\mathsf{pp}} \in \{\mathcal{R}_\lambda\}_\lambda$ and $(x, w) \in \mathcal{R}_{\mathsf{pp}}$. We say that $\Pi = (\mathsf{CRS\text{-}Gen}, \mathsf{Prove}, \mathsf{Verify})$ is a NIZK argument for $\mathcal{R}^*$ if it satisfies the properties defined as follows.

Completeness: For any $\lambda \in \mathbb{N}$, any (not necessarily efficient) adversary $\mathcal{A}$, there is a negligible function $\mathsf{negl} : \mathbb{N} \to \mathbb{N}$ such that

$$\Pr\big[\mathsf{Verify}_{\mathsf{pp}}(x, \pi) = 1 \ \wedge \ (x, w) \in \mathcal{R}_{\mathsf{pp}} \ \mid \ (\mathsf{pp}, \tau) \leftarrow \mathsf{CRS\text{-}Gen}(1^\lambda, \mathsf{lpp}), \\ (x, w) \leftarrow \mathcal{A}(\mathsf{pp}) \ , \ \pi \leftarrow \mathsf{Prove}_{\mathsf{pp}}(x, w)\big] = 1 - \mathsf{negl}(\lambda).$$

Knowledge-soundness: For any PPT adversary $\mathcal{A}$, there is a PPT extractor $\mathcal{E}_\mathcal{A}$ that has access to $\mathcal{A}$'s internal state and random coins ρ such that

$$\Pr\big[\mathsf{Verify}_{\mathsf{pp}}(x, \pi) = 1 \ \wedge \ (x, w) \notin \mathcal{R}_{\mathsf{pp}} \ \mid \ (\mathsf{pp}, \tau) \leftarrow \mathsf{CRS\text{-}Gen}(1^\lambda, \mathsf{lpp}), \\ (x, \pi) \leftarrow \mathcal{A}(\mathsf{pp}; \rho), \ w \leftarrow \mathcal{E}_\mathcal{A}(\mathsf{pp}, (x, \pi), \rho)\big] = \mathsf{negl}(\lambda).$$

(Statistical) Zero-knowledge: There is a PPT simulator Sim such that, for any $\lambda \in \mathbb{N}$ and any (not necessarily efficient) adversary $\mathcal{A}$ and any $b \in \{0, 1\}$,

$$\Pr\big[b \leftarrow \mathcal{A}^{\mathcal{O}_b}(\mathsf{pp}) \mid (\mathsf{pp}, \tau) \leftarrow \mathsf{CRS\text{-}Gen}(1^\lambda, \mathsf{lpp})\big] = 1/2 + \mathsf{negl}(\lambda).$$

where $\mathcal{O}_1$ is an oracle that inputs (x, w) and returns $\pi \leftarrow \mathsf{Prove}_{\mathsf{pp}}(x, w)$ if $(x, w) \in \mathcal{R}_{\mathsf{pp}}$ and $\perp$ otherwise; $\mathcal{O}_0$ is oracle that inputs (x, w) and returns $\pi \leftarrow \mathsf{Sim}(\mathsf{pp}, \tau, x)$ if $(x, w) \in \mathcal{R}_{\mathsf{pp}}$ and $\perp$ otherwise.

For many applications, it is desirable to strengthen knowledge-soundness by considering an adversary that can observe simulated proofs (for possibly false statements) and exploit some malleability of these proofs to generate a fake proof of its own. The notion of simulation-extractability prevent such attacks.

Simulation-Extractability: For any PPT adversary $\mathcal{A}$, there is a PPT extractor $\mathcal{E}_{\mathcal{A}}$ that has access to $\mathcal{A}$'s internal state/randomness ρ such that

$$\Pr\big[\mathsf{Verify}_{\mathsf{pp}}(x,\pi) = 1 \ \wedge\ (x,w) \notin \mathcal{R}_{\mathsf{pp}} \ \wedge\ (x,\pi) \notin Q \mid (\mathsf{pp},\tau) \leftarrow \mathsf{CRS\text{-}Gen}(1^\lambda, \mathsf{lpp}),$$
$$(x,\pi) \leftarrow \mathcal{A}^{\mathsf{SimProve}}(\mathsf{pp};\rho),\ w \leftarrow \mathcal{E}_{\mathcal{A}}(\mathsf{pp},(x,\pi),\rho,Q)\big] = \mathsf{negl}(\lambda),$$

where $\mathsf{SimProve}(\mathsf{pp},\tau,\cdot)$ is an oracle that returns a simulated proof $\pi \leftarrow \mathsf{Sim}(\mathsf{pp},\tau,x)$ for a given statement x and $Q = \{(x_i,\pi_i)\}_i$ denotes the set of queried statements and the simulated proofs returned by $\mathsf{SimProve}$.

In the following sections, we extend the syntax with an algorithm Com that inputs a vector $\boldsymbol{x} \in D^n$ over a domain D and outputs a commitment C. This commitment will be incorporated in the specific relation $\mathcal{R}_{\mathsf{pp}}$ defined by $\mathsf{CRS\text{-}Gen}$.

2.3 Algebraic Group Model

The algebraic group model (AGM) [40] is an idealized model, where all algorithms are assumed to be algebraic. Algebraic algorithms [11,73] generalize the notion of a generic algorithm [76] in that, whenever they compute a group element, they do it using generic operations, by taking linear combinations of available group elements so far. Hence, whenever they output a group element $X \in \mathbb{G}$, they also output a representation $\{\alpha_i\}_{i=1}^N$ of $X = \prod_{i=1}^N g_i^{\alpha_i}$ as a function of previously observed group elements $(g_1,\ldots,g_N) \in \mathbb{G}^N$ in the same group.

In contrast with generic algorithms, algebraic algorithms can exploit the structure of the group and obtain more information than they would in the generic group model. Although its relation with the generic group model is unclear [61], the AGM provides a powerful framework to analyze the security of efficient protocols via reductions. In particular, it has been widely used in the context of SNARKs [8,40,42–44,70].

3 Short Proofs that a Committed Vector Is Binary

Our construction for binary strings is defined for the relation

$$\mathcal{R}_{\mathsf{pp}} = \left\{ (\mathbf{x},\mathbf{w}) = \Big(\hat{V} = \hat{g}^{\gamma} \cdot \prod_{i=1}^{n} \hat{g}_1^{x_i} \in \hat{\mathbb{G}},\ \ (\gamma,(x_1,\ldots,x_n)) \in \mathbb{Z}_p \times \{0,1\}^n\Big) \right\}$$

where pp denotes the CRS containing the commitment key $(\hat{g},\{\hat{g}_i\}_{i=1}^n)$ and the description of groups $(\mathbb{G},\hat{\mathbb{G}},\mathbb{G}_T)$. Since the commitment is perfectly-hiding, the proven relation is trivially satisfied because, for any group element $\hat{V}$, there exists a string $\boldsymbol{x} \in \{0,1\}^n$ and a corresponding $\gamma \in \mathbb{Z}_p$ such that $\hat{V} = \hat{g}^{\gamma} \cdot \prod_{i=1}^n \hat{g}_i^{x_i}$. However, we can prove that the scheme is an argument of knowledge.

$\mathsf{CRS\text{-}Gen}(1^\lambda, 1^n)$: On input of a security parameter λ and the maximal dimension $n \in \mathsf{poly}(\lambda)$ of committed vectors, do the following:

1. Choose asymmetric bilinear groups $(\mathbb{G}, \hat{\mathbb{G}}, \mathbb{G}_T)$ of prime order $p > 2^{l(\lambda)}$, for some function $l : \mathbb{N} \to \mathbb{N}$, and $g \xleftarrow{R} \mathbb{G}$, $\hat{g} \xleftarrow{R} \hat{\mathbb{G}}$.
2. Pick $\alpha \xleftarrow{R} \mathbb{Z}_p$. Compute $g_1, \ldots, g_n, g_{n+2}, \ldots, g_{2n} \in \mathbb{G}$ and $\hat{g}_1, \ldots, \hat{g}_n \in \hat{\mathbb{G}}$, where $g_i = g^{(\alpha^i)}$ for each $i \in [2n] \setminus \{n+1\}$ and $\hat{g}_i = \hat{g}^{(\alpha^i)}$ for each $i \in [n]$.
3. Choose hash functions $H, H_t : \{0,1\}^* \to \mathbb{Z}_p^n$ and $H_{\mathsf{agg}} : \{0,1\}^* \to \mathbb{Z}_p^2$.

The public parameters are

$$\mathsf{pp} = \Big((\mathbb{G}, \hat{\mathbb{G}}, \mathbb{G}_T), g, \hat{g}, \{g_i\}_{i \in [2n] \setminus \{n+1\}}, \{\hat{g}_i\}_{i \in [n]}, \mathbf{H} = \{H, H_t, H_{\mathsf{agg}}\} \Big) .$$

Com$_{\mathsf{pp}}(\boldsymbol{x})$: To commit to a vector $\boldsymbol{x} = (x_1, \ldots, x_n) \in \mathbb{Z}_p^n$, choose a random $\gamma \xleftarrow{R} \mathbb{Z}_p$ and compute $\hat{C} = \hat{g}^\gamma \cdot \prod_{j=1}^n \hat{g}_j^{x_j}$. Return $\hat{C} \in \hat{\mathbb{G}}$ and the opening information $\mathsf{aux} = \gamma \in \mathbb{Z}_p$.

Prove$_{\mathsf{pp}}(\hat{C}, (\boldsymbol{x}, \mathsf{aux}))$: given a commitment $\hat{C}$ and witnesses $(\boldsymbol{x}; \mathsf{aux})$ consisting of a vector $\boldsymbol{x} = (x_1, \ldots, x_n) \in \mathbb{Z}_p^n$ and randomness $\mathsf{aux} = \gamma \in \mathbb{Z}_p$, return $\perp$ if $(x_1, \ldots, x_n) \notin \{0,1\}^n$. Otherwise, do the following:

1. Compute $\boldsymbol{y} = (y_1, \ldots, y_n) = H(\hat{C}) \in \mathbb{Z}_p^n$. Choose $\gamma_y \xleftarrow{R} \mathbb{Z}_p$ and compute
$$C_y = g^{\gamma_y} \cdot \prod_{j=1}^n g_{n+1-j}^{y_j \cdot x_j}$$
Then, compute $\boldsymbol{t} = (t_1, \ldots, t_n) = H_t(\boldsymbol{y}, \hat{C}, C_y) \in \mathbb{Z}_p^n$.
2. Generate a proof
$$\pi_{eq} = \frac{\prod_{i=1}^n \Big(g_{n+1-i}^{\gamma} \cdot \prod_{j \in [n] \setminus \{i\}} g_{n+1-i+j}^{x_j} \Big)^{t_i \cdot y_i}}{\prod_{i=1}^n \Big(g_i^{\gamma_y} \cdot \prod_{j \in [n] \setminus \{i\}} g_{n+1-j+i}^{y_j \cdot x_j} \Big)^{t_i}} \tag{12}$$
which satisfies
$$\frac{e(\prod_{i=1}^n g_{n+1-i}^{t_i \cdot y_i}, \hat{C})}{e(C_y, \prod_{i=1}^n \hat{g}_i^{t_i})} = e(\pi_{eq}, \hat{g}) , \tag{13}$$
and argues that C_y commits to $(y_n \cdot x_n, \ldots, y_1 \cdot x_1) \in \mathbb{Z}_p^n$.
3. Compute a proof
$$\pi_y = g^{\gamma \cdot \gamma_y} \cdot \prod_{j=1}^n g_{n+1-j}^{\gamma \cdot y_j \cdot (x_j - 1)} \cdot \prod_{i=1}^n \big(g_i^{\gamma_y} \cdot \prod_{j \in [n] \setminus \{i\}} g_{n+1-j+i}^{y_j \cdot (x_j - 1)} \big)^{x_i} \tag{14}$$
showing that $\sum_{i=1}^n y_i \cdot x_i \cdot (x_i - 1) = 0$ and satisfying
$$e\big(C_y \cdot \prod_{j=1}^n g_{n+1-j}^{-y_j}, \hat{C}\big) = e(\pi_y, \hat{g}) \tag{15}$$
4. Compute $(\delta_{eq}, \delta_y) = H_{\mathsf{agg}}(\hat{C}, C_y) \in \mathbb{Z}_p^2$ and then $\pi = \pi_{eq}^{\delta_{eq}} \cdot \pi_y^{\delta_y}$.

Output the final proof $\boldsymbol{\pi} := (C_y, \pi) \in \mathbb{G}^2$.

Verify$_{\mathsf{pp}}(\hat{C}, \boldsymbol{\pi})$: Given $\hat{C} \in \hat{\mathbb{G}}$ and a purported proof $\boldsymbol{\pi} = (C_y, \pi) \in \mathbb{G}^2$,

1. Compute $\boldsymbol{y} = H(\hat{C}) \in \mathbb{Z}_p^n$, $(\delta_{eq}, \delta_y) = H_{\text{agg}}(\hat{C}, C_y) \in \mathbb{Z}_p^2$ and $\boldsymbol{t} = H_t(\boldsymbol{y}, \hat{C}, C_y) \in \mathbb{Z}_p^n$.
2. Return 1 if the following equations is satisfied and 0 otherwise:

$$\frac{e\left(C_y^{\delta_y} \cdot \prod_{i=1}^{n} g_{n+1-i}^{(\delta_{eq}\cdot t_i - \delta_y)\cdot y_i}, \hat{C}\right)}{e\left(C_y, \prod_{i=1}^{n} \hat{g}_i^{\delta_{eq}\cdot t_i}\right)} = e(\pi, \hat{g}). \tag{16}$$

Correctness follows from the observation that equation (16) is obtained by aggregating (13)-(15), for which a detailed proof of correctness can be found in the full version of the paper.

We note that the prover can compute the entire proof using $O(n)$ exponentiations instead of computing π_{eq} and π_y using $O(n^2)$ exponentiations. To do this, we note that the left-hand-side member of (16) can be written $e(g, \hat{g})^{P_\pi(\alpha)}$, where $P_\pi[X]$ is a degree-$2n$ polynomial obtained as

$$P_\pi[X] = \Big(\delta_y \cdot \gamma_y + \sum_{i=1}^{n} (\delta_y \cdot x_i \cdot y_i + (\delta_{eq} \cdot t_i - \delta_y) \cdot y_i) \cdot X^{n+1-i}\Big) \cdot (\gamma + \sum_{i=1}^{n} x_j \cdot X^j)$$
$$- (\gamma_y + \sum_{i=1}^{n} y_i \cdot x_i \cdot X^{n+1-i}) \cdot (\sum_{i=1}^{n} \delta_{eq} \cdot t_i \cdot X^i) = \sum_{i=0}^{2n} \nu_i \cdot X^i,$$

where the degree-$(n+1)$ coefficient is $\nu_{n+1} = \delta_y \cdot \sum_{i=1}^{n} y_i \cdot (x_i^2 - x_i) = 0$. From $\{\nu_i\}_{i=0, i\neq n+1}^{2n}$, the prover can compute $\pi = g^{\nu_0} \cdot \prod_{i=1, i\neq n+1}^{2n} g_i^{\nu_i}$, which is the unique $\pi \in \mathbb{G}$ such that $e(g, \hat{g})^{P_\pi(\alpha)} = e(\pi, \hat{g})$.

In the algebraic group model, the construction can be proven zero-knowledge and knowledge-sound (the zero-knowledge simulator actually needs an algebraic representation of the adversarially-chosen commitment $\hat{C}$ but this requirement can be removed by swapping the groups where $\hat{C}$ and C_y live). The proof of knowledge-soundness can be inferred from the proof of Theorem 2 (in Sect. 4), of which it is a sub-case. In the upcoming sections, we will combine the system with other components in such a way that the combined arguments satisfy the stronger notion of simulation-extractability.

In the full version of the paper, we give a detailed comparison with the construction of Das *et al.* [33] and show that our scheme yields more compact range proofs. We also explain how to prove the exact Hamming weight (or an upper bound thereof) of committed binary/ternary vectors using 4 group elements.

4 A Range Proof with Very Short Proofs

Using the non-interactive argument for binary vectors from Sect. 3, we can build range arguments made of a constant number of group elements.

In the description below, we assume ranges $[0, B]$ such that $B+1$ is a power of 2 but the approach easily extends to general ranges. The standard approach to this problem is to consider the integer $\ell \in \mathbb{N}$ such that $2^{\ell-1} \leq B < 2^\ell$ and generate two range proofs showing that $x \in [0, 2^\ell - 1]$ and $x + (2^\ell - 1 - B) \in [0, 2^\ell - 1]$, where the second part is proven by leveraging the additive homomorphic property of the commitment. Instead of generating two independent range proofs, we can double the size of the CRS (by setting $n = 2\bar{\ell}$, where $\bar{\ell} \geq \ell$ is the maximal bitlength of the range) and avoid increasing the proof size.

4.1 Description

We assume that the initial Pedersen commitment $\hat{V} = \hat{g}^r \cdot \hat{g}_1^x$ to the witness $x \in [0, 2^\ell - 1]$ lives in the second source group $\hat{\mathbb{G}}$ of the pairing.[3]

The range membership relation is formally defined as

$$\mathcal{R}_{\mathsf{pp}} = \Big\{(\mathbf{x}, \mathbf{w}) = \big((\hat{V} = \hat{g}^r \cdot \hat{g}_1^x, \ell) \in \hat{\mathbb{G}} \times \mathbb{N},\ (r, x) \in \mathbb{Z}_p \times [0, 2^\ell - 1]\big)\Big\}$$

where the CRS pp specifies the commitment key $(\hat{g}, g_1)$ and the groups $(\mathbb{G}, \hat{\mathbb{G}}, \mathbb{G}_T)$.

$\mathsf{CRS\text{-}Gen}(1^\lambda, 1^n)$: On input of a security parameter λ and the maximal bitlength $n \in \mathsf{poly}(\lambda)$ of ranges, do the following:

1. Choose asymmetric bilinear groups $(\mathbb{G}, \hat{\mathbb{G}}, \mathbb{G}_T)$ of prime order $p > 2^{l(\lambda)}$, for some polynomial function $l : \mathbb{N} \to \mathbb{N}$, and $g \stackrel{R}{\leftarrow} \mathbb{G}$, $\hat{g} \stackrel{R}{\leftarrow} \hat{\mathbb{G}}$.
2. Pick a random $\alpha \stackrel{R}{\leftarrow} \mathbb{Z}_p$ and compute $g_1, \ldots, g_n, g_{n+2}, \ldots, g_{2n} \in \mathbb{G}$ as well as $\hat{g}_1, \ldots, \hat{g}_n \in \hat{\mathbb{G}}$, where $g_i = g^{(\alpha^i)}$ for each $i \in [2n] \setminus \{n+1\}$ and $\hat{g}_i = \hat{g}^{(\alpha^i)}$ for each $i \in [n]$.
3. Choose hash functions $H, H_t : \{0,1\}^* \to \mathbb{Z}_p^n$, $H_s : \{0,1\}^* \to \mathbb{Z}_p$ and $H_{\mathsf{agg}} : \{0,1\}^* \to \mathbb{Z}_p^4$ that will be modeled as random oracles.

The public parameters are defined to be

$$\mathsf{pp} = \Big((\mathbb{G}, \hat{\mathbb{G}}, \mathbb{G}_T), g, \hat{g}, \{g_i\}_{i \in [2n] \setminus \{n+1\}}, \{\hat{g}_i\}_{i \in [n]}, \mathbf{H} = \{H, H_s, H_t, H_{\mathsf{agg}}\}\Big)$$

$\mathsf{Com}_{\mathsf{pp}}(x)$: To commit to an integer $x \in \mathbb{Z}$, choose a random $r \stackrel{R}{\leftarrow} \mathbb{Z}_p$ and compute a Pedersen commitment $\hat{V} = \hat{g}^r \cdot \hat{g}_1^x \in \hat{\mathbb{G}}$. Return $\mathsf{com} = \hat{V} \in \hat{\mathbb{G}}$ and the opening information $\mathsf{aux} = r \in \mathbb{Z}_p$.

$\mathsf{Prove}_{\mathsf{pp}}(\mathsf{com}, (x, \mathsf{aux}))$: given $\mathsf{com} = \hat{V}$ and witnesses $(x; \mathsf{aux})$ consisting of an integer $x \in [0, 2^\ell - 1]$ with binary expansion $(x_1, \ldots, x_\ell) \in \{0,1\}^\ell$, where $\ell \leq n$, and $\mathsf{aux} = r \in \mathbb{Z}_p$ such that $\hat{V} = \hat{g}^r \cdot \hat{g}_1^x$, do the following:

[3] Committing x to a different, pairing-free, group $\mathbb{G}$ would not strengthen security since an adversary that would be able to compute α from pp would still break knowledge-soundness. The construction of [9] similarly assumes that the integer x is committed as a polynomial $f[X]$ such that $f(1) = x$.

1. Set $(x_{\ell+1}, \ldots, x_n) = \mathbf{0}^{n-\ell}$. Choose $\gamma \xleftarrow{R} \mathbb{Z}_p$ and compute

$$\hat{C} = \hat{g}^{\gamma} \cdot \prod_{j=1}^{\ell} \hat{g}_j^{x_j}$$

together with a proof $\pi_x \in \mathbb{G}$ that $\hat{C}$ commits to $(x_1, \ldots, x_n) \in \mathbb{Z}_p^n$ such that $\sum_{i=1}^{\ell} x_i \cdot 2^{i-1} = x$. This proof π_x satisfies

$$\frac{e(\prod_{i=1}^{\ell} g_{n+1-i}^{2^{i-1}}, \hat{C})}{e(g_n, \hat{V})} = e(\pi_x, \hat{g}) \tag{17}$$

and is obtained as

$$\pi_x = g_n^{-r} \cdot \prod_{i=1}^{\ell} \Big(g_{n+1-i}^{\gamma} \cdot \prod_{j \in [\ell] \setminus \{i\}} g_{n+1-i+j}^{x_j} \Big)^{2^{i-1}}.$$

2. Compute $\boldsymbol{y} = (y_1, \ldots, y_n) = H(\hat{V}, \hat{C}) \in \mathbb{Z}_p^n$. Pick $\gamma_y \xleftarrow{R} \mathbb{Z}_p$ and compute

$$C_y = g^{\gamma_y} \cdot \prod_{j=1}^{\ell} g_{n+1-j}^{y_j \cdot x_j}$$

Then, compute $\boldsymbol{t} = (t_1, \ldots, t_n) = H_t(\boldsymbol{y}, \hat{V}, \hat{C}, C_y) \in \mathbb{Z}_p^n$.

3. Prove that C_y commits to $(y_1 \cdot x_1, \ldots, y_n \cdot x_n) \in \mathbb{Z}_p^n$ by computing a short $\pi_{eq} \in \mathbb{G}$ (as specified in (12)) satisfying

$$\frac{e(\prod_{i=1}^{n} g_{n+1-i}^{t_i \cdot y_i}, \hat{C})}{e(C_y, \prod_{i=1}^{n} \hat{g}_i^{t_i})} = e(\pi_{eq}, \hat{g}). \tag{18}$$

4. Prove that $\sum_{i=1}^{n} y_i \cdot x_i \cdot (x_i - 1) = 0$ by computing $\pi_y \in \mathbb{G}$ via (14), which satisfies

$$e\big(C_y \cdot \prod_{j=1}^{n} g_{n+1-j}^{-y_j}, \hat{C}\big) = e(\pi_y, \hat{g}) \tag{19}$$

5. Generate an aggregated proof that $\hat{V} = \hat{g}^r \cdot \hat{g}_1^x$ is a commitment to a vector that contains 0 in its last $n-1$ coordinates. Namely, compute $\pi_v = \prod_{i=2}^{n} \left(g_{n+1-i}^r \cdot g_{n+2-i}^x \right)^{s_i} \in \mathbb{G}$ such that

$$e\big(\prod_{i=2}^{n} g_{n+1-i}^{s_i}, \hat{V}\big) = e(\pi_v, \hat{g}). \tag{20}$$

where $s_i = H_s(i, [2, n], \hat{V}, \hat{C}, C_y) \in \mathbb{Z}_p$ for each $i \in [2, n]$.

6. Compute $(\delta_x, \delta_{eq}, \delta_y, \delta_v) = H_{\text{agg}}(\hat{V}, \hat{C}, C_y) \in \mathbb{Z}_p^4$ and an aggregated proof

$$\pi = \pi_x^{\delta_x} \cdot \pi_y^{\delta_y} \cdot \pi_{eq}^{\delta_{eq}} \cdot \pi_v^{\delta_v}.$$

Output the final range argument which consists of

$$\boldsymbol{\pi} := (\hat{C}, C_y, \pi). \tag{21}$$

Verify$_{\text{pp}}$(com, $\boldsymbol{\pi}$): Given com $= \hat{V} \in \hat{\mathbb{G}}$ and a purported proof $\boldsymbol{\pi} = (\hat{C}, C_y, \pi)$,

1. Compute $\boldsymbol{y} = H(\hat{V}, \hat{C}) \in \mathbb{Z}_p^n$, $(\delta_x, \delta_{eq}, \delta_y, \delta_v) = H_{\text{agg}}(\hat{V}, \hat{C}, C_y) \in \mathbb{Z}_p^4$, $\boldsymbol{t} = H_t(\boldsymbol{y}, \hat{V}, \hat{C}, C_y) \in \mathbb{Z}_p^n$. Set $s_1 = 0$ and $s_i = H_s(i, [2, n], \hat{V}, \hat{C}, C_y)$ for all indices $i \in [2, n]$.
2. Return 1 if and only if

$$\frac{e\big(C_y^{\delta_y} \cdot \prod_{i=1}^{n} g_{n+1-i}^{\delta_{x,i} \cdot 2^{i-1} + (\delta_{eq} \cdot t_i - \delta_y) \cdot y_i}, \hat{C}\big)}{e\big(g_n^{\delta_x} \cdot \prod_{i=2}^{n} g_{n+1-i}^{-\delta_v \cdot s_i}, \hat{V}\big) \cdot e\big(C_y, \prod_{i=1}^{n} \hat{g}_i^{\delta_{eq} \cdot t_i}\big)} = e(\pi, \hat{g}), \tag{22}$$

where $\delta_{x,i} = \delta_x$ if $i \in [\ell]$ and $\delta_{x,i} = 0$ if $i \in [\ell + 1, n]$.

Correctness. The verification equation (22) is obtained by raising equalities (17), (18), (19) and (20) to the powers δ_x, δ_{eq}, δ_y, and δ_v, respectively, and multiplying the results together. In the full version of the paper, we provide detailed proofs of correctness for individual verification equations (17)-(20).

Efficiency. The cost of the prover is dominated by $3n$ exponentiations in $\mathbb{G}$ and two exponentiations in $\hat{\mathbb{G}}$. Indeed, computing $\hat{C}$ at step 1 only requires one exponentiation and a subset product (which is cheaper than an exponentiation) in $\hat{\mathbb{G}}$. Step 2 requires $n+1$ exponentiations in $\mathbb{G}$. Instead of individually computing the proof elements $(\pi_x, \pi_{eq}, \pi_y, \pi_v)$, the prover can directly compute the entire product π at step 6 using only $2n$ exponentiations since the aggregation coefficients $(\delta_x, \delta_{eq}, \delta_y, \delta_v)$, $\boldsymbol{y}$ and $\boldsymbol{t}$ only depend on the commitments $(\hat{V}, \hat{C}, C_y)$. This allows the prover to obtain the coefficients allowing to compute π from $\{g_i\}_{i \neq n+1}$ via 3 polynomial products by proceeding in the same way as in Sect. 3. Overall, the prover's overhead amounts to $3n$ exponentiations in $\mathbb{G}$, 2 exponentiations in $\hat{\mathbb{G}}$, and $O(n \log n)$ multiplications over $\mathbb{Z}_p$. The verifier's work is dominated by $2n + 1$ exponentiations in $\mathbb{G}$, n exponentiations in $\hat{\mathbb{G}}$ and 4 pairings.

In terms of proof length, $\boldsymbol{\pi}$ only requires one element of $\hat{\mathbb{G}}$, and 2 element of $\mathbb{G}$, which matches the optimal size of simulation-extractable pairing-based SNARKs [56]. Using the KSS18 family of pairing-friendly curves suggested by Kachisa *et al.* [59], each element of $\mathbb{G}$ (resp. $\hat{\mathbb{G}}$) can have a 348-bit (resp. 1044-bit) representation at the 128-bit security level according to [37]. Assuming that elements of $\hat{\mathbb{G}}$ are three times as large as those of $\mathbb{G}$, the overall proof length does not exceed the equivalent of 5 elements of $\mathbb{G}$, which amounts to 1740 bits.

In Sect. 4.4, we give a detailed comparison among existing constant-size range proofs. As shown in Table 1, our scheme provides the shortest proof length and the smallest computational cost at the prover.

4.2 Security in the AGM and ROM

We first prove the zero-knowledge property in the random oracle model.

Theorem 1. *The construction provides statistical zero-knowledge in the ROM.* (The proof is given in the full version of the paper.)

The simulator in the proof of Theorem 1 proceeds by programming the random oracles and also uses the trapdoor of the CRS. On the other hand, it works for any given $\hat{V} \in \hat{\mathbb{G}}$ without knowing an algebraic representation of $\hat{V}$. If we restrict $\hat{V}$ to be chosen by an algebraic adversary, it is possible to build an algebraic simulator that does not rely on random oracles.

In the proof of simulation-extractability, we need to build a trapdoor-less simulator, which does not use the trapdoor α of the common reference string.

Theorem 2. *Under the $(2n, n)$-DLOG assumption, the scheme is simulation-extractable in the algebraic group model and in the random oracle model.*

Proof. In the AGM+ROM model, we show that, unless the $(2n, n)$-DLOG assumption is false, there exists an extractor that can extract a witness from any adversarially-generated proof $\boldsymbol{\pi} = (\hat{C}, C_y, \pi)$ and statement $(\hat{V}, [0, 2^\ell - 1])$. Specifically, we give an algorithm $\mathcal{B}$ that can either extract a witness (x, r) with $x \in [0, 2^\ell - 1]$ or solve an $(2n, n)$-DLOG instance by computing $\alpha \in \mathbb{Z}_p$ from $\{(g, g_1, \ldots, g_{2n}), (\hat{g}_1, \ldots, \hat{g}_n)\}$, where $g_i = g^{(\alpha^i)}$ and $\hat{g}_i = \hat{g}^{(\alpha^i)}$ for all i.

The given problem instance $\{(g, g_1, \ldots, g_{2n}), (\hat{g}_1, \ldots, \hat{g}_n)\}$ is used to define the CRS pp. Note that $g_{n+1} = g^{(\alpha^{n+1})}$ is *not* included in pp and will never be used by $\mathcal{B}$. Our reduction/extractor $\mathcal{B}$ then interacts with $\mathcal{A}$ as follows.

Queries: At each random oracle query, $\mathcal{B}$ returns a random element in the appropriate range. When $\mathcal{A}$ queries a hash value $H_{\text{agg}}(\hat{V}, \hat{C}, C_y)$, $\mathcal{B}$ makes the corresponding queries $\boldsymbol{y} = H(\hat{V}, \hat{C})$, $\boldsymbol{t} = H_t(\boldsymbol{y}, \hat{V}, \hat{C}, C_y)$, $\{s_i = H_s(i, \hat{V}, [2, n])\}_{i=2}^n$ for itself before returning a tuple $(\delta_x, \delta_{eq}, \delta_y, \delta_v)$. At the first query involving a group element, $\mathcal{A}$ provides a representation of this group element as a linear combination of all the group elements that it observed so far in the same group.

At any time, $\mathcal{A}$ can choose a commitment $\mathsf{com} = \hat{V}$ and ask for a simulated proof that $\hat{V}$ is a commitment to some integer in $[0, 2^\ell - 1]$ for some $\ell \leq n$ of its choice. Since $\mathcal{A}$ is algebraic, it provides a representation of $\hat{V}$ w.r.t. $\{\hat{g}_i\}_{i \in [0,n]}$ and the commitments $\hat{C}$ contained in earlier simulated proofs. However, the simulator used by $\mathcal{B}$ is itself algebraic and always simulates proofs by computing $\hat{C}$ as a linear combination of $\{\hat{g}_i\}_{i \in [0,n]}$ for coefficients of its choice. Hence, for any $\hat{V}$ chosen by $\mathcal{A}$, $\mathcal{B}$ can always compute a representation $\{v_i\}_{i=0}^n$ such that $\hat{V} = \hat{g}^{v_0} \cdot \prod_{i=1}^n \hat{g}_i^{v_i}$. We assume w.l.o.g. that either $v_1 \notin [0, 2^\ell - 1]$ or $(v_2, \ldots, v_n) \neq \mathbf{0}$ since, otherwise, $\mathcal{B}$ can generate a real proof using (v_1, v_0). Then, $\mathcal{B}$ simulates a proof as follows without using g_{n+1}:

1. Choose random vectors $\boldsymbol{\delta} = (\delta_x, \delta_{eq}, \delta_y, \delta_v) \xleftarrow{R} \mathbb{Z}_p^4$, $\boldsymbol{y} = (y_1, \ldots, y_n) \xleftarrow{R} \mathbb{Z}_p^n$, $\boldsymbol{t} = (t_1, \ldots, t_n) \xleftarrow{R} \mathbb{Z}_p^n$.

2. Let $f_{n+1} = \sum_{i=2}^{n} v_i \cdot s_i$ for random $s_2, \ldots, s_n \stackrel{R}{\leftarrow} \mathbb{Z}_p$. Define $z_n = y_1$ and
$$a_1 = v_1 - \frac{\delta_v \cdot f_{n+1}}{\delta_x} \qquad\qquad \forall i \in [2, n] \; : \; a_i = 0$$
Note that $a_1 \notin \{0, 1\}$ w.h.p. if $v_1 \notin [0, 2^\ell - 1]$ or $(v_2, \ldots, v_n) \neq \mathbf{0}$. Then, compute an arbitrary vector $(z_1, \ldots, z_{n-1}) \in \mathbb{Z}_p^{n-1}$ satisfying the equality $\sum_{i=2}^{n} t_i \cdot z_{n+1-i} = t_1 \cdot (a_1 \cdot y_1 - y_1)$.
3. Choose random $a_0, z_0 \stackrel{R}{\leftarrow} \mathbb{Z}_p$ and compute simulated commitments
$$\hat{C} = \hat{g}^{a_0} \cdot \prod_{i=1}^{n} \hat{g}_i^{a_i} = \hat{g}^{a_0} \cdot \hat{g}^{a_1}, \qquad\qquad C_y = g^{z_0} \cdot \prod_{i=1}^{n} g_i^{z_i}.$$
4. If one of the random oracle values $H_{\mathrm{agg}}(\hat{V}, \hat{C}, C_y)$, $H(\hat{V}, \hat{C})$, $H_t(\boldsymbol{y}, \hat{V}, \hat{C}, C_y)$ or $\{H_s(i, [2, n], \hat{V}, \hat{C}, C_y)\}_{i=2}^{n}$ was already defined, then abort and report failure. Otherwise, set $\boldsymbol{y} = H(\hat{V}, \hat{C})$, $\boldsymbol{t} = H_t(\boldsymbol{y}, \hat{V}, \hat{C}, C_y)$, $\boldsymbol{\delta} = H_{\mathrm{agg}}(\hat{V}, \hat{C}, C_y)$ and $s_i = H_s(i, [2, n], \hat{V}, \hat{C}, C_y)$ for each $i \in [2, n]$.
5. Define the polynomials
$$Q_x[X] = \Big(\sum_{i=0}^{n} a_i \cdot X^i\Big) \cdot \Big(\sum_{i=1}^{\ell} 2^{i-1} \cdot X^{n+1-i}\Big) - \Big(\sum_{i=0}^{n} v_i \cdot X^{i+n}\Big) = \sum_{i=0}^{n+\ell} q_i \cdot X^i,$$
$$Q_y[X] = \Big(\sum_{i=0}^{n} z_i \cdot X^i - \sum_{i=1}^{n} y_i \cdot X^{n+1-i}\Big) \cdot \Big(\sum_{i=0}^{n} a_i \cdot X^i\Big) = \sum_{i=0}^{2n} \sigma_i \cdot X^i$$
$$Q_{eq}[X] = \Big(\sum_{i=0}^{n} a_i \cdot X^i\Big) \cdot \Big(\sum_{i=1}^{n} t_i \cdot y_i \cdot X^{n+1-i}\Big) - \Big(\sum_{i=0}^{n} z_i \cdot X^i\Big) \cdot \Big(\sum_{i=1}^{n} t_i \cdot X^i\Big) = \sum_{j=0}^{2n} e_j \cdot X^j,$$
$$Q_v[X] = \Big(\sum_{i=0}^{n} v_i \cdot X^i\Big) \cdot \Big(\sum_{i=2}^{n} s_i \cdot X^{n+1-i}\Big) = \sum_{j=0}^{2n} f_j \cdot X^j.$$
Their degree-$(n+1)$ coefficients are $f_{n+1} = \sum_{i=2}^{n} v_i \cdot s_i$ and
$$q_{n+1} = -v_1 + \sum_{i=1}^{\ell} a_i \cdot 2^{i-1} = -v_1 + a_1 = -\frac{\delta_v \cdot f_{n+1}}{\delta_x},$$
$$\sigma_{n+1} = \sum_{i=1}^{n} a_i \cdot (z_{n+1-i} - y_i) = a_1 \cdot (z_n - y_1) = 0$$
$$e_{n+1} = \sum_{i=1}^{n} t_i \cdot (a_i \cdot y_i - z_{n+1-i}) = t_1 \cdot (a_1 \cdot y_1 - y_1) - \sum_{i=2}^{n} t_i \cdot z_{n+1-i} = 0$$
due to the definition of $\boldsymbol{a} = (a_1, \ldots, a_n)$ and $\boldsymbol{z} = (z_1, \ldots, z_n)$. Note that
$$\delta_x \cdot q_{n+1} + \delta_{eq} \cdot e_{n+1} + \delta_y \cdot \sigma_{n+1} + \delta_v \cdot f_{n+1} = 0 \tag{23}$$

6. Define the polynomial

$$Q_{\mathsf{agg}}[X] = \delta_x \cdot Q_x[X] + \delta_{eq} \cdot Q_{eq}[X] + \delta_y \cdot Q_y[X] + \delta_v \cdot Q_v[X] = \sum_{i=0}^{2n} \eta_i \cdot X^i$$

for which $\eta_{n+1} = 0$ by construction. Compute $\pi = \prod_{i=1,i\neq n+1}^{2n} g_i^{\eta_i}$ using $(g, \{g_i\}_{i\in[2n]\setminus\{n+1\}})$ and return the simulated proof $\boldsymbol{\pi} = (\hat{C}, C_y, \pi)$.

Note that the simulated π satisfies the verification equation

$$\frac{e\big(C_y^{\delta_y} \cdot \prod_{i=1}^{\ell} g_{n+1-i}^{\delta_x \cdot 2^{i-1} + (\delta_{eq}\cdot t_i - \delta_y)\cdot y_i} \cdot \prod_{i=\ell+1}^{n} g_{n+1-i}^{(\delta_{eq}\cdot t_i - \delta_y)\cdot y_i}, \hat{C}\big)}{e\big(g_n^{\delta_x} \cdot \prod_{i=2}^{n} g_{n+1-i}^{-\delta_v \cdot s_i}, \hat{V}\big) \cdot e\big(C_y, \prod_{i=1}^{n} \hat{g}_i^{\delta_{eq}\cdot t_i}\big)} = e(\pi, \hat{g}). \quad (24)$$

and $\boldsymbol{\pi}$ has the same distribution as a proof generated by the zero-knowledge simulator in the proof of Theorem 1. Indeed, π is uniquely determined by the commitments $(\hat{C}, \hat{V}, C_y)$ and the $\mathbb{Z}_p$-elements $\boldsymbol{y}, \boldsymbol{t}$, $\{s_i\}_{i=2}^{n}$, and $\boldsymbol{\delta}$ in (24). Also, while the committed vectors $\boldsymbol{a}, \boldsymbol{z} \in \mathbb{Z}_p^n$ are programmed in a special way, they are perfectly hidden by the randomness a_0 and z_0 in $\hat{C}$ and C_y.

Consequently, the simulation is perfect, unless a collision occurs when random oracles are programmed in one of the simulation queries. If Q_S (reps. Q_H) denotes the number of queries made by $\mathcal{A}$ to the simulator (resp. to random oracles), this happens with probability at most $(Q_S + Q_H) \cdot Q_H/p$.

Output: When $\mathcal{A}$ halts, it outputs a statement $(\hat{V}, [0, 2^{\ell-1}])$, for some $\ell \in [1, n]$, together with a verifying proof $\boldsymbol{\pi} = \big(\hat{C}, C_y, \pi\big)$.

Any malicious algebraic prover that comes up with a commitment $\mathsf{com} = \hat{V}$ and a proof $\boldsymbol{\pi} = \big(\hat{C}, C_y, \pi\big)$ also gives a representation of each group element w.r.t. the group elements that have been observed so far.[4] In particular, $\mathcal{A}$ must provide a representation of C_y w.r.t to $(g, \{g_i\}_{i\in[2n]\setminus\{n+1\}})$ and the group elements $\{C_y^{(i)}, \pi^{(i)}\}_{i\in[Q_S]}$ contained in simulated proofs $\{\pi^{(i)}\}_{i\in[Q_S]}$. Likewise, $\mathcal{A}$ must provide a representation of $\hat{C}$ w.r.t $(\hat{g}, \{\hat{g}_i\}_{i\in[n]})$ and the commitments $\{\hat{C}^{(i)}\}_{i\in[Q_S]}$ contained in $\{\pi^{(i)}\}_{i\in[Q_S]}$. However, for each $i \in [Q_S]$, $\mathcal{B}$ knows a representation of $\hat{C}^{(i)}$ w.r.t. $(\hat{g}, \{\hat{g}_i\}_{i\in[n]})$ and a representation of C_y w.r.t. $(g, \{g_i\}_{i=1}^{n})$. It also knows a representation of each $\pi^{(i)}$ w.r.t $(g, \{g_i\}_{i\in[2n]\setminus\{n+1\}})$. From $\mathcal{A}$'s output and the random coins of the simulation, $\mathcal{B}$ can compute scalars $\{(\theta_i, z_i) \in \mathbb{Z}_p^2\}_{i\in[0,2n]\setminus\{n+1\}}$, $\{(a_i, v_i) \in \mathbb{Z}_p^2\}_{i\in[0,n]}$ such that

$$\hat{C} = \prod_{i=0}^{n} \hat{g}_i^{a_i}, \qquad C_y = \prod_{i=0,i\neq n+1}^{2n} g_i^{z_i}, \qquad \hat{V} = \prod_{i=0}^{n} \hat{g}_i^{v_i}, \qquad \pi = \prod_{i=0,i\neq n+1}^{2n} g_i^{\theta_i},$$

where we define $g_0 = g$ and $\hat{g}_0 = \hat{g}$ for convenience.

4 These representations are supplied by $\mathcal{A}$ at the first query involving the corresponding group elements.

If the representation $(v_0, v_1, \ldots, v_n) \in \mathbb{Z}_p^2$ of $\hat{V}$ is such that $v_1 \in [0, 2^\ell - 1]$ and $v_i = 0$ for all $i \in [2, n]$, then $\mathcal{B}$ is done as it can simply output $(v_1, v_0) \in \mathbb{Z}_p^2$ as a valid opening of the Pedersen commitment $\hat{V}$ to an integer v_1 in the proper range. We now assume that either $v_1 \notin [0, 2^\ell - 1]$ or $(v_2, \ldots, v_n) \neq \mathbf{0}^{n-1}$.

Solving $(2n, n)$-DLOG: By hypothesis, $\mathcal{A}$'s statement $(\mathsf{com} = \hat{V}, [0, 2^{\ell-1}])$ and proof $\boldsymbol{\pi} = \big(\hat{C}, C_y, \pi\big)$ satisfy (24), where $\boldsymbol{y} = H(\hat{V}, \hat{C})$, $\boldsymbol{t} = H_t(\boldsymbol{y}, \hat{V}, \hat{C}, C_y)$, $s_0 = 0$, $s_i = H_s(i, [2, n], \hat{V}, \hat{C}, C_y)$ for $i \in [2, n]$, and $(\delta_x, \delta_{eq}, \delta_y, \delta_v) = H_{\text{agg}}(\hat{V}, \hat{C}, C_y)$.

We first note that a non-trivial valid $\boldsymbol{\pi}$ cannot recycle $(\hat{V}, \hat{C}, C_y)$ obtained from the simulation oracle (namely, we must have $(\hat{V}, \hat{C}, C_y) \neq (\hat{V}^{(i)}, \hat{C}^{(i)}, C_y)$ for all $i \in [Q_S]$) since the left-hand-side member of (24) is uniquely determined by $(\hat{V}^{(i)}, \hat{C}^{(i)}, C_y^{(i)})$ and it in turn determines a unique valid $\pi^{(i)}$. Consequently, the hash values $H_{\text{agg}}(\hat{V}, \hat{C}, C_y)$, $H_t(\boldsymbol{y}, \hat{V}, \hat{C}, C_y)$ and $\{H_s(i, [2, n], \hat{V}, \hat{C}, C_y)\}_{i=2}^n$ were *not* programmed by the simulator in a simulation query.

We also note that the left-hand-side member of (24) is obtained by raising those of (17)-(20) to the powers $(\delta_x, \delta_{eq}, \delta_y, \delta_v)$ and multiplying the results together. Hence, it can be written $e(g, \hat{g})^{P_{\text{agg}}(\alpha)}$, where $P_{\text{agg}}[X]$ is the polynomial

$$P_{\text{agg}}[X] = \delta_x \cdot P_x[X] + \delta_y \cdot P_y[X] + \delta_{eq} \cdot P_{eq}[X] + \delta_v \cdot P_v[X]$$

obtained as a linear combination of the polynomials

$$P_x[X] = \Big(\sum_{i=0}^{n} a_i \cdot X^i\Big) \cdot \Big(\sum_{i=1}^{\ell} 2^{i-1} \cdot X^{n+1-i}\Big) - \big(\sum_{i=0}^{n} v_i \cdot X^{n+i}\big) = \sum_{i=0}^{n+\ell} \omega_i \cdot X^i,$$

$$P_y[X] = \Big(z_0 + \sum_{i=1}^{n} (z_{n+1-i} - y_i) \cdot X^{n+1-i} + \sum_{i=n+2}^{2n} z_i \cdot X^i\Big) \cdot \Big(\sum_{i=0}^{n} a_i \cdot X^i\Big) = \sum_{i=0}^{3n} \gamma_i \cdot X^i$$

$$P_{eq}[X] = \Big(\sum_{i=0}^{n} a_i \cdot X^i\Big) \cdot \Big(\sum_{i=1}^{n} t_i \cdot y_i \cdot X^{n+1-i}\Big) - \Big(\sum_{i=0, i\neq n+1}^{2n} z_i \cdot X^i\Big) \cdot \Big(\sum_{i=1}^{n} t_i \cdot X^i\Big) = \sum_{j=0}^{3n} \beta_j \cdot X^j,$$

$$P_v[X] = \Big(\sum_{i=0}^{n} v_i \cdot X^i\Big) \cdot \Big(\sum_{i=2}^{n} s_i \cdot X^{n+1-i}\Big) = \sum_{j=0}^{2n} \mu_j \cdot X^j$$

for which the left-hand-side members of (17)-(20) can be written $e(g, \hat{g})^{P_x(\alpha)}$, $e(g, \hat{g})^{P_{eq}(\alpha)}$, $e(g, \hat{g})^{P_y(\alpha)}$, and $e(g, \hat{g})^{P_v(\alpha)}$, respectively.

Letting $P_{\text{agg}}[X] = \sum_{i=0}^{3n} \nu_i \cdot X^i$, the coefficient of its degree-$(n+1)$ term is

$$\nu_{n+1} = \underbrace{\delta_x \cdot \big(\sum_{i=1}^{\ell} a_i \cdot 2^{i-1} - v_1\big)}_{\triangleq\, \omega_{n+1}} + \underbrace{\delta_y \cdot \sum_{i=1}^{n} \big(z_{n+1-i} - y_i\big) \cdot a_i}_{\triangleq\, \gamma_{n+1}} + \underbrace{\delta_{eq} \cdot \sum_{i=1}^{n} t_i \cdot (a_i \cdot y_i - z_{n+1-i})}_{\triangleq\, \beta_{n+1}} + \underbrace{\delta_v \cdot \sum_{i=2}^{n} v_i \cdot s_i}_{\triangleq\, \mu_{n+1}},$$

where $(\omega_{n+1}, \gamma_{n+1}, \beta_{n+1}, \mu_{n+1})$ are the coefficients of the degree-$(n+1)$ terms of $(P_x[X], P_y[X], P_{eq}[X], P_v[X])$, respectively. We argue that, if $v_1 \notin [0, 2^\ell - 1]$ or $(v_2, \ldots, v_n) \neq \mathbf{0}^{n-1}$, we cannot have $\nu_{n+1} = 0$, except with negligible probability. This follows from the following two arguments:

- The probability that $\boldsymbol{\rho} \triangleq (\omega_{n+1}, \gamma_{n+1}, \beta_{n+1}, \mu_{n+1}) = \mathbf{0}$ is negligible if $v_1 \notin [0, 2^\ell - 1]$ or $(v_2, \ldots, v_n) \neq \mathbf{0}^{n-1}$. Indeed, when $(v_2, \ldots, v_n) \neq \mathbf{0}^{n-1}$, we have $\mu_{n+1} = 0$, with probability $1/p$ over the random choice of $\{s_i\}_{i=2}^n$ since $\{s_i = H_s(i, [2, n], \hat{V}, \hat{C}, C_y)\}_{i=2}^n$ are derived uniformly *after* the choice of $\{v_i\}_{i=2}^n$. Likewise, when $z_{n+1-i} \neq a_i \cdot y_i$ for some $i \in [n]$, we have $\beta_{n+1} = 0$ with probability $1/p$ since $\boldsymbol{t} = H_t(\boldsymbol{y}, \hat{V}, \hat{C}, C_y)$ is derived *after* the choice of $\boldsymbol{y}$, $\{a_i\}_{i=0}^n$ and $\{z_i\}_{i \in [0,2n] \setminus \{n+1\}}$. Then, if $z_{n+1-i} = a_i \cdot y_i$ for all $i \in [n]$, we have $\gamma_{n+1} = \sum_{i=1}^n y_i \cdot (a_i - 1) \cdot a_i$, which cancels with probability $1/p$ if there exists $i \in [n]$ such that $a_i \notin \{0, 1\}$. To see this, we distinguish two cases:
    a. If $\boldsymbol{y} = H(\hat{V}, \hat{C})$ was programmed in a simulation query, we only have $\gamma_{n+1} = 0$ with probability $1/p$ since $\mathcal{B}$ chose $(a_1, \ldots, a_n)$ so as to have $\gamma_{n+1} = \sum_{i=1}^n y_i \cdot a_i \cdot (a_i - 1) = y_1 \cdot a_1 \cdot (a_1 - 1)$ with $y_1 \in_R \mathbb{Z}_p$ and $a_1 \notin \{0, 1\}$. This covers the case of $\mathcal{A}$ attempting to recycle $(\hat{V}, \hat{C}) = (\hat{V}^{(i)}, \hat{C}^{(i)})$ from a simulated $\boldsymbol{\pi}^{(i)} = (\hat{C}^{(i)}, C_y^{(i)}, \pi^{(i)})$, with a modified $C_y \neq C_y^{(i)}$.
    b. If $H(\hat{V}, \hat{C})$ was not programmed by the simulator, then $\boldsymbol{y} = H(\hat{V}, \hat{C})$ was defined after $\mathcal{B}$ obtained the representation $\{a_i\}_{i=0}^n$ of $\hat{C}$. Over the choice of $\boldsymbol{y}$, we have $\sum_{i=1}^n y_i \cdot (a_i - 1) \cdot a_i = 0$ with probability $1/p$.

  If none of the above events occurs and $\omega_{n+1} = 0$, we have $v_1 = \sum_{i=1}^\ell a_i \cdot 2^{i-1}$ and $a_i \in \{0, 1\}$ for all $i \in [\ell]$, which contradicts the hypothesis $v_1 \notin [0, 2^\ell - 1]$.

- If $\boldsymbol{\rho} \neq \mathbf{0}$, then $\nu_{n+1} \neq 0$ with probability $1 - 1/p$ since $\boldsymbol{\delta} = H_{\text{agg}}(\hat{V}, \hat{C}, C_y)$ is derived *after* the choice of $\{(a_i, v_i)\}_{i=0}^n$, and $\{z_i\}_{i \in [0,2n] \setminus \{n+1\}}$, which determine $\boldsymbol{\rho}$. So, a random $\boldsymbol{\delta} \in \mathbb{Z}_p^4$ satisfies $\langle \boldsymbol{\delta}, \boldsymbol{\rho} \rangle = 0$ with probability $1/p$.

If $\nu_{n+1} \neq 0$, $\mathcal{B}$ can compute $\alpha \in \mathbb{Z}_p$ by observing that the aggregated verification equation (24) implies

$$\pi = g_{n+1}^{\nu_{n+1}} \cdot \prod_{i \in [0,3n] \setminus \{n+1\}} g_i^{\nu_i}, \tag{25}$$

where $g_{2n+1} = g^{(\alpha^{2n+1})}, \ldots, g_{3n} = g^{(\alpha^{3n})}$ are not available. However, $\mathcal{B}$ knows $\{\nu_i\}_{i=0}^{3n}$. Since $\nu_{n+1} \neq 0$, we are guaranteed that the representation (25) of π differs from its representation $\pi = \prod_{i=0, i \neq n+1}^{2n} g_i^{\theta_i}$ revealed by $\mathcal{A}$ as part of its output. This means that $\alpha \in \mathbb{Z}_p$ can be found among the roots of the non-zero

$$R[X] = \sum_{i \in [0,2n] \setminus \{n+1\}} (\nu_i - \theta_i) \cdot X^i + \nu_{n+1} \cdot X^{n+1} + \sum_{i=2n+1}^{3n} \nu_i,$$

□

4.3 Batched Range Proofs and Proving the Smallness of Vectors

As detailed in the full version of the paper, the construction extends to prove multiple ranges at once for a committed vector $\hat{V} = \hat{g}^r \cdot \prod_{k=1}^m \hat{g}_k^{x_k}$ of integers. Namely, $\hat{C}$ commits to concatenation of the binary decompositions of all $\{x_k\}_{k=1}^m$. Then, a single group element allows proving that, for each $k \in [m]$, the k-th sub-vector $\boldsymbol{x}_k = (x_{k,1}, \ldots, x_{k,\ell}, 0, \ldots, 0)$ hidden by $\hat{C}$ is a binary vector satisfying $x_k = \sum_{i=1}^{\ell} x_{k,i} \cdot 2^{i-1}$. For the k-th slot, the prover computes $\pi_k \in \mathbb{G}$ such that

$$e\big(\prod_{i=1}^{\ell} g_{n+1-((k-1)\ell+i)}^{2^{i-1}}, \hat{C}\big) = e(g_1, \hat{g}_n)^{x_k} \cdot e(\pi_k, \hat{g}) \tag{26}$$

Since $\hat{V}$ is itself a vector commitment, the prover can compute $\pi_{v,k}$ such that

$$e\big(g_k, \hat{V}\big) = e(g_1, \hat{g}_n)^{x_k} \cdot e(\pi_{v,k}, \hat{g}) \tag{27}$$

Then, by dividing (27) from (26), raising the result to a random power $\xi_k \in \mathbb{Z}_p$ and taking the product over all indices $k \in [m]$, we find that the prover is able to compute a short $\pi = \prod_{k=1}^m (\pi_k / \pi_{v,k})^{\xi_k}$ such that

$$\frac{e\big(\prod_{k=1}^m \big(\prod_{i=1}^{\ell} g_{n+1-((k-1)\ell+i)}^{2^{i-1}}\big)^{\xi_k}, \hat{C}\big)}{e\big(\prod_{k=1}^m g_k^{\xi_k}, \hat{V}\big)} = e(\pi, \hat{g}), \tag{28}$$

which argues that $x_k = \sum_{i=1}^{\ell} x_{k,i} \cdot 2^{i-1}$ for all $k \in [m]$. Indeed, otherwise, we have $\sum_{k=1}^m \xi_k \cdot (x_k - \sum_{i=1}^{\ell} x_{k,i} \cdot 2^{i-1}) = 0$ with negligible probability $1/p$ as long as $(\xi_1, \ldots, \xi_m)$ are chosen uniformly after the commitments $\hat{V}$ and $\hat{C}$.

The remaining proof elements are computed exactly as in the single-slot setting, so that the final proof $\boldsymbol{\pi}$ still lives in $\hat{\mathbb{G}} \times \mathbb{G}^2$. This immediately provides a short proof that a committed vector has small infinity norm. By introducing a few more group elements in the proof, we can also prove small Euclidean norms.

4.4 Comparisons

Our construction assumes that the witness x is committed using a Pedersen commitment in the pairing-friendly group specified by the CRS of the range proof. The range proof of [9] similarly requires x to be committed as a constant polynomial using the CRS of a polynomial commitment scheme.

The BFGW range proofs [9] were the shortest ones so far and they also feature constant verification time (whereas our verifier computes $O(n)$ exponentiations, where n is the maximal bitlength of the range, as in BulletProofs). When instantiated with KZG commitments [60] and the cross-commitment evaluation techniques of [8, Section 4.1], BFGW proofs consist of 2 commitments to polynomials (each of which takes an element of $\mathbb{G}$), 3 elements of $\mathbb{Z}_p$ representing evaluations of committed polynomials, and a batched evaluation proof comprised of a group element and at least one scalar.[5] If their construction is instantiated with the polynomial commitment of [65, Section 4.1][6] and the batched evaluation protocol of [8, Section 4.1], the communication cost decreases to 2 elements of $\mathbb{G}$ (which commit to polynomials), 3 scalars (for polynomial evaluations) and a single element of $\mathbb{G}$ for the batched evaluation proof. In the latter case, the range proof of [9] only requires 3 elements of $\mathbb{G}$ and 3 elements of $\mathbb{Z}_p$. On the downside, combining [9,65] induces $2n$ exponentiations in $\hat{\mathbb{G}}$ at the verifier (instead of $O(1)$ using KZG commitments) and increases the prover's overhead to $7n$ exponentiations in $\mathbb{G}$.

Not only does our construction ensure simulation-extractability in the AGM, it also features the smallest number of exponentiations at the prover (which is reduced by at least 40%) while matching the shortest proof length of SNARKs.In terms of space, our construction also improves upon BulletProofs [16], which requires the prover to send $2\lceil \log \ell \rceil + 4$ group elements and 5 elements of $\mathbb{Z}_p$. If we compare with SNARKs, we obtain the same proof size as optimally short candidates [55,56] with the advantage that our CRS size is much shorter: It only depends on the maximal bitlength n of a range rather than the size of a circuit representation of the statement. Also, our prover only needs to compute $O(n)$

Table 1. Efficiency comparisons between constant-size range proofs

Schemes	Proof size	CRS size	Prover cost	Verifier cost
BFGW [9]	$3 \times \lvert\mathbb{G}\rvert$	$(4n+2) \times \lvert\mathbb{G}\rvert$	$5n\ \exp_{\mathbb{G}}$	$3P + 4\exp_{\hat{\mathbb{G}}}$
+ KZG [60, Section 3.3]	$4 \times \lvert\mathbb{Z}_p\rvert$	$4 \times \lvert\hat{\mathbb{G}}\rvert$		$1\exp_{\mathbb{G}}$
BFGW	$4 \times \lvert\mathbb{G}\rvert$	$(2n+1) \times \lvert\mathbb{G}\rvert$	$5n\ \exp_{\mathbb{G}}$	$3P + 4\exp_{\hat{\mathbb{G}}}$
+ Zhang *et al.* [83]	$3 \times \lvert\mathbb{Z}_p\rvert$	$3 \times \lvert\hat{\mathbb{G}}\rvert$		$1\exp_{\mathbb{G}}$
BFGW	$3 \times \lvert\mathbb{G}\rvert$	$4n \times \lvert\mathbb{G}\rvert$	$7n\ \exp_{\mathbb{G}}$	$3P + 2n\exp_{\hat{\mathbb{G}}}$
+ LRY [65]	$3 \times \lvert\mathbb{Z}_p\rvert$	$2n \times \lvert\hat{\mathbb{G}}\rvert$		$2\exp_{\mathbb{G}}$
Groth16 [55]	$1 \times \lvert\hat{\mathbb{G}}\rvert$	$3\lvert\mathcal{C}\rvert \times \lvert\mathbb{G}\rvert$	$4\lvert\mathcal{C}\rvert\ \exp_{\mathbb{G}}$	$3P + O(1)\exp_{\mathbb{G}}$
	$2 \times \lvert\mathbb{G}\rvert$	$\lvert\mathcal{C}\rvert \times \lvert\hat{\mathbb{G}}\rvert$	$\lvert\mathcal{C}\rvert\ \exp_{\hat{\mathbb{G}}}$	
New construction	$1 \times \lvert\hat{\mathbb{G}}\rvert$	$2n \times \lvert\mathbb{G}\rvert$	$3n\ \exp_{\mathbb{G}}$	$4P + 2n\exp_{\mathbb{G}}$
(Sect. 4)	$2 \times \lvert\mathbb{G}\rvert$	$n \times \lvert\hat{\mathbb{G}}\rvert$	$1\exp_{\hat{\mathbb{G}}}$	$n\exp_{\hat{\mathbb{G}}}$
			$n\ \text{mult}_{\hat{\mathbb{G}}}$	

$\exp_{\mathbb{G}}$ and $\exp_{\hat{\mathbb{G}}}$ denote exponentiations in $\mathbb{G}$ and $\hat{\mathbb{G}}$ while $\text{mult}_{\hat{\mathbb{G}}}$ denotes a multiplication in $\hat{\mathbb{G}}$; n denotes the bitlength of the range; P stands for a pairing computation; $\lvert\mathcal{C}\rvert$ is the size of the arithmetic circuit verifying a commitment opening.

[5] In randomized versions of the KZG commitment (described in [60, Section 3.3], [8, Appendix B.2] and [83]), each evaluation proof consists of an element of $\mathbb{G}$ and at least one scalar or an additional element of $\mathbb{G}$.

[6] In order to prove the knowledge soundness of the range proof of [9] when the polynomial commitment of [65] is used, it is necessary to rely on the latter's knowledge soundness in the AGM (as defined in [8, Appendix C.1.3]) but we believe this property holds under the $(2n, n)$-DLOG assumption.

exponentiations instead of a number of exponentiations growing with the size of an arithmetic circuit that computes a commitment opening (which would be very large as the circuit would have to compute modular exponentiations).

In Table 1, we compare our constant-size range proofs with existing pairing-based solutions featuring similarly short proofs. Several instantiations of [9] are considered for different polynomial commitment schemes that are known to provide constant-size evaluation proofs. Among schemes that do not generically rely on SNARKs, we only consider those where the CRS size is at most logarithmic in the maximal range magnitude $N = 2^n$ (i.e., linear in n). For example, Table 1 does not include range proofs based on lookup arguments [41,82] as they would require a CRS of size $O(N) = O(2^n)$. For a range $[0, 2^{30}]$, this would translate into a CRS of about 30 GB instead of 6 KB in our construction.

References

1. Albrecht, M.R., Cini, V., Lai, R.W.F., Malavolta, G., Thyagarajan, S.A.: Lattice-based SNARKs: publicly verifiable, preprocessing, and recursively composable: (extended abstract). In: Dodis, Y., Shrimpton, T. (eds.) Advances in Cryptology. CRYPTO 2022. LNCS, vol. 13508, pp. 102–132. Springer, Cham (2022). https://doi.org/10.1007/978-3-031-15979-4_4
2. Arun, A., Ganesh, C., Lokam, S., Mopuri, T., Sridhar, S.: Dew: a transparent constant-sized polynomial commitment scheme. In: Boldyreva, A., Kolesnikov, V. (eds.) Public-Key Cryptography. PKC 2023. LNCS, vol. 13941, pp. 542–571. Springer, Cham (2023). https://doi.org/10.1007/978-3-031-31371-4_19
3. Baghery, K., Kohlweiss, M., Siim, J., Volkhov, M.: Another look at extraction and randomization of Groth's zk-SNARK. In: Borisov, N., Diaz, C. (eds.) Financial Cryptography and Data Security: 25th International Conference. FC 2021. LNCS, vol. 12674, pp. 457–475. Springer, Heidelberg (2021). https://doi.org/10.1007/978-3-662-64322-8_22
4. Baghery, K., Pindado, Z., Ràfols, C.: Simulation extractable versions of Groth's zk-SNARK revisited. In: Krenn, S., Shulman, H., Vaudenay, S. (eds.) Cryptology and Network Security. LNCS, 12579, pp. 453–461. Springer, Cham (2020). https://doi.org/10.1007/978-3-030-65411-5_22
5. Balbas, D., Catalano, D., Fiore, D., Lai, R.-F.: Chainable functional commitments: from quadratic polynomials to unbounded-depth circuits. In: Rothblum, G., Wee, H. (eds.) Theory of Cryptography. TCC 2023. LNCS, vol. 14371, pp. 363–393. Springer, Cham (2023). https://doi.org/10.1007/978-3-031-48621-0_13
6. Boneh, D., Bünz, B., Fisch, B.: Batching techniques for accumulators with applications to IOPs and stateless blockchains. In: Boldyreva, A., Micciancio, D. (eds.) Advances in Cryptology. CRYPTO 2019. LNCS, vol. 11692, pp. 561–586. Springer, Cham (2019). https://doi.org/10.1007/978-3-030-26948-7_20
7. Boneh, D., Drake, J., Fisch, B., Gabizon, A.: Efficient polynomial commitment schemes for multiple points and polynomials. Cryptology ePrint Archive Report 2020/81 (2020)
8. Boneh, D., Drake, J., Fisch, B., Gabizon, A.: Halo infinite: proof-carrying data from additive polynomial commitments. In: Malkin, T., Peikert, C. (eds.) Advances in Cryptology. CRYPTO 2021. LNCS, vol. 12825, pp. 649–680. Springer, Cham (2021). https://doi.org/10.1007/978-3-030-84242-0_23

9. Boneh, D., Fisch, B., Gabizon, A., Williamson, Z.: A simple range proof from polynomial commitments (2020). https://hackmd.io/@dabo/B1U4kx8XI
10. Boneh, D., Nguyen, W., Ozdemir, A.: Efficient functional commitments: how to commit to a private function. Cryptology ePrint Archive Report 2021/1342
11. Boneh, D., Venkatesan, R.: Breaking RSA may not be equivalent to factoring: extended abstract. In: Nyberg, K. (ed.) Advances in Cryptology. EUROCRYPT 1998. LNCS, vol. 1403, pp. 59–71. Springer, Heidelberg (1998). https://doi.org/10.1007/BFb0054117
12. Boudot, F.: Efficient proofs that a committed number lies in an interval. In: Preneel, B. (ed.) Advances in Cryptology. EUROCRYPT 2000. LNCS, vol. 1807, pp. 431–444. Springer, Heidelberg (2000). https://doi.org/10.1007/3-540-45539-6_31
13. Bowe, S., Gabizon, A.: Making Groth's zk-SNARK simulation extractable in the random oracle model. Cryptology ePrint Archive Report 2018/187
14. Brakerski, Z., Gentry, C., Vaikuntanathan, V.: (Leveled) Fully Homomorphic Encryption without Bootstrapping. In: ITCS (2012)
15. Brickell, E.F., Chaum, D., Damgård, I.B., van de Graaf, J.: Gradual and verifiable release of a secret (Extended Abstract). In: Pomerance, C. (ed.) Advances in Cryptology. CRYPTO 1987. LNCS, vol. 293, pp. 156–166. Springer, Heidelberg (1988). https://doi.org/10.1007/3-540-48184-2_11
16. Bünz, B., Bootle, J., Boneh, D., Poelstra, A., Wuille, P., Maxwell, G.: Bulletproofs: short proofs for confidential transactions and more. In: IEEE S&P (2018)
17. Bünz, B., Fisch, B., Szepieniec, A.: Transparent SNARKs from DARK compilers. In: Canteaut, A., Ishai, Y. (eds.) Advances in Cryptology. EUROCRYPT 2020. LNCS, vol. 12105, pp. 677–706. Springer, Cham (2020). https://doi.org/10.1007/978-3-030-45721-1_24
18. Camenisch, J., Chaabouni, R., Shelat, A.: Efficient protocols for set membership and range proofs. In: Pieprzyk, J. (ed.) Advances in Cryptology. ASIACRYPT 2008. LNCS, vol. 5350, pp. 234–252. Springer, Heidelberg (2008). https://doi.org/10.1007/978-3-540-89255-7_15
19. Camenisch, J., Dubovitskaya, M., Haralambiev, K., Kohlweiss, M.: Composable and modular anonymous credentials: definitions and practical constructions. In: Iwata, T., Cheon, J. (eds.) Advances in Cryptology. ASIACRYPT 2015. LNCS, vol. 9453, pp. 262–288. Springer, Heidelberg (2015). https://doi.org/10.1007/978-3-662-48800-3_11
20. Campanelli, M., Fiore, D., Greco, N., Kolonelos, D., Nizzardo, L.: Incrementally aggregatable vector commitments and applications to verifiable decentralized storage. In: Moriai, S., Wang, H. (eds.) Advances in Cryptology. ASIACRYPT 2020. LNCS, vol. 12492, pp. 3–35. Springer, Cham (2020). https://doi.org/10.1007/978-3-030-64834-3_1
21. Campanelli, M., Nitulescu, A., Ràfols, C., Zacharakis, A., Zapico, A.: Linear-map vector commitments and their practical applications. In: Agrawal, S., Lin, D. (eds.) Advances in Cryptology. ASIACRYPT 2022. LNCS, vol. 13794, pp. 189–219. Springer, Cham (2022). https://doi.org/10.1007/978-3-031-22972-5_7
22. Catalano, D., Fiore, D.: Vector commitments and their applications. In: Kurosawa, K., Hanaoka, G. (eds.) Public-Key Cryptography. PKC 2013. LNCS, vol. 7778, pp. 55–72. Springer, Heidelberg (2013). https://doi.org/10.1007/978-3-642-36362-7_5
23. Catalano, D., Fiore, D., Gennaro, R., Giunta, E.: On the impossibility of algebraic vector commitments in pairing-free groups. In: Kiltz, E., Vaikuntanathan, V. (eds.) Theory of Cryptography: 20th International Conference. TCC 2022. LNCS, vol. 13748, pp. 274–299. Springer, Cham (2022). https://doi.org/10.1007/978-3-031-22365-5_10

24. Catalano, D., Fiore, D., Tucker, I.: Additive-homomorphic functional commitments and applications to homomorphic signatures. In: Agrawal, S., Lin, D. (eds.) Advances in Cryptology. ASIACRYPT 2022. LNCS, vol. 13794, pp. 159–188. Springer, Cham (2022). https://doi.org/10.1007/978-3-031-22972-5_6
25. Chaabouni, R., Lipmaa, H., Zhang, B.: A non-interactive range proof with constant communication. In: Keromytis A.D. (ed.) Financial Cryptography and Data Security. LNCS, vol. 7397, pp. 179–199. Springer, Heidelberg (2012). https://doi.org/10.1007/978-3-642-32946-3_14
26. Chan, A., Frankel, Y., Tsiounis, Y.: Easy come — Easy go divisible cash. In: Nyberg, K. (ed.) Advances in Cryptology. EUROCRYPT 1998. LNCS, vol. 1403, pp. 561–575. Springer, Heidelberg (1998). https://doi.org/10.1007/BFb0054154
27. Chillotti, I., Gama, N., Georgieva, M., Izabachène, M.: TFHE: fast fully homomorphic encryption over the torus. J. Cryptol. **33**(1), 34–91 (2020)
28. Chu, H., Fiore, D., Kolonelos, D., Schröder, D.: Inner product functional commitments with constant-size public parameters and openings. In: Galdi, C., Jarecki, S. (eds.) Security and Cryptography for Networks: 13th International Conference. SCN 2022. LNCS, vol. 13409, pp. 639–662. Springer, Cham (2022). https://doi.org/10.1007/978-3-031-14791-3_28
29. Couteau, G., Goudarzi, D., Klooß, M., Reichle, M.: Sharp: short relaxed range oroofs. In: ACM-CCS (2022)
30. Couteau, G., Klooß, M., Lin, H., Reichle, M.: Efficient range proofs with transparent setup from bounded integer commitments. In: Canteaut, A., Standaert, F.-X. (eds.) Advances in Cryptology. EUROCRYPT 2021. LNCS, vol. 12698, pp. 247–277. Springer, Cham (2021). https://doi.org/10.1007/978-3-030-77883-5_9
31. Couteau, G., Peters, T., Pointcheval, D.: Removing the strong RSA assumption from arguments over the integers. In: Coron, J.-S., Nielsen, J.B. (eds.) Advances in Cryptology. EUROCRYPT 2017. LNCS, vol. 10211, pp. 321–350. Springer, Cham (2017). https://doi.org/10.1007/978-3-319-56614-6_11
32. Dai, W.: PESCA: a privacy-enhancing smart-contract architecture. Manuscript
33. Das, S., Camacho, P., Xiang, Z., Nieto, J., Bünz, B., Ren, L.: Threshold signatures from inner product argument: succinct, weighted, and multi-threshold. In: ACM-CCS (2023)
34. de Castro, L., Peikert, C.: Functional commitments for all functions, with transparent setup and from SIS. In: Hazay, C. , Stam, M. (eds.) Advances in Cryptology. EUROCRYPT 2023. LNCS, vol. 14006, pp. 287–320. Springer, Cham (2023). https://doi.org/10.1007/978-3-031-30620-4_10
35. del Pino, R., Lyubashevsky, V., Seiler, G.: Short discrete log proofs for FHE and ring-LWE ciphertexts. In: Lin, D., Sako, K. (eds.) Public-Key Cryptography. PKC 2019. LNCS, vol. 11442, pp. 344–373. Springer, Cham (2019). https://doi.org/10.1007/978-3-030-17253-4_12
36. Dolev, D., Dwork, C., Naor, M.: Non-malleable cryptography. In: STOC (1991)
37. El Housni, Y., Guillevic, A.: Optimized and secure pairing-friendly elliptic curves suitable for one layer proof composition. In: Krenn, S., Shulman, H., Vaudenay, S. (eds.) Cryptology and Network Security. CANS 2020. LNCS, vol. 12579, pp. 259–279. Springer, Cham (2020). https://doi.org/10.1007/978-3-030-65411-5_13
38. Feneuil, T., Maire, J., Rivain, M., Vergnaud, D.: Zero-knowledge protocols for the subset sum problem from MPC-in-the-head with rejection. In: Agrawal, S., Lin, D. (eds.) Advances in Cryptology. ASIACRYPT 2022. LNCS, vol. 13792, pp. 371–402. Springer, Cham (2022). https://doi.org/10.1007/978-3-031-22966-4_13

39. Fiore, D., Nitulescu, A., Pointcheval, D.: Boosting verifiable computation on encrypted data. In: Kiayias, A., Kohlweiss, M., Wallden, P., Zikas, V. (eds.) Public-Key Cryptography. PKC 2020. LNCS, vol. 12111, pp. 124–154. Springer, Cham (2020). https://doi.org/10.1007/978-3-030-45388-6_5
40. Fuchsbauer, G., Kiltz, E., Loss, J.: The algebraic group model and its applications. In: Shacham, H., Boldyreva, A. (eds.) Advances in Cryptology. CRYPTO 2018. LNCS, vol. 10992, pp. 33–62. Springer, Cham (2018). https://doi.org/10.1007/978-3-319-96881-0_2
41. Gabizon, A., Williamson, Z.: Plookup: a simplified polynomial protocol for lookup tables. Cryptology ePrint Archive Report 2020/315
42. Gabizon, G., Williamson, Z., Ciobotaru, O.: PLONK: permutations over lagrange-bases for oecumenical noninteractive arguments of knowledge. Cryptology ePrint Archive, Report 2019/953,2019
43. Ganesh, C., Khoshakhlagh, H., Kohlweiss, M., Nitulescu, A., Zajkac, M.: What makes Fiat–Shamir zkSNARKs (Updatable SRS) simulation extractable? In: Galdi, C., Jarecki, S. (eds.) Security and Cryptography for Networks. SCN 2022. LNCS, vol. 13409, pp. 735–760. Springer, Cham (2022). https://doi.org/10.1007/978-3-031-14791-3_32
44. Ganesh, C., Orlandi, C., Pancholi, M., Takahashi, A., Tschudi, D.: Fiat–Shamir bulletproofs are non-Malleable (in the Algebraic Group Model). In: Dunkelman, O., Dziembowski, S. (eds.) Advances in Cryptology. EUROCRYPT 2022. LNCS, vol. 13276, pp. 397–426. Springer, Cham (2022). https://doi.org/10.1007/978-3-031-07085-3_14
45. Gennaro, R., Gentry, C., Parno, B., Raykova, M.: Quadratic span programs and succinct NIZKs without PCPs. In: Johansson, T., Nguyen, P.Q. (eds.) Advances in Cryptology. EUROCRYPT 2013. LNCS, vol. 7881, pp. 626–645. Springer, Heidelberg (2013). https://doi.org/10.1007/978-3-642-38348-9_37
46. Gentry, C., Wichs, D.: Separating succinct non-interactive arguments from all falsifiable assumptions. In: STOC (2011)
47. González, A.: Efficient non-interactive zero-knowledge proofs. Ph.D. thesis Universidad De Chile, Santiago (2017)
48. González, A., Hevia, A., Ràfols, C.: QA-NIZK arguments in asymmetric groups: new tools and new constructions. In: Iwata, T., Cheon, J.H. (eds.) Advances in Cryptology. ASIACRYPT 2015. LNCS, vol. 9452, pp. 605–629. Springer, Heidelberg (2015). https://doi.org/10.1007/978-3-662-48797-6_25
49. González, A., Ráfols, C.: New techniques for non-interactive shuffle and range arguments. In: Manulis, M., Sadeghi, A.-R., Schneider, S. (eds.) Applied Cryptography and Network Security. ACNS 2016. LNCS, vol. 9696, pp. 427–444. Springer, Cham (2016). https://doi.org/10.1007/978-3-319-39555-5_23
50. Gorbunov, S., Reyzin, L., Wee, H., Zhang, Z.: PointProofs: aggregating proofs for multiple vector commitments. In: ACM-CCS (2020)
51. Gorbunov, S., Vaikuntanathan, V., Wichs, D.: Leveled fully homomorphic signatures from standard lattices. In: STOC (2015)
52. Groth, J.: Non-interactive zero-knowledge arguments for voting. In: Ioannidis, J., Keromytis, A., Yung, M. (eds.) Applied Cryptography and Network Security. ACNS 2005. LNCS, vol. 3531, pp. 467–482. Springer, Heidelberg (2005). https://doi.org/10.1007/11496137_32
53. Groth, J.: Pairing-based non-interactive zero-knowledge proofs. In: Joye, M., Miyaji, A., Otsuka, A. (eds.) Pairing-Based Cryptography. Pairing 2010. LNCS, vol. 6487, pp. 206–206. Springer, Heidelberg (2010). https://doi.org/10.1007/978-3-642-17455-1_13

54. Groth, J.: Efficient zero-knowledge arguments from two-tiered homomorphic commitments. In: Lee, D.H., Wang, X. (eds.) Advances in Cryptology. ASIACRYPT 2011. LNCS, vol. 7073, pp. 431–448. Springer, Heidelberg (2011). https://doi.org/10.1007/978-3-642-25385-0_23
55. Groth, J.: On the size of pairing-based non-interactive arguments. In: Fischlin, M., Coron, J.-S. (eds.) Advances in Cryptology. EUROCRYPT 2016. LNCS, vol. 9666, pp. 305–326. Springer, Heidelberg (2016). https://doi.org/10.1007/978-3-662-49896-5_11
56. Groth, J., Maller, M.: Snarky signatures: minimal signatures of knowledge from simulation-extractable SNARKs. In: Katz, J., Shacham, H. (eds.) Advances in Cryptology. CRYPTO 2017. LNCS, vol. 10402, pp. 581–621. Springer, Cham (2017). https://doi.org/10.1007/978-3-319-63715-0_20
57. Groth, J., Sahai, A.: Efficient non-interactive proof systems for bilinear groups. In: Smart, N. (ed.) Advances in Cryptology. EUROCRYPT 2008. LNCS, vol. 4965, pp. 415–432. Springer, Heidelberg (2008). https://doi.org/10.1007/978-3-540-78967-3_24
58. Ishai, Y., Kushilevitz, E., Ostrovsky, R.: Efficient arguments without short PCPs. In: CCC (2007)
59. Kachisa, E.J., Schaefer, E.F., Scott, M.: Constructing Brezing-Weng pairing-friendly elliptic curves using elements in the cyclotomic field. In: Galbraith, S.D., Paterson, K.G. (eds.) Pairing-Based Cryptography. Pairing 2008. LNCS, vol. 5209, pp. 126–135. Springer, Heidelberg (2008). https://doi.org/10.1007/978-3-540-85538-5_9
60. Kate, A., Zaverucha, G.M., Goldberg, I.: Constant-size commitments to polynomials and their applications. In: Abe, M. (ed.) Advances in Cryptology. ASIACRYPT 2010. LNCS, vol. 6477, pp. 177–194. Springer, Heidelberg (2010). https://doi.org/10.1007/978-3-642-17373-8_11
61. Zhang, C., Zhou, HS., Katz, J.: An analysis of the algebraic group model. In: Agrawal, S., Lin, D. (eds.) Advances in Cryptology. ASIACRYPT 2022. LNCS, vol. 13794, pp. 310–322. Springer, Cham (2022). https://doi.org/10.1007/978-3-031-22972-5_11
62. Krupp, J., Schröder, D., Simkin, M., Fiore, D., Ateniese, G., Nuernberger, S.: Nearly optimal verifiable data streaming. In: PKC (2016)
63. Lai, R.W.F., Malavolta, G.: Subvector commitments with application to succinct arguments. In: Boldyreva, A., Micciancio, D. (eds.) Advances in Cryptology. CRYPTO 2019. LNCS, vol. 11692, pp. 530–560. Springer, Cham (2019). https://doi.org/10.1007/978-3-030-26948-7_19
64. Lee, J.: Dory: efficient, transparent arguments for generalised inner products and polynomial commitments. In: Nissim, K., Waters, B. (eds.) Theory of Cryptography. TCC 2021. LNCS, vol. 13043, pp. 1–34. Springer, Cham (2021). https://doi.org/10.1007/978-3-030-90453-1_1
65. Libert, B., Ramanna, S., Yung, M.: Functional commitment schemes: from polynomial commitments to pairing-based accumulators from simple assumptions. In: ICALP (2016)
66. Libert, B., Yung, M.: Concise mercurial vector commitments and independent zero-knowledge sets with short proofs. In: Micciancio, D. (ed.) Theory of Cryptography. TCC 2010. LNCS, vol. 5978, pp. 499–517. Springer, Heidelberg (2010). https://doi.org/10.1007/978-3-642-11799-2_30
67. Lipmaa, H.: On diophantine complexity and statistical zero-knowledge arguments. In: Laih, C.S. (ed.) Advances in Cryptology. ASIACRYPT 2003. LNCS, vol.

2894, pp. 398–415. Springer, Heidelberg (2003). https://doi.org/10.1007/978-3-540-40061-5_26
68. Lipmaa, H., Pavlyk, K.: Succinct functional commitment for a large class of arithmetic circuits. In: Moriai, S., Wang, H. (eds.) Advances in Cryptology. ASIACRYPT 2020. LNCS, vol. 12493, pp. 686–716. Springer, Cham (2020). https://doi.org/10.1007/978-3-030-64840-4_23
69. Lyubashevsky, V., Peikert, C., Regev, O.: On ideal lattices and learning with errors over rings. In: Gilbert, H. (ed.) Advances in Cryptology. EUROCRYPT 2010. LNCS, vol. 6110, pp. 1–23. Springer, Heidelberg (2010). https://doi.org/10.1007/978-3-642-13190-5_1
70. Maller, M., Bowe, S., Kohlweiss, M., Meiklejohn, S.: Sonic: zero-knowledge SNARKs from linear-size universal and updateable structured reference strings. In: ACM-CCS (2019)
71. Merkle, R.: A certified digital signature. In: Crypto (1989)
72. Micali, S.: Computationally sound proofs. SIAM J. Comput. **30**(4) (2000)
73. Paillier, P., Vergnaud, D.: Discrete-log-based signatures may not be equivalent to discrete log. In: Roy, B. (ed.) Advances in Cryptology. ASIACRYPT 2005. LNCS, vol. 3788, pp. 1–20. Springer, Heidelberg (2005). https://doi.org/10.1007/11593447_1
74. Pedersen, T.P.: Non-interactive and information-theoretic secure verifiable secret sharing. In: Feigenbaum, J. (ed.) Advances in Cryptology. CRYPTO 1991. LNCS, vol. 576, pp. 129–140. Springer, Heidelberg (1992). https://doi.org/10.1007/3-540-46766-1_9
75. Peikert, C., Pepin, Z., Sharp, C.: Vector and functional commitments from lattices. In: Nissim, K., Waters, B. (eds.) Theory of Cryptography. TCC 2021. LNCS, vol. 13044, pp. 480–511. Springer, Cham (2021). https://doi.org/10.1007/978-3-030-90456-2_16
76. Shoup, V.: Lower bounds for discrete logarithms and related problems. In: Fumy, W. (ed.) Advances in Cryptology. EUROCRYPT 1997. LNCS, vol. 1233, pp. 256–266. Springer, Heidelberg (1997). https://doi.org/10.1007/3-540-69053-0_18
77. Solomon, R., Weber, R., Almashaqbeh, G.: smartFHE: privacy-preserving smart contracts from fully homomorphic encryption. In: EuroS&P (2023)
78. Srinivasan, S., Chepurnoy, A., Papamanthou, C., Tomescu, A., Zhang, Y.: Hyperproofs: aggregating and maintaining proofs in vector commitments. In: USENIX Security (2022)
79. Tomescu, A., Abraham, I., Buterin, V., Drake, J., Feist, D., Khovratovich, D.: Aggregatable subvector commitments for stateless cryptocurrencies. In: Galdi, C., Kolesnikov, V. (eds.) Security and Cryptography for Networks. SCN 2020. LNCS, vol. 12238, pp. 45–64. Springer, Cham (2020). https://doi.org/10.1007/978-3-030-57990-6_3
80. Tomescu, A., Xia, Y., Newman, Z.: Authenticated dictionaries with cross-incremental proof (DIS)aggregation. Cryptology ePrint Archive Report 2020/1239
81. Wee, H., Wu, D.J.: Succinct vector, polynomial, and functional commitments from lattices. In: Hazay, C., Stam, M. (eds.) Advances in Cryptology. EUROCRYPT 2023. LNCS, vol. 14006, pp. 385–416. Springer, Cham (2023). https://doi.org/10.1007/978-3-031-30620-4_13
82. Zapico, A, Buterin, V., Khovratovich, D., Maller, M., Nitulescu, A., Simkin, M.: Caulk: lookup arguments in sublinear time. In: ACM-CCS (2022)
83. Zhang, Y., Genkin, D., Katz, J., Papadopoulos, D., Papamanthou, C.: A zero-knowledge version of vSQL. Cryptology ePrint Archive Report 2017/1146

Simulation-Extractable KZG Polynomial Commitments and Applications to HyperPlonk

Benoît Libert(✉)

Zama, Paris, France
benoit.libert@zama.ai

Abstract. HyperPlonk is a recent SNARK proposal (Eurocrypt'23) that features a linear-time prover and supports custom gates of larger degree than Plonk. For the time being, its instantiations are only proven to be knowledge-sound (meaning that soundness is only guaranteed when the prover runs in isolation) while many applications motivate the stronger notion of simulation-extractability (SE). Unfortunately, the most efficient SE compilers are not immediately applicable to multivariate polynomial interactive oracle proofs. To address this problem, we provide an instantiation of HyperPlonk for which we can prove simulation-extractability in a strong sense. As a crucial building block, we describe KZG-based commitments to multivariate polynomials that also provide simulation-extractability while remaining as efficient as malleable ones. Our proofs stand in the combined algebraic group and random oracle model and ensure straight-line extractability (i.e., without rewinding).

Keywords: Polynomial commitments · SNARKs · zero-knowledge · simulation-extractability

1 Introduction

A standard technique to obtain succinct non-interactive arguments of knowledge (SNARKs) is to compile a polynomial interactive oracle proof (PIOP) [10] using a polynomial commitment scheme (PCS) [37]. The resulting interactive argument system can then be made non-interactive using the Fiat-Shamir heuristic [25]. Many popular SNARKs (including Sonic [44], Plonk [28], STARK [9], Marlin [18] or Gemini [12]) were designed using this methodology. In order to obtain concretely efficient SNARKs, two widely used polynomial commitment schemes (PCS) are KZG [37] and FRI [8].

Most SNARKs are proven to be knowledge-sound, which only guarantees soundness against a stand-alone prover. In practical applications, however, cheating provers can copy proofs from one another and even tamper with proofs generated by honest parties in an attempt to prove a related statement without knowing underlying witnesses. The notions of simulation-soundness [46] and simulation-extractability [21] rule out these malleability attacks. In particular, simulation-extractability (SE) ensures knowledge-soundness even when

Q. Tang and V. Teague (Eds.): PKC 2024, LNCS 14602, pp. 68–98, 2024.
https://doi.org/10.1007/978-3-031-57722-2_3

the adversary can observe proofs generated by honest parties and try to create a proof of its own by mauling honestly generated proofs. Simulation-extractability is thus an important security property in all applications where succinct arguments are widely available online.

The most efficient simulation-extractable SNARKs often require a scheme-specific analysis [3,36] or, in instantiations of the PIOP paradigm, require specific conditions on the underlying PIOP and polynomial commitments [23,29,39]. To our knowledge, existing generic approaches either fail to preserve succinctness [41] or introduce significant overhead [2] by relying on additional primitives.

In this paper, we further investigate the (non-black-box) simulation-extractability of SNARKs obtained by compiling multivariate PIOPs using pairing-based polynomial commitments like KZG. We focus on the recent HyperPlonk construction of Chen *et al.* [17], which improves Plonk so as to obtain a linear-time prover and larger-degree custom gates by working over the Boolean hypercube. We provide a simulation-extractable instantiation of HyperPlonk in the combined algebraic group and random oracle (AGM+ROM) model using appropriate polynomial commitments that are themselves proven simulation-extractable. Our security proof features a straight-line knowledge extractor that extracts witnesses without rewinding in order to make the reduction tighter.

To this end, we build suitable simulation-extractable polynomial commitments to multivariate polynomials since HyperPlonk heavily relies on multilinear polynomial commitments over the Boolean hypercube.

1.1 Contributions

We first construct pairing-based simulation-extractable polynomial commitments (SE-PCS) in the combined algebraic group and random oracle model. For multivariate and univariate polynomials, we obtain these by tweaking KZG-based commitments [37,52] and prove simulation-extractability in a strong sense.

Our multivariate PCS is obtained by modifying a multivariate PCS suggested by Zhang *et al.* [52], which is itself a randomized variant the multivariate extension of KZG from [45]. Just like its deterministic version [45], the multivariate PCS of [52] is actually malleable. However, we show that it can be made simulation-extractable (by introducing a random oracle) at a moderate cost using an approach of "proving knowledge of an evaluation proof" via the Fiat-Shamir paradigm [25]. This approach only slightly increases the complexity of the scheme (by introducing only one additional scalar in the proof without significantly affecting computational costs) and leverages the non-malleability properties [24] of the Fiat-Shamir transform. Despite the use of Fiat-Shamir, we can prove simulation-extractability in the AGM+ROM without rewinding.

Along the way, we also provide a new security proof (in the algebraic group model) for the multivariate PCS of Zhang *et al.* [52], in its simplest variant where commitments only consist of one group element. While the original proof was given under a knowledge assumption (more precisely, a parameterized variant of the knowledge-of-exponent assumption [19]) in the standard model and for a less efficient variant of the scheme, it was recently shown to be incorrect [40].

Our new proof stands in the algebraic group model and generalizes the result Kohrita and Towa [40] who gave a new proof in the univariate case.

Using our simulation-extractable multivariate PCS, we then give a simulation-extractable variant of HyperPlonk which preserves its linear complexity at the prover. Again, we can prove security in the AGM+ROM without rewinding.

As a result of independent interest, we describe a new randomized variant of univariate KZG commitments, which is more efficient than the standard randomized variant (described in [37]) of KZG commitments. In particular, its hiding and zero-knowledge properties do not require the commitment randomness to be as large as the degree of the committed polynomial, even when many evaluations are given out. This variant is proven simulation-extractable and is more efficient than the one implied by our simulation-extractable variant of [52].

1.2 Technical Overview

In SNARK constructions relying on a trusted setup, proving SE via the modular frameworks of [29,39] requires to provide a trapdoor-less zero-knowledge simulator, which does not use the trapdoor of the SRS but proceeds by only programming random oracles. In the zero-knowledge version of HyperPlonk [17, Appendix A], the simulator uses a ZK simulator described in [51] for sumcheck protocols [43]. However, the latter zero-knowledge sumcheck simulator assumes that the underlying multivariate PCS has zero-knowledge evaluation proofs (see [17, Lemma A.2] and [51, Theorem 3]). While the commitment scheme of Zhang *et al.* [52] satisfies this property, its simulator is not trapdoor-less. Moreover, it does not provide the weak unique response property required by [39] because its evaluation proofs are publicly randomizable. For the same reason, we cannot easily extend the ideas of [23] to the multivariate setting since they require an even stronger property on behalf of the polynomial commitment.

To overcome the above hurdle, we construct a variant of the multivariate PCS of [52] which is trapdoor-less zero-knowledge and satisfies a strong flavor of simulation-extractability.

Our multivariate PCS system commits to polynomials in the same way as its malleable counterpart [52]. However, we use a different non-interactive evaluation protocol, which proceeds by having the committer prove knowledge of an evaluation proof of the original PCS scheme [52]. This can be done efficiently by exploiting the malleability of the initial evaluation proofs. In groups $(\mathbb{G}, \hat{\mathbb{G}}, \mathbb{G}_T)$ endowed with a bilinear map $e : \mathbb{G} \times \hat{\mathbb{G}} \to \mathbb{G}_T$, the malleable PCS of [52] commits to polynomials $f \in \mathbb{Z}_p[X_1, \ldots, X_\ell]$ via commitments of the form $C = g^{f(\alpha_1,\ldots,\alpha_\ell)+r\cdot\alpha_r}$, for a random $r \in \mathbb{Z}_p$ and where $(\alpha_1, \ldots, \alpha_\ell, \alpha_r)$ are secrets hidden in the structured reference string (SRS). The correctness of evaluations $y = f(z_1, \ldots, z_\ell)$ is proven via group elements $\boldsymbol{\pi} = (\pi_1, \ldots, \pi_\ell, \pi_r) \in \mathbb{G}^{\ell+1}$ satisfying a pairing-product equation of the form

$$F(\mathsf{srs}, C, y) = \prod_{i=1}^{\ell} e(\pi_i, \hat{g}^{\alpha_i} \cdot \hat{g}^{-z_i}) \cdot e(\pi_r, \hat{g}^{\alpha_r}), \tag{1}$$

where F is a function of the SRS, C is the commitment and $y \in \mathbb{Z}_p$ is the claimed output. Instead of revealing $\boldsymbol{\pi}$ as the original scheme does, we exploit the linearity properties of equation (1) which make it possible to efficiently prove knowledge of $(\pi_1, \ldots, \pi_\ell, \pi_r) \in \mathbb{G}^{\ell+1}$ satisfying (1) via a standard Schnorr-like Σ-protocol [47] allowing to prove knowledge of homomorphism pre-images. Although the product (1) allows randomizing the underlying $\boldsymbol{\pi}$, we can achieve simulation-extractability by exploiting the non-malleability [24] of Fiat-Shamir when $(C, y, \boldsymbol{z} = (z_1, \ldots, z_\ell))$ are included in the inputs of the random oracle.

While the above idea is simple, proving the simulation-extractability of the Fiat-Shamir-compiled evaluation proof is non-trivial when it comes to achieving straight-line extraction. To this end, we extend an observation from [27] which shows that, in the AGM, Schnorr signatures can be proven secure without rewinding. In our SE-PCS, in order to prove knowledge of $(\pi_1, \ldots, \pi_\ell, \pi_r)$ satisfying (1), we reveal $(\pi_1, \ldots, \pi_\ell)$ in the clear but we prove knowledge of π_r. The Σ-protocol has a verification equation of the form

$$R = e(S_\pi, \hat{g}^{\alpha_r}) \cdot \left(F(\mathsf{srs}, C, y) \cdot \prod_{i=1}^{\ell} e(\pi_i, \hat{g}^{\alpha_i} \cdot \hat{g}^{-z_i})^{-1} \right)^{-c} .$$

where S_π is a blinded version of π_r and $c \in \mathbb{Z}_p$ is a Fiat-Shamir challenge obtained by hashing $R \in \mathbb{G}_T$ along with $(C, y, \boldsymbol{z})$ and $(\pi_1, \ldots, \pi_\ell)$. In the combined AGM+ROM model, when the adversary makes a random oracle query involving a tuple (R, C, y, z), it has to provide algebraic representations of group elements R and C with respect to previously observed elements of the same group. From these representations, the knowledge extractor can infer polynomials $R[X_1, \ldots, X_\ell, X_r]$, $\{A_i[X_1, \ldots, X_\ell, X_r]\}_{i=1}^{\ell}$ and $f[X_1, \ldots, X_\ell]$ such that $C = g^{f(\alpha_1, \ldots, \alpha_\ell) + r \cdot \alpha_r}$, $R = e(g, \hat{g})^{R(\alpha_1, \ldots, \alpha_\ell, \alpha_r)}$, and $\pi_i = g^{A_i(\alpha_1, \ldots, \alpha_\ell, \alpha_r)}$ for each $i \in [\ell]$. If $y \neq f(z_1, \ldots, z_\ell)$, we can use an argument reminiscent of Katz-Wang signatures [38] and argue that a certain $(\ell+1)$-variate polynomial – which is computable from $R[X_1, \ldots, X_\ell, X_r]$, $\{A_i[X_1, \ldots, X_\ell, X_r]\}_{i=1}^{\ell}$ and $f[X_1, \ldots, X_\ell]$ – is non-zero with overwhelming probability. In turn, this non-zero polynomial determines a univariate polynomial whose roots contain the discrete logarithm $\alpha \in \mathbb{Z}_p$ hidden in the structured CRS $(g, (g^{(\alpha^i)})_{i=1}^{m}, (\hat{g}^{(\alpha^i)})_{i=1}^{n})$.

In order to build an SE variant of HyperPlonk, we use our SE-PCS in the following way. Like Plonk [28], HyperPlonk proceeds by having the prover define an $N \times 3$ matrix of which the rows $\mathbf{M} = \{(L_i, R_i, O_i)\}_{i=1}^{N}$ contain the left/right inputs and the output of each gate. It commits to a multilinear $M[X_1, \ldots, X_\ell]$ whose evaluations over the Boolean hypercube are the entries of $\mathbf{M}$. Then, it proves that $M[\boldsymbol{X}]$ satisfies a "gate identity" by showing that some polynomial $f[\boldsymbol{X}]$ defined as a function of $M[\boldsymbol{X}]$ and circuit-dependent polynomials cancels everywhere on the hypercube $\{0,1\}^\ell$. Next, in order to prove that $\mathbf{M}$ is consistent with the wiring of the circuit, it proves that $M[\boldsymbol{X}]$ satisfies a "wiring identity" $M(\boldsymbol{x}) = M(\hat{\sigma}(\boldsymbol{x}))$ for all $x \in \{0,1\}^\ell$, for some circuit-dependent permutation $\hat{\sigma}$. This is done by showing that $M[\boldsymbol{X}]$ satisfies a product argument over $\{0,1\}^\ell$, by adapting a technique used in Plonk [28] and inspired from [7]. In turn, the product relation is proven by showing that another polynomial vanishes over $\{0,1\}^\ell$ and that some related polynomial $\tilde{v}[\boldsymbol{X}]$ evaluates to 1 on the input $(1, 1, \ldots, 1, 0)$.

In order to obtain a trapdoor-less simulator for HyperPlonk, we choose a multilinear polynomial $\hat{M}[\boldsymbol{X}]$ that satisfies the gate identity, but not the wiring identity (which is always possible without knowing a witness). Then, we can easily prove that the appropriate polynomials vanish everywhere on $\{0,1\}^\ell$ (since $\hat{M}[\boldsymbol{X}]$ is a valid witness for the zerocheck arguments) but, since $\hat{M}[\boldsymbol{X}]$ does not satisfy the wiring identity and the underlying product relation, the corresponding polynomial $\tilde{v}[\boldsymbol{X}]$ does not evaluate to 1 on $(1, 1, \ldots, 1, 0)$. However, we can simulate a proof of the latter false statement using our SE-PCS construction.

1.3 Related Work

Simulation-soundness was first introduced by Sahai [46] and strengthened by De Santis *et al.* [21] so as to further ensure extractability. Several techniques based on OR proofs [21,34] have been proposed to generically build simulation-extractable NIZK proofs by upgrading NIZK proofs satisfying the standard notion of soundness. Among these, the technique of De Santis *et al.* [21] makes non-black-box use of additional building blocks such as one-time signatures and pseudorandom functions, which is generally very expensive. Optimizations of this approach were considered in [1,2,41]. The compiler of Kosba *et al.* [41] fails to preserve succinctness in the SNARK setting. While the lifting techniques of [1,2] retain succcinctness, they introduce additional components such as key-homomorphic signatures, which still introduce a significant overhead in terms of proving/verification time or SRS size. The compilers of [1,30] further achieve universal composability [16]. Ganesh *et al.* [30] notably achieve full succinctness via a generic construction allowing to achieve UC security on top of simulation-extractable SNARKs (in the non-programmable ROM).

A different approach proceeds via direct, scheme-specific security analyzes. Groth and Maller [36] gave a simulation-extractable SNARK where proofs only consist of 3 group elements. SE variants of Groth16 [35] were given in [3,4,6,13] while the original version of the scheme [35] was proven [5] weakly simulation-extractable (meaning that the adversary can randomize existing proofs but not come up with a fake proof for a new statement). Lipmaa [42] gave a general framework for constructing SE-SNARKs for R1CS statements [33] in an extension of the AGM allowing to oblivious sample group elements. The constructions of [3,4,13,35,36,42] rely on a non-universal (i.e., circuit-dependent) CRS.

BulletProofs [14] was shown to provide simulation-extractability in the AGM [32] and in the random oracle model [20,31]. Ganesh *et al.* [29] proved the simulation-extractability of Plonk [28], Sonic [44] and Marlin [18] in the combined random oracle and algebraic group model (AGM) [26] using a rewinding-based proof. One disadvantage of their framework is the use of rewinding, which results in non-tight reductions. Also, the proof of simulation-extractability given in [29] for Plonk was recently found [39] to be flawed since the original Plonk uses a deterministic variant of KZG commitments [37]. Specifically, the trapdoor-less simulator of [29] was shown [39] to not provide statistical zero-knowledge.[1] In [39], the authors showed that this problem can be fixed using a randomized version of KZG commitments. A closer inspection suggests that, when instantiated with randomized KZG commitments, Plonk can be proven simulation-extractable without rewinding by applying the compiler of [39] since its knowledge soundness can be argued via a straight-line extractor in the AGM.

A third approach builds SE-SNARKs using the PIOP paradigm by formalizing specific requirements on the underlying PIOP and PCS systems. A recent work of Faonio *et al.* [23] suggests to use a weak form of simulation-extractable polynomial commitments. While they prove such a weak form of simulation-extractability for randomized KZG commitments, they only do it in the univariate case and their techniques are not known to carry over to existing multivariate PCS. The same holds for the framework of [39] as it requires a PCS satisfying a notion of weak uniqueness, meaning that no PPT adversary should be able to randomize a proof obtained from the simulator for the same evaluation pair $(\boldsymbol{z}, y)$. Unfortunately, the most widely used multivariate extensions [45,52] of KZG commitments do not satisfy the latter property since their proofs are publicly randomizable. As it turns out, none of the results of [23,29,39] readily applies to HyperPlonk [17], let alone with straight-line simulation extractability.

In the relaxed notion of SE-PCS formalized by Faonio *et al.* [23], simulation-extractability is defined with respect to a policy. They showed that KZG commitments satisfy their relaxed security notion for random evaluation inputs, which suffices to build simulation-extractable SNARKs. Here, we show that a stronger and simpler-to-state flavor of SE-PCS is achievable at a quite moderate cost in the combined algebraic group and random oracle model. Compared to the underlying malleable randomized commitment (of which we prove knowledge of an evaluation proof), we just need to introduce one more scalar in the evaluation proof and the number of pairings at the verifier remains exactly the same.

Unlike [23,39], our approach is not generic as we only apply it to HyperPlonk, which is one of the most appealing candidates in terms of efficiency. However, we believe that our multivariate SE-PCS can be applied to other PIOPs that proceed by proving sumcheck relations. A common feature of our construction and [23] is that they both impose stronger (yet, efficiently achievable) requirements on behalf of the underlying PCS instead of relying on PIOPs satisfying unique response properties. At the same time, we depart from [23] in that our SE-PCS candidates have a trapdoor-less simulator while [23] simulates evaluation proofs using "programmable" trapdoors in randomized KZG commitments.

Campanelli *et al.* [15] recently described a SNARK featuring a linear-time prover, $O(1)$-size proofs and a universal SRS whose size only grows with the square root of the circuit size. Their approach consists in proving knowledge of a Spartan proof [48] using Groth16 [35]. It is plausible that existing techniques [3,6,13] allowing to make Groth16 simulation-extractable carry over to achieve simulation-extractability in Testudo [15]. Compared to HyperPlonk, Testudo [15]

---

[1] This does not contradict the stated zero-knowledge property of Plonk since the simulator outlined in [28] uses the trapdoor of the CRS (unlike the one from [29]).

provides shorter proof/SRS sizes. On the other hand, its R1CS arithmetization does not immediately support custom gates as HyperPlonk does.

In the context of polynomial commitments, Kohrita and Towa [40, Appendix B.2.2] recently reported an error in the original security proof of Zhang *et al.*'s randomized variant [52] of [45]. A new security proof in the AGM was given in [40, Appendix B] in the univariate case. Our security proof differs from theirs (but relies on the same assumption in the AGM) and carries over to the multivariate case. In [40], Kohrita and Towa [40] also gave a generic construction of multilinear polynomial commitments from additively homomorphic univariate polynomial commitments. Their multilinear PCS scheme has a faster verification algorithm than [52] with only 3 pairing evaluations instead of $O(\mu)$, where μ is the number of variables. They also provide a randomized variant of KZG commitments where the prover's randomness consists of a constant number of field elements, but proofs are randomizable. In this paper, we provide a simulation-extractable variant of the multilinear PCS from [52] whereas [40] does not consider simulation-extractability. It may be possible to combine the univariate-to-multilinear transformation of [40] with our simulation-extractable univariate PCS (described in the full version of the paper) to obtain a more efficient SE-PCS to multilinear polynomials with a constant number of pairing evaluations at the verifier. This requires a simulation-extractable variant of the batch-degre-check argument of [40] and we leave it for future work.

2 Background and Definitions

For any positive integer ℓ, we denote by $[\ell]$ the set $\{1, \ldots, \ell\}$. For a positive integer x, we denote by $\langle x \rangle$ its binary representation. When $\boldsymbol{x} = x_1 \ldots x_\mu \in \{0,1\}^\mu$, we denote by $[x]$ the integer $[x] = \sum_{i=1}^{\mu} 2^{i-1} \cdot x_i$.

For a positive integer μ, we denote by $B_\mu = \{0,1\}^\mu$ the Boolean hypercube of dimension μ. For an integer $d > 0$, we define $\mathcal{W}_{d,\ell} = \{0, \ldots, d\}^\ell$. For convenience, we also define the set

$$\mathcal{U}_{d,\ell} = \{(i_1, \ldots, i_\ell) \in \{0, \ldots, d\} \times \{0,1\}^{\ell-3} \times \{0,1,2\} \times \{0,1,2,3\}\}.$$

2.1 Definitions for Polynomials

In the following, we denote by $\mathbb{Z}_p^{(\leq d)}[X]$ the set of polynomials of degree at most $d \in \mathbb{N}$ with coefficients in $\mathbb{Z}_p$. In the case of ℓ-variate polynomials, we denote by $\mathbb{Z}_p^{(\leq d)}[X_1, \ldots, X_\ell]$ the set of polynomials that have degree $\leq d$ in each variable.

Definition 1. *For every function $f : B_\mu \rightarrow \mathbb{Z}_p$, there exists a unique multilinear polynomial $\tilde{f} \in \mathbb{Z}_p^{(\leq 1)}[X_1, \ldots, X_\mu]$ such that $\tilde{f}(\boldsymbol{b}) = f(\boldsymbol{b})$ for all $\boldsymbol{b} \in B_\mu$. This polynomial $\tilde{f}$ is called the multilinear extension of the function f and it is obtained as $\tilde{f}[X_1, \ldots, X_\mu] = \sum_{\boldsymbol{b} \in B_\mu} f(\boldsymbol{b}) \cdot eq_{\boldsymbol{b}}[X_1, \ldots, X_\mu]$, for the multilinear polynomial $eq_{\boldsymbol{b}}[X_1, \ldots, X_\mu] = \prod_{i=1}^{\mu}(b_i \cdot X_i + (1 - b_i) \cdot (1 - X_i))$*

2.2 Hardness Assumptions

Let $(\mathbb{G}, \hat{\mathbb{G}}, \mathbb{G}_T)$ be cyclic groups of prime order p that are equipped with a bilinear map $e : \mathbb{G} \times \hat{\mathbb{G}} \rightarrow \mathbb{G}_T$. We rely on the hardness of the following problem, which has been widely used in pairing-based SNARKs.

Definition 2 ([26]). *Let $(\mathbb{G}, \hat{\mathbb{G}}, \mathbb{G}_T)$ be asymmetric bilinear groups of prime order p. For integers m, n, the (m, n)-***Discrete Logarithm** *((m, n)-DLOG) problem is, given $(g, g^\alpha, g^{(\alpha^2)}, \ldots, g^{(\alpha^m)}, \hat{g}, \hat{g}^\alpha, \ldots, \hat{g}^{(\alpha^n)})$ where $\alpha \xleftarrow{R} \mathbb{Z}_p$, $g \xleftarrow{R} \mathbb{G}$, $\hat{g} \xleftarrow{R} \hat{\mathbb{G}}$, to compute $\alpha \in \mathbb{Z}_p$.*

2.3 Succinct Non-interactive Arguments

An indexed relation is a set of triples $(\mathbb{i}, \mathbb{x}, \mathbb{w})$ where $\mathbb{i}$ is the index, $\mathbb{x}$ is the instance and $\mathbb{w}$ is the witness. Given an index $\mathbb{i}$, $\mathcal{R}_\mathbb{i}$ denotes the restriction of $\mathcal{R}$ to $\{(\mathbb{x}, \mathbb{w}) : (\mathbb{i}, \mathbb{x}, \mathbb{w}) \in \mathcal{R}\}$. Typically, $\mathbb{i}$ is an arithmetic circuit over a finite field, $\mathbb{x}$ is the public input and $\mathbb{w}$ is the private input.

A (preprocessing) succinct non-interactive zero-knowledge argument of knowledge (SNARK) consists of algorithms ($\mathsf{CRS\text{-}Gen}$, $\mathsf{PreProcess}$, Prove, Verify) with the following specifications. On input of a security parameter $\lambda \in \mathbb{N}$ and (optionally) other parameters, $\mathsf{CRS\text{-}Gen}$ generates a universal common reference string srs and a simulation trapdoor τ; $\mathsf{PreProcess}$ is a deterministic algorithm that takes as input the universal common references string srs and an index $\mathbb{i}$ describing a circuit $\mathcal{C}$ in order to generate a short circuit-dependent reference string vp (which can be seen as a digest of $\mathbb{i}$) and a longer one pp; Algorithm Prove takes as input the common reference string pp, an index $\mathbb{i}$, a statement $\mathbb{x}$ and a witness $\mathbb{w}$ and outputs a proof π; Verify takes as input vp, a statement $\mathbb{x}$ and a proof π and returns 0 or 1. Correctness requires that proofs honestly generated by the prover are always (or with overwhelming probability) accepted by the verifier.

The $\mathsf{PreProcess}$ algorithm is run exactly once for each circuit (in contrast with the $\mathsf{CRS\text{-}Gen}$ algorithm which generates a universal SRS that can be re-used for any circuit of a priori bounded size). The verifier's preprocessed reference string vp is required to have at most poly-logarithmic length in the size of $\mathcal{C}$. We assume that pp and vp are uniquely determined by srs and $\mathcal{C}$.

From a security point of view, NIZK argument systems should satisfy two properties. The *zero-knowledge* property requires that proofs leak no information about the witness. This is formalized by asking that the trapdoor τ (hidden in pp) allows simulating proofs that are (statistically or computationally) indistinguishable from real proofs. The (non-black-box) *knowledge-soundness* property requires that there exists an extractor that can compute a witness whenever the adversary generates a valid proof. The extractor has access to the adversary's internal state, including its random coins. In a NIZK argument for a relation $\mathcal{R}$, these properties are defined below.

Completeness: For any $\lambda \in \mathbb{N}$, any index $\mathbb{i}$, and any statement-witness pair $(\mathbb{x}, \mathbb{w}) \in \mathcal{R}_{\mathbb{i}}$, we have

$$\Pr\big[\mathsf{Verify}_{\mathsf{vp}}(\mathbb{i}, \mathbb{x}, \pi) = 1 \mid (\mathsf{srs}, \tau) \leftarrow \mathsf{CRS\text{-}Gen}(1^\lambda),\\ \pi \leftarrow \mathsf{Prove}_{\mathsf{pp}}(\mathbb{i}, \mathbb{x}, \mathbb{w})\big] = 1 - \mathsf{negl}(\lambda)$$

for some negligible function $\mathsf{negl} : \mathbb{N} \rightarrow \mathbb{N}$.

Knowledge-Soundness: For any PPT adversary $\mathcal{A}$, there is a PPT extractor $\mathcal{E}_{\mathcal{A}}$ that has access to $\mathcal{A}$'s internal state and random coins ρ such that

$$\Pr\big[\mathsf{Verify}_{\mathsf{vp}}(\mathbb{i}, \mathbb{x}, \pi) = 1 \ \wedge \ (\mathbb{i}, \mathbb{x}, \mathbb{w}) \notin \mathcal{R} \ \mid \ (\mathsf{srs}, \tau) \leftarrow \mathsf{CRS\text{-}Gen}(1^\lambda),\\ (\mathbb{i}, \mathbb{x}, \pi) \leftarrow \mathcal{A}(\mathsf{srs}; \rho), \ w \leftarrow \mathcal{E}_{\mathcal{A}}(\mathsf{srs}, (\mathbb{i}, \mathbb{x}, \pi), \rho)\big] = \mathsf{negl}(\lambda).$$

(Statistical) Zero-knowledge: There exists a PPT simulator Sim such that, for any $\lambda \in \mathbb{N}$, and any pair $(\mathbb{i}, \mathbb{x}, \mathbb{w}) \in \mathcal{R}$, the distributions $D_0 = \{\pi \leftarrow \mathsf{Prove}_{\mathsf{pp}}(\mathbb{i}, \mathbb{x}, \mathbb{w}) : (\mathsf{srs}, \tau) \leftarrow \mathsf{CRS\text{-}Gen}(1^\lambda)\}$ and $D_1 = \{\pi \leftarrow \mathsf{Sim}(\mathsf{srs}, \tau, \mathbb{i}, \mathbb{x}) : (\mathsf{srs}, \tau) \leftarrow \mathsf{CRS\text{-}Gen}(1^\lambda)\}$ are statistically close.

Simulation-extractability strengthens knowledge-soundness by giving the adversary access to an oracle that simulates proofs for possibly false statements.

Simulation-Extractability: For any PPT adversary $\mathcal{A}$, there is a PPT extractor $\mathcal{E}_{\mathcal{A}}$ that has access to $\mathcal{A}$'s internal state/randomness ρ such that

$$\Pr\big[\mathsf{Verify}_{\mathsf{vp}}(\mathbb{i}, \mathbb{x}, \pi) = 1 \ \wedge \ (\mathbb{i}, \mathbb{x}, \mathbb{w}) \notin \mathcal{R} \ \wedge \ (\mathbb{i}, \mathbb{x}, \pi) \notin Q \mid\\ (\mathsf{srs}, \tau) \leftarrow \mathsf{CRS\text{-}Gen}(1^\lambda), \ (\mathbb{i}, \mathbb{x}, \pi, \mathsf{lbl}) \leftarrow \mathcal{A}^{\mathsf{SimProve}}(\mathsf{srs}; \rho),\\ \mathbb{w} \leftarrow \mathcal{E}_{\mathcal{A}}(\mathsf{srs}, (\mathbb{i}, \mathbb{x}, \pi), \rho, Q)\big] = \mathsf{negl}(\lambda) \ ,$$

where $\mathsf{SimProve}(\mathsf{srs}, \tau, \cdot, \cdot)$ is an oracle that returns a simulated proof $\pi \leftarrow \mathsf{Sim}(\mathsf{srs}, \tau, \mathbb{i}, \mathbb{x})$ for a given $(\mathbb{i}, \mathbb{x})$ and $Q = \{(\mathbb{i}_j, \mathbb{x}_j, \pi_j)\}_j$ denotes the set of queried statements and the simulated proofs returned by $\mathsf{SimProve}$.

2.4 Algebraic Group Model

The algebraic group model (AGM) [26] is an idealized model, where the adversary is modeled as an algebraic algorithm. Algebraic algorithms generalize generic algorithms in the sense that they only compute group elements as linear combinations of group elements observed so far. Therefore, whenever they output a group element $X \in \mathbb{G}$, they also provide a representation $\{\alpha_i\}_{i=1}^N$ of $X = \prod_{i=1}^N g_i^{\alpha_i}$ as a function of previously seen elements $(g_1, \ldots, g_N) \in \mathbb{G}^N$ of the same group. Unlike generic algorithms, algebraic ones can freely exploit the structure of the group. Due to its generality and because it provides a powerful framework that simplifies the security analyzes of complex protocols, the AGM has been widely used to prove the security of SNARKs.

2.5 Polynomial Commitments

We first recall the syntax of polynomial commitments [37]. We restrict ourselves to polynomials over a field and where the evaluation protocol Eval is non-interactive. We allow Eval and Verify to take as input a label consisting of public data that should be bound to evaluation proofs in a non-malleable way.

Definition 3. *A polynomial commitment scheme (PCS)* $\Gamma = (\mathsf{CRS\text{-}Gen}, \mathsf{Com}, \mathsf{Eval}, \mathsf{Verify})$ *is a tuple of (possibly randomized) algorithms where:*

- $\mathsf{CRS\text{-}Gen}$ *inputs a security parameters and (optionally) the number ℓ of variables and an upper bound d on the degree of committed polynomials in each variable. It outputs a common reference string* srs *that specifies the field $\mathbb{F}$ for which committed polynomials live in $\mathbb{F}^{(\leq d)}[X_1, \ldots, X_\ell]$ and (optionally) a simulator trapdoor τ. The reference string* srs *is implicitly taken as input by all other algorithms hereunder.*
- $\mathsf{Com}_{\mathsf{srs}}$ *is a (possibly randomized) algorithm that takes as input a polynomial $f \in \mathbb{F}^{(\leq d)}[X_1, \ldots, X_\ell]$ and outputs a commitment C to f, together with the state information* aux *allowing to open C. We assume that* aux *contains the randomness allowing to compute the commitment C.*
- $\mathsf{Eval}_{\mathsf{srs}}$ *is a (possibly randomized) algorithm that inputs a commitment C together its the corresponding state information* aux*, an input $\boldsymbol{z} \in \mathbb{F}^\ell$, an output $y \in \mathbb{F}$ and (optionally) a label* lbl*. If $y = f(\boldsymbol{z})$, it outputs a proof $\boldsymbol{\pi}$ that $y = f(\boldsymbol{z})$. If $y \neq f(\boldsymbol{z})$, it returns $\perp$.*
- $\mathsf{Verify}_{\mathsf{srs}}$ *is a (usually deterministic) algorithm that inputs a commitment C, an input $\boldsymbol{z} \in \mathbb{F}^\ell$, a claimed output $y \in \mathbb{F}$, a candidate proof $\boldsymbol{\pi}$, and (optionally) a label* lbl*. It outputs 0 or 1.*

A PCS is called *succinct* if the size of commitments C and evaluation proofs $\boldsymbol{\pi}$ grows at most logarithmically with the degree d of committed polynomials.

In terms of security, a PCS should satisfy the binding property of standard commitment schemes, which is the infeasiliby of opening a given commitment to distinct polynomials f, f'. The construction of SNARKs requires a PCS satisfying a notion of knowledge-soundness, which is formalized in the same way as in Sect. 2.3 but we explicitly write it in order to clearly parse statements and witnesses. Together with the binding property, knowledge soundness implies *evaluation-binding*, which captures the adversary's inability to prove two distinct evaluations of a committed polynomial on a given input.

Definition 4. *A PCS is* **knowledge-sound** *if, for any* $\mathsf{srs} \leftarrow \mathsf{CRS\text{-}Gen}(1^\lambda, 1^\ell, 1^d)$, Eval *is a non-interactive argument of knowledge for the relation*

$$\mathcal{R}_{\mathsf{Eval}}(\mathsf{srs}, 1^\ell, 1^d) := \{ (\underbrace{(C, y, \boldsymbol{z})}_{\triangleq \mathbb{x}}, \underbrace{(f, \mathsf{aux})}_{\triangleq \mathbb{w}}) : f \in \mathbb{F}^{(\leq d)}[X_1, \ldots, X_\ell]$$
$$\wedge \quad f(\boldsymbol{z}) = y \quad \wedge \quad C = \mathsf{Com}_{\mathsf{srs}}(f; r) \}$$

where r is the randomness contained in aux.

For our purposes, we also consider a notion of *extended knowledge-soundness* that stands between knowledge-soundness and simulation-extractability, which will be defined shortly.

In order to build *zero-knowledge* SNARKs, it is useful to have PCS constructions satisfying the hiding property.

Definition 5. *A PCS is* **hiding** *if, for any PPT adversary $\mathcal{A} = (\mathcal{A}_0, \mathcal{A}_1)$,*

$$\Big| \Pr\Big[b' = b : \mathsf{srs} \leftarrow \mathsf{CRS\text{-}Gen}(1^\lambda, 1^\ell, 1^d);\ (st, f_0, f_1) \leftarrow \mathcal{A}_0(\mathsf{srs}); \\ b \stackrel{R}{\leftarrow} \{0,1\}; C \leftarrow \mathsf{Com}_{\mathsf{srs}}(f_b); b' \leftarrow \mathcal{A}_1(st, C)\Big] - 1/2\Big| \leq \mathsf{negl}(\lambda)$$

A PCS is zero-knowledge if its evaluation protocol Eval is zero-knowledge. In the case of a non-interactive Eval, there is a simulator that can use a trapdoor hidden in pp to simulate proofs without using witnesses. Our definition of zero-knowledge is almost identical to the notion called *hiding* in [39] (the main difference is that their definition also involves a simulated setup algorithm).

Definition 6. *A PCS for parameters $d, \ell \in \mathsf{poly}(\lambda)$ is* **zero-knowledge** *if, for any polynomial $Q \in \mathsf{poly}(\lambda)$, and any adversary $\mathcal{A}$, there is a simulator $\mathcal{S} = (\mathsf{SimCom}, \mathsf{Sim})$ s.t. $|\Pr[\mathbf{Real}_{\mathcal{A},Q}(1^\lambda) \Rightarrow 1] - \Pr[\mathbf{Ideal}_{\mathcal{A},Q}(1^\lambda) \Rightarrow 1]| \leq \mathsf{negl}(\lambda)$ for the following experiments.*

$\mathbf{Real}_{\mathcal{A},Q}(1^\lambda)$:
1. $(\mathsf{srs}, \tau) \leftarrow \mathsf{CRS\text{-}Gen}(1^\lambda, 1^\ell, 1^d)$
2. $ctr = 0$; $st = \varepsilon$
3. $(f, st) \leftarrow \mathcal{A}(\mathsf{srs}, st)$
   If $f \notin \mathbb{F}^{(\leq d)}[X_1, \ldots, X_\ell]$ *return* 0.
4. $(C, \mathsf{aux}) \leftarrow \mathsf{Com}_{\mathsf{srs}}(f; r_f)$
5. $(k, st) \leftarrow \mathcal{A}(\mathsf{srs}, C, st)$
6. *For* $i = 1$ *to* k
   a. $(\boldsymbol{z}_i, \mathsf{lbl}_i, st) \leftarrow \mathcal{A}(\mathsf{srs}, \{f(\boldsymbol{z}_j), \pi_j\}_{j=1}^{i-1}, st)$
   b. $\pi_i \leftarrow \mathsf{Eval}_{pp}(C, \boldsymbol{z}_i, f(\boldsymbol{z}_i), \mathsf{aux}, \mathsf{lbl}_i)$
7. *If* $ctr < Q$, *set* $ctr = ctr + 1$ *and go to step 3*
8. $d \leftarrow \mathcal{A}(C, f(\boldsymbol{z}_k), \pi_k, st)$
9. *Return* d.

$\mathbf{Ideal}_{\mathcal{A},Q}(1^\lambda)$:
1. $(\mathsf{srs}, \tau) \leftarrow \mathsf{CRS\text{-}Gen}(1^\lambda, 1^\ell, 1^d)$
2. $ctr = 0$; $st = \varepsilon$
3. $(f, st) \leftarrow \mathcal{A}(\mathsf{srs}, st)$
   If $f \notin \mathbb{F}^{(\leq d)}[X_1, \ldots, X_\ell]$ *return* 0.
4. $(C, \widetilde{\mathsf{aux}}) \leftarrow \mathsf{SimCom}_{\mathsf{srs}}(\tau)$
5. $(k, st) \leftarrow \mathcal{A}(\mathsf{srs}, C, st)$
6. *For* $i = 1$ *to* k
   a. $(\boldsymbol{z}_i, \mathsf{lbl}_i, st) \leftarrow \mathcal{A}(\mathsf{srs}, \{f(\boldsymbol{z}_j), \pi_j\}_{j=1}^{i-1}, st)$
   b. $\pi_i \leftarrow \mathsf{Sim}_{pp}(\tau, \boldsymbol{z}_i, f(\boldsymbol{z}_i), \widetilde{\mathsf{aux}}, \mathsf{lbl}_i)$
7. *If* $ctr < Q$, *set* $ctr = ctr + 1$ *and go to step 3*
8. $d \leftarrow \mathcal{A}(C, f(\boldsymbol{z}_k), \pi_k, st)$
9. *Return* d.

REMARK. In the ideal experiment of Definition 6, we assume that the output of SimCom contains the state information $\widetilde{\mathsf{aux}}$ allowing to re-compute C. If $(C, \widetilde{\mathsf{aux}})$ is a possible output of SimCom, we say that aux is *consistent* with C.

The notion of simulation-extractability is formalized for PCS in the same way as in general succinct NIZK arguments.

Definition 7. *A PCS is* **simulation-extractable** *if, for any PPT adversary $\mathcal{A}$, there is a PPT extractor $\mathcal{E}_{\mathcal{A}}$ that has access to $\mathcal{A}$'s internal state/randomness ρ such that*

$$\Pr\Big[\mathsf{Verify}_{\mathsf{srs}}(C, \boldsymbol{z}, y, \pi, \mathsf{lbl}) = 1 \\ \wedge \ \big((C, y, \boldsymbol{z}), (f, \mathsf{aux})\big) \notin \mathcal{R}_{\mathsf{Eval}}(\mathsf{srs}, 1^{\ell}, 1^{d}) \ \wedge \ \big((C, y, \boldsymbol{z}), \pi, \mathsf{lbl}\big) \notin Q \mid \\ (\mathsf{srs}, \tau) \leftarrow \mathsf{CRS\text{-}Gen}(1^{\lambda}), \ \big((C, y, \boldsymbol{z}), \pi, \mathsf{lbl}\big) \leftarrow \mathcal{A}^{\mathsf{Sim}_{\mathsf{srs}}(\tau,\cdot,\cdot,\cdot)}(\rho), \\ (f, \mathsf{aux}) \leftarrow \mathcal{E}_{\mathcal{A}}(\mathsf{srs}, ((C, y, z), \pi, \mathsf{lbl}), \rho, Q)\Big] = \mathsf{negl}(\lambda) \ ,$$

where $\mathsf{Sim}_{\mathsf{srs}}(\tau, \cdot, \cdot, \cdot)$ *is a simulation oracle that takes as input a statement-label pair* $(\mathbb{x} = (C, \boldsymbol{z}, y), \mathsf{lbl})$ *and an auxiliary information* $\widetilde{\mathsf{aux}}$*. If* $\widetilde{\mathsf{aux}}$ *is inconsistent with* C*, it returns* $\perp$*. Otherwise, it returns a simulated proof* $\pi \leftarrow \mathsf{Sim}_{\mathsf{srs}}(\tau, (C, \boldsymbol{z}, y), \mathsf{lbl}, \widetilde{\mathsf{aux}})$ *and* $Q = \{(\mathbb{x}_i = (C_i, \boldsymbol{z}_i, y_i), \pi_i, \mathsf{lbl}_i)\}_i$ *denotes the set of queried statements and the simulated proofs returned by* $\mathsf{Sim}_{\mathsf{srs}}$.

Faonio *et al.* [23] considered relaxed notion of simulation-extractable PCS, which is defined w.r.t. policies. In their definition, the forgery is required to be made on a random evaluation point $\boldsymbol{z}$ (derived from a random oracle) and simulation-queries are made selectively, before the generation of the commitment key. Although we could also use a relaxed notion of SE for our purposes, we chose to work with Definition 7 since it can be achieved efficiently in the AGM+ROM.

Extended Knowledge-Soundness. The notion of extended knowledge-soundness is weaker than simulation-extractability and only preserves extractability when the adversary can see honestly generated proofs. It is thus similar to *true simulation-extractability* [22], except that the adversary obtains real proofs (instead of simulated ones) of true statements. The definition is identical to Definition 7 but, instead of having oracle access to a simulator, the adversary is given a $\mathsf{Prove}(\cdot)$ oracle taking as input a polynomial f and a set $S \subset \mathbb{F}^{\ell}$ of evaluation inputs and returning a commitment C to f (obtained as $(C, \mathsf{aux}) \leftarrow \mathsf{Com}_{\mathsf{srs}}(f)$) together with real evaluation proofs $\{\pi_i \leftarrow \mathsf{Eval}_{\mathsf{srs}}(C, z_i, f(z_i), \mathsf{aux})\}_{z_i \in S}$. In the AGM, it is easy to see that extended knowledge-soundness is equivalent to standard knowledge-soundness when Com and Eval are algebraic algorithms that compute linear combinations of group elements contained in the SRS.

3 Commitments to Multivariate Polynomials

We first prove the security of the multivariate PCS of Zhang *et al.* [52] in the AGM under the (m,n)-DLOG assumption. In [52], a less simple variant of the scheme was considered. In this variant (which was also used in [51]), each commitment consists of a pair $(g^{f(\alpha_1,\ldots,\alpha_\ell)+r\cdot\alpha_{\ell+1}}, h^{f(\alpha_1,\ldots,\alpha_\ell)+r\cdot\alpha_{\ell+1}})$, where g, h are public generators, in order to extract the coefficients of the committed $f[X_1, \ldots, X_\ell]$ using a variant of the knowledge-of-exponent assumption [19]. In the AGM, we give a security proof for the simpler scheme where each commitment consists of only one group element. Our proof generalizes the one given by Kohrita and Towa [40] to the multivariate case. In Sect. 4, we will modify the scheme to achieve simulation-extractability. We assume that committed polynomials have bounded degree $\leq d$ in each variable.

3.1 The Multivariate PCS of Zhang et al.

When it comes to committing to polynomials in $\mathbb{Z}_p^{(\leq d)}[X_1,\ldots,X_\ell]$, the multivariate PCS of [52] can be described as follows.

In order to use the scheme in HyperPlonk, we need to allow the prover to commit to (and generate proofs for) polynomials where the number of variables may be smaller than the maximal number ℓ of variables allowed by the SRS. For this reason, when the actual number of variables μ is strictly smaller than ℓ in the verification algorithm, the knowledge extractor does not extract an opening of the commitment C to an μ-variate polynomial $f[X_1,\ldots,X_\mu]$ such that $f(\boldsymbol{z}) = y$ in general. It only extracts an opening of C to an ℓ-variate polynomial $f \in \mathbb{Z}_p^{(\leq d)}[X_1,\ldots,X_\ell]$ such that $f(\boldsymbol{z}, x_{\mu+1},\ldots,x_\ell) = y$ for all assignments of $(x_{\mu+1},\ldots,x_\ell) \in \mathbb{Z}_p^{\ell-\mu}$ (i.e., $f[\boldsymbol{z}, X_{\mu+1},\ldots,X_\ell] - y$ is the zero polynomial). However, it still ensures that the prover knows a polynomial $\bar{f}[X_1,\ldots,X_\mu] = f[X_1,\ldots,X_\mu,0,\ldots,0]$ such that $\bar{f}(\boldsymbol{z}) = y$. Moreover, when $\boldsymbol{z} \in \mathbb{Z}_p^\mu$ is a random evaluation point (as is the case in sumcheck protocols), the knowledge extractor *does* extract (with overwhelming probability) an opening of C to an μ-variate polynomial $f[X_1,\ldots,X_\mu]$ such that $f(\boldsymbol{z}) = y$.

The multivariate PCS of [52] is a probabilistic version of PST commitments [45]. Its simplified version goes as follows.

CRS-Gen$(1^\lambda, 1^d, 1^\ell)$: On input of a security parameter λ, a number of variables ℓ and a degree d such that $(d+1)^\ell \in \mathsf{poly}(\lambda)$, generate the SRS as follows:

1. Choose asymmetric bilinear groups $(\mathbb{G}, \hat{\mathbb{G}}, \mathbb{G}_T)$ of prime order $p > 2^{l(\lambda)}$, for some function $l : \mathbb{N} \rightarrow \mathbb{N}$, and $g \xleftarrow{R} \mathbb{G}$, $\hat{g} \xleftarrow{R} \hat{\mathbb{G}}$.
2. Pick $\alpha_1,\ldots,\alpha_\ell,\alpha_r \xleftarrow{R} \mathbb{Z}_p$ and compute $\hat{g}_1,\ldots,\hat{g}_\ell \in \mathbb{G}$, where $\hat{g}_i = \hat{g}^{\alpha_i}$ for each $i \in [\ell]$. Compute $g_r = g^{\alpha_r}$ and $\hat{g}_r = \hat{g}^{\alpha_r}$.
3. For each tuple $\mathcal{I} = (i_1,\ldots,i_\ell) \in \mathcal{W}_{d,\ell}$, compute $g_{\mathcal{I}} = g^{\prod_{j=1}^{\ell} \alpha_j^{i_j}}$.

The public parameters are defined to be

$$\mathsf{srs} = \Big((\mathbb{G}, \hat{\mathbb{G}}, \mathbb{G}_T), \{g_{\mathcal{I}}\}_{\mathcal{I} \in \mathcal{W}_{d,\ell}}, g_r, \hat{g}_r, \hat{g}, \{\hat{g}_i\}_{i \in [\ell]} \Big)$$

Com$_{\mathsf{srs}}(f)$: To commit to $f[X_1,\ldots,X_\mu] \in \mathbb{Z}_p^{(\leq d)}[X_1,\ldots,X_\mu]$, where $\mu \leq \ell$, choose a random $r \xleftarrow{R} \mathbb{Z}_p$ and compute $C = g^{f(\alpha_1,\ldots,\alpha_\mu)+r\cdot\alpha_r}$ using $\{g_{\mathcal{I}}\}_{\mathcal{I} \in \mathcal{W}_{d,\ell}}$ and g_r. Then, output C and $(\mathsf{aux}, f) = (r, f)$.

Eval$_{\mathsf{srs}}(C, \boldsymbol{z}, y, \mathsf{aux})$: given a commitment C, a witness $\mathsf{aux} = (r, f)$, an input $\boldsymbol{z} = (z_1,\ldots,z_\mu) \in \mathbb{Z}_p^\mu$ of dimension $\mu \leq \ell$, and an output $y = f(\boldsymbol{z}) \in \mathbb{Z}_p$, return $\perp$ if $y \neq f(\boldsymbol{z})$. Otherwise, do the following:

1. Using [45, Lemma 1], compute $\{Q_i[X_1,\ldots,X_\mu]\}_{i=1}^\mu$ such that

$$f[X_1,\ldots,X_\mu] - y = \sum_{i=1}^{\mu} Q_i[X_1,\ldots,X_\mu] \cdot (X_i - z_i)$$

2. Choose $s_1,\ldots,s_\mu \xleftarrow{R} \mathbb{Z}_p$ and compute $\pi_{1,i} = g^{Q_i(\alpha_1,\ldots,\alpha_\mu)+s_i\cdot\alpha_r}$ for each $i \in [\mu]$ together with $\pi_2 = g^{r-\sum_{i=1}^{\mu} s_i\cdot(\alpha_i - z_i)}$.

Return the proof $\boldsymbol{\pi} = \big((\pi_{1,i})_{i=1}^{\mu}, \pi_2\big) \in \mathbb{G}^{\mu+1}$.

Verify$_{\mathsf{srs}}(C, y, \boldsymbol{z}, \boldsymbol{\pi})$: Given $C \in \mathbb{G}$, an input $\boldsymbol{z} = (z_1, \ldots, z_\mu) \in \mathbb{Z}_p^\mu$, a claimed evaluation $y \in \mathbb{Z}_p$, and a purported proof $\boldsymbol{\pi}$, return 0 if $\boldsymbol{\pi}$ does not parse properly. Return 1 if the following equality holds and 0 otherwise:

$$e(C \cdot g^{-y}, \hat{g}) = \prod_{i=1}^{\mu} e(\pi_{i,1}, \hat{g}_i \cdot \hat{g}^{-z_i}) \cdot e(\pi_2, \hat{g}_r) \tag{2}$$

The scheme is correct since equation (2) uses the pairing to check the equality

$$f(\alpha_1, \ldots, \alpha_\mu) + r \cdot \alpha_r - y = \sum_{i=1}^{\mu} (\alpha_i - z_i) \cdot (Q_i(\alpha_1, \ldots, \alpha_\mu) + s_i \cdot \alpha_r) + \alpha_r \cdot \Big(r - \sum_{i=1}^{\mu} s_i \cdot (\alpha_i - z_i)\Big).$$

We now prove knowledge-soundness under the $(d\ell, d\ell)$-DLOG assumption in the AGM. The proof of Theorem 1 (which can be found in the full version of the paper) differs from the one given by [40] in the univariate case.

Theorem 1. *In the AGM and under the $(d\ell, d\ell)$-DLOG assumption, the scheme is an (extended) knowledge-sound argument of knowledge of a polynomial $f \in \mathbb{Z}_p^{(\leq d)}[X_1, \ldots, X_\ell]$ such that $f(z_1, \ldots, z_\mu, X_{\mu+1}, \ldots, X_\ell) = y$ for any assignment of $(X_{\mu+1}, \ldots, X_\ell)$, where $(y, \boldsymbol{z}) \in \mathbb{Z}_p \times \mathbb{Z}_p^\mu$. Moreover, if $\boldsymbol{z} = (z_1, \ldots, z_\mu)$ is a random input, the knowledge extractor outputs $f \in \mathbb{Z}_p^{(\leq d)}[X_1, \ldots, X_\mu]$ and $r \in \mathbb{Z}_p$ such that $C = g^{f(\alpha_1, \ldots, \alpha_\mu) + r \cdot \alpha_r}$ with overwhelming probability.*

Using standard batching techniques, multiple evaluations of committed polynomials can be proven at once on a common input. The scheme and the proof of Theorem 1 easily extend, as explained in the full version of the paper.

Zero-Knowledge. We note that the trapdoor $\alpha_r \in \mathbb{Z}_p^*$ can be used to simulate proofs for a given commitment C and a given pair $(y, \boldsymbol{z})$. Indeed, the simulator can choose $\theta_{i,1} \stackrel{R}{\leftarrow} \mathbb{Z}_p$ for each $i \in [\mu]$ in order to compute $\pi_{i,1} = g^{\theta_{i,1}}$ for all $i \in [\mu]$ and $\pi_2 = \big(C \cdot g^{-y} \cdot \prod_{i=1}^{\mu} (g_i \cdot g^{-z_i})^{-\theta_{i,1}}\big)^{1/\alpha_r}$. This yields a simulated $\big((\pi_{1,i})_{i=1}^{\mu}, \pi_2\big)$ that is distributed as a real proof.

While the use of α_r yields a zero-knowledge simulator, it is not trapdoor-less and cannot be used to obtain simulation-extractability Moreover, the scheme is clearly not simulation-extractable as it is since a proof for $(C, y, \boldsymbol{z})$ is also a proof for $(C \cdot g, y + 1, \boldsymbol{z})$. In Sect. 4, we show how to thwart such attacks.

3.2 Enforcing a Special Shape for Committed Polynomials

In order to achieve zero-knowledge at the PIOP level, HyperPlonk [17, Appendix A] suggests to transform ℓ-variate multilinear polynomials into polynomials that agree with the original polynomials everywhere on the hypercube B_ℓ but evaluate to random-looking values outside B_ℓ. These "almost multilinear" polynomials (where all variables have degree 1, except one) can be written as a sum

$$f[X_1,\dots,X_\ell] = f'[X_1,\dots,X_\ell] + R[X_\mu]\cdot X_\mu \cdot (X_\mu - 1), \tag{3}$$

for some $\mu \in [\ell]$, where $f' \in \mathbb{Z}_p^{(\leq 1)}[X_1,\dots,X_\ell]$ is the original multilinear polynomial and $R[X_\mu]$ is univariate of degree t for some $t \geq 0$. In order to achieve zero-knowledge in sumcheck-based protocols, polynomials of the form (3) have the properties that: (i) f and f' agree everywhere on B_ℓ; (ii) Any set of $t+1$ evaluations of f outside B_ℓ are random and independent (since $R[X_\mu]$ has degree t) and can be easily simulated in zero-knowledge.

In the case of HyperPlonk, the verifier has to obtain evaluation proofs on correlated inputs sharing the same value of X_μ, in which case the above masking technique does not quite suffice to ensure that evaluations look independent. Therefore we need to slightly modify the masking technique (3) and encode the original $f' \in \mathbb{Z}_p^{(\leq 1)}[X_1,\dots,X_\ell]$ as

$$f[X_1,\dots,X_\ell] = f'[X_1,\dots,X_\ell] + R[X_1 + X_{\mu+1}]\cdot X_\mu \cdot (X_\mu - 1), \tag{4}$$

where $\mu + 1 < \ell$ (the reason why this modification works will become clear in the proof of Theorem 5 in Sect. 5.1).

In the following, we need to consider multivariate PCS schemes where the SRS allows committing to polynomials of the form (4). For the soundness analysis, the verifier should be convinced that a committed polynomial is really of this form. This can be ensured by a careful choice of the group elements available in the SRS. At the same time, we need to preserve the prover's ability to commit to both univariate and multivariate polynomials of larger degree $d > 1$. Our solution is to have the prover commit to these polynomials in $\mathbb{G}$ (instead of $\hat{\mathbb{G}}$).

The Modified PCS. We now describe a variant of the scheme in Sect. 3.1 where we force each committed polynomial to be of the form (4), where the number of evaluations t is set to $t = 3$. Although, the committer is meant to commit to almost multilinear polynomials, the CRS-Gen algorithm still inputs a parameter $\bar{d} > 1$ which is the maximal variable-degree of commitments to be committed in the first source group $\mathbb{G}$. We also assume that $\bar{d} \geq t+2$ in order to allow the prover to compute evaluation proofs in $\mathbb{G}$.

In the notations, the set $\mathcal{U}_{\bar{d},\ell} \subset \mathcal{W}_{\bar{d},\ell}$ determines a set of monomials in the exponent and is defined in Sect. 2 to retain a linear-size SRS in Sect. 5.

CRS-Gen$(1^\lambda, 1^d, 1^\ell)$**:** On input of a security parameter λ, a number of variables ℓ and a degree $\bar{d}$ such that $\bar{d}\cdot 2^\ell \in \mathsf{poly}(\lambda)$, generate the SRS as follows:

1. Choose asymmetric bilinear groups $(\mathbb{G}, \hat{\mathbb{G}}, \mathbb{G}_T)$ of prime order $p > 2^{l(\lambda)}$, for some function $l : \mathbb{N} \to \mathbb{N}$, and $g \xleftarrow{R} \mathbb{G}$, $\hat{g} \xleftarrow{R} \hat{\mathbb{G}}$.
2. Pick $\alpha_1,\dots,\alpha_\ell,\alpha_r \xleftarrow{R} \mathbb{Z}_p$. Compute $g_r = g^{\alpha_r}$ and $\hat{g}_r = \hat{g}^{\alpha_r}$.
3. For each $\mathcal{I} = (i_1,\dots,i_\ell) \in \mathcal{U}_{\bar{d},\ell}$, compute $g_{\mathcal{I}} = g^{\prod_{j=1}^{\ell} \alpha_j^{i_j}}$.

4. For each $\mathcal{I} = (i_1, \ldots, i_\ell) \in \mathcal{W}_{1,\ell}$, compute $\hat{g}_\mathcal{I} = \hat{g}^{\prod_{j=1}^{\ell} \alpha_j^{i_j}}$. Compute $\{\hat{g}^{(\alpha_1+\alpha_{\mu+1})^i \cdot \alpha_\mu \cdot (\alpha_\mu - 1)}\}_{i=0}^{3}$, where $\mu = \ell - 1$.

The public parameters are defined to be

$$\mathsf{srs} = \Big((\mathbb{G}, \hat{\mathbb{G}}, \mathbb{G}_T), g_r, \hat{g}_r, \{g_\mathcal{I}\}_{\mathcal{I} \in \mathcal{U}_{\bar{d},\ell}}, \{\hat{g}_\mathcal{I}\}_{\mathcal{I} \in \mathcal{W}_{1,\ell}}, \{\hat{g}^{(\alpha_1+\alpha_{\mu+1})^i \cdot \alpha_\mu \cdot (\alpha_\mu - 1)}\}_{i=0}^{3} \Big).$$

$\mathsf{Com}_{\mathsf{srs}}(f)$: To commit to a polynomial $f[X_1, \ldots, X_{\mu'}] \in \mathbb{Z}_p[X_1, \ldots, X_{\mu'}]$ of the form (4), where $\mu' \leq \ell$, choose $r \stackrel{R}{\leftarrow} \mathbb{Z}_p$ and compute $\hat{C} = \hat{g}^{f(\alpha_1, \ldots, \alpha_{\mu'}) + r \cdot \alpha_r}$. Then, output $\hat{C}$ and $(\mathsf{aux}, f) = (r, f)$.

$\mathsf{Eval}_{\mathsf{srs}}(\hat{C}, \boldsymbol{z}, y, \mathsf{aux})$: given a commitment $\hat{C}$, a witness $\mathsf{aux} = (r, f)$, an input $\boldsymbol{z} = (z_1, \ldots, z_{\mu'}) \in \mathbb{Z}_p^{\mu'}$ of dimension $\mu' \leq \ell$, and an output $y = f(\boldsymbol{z}) \in \mathbb{Z}_p$, return $\perp$ if $y \neq f(\boldsymbol{z})$. Otherwise, do the following:

1. Using [45, Lemma 1], compute polynomials $\{Q_i[X_1, \ldots, X_{\mu'}]\}_{i=1}^{\mu'}$ such that $f[X_1, \ldots, X_{\mu'}] - y = \sum_{i=1}^{\mu'} Q_i[X_1, \ldots, X_{\mu'}] \cdot (X_i - z_i)$.
2. Choose $s_1, \ldots, s_{\mu'} \stackrel{R}{\leftarrow} \mathbb{Z}_p$ and compute $\pi_{1,i} = g^{Q_i(\alpha_1, \ldots, \alpha_{\mu'}) + s_i \cdot \alpha_r}$ for each $i \in [\mu']$ together with $\pi_2 = g^{r - \sum_{i=1}^{\mu'} s_i \cdot (\alpha_i - z_i)}$.

Return the proof $\boldsymbol{\pi} = \big((\pi_{1,i})_{i=1}^{\mu'}, \pi_2 \big) \in \mathbb{G}^{\mu'+1}$.

$\mathsf{Verify}_{\mathsf{srs}}(\hat{C}, y, \boldsymbol{z}, \boldsymbol{\pi})$: Given $\hat{C} \in \hat{\mathbb{G}}$, an input $\boldsymbol{z} = (z_1, \ldots, z_{\mu'}) \in \mathbb{Z}_p^{\mu'}$, a claimed evaluation $y \in \mathbb{Z}_p$, and a candidate proof $\boldsymbol{\pi}$, return 0 if $\boldsymbol{\pi}$ does not parse properly. Then, return 1 if the following equation holds and 0 otherwise:

$$e(g, \hat{C} \cdot \hat{g}^{-y}) = \prod_{i=1}^{\mu'} e(\pi_{i,1}, \hat{g}^{\alpha_i} \cdot \hat{g}^{-z_i}) \cdot e(\pi_2, \hat{g}_r) \tag{5}$$

Although the commitment lives in a different group than evaluation proofs, the proof of Theorem 1 easily extends to give the following result.

Theorem 2. *In the AGM+ROM, under the $(d\ell, d\ell)$-DLOG assumption, the scheme is a knowledge-sound argument of knowledge of an ℓ-variate polynomial $f \in \mathbb{Z}_p[X_1, \ldots, X_\ell]$ of the form (4) such that $f(z_1, \ldots, z_{\mu'}, X_{\mu'+1}, \ldots, X_\ell) = y$ for any assignment of $(X_{\mu'+1}, \ldots, X_\ell)$, where $(y, \boldsymbol{z}) \in \mathbb{Z}_p \times \mathbb{Z}_p^{\mu'}$. Moreover, if the tuple $\boldsymbol{z} = (z_1, \ldots, z_{\mu'})$ is a random evaluation input, the knowledge extractor outputs an f of the form (4) and $r \in \mathbb{Z}_p$ such that $\hat{C} = \hat{g}^{f(\alpha_1, \ldots, \alpha_{\mu'}) + r \cdot \alpha_r}$ with overwhelming probability.* (The proof is given in the full version of the paper.)

4 A Simulation-Extractable Variant of Zhang et al.'s Polynomial Commitment

We now apply the Fiat-Shamir transform to build a simulation-extractable multivariate PCS. We apply the idea to the scheme of Sect. 3.2 because it is the version that we need to compile the HyperPlonk PIOP in its zero-knowledge version. However, the same technique applies to the PCS of Sect. 3.1 and the batch version described in the full version of the paper.

4.1 Description

The construction is almost as efficient as the one of Sect. 3.1. Indeed, proofs are only longer by one element of $\mathbb{Z}_p$ and the verifier computes the same number of pairings and exponentiations.

CRS-Gen$(1^\lambda, 1^{\bar{d}}, 1^\ell)$**:** On input of a security parameter λ, a number of variables ℓ and a degree d such that $\bar{d} \cdot 2^\ell \in \mathsf{poly}(\lambda)$, generate the SRS as follows:

1. Choose asymmetric bilinear groups $(\mathbb{G}, \hat{\mathbb{G}}, \mathbb{G}_T)$ of prime order $p > 2^{l(\lambda)}$, for some function $l : \mathbb{N} \to \mathbb{N}$, and $g \stackrel{R}{\leftarrow} \mathbb{G}$, $\hat{g} \stackrel{R}{\leftarrow} \hat{\mathbb{G}}$.
2. Pick $\alpha_1, \ldots, \alpha_\ell, \alpha_r \stackrel{R}{\leftarrow} \mathbb{Z}_p$. Compute $g_r = g^{\alpha_r}$ and $\hat{g}_r = \hat{g}^{\alpha_r}$.
3. For each $\mathcal{I} = (i_1, \ldots, i_\ell) \in \mathcal{U}_{\bar{d},\ell}$, compute $g_{\mathcal{I}} = g^{\prod_{j=1}^{\ell} \alpha_j^{i_j}}$, where $\mathcal{U}_{\bar{d},\ell}$ is defined as in Sect. 2.
4. For each $\mathcal{I} = (i_1, \ldots, i_\ell) \in \mathcal{W}_{1,\ell}$, compute $\hat{g}_{\mathcal{I}} = \hat{g}^{\prod_{j=1}^{\ell} \alpha_j^{i_j}}$. Compute $\{\hat{g}^{(\alpha_1+\alpha_{\mu+1})^i \cdot \alpha_\mu \cdot (\alpha_\mu - 1)}\}_{i=0}^{3}$ for an arbitrary index $\mu \in [2, \ell-1]$.
5. Choose a hash function $H_{\mathsf{PCS}} : \{0,1\}^* \to \mathbb{Z}_p$ modeled as a random oracle.

The public parameters are defined to be

$$\mathsf{srs} = \Big((\mathbb{G}, \hat{\mathbb{G}}, \mathbb{G}_T), g_r, \hat{g}_r, \{g_{\mathcal{I}}\}_{\mathcal{I} \in \mathcal{U}_{\bar{d},\ell}}, \\ \{\hat{g}_{\mathcal{I}}\}_{\mathcal{I} \in \mathcal{W}_{1,\ell}}, \{\hat{g}^{(\alpha_1+\alpha_{\mu+1})^i \cdot \alpha_\mu \cdot (\alpha_\mu - 1)}\}_{i=0}^{3}, H_{\mathsf{PCS}} \Big)$$

Com$_{\mathsf{srs}}(f)$**:** To commit to a polynomial $f[X_1, \ldots, X_{\mu'}] \in \mathbb{Z}_p[X_1, \ldots, X_{\mu'}]$ of the form (4), for some $\mu' \leq \ell$, choose $r \stackrel{R}{\leftarrow} \mathbb{Z}_p$ and compute $\hat{C} = \hat{g}^{f(\alpha_1, \ldots, \alpha_{\mu'}) + r \cdot \alpha_r}$. Then, output $\hat{C}$ and $(\mathsf{aux}, f) = (r, f)$.

Eval$_{\mathsf{srs}}(\hat{C}, \boldsymbol{z}, y, \mathsf{aux}, \mathsf{lbl})$**:** given a commitment $\hat{C}$, a witness $\mathsf{aux} = (r, f)$, an input $\boldsymbol{z} = (z_1, \ldots, z_{\mu'}) \in \mathbb{Z}_p^{\mu'}$, an output $y = f(\boldsymbol{z}) \in \mathbb{Z}_p$, and a label lbl, return $\perp$ if $y \neq f(\boldsymbol{z})$. Otherwise, do the following:

1. Compute $((\pi_{1,i})_{i=1}^{\mu'}, \pi_2) \in \mathbb{G}^{\mu'+1}$ satisfying (5) by running the Eval algorithm of Sect. 3.2.
2. Generate a NIZK proof of knowledge of $\pi_2 \in \mathbb{G}$ satisfying

$$\frac{e(g, \hat{C} \cdot \hat{g}^{-y})}{\prod_{i=1}^{\mu'} e(\pi_{i,1}, \hat{g}_i \cdot \hat{g}^{-z_i})} = e(\pi_2, \hat{g}_r) \tag{6}$$

Namely,

a. Choose $R_\pi \stackrel{R}{\leftarrow} \mathbb{G}$ and compute[2] $R = e(R_\pi, \hat{g}_r)$.
b. Compute $c = H_{\mathsf{PCS}}(\mathsf{lbl}, C, y, \boldsymbol{z}, (\pi_{1,i})_{i=1}^{\mu'}, R) \in \mathbb{Z}_p$.
c. Compute the response $S_\pi = R_\pi \cdot \pi_2^c$.

Return the proof $\boldsymbol{\pi} = (c, (\pi_{1,i})_{i=1}^{\mu'}, S_\pi) \in \mathbb{Z}_p \times \mathbb{G}^{\mu'+1}$.

[2] The pairing evaluation can be avoided by computing $R_\pi = g^{r_\pi}$ and $R = e(g, \hat{g}_r)^{r_\pi}$.

Verify$_{\mathsf{srs}}(\hat{C}, y, \boldsymbol{z}, \boldsymbol{\pi}, \mathsf{lbl})$: Given $\hat{C} \in \hat{\mathbb{G}}$, an input $\boldsymbol{z} = (z_1, \ldots, z_{\mu'}) \in \mathbb{Z}_p^{\mu'}$, a purported evaluation $y \in \mathbb{Z}_p$, and a candidate proof $\boldsymbol{\pi}$ with a label lbl, return 0 if $\boldsymbol{\pi}$ does not parse correctly. Otherwise, compute

$$R = e(S_\pi, \hat{g}_r) \cdot \left(\frac{e(g, \hat{C} \cdot \hat{g}^{-y})}{\prod_{i=1}^{\mu'} e(\pi_{i,1}, \hat{g}^{\alpha_i} \cdot \hat{g}^{-z_i})} \right)^{-c}. \tag{7}$$

If $c = H_{\mathsf{PCS}}(\mathsf{lbl}, \hat{C}, y, \boldsymbol{z}, (\pi_{1,i})_{i=1}^{\mu'}, R)$, return 1. Otherwise, return 0.

We now prove that the above variant provides (straight-line) simulation-extractability in the combined algebraic group and random oracle model.

Theorem 3. *In the AGM+ROM model and under the $(d\ell, d\ell)$-DLOG assumption, the scheme is a simulation-extractable argument of knowledge of a polynomial $f \in \mathbb{Z}_p[X_1, \ldots, X_\ell]$ of the form (4) such that $\hat{C} = \hat{g}^{f(\alpha_1,\ldots,\alpha_\ell)+\alpha_r \cdot r}$ and $f(\boldsymbol{z}, x_{\mu'+1}, \ldots, x_\ell) = y$ for any $(x_{\mu'+1}, \ldots, x_\ell) \in \mathbb{Z}_p^{\ell-\mu'}$, where $(y, \boldsymbol{z}) \in \mathbb{Z}_p \times \mathbb{Z}_p^{\mu'}$.*

Proof. Given an algebraic adversary $\mathcal{A}$ in the experiment of Definition 7, we build an algorithm $\mathcal{B}$ that either extracts a witness or, if the extraction fails, solves a $(\bar{d\ell}, \bar{d\ell})$-DLOG instance $\mathsf{inst} = \left(g, \{g^{(\alpha^i)}\}_{i=1}^{\bar{d\ell}}, \hat{g}, \{\hat{g}^{(\alpha^i)}\}_{i=1}^{\bar{d\ell}}\right)$ w.h.p.

Algorithm $\mathcal{B}$ first chooses $\boldsymbol{\rho} = (\rho_1, \ldots, \rho_\ell, \rho_r) \stackrel{R}{\leftarrow} \mathbb{Z}_p^{\ell+1}$, $\boldsymbol{\theta} = (\theta_1, \ldots, \theta_\ell, \theta_r) \stackrel{R}{\leftarrow} \mathbb{Z}_p^{\ell+1}$. It implicitly sets $\alpha_i = \rho_i \cdot \alpha + \theta_i$ for each $i \in [\ell]$ and $\alpha_r = \rho_r \cdot \theta + \theta_r$. It can simulate srs from inst and $\{(\rho_i, \theta_i)\}_{i=1}^{\ell}$, (ρ_r, θ_r).

Queries: When $\mathcal{A}$ queries the random oracle, $\mathcal{B}$ returns the previously defined output if it exists and a random element of $\mathbb{Z}_p$ otherwise.

At any time, $\mathcal{A}$ can choose a commitment $\hat{C} \in \mathbb{G}$ and a pair $(y, \boldsymbol{z}) \in \mathbb{Z}_p \times \mathbb{Z}_p^{\mu'}$ and ask for a simulated proof, for some label lbl, that $\hat{C}$ commits to some polynomial $f \in \mathbb{Z}_p[X_1, \ldots, X_{\mu'}]$ of the form (4) such that $f[\boldsymbol{z}, X_{\mu'+1}, \ldots, X_\ell] - y$ is the zero-polynomial. Then, $\mathcal{B}$ simulates a proof by running the HVZK simulator of the Σ-protocol. Namely, it samples $c, t_0, \ldots, t_{\mu'} \stackrel{R}{\leftarrow} \mathbb{Z}_p$, computes

$$S_\pi = g^{t_0} \qquad \text{and} \qquad \pi_{1,i} = g^{t_i} \qquad \forall i \in [\mu']$$

together with $R = e(S_\pi, \hat{g}_r) \cdot \left(e(g, \hat{C} \cdot \hat{g}^{-y}) / \prod_{i=1}^{\mu'} e(\pi_{i,1}, \hat{g}_i \cdot \hat{g}^{-z_i})\right)^{-c}$ before programming $c = H_{\mathsf{PCS}}(\mathsf{lbl}, \hat{C}, y, \boldsymbol{z}, (\pi_{1,i})_{i=1}^{\mu'}, R) \in \mathbb{Z}_p$. If H_{PCS} was already defined for this input, $\mathcal{B}$ aborts. Since R is uniformly distributed over $\mathbb{G}_T$, this only happens with probability $< (Q_H + Q_S)/p$ if Q_H (resp. Q_S) denotes the number of random oracle (resp. simulation) queries. Unless a collision occurs on H_{PCS} in a simulation query, the simulation is perfect since the simulated $\left(c, (\pi_{1,i})_{i=1}^{\mu'}, S_\pi\right) \in \mathbb{Z}_p \times \mathbb{G}^{\mu'+1}$ has the same distribution as a real proof. The probability of a such a collision during the entire game is at most $Q_S(Q_S + Q_H)/p$.

Since $\mathcal{A}$ is algebraic, at each hash query $H_{\mathsf{PCS}}(\mathsf{lbl}, \hat{C}, y, \boldsymbol{z}, (\pi_{1,i})_{i=1}^{\mu'}, R)$, it must provide a representation of $\hat{C}$ w.r.t. the $\hat{\mathbb{G}}$-elements contained in srs as well as an algebraic representation of each $\{\pi_{1,i}\}_{i=1}^{\ell}$ w.r.t. the $\mathbb{G}$-elements of srs and a representation $\{\omega_{\mathcal{I},\hat{\mathcal{I}}}\}_{\mathcal{I}\in\mathcal{G},\hat{\mathcal{I}}\in\hat{\mathcal{G}}}$ of R as

$$R = \prod_{\mathcal{I}\in\mathcal{G},\hat{\mathcal{I}}\in\hat{\mathcal{G}}} e(g_{\mathcal{I}}, \hat{g}_{\hat{\mathcal{I}}})^{\omega_{\mathcal{I},\hat{\mathcal{I}}}} \tag{8}$$

where $\mathcal{G}$ (resp. $\hat{\mathcal{G}}$) denotes the set of $\mathbb{G}$-elements (resp. $\hat{\mathbb{G}}$-elements) contained in srs. While the representation given by $\mathcal{A}$ can also depend on elements of $\mathbb{G}$ contained in simulated proofs, $\mathcal{B}$ can always find a representation of the form (8) since it computes S_π and $\{\pi_{1,i}\}_{i=1}^{\mu}$ by sampling their logarithms w.r.t. g.

Output: When $\mathcal{A}$ halts, it outputs a commitment $\hat{C}$ and a pair $(y, \boldsymbol{z}) \in \mathbb{Z}_p \times \mathbb{Z}_p^{\mu'}$, for some $\mu' \in [\ell]$, together with a label lbl and a verifying proof $\boldsymbol{\pi}$ that $\hat{C}$ commits to $f[X_1, \ldots, X_\ell]$ such that $y = f[\boldsymbol{z}, X_{\mu'+1}, \ldots, X_\ell]$ for all assignments of $(X_{\mu'+1}, \ldots, X_\ell)$. The winning conditions of the simulation-extractability game impose that the tuple $(\mathsf{lbl}, \hat{C}, y, \boldsymbol{z}, \boldsymbol{\pi})$ be different from those defined by inputs/outputs of all simulation queries. Together with its output, $\mathcal{A}$ also provides a representation of $\hat{C}$ w.r.t. the group elements in $\hat{\mathbb{G}}$ that are contained in srs. From this representation, $\mathcal{B}$ can infer a polynomial

$$F[X_1, \ldots, X_\ell] = f[X_1, \ldots, X_\ell] + r \cdot X_r$$

such that $\hat{C} = \hat{g}^{F(\alpha_1, \ldots, \alpha_\ell)}$ and where f is of the form (4). At this point, if $f[\boldsymbol{z}, X_{\mu'+1}, \ldots, X_\ell] - y$ is the zero polynomial, then $\mathcal{B}$ is a successful extractor (meaning that $\mathcal{A}$ did not succeed in the experiment) since $(f[X_1, \ldots, X_\ell], r)$ is a valid witness. We henceforth assume that $f[\boldsymbol{z}, X_{\mu'+1}, \ldots, X_\ell] - y$ is non-zero.

Along with its forgery $\boldsymbol{\pi}$, $\mathcal{A}$ also outputs representations of $\{\pi_{1,i}\}_{i=1}^{\mu'}$ and S_π, which define polynomials $\{A_i[X_1, \ldots, X_\ell, X_r]\}_{i\in[\mu']}$, and $S[X_1, \ldots, X_\ell, X_r]$ such that $S_\pi = g^{S(\alpha_1, \ldots, \alpha_\ell, \alpha_r)}$ and $\pi_{1,i} = g^{A_i(\alpha_1, \ldots, \alpha_\ell, \alpha_r)}$ for each $i \in [\mu']$. Let

$$R = e(S_\pi, \hat{g}_r) \cdot \left(\frac{e(g, \hat{C} \cdot \hat{g}^{-y})}{\prod_{i=1}^{\mu'} e(\pi_{i,1}, \hat{g}_i \cdot \hat{g}^{-z_i})} \right)^{-c}. \tag{9}$$

If $\boldsymbol{\pi}$ verifies, $c = H_{\mathsf{PCS}}(\mathsf{lbl}, \hat{C}, y, \boldsymbol{z}, (\pi_{1,i})_{i=1}^{\mu'}, R)$. If the latter hash query was not made, $\mathcal{B}$ aborts. However, $\boldsymbol{\pi}$ can only be valid with probability $1/p$ in this case.

We now distinguish two cases: (i) The tuple $(\mathsf{lbl}, \hat{C}, y, \boldsymbol{z}, c, (\pi_{1,i})_{i=1}^{\mu'})$ was recycled from simulation query involving a different Fiat-Shamir response $\bar{S}_\pi$; (ii) $(\mathsf{lbl}, \hat{C}, y, \boldsymbol{z}, c, (\pi_{1,i})_{i=1}^{\mu'})$ is a fresh tuple. In case (i), we would have a collision

$$c = H_{\mathsf{PCS}}(\mathsf{lbl}, \hat{C}, y, \boldsymbol{z}, (\pi_{1,i})_{i=1}^{\mu'}, R) = H_{\mathsf{PCS}}(\mathsf{lbl}, \hat{C}, y, \boldsymbol{z}, (\pi_{1,i})_{i=1}^{\mu'}, \bar{R})$$

where $\bar{R} = e(\bar{S}_\pi, \hat{g}_r) \cdot \left(e(g, \hat{C} \cdot \hat{g}^{-y}) / \prod_{i=1}^{\mu'} e(\pi_{i,1}, \hat{g}_i \cdot \hat{g}^{-z_i})\right)^{-c}$ and

$$R = e(S_\pi, \hat{g}_r) \cdot \left(e(g, \hat{C} \cdot \hat{g}^{-y}) / \prod_{i=1}^{\mu'} e(\pi_{i,1}, \hat{g}_i \cdot \hat{g}^{-z_i})\right)^{-c}$$

since, for a given $(\hat{C}, R, y, \boldsymbol{z}, c, (\pi_{1,i})_{i=1}^{\mu'})$, there is a unique S_π satisfying (9). Since H_{PCS} is a random oracle, case (i) happens with probability $(Q_H + Q_S)^2/p$.

In case (ii), $c = H_{\mathsf{PCS}}(\mathsf{lbl}, \hat{C}, y, \boldsymbol{z}, (\pi_{1,i})_{i=1}^{\mu'}, R)$ must be fresh as well except with probability $(Q_H + Q_S)^2/p$ since, if it had been a hash value programmed by the simulator, we would have a collision

$$c = H_{\mathsf{PCS}}(\mathsf{lbl}, \hat{C}, y, \boldsymbol{z}, (\pi_{1,i})_{i=1}^{\mu'}, R) = H_{\mathsf{PCS}}(\mathsf{lbl}^{(0)}, \hat{C}^{(0)}, y^{(0)}, \boldsymbol{z}^{(0)}, (\pi_{1,i}^{(0)})_{i=1}^{\mu'}, R^{(0)}).$$

If c is fresh (i.e., it is not a programmed random oracle value), $\mathcal{B}$ can solve its $(\bar{d}\ell, \bar{d}\ell)$-DLOG instance by recalling the representation of R as $\{\omega_{\mathcal{I},\hat{\mathcal{I}}}\}_{\mathcal{I}\in\mathcal{G},\hat{\mathcal{I}}\in\hat{\mathcal{G}}}$ satisfying (8), which must have been supplied by $\mathcal{A}$ when it queried the hash value $H_{\mathsf{PCS}}(\mathsf{lbl}, \hat{C}, y, \boldsymbol{z}, (\pi_{1,i})_{i=1}^{\mu'}, R)$. From this representation, $\mathcal{B}$ can compute an $(\ell+1)$-variate polynomial $R[X_1, \ldots, X_\ell, X_r]$ such that $R = e(g, \hat{g})^{R(\alpha_1,\ldots,\alpha_\ell,\alpha_r)}$. The verification equation (9) then implies

$$\begin{aligned} R(\alpha_1, \ldots, \alpha_\ell, \alpha_r) &= S(\alpha_1, \ldots, \alpha_\ell, \alpha_r) \cdot \alpha_r \\ &\quad - c \cdot \Big(F(\alpha_1, \ldots, \alpha_\ell, \alpha_r) - y - \sum_{i=1}^{\mu'} A_i(\alpha_1, \ldots, \alpha_\ell, \alpha_r) \cdot (\alpha_i - z_i)\Big), \end{aligned} \tag{10}$$

which means that the $(\ell+1)$-variate polynomial

$$\begin{aligned} T[X_1, \ldots, X_\ell, X_r] &\triangleq R[X_1, \ldots, X_\ell, X_r] - S[X_1, \ldots, X_\ell, X_r] \cdot X_r \\ &\quad + c \cdot \Big(F[X_1, \ldots, X_\ell, X_r] - y - \sum_{i=1}^{\mu'} A_i[X_1, \ldots, X_\ell, X_r] \cdot (X_i - z_i)\Big), \end{aligned} \tag{11}$$

vanishes on $(\alpha_1, \ldots, \alpha_\ell, \alpha_r) \in \mathbb{Z}_p^{\ell+1}$. We argue that this polynomial is non-zero w.h.p. if $f[\boldsymbol{z}, X_{\mu'+1}, \ldots, X_\ell] - y$ is a non-zero polynomial. If $T[X_1, \ldots, X_\ell, X_r]$ is identically zero, so is $T[z_1, \ldots, z_{\mu'}, X_{\mu'+1}, \ldots, X_\ell, 0]$, in which case we have

$$R[z_1, \ldots, z_{\mu'}, X_{\mu'+1}, \ldots, X_\ell, 0] = -c \cdot (f[\boldsymbol{z}, X_{\mu'+1}, \ldots, X_\ell] - y) \tag{12}$$

since $F[\boldsymbol{z}, X_{\mu'+1}, \ldots, X_\ell, 0] = f[\boldsymbol{z}, X_{\mu'+1}, \ldots, X_\ell]$. We claim that, if the polynomial $f[\boldsymbol{z}, X_{\mu'+1}, \ldots, X_\ell] - y$ is non-zero, the identity (12) holds with probability at most Q_H/p. Indeed, $c = H_{\mathsf{PCS}}(\mathsf{lbl}, \hat{C}, y, \boldsymbol{z}, (\pi_{1,i})_{i=1}^{\mu'}, R)$ is a non-programmed random oracle output and is thus defined after R (whose algebraic representation uniquely determines the coefficients of $R[X_1, \ldots, X_\ell, X_r]$), the extracted polynomial $f[X_1, \ldots, X_\ell]$ (which is determined by the representation of $\hat{C}$) and the statement $(\boldsymbol{z}, y)$. So, for any non-programmed $H_{\mathsf{PCS}}(\mathsf{lbl}, \hat{C}, y, \boldsymbol{z}, (\pi_{1,i})_{i=1}^{\mu'}, R)$ where the polynomials $(f[X_1, \ldots, X_\ell], R[X_1, \ldots, X_\ell, X_r])$ defined by $(\hat{C}, R)$ are such that $f[\boldsymbol{z}, X_{\mu'+1}, \ldots, X_\ell] - y \not\equiv 0$, (12) holds for at most one scalar $c \in \mathbb{Z}_p$. The probability that the output of H_{PCS} hits this bad $c \in \mathbb{Z}_p$ is thus $1/p$.

We now assume that $T[X_1, \ldots, X_\ell, X_r]$ is non-zero and define the univariate

$$L[X] \triangleq T[\rho_1 X + \theta_1, \ldots, \rho_\ell X + \theta_\ell, \rho_r X + \theta_r]$$

Note that $L(\alpha) = T(\alpha_1, \ldots, \alpha_\ell, \alpha_r) = 0$, so that $\alpha \in \mathbb{Z}_p$ is computable by factoring $L[X]$ if it is a non-zero polynomial. Let zero_L the event that the polynomial $L[X]$ is identically zero given that $T[X_1, \ldots, X_{\ell+1}]$ is not. We show that $\Pr[\mathsf{zero}_L]$ is negligible.

If $L[X]$ is identically zero, we have $L(0) = T(\theta_1, \ldots, \theta_\ell, \theta_r) = 0$. However, $(\theta_1, \ldots, \theta_\ell, \theta_r)$ was sampled uniformly in $\mathbb{Z}_p^{\ell+1}$ and remains independent of $\mathcal{A}$'s view during the entire experiment. Indeed, srs only depends on $\alpha_r = \rho_r \cdot \alpha + \theta_r$ and $\{\alpha_i = \rho_i \cdot \alpha + \theta_i\}_{i=1}^r$ and $\mathcal{A}$ never gets to see any information about $\{\theta_i\}_{i \in [\ell]}$ nor θ_r. Since the total degree of $T[X_1, \ldots, X_\ell, X_r]$ is $\leq d\ell + 1$, the Schwartz-Zippel lemma implies $\Pr[\mathsf{zero}_L] \leq \Pr_{(\theta_1, \ldots, \theta_\ell, \theta_r)}[T(\theta_1, \ldots, \theta_\ell, \theta_r) = 0] \leq (d\ell + 1)/p$. □

4.2 Extensions

The scheme and the proof of Theorem 3 easily extend to the batch evaluation setting when we prove evaluations of multiple committed polynomials on a common input. The details are given in the full version of the paper.

In the univariate case, we can construct a simulation-extractable variant of KZG commitments with a better efficiency than by setting $\ell = 1$ in the above construction. The details are given in the full version of the paper.

5 A Simulation-Extractable Variant of HyperPlonk

Let $\mathcal{C}[G] : \mathbb{Z}_p^n \to \mathbb{Z}_p$ an arithmetic circuit of N gates, where each gate has fan-in two and can be an addition gate, a multiplication gate, or a custom gate $G : \mathbb{Z}_p^2 \to \mathbb{Z}_p$. The public input of the circuit is denoted by $\mathbb{x} \in \mathbb{Z}_p^n$ and we assume as in [17] that $n + N + 1 = 2^\mu$ is a power of 2. The Plonk arithmetization [28] represents the trace of the computation by a set $\hat{M}$ of triples $\{(L_i, R_i, O_i) \in \mathbb{Z}_p^3\}_{i=0}^{n+N}$, where (L_i, R_i, O_i) contains the left input, the right input and the output of the i-th gate. In HyperPlonk [17], the prover interpolates $\hat{M}$ by defining a multilinear polynomial $M \in \mathbb{Z}_p^{(\leq 1)}[X_1, \ldots, X_{\mu+2}]$ such that, for each $i \in \{0, \ldots, n+N\}$,

$$M(\langle i \rangle, 0, 0) = L_i, \qquad M(\langle i \rangle, 0, 1) = R_i, \qquad M(\langle i \rangle, 1, 0) = O_i.$$

In a pre-processing phase, the $\mathsf{PreProcess}$ algorithm takes as input the circuit and creates the verifier's public parameters vp. These parameters consist of deterministic commitments to selector polynomials $S_1, S_2, S_3 \in \mathbb{Z}_p^{(\leq 1)}[X_1, \ldots, X_\mu]$, and a wiring polynomial $\sigma \in \mathbb{Z}_p^{(\leq 1)}[X_1, \ldots, X_{\mu+2}]$, which is actually encoded as 3 partial polynomials in (15). These polynomials only depend on the circuit and are computed only once by the verifier.

Each verification requires to compute an input-dependent multilinear polynomial $I[X_1, \ldots, X_\mu]$ such that $I(\langle i \rangle, 0, \ldots, 0) = \mathbb{x}_i$ for each $i \in [n]$ and $I(\boldsymbol{x}) = 0$ for all $\boldsymbol{x} \in B_\mu \setminus \{(\langle i \rangle, 0, \ldots, 0)\}_{i \in [n]}$.

To generate a proof, the prover defines the virtual μ-variate polynomial

$$\begin{aligned} f[\boldsymbol{X}] = S_1[\boldsymbol{X}] \cdot \big(M[\boldsymbol{X}, 0, 0] + M_1[\boldsymbol{X}, 0, 1]\big) \\ + S_2[\boldsymbol{X}] \cdot \big(M[\boldsymbol{X}, 0, 0] \cdot M_1[\boldsymbol{X}, 0, 1]\big) \\ + S_3[\boldsymbol{X}] \cdot \boldsymbol{G}\big(M[\boldsymbol{X}, 0, 0], M_1[\boldsymbol{X}, 0, 1]\big) - M[\boldsymbol{X}, 1, 0] + I[\boldsymbol{X}], \quad (13) \end{aligned}$$

and convinces the verifier that $f[\boldsymbol{X}]$ vanishes everywhere on the hypercube B_μ.

The selector polynomials are defined such that, for extremal gates $i < n$ and $i = n + N$, we have $S_1(\langle i\rangle) = S_2(\langle i\rangle) = S_3(\langle i\rangle) = 0$ so that $M(\langle i\rangle, 1, 0) = I(\langle i\rangle)$ for each $i \in [0, n-1]$ while the constraint $M(\langle n + N\rangle) = 0$ ensures that the arithmetic circuit outputs 0. For internal gates $i \in [n, n+N-1]$, we have $S_1(\langle i\rangle) = 1$ and $S_2(\langle i\rangle) = S_3(\langle i\rangle) = 0$ for each addition gate i; $S_2(\langle i\rangle) = 1$ and $S_1(\langle i\rangle) = S_3(\langle i\rangle) = 0$ for each multiplication gate i; $S_3(\langle i\rangle) = 1$ and $S_1(\langle i\rangle) = S_2(\langle i\rangle) = 0$ for each custom gate i.

Then, the prover must also convince the verifier that $M[X_1, \ldots, X_\ell]$ correctly encodes the circuit. This is done by defining the "extended hypercube" $\mathcal{H} \triangleq B_\mu \times \{\langle i\rangle\}_{i=0}^2$ and proving that the wiring identity $M(\boldsymbol{x}) = M(\hat{\sigma}(\boldsymbol{x}))$ holds for all $\boldsymbol{x} \in \mathcal{H}$, where $\hat{\sigma} : \mathcal{H} \to \mathcal{H}$ is the circuit-dependent permutation.

The pre-processing algorithm thus commits to an additional multilinear polynomial $s_\sigma[X_1, \ldots, X_{\mu+2}]$ such that, for all $(\boldsymbol{x}, \langle i\rangle) \in \mathcal{H}$,

$$s_\sigma(\boldsymbol{x}, \langle i\rangle) = s_{\mathsf{id}}(\hat{\sigma}(\boldsymbol{x}, \langle i\rangle)) \tag{14}$$

where $s_{\mathsf{id}}[X_1, \ldots, X_{\mu+2}] = \sum_{i=1}^{\mu+2} 2^{i-1} \cdot X_i$.

In order to prove the wiring identity, HyperPlonk relies on a product argument over the Boolean hypercube which builds on the following lemma. Given commitments $C_1 = g^{f_1(\alpha_1, \ldots, \alpha_\mu) + r_1 \cdot \alpha_r}$, $C_2 = g^{f_2(\alpha_1, \ldots, \alpha_\mu) + r_2 \cdot \alpha_r}$ to polynomials $f_1, f_2 \in \mathbb{Z}_p^{(\leq d)}[X_1, \ldots, X_\mu]$, it allows a prover to convince the verifier that $f_b[X_1, \ldots, X_\mu] \in \mathbb{Z}_p^{(\leq d)}[X_1, \ldots, X_\mu]$ for each $b \in \{1, 2\}$ and $\prod_{\boldsymbol{x} \in B_\mu} f'(\boldsymbol{x}) = s$, for a given $s \in \mathbb{Z}_p$, where $f'(\boldsymbol{x}) = f_1(\boldsymbol{x})/f_2(\boldsymbol{x})$.

Lemma 1 ([49, Lemma 5.1]). *For a rational function $f' : \mathbb{Z}_p^\mu \to \mathbb{Z}_p$ and a scalar $s \in \mathbb{Z}_p$, the equality $s = \prod_{\boldsymbol{x} \in B_\mu} f'(\boldsymbol{x})$ holds if and only if there exists a multilinear polynomial $\tilde{v} \in \mathbb{Z}_p^{(\leq 1)}[X_1, \ldots, X_{\mu+1}]$ such that $\tilde{v}(1, 1, \ldots, 1, 0) = s$ and, for all $\boldsymbol{x} \in B_\mu$, $\tilde{v}(0, \boldsymbol{x}) = f'(\boldsymbol{x})$ and $\tilde{v}(1, \boldsymbol{x}) = \tilde{v}(\boldsymbol{x}, 0) \cdot \tilde{v}(\boldsymbol{x}, 1)$.*

5.1 Description

The description below is almost identical to the original HyperPlonk [17]. The main difference is that some multivariate PCS evaluation proofs have to be generated with the simulation-extractable polynomial commitment of Sect. 4.

Also, in order to obtain straight-line simulation-extractability in the AGM (and even knowledge-soundness), we need to carefully choose the groups where the different commitments live. Specifically, the knowledge soundness analysis sometimes requires committed polynomials to be of the form described in Sect. 3.2. For this reason, we chose to have those commitments live in the second source group $\hat{\mathbb{G}}$ for which the available generators contained in srs ensure that the AGM-extractor will be able to extract a polynomial of the form described in Sect. 3.2. As for commitments to univariate polynomials and the group elements contained in PCS evaluation proofs, they can live in $\mathbb{G}$.

As in [17], the batched zero-check protocol applies the sumcheck protocol to

$$F_\gamma[X_1, \ldots, X_\mu] = f[X_1, \ldots, X_\mu] \cdot eq_\gamma[X_1, \ldots, X_\mu],$$

using the multilinear $eq_\gamma[X_1,\ldots,X_\mu] = \prod_{i=1}^{\mu}\big(\gamma_i \cdot X_i + (1-\gamma_i)\cdot(1-X_i)\big)$ where $\gamma = (\gamma_1,\ldots,\gamma_\mu)$ is a random vector obtained by hashing the transcript so far.

CRS-Gen$(1^\lambda, 1^d, 1^\mu)$**:** On input of λ, a parameter $\mu = \log(n+N+1)$ specifying the circuit size, and a bound d on the degree of custom gates such that $d \cdot 2^\mu \in \mathsf{poly}(\lambda)$, set $\ell = \mu + 1$ and $\bar{d} = \max(2d+1, 9)$. Then,

1. Choose asymmetric bilinear groups $(\mathbb{G}, \hat{\mathbb{G}}, \mathbb{G}_T)$ of prime order $p > 2^{l(\lambda)}$, for some function $l : \mathbb{N} \to \mathbb{N}$, and $g \xleftarrow{R} \mathbb{G}$, $\hat{g} \xleftarrow{R} \hat{\mathbb{G}}$.
2. Pick $\alpha_1,\ldots,\alpha_\ell,\alpha_r \xleftarrow{R} \mathbb{Z}_p$. Compute $g_r = g^{\alpha_r}$ and $\hat{g}_r = \hat{g}^{\alpha_r}$.
3. For each $\mathcal{I} = (i_1,\ldots,i_\ell) \in \mathcal{U}_{\bar{d},\ell}$, compute $g_{\mathcal{I}} = g^{\prod_{j=1}^{\ell}\alpha_j^{i_j}}$.
4. For each $\mathcal{I} = (i_1,\ldots,i_\ell) \in \mathcal{W}_{1,\ell}$, compute $\hat{g}_{\mathcal{I}} = \hat{g}^{\prod_{j=1}^{\ell}\alpha_j^{i_j}}$. Then, compute $\{\hat{g}^{(\alpha_1+\alpha_{\mu+1})^i\cdot\alpha_\mu\cdot(\alpha_\mu-1)}\}_{i=0}^{3}$.
5. Choose hash functions $H, H_{\mathsf{PCS}}, H_{\mathsf{batch}}, H_\delta : \{0,1\}^* \to \mathbb{Z}_p$, $H_\xi : \{0,1\}^* \to \mathbb{Z}_p^*$, $H_\beta, H_\zeta : \{0,1\}^* \to \mathbb{Z}_p^2$ and $H_\gamma : \{0,1\}^* \to \mathbb{Z}_p^\mu$.

Let $\mathbf{H} = \{H, H_{\mathsf{PCS}}, H_{\mathsf{batch}}, H_\beta, H_\zeta, H_\xi, H_\delta\}$ and define the universal SRS

$$\mathsf{srs} = \Big((\mathbb{G}, \hat{\mathbb{G}}, \mathbb{G}_T), g_r, \hat{g}_r, \{g_{\mathcal{I}}\}_{\mathcal{I}\in\mathcal{U}_{\bar{d},\ell}}, \{\hat{g}_{\mathcal{I}}\}_{\mathcal{I}\in\mathcal{W}_{1,\ell}}, \{\hat{g}^{(\alpha_1+\alpha_{\mu+1})^i\cdot\alpha_\mu\cdot(\alpha_\mu-1)}\}_{i=0}^{3}, \mathbf{H}\Big).$$

PreProcess$_{\mathsf{srs}}(\mathbb{i})$**:** On input of the universal SRS srs and an arithmetic circuit $\mathbb{i} = \mathcal{C}[G] : \mathbb{Z}_p^n \to \mathbb{Z}_p$ of size N such that $n + N + 1 = 2^\mu$, do the following:

1. Let the selector polynomials $S_1, S_2, S_3 : \{0,1\}^\mu \to \mathbb{Z}_p$. Deterministically compute a multilinear polynomial $s_\sigma \in \mathbb{Z}_p^{(\leq 1)}[X_1,\ldots,X_\ell]$ that encodes the wiring of $\mathcal{C}$. Define the multilinear $s_{\mathsf{id}}[X_1,\ldots,X_\ell] = \sum_{i=1}^{\ell} 2^{i-1}\cdot X_i$. Let the partial permutation polynomials
$$s_\sigma[X_1,\ldots,X_\mu,0,0], \quad s_\sigma[X_1,\ldots,X_\mu,0,1], \quad s_\sigma[X_1,\ldots,X_\mu,1,0] \qquad (15)$$
2. For each $i \in \{0,1,2\}$, compute $C_{\sigma,\langle i\rangle} = g^{s_\sigma(\alpha_1,\ldots,\alpha_\mu,\langle i\rangle)}$.
3. For each $i \in \{1,2,3\}$, compute $C_{s,i} = g^{S_i(\alpha_1,\ldots,\alpha_\mu)}$.

Return $\mathsf{pp} = \mathsf{srs}$ and

$$\mathsf{vp} = \Big((\mathbb{G}, \hat{\mathbb{G}}, \mathbb{G}_T), g, \hat{g}, \hat{g}_r, \{\hat{g}_i = \hat{g}^{\alpha_i}\}_{i=1}^{\mu}, \{C_{\sigma,\langle i\rangle}\}_{i=0}^{2}, \{C_{s,i}\}_{i=1}^{3}, \mathbf{H}\Big).$$

Prove$_{\mathsf{pp}}(\mathbb{i}, \mathbb{x}, \mathbb{w})$**:** Given an arithmetic circuit $\mathbb{i} = \mathcal{C}[G] : \mathbb{Z}_p^n \to \mathbb{Z}_p$, a public input $\mathbb{x}$ and a witness $\mathbb{w}$ consisting of a wire assignment leading to the output 0,

1. Compute $I[\boldsymbol{X}]$, which encodes $\mathbb{x}$, as well as the circuit-dependent polynomials $\{S_i[\boldsymbol{X}]\}_{i=1}^{3}$, $\{s_\sigma[\boldsymbol{X},\langle i\rangle]\}_{i=0}^{2}$.
2. Compute the polynomial $M \in \mathbb{Z}_p^{(\leq 1)}[X_1,\ldots,X_\ell]$ satisfying the gate identity (13). For each $i \in [0,2]$, choose $R_i \xleftarrow{R} \mathbb{Z}_p$ (viewed as a constant univariate polynomial) and commit to
$$\bar{M}_i[X_1,\ldots,X_\mu] \triangleq M[X_1,\ldots,X_\mu,\langle i\rangle] + R_i\cdot X_\mu\cdot(X_\mu - 1),$$

by choosing $r_{M,i} \xleftarrow{R} \mathbb{Z}_p$ and computing

$$\hat{C}_{M,i} = \hat{g}^{M(\alpha_1,\ldots,\alpha_\mu,\langle i\rangle)+R_i\cdot\alpha_\mu\cdot(\alpha_\mu-1)+r_{M,i}\cdot\alpha_r}.$$

3. Compute the challenge $(\beta_1, \beta_2) = H_\beta(\mathbb{x}, \mathsf{vp}, (\hat{C}_{M,i})_{i=0}^2) \in \mathbb{Z}_p^2$. Compute a multilinear $\tilde{v} \in \mathbb{Z}_p^{(\le 1)}[X_1, \ldots, X_{\mu+1}]$ satisfying the conditions of Lemma 1 and such that

$$\tilde{v}(0, \boldsymbol{x}) = \prod_{i=0}^{2} \frac{\bar{M}_i(\boldsymbol{x}) + \beta_2 \cdot s_{\mathrm{id}}(\boldsymbol{x}, \langle i\rangle) + \beta_1}{\bar{M}_i(\boldsymbol{x}) + \beta_2 \cdot s_\sigma(\boldsymbol{x}, \langle i\rangle) + \beta_1} \qquad \forall \boldsymbol{x} \in B_\mu,$$

where $\langle i\rangle \in \{0,1\}^2$ is the binary representation of $i \in [0, 2]$.
4. Choose a random degree-3 polynomial $R_v \in \mathbb{Z}_p[X]$ and define

$$\bar{v}[X_1, \ldots, X_{\mu+1}] = \tilde{v}[X_1, \ldots, X_{\mu+1}] + R_v[X_1 + X_{\mu+1}] \cdot X_\mu \cdot (X_\mu - 1)$$

Commit to $\bar{v}[X_1, \ldots, X_{\mu+1}]$ by choosing $r_v \xleftarrow{R} \mathbb{Z}_p$ and computing

$$\hat{C}_v = \hat{g}^{\bar{v}(\alpha_1,\ldots,\alpha_{\mu+1})+R_v(\alpha_1+\alpha_{\mu+1})\cdot\alpha_\mu\cdot(\alpha_\mu-1)+r_v\cdot\alpha_r}$$

5. Compute $(\zeta_1, \zeta_2) = H_\zeta(\mathbb{x}, \mathsf{vp}, (\hat{C}_{M,i})_{i=0}^2, \hat{C}_v) \in \mathbb{Z}_p^2$. Define the following virtual (i.e., not explicitly computed) polynomials in $\boldsymbol{X} = (X_1, \ldots, X_\mu)$:

$$Q_1[\boldsymbol{X}] = \bar{v}[1, \boldsymbol{X}] - \bar{v}[\boldsymbol{X}, 0] \cdot \bar{v}[\boldsymbol{X}, 1]$$

$$Q_2[\boldsymbol{X}] = \prod_{i=0}^{2} \left(\bar{M}_i[\boldsymbol{X}] + \beta_2 \cdot s_{\mathrm{id}}[\boldsymbol{X}, \langle i\rangle] + \beta_1\right) - \bar{v}[0, \boldsymbol{X}] \cdot \prod_{i=0}^{2} \left(\bar{M}_i[\boldsymbol{X}] + \beta_2 \cdot s_\sigma[\boldsymbol{X}, \langle i\rangle] + \beta_1\right)$$

$$\begin{aligned} f[\boldsymbol{X}] &= S_1[\boldsymbol{X}] \cdot \left(\bar{M}_0[\boldsymbol{X}] + \bar{M}_1[\boldsymbol{X}]\right) \\ &+ S_2[\boldsymbol{X}] \cdot \left(\bar{M}_0[\boldsymbol{X}] \cdot \bar{M}_1[\boldsymbol{X}]\right) \\ &+ S_3[\boldsymbol{X}] \cdot \boldsymbol{G}\left(\bar{M}_0[\boldsymbol{X}], \bar{M}_1[\boldsymbol{X}]\right) - \bar{M}_2[\boldsymbol{X}] + I[\boldsymbol{X}], \end{aligned} \tag{16}$$

6. Prove that $F[\boldsymbol{X}] = f[\boldsymbol{X}] + \zeta_1 \cdot Q_1[\boldsymbol{X}] + \zeta_2 \cdot Q_2[\boldsymbol{X}]$ vanishes over B_μ. To this end, compute $\boldsymbol{\gamma} = H_\gamma(\mathbb{x}, \mathsf{vp}, (\hat{C}_{M,i})_{i=0}^2, \hat{C}_v) \in \mathbb{Z}_p^\mu$ and prove the statement $\sum_{\boldsymbol{x}\in B_\mu} F(\boldsymbol{x}) \cdot eq_{\boldsymbol{\gamma}}(\boldsymbol{x}) = 0$ via a zero-knowledge sumcheck protocol. Namely, let $\bar{d}' = \min(\bar{d}, 3) = 3$ and do the following.
   a. Choose a polynomial $a[X_1, \ldots, X_\mu] = a_0 + \sum_{i=1}^{\mu} a_i[X_i]$ such that, for each $i \in [\mu]$, $a_i[X_i] = \sum_{j=1}^{\bar{d}'} a_{i,j} \cdot X_i^j$, for random a_0, $\{a_{i,j}\}_{i,j}$, and compute a commitment $C_a = g^{a(\alpha_1,\ldots,\alpha_\mu)+r_a\cdot\alpha_r}$, where $r_a \xleftarrow{R} \mathbb{Z}_p$, using $\{g_{\mathcal{I}}\}_{\mathcal{I}\in\mathcal{W}_{\bar{d},\ell}}$. Compute $y_a = \sum_{\boldsymbol{x}\in B_\mu} a(\boldsymbol{x})$.
   b. Compute $\xi = H_\xi(\mathbb{x}, \mathsf{vp}, (\hat{C}_{M,i})_{i=0}^2, \hat{C}_v, C_a, y_a, (\zeta_1, \zeta_2), (\beta_1, \beta_2), \boldsymbol{\gamma}) \in \mathbb{Z}_p^*$. Let the virtual polynomial (of degree $\le \bar{d} = \max(2d + 1, 9)$)

$$F_{zk}[X_1, \ldots, X_\mu] \triangleq F[X_1, \ldots, X_\mu] \cdot eq_{\boldsymbol{\gamma}}[X_1, \ldots, X_\mu] + \xi \cdot a[X_1, \ldots, X_\mu]$$

c. Prove that $\sum_{\boldsymbol{x} \in B_\mu} F_{zk}(\boldsymbol{x}) = \xi \cdot y_a$. Namely, for $i = \mu$ to 1,
   1. Compute a commitment $C_{\theta,i} = g^{\theta_i(\alpha_1)}$ to the univariate

$$\theta_i[X] = \sum_{\boldsymbol{b} \in B_{i-1}} \Big(f[\boldsymbol{b}, X, r_{i+1}, \ldots, r_\mu] + \zeta_1 \cdot Q_1[\boldsymbol{b}, X, r_{i+1}, \ldots, r_\mu] \\ + \zeta_2 \cdot Q_2[\boldsymbol{b}, X, r_{i+1}, \ldots, r_\mu] \Big) \cdot eq_\gamma[\boldsymbol{b}, X, r_{i+1}, \ldots, r_\mu] \\ + \xi \cdot \sum_{\boldsymbol{b} \in B_{i-1}} a[\boldsymbol{b}, X, r_{i+1}, \ldots, r_\mu] \tag{17}$$

   2. Compute

$$r_i = H\big(\mathbb{x}, \mathsf{vp}, (\hat{C}_{M,i})_{i=0}^2, \hat{C}_v, C_a, y_a, \boldsymbol{\gamma}, (\beta_1, \beta_2), (\zeta_1, \zeta_2), \\ \{C_{\theta,j}, \theta_j(0), \theta_j(1)\}_{j \in [i,\mu]}, (r_j)_{j \in [i+1,\mu]}\big) \in \mathbb{Z}_p.$$

d. Generate a batch proof $\boldsymbol{\pi}_{\mathsf{batch}}$ that $(C_{\theta,i})_{i\in[\mu]}$ commit to polynomials $(\theta_i[X])_{i\in[\mu]}$ evaluating to $\{\theta_i(0), \theta_i(1), \theta_{i,r} \triangleq \theta_i(r_i)\}$ for the inputs $\Omega_i = \{0, 1, r_i\}$.
e. Generate multivariate PCS evaluation proofs. Namely,
   1. Using the PCS of Sect. 3.1, generate a batch proof $\boldsymbol{\pi}_{C,a}$ for the commitments $\big\{\{C_{s,i}\}_{i=1}^3, \{C_{\sigma,\langle i\rangle}\}_{i=0}^2, C_a\big\}$ showing that
      - For each $i \in [3]$, the selector polynomial $S_i[\boldsymbol{X}]$ evaluates to $s_{i,r} = S_i(r_1, \ldots, r_\mu)$
      - For each $i \in \{0, 1, 2\}$, the partial permutation polynomial $s_\sigma[\boldsymbol{X}, \langle i\rangle]$ evaluates to $\sigma_{i,r} \triangleq s_\sigma(r_1, \ldots, r_\mu, \langle i\rangle)$.
      - C_a commits to a polynomial that evaluates to $a_r \triangleq a(r_1, \ldots, r_\mu)$.
   2. Using the PCS of Sect. 4, generate a batch proof $\boldsymbol{\pi}_M$ showing that $\{\hat{C}_{M,i}\}_{i=0}^2$ commit to polynomials $\{\bar{M}_i[\boldsymbol{X}]\}_{i=0}^2$ that evaluate to $m_{i,r} \triangleq \bar{M}_i(r_1, \ldots, r_\mu)$ for each $i \in [0, 2]$. This proof is generated for a label lbl_1 containing the entire transcript so far.
   3. For the commitment $\hat{C}_v$, compute simulation-extractable proofs $(\boldsymbol{\pi}_{v,x,b}, \boldsymbol{\pi}_{v,b,x})_{b=0}^1$ that

$$\forall b \in \{0,1\} \ : \ \bar{v}(r_1, \ldots, r_\mu, b) = v_{r,b}, \quad \wedge \quad \bar{v}(b, r_1, \ldots, r_\mu) = v_{b,r},$$

      for labels $\{\mathsf{lbl}_{2,i}\}_{i=1}^4$ containing the entire transcript so far.
   4. For $\hat{C}_v$, prove that $\bar{v}(1, \ldots, 1, 0) = 1$ via a simulation-extractable proof $\boldsymbol{\pi}_{v,s}$ for a label lbl_3 containing the entire transcript so far.

Let

$$\boldsymbol{\pi}_r = \Big(\boldsymbol{\pi}_{C,a}, (\boldsymbol{\pi}_M, (\boldsymbol{\pi}_{v,x,b}, \boldsymbol{\pi}_{v,b,x})_{b=0}^1, \boldsymbol{\pi}_{v,s}\Big) \tag{18}$$

the vector of evaluation proofs and let the batched zero-check proof

$$\boldsymbol{\pi}_{\mathsf{zero}} = \big(C_a, a_r, y_a, \{m_{i,r}, \sigma_{i,r}\}_{i=0}^2, \{s_{i,r}\}_{i=1}^3, \{v_{r,b}, v_{b,r}\}_{b=0}^1, \\ \{C_{\theta,i}, \theta_i(0), \theta_i(1)\}_{i\in[\mu]}, \boldsymbol{\pi}_{\mathsf{batch}}, \boldsymbol{\pi}_r\big)$$

Return the proof $\boldsymbol{\pi} = \big((\hat{C}_{M,i})_{i=0}^{2}, \hat{C}_v, \boldsymbol{\pi}_{\mathsf{zero}}\big)$.

Verify$_{\mathsf{vp}}(\mathbb{i}, \mathbb{x}, \boldsymbol{\pi})$: Given a statement $(\mathbb{i}, \mathbb{x})$, a compressed version vp of $\mathbb{i} = \mathcal{C}[G]$, and a candidate proof $\boldsymbol{\pi}$, return 0 if $\boldsymbol{\pi}$ does not parse properly. Otherwise,

1. Compute $\gamma = H_\gamma\big(\mathbb{x}, \mathsf{vp}, (\hat{C}_{M,i})_{i=0}^{2}, \hat{C}_v\big) \in \mathbb{Z}_p^{\mu}$ and
$$(\beta_1, \beta_2) = H_\beta\big(\mathbb{x}, \mathsf{vp}, (\hat{C}_{M,i})_{i=0}^{2}\big), \qquad (\zeta_1, \zeta_2) = H_\zeta\big(\mathbb{x}, \mathsf{vp}, (\hat{C}_{M,i})_{i=0}^{2}, \hat{C}_v\big)$$
2. Compute the polynomial $I[X_1, \ldots, X_\mu]$ such that $I(\langle i \rangle, 0, \ldots, 0) = \mathbb{x}[i]$ for each $i \in [0, n-1]$ and $I(\boldsymbol{x}) = 0$ everywhere else.
3. For each $i = \mu$ to 1, compute
$$r_i = H\big(\mathbb{x}, \mathsf{vp}, (\hat{C}_{M,i})_{i=0}^{2}, \hat{C}_v, C_a, y_a, \gamma, (\beta_1, \beta_2), (\zeta_1, \zeta_2), \{C_{\theta,j}, \theta_j(0), \theta_j(1)\}_{j \in [i,\mu]}, (r_j)_{j \in [i+1,\mu]}\big) \in \mathbb{Z}_p. \quad (19)$$
4. Compute $\xi = H_\xi\big(\mathbb{x}, \mathsf{vp}, (\hat{C}_{M,i})_{i=0}^{2}, \hat{C}_v, C_a, y_a, (\zeta_1, \zeta_2), (\beta_1, \beta_2), \gamma\big) \in \mathbb{Z}_p^*$ and return 0 if $\theta_\mu(0) + \theta_\mu(1) \neq \xi \cdot y_a$.
5. Let $I_{\boldsymbol{r}} = I(r_1, \ldots, r_\mu)$ and
$$\begin{aligned}\theta_{1,\boldsymbol{r}} \triangleq \Big[\Big(&s_{1,\boldsymbol{r}} \cdot (m_{0,\boldsymbol{r}} + m_{1,\boldsymbol{r}}) + s_{2,\boldsymbol{r}} \cdot (m_{0,\boldsymbol{r}} \cdot m_{1,\boldsymbol{r}}) + s_{3,\boldsymbol{r}} \cdot G(m_{0,\boldsymbol{r}}, m_{1,\boldsymbol{r}}) - m_{2,\boldsymbol{r}} + I_{\boldsymbol{r}}\Big) \\ &+ \zeta_1 \cdot \big(v_{1,\boldsymbol{r}} - v_{\boldsymbol{r},0} \cdot v_{\boldsymbol{r},1}\big) + \zeta_2 \cdot \Big(\prod_{i=0}^{2} (m_{i,\boldsymbol{r}} + \beta_2 \cdot s_{\mathsf{id}}(\boldsymbol{r}, \langle i \rangle) + \beta_1) \\ &- v_{0,\boldsymbol{r}} \cdot \prod_{i=0}^{2} (m_{i,\boldsymbol{r}} + \beta_2 \cdot \sigma_{i,\boldsymbol{r}} + \beta_1)\Big)\Big] \cdot eq_\gamma(r_1, \ldots, r_\mu) + \xi \cdot a_{\boldsymbol{r}}\end{aligned}$$
Then, for each $i \in [2, \mu]$, define $\theta_{i,\boldsymbol{r}} \triangleq \theta_{i-1}(0) + \theta_{i-1}(1)$. Return 0 if $\boldsymbol{\pi}_{\mathsf{batch}}$ is not a valid univariate batch proof for commitments $(C_{\theta,i})_{i \in [\mu]}$, evaluations $(\theta_i(0), \theta_i(1), \theta_{i,\boldsymbol{r}})_{i=1}^{\mu}$, and inputs $\{\Omega_i = \{0, 1, r_i\}\}_{i=1}^{\mu}$.
6. Return 0 if the PCS evaluation proofs in $\boldsymbol{\pi}_{\boldsymbol{r}}$ do not verify for the commitments $((\hat{C}_{M,i})_{i=0}^{2}, \{C_{\sigma,\langle i \rangle}\}_{i=0}^{2}, \{C_{s,i}\}_{i=1}^{3}, C_a)$, the label lbl_1, and the claimed evaluations in $\boldsymbol{\pi}_{\mathsf{zero}}$ for the inputs $\boldsymbol{r}$, $\{(\boldsymbol{r}, b), (b, \boldsymbol{r})\}_{b \in \{0,1\}}$. Return 0 if $(\boldsymbol{\pi}_{v,x,b}, \boldsymbol{\pi}_{v,b,x})_{b=0}^{1}$ do not verify for the labels $\{\mathsf{lbl}_{2,i}\}_{i=1}^{4}$ and the inputs specified at step 6.e.2. Return 0 if $\boldsymbol{\pi}_{v,s}$ does not verify for the claimed evaluation $\tilde{v}(1, 1, \ldots, 1, 0) = 1$ and the label lbl_3.

If none of the previous checks failed, return 1.

We note that, at step 6 of Prove, the virtual polynomial $F[\boldsymbol{X}]$ has maximal degree $\max(2d+1, 9)$ since $Q_2[\boldsymbol{X}]$ has degree ≤ 9 in X_μ and $f[\boldsymbol{X}]$ has degree $\leq 2d+1$ in X_μ, where d is the degree of $\boldsymbol{G}$.

At step 6.c.1, the prover runs in linear time in 2^μ by using the algorithm of [17, Section 3] (see also [50] and [51, Section 3.2]). Since $eq_\gamma[X_1, \ldots, X_\mu]$, $\{\bar{M}_i[X_1, \ldots, X_\mu]\}_{i=0}^{2}$, $\tilde{v} \in \mathbb{Z}_p[X_1, \ldots, X_{\mu+1}]$, $\{S_i[X_1, \ldots, X_\mu]\}_{i=1}^{3}$ and the partial permutation polynomials (15) are multilinear polynomials in $(X_1, \ldots, X_{\mu+1})$, the virtual $F[\boldsymbol{X}]$ of step 6 can be written[3] as a composition $F[X_1, \ldots, X_\mu] =$

[3] This remains true after having added $R_v[X_1 + X_{\mu+1}] \cdot X_\mu(X_\mu - 1)$ to $\tilde{v}$.

$g(h_1, \ldots, h_c)$ of a c-variate function g of total degree d with multilinear polynomials $\{h_i[X_1, \ldots, X_\mu]\}_{i=1}^c$. When $c \approx d$, the round polynomials $\{\theta_i[X]\}_{i=1}^\mu$ of the sumcheck protocol are computable in time $O(2^\mu \cdot d \cdot \log^2 d)$.

On the SRS and Proof Sizes. The above instantiation is not optimized in terms of space. In order to enable custom gates of degree d, the common reference string srs must contain $O(d \cdot 2^\mu) = O(d \cdot |\mathcal{C}|)$ group elements. It is possible to optimize the scheme and reduce the SRS size to $O(d + |\mathcal{C}|)$ group elements by committing to all multivariate polynomials as multilinear polynomials. The linearization of multivariate polynomials also allows using the batch evaluation protocol of [17, Section 3.8] so as to reduce the proof size. We did not include these optimizations in the description in order to keep it as simple as possible.

5.2 Security

We first give a proof of knowledge-soundness. In a second step, we will describe a zero-knowledge simulator and argue that the knowledge extractor still works (without rewinding) when the adversary can observe many simulated proofs.

Knowledge-Soundness. Knowledge-soundness was proven in [17] for the underlying PIOP. Here, we adapt the proof to the instantiation from KZG/PST-based commitments since we aim at a non-rewinding extractor (in the AGM) that will also be used in the proof of Theorem 6. In particular, since our instantiation uses both multivariate and univariate commitments sharing the same SRS, we need to account for the fact that the algebraic representations of univariate commitments can depend on SRS components related to multivariate ones. In the full version of the paper, we show that the batch evaluation protocol of [11] still provides the suitable extractability properties when KZG commitments are used on a larger SRS allowing commitments to multivariate polynomials.

Theorem 4. *In the AGM+ROM model and under the $(d\ell, d\ell)$-DLOG assumption, the above instantiation of HyperPlonk provides knowledge-soundness with straight-line extractability.* (The proof is given in the full version of the paper.)

Zero-Knowledge. The proof of Theorem 5 provides a trapdoor-less ZK simulator which will be used in the proof of simulation-extractability. The simulator proceeds by sampling a "fake witness" consisting of a mutlilinear polynomial $M[X_1, \ldots, X_{\mu+2}]$ that induces a polynomial $F[\boldsymbol{X}] = f[\boldsymbol{X}] + \zeta_1 \cdot Q_1[\boldsymbol{X}] + \zeta_2 \cdot Q_2[\boldsymbol{X}]$ for which $F[\boldsymbol{x}] = 0$ for all $\boldsymbol{x} \in B_\mu$ at step 6 of the prover. Since the wiring identity $M(\boldsymbol{x}, \langle i \rangle) = M(\hat{\sigma}(\boldsymbol{x}, \langle i \rangle))$ is not satisfied for all $\boldsymbol{x} \in B_\mu$, the corresponding polynomial $\tilde{v}[X_1, \ldots, X_{\mu+1}]$ (defined at step 3) does not satisfy the condition $\tilde{v}(1, \ldots, 1, 0) = 1$ when we apply Lemma 1. As a loophole, we can simulate a fake PCS evaluation proof that $\tilde{v}(1, \ldots, 1, 0) = 1$. To make sure that no information leaks about the internal wires of the circuit, the simulator also simulates PCS proofs of random evaluations (instead of the real evaluations) for the partial polynomials $\{\bar{M}_i[X_1,\ldots,X_\mu]\}_{i=0}^2$ and $\{\bar{v}[X_1,\ldots,X_\mu,b],\bar{v}[b,X_1,\ldots,X_\mu]\}_{b=0}^1$ on inputs outside the Boolean hypercube. For this reason, the PCS evaluation proofs at steps 6.e.2-6.e.4 are generated using the PCS of Sect. 4. Thanks to the masking technique of (4), these evaluations can be proven statistically indistinguishable from real evaluations. The proof relies on the fact that $R_v[X_1+X_{\mu+1}]$ is evaluated on four distinct inputs when $\bar{v}[X_1,\ldots,X_{\mu+1}]$ is evaluated on the inputs $\{(r_1,\ldots,r_\mu,b),(b,r_1,\ldots,r_\mu)\}_{b=0}^1$ at step 6.e.3.

Theorem 5. *The above HyperPlonk protocol provides statistical zero-knowledge in the ROM.* (The proof is given in the full version of the paper.)

Simulation-Extractability. The only obstacle that prevents from applying the same analysis as in the proof of Theorem 4 is that the simulator $\mathcal{S}$ creates simulated proofs of false statements by programming random oracles, which is the only case where the outputs of random oracles are determined before their inputs (and the algebraic representations thereof). However, the only random oracle that is ever programmed is H_{PCS}, which is used in the polynomial commitment of Sect. 4.1 (or its batch version, where the security proof does not program any other hash function than H_{PCS}). In particular, evaluation proofs of univariate commitments are faithfully generated by $\mathcal{S}$. Therefore we only need to worry about proofs for incorrect evaluations of multivariate polynomials.

In the treatment of multivariate evaluation proofs, we need to rely either on the simulation-extractability of the PCS from Sect. 4 or the knowledge-soundness of the one from Sect. 3.2.

Theorem 6. *In the AGM+ROM, the above instantiation of HyperPlonk provides (straight-line) simulation-extractability under the $(d\ell, d\ell)$-DLOG assumption.* (The proof is given in the full version of the paper.)

References

1. Abdolmaleki, B., Glaes, N., Ramacher, S., Slamanig, D.: Universally composable NIZKs: Circuit-succinct, non-malleable and CRS-updatable. Cryptology ePrint Archive Report 2023/097 (2023)
2. Abdolmaleki, B., Ramacher, S., Slamanig, D.: Lift-and-shift: Obtaining simulation extractable subversion and updatable SNARKs generically. In: ACM-CCS 2020 (2020)
3. Baghery, K., Pindado, Z., Ràfols, C.: Simulation extractable versions of Groth's zk-SNARK revisited. In: Krenn, S., Shulman, H., Vaudenay, S. (eds.) CANS 2020. LNCS, vol. 12579, pp. 453–461. Springer, Cham (2020). https://doi.org/10.1007/978-3-030-65411-5_22
4. Atapoor, S., Baghery, K.: Simulation extractability in Groth's zk-SNARK. In: ESORICS 2019 (2019)
5. Baghery, K., Kohlweiss, M., Siim, J., Volkhov, M.: Another look at extraction and randomization of Groth's zk-SNARK. In: FC 2021 (2021)
6. Baghery, K., Pindado, Z., Ràfols, C.: Simulation extractable versions of Groth's zk-SNARK revisited. In: CANS 2020 (2020)

7. Bayer, S., Groth, J.: Efficient zero-knowledge argument for correctness of a shuffle. In: Pointcheval, D., Johansson, T. (eds.) EUROCRYPT 2012. LNCS, vol. 7237, pp. 263–280. Springer, Heidelberg (2012). https://doi.org/10.1007/978-3-642-29011-4_17
8. Ben-Sasson, E., Bentov, I., Horesh, Y., Riabzev, M.: Fast Reed-Solomon interactive oracle proofs of proximity. In: ICALP 2018 (2018)
9. Ben-Sasson, E., Bentov, I., Horesh, Y., Riabzev, M.: Scalable zero knowledge with no trusted setup. In: Boldyreva, A., Micciancio, D. (eds.) CRYPTO 2019. LNCS, vol. 11694, pp. 701–732. Springer, Cham (2019). https://doi.org/10.1007/978-3-030-26954-8_23
10. Ben-Sasson, E., Chiesa, A., Spooner, N.: Interactive oracle proofs. In: TCC 2016B (2016)
11. Boneh, D., Drake, J., Fisch, B., Gabizon, A.: Halo infinite: recursive zk-SNARKs from any additive polynomial commitment scheme. In: Crypto 2021 (2021)
12. Bootle, J., Chiesa, A., Hu, Y., Orrú, M.: Gemini: elastic SNARKs for diverse environments. In: Dunkelman, O., Dziembowski, S. (eds.) Advances in Cryptology–EUROCRYPT 2022. EUROCRYPT 2022. LNCS, vol. 13276, pp. 427–457. Springer, Cham (2022). https://doi.org/10.1007/978-3-031-07085-3_15
13. Bowe, S., Gabizon, A.: Making Groth's zk-SNARK simulation extractable in the random oracle model. Cryptology ePrint Archive Report 2018/187 (2018)
14. Bünz, B., Bootle, J., Boneh, D., Poelstra, A., Wuille, P., Maxwell, G.: Bulletproofs: short proofs for confidential transactions and more. In: IEEE S&P 2018 (2018)
15. Campanelli, M., Gailly, N., Gennaro, R., Jovanovic, M., Mihali, P., Thaler, J.: Testudo: linear time prover SNARKs with constant size proofs and square root size universal setup. In: Latincrypt 2023 (2023)
16. Canetti, R.: Universally composable security: a new paradigm for cryptographic protocols. In: FOCS 2001 (2001)
17. Chen, B., Bünz, B., Boneh, D., Zhang, Z.: HyperPlonk: plonk with linear-time prover and high-degree custom gates. In: Hazay, C., Stam, M. (eds.) Advances in Cryptology–EUROCRYPT 2023. EUROCRYPT 2023. LNCS, vol. 14005, pp. 499-530. Springer, Cham (2023). https://doi.org/10.1007/978-3-031-30617-4_17
18. Chiesa, A., Hu, Y., Maller, M., Mishra, P., Vesely, N., Ward, N.: Marlin: preprocessing zkSNARKs with universal and updatable SRS. In: Canteaut, A., Ishai, Y. (eds.) EUROCRYPT 2020. LNCS, vol. 12105, pp. 738–768. Springer, Cham (2020). https://doi.org/10.1007/978-3-030-45721-1_26
19. Damgård, I.: Towards practical public key systems secure against chosen ciphertext attacks. In: Feigenbaum, J. (ed.) CRYPTO 1991. LNCS, vol. 576, pp. 445–456. Springer, Heidelberg (1992). https://doi.org/10.1007/3-540-46766-1_36
20. Dao, Q., Grubbs, P.: Spartan and bulletproofs are simulation-extractable (for free!). In: Hazay, C., Stam, M. (eds.) Advances in Cryptology–EUROCRYPT 2023. EUROCRYPT 2023. LNCS, vol. 14005, pp. 531–562. Springer, Cham (2023). https://doi.org/10.1007/978-3-031-30617-4_18
21. De Santis, A., Di Crescenzo, G., Ostrovsky, R., Persiano, G., Sahai, A.: Robust non-interactive zero knowledge. In: Kilian, J. (ed.) CRYPTO 2001. LNCS, vol. 2139, pp. 566–598. Springer, Heidelberg (2001). https://doi.org/10.1007/3-540-44647-8_33
22. Dodis, Y., Haralambiev, K., López-Alt, A., Wichs, D.: Efficient public-key cryptography in the presence of key leakage. In: Abe, M. (ed.) ASIACRYPT 2010. LNCS, vol. 6477, pp. 613–631. Springer, Heidelberg (2010). https://doi.org/10.1007/978-3-642-17373-8_35
23. Faonio, A., Fiore, D., Kohlweiss, M., Russo, L., Zajac, M.: From polynomial IOP and commitments to non-malleable zkSNARKs. In: TCC 2023 (2023)

24. Faust, S., Kohlweiss, M., Marson, G., Venturi, D.: On the non-malleability of the Fiat-Shamir transform. In: Indocrypt 2012 (2012)
25. Fiat, A., Shamir, A.: How to prove yourself: practical solutions to identification and signature problems. In: Odlyzko, A.M. (ed.) CRYPTO 1986. LNCS, vol. 263, pp. 186–194. Springer, Heidelberg (1987). https://doi.org/10.1007/3-540-47721-7_12
26. Fuchsbauer, G., Kiltz, E., Loss, J.: The algebraic group model and its applications. In: Shacham, H., Boldyreva, A. (eds.) CRYPTO 2018. LNCS, vol. 10992, pp. 33–62. Springer, Cham (2018). https://doi.org/10.1007/978-3-319-96881-0_2
27. Fuchsbauer, G., Plouviez, A., Seurin, Y.: Blind Schnorr signatures and signed ElGamal encryption in the algebraic group model. In: Canteaut, A., Ishai, Y. (eds.) EUROCRYPT 2020. LNCS, vol. 12106, pp. 63–95. Springer, Cham (2020). https://doi.org/10.1007/978-3-030-45724-2_3
28. Gabizon, G., Williamson, Z., Ciobotaru, O.: PLONK: permutations over Lagrange-bases for oecumenical noninteractive arguments of knowledge. Cryptology ePrint Archive, Report 2019/953 (2019)
29. Ganesh, C., Khoshakhlagh, H., Kohlweiss, M., Nitulescu, A., Zajac, M.: What makes Fiat-Shamir zkSNARKs (Updatable SRS) simulation extractable? In: SCN 2022 (2022)
30. Ganesh, C., Kondi, Y., Orlandi, C., Pancholi, M., Takahashi, A., Tschudi, D.: Witness-succinct universally-composable SNARKs. In: Hazay, C., Stam, M. (eds.) Advances in Cryptology–EUROCRYPT 2023. EUROCRYPT 2023. LNCS, vol. 14005, pp. 315–346. Springer, Cham (2023). https://doi.org/10.1007/978-3-031-30617-4_11
31. Ganesh, C., Orlandi, C., Pancholi, M., Takahashi, A., Tschudi, D.: Fiat-Shamir Bulletproofs are non-malleable (in the random oracle model). Cryptology ePrint Archive Report 2023/147 (2023)
32. Ganesh, C., Orlandi, C., Pancholi, M., Takahashi, A., Tschudi, D.: Fiat-Shamir bulletproofs are non-malleable (in the algebraic group model). In: Dunkelman, O., Dziembowski, S. (eds.) Advances in Cryptology–EUROCRYPT 2022. EUROCRYPT 2022. LNCS, vol. 13276, pp. 397–426. Springer, Cham (2022). https://doi.org/10.1007/978-3-031-07085-3_14
33. Gennaro, R., Gentry, C., Parno, B., Raykova, M.: Quadratic span programs and succinct NIZKs without PCPs. In: Johansson, T., Nguyen, P.Q. (eds.) EUROCRYPT 2013. LNCS, vol. 7881, pp. 626–645. Springer, Heidelberg (2013). https://doi.org/10.1007/978-3-642-38348-9_37
34. Groth, J.: Simulation-sound NIZK proofs for a practical language and constant size group signatures. In: Lai, X., Chen, K. (eds.) ASIACRYPT 2006. LNCS, vol. 4284, pp. 444–459. Springer, Heidelberg (2006). https://doi.org/10.1007/11935230_29
35. Groth, J.: On the size of pairing-based non-interactive arguments. In: Fischlin, M., Coron, J.-S. (eds.) EUROCRYPT 2016. LNCS, vol. 9666, pp. 305–326. Springer, Heidelberg (2016). https://doi.org/10.1007/978-3-662-49896-5_11
36. Groth, J., Maller, M.: Snarky signatures: minimal signatures of knowledge from simulation-extractable snarks. In: Katz, J., Shacham, H. (eds.) CRYPTO 2017. LNCS, vol. 10402, pp. 581–612. Springer, Cham (2017). https://doi.org/10.1007/978-3-319-63715-0_20
37. Kate, A., Zaverucha, G.M., Goldberg, I.: Constant-size commitments to polynomials and their applications. In: Abe, M. (ed.) ASIACRYPT 2010. LNCS, vol. 6477, pp. 177–194. Springer, Heidelberg (2010). https://doi.org/10.1007/978-3-642-17373-8_11
38. Katz, J., Nang, N.: Efficiency improvements for signature schemes with tight security reductions. In: ACM-CCS 2003 (2003)

39. Kohlweiss, M., Pancholi, M., Takahashi, A.: How to compile polynomial IOP into simulation-extractable SNARKs: a modular approach. In: TCC 2023 (2023)
40. Kohrita, T., Towa, P.: Zeromorph: zero-knowledge multilinear-evaluation proofs from homomorphic univariate commitments. Cryptology ePrint Archive Report 2023/917 (2023)
41. Kosba, A., et al.: C∅c∅: A framework for building composable zero-knowledge proofs. Cryptology ePrint Archive Report 2015/1093 (2015)
42. Lipmaa, H.: A unified framework for non-universal SNARKs. In: PKC 2022 (2022)
43. Lund, C., Fortnow, L., Karlo, H., Nisan, N.: Algebraic methods for interactive proof systems. J. ACM. **39**(4), 859–868 (1992)
44. Maller, M., Bowe, S., Kohlweiss, M., Meiklejohn, S.: Sonic: Zero-knowledge SNARKs from linear-size universal and updateable structured reference strings. In: ACM-CCS 2019 (2019)
45. Papamanthou, C., Shi, E., Tamassia, R.: Signatures of correct computation. In: TCC 2013 (2013)
46. Sahai, A.: Non-malleable non-interactive zero knowledge and adaptive chosen-ciphertext security. In: FOCS 1999 (1999)
47. Schnorr, C.P.: Efficient identification and signatures for smart cards. In: Brassard, G. (ed.) CRYPTO 1989. LNCS, vol. 435, pp. 239–252. Springer, New York (1990). https://doi.org/10.1007/0-387-34805-0_22
48. Setty, S.: Spartan: efficient and general-purpose zkSNARKs without trusted setup. In: Micciancio, D., Ristenpart, T. (eds.) CRYPTO 2020. LNCS, vol. 12172, pp. 704–737. Springer, Cham (2020). https://doi.org/10.1007/978-3-030-56877-1_25
49. Setty, S., Lee, J.: Quarks: quadruple-efficient transparent zkSNARKs. Cryptology ePrint Archive 2020/1275 (2020)
50. Thaler, J.: Time-optimal interactive proofs for circuit evaluation. In: Canetti, R., Garay, J.A. (eds.) CRYPTO 2013. LNCS, vol. 8043, pp. 71–89. Springer, Heidelberg (2013). https://doi.org/10.1007/978-3-642-40084-1_5
51. Xie, T., Zhang, J., Zhang, Y., Papamanthou, C., Song, D.: Libra: succinct zero-knowledge proofs with optimal prover computation. In: Boldyreva, A., Micciancio, D. (eds.) CRYPTO 2019. LNCS, vol. 11694, pp. 733–764. Springer, Cham (2019). https://doi.org/10.1007/978-3-030-26954-8_24
52. Zhang, Y., Genkin, D., Katz, J., Papadopoulos, D., Papamanthou, C.: A zero-knowledge version of vSQL. Cryptology ePrint Archive Report 2017/1146 (2017)

Oblivious Accumulators

Foteini Baldimtsi[1(✉)], Ioanna Karantaidou[1], and Srinivasan Raghuraman[2]

[1] George Mason University, Fairfax, USA
{foteini,ikaranta}@gmu.edu
[2] Visa Research and MIT, Cambridge, USA

Abstract. A cryptographic accumulator is a succinct set commitment scheme with efficient (non-)membership proofs that typically supports updates (additions and deletions) on the accumulated set. When elements are added to or deleted from the set, an update message is issued. The collection of all the update messages essentially leaks the underlying accumulated set which in certain applications is not desirable.

In this work, we define *oblivious accumulators*, a set commitment with concise membership proofs that *hides the elements and the set size* from every entity: an outsider, a verifier or other element holders. We formalize this notion of privacy via two properties: *element hiding* and *add-delete indistinguishability*. We also define *almost-oblivious accumulators*, that only achieve a weaker notion of privacy called *add-delete unlinkability*. Such accumulators hide the elements but not the set size. We consider the trapdoorless, decentralized setting where different users can add and delete elements from the accumulator and compute membership proofs.

We then give a generic construction of an oblivious accumulator based on key-value commitments (KVC). We also show a generic way to construct KVCs from an accumulator and a vector commitment scheme. Finally, we give lower bounds on the communication (size of update messages) required for oblivious accumulators and almost-oblivious accumulators.

Keywords: accumulators · oblivious · key-value commitments

1 Introduction

A cryptographic *accumulator* [6,7] is a set commitment, i.e., a compact representation of a set of elements, as a short digest C. It allows a *prover* to generate a short proof of membership w_x, often called a witness, for any element x that has been accumulated, or non-membership proof for any element in the accumulator domain that has not been accumulated. A *verifier* can efficiently verify such

F. Baldimtsi and I. Karantaidou are supported by NSF Awards #2143287 and #2247304, as well as a Google Faculty Award. Ioanna Karantaidou is additionally supported by a Protocol Labs Fellowship.
I. Karantaidou—Part of this work was done while the second author was an intern at Visa Research.

Q. Tang and V. Teague (Eds.): PKC 2024, LNCS 14602, pp. 99–131, 2024.
https://doi.org/10.1007/978-3-031-57722-2_4

proofs using the digest alone without the need to access the entire set. Since their inception, accumulators have been considered in various settings with varying capabilities, leading to a rich taxonomy. Accumulators that only support membership proofs are called *positive*, while those supporting only non-membership proofs are called *negative*. An accumulator that supports both membership and non-membership proofs is called *universal*. Regarding updating the accumulated set, accumulators are called *additive* if they only allow for additions of new elements, *negative* or *subtractive* if they only allow for deletions, and *dynamic* if they support both operations. There exist a variety of accumulator constructions proposed in the literature with different properties and under different computational assumptions [3,11,12,20,27,30,37].

Accumulators have also been classified into two main categories based on the entity who is responsible for updating the accumulated set: *trapdoor-based* accumulators managed by a trusted party, and *trapdoorless* or *strong* accumulators. In a trapdoor-based accumulator, a trusted entity known as the *accumulator manager*, holds some secret information/trapdoor and has the ability to efficiently add or delete elements and create witnesses. Whenever a new element is added to the accumulator, the accumulator manager issues the corresponding membership proof w_x. On the other hand, trapdoorless accumulators allow for public additions or deletions of elements without relying on a trusted entity. Users adding new elements to the accumulator can compute (and later update) their corresponding witnesses themselves. Finally, some accumulator constructions have an interesting property called proof batching [9,32]. In this case, the prover can further compact proofs for multiple elements into one proof of size sublinear in the number of elements, that verifies faster than when compared to verifying each individual proof.

Accumulators have found numerous applications, with the most popular being anonymous credentials [1,4,11,12,21], group signatures [13,28,31], cloud storage [34,37], and more recently, stateless [9,18] and privacy-preserving cryptocurrencies such as ZCash [29] and RingCT 2.0 [33] proposed for Monero. Revocation of anonymous credentials is one of the most prominent applications of trapdoor-based accumulators. The credential issuing authority, that is responsible for granting credentials, also serves as the accumulator manager and maintains a list of valid credentials in the form of an accumulator. When a new credential is issued, it is added to the accumulated set by the issuing authority and the corresponding witness is sent to the user along with the credential. To use the credential, the user will have to prove membership in the accumulator in order to demonstrate to the verifier that the credential is still valid. The issuing authority/accumulator manager is responsible for removing revoked credentials from the accumulated set. Trapdoorless accumulators are mostly used in applications where set updates and witness creation are performed by an untrusted party, for example a cloud storage provider. Recently, trapdoorless accumulators have been proposed for data compression in decentralized settings. An accumulator can be used to construct a stateless blockchain, where anyone can add elements, as long as they can prove that their update is consistent with the previous state of the chain.

Privacy in Accumulators. The classic definition of a cryptographic accumulator does not offer any privacy preserving properties: an accumulator is not a hiding commitment and can leak information about the set. Information can be leaked from the accumulator digest itself, a membership proof, and most importantly from the update messages, that usually describe explicitly which element was added or deleted. This information can be used by any entity (proof holders and verifiers) in order to update their proof and/or the accumulator value. However, accumulators are often used in applications where privacy is needed for specific operations carried out on the accumulated set. A common example is in the context of anonymous credentials, where users may wish to hide the specific credential for which they are proving membership. To achieve this, a user can present a commitment to the credential and subsequently provide a zero-knowledge (ZK) proof, demonstrating that the committed value is indeed present in the accumulator. ZK proofs of (non-)membership for accumulators have been previously studied in the literature in the form of individual proofs [4,8,12] and batched proofs [14,32]. In the context of anonymous credentials, the notion of join-revoke unlinkability was previously introduced [5] which guarantees that the addition and revocation of the same credential should not be linkable. This idea could be extended to direct accumulator property of add-delete unlinikability and it is achieved by modular constructions as explained below. Finally, another flavor of privacy for accumulators is that of zero-knowledge accumulators for set operations [17,23,25,37]. In that setting, the guarantees provided by zero-knowledge assures that an external entity, such as a verifier, that gets to see *only* (non-)membership proofs and the accumulator digest, learns nothing else about the accumulated set.

Beyond the privacy-preserving accumulator application of anonymous credentials mentioned above, there are other scenarios where there is a need to conceal the elements of the accumulated set from *all participants*, including witness holders (and the accumulator manager in the case of trapdoor-based constructions), and additionally *hide the size* of the accumulated set. Consider for example a smart contract that is executed on a public blockchain and is using an accumulator to hold the credentials for all the customers of an organization in order to efficiently check (non-)membership. In such a scenario, it is crucial to hide the accumulated elements, since having access to the credentials of a user might allow for unauthorized access. At the same time, it would also be useful to hide the total number of the elements accumulated in order to conceal the size of the "customer base" of the organization. This brings us to the following interesting question:

Is it possible to construct a dynamic accumulator that hides the accumulated set (both its elements and its size)?

In this work we answer this question affirmatively. For the first time, we define the notion of *oblivious accumulators*, that achieve all the above properties and we provide a construction that achieves our definition. We also show that our construction meets the standard information-theoretic lower bounds. We prove communication costs for oblivious accumulators, along the lines of similar bounds that have been shown for dynamic accumulators [10] and revocable proof systems [19]. More specifically, we show that the total communication cost in the form of updates in our construction is equal to what must necessarily be stored as a state for an oblivious accumulator with the privacy properties that we propose.

1.1 Our Contributions

In Sect. 4 we define a dynamic positive trapdoorless oblivious accumulator. At a high level, an oblivious accumulator supports the typical accumulator operations. Setup generates the parameters and the initial accumulator C. Add inserts a new element x into the accumulator and computes its membership proof w_x and the new accumulator C'. Similarly, Del deletes an element from the accumulator and computes the new accumulator C'. The addition and deletion processes also release an update message u. The rest of the proof holders run MemProofUpdate with u as input and update their proofs. The digest U of all update messages can be used to update membership proofs at any point in time, thus alleviating the need for parties to always be online and process update messages as they come in. Anyone can check whether x has been accumulated by running MemVer, given the proof w_x and the accumulator C. A feature specific to our oblivious accumulator is the following: in order to add x, Add also generates auxiliary information aux (only known to the user that holds x), which is necessary in order to later construct a membership proof for x or to delete x.[1]

On top of the typical accumulator security properties, we define new privacy-related properties. The first property, *element hiding*, guarantees that one cannot learn x by looking at the corresponding update message u. Then we define *add-delete indistinguishability* which guarantees that one cannot even tell what type of operation, i.e., an add or a delete, took place, even with the knowledge of the accumulated set before the update. This property is equivalent to hiding the size of the set since, if one could track the number of additions and deletions, they could infer the current size of the set. We also formalize the notion of *add-delete unlinkability* as an intermediate privacy goal (this property was previously discussed in [5] under the term "join-revoke" unlinkability for a revocation system and not directly for an accumulator). Add-delete unlinkability states that despite having access to addition update messages, that may not hide the element, and with the knowledge that an update u corresponds to a deletion, one can still not link which updates refer to the same element. We note that add-delete indistinguishability implies add-delete unlinkability.

An Almost-Oblivious Accumulator. After defining the privacy properties of an oblivious accumulator, we focus on constructions that satisfy these properties. In order to build some intuition, we start by describing a construction, called *almost-oblivious* accumulator, that supports element hiding and add-delete unlinkability but not add-deleted indistinguishability. An intuitive way to achieve element hiding: is to accumulate hiding commitments of the element

[1] In a sense, aux is a summary of how x was hidden in order to achieve the privacy properties that we discuss ahead.

instead of adding them in the clear. Achieving add-delete unlinkability though is a bit more complex. An implicit solution for unlinkable additions and deletions was presented as Construction A in [5] and describes a modular construction of two accumulators $\mathsf{Acc} = (\mathsf{Acc}_1, \mathsf{Acc}_2)$, Acc_1 is additive and used for added elements and Acc_2 is additive and used for storing deleted elements. Acc_1 supports membership proofs and Acc_2 supports non-membership proofs, in order for the overall accumulator Acc to support membership proofs. To prove membership of x in Acc, one has to present a membership proof for x in Acc_1 and a non-membership proof for x in Acc_2. To get add-delete unlinkability in this modular accumulator, one can, instead of adding x in Acc_1, add c_1, a hiding commitment to x. We can delete x by adding a different commitment c_2 in Acc_2. A membership proof w_x in Acc now consists of a membership proof of c_1 in Acc_1 and a non-membership proof of c_2 in Acc_2, together with openings of c_1, c_2 to the same element x. An observer is not able to link c_1, c_2 unless they see w_x.

A more generic way to describe the modular structure is with two sets, without specifying compression techniques: the set of added elements (previously described as Acc_1) and the set of deleted elements (previously Acc_2). The anonymous cryptocurrency ZCash initially emerged as Zerocoin [29], an accumulator-based system for compressing the set of valid coins. ZCash follows the same modular structure. Random elements (serial numbers) are added as hiding commitments in the first set and then added in the clear in the second set. The first set is further compressed using a Merkle tree and proofs of membership. The second set is kept as a list and in order to ensure that an element has not been deleted, a lookup operation is performed. The trade-off compared to using compression and non-membership proofs in order to save in space is that storing the whole list, allows for concurrency. Concurrency of operations is a special property that comes up in cryptocurrencies. In this case, a transaction for spending a valid coin x is a membership proof w_x together with a deletion for x. If deletions are compressed, then w_x needs to be updated to reflect the new digest and as a result, transactions cannot be submitted and validated in parallel.

These constructions, which we call *almost-oblivious* accumulators achieve element hiding and add-delete unlinkability. However, since the two sets of added and deleted elements are distinct, such constructions inherently fail to satisfy add-delete indistinguishability (and thus these constructions reveal the size of the accumulated set).

Our Construction. Our goal is to build an oblivious accumulator that achieves element hiding and the stronger property of add-delete indistinguishability which will allow for hiding the size of the accumulated set. In order to achieve add-delete indistinguishability, we will use a single data structure for both additions and deletions, as opposed to the modular constructions from above. Both addition and deletion operations will result in new elements being added in the data structure in a way that is indistinguishable yet sound when it comes to proving (non-)membership. A first idea is to insert flags in random-looking positions of a vector commitment (VC) scheme. The positions are derived from the inserted element x and some randomness. However, a VC has to commit to a specified number of positions when initialized. Even if the VC supported a procedure that allows to extend the length of the vector (which some VCs do), this would not be enough, as we would need the random-looking positions to have high entropy, i.e., come from a very large space, which would mean that the length of the vector would have to be exponentially large. For VCs that we know today, this would be grossly inefficient if not impossible. Instead, our approach is to use Key-Value Commitments (KVC) [2,35]. A KVC is a dynamic length, sparse vector commitment with elements (k, v), k being the key and v being the inserted value. Its security property is key binding, meaning that proof of opening for (k, v) guarantees that there is a tuple of the form $(k, \cdot)$ and it is impossible to find a different proof for (k, v'), and $v \neq v'$. At the same time, KVC can support key non-membership proofs (i.e., proofs that a key k' was never inserted), a property that will be used by our construction in order to prove that an element has not been deleted. Looking ahead, the keys that we will use are essentially the random-looking positions from our prior discussion.

In Sect. 5, we present a generic trapdoorless, positive, dynamic oblivious accumulator from any KVC scheme that supports non-membership. Our construction is proven secure in the Random Oracle Model. Our construction briefly works as follows. The position of addition is decided by the output of a commitment using a hash function H_1 and the position of a deletion is decided by H_2. More specifically, the user who wishes to add x, generates randomness r and adds a value $v = 1$ in position $H_1(x, r)$. It also sets auxiliary information $\mathsf{aux} = r$ that allows them to delete x and compute a proof of membership on x. A proof of membership includes a proof of opening for key-value pair $(H_1(x, r), 1)$. We complete our oblivious accumulator construction with a non-membership proof for key $H_2(x, r)$, used by the prover to prove that x has not been deleted. Finally, a deletion for x happens with adding the key-value pair $(H_2(x, r), 1)$. This makes a membership proof invalid. In Sect. 5.5 we briefly discuss an extension of our constructions that allows for the accumulation of unique elements.

Since our construction is KVC-based, we can use values other than $v = 1$. This value, which is revealed during additions/deletions, allows for more expressive application scenarios. Consider the smart contract application described above: our KVC-based oblivious accumulator could be used to hold the customer base obliviously, i.e., hiding the accumulated elements and the size of the set, but at the same time, it could allow for a public value like the value of assets of each customer to be added as "metadata" when the customer is added in the accumulator. This scheme for example, can be used to guarantee that all added customers are contributing at least some minimum amount of assets in the smart contract. Assuming that the assets are within some fixed set of values (and not completely arbitrary real numbers), this additional metadata does not downgrade the overall privacy of the scheme. Furthermore, since we are working with a KVC, we will be able to update the values of the assets over time.

In Sect. 3, we show, as a side result, how to construct a KVC scheme with non-membership, using a universal accumulator and vector commitment with extendable length. We add keys k in the accumulator and elements (k,v) in the vector sequentially. Our construction inherits the position binding properties and additive updates from the vector commitment and the non-membership proofs from the accumulator. Moreover, it preserves efficiency properties of the underlying schemes such as constant commitment and proof size, efficient updates, etc., or features such as proof batching and aggregation or cross-aggregation. This construction is of independent interest as it gives a generic way to build a KVC and can allow for constructions under different assumptions than the ones currently known.

Finally, we investigate the lower bounds for almost-oblivious and oblivious accumulators with constant proof size and constant digest. In more detail, in Sect. 6, we follow the analysis of [10,19] to prove lower bounds on the communication costs of deletions, and then show that the obliviousness properties of oblivious accumulators translate these bounds for arbitrary operations, not just deletions. In light of this result, our construction has optimal communication cost. In the case of almost-oblivious accumulators, we leverage add-delete unlinkability to show the lower bound, which implies that constructions such as ZCash are essentially optimal.

2 Preliminaries

2.1 Notation

For $n \in \mathbb{N}$, let $[n] = \{1, 2, \ldots, n\}$. Let $\lambda \in \mathbb{N}$ denote the security parameter. Symbols in boldface such as $\mathbf{a}$ denote vectors. By a_i we denote the i-th element of the vector $\mathbf{a}$. For a vector $\mathbf{a}$ of length $n \in \mathbb{N}$ and an index set $I \subseteq [n]$, we denote by $\mathbf{a}|_I$ the sub-vector of elements a_i for $i \in I$ induced by I. By $\text{poly}(\cdot)$, we denote any function which is bounded by a polynomial in its argument. An algorithm $\mathcal{A}$ is said to be PPT if it is modeled as a probabilistic Turing machine that runs in time polynomial in λ. Informally, we say that a function is negligible, denoted by negl, if it vanishes faster than the inverse of any polynomial. If S is a set, then $x \leftarrow_{\$} S$ indicates the process of selecting x uniformly at random from S (which in particular assumes that S can be sampled efficiently). Similarly, $x \leftarrow_{\$} \mathcal{A}(\cdot)$ denotes the random variable that is the output of a randomized algorithm $\mathcal{A}$.

2.2 Compressing Primitives

In this section, we briefly recall definitions of compressing primitives for sets (*accumulators*), vectors (*vector commitments*), and key-value maps (*key-value commitments*). We present the various algorithms underlying the primitives, along with their corresponding correctness and security properties. We include related work for each primitive in our supplementary material.

2.2.1 Accumulators

An accumulator (Acc) allows one to commit to a set in such a way that it is later possible to prove or disprove that elements are in the set. We require an accumulator to be *concise* in the sense that the size of the accumulator string C is independent of the size of the set. We describe the primitive in the universal (supports membership and non-membership proofs) dynamic (supports additions and deletions) setting. We also assume that we are in the trapdoorless setting, i.e., updates can be performed with publicly available information.

We denote a set $S \subseteq \mathcal{D}$ to be a collection of elements $x \in \mathcal{D}$ where $\mathcal{D}$ is the accumulator domain. We define an accumulator Acc as a non-interactive primitive that can be described via the following algorithms:

- $(\mathsf{pp}, C) \leftarrow_\$ \mathsf{Setup}(1^\lambda)$: On input the security parameter λ, the setup algorithm outputs some public parameters pp (which implicitly define the accumulator domain $\mathcal{D}$) and the initial accumulator string C to the empty set. All other algorithms have access to the public parameters.
- $(C, w_x, u) \leftarrow \mathsf{Add}(C, x)$: On input an accumulator string C and an element $x \in \mathcal{D}$, the addition algorithm outputs a new accumulator string C, a membership proof w_x (that $x \in S$), and update information u.
- $(C, u) \leftarrow \mathsf{Del}(C, x, U)$: On input an accumulator string C, an element $x \in \mathcal{D}$, and the digest of all update information U produced until the current point in time, the deletion algorithm outputs a new accumulator string C and update information u.
- $w_x \leftarrow \mathsf{MemProofUpdate}(w_x, u)$: On input a membership proof w_x and update information u, the membership proof update algorithm outputs an updated membership proof w_x.
- $\overline{w_x} \leftarrow \mathsf{NonMemProofCreate}(x, U)$: On input an element $x \in \mathcal{D}$ and the digest of all updated information U produced until the current point in time, the non-membership proof creation algorithm outputs a non-membership proof $\overline{w_x}$ (that $x \notin S$).
- $\overline{w_x} \leftarrow \mathsf{NonMemProofUpdate}(\overline{w_x}, u)$: On input a non-membership proof $\overline{w_x}$ and update information u, the non-membership proof update algorithm outputs an updated non-membership proof $\overline{w_x}$.
- $0/1 \leftarrow \mathsf{MemVer}(C, x, w_x)$: On input an accumulator string C, an element $x \in \mathcal{D}$, and a membership proof w_x, the membership verification algorithm either outputs 1 (denoting accept) or 0 (denoting reject).
- $0/1 \leftarrow \mathsf{NonMemVer}(C, x, \overline{w_x})$: On input an accumulator string C, an element $x \in \mathcal{D}$, and a non-membership proof $\overline{w_x}$, the non-membership verification algorithm either outputs 1 (denoting accept) or 0 (denoting reject).

For correctness, we require that for all $\lambda \in \mathbb{N}$, for all honestly generated public parameters $\mathsf{pp} \leftarrow_\$ \mathsf{Setup}(1^\lambda)$, if C is an accumulator to a set S, obtained by running a sequence of calls to Add and Del, w_x is a membership proof corresponding to an element $x \in \mathcal{D}$ for any $x \in S$, generated during the call to Add and updated by appropriate calls to $\mathsf{MemProofUpdate}$, then $\mathsf{MemVer}(C, x, w_x)$ outputs 1 with probability 1. Similarly, if $\overline{w_x}$ is a non-membership proof corresponding to an element $x \in \mathcal{D}$ for any $x \notin S$, generated by a call to $\mathsf{NonMemProofCreate}$ and updated by appropriate calls to $\mathsf{NonMemProofUpdate}$, then $\mathsf{NonMemVer}(C, x, \overline{w_x})$ outputs 1 with probability 1.

The security requirement for accumulators is that of *soundness*. We consider two notions of soundness, i.e., *weak* and *strong soundness*. To satisfy weak soundness, it must be computationally infeasible for any polynomially bounded adversary (with knowledge of pp) to come up with an *honestly generated*[2] accumulator and either a membership proof that certifies membership of an element that has not been added, or a non-membership proof that certifies non-membership of an element that has been added. To satisfy strong soundness, it must be computationally infeasible for any polynomially bounded adversary (with knowledge of pp) to come up with a *potentially adversarially generated* accumulator and a pair of membership and non-membership proofs that certify membership and non-membership, respectively, of the same element.

Alternative Formalization. Some works alternatively formalize the algorithms Del and $\mathsf{NonMemProofCreate}$ to take S as input instead of U, but in most cases, the two hold similar information.

2.2.2 Vector Commitments

A vector commitment (VC) allows one to commit to a vector in such a way that it is later possible to open the commitment with respect to any specific index. We require a vector commitment to be *concise* in the sense that the size of the vector commitment string C is independent of the size of the vector. Furthermore, it must be possible to update the vector by updating the value of the vector at a specific position. We also assume that we are in the trapdoorless setting, i.e., updates can be performed with publicly available information.

We set up the following notation for a vector: A vector $\mathbf{v} \in \mathcal{D}^q$ of length q is a collection of q elements $v_i \in \mathcal{D}$[3] for $i \in [q]$. We define a vector commitment VC as a non-interactive primitive that can be formally described via the following algorithms:

- $(\mathsf{pp}, C) \leftarrow_\$ \mathsf{Setup}(1^\lambda, q)$: On input the security parameter λ and a length q, the setup algorithm outputs some public parameters pp (which implicitly define the vector commitment domain $\mathcal{D}$ and the vector length q) and the initial vector commitment string C to the vector of all 0s. All other algorithms have access to the public parameters. All other algorithms also have access to the initial proofs Λ_i for all $i \in [q]$ (that $v_i = 0$).
- $(C, u) \leftarrow \mathsf{Update}(C, (i, \delta))$: On input a vector commitment string C, a position $i \in [q]$, and an *additive* update value $\delta \in \mathcal{D}$, the update algorithm outputs a new vector commitment string C and update information u.
- $\Lambda_i \leftarrow \mathsf{ProofUpdate}(\Lambda_i, u)$: On input a proof Λ_i and update information u, the proof update algorithm outputs an updated proof Λ_i.

---

[2] In the experiment defining security, we also assume that elements that have not yet been added are never requested to be deleted by the adversary.

[3] We assume that $0 \in \mathcal{D}$.

- $0/1 \leftarrow \mathsf{ProofVer}(C, (i, v), \Lambda_i)$: On input a vector commitment string C, a position $i \in [q]$, an element $v \in \mathcal{D}$, and a proof Λ_i, the proof verification algorithm either outputs 1 (denoting accept) or 0 (denoting reject).

For correctness, we require that for all $\lambda \in \mathbb{N}$, for all honestly generated public parameters $\mathsf{pp} \leftarrow_\$ \mathsf{Setup}(1^\lambda)$, if C is the vector commitment to a vector $\mathbf{v}$, obtained by running a sequence of calls to Update, Λ_i is a proof corresponding to a position $i \in [q]$, updated by appropriate calls to ProofUpdate, then $\mathsf{ProofVer}(C, i, v_i, \Lambda_i)$ outputs 1 with probability 1.

The security requirement for vector commitments is that of *position binding.* We consider two notions of soundness, i.e., *weak* and *strong position binding.* To satisfy weak position binding, it must be computationally infeasible for any polynomially bounded adversary (with knowledge of pp) to come up with an *honestly generated* vector commitment and a proof that certifies a value at any position different from the one in the vector that has been committed. To satisfy strong soundness, it must be computationally infeasible for any polynomially bounded adversary (with knowledge of pp) to come up with a *potentially adversarially generated* vector commitment and a pair of proofs that certify different values at the same position.

Alternative Formalization. Some works alternatively formalize a vector commitment to not generate an initial vector commitment to the vector of all 0s, but rather to have an initial Commit procedure that takes a vector and generates a vector commitment to it. This formalization would usually be paired with a ProofCreate algorithm that takes the initial committed vector and a position and outputs the initial proof for that position. Some works also assume that Update takes as input the old and new values at a position, as opposed to an additive update–we say that such an Update algorithm is *non-oblivious.*

Positive Length. Occasionally, we will also consider vector commitments which support a dynamic increase of the length of the vector that is being committed to. In this case, the vector commitment has an additional algorithm:

- $(\mathsf{pp}, C, u) \leftarrow_\$ \mathsf{Extend}(1^\lambda, C)$: On input the security parameter λ and a vector commitment string C for a vector $\mathbf{v}$ of length q, the extend algorithm outputs new public parameters pp (corresponding to vectors of length $q+1$), the new vector commitment string C to the vector $\mathbf{v}'$ of length $q+1$, where $\mathbf{v}'|_{[q]} = \mathbf{v}$ and $v'_{q+1} = 0$, and update information u. All other algorithms have access to the initial proof Λ_{q+1} (that $v'_{q+1} = 0$).

2.2.3 Key-Value Commitments

A key-value commitment (KVC) allows one to commit to a key-value map in such a way that it is later possible to open the commitment with respect to any specific key. We require a key-value commitment to be *concise* in the sense that the size of the commitment string C is independent of the size of the map. We describe the primitive in the universal (supports membership and non-membership proofs) setting. Furthermore, it must be possible to update the map, by either adding new key-value pairs or updating the value corresponding to an existing key We also assume that we are in the trapdoorless setting, i.e., updates can be performed with publicly available information.

We set up the following notation for a key-value map: A key-value map $\mathcal{M} \subseteq \mathcal{K} \times \mathcal{V}$ is a collection of key-value pairs $(k, v) \in \mathcal{K} \times \mathcal{V}$. Let $\mathcal{K}_{\mathcal{M}} \subseteq \mathcal{K}$ denote the set of keys for which values have been stored in the map $\mathcal{M}$. We define a key-value commitment KVC as a non-interactive primitive that can be formally described via the following algorithms:

- $(\mathsf{pp}, C) \leftarrow_{\$} \mathsf{Setup}(1^\lambda)$: On input the security parameter λ, the setup generation algorithm outputs some public parameters pp (which implicitly define the key space $\mathcal{K}$ and value space $\mathcal{V}$) and the initial commitment C to the empty key-value map. All other algorithms have access to the public parameters.
- $(C, \Lambda_k, u) \leftarrow \mathsf{Insert}(C, (k, v))$: On input a key-value commitment string C and a key-value pair $(k, v) \in \mathcal{K} \times \mathcal{V}$, the insertion algorithm outputs a new key-value commitment string C, a proof Λ_k (that $(k, v) \in \mathcal{M}$), and update information u.
- $(C, u) \leftarrow \mathsf{Update}(C, (k, \delta))$: On input a key-value commitment string C, a key $k \in \mathcal{K}$, and an *additive* update value $\delta \in \mathcal{V}$, the update algorithm outputs a new key-value commitment string C and update information u.
- $\Lambda_k \leftarrow \mathsf{ProofUpdate}(\Lambda_k, u)$: On input a proof Λ_k for some value corresponding to the key k and update information u, the proof update algorithm outputs an updated proof Λ_k.
- $\overline{\Lambda_k} \leftarrow \mathsf{NonMemProofCreate}(k, U)$: On input a key $k \in \mathcal{K}$ and the digest of all updated information U produced until the current point in time, the non-membership proof creation algorithm outputs a non-membership proof $\overline{\Lambda_k}$ (that $k \notin \mathcal{K}_{\mathcal{M}}$).
- $\overline{\Lambda_k} \leftarrow \mathsf{NonMemProofUpdate}(\overline{\Lambda_k}, u)$: On input a non-membership proof $\overline{\Lambda_k}$ and update information u, the non-membership proof update algorithm outputs an updated non-membership proof $\overline{\Lambda_k}$.
- $1/0 \leftarrow \mathsf{Ver}(C, (k, v), \Lambda_k)$: On input a key-value commitment string C, a key-value pair $(k, v) \in \mathcal{K} \times \mathcal{V}$, and a proof Λ_k, the verification algorithm either outputs 1 (denoting accept) or 0 (denoting reject).
- $0/1 \leftarrow \mathsf{NonMemVer}(C, k, \overline{\Lambda_k})$: On input a key-value commitment string C, a key $x \in \mathcal{K}$, and a non-membership proof $\overline{\Lambda_k}$, the non-membership verification algorithm either outputs 1 (denoting accept) or 0 (denoting reject).

For correctness, we require that for all $\lambda \in \mathbb{N}$, for all honestly generated public parameters $\mathsf{pp} \leftarrow_{\$} \mathsf{KeyGen}(1^\lambda)$, if C is the key-value commitment to a key-value map $\mathcal{M}$, obtained by running a sequence of calls to Insert and Update, Λ_k is a proof corresponding to a key $k \in \mathcal{K}$ for any $k \in \mathcal{K}_{\mathcal{M}}$, generated during the call to Insert and updated by appropriate calls to $\mathsf{ProofUpdate}$, then $\mathsf{Ver}(C, (k, v), \Lambda_k)$ outputs 1 with probability 1 if $(k, v) \in \mathcal{M}$. Similarly, if $\overline{\Lambda_k}$ is a non-membership proof corresponding to a key $k \in \mathcal{K}$ for any $k \notin \mathcal{K}_{\mathcal{M}}$, generated by a call to

NonMemProofCreate and updated by appropriate calls to NonMemProofUpdate, then $\mathsf{NonMemVer}(C, k, \overline{\Lambda_k})$ outputs 1 with probability 1.

The security requirement for key-value commitments is that of *key binding.* We consider two notions of soundness, i.e., *weak* and *strong key binding.* To satisfy weak key binding, it must be computationally infeasible for any polynomially bounded adversary (with knowledge of pp) to come up with an *honestly generated* key-value commitment and either a proof that certifies membership of a key or a key-value pair that has not been inserted, or a non-membership proof that certifies non-membership of a key that has been inserted. To satisfy strong key-binding, it must be computationally infeasible for any polynomially bounded adversary (with knowledge of pp) to come up with a *potentially adversarially generated* key-value commitment and either a pair of membership and non-membership proofs that certify membership and non-membership, respectively, of the same key, or a pair of proofs that certify different values for the same key.

Alternative Formalization. Some works alternatively formalize the algorithm NonMemProofCreate to take $\mathcal{M}$ as input instead of U, but in most cases, the two hold similar information. Some works also assume that Update takes as input the old and new values corresponding to a key, as opposed to an additive update–we say that such an Update algorithm is *non-oblivious.*

3 KVC Based on Acc and VC

In Sects. 3.1 and 3.2, we show how to generically construct a key-value commitment using an accumulator and a vector commitment. The idea is to maintain an accumulator of the keys and a vector commitment of the values, tied by the positions. In realizing this, we will need the property that the vector commitment supports the procedure Extend that can dynamically increase the length of the vector that is being committed to, as described in Sect. 2.2.2. The efficiency of the final key-value commitment crucially depends on how efficient Extend is. We highlight that our generic construction allows us to achieve all desired properties of a KVC, including non-membership proofs.[4] It also provides a holistic way to look at existing constructions of KVCs, as we describe in Sect. 3.3.

3.1 Construction I with Weak Key Binding

Let Acc be an accumulator as described in Sect. 2.2.1, and let VC be a vector commitment as described in Sect. 2.2.2 that supports the procedure Extend. In this section, we will be designing a key-value commitment with *weak key binding* for the space of keys $\mathcal{K}$ which is the same as the space of elements $\mathcal{D}$ of Acc, and the space of values $\mathcal{V}$, where the space of elements $\mathcal{D}$ of VC is $\mathcal{K} \times \mathcal{V}$. We construct our key-value commitment KVC as follows:

[4] One can also readily support *key-deletion*, but we ignore this in our presentation.

- $(\mathsf{pp}, C) \leftarrow_\$ \mathsf{Setup}(1^\lambda)$: On input the security parameter λ, the setup generation algorithm:
  - runs $(\mathsf{pp}_{\mathsf{Acc}}, C_{\mathsf{Acc}}) \leftarrow_\$ \mathsf{Acc.Setup}(1^\lambda)$
  - runs $(\mathsf{pp}_{\mathsf{VC}}, C_{\mathsf{VC}}) \leftarrow_\$ \mathsf{VC.Setup}(1^\lambda, 0)$

  and finally outputs the public parameters $\mathsf{pp} = (\mathsf{pp}_{\mathsf{Acc}}, \mathsf{pp}_{\mathsf{VC}})$ and the initial commitment $C = (C_{\mathsf{Acc}}, C_{\mathsf{VC}}, 0)$ to the empty key-value map. All other algorithms have access to the public parameters.
- $(C, \Lambda_k, u) \leftarrow \mathsf{Insert}(C, (k, v))$: On input a key-value commitment string C and a key-value pair $(k, v) \in \mathcal{K} \times \mathcal{V}$, the insertion algorithm:
  - parses $C = (C_{\mathsf{Acc}}, C_{\mathsf{VC}}, q)$
  - runs $(C_{\mathsf{Acc}}, w_k, u_{\mathsf{Acc}}) \leftarrow \mathsf{Acc.Add}(C_{\mathsf{Acc}}, k)$
  - runs $(\mathsf{pp}_{\mathsf{VC}}, C_{\mathsf{VC}}, u_{\mathsf{VC},1}) \leftarrow_\$ \mathsf{VC.Extend}(1^\lambda, C_{\mathsf{VC}})$
  - runs $(C_{\mathsf{VC}}, u_{\mathsf{VC},2}) \leftarrow \mathsf{VC.Update}(C_{\mathsf{VC}}, (q+1, (k, v)))$
  - runs $\Lambda_{q+1} \leftarrow \mathsf{VC.ProofUpdate}(\Lambda_{q+1}, u_{\mathsf{VC},2})$

  and finally outputs a new key-value commitment string $C = (C_{\mathsf{Acc}}, C_{\mathsf{VC}}, q{+}1)$, a proof $\Lambda_k = \Lambda_{q+1}$, and update information $u = (u_{\mathsf{Acc}}, u_{\mathsf{VC},1}, u_{\mathsf{VC},2})$.
- $(C, u) \leftarrow \mathsf{Update}(C, (k, \delta))$: On input a key-value commitment string C, a key $k \in \mathcal{K}$ along with a position q_k[5], and an *additive* update value $\delta \in \mathcal{V}$, the update algorithm:
  - parses $C = (C_{\mathsf{Acc}}, C_{\mathsf{VC}}, q)$
  - runs $(C_{\mathsf{VC}}, u_{\mathsf{VC}}) \leftarrow \mathsf{VC.Update}(C_{\mathsf{VC}}, (q_k, \delta))$[6]

  and finally outputs a new key-value commitment string $C = (C_{\mathsf{Acc}}, C_{\mathsf{VC}}, q)$ and update information $u = u_{\mathsf{VC}}$.
- $\Lambda_k \leftarrow \mathsf{ProofUpdate}(\Lambda_k, u)$: On input a proof Λ_k for some value corresponding to the key k and update information u, the proof update algorithm:
  - parses u as either $(\cdot, u_{\mathsf{VC},1}, u_{\mathsf{VC},2})$ or u_{VC}
  - runs $\Lambda_k \leftarrow \mathsf{VC.ProofUpdate}(\mathsf{VC.ProofUpdate}(\Lambda_k, u_{\mathsf{VC},1}), u_{\mathsf{VC},2})$ or $\Lambda_k = \mathsf{VC.ProofUpdate}(\Lambda_k, u_{\mathsf{VC}})$

  and finally outputs an updated proof Λ_k.
- $\overline{\Lambda_k} \leftarrow \mathsf{NonMemProofCreate}(k, U)$: On input a key $k \in \mathcal{K}$ and the digest of all updated information U produced until the current point in time, the non-membership proof creation algorithm:
  - parses $U = \{u\}$, where either $u = (u_{\mathsf{Acc}}, \cdot, \cdot)$ or $u = \cdot$
  - defines $U_{\mathsf{Acc}} = \{u_{\mathsf{Acc}}\}$, the set of all update information released for Acc
  - runs $\overline{w_k} \leftarrow \mathsf{Acc.NonMemProofCreate}(k, U_{\mathsf{Acc}})$

  and finally outputs a non-membership proof $\overline{\Lambda_k} = \overline{w_k}$.

---

5 This is an implementation detail and can be assumed to be available in practice.

6 We are slightly cheating here as we have stored the key-value pair as the element in the vector and we only wish to add δ to the value component of this pair. This can be realized in practice by carefully handling the sizes of $\mathcal{K}$ and $\mathcal{V}$ to simulate addition to the value component by performing regular addition and avoiding overflows. The alternative is to store just the value in VC, but then Acc would have to store the keys with the positions where their values are stored in VC, which would mean that a non-membership proof for our KVC would now have to be a batched non-membership proof of Acc, which is also a viable solution, but may be less efficient depending on how large $|\mathcal{K}_{\mathcal{M}}|$ becomes.

- $\overline{\Lambda_k} \leftarrow$ NonMemProofUpdate$(\overline{\Lambda_k}, u)$: On input a non-membership proof $\overline{\Lambda_k}$ and update information u, the non-membership proof update algorithm:
  - parses u as either $(u_{\mathsf{Acc}}, \cdot, \cdot)$ or $\cdot$, in the latter case, the algorithm makes no changes to $\overline{\Lambda_k}$
  - runs $\overline{\Lambda_k} \leftarrow$ Acc.NonMemProofUpdate$(\overline{\Lambda_k}, u_{\mathsf{Acc}})$

  outputs an updated non-membership proof $\overline{\Lambda_k}$.
- $1/0 \leftarrow$ Ver$(C, (k, v), \Lambda_k)$: On input a key-value commitment string C, a key-value pair $(k, v) \in \mathcal{K} \times \mathcal{V}$ along with a position q_k, and a proof Λ_k, the verification algorithm:
  - parses $C = (C_{\mathsf{Acc}}, C_{\mathsf{VC}}, q)$
  - checks that $q_k \leq q$
  - runs $b \leftarrow$ VC.ProofVer$(C_{\mathsf{VC}}, (q_k, (k, v)), \Lambda_k)$

  and finally outputs b.
- $0/1 \leftarrow$ NonMemVer$(C, k, \overline{\Lambda_k})$: On input a key-value commitment string C, a key $x \in \mathcal{K}$, and a non-membership proof $\overline{\Lambda_k}$, the non-membership verification algorithm:
  - parses $C = (C_{\mathsf{Acc}}, C_{\mathsf{VC}}, \cdot)$
  - runs $b \leftarrow$ Acc.NonMemVer$(C_{\mathsf{Acc}}, k, \overline{\Lambda_k})$

  and finally outputs b.

The correctness of the above scheme follows directly from the construction and the correctness of Acc and VC. Additionally, we have the following lemma with regard to key binding.

Lemma 1. *If* Acc *and* VC *have (any flavor of) soundness and position binding, then* KVC *has weak key binding.*

Proof. This is a fairly simple reduction. Indeed, suppose we have a PPT adversary $\mathcal{A}$ that can break the weak key binding of KVC. By definition, this means that $\mathcal{A}$, with knowledge of pp, can come up with an *honestly generated* key-value commitment and either a proof that certifies membership of a key or key-value pair that has not been inserted, or a non-membership proof that certifies non-membership of a key that has been inserted. Suppose it is the former. Recall that in our scheme, a membership proof Λ_k is simply a proof of VC. Therefore, if a membership proof breaks the key binding of KVC, it can be used to break the position binding of VC. In the latter case, note that a non-membership proof $\overline{\Lambda_k}$ is simply a non-membership proof of Acc. Therefore, if a non-membership proof breaks the key binding of KVC, it can be used to break the weak soundness of Acc. We note that this KVC construction only achieves weak key binding because the verification algorithm has no way to verify the mapping between key-value pair (k, v) and its position q_k. In particular, for an adversarially generated key-value commitment, it is possible that the same key was inserted with different values in two different positions in the VC. □

We thus have the following theorem.

Theorem 1. *Assuming the existence of an accumulator and vector commitment (supporting the procedure* Extend*) that satisfy correctness, and soundness and position binding respectively, then there exists a key-value commitment that satisfies correctness and weak key binding.*

3.2 Construction II with Strong Key Binding

As before, let Acc be an accumulator as described in Sect. 2.2.1, and let VC be a vector commitment as described in Sect. 2.2.2 that supports the procedure Extend. In this section, we will be designing a key-value commitment with *strong key binding* (assuming both Acc and VC have strong soundness) for the space of keys $\mathcal{K}$ where the space of elements $\mathcal{D}$ of Acc is $\mathcal{K} \times \{0,1\}^\lambda \times \{0,1\}^7$, and the space of values $\mathcal{V}$, where the space of elements $\mathcal{D}$ of VC is $\mathcal{K} \times \mathcal{V}$. To do this, we introduce what we call a *key position proof* which ties a key-value pair (actually, the key) with its corresponding position. These key position proofs can be created and updated similar to other membership and non-membership proofs. Specifically, $\mathsf{KeyPosProofCreate}$ would be called by Insert (with access to the digest of all update information U produced until the current point in time) and $\mathsf{KeyPosProofUpdate}$ would be called by $\mathsf{ProofUpdate}$. We construct our key-value commitment KVC as follows:

- $(\mathsf{pp}, C) \leftarrow_\$ \mathsf{Setup}(1^\lambda)$: On input the security parameter λ, the setup generation algorithm:
  - runs $(\mathsf{pp}_{\mathsf{Acc}}, C_{\mathsf{Acc}}) \leftarrow_\$ \mathsf{Acc.Setup}(1^\lambda)$
  - runs $(\mathsf{pp}_{\mathsf{VC}}, C_{\mathsf{VC}}) \leftarrow_\$ \mathsf{VC.Setup}(1^\lambda, 0)$

  and finally outputs the public parameters $\mathsf{pp} = (\mathsf{pp}_{\mathsf{Acc}}, \mathsf{pp}_{\mathsf{VC}})$ and the initial commitment $C = (C_{\mathsf{Acc}}, C_{\mathsf{VC}}, 0)$ to the empty key-value map. All other algorithms have access to the public parameters.
- $(C, \Lambda_k, u) \leftarrow \mathsf{Insert}(C, (k, v))$: On input a key-value commitment string C and a key-value pair $(k, v) \in \mathcal{K} \times \mathcal{V}$, the insertion algorithm:
  - parses $C = (C_{\mathsf{Acc}}, C_{\mathsf{VC}}, q)$
  - parses $q+1$ as a λ-bit string $b_1, \ldots, b_\lambda$, where b_1 is the least significant bit, and b_λ is the most significant bit of $q+1$
  - runs $(C_{\mathsf{Acc}}, w_{k,j}, u_{\mathsf{Acc},j}) \leftarrow \mathsf{Acc.Add}(C_{\mathsf{Acc}}, (k, j, b_j))$ for each $j \in [\lambda]$
  - runs $(\mathsf{pp}_{\mathsf{VC}}, C_{\mathsf{VC}}, u_{\mathsf{VC},1}) \leftarrow_\$ \mathsf{VC.Extend}(1^\lambda, C_{\mathsf{VC}})$
  - runs $(C_{\mathsf{VC}}, u_{\mathsf{VC},2}) \leftarrow \mathsf{VC.Update}(C_{\mathsf{VC}}, (q+1, (k, v)))$
  - runs $\Lambda_{q+1} \leftarrow \mathsf{VC.ProofUpdate}(\Lambda_{q+1}, u_{\mathsf{VC},2})$

  and finally outputs a new key-value commitment string $C = (C_{\mathsf{Acc}}, C_{\mathsf{VC}}, q+1)$, a proof $\Lambda_k = (\{w_{k,j}\}_{j\in[\lambda]}, \Lambda_{q+1})$, and update information $u = (\{u_{\mathsf{Acc},j}\}_{j\in[\lambda]}, u_{\mathsf{VC},1}, u_{\mathsf{VC},2})$.
- $(C, u) \leftarrow \mathsf{Update}(C, (k, \delta))$: On input a key-value commitment string C, a key $k \in \mathcal{K}$ along with a position q_k , and an *additive* update value $\delta \in \mathcal{V}$, the update algorithm:
  - parses $C = (C_{\mathsf{Acc}}, C_{\mathsf{VC}}, q)$
  - runs $(C_{\mathsf{VC}}, u_{\mathsf{VC}}) \leftarrow \mathsf{VC.Update}(C_{\mathsf{VC}}, (q_k, \delta))$

  and finally outputs a new key-value commitment string $C = (C_{\mathsf{Acc}}, C_{\mathsf{VC}}, q)$ and update information $u = u_{\mathsf{VC}}$.
- $\Lambda_k \leftarrow \mathsf{ProofUpdate}(\Lambda_k, u)$: On input a proof Λ_k for some value corresponding to the key k and update information u, the proof update algorithm:

[7] We assume that the number of key-value pairs that will ever be inserted into our KVC is less than 2^λ.

- parses $\Lambda_k = (\{\Lambda_{k,j}\}_{j\in[\lambda]}, \Lambda_{q_k})$
- parses u as either $(\{u_{\mathsf{Acc},j}\}_{j\in[\lambda]}, u_{\mathsf{VC},1}, u_{\mathsf{VC},2})$ or u_{VC}
- runs $\Lambda_{k,j} \leftarrow \mathsf{Acc.MemProofUpdate}(\Lambda_{k,j}, u_{\mathsf{Acc},j'})$ for each $j, j' \in [\lambda]$
- runs $\Lambda_k \leftarrow \mathsf{VC.ProofUpdate}(\mathsf{VC.ProofUpdate}(\Lambda_k, u_{\mathsf{VC},1}), u_{\mathsf{VC},2})$ or $\Lambda_k = \mathsf{VC.ProofUpdate}(\Lambda_k, u_{\mathsf{VC}})$

and finally outputs an updated proof $\Lambda_k = (\{\Lambda_{k,j}\}_{j\in[\lambda]}, \Lambda_{q_k})$.

- $\Lambda_{k,q_k} \leftarrow \mathsf{KeyPosProofCreate}(k, q_k, U)$: On input a key $k \in \mathcal{K}$ along with a position q_k, and the digest of all update information U produced until the current point in time, the key position proof creation algorithm:
  - parses q_k as a λ-bit string $b_1, \ldots, b_\lambda$, where b_1 is the least significant bit, and b_λ is the most significant bit of q_k
  - parses $U = \{u\}$, where either $u = (u_{\mathsf{Acc}}, \cdot, \cdot)$ or $u = \cdot$
  - defines $U_{\mathsf{Acc}} = \{u_{\mathsf{Acc}}\}$, the set of all update information released for Acc
  - runs $\overline{w_{k,q_k,j}} \leftarrow \mathsf{Acc.NonMemProofCreate}((k, j, \overline{b_j}), U_{\mathsf{Acc}})$ for each $j \in [\lambda]$

  and finally outputs a key position proof $\Lambda_{k,q_k} = \{\overline{w_{k,q_k,j}}\}_{j\in[\lambda]}$.
- $\Lambda_{k,q_k} \leftarrow \mathsf{KeyPosProofUpdate}(\Lambda_{k,q_k}, u)$: On input a non-membership proof $\overline{\Lambda_k}$ and update information u, the key position proof update algorithm:
  - parses u as either $(u_{\mathsf{Acc}}, \cdot, \cdot)$ or $\cdot$, in the latter case, the algorithm makes no changes to Λ_{k,q_k}
  - parses $\Lambda_{k,q_k} = \{\Lambda_{k,q_k,j}\}_{j\in[\lambda]}$
  - runs $\Lambda_{k,q_k,j} \leftarrow \mathsf{Acc.NonMemProofUpdate}(\Lambda_{k,q_k,j}, u_{\mathsf{Acc}})$ for each $j \in [\lambda]$

  outputs an updated key position proof $\Lambda_{k,q_k} = \{\Lambda_{k,q_k,j}\}_{j\in[\lambda]}$.
- $\overline{\Lambda_k} \leftarrow \mathsf{NonMemProofCreate}(k, U)$: On input a key $k \in \mathcal{K}$ and the digest of all update information U produced until the current point in time, the non-membership proof creation algorithm:
  - parses $U = \{u\}$, where either $u = (u_{\mathsf{Acc}}, \cdot, \cdot)$ or $u = \cdot$
  - defines $U_{\mathsf{Acc}} = \{u_{\mathsf{Acc}}\}$, the set of all update information released for Acc
  - runs $\overline{w_{k,b}} \leftarrow \mathsf{Acc.NonMemProofCreate}((k, 1, b), U_{\mathsf{Acc}})$ for each $b \in \{0, 1\}$

  and finally outputs a non-membership proof $\overline{\Lambda_k} = \{\overline{w_{k,b}}\}_{b\in\{0,1\}}$.
- $\overline{\Lambda_k} \leftarrow \mathsf{NonMemProofUpdate}(\overline{\Lambda_k}, u)$: On input a non-membership proof $\overline{\Lambda_k}$ and update information u, the non-membership proof update algorithm:
  - parses u as either $(u_{\mathsf{Acc}}, \cdot, \cdot)$ or $\cdot$, in the latter case, the algorithm makes no changes to $\overline{\Lambda_k}$
  - parses $\overline{\Lambda_k} = \{\overline{\Lambda_{k,b}}\}_{b\in\{0,1\}}$
  - runs $\overline{\Lambda_{k,b}} \leftarrow \mathsf{Acc.NonMemProofUpdate}(\overline{\Lambda_{k,b}}, u_{\mathsf{Acc}})$ for each $b \in \{0, 1\}$

  outputs an updated non-membership proof $\overline{\Lambda_k} = \{\overline{\Lambda_{k,b}}\}_{b\in\{0,1\}}$.
- $1/0 \leftarrow \mathsf{Ver}(C, (k, v), \Lambda_k)$: On input a key-value commitment string C, a key-value pair $(k, v) \in \mathcal{K} \times \mathcal{V}$ along with a position q_k and a position proof Λ_{k,q_k}[8], and a proof Λ_k, the verification algorithm:
  - parses $C = (C_{\mathsf{Acc}}, C_{\mathsf{VC}}, q)$
  - checks that $q_k \leq q$
  - parses q_k as a λ-bit string $b_1, \ldots, b_\lambda$, where b_1 is the least significant bit, and b_λ is the most significant bit of q_k
  - parses $\Lambda_k = (\{\Lambda_{k,j}\}_{j\in[\lambda]}, \Lambda_{q_k})$ and $\Lambda_{k,q_k} = \{\Lambda_{k,q_k,j}\}_{j\in[\lambda]}$

[8] This is obtained using $\mathsf{KeyPosProofCreate}(k, q_k, \cdot)$ and $\mathsf{KeyPosProofUpdate}(\Lambda_{k,q_k}, \cdot)$.

- runs $b_1 \leftarrow \bigwedge_{j\in[\lambda]} \mathsf{Acc.MemVer}(C_{\mathsf{Acc}}, (k, j, b_j), \Lambda_{k,j})$
- runs $b_2 \leftarrow \bigwedge_{j\in[\lambda]} \mathsf{Acc.NonMemVer}(C_{\mathsf{Acc}}, (k, j, \overline{b_j}), \Lambda_{k,q_k,j})$
- runs $b_3 \leftarrow \mathsf{VC.ProofVer}(C_{\mathsf{VC}}, (q_k, (k, v)), \Lambda_{q_k})$

and finally outputs $b_1 \wedge b_2 \wedge b_3$.

– $0/1 \leftarrow \mathsf{NonMemVer}(C, k, \overline{\Lambda_k})$: On input a key-value commitment string C, a key $x \in \mathcal{K}$, and a non-membership proof $\overline{\Lambda_k}$, the non-membership verification algorithm:
  - parses $C = (C_{\mathsf{Acc}}, C_{\mathsf{VC}}, \cdot)$
  - parses $\overline{\Lambda_k} = \{\overline{\Lambda_{k,b'}}\}_{b'\in\{0,1\}}$
  - runs $b \leftarrow \bigwedge_{b'\in\{0,1\}} \mathsf{Acc.NonMemVer}(C_{\mathsf{Acc}}, (k, 1, b'), \overline{\Lambda_{k,b'}})$

  and finally outputs b.

The correctness of the above scheme follows directly from the construction and the correctness of Acc and VC. Additionally, we have the following lemma with regard to key binding which leads to the subsequent theorem.

Lemma 2. *If* Acc *and* VC *have strong soundness and position binding, then* KVC *has strong key binding.*

Proof. This is a fairly simple reduction. Indeed, suppose we have a PPT adversary $\mathcal{A}$ that can break the strong key binding of KVC. By definition, this means that $\mathcal{A}$, with knowledge of pp, can come up with a *potentially adversarially generated* key-value commitment and either a proof that certifies membership of a key or key-value pair that has not been inserted, or a non-membership proof that certifies non-membership of a key that has been inserted. Suppose it is the former. Our verification algorithm ensures that the key k is bound to precisely the position q_k in Acc and that VC stores the right key-value pair at position q_k. Therefore, if a membership proof breaks the strong key binding of KVC, it can be used to break either the strong soundness of Acc or the strong position binding of VC. In the latter case, note that a non-membership proof $\overline{\Lambda_k}$ is simply a pair of non-membership proofs of Acc which cannot verify if the key k has been inserted. Therefore, if a non-membership proof breaks the strong key binding of KVC, it can be used to break the strong soundness of Acc. □

Theorem 2. *Assuming the existence of an accumulator and vector commitment (supporting the procedure* Extend*) that satisfy correctness, and strong soundness and strong position binding respectively, then there exists a key-value commitment that satisfies correctness and strong key binding.*

Constant Sized Proofs. In our construction, proofs are in general larger by a factor of $O(\lambda)$. If Acc supports batched membership and non-membership proofs, this can be brought down to $O(1)$ in a straightforward manner.

3.3 Relation to Existing Constructions

We now describe how existing KVC constructions relate to our generic construction. We focus on schemes that support key non-membership and updates.

Black-box KVC constructions have been proposed from stronger primitives such as functional commitments [15].[9]. Aardvark [26] is a generic construction that uses a plain VC scheme and performs sequential insertions. It differs in the way it implements key non-membership. In order to support non-membership, it stores elements $(k, v, succ(k))$, where $succ(k)$ is the smallest key in the list larger than k. To prove non-membership for k', one gives a proof of opening for an element with the same successor as k'. This approach complicates updates, because when a new key is inserted, multiple positions need to be updated. The same holds for the generic construction by Fiore et al. [22] that utilizes VC schemes and cuckoo hashing. Instead of sequential VC additions, keys and their corresponding values are placed in the same position inside two vectors, determined by the cuckoo hashing functions. Because of the heavy rearrangement of elements when a new key is inserted, there is no proof updates, instead, many proofs need to be computed from scratch (to reflect the new position). Compared to our strong KVC from Sect. 3.2, both [22,26] have a verifier state overhead (Aardvark uses multiple vector commitments and cuckoo hashing uses a stack) and they do not offer stateless updates. Beyond black box constructions, there exist a number of KVC constructions with key non-membership and updates which are based on specific RSA-related assumptions [2,35,36]. Our generic construction could give rise to concrete instantiations under different assumptions.

4 Oblivious Accumulators

In this section, we provide our definition of *oblivious accumulators*. The overarching goal of an oblivious accumulator is for its updates to be *completely oblivious*, i.e., hide the details of the underlying operation being performed on the accumulator. In particular, from the definition of the accumulator from Sect. 2.2.1, we would like for the public parameters pp, accumulator string C, and update any information u that is released by calls to Add or Del (and hence the digest of all update information at any point in time) to hide as much information about the underlying accumulated set S as possible[10].

Looking forward, we will formulate three properties that an oblivious accumulator must satisfy. These three properties combined will provide the guarantee that any publicly available information will hide as much information about S as possible. The three properties are:

1. *Element hiding.* Informally, this will mean that any publicly available information does not reveal anything about the elements in S.
2. Add-Del *unlinkability.* Informally, this will mean that any publicly available information does not reveal if two operations correspond to an add and a delete of the same element.

[9] KVC constructions have also been proposed from sparse VC schemes [9,16] but supporting key non-membership and updates at the same time is expensive.

[10] Indeed, note that if only one operation has been performed, we know that it must be an Add, but we don't necessarily know the element that has been added.

3. Add-Del *indistinguishability.* Informally, this will mean that any publicly available information does not reveal if an operation corresponds to an add or a delete, more than can be deduced given no update information.[11]

4.1 Definition

Recall that we will define the primitive in the positive (supports membership proofs) dynamic (supports additions and deletions) setting. We also assume that we are in the trapdoorless setting, i.e., updates can be performed with publicly available information. Much of our definition from Sect. 2.2.1 can be used to define oblivious accumulators, but crucially some changes are required. Essentially, any operation that is performed, in order to hide particulars of the operation such as the nature of the operation itself (Add or Del) and the associated element, must make use of some *secret* or *auxiliary information*, that we denote by aux. This auxiliary information must at the very least be used in the generation and verification of membership proofs.[12] Furthermore, since Adds and Dels are indistinguishable, it may become necessary for an Add to now take as input all past updates, just as Del does. Based on these observations, we modify our definition from 2.2.1 and define oblivious accumulators below. We define an *oblivious accumulator* OblvAcc as a non-interactive primitive that can be formally described via the following algorithms:

- $(\mathsf{pp}, C) \leftarrow_\$ \mathsf{Setup}(1^\lambda)$: On input the security parameter λ, the setup algorithm outputs some public parameters pp (which implicitly define the accumulator domain $\mathcal{D}$) and the initial accumulator string C to the empty set. All other algorithms have access to the public parameters.
- $(C, w_x, u, \mathsf{aux}) \leftarrow_\$ \mathsf{Add}(C, x, U)$: On input an accumulator string C, an element $x \in \mathcal{D}$, and the digest of all update information U produced until the current point in time, the addition algorithm outputs a new accumulator string C, a membership proof w_x (that $x \in S$), update information u, and auxiliary information aux.
- $(C, u) \leftarrow \mathsf{Del}(C, x, U, \mathsf{aux})$: On input an accumulator string C, an element $x \in \mathcal{D}$, the digest of all update information U produced until the current point in time, and auxiliary information aux, the deletion algorithm outputs a new accumulator string C and update information u.
- $w_x \leftarrow \mathsf{MemProofUpdate}(w_x, u)$: On input a membership proof w_x and update information u, the membership proof update algorithm outputs an updated membership proof w_x.
- $0/1 \leftarrow \mathsf{MemVer}(C, x, w_x, \mathsf{aux})$: On input an accumulator string C, an element $x \in \mathcal{D}$, a membership proof w_x, and auxiliary information aux, the membership verification algorithm either outputs 1 (denoting accept) or 0 (denoting reject).

---

[11] For example, if we have a sequence of four operations, they cannot be one Add and three Dels.

[12] One could imagine that they are also required for updating membership proofs, but we will not need this and so opt for the stronger definition where aux is only needed to generate membership proofs.

The correctness and soundness properties of an oblivious accumulator are identical to those of a regular accumulator, as defined in Sect. 2.2.1. We will define the three properties underlying the obliviousness of the accumulator in the next section.

4.2 Obliviousness Properties

In this section, we will define the three properties underlying the obliviousness of the accumulator.

4.2.1 Element Hiding

The property of element hiding is meant to provide the guarantee that an adversary that observes the publicly available information does not learn about the elements in the underlying accumulated set S. We define this property as a game between a challenger and an adversary. In the game, the adversary gets to see honestly generated public parameters and then pick two elements $x_0, x_1 \in \mathcal{D}$. The challenger then picks $b \leftarrow_\$ \{0,1\}$ and performs an Add of x_b, followed by a Del of x_b. The adversary is then given the update information generated by each of the operations and has to guess b. The oblivious accumulator is said to be element hiding if the adversary cannot guess b with non-negligible advantage over $\frac{1}{2}$. We extend the game in a natural left-or-right paradigm to extend it to support multiple queries (denoted by $\{\cdot\}_i$ where the queries are indexed by i). We define this formally below.

Definition 1 (Element hiding). *An oblivious accumulator is said to be element hiding if for any* PPT *adversary* $\mathcal{A}$*, the following probability is at most* $\frac{1}{2} + \mathrm{negl}(\lambda)$*:*

$$\Pr\left[b' = b \;\middle|\; \begin{array}{c} (\mathsf{pp}, C_0) \leftarrow_\$ \mathsf{Setup}(1^\lambda) \\ b \leftarrow_\$ \{0,1\}, \mathsf{inp} = (\mathsf{pp}, C_0), j = 0, U = \emptyset, J = \emptyset \\ \left\{ \begin{array}{c} \left\{ \begin{array}{c} j = j+1 \\ (\mathsf{add}, x_{0,j}, x_{1,j}) \leftarrow_\$ \mathcal{A}(\mathsf{inp}) \\ (C_i, \cdot, u_i, \mathsf{aux}_j) \leftarrow_\$ \mathsf{Add}(C_{i-1}, x_{b,j}, U) \\ \mathsf{inp} = \mathsf{inp} \| (\mathsf{add}, x_{0,j}, x_{1,j}, C_i), U = U \cup \{u_i\} \end{array} \right\} \\ \textbf{or} \\ \left\{ \begin{array}{c} (\mathsf{del}, j') \leftarrow_\$ \mathcal{A}(\mathsf{inp}) \\ \textbf{assert } j' \leq j \wedge j' \notin J \\ J = J \cup \{j'\} \\ (C_i, u_i) \leftarrow \mathsf{Del}(C_{i-1}, x_{b,j'}, U, \mathsf{aux}_{j'}) \\ \mathsf{inp} = \mathsf{inp} \| (\mathsf{del}, j', C_i), U = U \cup \{u_i\} \end{array} \right\} \end{array} \right\}_i \\ b' \leftarrow_\$ \mathcal{A}(\mathsf{inp}, U) \end{array} \right]$$

We note that while there are other games one could think of to define this property, they would not offer any advantages over our proposed game.

4.2.2 Add-Del Unlinkability

We first state a weaker flavor of privacy: Add-Del unlinkability, introduced by Baldimtsi et al. [5] in the context of manager-based anonymous revocation component (ARC) systems. We re-define this property in the context of a trapdoorless accumulator. Add-Del unlinkability is meant to provide the guarantee that an adversary that observes the publicly available information does not learn if two operations correspond to an Add and a Del of the same element. We define this property as a game between a challenger and an adversary. In the game, the adversary gets to see honestly generated public parameters and then pick two elements $x_0, x_1 \in \mathcal{D}$. The challenger first performs an Add of x_0 and x_1, in order. Then, the challenger picks $b \leftarrow_\$ \{0,1\}$ and performs a Del of x_b, followed by a Del of x_{1-b}. The adversary is then given the update information generated by each of the operations and has to guess b. The oblivious accumulator is said to be Add-Del unlinkable if the adversary cannot guess b with non-negligible advantage over $\frac{1}{2}$. We extend the game in a natural left-or-right paradigm to extend it to support multiple queries (denoted by $\{\cdot\}_i$ where the queries are indexed by i). We define this formally below.

Definition 2 (Add-Del unlinkability). *An oblivious accumulator is said to be* Add-Del *unlinkable if for any* PPT *adversary $\mathcal{A}$, the following probability is at most $\frac{1}{2} + \text{negl}(\lambda)$:*

$$\Pr\left[b' = b \;\middle|\; \begin{array}{c} (\mathsf{pp}, C_0) \leftarrow_\$ \mathsf{Setup}(1^\lambda) \\ b \leftarrow_\$ \{0,1\}, \mathsf{inp} = (\mathsf{pp}, C_0), j = 0, U = \emptyset, J = \emptyset \\ \\ \left\{ \begin{array}{c} \left\{ \begin{array}{c} j = j+1 \\ (\mathsf{add}, x_{0,j}, x_{1,j}) \leftarrow_\$ \mathcal{A}(\mathsf{inp}) \\ (C_{2i-1}, \cdot, u_{2i-1}, \mathsf{aux}_{2j-1}) \leftarrow_\$ \mathsf{Add}(C_{2i-2}, x_{0,j}, U) \\ (C_{2i}, \cdot, u_{2i}, \mathsf{aux}_{2j}) \leftarrow_\$ \mathsf{Add}(C_{2i-1}, x_{1,j}, U \cup \{u_{2i-1}\}) \\ \mathsf{inp} = \mathsf{inp} \| (\mathsf{add}, x_{0,j}, x_{1,j}, C_{2i-1}, C_{2i}) \\ U = U \cup \{u_{2i-1}, u_{2i}\} \end{array} \right\} \\ \textbf{or} \\ \left\{ \begin{array}{c} (\mathsf{del}, j') \leftarrow_\$ \mathcal{A}(\mathsf{inp}) \\ \textbf{assert } j' \leq j \wedge j' \notin J \\ J = J \cup \{j'\} \\ (C_{2i-1}, u_{2i-1}) \leftarrow \mathsf{Del}(C_{2i-2}, x_{b,j'}, U, \mathsf{aux}_{2j'-(1-b)}) \\ (C_{2i}, u_{2i}) \leftarrow \mathsf{Del}(C_{2i-1}, x_{1-b,j'}, U \cup \{u_{2i-1}\}, \mathsf{aux}_{2j'-b}) \\ \mathsf{inp} = \mathsf{inp} \| (\mathsf{del}, j', C_{2i-1}, C_{2i}) \\ U = U \cup \{u_{2i-1}, u_{2i}\} \end{array} \right\} \end{array} \right\}_i \\ \\ b' \leftarrow_\$ \mathcal{A}(\mathsf{inp}, U) \end{array} \right]$$

We note that while there are other games one could think of to define this property, they would not offer any advantages over our proposed game.

4.2.3 Add-Del Indistinguishability

We now define Add-Del indistinguishability, a stronger privacy property which implies Add-Del unlinkability as defined above. The property of Add-Del indistinguishability is meant to provide the guarantee that an adversary that observes the publicly available information does not learn if an operation is an Add or a Del, beyond what it can learn without even observing any update information. We define this property as a game between a challenger and an adversary. In the game, the adversary gets to see honestly generated public parameters and then pick an element $x_0 \in \mathcal{D}$. The challenger first performs an Add of x_0. Then, the challenger picks $b \leftarrow_\$ \{0, 1\}$. If $b = 0$, the challenger picks a random element $x_1 \in \mathcal{D}$ and performs an Add of x_1. Otherwise, the challenger performs a Del of x_0. The adversary is then given the update information generated by each of the operations and has to guess b. The oblivious accumulator is said to be Add-Del indistinguishable if the adversary cannot guess b with non-negligible advantage over $\frac{1}{2}$. We extend the game in a natural left-or-right paradigm to extend it to support multiple queries (denoted by $\{\cdot\}_i$ where the queries are indexed by i). We define this formally below.

Definition 3 (Add-Del indistinguishability). *An oblivious accumulator is said to be* Add-Del *indistinguishable if for any* PPT *adversary $\mathcal{A}$, the following probability is at most $\frac{1}{2} + \mathrm{negl}(\lambda)$:*

$$\Pr\left[b' = b \;\middle|\; \begin{array}{c} (\mathsf{pp}, C_0) \leftarrow_\$ \mathsf{Setup}(1^\lambda) \\ b \leftarrow_\$ \{0,1\}, \mathsf{inp} = (\mathsf{pp}, C_0), j = 0, U = \emptyset, J = \emptyset \\ \left\{ \begin{array}{c} \left\{ \begin{array}{c} j = j + 1 \\ (\mathsf{add}, x_j) \leftarrow_\$ \mathcal{A}(\mathsf{inp}) \\ (C_i, \cdot, u_i, \mathsf{aux}_j) \leftarrow_\$ \mathsf{Add}(C_{i-1}, x_j, U) \\ \mathsf{inp} = \mathsf{inp} \| (\mathsf{add}, x_j, C_i), U = U \cup \{u_i\} \end{array} \right\} \\ \textbf{or} \\ \left\{ \begin{array}{c} (\mathsf{del}, j') \leftarrow_\$ \mathcal{A}(\mathsf{inp}) \\ \textbf{assert } j' \le j \wedge j' \notin J \\ J = J \cup \{j'\}, y_i \leftarrow_\$ \mathcal{D} \\ \textbf{if } b = 0 : (C_i, \cdot, u_i, \cdot) \leftarrow_\$ \mathsf{Add}(C_{i-1}, y_i, U) \\ \textbf{if } b = 1 : (C_i, u_i) \leftarrow_\$ \mathsf{Del}(C_{i-1}, x_{j'}, U, \mathsf{aux}_{j'}) \\ \mathsf{inp} = \mathsf{inp} \| (\mathsf{del}, j', C_i) \\ U = U \cup \{u_i\} \end{array} \right\} \end{array} \right\}_i \\ b' \leftarrow_\$ \mathcal{A}(\mathsf{inp}, U) \end{array} \right]$$

We note that while there are other games one could think of to define this property, they would not offer any advantages over our proposed game.

Note that Add-Del indistinguishability implies Add-Del unlinkability. Intuitively, if an adversary cannot even tell Adds from Dels, then they certainly cannot identify a pair of updates that correspond to an Add and a Del, let along identifying that they are with respect to the same element. Formally, in the Add-Del unlinkability game, the two Dels can we be swapped with Adds, assuming Add-Del indistinguishability, and then back to Dels, but in the reverse order, again assuming Add-Del indistinguishability, and this would prove Add-Del unlinkability. We call accumulators that satisfy Add-Del unlinkability but not Add-Del indistinguishability as *almost-oblivious accumulators*, and ones that satisfy Add-Del indistinguishability as *oblivious accumulators*.

5 OblvAcc Based on KVC

In this section, we show how to generically construct an oblivious accumulator using a key-value commitment. The idea is to maintain an *indicator map* that reflects which elements are in the underlying accumulated set, but where the keys associated with each element are kept secret and hence not publicly known. This helps in the first step of achieving element hiding. To achieve Add-Del indistinguishability, we perform both Adds and Dels as Inserts of the key-value commitment, but with different keys. Finally, the fact that the correspondence between elements and keys is not publicly known will also lend itself to Add-Del unlinkability. We formally describe this construction in the next section.

5.1 Construction

Let KVC be a key-value commitment as described in Sect. 2.2.3. Let $H_1, H_2 : \{0,1\}^\lambda \times \mathcal{D} \rightarrow \mathcal{K}$ be two hash functions (that will be modeled as random oracles). Note that we will be designing an oblivious accumulator for elements from $\mathcal{D}$ and $\mathcal{K}$ denotes the space of keys for the key-value commitment, and $|\mathcal{K}| = 2^{2\lambda}$. If all we want is to accumulate elements, then the only requirement from the space of values $\mathcal{V}$ for the key-value commitment is that $1 \in \mathcal{V}$. However, if we would like to support a richer structure where elements in our accumulator are tagged by some public values that may change with time, we would require $\mathcal{V}$ to include these public tag values. We present our basic oblivious accumulator OblvAcc below:

- $(\mathsf{pp}, C) \leftarrow_\$ \mathsf{Setup}(1^\lambda)$: On input the security parameter λ, the setup algorithm runs $(\mathsf{pp}_{\mathsf{KVC}}, C_{\mathsf{KVC}}) \leftarrow_\$ \mathsf{KVC.Setup}(1^\lambda)$ and outputs the public parameters $\mathsf{pp} = (\mathsf{pp}_{\mathsf{KVC}}, H_1, H_2)$ and the initial accumulator string $C = C_{\mathsf{KVC}}$. All other algorithms have access to the public parameters.
- $(C, w_x, u, \mathsf{aux}) \leftarrow_\$ \mathsf{Add}(C, x, U)$: On input an accumulator string C, an element $x \in \mathcal{D}$, and the digest of all update information U produced until the current point in time, the addition algorithm:
  - samples $r \leftarrow_\$ \{0,1\}^\lambda$
  - computes $k_1 = H_1(r, x)$, $k_2 = H_2(r, x)$
  - runs $(C_{\mathsf{KVC}}, \Lambda_{k_1}, u_{\mathsf{KVC}}) \leftarrow \mathsf{KVC.Insert}(C, (k_1, 1))$
  - runs $\Lambda_{k_2} \leftarrow \mathsf{KVC.NonMemProofCreate}(k_2, U \cup \{u_{\mathsf{KVC}}\})$

and finally outputs a new accumulator string $C = C_{\mathsf{KVC}}$, a membership proof $w_x = (\Lambda_{k_1}, \overline{\Lambda_{k_2}})$, update information $u = u_{\mathsf{KVC}}$, and auxiliary information $\mathsf{aux} = r$.

- $(C, u) \leftarrow \mathsf{Del}(C, x, U, \mathsf{aux})$: On input an accumulator string C, an element $x \in \mathcal{D}$, the digest of all update information U produced until the current point in time, and auxiliary information aux, the deletion algorithm:
  - parses $\mathsf{aux} = r$
  - computes $k_2 = H_2(r, x)$
  - runs $(C_{\mathsf{KVC}}, \Lambda_{k_2}, u_{\mathsf{KVC}}) \leftarrow \mathsf{KVC.Insert}(C, (k_2, 1))$

  and finally outputs a new accumulator string $C = C_{\mathsf{KVC}}$ and update information $u = u_{\mathsf{KVC}}$.
- $w_x \leftarrow \mathsf{MemProofUpdate}(w_x, u)$: On input a membership proof w_x and update information u, the membership proof update algorithm:
  - parses $w_x = (\Lambda_{k_1}, \overline{\Lambda_{k_2}})$
  - runs $\Lambda_k \leftarrow \mathsf{KVC.ProofUpdate}(\Lambda_{k_1}, u)$
  - $\overline{\Lambda_{k_2}} \leftarrow \mathsf{KVC.NonMemProofUpdate}(\overline{\Lambda_{k_2}}, u)$

  and finally outputs an updated membership proof $w_x = (\Lambda_{k_1}, \overline{\Lambda_{k_2}})$.
- $0/1 \leftarrow \mathsf{MemVer}(C, x, w_x, \mathsf{aux})$: On input an accumulator string C, an element $x \in \mathcal{D}$, and a membership proof w_x, the membership verification algorithm:
  - parses $\mathsf{aux} = r$
  - computes $k_1 = H_1(r, x)$, $k_2 = H_2(r, x)$
  - parses $w_x = (\Lambda_{k_1}, \overline{\Lambda_{k_2}})$
  - runs $b_1 \leftarrow \mathsf{KVC.Ver}(C, (k_1, 1), \Lambda_{k_1})$
  - runs $b_2 \leftarrow \mathsf{KVC.NonMemVer}(C, k_2, \overline{\Lambda_{k_2}})$

  and finally outputs $b_1 \wedge b_2$.

Supporting Updatable Public Tags. As noted above, by using a value other than 1 while inserting into the KVC, we can tag elements in our accumulator with any public value from $\mathcal{V}$. Furthermore, we can update these public tags using the $\mathsf{Update}(\cdot)$ operation of KVC (recall the example of maintaining metadata for a customer base on a smart contract from Sect. 1.1). Indeed, if one does not care about such tags, we can replace the KVC in the above construction with an accumulator.

The correctness of the above scheme follows directly from the construction and the correctness of KVC. In the remainder of this section, we will prove the soundness and obliviousness properties of our oblivious accumulator. We thus have the following theorem.

Theorem 3. *Assuming the existence of a key-value commitment that satisfies correctness and weak (strong) key binding, then there exists an oblivious accumulator that satisfies correctness, weak (strong) soundness, element hiding, and* Add-Del *indistinguishability, in the random oracle model.*

5.2 Soundness

Lemma 3. *Assume that H_1, H_2 are random oracles. If* KVC *has weak (strong) key binding, then* OblvAcc *has weak (strong) soundness.*

Proof. Suppose we have a PPT adversary $\mathcal{A}$ that can break the weak (strong) soundness of OblvAcc. By definition, this means that $\mathcal{A}$, with knowledge of pp, can come up with an *honestly generated* (*potentially adversarially generated*) accumulator and either a membership proof that certifies membership of an element that has not been added, or a non-membership proof that certifies non-membership of an element that has been added. Suppose it is the former. Recall that in our scheme, a membership proof w_x consists of a proof Λ_{k_1} and non-membership proof $\overline{\Lambda_{k_2}}$ of KVC, where $k_1 = H_1(r, x)$, $k_2 = H_2(r, x)$. If it is the case that x has not been added, then there cannot exist an r such that both Λ_{k_1} and $\overline{\Lambda_{k_2}}$ verify (as if they do, by definition, x has been added, and not yet deleted). Therefore, if w_x certifies x that has not been added, at least one of Λ_{k_1} and $\overline{\Lambda_{k_2}}$ can be used to break the weak (strong) key binding of KVC. A similar argument can be made for the latter case. A final detail is we assume that H_1, H_2 exhibit no collisions over the inputs queried on by $\mathcal{A}$. Indeed, since $\mathcal{A}$ is PPT and $|\mathcal{K}| = 2^{2\lambda}$, this is true with probability all but $\text{negl}(\lambda)$. □

5.3 Element Hiding

Lemma 4. *Assume that H_1, H_2 are random oracles.* OblvAcc *is element hiding.*

Proof. For simplicity, we will show that for any PPT adversary $\mathcal{A}$,

$$\Pr\left[b' = b \;\middle|\; \begin{array}{c} (\mathsf{pp}, C_0) \leftarrow_\$ \mathsf{Setup}(1^\lambda) \\ x_0, x_1 \leftarrow_\$ \mathcal{A}(\mathsf{pp}, C_0) \\ b \leftarrow_\$ \{0,1\} \\ (C_1, w_{x_b}, u_1, \mathsf{aux}) \leftarrow_\$ \mathsf{Add}(C_0, x_b, \emptyset) \\ (C_2, u_2) \leftarrow \mathsf{Del}(C_1, x_b, \{u_1\}, \mathsf{aux}) \\ b' \leftarrow_\$ \mathcal{A}(C_1, C_2, u_1, u_2) \end{array} \right] \le \frac{1}{2} + \text{negl}(\lambda)$$

This is essentially the single-query version of the game in Definition 1. To extend the argument for the single-query version to prove the statement in Definition 1, one can essentially guess the query that the adversary uses to win the game in Definition 1 and use it, with appropriate bookkeeping, to break the single-query version above.

We assume that H_1, H_2 exhibit no collisions over the inputs queried on by $\mathcal{A}$. Indeed, since $\mathcal{A}$ is PPT and $|\mathcal{K}| = 2^{2\lambda}$, this is true with probability all but $\text{negl}(\lambda)$. Note that $(C_1, \cdot, u_1) \leftarrow \mathsf{KVC.Insert}(C_0, (k_{1,b}, 1))$, where $k_{1,b} = H_1(r_b, x_b)$, and $(C_2, \cdot, u_2) \leftarrow \mathsf{KVC.Insert}(C_1, (k_{2,b}, 1))$, where $k_{2,b} = H_2(r_b, x_b)$. Since r_b is sampled at random from $\{0,1\}^\lambda$ and H_1 and H_2 are random oracles, we have $(k_{1,b}, k_{2,b}) \equiv (k_{1,1-b}, k_{2,1-b}) \equiv (\alpha_1, \alpha_2)$, where $\alpha_1, \alpha_2 \leftarrow_\$ \mathcal{K}$. Since these are the only values needed by the challenger to play the above game, this means that (C_1, C_2, u_1, u_2) is distributed the same, regardless of b. Therefore, the claim of OblvAcc being element hiding follows. □

5.4 Add-Del Indistinguishability

Lemma 5. *Assume that* H_1, H_2 *are random oracles.* OblvAcc *is* Add-Del *indistinguishable.*

Proof. For simplicity, we will show that for any PPT adversary $\mathcal{A}$,

$$\Pr\left[b' = b \;\middle|\; \begin{array}{c} (\mathsf{pp}, C_0) \leftarrow_{\$} \mathsf{Setup}(1^\lambda) \\ x_0 \leftarrow_{\$} \mathcal{A}(\mathsf{pp}, C_0) \\ (C_1, w_{x_0}, u_1, \mathsf{aux}_0) \leftarrow_{\$} \mathsf{Add}(C_0, x_0, \emptyset) \\ b \leftarrow_{\$} \{0,1\}, x_1 \leftarrow_{\$} \mathcal{D} \\ \textbf{if } b = 0\text{: } (C_2, w_{x_1}, u_2, \mathsf{aux}_1) \leftarrow_{\$} \mathsf{Add}(C_1, x_1, \{u_1\}) \\ \textbf{if } b = 1\text{: } (C_2, u_2) \leftarrow \mathsf{Del}(C_1, x_0, \{u_1\}, \mathsf{aux}_0) \\ b' \leftarrow \mathcal{A}(C_1, C_2, u_1, u_2) \end{array} \right] \leq \frac{1}{2} + \text{negl}(\lambda)$$

This is essentially the single-query version of the game in Definition 3. To extend the argument for the single-query version to prove the statement in Definition 3, one can essentially guess the query that the adversary uses to win the game in Definition 3 and use it, with appropriate bookkeeping, to break the single-query version above.

We assume that H_1, H_2 exhibit no collisions over the inputs queried on by $\mathcal{A}$. Indeed, since $\mathcal{A}$ is PPT and $|\mathcal{K}| = 2^{2\lambda}$, this is true with probability all but negl(λ). Note that $(C_1, \cdot, u_1) \leftarrow \mathsf{KVC.Insert}(C_0, (k_{1,0}, 1))$, where $k_{1,0} = H_1(r_0, x_0)$, and $(C_2, \cdot, u_2) \leftarrow \mathsf{KVC.Insert}(C_1, (k_{1,1}, 1))$, where $k_{1,1} = H_1(r_1, x_1)$ if $b = 0$, and $(C_2, \cdot, u_2) \leftarrow \mathsf{KVC.Insert}(C_1, (k_{2,0}, 1))$, where $k_{2,1} = H_2(r_0, x_0)$ if $b = 1$. Since r_0, r_1 are sampled at random from $\{0,1\}^\lambda$ and H_1 and H_2 are random oracles, we have $(k_{1,0}, k_{1,1}) \equiv (k_{1,0}, k_{2,0}) \equiv (\alpha_1, \alpha_2)$, where $\alpha_1, \alpha_2 \leftarrow_{\$} \mathcal{K}$. Since these are the only values needed by the challenger to play the above game, this means that (C_1, C_2, u_1, u_2) is distributed the same, regardless of b. Therefore, the claim of OblvAcc being Add-Del indistinguishable follows. □

5.5 Extension for Unique Accumulation of Elements

Both our main construction of Sect. 5.1 and the modular construction of the *almost-oblivious* accumulator described in the introduction, do not guarantee that the accumulated elements are unique. This implies that the same element x can be accumulated more than once and this would go unnoticed because of the element hiding property[13].

To overcome this problem instead of accumulating commitments to x one could use a deterministic commitment (assuming also that the accumulated elements bare random and from a large enough domain to avoid guessing attacks). One approach to do so, would be to use a hash function as a commitment scheme. If guessing is still a concern, we could use a verifiable oblivious PRF (VOPRF) [24] for the generation of the committed value in the almost-oblivious construction (or for the selection of randomness r in the construction of Sect. 5.1). In

[13] In the almost-oblivious accumulator which reveals the size of the accumulated set, this might be more problematic if in the underlying application the size of the set is important and should only contain unique elements.

a high level, in a VOPRF protocol, when given a PRF F, a third party can communicate with a server holding a secret key k to evaluate an argument x and get back $y = F_k(x)$, while the server learns nothing about x. If F is also verifiable, there is a way to convince a third party that y is the true output of $F_k(x)$ without revealing k. Using this approach, has the trade off of requiring a server that holds the PRF key (thus, some point of centralization), however it makes such guessing attacks harder since an attacker would have to interact with a server in order to test for elements (which might imply some actual financial cost, i.e. the server could charge a fee for its given evaluation).

6 Lower Bounds

In this section, we will first show that for an oblivious accumulator, the digest of all update information cannot be compressed with time and must grow linearly with the number of operations that have been performed. This builds off of an information-theoretic argument in the style of [10,19] to argue the claim for deletions, and then uses the obliviousness properties to argue that the claim must hold for any sequence of operations. This result appears in Sect. 6.1.

Next, we show that a similar claim holds even for non-oblivious accumulators like ZCash that don't satisfy Add-Del indistinguishability but have have Add-Del unlinkability. For such accumulators, we show that the digest of all update information must grow in a sense with the number of deletions that have been performed. This result appears in Sect. 6.2.

6.1 Oblivious Accumulators

Lemma 6. *Let* OblvAcc *be an oblivious accumulator over the domain $\mathcal{D}$. Let $S \subseteq \mathcal{D}$ be a set of size n and let $T \subset S$ be a set of size $\frac{n}{2}$. Consider performing the following sequence of operations in order:*

1. $(\mathsf{pp}, C) \leftarrow_\$ \mathsf{Setup}(1^\lambda)$
2. $(C, w_x, u, \mathsf{aux}) \leftarrow_\$ \mathsf{Add}(C, x, U)$ *for each* $x \in S$
3. $(C, u) \leftarrow \mathsf{Del}(C, x, U, \mathsf{aux})$ *for each* $x \in T$

Let C be the accumulator string and U be the digest of all update information produced at the end of all the operations. Then,

$$|C| + |U| = \Omega(n)$$

Proof. We will show that if the theorem is false, then we can encode arbitrary subsets of S of size $\frac{n}{2}$ with $o(n)$ bits, which is impossible information-theoretically from Shannon's coding theorem, as there are $\binom{n}{\frac{n}{2}} = 2^{\Omega(n)}$ possible subsets of S of size $\frac{n}{2}$.

Let $T \subset S$ be a set of size $\frac{n}{2}$. Consider two parties A and B who know the set S, and suppose A knows T and wishes to encode T for B. A and B agree upon a mutual source of randomness and thus, we can assume that both parties toss the same random coins. A proceeds as follows. A runs $(\mathsf{pp}, C) \leftarrow_{\$} \mathsf{OblvAcc.Setup}(1^\lambda)$. Then, A runs $(C, w_x, u, \mathsf{aux}) \leftarrow_{\$} \mathsf{OblvAcc.Add}(C, x, U)$ for each $x \in S$, followed by $(C, u) \leftarrow \mathsf{OblvAcc.Del}(C, x, U, \mathsf{aux})$ for each $x \in T$. Let C be the final accumulator string and U be the final digest of all update information. A then sends along (C, U) to B.

We now claim that B can recover T. B can run $(\mathsf{pp}, C) \leftarrow_{\$} \mathsf{OblvAcc.Setup}(1^\lambda)$ and $(C, w_x, u, \mathsf{aux}) \leftarrow_{\$} \mathsf{OblvAcc.Add}(C, x, U)$ for each $x \in S$ (using the same random coins as A). Now, using $\mathsf{OblvAcc.MemProofUpdate}$, B can compute membership proofs w_x for each $x \in S$ after the sequence of $\mathsf{OblvAcc.Adds}$. Notice that this point, all those proofs would verify. Then, using $\mathsf{OblvAcc.MemProofUpdate}$ and U, B can compute updated membership proofs for each $x \in S$ after the sequence of $\mathsf{OblvAcc.Dels}$. From the correctness and soundness of $\mathsf{OblvAcc}$, only the membership proof of $x \in S \setminus T$ will now verify. Thus, by attempting to invoke $\mathsf{OblvAcc.MemVer}$ on each w_x, B can learn if $x \in T$ or not. Thus (C, U) encodes T and hence the claim in the lemma follows. □

For an oblivious accumulator, call a sequence of operations $\{O_i\}_i$ *valid*, where each O_i is an Add or Del, if and only if no operation attempts to Del an element that does not exist, i.e., has not been added or has already been deleted.

Lemma 7. *Let* $\mathsf{OblvAcc}$ *be an oblivious accumulator and let* $\ell \in \mathbb{N}$. *Let* $\{O_i\}_{i\in[\ell]}$ *and* $\{O'_i\}_{i\in[\ell]}$ *be two valid sequences of operations for* $\mathsf{OblvAcc}$. *Consider performing the following operations:*

1. $(\mathsf{pp}, C_0) \leftarrow_{\$} \mathsf{Setup}(1^\lambda)$
2. $(C_i, (\cdot), u_i, (\cdot)) \leftarrow_{\$} O_i(C_{i-1}, \cdot, \cdot, (\cdot))$ *for* $i \in [\ell]$
3. $(C'_i, (\cdot), u'_i, (\cdot)) \leftarrow_{\$} O'_i(C'_{i-1}, \cdot, \cdot, (\cdot))$ *for* $i \in [\ell]$, *where* $C'_0 = C_0$

Then, for any PPT adversary,

$$(C_1, \ldots, C_\ell, u_1, \ldots, u_\ell) \approx_c (C'_1, \ldots, C'_\ell, u'_1, \ldots, u'_\ell)$$

that is, the sequence of accumulator strings and update information released are computationally indistinguishable.

Proof. We can prove this by induction on ℓ. For $\ell = 1$, both O_1 and O'_1 must be Adds. In this case, by the element hiding of $\mathsf{OblvAcc}$, the claim of the lemma holds. Assume the claim holds for $\ell = k$, and let us consider the case of $\ell = k+1$.

For any sequence of operations $\mathsf{O} = \{\mathsf{O}_i\}_{i\in[k+1]}$, let $\mathsf{transcript}(\mathsf{O})$ denote the sequence of accumulator strings and update information released. In particular,

$$\mathsf{transcript}(\{O_i\}_{i\in[k+1]}) = (C_1, \ldots, C_{k+1}, u_1, \ldots, u_{k+1})$$

and

$$\mathsf{transcript}(\{O'_i\}_{i\in[k+1]}) = (C'_1, \ldots, C'_{k+1}, u'_1, \ldots, u'_{k+1})$$

Let O be an Add. First, note that

$$\mathsf{transcript}(\{O_i\}_{i\in[k+1]}) \approx_c \mathsf{transcript}(\{O_i\}_{i\in[k]} \cup \{O\})$$

This follows from just element hiding if O_{k+1} were an Add, and from Add-Del unlinkability and indistinguishability if O_{k+1} were a Del. Next, note that there is a function $f_{O,\mathsf{pp}}$ such that

$$\mathsf{transcript}(\{O_i\}_{i\in[k]} \cup \{O\}) \leftarrow_\$ f_{O,\mathsf{pp}}(\mathsf{transcript}(\{O_i\}_{i\in[k]}))$$

By our inductive hypothesis,

$$\mathsf{transcript}(\{O_i\}_{i\in[k]}) \approx_c \mathsf{transcript}(\{O'_i\}_{i\in[k]})$$

Therefore,

$$\mathsf{transcript}(\{O_i\}_{i\in[k]} \cup \{O\}) \approx_c \mathsf{transcript}(\{O'_i\}_{i\in[k]} \cup \{O\})$$

as

$$\mathsf{transcript}(\{O'_i\}_{i\in[k]} \cup \{O\}) \leftarrow_\$ f_{O,\mathsf{pp}}(\mathsf{transcript}(\{O'_i\}_{i\in[k]}))$$

Finally, note that

$$\mathsf{transcript}(\{O'_i\}_{i\in[k+1]}) \approx_c \mathsf{transcript}(\{O'_i\}_{i\in[k]} \cup \{O\})$$

which follows as before from just element hiding if O'_{k+1} were an Add, and from Add-Del unlinkability and indistinguishability if O'_{k+1} were a Del. This completes the proof of the lemma. □

Theorem 4. *Let* $\mathsf{OblvAcc}$ *be an oblivious accumulator. Let* $\{O_i\}_{i\in[n]}$ *be a valid sequence of operations for* $\mathsf{OblvAcc}$. *Consider performing the following sequence of operations in order:*

1. $(\mathsf{pp}, C_0) \leftarrow_\$ \mathsf{Setup}(1^\lambda)$
2. $(C_i, (\cdot), u_i, (\cdot)) \leftarrow_\$ O_i(C_{i-1}, \cdot, \cdot, (\cdot))$ *for* $i \in [n]$

Let C *be the accumulator string and* U *be the digest of all update information produced at the end of all the operations. Then,*

$$|C| + |U| = \Omega(n)$$

Proof. We combine Lemmas 6 and 7. We know from Lemma 6 that there is a sequence of valid operations for which the claim in this lemma is true. We claim that from Lemma 7, this claim is true for all sequences of valid operations. This follows because both (C, U) is some function of the $\mathsf{transcript}$ of a sequence of operations (as defined in Lemma 7), and since the $\mathsf{transcripts}$ are indistinguishable from Lemma 7, $|C| + |U|$ must be as well. □

6.2 Oblivious Accumulators Without Add-Del Indistinguishability

For an oblivious accumulator, define the $\mathsf{optrace}$ of a sequence of operations $\{O_i\}_i$ to be the sequence of operation types of each operation O_i as either an Add or a Del.

Lemma 8. *Let* $\mathsf{OblvAcc}$ *be an oblivious accumulator without* $\mathsf{Add\text{-}Del}$ *indistinguishability and let* $\ell \in \mathbb{N}$. *Let* $\{O_i\}_{i\in[\ell]}$ *and* $\{O'_i\}_{i\in[\ell]}$ *be two valid sequences of operations for* $\mathsf{OblvAcc}$ *with the same* $\mathsf{optrace}$. *Consider performing the following operations:*

1. $(\mathsf{pp}, C_0) \leftarrow_\$ \mathsf{Setup}(1^\lambda)$
2. $(C_i, (\cdot), u_i, (\cdot)) \leftarrow_\$ O_i(C_{i-1}, \cdot, \cdot, (\cdot))$ *for* $i \in [\ell]$
3. $(C'_i, (\cdot), u'_i, (\cdot)) \leftarrow_\$ O'_i(C'_{i-1}, \cdot, \cdot, (\cdot))$ *for* $i \in [\ell]$, *where* $C'_0 = C_0$

Then, for any PPT adversary,

$$(C_1, \ldots, C_\ell, u_1, \ldots, u_\ell) \approx_c (C'_1, \ldots, C'_\ell, u'_1, \ldots, u'_\ell)$$

that is, the sequence of accumulator strings and update information released are computationally indistinguishable.

Proof. The proof of this lemma is similar to the proof of Lemma 7, we defer it to our supplementary material.

For an oblivious accumulator, define the $\mathsf{delspace}$ of a sequence of operations $\{O_i\}_i$ as follows:

– For each i such that O_i is a Del, define

$$\mathsf{delspace}(O_i) = i - 1 - 2 \cdot |\{j < i : O_j \text{ is a } \mathsf{Del}\}|$$

– Define

$$\mathsf{delspace}(\{O_i\}_i) = \prod_{i:O_i \text{ is a } \mathsf{Del}} \mathsf{delspace}(O_i)$$

Based on the above definition and Lemma 8, we can prove the following theorem, just as we did Theorem 4.

Theorem 5. *Let* $\mathsf{OblvAcc}$ *be an oblivious accumulator without* $\mathsf{Add\text{-}Del}$ *indistinguishability. Let* $\{O_i\}_{i\in[n]}$ *be a valid sequence of operations for* $\mathsf{OblvAcc}$. *Consider performing the following sequence of operations in order:*

1. $(\mathsf{pp}, C_0) \leftarrow_\$ \mathsf{Setup}(1^\lambda)$
2. $(C_i, (\cdot), u_i, (\cdot)) \leftarrow_\$ O_i(C_{i-1}, \cdot, \cdot, (\cdot))$ *for* $i \in [n]$

Let C *be the accumulator string and* U *be the digest of all update information produced at the end of all the operations. Then,*

$$|C| + |U| = \Omega(\log \mathsf{delspace}(\{O_i\}_{i\in[n]}))$$

References

1. Acar, T., Nguyen, L.: Revocation for delegatable anonymous credentials. In: Catalano, D., Fazio, N., Gennaro, R., Nicolosi, A. (eds.) PKC 2011. LNCS, vol. 6571, pp. 423–440. Springer, Heidelberg (2011). https://doi.org/10.1007/978-3-642-19379-8_26
2. Agrawal, S., Raghuraman, S.: KVaC: key-value commitments for blockchains and beyond. In: Moriai, S., Wang, H. (eds.) ASIACRYPT 2020. LNCS, vol. 12493, pp. 839–869. Springer, Cham (2020). https://doi.org/10.1007/978-3-030-64840-4_28
3. Au, M.H., Tsang, P.P., Susilo, W., Mu, Y.: Dynamic universal accumulators for DDH groups and their application to attribute-based anonymous credential systems. In: Fischlin, M. (ed.) CT-RSA 2009. LNCS, vol. 5473, pp. 295–308. Springer, Heidelberg (2009). https://doi.org/10.1007/978-3-642-00862-7_20
4. Au, M.H., Tsang, P.P., Susilo, W., Mu, Y.: Dynamic universal accumulators for DDH groups and their application to attribute-based anonymous credential systems. In: Fischlin, M. (ed.) Topics in Cryptology - CT-RSA 2009, pp. 295–308. Springer, Berlin Heidelberg, Berlin, Heidelberg (2009). https://doi.org/10.1007/978-3-642-00862-7_20
5. Baldimtsi, F., et al.: Accumulators with applications to anonymity-preserving revocation. In: 2017 IEEE European Symposium on Security and Privacy (EuroS&P), pp. 301–315. IEEE (2017)
6. Barić, N., Pfitzmann, B.: Collision-free accumulators and fail-stop signature schemes without trees. In: Fumy, W. (ed.) EUROCRYPT 1997. LNCS, vol. 1233, pp. 480–494. Springer, Heidelberg (1997). https://doi.org/10.1007/3-540-69053-0_33
7. Benaloh, J., de Mare, M.: One-Way accumulators: a decentralized alternative to digital signatures. In: Helleseth, T. (ed.) Advances in Cryptology – EUROCRYPT '93, pp. 274–285. Springer, Berlin Heidelberg (1993). https://doi.org/10.1007/3-540-48285-7_24
8. Benarroch, D., Campanelli, M., Fiore, D., Gurkan, K., Kolonelos, D.: Zero-knowledge proofs for set membership: efficient, succinct, modular. In: International Conference on Financial Cryptography and Data Security, pp. 393–414. Springer (2021). https://doi.org/10.1007/s10623-023-01245-1
9. Boneh, D., Bünz, B., Fisch, B.: Batching techniques for accumulators with applications to IOPs and stateless blockchains. In: Boldyreva, A., Micciancio, D. (eds.) Advances in Cryptology - CRYPTO 2019, pp. 561–586. Springer, Cham (2019). https://doi.org/10.1007/978-3-030-26948-7_20
10. Camacho, P., Hevia, A.: On the impossibility of batch update for cryptographic accumulators. In: Progress in Cryptology–LATINCRYPT 2010: First International Conference on Cryptology and Information Security in Latin America, Puebla, Mexico, August 8-11, 2010, Proceedings 1, pp. 178–188. Springer (2010). https://doi.org/10.1007/978-3-642-14712-8_11
11. Camenisch, J., Kohlweiss, M., Soriente, C.: An accumulator based on bilinear maps and efficient revocation for anonymous credentials. In: Jarecki, S., Tsudik, G. (eds.) Public Key Cryptography - PKC 2009, pp. 481–500. Springer, Berlin, Heidelberg (2009). https://doi.org/10.1007/978-3-642-00468-1_27
12. Camenisch, J., Lysyanskaya, A.: Dynamic accumulators and application to efficient revocation of anonymous credentials. In: Yung, M. (ed.) Advances in Cryptology – CRYPTO 2002, pp. 61–76. Springer, Berlin, Heidelberg (2002). https://doi.org/10.1007/3-540-45708-9_5

13. Camenisch, J., Stadler, M.: Efficient group signature schemes for large groups. In: CRYPTO (1997)
14. Campanelli, M., Fiore, D., Han, S., Kim, J., Kolonelos, D., Oh, H.: Succinct zero-knowledge batch proofs for set accumulators. In: Proceedings of the 2022 ACM SIGSAC Conference on Computer and Communications Security, pp. 455–469 (2022)
15. de Castro, L., Peikert, C.: Functional commitments for all functions, with transparent setup and from sis. In: Annual International Conference on the Theory and Applications of Cryptographic Techniques. pp. 287–320. Springer, Cham (2023). https://doi.org/10.1007/978-3-031-30620-4_10
16. Catalano, D., Fiore, D.: Vector commitments and their applications. In: Kurosawa, K., Hanaoka, G. (eds.) PKC 2013. LNCS, vol. 7778, pp. 55–72. Springer, Heidelberg (2013). https://doi.org/10.1007/978-3-642-36362-7_5
17. Chen, B., et al.: Rotatable zero knowledge sets - post compromise secure auditable dictionaries with application to key transparency. In: Agrawal, S., Lin, D. (eds.) Advances in Cryptology - ASIACRYPT 2022 - 28th International Conference on the Theory and Application of Cryptology and Information Security, Taipei, Taiwan, December 5-9, 2022, Proceedings, Part III. Lecture Notes in Computer Science, vol. 13793, pp. 547–580. Springer (2022)
18. Chepurnoy, A., Papamanthou, C., Srinivasan, S., Zhang, Y.: EDRAX: a Cryptocurrency with Stateless Transaction Validation. Cryptology ePrint Archive, Report 2018/968 (2018)
19. Christ, M., Bonneau, J.: Limits on revocable proof systems, with applications to stateless blockchains. Cryptology ePrint Archive (2022)
20. Damgård, I., Triandopoulos, N.: Supporting non-membership proofs with bilinear-map accumulators. Cryptology ePrint Archive, Report 2008/538 (2008)
21. Dodis, Y., Kiayias, A., Nicolosi, A., Shoup, V.: Anonymous identification in ad hoc groups. In: Eurocrypt (2004)
22. Fiore, D., Kolonelos, D., de Perthuis, P.: Cuckoo commitments: registration-based encryption and key-value map commitments for large spaces. Cryptology ePrint Archive (2023)
23. Ghosh, E., Ohrimenko, O., Papadopoulos, D., Tamassia, R., Triandopoulos, N.: Zero-knowledge accumulators and set algebra. In: Asiacrypt (2016)
24. Jarecki, S., Kiayias, A., Krawczyk, H.: Round-optimal password-protected secret sharing and T-PAKE in the password-only model. In: Sarkar, P., Iwata, T. (eds.) ASIACRYPT 2014. LNCS, vol. 8874, pp. 233–253. Springer, Heidelberg (2014). https://doi.org/10.1007/978-3-662-45608-8_13
25. Karantaidou, I., Baldimtsi, F.: Efficient constructions of pairing based accumulators. In: 2021 IEEE 34th Computer Security Foundations Symposium (CSF), pp. 1–16. IEEE (2021)
26. Leung, D., Gilad, Y., Gorbunov, S., Reyzin, L., Zeldovich, N.: Aardvark: an asynchronous authenticated dictionary with applications to account-based cryptocurrencies. In: 31st USENIX Security Symposium (USENIX Security 22), pp. 4237–4254 (2022)
27. Li, J., Li, N., Xue, R.: Universal accumulators with efficient nonmembership proofs. In: Katz, J., Yung, M. (eds.) Applied Cryptography and Network Security, pp. 253–269. Springer, Berlin, Heidelberg (2007). https://doi.org/10.1007/978-3-540-72738-5_17
28. Libert, B., Ling, S., Nguyen, K., Wang, H.: Zero-knowledge arguments for lattice-based accumulators: logarithmic-size ring signatures and group signatures without trapdoors. In: Eurocrypt (2016)

29. Miers, I., Garman, C., Green, M., Rubin, A.D.: Zerocoin: anonymous distributed E-Cash from bitcoin. In: 2013 IEEE Symposium on Security and Privacy, pp. 397–411 (2013)
30. Nguyen, L.: Accumulators from bilinear pairings and applications. In: Menezes, A. (ed.) Topics in Cryptology - CT-RSA 2005, pp. 275–292. Springer, Berlin, Heidelberg (2005). https://doi.org/10.1007/978-3-540-30574-3_19
31. Nguyen, L., Safavi-Naini, R.: Efficient and provably secure trapdoor-free group signature schemes from bilinear pairings. In: Asiacrypt (2004)
32. Srinivasan, S., Karantaidou, I., Baldimtsi, F., Papamanthou, C.: Batching, aggregation, and zero-knowledge proofs in bilinear accumulators. In: Proceedings of the 2022 ACM SIGSAC Conference on Computer and Communications Security, pp. 2719–2733 (2022)
33. Sun, S.F., Au, M.H., Liu, J.K., Yuen, T.H.: RingCT 2.0: a compact accumulator-based (linkable ring signature) protocol for blockchain cryptocurrency Monero. In: ESORICS (2017)
34. Tomescu, A., Bhupatiraju, V., Papadopoulos, D., Papamanthou, C., Triandopoulos, N., Devadas, S.: Transparency logs via append-only authenticated dictionaries. In: Proceedings of the 2019 ACM SIGSAC Conference on Computer and Communications Security, pp. 1299–1316 (2019)
35. Tomescu, A., Xia, Y., Newman, Z.: Authenticated dictionaries with cross-incremental proof (dis) aggregation. Cryptology ePrint Archive (2020)
36. Tyagi, N., Fisch, B., Zitek, A., Bonneau, J., Tessaro, S.: VeRSA: verifiable registries with efficient client audits from RSA authenticated dictionaries. In: Proceedings of the 2022 ACM SIGSAC Conference on Computer and Communications Security, pp. 2793–2807 (2022)
37. Zhang, Y., Katz, J., Papamanthou, C.: An expressive (Zero-Knowledge) set accumulator. In: 2017 IEEE European Symposium on Security and Privacy (EuroS P), pp. 158–173 (2017)

Witness Encryption for Succinct Functional Commitments and Applications

Matteo Campanelli[1], Dario Fiore[2], and Hamidreza Khoshakhlagh[3](✉)

[1] Protocol Labs, San Francisco, USA
matteo@protocol.ai
[2] IMDEA Software Institute, Madrid, Spain
dario.fiore@imdea.org
[3] Concordium, Aarhus, Denmark
hk@concordium.com

Abstract. Witness encryption (WE), introduced by Garg, Gentry, Sahai, and Waters (STOC 2013) allows one to encrypt a message to a statement x for some NP language $\mathcal{L}$, such that any user holding a witness for $\mathsf{x} \in \mathcal{L}$ can decrypt the ciphertext. The extreme power of this primitive comes at the cost of its elusiveness: a *practical* construction from established cryptographic assumptions is currently out of reach.

In this work, we investigate a new notion of encryption that has a flavor of WE and that we can build only based on bilinear pairings, for interesting classes of computation. We do this by connecting witness encryption to functional commitments (FC). FCs are an advanced notion of commitments that allows fine-grained openings, that is non-interactive proofs to show that a commitment cm opens to v such that $y = G(v)$, with the crucial feature that both commitments and openings are succinct.

Our new WE notion, *witness encryption for (succinct) functional commitment* (WE-FC), allows one to encrypt a message with respect to a triple (cm, G, y), and decryption is unlocked using an FC opening that cm opens to v such that $y = G(v)$. This mechanism is similar to the notion of witness encryption for NIZK of commitments [Benhamouda and Lin, TCC'20], with the crucial difference that ours supports commitments and decryption time whose size and complexity do not depend on the length of the committed data v.

Our main contributions are therefore the formal definition of WE-FC, a generic methodology to compile an FC in bilinear groups into an associated WE-FC scheme (semantically secure in the generic group model), and a new FC construction for NC^1 circuits that yields a WE-FC for the same class of functions. Similarly to [Benhamouda and Lin, TCC'20], we show how to apply WE-FC to construct multiparty reusable non-interactive secure computation (mrNISC) protocols. Crucially, the efficiency profile of WE-FC yields mrNISC protocols whose offline stage has shorter communication (only a succinct commitment from each party).

Work done in part while the author was affiliated to Aarhus University.

Q. Tang and V. Teague (Eds.): PKC 2024, LNCS 14602, pp. 132–167, 2024.
https://doi.org/10.1007/978-3-031-57722-2_5

As an additional contribution, we discuss further applications of WE-FC and show how to extend this primitive to better suit these settings.

Keywords: Witness encryption · Functional commitments · Secure multiparty computation · Smooth projective hash functions

1 Introduction

Witness Encryption (WE) [29] is an encryption paradigm that allows one to encrypt a message under a hard problem—a statement x of an NP language $\mathcal{L}$—so that anyone knowing a solution to this problem—a witness w such that $(\mathsf{x}, \mathsf{w}) \in \mathcal{R}_{\mathcal{L}}$—can decrypt the ciphertext in an efficient manner. Witness encryption generalizes the classical notion of public-key encryption, where a user can encrypt a message m to any user who knows the (secret) decryption key $\mathsf{w} = \mathsf{sk}$ associated to some (public) encryption key $\mathsf{x} = \mathsf{pk}$.

A general-purpose WE, one for all NP, is a powerful tool: it can be used to construct several cryptographic primitives [11,24,51,52]. Yet, currently, all its general-purpose constructions rely on powerful and/or inefficient primitives, e.g., multilinear maps [29,31] or indistinguishability obfuscation (iO) [28]. An interesting question is whether the full power of WE is always needed. Perhaps some of the applications of WE can be obtained through primitives that are both more efficient and require weaker assumptions.

Some of the recent literature has indeed confirmed this intuition. A relevant work addressing this is that of Benhamouda and Lin [9] who apply the round-collapsing techniques of [34] to construct *multi-party reusable non-interactive secure computation* (or mrNISC), a type of MPC that requires no interaction among subsets of users, provided that users had earlier committed to their input on a public bulletin board (this offline stage is called "input encoding stage"). While work prior to [9] required full-blown WE to obtain this result, Benhamouda and Lin show its feasibility under a different type of WE called "WE for NIZK of commitments" ($\mathrm{WE}^{\text{ZK-CM}}$ for short). In $\mathrm{WE}^{\text{ZK-CM}}$, the encryption statement is (cm, G, y), and decryption requires as the witness a non-interactive zero-knowledge (NIZK) proof π proving that the evaluation of G on the value v committed in cm outputs y, i.e., "$\mathsf{cm} = \mathsf{Commit}(v)$ and $y = G(v)$". The interesting aspect of this weakening of WE is that [9] constructs $\mathrm{WE}^{\text{ZK-CM}}$ from well established assumptions over bilinear groups.

On the other hand, in [9], both the commitment and the proof size—and hence decryption time—grow linearly in the size of v. The latter represents a piece of potentially *large* data and whose commitment is *publicly shared* at an earlier time. We refer concisely to a construction not having this dependency in efficiency as having "input-independent (decryptor's) complexity". A scheme with input-independent complexity would be interesting to further minimize the communication complexity of applications of this type of WE. This can be relevant, for example, in the input encoding phase of mrNISC (as well as in other applications, see Sect. 7): commitments are stored on a bulletin board (e.g., a blockchain) forever and thus their size significantly affects its growth over time.

1.1 Our Work: WE for Succinct Functional Commitments

The work from [9] is encouraging: we may be able to use more familiar assumptions to obtain useful variants of witness encryption. Our work is motivated by pushing this avenue further, both practically and theoretically. We ask:

What are other weak-but-useful variants of WE that remain "as simple as possible" in terms of assumptions to build them and that can achieve input-independent complexity?

In this work, we address this question by generalizing $\mathrm{WE}^{\text{ZK-CM}}$, the primitive in [9], to support *succinct commitments with succinct arguments.* That is, where commitments are of fixed size—independent of the input's length—and so are the arguments about the correctness of computations on the committed inputs. We call our notion *"WE for functional commitments"* ($\mathrm{WE}^{\mathrm{FC}}$), as we define it on top of the notion of *functional commitments* [48].

Our main contributions are therefore to formally define the $\mathrm{WE}^{\mathrm{FC}}$ primitive, to propose a generic methodology to construct $\mathrm{WE}^{\mathrm{FC}}$ over bilinear groups, and to show applications of $\mathrm{WE}^{\mathrm{FC}}$ to mrNISC (with succinct offline phase) and to more scenarios. In the following section we discuss our contributions in detail.

1.2 Our Contributions

Defining $\mathrm{WE}^{\mathrm{FC}}$. We introduce and formally define the notion of witness encryption for functional commitments ($\mathrm{WE}^{\mathrm{FC}}$). A functional commitment (FC) allows a party to commit to a value v and to later open the commitment to $y = G(v)$ for some functions G, by generating an opening proof π. In terms of security, an FC should be *evaluation binding* and *hiding.* The former means that an adversary cannot open the commitment to two distinct outputs $y \neq y'$ for the same function G, while the latter is the standard hiding property of commitments. In addition, in our work we require FC to be *zero-knowledge*, which informally states that the opening proof π should not reveal any information about the committed value v. What makes FCs suitable to our scenario is that both the commitment and the opening proofs are succinct (in particular, throughout this work we always use the term 'functional commitments' to mean succinct ones). Similarly to the $\mathrm{WE}^{\text{ZK-CM}}$ of [9], in our $\mathrm{WE}^{\mathrm{FC}}$ one encrypts with respect to a triple (cm, G, y) and decryption is unlocked when using an opening proof of cm to $y = G(v)$.

Construction and Techniques. We present several realizations of $\mathrm{WE}^{\mathrm{FC}}$ based on bilinear pairings and secure in the generic group model. Our approach consists in a generic methodology that combines any functional commitment whose verification is a "linear" pairing equation (here by linear, we mean that it is linear in the group elements of the opening proof), together with a suitable variant of smooth projective hash functions (SPHFs, [22]), that we define in our work. To realize this approach, *we develop three main technical contributions* (and we refer to our technical overview in Sect. 1.3 for further details).

The first one is *finding a useful variant of projective hash function for our purposes.* While our approach follows the blueprint of [9] (i.e., combining a proof system with an SPHF for its verification language), we had to solve substantial challenges due to our shift from the "soundness against any adversary" of NIZKs to the "computational binding" of functional commitments. The $\mathsf{WE}^{\mathsf{ZK\text{-}CM}}$ construction of [9] crucially relies on statistically binding commitments and statistically sound NIZKs—we cannot. We solve this issue by using a different building block. We introduce a new notion, *extractable* PHFs (EPHF), in which every adversary that successfully computes the hash value for a statement must know the corresponding witness. We then propose a construction of this primitive in the generic group model.[1]

The second technical contribution is the generic construction of $\mathsf{WE}^{\mathsf{FC}}$ that combines an FC and an EPHF for its verification language. Notably, it turns out that we cannot encrypt following the same approach of [9] based on SPHF. For wrong statements, the EPHF values are only computationally hard to compute, hence we cannot use them as a mask for the message. We solve this issue via a *different methodology for building WE from* *<u>extractable</u>* *projective hash functions.* Instantiated with our EPHF construction, we obtain a $\mathsf{WE}^{\mathsf{FC}}$ in the generic group model.

Finally, our third technical contribution is the realization of a new FC scheme that supports the evaluation of circuits in the class NC^1 and that enjoys the linear verification requirement needed by our generic construction. Among prior work on FCs, only the schemes of [48,50] have the linear verification property. However, the class of functions supported by these schemes is insufficient to instantiate the mrNISC protocols, which need at least the support of circuits in NC^1. On the other hand, all the recent pairing-based constructions for NC^1 in [17] and general circuits in [5] have quadratic verification.

A Construction of mrNISC from $\mathbf{WE^{FC}}$. We show how our $\mathsf{WE}^{\mathsf{FC}}$ notion can be used to build mrNISC. The latter is a class of secure multiparty computation protocols in which parties work with minimal interaction. In a first round, each party posts an encoding of its inputs in a public bulletin board. This is done once and for all. Next, any subset of parties can compute a function of their private inputs by sending only one message each. This second phase can be repeated many times for different computations and different subsets of parties. Our construction for mrNISC confirms that our notion is not losing expressivity compared to $\mathsf{WE}^{\mathsf{ZK\text{-}CM}}$ from [9] and, thanks to our new FC, yields the first mrNISC protocols with a succinct input encoding phase.

Other Applications of $\mathbf{WE^{FC}}$. We provide additional applications beyond mrNISC where $\mathsf{WE}^{\mathsf{FC}}$ can be useful. As a first application, we show how $\mathsf{WE}^{\mathsf{FC}}$

[1] See Remark 2 for a discussion on the idealized models used in our realizations.

can be used for a simple construction of a variant of *targeted broadcast.* In targeted broadcast [36] we want a certain message to be conveyed only to authorized parties. An authorized party is one holding attributes satisfying a certain property (specified at encryption time). As an example, a streaming service may want to broadcast an encryption of a movie so that only users having purchased certain packages would be able to decrypt (and watch) it. There exist ways to build this primitive non-naively while satisfying basic desiderata of the application domain[2], for example through ciphertext-policy ABE [36]. We show how we can achieve targeted broadcast in a new (and simple) manner through $\mathsf{WE}^{\mathsf{FC}}$. We observe that our construction achieves some interesting properties absent in previous approaches: it achieves *flexible and secret attestation* and *without any master secret.* This means that decryption attributes may be granted to a user through different methods, that the latter can be kept secret and that there is no single party holding a key that can decrypt all messages in the system. We provide further details and motivation in Sect. 7.

As a second application, we show how, through $\mathsf{WE}^{\mathsf{FC}}$, we can achieve simple and non-interactive *contingent payment for services* [15] ("contingent payment" for short[3]). In a contingent payment a *payer* wants to provide a reward/payment to another user conditional to the user having performed a certain service. For example, a user may want to pay a cloud service conditionally to them storing their data. Ideally this protocol should require no interaction. We describe a simple way to instantiate the above through $\mathsf{WE}^{\mathsf{FC}}$. Our solution can be used, for example, to incentivize, in a fine-grained manner, portions of large committed data (for instance incentivizing storage of specific pages of Wikipedia or the Internet Archive of particular importance on IPFS[4]) [1]. Compared to other approaches [15], our solution is simple (e.g., does not require a blockchain with special properties or smart contracts) and is highly communication efficient. To achieve this solution we need to solve additional technical challenges: modeling and building an extractable variant of $\mathsf{WE}^{\mathsf{FC}}$. We provide further details in Sect. 7.

1.3 Technical Overview

We start with an overview of the techniques in [9]. Their notion of witness encryption called "WE for NIZK of Commitments" ($\mathsf{WE}^{\mathsf{ZK\text{-}CM}}$) is defined for an NP language whose statements are of the form $\mathsf{x} = (\mathsf{cm}, G, y)$ such that cm is a commitment, G is an arbitrary polynomial-size circuit, and y is a value (additionally, this language is parametrized by the common reference string, or crs, of the NIZK). The type of commitment assumed in [9] is perfectly binding;

[2] For example, sometimes a desideratum in such systems is that the broadcaster should not have to refer to a database of user authorizations each time a different item is to be encrypted for broadcast.

[3] Notice that "contingent payment" can also refer to payment for *goods*, rather than *services*. In this paper we only refer to payment for services.

[4] http://wikipedia.org, http://archive.org, http://ipfs.io.

therefore, a statement (cm, G, y) is true if there exists a NIZK proof π (as a witness) which proves w.r.t. crs that G evaluates to y on the value v committed in cm.

The definition of $\mathrm{WE}^{\mathrm{ZK\text{-}CM}}$ states that semantic security property should hold for ciphertexts created with respect to false claims (that is, commitments whose opening v is such that $G(v) \neq y$). To achieve this property, the idea in [9] relies on applying smooth projective hash functions on the verification algorithm of the NIZK. For the sake of this high-level overview, the reader can think of an SPHF as a form of WE itself and which we know how to realize for simple languages. The crux of the construction in [9] is that, if the NIZK verification algorithm is "simple enough", then we can leverage it to build $\mathrm{WE}^{\mathrm{ZK\text{-}CM}}$. In more detail, let $\boldsymbol{\Theta} = \mathbf{M}\pi$ be the linear equation corresponding to the verification of a NIZK for a statement $\mathsf{x} = (\mathsf{cm}, G, y)$, such that $\boldsymbol{\Theta}$ and $\mathbf{M}$ depend on x and crs, and hence are known at the time of encryption. To encrypt a message, one can use an SPHF for this relation such that only those who can compute the hash value using a valid witness π (i.e., π such that $\boldsymbol{\Theta} = \mathbf{M}\pi$) can retrieve the message. The work in [9] instantiates the above paradigm through Groth-Sahai NIZKs, which can be reduced to a linear verification for committed inputs (this is true for only a restricted class of computations which then [9] shows how to extend to all of P through randomized encodings). The commitments they rely on are statistically binding and thus not compressing.

Our General Construction of $\mathrm{WE}^{\mathrm{FC}}$. We now discuss how to go from this idea to our solutions. Recall that our goal is to have a type of witness encryption that works on succinct functional commitments. This implies that both the commitments and opening proofs for functional evaluation on them are compressing. This efficiency requirement is the main point of divergence between $\mathrm{WE}^{\mathrm{FC}}$ and $\mathrm{WE}^{\mathrm{ZK\text{-}CM}}$.

Moving from [9] to our approach is not unproblematic. In [9], in order to *(i)* effectively reduce the original relation ($G(v) = y$ for a correct opening v) to the verification of the NIZK, and *(ii)* to maintain semantic security at the same time—in order to simultaneously achieve these two points—it is crucial that the NIZK proof has unconditional soundness and that the underlying commitments are perfectly binding[5]. At a very high level, the switch from [9] to our work consists of the switch from a NIZK *proof* system [38], with *linear proof size*, to a *succinct certificate*, a succinct functional commitment. Simple as it may sound, however, this switch is not immediate and requires solving several new challenges on the way.

The main challenge arises when using arguments (as opposed to proofs) as witness in the witness encryption scheme. Recall that $\mathrm{WE}^{\mathrm{ZK\text{-}CM}}$ constructs WE

[5] Unconditional soundness of a proof system means: "for a false statement, *no* proof string will have a substantial probability of being accepted as valid". This is in contrast to the computational soundness of our building blocks: "for a false statement, no PPT adversary can produce a proof string with substantial probability of being accepted". The latter does not state that such proof string does not exist. .

for the augmented relation $\mathcal{R}$ corresponding to the verification algorithm of the NIZK proof and, as mentioned above, switching to $\mathcal{R}$ still preserves semantic security. However, the same idea does not work when using an argument system. This is because semantic security only guarantees security when the statement, under which the challenge ciphertext is generated, is *false*. Defining $\mathcal{R}$ as the relation specified by the verification of an argument system makes all statements potentially *true*. Hence, even though finding a witness (i.e., an argument) is computationally hard, semantic security holds vacuously and makes no guarantee about the encrypted message.

To solve this challenge, we observe that even though the relation is trivial here, finding the witness for a statement yields a contradiction to security properties of the commitment in use. To elaborate further, we note that the WE is constructed for the NP language corresponding to the verification algorithm of a functional commitment. Now, given a "false" statement $\bar{\mathsf{x}} = (\mathsf{cm}, G, y)$, where $G(v) \neq y$ for v committed in cm and chosen by the adversary, our construction is such that for any efficient adversary that distinguishes ciphertexts encrypted under the statement x corresponding to the verification circuit which (incorrectly) asserts the truth of $\bar{\mathsf{x}}$, there exists an efficient adversary that breaks the evaluation-binding property of the functional commitment by computing a valid opening proof op that satisfies the FC verification.

To build the above reduction, we make use of the Goldreich-Levin technique [33] by which we can transform a ciphertext distinguisher into an efficient algorithm that computes the hash value H (from a hash proof system) used as a *one-time pad* to mask the message. While this part of the reduction may seem straightforward, one challenge is how to compute a valid opening proof op from H. To this end, we observe that the underlying SPHF is for the same language $\mathcal{L}$ that we build our WE and thus op plays the role of the witness for x by which one can compute H. Thus, it seems like we would need a type of SPHF with a strong notion of *extractable* security. Namely, a type of projective hash function (PHF) that guarantees the existence of an extractor such that for any adversary that is able to compute a valid hash, the extractor can compute a witness for the corresponding problem statement[6].

Unfortunately, there exists no construction of extractable PHF in literature, even based on non-standard assumptions. The closest work is that of Wee [53] which suggests a similar notion but only for some relations not in NP that correspond to search problems. Therefore, we propose a new construction of extractable PHF and prove it secure under the discrete logarithm assumption in the algebraic group model.

---

[6] At the high-level SPHFs are also used as the main leveraging point in [9], but with one important difference (we skip some details for simplicity): their construction produces a hash through a standard SPHF, where security is only guaranteed *statistically* for false statements. Because of our switch from (statistically secure) NIZKs to succinct functional commitment, we cannot rely on the latter.

Our FC for NC1 with Linear Verification. To build an FC supporting the evaluation of circuits in the class NC^1, we build an FC for the language of (read-once) monotone span programs (MSP) [42], and then use standard transformations to turn it into one for NC^1. We construct our scheme by adapting the FC for MSP recently proposed by Catalano, Fiore and Tucker [17]. In particular, while the scheme of [17] has a quadratic verification (i.e., it needs to pair group elements in the opening between themselves), we give a variant of their technique with linear verification.

We begin by recalling that a read-once MSP is defined by a matrix $\mathbf{M}$ and

$$\mathbf{M}\text{accepts}\boldsymbol{x} \in \{0,1\}^n\text{iff}\exists \boldsymbol{w} : (\boldsymbol{x} \circ \boldsymbol{w}) \cdot \mathbf{M} = \boldsymbol{e}_1^\top = (1, 0, \ldots, 0) \quad (1)$$

where $\circ$ refers to entry-wise multiplication. In an FC for MSP, the commitment contains $\boldsymbol{x}$ and the opening to an MSP $\mathbf{M}$ should prove the existence of $\boldsymbol{w}$ that satisfies equation (1). To achieve this, the basic idea of [17] is to "linearize" the quadratic part of Eq. 1, so as to reduce the problem to that of proving satisfiability of a linear system and thus apply the techniques of Lai and Malavolta for linear map functional commitments [45]. In [17], this linearization is done by defining the matrix $\mathbf{M}_{\boldsymbol{x}} = (\boldsymbol{x}||\cdots||\boldsymbol{x}) \circ \mathbf{M}$, i.e., the matrix where each column of $\mathbf{M}$ is multiplied entry-wise with $\boldsymbol{x}$, so that proving equation (1) boils down to proving the satisfiability of the linear system $\exists \boldsymbol{w} : \mathbf{M}_{\mathbf{x}}^\top \cdot \boldsymbol{w} = \boldsymbol{e}_1$. However, the verifier only knows $\mathbf{M}$ and not $\boldsymbol{x}$. Thus [17] includes in the opening an element $\varPhi_{\boldsymbol{x}} \in \mathbb{G}_2$ which is a succinct encoding of $\mathbf{M}_{\boldsymbol{x}}$, and then they use a variant of [45]: they include a commitment $\pi_w \in \mathbb{G}_1$ to the witness $\boldsymbol{w}$ and a proof $\hat{\pi} \in \mathbb{G}_1$. The verifier in [17] needs to check that $\varPhi_{\boldsymbol{x}}$ is a valid encoding of $\mathbf{M}_{\boldsymbol{x}}$ w.r.t. the committed $\boldsymbol{x}$—this is done by testing $\hat{e}(\mathsf{cm}_{\boldsymbol{x}}, \varPhi) \stackrel{?}{=} \hat{e}([1]_1, \varPhi_{\boldsymbol{x}})$, where $\varPhi$ is an encoding of $\mathbf{M}$ and $\mathsf{cm}_{\boldsymbol{x}} := \sum_{j\in[n]} x_j \cdot [\rho_j]_2$ for some $[\rho_j]_2$-s part of the commitment key. Then the verifier checks the validity of the linear system by testing $\hat{e}(\pi_w, \varPhi_{\boldsymbol{x}}) \stackrel{?}{=} \hat{e}(\hat{\pi}, [1]_2) \cdot B$, for some element $B \in \mathbb{G}_T$ in the public parameters. This last equation is the issue why this scheme does not have a linear verification, that is one needs to compute the pairing $\hat{e}(\pi_w, \varPhi_{\boldsymbol{x}})$ where both inputs are part of the opening proof.

To get around this problem, we use an alternative linearization technique. In a nutshell, we include in the opening a commitment π_w to $\boldsymbol{w}$ (as in [17]) and a succinct commitment π_u of $\boldsymbol{u} = \boldsymbol{x} \otimes \boldsymbol{w}$. The verifier can test the validity of π_u by checking the linear pairing equation $\hat{e}(\pi_w, \mathsf{cm}_{\boldsymbol{x}}) \stackrel{?}{=} \hat{e}(\pi_u, [1]_2)$. Next, we propose a variant of the [45] technique to prove that, with respect to the commitment π_u, the linear system $(\mathbf{M}^\top \mid \boldsymbol{e}_1)$ is satisfied, but not by the full committed vector $\boldsymbol{u}$, but rather by the portion corresponding to the subvector $\boldsymbol{u}^* = \boldsymbol{w} \circ \boldsymbol{x} \subset \boldsymbol{w} \otimes \boldsymbol{x}$. This proof is a single group element π, which can be verified by a second linear pairing equation $\hat{e}(\pi_u, \varPhi) \stackrel{?}{=} \hat{e}(\hat{\pi}, [1]_2) \cdot B$.

Other Technical Points.

Reusability. By replacing NIZK of commitments with a functional commitment as described above and then following the same approach of [9,34], we can obtain a two-round MPC protocol. However, building a mrNISC protocol is more challenging as the construction may not necessarily provide reusability. To provide this property, we need functional commitment schemes that satisfy a strong form of zero-knowledge, wherein any number of opening proofs for a given commitment can be simulated. In other words, for a commitment cm broadcasted by a party in the first round of the protocol, running computation on different statements (cm, G_i, y_i) with the same commitment cm does not reveal any information about the committed value. This should be guaranteed by the existence of an efficient simulator that can generate simulated openings for any adversarially chosen computation.

Trusted Setup and Malicious Security. We note that both existing constructions of mrNISC from bilinear pairing groups [9] or from LWE [8] are in the plain model, whereas our construction requires a trusted setup. However, for security analysis of mrNISC construction in previous works, it is assumed that the corruption by the adversary is static. Further, the security in these works is only against semi-malicious adversaries where corrupted parties follow the protocol specification, except they are allowed to select their input and randomness from arbitrary distributions. This has been justified by the fact that providing stronger notion of malicious security for MPC in two rounds in the plain model is impossible and hence one should use either a trusted setup assumption or overcome this impossibility by relying on super-polynomial time simulation (See [25] for the second approach). We thus see the use of trusted setup in our construction, in a sense, at no cost as it is crucial for achieving malicious security[7]. We point out that the setup of our FC construction is also *updatable* (any party can add randomness to it).

1.4 Related Work

The first candidate construction of witness encryption was proposed by the seminal work of Garg et al. [29] based on multilinear maps. In a line of research, several other works [28,31,35] proposed constructions from similar strong assumptions; i.e., multilinear maps as in [29], or indistinguishability obfuscation (iO). Recently, Barta et al. [6] showed a witness encryption scheme based on a coding problem called *Gap Minimum Distance Problem* (GapMDP). However, they left it as an open problem whether their version of GapMDP is NP-hard. Another recent proposal based on new unexplored algebraic structures and with conjectured security is that in [20].

A recent line of work started by [40] builds iO—which implies a WE construction—from standard assumption. Asymptotically, this approach runs in polynomial time, but it still is impractical for two reasons. First, the polynomial describing its running time has a relatively high degree. On top of that, the WE

[7] Achieving malicious security by using NIZK proofs in the trust model is a folklore technique and has been used in many classical MPC works (e.g., See Lemma 7.5 in [9]). We thus omit details on malicious security and similarly to previous works focus only on semi-malicious security.

construction would need to indirectly invoke iO, which is a plausibly stronger primitive[8]. This indirect approach results in compounded efficiency costs.

The work of [9] defines a restricted flavour of witness encryption called *WE for NIZK of commitments* wherein parties first commit to their private inputs once and for all, and then later, an encryptor can produce a ciphertext so that any party with a NIZK showing that the committed input satisfies the relation can decrypt. Their construction relies on the SXDH assumption in bilinear pairings and Groth-Sahai commitments and NIZKs. Using NIZK proofs as the decryption key provides a "delegatability" property in [9], where the holder of a witness can delegate the decryption by publishing a NIZK proof for the truth of the statement. Recently, [12] formalize a similar notion but without delegation property, and give more efficient instantiations based on two-party Multi-Sender Non-Interactive Secure Computation (MS-NISC) protocols. The recent work of [43] also defines a similar notion of *Witness Encryption with Decryptor Privacy* that provides zero-knowledge, but not delegation property. Our approach is a follow-up to the work of [9]. Finally, we note that constructions with a flavor of witness-encryption-over-commitments [9,12] are also a viable solution to the problem of encrypting to who knows the opening of a commitment, but with the caveat of commitments having to be as large as the data (which is problematic if the data is large). This is not the case in our constructions.

If we turn our attention to NIZKs and succinct commitments, one may wonder whether one can adapt the results of [9] to work with (commit-and-prove) SNARKs. Although we cannot exclude this option, we argue this may be an overkill for two reasons. First, in terms of assumptions this approach would inherently require the use of non-falsifiable assumptions due to the impossibility result of Gentry and Wichs [32]. In particular, the semantic security definition of $\mathrm{WE}^{\mathrm{ZK\text{-}CM}}$ is falsifiable and thus could in principle be realized without these strong assumptions. Second, in terms of efficiency, if we want to rely on the SPHF construction blueprint we would need a SNARK with a linear verification over bilinear groups, but such schemes are likely impossible [37].

The primitive that we propose in this work is closely tied to functional commitments, first formalized by Libert et al. [48]. The functional commitment schemes in the state of the art support a variety of functions classes, which include linear maps [45,48], sparse polynomials [50], constant-degree polynomials [4,17], and NC^1 circuits [17]. Also, very recent works [5,16,54] propose FC schemes for virtually arbitrary computations. As we mentioned earlier, our construction of $\mathrm{WE}^{\mathrm{FC}}$ relies on FCs whose verification algorithm is a "linear" pairing-based equation. This property is achieved by the FC schemes for linear maps [48] [45] and sparse polynomials [50], which means we can obtain instantiations of $\mathrm{WE}^{\mathrm{FC}}$ for these classes of functions. The recent and more expressive constructions that are based on pairings [5,17] unfortunately do not support this linear verification, as they need to pair elements of the proof. Our new FC construction does not have this limitation and supports large classes of circuits.

[8] As shown in [35,55], under the LWE assumption, WE is equivalent to a very weak form of iO, called null-iO.

2 Preliminaries

Notation. We use DPT (resp. PPT) to mean a deterministic (resp. probabilistic) polynomial time algorithm. We denote by $[n]$ the set $\{1, \ldots, n\} \subseteq \mathbb{N}$. To represent matrices and vectors, we use bold upper-case and bold lower-case letters, respectively. We denote the security parameter by $\lambda \in \mathbb{N}$. For an algorithm $\mathcal{A}$, $\mathsf{RND}(\mathcal{A})$ is the random tape of $\mathcal{A}$ (for a fixed choice of λ), and $r \leftarrow_{\$} \mathsf{RND}(\mathcal{A})$ denotes the random choice of r from $\mathsf{RND}(\mathcal{A})$. By $y \leftarrow \mathcal{A}(\mathsf{x}; r)$ we denote that $\mathcal{A}$, given an input x and a randomizer r, outputs y. By $x \leftarrow_{\$} \mathsf{D}$ we denote that x is sampled according to distribution D or uniformly randomly if D is a set. Let $\mathsf{negl}(\lambda)$ be an arbitrary negligible function.

Pairings. Bilinear groups are defined by a tuple $\mathsf{bp} = (p, \mathbb{G}_1, \mathbb{G}_2, \mathbb{G}_T, \hat{e}, g_1, g_2)$ where $\mathbb{G}_1, \mathbb{G}_2, \mathbb{G}_T$ are groups of prime order p, g_1 (resp. g_2) is a generator of $\mathbb{G}_1$ (resp. $\mathbb{G}_2$), and $\hat{e} : \mathbb{G}_1 \times \mathbb{G}_2 \rightarrow \mathbb{G}_T$ is an efficient, non-degenerate bilinear map.

For group elements, we use the bracket notation in which, for $t \in \{1, 2, T\}$ and $a \in \mathbb{Z}_p$, $[a]_t$ denotes g_t^a. We use additive notation for $\mathbb{G}_1$ and $\mathbb{G}_2$ and multiplicative one for $\mathbb{G}_T$. For $t = 1, 2$, given an element $[a]_t$ and a scalar x, one can efficiently compute $x[a]_t = [xa]_t = g_t^{xa} \in \mathbb{G}_t$; and given group elements $[a]_1 \in \mathbb{G}_1$ and $[b]_2 \in \mathbb{G}_2$, one can efficiently compute $\hat{e}([a]_1, [b]_2) = [ab]_T$. For $\boldsymbol{u}, \boldsymbol{v}$ vectors we write $\hat{e}([\boldsymbol{u}]_1^\top, [\boldsymbol{v}]_2)$ for $\prod_j \hat{e}([u_j]_1, [v_j]_2)$. The same notation naturally extends to pairings between a matrix $[\boldsymbol{M}]_1$ and vector $[\boldsymbol{v}]_2$ where we return the vector of pairing products performed between each row of the matrix and $[\boldsymbol{v}]_2$, i.e., $\hat{e}([\boldsymbol{M}]_1, [\boldsymbol{v}]_2) = [\boldsymbol{M} \cdot \boldsymbol{v}]_T$.

Algebraic (Bilinear) Group Model. In the algebraic group model (AGM) [26], one assumes that every PPT algorithm $\mathcal{A}$ is algebraic in the sense that $\mathcal{A}$ is allowed to see and use the structure of the group, but is required to also output a representation of output group elements as a linear combination of the inputs. While the definition of AGM in [26] only captures regular groups, here we require an extension that captures asymmetric pairings as well. To formalize this notion, we use the following definition that is taken from [21], but adjusted for our setting where $\mathcal{A}$ only outputs target group elements. We note that the idea of proving statements with respect to algebraic adversaries has also been explored in earlier works [2,10].

Definition 1 (Algebraic Adversaries). *Let* $\mathsf{bp} = (p, \mathbb{G}_1, \mathbb{G}_2, \mathbb{G}_T, \hat{e}, g_1, g_2)$ *be a bilinear group and* $[\mathbf{x}]_1 = ([x_1]_1, \ldots, [x_n]_1) \in \mathbb{G}_1^n$, $[\mathbf{y}]_2 = ([y_1]_2, \ldots, [y_m]_2) \in \mathbb{G}_2^m$, $[\mathbf{z}]_T = ([z_1]_T, \ldots, [z_l]_T) \in \mathbb{G}_T^l$. *An algorithm* $\mathcal{A}$ *with input* $[\mathbf{x}]_1, [\mathbf{y}]_2, [\mathbf{z}]_T$ *is called algebraic if in addition to its output*

$$\mathbf{S} = ([S_1]_T \ldots, [S_{l'}]_T) \in \mathbb{G}_T^{l'},$$

$\mathcal{A}$ *also provides a vector*

$$\mathbf{s} = \left((A_{ijk})_{i \in [l'], j \in [n], k \in [m]}, (B_{ij})_{i \in [l'], j \in [l]} \right) \in \mathbb{Z}_p^\zeta \qquad \textit{with } \zeta = l' \cdot (l + n \cdot m)$$

$$\text{suchthat } [S_i]_T = \prod_{j=1}^{n} \prod_{k=1}^{m} \hat{e}\left([x_j]_1, [y_k]_2\right)^{A_{ijk}} \cdot \prod_{j=1}^{l} [z_i]_T^{B_{ij}} \quad \textit{for } i \in \{1, \ldots, l'\}$$

2.1 Functional Commitment Schemes

We recall the notion of functional commitments (FC) [48]. Let $\mathcal{D}$ be some domain and $\mathcal{F} := \{F : \mathcal{D}^n \rightarrow \mathcal{D}^\kappa\}$ be a class of functions over $\mathcal{D}$. In a functional commitment for $\mathcal{F}$, the committer first commits to an input vector $\mathbf{x} \in \mathcal{D}^n$, obtaining commitment cm; she can later open cm to $\mathbf{y} = F(\mathbf{x}) \in \mathcal{D}^\kappa$, for $F \in \mathcal{F}$.

Definition 2 (Functional Commitments [48]**).** *For a class $\mathcal{F}$ of functions $F : \mathcal{D}^n \rightarrow \mathcal{D}^\kappa$, a functional commitment scheme* FC *consists of four polynomial-time algorithms* $(\mathsf{Setup}, \mathsf{Commit}, \mathsf{Open}, \mathsf{Verify})$ *that satisfy correctness as described below.*

Setup. $\mathsf{Setup}(1^\lambda, \mathcal{F})$ *is a probabilistic algorithm that given a security parameter $\lambda \in \mathbb{N}$, and a function class $\mathcal{F}$, outputs a commitment key* ck *and a trapdoor key* td*. For simplicity of notation, we assume that* ck *contains the description of 1^λ and $\mathcal{F}$.*

Commitment. $\mathsf{Commit}(\mathsf{ck}, \mathbf{x}; r)$ *is a probabilistic algorithm that on input a commitment key* ck*, a message $\mathbf{x} \in \mathcal{D}^n$, and randomness r, outputs* $(\mathsf{cm}, \mathsf{d})$*, where* cm *is a commitment to $\mathbf{x}$ and* d *is a decommitment information.*

Opening. $\mathsf{Open}(\mathsf{ck}, \mathsf{d}, F)$ *is a deterministic algorithm that on input* ck*, a decommitment* d*, and a function $F \in \mathcal{F}$, outputs an opening* $\mathsf{op}_\mathbf{y}$ *to $\mathbf{y} = F(\mathbf{x})$.*

Verification. $\mathsf{Verify}(\mathsf{ck}, \mathsf{cm}, \mathsf{op}_\mathbf{y}, F, \mathbf{y})$ *is a deterministic algorithm that on input* ck*, a commitment* cm*, an opening* $\mathsf{op}_\mathbf{y}$*, a function $F \in \mathcal{F}$, and $\mathbf{y} \in \mathcal{D}^\kappa$, outputs 1 if* $\mathsf{op}_\mathbf{y}$ *is a valid opening for* cm *and outputs 0 otherwise.*

Correctness. FC *is correct if for any* $(\mathsf{ck}, \mathsf{td}) \leftarrow \mathsf{Setup}(1^\lambda, \mathcal{F})$*, any $F \in \mathcal{F}$, and any vector $\mathbf{x} \in \mathcal{D}^n$, if* $(\mathsf{cm}, \mathsf{d}) \leftarrow \mathsf{Commit}(\mathsf{ck}, \mathbf{x}; r)$*, then*

$$\Pr[\mathsf{Verify}(\mathsf{ck}, \mathsf{cm}, \mathsf{Open}(\mathsf{ck}, \mathsf{d}, F), F, F(\mathbf{x})) = 1] = 1.$$

Succinctness. We say that FC is succinct if the length of commitments and openings are poly-logarithmic in $|\mathbf{x}|$.

Evaluation Binding. FCs are required to be evaluation binding, which intuitively means that a PPT adversary cannot create valid openings for incorrect results. In [48], this concept is formalized by requiring that no PPT adversary can generate a commitment and opens it to two different outputs for the same function. In our work, we only need a weaker version of this property in which the adversary reveals the committed vector and wins if it creates a valid opening for an incorrect result. In [17] this notion is called *weak evaluation binding*; we recall it below.

Definition 3 (Weak evaluation-binding [17]). *A functional commitment scheme* $\mathsf{FC} = (\mathsf{Setup}, \mathsf{Commit}, \mathsf{Open}, \mathsf{Verify})$ *for* $\mathcal{F}$ *satisfies weak evaluation-binding if for any PPT adversary* $\mathcal{A}$, $\mathsf{Adv}^{\mathrm{bind}}_{\mathsf{FC},\mathcal{A}}(\lambda) = \mathsf{negl}(\lambda)$, *where*

$$\mathsf{Adv}^{\mathrm{bind}}_{\mathsf{FC},\mathcal{A}}(\lambda) := \Pr\left[\begin{array}{l|l} F \in \mathcal{F} \ \wedge \ \mathbf{y} \in \mathcal{D}^{\kappa} \ \wedge F(\mathbf{x}) \neq \mathbf{y} & \\ \wedge \ \mathsf{cm} = \mathsf{Commit}(\mathsf{ck}, \mathbf{x}; r) & \end{array} : \begin{array}{l} (\mathsf{ck}, \mathsf{td}) \leftarrow \mathsf{Setup}(1^{\lambda}, \mathcal{F}) \\ (\mathbf{x}, r, F, \mathbf{y}, \mathsf{op}_{\mathbf{y}}) \leftarrow \mathcal{A}(\mathsf{ck}) \end{array}\right.$$
$$\left.\mathsf{Verify}(\mathsf{ck}, \mathsf{cm}, \mathsf{op}_{\mathbf{y}}, F, \mathbf{y}) = 1\right]$$

Zero-knowledge. The zero-knowledge property can be seen as a simulation-based definition of hiding property, considerably stronger than the definition given in [48][9]. Further, compared to the zero-knowledge definition of [50], ours is stronger in the sense that the commitment and simulated openings are not generated at the same time. In other words, to make commitments reusable for our mrNISC application, we need two simulators $\mathcal{S}_1, \mathcal{S}_2$, where $\mathcal{S}_1$ generates a simulated commitment, and $\mathcal{S}_2$—given the simulated commitment—can produce any number of simulated openings for different adversarially chosen functions.

Definition 4 (Perfect zero-knowledge). *A functional commitment scheme* $\mathsf{FC} = (\mathsf{Setup}, \mathsf{Commit}, \mathsf{Open}, \mathsf{Verify})$ *for a class of functions* $\mathcal{F}$ *is perfectly zero-knowledge if there exists a PPT simulator* $\mathcal{S} = (\mathcal{S}_1, \mathcal{S}_2)$, *such that for any* λ, $(\mathsf{ck}, \mathsf{td}) \leftarrow \mathsf{Setup}(1^{\lambda}, \mathcal{F})$, *and any adversary* $\mathcal{A}$, *the following distributions are identical.*

$$\left\{\mathcal{A}^{\mathsf{O}_{\mathsf{Open}}}(\mathsf{st}) = 1 : (\mathsf{st}, \mathbf{x}) \leftarrow \mathcal{A}(\mathsf{td}), r \leftarrow_{\$} \mathsf{RND}_{\lambda}(\mathsf{Commit}), (\mathsf{cm}, \mathsf{d}) \leftarrow \mathsf{Commit}(\mathsf{ck}, \mathbf{x}; r)\right\}\}$$
$$\left\{\mathcal{A}^{\mathsf{O}_{\mathcal{S}}}(\mathsf{st}) = 1 : (\mathsf{st}, \mathbf{x}) \leftarrow \mathcal{A}(\mathsf{td}), (\mathsf{cm}, \mathit{aux}) \leftarrow \mathcal{S}_1(\mathsf{td})\right\}$$

where $\mathsf{O}_{\mathsf{Open}}(F) := \mathsf{Open}(\mathsf{ck}, \mathsf{d}, F)$ *and* $\mathsf{O}_{\mathcal{S}}(F) := \mathcal{S}_2(\mathsf{td}, \mathit{aux}, F, F(\mathbf{x}))$.

3 $\mathrm{WE}^{\mathrm{FC}}$: Witness Encryption for Functional Commitment

In this section we define our notion of witness encryption for functional commitments. In standard witness encryption, we require semantic security for false statements; in our notion we require semantic security for false statements on committed inputs. The decryption algorithm requires an opening proof of the functional commitment w.r.t. a function and output specified at encryption time. Like other variants of WE [9,12], loses the pure "non-deterministic" flavor of WE since it requires the existence of a commitment to the decryption witness. We refer to the introduction for further intuitions about the notion.

[9] The definition of hiding in [48] only guarantees that the commitment does not reveal any information about $\mathbf{x}$.

Definition 5 (Witness Encryption for Functional Commitments). *Let* $\mathsf{FC} = (\mathsf{Setup}, \mathsf{Commit}, \mathsf{Open}, \mathsf{Verify})$ *be a functional commitment scheme for a class of functions* $\mathcal{F}$. *A witness encryption for* FC, *denoted by* $\mathsf{WE}^{\mathsf{FC}}$, *is a tuple of polynomial-time algorithms* $\mathsf{WE}^{\mathsf{FC}} = (\mathsf{Setup}, \mathsf{Commit}, \mathsf{Open}, \mathsf{Verify}, \mathsf{Enc}, \mathsf{Dec})$, *where* Setup, Commit, Open, *and* Verify *are defined by* FC *and*

Encryption. $\mathsf{Enc}(\mathsf{ck}, \mathsf{cm}, F, \mathbf{y}, \mathsf{m})$ *is a probabilistic algorithm that takes as input the commitment key* ck, *a statement* $\mathsf{x} = (\mathsf{cm}, F, \mathbf{y})$, *and a bitstring* m, *and outputs an encryption* ct *of* m *under* x.

Decryption. $\mathsf{Dec}(\mathsf{ck}, \mathsf{ct}, \mathsf{cm}, F, \mathbf{y}, \mathsf{op}_\mathbf{y})$ *is a deterministic algorithm that on input* ck, *a ciphertext* ct, *a statement* $\mathsf{x} = (\mathsf{cm}, F, \mathbf{y})$, *and an opening proof* $\mathsf{op}_\mathbf{y}$, *decrypts* ct *into a message* m, *or returns* $\perp$.

We require two properties, *correctness* and *semantic security.*

(Perfect) Correctness. For all $\lambda \in \mathbb{N}$, $\mathsf{ck} \leftarrow \mathsf{Setup}(1^\lambda, \mathcal{F})$, $F \in \mathcal{F}$, message m, and vector $\mathbf{x}$ we have:

$$\Pr\left[\mathsf{Dec}(\mathsf{ck}, \mathsf{ct}, \mathsf{cm}, F, F(\mathbf{x}), \mathsf{op}) = \mathsf{m} \;:\; \begin{array}{l}(\mathsf{cm}, \mathsf{d}) \leftarrow \mathsf{Commit}(\mathsf{ck}, \mathbf{x}; r)\\ \mathsf{ct} \leftarrow \mathsf{Enc}(\mathsf{ck}, \mathsf{cm}, F, F(\mathbf{x}), \mathsf{m})\\ \mathsf{op} \leftarrow \mathsf{Open}(\mathsf{ck}, \mathsf{d}, F)\end{array}\right] = 1$$

Semantic Security. For any PPT adversary $\mathcal{A} = (\mathcal{A}_1, \mathcal{A}_2)$, $\mathsf{Adv}^{\mathsf{ss}}_{\mathsf{WE},\mathsf{FC},\mathcal{A}}(\lambda) = \mathsf{negl}(\lambda)$, where $\mathsf{Adv}^{\mathsf{ss}}_{\mathsf{WE},\mathsf{FC},\mathcal{A}}(\lambda) :=$

$$\left|\Pr\left[b' = b \;:\; \begin{array}{l}(\mathsf{ck}, \mathsf{td}) \leftarrow \mathsf{Setup}(1^\lambda, \mathcal{F}); (\mathbf{x}, r, F, \mathbf{y}, \mathsf{m}_0, \mathsf{m}_1) \leftarrow \mathcal{A}_1(\mathsf{ck})\\ (\mathsf{cm}, \mathsf{d}) \leftarrow \mathsf{Commit}(\mathsf{ck}, \mathbf{x}; r);\\ b \leftarrow_{\$} \{0,1\}; \mathsf{ct} \leftarrow \mathsf{Enc}(\mathsf{ck}, \mathsf{cm}, F, \mathbf{y}, \mathsf{m}_b)\\ \textbf{if } F(\mathbf{x}) = \mathbf{y} \textbf{ then } \mathsf{ct} := \perp; b' \leftarrow \mathcal{A}_2(\mathsf{ct})\end{array}\right] - 1/2\right|$$

4 Our $\mathrm{WE}^{\mathrm{FC}}$ Construction

We present our construction of $\mathrm{WE}^{\mathrm{FC}}$. The construction consists of two building blocks: Functional Commitments (see Sect. 2.1), and a flavor of Smooth Projective Hash Functions with *extractability* property.

We start by recalling the definition of SPHFs.

4.1 Smooth Projective Hash Functions

Let $\mathcal{L}_{\mathsf{lpar}} \subseteq \mathcal{X}_{\mathsf{lpar}}$ be a NP language, parametrized by a language parameter lpar, and $\mathcal{R}_{\mathsf{lpar}}$ be its corresponding relation. A Smooth projective hash functions (SPHFs, [22]) for $\mathcal{L}_{\mathsf{lpar}}$ is a cryptographic primitive with this property that given lpar and a statement x, one can compute a hash of x in two different ways: either by using a projection key hp and $(\mathsf{x}, \mathsf{w}) \in \mathcal{R}_{\mathsf{lpar}}$ as $\mathsf{pH} \leftarrow \mathsf{projhash}(\mathsf{lpar}, \mathsf{hp}, \mathsf{x}, \mathsf{w})$, or by using a hashing key hk and $\mathsf{x} \in \mathcal{X}_{\mathsf{lpar}}$ as $\mathsf{H} \leftarrow \mathsf{hash}(\mathsf{lpar}, \mathsf{hk}, \mathsf{x})$. The formal definition of SPHF follows.

Definition 6. *A SPHF for* $\{\mathcal{L}_{\mathsf{lpar}}\}$ *is a tuple of PPT algorithms* $(\mathsf{PGen}, \mathsf{hashkg}, \mathsf{projkg}, \mathsf{hash}, \mathsf{projhash})$*, which are defined as follows:*

$\mathsf{PGen}(1^\lambda)$**:** *Takes in a security parameter* λ *and generates the global parameters* pp *together with the language parameters* lpar*. We assume that all algorithms have access to* pp*.*

$\mathsf{hashkg}(\mathsf{lpar})$**:** *Takes in a language parameter* lpar *and outputs a hashing key* hk*.*

$\mathsf{projkg}(\mathsf{lpar}, \mathsf{hk}, \mathsf{x})$**:** *Takes in a hashing key* hk*,* lpar*, and a statement* x *and outputs a projection key* hp*, possibly depending on* x*.*

$\mathsf{hash}(\mathsf{lpar}, \mathsf{hk}, \mathsf{x})$**:** *Takes in a hashing key* hk*,* lpar*, and a statement* x *and outputs a hash value* H*.*

$\mathsf{projhash}(\mathsf{lpar}, \mathsf{hp}, \mathsf{x}, \mathsf{w})$**:** *Takes in a projection key* hp*,* lpar*, a statement* x*, and a witness* w *for* $\mathsf{x} \in \mathcal{L}_{\mathsf{lpar}}$ *and outputs a hash value* pH*.*

To shorten notation, we sometimes denote "$\mathsf{hk} \leftarrow \mathsf{hashkg}(\mathsf{lpar})$; $\mathsf{hp} \leftarrow \mathsf{projkg}(\mathsf{lpar}, \mathsf{hk}, \mathsf{x})$" by $(\mathsf{hp}, \mathsf{hk}) \leftarrow \mathsf{kgen}(\mathsf{lpar}, \mathsf{x})$. A SPHF must satisfy the following properties:

Correctness. It is required that $\mathsf{hash}(\mathsf{lpar}, \mathsf{hk}, \mathsf{x}) = \mathsf{projhash}(\mathsf{lpar}, \mathsf{hp}, \mathsf{x}, \mathsf{w})$ for all $\mathsf{x} \in \mathcal{L}_{\mathsf{lpar}}$ and their corresponding witnesses w.

Smoothness. It is required that for any lpar and any $\mathsf{x} \notin \mathcal{L}_{\mathsf{lpar}}$, the following distributions are statistically indistinguishable:

$$\{(\mathsf{hp}, \mathsf{H}) : (\mathsf{hp}, \mathsf{hk}) \leftarrow \mathsf{kgen}(\mathsf{lpar}, \mathsf{x}), \mathsf{H} \leftarrow \mathsf{hash}(\mathsf{lpar}, \mathsf{hk}, \mathsf{x})\}$$
$$\{(\mathsf{hp}, \mathsf{H}) : (\mathsf{hp}, \mathsf{hk}) \leftarrow \mathsf{kgen}(\mathsf{lpar}, \mathsf{x}), \mathsf{H} \leftarrow \Omega\} \ .$$

where Ω is the set of hash values.

Remark 1. For our application, we need a type of SPHF where hp depends on the statement. This type of SPHF with such "non-adaptivity" in the smoothness property was formally defined by Gennaro and Lindell in [30] and was later named GL-SPHF in [7]. Throughout this work, we always mean GL-SPHF when talking about SPHFs.

Existing constructions of SPHFs over groups are based on a framework called *diverse vector space* (DVS). Intuitively, a DVS [3,7,39] is a way to represent a language $\mathcal{L} \subseteq \mathcal{X}$ as a subspace $\hat{\mathcal{L}}$ of some vector space of some finite field. In the seminal work [22], Cramer and Shoup showed that such languages automatically admit SPHFs. To briefly recap the notion of DVS, let $\mathcal{R} = \{(\mathsf{x}, \mathsf{w})\}$ be a relation with $\mathcal{L} = \{\mathsf{x} : \exists \mathsf{w}, (\mathsf{x}, \mathsf{w}) \in \mathcal{R}\}$[10]. Let pp be system parameters, including say the description of a bilinear group. A (pairing-based) DVS $\mathcal{V}$ is defined as $\mathcal{V} = (\mathsf{pp}, \mathcal{X}, \mathcal{L}, \mathcal{R}, n, k, \mathbf{M}, \boldsymbol{\Theta}, \boldsymbol{\Lambda})$, where $\mathbf{M}(\mathsf{x})$ is an $n \times k$ matrix, $\boldsymbol{\Theta}(\mathsf{x})$ is an

[10] The reader who is uninterested in fully understanding the formal details of DVS can think of this formalism as a language to describe relations in (linear) algebraic terms. We refer the reader to [39] for more details on DVS.

n-dimensional vector, and $\boldsymbol{\Lambda}(\mathsf{x},\mathsf{w})$ a k-dimensional vector. In this work, we consider the case that the matrix $\mathbf{M}(\mathsf{x})$ may depend on x (i.e., GL-DVS similarly to GL-SPHF). Moreover, as long as the equation $\boldsymbol{\Theta}(\mathsf{x}) = \mathbf{M}(\mathsf{x}) \cdot \boldsymbol{\Lambda}(\mathsf{x},\mathsf{w})$ is consistent, it could be that different coefficients of $\boldsymbol{\Theta}(\mathsf{x})$, $\mathbf{M}(\mathsf{x})$, and $\boldsymbol{\Lambda}(\mathsf{x},\mathsf{w})$ belong to different algebraic structures. The most common case is that for a given bilinear group $\mathsf{pp} = (p, \mathbb{G}_1, \mathbb{G}_2, \mathbb{G}_T, \hat{e}, g_1, g_2)$, these coefficients belong to either $\mathbb{Z}_p$, $\mathbb{G}_1$, $\mathbb{G}_2$, or $\mathbb{G}_T$ as long as the consistency is preserved.

For our $\mathrm{WE}^{\mathrm{FC}}$, we are interested in SPHFs defined over bilinear groups. Namely, SPHFs for languages $\mathcal{L}_{\mathsf{lpar}}$ with $\mathsf{lpar} = (\mathbf{M}, \boldsymbol{\Theta}, \boldsymbol{\Lambda})$, such that the coefficients of $[\mathbf{M}(\mathsf{x})]_\iota$ (resp. $[\boldsymbol{\Lambda}(\mathsf{x},\mathsf{w})]_{3-\iota}$) belong to the group $\mathbb{G}_\iota$ (resp. $\mathbb{G}_{3-\iota}$, i.e. the other group) for some $\iota \in \{1,2\}$, and that $[\boldsymbol{\Theta}(\mathsf{x})]_T \in \mathbb{G}_T$ is the pairing of $[\mathbf{M}(\mathsf{x})]_\iota$ and $[\boldsymbol{\Lambda}(\mathsf{x},\mathsf{w})]_{3-\iota}$. For notational simplicity, we specifically pick $\iota = 1$ in the rest of the paper. We define $\mathcal{L}_{\mathsf{lpar}}$ therefore as

$$\mathcal{L}_{\mathsf{lpar}} = \Big\{[\boldsymbol{\Theta}(\mathsf{x})]_T : \exists[\boldsymbol{\Lambda}(\mathsf{x},\mathsf{w})]_2 \mathrm{s.t} [\boldsymbol{\Theta}(\mathsf{x})]_T = \hat{e}([\mathbf{M}(\mathsf{x})]_1, [\boldsymbol{\Lambda}(\mathsf{x},\mathsf{w})]_2)\Big\}.$$

Given a GL-DVS for $\mathcal{L}_{\mathsf{lpar}}$, one can construct an efficient GL-SPHF for $\mathcal{L}_{\mathsf{lpar}}$ as depicted in Fig. 1.

Extractable PHF. In the definition of SPHF, smoothness is guaranteed only for false statements. Hence, for trivial languages where all statements are true, such notion of smoothness is vacuous. To argue security in this case, a stronger notion of knowledge-smoothness is required which guarantees that if an adversary can compute the hash value with non-negligible probability, it must *know* a

- $\mathsf{hashkg}(\mathsf{lpar})$: sample $\boldsymbol{\alpha} \leftarrow\!\$\, \mathbb{Z}_p^n$, and output $\mathsf{hk} \leftarrow \boldsymbol{\alpha}$;
- $\mathsf{projkg}(\mathsf{lpar}, \mathsf{hk}, \mathsf{x})$: $[\boldsymbol{\gamma}]_1^\top \leftarrow \boldsymbol{\alpha}^\top [\mathbf{M}(\mathsf{x})]_1 \in \mathbb{G}_1^{1\times k}$; return $\mathsf{hp} \leftarrow [\boldsymbol{\gamma}]_1$;
- $\mathsf{hash}(\mathsf{lpar}, \mathsf{hk}, \mathsf{x})$: return $[\mathsf{H}]_T \leftarrow \boldsymbol{\alpha}^\top [\boldsymbol{\Theta}(\mathsf{x})]_T$;
- $\mathsf{projhash}(\mathsf{lpar}, \mathsf{hp}, \mathsf{x}, \mathsf{w})$: return $[\mathsf{pH}]_T \leftarrow \hat{e}([\boldsymbol{\gamma}]_1^\top, [\boldsymbol{\Lambda}(\mathsf{x},\mathsf{w})]_2)$

Fig. 1. DVS-based SPHF construction $\mathsf{HF}_{\mathsf{dvs}}$ for $\mathcal{L}_{\mathsf{lpar}}$ with $\mathsf{lpar} = (\mathbf{M}, \boldsymbol{\Theta}, \boldsymbol{\Lambda})$.

1. $(\mathsf{pp}, \mathsf{lpar}) \leftarrow \mathsf{PGen}(1^\lambda)$;
2. $\mathsf{aux} \leftarrow \mathcal{A}_1(\mathsf{lpar})$; $\mathsf{x} \leftarrow \mathsf{IG}(\mathsf{aux})$;
3. **if** $\mathsf{x} = \bot$, **return** 0; **else** $\mathsf{x}' \leftarrow [\boldsymbol{\Theta}(\mathsf{x})]_T$;
4. $(\mathsf{hp}, \mathsf{hk}) \leftarrow \mathsf{kgen}(\mathsf{lpar}, \mathsf{x})$; $\mathsf{H} \leftarrow \mathcal{A}_2(\mathsf{lpar}, \mathsf{hp}, \mathsf{aux})$;
5. $\mathsf{w}' \leftarrow \mathsf{Ext}_{\mathcal{A}}(\mathsf{lpar}, \mathsf{hp})$; $\mathsf{H}' = \mathsf{hash}(\mathsf{lpar}, \mathsf{hk}, \mathsf{x})$;
6. **return** $\big((\mathsf{H} = \mathsf{H}') \wedge (\mathsf{x}', \mathsf{w}') \notin \mathcal{R}_{\mathsf{lpar}}\big)$;

Fig. 2. Knowledge smoothness experiment $\mathsf{Exp}^{\mathsf{KS}}_{\mathsf{PHF},\mathsf{IG}}(\mathcal{A}, \lambda)$

witness of the statement used in the hash computation. In the following, we state the definition of knowledge smoothness for languages of our interest, and prove that $\mathsf{HF}_{\mathsf{dvs}}$ in Fig. 1 has this property in the algebraic bilinear group model.

Knowledge Smoothness. A projective hash function $\mathsf{PHF} = (\mathsf{PGen}, \mathsf{hashkg}, \mathsf{projkg}, \mathsf{hash}, \mathsf{projhash})$ for $\{\mathcal{L}_{\mathsf{lpar}}\}$ defined by $\mathsf{lpar} = (\mathbf{M}, \boldsymbol{\Theta}, \boldsymbol{\Lambda})$ is knowledge smooth if for any λ, for any PPT adversary $\mathcal{A} = (\mathcal{A}_1, \mathcal{A}_2)$, there exists a PPT extractor $\mathsf{Ext}_{\mathcal{A}}$ such that $\Pr[\mathsf{Exp}^{\mathsf{KS}}_{\mathsf{PHF},\mathsf{IG}}(\mathcal{A}, \lambda)] \le \mathsf{negl}(\lambda)$, where $\mathsf{Exp}^{\mathsf{KS}}_{\mathsf{PHF},\mathsf{IG}}(\mathcal{A}, \lambda)$ is defined in Fig. 2.

We call a PHF with knowledge-smoothness an *extractable PHF*. Note that by the definition, the extractor is supposed to extract only $\mathsf{w}' = [\boldsymbol{\Lambda}(\mathsf{x}, \mathsf{w})]_2$ (and not w) such that $([\boldsymbol{\Theta}(\mathsf{x})]_T, \mathsf{w}') \in \mathcal{R}_{\mathsf{lpar}}$. The security guarantee is that for any PPT adversary $\mathcal{A} = (\mathcal{A}_1, \mathcal{A}_2)$ that can compute a valid hash value for an adversarially chosen statement, there exists an efficient extractor that can extract a valid witness for the statement. Furthermore, since in our application we need to make sure that the statement chosen by $\mathcal{A}$ satisfies some predicate[11], we let $\mathcal{A}_1$ to select the statement by revealing the random coins aux of the statement, instead. The actual statement is then generated by a deterministic instance generator IG that takes aux as input and returns an instance x if the predicate holds.

Theorem 1. *Let $\mathcal{L}_{\mathsf{lpar}}$ be a language defined by $\mathsf{lpar} = (\mathbf{M}, \boldsymbol{\Theta}, \boldsymbol{\Lambda})$. Under the discrete logarithm assumption, $\mathsf{HF}_{\mathsf{dvs}}$ in Fig. 1 is an extractable PHF against all PPT adversaries $\mathcal{A} = (\mathcal{A}_1, \mathcal{A}_2)$, where $\mathcal{A}_2$ is algebraic.*

Proof. We prove the theorem for $\iota = 1$; the other case goes exactly in the same way. Let $\mathcal{A} = (\mathcal{A}_1, \mathcal{A}_2)$ be any PPT adversary against the knowledge smoothness of $\mathsf{HF}_{\mathsf{dvs}}$ and assume that $\mathcal{A}_2$ is algebraic. Let x be the statement output by $\mathcal{A}_1$ on input $\mathsf{lpar} = (\mathbf{M}, \boldsymbol{\Theta}, \boldsymbol{\Lambda})$. $\mathcal{A}_2$ returns a hash value $\mathsf{H} \in \mathbb{G}_T$, and by its algebraic nature, $\mathcal{A}_2$ also provides coefficients that "explain" these elements as linear combinations of the input. Let $[\mathbf{x}]_1 = [1, \boldsymbol{\gamma}, \mathbf{M}(\mathsf{x})]_1$[12] be $\mathcal{A}_2$'s input in $\mathbb{G}_1$. Let $[y]_2 = [1]_2$ be $\mathcal{A}_2$'s input in $\mathbb{G}_2$, and $[\mathbf{z}]_T = [\boldsymbol{\Theta}(\mathsf{x})]_T$ its input in $\mathbb{G}_T$. The coefficients returned by $\mathcal{A}_2([\mathbf{x}]_1, [y]_2, [\mathbf{z}]_T)$ are $A_0, (A_i)_{i \in [k]}, (B_{ij})_{i \in [n], j \in [k]}, (C_i)_{i \in [n]} \in \mathbb{Z}_p$ such that

$$\mathsf{H} = \prod_{i=0}^{k} \hat{e}\left([x_i]_1, [y]_2\right)^{A_i} \cdot \prod_{i=1}^{n} \prod_{j=1}^{k} \hat{e}\left([\mathbf{M}_{ij}(\mathsf{x})]_1, [y]_2\right)^{B_{ij}} \cdot \prod_{i=1}^{n} [z_i]_T^{C_i}.$$

Let Ext be the extractor that runs the algebraic adversary $\mathcal{A}_2$ and returns $[\boldsymbol{\Lambda}(\mathsf{x}, \mathsf{w})]_2 = ([A_1]_2, \ldots, [A_k]_2)$. We can show that this is a valid witness for $[\boldsymbol{\Theta}(\mathsf{x})]_T$ as long as the hash value H returned by $\mathcal{A}_2$ is a correct hash. In other words, if $\mathcal{A}_2$ can output H such that $\mathsf{H} = \boldsymbol{\alpha}^\top [\boldsymbol{\Theta}(\mathsf{x})]_T$, and $\boldsymbol{\Theta}(\mathsf{x}) \neq \mathbf{M}(\mathsf{x})\boldsymbol{\Lambda}(\mathsf{x}, \mathsf{w})$,

[11] For example, for $\mathsf{x} = (\mathsf{cm}, G, y)$, the predicate checks if $G(v) \neq y$, where v is committed in cm.

[12] $x_0 = 1$ and $x_i = \gamma_i$ for $1 \le i \le k$.

we can construct an algorithm $\mathcal{B}$ that exploits $\mathcal{A}_2$ and breaks the discrete logarithm problem. To do this, $\mathcal{B}$ on challenge input $Z = [z]_1$ proceeds as follows. First, it uses $\mathsf{D}_{\mathsf{lpar}}$ to sample $\mathsf{lpar} = (\mathbf{M}, \mathbf{\Theta}, \boldsymbol{\Lambda})$. Second, it samples $\mathbf{r}, \mathbf{s} \leftarrow_{\$} \mathbb{Z}_p^n$ and implicitly sets $\boldsymbol{\alpha} := z \cdot \mathbf{r} + \mathbf{s}$. Third, it computes $\mathsf{hp} = [\boldsymbol{\gamma}]_1 = [\mathbf{M}(\mathsf{x})^\top \boldsymbol{\alpha}]_1$ and runs $\mathcal{A}_2(\mathsf{lpar}, \mathsf{hp}, \mathsf{x})$. Once received $\mathcal{A}_2$'s output H, $\mathcal{B}$ returns z computed from the following equation.

$$\boldsymbol{\alpha}^\top \mathbf{\Theta}(\mathsf{x}) - \boldsymbol{\gamma}^\top \mathbf{A} = A_0 + \sum_{i=1}^{n} \sum_{j=1}^{k} \mathbf{M}_{ij}(\mathsf{x}) B_{ij} + \mathbf{\Theta}(\mathsf{x})^\top \mathbf{C}$$

$$\Rightarrow \boldsymbol{\alpha}^\top (\mathbf{\Theta}(\mathsf{x}) - \mathbf{M}(\mathsf{x})\mathbf{A}) = A_0 + \sum_{i=1}^{n} \sum_{j=1}^{k} \mathbf{M}_{ij}(\mathsf{x}) B_{ij} + \mathbf{\Theta}(\mathsf{x})^\top \mathbf{C}$$

where $\mathbf{A} = (A_1, \ldots, A_k)$ and $\mathbf{C} = (C_1, \ldots, C_n)$. Note that z is the only unknown in the equation and can be computed by the assumption that $\mathbf{\Theta}(\mathsf{x}) \neq \mathbf{M}(\mathsf{x})\mathbf{A}$. □

In the following corollary, we argue the extractability of $\mathsf{HF}_{\mathsf{dvs}}$ also in the GGM, which we use to enable the instantiation of our Theorem 2 (see Remark 2).

Corollary 1. $\mathsf{HF}_{\mathsf{dvs}}$ *in Fig. 1 is an extractable PHF in the generic group model.*

Proof. The proof follows straightforwardly from theorem 1 and lemma 2.2 in [26].

4.2 Our Construction

Let $\mathsf{FC} = (\mathsf{Setup}, \mathsf{Commit}, \mathsf{Open}, \mathsf{Verify})$ be a succinct functional commitment scheme for $\mathcal{F}$, where the verification circuit is linear (i.e., of degree one) in the opening proof. Let $\mathsf{EPHF} = (\mathsf{PGen}, \mathsf{hashkg}, \mathsf{projkg}, \mathsf{hash}, \mathsf{projhash})$ be an extractable projective hash function. The key idea of the construction is to use EPHF for the language defined by the verification circuit of FC. Since this circuit is affine in the opening proof op, and we know how to construct PHF for affine languages, the witness encryption just uses EPHF in a straightforward way. Note that because the language is trivial, we need knowledge smoothness rather than standard smoothness.

Construction. Let $\mathsf{lpar} = (\mathsf{ck}, \mathbf{M}, \mathbf{\Theta})$ be the language parameter that defines $\mathcal{L}_{\mathsf{lpar}}$ corresponding to the verification circuit of FC as follows:

$$\mathcal{L}_{\mathsf{lpar}} = \{\mathsf{x} = (\mathsf{cm}, \boldsymbol{\beta}, \mathbf{y}) | \exists \mathsf{op} : \mathsf{Verify}(\mathsf{ck}, \mathsf{cm}, \mathsf{op}, \boldsymbol{\beta}, \mathbf{y}) = 1\}$$

Note that due to the linearity of verification circuit in the opening op, there should exist a matrix $[\mathbf{M}(\mathsf{x})]_\star$[13] and a vector $[\mathbf{\Theta}(\mathsf{x})]_T$ such that

$$[\mathbf{\Theta}(\mathsf{x})]_T = [\mathbf{M}(\mathsf{x}) \cdot \widetilde{\mathsf{op}}]_T$$

[13] The star $\star$ means that the elements are not necessarily in the same group.

where $\widetilde{\mathsf{op}}$ is derived from op by replacing its group elements with their discrete logarithms. Let $\sigma : G_T \rightarrow \{0,1\}^\ell$ be a generic deterministic injective encoding that maps group elements in $\mathbb{G}_T$ into ℓ-bit strings, and that has an efficient inversion algorithm σ^{-1}. Our WE for functional commitments $\mathsf{WE}^{\mathsf{FC}} = (\mathsf{Setup}, \mathsf{Commit}, \mathsf{Open}, \mathsf{Verify}, \mathsf{Enc}, \mathsf{Dec})$ for $\mathcal{L}_{\mathsf{lpar}}$ can be described as follows:

$\mathsf{Setup}, \mathsf{Commit}, \mathsf{Open}, \mathsf{Verify}$ are defined by FC, and specify $\mathsf{lpar} = (\mathsf{ck}, \mathbf{M}, \mathbf{\Theta})$.

$\mathsf{Enc}(\mathsf{ck}, \mathsf{cm}, \boldsymbol{\beta}, \mathbf{y}, \mathsf{m})$. Let $\mathsf{x} = (\mathsf{cm}, \boldsymbol{\beta}, \mathbf{y})$. To encrypt a bit message $\mathsf{m} \in \{0,1\}$, select a uniformly random vector $\mathsf{hk} \in \mathbb{Z}_p^{1\times\nu}$, where ν is the number of rows of $\mathbf{M}(\mathsf{x})$, sample a random $r \leftarrow_{\$} \{0,1\}^\ell$, and compute the ciphertext $\mathsf{ct} = (\mathsf{hp}, r, \widehat{\mathsf{ct}})$, where

$$\mathsf{hp} = [\mathsf{hk} \cdot \mathbf{M}(\mathsf{x})]_\star, \qquad \mathsf{H} = [\mathsf{hk} \cdot \mathbf{\Theta}(\mathsf{x})]_T, \qquad \widehat{\mathsf{ct}} = \langle \sigma(\mathsf{H}), r \rangle \oplus \mathsf{m}$$

$\mathsf{Dec}(\mathsf{ck}, \mathsf{ct}, \mathsf{cm}, \boldsymbol{\beta}, \mathbf{y}, \mathsf{op})$. On input a ciphertext $\mathsf{ct} = (\mathsf{hp}, r, \widehat{\mathsf{ct}})$, first compute $\mathsf{pH} = [\mathsf{hp} \cdot \widetilde{\mathsf{op}}]_T$ using op, and then output the message $\mathsf{m} \in \{0,1\}$ computed as $\mathsf{m} = \langle \sigma(\mathsf{pH}), r \rangle \oplus \widehat{\mathsf{ct}}$.

Theorem 2. *Let* FC *be a functional commitment scheme for functions* $\mathcal{F}$ *that is evaluation-binding. Let* EPHF *be an extractable PHF. Then* $\mathsf{WE}^{\mathsf{FC}}$ *described above is a* $\mathrm{WE}^{\mathrm{FC}}$ *for* $\mathcal{F}$*. Furthermore, if* EPHF *is extractable in the generic group model (GGM), then* $\mathsf{WE}^{\mathsf{FC}}$ *is semantically secure in the GGM.*

Proof. Perfect correctness follows directly from correctness of FC and EPHF. To prove semantic security, we show a reduction from evaluation-binding of FC to semantic security of $\mathsf{WE}^{\mathsf{FC}}$. To do so, let us assume that $\mathsf{WE}^{\mathsf{FC}}$ is not semantically secure. By definition, there exists an efficient adversary $\mathcal{A}$ that, for a maliciously chosen (false) statement $\mathsf{x} = (\mathsf{cm}, \boldsymbol{\beta}, \mathbf{y})$[14], where $\mathsf{cm} = \mathsf{Commit}(\mathsf{ck}, \boldsymbol{\alpha}; r)$ (all known to $\mathcal{A}$), it can distinguish, with non-negligible advantage, encryptions of 0 and 1 under x. We first show how to construct an efficient algorithm $\mathcal{B}$ that uses $\mathcal{A}$ to compute a hash value $\mathsf{H} = \mathsf{hash}(\mathsf{lpar}, \mathsf{hk}, \mathsf{x})$.

Before giving the description of $\mathcal{B}$, let us first recall the classic Goldreich-Levin theorem [33] based on which we construct $\mathcal{B}$.

Theorem 3 (Goldreich-Levin). *Let* $\epsilon > 0$*. Fix some* $x \in \{0,1\}^n$ *and let* $\mathcal{A}_x$ *be a PPT algorithm such that* $\Pr[\mathcal{A}_x(r) = \langle r, x\rangle | r \leftarrow_{\$} \{0,1\}^n] \geq 1/2 + \epsilon$*. There exists a decoding algorithm* $D^{\mathcal{A}_x(\cdot)}$ *with oracle access to* $\mathcal{A}_x$ *that runs in* $\mathsf{poly}(n, 1/\epsilon)$*-time and outputs a list* $L \subseteq \{0,1\}^n$ *such that* $|L| = \mathsf{poly}(n, 1/\epsilon)$ *and* $x \in L$ *with probability at least* $1/2$*.*

The fact that $\mathcal{A}$ can distinguishes ct_0 and ct_1 under $\mathsf{x} = (\mathsf{cm}, \boldsymbol{\beta}, \mathbf{y})$ with non-negligible advantage implies that

[14] Note that x is false in the sense that for $\mathsf{cm} = \mathsf{Commit}(\mathsf{ck}, \boldsymbol{\alpha}; r)$, we have $F(\boldsymbol{\alpha}, \boldsymbol{\beta}) \neq \mathbf{y}$. With respect to the language $\mathcal{L}_{\mathsf{lpar}}$ corresponding to the verification of functional commitments, such statements are always true however.

$$\Pr\left[\begin{array}{ll} & b \leftarrow_{\$} \{0,1\}; \mathsf{hk} \leftarrow_{\$} \mathbb{Z}_p^{1\times\nu}; r \leftarrow_{\$} \{0,1\}^{\ell}; \\ b' = b \ : & \mathsf{hp} = [\mathsf{hk}\cdot\mathbf{M}(\mathsf{x})]_{\star}; \mathsf{H} = [\mathsf{hk}\cdot\mathbf{\Theta}(\mathsf{x})]_T; \widehat{\mathsf{ct}} = \langle\sigma(\mathsf{H}), r\rangle \oplus b; \\ & b' \leftarrow \mathcal{A}(\mathsf{hp}, r, \widehat{\mathsf{ct}}) \end{array}\right] \geq 1/2+\epsilon$$

for some $\epsilon = 1/p(\lambda)$, where p is a polynomial. We first construct an algorithm $\bar{\mathcal{B}}$ that on input (hp, r) for $r \leftarrow_{\$} \{0,1\}^{\ell}$, it uses $\mathcal{A}$ to predict the value of $\langle r, \sigma(\mathsf{H})\rangle$. $\bar{\mathcal{B}}$ proceeds as follows: on input (hp, r), it samples $b \leftarrow_{\$} \{0,1\}$ and runs $\mathcal{A}$ on input (hp, r, b). If $\mathcal{A}$ correctly guesses b, $\bar{\mathcal{B}}$ outputs 0, and otherwise 1. By construction, it is easy to see that $\bar{\mathcal{B}}$ outputs $\langle r, \sigma(\mathsf{H})\rangle$ with probability at least $1/2+\epsilon$. Using $\bar{\mathcal{B}}$ and Goldreich-Levin decoding algorithm $D^{\bar{\mathcal{B}}(\mathsf{hp},\cdot)}$ in theorem 3, we now construct $\mathcal{B}$ that on input lpar, hp and x, computes $\sigma(\mathsf{H})$ as follows:

- Runs $D^{\bar{\mathcal{B}}(\mathsf{hp},\cdot)}$ so that to answer an oracle query $r \in \{0,1\}^{\ell}$, $\mathcal{B}$ outputs $\bar{\mathcal{B}}(\mathsf{hp}, r)$.
- Let $L \subseteq \{0,1\}^{\ell}$ be the list that $D^{\bar{\mathcal{B}}(\mathsf{hp},\cdot)}$ outputs. $\mathcal{B}$ returns $\sigma(\mathsf{H}) \leftarrow_{\$} L$.

To analyze the success probability of $\mathcal{B}$, let K be the set of hashing keys $\mathsf{hk} \in \mathbb{Z}_p^{1\times\nu}$ such that for $\mathsf{hp} \leftarrow \mathsf{projkg}(\mathsf{lpar}, \mathsf{hk}, \mathsf{x})$, and $\mathsf{H} \leftarrow \mathsf{hash}(\mathsf{lpar}, \mathsf{hk}, \mathsf{x})$,

$$\Pr[\bar{\mathcal{B}}(\mathsf{hp}, r) = \langle r, \sigma(\mathsf{H})\rangle | r \leftarrow_{\$} \{0,1\}^{\ell}] \geq 1/2 + \epsilon/2.$$

By an averaging argument, the probability that a random $\mathsf{hk} \leftarrow_{\$} \mathbb{Z}_p^{1\times\nu}$ is in K is at least ϵ. This indicates that with probability at least ϵ, the hashing key hk chosen in the knowledge smoothness experiment of EPHF lies in K and hence the oracle $\bar{\mathcal{B}}(\mathsf{hp}, \cdot)$ satisfies the requirement in theorem 3. This subsequently indicates that the list L returned by $D^{\bar{\mathcal{B}}(\mathsf{hp},\cdot)}$ contains $\sigma(\mathsf{H})$ with probability at least 1/2. Therefore, $\mathcal{B}$ computes $\sigma(\mathsf{H})$, and thus H with probability at least $\epsilon \cdot \frac{1}{2} \cdot \frac{1}{|L|}$ which is $\frac{1}{q(\lambda)}$ for some polynomial q. Due to extractability of the EPHF, there should exist an efficient extractor $\mathsf{Ext}_{\mathcal{B}}$ for $\mathcal{B}$ such that for $\mathsf{cm} = \mathsf{Commit}(\mathsf{ck}, \boldsymbol{\alpha}; r)$ and $\mathsf{x} = (\mathsf{cm}, \boldsymbol{\beta}, \mathbf{y})$, $\mathsf{Ext}_{\mathcal{B}}$ can extract a valid witness $\mathsf{w}' = \mathsf{op}$ such that $([\mathbf{\Theta}(\mathsf{x})]_T, \mathsf{w}') \in \mathcal{R}_{\mathsf{lpar}}$ with probability at least $\frac{1}{q(\lambda)}$. The above reduction can subsequently be invoked by a computational evaluation-binding adversary to break this property with non-negligible probability by outputting $(\boldsymbol{\alpha}, r, \boldsymbol{\beta}, \mathbf{y}, \mathsf{op})$. Note that the reduction is generic and thus a GGM adversary against semantic security of $\mathsf{WE}^{\mathsf{FC}}$ yields a GGM adversary against EPHF.

□

Remark 2 (Instantiating our $\mathsf{WE}^{\mathsf{FC}}$ *scheme using the* EPHF *of Fig. 1).* Due to a subtle technicality (and an intriguing gap between AGM and GGM), we cannot apply Theorem 2 to an EPHF that is extractable in the AGM and then argue that the semantic security of the resulting WE scheme holds in the AGM. The strategy to prove the semantic security of the WE scheme is to reduce a distinguisher $\mathcal{A}$ against the WE to a PHF adversary $\mathcal{B}$ that returns the correct PHF output. To do this reduction in the AGM, we would have to construct an *algebraic* PHF adversary that, along with the PHF output, returns an algebraic explanation of it. However, we do not see a way to build this algebraic adversary from the WE one. The reason is that, before using the Goldreich-Levin technique, the WE adversary $\mathcal{A}$ only returns a bit (thus, even if we assume it is algebraic, we cannot extract any algebraic representations from $\mathcal{A}$ because it does not return group elements). Therefore, even if eventually we can build a PHF adversary $\mathcal{B}$ that, with good probability, returns the correct group elements, we cannot return their algebraic representation. This issue does not arise in the GGM, where we can reduce a generic WE adversary $\mathcal{A}$ into a generic PHF adversary $\mathcal{B}$ by letting $\mathcal{B}$ relay $\mathcal{A}$'s GGM oracle queries to its own GGM oracle. It is an interesting future direction to find a non-GGM based EPHF construction.

5 Our WE^{FC} Instantiations

In this section, we present succinct FC schemes that are compatible with the requirements of our WE^{FC} construction of Sect. 4.2, namely they are pairing-based schemes whose verification algorithm can be expressed as a system of equations linear in opening elements. Our main contribution is a new FC scheme for the language of *monotone span programs* (MSP) which, using known transformations can be turned into an FC for circuits in the class NC^1.[15] Next, in Sect. 5.2 we show that also the functional commitments of Libert, Ramanna and Yung [48] for linear functions, and that of Lipmaa and Pavlyk for semi-sparse polynomials [50] satisfy the required properties.

5.1 Our FC for Monotone Span Programs

We construct our scheme by adapting the FC proposed by Catalano, Fiore and Tucker [17]. In particular, while the scheme of [17] has a quadratic verification (i.e., it needs to pair group elements in the opening between themselves), we show a variant of their technique with linear verification.

We start by recalling the notion of (monotone) span programs (MSP) [42].

Definition 7 (Monotone Span Programs [42]). *A monotone span program for attribute universe* $[n]$ *is a pair* $(\mathbf{M}, \rho)$ *where* $\mathbf{M} \in \mathbb{Z}_p^{\ell \times m}$ *and* $\rho : [\ell] \to [n]$. *Let* $\mathbf{M}_i$ *denote the i-th row of* $\mathbf{M}$. *For an input* $\boldsymbol{x} \in \{0,1\}^n$, *we say that*

$$(\mathbf{M}, \rho)\text{accepts}\boldsymbol{x}\text{iff } \exists \boldsymbol{w} \in \mathbb{Z}_p^{\ell} : \sum_{i:x_{\rho(i)}=1} w_i \cdot \mathbf{M}_i = (1, 0, \dots, 0)$$

MSPs are in the class $\mathcal{P}$ as one can use Gaussian elimination to find $\boldsymbol{w}$ in polynomial time. As in other works [18,19,46], we use a restricted version of MSPs where every input x_i is read only once, and thus $\ell = n$ and ρ is a permutation (which up to reordering the rows of $\mathbf{M}$ can be assumed the identity function).

[15] One can convert a circuit in NC^1 into a polynomial-size boolean formula, and then turn this one into a MSP of equivalent size [47, Appendix G].

The one-use restriction can be removed by working with larger inputs of length $n' = k \cdot n$ in which each entry x_i is repeated k times, where k is an upper bound on the input's fan out. Therefore, without loss of generality in our FC we work with MSPs defined by $\mathbf{M} \in \mathbb{Z}_p^{n \times m}$ such that

$$\mathbf{M} \text{accepts} \boldsymbol{x} \ \text{ iff } \ \exists \boldsymbol{w} \in \mathbb{Z}_p^n : (\boldsymbol{w} \circ \boldsymbol{x})^\top \cdot \mathbf{M} = (1, 0 \ldots, 0) \tag{2}$$

Our FC for MSP. For simplicity, we present our FC with deterministic commitments and openings. At the end of this section, we discuss how to easily change it to achieve zero-knowledge.

In the scheme, for a vector $\boldsymbol{v}$ we denote by $p_{\boldsymbol{v}}(Z)$ the polynomial $\sum_{j \in [n]} v_j Z^j$. Our scheme assumes a bilinear group description $\mathsf{bp} := (p, \mathbb{G}_1, \mathbb{G}_2, \mathbb{G}_T, \hat{e}, g_1, g_2)$ associated to the security parameter λ and works as follows.

Setup$(1^\lambda, n, m)$ takes as input two integers $m, n \geq 1$ that bound the size of the MSPs supported by the scheme (i.e., matrices in $\mathbb{Z}_p^{m \times n}$) and the length of the inputs. It samples random $\alpha, \gamma, \eta \leftarrow_\$ \mathbb{Z}_p, \boldsymbol{\beta} \leftarrow_\$ \mathbb{Z}_p^m$ and outputs

$$\mathsf{ck} := \begin{pmatrix} \{[\alpha^j]_1, [\eta\gamma^j]_2\}_{j \in [n]}, \{[\eta\alpha^j\gamma^\ell]_1\}_{j,\ell \in [n]}, \left\{\left[\alpha^j \beta_i \gamma^\ell\right]_1\right\}_{i \in [m], j, \ell \in [2n]: \ell \neq n+1} \\ [(\alpha\gamma)^n]_2, \left\{\left[\frac{(\alpha\gamma)^j \beta_i}{\eta}\right]_2\right\}_{i \in [m], j \in [n]} \end{pmatrix}$$

Commit$(\mathsf{ck}, \boldsymbol{x})$ returns $\mathsf{cm} := \sum_{j \in [n]} x_j \cdot [\eta\gamma^j]_2 = [\eta p_{\boldsymbol{x}}(\gamma)]_2$ and $\mathsf{d} := \boldsymbol{x}$.

Open$(\mathsf{ck}, \mathsf{d}, \mathbf{M})$ Let $\mathbf{M} \in \mathbb{Z}_p^{n \times m}$ be an MSP which accepts the input $\boldsymbol{x}$ in d. The algorithm computes a witness $\boldsymbol{w} \in \mathbb{Z}_p^n$ such that $\mathbf{M}^\top \cdot (\boldsymbol{w} \circ \boldsymbol{x}) = \boldsymbol{e}_1$, where $\boldsymbol{e}_1^\top = (1, 0, \ldots, 0)$, and then returns the opening $\mathsf{op} := (\pi_w, \pi_u, \hat{\pi}) \in \mathbb{G}_1^3$ computed as follows:

$$\begin{aligned}
\pi_w &:= \sum_{j \in [n]} w_j \cdot [\alpha^j]_1 = [p_{\boldsymbol{w}}(\alpha)]_1 \\
\pi_u &:= \sum_{j,\ell \in [n]} w_j \cdot x_\ell \cdot [\eta\alpha^j\gamma^\ell]_1 = [\eta \cdot p_{\boldsymbol{w}}(\alpha) \cdot p_{\boldsymbol{x}}(\gamma)]_1 \\
\hat{\pi} &:= \sum_{\substack{i \in [m] \\ j,k \in [n]: j \neq k}} M_{j,i} \cdot x_j \cdot w_k \cdot [\alpha^{n+1-j+k} \beta_i \gamma^{n+1}]_1 \\
&\quad + \sum_{\substack{i \in [m] \\ j,k,\ell \in [n]: \ell \neq j}} M_{j,i} \cdot x_\ell \cdot w_k \cdot \left[\alpha^{n+1-j+k} \beta_i \gamma^{n+1-j+\ell}\right]_1
\end{aligned}$$

Above, π_w represents a commitment to the witness $\boldsymbol{w} = [p_{\boldsymbol{w}}(\alpha)]_1$, $\pi_u = [\eta p_{\boldsymbol{w}}(\alpha) p_{\boldsymbol{x}}(\gamma)]_1$ is an encoding of $\boldsymbol{u} = \boldsymbol{w} \circ \boldsymbol{x}$. Finally, $\hat{\pi}$ can be seen as an evaluation proof for the linear map FC of [45] which shows that the vector $\boldsymbol{w}$ committed in π_w is a solution to the linear system $((\boldsymbol{x}||\cdots||\boldsymbol{x}) \circ \mathbf{M})^\top \cdot \boldsymbol{w} = \mathbf{M}^\top \cdot (\boldsymbol{w} \circ \boldsymbol{x}) = \boldsymbol{e}_1$.

<u>$\mathsf{Verify}(\mathsf{ck}, \mathsf{cm}, \mathsf{op}, \mathbf{M}, \mathsf{true})$</u> Compute $\Phi \leftarrow \sum_{i\in[m],j\in[m]} M_{j,i} \cdot \left[\frac{(\alpha\gamma)^{n+1-j}\beta_i}{\eta}\right]_2$, and output 1 iff the following checks are both satisfied:

$$\hat{e}(\pi_w, \mathsf{cm}) \stackrel{?}{=} \hat{e}(\pi_u, [1]_2) \tag{3}$$
$$\hat{e}(\pi_u, \Phi) \stackrel{?}{=} \hat{e}(\hat{\pi}, [1]_2) \cdot \hat{e}([\alpha\beta_1\gamma]_1, [(\alpha\gamma)^n]_2) \tag{4}$$

Remark 3. In the FC scheme above one can only create an opening if the MSP $\mathbf{M}$ accepts the committed input $\boldsymbol{x}$, but not if it rejects. This functionality is enough to build an FC for NC^1 circuits with a single output. If one wants to open for a circuit C such that $C(\boldsymbol{x})$ outputs 1 then uses the MSP $\mathbf{M}_C$ associated to C. If on the other hand, one wants to open to C such that $C(\boldsymbol{x}) = 0$ then one can instead prove that $\bar{C}(\boldsymbol{x}) = 1$, where $\bar{C}$ is the same as C with a negated output, and then use the MSP $\mathbf{M}_{\bar{C}}$ and show that it accepts.

Proof of Security. In the full version [13], we prove the weak evaluation binding of our FC based on the following (falsifiable) assumption. This is a variant of the assumption used in [17], which we justify in the generic group model in the full version[13].

Definition 8 ((n,m)-QP-BDHE assumption). *Let* $\mathsf{bp} = (p, \mathbb{G}_1, \mathbb{G}_2, \mathbb{G}_T, \hat{e}, g_1, g_2)$ *be a bilinear group setting. The (n,m)-QP-BDHE holds if for every $n, m = \mathsf{poly}$ and any PPT $\mathcal{A}$, the following advantage is negligible*

$$\mathbf{Adv}_{\mathcal{A}}^{(n,m)\text{-}QP\text{-}BDHE}(\lambda) = \Pr[\mathcal{A}(\mathsf{bp}, \Omega) => \alpha^{n+1}\gamma^{n+1}\delta] \quad \text{where}$$

$$\Omega := \begin{pmatrix} \{[\alpha^j]_1, [\eta\gamma^j]_2\}_{j\in[n]}, \{[\eta\alpha^j\gamma^\ell]_1\}_{j,\ell\in[n]}, \left\{\left[\alpha^j\beta_i\gamma^\ell\right]_1\right\}_{i\in[m],j,\ell\in[2n]:\ell\neq n+1} \\ [(\alpha\gamma)^n]_2, \left\{\left[\frac{(\alpha\gamma)^j\beta_i}{\eta}\right]_2\right\}_{i\in[m],j\in[n]} \\ \left\{\left[\frac{\delta}{\beta_k}\right]_2\right\}_{k\in[m]}, \left\{\left[\frac{\alpha^j\beta_i\gamma^{n+1}\delta}{\beta_k}\right]_2\right\}_{\substack{j\in[n],i,k\in[m]\\ i\neq k}}, \left\{\left[\frac{\alpha^j\beta_i\gamma^\ell\delta}{\beta_k}\right]_2\right\}_{\substack{i,k\in[m],j\in[n]\\ \ell\in[2n]\setminus\{n+1\}}} \end{pmatrix}$$

and the probability is over the random choices of $\alpha, \gamma, \delta, \eta \leftarrow_\$ \mathbb{Z}_q$, $\boldsymbol{\beta} \leftarrow_\$ \mathbb{Z}_q^m$ and $\mathcal{A}$'s random coins.

Zero-Knowledge. We discuss how to tweak the FC scheme in such a way that the commitment is hiding and the openings are zero-knowledge.

To do this, we consider an instantiation of the FC for vectors of length $n+1$. Then, a commitment to $\boldsymbol{x}$ is a commitment to $\tilde{\boldsymbol{x}} = (r, \boldsymbol{x})$ where $r \leftarrow_\$ \mathbb{Z}_p$. This way the group element cm is distributed like a uniformly random group element. The second change in the scheme is that in both Open and Verify, given an MSP matrix $\mathbf{M}$, one runs the same algorithms with a matrix $\tilde{\mathbf{M}} = (\mathbf{0} \mid \mathbf{M}^\top)^\top$, i.e., $\mathbf{M}$ with a zero row on top. This way the linear system remains functionally equivalent as r is ignored; this preserves both correctness and binding.

The third change is that Open computes π_w as a commitment to the vector $\tilde{\boldsymbol{w}} = (s, \boldsymbol{w})$ for a random $s \leftarrow_\$ \mathbb{Z}_p$. This way, π_w is uniformly distributed. Thanks to the row of zeros in $\tilde{\mathbf{M}}$, correctness is preserved.

Finally, to argue that this modified FC satisfies zero-knowledge, we show the simulators (that are assumed to know as trapdoors the values $\alpha, \gamma, \eta, \boldsymbol{\beta}$). $\mathcal{S}_1$ outputs cm as a commitment to $(r, \mathbf{0})$ using a random $r \leftarrow_\$ \mathbb{Z}_p$, and stores r in aux. $\mathcal{S}_2$ samples $\pi_w \leftarrow_\$ \mathbb{G}_1$, computes $\pi_u \leftarrow (\eta\gamma r) \cdot \pi_w$ and computes the simulated proof $\hat{\pi}$ as

$$\hat{\pi} := \left(\sum_{i \in [m], j \in [m]} M_{j,i} \cdot \frac{(\alpha\gamma)^{n+1-j} \beta_i}{\eta} \right) \cdot \pi_u - [(\alpha\gamma)^{n+1} \beta_1]_1$$

which is the unique value satisfying equation (4).

5.2 Other Instantiations

Libert et al.'s FC. The seminal work of Libert et al. [48] constructs FC for linear functions $\mathcal{F} := \{F : \mathbb{Z}_p^n \to \mathbb{Z}_p\}$, such that each F is defined by a vector $\boldsymbol{\beta}$ and $F_{\boldsymbol{\beta}}(\mathbf{x}) = \sum_{i=1}^{n} \mathbf{x}_i \boldsymbol{\beta}_i$. Consider a bilinear group setting $\mathsf{bp} := (p, \mathbb{G}_1, \mathbb{G}_2, \mathbb{G}_T, e, g_1, g_2)$. The construction is as follows.

$\mathsf{Setup}(1^\lambda, n)$ samples $u \leftarrow_\$ \mathbb{Z}_p$ and returns ck as

$$\mathsf{ck} := \left(\{[u^j]_1\}_{j \in [2n] \setminus \{n+1\}}, \{[u^j]_2\}_{j \in [n]} \right).$$

The trapdoor key is defined as $\mathsf{td} := [u^{n+1}]_1$.

$\mathsf{Commit}(\mathsf{ck}, \mathbf{x}; r)$ returns $\mathsf{cm} = [r]_1 + \sum_{j \in [n]} \mathbf{x}_j \cdot [u^j]_1$ and $\mathsf{d} = (\mathbf{x}, r)$.

$\mathsf{Open}(\mathsf{ck}, \mathsf{d}, \boldsymbol{\beta})$ parses d as $\mathsf{d} = (\mathbf{x}, r)$ and for $y = \langle \mathbf{x}, \boldsymbol{\beta} \rangle$, returns $\mathsf{op}_y = \sum_{i \in [n]} \boldsymbol{\beta}_i \cdot W_i$, where $W_i = r \cdot [u^{n-i+1}]_1 + \sum_{j \in [n], j \neq i} \mathbf{x}_j \cdot [u^{n+1-i+j}]_1$.

$\mathsf{Verify}(\mathsf{ck}, \mathsf{cm}, \mathsf{op}_y, \boldsymbol{\beta}, y)$ returns 1 if

$$\hat{e}(\mathsf{cm}, \sum_{i \in [n]} \boldsymbol{\beta}_i \cdot [u^{n+1-i}]_2) \stackrel{?}{=} \hat{e}(\mathsf{op}_y, [1]_2) \cdot \hat{e}([u]_1, [u^n]_2)^y$$

It is clear that the verification is linear in the opening proof. To show the construction provides perfect ZK, an efficient simulator $\mathcal{S} = (\mathcal{S}_1, \mathcal{S}_2)$ can be constructed as follows: $\mathcal{S}_1(\mathsf{td})$ first generates $\mathsf{cm} := \mathsf{Commit}(\mathsf{ck}, \mathbf{0}; r)$ and defines $\mathsf{aux} := r$. Now, for any adversarially chosen vector $\mathbf{x}$, and any query $\boldsymbol{\beta}$, $\mathcal{S}_2(\mathsf{td}, \mathsf{aux}, \boldsymbol{\beta}, y = \langle \mathbf{x}, \boldsymbol{\beta} \rangle)$ returns $\mathsf{op} = r \cdot (\sum_{i \in [n]} \boldsymbol{\beta}_i \cdot [u^{n+1-i}]_1) - y \cdot [u^{n+1}]_1 \in \mathbb{G}_1$.

Lipmaa and Pavlyk's FC. Limpaa and Pavlyk [50] proposed an FC for a class of circuits $\mathcal{F} := \{F : \mathcal{D}^n \to \mathcal{D}^\kappa\}$ where each $\mathcal{F}$ is defined by a vector $\boldsymbol{\beta} \in \mathcal{D}^{\mu_\beta}$. Their scheme is based on the SNARK construction of Groth16 [37] for F^*—a compiled version of F. In Groth's SNARK, the argument consists of three group elements $\pi = ([A]_1, [B]_2, [C]_1)$. The key idea in SFC of [50] is as follows: first, express the first two elements $[A]_1, [B]_2$ as sums of two elements where the first depends only on the secret data and the second depends only on the public data (i.e., $\boldsymbol{\beta}$ and the output $F(\mathbf{x}, \boldsymbol{\beta})$). That is, $[A]_1 = [A_s]_1 + [A_p]_1$ and $[B]_2 = [B_s]_2 + [B_p]_2$. Next, write $[C]_1$ as $[C_{sp}]_1 + [C_p]_1$, where $[C_p]_1$ depends only on the public data and $[C_{sp}]_1$ depends on both the public and the secret data. Now, a functional commitment to $\mathbf{x}$ is $\mathsf{cm} = ([A_s]_1, [B_s]_2)$ and the opening to $F(\cdot, \boldsymbol{\beta})$ is $\mathsf{op} = [C_{sp}]_1$. To verify an opening op, the verifier computes $[A_p]_1$, $[B_p]_2$, and $[C_p]_1$, and then runs the SNARK verifier on the argument $([A_s]_1 + [A_p]_1, [B_s]_2 + [B_p]_2, [C_{sp}]_1 + [C_p]_1)$. The construction is shown to be perfectly zero-knowledge as defined in [50], but it is not hard to show that it satisfies our stronger definition (i.e., definition 4) as well. In fact, given $\mathsf{td} = (u, v)$ as the trapdoor of the commitment key, $\mathcal{S}_1(\mathsf{td})$ generates the commitment as the first step of the SNARK simulation in [50] and defines aux as the discrete logarithm of the commitment. Now, $\mathcal{S}_2$ can utilises aux and answer oracle queries for different circuits $F(\cdot, \boldsymbol{\beta})$ by performing the rest of the SNARK simulation. Given that the verification in the SNARK of [37] is linear in the opening $[C_{sp}]_1$ makes this functional commitment an appropriate instantiation for our construction of $\mathrm{WE}^{\mathrm{FC}}$.

6 From $\mathrm{WE}^{\mathrm{FC}}$ to Reusable Non-interactive MPC

6.1 Preliminaries on mrNISC

Here we first recall the definition of mrNISC schemes in [9] and their construction based on $\mathrm{WE}^{\mathrm{ZK\text{-}CM}}$. We then show how our notion of $\mathrm{WE}^{\mathrm{FC}}$ can be used as a replacement of $\mathrm{WE}^{\mathrm{ZK\text{-}CM}}$ in their construction.

There are two rounds in mrNISC-style variant of secure multiparty computation protocols, *input encoding phase* and *evaluation phase*. In the first round, parties publish encodings of their secret inputs on a public bulletin board, without any coordination with other parties. This happens once and for all. Next, in the second round, any subset of parties can compute a function on their inputs by publishing only one message each. More formally, a mrNISC scheme is defined by the following three algorithms:

Input Encoding $(\hat{x}_i, s_i) \leftarrow \mathsf{Commit}(1^\lambda, x_i)$ by which a party P_i encodes its private input x_i and publishes the encoding $\hat{x}_i$.

Computation Encoding $\eta_i \leftarrow \mathsf{Encode}(z, \{\hat{x}_j\}_{j \in J}, s_i)$ by which each party P_i among a subset of parties $\{P_j\}_{j \in J}$ generates and publishes a computation encoding η_i. This allows parties in J to compute a functionality f described by z (i.e., $f(z, \star)$) on their private inputs.

Output $y = \mathsf{Eval}(z, \{\hat{x}_j\}_{j \in J}, \{\eta_j\}_{j \in J})$ which deterministically computes the output y (required to be $f(z, \{x_j\}_{j \in J})$ by the correctness property).

The construction of mrNISC in [9] is based upon the work of [34], where they follow the *round collapsing* approach for constructing 2-round MPC protocols used in [27]. Let $\prod$ be an L-round MPC protocol. The round collapsing approach collapses $\prod$ into a 2-round protocol $\overline{\prod}$ as follows. For $\ell \in [L]$, let m_i^ℓ denote the message published by party P_i in round ℓ of $\prod$. Let x_i and r_i be respectively the secret input and random tape of P_i used to execute $\prod$. In the first round of $\overline{\prod}$, each party P_i commits to its private input (x_i, r_i) and broadcasts the resulting commitment cm_i. In the second round, each party P_i garbles its next-step message function F_i^ℓ in $\prod$ for each round $\ell \in [L]$. Note that the resulting garbled circuit, denoted by $\hat{F}_i^\ell$, should take as input all the messages $\mathbf{m}^{<\ell} = \{m_j^\ell\}_{l<\ell, j\in[n]}$ of all parties up to round $\ell - 1$, and outputs the next message m_i^ℓ of P_i in $\prod$. To do so, each P_i should provide a way for other parties to compute the labels of $\hat{F}_i^\ell$ that correspond to the correct messages in $\prod$, where a message m_j^l is correct if it is computed from P_i's committed messages (x_i, r_i) in the first round. To this end, [34] suggests the following mechanism: let k_0 and k_1 be two labels for an input wire in P_i's garbled circuit $\hat{F}_i^\ell$. Suppose that $\hat{F}_i^\ell$ takes as input the t'th bit $y = m_{j,t}^l$ of a message from P_j (where m_j^l is output by P_j's garbled circuit $\hat{F}_j^l$), and provides a way for all parties to obtain the valid label k_y. The key idea in [34] is to use a general-purpose WE to produce a ciphertext $\mathsf{ct}_y \leftarrow \mathsf{WE.Enc}(\mathsf{x}_y, k_y)$ for $y \in \{0, 1\}$ under the statement x_y that "there exists a NIZK proof π_y that proves $y = m_{j,t}^l$ is computed correctly". Again, correct computation here means that y is computed from P_j's committed messages (x_i, r_i) in the first round, and in accordance to the partial transcript of messages $\mathbf{m}^{<l}$. The two ciphertexts $(\mathsf{ct}_0, \mathsf{ct}_1)$ are part of what P_i in the garbled circuit $\hat{F}_i^l$ outputs. Furthermore, to allow all parties to (publicly) obtain the correct label k_y, P_j's garbled circuit $\hat{F}_j^l$ additionally outputs a NIZK proof π_y that $y = m_{j,t}^l$ is correctly computed. Correctness of $\overline{\prod}$ follows from correctness of WE. Security also follows from the fact that k_{1-y} remains hidden by the soundness of NIZK and semantic security of WE. Furthermore, the ZK property of NIZK guarantees the privacy of parties.

The main problem in the above construction of [34] is the lack of general-purpose WE from standard assumptions. Benhamouda and Lin [9] overcome this problem by observing that not a WE for general NP language, but a WE scheme for a particular language corresponding to the verification circuit of a NIZK proof that proves the correctness of computation over committed information suffices to realize the above construction. This variant of WE, denoted by WE$^{\text{ZK-CM}}$ in this work, consists of a triple $\mathsf{WE}^{\mathsf{ZK\text{-}CM}} = (\mathsf{COM}, \mathsf{NIZK}, \mathsf{WE})$ and is defined for a NP language $\mathcal{L}$ such that a statement $\mathsf{x} = (\mathsf{cm}, G, y)$ is in $\mathcal{L}$ iff there exists an accepting NIZK proof π (as the witness for x) w.r.t. crs that proves cm is a commitment of some value v and that $G(v) = y$. As provided in the construction of [34] (but based on stronger assumption of general-purpose WE), WE$^{\text{ZK-CM}}$ should support all polynomial computations; i.e., it should be that G in the statements $\mathsf{x} = (\mathsf{cm}, G, y)$ can be any arbitrary polynomial-sized circuit. Moreover, the commitments in WE$^{\text{ZK-CM}}$ should be reusable in the sense that generating unbounded number of NIZK proofs and WE ciphertexts w.r.t. commitments should not reveal any information about the committed (secret) values, except what is revealed by the statements. Equipped with this property then allows to make the construction of [34] reusable by replacing r_i with a

PRF seed s_i that generates pseudo-random tapes for an unbounded number of computations. The key idea in the construction of $\mathrm{WE}^{\mathrm{ZK\text{-}CM}}$ in [9] is to use a NIZK proof system that has a linear-decision verification. Given such NIZK is then sufficient to realize $\mathrm{WE}^{\mathrm{ZK\text{-}CM}}$ using a WE for linear languages which can be constructed efficiently based on SPHFs. In more details, let $\boldsymbol{\Theta} = \mathbf{M}\pi$ be the linear equation corresponding to the verification of NIZK for a statement $\mathsf{x} = (\mathsf{cm}, G, y)$, such that $\boldsymbol{\Theta}$ and $\mathbf{M}$ depend on x and thus are known at the time of encryption. One can now encrypt a message straightforwardly by using an SPHF for this relation such that only one who can compute the hash value using a valid witness π can retrieve the message.

6.2 Our mrNISC Construction

We now show how one can replace $\mathrm{WE}^{\mathrm{ZK\text{-}CM}}$ with $\mathrm{WE}^{\mathrm{FC}}$ in the aforementioned construction. Let FC be a succinct functional commitment for circuit class $\mathcal{F}$, and $\mathsf{WE}^{\mathsf{FC}} = (\mathsf{Setup}, \mathsf{Commit}, \mathsf{Open}, \mathsf{Verify}, \mathsf{Enc}, \mathsf{Dec})$ be a $\mathrm{WE}^{\mathrm{FC}}$ for $\mathcal{F}$ constructed as in Sect. 4.2. Besides $\mathsf{WE}^{\mathsf{FC}}$, the construction uses the following building blocks, formally defined in the full version [13]:

- A semi-malicious output-delayed simulatable L-round MPC protocol $\prod = (\mathsf{Next}, \mathsf{Output})$ for f.
- A garbled circuit $\mathsf{GC} = (\mathsf{Gen}, \mathsf{Garble}, \mathsf{Eval}, \mathsf{Sim})$ for $\mathcal{F}$.

The construction is as follows:

Input Encoding. For a binary input x_i and PRF key $fk_i \leftarrow_{\$} \{0,1\}^\lambda$, party P_i commits to $x_i||fk_i$ as $(\mathsf{cm}_i, \mathsf{d}_i) \leftarrow \mathsf{Commit}(\mathsf{ck}, (x_i||fk_i); r_i)$. It then sets $\hat{x}_i := \mathsf{cm}_i$ and $s_i := (x_i, fk_i, \mathsf{d}_i)$.

Computation Encoding. To encode a computation $f(z, \star)$, each party P_i for $\ell \in [L]$ generates input labels $(\mathbf{stE}_i^\ell, \{\mathbf{msgE}_{i,j}^\ell\}_{j\in J}) \leftarrow \mathsf{Gen}(1^\lambda)$ and garbles the evaluation function $\mathbf{F}_i^\ell$ (defined in Fig. 3) as $\hat{\mathbf{F}}_i^\ell \leftarrow \mathsf{Garble}((\mathbf{stE}_i^\ell, \{\mathbf{msgE}_{i,j}^\ell\}_{j\in J}), \mathbf{F}_i^\ell)$. Finally, it sets $\eta_i := \{\hat{\mathbf{F}}_i^\ell\}_{\ell\in[L]}$.

Output. The output is computed by recovering the input labels and then evaluating the garbled circuits on them in L iteration. That is, for $\ell = 1, \ldots, L$:

1. For $i \in J$,

$$\left(\mathbf{stE}_i^{\prime\ell+1}, \{\mathsf{ct}_{i,j,k,b}^\ell\}_{j,k,b}, m_i^\ell, \{\mathsf{op}_{i,k}^\ell\}_k\right) := \mathsf{Eval}(\hat{\mathbf{F}}_i, (\mathbf{stE}_i^{\prime\ell}, \{\mathbf{msgE}_{i,j}^\ell[m_j^{\ell-1}]\}_{j\in J})).$$

2. If $\ell \neq L$, then for $i, j \in J$ and $k \in [\nu_m]$,

$$\mathbf{msgE}_{i,j}^{\ell+1}[m_j^\ell] := \left\{\mathsf{Dec}(\mathsf{ck}, \mathsf{ct}_{i,j,k,m_{j,k}^\ell}^{\ell+1}, \mathsf{cm}_j, G_{j,k}^\ell, m_{j,k}^\ell, \mathsf{op}_{i,j,k}^\ell)\right\}$$

After all the messages $\mathbf{m} = \{m_j^\ell\}_{j\in J,\ell\in[L]}$ of the inner MPC are recovered, the final output is computed as $y := \mathsf{Output}(z, \mathbf{m})$.

Hardwired Values:
$(1^\lambda, \ell, i, z, \{\hat{x}_j = \mathsf{cm}_j\}_{j\in J}, s_i = (x_i, fk_i, \mathsf{d}_i), \mathbf{stE}_i^{\ell+1}, \{\mathbf{msgE}_{i,j}^{\ell+1}\}_{j\in J})$.

Circuit Inputs. $(\mathbf{m}^{<\ell-1}, \mathbf{m}^{\ell-1})$, where $\mathbf{m}^{<\ell-1}$ are the protocol messages of the first $\ell-2$ rounds with corresponding garble labels $\mathbf{stE}_i^{\ell}$, and $\mathbf{m}^{\ell-1}$ are the messages of the $\ell-1$ round with corresponding garble labels $\{\mathbf{msgE}_{i,j}^{\ell}\}_{j\in J}$.

Procedure. 1. For $j \in J$ and $k \in [\nu_m]$, define the circuits G_j^ℓ and $G_{j,k}^\ell$ as follows:

$$G_j^\ell(x_j, fk_j) = \mathsf{Next}_j(z, x_j, \mathsf{PRF}(fk_j, z\|[\nu_r]), \mathbf{m}^{<\ell-1}, \mathbf{m}^{\ell-1})\,; \qquad G_{j,k}^\ell := k\text{-th bit of } G_j^\ell$$

2. Compute the ℓ-th round message $m_i^\ell = m_{i,1}^\ell\|\ldots\|m_{i,\nu_m}^\ell$ of P_i, and proofs of correct openings $\mathsf{op}_{i,k}^\ell$ for each bit $k \in [\nu_m]$:

$$m_i^\ell := G_i^\ell(x_i, fk_i)\ ; \mathsf{op}_{i,k}^\ell \leftarrow \mathsf{Open}(\mathsf{ck}, s_i, G_{i,k}^\ell) \qquad \textbf{for } k \in [\nu_m].$$

3. For $j \in J$ and $k \in [\nu_m]$, encrypt labels $\mathbf{msgE}_{i,j}^{\ell+1}[k,b]$ so that the valid message m_j^ℓ can be used to obtain $\mathbf{msgE}_{i,j}^{\ell+1}[m_j^\ell] = \{\mathbf{msgE}_{i,j}^{\ell+1}[k, m_{j,k}^\ell]\}_{k\in[\nu_m]}$:

$$\mathsf{ct}_{i,j,k,b}^{\ell+1} \leftarrow \mathsf{Enc}(\mathsf{ck}, \mathsf{cm}_j, G_{j,k}^\ell, b, \mathbf{msgE}_{i,j}^{\ell+1}[k,b])^a \qquad \textbf{for } b \in \{0,1\}.$$

Circuit Output. $(\mathbf{stE}_i^{\ell+1}[\mathbf{m}^{<\ell-1}\|\mathbf{m}^{\ell-1}], \{\mathsf{ct}_{i,j,k,b}^{\ell+1}\}_{j,k,b}, m_i^\ell, \{\mathsf{op}_{i,k}^\ell\}_k)$.

[a] The ciphertexts are set to be empty strings for $\ell = L$.

Fig. 3. Circuit $\mathbf{F}_i^\ell$ for the construction of mrNISC based on $\mathrm{WE}^{\mathrm{FC}}$

The correctness of the construction follows straightforwardly from the correctness of the underlying building blocks. For security, we refer to [9] as the proof is similar to the security of the mrNISC construction in [9]. Here, we only state the theorem.

Theorem 4. *Let* PRF *be a pseudorandom function,* GC *be a garbled circuit with simulatability property,* $\prod$ *be a semi-malicious output-delayed simulatable MPC protocol, and* $\mathsf{WE}^{\mathsf{FC}}$ *be a* $\mathrm{WE}^{\mathrm{FC}}$ *with semantic security. The* mrNISC scheme described above is semi-maliciously private.

On the Efficiency of our mrNISC Construction. The main advantage of our mrNISC construction compared to the one in [9] is that our approach admits an input encoding phase with much shorter communication since we use succinct commitments. This is especially important since commitments are supposed to be stored in a public bulletin board to be re-used in several future computations.

Remark 4. While our FC construction can be used to instantiate our $\mathrm{WE}^{\mathrm{FC}}$ for NC^1, we need one to support arbitrary circuits to instantiate our mrNISC (roughly, this corresponds to the round function of the "lifted" MPC, plus PRFs). To achieve this, we notice we can use the same generic bootstrapping technique used in [9] to obtain $\mathrm{WE}^{\mathrm{FC}}$ for all polynomial-size circuits. For a polynomial-size computation $G(v) = y$, the bootstrapping technique encodes the computation into a randomized encoding $o = \mathsf{RE}(G, v, \mathsf{PRF}(k))$ (for some PRF seed k) that reveals y. Given that both RE and PRF are computable in NC^1, our $\mathrm{WE}^{\mathrm{FC}}$ for NC^1 can be used to verify if the computation of o from (v, k)—committed in a commitment cm—is correct. There is still one issue left that verifying that o decodes to y is still in P. To get around this, a garbled circuit is instead used to verify if a given input o' decodes to y.

We observe that this technique preserves the succinctness of the encoding (commitments) in the context of mrNISC protocols.

7 Other Application Scenarios

In this section we show that our notion of $\mathrm{WE}^{\mathrm{FC}}$can be versatile; we describe how it can be used in other scenarios besides mrNISC.

7.1 Targeted Broadcast

As a first application scenario, we discuss how to apply $\mathrm{WE}^{\mathrm{FC}}$ to a targeted broadcast with "special properties". See last item in Sect. 1.2 for a description of the problem, but a quick summary is: we aim at encrypting a message with respect to some attributes (not necessarily known before encryption time); only users holding those attributes can decrypt (we discuss later how they are granted).

This subsection proceeds in three parts. We first give a flavor of our approach template, which we call "commit-and-receive" since it involves a commitment to user attributes which allows them to decrypt to compatible messages. We then argue what properties make this approach interesting compared to the more standard targeted broadcast setting. Finally we compare to alternative approaches in more detail. Due to the lack of space, the last two parts are deferred to the full version [13].

Our Approach: Commit-and-Receive. We now describe our general approach. To better provide an intuition for it, we start with a flavor of which *settings* it is suitable for; this is best introduced through a specific toy example. Consider a sophisticated programming contest where participants are asked to write a program solving a specific algorithmic problem. To evaluate each submission, it is common for the organizers to execute the program against several test cases (not public before submission deadline). If submission passes enough test-cases, the sender can receive instructions to move on to the next stage (or receive a digital prize, e.g. a full copy of TAOCP[16]). If the participants want to keep their

[16] The Art Of Computer Programming (TAOCP) by Donald E. Knuth https://www-cs-faculty.stanford.edu/~knuth/taocp.html.

code secret, can their program still be tested and receive the instructions/prize? There are arguably other natural settings besides this one[17].

We aim at providing a solution for a generalized version of the setting above with particular attention at *minimizing round interaction.* We call our approach "Commit-and-Receive"[18] and we show how it can be naturally built through our primitive $\mathsf{WE}^{\mathsf{FC}}$.

Our approach, described through the lens of the application example above: consider a party R interested in receiving some message (e.g. a digital good) from a sender S. The latter would like the message to be received by R only if some data D_R held by R satisfy a certain policy (e.g. the tests determined which programs will pass the contest or the drawn lottery number). The data D_R are committed beforehand and the policy is not chosen adaptively and thus possibly not known at commitment time. After each participant has published a commitment cm_i to their program, the organizers can broadcast $\mathbf{ct} := (\mathsf{ct}_1, \ldots, \mathsf{ct}_\ell)$ with $\mathsf{ct}_i \leftarrow \mathsf{WE}^{\mathsf{FC}}.\mathsf{Enc}(\mathsf{ck}, \mathsf{cm}_i, F_{\mathsf{tests}}, m)$, where m contains further instructions or a digital prize and F_{tests} is a function checking if tests are passed. The participants whose solutions do not pass the tests will not be able to decrypt their respective ciphertext.

7.2 Simple Contingent Payment for Services

The next application setting we describe has to do with a form of conditional payments. Imagine we want to incentivize the availability of some large data (Internet Archive, Wikipedia, etc.). One approach to (publicly) check data availability uses some variant of this approach: for the data D there exists a public, *succinct* commitment (e.g., a Merkle Tree or a functional commitment compatible with $\mathsf{WE}^{\mathsf{FC}}$ in our case); once every epoch, a verifier samples random indices $r_1, \ldots, r_m \leftarrow_{\$} [|D|]$; a storage provider shows an opening (e.g., Merkle tree paths) to the values $D[r_1], \ldots, D[r_m]$. If carried out enough times and appropriately choosing m, this procedure can guarantee data availability with low communication [41]. Notice that the use of succinct commitments is essential in such an application: if verification requires the same amount of storage as the data D, one may be better off storing D.

There are several approaches to incentivizing availability without the need of interaction from the party interested in keeping the data available (which we call stakeholder in the remainder). Several of these approaches involve embedding

[17] Another straightforward example for our setting is that of *lotteries.* Each party commits to a lottery number (or through an identifier sampled in some manner), then a draw occurs and only the winner(s) can obtain a certain message, e.g., a digital prize or some other message. The lottery setting while simple is actually quite concretely practical, for instance in *proofs of stake* [23]. The problem of commit-and-receive can be seen as a a more general version of the primitive "Encryption to the Current Winner" (ECW) defined in [12] in the context of proofs of stake. In fact the solution described in this section can be leveraged as a construction for ECW with short commitments.

[18] The name is a variant of "commit-and-prove" as used in [14,49].

incentives in the mining process in a blockchain (e.g., Filecoin) or letting a smart contract (e.g., on Ethereum) unlock a reward[19] if the verification process above succeeds. Other solutions apply threshold cryptography requiring a set of parties to be available and act as decryptor oracles [44]. Through $\mathrm{WE}^{\mathrm{FC}}$, we can achieve a simpler solution that does not rely on threshold networks, a specific blockchain architecture or smart contracts (convenient both in terms of gas costs, simplicity and communication complexity on chain) . The solution is as follows. The stakeholder produces a vector of random indices $\boldsymbol{r}$ as above and produces the ciphertext $\mathsf{ct} \leftarrow \mathsf{WE}^{\mathsf{FC}}.\mathsf{Enc}(\mathsf{ck}, \mathsf{cm}_D, F_{\boldsymbol{r}}, \mathsf{k}_{\mathrm{ca\$h}})$ where cm_D is a commitment to the data, $F_{\boldsymbol{r}}$ is a selector function—$F_{\boldsymbol{r}}(D) := (D[r_1], \ldots, D[r_m])$—and $\mathsf{k}_{\mathrm{ca\$h}}$ is the message we are encrypting, that is a secret that allows access to the reward (e.g., a Bitcoin private key). Further subtleties of this approach are discussed in the full version [13]. We believe the solution above can be applied generically to other natural settings.

An important note is that for the approach above to work we need a stronger variant of $\mathrm{WE}^{\mathrm{FC}}$ in which (a) the encryptor does not need to know the output of the function used in the statement, and (2) security has an *extractability* flavor which ensures that a successful decryptor will actually know the output of $F_{\boldsymbol{r}}(D)$ for committed data D. In the full version [13], we define this variant of $\mathrm{WE}^{\mathrm{FC}}$ and prove that our same construction of Sect. 4 satisfies this stronger property.

Acknowledgements. This work has received funding from the European Research Council (ERC) under the European Union's Horizon 2020 research and innovation programme under project PICOCRYPT (grant agreement No. 101001283), and from the Spanish Government MCIN/AEI/10.13039/501100011033/ under projects PRODIGY (TED2021-132464B-I00) and ESPADA (PID2022-142290OB-I00). The last two projects are co-funded by European Union FEDER and NextGenerationEU/PRTR funds.

References

1. Decentralized storage. https://ethereum.org/en/developers/docs/storage/ (2022)
2. Abdalla, M., Benhamouda, F., MacKenzie, P.: Security of the J-PAKE password-authenticated key exchange protocol. In: 2015 IEEE Symposium on Security and Privacy, pp. 571–587. IEEE Computer Society Press (2015). https://doi.org/10.1109/SP.2015.41
3. Abdalla, M., Benhamouda, F., Pointcheval, D.: Disjunctions for hash proof systems: new constructions and applications. In: Oswald, E., Fischlin, M. (eds.) EUROCRYPT 2015. LNCS, vol. 9057, pp. 69–100. Springer, Heidelberg (2015). https://doi.org/10.1007/978-3-662-46803-6_3

[19] See respectively https://docs.filecoin.io/about-filecoin/what-is-filecoin/ and https://thegraph.com/docs/en/about/.

4. Albrecht, M.R., Cini, V., Lai, R.W.F., Malavolta, G., Thyagarajan, S.A.K.: Lattice-based SNARKs: publicly verifiable, preprocessing, and recursively composable: (extended abstract). In: Dodis, Y., Shrimpton, T. (eds.) Advances in Cryptology – CRYPTO 2022: 42nd Annual International Cryptology Conference, CRYPTO 2022, Santa Barbara, CA, USA, August 15–18, 2022, Proceedings, Part II, pp. 102–132. Springer, Cham (2022). https://doi.org/10.1007/978-3-031-15979-4_4
5. Balbás, D., Catalano, D., Fiore, D., Lai, R.W.F.: Chainable functional commitments for unbounded-depth circuits. In: Rothblum, G., Wee, H. (eds.) Theory of Cryptography: 21st International Conference, TCC 2023, Taipei, Taiwan, November 29–December 2, 2023, Proceedings, Part III, pp. 363–393. Springer, Cham (2023). https://doi.org/10.1007/978-3-031-48621-0_13
6. Barta, O., Ishai, Y., Ostrovsky, R., Wu, D.J.: On succinct arguments and witness encryption from groups. In: Micciancio, D., Ristenpart, T. (eds.) Advances in Cryptology – CRYPTO 2020: 40th Annual International Cryptology Conference, CRYPTO 2020, Santa Barbara, CA, USA, August 17–21, 2020, Proceedings, Part I, pp. 776–806. Springer, Cham (2020). https://doi.org/10.1007/978-3-030-56784-2_26
7. Benhamouda, F., Blazy, O., Chevalier, C., Pointcheval, D., Vergnaud, D.: New techniques for SPHFs and efficient one-round PAKE protocols. In: Canetti, R., Garay, J.A. (eds.) Advances in Cryptology – CRYPTO 2013, pp. 449–475. Springer, Berlin, Heidelberg (2013). https://doi.org/10.1007/978-3-642-40041-4_25
8. Benhamouda, F., Jain, A., Komargodski, I., Lin, H.: Multiparty reusable non-interactive secure computation from LWE. In: Canteaut, A., Standaert, F.-X. (eds.) Advances in Cryptology – EUROCRYPT 2021: 40th Annual International Conference on the Theory and Applications of Cryptographic Techniques, Zagreb, Croatia, October 17–21, 2021, Proceedings, Part II, pp. 724–753. Springer, Cham (2021). https://doi.org/10.1007/978-3-030-77886-6_25
9. Benhamouda, F., Lin, H.: Mr NISC: multiparty reusable non-interactive secure computation. In: Pass, R., Pietrzak, K. (eds.) Theory of Cryptography: 18th International Conference, TCC 2020, Durham, NC, USA, November 16–19, 2020, Proceedings, Part II, pp. 349–378. Springer, Cham (2020). https://doi.org/10.1007/978-3-030-64378-2_13
10. Bernhard, D., Fischlin, M., Warinschi, B.: On the hardness of proving CCA-security of signed ElGamal. In: Cheng, C.-M., Chung, K.-M., Persiano, G., Yang, B.-Y. (eds.) Public-Key Cryptography – PKC 2016: 19th IACR International Conference on Practice and Theory in Public-Key Cryptography, Taipei, Taiwan, March 6-9, 2016, Proceedings, Part I, pp. 47–69. Springer, Berlin, Heidelberg (2016). https://doi.org/10.1007/978-3-662-49384-7_3
11. Boneh, D., Franklin, M.K.: Identity based encryption from the Weil pairing. SIAM J. Comput. **32**(3), 586–615 (2003)
12. Campanelli, M., David, B., Khoshakhlagh, H., Kristensen, A.K., Nielsen, J.B.: Encryption to the future: a paradigm for sending secret messages to future (anonymous) committees. In: IACR Cryptology ePrint Archive, p. 1423 (2021). https://eprint.iacr.org/2021/1423
13. Campanelli, M., Fiore, D., Khoshakhlagh, H.: Witness encryption for succinct functional commitments and applications. IACR Cryptol. ePrint Arch., p. 1510 (2022). https://eprint.iacr.org/2022/1510

14. Campanelli, M., Fiore, D., Querol, A.: LegoSNARK: modular design and composition of succinct zero-knowledge proofs. In: Cavallaro, L., Kinder, J., Wang, X., Katz, J. (eds.) ACM CCS 2019, pp. 2075–2092. ACM Press (2019). https://doi.org/10.1145/3319535.3339820
15. Campanelli, M., Gennaro, R., Goldfeder, S., Nizzardo, L.: Zero-knowledge contingent payments revisited: attacks and payments for services. In: Thuraisingham, B.M., Evans, D., Malkin, T., Xu, D. (eds.) ACM CCS 2017, pp. 229–243. ACM Press (2017). https://doi.org/10.1145/3133956.3134060
16. de Castro, L., Peikert, C.: Functional commitments for all functions, with transparent setup and from SIS. In: Hazay, C., Stam, M. (eds.) Advances in Cryptology – EUROCRYPT 2023: 42nd Annual International Conference on the Theory and Applications of Cryptographic Techniques, Lyon, France, April 23-27, 2023, Proceedings, Part III, pp. 287–320. Springer, Cham (2023). https://doi.org/10.1007/978-3-031-30620-4_10
17. Catalano, D., Fiore, D., Tucker, I.: Additive-homomorphic functional commitments and applications to homomorphic signatures. In: Agrawal, S., Lin, D. (eds.) Advances in Cryptology – ASIACRYPT 2022: 28th International Conference on the Theory and Application of Cryptology and Information Security, Taipei, Taiwan, December 5–9, 2022, Proceedings, Part IV, pp. 159–188. Springer, Cham (2022). https://doi.org/10.1007/978-3-031-22972-5_6
18. Chen, J., Gay, R., Wee, H.: Improved dual system ABE in prime-order groups via predicate encodings. In: Oswald, E., Fischlin, M. (eds.) Advances in Cryptology - EUROCRYPT 2015: 34th Annual International Conference on the Theory and Applications of Cryptographic Techniques, Sofia, Bulgaria, April 26-30, 2015, Proceedings, Part II, pp. 595–624. Springer, Berlin, Heidelberg (2015). https://doi.org/10.1007/978-3-662-46803-6_20
19. Chen, J., Gong, J., Kowalczyk, L., Wee, H.: Unbounded ABE via bilinear entropy expansion, revisited. In: Nielsen, J.B., Rijmen, V. (eds.) Advances in Cryptology – EUROCRYPT 2018: 37th Annual International Conference on the Theory and Applications of Cryptographic Techniques, Tel Aviv, Israel, April 29 - May 3, 2018 Proceedings, Part I, pp. 503–534. Springer, Cham (2018). https://doi.org/10.1007/978-3-319-78381-9_19
20. Chen, Y., Vaikuntanathan, V., Wee, H.: GGH15 beyond permutation branching programs: proofs, attacks, and candidates. In: Shacham, H., Boldyreva, A. (eds.) Advances in Cryptology – CRYPTO 2018: 38th Annual International Cryptology Conference, Santa Barbara, CA, USA, August 19–23, 2018, Proceedings, Part II, pp. 577–607. Springer, Cham (2018). https://doi.org/10.1007/978-3-319-96881-0_20
21. Couteau, G., Hartmann, D.: Shorter non-interactive zero-knowledge arguments and ZAPs for algebraic languages. In: Micciancio, D., Ristenpart, T. (eds.) Advances in Cryptology – CRYPTO 2020: 40th Annual International Cryptology Conference, CRYPTO 2020, Santa Barbara, CA, USA, August 17–21, 2020, Proceedings, Part III, pp. 768–798. Springer, Cham (2020). https://doi.org/10.1007/978-3-030-56877-1_27
22. Cramer, R., Shoup, V.: Universal hash proofs and a paradigm for adaptive chosen ciphertext secure public-key encryption. In: Knudsen, L.R. (ed.) Advances in Cryptology—EUROCRYPT 2002, pp. 45–64. Springer, Berlin, Heidelberg (2002). https://doi.org/10.1007/3-540-46035-7_4

23. Daian, P., Pass, R., Shi, E.: Snow White: robustly reconfigurable consensus and applications to provably secure proof of stake. In: Goldberg, I., Moore, T. (eds.) Financial Cryptography and Data Security: 23rd International Conference, FC 2019, Frigate Bay, St. Kitts and Nevis, February 18–22, 2019, Revised Selected Papers, pp. 23–41. Springer, Cham (2019). https://doi.org/10.1007/978-3-030-32101-7_2
24. Diffie, W., Hellman, M.E.: New directions in cryptography. IEEE Trans. Inf. Theory **22**(6), 644–654 (1976). https://doi.org/10.1109/TIT.1976.1055638
25. Fernando, R., Jain, A., Komargodski, I.: Maliciously-secure MrNISC in the plain model. In: IACR Cryptology ePrint Archive, p. 1319 (2021). https://eprint.iacr.org/2021/1319
26. Fuchsbauer, G., Kiltz, E., Loss, J.: The algebraic group model and its applications. In: Shacham, H., Boldyreva, A. (eds.) Advances in Cryptology – CRYPTO 2018: 38th Annual International Cryptology Conference, Santa Barbara, CA, USA, August 19–23, 2018, Proceedings, Part II, pp. 33–62. Springer, Cham (2018). https://doi.org/10.1007/978-3-319-96881-0_2
27. Garg, S., Gentry, C., Halevi, S., Raykova, M.: Two-round secure MPC from indistinguishability obfuscation. In: Lindell, Y. (ed.) Theory of Cryptography, pp. 74–94. Springer, Berlin, Heidelberg (2014). https://doi.org/10.1007/978-3-642-54242-8_4
28. Garg, S., Gentry, C., Halevi, S., Raykova, M., Sahai, A., Waters, B.: Candidate indistinguishability obfuscation and functional encryption for all circuits. In: 54th FOCS, IEEE Computer Society Press, pp. 40–49 (2013). https://doi.org/10.1109/FOCS.2013.13
29. Garg, S., Gentry, C., Sahai, A., Waters, B.: Witness encryption and its applications. In: Boneh, D., Roughgarden, T., Feigenbaum, J. (eds.) In: 45th ACM STOC, pp. 467–476. ACM Press (2013). https://doi.org/10.1145/2488608.2488667
30. Gennaro, R., Lindell, Y.: A framework for password-based authenticated key exchange. ACM Trans. Inf. Syst. Secur. **9**(2), 181–234 (2006)
31. Gentry, C., Lewko, A., Waters, B.: Witness encryption from instance independent assumptions. In: Garay, J.A., Gennaro, R. (eds.) CRYPTO 2014. LNCS, vol. 8616, pp. 426–443. Springer, Heidelberg (2014). https://doi.org/10.1007/978-3-662-44371-2_24
32. Gentry, C., Wichs, D.: Separating succinct non-interactive arguments from all falsifiable assumptions. In: Fortnow, L., Vadhan, S.P. (eds.) 43rd ACM STOC, pp. 99–108. ACM Press (2011). https://doi.org/10.1145/1993636.1993651
33. Goldreich, O., Levin, L.A.: A hard-core predicate for all one-way functions. In: 21st ACM STOC, pp. 25–32. ACM Press (1989). https://doi.org/10.1145/73007.73010
34. Dov Gordon, S., Liu, F.-H., Shi, E.: Constant-round MPC with fairness and guarantee of output delivery. In: Gennaro, R., Robshaw, M. (eds.) CRYPTO 2015. LNCS, vol. 9216, pp. 63–82. Springer, Heidelberg (2015). https://doi.org/10.1007/978-3-662-48000-7_4
35. Goyal, R., Koppula, V., Waters, B.: Lockable obfuscation. In: Umans, C. (ed.) 58th FOCS, pp. 612–621. IEEE Computer Society Press (2017). https://doi.org/10.1109/FOCS.2017.62
36. Goyal, V., Pandey, O., Sahai, A., Waters, B.: Attribute-based encryption for fine-grained access control of encrypted data. In: Juels, A., Wright, R.N., De Capitani di Vimercati, S. (eds.) ACM CCS 2006, pp. 89–98. ACM Press (2006). https://doi.org/10.1145/1180405.1180418, available as Cryptology ePrint Archive Report 2006/309

37. Groth, J.: On the size of pairing-based non-interactive arguments. In: Fischlin, M., Coron, J.-S. (eds.) EUROCRYPT 2016. LNCS, vol. 9666, pp. 305–326. Springer, Heidelberg (2016). https://doi.org/10.1007/978-3-662-49896-5_11
38. Groth, J., Sahai, A.: Efficient non-interactive proof systems for bilinear groups. In: Smart, N. (ed.) EUROCRYPT 2008. LNCS, vol. 4965, pp. 415–432. Springer, Heidelberg (2008). https://doi.org/10.1007/978-3-540-78967-3_24
39. Hamouda-Guichoux, F.B.: Diverse modules and zero-knowledge. Ph.D. thesis, École Normale Supérieure, Paris, France (2016). https://tel.archives-ouvertes.fr/tel-01399476
40. Jain, A., Lin, H., Sahai, A.: Indistinguishability obfuscation from well-founded assumptions. In: Proceedings of the 53rd Annual ACM SIGACT Symposium on Theory of Computing, pp. 60–73 (2021)
41. Juels, A., Kaliski Jr., B.S.: PORs: proofs of retrievability for large files. In: Ning, P., De Capitani di Vimercati, S., Syverson, P.F. (eds.) ACM CCS 2007, pp. 584–597. ACM Press (2007). https://doi.org/10.1145/1315245.1315317
42. Karchmer, M., Wigderson, A.: On span programs. In: [1993] Proceedings of the Eighth Annual Structure in Complexity Theory Conference, pp. 102–111 (1993)
43. Khoshakhlagh, H.: (Commit-and-prove) predictable arguments with privacy. In: Ateniese, G., Venturi, D. (eds.) ACNS 22. LNCS, vol. 13269, pp. 542–561. Springer, Heidelberg (2022). https://doi.org/10.1007/978-3-031-09234-3_27
44. Kokoris-Kogias, E., et al.: CALYPSO: auditable sharing of private data over blockchains. Cryptology ePrint Archive, Report 2018/209 (2018). https://eprint.iacr.org/2018/209
45. Lai, R.W.F., Malavolta, G.: Subvector commitments with application to succinct arguments. In: Boldyreva, A., Micciancio, D. (eds.) CRYPTO 2019. LNCS, vol. 11692, pp. 530–560. Springer, Cham (2019). https://doi.org/10.1007/978-3-030-26948-7_19
46. Lewko, A., Okamoto, T., Sahai, A., Takashima, K., Waters, B.: Fully secure functional encryption: attribute-based encryption and (hierarchical) inner product encryption. In: Gilbert, H. (ed.) EUROCRYPT 2010. LNCS, vol. 6110, pp. 62–91. Springer, Heidelberg (2010). https://doi.org/10.1007/978-3-642-13190-5_4
47. Lewko, A., Waters, B.: Unbounded HIBE and attribute-based encryption. In: Paterson, K.G. (ed.) EUROCRYPT 2011. LNCS, vol. 6632, pp. 547–567. Springer, Heidelberg (2011). https://doi.org/10.1007/978-3-642-20465-4_30
48. Libert, B., Ramanna, S.C., Yung, M.: Functional commitment schemes: from polynomial commitments to pairing-based accumulators from simple assumptions. In: Chatzigiannakis, I., Mitzenmacher, M., Rabani, Y., Sangiorgi, D. (eds.) ICALP 2016. LIPIcs, vol. 55, pp. 30:1–30:14. Schloss Dagstuhl (2016). https://doi.org/10.4230/LIPIcs.ICALP.2016.30
49. Lipmaa, H.: Prover-efficient commit-and-prove zero-knowledge SNARKs. In: Pointcheval, D., Nitaj, A., Rachidi, T. (eds.) AFRICACRYPT 2016. LNCS, vol. 9646, pp. 185–206. Springer, Cham (2016). https://doi.org/10.1007/978-3-319-31517-1_10
50. Lipmaa, H., Pavlyk, K.: Succinct functional commitment for a large class of arithmetic circuits. In: Moriai, S., Wang, H. (eds.) ASIACRYPT 2020. LNCS, vol. 12493, pp. 686–716. Springer, Cham (2020). https://doi.org/10.1007/978-3-030-64840-4_23
51. Sahai, A., Waters, B.: Fuzzy identity-based encryption. In: Cramer, R. (ed.) EUROCRYPT 2005. LNCS, vol. 3494, pp. 457–473. Springer, Heidelberg (2005). https://doi.org/10.1007/11426639_27

52. Shamir, A.: Identity-based cryptosystems and signature schemes. In: Blakley, G.R., Chaum, D. (eds.) CRYPTO 1984. LNCS, vol. 196, pp. 47–53. Springer, Heidelberg (1985). https://doi.org/10.1007/3-540-39568-7_5
53. Wee, H.: Efficient chosen-ciphertext security via extractable hash proofs. In: Rabin, T. (ed.) CRYPTO 2010. LNCS, vol. 6223, pp. 314–332. Springer, Heidelberg (2010). https://doi.org/10.1007/978-3-642-14623-7_17
54. Wee, H., Wu, D.J.: Succinct vector, polynomial, and functional commitments from lattices. In: Hazay, C., Stam, M. (eds.) EUROCRYPT 2023, Part III. LNCS, vol. 14006, pp. 385–416. Springer, Heidelberg (2023). https://doi.org/10.1007/978-3-031-30620-4_13
55. Wichs, D., Zirdelis, G.: Obfuscating compute-and-compare programs under LWE. In: Umans, C. (ed.) 58th FOCS, pp. 600–611. IEEE Computer Society Press (2017). https://doi.org/10.1109/FOCS.2017.61

Multiparty Computation

Network-Agnostic Multi-party Computation Revisited (Extended Abstract)

Nidhish Bhimrajka, Ashish Choudhury(✉), and Supreeth Varadarajan

International Institute of Information Technology Bangalore, Bengaluru, India
{nidhish.bhimrajka,ashish.choudhury,supreeth.varadarajan}@iiitb.ac.in

Abstract. We study network-agnostic *secure multi-party computation* (MPC) in the presence of *computationally-bounded* adversaries. A network-agnostic protocol provides the best possible security guarantees, irrespective of the type of underlying communication network. Previous MPC protocols in this regime either assume a setup for a common reference string (CRS) and a threshold additively homomorphic encryption (Blum et al. CRYPTO 2020) or a plain public-key infrastructure (PKI) setup (Bacho et al. CRYPTO 2023). Both these MPC protocols perform circuit-evaluation over encrypted data and also deploy different forms of zero-knowledge (ZK) proofs, along with other computationally-expensive cryptographic machinery. We aim to build an MPC protocol based on circuit evaluation on secret-shared data, *avoiding* ZK proofs and other computationally-expensive cryptographic machinery and based on a *plain* PKI setup.

To achieve our goal, we present the *first* network-agnostic *verifiable secret sharing* (VSS) protocol with the *optimal* threshold conditions, which is of independent interest. Previously, network-agnostic VSS is known either with *perfect* security (Appan et al. IEEE IT 2023) where the threshold conditions are *not* known to be optimal or with *statistical security* (Appan et al. TCC 2023) where the threshold conditions are optimal, but the parties need to perform *exponential* amount of computation and communication. Although our proposed MPC protocol incurs higher communication complexity compared to state-of-the-art network-agnostic MPC protocols, it offers valuable insights and motivates alternative directions for designing *computationally inexpensive* MPC protocols, based on a plain PKI setup, which has not been explored in the domain of network-agnostic MPC.

Keywords: Cryptographic security · Multiparty Computation · Verifiable Secret Sharing · Network-agnostic · Public Key Infrastructure

This research is an outcome of the R&D work undertaken in the project under the Visvesvaraya PhD Scheme of the Ministry of Electronics & Information Technology, Government of India, being implemented by Digital India Corporation.

Q. Tang and V. Teague (Eds.): PKC 2024, LNCS 14602, pp. 171–204, 2024.
https://doi.org/10.1007/978-3-031-57722-2_6

1 Introduction

A *secure multi-party computation* (MPC) protocol [11,32,39,41] allows a set of n mutually distrusting parties $\mathcal{P} = \{P_1, ..., P_n\}$ with private inputs, to securely compute any function of their inputs, without revealing any additional information, even if a subset of the parties are under the control of an adversary who may behave arbitrarily during the protocol execution. In any MPC protocol, the parties exchange messages over an underlying communication network and the network behaviour is assumed to be *known beforehand* to the parties. The more popular synchronous MPC (SMPC) protocols are designed for a *synchronous* network where the local clocks of the parties are assumed to be synchronized and where there is a *publicly-known* upper bound on message delays. Unfortunately, the security of such protocols breaks down completely even if a single expected message fails to get delivered within the expected time-out. To deal with this shortcoming, there is another category of MPC protocols, designed for the *asynchronous* network model [9,10,37], where no assumption is made on the message delays and where the messages can be delayed arbitrarily yet finitely, with the guarantee that every message being sent is delivered *eventually*. Apart from better modelling of real-world networks like the Internet, *asynchronous* MPC (AMPC) protocols also have the advantage of running at the "actual" speed of the underlying network. The downside is that AMPC protocols are more complex, since in the *absence* of any known time-outs, the parties do not know how long to wait for an expected message and waiting for messages from all the parties may turn out to be an endless wait. Consequently, as soon a party receives messages from a "subset" of parties, it has to process them and in the process, messages from a subset of "slow" but potentially honest parties may get ignored. Moreover, the *resilience* (namely the maximum number of allowed corruptions) of AMPC protocols is poor compared to SMPC protocols. A very recent and highly practically-motivated category of MPC protocols is that of *network-agnostic* protocols [3,5,15,27], where the parties *need not* know the behaviour of the underlying network and which provides the best possible security guarantees, irrespective of the behaviour of the network.

Our Motivation: In this work, we focus on network-agnostic MPC protocols with *cryptographic* security, where the adversary is assumed to be *computationally bounded.* Let t_s and t_a be the maximum number of parties which can be corrupted by the adversary in the *synchronous* and *asynchronous* network respectively, where $t_s < \frac{n}{2}$ and $t_a < \frac{n}{3}$.[1] The pioneering work of Blum et al. [15] has shown that network-agnostic MPC protocols with cryptographic security is possible only if $t_a + 2t_s < n$ is satisfied. They also present a network-agnostic MPC protocol with the condition $t_a + 2t_s < n$. The work of Blum et al. is followed by the work of Deligios et al. [27] and Bacho et al. [5], who also present

[1] The conditions $t_s < \frac{n}{2}$ and $t_a < \frac{n}{3}$ are necessary and sufficient for cryptographically-secure SMPC [23] and AMPC protocols [33] respectively with full security. By full security, we mean that the honest parties always get the correct output.

network-agnostic MPC protocols with the condition $t_a + 2t_s < n$. All these protocols let the parties jointly perform secure *circuit-evaluation*. Namely, in all these protocols the function to be securely computed is abstracted as an arithmetic circuit over some algebraic structure, which could be a ring or a field and then the parties securely and jointly evaluate each gate in the circuit. The evaluation happens in such a way that the adversary does not learn any additional information about the inputs of the honest parties, beyond what can be inferred from the input and output of the corrupt parties. These protocols can be broadly classified into *two* categories.

- **Threshold-Encryption Based Approach**: This approach was first pioneered for SMPC protocols in [23] and later also used for AMPC protocols in [20,33,34]. The network-agnostic protocols of [5,15] follow this approach. Here the circuit-evaluation happens over encrypted values, where each value during the evaluation remains encrypted under some threshold linearly-homomorphic encryption scheme. Informally, it is a special form of public-key encryption scheme, where the encryption key is *publicly available*, but the decryption key remains secret-shared among the parties, with each party holding a *private* secret-share of the decryption key. Such a setup (of *public* encryption key and *private* decryption-key shares) is assumed to be *already* available to the parties, through some *trusted* entity. Doing circuit-evaluation using this approach is computationally expensive and apart from the expensive setup of threshold encryption, the protocols deploy other heavy cryptographic machinery such as zero-knowledge (ZK) proofs, which are used to prove the "correctness" of each message exchanged by the parties during the circuit evaluation.
  The protocol of [15] deploys threshold homomorphic encryption and also assumes a *trusted* setup for a *common reference string* (CRS). The CRS is utilized to instantiate *non-interactive* ZK (NIZK) proofs for various tasks. The protocol of [5] also deploys threshold homomorphic encryption and NIZK proofs, but gets rid of the CRS setup assumption and instead assumes a *plain* public-key infrastructure (PKI) set-up. The number of communication rounds in these protocols is proportional to the multiplicative depth of the underlying circuit.
- **Garbled-Circuit Based Approach**: This approach was first pioneered for SMPC protocols in [8,25,41] and later for AMPC protocols in [22]. The network-agnostic protocol of [27] uses this approach. This approach yields a *constant* round protocol. To deploy this approach, the protocol of [27] requires a *trusted* setup of a threshold homomorphic encryption scheme. Additionally, the protocol also uses ZK proofs.

Evidently, the known protocols assume strong setup assumptions such as threshold homomorphic encryption and deploy computationally-expensive cryptographic machinery, such as ZK proofs, to name a few. Apart from the above two approaches for secure circuit-evaluation, another well-known approach is that of secret-shared circuit evaluation, used heavily both by SMPC [11,39] and AMPC [9,10] protocols. In this approach, each value during the circuit-evaluation remains verifiably secret-shared among the parties in such a way that the shares of the corrupt parties do not reveal any additional information to the adversary. Such protocols are conceptually much simpler and typically *do not* require any trusted setup. Moreover, they are computationally inexpensive, based on the properties of polynomials over fields and avoid costly machinery like ZK protocols for proving the correctness during circuit-evaluation. The *unconditionally-secure* network-agnostic protocols of [2,3] are based on the approach of the secret-shared circuit-evaluation. Even though the approach is well studied in the literature, surprisingly, to the best of our knowledge, no one has yet explored the feasibility of network-agnostic MPC protocols with *cryptographic security* based on the approach of secret-shared circuit evaluation. This motivates us to ask the following central question:

Does there exist an efficient network-agnostic MPC protocol with cryptographic security and optimal threshold conditions, based on secret-shared circuit-evaluation, without deploying any computationally-expensive cryptographic machinery, such as ZK and any expensive setup such as threshold homomorphic encryption?

Our Results. In this work, we make inroads to answer the above question by presenting a network-agnostic MPC with the condition $t_a + 2t_s < n$, based on the approach of secret-shared circuit-evaluation. Our protocol is in the *plain* PKI model and requires the setup of only a linearly-homomorphic commitment scheme. For simplicity, we use Pedersen's commitment scheme, whose security is based on the standard *discrete log* assumption in a cyclic group. To instantiate the scheme, the only setup needed is the *public* knowledge of a generator of a cyclic group, along with the *public* knowledge of a random element of the group. We stress that *unlike* the setup of threshold homomorphic encryption which has to generate both *public* as well as *private* components, the setup for Pedersen's scheme is relatively simpler, since it has to generate only *public* components. Our protocol also *avoids* any kind of ZK proofs (and the associated setup assumptions) for proving the correctness of the messages exchanged among the parties. A central pillar in our protocol is the *first* network-agnostic *Verifiable Secret Sharing* (VSS) protocol [19] with *cryptographic security*, which is of independent interest. VSS is in itself a very important cryptographic primitive and used for a variety of important secure distributed-computing tasks. For example, it can be used to instantiate a *common-coin* primitive [18,29] from scratch *without* any setup, which is a central tool for designing Byzantine agreement (BA) protocols with a constant expected time [29]. VSS also constitutes an important building block for designing *distributed key-generation* (DKG) protocols [35]. Previously, network-agnostic VSS is known either with *perfect-security* but with condition $t_a + 3t_s < n$ [3] or with *statistical-security* and condition $t_a + 2t_s < n$ [2], but where the parties need to perform an exponential amount of computation and communication.

We outline our MPC protocol and compare it with the relevant MPC protocols in Table 1. In the table, **Rounds** denotes the (expected) round complexity, while D_M and c_M denote the multiplicative depth and the number of multiplication gates in the underlying circuit, representing the function to be securely computed. **Communication Complexity (CC)** denotes the number of bits communicated by the parties in the protocol for evaluating the multiplication gates in the underlying circuit and κ denotes the computational security parameter. **Setup** denotes the setup assumptions, which include a plain public-key infrastructure (PKI), a common reference string (CRS), a threshold homomorphic cryptosystem, or a homomorphic commitment.

Table 1. Summary of network-agnostic MPC protocols with cryptographic security.

Reference	Rounds	CC	Setup
[15]	$\mathcal{O}(D_M)$	$\mathcal{O}(c_M \cdot n^3 \cdot \kappa)$	CRS, PKI, Threshold Encryption
[27]	$\mathcal{O}(\kappa)$	$\mathcal{O}(c_M \cdot n^3 \cdot \kappa)$	CRS, PKI, Threshold Encryption
[5]	$\mathcal{O}(D_M)$	$\mathcal{O}(c_M \cdot n^3 \cdot \mathsf{poly}(\kappa))$	PKI, Threshold Encryption
This work	$\mathcal{O}(D_M)$	$\mathcal{O}(c_M \cdot n^7 \cdot \kappa)$	PKI, Homomorphic Commitment

Although our protocol incurs higher communication complexity, it demonstrates the feasibility of achieving MPC *without* relying on complex setup assumptions, as well as computationally expensive cryptographic machinery. Moreover, during the design of our protocol, we get an independent and important cryptographic primitive, namely VSS. As explained in the next section, our work shows the feasibility of performing secure circuit-evaluation on secret-shared data with the condition $t_a + 2t_s < n$ and that too without deploying complex cryptographic machinery. Prior secret-shared based protocols were either with condition $t_a + 3t_s < n$ [3] or with the condition $t_a + 2t_s < n$ but requiring exponential computation and communication [2].

1.1 Technical Overview

We assume that the function to be securely computed is abstracted as an arithmetic circuit cir over a finite field, consisting of linear and non-linear (multiplication) gates. The idea is then to securely evaluate cir in a *secret-shared* manner, based on the paradigm of [11]. In this approach, each value during the evaluation of cir is (verifiably) t-shared according to Shamir's secret-sharing scheme [40], where t denotes the maximum number of corrupt parties. Essentially, this guarantees that an adversary controlling up to t parties gains no additional information throughout the circuit evaluation process, as the shares held by the corrupt parties do not reveal additional details about the underlying shared values. Since the parties will be unaware of the network type, the *degree-of-sharing* t has to be set to *always* $t = t_s$.

The linearity of Shamir's secret-sharing guarantees that the linear gates in cir can be evaluated non-interactively over secret-shared gate inputs. For evaluating the multiplication gates over secret-shared inputs, we deploy the standard Beaver's paradigm [7]. According to this paradigm, multiplication gates are evaluated using randomly generated t_s-shared *multiplication-triples*. The secret-shared multiplication-triples are generated leveraging the framework proposed in [21]. This framework demonstrates how to utilize any polynomial-based VSS and a BA protocol to generate shared random multiplication-triples. Importantly, the framework operates in both synchronous and asynchronous networks, assuming that the participating parties possess knowledge of the *exact* network type. The work by [3] introduces techniques for adapting the framework to achieve *perfect* security with condition $t_a + 3t_s < n$ in a network-agnostic context. For our purpose, we adapt the framework with condition $t_a + 2t_s < n$ to achieve *cryptographic* security. This requires network-agnostic BA and VSS protocols with condition $t_a + 2t_s < n$. The BA protocol presented in [14] aligns well with our objectives. The main challenge however is finding a network-agnostic VSS protocol.

Informally, in a (polynomial-based) VSS protocol, there exists a designated *dealer* $\mathsf{D} \in \mathcal{P}$ with a t-degree polynomial as input, where t represents the maximum number of *corrupt* parties, possibly including D. The protocol allows D to distribute points on this polynomial to the parties in a "verifiable" manner, such that the view of the adversary remains independent of D's polynomial for an *honest* D (*privacy* property). In a *synchronous* VSS (SVSS) protocol, every party has the correct point on the polynomial after some known time-out, say T (*correctness* property). The *verifiability* ensures that even if D is corrupt, it is bound to distribute points on some t-degree polynomial within time T (*strong-commitment* property). It is well-known that cryptographically-secure SVSS is possible iff $t < \frac{n}{2}$ [39]. In an *asynchronous* VSS (AVSS) protocol, the *correctness* property guarantees that when D is *honest*, the honest parties will *eventually* receive points on D's polynomial. However, a corrupt D may choose not to invoke the protocol, and the parties *cannot* distinguish this situation from when D's messages are arbitrarily delayed. Therefore, the *strong-commitment* of AVSS ensures that if D is *corrupt* and if at least one honest party obtains a point on D's polynomial, then all honest parties will eventually obtain their respective points on this polynomial. It is well-known that cryptographically-secure AVSS is possible iff $t < \frac{n}{3}$ [17].

Existing SVSS protocols become completely insecure in an *asynchronous* network, even if a single anticipated message from an *honest* party encounters a delay. Conversely, existing AVSS protocols work only when at most $t < \frac{n}{3}$ parties are corrupt, and become insecure if the number of corruptions exceeds $\frac{n}{3}$ (which can happen in our context when the network behaves *synchronously* where $t < \frac{n}{2}$). We are currently unaware of any cryptographically-secure VSS protocol that provides the specific guarantees we seek, all while adhering to the minimally intensive computational requirements. We propose a network-agnostic cryptographically-secure VSS protocol that meets the aforementioned requirements, given that the condition $t_a + 2t_s < n$ is met. Our VSS protocol satisfies the *correctness* requirement of SVSS and AVSS in a synchronous and an asynchronous network, respectively. However, it *only* satisfies the *strong-commitment* requirement of AVSS, even in a synchronous network. This is because a potentially *corrupt* D may choose *not* to invoke the protocol, and the parties will *not* be aware of the exact network type. We stress that this does not hinder us from deploying our VSS protocol in the framework of [21]. Given that our VSS protocol involves technical intricacies, we defer its explanation to Sect. 4 of our paper.

The construction of the aforementioned VSS protocol necessitates the implementation of a Byzantine Broadcast protocol. Informally, a broadcast protocol allows a designated party called a *Sender* to consistently distribute a message among a set of parties which guarantees security in a synchronous network where the adversary can corrupt up to $t < \frac{n}{2}$ parties, and also in an asynchronous network, where the adversary can corrupt up to $t < \frac{n}{3}$ parties. Previous research has presented secure broadcast protocols for both synchronous [28] and asynchronous [16] networks. Additionally, previous studies by [5,15,27] have also leveraged broadcast protocols in the network-agnostic setting. However, their proposed protocols offer comparatively weaker consistency assurances in asynchronous networks. For instance, the protocol introduced by [15] only ensures that even though every honest party outputs some value, only a subset of honest parties output the desired value, while the rest output some default value in an asynchronous network. Consequently, we introduce an additional broadcast protocol designed to ensure security in both synchronous and asynchronous networks, which can be safely integrated into our VSS protocol.

Other Related Works. As mentioned earlier, the domain of network-agnostic cryptographic protocols is relatively new. The works of [1,13] present network-agnostic cryptographically-secure atomic broadcast protocol. The work of [36] studies Byzantine fault tolerance and state machine replication protocols for multiple thresholds, including t_s and t_a. The works of [30,31] study network-agnostic protocol for the task of approximate agreement. The works of [12,26] have studied the problem of network-agnostic secure message transmission (SMT) over *incomplete* graphs.

Paper Organization. The major contribution of the paper is the network-agnostic VSS and so we mostly focus on it; the design of the preprocessing phase protocol for generating the secret-shared multiplication-triples and the MPC protocol mostly follows from [3] by adapting the techniques to the setting of $t_a + 2t_s < n$. Due to space constraints, the detailed formal security proofs are not presented in this extended abstract and are deferred to the full version of the paper.

2 Preliminaries and Definitions

We consider a network of n parties $\mathcal{P} = \{P_1, \ldots, P_n\}$, where the distrust in the system is modelled by a *computationally bounded* Byzantine (malicious) adversary Adv, who can corrupt a subset of parties and force them to behave in any *arbitrary* fashion during the execution of a protocol. We assume a *static* adversary, who decides the set of corrupt parties at the beginning of the protocol execution.

We consider a communication model where the parties have access to *local* clocks and are *not aware* apriori about the network conditions when executing any protocol, where the underlying network could behave either in a *synchronous* fashion or in an *asynchronous* fashion. In a *synchronous* network, every sent message is delivered within some *known* time bound Δ. The protocols in this model can be conveniently described as a sequence of communication *rounds*, where for every $r \in \mathbb{N}$ with $r \geq 1$, any message received in the time slot $[r\Delta, (r+1)\Delta]$ as per the local clock of the receiving party is regarded as a round-r message. Moreover, in this model, it is assumed that the adversary Adv can control up to t_s parties.

In an *asynchronous* network, the local clocks of the parties are *not* synchronised, and there is *no known* upper bound on message delays. To model the worst-case scenario, the adversary is allowed to schedule the delivery of messages *arbitrarily*, with the restriction that every message being sent is *eventually* delivered. The protocols in this model are described in an *event-based* fashion. That is, upon receiving a message, the receiving party adds the message to a pool of received messages and checks whether a list of conditions specified in the underlying protocol is satisfied to decide its next set of actions. In this model, it is assumed that Adv can corrupt at most t_a parties.

We assume that $t_a < t_s$ and $t_a + 2t_s < n$ holds. This automatically implies that $t_s < \frac{n}{2}$ and $t_a < \frac{n}{3}$ holds, which are necessary for any cryptographically-secure SMPC and AMPC protocol, respectively. We assume that the function to be securely computed is abstracted as an arithmetic circuit cir over the prime field $\mathbb{F}_p$, where p is a κ-bit long prime and where κ is the security parameter. Moreover, we assume that $|\mathbb{F}_p| > n$ and each party P_i is publicly associated with the evaluation point i at which all the shares are computed for P_i. For simplicity and without loss of generality, we assume that each P_i has a private input $x^{(i)} \in \mathbb{F}_p$, and the parties want to securely compute a function $f : \mathbb{F}_p^n \rightarrow \mathbb{F}_p$. Without loss of generality, f is represented by an arithmetic circuit cir over $\mathbb{F}_p$, consisting of linear and non-linear (multiplication) gates, where cir has c_M number of multiplication gates and has a multiplicative depth of D_M.

Termination Guarantees of Our Sub-protocols. As done in [3], for simplicity, we will not be specifying any termination criteria for our sub-protocols. And the parties will keep on participating in these sub-protocol instances, even after receiving their outputs. The termination criteria of our MPC protocol will ensure that once a party terminates the MPC protocol, it terminates all underlying sub-protocol instances.

2.1 Primitives and Definitions

We next present the definitions and primitives used in our protocols.

Polynomials Over a Field. A d-degree univariate polynomial over $\mathbb{F}_p$ is of the form $f(x) = a_0 + a_1 x + ... + a_d x^d$, where each $a_i \in \mathbb{F}_p$. A (d,d)-degree bivariate polynomial over $\mathbb{F}_p$ is of the form

$$F(x,y) = \sum_{i,j=0}^{i=d,j=d} r_{ij} x^i y^j,$$

where each $r_{ij} \in \mathbb{F}_p$. The polynomial is called *symmetric* if $r_{ji} = r_{ij}$ holds for all i,j. This automatically implies that $F(i,j) = F(j,i)$ holds for all $i,j \in \{1,\ldots,n\}$. Given $i \in \{1,\ldots,n\}$ and a d-degree polynomial $F_i(x)$, we say that $F_i(x)$ *lies* on a (d,d)-degree symmetric bivariate polynomial $F(x,y)$, if $F(x,i) = F_i(x)$ holds. The following properties for bivariate polynomials are standard.

Lemma 1 ([4,24])(Pairwise Consistency Lemma). *Let $f_{i_1}(x),\ldots,f_{i_q}(x)$ be d-degree univariate polynomials over $\mathbb{F}_p$, where $q \geq d+1$ and $i_1,\ldots,i_q \in \{1,\ldots,n\}$, such that $f_i(j) = f_j(i)$ holds for all $i,j \in \{i_1,\ldots,i_q\}$. Then $f_{i_1}(x),\ldots,f_{i_q}(x)$ lie on a unique (d,d)-degree symmetric bivariate polynomial, say $F^\star(x,y)$.*

Lemma 2 ([4,24]). *Let $\mathcal{C} \subset \mathcal{P}$ and $q_1(\cdot) \neq q_2(\cdot)$ be d-degree polynomials where $d \geq |\mathcal{C}|$ such that $q_1(i) = q_2(i)$ holds for all $P_i \in \mathcal{C}$. Then the probability distributions $\left\{\{F(x,i)\}_{P_i \in \mathcal{C}}\right\}$ and $\left\{\{F'(x,i)\}_{P_i \in \mathcal{C}}\right\}$ are identical, where $F(x,y)$ and $F'(x,y)$ are random (d,d)-degree symmetric bivariate polynomials, such that $F(0,y) = q_1(\cdot)$ and $F'(0,y) = q_2(\cdot)$ holds.*

In our protocols, we deploy a homomorphic commitment scheme, which is instantiated with Pedersen's commitment scheme [38]. Informally, the scheme enables a party to *commit* a value such that later it can be *opened* uniquely.

Pedersen Commitment Scheme [38]. The scheme consists of a two-phase protocol involving a *committer* and a *verifier*. The first phase is known as the "commit" phase, executed through a protocol denoted as Commit, while the second phase is the "opening" phase, implemented via the protocol Open. In the Commit protocol, the committer possesses a private input value $m \in \mathbb{F}_p$, which it commits to the verifier by publicly disclosing a commitment denoted as Com_m. During the Open protocol, the committer reveals the actual value m that was committed in Com_m. Subsequently, the verifier verifies whether m was indeed the value committed in Com_m during the Commit phase. The verifier's output is either 1 if the commitment is valid or 0 if it is not. Pedersen's commitment scheme offers the *hiding* property, which implies that if the committer is *honest*, the verifier gains no information about the value m. The verifier's view remains independent of the specific value m committed in Com_m, and this independence holds even when the verifier is *computationally unbounded.* Additionally, the scheme adheres to the *binding* property, which means that if the committer is *corrupt* and the verifier is *honest*, then except with a negligible probability, it is impossible for the committer to commit a value m in Com_m during the Commit phase and subsequently reveal a different value $m^\star \neq m$ during the Open phase, leading to the verifier outputting 1. The detailed formal description of the scheme is as follows.

As part of the setup, the parties are equipped with essential information: a generator g of $\mathbb{F}_p$ and a randomly chosen element $h \in \mathbb{F}_p$. To commit a value $m \in \mathbb{F}_p$, the committer first selects a random value r from $\mathbb{F}_p$ and computes the commitment $\mathsf{Com}_m = \mathsf{Commit}(m, r) \stackrel{def}{=} g^m h^r \bmod p$. During the Open protocol, the committer discloses $m^\star$ and $r^\star$ (which are supposed to be m and r respectively for an *honest* committer), after which the verifier decides to output either 1 or 0, contingent upon the equality check $\mathsf{Com}_m \stackrel{?}{=} g^{m^\star} h^{r^\star} \bmod p$. Both the Commit and Open protocols incur a communication complexity of $\mathcal{O}(\kappa)$ bits. It is a well-established fact that if the committer is honest, then the view of a corrupt verifier remains identically distributed for any potential combination of (m, r), even when the verifier possesses unbounded computational capabilities. Conversely, assuming that solving the Discrete logarithm problem in $\mathbb{F}_p$ is computationally challenging, it becomes infeasible for a corrupt committer to reveal $(m^\star, r^\star) \neq (m, r)$ during the Open phase in such a way that an honest verifier would output 1. Throughout the remainder of this paper, we say that (m, r) is *consistent* with Com_m if and only if $\mathsf{Com}_m = g^m h^r \bmod p$ holds.

The Pedersen commitment scheme exhibits homomorphic properties. Given commitments $\mathsf{Com}_{m_1} = \mathsf{Commit}(m_1, r_1)$ and $\mathsf{Com}_{m_2} = \mathsf{Commit}(m_2, r_2)$, as well as publicly-known constants $c_1, c_2 \in \mathbb{F}_p$, it is feasible to compute a commitment $\mathsf{Com}_{c_1 m_1 + c_2 m_2}$ for the sum $c_1 m_1 + c_2 m_2$ under the randomness $c_1 r_1 + c_2 r_2$ through local computations performed on Com_{m_1} and Com_{m_2}. Specifically, we can express this as $(\mathsf{Com}_{m_1})^{c_1} \cdot (\mathsf{Com}_{m_2})^{c_2} = g^{c_1 m_1 + c_2 m_2} \cdot h^{c_1 r_1 + c_2 r_2} = \mathsf{Com}_{c_1 m_1 + c_2 m_2}$. In general, let $q : \mathbb{F}_p^l \rightarrow \mathbb{F}_p^m$ be an arbitrary linear function where $q(x_1, \ldots, x_l) = (y_1, \ldots, y_m)$. Then given commitments $\mathsf{Com}_{x_1}, \ldots, \mathsf{Com}_{x_l}$ for $x_1, \ldots, x_l$ respectively, it is possible to locally compute commitments $\mathsf{Com}_{y_1}, \ldots, \mathsf{Com}_{y_m}$ for $y_1, \ldots, y_m$, respectively, using only $\mathsf{Com}_{x_1}, \ldots, \mathsf{Com}_{x_l}$. Throughout the paper, we use the term parties locally compute $\mathsf{Com}_{y_1}, \ldots, \mathsf{Com}_{y_m} = q(\mathsf{Com}_{x_1}, \ldots, \mathsf{Com}_{x_l})$ to refer to this process of leveraging the above linearity properties for such computations.

We will now revisit the definition of t-sharing with publicly committed shares as outlined in [6].

Definition 1 (t-Sharing with Publicly Committed Shares [6]). *A value $s \in \mathbb{F}_p$ is said to be t-shared with publicly committed shares, if there exists a t-degree polynomial $f(x)$ over $\mathbb{F}_p$ with $f(0) = s$, such that each (honest) $P_i \in \mathcal{P}$ holds (s_i, r_i) and a vector of commitments $(\mathsf{Com}_{s_1}, \ldots, \mathsf{Com}_{s_n})$, where $s_i = f(i)$ and $\mathsf{Com}_{s_j} = \mathsf{Commit}(s_j, r_j)$, for $j = 1, \ldots, n$.*

In our notation, we use $[s]$ to represent a vector of shares and the publicly known commitment of these shares. Additionally, we use $[s]_i$ to represent P_i's share, (s_i, r_i) and the public commitments. We will use the term "a value s is $[\cdot]$-shared among the parties", to describe a scenario where s is t_s-shared (unless specified otherwise) with publicly committed shares.

Note that $[\cdot]$-sharing satisfies the linearity property, which arises from the linearity property of Pedersen's commitment scheme. In other words, given shared values $[a]$ and $[b]$ along with public constants c_1 and c_2, each party P_i can locally compute its information corresponding to $[c_1a + c_2b]$. In a more general context, suppose we have a linear function $q : \mathbb{F}_p^l \rightarrow \mathbb{F}_p^m$ and let $q(x_1, \ldots, x_l) = (y_1, \ldots, y_m)$. Then given the secret-shared values $[x_1], \ldots, [x_l]$, each party can locally compute its information corresponding to $[y_1], \ldots, [y_m]$. Throughout the rest of the paper, we use the phrase parties locally compute $([y_1], \ldots, [y_m]) = q([x_1], \ldots, [x_l])$ to signify this property.

Digital Signature Scheme. We assume a Public Key Infrastructure (PKI) setup, where each party P_i within the set $\mathcal{P}$ possesses a pair of keys for a digital signature scheme, specifically a signing key sk_i and a verification key vk_i. Importantly, the verification keys $\mathsf{vk}_1, \ldots, \mathsf{vk}_n$ for all parties are publicly accessible, while the signing key sk_i is kept private and known only to P_i (malicious parties may choose their keys arbitrarily). We further assume that the digital signature scheme adheres to the standard security notion of *unforgeability*. This means that, except with a negligible probability in κ, the adversary cannot produce a valid signature of an honest party P_i on any message m that was never signed by P_i. Each signature generated using this scheme has a fixed size of κ bits, where κ represents the security parameter. In the paper, we use the notation $\langle m \rangle_{P_i}$ to indicate party P_i's signature on a message m. Additionally, we refer to a signature $\langle m \rangle_{P_i}$ on message m as *valid* if, along with the message m, it successfully passes the verification process using the verification key vk_i corresponding to P_i.

Definition 2 (Byzantine Agreement (BA) [14]). *Let Π be a protocol for $\mathcal{P}$, where every party P_i has an input $b_i \in \{0, 1\}$ and a possible output from $\{0, 1\} \cup \{\bot\}$. Moreover, let* Adv *be a computationally-bounded adversary, which can corrupt up to t parties in $\mathcal{P}$ during the execution of Π.*

- **t-liveness:** *Π has t-liveness if all honest parties obtain an output.*
- **t-validity:** *Π has t-validity if the following holds: If all honest parties have input b, then every honest party with an output, outputs b.*
- **t-weak validity:** *Π has t-weak validity if the following holds: If all honest parties have input b, then every honest party with an output, outputs b or $\bot$.*
- **t-consistency:** *Π has t-consistency if all honest parties with an output, output the same value (which can be $\bot$).*
- **t-weak consistency:** *Π has t-weak consistency if all honest parties with an output, output either a common $v \in \{0, 1\}$ or $\bot$.*

A protocol Π is said to be a *t-secure Byzantine Agreement* (BA) protocol if it guarantees *t-liveness*, *t-validity* and *t-consistency*.

Definition 3 (Byzantine Broadcast [14]). *Let Π be a protocol for $\mathcal{P}$, where a designated sender* $\mathsf{S} \in \mathcal{P}$ *has input $m \in \{0, 1\}$, and parties obtain a possible output from $\{0, 1\} \cup \{\bot\}$. Moreover, let* Adv *be a computationally-bounded adversary, which can corrupt up to t parties in $\mathcal{P}$ during the execution of Π.*

- t-**liveness**: *Π has t-liveness, if all honest parties obtain an output.*
- t-**validity**: *Π has t-validity if the following holds: if S is honest, then every honest party with an output, outputs m.*
- t-**weak validity**: *has t-weak validity if the following holds: if S is honest, then every honest party outputs either m or $\perp$.*
- t-**consistency**: *Π has t-consistency if the following holds: if S is corrupt, then every honest party with an output, has a common output.*
- t-**weak consistency**: *Π has t-weak consistency if the following holds: if S is corrupt, then every honest party with an output, outputs either a common $m^\star \in \{0,1\}$ or $\perp$.*

A protocol Π is said to be a *t-secure Broadcast* protocol if it guarantees *t-liveness*, *t-validity* and *t-consistency*.

2.2 Existing Building Blocks

Network-Agnostic Byzantine Agreement. The work of [14] presents a network-agnostic BA protocol Π_{BA} with $t_a + 2t_s < n$ that achieves *t_s-security* when run in a synchronous network and *t_a-security* when run in an asynchronous network. The protocol is obtained cleverly by combining a t_s-secure *synchronous* BA (SBA) protocol which also provides certain guarantees in an asynchronous network and a t_a-secure *asynchronous* BA (ABA) protocol which also provides certain guarantees in a synchronous network (against t_s corruptions). The detailed description is omitted due to brevity, but interested readers can refer to [14] for further detail and clarification.

In our VSS protocol, we use several standard procedures to verify certain properties of univariate polynomials and points lying on a bivariate polynomial, where the bivariate polynomial is publicly committed. All these procedures are based on the homomorphic properties of Pedersen's commitment scheme. We next describe these procedures.

Verifying Committed Bivariate Polynomial. This procedure takes input the commitments of the coefficients of n univariate polynomials, supposedly lying on a (d,d)-degree symmetric bivariate polynomial, where $d < n$. The procedure outputs 1 iff the committed polynomials lie on a (d,d)-degree symmetric bivariate polynomial. In more detail, the procedure $\mathsf{VerifyPoly}(\mathbf{C}, d)$ takes input a matrix $\mathbf{C}$ of commitments of size $n \times (d+1)$, where for $i = 1, \ldots, n$, the ith row consists of the commitments $\{\mathsf{Com}_{ij}\}_{j=0,\ldots,d}$. The output of the procedure is 1 iff there exists (d,d)-degree *symmetric* bivariate polynomials $H(x,y)$ and $R(x,y)$ over $\mathbb{F}_p$, such that the following condition is satisfied for $i = 1, \ldots, n$:

- Let $h_i(x) = H(x,i) = h_{i0} + h_{i1} \cdot x + \ldots + h_{id} \cdot x^d$ and $r_i(x) = R(x,i) = r_{i0} + r_{i1} \cdot x + \ldots + r_{id} \cdot x^d$. Then $\mathsf{Com}_{ij} = \mathsf{Commit}(h_{ij}, r_{ij})$ should hold, for $j = 0, \ldots, d$.

The procedure is very simple and *homomorphically* checks if the pairwise consistency lemma (Lemma 1) is satisfied for each $i, j \in \{1, \ldots, n\}$. In more detail, consider the commitments $\mathsf{Com}_{i0}, \ldots, \mathsf{Com}_{id}$ along the ith row of $\mathbf{C}$. Let $h_i^\star(x) = h_{i0}^\star + h_{i1}^\star \cdot x + \ldots + h_{id}^\star \cdot x^d$ and $r_i^\star(x) = r_{i0}^\star + r_{i1}^\star \cdot x + \ldots + r_{id}^\star \cdot x^d$ be d-degree polynomials, such that $\mathsf{Com}_{ij} = \mathsf{Commit}(h_{ij}^\star, r_{ij}^\star)$ holds for $j = 0, \ldots, d$. We wish to check whether $h_i^\star(j) = h_j^\star(i)$ and $r_i^\star(j) = r_j^\star(i)$ holds for each $i, j \in \{1, \ldots, n\}$. For this, we check the above relation over the commitments of $h_i^\star(j)$ and $h_j^\star(i)$, under the randomness $r_i^\star(j)$ and $r_j^\star(i)$ respectively. This is possible since the commitment of $h_i^\star(j)$ and $h_j^\star(i)$ can be homomorphically computed, as these points can be computed as a publicly-known *linear* function of the coefficients of $h_i^\star(x)$ and $h_j^\star(x)$ respectively. In more detail, $h_i^\star(j) = h_{i0}^\star + h_{i1}^\star \cdot j + \ldots + h_{id}^\star \cdot j^d$. and $r_i^\star(j) = r_{i0}^\star + r_{i1}^\star \cdot j + \ldots + r_{id}^\star \cdot j^d$. Consequently, $\mathsf{Commit}(h_i^\star(j), r_i^\star(j)) = \mathsf{Com}_{i0} \cdot (\mathsf{Com}_{i1})^j \cdot (\mathsf{Com}_{i2})^{j^2} \cdot \ldots \cdot (\mathsf{Com}_{id})^{j^d}$ holds and similarly $\mathsf{Commit}(h_j^\star(i), r_j^\star(i)) = \mathsf{Com}_{j0} \cdot (\mathsf{Com}_{j1})^i \cdot (\mathsf{Com}_{j2})^{i^2} \cdot \ldots \cdot (\mathsf{Com}_{jd})^{i^d}$ holds. Hence instead of checking $h_i^\star(j) = h_j^\star(i)$ and $r_i^\star(j) = r_j^\star(i)$, the procedure actually checks if the following holds for each $i, j \in \{1, \ldots, n\}$:

$$\mathsf{Com}_{i0} \cdot (\mathsf{Com}_{i1})^j \cdot \ldots \cdot (\mathsf{Com}_{id})^{j^d} = \mathsf{Com}_{j0} \cdot (\mathsf{Com}_{j1})^i \cdot \ldots \cdot (\mathsf{Com}_{jd})^{i^d}.$$

Verifying Point on a Committed Polynomial. The next procedure $\mathsf{VerifyPoint}(\{\mathsf{Com}_0, \ldots, \mathsf{Com}_d\}, (\mathbf{h}, \mathbf{r}), j)$ takes input a set of $d+1$ commitments, an index $j \in \{1, \ldots, n\}$ and a pair of values $(\mathbf{h}, \mathbf{r})$, where the commitments are already *known* to be the commitments of the coefficients of a d-degree polynomial. That is, there exist d-degree polynomials, say $h(x) = h_0 + h_1 \cdot x + \ldots + h_d \cdot x^d$ and $r(x) = r_0 + r_1 \cdot x + \ldots + r_d \cdot x^d$, where it is *already known* that $\mathsf{Com}_i = \mathsf{Commit}(h_i, r_i)$ holds, for $i = 0, \ldots, d$. The procedure outputs 1 iff $\mathbf{h}$ and $\mathbf{r}$ constitutes the jth point on $h(x)$ and $r(x)$ respectively; i.e. iff $h(j) = \mathbf{h}$ and $r(j) = \mathbf{r}$ holds. Similar to the previous procedure, the verification here happens homomorphically over the commitments. That is, the procedure checks if the following relation holds:

$$\mathsf{Commit}(\mathbf{h}, \mathbf{r}) = \mathsf{Com}_0 \cdot (\mathsf{Com}_1)^j \cdot (\mathsf{Com}_2)^{j^2} \cdot \ldots \cdot (\mathsf{Com}_d)^{j^d}.$$

Robust Reconstruction of a $[\cdot]$-Shared Value. Let s be a value which is $[\cdot]$-shared among the parties, where the degree of sharing is t_s, with each (honest) P_i having its share (s_i, r_i) and all the parties having the commitments $\mathsf{Com}_{s_1}, \ldots, \mathsf{Com}_{s_n}$, where $\mathsf{Com}_{s_i} = \mathsf{Commit}(s_i, r_i)$. Protocol $\Pi_{\mathsf{RecPub}}([s])$ then allows the parties in $\mathcal{P}$ to publicly reconstruct s irrespective of the network type, provided $t_s < \frac{n}{2}$. The protocol is standard and straightforward. Every P_i provides its share (s_i, r_i) to every party, which is verified with respect to Com_{s_i}. Once $t_s + 1$ correct shares are identified, they are used to interpolate the underlying t_s-degree sharing polynomial and its constant term is taken as the output. The protocol requires Δ time in a synchronous network and irrespective of the network type, incurs a communication of $\mathcal{O}(n^2 \cdot \kappa)$ bits. Since the protocol is standard, we avoid presenting its formal description.

3 Network-Agnostic Byzantine Broadcast

We wish to design a cryptographically-secure network-agnostic broadcast protocol which is t_s-secure in a synchronous network and t_a-secure in an asynchronous network. For doing so, we assume a PKI setup. Our protocol follows the design of the *perfectly-secure* network-agnostic broadcast protocol from [3] which makes use of *two* primitives, which we discuss first.

3.1 Asynchronous Broadcast with Weaker Synchronous Guarantees

The first primitive is a protocol Π_{ABC}, which is a t_a-secure broadcast in an asynchronous network. The primitive also achieves the properties of broadcast in a *synchronous* network against t_s corruptions for an *honest* sender but fails if the sender is *corrupt*. Namely, in the latter case, there is *no* guarantee that the honest parties obtain any output. Moreover, even if the honest parties obtain an output, they *may not* do so at the same (local) time.

The work of [3] uses the famous *perfectly-secure* asynchronous broadcast protocol (or Acast) of [16] as an instantiation of Π_{ABC}. The protocol can tolerate up to $t < \frac{n}{3}$ corruptions, irrespective of the network type and hence fits the bill in [3]; this is because for *perfect* security, $t_s < \frac{n}{3}$ holds. However, in our context, $t_s < \frac{n}{2}$ and so we *cannot* use the Acast protocol of [16] as instantiation of Π_{ABC}. However, we notice that the reliable broadcast protocol of [36] realises the exact requirements we demand from an instantiation of Π_{ABC}. The protocol achieves *cryptographic* security, assuming a PKI setup. For completeness, the protocol is given in Fig. 1.

Protocol Π_{ABC}

- **Sending the Input** — Sender S, on having input m, sends (propose, m, $\langle m\rangle_S$) to all the parties.
- **Forwarding the Input** — Each $P_i \in \mathcal{P}$ does the following:
  - Upon receiving the first (propose, m, $\langle m\rangle_S$) message with a valid signature from S, send (propose, m, $\langle m\rangle_S$) to all $P_j \in \mathcal{P}$, and wait till local time becomes an integer multiple of Δ.
- **Sending Vote** — Each $P_i \in \mathcal{P}$ does the following:
  - If (propose, m', $\langle m'\rangle_S$) for $m' \neq m$ is not received, then send (vote, m, $\langle m\rangle_{P_i}$) to all the parties.
- **Sending Quorum and Output computation** — Each $P_i \in \mathcal{P}$ does the following:
  - Upon receiving a quorum of $n - t_s$ messages (vote, m, $\langle m\rangle_\star$) with valid signatures, denote these by $V(m)$, send $V(m)$ to all the parties and output the value m.

Fig. 1. Asynchronous broadcast with weaker synchronous guarantees

The properties of the protocol Π_{ABC} are stated in Lemma 3.

Lemma 3. *Let $t_a < t_s$ and $t_a + 2t_s < n$ and let* S *have a message m as input for Π_{ABC}. Then, the protocol Π_{ABC} satisfies the following properties.*

- *In a Synchronous Network:*
  - *t_s-liveness: If* S *is honest, then all honest parties obtain an output within time 3Δ.*
  - *t_s-validity: If* S *is honest, then every honest party outputs m.*
  - *t_s-consistency: If* S *is corrupt and some honest party outputs $m^\star$ at time T, then every honest party outputs $m^\star$ at time $T + \Delta$.*
- *In an Asynchronous Network:*
  - *t_a-liveness: If* S *is honest, then all honest parties eventually obtain an output.*
  - *t_a-validity: If* S *is honest, then every honest party with an output, outputs m.*
  - *t_a-consistency: If* S *is corrupt and some honest party outputs $m^\star$, then every honest party eventually outputs $m^\star$.*
- *Irrespective of the network type, the protocol incurs a communication of $\mathcal{O}(n^3 \cdot |m|)$ bits from the honest parties, where $|m|$ denotes the size of m in bits.*

In our description, we will say that S *acasts* m to mean that S invokes an instance of Π_{ABC} with input m and the parties participate in this instance. Similarly, we will say that the *parties receive m through the acast of* S to denote that the output of the parties in the Π_{ABC} instance is m.

3.2 Synchronous Byzantine Agreement

The second component used in [3] is a t_s-secure *synchronous* BA (SBA) protocol Π_{SBA}, that additionally guarantees *liveness* in an *asynchronous* network against t_a corruptions. The instantiation of Π_{SBA} is with *perfect* security where $t_s < \frac{n}{3}$ and will *not* work for our setting where $t_s < \frac{n}{2}$. Instead, our instantiation of Π_{SBA} is the Dolev-Strong BA protocol [28] based on the PKI setup, which requires $t_s + 1$ rounds (in a *synchronous* network). To achieve liveness in the *asynchronous* network, it suffices to have the parties execute the protocol for local time $T_{\mathsf{SBA}} = (t_s + 1) \cdot \Delta$ time and check if an output is computed at time T_{SBA}. If no output is computed, then the parties output $\bot$, else they take the output as determined by the protocol. The protocol incurs a communication of $\mathcal{O}(n^3 \cdot |m|)$ bits from the honest parties, where $|m|$ is the size of m in bits. The detailed protocol and proofs are omitted due to brevity.

3.3 $\Pi_{\mathsf{ABC}} + \Pi_{\mathsf{SBA}} \rightarrow$ Network-Agnostic BC

Once we have instantiations of Π_{ABC} and Π_{SBA}, we obtain a network-agnostic broadcast protocol following [3] as follows: first, S invokes an instance of Π_{ABC} to broadcast its input. If the network is *synchronous* then all honest parties should have the sender's input at the time 3Δ. To check the same, the parties run an instance of Π_{SBA} on the outputs obtained from the Π_{ABC} instance at time 3Δ. Finally, at time $3\Delta + T_{\mathsf{SBA}}$, the parties check the output from the Π_{SBA} instance. The parties then decide their output at time $3\Delta + T_{\mathsf{SBA}}$, based on the output they obtained from the instance of Π_{ABC} and Π_{SBA}. This will ensure that the resultant protocol achieves t_s-security in a *synchronous* network. However, if the network is *asynchronous*, then it might be possible that at the local time $3\Delta + T_{\mathsf{SBA}}$, different honest parties have different outputs. Namely some honest parties may output $\perp$, while others may have an output $m^\star$, *different* from $\perp$. Consequently, as done in [3], we provide a provision for the former set of parties to continue running the protocol, so that they also eventually obtain the output $m^\star$. Following the terminology of [3], we denote the two different methods of computing the outputs as *regular* and *fallback* mode. The protocol is formally presented in Fig. 2.

Protocol Π_{BC}

Regular Mode

- **Acasting the Input** — Sender S, on having input m, acasts it.
- **Agreeing on the Acast Output** — Each party $P_i \in \mathcal{P}$ does the following at time 3Δ:
  - Set the input to an instance of Π_{SBA} as follows:
    - If an $m^\star$ is received from the acast of S then set it as the input;
    - Otherwise, set $\perp$ as the input.
  - Participate in the instance of Π_{SBA} with the set input.
- **Local Output Computation** — At time $3\Delta + T_{\mathsf{SBA}}$ each $P_i \in \mathcal{P}$ computes the output through *regular* mode as follows:
  - Output $m^\star \neq \perp$, if $m^\star$ is received from the acast of S *and* computed as the output during the instance of Π_{SBA}.
  - Else, output $\perp$.

Fallback Mode

Every $P_i \in \mathcal{P}$ who computed the output $\perp$ at time $3\Delta + T_{\mathsf{SBA}}$ does the following: if $m^\star$ received from the acast of S then change the output from $\perp$ to $m^\star$.

Fig. 2. Network-agnostic broadcast protocol

The properties of the protocol Π_{BC} stated in Lemma 4 can be proved in the same way as in [3].

Lemma 4. *Let $t_a < t_s$ and $t_a + 2t_s < n$ and let* S *have an input m for Π_{BC}. Then, the protocol Π_{BC} satisfies the following properties, where $T_{\mathsf{BC}} = 3\Delta + T_{\mathsf{SBA}}$.*

- *In a Synchronous Network:*
  - *t_s-liveness: If* S *is honest, then all honest parties obtain an output within time T_{BC}.*
  - *t_s-validity: If* S *is honest, then every honest party outputs m.*
  - *t_s-consistency: If* S *is corrupt, then*
    - *If some honest party outputs $m^\star$ at time T_{BC}, then every honest party outputs $m^\star$ at time T_{BC}.*

  - *If some honest party outputs $m^\star$ at time $T > T_{\mathsf{BC}}$, then every honest party outputs $m^\star$ at time $T + \Delta$.*
- *In an Asynchronous Network:*
  - *t_a-liveness: If* S *is honest, then all honest parties eventually obtain an output.*
  - *t_a-validity: If* S *is honest, then every honest party with an output, outputs m.*
  - *t_a-consistency: If* S *is corrupt and some honest party outputs $m^\star$, then every honest party eventually outputs $m^\star$.*
- *Irrespective of the network type, the protocol incurs a communication of $\mathcal{O}(n^3 \cdot |m|)$ bits from the honest parties.*

As in [3], we use the following terminologies for Π_{BC} in the rest of the paper.

Terminologies for Π_{BC}. When we say that "*P_i broadcasts m*", we mean that P_i invokes an instance of Π_{BC} as S with input m and the parties participate in this instance. Similarly, when we say that "*P_j receives m from the broadcast of P_i through regular mode*", we mean that P_j has the output m at time T_{BC}, during the instance of Π_{BC}. Finally, when we say that "*P_j receives m from the broadcast of P_i through fallback mode*", we mean that P_j has the output m after time T_{BC} during the instance of Π_{BC}.

4 Network-Agnostic VSS

In this section, we present our network-agnostic VSS protocol Π_{VSS}, which allows a designated dealer D to *verifiably* $[\cdot]$-share its input s, where the degree of sharing will be t_s, irrespective of the network type. For an *honest* D, the value s will be $[\cdot]$-shared *eventually* in an *asynchronous* network, while s will be $[\cdot]$-shared after a *fixed* known time, if the network behaves *synchronously*. The *verifiability* here ensures that if D is *corrupt*, then either no honest party obtains any output (if D does not invoke the protocol), or there exists some value which gets $[\cdot]$-shared among the parties. Note that in the latter case, we *cannot* bound the time within which honest parties will have their shares, even if the network is *synchronous*. This is because a *corrupt* D may delay sending the designated messages arbitrarily, and the parties will *not* know the exact network type.

The idea behind Π_{VSS} is as follows: D embeds s in a random t_s-degree polynomial $q(\cdot)$ in its constant term, where the polynomial $q(\cdot)$ is further embedded in a random (t_s, t_s)-degree symmetric bivariate polynomial, say $F(x, y)$, at $x = 0$. The goal is then to verifiably distribute the point $q(i)$ to each party P_i and make public the commitments of these points. To achieve this, D further picks a random (t_s, t_s)-degree symmetric bivariate polynomial, say $R(x, y)$, and publicly commits the coefficients of the polynomials $f_i(x)$ using the coefficients of the polynomial $r_i(x)$ as randomness, where $f_i(x) = F(x, i)$ and $r_i(x) = R(x, i)$. The matrix of coefficients $\mathbf{C}$ which is of size $n \times (t_s + 1)$ is made public through an instance of our network-agnostic broadcast protocol Π_{BC}. Additionally, each party P_i is also provided the pair of points $\{f_i(j), r_i(j)\}_{j=1,\ldots,n}$. Every party

P_i upon receiving the points $\{f_i(j), r_i(j)\}_{j=1,\ldots,n}$ and the matrix $\mathbf{C}$ can check for their "consistency". That is, P_i can check if $\mathbf{C}$ constitutes commitments of the coefficients of some (t_s, t_s)-degree symmetric bivariate polynomial (using the procedure $\mathsf{VerifyPoly}$) and if the points $\{f_i(j), r_i(j)\}_{j=1,\ldots,n}$ lie on the ith univariate polynomial committed in $\mathbf{C}$ (using the procedure $\mathsf{VerifyPoint}$). If both the tests are positive, then P_i notifies this publicly, through an instance of the broadcast protocol Π_{BC}. The dealer D then looks for a candidate "core" set of parties $\mathcal{CS}$ of size at least $n - t_s$ who responded *positively* and upon finding a $\mathcal{CS}$, D makes it public (again through an instance of Π_{BC}).

For simplicity, let us assume that the network behaves *synchronously* and D is *honest*. Then all *honest* parties (which are at least $n - t_s$ in number), should respond positively by time $2T_{\mathsf{BC}}$. This is because each instance of Π_{BC} takes T_{BC} time to generate an output. Consequently, D should find a candidate $\mathcal{CS}$ and hence all honest parties should have this $\mathcal{CS}$ at time $3T_{\mathsf{BC}}$. Based on this observation, at (local) time $3T_{\mathsf{BC}}$, the parties check if D made public a candidate core set of size at least $n - t_s$ (who have responded positively). Since different parties may have different opinions about the existence of a candidate core set, the parties execute an instance of the network-agnostic BA protocol Π_{BA} to have a common opinion. Based on the output of the Π_{BA} instance, the parties can conclude about the type of the network and behaviour of D.

Let us *first* consider the case when the output of the Π_{BA} instance is *positive*, implying that at least one honest party has seen a candidate $\mathcal{CS}$ at (local) time $3T_{\mathsf{BC}}$. Let $\mathcal{H}$ be the set of *honest* parties and let $\mathcal{H}_{\mathcal{CS}}$ be the set of honest parties in $\mathcal{CS}$. Note that $\mathcal{H}_{\mathcal{CS}} \neq \emptyset$, *irrespective* of the network type, since $|\mathcal{CS}| \geq n - t_s \geq t_s + t_a + 1$. Since the parties in $\mathcal{H}_{\mathcal{CS}}$ have verified $\mathbf{C}$ using the procedure $\mathsf{VerifyPoly}$, it implies that there exists a (t_s, t_s)-degree *symmetric* bivariate polynomial, say $F^\star(x, y)$ and a (t_s, t_s)-degree bivariate polynomial, say $R^\star(x, y)$, such that coefficients of the polynomials $\{F^\star(x, i)\}_{i=1,\ldots,n}$ are committed by D in $\mathbf{C}$, using the coefficients of the polynomials $\{R^\star(x, i)\}_{i=1,\ldots,n}$ as randomness. We call $F^\star(x, y)$ as D's *committed* bivariate polynomial and note that $F^\star(x, y) = F(x, y)$ holds, if D is *honest*. Let $q^\star(\cdot) \stackrel{def}{=} F^\star(0, y)$ and let $s^\star \stackrel{def}{=} F^\star(0, 0)$. Again note that if D is *honest*, then $s^\star = s$, since $q^\star(\cdot) = q(\cdot)$ holds. Let $F_i^\star(x) = F^\star(x, i)$ and $R_i^\star(x) = R^\star(x, i)$. The next goal will be to ensure that $s^\star$ gets $[\cdot]$-shared, for which it is sufficient to have each $P_i \in \mathcal{H}$ have the pair of points $(F_i^\star(0), R_i^\star(0))$, since the commitment of these points are *already* available through $\mathbf{C}$. We also know that each party in $\mathcal{H}_{\mathcal{CS}}$ *already* has received the designated pair of points $(F_i^\star(0), R_i^\star(0))$ from D, since they responded positively after verifying the pairs of points received from D using the procedure $\mathsf{VerifyPoint}$. So what is left to ensure that the potentially honest parties P_i *outside* $\mathcal{CS}$ get their designated pair of points $(F_i^\star(0), R_i^\star(0))$. We stress that there *might* be such potential honest parties outside $\mathcal{CS}$. While this can always happen in an asynchronous network (even if D is honest) where the designated messages for a subset of honest parties may be delayed, the same can happen in a synchronous network where a *corrupt* D may not send the designated messages to a subset of honest parties.

One option to enable the parties P_i *outside* $\mathcal{CS}$ to get their respective pair of points $(F_i^{\star}(0), R_i^{\star}(0))$ is to let the parties *inside* $\mathcal{CS}$ provide P_i the supposedly common points on the polynomials $F_i^{\star}(x)$ and $R_i^{\star}(x)$, which P_i can verify using $\mathbf{C}$. And once P_i has at least $t_s + 1$ correct points on these polynomials, it can interpolate them and get $(F_i^{\star}(0), R_i^{\star}(0))$. This idea will certainly work, if the network is *guaranteed* to be *asynchronous*, since in this case $|\mathcal{H}_{\mathcal{CS}}| \geq n - t_s - t_a > t_s$. Unfortunately, the network type will be *unknown* and it may so happen that the network is *synchronous* and D is *corrupt*, in which case we are guaranteed to have $|\mathcal{H}_{\mathcal{CS}}| \geq n - t_s - t_s > t_a$, which is *not* sufficient to implement the above idea. Instead, we follow a different approach, which constitutes the crux of the protocol.

Once $\mathcal{CS}$ is publicly identified, D next *freshly* secret-shares the points $F_i^{\star}(0)$ and $R_i^{\star}(0)$, for every $P_i \notin \mathcal{CS}$. The crucial point here is that the degree of sharing now is *only* t_a and *not* t_s. We stress that this *does not* violate the privacy of the points $F_i^{\star}(0)$ and $R_i^{\star}(0)$ in any network for an *honest* D. This is because if the network is *synchronous*, then *every* party $P_i \notin \mathcal{CS}$ is *guaranteed* to be *corrupt* for an *honest* D and so the adversary will already be *knowing* the points $F_i^{\star}(0)$ and $R_i^{\star}(0)$. On the other hand, if the network is *asynchronous*, then the fresh sharing will not violate the privacy, since there will be at most t_a corrupt parties and the degree of the new sharing is t_a. To secret-share the points $F_i^{\star}(0)$ and $R_i^{\star}(0)$, the dealer embeds them in random t_a-degree polynomials at their constant term, distribute distinct points on these polynomials to respective parties and also publicly commit the coefficients of these polynomials. The parties then verify the received points with respect to the commitments using the procedure $\mathsf{VerifyPoint}$. Moreover, they also verify whether the points which are freshly secret-shared are the *same* which are committed in the existing matrix $\mathbf{C}$. Every party upon verifying both these conditions positively, notifies it in public. The goal is then to let D publicly identify a "qualified" subset of parties $\mathcal{Q}$ of size $n - t_s$ (who could be different from $\mathcal{CS}$), who responded positively for the fresh secret-sharings done by D. Note that an *honest* D will always find such a candidate set $\mathcal{Q}$, irrespective of the network type, since $\mathcal{H}$ will always constitute a candidate $\mathcal{Q}$ set. Once the set $\mathcal{Q}$ is identified, then the parties in $\mathcal{Q}$ enable the parties $P_i \notin \mathcal{CS}$ to interpolate the t_a-degree polynomials using which D has freshly shared $F_i^{\star}(0)$ and $R_i^{\star}(0)$. For this, the parties in $\mathcal{Q}$ provide their respective points on these fresh polynomials to P_i, who can identify the correct points by using the procedure $\mathsf{VerifyPoint}$. Note that P_i will need only $t_a + 1$ correct points now, which are bound to arrive in *any* network, since $\mathcal{Q}$ is bound to have at least $t_a + 1$ honest party in any network. This completes the description of the protocol for the case when a candidate $\mathcal{CS}$ is identified within the designated time of $3T_{\mathsf{BC}}$.

Let us now consider the *second* case when *no* candidate $\mathcal{CS}$ is identified within the designated time of $3T_{\mathsf{BC}}$. This case is relatively simpler. In this case we already know that either D is *corrupt* or the network is *asynchronous*. Consequently, D is now asked to look for a candidate $\mathcal{CS}$ of size at least $n - t_a$, who responded positively for the matrix $\mathbf{C}$ and the points received from D. Note that an *honest* D is guaranteed to get such a $\mathcal{CS}$ because in this case the network is *asynchronous* and so $|\mathcal{H}| \geq n - t_a$ and hence $\mathcal{H}$ will eventually constitute a candidate $\mathcal{CS}$. Once $\mathcal{CS}$ (of size at least $n - t_a$) is identified, then the parties *inside* $\mathcal{CS}$ can help the parties P_i *outside* $\mathcal{CS}$ to get their respective pair of points $(F_i^\star(0), R_i^\star(0))$ by supplying them the supposedly common points on the polynomials $F_i^\star(x)$ and $R_i^\star(x)$. Party P_i can then identify the correct points (using $\mathbf{C}$ and procedure $\mathsf{VerifyPoint}$) and once P_i has $t_s + 1$ correct points, it can interpolate them and get $(F_i^\star(0), R_i^\star(0))$. Interestingly, the availability of at least $t_s + 1$ correct points from the parties in the *new* $\mathcal{CS}$ is *always* guaranteed, even if the network is *synchronous*. This is because now $|\mathcal{CS}| \geq n - t_a$ and hence has $n - t_a - t_s > t_s$ honest parties even in a *synchronous* network.

This completes the description of the protocol Π_{VSS}, which is presented in Fig. 3. There are *two* cases in the protocol, depending upon whether the parties identify a candidate core set of size at least $n - t_s$ within the designated time $3T_{\mathsf{BC}}$. For the *first* case, D has to secret-share values *two* times, first while distributing points on bivariate polynomials and second while again secret-sharing the shares of the parties who are outside the candidate core set. To distinguish between these two types of sharing, we use the terms *primary* and *secondary* sharing respectively.

The properties of the protocol Π_{VSS} are stated in Theorem 1.

Theorem 1. *Let $t_a < t_s$ and $t_a + 2t_s < n$ and let D has an input $s \in \mathbb{F}_p$ for Π_{VSS}. Moreover, let $T_{\mathsf{VSS}} = 6T_{\mathsf{BC}} + T_{\mathsf{BA}} + \Delta$. Then, the protocol Π_{VSS} achieves the following properties.*

- *If D is honest, then the following hold.*
  - *t_s-correctness: In a synchronous network, s is $[\cdot]$-shared at time T_{VSS}.*
  - *t_a-correctness: In an asynchronous network, s is eventually $[\cdot]$-shared.*
  - *t_s-privacy: Irrespective of the network type, the view of the adversary remains independent of s.*
- *If D is corrupt, then either no honest party computes any output, or there exists some $s^\star \in \mathbb{F}_p$ such that the following holds.*
  - *t_s-strong commitment: In a synchronous network, $s^\star$ is $[\cdot]$-shared, such that one of the following holds.*
    - *If any honest party computes its output at time T_{VSS}, then all honest parties compute its output at time T_{VSS}.*
    - *If any honest party computes its output at time $T > T_{\mathsf{VSS}}$, then every honest party computes its output by time $T + \Delta$.*
  - *t_a-strong commitment: In an asynchronous network, $s^\star$ is eventually $[\cdot]$-shared.*
- *Irrespective of the network type, the protocol incurs a communication of $\mathcal{O}(n^5 \cdot \kappa)$ bits from the honest parties and invokes 1 instance of Π_{BA}.*

Protocol Π_{VSS} for L Inputs. Protocol Π_{VSS} can be easily modified to handle the case when D has L inputs where $L \geq 1$, such that the number of Π_{BA} instances in the protocol is *only* one and remains *independent* of L. The idea is to execute the steps of the protocol Π_{VSS} L times, once on behalf of each input of D. However, *instead* of finding L candidate $\mathcal{CS}$ or $\mathcal{Q}$ sets, the dealer D finds a

Protocol Π_{VSS}

- **Phase I: Primary-Share Distribution** — D on having the input s, does the following:
  - Pick a random t_s-degree polynomial $q(\cdot)$, such that $q(0) = s$.
  - Pick two random (t_s, t_s)-degree symmetric bivariate polynomials $F(x, y)$ and $R(x, y)$, such that $F(0, y) = q(\cdot)$.
  - For $i = 1, \ldots, n$, let $f_i(x) = F(x, i) = a_{i0} + a_{i1}x + \ldots + a_{it_s}x^{t_s}$ and let $r_i(x) = R(x, i) = b_{i0} + b_{i1}x + \ldots + b_{it_s}x^{t_s}$. For $j = 0, \ldots, t_s$, compute the commitment $\mathsf{Com}_{ij} = \mathsf{Commit}(a_{ij}, b_{ij})$.
  - For $i = 1, \ldots, n$, send the vector of values $(f_{i1}, \ldots, f_{in})$ and $(r_{i1}, \ldots, r_{in})$ to P_i, where for $j = 1, \ldots, n$, the condition $f_{ij} = f_i(j)$ and $r_{ij} = r_i(j)$ holds.
  - Let $\mathbf{C}$ be the $n \times (t_s + 1)$ matrix, where for $i = 1, \ldots, n$ the ith row consists of $(\mathsf{Com}_{i0}, \ldots, \mathsf{Com}_{it_s})$. Broadcast the matrix $\mathbf{C}$.
- **Phase II: Publicly Declaring the Consistency of Primary-Shares** — Each $P_i \in \mathcal{P}$ (including D) upon receiving the vector of values $(f_{i1}, \ldots, f_{in})$ and $(r_{i1}, \ldots, r_{in})$ from D, and the matrix $\mathbf{C}$ from D's broadcast through *regular* mode, wait till the current local time becomes an integer multiple of Δ. It then broadcasts $(\mathsf{ReceivedPrimary}, i)$ if *all* the following holds:
  - $\mathbf{C}$ is an $n \times (t_s + 1)$ matrix.
  - $\mathsf{VerifyPoly}(\mathbf{C}, t_s)$ outputs 1.
  - For $i = 1, \ldots, n$, let $(\mathsf{Com}_{i0}, \ldots, \mathsf{Com}_{it_s})$ be the ith row of $\mathbf{C}$. Then $\mathsf{VerifyPoint}(\{\mathsf{Com}_{i0}, \ldots, \mathsf{Com}_{it_s}\}, (f_{ij}, r_{ij}), j)$ outputs 1, for $j = 1, \ldots, n$.
- **Phase III: Publicly Declaring the Core Set** — D does the following at time $2T_{\mathsf{BC}}$:
  - Initialize a set $\mathcal{CS} = \emptyset$.
  - Include P_i to $\mathcal{CS}$, if $(\mathsf{ReceivedPrimary}, i)$ is received from the broadcast of P_i through *regular* mode.
  - If $|\mathcal{CS}| \geq n - t_s$, then broadcast $\mathcal{CS}$.
- **Local Computation: Verifying and Accepting the Core Set** — Each $P_i \in \mathcal{P}$ (including D) does the following at time $3T_{\mathsf{BC}}$:
  - If a set $\mathcal{CS}$ is received from D's broadcast through *regular* mode, such that $|\mathcal{CS}| \geq n - t_s$, then *accept* it if $(\mathsf{ReceivedPrimary}, j)$ *was* received from the broadcast of every $P_j \in \mathcal{CS}$, through *regular* mode at time $2T_{\mathsf{BC}}$.
- **Phase IV: Deciding Whether to Go for a Core Set of Size** $(n - t_a)$ — At time $3T_{\mathsf{BC}}$, each $P_i \in \mathcal{P}$ participates in an instance of Π_{BA} with input $b_i = 1$ if a $\mathcal{CS}$ is accepted, else with input $b_i = 0$, and waits for time T_{BA}.

Case I (If a Core Set of Size $n - t_s$ is Found)

This part is executed if the output of Π_{BA} is 1.

- **Phase V: Distributing Secondary-Shares of Non-Core Parties by** D —For each $P_i \notin \mathcal{CS}$, D does the following:
  - Select a random t_a-degree polynomial $m_i(x)$ such that $m_i(0) = f_i(0) = a_{i0}$. Let $m_i(x) = a_{i0} + e_{i1}x + \ldots + e_{it_a}x^{t_a}$.
  - Select a random t_a-degree polynomial $c_i(x)$ such that $c_i(0) = r_i(0) = b_{i0}$. Let $c_i(x) = b_{i0} + u_{i1}x + \ldots + u_{it_a}x^{t_a}$.
  - For $k = 1, \ldots, t_a$, compute the commitment $\mathsf{Sec\text{-}Com}_{ik} = \mathsf{Commit}(e_{ik}, u_{ik})$.
  - For $j = 1, \ldots, n$, send m_{ij} and c_{ij} to party P_j, where $m_{ij} = m_i(j)$ and $c_{ij} = c_i(j)$.

  D then broadcasts the commitments $\{\mathsf{Sec\text{-}Com}_{ik}\}_{P_i \notin \mathcal{CS}, k=1,\ldots,t_a}$.
- **Phase VI: Publicly Declaring the Consistency of Secondary-Shares** — Each $P_j \in \mathcal{P}$ does the following:
  - If $\mathcal{CS}$ and $\mathbf{C}$ is not yet received from D's broadcast, then wait to receive them from D's broadcast through *fallback* mode.
  - Upon receiving the points $\{m_{ij}, c_{ij}\}_{P_i \notin \mathcal{CS}}$ from D and the commitments $\{\mathsf{Sec\text{-}Com}_{ik}\}_{P_i \notin \mathcal{CS}, k=1,\ldots,t_a}$ from D's broadcast (through *any* mode), wait till the current local time becomes an integer multiple of Δ and then broadcast $(\mathsf{ReceivedSecondary}, j)$ if the following holds for *every* $P_i \notin \mathcal{CS}$:
    - $\mathsf{VerifyPoint}(\{\mathsf{Com}_{i0}, \mathsf{Sec\text{-}Com}_{i1}, \ldots, \mathsf{Sec\text{-}Com}_{it_a}\}, (m_{ij}, c_{ij}), j)$ outputs 1. Here $(\mathsf{Com}_{i0}, \ldots, \mathsf{Com}_{it_s})$ denotes the ith row of $\mathbf{C}$.

Fig. 3. Network-agnostic VSS protocol

- **Phase VII: Publicly Declaring the** Qualified set — D does the following after (local) time $5T_{\mathsf{BC}} + T_{\mathsf{BA}}$:
  - Initialize a set $\mathcal{Q} = \emptyset$.
  - Include P_j to $\mathcal{Q}$, if $(\mathsf{ReceivedSecondary}, j)$ is received from the broadcast of P_j (through *any* mode).
  - If $|\mathcal{Q}| \geq n - t_s$, then broadcast $\mathcal{Q}$.
- **Local Computation: Verifying and Accepting the** Qualified Set — Every party in $\mathcal{P}$ (including D) does the following at time $6T_{\mathsf{BC}} + T_{\mathsf{BA}}$:
  - If a set $\mathcal{Q}$ is received from D's broadcast (through *any* mode) such that $|\mathcal{Q}| \geq n - t_s$, then *accept* it if $(\mathsf{ReceivedSecondary}, j)$ is received from the broadcast of every $P_j \in \mathcal{Q}$ (through *any* mode).
- **Phase VIII: Sending Secondary-Shares to the Non-Core Parties** — Each $P_j \in \mathcal{P}$ (including D) does the following:
  - If $P_j \in \mathcal{Q}$ and P_j has *accepted* $\mathcal{Q}$, then send (m_{ij}, c_{ij}) to every $P_i \notin \mathcal{CS}$.
- **Output Computation** — Each $P_i \in \mathcal{P}$ waits till the current local time becomes an integer multiple of Δ and then does the following:
  - If $P_i \in \mathcal{CS}$, then output $(f_i(0), r_i(0))$ and the commitments $\{\mathsf{Com}_{k0}\}_{k=1,\ldots,n}$.
  - Else if $P_i \notin \mathcal{CS}$ and if P_i has *accepted* $\mathcal{Q}$, then do the following:
    - Initialize a set $\mathcal{SS}_i = \emptyset$.
    - Upon receiving (m_{ij}, c_{ij}) from $P_j \in \mathcal{Q}$, include P_j to $\mathcal{SS}_i$ if $\mathsf{VerifyPoint}(\{\mathsf{Com}_{i0}, \mathsf{Sec\text{-}Com}_{i1}, \ldots, \mathsf{Sec\text{-}Com}_{it_a}\}, (m_{ij}, c_{ij}), j)$ outputs 1.
    - If $|\mathcal{SS}_i| > t_a$, interpolate the points $\{(j, m_{ij})\}_{P_j \in \mathcal{SS}_i}$ and $\{(j, c_{ij})\}_{P_j \in \mathcal{SS}_i}$ to obtain t_a-degree polynomials $m_i(x)$ and $c_i(x)$ respectively. Set $f_i(0) = m_i(0)$ and $r_i(0) = c_i(0)$, then output $(f_i(0), r_i(0))$ and $\{\mathsf{Com}_{k0}\}_{k=1,\ldots,n}$.

Case II (If a Core Set of Size $n - t_s$ is Not Found)

This part is executed if the output of Π_{BA} is 0

- **Phase V: Broadcasting a Core Set of Size** $(n - t_a)$ —D does the following:
  - Upon receiving $(\mathsf{ReceivedPrimary}, i)$ from the broadcast of P_i (through *any* mode) include P_i to $\mathcal{CS}$.
  - If $|\mathcal{CS}| \geq n - t_a$, then broadcast $\mathcal{CS}$.
- **Local Computation: Verifying and Accepting the Core Set of Size** $(n - t_a)$ — Each $P_i \in \mathcal{P}$ does the following:
  - Participate in any instance of Π_{BC} invoked by D for broadcasting $\mathcal{CS}$ *only* after time $6T_{\mathsf{BC}} + T_{\mathsf{BA}} + \Delta$. Wait till some $\mathcal{CS}$ is obtained from D's broadcast (through *any* mode) and *accept* it if the following holds:
    - $|\mathcal{CS}| \geq n - t_a$.
    - $(\mathsf{ReceivedPrimary}, j)$ is received from the broadcast of all $P_j \in \mathcal{CS}$ (through *any* mode).
- **Phase VI: Sending Common Points to the Parties Outside** $\mathcal{CS}$ — Each $P_i \in \mathcal{P}$ does the following:
  - If $P_i \in \mathcal{CS}$ and P_i has *accepted* $\mathcal{CS}$, then send (f_{ij}, r_{ij}) to each $P_j \notin \mathcal{CS}$.
- **Output Computation** — Each $P_i \in \mathcal{P}$ waits till the current local time becomes an integer multiple of Δ and then does the following:
  - If $P_i \in \mathcal{CS}$, then output $(f_i(0), r_i(0))$ and the commitments $\{\mathsf{Com}_{k0}\}_{k=1,\ldots,n}$.
  - Else if P_i has *accepted* $\mathcal{CS}$, then do the following:
    - Initialize a set $\mathcal{SS}_i = \emptyset$.
    - Upon receiving (f_{ji}, r_{ji}) from $P_j \in \mathcal{CS}$, include P_j to $\mathcal{SS}_i$ if the following holds:
      - $\mathsf{VerifyPoint}(\{\mathsf{Com}_{j0}, \mathsf{Com}_{j1}, \ldots, \mathsf{Com}_{jt_s}\}, (f_{ji}, r_{ji}), i)$ outputs 1.
    - If $|\mathcal{SS}_i| \geq t_s + 1$, interpolate the points $\{(j, f_{ji})\}_{P_j \in \mathcal{SS}_i}$ and $\{(j, r_{ji})\}_{P_j \in \mathcal{SS}_i}$ to obtain t_s-degree polynomials $f_i(x)$ and $r_i(x)$ respectively. Then output $(f_i(0), r_i(0))$ and $\{\mathsf{Com}_{k0}\}_{k=1,\ldots,n}$.

Fig. 3. (*continued*)

single $\mathcal{CS}$ or $\mathcal{Q}$ set. For this, each party broadcasts a *single* (ReceivedPrimary, $\star$) message or (ReceivedSecondary, $\star$) message (instead of L such messages), if the conditions for broadcasting these messages are satisfied on behalf of *all* the L inputs of D. As the modifications are straightforward, we avoid the details and note that the protocol incurs a communication of $\mathcal{O}(n^5 \cdot L \cdot \kappa)$ bits from the honest parties and invokes 1 instance of Π_{BA}.

5 Agreement on a Common Subset (ACS)

In this section, we adapt the ACS protocol proposed by [3] to our specific setting by incorporating our network-agnostic VSS protocol Π_{VSS} and the network-agnostic BA protocol Π_{BA} of [14]. The ACS protocol, denoted as Π_{ACS}, will be utilized in both our preprocessing phase protocol and the circuit-evaluation protocol. In the protocol, each party is supposed to $[\cdot]$-share L input values using instances of Π_{VSS}.[2] The goal of Π_{ACS} is to enable the parties to agree upon a common subset of parties CS of size at least $n - t_s$, such that the inputs of all the parties in CS are $[\cdot]$-shared. Additionally, in a synchronous network, all honest parties are present in CS.

The underlying idea of Π_{ACS} is as follows: Each party $P_i \in \mathcal{P}$ acts as a dealer and invokes an instance $\Pi_{\mathsf{VSS}}^{(i)}$ of the protocol, Π_{VSS}, to verifiably $[\cdot]$-share its inputs. In a *synchronous* network, after time T_{VSS}, the inputs of all *honest* parties should be $[\cdot]$-shared. Consequently, after (local) time T_{VSS}, the parties examine the instances of Π_{VSS} in which they computed their respective outputs. Based on this information, the parties engage in n instances of the protocol Π_{BA}, where the jth instance is to determine whether P_j should be included in CS. The input criteria for these Π_{BA} instances are as follows: if a party has computed output during the instance $\Pi_{\mathsf{VSS}}^{(j)}$, then it participates with input 1 in the jth instance $\Pi_{\mathsf{BA}}^{(j)}$ of Π_{BA}. Once at least $n - t_s$ instances of Π_{BA} yield an output of 1, the parties participate with input 0 in any remaining Π_{BA} instances for which they have not yet provided any input. Finally, after obtaining outputs from all n instances of Π_{BA}, party P_j is included in CS iff the output of the $\Pi_{\mathsf{BA}}^{(j)}$ instance is 1. Since the parties wait for time T_{VSS} before initiating the Π_{BA} instances, it is guaranteed that all honest dealers are included in CS in a synchronous network.

The properties of the protocol Π_{ACS} stated in Lemma 5 follows from [3].

Lemma 5. *Let $t_a < t_s$ and $t_a + 2t_s < n$. Then, the protocol Π_{ACS} achieves the following properties, where every party P_i has L values $(s_{(i,1)}, \ldots, s_{(i,L)})$ from $\mathbb{F}_p$ as input.*

- *t_s-correctness: If the network is synchronous, then at time $T_{\mathsf{ACS}} = T_{\mathsf{VSS}} + 2T_{\mathsf{BA}}$, the honest parties have a common subset* CS *of size at least $n - t_s$, such that all the following holds:*
  - *All honest parties will be present in* CS.

[2] The exact inputs depend upon the underlying context.

  - *Corresponding to every $P_i \in \mathsf{CS}$, there exist L values $(s^\star_{(i,1)}, \ldots, s^\star_{(i,L)})$, which are same as $(s_{(i,1)}, \ldots, s_{(i,L)})$ for an honest P_i, such that $s^\star_{(i,1)}, \ldots, s^\star_{(i,L)}$ are $[\cdot]$-shared among the parties at time T_{ACS}.*
- *t_a-correctness: If the network is asynchronous, then the honest parties eventually output a common subset CS of size at least $n - t_s$. Moreover, corresponding to every $P_i \in \mathsf{CS}$, there exist L values $(s^\star_{(i,1)}, \ldots, s^\star_{(i,L)})$, which are same as $(s_{(i,1)}, \ldots, s_{(i,L)})$ for an honest P_i, such that $s^\star_{(i,1)}, \ldots, s^\star_{(i,L)}$ are eventually $[\cdot]$-shared among the parties.*
- *t_s-privacy: Irrespective of the network type, the view of the adversary remains independent of the inputs of the honest parties.*
- *Irrespective of the network type, the protocol incurs a communication of $\mathcal{O}(n^6 \cdot L \cdot \kappa)$ bits from the honest parties and invokes $\mathcal{O}(n)$ instances of Π_{BA}.*

6 The Preprocessing Phase Protocol

We now present our network-agnostic preprocessing protocol in this section. The protocol aims to produce c_M number of $[\cdot]$-shared multiplication-triples that are random from the adversary's point of view. The protocol is obtained by adapting a similar protocol from [3] to the setting where $t_a + 2t_s < n$.[3] We begin by describing the various building blocks used in the protocol. The current description is mostly taken from [3] and we refer to [3] for the complete proofs.

6.1 Network-Agnostic Beaver's Multiplication Protocol

Protocol $\Pi_{\mathsf{Beaver}}(([x],[y]),([a],[b],[c]))$ takes as inputs $[\cdot]$-shared x, y and a $[\cdot]$-shared triple (a, b, c) and outputs a $[\cdot]$-shared z, where $z = x \cdot y$, if and only if $c = a \cdot b$. During the protocol, the parties first locally compute $[e] = [x] - [a]$ and $[d] = [y] - [b]$ and then publicly reconstruct e and d, using the reconstruction protocol Π_{RecPub}. Using these values, a $[\cdot]$-sharing of z is then computed locally as $[z] = e \cdot d + e \cdot [b] + d \cdot [a] + [c]$. One can see that if (a, b, c) is random from the adversary's point of view, then x and y will remain private from the point of view of the adversary. The protocol takes Δ time to output $[z]$ in a synchronous network, while it outputs $[z]$ eventually in an asynchronous network. Irrespective of the network type, the protocol incurs a communication of $\mathcal{O}(n^2 \cdot \kappa)$ bits from the honest parties.

6.2 Network-Agnostic Triple-Transformation Protocol

Protocol $\Pi_{\mathsf{TripTrans}}$ takes as input a set of $2d + 1$ $[\cdot]$-shared triples $\{([x^{(i)}],[y^{(i)}],[z^{(i)}])\}_{i=1,\ldots,2d+1}$, where the triples may not be "related". The protocol outputs "co-related" $[\cdot]$-shared triples $\{([\mathsf{x}^{(i)}],[\mathsf{y}^{(i)}],[\mathsf{z}^{(i)}])\}_{i=1,\ldots,2d+1}$, satisfying the following properties *regardless* of the network type:

[3] In [3], the protocol was presented for the condition $t_a + 3t_s < n$.

- There exist d-degree polynomials $\mathsf{X}(\cdot), \mathsf{Y}(\cdot)$ and a $2d$-degree polynomial $\mathsf{Z}(\cdot)$, such that $\mathsf{X}(i) = \mathsf{x}^{(i)}$, $\mathsf{Y}(i) = \mathsf{y}^{(i)}$ and $\mathsf{Z}(i) = \mathsf{z}^{(i)}$ holds for $i = 1, \ldots, 2d + 1$.
- The triple $(\mathsf{x}^{(i)}, \mathsf{y}^{(i)}, \mathsf{z}^{(i)})$ is a multiplication-triple if and only if $(x^{(i)}, y^{(i)}, z^{(i)})$ is a multiplication-triple. Consequently, $\mathsf{Z}(\cdot) = \mathsf{X}(\cdot) \cdot \mathsf{Y}(\cdot)$ holds iff all the $2d+1$ input triples are multiplication-triples.
- The adversary learns the triple $(\mathsf{x}^{(i)}, \mathsf{y}^{(i)}, \mathsf{z}^{(i)})$ iff it knows the input triple $(x^{(i)}, y^{(i)}, z^{(i)})$.

The protocol is *identical* to a same protocol with *perfect security* proposed in [3]; the only difference is that they use a *perfectly-secure* version of the Beaver's multiplication protocol (since $t_s < \frac{n}{3}$ holds for them), while we use a cryptographically-secure version of the Beaver's multiplication protocol (since $t_s < \frac{n}{2}$ holds for our setting). In a synchronous network, the protocol outputs the transformed triples by time Δ, while in an asynchronous network, the parties eventually output the transformed triples. The protocol incurs a communication of $\mathcal{O}(n^2 \cdot d \cdot \kappa)$ bits.

The protocol proceeds as follows: the first and second components of the first $d + 1$ input triples are used to define the d-degree polynomials $\mathsf{X}(\cdot)$ and $\mathsf{Y}(\cdot)$. These points define the first $d + 1$ points on these polynomials. Then, using the shares of the first $d + 1$ triples, the parties locally compute $[\cdot]$-sharings of d new points on these polynomials. The remaining d input triples are then utilized to calculate the $[\cdot]$-sharing of the product of these new points using the Beaver's multiplication protocol. Consequently, the $\mathsf{Z}(\cdot)$ polynomial is defined by the d computed products and the third component of the first $d + 1$ input triples.

6.3 Network-Agnostic Protocol for Generating a Random Value

Protocol Π_{Rand} is a cryptographically-secure network-agnostic protocol which enables the parties to generate a random value $r \in \mathbb{F}_p$, which will be known to all the parties at the end of the protocol. The instantiation of Π_{Rand} is based on a random value generation protocol described in [21]. The protocol proceeds as follows: the parties invoke an instance of the protocol Π_{ACS}, where the input of each party is a random element from $\mathbb{F}_p$. Protocol Π_{ACS} ensures that a common subset CS of at least $n - t_s$ parties is agreed upon, such that all the parties in CS have $[\cdot]$-shared their (random) values. The value r is then set to the sum of the values shared by the parties in CS, which will be available in a $[\cdot]$-shared fashion. The parties then publicly reconstruct r using an instance of Π_{RecPub}. Since at least one honest party is guaranteed in CS (irrespective of the network type), whose secret-shared input will be random and unknown to the adversary, it follows that r will be indeed random. The protocol takes $T_{\mathsf{Rand}} = T_{\mathsf{ACS}} + \Delta$ time in a *synchronous* network to generate the output, while in an *asynchronous* network, the honest parties eventually get their output. Irrespective of the network type, the protocol incurs a communication of $\mathcal{O}(n^6 \cdot \kappa)$ bits from the honest parties and invokes $\mathcal{O}(n)$ instances of Π_{BA}.

6.4 Network-Agnostic Polynomial-Verification Protocol

We next describe a network-agnostic polynomial-verification protocol, Π_{PolyVer}. In the protocol, there exists a triplet of polynomials $(\mathsf{X}(\cdot), \mathsf{Y}(\cdot), \mathsf{Z}(\cdot))$. Polynomials $\mathsf{X}(\cdot)$ and $\mathsf{Y}(\cdot)$ are d-degree polynomials, while $\mathsf{Z}(\cdot)$ is a $2d$-degree polynomial. There will be $2d+1$ distinct points on these polynomials, which will be $[\cdot]$-shared among the parties. The goal of Π_{PolyVer} is to probabilistically verify if $\mathsf{Z}(\cdot) \stackrel{?}{=} \mathsf{X}(\cdot) \cdot \mathsf{Y}(\cdot)$ holds. The instantiation of Π_{PolyVer} is based on a polynomial verification protocol presented in [21].

The basic idea of the protocol is as follows: first, a random value α is generated using an instance of Π_{Rand}. The parties then check if $\mathsf{Z}(\alpha) \stackrel{?}{=} \mathsf{X}(\alpha) \cdot \mathsf{Y}(\alpha)$ holds. For this, the parties compute $\mathsf{X}(\alpha), \mathsf{Y}(\alpha)$ and $\mathsf{Z}(\alpha)$ in a $[\cdot]$-shared fashion, followed by publicly reconstructing these values using instances of Π_{RecPub}. Since α is selected randomly, if the polynomials $(\mathsf{X}(\cdot), \mathsf{Y}(\cdot), \mathsf{Z}(\cdot))$ *do not* satisfy the multiplicative relationship, then the above test will fail, except with probability at most $\frac{2d}{|\mathbb{F}_p|}$. During the verification process, the only information learnt by the adversary are the points $\mathsf{X}(\alpha)$, $\mathsf{Y}(\alpha)$ and $\mathsf{Z}(\alpha)$. In a *synchronous* network, the protocol will generate output after time $T_{\mathsf{PolyVer}} = T_{\mathsf{Rand}} + \Delta$, while in an *asynchronous* network, the parties get output eventually. The protocol incurs a communication of $\mathcal{O}(n^6 \cdot \kappa)$ bits from the honest parties.

6.5 Network-Agnostic Triple-Sharing Protocol

The network-agnostic triple-sharing protocol Π_{TripSh} allows a designated *dealer* D to verifiably $[\cdot]$-share t_s multiplication-triples. The protocol ensures that if the dealer is *honest* then the triples remain random from the adversary's view and all honest parties output the shares of the dealer's multiplication-triples. The "verifiability" here guarantees that if D is *corrupt*, then either no honest party computes any output (if D *does not* invoke the protocol) or there exist t_s multiplication-triples, which are $[\cdot]$-shared among the parties. The protocol is borrowed from [3,21].

The protocol begins with the dealer $[\cdot]$-sharing $2t_s+1$ random multiplication-triples, denoted as $(x^{(j)}, y^{(j)}, z^{(j)})_{j=1,\ldots,2t_s+1}$, using an instance of Π_{VSS}. The verifiability property of Π_{VSS} ensures that the shared triples are $[\cdot]$-shared. However, there is no guarantee that these shared triples are actually multiplication-triples. To verify if the $[\cdot]$-shared triples are indeed multiplication-triples, the $[\cdot]$-sharing of these triples is transformed to $[\cdot]$-sharing of triples $(\mathsf{x}^{(j)}, \mathsf{y}^{(j)}, \mathsf{z}^{(j)})_{j=1,\ldots,2t_s+1}$ using an instance of $\Pi_{\mathsf{TripTrans}}$. The transformed triples have associated polynomials $\mathsf{X}(\cdot)$, $\mathsf{Y}(\cdot)$, and $\mathsf{Z}(\cdot)$, with degrees t_s, t_s, and $2t_s$, respectively. If the dealer is honest, the adversary learns no information about $\mathsf{X}(\cdot)$, $\mathsf{Y}(\cdot)$, and $\mathsf{Z}(\cdot)$.

Next, the relationship $\mathsf{Z}(\cdot) \stackrel{?}{=} \mathsf{X}(\cdot) \cdot \mathsf{Y}(\cdot)$ is verified by executing the Π_{PolyVer} protocol. It follows from the properties of $\Pi_{\mathsf{TripTrans}}$ and Π_{PolyVer} that Π_{PolyVer} outputs 1 iff all the input triples $(x^{(j)}, y^{(j)}, z^{(j)})_{j=1,\ldots,2t_s+1}$ are multiplication-triples, except with an error probability of $\frac{2t_s}{|\mathbb{F}_p|}$. This is because a corrupt dealer will only learn the random verification point used for verifying the multiplicative relationship during Π_{PolyVer} after sharing the triples.

If D is *honest* then the adversary learns only one point on $\mathsf{X}(\cdot)$, $\mathsf{Y}(\cdot)$, and $\mathsf{Z}(\cdot)$ during the verification process. This leaves $t_s + 1 - 1 = t_s$ degrees of freedom in these polynomials. If Π_{PolyVer} outputs 1, the parties output t_s $[\cdot]$-shared triples $([a^{(i)}], [b^{(i)}], [c^{(i)}])$ on behalf of the dealer D, where $a^{(i)} = \mathsf{X}(\beta^{(i)})$, $b^{(i)} = \mathsf{Y}(\beta^{(i)})$, and $c^{(i)} = \mathsf{Z}(\beta^{(i)})$. Here $\beta^{(1)}, \ldots, \beta^{(t_s)}$ are distinct elements from $\mathbb{F}_p$, which are *different* from the random verification point, used during Π_{PolyVer} and also from the evaluation points of the parties. The shared triples $\{([a^{(i)}], [b^{(i)}], [c^{(i)}])\}_{i=1,\ldots,t_s}$ constitute the actual multiplication-triples that are $[\cdot]$-shared on behalf of the dealer. If Π_{PolyVer} outputs 0, then the parties output a default $[\cdot]$-sharing of $(0, 0, 0)$ t_s times on behalf of the dealer. In a *synchronous* network, the protocol generates output after time $T_{\mathsf{TripSh}} = T_{\mathsf{VSS}} + T_{\mathsf{PolyVer}} + \Delta$, while in an *asynchronous* network, the parties get their output eventually. The protocol incurs a communication of $\mathcal{O}(n^6 \cdot \kappa)$ bits and invokes 1 instance of Π_{BA}.

6.6 Network-Agnostic Triple-Extraction Protocol

The next protocol Π_{TripExt} takes as input a publicly known set of $2d + 1$ parties denoted as $\mathcal{CS}$, where $d \geq t_s$, and where each party in $\mathcal{CS}$ has $[\cdot]$-shared a multiplication-triple. Notably, the multiplication-triples shared by honest parties in $\mathcal{CS}$ are random for the adversary. The output of the protocol consists of $d+1-t_s$ $[\cdot]$-shared multiplication-triples, which remain random from the view of the adversary. The protocol is *identical* to a similar protocol with *perfect security* proposed in [3]; the only difference is that they used a *perfectly-secure* version of the triple-transformation protocol, while we use our cryptographically-secure instantiation of the same.

The underlying idea of the protocol is as follows: the parties invoke an instance of $\Pi_{\mathsf{TripTrans}}$ to "transform" the input triples into a set of correlated triples. Since the input for the protocol consists of multiplication-triples, this transformation process ensures that the output triples are also multiplication-triples. Let $\mathsf{X}(\cdot)$, $\mathsf{Y}(\cdot)$, and $\mathsf{Z}(\cdot)$ represent the polynomials associated with the transformed triples. The properties of $\Pi_{\mathsf{TripTrans}}$ guarantee that the adversary has knowledge of at most t_s points on these polynomials, thereby implying that a minimum of $d+1-t_s$ points on these polynomials are random from the adversary's view. Consequently, the parties locally compute and generate $d + 1 - t_s$ "new" points on these polynomials, which are guaranteed to appear random to the adversary.

In a *synchronous* network, the protocol takes Δ time to generate the output, while in *asynchronous* network, the honest parties eventually get their output. The protocol incurs a communication of $\mathcal{O}(n^2 \cdot d \cdot \kappa)$ bits from the honest parties.

6.7 The Network-Agnostic Preprocessing Phase Protocol

We finally present our cryptographically-secure network-agnostic preprocessing phase protocol, which generates $[\cdot]$-sharing of c_M multiplication-triples, which are random from the point of view of the adversary. The protocol is similar to the preprocessing phase protocol of [3] with *perfect security*; the only difference is that we now use various components which are cryptographically-secure. Moreover, we also use a trick to get a *better* communication complexity, compared to [3].

The protocol proceeds as follows: each party P_i acts as a dealer and invokes an instance $\Pi^{(i)}_{\mathsf{TripSh}}$ of Π_{TripSh} to share c_M random multiplication-triples on its behalf. Corrupt parties P_j may choose not to invoke their $\Pi^{(j)}_{\mathsf{TripSh}}$ instances. Consequently, the parties employ a similar approach as in the protocol Π_{ACS} to agree on a common subset of parties $\mathcal{CS}$ of size $n - t_s$, whose multiplication-triples will be $[\cdot]$-shared. For this, the parties invoke instances of the network-agnostic BA protocol Π_{BA}. Since the adversary will not know the multiplication-triples shared by the honest parties in $\mathcal{CS}$, the parties execute c_M instances of Π_{TripExt} on the multiplication-triples shared by the parties in $\mathcal{CS}$ to extract random $[\cdot]$-shared multiplication-triples.

For simplicity and without loss of generality, let $|\mathcal{CS}| = 2d + 1$. Note that $d \geq t_s$ *need not* hold here, since $n - t_s \geq t_s + t_a + 1$ and $t_a < t_s$.[4] Consequently, by applying the procedure Π_{TripExt}, it is *not* guaranteed that the resultant extracted secret-shared multiplication-triples will be indeed random for the adversary.[5] To get rid of this, we deploy the following trick: if $|\mathcal{CS}| < 2t_s + 1$, then we add *dummy* parties in $\mathcal{CS}$ and consider a default $[\cdot]$-sharing of $(0, 0, 0)$ on their behalf, followed by applying the procedure Π_{TripExt} on the multiplication-triples of the "extended" $\mathcal{CS}$. This will *always* result in $[\cdot]$-sharing of c_M random multiplication-triples. For instance, if the network is *synchronous*, then we know that *all honest* parties are guaranteed to be in $\mathcal{CS}$, since the parties start executing the instances of Π_{BA} *only after* time T_{TripSh}, ensuring that the multiplication-triples of all honest parties are $[\cdot]$-shared through their respective Π_{TripSh} instances. Consequently, the dummy parties added in a *synchronous* network are *guaranteed* to be corrupt. On the other hand, if the network is *asynchronous*, then the dummy parties added to $\mathcal{CS}$ might be honest; however, in this case, there will be at least $n - t_s - t_a > t_s$ honest parties *already* present in the "non-extended" $\mathcal{CS}$. Hence, irrespective of the network type, it is always guaranteed that even after adding dummy parties to $\mathcal{CS}$, there are at least $t_s + 1$ honest parties in $\mathcal{CS}$, whose secret-shared multiplication-triples are random for the adversary. Consequently, the parties will now be able to extract c_M random secret-shared multiplication-triples. The preprocessing phase protocol is presented in Fig. 4.

The properties of the protocol $\Pi_{\mathsf{PreProcessing}}$ stated in Lemma 6 follows from [3].

Lemma 6. *Let $t_a < t_s$ and $t_a + 2t_s < n$. Then, the protocol $\Pi_{\mathsf{PreProcessing}}$ achieves the following properties. In a synchronous network, by time $T_{\mathsf{TripGen}} = T_{\mathsf{TripSh}} +$*

[4] Recall that for Π_{TripExt}, it is *necessary* that $d \geq t_s$ holds.

[5] Note that in [3], the condition $t_a + 3t_s < n$ holds and consequently, $n - t_s \geq 2t_s + t_a + 1$ holds; hence the triple-extraction on the multiplication-triples shared by the parties in $\mathcal{CS}$ is *guaranteed* to result in random secret-shared multiplication-triples in their case.

Protocol $\Pi_{\mathsf{PreProcessing}}$

- **Phase I - Sharing Random Multiplication-Triples**: Each $P_i \in \mathcal{P}$ does the following:
  - Act as a dealer D and invoke an instance $\Pi^{(i)}_{\mathsf{TripSh}}$ of Π_{TripSh}, so that c_M multiplication-triples are shared on its behalf.
  - For $j = 1, \ldots, n$, participate in the instance $\Pi^{(j)}_{\mathsf{TripSh}}$ invoked by P_j and wait for time T_{TripSh}.
  - Initialize a set $\mathcal{C}_i = \emptyset$ and include P_j in $\mathcal{C}_i$, if an output is computed during the instance $\Pi^{(j)}_{\mathsf{TripSh}}$.
- **Phase II - Agreement on a Common Subset of Triple-Providers**: Each $P_i \in \mathcal{P}$ does the following:
  - For $j = 1, \ldots, n$, participate in an instance $\Pi^{(j)}_{\mathsf{BA}}$ of Π_{BA} with input 1, if $P_j \in \mathcal{C}_i$.
  - Once $n - t_s$ instances of Π_{BA} have produced an output 1, then participate with input 0 in all the Π_{BA} instances $\Pi^{(j)}_{\mathsf{BA}}$, such that $P_j \notin \mathcal{C}_i$.
  - Once an output is computed in all the n instances of Π_{BA}, set $\mathcal{CS}$ to be the set of parties P_j, such that 1 is obtained as the output in the instance of $\Pi^{(j)}_{\mathsf{BA}}$.
  - If $|\mathcal{CS}| \geq 2t_s + 1$, then select the first $2t_s + 1$ least-indexed parties in $\mathcal{CS}$ and discard the rest. Else if $|\mathcal{CS}| < 2t_s + 1$, then include sufficiently many parties P_j to $\mathcal{CS}$ (least indices parties not in $\mathcal{CS}$), such that $|\mathcal{CS}| = 2t_s + 1$, and assume a default-sharing of c_M number of $[\cdot]$-shared triples $([0], [0], [0])$ on the behalf of P_j.
- **Phase III - Extracting Random Multiplication-Triples**: The parties do the following:
  - For every $P_j \in \mathcal{CS}$, let $\{([x^{(j,l)}], [y^{(j,l)}], [z^{(j,l)}])\}_{l=1,\ldots,c_M}$ be the $[\cdot]$-shared multiplication-triples, shared on P_j's behalf.
  - For $l = 1, \ldots, c_M$, the parties participate in the instance $\Pi_{\mathsf{TripExt}}(\mathcal{CS}, \{([x^{(j,l)}], [y^{(j,l)}], [z^{(j,l)}])\}_{P_j \in \mathcal{CS}})$ of Π_{TripExt} and compute the output $([\mathsf{a}^{(l)}], [\mathsf{b}^{(l)}], [\mathsf{c}^{(l)}])$.
  - Output the shared triples $\{([\mathsf{a}^{(l)}], [\mathsf{b}^{(l)}], [\mathsf{c}^{(l)}])\}_{l=1,\ldots,c_M}$.

Fig. 4. Network-agnostic preprocessing phase protocol

$2T_{\mathsf{BA}} + \Delta$, the honest parties output a $[\cdot]$-sharing of c_M multiplication-triples, while in an asynchronous network, the honest parties eventually output a $[\cdot]$-sharing of c_M multiplication-triples. Irrespective of the network type, the view of the adversary remains independent of the output multiplication-triples. The protocol incurs a communication of $\mathcal{O}(c_M \cdot n^6 \cdot \kappa)$ bits from the honest parties and invokes $\mathcal{O}(n)$ instances of Π_{BA}.

7 The Network-Agnostic Circuit-Evaluation Protocol

The network-agnostic circuit evaluation protocol Π_{CirEval} (Fig. 5) is standard and is similar to the circuit-evaluation protocol of [3], except that we now use cryptographically-secure building blocks. The protocol consists of *four* phases. In the first phase, the parties generate c_M random $[\cdot]$-shared multiplication-triples using an instance of the $\Pi_{\mathsf{PreProcessing}}$ protocol. Simultaneously, the parties execute an instance of the Π_{ACS} protocol to generate $[\cdot]$-sharing of their respective inputs for the function f. The instance of Π_{ACS} will output a common subset CS

Protocol Π_{CirEval}

- **Preprocessing and Input-Sharing**: The parties do the following:
  - Each $P_i \in \mathcal{P}$ on having the input $x^{(i)}$ for f, participates in an instance of Π_{ACS} with input $x^{(i)}$. Let CS be the common subset of parties, computed as an output during the instance of Π_{ACS}, where $|\mathsf{CS}| \geq n - t_s$. Corresponding to every $P_j \notin \mathsf{CS}$, set $x^{(j)} = 0$ and set $[x^{(j)}]$ to a default $[\cdot]$-sharing of 0.
  - In parallel, participate in an instance of $\Pi_{\mathsf{PreProcessing}}$. Let $\{([\mathsf{a}^{(j)}], [\mathsf{b}^{(j)}], [\mathsf{c}^{(j)}])\}_{j=1,\ldots,c_M}$ be the $[\cdot]$-shared multiplication-triples, computed as an output during the instance of $\Pi_{\mathsf{PreProcessing}}$.
- **Circuit Evaluation**:
  - Let $G_1, \ldots, G_m$ be a publicly-known topological ordering of the gates of cir. For $k = 1, \ldots, m$, the parties do the following for gate G_k:
    - *If G_k is an addition gate:* the parties locally compute $[w] = [u] + [v]$, where u and v are gate-inputs and w is the gate-output.
    - *If G_k is a multiplication-with-a-constant gate with constant c:* the parties locally compute $[v] = c \cdot [u]$, where u is the gate-input and v is the gate-output.
    - *If G_k is an addition-with-a-constant gate with constant c:* the parties locally compute $[v] = c + [u]$, where u is the gate-input and v is the gate-output.
    - *If G_k is a multiplication gate:* let G_k be the lth multiplication gate in cir where $l \in \{1, \ldots, c_M\}$ and let $([\mathsf{a}^{(l)}], [\mathsf{b}^{(l)}], [\mathsf{c}^{(l)}])$ be the lth $[\cdot]$-shared multiplication-triple, generated from $\Pi_{\mathsf{PreProcessing}}$. Moreover, let $[u]$ and $[v]$ be the shared gate-inputs of G_k. Then the parties participate in an instance $\Pi_{\mathsf{Beaver}}(([u], [v]), ([\mathsf{a}^{(l)}], [\mathsf{b}^{(l)}], [\mathsf{c}^{(l)}]))$ of Π_{Beaver} and compute the output $[w]$.
- **Output Computation**:
  - Let $[y]$ be the $[\cdot]$-shared circuit-output. The parties participate in an instance $\Pi_{\mathsf{RecPub}}([y])$ of Π_{RecPub} to reconstruct y.
- **Termination**: Each $P_i \in \mathcal{P}$ concurrently executes the following steps during the protocol:
  - Upon computing circuit output y, send the message (ready, y) to all the parties in $\mathcal{P}$.
  - Upon receiving the message (ready, y) from at least $t_s + 1$ parties, send the message (ready, y) to all the parties in $\mathcal{P}$, provided no $(\mathsf{ready}, \star)$ message has been sent yet.
  - Upon receiving the message (ready, y) from at least $n - t_s$ parties, output y and terminate.

Fig. 5. Network-agnostic circuit-evaluation protocol

of at least $n - t_s$ parties, whose inputs are $[\cdot]$-shared. For the parties outside of CS, a default $[\cdot]$-sharing of 0 is considered as their input. Note that the properties of Π_{ACS} would guarantee that all honest parties are included in CS, ensuring the consideration of inputs from *all honest* parties (namely *input provision*). The second phase involves joint secret-shared evaluation of each gate in the circuit cir, with the resulting output being publicly reconstructed during the *third* phase. Note that once an honest party reconstructs the circuit output, it *cannot* afford to immediately terminate the protocol if the network is *asynchronous* since its participation might be required in various subprotocols to generate output for the other honest parties. Consequently, the last phase is the termination phase, whereupon reconstructing the circuit output, the parties circulate it and check whether it is "safe" to terminate the protocol. The steps for this phase are similar to the Bracha's Acast protocol [16]. Once it is confirmed that it is safe to terminate the protocol, the parties terminate the protocol and all underlying subprotocols.

The properties of the protocol Π_{CirEval} stated in Theorem 2 follows from [2,3].

Theorem 2. *Let $t_a < t_s$, such that $t_a + 2t_s < n$. Moreover, let $f : \mathbb{F}_p^n \rightarrow \mathbb{F}_p$ be a publicly-known function represented by an arithmetic circuit cir over $\mathbb{F}_p$ consisting of c_M number of multiplication gates, and whose multiplicative depth is D_M. Moreover, let party P_i has input $x^{(i)}$ for f. Then, Π_{CirEval} achieves the following.*

- *In a synchronous network, all honest parties output $y = f(x^{(1)}, ..., x^{(n)})$ at time $6T_{\mathsf{BA}} + (12n + 56 + D_M)\Delta$, where $x^{(j)} = 0$ for every $P_j \notin \mathsf{CS}$, such that $|\mathsf{CS}| \geq n - t_s$ and every honest party $P_j \in \mathcal{P}$ is present in CS.*
- *In an asynchronous network, the honest parties eventually output $y = f(x^{(1)}, ..., x^{(n)})$, where $x^{(j)} = 0$ for every $P_j \notin \mathsf{CS}$, such that $|\mathsf{CS}| \geq n - t_s$.*
- *Irrespective of the network type, the view of the adversary will be independent of the inputs of the honest parties in CS.*
- *The protocol incurs a communication of $\mathcal{O}(c_M \cdot n^7 \cdot \kappa)$ bits from the honest parties and invokes $\mathcal{O}(n)$ instances of Π_{BA}.*

8 Conclusion and Open Problems

In this paper, we presented a network-agnostic MPC protocol with *optimal* threshold conditions within the plain PKI model. Our protocol is designed by introducing a network-agnostic VSS protocol, resulting in a computationally simpler MPC protocol compared to existing protocols relying on zero-knowledge proofs, threshold homomorphic encryption, and other setups. There are several interesting research directions to pursue in this domain. We outline a few of them below.

- The communication complexity of our MPC protocol does not currently match that of the state-of-the-art network-agnostic protocol of [5]. It would be interesting to develop MPC protocols based on VSS that achieve the same level of communication complexity as the state-of-the-art.
- In this work we have considered the plain PKI model. It will be interesting to apply the methodologies presented in this paper to develop a network-agnostic MPC protocol that incorporates trusted setups.
- Obtaining a packed version of our network-agnostic VSS protocol would be of great interest, as it would subsequently contribute to reducing the communication complexity of the MPC protocol.

Acknowledgement. We would sincerely like to thank the anonymous reviewers whose comments and feedback helped to tremendously improve the overall paper. Additionally, we would like to thank PKC 2024, ACM IARCS, and Silence Laboratories for providing conference and travel support.

References

1. Alexandru, A.B., Blum, E., Katz, J., Loss, J.: State machine replication under changing network conditions. In: Agrawal, S., Lin, D. (eds.) ASIACRYPT 2022. LNCS, vol. 13791, pp. 681–710. Springer, Cham (2022). https://doi.org/10.1007/978-3-031-22963-3_23
2. Appan, A., Choudhury, A.: Network agnostic MPC with statistical security. In: Rothblum, G., Wee, H. (eds.) TCC 2023. LNCS, vol. 14370, pp. 63–93. Springer, Cham (2023). https://doi.org/10.1007/978-3-031-48618-0_3
3. Appan, A., Chandramouli, A., Choudhury, A.: Perfectly-secure synchronous MPC with asynchronous fallback guarantees. In: Proceedings of the 2022 ACM Symposium on Principles of Distributed Computing. PODC'22, pp. 92–102. Association for Computing Machinery (2022). https://doi.org/10.1145/3519270.3538417
4. Asharov, G., Lindell, Y.: A full proof of the BGW protocol for perfectly secure multiparty computation. J. Cryptol. **30**(1), 58–151 (2017).https://doi.org/10.1007/s00145-015-9214-4
5. Bacho, R., Collins, D., Liu-Zhang, C.D., Loss, J.: Network-agnostic security comes (almost) for free in DKG and MPC. In: Handschuh, H., Lysyanskaya, A. (eds.) CRYPTO 2023. LNCS, vol. 14081, pp. 71–106. Springer, Cham (2023). https://doi.org/10.1007/978-3-031-38557-5_3
6. Bangalore, L., Choudhury, A., Garimella, G.: Round efficient computationally secure multi-party computation revisited. In: Proceedings of the 20th International Conference on Distributed Computing and Networking. ICDCN '19, pp. 292–301. Association for Computing Machinery, New York, NY, USA (2019). https://doi.org/10.1145/3288599.3288600
7. Beaver, D.: Efficient multiparty protocols using circuit randomization. In: Feigenbaum, J. (ed.) CRYPTO 1991. LNCS, vol. 576, pp. 420–432. Springer, Heidelberg (1992). https://doi.org/10.1007/3-540-46766-1_34
8. Beaver, D., Micali, S., Rogaway, P.: The round complexity of secure protocols. In: Proceedings of the Twenty-Second Annual ACM Symposium on Theory of Computing. STOC '90, pp. 503–513. Association for Computing Machinery (1990). https://doi.org/10.1145/100216.100287
9. Ben-Or, M., Canetti, R., Goldreich, O.: Asynchronous secure computation. In: STOC, pp. 52–61. ACM (1993). https://doi.org/10.1145/167088.167109
10. Ben-Or, M., Kelmer, B., Rabin, T.: Asynchronous secure computations with optimal resilience (extended abstract). In: PODC, pp. 183–192. ACM (1994). https://doi.org/10.1145/197917.198088
11. Ben-Or, M., Goldwasser, S., Wigderson, A.: Completeness theorems for non-cryptographic fault-tolerant distributed computation (extended abstract), pp. 1–10 (1988). https://doi.org/10.1145/62212.62213
12. Bhimrajka, N., Choudhury, A., Varadarajan, S.: Network-agnostic perfectly secure synchronous message transmission revisited. In: INDOCRYPT (2023). https://doi.org/10.1007/978-3-031-56235-8_2
13. Blum, E., Katz, J., Loss, J.: Tardigrade: an atomic broadcast protocol for arbitrary network conditions. In: Tibouchi, M., Wang, H. (eds.) ASIACRYPT 2021. LNCS, vol. 13091, pp. 547–572. Springer, Cham (2021). https://doi.org/10.1007/978-3-030-92075-3_19
14. Blum, E., Katz, J., Loss, J.: Synchronous consensus with optimal asynchronous fallback guarantees. In: Hofheinz, D., Rosen, A. (eds.) TCC 2019. LNCS, vol. 11891, pp. 131–150. Springer, Cham (2019). https://doi.org/10.1007/978-3-030-36030-6_6

15. Blum, E., Liu-Zhang, C.D., Loss, J.: Always have a backup plan: fully secure synchronous MPC with asynchronous fallback. In: Micciancio, D., Ristenpart, T. (eds.) CRYPTO 2020. LNCS, vol. 12171, pp. 707–731. Springer, Cham (2020). https://doi.org/10.1007/978-3-030-56880-1_25
16. Bracha, G.: An asynchronous [(n - 1)/3]-resilient consensus protocol. In: Proceedings of the Third Annual ACM Symposium on Principles of Distributed Computing. PODC '84, pp. 154–162. Association for Computing Machinery (1984). https://doi.org/10.1145/800222.806743
17. Cachin, C., Kursawe, K., Lysyanskaya, A., Strobl, R.: Asynchronous verifiable secret sharing and proactive cryptosystems. In: CCS, pp. 88–97. ACM (2002). https://doi.org/10.1145/586110.586124
18. Canetti, R., Rabin, T.: Fast asynchronous byzantine agreement with optimal resilience. In: STOC, pp. 42–51 (1993). https://doi.org/10.1145/167088.167105
19. Chor, B., Goldwasser, S., Micali, S., Awerbuch, B.: Verifiable secret sharing and achieving simultaneity in the presence of faults (extended abstract). In: FOCS, pp. 383–395. IEEE Computer Society (1985). https://doi.org/10.1109/SFCS.1985.64
20. Choudhury, A., Patra, A.: Optimally resilient asynchronous MPC with linear communication complexity. In: ICDCN. ACM (2015). https://doi.org/10.1145/2684464.2684470
21. Choudhury, A., Patra, A.: An efficient framework for unconditionally secure multiparty computation. IEEE Trans. Inf. Theory **63**(1), 428–468 (2017). https://doi.org/10.1109/TIT.2016.2614685
22. Coretti, S., Garay, J., Hirt, M., Zikas, V.: Constant-round asynchronous multiparty computation based on one-way functions. In: Cheon, J.H., Takagi, T. (eds.) ASIACRYPT 2016. LNCS, vol. 10032, pp. 998–1021. Springer, Heidelberg (2016). https://doi.org/10.1007/978-3-662-53890-6_33
23. Cramer, R., Damgård, I., Nielsen, J.B.: Multiparty computation from threshold homomorphic encryption. In: Pfitzmann, B. (ed.) EUROCRYPT 2001. LNCS, vol. 2045, pp. 280–300. Springer, Heidelberg (2001). https://doi.org/10.1007/3-540-44987-6_18
24. Cramer, R., Damgård, I.: Multiparty Computation, an Introduction, pp. 41–87. Birkhäuser Basel (2006). https://doi.org/10.1007/3-7643-7394-6_2
25. Damgård, I., Ishai, Y.: Scalable secure multiparty computation. In: Dwork, C. (ed.) CRYPTO 2006. LNCS, vol. 4117, pp. 501–520. Springer, Heidelberg (2006). https://doi.org/10.1007/11818175_30
26. Deligios, G., Liu-Zhang, C.: Synchronous perfectly secure message transmission with optimal asynchronous fallback guarantees. In: Baldimtsi, F., Cachin, C. (eds.) FC 2023, Part I. Lecture Notes in Computer Science, vol. 13950, pp. 77–93. Springer, Cham (2023). https://doi.org/10.1007/978-3-031-47754-6_5
27. Deligios, G., Hirt, M., Liu-Zhang, C.-D.: Round-efficient byzantine agreement and multi-party computation with asynchronous fallback. In: Nissim, K., Waters, B. (eds.) TCC 2021. LNCS, vol. 13042, pp. 623–653. Springer, Cham (2021). https://doi.org/10.1007/978-3-030-90459-3_21
28. Dolev, D., Strong, H.R.: Authenticated algorithms for byzantine agreement. SIAM J. Comput. **12**(4), 656–666 (1983). https://doi.org/10.1137/0212045
29. Feldman, P., Micali, S.: Optimal algorithms for byzantine agreement. In: STOC, pp. 148–161. ACM (1988). https://doi.org/10.1145/62212.62225
30. Ghinea, D., Liu-Zhang, C., Wattenhofer, R.: Optimal synchronous approximate agreement with asynchronous fallback. In: PODC '22: ACM Symposium on Principles of Distributed Computing, Salerno, Italy, 25–29 July 2022, pp. 70–80. ACM (2022). https://doi.org/10.1145/3519270.3538442

31. Ghinea, D., Liu-Zhang, C., Wattenhofer, R.: Multidimensional approximate agreement with asynchronous fallback. In: Proceedings of the 35th ACM Symposium on Parallelism in Algorithms and Architectures, SPAA 2023, Orlando, FL, USA, 17–19 June 2023, pp. 141–151. ACM (2023). https://doi.org/10.1145/3558481.3591105
32. Goldreich, O., Micali, S., Wigderson, A.: How to play any mental game or a completeness theorem for protocols with honest majority. In: Aho, A.V. (ed.) Proceedings of the 19th Annual ACM Symposium on Theory of Computing, New York, New York, USA, pp. 218–229. ACM (1987). https://doi.org/10.1145/28395.28420
33. Hirt, M., Nielsen, J.B., Przydatek, B.: Cryptographic asynchronous multi-party computation with optimal resilience. In: Cramer, R. (ed.) EUROCRYPT 2005. LNCS, vol. 3494, pp. 322–340. Springer, Heidelberg (2005). https://doi.org/10.1007/11426639_19
34. Hirt, M., Nielsen, J.B., Przydatek, B.: Asynchronous multi-party computation with quadratic communication. In: Aceto, L., Damgård, I., Goldberg, L.A., Halldórsson, M.M., Ingólfsdóttir, A., Walukiewicz, I. (eds.) ICALP 2008. LNCS, vol. 5126, pp. 473–485. Springer, Heidelberg (2008). https://doi.org/10.1007/978-3-540-70583-3_39
35. Kate, A., Goldberg, I.: Distributed key generation for the internet. In: 29th IEEE International Conference on Distributed Computing Systems (ICDCS 2009), 22–26 June 2009, Montreal, Québec, Canada, pp. 119–128. IEEE Computer Society (2009). https://doi.org/10.1109/ICDCS.2009.21
36. Momose, A., Ren, L.: Multi-threshold byzantine fault tolerance. In: Proceedings of the 2021 ACM SIGSAC Conference on Computer and Communications Security. CCS '21, pp. 1686–1699. Association for Computing Machinery (2021).https://doi.org/10.1145/3460120.3484554
37. Patra, A., Choudhury, A., Pandu Rangan, C.: Efficient asynchronous verifiable secret sharing and multiparty computation. J. Cryptol. **28**(1), 49–109 (2015). https://doi.org/10.1007/s00145-013-9172-7
38. Pedersen, T.P.: Non-interactive and information-theoretic secure verifiable secret sharing. In: Feigenbaum, J. (ed.) CRYPTO 1991. LNCS, vol. 576, pp. 129–140. Springer, Heidelberg (1992). https://doi.org/10.1007/3-540-46766-1_9
39. Rabin, T., Ben-Or, M.: Verifiable secret sharing and multiparty protocols with honest majority (extended abstract). In: Johnson, D.S. (ed.) Proceedings of the 21st Annual ACM Symposium on Theory of Computing, 14–17 May 1989, Seattle, Washington, USA, pp. 73–85. ACM (1989). https://doi.org/10.1145/73007.73014
40. Shamir, A.: How to share a secret. Commun. ACM **22**(11), 612–613 (1979). https://doi.org/10.1145/359168.359176
41. Yao, A.C.: Protocols for secure computations (extended abstract). In: FOCS, pp. 160–164. IEEE Computer Society (1982). https://doi.org/10.1109/SFCS.1982.38

On Information-Theoretic Secure Multiparty Computation with Local Repairability

Daniel Escudero[1(✉)], Ivan Tjuawinata[2], and Chaoping Xing[3]

[1] J.P. Morgan AI Research, New York, USA
daniel.escudero@protonmail.com
[2] Strategic Centre for Research on Privacy-Preserving Technologies and Systems, Nanyang Technological University, Singapore, Singapore
ivan.tjuawinata@ntu.edu.sg
[3] Shanghai Jiao Tong University, Shanghai, China
xingcp@sjtu.edu.cn

Abstract. In this work we consider the task of designing information-theoretic MPC protocols for which the state of a given party can be recovered from a small amount of parties, a property we refer to as *local repairability.* This is useful when considering MPC over dynamic settings where parties leave and join a computation, a scenario that has gained notable attention in recent literature. Thanks to the results of (Cramer *et al.* EUROCRYPT'00), designing such protocols boils down to constructing a linear secret-sharing scheme (LSSS) with good locality, that is, each share is determined by only a small amount of other shares, that also satisfies the so-called multiplicativity property. Previous constructions that achieve locality (*e.g.* using locally recoverable codes—LRCs) do not enjoy multiplicativity, and LSSS that are multiplicative (*e.g.* Shamir's secret-sharing) do not satisfy locality. Our construction bridges this literature gap by showing the existence of an LSSS that achieves both properties simultaneously.

Our results are obtained by making use of well known connection between error correcting codes and LSSS, in order to adapt the LRC construction by (Tamo & Barg, IEEE Transactions on Information Theory 2014) to turn it into a LSSS. With enough care, such coding-theoretic construction yields our desired locality property, but it falls short at satisfying multiplicativity. In order to address this, we perform an extensive analysis of the privacy properties of our scheme in order to identify parameter regimes where our construction satisfies multiplicativity.

Finally, since our LSSS satisfies locality, every share is determined by a small amount of shares. However, in an MPC context it is not enough to let the (small set of) parties to send their shares to the repaired party, since this may leak more information than the regenerated share. To obtain our final result regarding MPC with local repairability, we construct a lightweight MPC protocol that performs such repairing process without any leakage. We provide both a passively secure construction (for the *plain* multiplicative regime) and an actively secure one (for *strong* multiplicativity).

Q. Tang and V. Teague (Eds.): PKC 2024, LNCS 14602, pp. 205–239, 2024.
https://doi.org/10.1007/978-3-031-57722-2_7

1 Introduction

Secure multiparty computation (MPC) is a set of techniques that enables a set of n mutually distrustful parties $P_1, \dots, P_n$ to securely compute a function on secret data, while revealing only its output, even if some unknown subset t of the parties is corrupted by an adversary. Let us represent the function to be computed securely as an arithmetic circuit comprised of addition and multiplication gates over a finite field $\mathbb{F}$. A popular and successful approach to building MPC protocols consists of letting the parties obtain *secret-shared* versions of the inputs, that is, each party holds a *share* of each input to the computation in such a way that the shares of the corrupted parties collectively leak nothing about the inputs, and yet, certain allowed sets of shares can reconstruct the underlying secret. Then, the parties engage in some interactions in order to securely compute shares of each intermediate wire in the circuit until they reach shares of the output, at which point they use the reconstruction procedure to learn the result. Many notable protocols follow this paradigm, both in the honest majority setting [9,20,32–34] (where the adversary corrupts at most a minority of the parties) and also with dishonest majority [4,6,23,24,43,44] (where, in contrast, the adversary may control all but one of the parties). Furthermore, MPC protocols are also categorized by the level of security they achieve (e.g. computational or information-theoretic), or by the type of adversary they tolerate (e.g. passive/semi-honest or active/malicious).

In this work we focus specifically in the context of passive security with $t < n/2$ and active security with $t < n/3$, both with perfect security. In this case, a common template is to use Shamir's secret-sharing [8,65], where the shares of a secret $s \in \mathbb{F}$ are given by $(f(1), \dots, f(n))$, where $f(\mathtt{X})$ is a random polynomial over $\mathbb{F}$ of degree $\leq t$, subject to $f(0) = s$. This scheme satisfies t-privacy (meaning any t shares do not leak any information about the secret, which ensures the adversary does not learn any sensitive information) and $(t+1)$-reconstruction (meaning that any $t+1$ shares together can reconstruct the secret). Furthermore, this scheme is *linear*, which means that the parties can locally add their shares of two secrets to obtain shares of the sum; this property enables the parties to process addition gates non-interactively. Finally, another important property is that the parties can locally multiply their shares of two secrets to obtain degree-$2t$ sharings of their product; in particular, if $t < n/2$, so $2t < n$, all the parties together can still reconstruct the product of the secrets, and if $t < n/3$ the $n - t$ honest parties on their own can do this, without the help of the t corrupt parties. These properties are accordingly called *multiplicativity* and *strong multiplicativity*, and they are key in obtaining MPC for $t < n/2$ with passive security and $t < n/3$ with active security, respectively, and in fact there is a long series of works that relies specifically on this construction (*e.g.* [5,16], to cite a few). Even more, it was shown in [18] that MPC is in general possible from *any* linear secret-sharing scheme (LSSS) that satisfies multiplicativity (for $t < n/2$ with passive security) and strong multiplicativity (for $t < n/3$ with active security) and in fact, it is currently unknown whether we can obtain this type of MPC without using these properties.

MPC with Repairing Parties. In protocols that follow the secret-sharing paradigm, the "state" of a party during a protocol execution is typically given by the set of shares it holds. Depending on the secret-sharing scheme used and the adversarial setting, this "state" is usually determined by the shares held by the other parties. For example, in Shamir's secret-sharing any $t + 1$ sharings together determine the polynomial $f(\mathtt{X})$ and hence determine the secret $s = f(0)$, but even more interestingly, they also determine *any other share* $f(i)$. This way, if a party P_i needs to learn its "state" $f(i)$, the other parties can engage in a lightweight MPC protocol where each party P_j for $j \neq i$ inputs its share $f(j)$, and P_i learns precisely $f(i)$. We will refer to the task of reconstructing P_i's share as *repairing* or *regenerating* this share.

The ability to restore a party's state from the other parties' information is useful once we factor in the fact that, depending on the setting and the function being computed, the execution of an MPC protocol can take a considerable amount of resources and time. During such period of time it is not unreasonable for a party to have the need to learn its state: perhaps the party crashed and lost its state, or it had network issues and got disconnected, or possibly a new party is joining the computation (which is useful for example to add diversity to the computation, preventing collusions). However, the simple idea sketched above suffers from a massive drawback: the party joining must receive messages from *all* of the other computing parties in order to obtain its share. This is a huge blocker, especially in large-scale scenarios. Compare this to, for example, other large-scale distributed scenarios such as permissionless blockchains: consensus is maintained by letting multiple parties hold the same view of the underlying ledger, and whenever a new participant wishes to join the network, he or she only needs to contact a small subset of nodes in order to receive the current state, at which point the new node can become an active member. In fact, one can argue that part of the scalability of such systems comes from the fact that their underlying networks are comprised of "local" committees, where each party connects to a subset of the nodes, and messages are propagated via network flooding and echoing.

The above discussion sets the stage for the following question:

> *Is it possible to design MPC protocols with repairing ability, in such a way that regenerating the state of a party does not require communication from all of the other computing parties?*

1.1 Our Contribution

Our work makes substantial progress in addressing the question above by introducing a linear secret-sharing scheme that simultaneously (1) allows for efficient share repairing and (2) is suitable for the design of honest majority MPC protocols. Shamir's secret-sharing as described previously is a good example of a scheme that satisfies (2)—and in fact is one of the most widely used building blocks in honest majority MPC—but it does not satisfy (1) as repairing requires communication from a large amount of parties. In contrast, the literature of secure distributed storage (see for example [28,45,70]), where multiple parties hold shares of a secret but only for the purpose of storing it (in contrast to *computing* on it as in MPC), already considers secret-sharing schemes that satisfy (1). Efficient regeneration of shares is crucial in this context in order to preserve data availability and to achieve this, multiple works make use of *locally recoverable codes* (LRC), which enable shares to be regenerated only from a small subset of shares. Unfortunately, such works did not consider multiplicativity—needed for item (2)—when using the efficient LRC constructions from [52,53,66,69].

We reconcile the state of affairs from above by considering a linear secret sharing scheme that satisfies the two items required, which makes it suitable in the context of MPC where parties leave (*e.g.* due to crashing) and rejoin a given computation. We achieve this by proposing an efficient and secure share repairing lightweight protocol, and we also investigate the multiplicativity and strong multiplicativity properties of our lsss, for certain corruption regimes. Our scheme, unlike Shamir's secret-sharing, is not a *threshold* scheme, meaning that while its privacy threshold is t, its reconstruction threshold r is strictly larger than $t+1$. Such schemes are called *ramp.* Given the context above, we state the following result pertaining the properties of our LSSS:

Corollary 1 (Simplification of Theorems 1 and 2). *For any prime power q and positive integers v, n such that $v \mid n$, there exists a secure repairable linear ramp secret-sharing Σ for n players over $\mathbb{F}_q$ with reconstruction threshold r and privacy threshold t, where the gap is $r - t = O\left(\frac{n}{v}\right)$, and such that any share can be recovered by contacting v other players. Furthermore*

- *There exists a family of instantiations of Σ with $t < r \leq \frac{n}{2}$ that is multiplicative where $t = n\left(\frac{1}{2} - O\left(\frac{1}{v}\right)\right) + O(1)$.*
- *There exists a family of instantiations of Σ with $t < r \leq \frac{n}{3}$ that is strongly multiplicative where $t = n\left(\frac{1}{3} - O\left(\frac{1}{v}\right)\right) + O(1)$.*

By setting $v \approx n$ we obtain parameters comparable to Shamir's: multiplicativity for $t \approx n/2$ and strong multiplicativity for $t \approx n/3$, but we do not save in terms of repairing since essentially all shares are needed to regenerate an additional share. Interesting regimes occur when we take $v \ll n$. For example, by taking $v \approx n/c$ we obtain multiplicativity with $t \approx n/2 - c$, and strong multiplicativity with $t \approx n/3 - c$. This shows we can save a *multiplicative* factor of c in terms of locality, while only sacrificing the corruption tolerance by an *additive* term of c. We remark that our actual construction involves several parameters, and Corollary 1 is a concrete instantiation of the family of LSSSs we construct. For details, we refer the reader to Sect. 3 where we present our construction and present its parameters more thoroughly.

On Share Privacy and Static Adversaries. In our LSSS, each share is determined by at most v other shares, where v can be chosen to be much smaller than n. More precisely, the set of n parties will be partitioned in a series of groups of size $v+1$, where v shares within a group can be used to reconstruct the remaining share of the group. However, this means that if an adversary corrupts v parties of a single group, then via locality the adversary can learn the share of the remaining uncorrupted party. This may not affect privacy of the secret since even with these extra shares the adversary may not have enough information to reconstruct the secret, but still violates the privacy of the honest party, whose share has been revealed. We consider the notion of *share privacy*, where the share of each honest party must also be kept secret from the adversary, and similar to committee-based approaches in MPC (e.g. [22]), we achieve it by assuming that the adversary is *static*, meaning that he chooses which parties to corrupt before the actual protocol execution starts, and that the assignment of parties into groups is done uniformly at random. From this, via a careful choice of parameters and a non-trivial analysis of probabilities, we are able to show our repairing protocol and hence the whole secret sharing scheme is statistically secure, when the group size (and hence the number of parties) is sufficiently large. We remark that the restriction of the adversary being static is required for any repairable secret sharing scheme that provides share privacy. In fact, the same assumption of a static adversary can also be found in other works on repairable secret sharing (see, for example [1,42,46,48,60]).

Secure Protocols for Regenerating Shares. In the context of repairing a given share, sending the v needed shares for regeneration *in the clear* may leak more than the intended share to regenerate, and in fact it may violate share privacy as considered above. To address this, instead of the v parties sending their shares directly to the party being repaired, these parties run a lightweight MPC protocol in which the v parties input their shares and the receiving party receives *only* its own regenerated share. We refer to such procedure as a *repairing protocol with locality* v. In this work we also present explicit and efficient repairing protocols for our secret-sharing scheme, which enables a party to learn its share while communicating with only v parties, and without leaking anything beyond this share. As above, our repairing protocols only tolerate *static adversaries*, where the set of corrupt parties is fixed before any protocol execution.

MPC Results. Coupling the properties of our LSSS together with our repairing protocols and the results in [18], we obtain the following as corollaries:

Corollary 2 (MPC with efficient repairing). *Let q be a prime power, and let v, n be positive integers such that $v \mid n$ and $v = \ln^{(1+\varepsilon)} n$ for some $\varepsilon > 0$. Assume that $n = \Omega(\kappa)$, where κ is the statistical security parameter. Then there exist statistically secure MPC protocols for general arithmetic circuits, protecting against a static adversary corrupting t parties, and having repairing protocols with locality v, with either one of the following properties:*

- *Passive security with* $t = n\left(\frac{1}{2} - O\left(\frac{1}{v}\right)\right) + O(1)$.
- *Active security with* $t = n\left(\frac{1}{3} - O\left(\frac{1}{v}\right)\right) + O(1)$.

1.2 Related Work

Repairable Secret-Sharing. The notion of locally repairable codes, which implicitly lies at the core of our construction, is used in a wide variety of scenarios such as distributed storage systems, or DSS, for short. In this context, a piece of data is encoded and stored in several nodes with the goal of ensuring its availability even if some nodes fail/crash, and at the same time, possibly, providing some notion of privacy. Among the desired properties for such system we find repairability (see, for example, [14,15,49,73]), which, intuitively, allows any entry of a given codeword to be determined by partial information obtained from some of the other entries of the codeword. When translating these notions to the secret-sharing setting, we arrive at the concept of repairable secret sharing.

The study of secure repairable secret sharing was firstly proposed by Herzberg *et al.* [39].[1] In that work, the authors proposed a reparing mechanism to enroll new parties based on Shamir's secret sharing. Since then, there have been studies that follow a similar direction with the help of error correcting codes, publicly-verifiable secret sharing schemes, bivariate polynomial secret sharing scheme and vector space secret sharing schemes (see, for example, [62,71,74]). A survey on the study of repairable secret sharing schemes can be found in [46].

Repairable Error-Correcting Codes. The concept of repairability has been well-studied in the field of error correcting codes, in particular in its relation with distributed storage systems. Regenerating codes constitute a family of error correcting codes that was proposed by Dimakis *et al.* [26] where, given any codeword of the code, any of its entries can be recovered from some partial information from some of the other entries. Such property enables regenerating codes to be used to encode data in several nodes where failure in a node can be repaired by downloading some information from some other nodes. A bit more precisely, we may encode a piece of data $\mathfrak{D}$ in N nodes where each node stores δ bits of data in such a way that $\mathfrak{D}$ can be recovered by downloading the information stored in any $K \leq N$ nodes, with K ideally being much smaller than N. The regenerating capability ensures that if a node fails, it can contact $K \leq D < N$ nodes and download κ bits from each of the contacted node to regenerate the data to be stored in the failed node. Here the *repair bandwidth* is the total amount of bits needed to perform a repair process, which is $D \cdot \kappa$ in the case above.

Some families of regenerating codes that are constructed with the objective of minimizing either storage or bandwidth are called Minimum Storage Regenerating (MSR for short) codes and Minimum Bandwidth Regenerating (MBR for short) codes, respectively. There have been numerous studies investigating both MSR and MBR codes. It was shown that we can construct codes from both families using product-matrix constructions [57]. There have also been some

[1] More precisely, [39] studies *proactive secret-sharing schemes* in which shares of a given secret must be "refreshed". However, in Sect. 4 of their paper, the authors argue that share recovery is essential to have a secure proactive SS. In addition, in several other references on repairable secret-sharing schemes, [39] is credited to be the first to propose the concept of repairing shares (which is either corrupt or lost).

studies on regenerating codes in various other directions such as impossibility results (e.g. [64]), existential bounds (e.g. [3,10,61,68]) and explicit constructions (e.g. [31,58,72]).

Note that in practice, the nodes may be spread around the world, and in such a case the distance between nodes may become very large. Hence, instead of just focusing on the repair bandwidth, we may also be interested in keeping the amount of contacted nodes small. This is captured by the metric of *locality*. The study of this concept, together with the construction of codes with small locality, were first pioneered in [30,38,40]. There have then been many studies on both bounds and constructions of locally repairable codes; see for example [11, 37,41,50,51,69].

Securely Repairing Shares in Repairable Secret-Sharing. Despite the numerous studies on the concept of repairable error correcting codes, such studies only focus on repairing failing nodes without considering the privacy of either the original data being encoded, or the data stored in different nodes. Furthermore, since these studies are typically set in the domain of distributed storage systems, they consider *static* data that is not manipulated to perform arbitrary computations,[2] which is the case in the field of secure MPC.

Due to the close relation between error correcting codes and secret sharing schemes, the concept of repairability has also been considered in the latter. To enable this, some notion of *security* has been added to the concept of regenerating codes, (e.g. [1,42,60]) This study was first initialized by Pawar *et al.* [54]. Secure repairable secret sharing schemes have subsequently been proposed based on various techniques such as enrollment protocols [35,67], combinatorial design [67], linearized polynomials [63] and regenerating codes [57,59,63]. However, in all these studies, the adversary model that is considered is that of a passive adversary who can learn the data stored in a set of players and the messages received by a different set of players, without the ability to arbitrarily modify the behaviour of those players.

To the best of our knowledge, there has only been one work on the construction of regenerating codes having security against somewhat "active" adversaries [48]. In this work, Li *et al.* constructed a repairable secret sharing scheme by first masking the message with the output stream of a linear feedback shift register (LFSR) before encoding the masked message with an MSR encoding. In their work, they show that the resulting regenerating code is secure against a passive eavesdropper, but enhanced so that any malicious modification of any message can be detected and corrected with probability of at least $1 - \frac{1}{q}$, where q is the order of the underlying finite field. However, in that work, the privacy of the shares is not considered during the repairing process, while the privacy of the secret is obtained via the security guarantee of the underlying block cipher. Furthermore, the authors do not consider the multiplicative property of the scheme,

[2] If the encoding process is linear then computation represented by simple linear operations is possible. However, the calculation of the product of two encoded values is not easy to achieve, which is where the concepts of multiplicativity and strong multiplicativity become useful.

which is an essential property for the application of secret sharing scheme in the design of actively secure MPC schemes. Such property is most likely not satisfied due to the encryption step before the share generation. In other words, to the best of our knowledge, our construction from Sect. 5 constitutes the first repairable secret sharing scheme suitable for secure multiparty computation, satisfying security against an active adversary.

Enabling Parties to Join a Secure Computation. The problem of handling involuntary crashes in MPC has received quite some attention recently, and several works are dedicated to the study of such protocols [2,17,21,27,29,36]. However, among those, to the best of our knowledge, only [17,21,29] enable parties to rejoin the computation, and moreover, only [21] allows parties to rejoin while possibly missing all the intermediate messages sent to them while being offline. Our work enables parties to join a computation not only if they miss messages while being offline, but even if they were never a previous participant in the protocol to begin with. However, we do not achieve optimal privacy and reconstruction parameters (in fact, our scheme is a ramp scheme, which has a gap between the privacy and reconstruction thresholds), while the works mentioned above show and achieve lower bounds. Furthermore, these works build on top of "standard" Shamir's secret-sharing and hence require communication from essentially all the parties, while our work considers a substantial modification to this scheme that enables local repairability.

Remark 3 (On "YOSO-fying" or "Fluidifying" our protocols). *Both the YOSO and Fluid MPC [17,29] and their follow-ups [7,12,25,55] consider MPC in a setting where the set of parties change dynamically in every round. Furthermore, YOSO focuses on removing the static-corruption assumption from committee-based MPC protocols, and an interesting research direction involves using YOSO-like protocols to remove the static-adversary assumption from our work. Another interesting direction consists of using our secret-sharing scheme to improve the efficiency of YOSO/Fluid protocols, in particular, reducing the communication overhead of the re-sharing step (whereby a committee passes a shared secret to the next committee), which is typically the bottleneck in these protocols. Our scheme allows for each share to be determined from a small amount of shares, which may indeed improve efficiency. We leave this for future work.*

1.3 Organization

This paper is organized as follows. In Sect. 2, we briefly define some basic notations and discuss some basic concepts that will be useful in our discussion. Section 3 contains our main LSSS Σ as Algorithm 1, together with the analysis of its main properties. Next, we consider how to securely repair shares for the multiplicative variant of our construction with passive security in Sect. 4. This is then extended to active adversaries for the strongly multiplicative variant of our scheme in Sect. 5. Finally, we provide some discussion on related work in Sect. 1.2.

Table 1. Table of Notations

q	Prime power, number of field elements
$\mathbb{F}_q$	The finite field with q elements
n	Number of players
τ	Number of corrupted players
P_i	The i-th player, $1 \leq i \leq n$
v	Number of involved parties in secure repairing scheme (size of each local group: $v+1$, which divides $q+1$)
H	Multiplicative subgroup of $\mathbb{F}_q^*$ of size $v+1$
m	Number of cosets of H considered, or number of local groups, where $m \leq \frac{q-1}{v+1}, n = m(v+1)$
$\beta_1, \ldots, \beta_m$	Coset leaders of H
$\ell(x)$	$\ell(x) = \prod_{\alpha \in H}(x - \alpha)$
ρ	$\rho \in \mathbb{F}_q \setminus \ell(\mathbb{F}_q)$
$g(x)$	$g(x) = \ell(x) + \rho$
$\gamma_0, \gamma_1, \ldots, \gamma_n$	Evaluation points belonging to $\{0\} \cup \left(\bigcup_{i=1}^m \beta_i H\right)$, where $\gamma_0 = 0$
$f(x)$	Polynomial used to share s, $s = \sum_{j=0}^{w} a_{0j} g(0)^j$. It holds that $f(x) = \sum_{i=0}^{d-1} \left(\sum_{j=0}^{w} a_{i,j} g(x)^j\right) x^i \in \mathbb{F}_q[x]$
d	Degree of $f(x)$ (plus one) when $g(x)$ is fixed to be a constant, upper bound on corrupted parties in each local group, $d \leq v$
w	$w+1$ is the minimum number of local groups required to recover the secret, $w < m$
$s \in \mathbb{F}_q$	Secret
t	Privacy level
r	Reconstruction level
$h(x)$	Polynomial mask for repairing process
$h_i(x)$	Share of polynomial mask generated by P_i

2 Preliminaries

In this section, we briefly discuss some notations that are used throughout the manuscript. As a useful reference, a complete table of notations can be found in Table 1.

For a prime power q, we denote by $\mathbb{F}_q$ the finite field with q elements. We also define $\mathbb{F}_q[\mathtt{X}]$ to be the set of polynomials over $\mathbb{F}_q$. For any positive integer N, define $\mathbb{F}_q^N$ the set of vectors of length N over $\mathbb{F}_q$. Also, for any positive integer n, we denote by $[n] = \{1, \ldots, n\}$. Let $v \geq 2$ be a positive integer such that $(v+1)|(q-1)$. This implies that there exists a unique multiplicative subgroup H of $\mathbb{F}_q^*$ of size $v+1$. Observe that H partitions $\mathbb{F}_q^*$ to $\frac{q-1}{v+1}$ disjoint cosets. Let such cosets be $\beta_1 H, \beta_2 H, \ldots, \beta_{\frac{q-1}{v+1}} H$.

In the following, we define a function that is a constant in each coset, which will be used as an ingredient in our secret sharing construction.

Lemma 4. *Let $\ell(\mathtt{X}) = \prod_{\alpha \in H}(\mathtt{X} - \alpha)$. Then $\ell(\mathtt{X})$ is a constant in each coset and $\ell(0) \neq 0$. Furthermore, for any $\beta, \gamma \in \mathbb{F}_q, \ell(\beta) = \ell(\gamma)$ if and only if either β, γ belong to the same coset or $\beta = \gamma = 0$.*

Proof. Indeed, for any $\beta_i \alpha' \in \beta_i H$ with $\alpha' \in H$, we have

$$\ell(\beta_i \alpha') = \prod_{\alpha \in H} (\beta_i \alpha' - \alpha) = (\alpha')^{v+1} \prod_{\alpha \in H} (\beta_i - \alpha(\alpha')^{-1}) = \prod_{\alpha \in H} (\beta_i - \alpha) = \ell(\beta_i).$$

This proves the first part.

Now suppose that $\ell(\beta) = \ell(\gamma)$ and at least one of β, γ is a nonzero element. Then, from the first statement we already proved, $\ell(\lambda) - \ell(\beta) = 0$ for all $\lambda \in \beta H \cup \gamma H$. As $\deg(\ell(\mathtt{X}) - \ell(\beta)) = |H|$, we must have $|\beta H \cup \gamma H| \leqslant |H|$. This implies that both β, γ are nonzero and they belong to the same coset. □

2.1 Secret Sharing Schemes

Let $\mathsf{P} = \{P_1, \ldots, P_n\}$ be a finite set of players. A *forbidden set* $\mathcal{F}$ is a family of subsets of P such that for any $A \in \mathcal{F}$ and $A' \subseteq A$, we must have $A' \in \mathcal{F}$. For any $t < n$, we define $\mathcal{F}_{t,n}$ to be the forbidden set containing all subsets of P of size at most t. On the other hand, a *qualified set* Γ is a family of subsets of P such that for any $B \in \Gamma$ and $B \subseteq B'$, we must have $B' \in \Gamma$. For any $r \leq n$, we define $\Gamma_{r,n}$ to be the qualified set containing all subsets of P of size at least r. For any forbidden set $\mathcal{F}$ and a qualified set Γ over P such that $\mathcal{F} \cap \Gamma = \emptyset$, the pair $(\mathcal{F}, \Gamma)$ is called an *access structure.*

A secret sharing scheme with access structure $(\mathcal{F}, \Gamma)$ over $\mathbb{F}_q$ on P is a pair of functions $(\mathsf{Share}, \mathsf{Rec})$ where Share is a probabilistic function that calculates the random shares for the n players given the secret. For any secret $S \in \mathbb{F}_q$, if $(\mathbf{S}_1, \ldots, \mathbf{S}_n) = \mathsf{Share}(S)$, for any $A \subseteq \mathsf{P}$, we denote by $\mathbf{S}^A = (\mathbf{S}_i)_{P_i \in A}$, the vector containing the shares of all players $P_i \in A$. On the other hand, Rec accepts shares from a set of players in P and attempt to recover the original secret that satisfies the following requirements:

1. For any $B \in \Gamma$, given the shares of all players $P_i \in B$, Rec returns the original secret S.
2. For any $A \in \mathcal{F}$, the shares of $P_i \in A$ does not give any information regarding the secret. That is, the distribution of the shares $\mathbf{S}^A$ of players in A is independent of the original secret S.

A secret sharing scheme with access structure $(\mathcal{F}, \Gamma)$ such that $\mathcal{F}_{t,n} \subseteq \mathcal{F}$ and $\Gamma_{r,n} \subseteq \Gamma$ for some $0 < t < r < n$ is called a *ramp secret sharing scheme providing t-privacy and r-reconstruction.* If $r = t+1$, we call it a threshold secret sharing scheme.

Next we discuss the notions of linearity, multiplicativity and strong multiplicativity. We follow the definitions given in [19].

A *linear secret sharing scheme* over $\mathbb{F}_q$ on n players with secret space and share space $\mathbb{F}_q$ is a pair $(\mathsf{Share} : \mathbb{F}_q \to \mathbb{F}_q^n,\ \mathsf{Rec} : \mathbb{F}_q^* \to \mathbb{F}_q \cup \{\perp\})$ such that the set $\{(s, \mathsf{Share}(s)) : s \in \mathbb{F}_q\}$ is an $\mathbb{F}_q$-subspace of $\mathbb{F}_q \times \mathbb{F}_q^n$ and for any $s \in \mathbb{F}_q, \mathsf{Rec}(\mathsf{Share}(s)) = s$. A linear secret sharing scheme Σ is said to be multiplicative if there is a vector $\mathbf{r} \in \mathbb{F}_q^n$ such that for any two secrets $s, s' \in \mathbb{F}_q$ with their respective shares $\mathsf{Share}(s) = (s_1, \ldots, s_n)$ and $\mathsf{Share}(s') = (s'_1, \ldots, s'_n)$ where $s_i, s'_i \in \mathbb{F}_q$ for any $i = 1, \ldots, n$, $\mathbf{r} \circ (s_1 s'_1, \ldots, s_n s'_n) = s \cdot s'$ where $\circ$ represents the standard inner product.

Lastly, a linear secret sharing Σ is said to be t-strongly multiplicative if it has t-privacy and for any two secrets $s, s' \in \mathbb{F}_q$ such that $(s_1, \ldots, s_n) = \mathsf{Share}(s), (s'_1, \ldots, s'_n) = \mathsf{Share}(s'), ss'$ can be recovered from any $n - t$ entries of $(s_1 s'_1, \ldots, s_n s'_n)$.

A well-known example of a linear threshold secret sharing scheme is Shamir's secret sharing scheme. For two positive integers t and n such that $t < n < q$, a (t, n)-Shamir's secret sharing scheme over $\mathbb{F}_q$ is a linear secret sharing scheme for n parties with providing t-privacy and $t+1$ reconstruction with both secrets and shares being elements of $\mathbb{F}_q$. The share generation is done in the following way. First, we choose n non-zero pairwise distinct elements of $\mathbb{F}_q$, say $\alpha_1, \ldots, \alpha_n$, and assign each element to different players. Given the secret $s \in \mathbb{F}_q$, first, we randomly choose a polynomial $f(\mathtt{X}) \in \mathbb{F}_q[\mathtt{X}]$ of degree t such that $f(0) = s$. Then the share for the player assigned to the element α_i is defined to be $f(\alpha_i) \in \mathbb{F}_q$. It can be shown that this secret sharing scheme provides t-privacy and $t + 1$ reconstruction. Furthermore, such secret sharing scheme is linear, multiplicative when $t < \frac{n}{2}$ and strongly multiplicative when $t < \frac{n}{3}$.

2.2 Linear Codes

In this section, we briefly discuss the concept of linear codes.

Definition 1 (Linear Codes). *Let n, k, d be non-negative integers such that d and k are at most n. A linear code C over $\mathbb{F}_q$ with parameter $[n, k, d]$ is a subspace $C \subseteq \mathbb{F}_q^n$ of dimension k such that for any non-zero $\mathbf{c} \in C \setminus \{\mathbf{0}\}, wt_H(\mathbf{c}) \geq d$ where for any vector $\mathbf{x} = (x_1, \ldots, x_n), wt_H(\mathbf{x})$ is defined to be the Hamming weight of $\mathbf{x}$, i.e., $wt_H(\mathbf{x}) = |\{i : x_i \neq 0\}|$. It is well known that a code of minimum distance d can uniquely correct any error of Hamming weight $\lfloor \frac{d-1}{2} \rfloor$.*

Next, we recall the definition of Reed-Solomon codes.

Definition 2. *Let q be a prime power and let n and k be positive integers such that $k \leq n \leq q$. Fix $\boldsymbol{\alpha} = (\alpha_1, \ldots, \alpha_n) \in \mathbb{F}_q^n$ where α_i is pairwise distinct. We define $\mathbb{F}_q[\mathtt{X}]_{<k}$ to be the set of polynomials over $\mathbb{F}_q$ of degree at most $k - 1$. For any $f(\mathtt{X}) \in \mathbb{F}_q[\mathtt{X}]$, define $\mathbf{c}_{f,\boldsymbol{\alpha}} = (f(\alpha_1), \ldots, f(\alpha_n)) \in \mathbb{F}_q^n$. The Reed-Solomon code $RS_{n,k,\boldsymbol{\alpha}}$ is defined to be the set of vectors $\mathbf{c}_{f,\boldsymbol{\alpha}}$ with $f(\mathtt{X}) \in \mathbb{F}_q[\mathtt{X}]_{<k}$, that is,*

$$\mathsf{RS}_{n,k,\boldsymbol{\alpha}} = \{(f(\alpha_1), \ldots, f(\alpha_n)) : f(\mathtt{X}) \in \mathbb{F}_q[\mathtt{X}]_{<k}\}.$$

It is well known that for any choice of $\boldsymbol{\alpha}$, the minimum Hamming distance of $RS_{n,k,\boldsymbol{\alpha}}$ is $n-k+1$. Hence, it can uniquely correct up to $\lfloor \frac{n-k}{2} \rfloor$ Hamming errors.

2.3 Security Model

In this work, we consider security against a computationally-unbounded adversary controlling τ out of the n players. In other words, throughout this work, we consider constructions in information-theoretical security setting. Here we consider two types of adversaries depending on the extent of control it has on the players. Firstly, we focus on a semi-honest adversary which learns all the values stored by the players it controls. Secondly, we also consider a malicious adversary which means that the corrupted players do not have to follow the protocol. In either case we assume the corruption is static, i.e. the adversary chooses the parties to corrupt at the beginning of the protocol, and no more parties are corrupted once the execution of the protocol starts.

3 Our Linear Secret-Sharing Scheme with Good Locality

Let q be a prime power, and let $v \geq 2$ be a positive integer such that $(v+1) \mid (q-1)$. Let $n = (v+1)m$ for some integer $m \in \left\{1, \ldots, \frac{q-1}{v+1}\right\}$, and let $r = w(v+1)+d$ for some chosen positive integer $w \leq m-1$ and $d \leq v$. In this section, we discuss the construction of a repairable secret sharing scheme with n players and reconstruction level r. The scheme has t-privacy, where t depends on the value of w: if $w = m-1$ then $t = v(w+1)-1 = vm-1$, and if $w < m-1$ then $t = (v-1)(w+1)$.

Let H be the unique multiplicative subgroup H of $\mathbb{F}_q^*$ of size $v+1$. Observe that H partitions $\mathbb{F}_q^*$ to $m = \frac{q-1}{v+1}$ disjoint cosets $\beta_1 H, \beta_2 H, \ldots, \beta_m H$. It can be proven (see Lemma 4 in Sect. 2) that if $\ell(\mathtt{X}) = \prod_{\alpha \in H}(\mathtt{X}-\alpha)$, then for any $\beta, \gamma \in \mathbb{F}_q$, $\ell(\beta) = \ell(\gamma)$ if and only if either β, γ belong to the same coset or $\beta = \gamma = 0$; furthermore, $\ell(0) \neq 0$. Choose m distinct cosets of H and let $\beta_1, \ldots, \beta_m$ be their coset representatives. We denote the set $\{0\} \cup (\bigcup_{i=1}^{m} \beta_i H)$ by $\{\gamma_0 = 0, \gamma_1, \ldots, \gamma_n\}$. Let $\ell(\mathtt{X})$ be the polynomial defined in Lemma 4. Note that $\ell(\mathbb{F}_q)$ is a subset of $\mathbb{F}_q$ of size $1 + \frac{q-1}{v+1} < q$. Hence there exists $\rho \in \mathbb{F}_q$ such that $-\rho \notin \ell(\mathbb{F}_q)$. Define $g(\mathtt{X}) = \ell(\mathtt{X}) + \rho$. Then $0 \notin g(\mathbb{F}_q)$, and $g(\beta) = g(\gamma)$ if and only if either they belong to the same coset or $\beta = \gamma = 0$. In our LSSS construction each party P_i gets assigned a random element $\gamma_{\pi(i)}$, for some random permutation $\pi : [n] \to [n]$ that is sampled before the adversary sets τ of the parties to be corrupt (recall we only consider *static* adversaries). Note that such random assignment is only done once before the sharing of the first secret and the same assignment will be used for all the subsequent sharings. In an MPC setting, such randomization can be done in the clear by the n parties as a part of the initialization phase; for example, the parties can use a publicly available randomness beacon (see for example [13,47,56]) to generate a random assignment of the parties to their IDs. For notational simplicity we will assume π is the identity function, that is, each P_i gets assigned to γ_i.

Now we are ready to discuss our construction, which can be found in Construction 1. For simplicity in the description we fix the parities (odd/even) of some of the parameters involved. This can be easily generalized to remove such restriction. At a high level, our LSSS follows a re-interpretation of the local-repairable codes proposed by Tamo and Barg [69], in the context of secret-sharing. As we have already pointed out, the authors in [69] are not concerned with privacy, nor computation, and hence concepts such as t-privacy, multiplicativity or strong multiplicativity is not within the scope of their work. We further note that although the construction of local-repairable codes allows codeword entries to be repaired by the use of small numbers of other entries, such repairing process is designed without privacy as a factor. As it turns out, it is highly non-trivial to perform such analysis, and we do this in Sects. 3.1, 3.2, and 4 respectively.

Construction 1. *Let q and v be chosen such that $3 \mid (v+1)$ and v is odd. Let n and m be as defined above, with n odd. We also let d be a positive integer such that $d \leq v$. Lastly, we let $w \leq m-1, r = w(v+1)+d$ and we also fix the m distinct cosets of H as well as their coset leaders $\beta_1, \ldots, \beta_m$. The construction is presented as Algorithm 1.*

Algorithm 1. Repairable Secret Sharing Scheme

Require: $S \in \mathbb{F}_q$: the secret to be secretly shared;
1: Randomly select $a_{i,j} \in \mathbb{F}_q$ for $i = 0, 1, \ldots, w$ and $j = 0, 1, \ldots, d-1$ subject to $S = \sum_{j=0}^{w} a_{0j} g(0)^j$;
2: Define $f(\mathtt{X}) = \sum_{i=0}^{d-1} \left(\sum_{j=0}^{w} a_{i,j} g(\mathtt{X})^j \right) \mathtt{X}^i$;
3: **Secret and shares:** Calculate and distribute the shares to the n players where the share for the player assigned γ_i is $S_i = f(\gamma_i)$ for $i = 1, \ldots, n$;

Remark 1 (On two-level Shamir's secret-sharing). A related and simpler construction is to split the parties into groups, use Shamir's secret-sharing to obtain one sharing per group, and secret-share each of these shares, again using Shamir's secret-sharing, among the members of the corresponding group. This scheme has good locality since each "two-level share" is determined by the shares of the parties in the given group. However, it turns out that our scheme can be regarded a refined version of this simple and naive construction, and by our more elaborate analysis we are able to obtain much better parameters. We expand on this discussion in Sect. A in the Appendix.

3.1 Reconstruction, Multiplicativity and Strong Multiplicativity

Now we consider the reconstruction, multiplicative and strong multiplicative properties of our LSSS. We analyze privacy in Sect. 3.2. The repairing process for different adversary settings are analyzed in Sect. 4.

Theorem 1. *Let $\mathbb{F}_q$ be a finite field of q elements, v, m, w, d be positive integers such that $v+1$ divides $q-1, m \leq \frac{q-1}{v+1}, w \leq m-1$ and $d \leq v$. Then the secret sharing scheme Σ for $n = (v+1)m$ players over $\mathbb{F}_q$ constructed in Construction 1 using the parameters q, v, n, m, d, w has the following properties:*

(i) **Reconstruction**: *It has r-reconstruction with $r = w(v+1) + d$,*
(ii) **Multiplicativity**: *The product of two secrets can be recovered as a linear combination of the product of the corresponding shares if $2w(v+1) + 2d - 1 \leq n$*
(iii) **Strong Multiplicativity**: *Σ is t'-strongly multiplicative if and only if Σ is t'-private and $t' \leq n - (2w(v+1) + 2d - 1)$.*

Proof. (i) As the degree of g is v, the total degree of $f(\mathtt{X})$ is $w(v+1) + d - 1$. Hence, the secret can be reconstructed by any $w(v+1) + d$ shares.

(ii) The product of the corresponding shares forms a Reed-Solomon code with length n and dimension $2(w(v+1) + d - 1) + 1 = 2w(v+1) + 2d - 1$. It is only well defined if $2w(v+1) + 2d - 1 \leq n$. Hence Σ is multiplicative if and only if $2w(v+1) + 2d - 1 \leq n$.

(iii) By definition, Σ is t' strongly multiplicative if and only if Σ is t'-private and for any two secrets $s, s' \in \mathbb{F}_q$ such that $(s_1, \ldots, s_n) = \mathsf{Share}(s) = (s_1, \ldots, s_n)$ and $(s'_1, \ldots, s'_n) = \mathsf{Share}(s'), ss'$ can be recovered from any $n - t'$ entries of $(s_1 s'_1, \ldots, s_n s'_n)$. As discussed above, $(s_1 s'_1, \ldots, s_n s'_n)$ is a codeword of a Reed-Solomon code with length n and dimension $2w(v+1) + 2d - 1$. Hence it has $2w(v+1) + 2d - 1$-reconstruction. So Σ is t'-strongly multiplicative if and only if Σ is t'-private and $t' \leq n - 2w(v+1) - 2d + 1$, concluding the proof. □

Parameters for Multiplicativity. To understand better what parameter regimes are attainable with our construction, we discuss some concrete parameter choices that lead to our scheme being multiplicative. We also discuss below the strongly multiplicative case. From Theorem 1, for Σ to be multiplicative, we require $2w(v+1) + 2d - 1 \leq n$. Since $d \geq 1$, we have $2w(v+1) + 2d - 1 > 2w(v+1)$. Hence, using $n = m(v+1)$, we must have $w \leq \frac{m}{2} < m$, which implies that (a lower bound on) the privacy threshold is $t = (d-1)(w+1)$. For any choice of $\delta > 0$, assuming that $v + 1 \geq \frac{3}{2\delta}$, we may set $d \approx (1-\delta)(v+1) + \frac{1}{2} \leq v$ and $w \approx \frac{m}{2} - (1-\delta)$. For such choice of d and w, when both v and m are sufficiently large, we have $\frac{t}{n} = \frac{1}{2}(1-\delta) + O\left(\max\left(\frac{1}{m}, \frac{1}{v}\right)\right)$, which approaches 1/2, the optimal fraction of players a passive adversary can corrupt for a multiplicative secret sharing scheme. Alternatively, we may also set $w = \frac{m}{2} - 1$ and $d = v$. Then if $v + 1 \geq \frac{1}{\delta}$, we may also have $\frac{t}{n} \geq \frac{1}{2} - \delta$, providing an asymptotically optimal multiplicative instance of Σ.

Parameters for Strong-Multiplicativity. For Σ to be t-strongly multiplicative, we need $t \leq (m-2w)(v+1)+2d-1$. Note that if $w \geq \frac{m}{2}+1$, for a sufficiently large v, the upper bound $(m-2w)(v+1)+2d-1$ is negative. Hence, for a positive value of t, we need $w \leq \frac{m}{2}+1 < m$ for a sufficiently large m. Hence, as before, for Σ to be t-strongly multiplicative, we have $t = (d-1)(w+1)$. For any choice of $\delta > 0$, we may set $d \approx 1 + \frac{(1-\delta)w(v+1)-1}{w+3} < 1 + (1-\delta)(v+1)$ which is at most v assuming $v \geq \frac{2-\delta}{\delta}$. Furthermore, we may set $w \approx \frac{m}{3-\delta}$. For such choice of d and w, when v and m are sufficiently large, we have $\frac{t}{n} = \frac{1}{3}(1-\delta) + O\left(\frac{1}{mv}\right)$, which approaches 1/3, the optimal number of corrupted players for a strongly-multiplicative secret sharing scheme.

3.2 Privacy Analysis

We have already determined under which choice of parameters our LSSS satisfies r-reconstruction, multiplicativity and strong multiplicativity. Another crucial aspect of an LSSS is its privacy threshold, that is, how many shares can an adversary know in such a way that they do not leak anything about the underlying secret. As we have mentioned, our scheme is a secret-sharing-based interpretation of the codes from [69], but in that work the authors did not consider privacy, and hence did not analyze this property. As it turns out, determining the privacy level of this scheme is not an easy task.

To better understand the complications of analyzing the privacy of our LSSS, we first perform a simple analysis that turns out to be far from what we can actually achieve. Consider an adversary that sees shares associated with a subset A of $\bigcup_{i=1}^{m} \beta_i H = \{\gamma_1, \dots, \gamma_n\}$, and let us denote by A_i the intersection $A \cap \beta_i H$. Consider sharings $(s_1, \dots, s_n)$ of a secret $s \in \mathbb{F}_q$, that is, $s_\ell = h(\gamma_\ell) = \sum_{i=0}^{d-1} \left(\sum_{j=0}^{w} b_{i,j} g(\gamma_\ell)^j \right) \gamma_\ell^i$. For every $\gamma_\ell \in A$ the adversary learns s_ℓ, but suppose temporarily that the adversary actually learns the "inner summands" $\{\sum_{j=0}^{w} b_{i,j} g(\gamma_\ell)^j\}_{i=0}^{d-1}$, which is *more information* than what is actually leaked to the adversary. Since $g(\mathtt{X})$ is constant in all of A_ℓ, we have that for every $\gamma \in A_\ell$: $\sum_{j=0}^{w} b_{i,j} g(\gamma)^j = \sum_{j=0}^{w} b_{i,j} g(\beta_\ell)^j$, which is a random polynomial of degree $\leq w$ in $g(\beta_\ell)$.

If we denote by A_{non} the set $\{i \in [m] : A_i \neq \emptyset\}$ (which corresponds to the amount of "groups" $\{\beta_i H\}_i$ for which the adversary has *at least* one share) we see that the only information the adversary sees is $|A_{non}|$ evaluations of each of the random degree-w polynomials $\sum_{j=0}^{w} b_{i,j} \mathtt{X}^j$, for $i = 0, \dots, d-1$. If it happens to be the case that $|A_{non}| \leq w$, each of these evaluations leak nothing about $\sum_{j=0}^{w} b_{i,j} g(0)^j$, so in particular they leak nothing about the secret $s = \sum_{j=0}^{w} b_{0,j} g(0)^j$. One way in which it can happen that $|A_{non}| \leq w$ is if $|A| \leq w$ to begin with, which shows that, if the adversary corrupts at most w parties, then the shares of the corrupted parties leak nothing about the underlying secret. In other words, our LSSS has w-privacy, or equivalently, its privacy level is *at least* w.

The lower bound of w on the privacy level of our scheme obtained above is relatively easy to derive, but it is unfortunately too pessimistic. One way to see why this should be the case is by noticing that $|A| \leq w$ is a sufficient condition for $|A_{non}| \leq w$, but it is far from being necessary. It could be the case that $|A_{non}| \leq w$ in spite of $|A|$ being much larger than w, for example, if the adversary gets unlucky and all of his corrupted parties happen to be randomly assigned to the same coset (recall the adversary is static and the random assigments are done after the corrupted parties are set). Furthermore, in our analysis above we assumed that the adversary got $\{\sum_{j=0}^{w} b_{i,j} g(\gamma_\ell)^j\}_{i=0}^{d-1}$ for every $\gamma_\ell \in A$, while in reality he does not get these individual terms but rather the sum $s_\ell = \sum_{i=0}^{d-1} \sum_{j=0}^{w} b_{i,j} g(\gamma_\ell)^j \gamma_\ell^i$.

In what follows we perform a more extensive and accurate analysis that takes into account the observations above, together with several other extra considerations. As we will see, we are able to obtain the following theorem.

Theorem 2. *Let $\mathbb{F}_q$ be a finite field of q elements, v, m, w, d be positive integers such that $v+1$ divides $q-1, m \leq \frac{q-1}{v+1}, w \leq m-1$ and $d \leq v$. The secret sharing scheme Σ constructed in Construction 1 using the parameters q, v, n, m, d, w has t-privacy where*

$$t = \begin{cases} md-1, & \text{if } w = m-1 \\ (d-1)(w+1), & \text{otherwise} \end{cases}.$$

We see then that the privacy threshold can be actually lower bounded by $\approx w \cdot d$, which is around d times better than the pessimistic lower bound of w we obtained previously. In fact, as we will see later in Proposition 8, the privacy level of our construction can also be upper bounded by $\approx w \cdot d$, which shows that our improved analysis is closer to being optimal (however, there is still a *constant* gap between the lower and the upper bounds).

We will prove Theorem 2 in multiple steps. First, we provide a supporting proposition that is essential in the analysis of the privacy level for our LSSS.

Proposition 5. *Let $A \subseteq \bigcup_{i=1}^m \beta_i H$ of size at most $d(w+1)-1$ and $A_i = A \cap \beta_i H$. Without loss of generality, we assume $|A_1| \geq |A_2| \geq \cdots \geq |A_m|$. Then there exists a non-negative integer $M \leq w$, a vector $\boldsymbol{u} \in \mathbb{F}_q^{d(w-M+1)}$ and a matrix $\mathcal{A} \in \mathbb{F}_q^{(\sum_{i=M+1}^m |A_i|)\times(d(w-M+1))}$ satisfying the following: in order to show that the shares of A contain no information on the secret, it is sufficient to show that $\boldsymbol{u}$ does not belong to the row span of $\mathcal{A}$. More specifically, if $\boldsymbol{u}$ does not belong to the row span of $\mathcal{A}$, the distribution of the shares of A is independent of the secret.*

Proof. Each $\alpha \in A_i$ provides one evaluation point to the polynomial $f(\mathtt{X})|_{\beta_i H}$ which has degree $d-1$. Hence if $|A_i| \geq d$, the shares in A_i can be used to recover the values of $\sum_{j=0}^w a_{k,j} g(\beta_k)^j$ for $k = 0, \ldots, d-1$. Assuming that there are M different values of i such that $|A_i| \geq d$, this information provides M different evaluation points to the polynomial $f_k(\mathtt{Y}) \triangleq \sum_{j=0}^w a_{k,j} \mathtt{Y}^j$ for $k = 0, \ldots, d-1$. By assumption, we have $|A| \leq (w+1)d - 1$. Hence we must have $M \leq w$.

Since we want to show that shares of A contain no information on the secret, we want to find the values of $b_{i,j}$ for $i = 0, \ldots, d-1$ and $j = 0, \ldots, w$ such that the polynomial $h(\mathtt{X}) = \sum_{i=0}^{d-1} \left(\sum_{j=0}^w b_{i,j} g^j(\mathtt{X})\right) \mathtt{X}^i$ satisfies $h(0) = 1$ and $h(\gamma) = 0$ for any $\gamma \in A$. For $k = 0, \ldots, d-1$, we denote by $h_k(\mathtt{X}) \triangleq \sum_{j=0}^w b_{k,j} \mathtt{X}^j$. Note that for the M distinct values of i such that $|A_i| \geq d$, we have $h_k(g(\beta_i)) = 0$ for $k = 0, \ldots, d-1$. Hence we have $(\mathtt{Y} - g(\beta_i)) \mid h_k(\mathtt{Y})$ for any of such i and $k = 0, \ldots, d-1$. So $\prod_{i=1}^M (\mathtt{Y} - g(\beta_i)) \mid h_k(\mathtt{Y})$. For $k = 0, \ldots, d-1$, we denote by $H_k(\mathtt{Y}) \triangleq \frac{h_k(\mathtt{Y})}{\prod_{i=1}^M (\mathtt{Y} - g(\beta_i))}$. Note that to find the values of $b_{k,j}$, it is equivalent to find $H_k(\mathtt{Y}) \triangleq \sum_{j=0}^{w-M} B_{k,j} \mathtt{Y}^j$ for $k = 0, \ldots, d-1$ such that $H_0(g(0)) = 1$ and $\sum_{k=0}^{d-1} H_k(g(\gamma))\gamma^k = 0$ for any $\gamma \in \bigcup_{i=M+1}^m A_i$.

These new requirements can be represented as a problem of finding a solution of the matrix equation $\mathcal{M}\mathtt{X} = \boldsymbol{y}$. Here $\mathtt{X} \in \mathbb{F}_q^{d(w-M+1)}$ is defined as

$$\boldsymbol{x} = (B_{0,0}, B_{0,1}, \ldots, B_{0,w-M}, \ldots, B_{d-1,0}, \ldots, B_{d-1,w-M})^T$$

while $\boldsymbol{y}$ is a vector of length $1 + \sum_{i=M+1}^{m} |A_i|$ defined as $\boldsymbol{y} = (1, 0, 0, \ldots, 0)^T$. Lastly, $\mathcal{M}$ is a matrix with $1 + \sum_{i=M+1}^{m} |A_i|$ rows and $d(w - M + 1)$ columns corresponding to the requirements defined by the system of equations where

$$\mathcal{M} = \begin{bmatrix} \boldsymbol{u} \\ \mathcal{A} \end{bmatrix} \in \mathbb{F}_q^{(1+\sum_{i=M+1}^{m} |A_i|) \times (d(w-M+1)))}.$$

Here $\boldsymbol{u}$, the first row of $\mathcal{M}$, corresponds to the equation related to the secret, i.e. $\sum_{j=0}^{w-M} b_{0,j} g(0)^j = 1$. The remaining rows of $\mathcal{M}$ corresponds to the shares of $\bigcup_{i=M+1}^{m} A_i$. More specifically, for any $\gamma \in A_i = A \cap \beta_i H \subseteq \bigcup_{i=M+1}^{m} A_i$, the row of $\mathcal{A}$ corresponding to γ is the following vector of length $d(w - M + 1)$:

$$\mathcal{A}_\gamma = \left(1 \cdot \boldsymbol{g}(\beta_i) \| \gamma \cdot \boldsymbol{g}(\beta_i) \| \ldots \| \gamma^{d-1} \cdot \boldsymbol{g}(\beta_i)\right)$$

where $\boldsymbol{g}(\beta_i) = (1, g(\beta_i), g^2(\beta_i), \ldots, g^{w-M}(\beta_i))$.

We claim that if $\boldsymbol{u}$ does not belong to the row span of $\mathcal{A}$, then the required vector $\boldsymbol{x}$ exists, proving that the shares of A contain no information on the secret. Indeed, if $\boldsymbol{u}$ does not belong to the row span of $\mathcal{A}$, then there exists $\boldsymbol{z}$ that belongs to the dual of the row span of $\mathcal{A}$ such that $\boldsymbol{u} \cdot \boldsymbol{z} \neq 0$. Hence by using an appropriate scalar multiplication, we can find $\boldsymbol{x}$ belonging to the dual of the row span of $\mathcal{A}$ such that $\boldsymbol{u} \cdot \boldsymbol{x} = 1$ as required. □

Now we are ready to prove Theorem 2.

Proof (of Theorem 2). Let $A \subseteq \bigcup_{i=1}^{m} \beta_i H$ of size t and $A_i = A \cap \beta_i H$. Without loss of generality, we assume that $|A_1| \geq |A_2| \geq \cdots \geq |A_m|$. By Proposition 5, in order to show that the shares of A do not provide any information on the secret, it is sufficient to show that the vector $\boldsymbol{u} \triangleq (1, g(0), g^2(0), \ldots, g^{w-M}(0), 0, \ldots, 0) \in \mathbb{F}_q^{d(w-M+1)}$ does not belong to the span of the set $\{\mathcal{A}_\gamma \triangleq (1, g(\beta_i), \ldots, g^{w-M}(\beta_i), \gamma \cdot 1, \ldots, \gamma \cdot g^{w-M}(\beta_i), \ldots, \gamma^{d-1} \cdot 1, \ldots, \gamma^{d-1} \cdot g^{w-M}(\beta_i)) : i = M+1, \ldots, m \gamma \in A_i\}$.

We prove this by contradiction. Suppose that there exist $\lambda_\gamma \in \mathbb{F}_q$ for $\gamma \in A$ such that $\boldsymbol{u} = \sum_{\gamma \in A} \lambda_\gamma \mathcal{A}_\gamma$. Since the first entry of $\boldsymbol{u}$ is 1, we must have λ_γ to not all be zero. This shows that the set $\{(\gamma \cdot 1, \ldots, \gamma \cdot g^{w-M}(\beta_i), \ldots, \gamma^{d-1} \cdot 1, \ldots, \gamma^{d-1} \cdot g^{w-M}(\beta_i)) : i = M+1, \ldots, m, \gamma \in A_i\}$ is not linearly independent. More specifically, for $j = 1, \ldots, d-1$, we have $(0, \cdots, 0) = \sum_{i=M+1}^{m} \left(\sum_{\gamma \in A_i} \lambda_\gamma \gamma^j\right) \cdot (1, \ldots, g^{w-M}(\beta_i))$.

For each j, this defines a homogeneous system of linear equation that can be represented as a matrix equation with the matrix being a Vandermonde-like matrix with $w - M + 1$ rows and $m - M$ columns. Now we divide the argument into two cases based on the value of w.

1. When $w = m - 1$, each matrix is a square and hence invertible. This implies that for any $j = 1, \ldots, d-1$ and $i = M+1, \ldots, m$, we have $\sum_{\gamma \in A_i} \lambda_\gamma \gamma^j = 0$. For each $i = M+1, \ldots, m$, we have $\sum_{\gamma \in A_i} \lambda_\gamma \gamma^j = 0$ for $j = 1, \ldots, d-1$. This again defines a homogeneous system of linear equations with $|A_i|$ unknowns and $d-1$ equations with the corresponding matrix being a Vandermonde-like matrix. By the argument provided in the proof of Proposition 5, we have $|A_i| \leq d-1$. Hence for each $i = M+1, \ldots, m$, the system is overdefined. Because of this, we must have $\lambda_\gamma = 0$ for any $\gamma \in A_i$ for any $i = M+1, \ldots, m$. However, this is a contradiction with the earlier observation that λ_γ cannot be all zero. This shows that if $w = m-1$, for any $A \subseteq \bigcup_{i=1}^m \beta_i H$ such that $|A| = md-1$, the shares of A do not contain any information about the secret, proving that Σ provides at least $md-1$ privacy when we set $w = m-1$.
2. Next, we assume that $w < m-1$. Recall that we assumed the existence of $(\lambda_\gamma)_{\gamma \in A}$ that are not identically zero such that for any $j = 1, \ldots, d-1$ and $\ell = 0, \ldots, w-M$, we have $\sum_{i=M+1}^m \left(\sum_{\gamma \in A_i} \lambda_\gamma \gamma^j\right) g^\ell(\beta_i) = 0$. Note that this defines a homogeneous system of linear equations with $(d-1)(w-M+1)$ equations and $\sum_{i=M+1}^m |A_i| = t - \sum_{i=1}^M |A_i| \leq t - Md$ unknowns. By the choice of t, we have $(d-1)(w-M+1) \geq t - Md$.

We derive a contradiction by showing that this system of linear equations can only have a zero solution, which is a contradiction to the assumption that $(\lambda_\gamma)_{\gamma \in A}$ are not all zero. We define the matrix $\mathcal{N}$ over $\mathbb{F}_q$ with $(d-1)(w-M+1)$ rows and $\sum_{i=M+1}^m |A_i|$ columns, which corresponds to the system of linear equations discussed above. For the matrix $\mathcal{N}$, we group the rows to $w-M+1$ distinct groups based on the value of ℓ. This means that each group consists of $d-1$ rows with various values of $j \in \{1, \ldots, d-1\}$.

We further note that each column of $\mathcal{N}$ corresponds to some $\gamma \in A$. Based on this correspondence, we further group the columns of $\mathcal{N}$ to $m-M$ column groups based on the cosets $\beta_i H$ that contains the corresponding γ. By using this grouping method, we can represent $\mathcal{N}$ as a block matrix. For $1 \leq i \leq w-M+1$ and $1 \leq j \leq m-M$ we denote by $\mathcal{N}_{i,j}^{(1)}$ the block matrix belonging to the i-th row group and j-th column group. More specifically, for $\ell = 1, \ldots, d-1$, the ℓ-th row of $\mathcal{N}_{i,j}^{(1)}$ is $\left[\left(\gamma^\ell g^{i-1}(\beta_{j+M})\right)_{\gamma \in \beta_{j+M} H}\right]$. Hence $\mathcal{N}_{i,j}^{(1)}$ can be written as $\mathcal{N}_{i,j}^{(1)} = g^{i-1}(\beta_{j+M}) \cdot \left[(\gamma)_{\beta_{j+M} H}^T, (\gamma^2)_{\gamma \in \beta_{j+M} H}, \ldots, \left(\gamma^{d-1}\right)_{\gamma \in \beta_{j+M} H}\right]^T$. So $\mathcal{N}_{i,j}^{(1)}$ is a non-zero multiple of a Vandermonde-like matrix with $d-1$ rows and $|A_{j+M}| \leq d-1$ columns. Hence any square sub-matrix of $\mathcal{N}_{i,j}^{(1)}$ is invertible. Our argument is based on the following claim that can be easily verified.

Claim 6. *Suppose that $\mathcal{N}$ has an alternative representation as a block matrix $(\mathcal{N}_{i,j})$ with more row groups than column groups such that $\mathcal{N}_{i,i}$ is an invertible square matrix for all i. Then the only solution of $\mathcal{N}\boldsymbol{x} = \mathbf{0}$ is $\boldsymbol{x} = \mathbf{0}$.*

By Claim 6, to derive the contradiction, it is sufficient to construct such alternative representation $(\mathcal{N}_{i,j})$ of $\mathcal{N}$ as a block matrix satisfying the requirement provided. We will keep the partition of the column as before. However, we will partition the row following the number of columns in each column group. More specifically, we define the first row group to be the first $|A_{m+1}|$ rows of $\mathcal{N}$, the second row group to be the next $|A_{m+2}|$ rows of $\mathcal{N}$ and so on while the $(m-M+1)$-st row group to contain the remaining rows. Note that this can always be done since $\mathcal{N}$ has more rows than columns. Furthermore, since $|A_i| \leq d-1$ for any $i = M+1, \ldots, m$, there exists a value $\ell = 1, \ldots, w-M+1$ such that the square submatrix $\mathcal{N}_{i,i}$ has all its rows to belong to $\mathcal{N}_{i,\ell}^{(1)}$ and possibly $\mathcal{N}_{i,\ell+1}^{(1)}$. So there exists $s, u \in \{1, \ldots, d-1\}$ such that

$$\mathcal{N}_{i,i} = \begin{bmatrix} (g^{i-1}(\beta_{i+M})\gamma^s)_{\gamma\in\beta_{i+M}H} \\ (g^{i-1}(\beta_{i+M})\gamma^{s+1})_{\gamma\in\beta_{i+M}H} \\ \vdots \\ (g^{i-1}(\beta_{i+M})\gamma^{d-1})_{\gamma\in\beta_{i+M}H} \\ \hline (g^{i}(\beta_{i+M})\gamma)_{\gamma\in\beta_{i+M}H} \\ (g^{i}(\beta_{i+M})\gamma^2)_{\gamma\in\beta_{i+M}H} \\ \vdots \\ (g^{i}(\beta_{i+M})\gamma^u)_{\gamma\in\beta_{i+M}H} \end{bmatrix}.$$

Recall that $\mathcal{N}_{i,i}$ is a square matrix. Hence, we can partition $\beta_{i+M}H$ to two sets L_i, R_i such that $|L_i| = d-s$ and $|R_i| = u$. Hence we can rewrite $\mathcal{N}_{i,i}$ to

$$\mathcal{N}_{i,i} = \left[\begin{array}{c|c} (g^{i-1}(\beta_{i+M})\gamma^s)_{\gamma\in L_i} & (g^{i-1}(\beta_{i+M})\gamma^s)_{\gamma\in R_i} \\ (g^{i-1}(\beta_{i+M})\gamma^{s+1})_{\gamma\in L_i} & (g^{i-1}(\beta_{i+M})\gamma^{s+1})_{\gamma\in R_i} \\ \vdots & \vdots \\ (g^{i-1}(\beta_{i+M})\gamma^{d-1})_{\gamma\in L_i} & (g^{i-1}(\beta_{i+M})\gamma^{d-1})_{\gamma\in R_i} \\ \hline (g^{i}(\beta_{i+M})\gamma)_{\gamma\in L_i} & (g^{i}(\beta_{i+M})\gamma)_{\gamma\in R_i} \\ (g^{i}(\beta_{i+M})\gamma^2)_{\gamma\in L_i} & (g^{i}(\beta_{i+M})\gamma^2)_{\gamma\in R_i} \\ \vdots & \vdots \\ (g^{i}(\beta_{i+M})\gamma^u)_{\gamma\in L_i} & (g^{i}(\beta_{i+M})\gamma^u)_{\gamma\in R_i} \end{array}\right].$$

It is easy to see that the top left and bottom right sub-matrices of $\mathcal{N}_{i,i}$ are square matrices that can be rewritten as non-zero constant multiples of a Vandermonde-like matrix. Hence by Claim 6, $\mathcal{N}_{i,i}$ is also invertible for all $i = M+1, \ldots, m$. We can use Claim 6 again to conclude that we must have $(\lambda_\gamma)_{\gamma\in A}$ to be identically zero, contradicting the assumption that it cannot be a zero vector, completing the proof for the privacy level of the secret sharing scheme defined in Construction 1 when $w < m-1$. □

Remark 7. *In general, the privacy threshold that is claimed in Theorem 2 is not guaranteed to be the largest possible privacy threshold of the scheme. On the other hand, Proposition 8 below provides an upper bound on the largest possible privacy threshold of the scheme. So in particular, when $w = m-1$, the privacy threshold provided in Theorem 2 is the largest possible privacy threshold of the secret sharing scheme Σ proposed in Construction 1, and when $w < m-1$, the lower and upper bounds are off by a constant term.*

Proposition 8. *If the secret sharing scheme constructed in Construction 1 provides t-privacy, then* $t \leq d(w+1)-1$.

Proof. Set $A \subseteq \bigcup_{i=1}^{w+1} \beta_i H$ such that for each $i = 1, \ldots, w+1$, we have $|A_i| = d$. Since each $\gamma \in A_i$ provides an evaluation point to the polynomial $f(\mathtt{X})|_{\beta_i H}$ which has degree $d-1$, the shares of A_i can be used to recover the value of $\sum_{j=0}^{w} a_{k,j} g^j(\beta_k)$ for $k = 0, \ldots, d-1$. In particular, it provides an evaluation point of $\sum_{j=0}^{w} a_{0,j} y^j$ where the evaluation point is $y = g(\beta_i)$. Note that this is a polynomial of degree w and we are given the value of the polynomial in $w+1$ evaluation points which are pairwise distinct by Lemma 4. Hence, this information can be used to recover the polynomial $\sum_{j=0}^{w} a_{0,j} y^j$, which can then be used to calculate $\sum_{j=0}^{w} a_{0,j} g^j(0) = S$, proving that if we allow $A \geq d(w+1)$, it is possible for such set to not only learn some information about the secret but also fully recover it. Hence, if the secret sharing scheme provides t-privacy, we must have $t \leq d(w+1)-1$. □

4 Passively Secure Repairing Protocol for Multiplicative Variants of Σ

In this section, we discuss the secure repairing capability of multiplicative instances of Σ in the scenario that a set of τ players is corrupted by a semi-honest adversary. Here we set $w - 1 \leq \frac{m}{2}$ so that multiplicativity is achieved, and we require τ, the number of corrupted parties, to be upper-bounded by the privacy level of the secret sharing scheme, which, from Theorem 2, equals $(d-1)(w+1)$ (since $w < m-1$).

In this section we are interested in different metrics/properties such as privacy of the secret after some shares have been repaired, the number of players contacted during the repairing process and the bandwidth required for the repairing process. First we restate the repairable claim as stated in Theorem 3. We note that for simplicity of discussion, we consider one of the instantiations where we set $d = v$ and $w = \frac{m}{2} - 1$.

Theorem 3. *Consider the secret sharing scheme Σ presented in Construction 1 with $d = v, w \leq \frac{m}{2} - 1, r = w(v+1) + v$ and $t = (v-1)(w+1)$. Without loss of generality, suppose that the player P_1 identified by γ_1 loses his share $f(\gamma_1)$. Then he can recover the value of $f(\gamma_1)$ by contacting v other players. The repairing process requires the v contacted players to send in total $2v \log q$ bits of data to each other and P_1, while P_1 needs to send $v \log q$ bits of data to the v contacted players. Furthermore, assuming that $v = \ln^{(1+\varepsilon)} n$ for some $\varepsilon > 0$, and that the adversary corrupts only t parties, such repair scheme does not leak any information about either the secret or the shares of the contacted players except with negligible probability in n.*

Proof. Assume that $\gamma_1 = \beta_1 \alpha_1$ for some $\alpha_1 \in H$. Consider $f(\mathtt{X})|_{\beta_1 H}$, the restriction of $f(\mathtt{X})$ to $\beta_1 H$. It is easy to see that $f(\mathtt{X})|_{\beta_1 H} = \sum_{i=0}^{v-1} \left(\sum_{j=0}^{w} a_{i,j} g(\beta_1)^j \right) \mathtt{X}^i$, which is a polynomial of degree at most $v-1$. Label the other v elements in $\beta_1 H$ by $\gamma_2, \ldots, \gamma_{v+1}$ and the $v+1$ corresponding players by $P_1, \ldots, P_{v+1}$. First, these $v+1$ players execute a simple multiparty computation protocol to generate a random shared mask, denoted by MaskGen. Its full specification can be found in Algorithm 2.

Algorithm 2. Random Mask Generation $(h(\gamma_1), \ldots, h(\gamma_{v+1})) \leftarrow \mathsf{MaskGen}()$

for $i = 1, \ldots, v+1$ **do**
  Player P_i randomly selects a polynomial $h_i(\mathtt{X}) \in \mathbb{F}_q[\mathtt{X}]_{<v}$ of degree at most $v-1$ and sends $h_i(\gamma_j)$ to player P_j for $j = 1, \ldots, v+1$;
  Upon receiving $h_j(\gamma_i)$ for $j = 1, \ldots, v+1$, player P_i defines $h(\gamma_i) = \sum_{j=1}^{v+1} h_j(\gamma_i)$;
end for
The generated mask is $h(x)$, which is shared as $(h(\gamma_1), \ldots, h(\gamma_{v+1}))$;

Note that since h has degree $\leq v-1$, if the adversary only corrupts up to $v-1$ of the $v+1$ players, he learns no information about the polynomial $h(\mathtt{X})$. Now we define the repairing process conducted by $P_1, \ldots, P_{v+1}$ to repair the share of P_1. We denote such algorithm by Repair, which can be found in Algorithm 3. It is easy to see that Algorithm 3 correctly recovers $f(\gamma_1)$ for P_1 when the adversary is semi-honest. Now we analyze in more detail that the privacy of the secret and the privacy of the shares of honest parties is maintained. Let A_1 be the set of corrupted parties in $\beta_1 H$. Note that since $P_2, \ldots, P_{v+1}$ receive no additional information from the execution of Repair, a possible leak of information is only possible if $P_1 \in A_1$. Note that since Repair only involves players in the same coset, if $A_1 = \beta_1 H$, then the amount of information that the adversary learns will not change after the execution of Repair. Given this, we can assume that $|A_1| \leq v$.

Algorithm 3. Share Repair $(f(\gamma_1), -, \ldots, -) \leftarrow \mathsf{Repair}(-, f(\gamma_2), \ldots, f(\gamma_{v+1}))$

The $v+1$ players execute MaskGen to generate a random mask $(h(\gamma_1), \ldots, h(\gamma_{v+1}))$ where $h(\gamma_i)$ is held by P_i;
for $i = 2, \ldots, v+1$ **do**
  P_i calculates $f(\gamma_i)|_{\beta_1 H} + h(\gamma_i)$ and sends it to P_1;
end for
Since $f(\mathtt{X})|_{\beta_1 H} + h(\mathtt{X})$ is a polynomial of degree at most $v-1$ and P_1 obtains v of its evaluation points, P_1 can recover the polynomial and in particular, she can recover $f(\gamma_1)|_{\beta_1 H} + h(\gamma_1)$;
Since P_1 knows $h(\gamma_1)$, she can then recover $f(\gamma_1)$;

First, suppose that $|A_1| \leq v-1$. In this case, P_1 learns the polynomial $f|_{\beta_1 H} + h$ along with at most $v-1$ evaluation points of $h(x)$. Since the degree of $h(\mathtt{X})$ is $v-1$, the adversary learns no information on $h(\gamma_i)$ for $\gamma_i \notin A_1$. So aside from the information about $f(\gamma_1)$, the adversary learns no further information about the shares of the other honest parties. This also implies that the repairing process does not increase the amount of information the adversary has on the other shares. So as long as the total number of corrupted parties in A_1 is at most $v-1$, no information on the secret is leaked from the execution of Repair.

From the above, we see that leakage on either the shares of the honest parties or the secret, when repairing P_1's share, is possible only if $|A_1| = v$. More generally, other parties might be repaired during a protocol execution, so leakage is only possible if there exists i such that $|A_i| = v$. The rest of this proof is devoted to showing that this event happens with low probability, taking as a starting point the fact that the adversary is assumed static and the random assignments of the n field elements is performed after the corruptions have been established.

Let $\mathcal{E}$ be the event that there exists at least one i such that $|A_i| = v$, and let $\mathcal{E}^c$ be the event that $|A_i| \neq v$ for every $i = 1, \ldots, m$. We aim to show that $\Pr(\mathcal{E})$ is negligible. We define $\mathcal{E}_i$ to be the event that $|A_i| = v$. It is easy to see that $P(\mathcal{E}_i) = \frac{\binom{t}{v}\cdot(n-t)}{\binom{m(v+1)}{v+1}}$. We assume that as n goes to infinity, we also have both m and v to also approach infinity. Then, by union bound, $\Pr(\mathcal{E})$ is at most $m(n-t)\frac{\binom{t}{v}}{\binom{m(v+1)}{v+1}} \leq n^2\frac{\binom{t}{v}}{\binom{n}{v}}$.

Recall that for any integers $0 < b < a$, we have the following approximation by the use of Stirling's approximation, $\binom{a}{b} \approx \frac{1}{\sqrt{2\pi b}}\sqrt{\frac{a}{a-b}}\left(\frac{a}{a-b}\right)^a\left(\frac{a-b}{b}\right)^b$. Then if $b = o(a)$, there exist two positive constants $0 < \lambda_1 < \lambda_2$ such that $\lambda_1 < \sqrt{\frac{a}{2\pi(a-b)}} < \lambda_2$. Hence we have that if $b = o(a)$, $\frac{\lambda_1}{\sqrt{b}}\left(\frac{a}{a-b}\right)^a\left(\frac{a-b}{b}\right)^b < \binom{a}{b} < \frac{\lambda_2}{\sqrt{b}}\left(\frac{a}{a-b}\right)^a\left(\frac{a-b}{b}\right)^b$.

Assuming that w also approaches infinity as n does, $\Pr(\mathcal{E})$ can be upper bounded by $\frac{\lambda_2}{\lambda_1}n^2\left(\frac{t-v}{n-v}\right)^v\left(\frac{t}{t-v}\right)^t\left(\frac{n-v}{n}\right)^n$. Hence $\ln(\Pr(\mathcal{E})) \leq \ln\left(\frac{\lambda_2}{\lambda_1}\right) + 2\ln n + v\ln\frac{t-v}{n-v} + t\ln\left(1+\frac{v}{t-v}\right) + n\ln\left(1-\frac{v}{n}\right)$. Note that for any $v > 0$, we have $\frac{t-v}{n-v} < \frac{t}{n}$. We denote $\theta = \frac{t}{n}$, which is a constant that is smaller than 1. Recall that for $|x| < 1$, we have $\ln(1+x) = \sum_{i\geq 1}(-1)^{i+1}\frac{x^i}{i}$. Since $v = o(t)$ and $t < n$, we can approximate $\ln\left(1+\frac{v}{t-v}\right) = \frac{v}{t-v} + O\left(\left(\frac{v}{t-v}\right)^2\right) \approx \frac{v}{t}$ and $\ln\left(1-\frac{v}{n}\right) = -\frac{v}{n} + O\left(\left(\frac{v}{n}\right)^2\right) \approx -\frac{v}{n}$.

Hence we have $\ln(\Pr(\mathcal{E})) \leq \ln\left(\frac{\lambda_2}{\lambda_1}\right) + 2\ln n + v\ln\theta$. By assumption, since $v = \Omega(\ln^{(1+\varepsilon)} n)$, we have $\ln(\Pr(\mathcal{E})) = -\Omega\left(\ln^{(1+\varepsilon)} n\right)$, which implies that $\Pr(\mathcal{E}) = e^{-\Omega\left(\ln^{(1+\varepsilon)} n\right)}$ which is negligibly small when n grows sufficiently large. □

5 Actively Secure Repairing Protocol for Strongly-Multiplicative Variants of Σ

In this section, we discuss the repairability of a strongly-multiplicative instance of Σ in the scenario that a set of τ players is corrupted by an active adversary. As discussed before, to achieve strong multiplicativity, we must have $w < m-1$. Furthermore, similar to the discussion in Sect. 4, we require τ to be at most the privacy threshold, which equals $(d-1)(w+1)$. In general, our actively secure repairing process is very similar to the passively secure process defined in Sect. 4. The crucial difference here is the need of the participants to perform verification process to the generated random mask which is done through the protocol described in [5]. We restate and prove the repairable claim for Σ, as stated in Theorem 4.

Theorem 4. *Let Σ be the secret sharing scheme constructed in Algorithm 1 with $w \approx \frac{m}{3}, r = w(v+1)+d$ and $t \approx \frac{1}{3}n$. Without loss of generality, suppose that the player P_1 identified by γ_1 loses his share $f(\gamma_1)$. Then he can recover the value of $f(\gamma_1)$ by contacting v other players where each involved player needs to send $O(v \log q)$ bits of data to each other. Furthermore, assuming that $v = \Omega(\ln^{(1+\varepsilon)} n)$ for some $\varepsilon > 0$, such repair scheme is unconditionally secure with overwhelming probability with respect to both the secret and the shares of the players against an active adversary controlling up to t players.*

Proof. We first start by defining two algorithms, which are analogues of MaskGen and Repair described in Theorem 3. We will use the notations described in the first paragraph of the proof of Theorem 3 except that $f(\mathtt{X})|_{\beta_1 H}$ is a polynomial of degree at most $d-1$ instead of $v-1$. The full specification of the protocol ActMaskGen, which is a variant of MaskGen, can be found in Algorithm 4. Here, we take $d = \frac{v+1}{3}$. Note that since h has degree $\frac{v+1}{3} - 1$, if the adversary only corrupts up to $\frac{v+1}{3} - 1$ of the $v+1$ players, he learns no information about the polynomial $h(\mathtt{X})$. Furthermore, since such sharing can be seen as a codeword of a Reed-Solomon code of length $v+1$ and dimension $\frac{v+1}{3}$, it can correct up to $\frac{v+1}{3}$ errors. So in particular, it can correct any malicious behavior of an adversary controlling up to $\frac{v+1}{3} - 1$ of the $v+1$ players. Now we define the repairing process conducted by $P_1, \dots, P_{v+1}$ to repair the share of P_1. We denote such algorithm by Repair, which can be found in Algorithm 3.

It is easy to see that Algorithm 3 correctly recovers $f(\gamma_1)$ for P_1 when the adversary is malicious and controls up to $\frac{v+1}{3} - 1$ out of the $v+1$ involved players. Now, we consider the security of the secret and the shares of honest participating parties against the active adversary. Let A_1 be the set of corrupted parties in $\beta_1 H$. Note that since $P_2, \dots, P_{v+1}$ learns no additional information either from the execution of Repair, a possible leak of information is only possible if $P_1 \in A_1$. Note that since Repair only involves players in the same coset, if $A_1 = \beta_1 H$, the amount of information that the adversary learns will not change after the execution of Repair. So we can assume that $|A_1| \leq v$. Suppose that $|A_1| \leq \frac{v+1}{3} - 1$.

Algorithm 4. Actively Secure Random Mask Generation $(h(\gamma_1), \ldots, h(\gamma_{v+1})) \leftarrow \mathsf{ActMaskGen}()$

for $i = 1, \ldots, v+1$ **do**
  Player P_i randomly selects a polynomial $h_i(\mathtt{X}) \in \mathbb{F}_q[\mathtt{X}]_{<\frac{v+1}{3}}$ of degree at most $\frac{v+1}{3} - 1$ and sends $h_i(\gamma_j)$ to player P_j for $j = 1, \ldots, v+1$;
  Player P_i follows the verification process described in [5] to prove to the other players that $h_i(\gamma_j)$ is indeed an evaluation of some polynomial of degree at most $\frac{v+1}{3} - 1$;
  If the verification protocol fails, the protocol aborts;
  If the verification protocol is successful, having $h_j(\gamma_i)$ for $j = 1, \ldots, v+1$, player P_i defines $h(\gamma_i) = \sum_{j=1}^{v+1} h_j(\gamma_i)$;
end for
The generated mask is $h(x)$, which is shared as $(h(\gamma_1), \ldots, h(\gamma_{v+1}))$;

Algorithm 5. Share Repair $(f(\gamma_1), -, -, \ldots, -) \leftarrow \mathsf{ActRepair}(-, f(\gamma_2), \ldots, f(\gamma_{v+1}))$

The $v+1$ players executes $\mathsf{MaskGen}$ to generate a random mask $(h(\gamma_1), \ldots, h(\gamma_{v+1}))$ where $h(\gamma_i)$ is held by P_i;
for $i = 2, \ldots, v+1$ **do**
  P_i calculates $f(\gamma_i)|_{\beta_1 H} + h(\gamma_i)$ and sends it to P_1;
end for
Since $f(\mathtt{X})|_{\beta_1 H} + h(\mathtt{X})$ is a polynomial of degree at most $\frac{v+1}{3} - 1$ and P_1 obtains v of its evaluation points, P_1 can recover and correct the polynomial and in particular, she can recover $f(\gamma_1)|_{\beta_1 H} + h(\gamma_1)$ as long as the adversary only controls up to $\frac{v+1}{3} - 1$ out of the $v+1$ players.
Since P_1 knows $h(\gamma_1)$, she can then recover $f(\gamma_1)$;

In this case, P_1 learns the polynomial $f|_{\beta_1 H} + h$ along with at most $\frac{v+1}{3} - 1$ evaluation points of $h(x)$. Since the degree of $h(x)$ is $\frac{v+1}{3} - 1$, the adversary learns no information on $h(\gamma_i)$ for $\gamma_i \notin A_1$. So aside from the information about $f(\gamma_1)$, the adversary learns no further information about the shares of the other honest parties. This also implies that the repairing process does not increase the amount of information the adversary has on the other shares. So as long as the total number of corrupted parties in each coset is at most $\frac{v+1}{3}$, no information on the secret is leaked from the execution of Repair. So leakage of information of either the share of honest parties or the secret is possible if there exists i such that $|A_i| \geq \frac{v+1}{3}$. So the probability that the execution of Repair leaks information about either the secret or the share of honest parties is at most the probability that during the random assignments of the n field elements, there exists $i \in [m]$ such that $\frac{v+1}{3} \leq |A_i| \leq v$.

Let $\mathcal{F}$ be the event that there exists at least one i such that $\frac{v+1}{3} \leq |A_i| \leq v$ and $\mathcal{F}^c$ be the event that $|A_i| < \frac{v+1}{3}$ for any $i = 1, \ldots, m$. We aim to show that $\Pr(\mathcal{F})$ is negligible. We define $\mathcal{F}_i$ to be the event that $\frac{v+1}{3} \leq |A_i| \leq v$. Then we have $\Pr(\mathcal{F}_i) = \frac{\sum_{\kappa=\frac{v+1}{3}}^{v} \binom{t}{\kappa}\binom{n-t}{v+1-\kappa}}{\binom{n}{v+1}}$.

Claim 9. *Let* $0 < v < t < n$ *such that* $t \leq \frac{1}{3}n$ *and* $\kappa \in \left\{\frac{v+1}{3}, \frac{v+1}{3}+1, \ldots, v\right\}$. *Then* $\binom{t}{\kappa}\binom{n-t}{v+1-\kappa}$ *achieves its maximum of* $\binom{t}{\frac{v+1}{3}}\binom{n-t}{\frac{2(v+1)}{3}}$ *when* $\kappa = \frac{v+1}{3}$.

Proof. Let $\kappa \geq \frac{v+1}{3}$. Then $\rho \triangleq \frac{\binom{t}{\kappa+1}\binom{n-t}{v-\kappa}}{\binom{t}{\kappa}\binom{n-t}{v+1-\kappa}} = \frac{(t-\kappa)(v+1-\kappa)}{(\kappa+1)(n-t-v+\kappa)}$ is upper bounded by

$$\rho \leq \frac{\left(t - \frac{v+1}{3}\right)\left(\frac{2}{3}(v+1)\right)}{\left(\frac{v+1}{3}\right)\left(n - t - (v+1) + \frac{v+1}{3}\right)} \leq 2\frac{(v+1)\left(\frac{1}{3}m - \frac{1}{3}\right)}{(v+1)\left(\frac{2}{3}m - \frac{2}{3}\right)} = 1.$$

This shows that if $t \leq \frac{1}{3}n$ and $\kappa \geq \frac{v+1}{3}$, the term $\binom{t}{\kappa}\binom{n-t}{v+1-\kappa}$ is decreasing. Hence, it achieves its maximum of $\binom{t}{\frac{v+1}{3}}\binom{n-t}{\frac{2(v+1)}{3}}$ when $\kappa = \frac{v+1}{3}$. □

Following the discussion in Sect. 3.1 regarding the parameter choices, for Σ to be t'-strongly multiplicative where t' is sufficiently close to $\frac{1}{3}n$, for $\delta \in (0,1)$ and sufficiently large m and v, we may choose $d \approx 1 + (1-\delta)(v+1) \leq v$ and $w \approx \frac{m}{3-\delta}$. So we have $t \approx \frac{1}{3}(1-\delta)n$.

Then by union bound, we have the following upper bound

$$\Pr(\mathcal{F}) \leq \frac{2n}{3}\frac{\binom{(v+1)(w+1)}{\frac{v+1}{3}}\binom{(m-w+1)(v+1)}{\frac{2(v+1)}{3}}}{\binom{m(v+1)}{v+1}}.$$

Recall that by the discussion in the proof of Theorem 3, if $b = o(a)$, there exist positive constants $0 < \lambda_1 < \lambda_2$ such that

$$\frac{\lambda_1}{\sqrt{b}}\left(\frac{a}{a-b}\right)^a\left(\frac{a-b}{b}\right)^b < \binom{a}{b} < \frac{\lambda_2}{\sqrt{b}}\left(\frac{a}{a-b}\right)^a\left(\frac{a-b}{b}\right)^b.$$

So we have the following upper bound

$$\begin{aligned}
\Pr(\mathcal{F}) \quad &\leq \frac{2}{3}n\frac{\lambda_2^2}{\lambda_1}\sqrt{\frac{v+1}{\frac{v+1}{3}\frac{2(v+1)}{3}}}\frac{(w+1)^{(v+1)(w+1)}3^{\frac{v+1}{3}}}{\left(w+\frac{2}{3}\right)^{(v+1)\left(w+\frac{2}{3}\right)}} \\
&\cdot\left(\frac{3}{2}\right)^{\frac{2}{3}(v+1)}\cdot\frac{(m-w+1)^{(m-w+1)(v+1)}}{\left(m-w+\frac{1}{3}\right)^{(v+1)\left(m-w+\frac{1}{3}\right)}} \\
&\cdot\frac{(m-1)^{(m-1)(v+1)}}{m^{m(v+1)}} \\
&= \sqrt{2}\frac{n}{\sqrt{v+1}}\frac{\lambda_2^2}{\lambda_1}\cdot\frac{3^{v+1}}{2^{\frac{2}{3}(v+1)}}\cdot\left(\frac{w+1}{w+\frac{2}{3}}\right)^{\left(w+\frac{2}{3}\right)(v+1)} \\
&\cdot\left(\frac{m-1}{m}\right)^{(m-1)(v+1)}\cdot\frac{(w+1)^{\frac{v+1}{3}}(m-w+1)^{\frac{2}{3}(v+1)}}{m^{v+1}} \\
&\cdot\left(\frac{m-w+1}{m-w+\frac{1}{3}}\right)^{\left(m-w+\frac{1}{3}\right)(v+1)}
\end{aligned}$$

Then for a sufficiently large m, we have

$$\left(\frac{w+1}{w+\frac{2}{3}}\right)^{(w+\frac{2}{3})(v+1)} \cdot \left(\frac{m-1}{m}\right)^{(m-1)(v+1)} \cdot \left(\frac{m-w+1}{m-w+\frac{1}{3}}\right)^{(m-w+\frac{1}{3})(v+1)} \leq 1+\delta.$$

Furthermore, for a sufficiently large m and v, we have

$$\frac{(w+1)^{\frac{v+1}{3}}(m-w+1)^{\frac{2}{3}(v+1)}}{m^{v+1}} \leq \frac{(2-\delta)^{\frac{2}{3}(v+1)}}{(3-\delta)^{v+1}}.$$

So the upper bound above can be simplified to the following

$$\Pr(\mathcal{F}) \leq \sqrt{2}(1+\delta)\frac{n}{\sqrt{v+1}}\frac{\lambda_2^2}{\lambda_1}\left(\frac{3}{3-\delta}\cdot\left(\frac{2-\delta}{2}\right)^{\frac{2}{3}}\right)^{v+1}.$$

Note that by the choice of δ, $\frac{3}{3-\delta}\cdot\left(\frac{2-\delta}{2}\right)^{\frac{2}{3}} < 1$. Hence, there exists $C > 0$ such that $\ln\left(\frac{3}{3-\delta}\cdot\left(\frac{2-\delta}{2}\right)^{\frac{2}{3}}\right) < -C$. Then we have $\ln\Pr(\mathcal{F}) \leq \frac{1}{2}\ln 2 + \ln(1+\delta) + \ln n - \frac{1}{2}\ln(v+1) + \ln\left(\frac{\lambda_2^2}{\lambda_1}\right) - C(v+1)$.

By assumption, $v+1 = \ln^{(1+\varepsilon)} n$. Then $\ln Pr(\mathcal{F}) = -\Omega(\ln^{(1+\varepsilon)} n)$. This implies that $\Pr(\mathcal{F}) = e^{-\Omega(\ln^{(1+\varepsilon)} n)}$ which is negligibly small when n is sufficiently large.

Acknowledgments. This research is supported by the National Research Foundation, Singapore under its Strategic Capability Research Centres Funding Initiative. Any opinions, findings and conclusions or recommendations expressed in this material are those of the author(s) and do not reflect the views of National Research Foundation, Singapore.

The work of Chaoping Xing was supported in part by the National Key Research and Development Project under Grant 2022YFA1004900, in part by the National Natural Science Foundation of China under Grants 12031011, 12361141818 and 12271084.

This paper was prepared in part for information purposes by the Artificial Intelligence Research Group and the AlgoCRYPT CoE of JPMorgan Chase & Co and its affiliates ("JP Morgan") and is not a product of the Research Department of JP Morgan. JP Morgan makes no representation and warranty whatsoever and disclaims all liability, for the completeness, accuracy, or reliability of the information contained herein. This document is not intended as investment research or investment advice, or a recommendation, offer, or solicitation for the purchase or sale of any security, financial instrument, financial product, or service, or to be used in any way for evaluating the merits of participating in any transaction, and shall not constitute a solicitation under any jurisdiction or to any person, if such solicitation under such jurisdiction or to such person would be unlawful.

Appendix

A Comparison with a Two-Level Shamir's Secret Sharing Scheme

In this section, we will compare our construction presented in Construction 1, which we will denote by Σ with a more natural two-level Shamir's secret sharing scheme, which we denote by Σ'. For completeness, first, we discuss the two-level Shamir's secret sharing scheme Σ'. Let n be the number of parties and consider two integers v and m such that $n = (v+1)m$. Split the parties into m groups of $v+1$ parties each. Let q be a prime number, d, w integers with $d \leq v$ and $w \leq m-1$. Consider a linear secret-sharing scheme that, to distribute a secret $s \in \mathbb{F}_q$, proceeds as follows.

1. Generate m shares of the secret s using a (w, m)–Shamir's secret sharing scheme where the m shares are denoted as $s_1, \ldots, s_m$. Here for positive integers $a < b$, we use the notation (a, b)–Shamir's secret sharing scheme to denote the Shamir's secret sharing scheme providing a privacy where shares are evaluations of a polynomial of degree a in b distinct evaluation points. Suppose that this is done by using a degree w polynomial $F(\mathtt{X}) = \sum_{i=0}^{w} F_i \mathtt{X}^i$ with set of evaluation points $\{\alpha_1, \ldots, \alpha_m\}$.
2. For each $i = 1, \ldots, m$, generate $v+1$ shares for the local secret s_i using a $(d-1, v+1)$– Shamir's secret sharing scheme where the $v+1$ shares are denoted as $s_{i,1}, \ldots, s_{i,v+1}$. Suppose that such share generation is done using a degree $d-1$ polynomial $F^{(i)}(\mathtt{X}) = \sum_{j=0}^{d-1} F_j^{(i)} \mathtt{X}^j$ with $\{\gamma_{i,1}, \ldots, \gamma_{i,v+1}\}$ as the set of evaluation points.
3. For $i = 1, \ldots, m$ and $j = 1, \ldots, v+1$, assign the share $s_{i,j}$ to the j-th party in group i.

Note that we have in total m local groups, each with $v+1$ players where the threshold for the local group is $d-1$. On the other hand, when we consider each group as one player, our construction is reduced to a (w, m)- Shamir's secret sharing scheme. In order to have a comparable scheme, for the second

---

Algorithm 6. Two-Step Shamir's Secret Sharing Scheme

Require: $S \in \mathbb{F}_q$: the secret to be secretly shared.
1: Randomly select $F_0, \ldots, F_w \in \mathbb{F}_q$ such that $S = \sum_{i=0}^{w} F_i \alpha_0^i$;
2: **for** $K = 1, \ldots, m$ **do**
3:     Define $S_K = \sum_{i=0}^{w} F_i \alpha_K^i$;
4:     Randomly select $f_0^{(K)}, \ldots, f_{d-1}^{(K)}$ such that $S_K = f_0^{(K)}$;
5:     Define $f^{(K)}(\mathtt{X}) = \sum_{j=0}^{d-1} f_j^{(K)} \mathtt{X}^j$;
6:     **Secret and shares:** Calculate and distribute the shares to the $v+1$ players where the share for the player assigned $\gamma_i^{(K)}$ is $S_i^{(K)} = f^{(K)}(\gamma_i^{(K)})$;
7: **end for**

---

construction, which is based on two-steps of Shamir's secret sharing, we assume that the first step uses a (w, m)-Shamir's secret sharing scheme where each of its share is further secretly shared using a $(d-1, v+1)$-Shamir's secret sharing scheme. Furthermore, for the first step of the sharing, we assume that the chosen evaluation points are $\alpha_0, \ldots, \alpha_m$ where α_0 is used as the evaluation point for the secret. Furthermore, for $K = 1, \ldots, M$, each such share is further secretly shared using evaluation points $\gamma_1^{(K)}, \ldots, \gamma_{v+1}^{(K)}$. The complete specification of the secret sharing scheme Σ' is specified in Algorithm 6.

Note that in this definition, we assume that the m instantiations of the secret sharing schemes used to secretly share S_K to $v+1$ players using the polynomial $f^{(K)}$ encodes S_K as $f^{(K)}(0)$. However, it is easy to see that a simple shifting operation can be used to have S_K to be $f^{(K)}(y_K)$ for any choice of $y_K \in \mathbb{F}_q$ without changing any of the shares $S_i^{(K)}$.

First we show that for any secret sharing scheme Σ constructed using Algorithm 1, it is equivalent to Σ', which is obtained from Algorithm 6 with some choice of the parameters.

Lemma 10. *Let* $(S_{i,j} : 1 \leq i \leq m, 1 \leq j \leq v+1)$ *be the shares for the* n *players in a secret sharing scheme* Σ *constructed using Algorithm 1 with a fixed secret* $S \in \mathbb{F}_q$*. Then there exists some assignments of the variables such that the shares generated by a secret sharing scheme* Σ' *following Algorithm 6 are* $(S_{i,j} : 1 \leq i \leq m, 1 \leq j \leq v+1)$.

Proof. Let $\alpha_0 = g(0)$ and for $i = 1, \ldots, m, \alpha_i = g(\beta_i)$. For each $K = 1, \ldots, M$ and $j = 1, \ldots, v+1$, we define $\gamma_j^{(K)} = \gamma_{K,j}$. We aim to show that for any $K = 1, \ldots, M$ and $j = 1, \ldots, v+1$, we have $S_i^{(K)} = S_{K,i}$. For $i = 0, \ldots, w$, we set $F_i = a_{0i}$. Then we have $\sum_{i=0}^{w} F_i \alpha_0^i = \sum_{i=0}^{w} a_{0i} g(0)^i = S$ as required. Furthermore, we have $S_K = \sum_{i=0}^{w} F_i \alpha_K^i = \sum_{i=0}^{w} a_{0i} g(\beta_K)^i$. Lastly, we set $f_0^{(K)} = S_K$ and for $j = 1, \ldots, d-1$ and $K = 1, \ldots, m$, let $f_j^{(K)} = \sum_{i=0}^{w} a_{ji} g(\beta_K)^i$.

Then for each group $K = 1, \ldots, m$, the player assigned to $\gamma_i^{(k)}$ receives the share

$$
\begin{aligned}
S_i^{(K)} = f^{(K)}(\gamma_i^{(K)}) = \sum_{j=0}^{d-1} f_j^{(K)} \left(\gamma_i^{(K)}\right)^j = \sum_{i=0}^{w} a_{0i} g(\beta_K)^i \\
+ \sum_{j=1}^{d-1} \left(\sum_{i=0}^{w} a_{ji} g(\beta_K)^i \right) \left(\gamma_i^{(K)}\right)^j = \sum_{j=0}^{d-1} \sum_{i=0}^{w} a_{ji} g(\gamma_i^{(K)})^j \left(\gamma_i^{(K)}\right)^j = S_{K,i}
\end{aligned}
$$

completing the proof. □

Next we show that a secret sharing scheme Σ' obtained from Algorithm 6 is also equivalent to a secret sharing scheme Σ obtained from Algorithm 1 with some possible changes of parameters.

Lemma 11. *Let* $(S_i^{(K)} : K = 1, \ldots, m, i = 1, \ldots, v+1)$ *be the shares for the* n *players generated by Algorithm 6 with a fixed secret* $S \in \mathbb{F}_q$ *and the evaluation* *points* $\gamma_i^{(K)}$ *that are pairwise distinct. Then there exists some assignments of the variables such that* $(S_i^{(K)} : K = 1, \ldots, m, i = 1, \ldots, v+1)$ *are generated using Algorithm 1 with some possibly changed parameters.*

Proof. Recall that we have $S = \sum_{i=0}^{w} F_i \alpha_0^i$. Next, for $K = 1, \ldots, m$, we have $f_0^{(K)} = s_K = \sum_{i=0}^{w} F_i \alpha_K^i$. Furthermore, we define $f_1^{(K)}, \ldots, f_{d-1}^{(K)}$ such that $S_i^{(K)} = \sum_{j=0}^{d-1} f_j^{(K)} \left(\gamma_i^{(K)}\right)^j$.

Then for $K = 1, \ldots, m$, we have $f^{(K)}(\mathtt{X}) = \sum_{i=0}^{w} F_i \alpha_K^i + \sum_{j=1}^{d-1} f_j^{(K)} \mathtt{X}^j$. Now for $j = 1, \ldots, d-1$, there exists $d_j \in \{0, \ldots, m-1\}$ and $a_{0,j}, \ldots, a_{d_j,j} \in \mathbb{F}_q$ such that for any $K = 1, \ldots, m$, $f_j^{(K)} = \sum_{i=0}^{d_j} a_{i,j} \alpha_K^i$. We further define $d_0 = w$ and $a_{i,0} = F_i$ for $i = 0, \ldots, w$. Lastly, we define $D_1 = \max\{d_0, \ldots, d_{d-1}\}$. For any $i = 0, \ldots, D_1$ and $j = 1, \ldots, d-1$, such that $a_{i,j}$ is not yet defined, we set $a_{i,j} = 0$.

Then we have $f^{(K)}(\mathtt{X}) = \sum_{j=0}^{d-1} \left(\sum_{i=0}^{D_1} a_{i,j} \alpha_K^i\right) \mathtt{X}^j$ where for any $i = 1, \ldots, v+1$, we have $S_i^{(K)} = f^{(K)}(\gamma_i^{(K)}) = \sum_{j=0}^{d-1} \left(\sum_{i=0}^{D_1} a_{i,j} \alpha_K^i\right) \left(\gamma_i^{(K)}\right)^j$. This shows that if we want to have one polynomial $f^*(\mathtt{X})$ such that for any $K = 1, \ldots, m$ and $i = 1, \ldots, v+1, f^*(\gamma_i^{(K)}) = S_i^{(K)}$, we need to have some polynomial $g^*(\mathtt{X})$ such that for any $K = 1, \ldots, m$ and $i = 1, \ldots, v+1, g^*(\gamma_i^{(K)}) = \alpha_K$. Note that such $g^*(\mathtt{X})$ is guaranteed to exist with degree of at most n. Then with such $g^*(\mathtt{X})$, we can define $f^*(\mathtt{X}) = \sum_{j=0}^{d-1} \left(\sum_{i=0}^{D_1} a_{i,j} g * (\mathtt{X})^i\right) x^j$. So letting $\gamma_{i,j} = \gamma_j^{(i)}$ for $i = 1, \ldots, M, j = 1, \ldots, v+1$, for such specific instances of the secret sharing schemes obtained by Algorithm 6 it can also be generated using Algorithm 1. □

Remark 2. We note that based on the form of f^* which requires the polynomial $g^*(x)$, for two players belonging to different local groups, they cannot possess the same evaluation points. Otherwise, they will have exactly the same share. So this is the reason why we require such restriction in the statement of Lemma 11.

Lemma 11 shows that if all the evaluation points in the second step of Algorithm 6 are pairwise distinct, then we can transform it to a one-step secret sharing which follows Algorithm 1 with a possible change in the degree of $g(\mathtt{X})$ from $v+1$ to a positive integer, say D_2, and the inner degree from w to D_1. We claim that $v+1 \leq D_2$. Indeed, we note that $g^*(\mathtt{X})$ cannot be a constant since we have at least m distinct evaluation points evaluated to m distinct values. Furthermore, recall that $g^*(\gamma_i^{(1)}) = \alpha_1$ for $i = 1, \ldots, v+1$. Consider $\hat{g}(\mathtt{X}) = g^*(\mathtt{X}) - \alpha_1$. It is easy to see that $\hat{g}(\mathtt{X})$ has the same degree as $g^*(\mathtt{X})$ and neither is a constant function. However, we have $\hat{g}(\gamma_i^{(1)}) = 0$ for $i = 1, \ldots, v+1$. Hence we have $\prod_{i=1}^{v+1}(\mathtt{X} - \gamma_i^{(1)}) | \hat{g}(\mathtt{X})$, proving that its degree, and hence the degree of $g^*(\mathtt{X})$, is at least $v+1$ as claimed.

Consider Σ a secret sharing scheme following Algorithm 1. By Theorems 1 and 2, Σ is shown to have t_1 privacy and r_1 recovery where $(d-1)(w+1) \leq t_1 \leq d(w+1) - 1$ and $r_1 \leq w(v+1) + d$.

Now suppose that we generate a secret sharing scheme Σ' following Algorithm 6. First we consider its recovery level r_2. Note that by Lemma 11, the degree of the constructed $f^*(\mathtt{X})$ is $D_1 \cdot \deg(g^*(\mathtt{X})) + d - 1$ where $\deg(g^*(\mathtt{X}))$ is the degree of $g^*(\mathtt{X})$. Recall that $D_1 = \max\{d_0, d_1, \ldots, d_{d-1}\}$ where $d_0 = w$ while for any $j = 1, \ldots, d-1$, the polynomial $\sum_{i=0}^{d_j} a_{i,j}\mathtt{X}^i$ maps α_K^i to $f_j^{(K)}$ for each $K = 1, \ldots, m$. Note that since $f_j^{(K)}$ is also unknown, each of such d_j can be as large as $m-1$. Hence, in general, $d_j = m-1$ for $j = 1, \ldots, d-1$, which implies $D_1 = m-1$. Furthermore, as we have established, the degree of $g^*(\mathtt{X})$ is at least $v+1$, which implies that $\deg(f^*(\mathtt{X})) \geq (m-1)(v+1) + (d-1) = m(v+1) - (v+2-d)$.

Consider a group of players containing $v+1$ players from the first w groups and $d-1$ players from the remaining $m-w$ groups. Note that such group has size $(v+1)w + (d-1)(m-w) \leq \deg(f^*(\mathtt{X}))$. We claim that it is possible to have a share generation such that the original secret $s = 1$ while all the shares of these players to be 0. Note that by linearity of Σ', this means that the shares from such group of size $m(v+1) + (m-w)(d-v-2)$ contains no information about s, proving that it provides privacy from such group. This would imply that $r_2 \geq (v+1)w + (d-1)(m-w) + 1$.

First, for the first w groups, since we have the shares of all $v+1$ players from such group, we would be able to recover the local secret s_i from the shares of these players. Since their shares are 0, we can conclude that $s_i = 0$ for $i = 1, \ldots, w$. Next, note that since s_i is a valid share from a (w, m)-Shamir's secret sharing scheme, by the w-privacy guarantee of the (w, m)-Shamir's secret sharing scheme, there is a valid share generation of 1 such that $s_i = 0$ for $i = 1, \ldots, w$. This will also fix the values of s_i for $i = w+1, \ldots, m$. Next, we consider the sharing of the players in the i-th group for $i = w+1, \ldots, m$. Note that since $s_{i,j}$ is a valid secret share of s_i using $(d-1, v+1)$-Shamir's secret sharing scheme, by its $d-1$-privacy guarantee, it is possible to have a valid share generation of s_i such that $s_{i,j} = 0$ for $d-1$ of such j. This shows that it is possible to have a valid share generation of $s = 1$ such that the share of all the players belonging to the group described above to be zero. This proves that $r_2 \geq (v+1)w + (d-1)(m-w) + 1$. Combined with the upper bound established for r_1, we obtain $r_2 - r_1 \geq (d-1)(m-w-1)$.

Next, we consider the privacy level of Σ', which we denote by t_2. Consider the group of players consisting of d players from each of the first $w+1$ groups. It is easy to see that such group can recover the original secret. This shows that $t_2 \leq d(w+1) - 1$. So combined with the fact that $(d-1)(w+1) \leq t_1$, we have $t_2 - t_1 \leq d - 1$. It is easy to see that when $w - 1 < m$, the increase of recovery level, which is at least $(m-w-1)(d-1)$ is at least the increase in the privacy level, which is at most $d-1$. This gap becomes much larger especially in the scenario where the secret sharing scheme is (strongly) multiplicative with repairing process that provides statistical security for the privacy of the shares. Note that in this case, since $w \leq \frac{m}{2}$ and $m = O\left(\frac{n}{v}\right) = O\left(\frac{n}{\ln^{(1+\varepsilon)} n}\right)$ for some $\varepsilon > 0$, the gap is $O\left(\frac{n}{\ln^{(1+\varepsilon)} n}\right)$. This shows that in general, a secret sharing scheme generated by Algorithm 6 comes with a larger gap between the privacy level and recovery level. So if we maintain the recovery level to be the same, the privacy level provided by Σ' is much smaller than what can be guaranteed from the construction following Algorithm 1. Such limitation of Algorithm 6 provides us with a justification on considering the one-step construction in Algorithm 1 instead of the more natural Algorithm 6.

References

1. Agarwal, A., Mazumdar, A.: Security in locally repairable storage. IEEE Trans. Inf. Theory **62**(11), 6204–6217 (2016)
2. Badrinarayanan, S., Jain, A., Manohar, N., Sahai, A.: Secure MPC: laziness leads to GOD. In: Moriai, S., Wang, H. (eds.) ASIACRYPT 2020. LNCS, vol. 12493, pp. 120–150. Springer, Cham (2020). https://doi.org/10.1007/978-3-030-64840-4_5
3. Balaji, S.B., Kumar, P.V.: A tight lower bound on the sub- packetization level of optimal-access MSR and MDS codes. In: 2018 IEEE International Symposium on Information Theory (ISIT), pp. 2381–2385 (2018)
4. Baum, C., Cozzo, D., Smart, N.P.: Using TopGear in overdrive: a more efficient ZKPoK for SPDZ. In: Paterson, K.G., Stebila, D. (eds.) SAC 2019. LNCS, vol. 11959, pp. 274–302. Springer, Cham (2020). https://doi.org/10.1007/978-3-030-38471-5_12
5. Ben-Or, M., Goldwasser, S., Wigderson, A.: Completeness theorems for non-cryptographic fault-tolerant distributed computation. In: Proceedings of the Twentieth Annual ACM Symposium on Theory of Computing, STOC 1988, pp. 1–10. Association for Computing Machinery, New York, NY, USA (1988)
6. Bendlin, R., Damgård, I., Orlandi, C., Zakarias, S.: Semi-homomorphic encryption and multiparty computation. In: Paterson, K.G. (ed.) EUROCRYPT 2011. LNCS, vol. 6632, pp. 169–188. Springer, Heidelberg (2011). https://doi.org/10.1007/978-3-642-20465-4_11
7. Bienstock, A., Escudero, D., Polychroniadou, A.: On linear communication complexity for (maximally) fluid MPC. In: Handschuh, H., Lysyanskaya, A. (eds.) Advances in Cryptology - CRYPTO 2023, pp. 263–294. Springer, Cham (2023). https://doi.org/10.1007/978-3-031-38557-5_9
8. Blakley, G.R.: Safeguarding cryptographic keys. In: International Workshop on Managing Requirements Knowledge, p. 313. IEEE Computer Society (1979)
9. Boyle, E., Gilboa, N., Ishai, Y., Nof, A.: Efficient fully secure computation via distributed zero-knowledge proofs. In: Moriai, S., Wang, H. (eds.) ASIACRYPT 2020. LNCS, vol. 12493, pp. 244–276. Springer, Cham (2020). https://doi.org/10.1007/978-3-030-64840-4_9
10. Cadambe, V.R., Jafar, S.A., Maleki, H.: Distributed data storage with minimum storage regenerating codes - exact and functional repair are asymptotically equally efficient (2010)
11. Cai, H., Miao, Y., Schwartz, M., Tang, X.: On optimal locally repairable codes with super-linear length. IEEE Trans. Inf. Theory **66**(8), 4853–4868 (2020)
12. Cascudo, I., David, B., Garms, L., Konring, A.: YOLO YOSO: fast and simple encryption and secret sharing in the YOSO model. In: Agrawal, S., Lin, D. (eds) ASIACRYPT 2022. LNCS, vol. 13791, pages 651–680. Springer, Cham (2022). https://doi.org/10.1007/978-3-031-22963-3_22
13. Cascudo, I., David, B., Shlomovits, O., Varlakov, D.: Mt. Random: multi-tiered randomness beacons. Cryptology ePrint Archive, Paper 2021/1096 (2021). https://eprint.iacr.org/2021/1096

14. Chen, B., Fang, W., Xia, S.-T., Fu, F.-W.: Constructions of optimal (r, δ) locally repairable codes via constacyclic codes. IEEE Trans. Commun. **67**(8), 5253–5263 (2019)
15. Chen, B., Fang, W., Xia, S.-T., Hao, J., Fu, F.-W.: Improved bounds and Singleton-optimal constructions of locally repairable codes with minimum distance 5 and 6. IEEE Trans. Inf. Theory **67**(1), 217–231 (2020)
16. Chida, K., et al.: Fast large-scale honest-majority MPC for malicious adversaries. In: Shacham, H., Boldyreva, A. (eds.) CRYPTO 2018. LNCS, vol. 10993, pp. 34–64. Springer, Cham (2018). https://doi.org/10.1007/978-3-319-96878-0_2
17. Choudhuri, A.R., Goel, A., Green, M., Jain, A., Kaptchuk, G.: Fluid MPC: secure multiparty computation with dynamic participants. In: Malkin, T., Peikert, C. (eds.) CRYPTO 2021. LNCS, vol. 12826, pp. 94–123. Springer, Cham (2021). https://doi.org/10.1007/978-3-030-84245-1_4
18. Cramer, R., Damgård, I., Maurer, U.: General secure multi-party computation from any linear secret-sharing scheme. In: Preneel, B. (ed.) EUROCRYPT 2000. LNCS, vol. 1807, pp. 316–334. Springer, Heidelberg (2000). https://doi.org/10.1007/3-540-45539-6_22
19. Cramer, R., Xing, C., Yuan, C.: On the complexity of arithmetic secret sharing. In: Pass, R., Pietrzak, K. (eds.) TCC 2020. LNCS, vol. 12552, pp. 444–469. Springer, Cham (2020). https://doi.org/10.1007/978-3-030-64381-2_16
20. Dalskov, A., Escudero, D.: Honest majority MPC with abort with minimal online communication. In: Longa, P., Ràfols, C. (eds.) LATINCRYPT 2021. LNCS, vol. 12912, pp. 453–472. Springer, Cham (2021). https://doi.org/10.1007/978-3-030-88238-9_22
21. Damgård, I., Escudero, D., Polychroniadou, A.: Phoenix: secure computation in an unstable network with dropouts and comebacks. Cryptology ePrint Archive (2021)
22. Damgård, I., Ishai, Y., Krøigaard, M., Nielsen, J.B., Smith, A.: Scalable multiparty computation with nearly optimal work and resilience. In: Wagner, D. (ed.) CRYPTO 2008. LNCS, vol. 5157, pp. 241–261. Springer, Heidelberg (2008). https://doi.org/10.1007/978-3-540-85174-5_14
23. Damgård, I., Keller, M., Larraia, E., Pastro, V., Scholl, P., Smart, N.P.: Practical covertly secure MPC for dishonest majority – or: breaking the SPDZ limits. In: Crampton, J., Jajodia, S., Mayes, K. (eds.) ESORICS 2013. LNCS, vol. 8134, pp. 1–18. Springer, Heidelberg (2013). https://doi.org/10.1007/978-3-642-40203-6_1
24. Damgård, I., Pastro, V., Smart, N., Zakarias, S.: Multiparty computation from somewhat homomorphic encryption. In: Safavi-Naini, R., Canetti, R. (eds.) CRYPTO 2012. LNCS, vol. 7417, pp. 643–662. Springer, Heidelberg (2012). https://doi.org/10.1007/978-3-642-32009-5_38
25. David, B., et al.: Perfect MPC over layered graphs. In: Handschuh, H., Lysyanskaya, A. (eds.) CRYPTO 2023. LNCS, vol. 14081, pp. 360–392. Springer, Cham (2023). https://doi.org/10.1007/978-3-031-38557-5_12
26. Dimakis, A.G., Godfrey, P.B., Wu, Y., Wainwright, M.J., Ramchandran, K.: Network coding for distributed storage systems. IEEE Trans. Inf. Theory **56**(9), 4539–4551 (2010)
27. Fitzi, M., Hirt, M., Maurer, U.: Trading correctness for privacy in unconditional multi-party computation. In: Krawczyk, H. (ed.) CRYPTO 1998. LNCS, vol. 1462, pp. 121–136. Springer, Heidelberg (1998). https://doi.org/10.1007/BFb0055724
28. Garay, J.A., Gennaro, R., Jutla, C., Rabin, T.: Secure distributed storage and retrieval. Theoret. Comput. Sci. **243**(1), 363–389 (2000)

29. Gentry, C., et al.: YOSO: you only speak once. In: Malkin, T., Peikert, C. (eds.) CRYPTO 2021. LNCS, vol. 12826, pp. 64–93. Springer, Cham (2021). https://doi.org/10.1007/978-3-030-84245-1_3
30. Gopalan, P., Huang, C., Simitci, H., Yekhanin, S.: On the locality of codeword symbols. IEEE Trans. Inf. Theory **58**(11), 6925–6934 (2012)
31. Goparaju, S., Fazeli, A., Vardy, A.: Minimum storage regenerating codes for all parameters. IEEE Trans. Inf. Theory **63**(10), 6318–6328 (2017)
32. Goyal, V., Li, H., Ostrovsky, R., Polychroniadou, A., Song, Y.: ATLAS: efficient and scalable MPC in the honest majority setting. In: Malkin, T., Peikert, C. (eds.) CRYPTO 2021. LNCS, vol. 12826, pp. 244–274. Springer, Cham (2021). https://doi.org/10.1007/978-3-030-84245-1_9
33. Goyal, V., Polychroniadou, A., Song, Y.: Unconditional communication-efficient MPC via Hall's marriage theorem. In: Malkin, T., Peikert, C. (eds.) CRYPTO 2021. LNCS, vol. 12826, pp. 275–304. Springer, Cham (2021). https://doi.org/10.1007/978-3-030-84245-1_10
34. Goyal, V., Song, Y., Zhu, C.: Guaranteed output delivery comes free in honest majority MPC. In: Micciancio, D., Ristenpart, T. (eds.) CRYPTO 2020. LNCS, vol. 12171, pp. 618–646. Springer, Cham (2020). https://doi.org/10.1007/978-3-030-56880-1_22
35. Guang, X., Lu, J., Fu, F.: Repairable threshold secret sharing schemes. CoRR, abs/1410.7190 (2014)
36. Guo, Y., Pass, R., Shi, E.: Synchronous, with a chance of partition tolerance. In: Boldyreva, A., Micciancio, D. (eds.) CRYPTO 2019. LNCS, vol. 11692, pp. 499–529. Springer, Cham (2019). https://doi.org/10.1007/978-3-030-26948-7_18
37. Guruswami, V., Xing, C., Yuan, C.: How long can optimal locally repairable codes be? IEEE Trans. Inf. Theory **65**(6), 3662–3670 (2019)
38. Han, J., Lastras-Montano, L.A.: Reliable memories with subline accesses. In: 2007 IEEE International Symposium on Information Theory, pp. 2531–2535 (2007)
39. Herzberg, A., Jarecki, S., Krawczyk, H., Yung, M.: Proactive secret sharing or: how to cope with perpetual leakage. In: Coppersmith, D. (ed.) CRYPTO 1995. LNCS, vol. 963, pp. 339–352. Springer, Heidelberg (1995). https://doi.org/10.1007/3-540-44750-4_27
40. Huang, C., Chen, M., Li, J.: Pyramid codes: flexible schemes to trade space for access efficiency in reliable data storage systems. In: Sixth IEEE International Symposium on Network Computing and Applications (NCA 2007), pp. 79–86 (2007)
41. Jin, L., Ma, L., Xing, C.: Construction of optimal locally repairable codes via automorphism groups of rational function fields. IEEE Trans. Inf. Theory **66**(1), 210–221 (2020)
42. Kadhe, S., Sprintson, A.: Security for minimum storage regenerating codes and locally repairable codes. In: 2017 IEEE International Symposium on Information Theory (ISIT), pp. 1028–1032 (2017)
43. Keller, M., Orsini, E., Scholl, P.: MASCOT: faster malicious arithmetic secure computation with oblivious transfer. In: Proceedings of the 2016 ACM SIGSAC Conference on Computer and Communications Security, pp. 830–842 (2016)
44. Keller, M., Pastro, V., Rotaru, D.: Overdrive: making SPDZ great again. In: Nielsen, J.B., Rijmen, V. (eds.) EUROCRYPT 2018. LNCS, vol. 10822, pp. 158–189. Springer, Cham (2018). https://doi.org/10.1007/978-3-319-78372-7_6
45. Kher, V., Kim, Y.: Securing distributed storage: challenges, techniques, and systems. In: Proceedings of the 2005 ACM Workshop on Storage Security and Survivability, StorageSS 2005, pp. 9–25. Association for Computing Machinery, New York, NY, USA (2005)

46. Laing, T.M., Stinson, D.R.: A survey and refinement of repairable threshold schemes. J. Math. Cryptol. **12**(1), 57–81 (2018)
47. Lavaur, T., Lacan, J.: zkBeacon: proven randomness beacon based on zero-knowledge verifiable computation. In: di Vimercati, S.D.C., Samarati, P. (eds.) Proceedings of the 19th International Conference on Security and Cryptography, SECRYPT 2022, Lisbon, Portugal, 11–13 July 2022, pp. 406–414. SCITEPRESS (2022)
48. Li, J., Li, T., Ren, J.: Secure regenerating code. In: 2014 IEEE Global Communications Conference, pp. 770–774 (2014)
49. Li, R., Yang, S., Rao, Y., Fu, Q.: On binary locally repairable codes with distance four. Finite Fields Appl. **72**, 101793 (2021)
50. Li, X., Ma, L., Xing, C.: Optimal locally repairable codes via elliptic curves. IEEE Trans. Inf. Theory **65**(1), 108–117 (2019)
51. Ma, L., Xing, C.: A survey on optimal locally repairable codes (in Chinese). SCIENTIA SINICA Mathematica, 1–18, 2–21 (2021)
52. Martínez-Peñas, U., Kschischang, F.R.: Universal and dynamic locally repairable codes with maximal recoverability via sum-rank codes. IEEE Trans. Inf. Theory **65**(12), 7790–7805 (2019)
53. Papailiopoulos, D.S., Dimakis, A.G.: Locally repairable codes. IEEE Trans. Inf. Theory **60**(10), 5843–5855 (2014)
54. Pawar, S., El Rouayheb, S., Ramchandran, K.: On secure distributed data storage under repair dynamics. In: 2010 IEEE International Symposium on Information Theory, pp. 2543–2547 (2010)
55. Rachuri, R., Scholl, P.: Le Mans: dynamic and fluid MPC for dishonest majority. In: Dodis, Y., Shrimpton, T. (eds.) CRYPTO 2022. LNCS, vol. 13507, pp. 719–749. Springer, Cham (2022). https://doi.org/10.1007/978-3-031-15802-5_25
56. Raikwar, M., Gligoroski, D.: SoK: decentralized randomness beacon protocols. In: Nguyen, K., Yang, G., Guo, F., Susilo, W. (eds.) ACISP 2022. LNCS, vol. 13494, pp. 420–446. Springer, Cham (2022). https://doi.org/10.1007/978-3-031-22301-3_21
57. Rashmi, K.V., Shah, N.B., Kumar, P.V.: Optimal exact-regenerating codes for distributed storage at the MSR and MBR points via a product-matrix construction. IEEE Trans. Inf. Theory **57**(8), 5227–5239 (2011)
58. Raviv, N., Silberstein, N., Etzion, T.: Constructions of high-rate minimum storage regenerating codes over small fields. In: 2016 IEEE International Symposium on Information Theory (ISIT), pp. 61–65 (2016)
59. Rawat, A.S.: A note on secure minimum storage regenerating codes. CoRR, abs/1608.01732 (2016)
60. Rawat, A.S.: Secrecy capacity of minimum storage regenerating codes. In: 2017 IEEE International Symposium on Information Theory (ISIT), pp. 1406–1410 (2017)
61. Sasidharan, B., Agarwal, G.K., Kumar, P.V.: A high-rate MSR code with polynomial sub-packetization level. In: 2015 IEEE International Symposium on Information Theory (ISIT), pp. 2051–2055 (2015)
62. Saxena, N., Tsudik, G., Yi, J.H.: Efficient node admission and certificateless secure communication in short-lived MANETs. IEEE Trans. Parallel Distrib. Syst. **20**(2), 158–170 (2008)
63. Shah, N.B., Rashmi, K.V., Kumar, P.V.: Information-theoretically secure regenerating codes for distributed storage. In: 2011 IEEE Global Telecommunications Conference - GLOBECOM 2011, pp. 1–5 (2011)

64. Shah, N.B., Rashmi, K.V., Kumar, P.V., Ramchandran, K.: Distributed storage codes with repair-by-transfer and nonachievability of interior points on the storage-bandwidth tradeoff. IEEE Trans. Inf. Theory **58**(3), 1837–1852 (2012)
65. Shamir, A.: How to share a secret. Commun. ACM **22**(11), 612–613 (1979)
66. Silberstein, N., Rawat, A.S., Koyluoglu, O.O., Vishwanath, S.: Optimal locally repairable codes via rank-metric codes. In: 2013 IEEE International Symposium on Information Theory, pp. 1819–1823 (2013)
67. Stinson, D.R., Wei, R.: Combinatorial repairability for threshold schemes. Des. Codes Cryptography **86**(1), 195–210 (2018)
68. Suh, C., Ramchandran, K.: On the existence of optimal exact-repair MDS codes for distributed storage (2010)
69. Tamo, I., Barg, A.: A family of optimal locally recoverable codes. IEEE Trans. Inf. Theory **60**(8), 4661–4676 (2014)
70. Tandon, R., Amuru, S., Clancy, T.C., Buehrer, R.M.: Toward optimal secure distributed storage systems with exact repair. IEEE Trans. Inf. Theory **62**(6), 3477–3492 (2016)
71. Wu, Y., Li, D., Wang, F.: Secret sharing member expansion protocol based on ECC. Open Cybern. Systemics J. **8**(1) (2014)
72. Ye, M., Barg, A.: Explicit constructions of optimal-access MDS codes with nearly optimal sub-packetization. IEEE Trans. Inf. Theory **63**(10), 6307–6317 (2017)
73. Ye, M., Qiu, H., Wang, Y., Zhou, Z., Zheng, F., Ma, T.: A method of repairing single node failure in the distributed storage system based on the regenerating-code and a hybrid genetic algorithm. Neurocomputing (2020)
74. Yu, J., Kong, F., Hao, R.: Publicly verifiable secret sharing with enrollment ability. In: Eighth ACIS International Conference on Software Engineering, Artificial Intelligence, Networking, and Parallel/Distributed Computing (SNPD 2007), vol. 3, pp. 194–199. IEEE (2007)

Zero Knowledge Proofs

Zero Knowledge Protocols and Signatures from the Restricted Syndrome Decoding Problem

Marco Baldi[1], Sebastian Bitzer[2], Alessio Pavoni[1], Paolo Santini[1(✉)], Antonia Wachter-Zeh[2], and Violetta Weger[2]

[1] Department for Information Engineering, Polytechnic University of Marche, Brecce Bianche 12, 60131 Ancona, Italy
{m.baldi,p.santini}@staff.univpm.it

[2] Institute for Communications Engineering, Technical University of Munich, Theresienstraße 90, 80333 Munich, Germany
{sebastian.bitzer,antonia.wachter-zeh,violetta.weger}@tum.de

Abstract. The Restricted Syndrome Decoding Problem (R-SDP) corresponds to the Syndrome Decoding Problem (SDP) with the additional constraint that all entries of the solution error vector must live in a fixed subset of the finite field. In this paper, we study how this problem can be applied to the construction of signatures derived from Zero-Knowledge (ZK) protocols. First, we show that R-SDP appears to be well-suited for this type of application: ZK protocols relying on SDP can easily be modified to use R-SDP, resulting in significant reductions in the communication cost. We then introduce and analyze a variant of R-SDP, which we call R-SDP(G), with the property that solution vectors can be represented with a number of bits that is slightly larger than the security parameter (which clearly provides an ultimate lower bound). This enables the design of competitive ZK protocols. We show that existing ZK protocols can greatly benefit from the use of R-SDP, achieving signature sizes in the order of 7 kB, which are smaller than those of several other schemes submitted to NIST's additional call for post-quantum digital signatures.

Keywords: Code-based Cryptography · Post-Quantum Cryptography · Restricted Errors · Signature Scheme · Syndrome Decoding Problem

1 Introduction

In 2023, the National Institute of Standards and Technology (NIST) reopened the standardization call for post-quantum cryptography, targeting solely signa-

The original version of the chapter has been revised. The acknowledgment section have been corrected. A correction to this chapter can be found at
https://doi.org/10.1007/978-3-031-57722-2_15

Q. Tang and V. Teague (Eds.): PKC 2024, LNCS 14602, pp. 243–274, 2024.
https://doi.org/10.1007/978-3-031-57722-2_8

ture schemes, preferably not based on structured lattices.[1] Arguably, this additional call has shifted the focus of the cryptographic community to finding new and efficient post-quantum signature schemes.

In particular, over the last years, significant attention has been dedicated to schemes obtained via the Fiat-Shamir transform of a Zero-Knowledge (ZK) interactive protocol. As a matter of fact, signatures derived from this paradigm are now perceived as one of the most promising solutions. This is visible within the round 1 submissions to NIST's additional call: out of the 40 submitted schemes, 15 candidates are based on such a paradigm.

The Fiat-Shamir transform works by making a ZK protocol non-interactive: the signer simulates an execution of the protocol, binding it to the message-to-be-signed (thanks to the one-wayness of hash functions), and the signature is composed by the *transcript*, i.e., the list of messages that are exchanged during the protocol execution. When the *soundness error* of the considered protocol is too high, a certain number of repetitions is needed to avoid efficient forgeries; in such a case, the number of exchanged messages increases, and the signature size grows, as well. Historically, the large signature size has been the Achilles' heel of these types of signature schemes. However, the panorama has greatly changed in the past few years thanks to various techniques and optimizations capable of compressing signatures. One of the most popular approaches consists of designing protocols with very low soundness error; this reduces the number of repetitions and, consequently, leads to shorter transcripts. In particular, for problems related to decoding (e.g., the Syndrome Decoding Problem (SDP) and the Permuted Kernel Problem (PKP)), popular approaches are the so-called protocol-with-helper [14] and the Multi-Party Computation (MPC) in-the-Head (MPCitH) paradigm [28].

1.1 Our Contribution

In this paper, we study ZK protocols derived from the Restricted Syndrome Problem (R-SDP), introduced in [8][2], which adds to the classical SDP the constraint that each entry must live in a fixed subset $\mathbb{E}$ of the underlying finite field. We first describe the problem in its full generality and then move to the particular version with full Hamming weight and $\mathbb{E}$ being a cyclic subgroup of the multiplicative group.

We show that the restricted setting can be tailored so that many existing ZK protocols receive a significant reduction in the communication cost. This happens because of two phenomena. First, in R-SDP the error can have a much larger Hamming weight, even maximum (that is, no null entry), while still having a unique solution to the problem. This increases the cost of Information Set Decoding (ISD) algorithms, and, as a matter of fact, with R-SDP we can achieve the same security level using smaller codes. Another important improvement is due to the transformations used in ZK protocols. For the classical SDP, they

[1] See, e.g., the official NIST call https://csrc.nist.gov/csrc/media/Projects/pqc-dig-sig/documents/call-for-proposals-dig-sig-sept-2022.pdf.

[2] A similar idea was already mentioned in [37], but it was not used in conjunction with a decoding problem.

are given by a monomial transformation (a permutation with scaling factors), as these are the transitive linear maps acting on the Hamming sphere. For the new R-SDP, component-wise multiplication with restricted vectors is enough since these linear maps act transitively on the set of restricted vectors. This yields another significant reduction in the communication cost.

Then, we derive a special version of R-SDP, called R-SDP(G), with which the performances of ZK protocols can be further boosted. With R-SDP(G), the solution space is a subgroup $G \leq \mathbb{E}^n$, whose size can be tuned to minimize the communication cost. Namely, for a security of λ bits, R-SDP(G) uses a solution space G of size $2^{(1+\alpha)\lambda}$, where $\alpha \geq 0$ is a small constant (say, $\alpha \leq 1$). From a mathematical point of view, G is a group that acts transitively and freely on itself: this implies that we can sample any restricted object (i.e., secret keys and hiding transformations) from G and represent its elements using only $(1+\alpha)\lambda \leq 2\lambda$ bits. The value of α is chosen from a conservative perspective so that existing attacks cannot be sped up considering the knowledge of G.

Finally, we apply R-SDP and R-SDP(G) to modern ZK protocols, namely the GPS scheme [26] and BG scheme for the Permuted Kernel Problem (PKP) [15]. We call the newly derived schemes R-GPS and R-BG, respectively, and show that moving to R-SDP and R-SDP(G) leads to significant reductions in the communication cost and in signature sizes, as well. In fact, for R-GPS, we almost halve the signature sizes, while for R-BG we achieve important savings: using R-SDP(G), we obtain signatures with a size of 7.8 kB (instead of 10.0 kB) for the fast variant, and 7.2 kB (instead of 8.9 kB) for the short variant. We also provide timings for a (non-optimized) Proof of concept implementation for R-BG, which confirms that the proposed protocols are practical.

The work in this paper lies the foundation of CROSS [7], one of the schemes submitted to the NIST call for additional signatures. CROSS uses R-SDP and R-SDP(G), applied to a basic ZK protocol inspired from [17], with soundness error $\approx 1/2$. Signature sizes are in the same ballpark as those of other ZK/M-PCitH schemes, but CROSS is one of the fastest schemes in this category. This is made possible by using R-SDP and R-SDP(G). Indeed, techniques to reduce the soundness error normally come with the price of some significant computational overhead. Since using R-SDP and R-SDP(G) leads to very compact messages, CROSS can use a simple but highly efficient protocol and still achieve sufficiently short signatures.

1.2 Paper Organization

Section 2 settles the notation we use and gives (minimal) preliminaries about linear codes and ZK protocols. In Sect. 3, we formally introduce R-SDP, show how it can be solved using Information Set Decoding (ISD), and show that R-SDP can be much harder than SDP. We then move to the special case of full-weight vectors and $\mathbb{E}$ being a subgroup of $\mathbb{F}_q^*$, describing generic decoders tailored to this setting. In Sect. 4, we show how R-SDP can be applied to ZK protocols, using the well-known example of CVE [17], and argue why this leads to very promising schemes. In Sect. 5, we introduce another variant of R-SDP, called R-SDP(G), and analyze its security. In Sect. 6, we apply R-SDP and R-SDP(G) to the GPS [26] and BG [15] protocols, resulting in the schemes called

R-GPS and R-BG. We compare the two schemes to existing ones in Sect. 7 and show their competitiveness. Finally, Sect. 8 concludes the paper.

2 Notation and Preliminaries

We use $[a; b]$ to denote the set of all reals $x \in \mathbb{R}$ such that $a \leq x \leq b$. For a finite set A, the expression $a \xleftarrow{\$} A$ means that a is chosen uniformly at random from A. In addition, we denote by $|A|$ the cardinality of A, by A^C its complement and by $A_0 = A \cup \{0\}$. As usual, for q being a positive integer, we denote by $\mathbb{Z}_q = \mathbb{Z}/q\mathbb{Z}$ the ring of integers modulo q. For a prime power q, we denote by $\mathbb{F}_q$ the finite field of order q and by $\mathbb{F}_q^*$ its multiplicative group. For $g \in \mathbb{F}_q^*$, we denote by $\mathrm{ord}(g)$ its multiplicative order.

We use uppercase (resp. lowercase) bold letters to indicate matrices (resp. vectors). If J is a set, we use $\mathbf{A}_J$ to denote the matrix formed by the columns of $\mathbf{A}$ indexed by J; analogous notation is used for vectors. The identity matrix of size m is denoted as $\mathbf{I}_m$. We use $\mathbf{0}$ to denote the null matrix or the null vector without specifying dimensions (which will always be clear from the context). We denote by S_n the symmetric group of order n. Finally, we denote by $h_q(x) = x\log_q(q-1) - x\log_q(x) - (1-x)\log_q(1-x)$ the q-ary entropy function.

2.1 Cryptographic Tools

Throughout the paper, we adopt conventional cryptographic notations, e.g., λ indicates the security parameter. Standard functions are always implicitly defined, e.g., Hash indicates a secure hash function with digests of size 2λ. We focus on Zero-Knowledge (ZK) protocols, that is, interactive protocols in which a *prover* aims to convince a *verifier* that she knows a secret that verifies some public statement. Informally, a protocol achieves the ZK property when the interaction between the two parties reveals no information about the specific secret held by the prover. We say that a protocol has *soundness error* ε if a cheating prover, i.e., someone that does not know the secret, can convince the honest verifier with probability ε. When t parallel repetitions of a (public coin) ZK protocol with soundness error ε are considered, and the verifier only accepts if each of the repetitions is accepted, we obtain a new protocol with soundness error ε^t. Due to lack of space, we do not provide formal definitions for such properties, as they are standard and can be found in the literature (e.g., [24] nicely recaps all the necessary background).

ZK protocols can be turned into signature schemes with the Fiat-Shamir transform [25]. For 5-pass protocols (i.e., the number of messages that are exchanged in each execution is 5), the number of parallel executions shall be chosen taking into account the attack in [30]. Namely, setting $\varepsilon^t < 2^{-\lambda}$ may not be enough to protect against forgery attacks. The authors of [30] describe how to properly choose t, and when needed, we use their formula (e.g., Eq. (9)).

2.2 Linear Codes

A *linear code* $\mathscr{C}$ over the finite field $\mathbb{F}_q$ with length n and dimension $k \leq n$ is a k-dimensional linear subspace of $\mathbb{F}_q^n$. We say that a code of length n and dimension k has rate $R = \frac{k}{n}$ and redundancy $r = n - k$.

A compact representation for a code is a *generator matrix*, that is, a full-rank $\mathbf{G} \in \mathbb{F}_q^{k \times n}$ such that $\mathscr{C} = \{\mathbf{uG} \mid \mathbf{u} \in \mathbb{F}_q^k\}$. Equivalently, one can represent a code through a full-rank $\mathbf{H} \in \mathbb{F}_q^{r \times n}$, called *parity-check matrix*, such that $\mathscr{C} = \{\mathbf{c} \in \mathbb{F}_q^n \mid \mathbf{cH}^\top = \mathbf{0}\}$. The *syndrome* of some $\mathbf{x} \in \mathbb{F}_q^n$ is the length-r vector $\mathbf{s} = \mathbf{xH}^\top$. A set $J \subseteq \{1, \ldots, n\}$ of size k is called *information set* for $\mathscr{C}$ if $|\mathscr{C}_J| = q^k$, where $\mathscr{C}_J = \{\mathbf{c}_J \mid \mathbf{c} \in \mathscr{C}\}$. It directly follows that $\mathbf{G}_J$ and $\mathbf{H}_{J^C}$ are invertible matrices. We say that a generator matrix, respectively, a parity-check matrix, is in systematic form (with respect to the information set J), if $\mathbf{G}_J = \mathbf{I}_k$, respectively $\mathbf{H}_{J^C} = \mathbf{I}_r$.

We endow the vector space $\mathbb{F}_q^n$ with the *Hamming metric*: given $\mathbf{x} \in \mathbb{F}_q^n$, its Hamming weight $\mathrm{wt}(\mathbf{x})$ is the number of non-zero entries. The *minimum distance* of a linear code is given by $d(\mathscr{C}) = \min\{\mathrm{wt}(\mathbf{c}) \mid \mathbf{c} \in \mathscr{C}, \mathbf{c} \neq \mathbf{0}\}$. The *relative minimum distance* of a code is then denoted by $\delta = d(\mathscr{C})/n$. It is well known that random codes with sufficiently large length n attain the Gilbert-Varshamov (GV) bound: for a random code, we may assume $\delta = h_q^{-1}(1 - R)$.

Code-based cryptography usually relies on the following NP-complete problem [11,13].

Problem 1 Syndrome Decoding Problem (SDP)
Given $\mathbf{H} \in \mathbb{F}_q^{r \times n}, t \in \mathbb{N}, \mathbf{s} \in \mathbb{F}_q^r$, *decide if there exists* $\mathbf{e} \in \mathbb{F}_q^n$, *such that* $wt(\mathbf{e}) \leq t$ *and* $\mathbf{eH}^\top = \mathbf{s}$?

The hardest instances of SDP are typically those with the largest value of t and, at the same time, an expected unique solution. When random codes are employed (i.e., $\mathbf{H}$ is uniformly random over $\mathbb{F}_q$), this corresponds to choosing $t = \delta n$, as the average number of solutions is given by $q^{n(h_q(\delta)-1+R)}$.

3 The Restricted Syndrome Decoding Problem

Let us consider some subset $\mathbb{E}$ of $\mathbb{F}_q^*$, denote by $\mathbb{E}_0 = \mathbb{E} \cup \{0\}$ and by

$$\mathscr{S}_w^{\mathbb{E}} := \{\mathbf{x} \in \mathbb{E}_0^n \mid \mathrm{wt}(\mathbf{x}) = w\}$$

the *Hamming sphere with radius w and restriction* $\mathbb{E}$. Clearly, for $\mathbb{E}$ of size z, we have $\left|\mathscr{S}_w^{\mathbb{E}}\right| = \binom{n}{w} z^w$. The Restricted Syndrome Decoding Problem (R-SDP), introduced in [8], reads as follows.

Problem 2 Restricted Syndrome Decoding Problem (R-SDP)
Given $\mathbf{H} \in \mathbb{F}_q^{r \times n}$, $\mathbf{s} \in \mathbb{F}_q^r$ *and* $w \in \mathbb{N}$, *decide if there exists* $\mathbf{e} \in \mathscr{S}_w^{\mathbb{E}}$, *such that* $\mathbf{eH}^\top = \mathbf{s}$.

It is easy to see that R-SDP is strongly related to other well-known hard problems. For instance, when $\mathbb{E} = \mathbb{F}_q^*$, the R-SDP corresponds to the classical SDP and if $\mathbb{E} = \{1\}$, the R-SDP is similar to the Subset Sum Problem (SSP) over finite fields.

Consequently, it is unsurprising that R-SDP is NP-complete for any choice of $\mathbb{E}$. The proof is essentially the same as in [8], where the authors focus on the case $\mathbb{E} = \{\pm x_1, \pm x_2, \cdots, \pm x_a\}$. Another proof can be immediately obtained from [38], whenever $1 \in \mathbb{E}$.

We always consider that the R-SDP instance is chosen uniformly at random. We expect to have on average (at most) a unique solution if w is such that

$$\binom{n}{w} z^w q^{k-n} \leq 1. \tag{1}$$

Let $W = w/n \in [0;1]$; since $\binom{n}{w} = 2^{n \cdot h_2(W) \cdot \left(1+o(1)\right)}$, we rewrite Eq. (1) as

$$2^{n(h_2(W)+W\log_2(z)-(1-R)\log_2(q))} \leq 1.$$

Let W^* be the maximum value of W for which a random instance of R-SDP is expected to have a unique solution, that is

$$W^* = \max\left\{W \in [0;1] \mid h_2(W) + W\log_2(z) - (1-R)\log_2(q) \leq 0\right\}. \tag{2}$$

Comparing this to the GV bound, we can see that with the R-SDP, we can choose a much larger weight w and still guarantee the uniqueness of the solution. This is a crucial difference with SDP, since a high Hamming weight corresponds to an exponentially large number of solutions [21]. Note that if $\log_2(z) \leq (1-R)\log_2(q)$, we even have uniqueness for full-weight vectors.

3.1 Solving R-SDP

To compare the computational complexity of R-SDP with classical SDP, we provide an adaption of the Stern/Dumer algorithm [23,35], which works for any choice of $\mathbb{E}$. Notice that, depending on the structure of $\mathbb{E}$, this algorithm can be improved using *representations*. For this, we refer to the extended version [9] of this manuscript.

For the sake of completeness, we provide full details for the Stern/Dumer algorithm to solve R-SDP in the following. As a first step, we choose a set $J \subset \{1, \ldots, n\}$ of size $k+\ell$ which contains an information set and perform a Partial Gaussian Elimination (PGE) on $\mathbf{H}$ in the columns indexed by J, obtaining $\widetilde{\mathbf{H}}$, and perform the same operations on the syndrome. For simplicity, let us assume that J is chosen in the first $k+\ell$ positions, thus

$$\mathbf{e}\widetilde{\mathbf{H}}^\top = (\mathbf{e}_1, \mathbf{e}_2)\begin{pmatrix} \mathbf{H}_1 & \mathbf{I}_{r-\ell} \\ \mathbf{H}_2 & \mathbf{0} \end{pmatrix}^\top = (\mathbf{s}_1, \mathbf{s}_2),$$

where $\mathbf{e}_1 \in \mathbb{E}_0^{k+\ell}, \mathbf{e}_2 \in \mathbb{E}_0^{r-\ell}, \mathbf{H}_1 \in \mathbb{F}_q^{(r-\ell)\times(k+\ell)}, \mathbf{H}_2 \in \mathbb{F}_q^{\ell\times(k+\ell)}, \mathbf{s}_1 \in \mathbb{F}_q^{r-\ell}$ and $\mathbf{s}_2 \in \mathbb{F}_q^{\ell}$. Thus, we get two syndrome equations, being

$$\mathbf{e}_1\mathbf{H}_1^\top + \mathbf{e}_2 = \mathbf{s}_1, \quad \mathbf{e}_1\mathbf{H}_2^\top = \mathbf{s}_2.$$

We solve these equations by requiring that $\mathbf{e}_1$ has weight v; for each such $\mathbf{e}_1$, it is enough to check that $\mathbf{s}_1 - \mathbf{e}_1\mathbf{H}_1^\top$ has weight $w - v$ and entries in $\mathbb{E}_0$. To solve the smaller instance given by $\mathbf{H}_2, \mathbf{s}_2$ and v, we use a collision search.

To improve readability, we drop any rounding operations and implicitly assume that all parameters can be chosen as integers. For this, we write $\mathbf{e}_1 = (\mathbf{x}_1, \mathbf{x}_2)$ with $\mathbf{x}_i$ of length $(k+\ell)/2$ and weight $v/2$. Thus, we also split $\mathbf{H}_2 = (\mathbf{A}_1, \mathbf{A}_2)$ and construct the two lists

$$\mathscr{L}_1 := \{(\mathbf{x}_1, \mathbf{x}_1\mathbf{A}_1^\top) \mid \mathbf{x}_1 \in \mathbb{E}_0^{(k+\ell)/2}, \mathrm{wt}(\mathbf{x}_1) = v/2\},$$
$$\mathscr{L}_2 := \{(\mathbf{x}_2, \mathbf{s}_2 - \mathbf{x}_2\mathbf{A}_2^\top) \mid \mathbf{x}_2 \in \mathbb{E}_0^{(k+\ell)/2}, \mathrm{wt}(\mathbf{x}_2) = v/2\}.$$

We then check for collisions, that is, all pairs $(\mathbf{x}_1, \mathbf{a}) \in \mathscr{L}_1$, $(\mathbf{x}_2, \mathbf{a}) \in \mathscr{L}_2$. The two lists are of size $L = \binom{(k+\ell)/2}{v/2} z^{v/2}$ and the collision search costs approximately $L^2 q^{-\ell} = \binom{k+\ell}{v} z^v q^{-\ell}$. The cost of this restricted Stern/Dumer algorithm is then in

$$O\left(\binom{n}{w}\binom{(k+\ell)/2}{v/2}^{-2}\binom{r-\ell}{w-v}^{-1} \cdot \left(\binom{(k+\ell)/2}{v/2} z^{v/2} + \binom{k+\ell}{v} z^v q^{-\ell}\right)\right).$$

Remark 1. Let $L = \ell/n$, then in the case of $w = n$, the optimized cost of Stern's algorithm is in $O\left(2^{F(R,q,z)n}\right)$, where

$$F(R, q, z) = \min_{0 \le L \le 1-R} \left\{\left(\tfrac{R+L}{2}\right)\log_2(z),\ (R+L)\log_2(z) - L\log_2(q)\right\}.$$

In Fig. 1, we give the cost of Stern's algorithm for random R-SDP instances, where we choose $W = W^*$, i.e., the maximal weight that guarantees uniqueness. Note that the cost at the point $z = q-1$ corresponds to the cost of Stern on a random SDP instance and thus, we can see that R-SDP with $z < q-1$ has a much larger cost than the SDP with the same parameters q, n, R.

The security of R-SDP highly depends on the exact shape of $\mathbb{E}$. There are, indeed, several choices that lead to a somewhat easier problem. For instance, one can choose an extension field $\mathbb{F}_{p^m}$, for some prime p and integer m and $\mathbb{E} \subset \mathbb{F}_{p^m}^*$. In this case, several choices of $\mathbb{E}$ lead to an easier problem, e.g. $\mathbb{E} = \mathbb{F}_p^*$. To avoid this possibility, we directly restrict our considerations to prime fields. As another suboptimal choice, one can choose rather large values for q and $\mathbb{E}_0 = \{0, 1\}$. Thus, solvers for subset sum problems may be used [12], where one adds some elements to the search space.

To circumvent possible speedups from such techniques, we restrict ourselves to particular choices of error sets $\mathbb{E}$ of relatively large size. For more details on safe choices of $\mathbb{E}$ and attacks using [12], we refer to the extended version [9] of this manuscript.

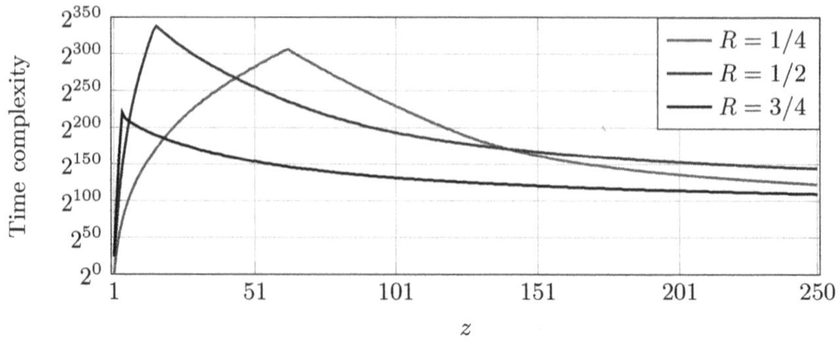

Fig. 1. Cost of Stern's algorithm for random R-SDP instances with $q = 251$, $n = 256$, $W = W^*$ and several rates R.

Let us also quickly comment on other solvers for R-SDP. Note that statistical decoding for SDP [16,22,29] is based on the bias towards 0 of $\langle \mathbf{e}, \mathbf{h} \rangle$ for sparse vectors $\mathbf{e}$ and $\mathbf{h}$. For R-SDP with full weight vectors, the sought error vector $\mathbf{e}$ is not sparse, and the multiplicative structure of $\mathbb{E}$ is lost in the additions of the inner product. On the other hand, algebraic attacks that exploit the small order of the entries of $\mathbf{e}$ cannot be mounted straightforwardly, as the multiplicative structure of $\mathbb{E}$ is incompatible with the additive linearity of the syndrome computation. Also, Gröbner bases attacks do not give, apparently, any speed up over the considered ISD algorithms as observed in [7].

4 Building ZK Protocols from the R-SDP: A Preliminary Analysis

This section describes how standard approaches to building ZK protocols can be converted to use R-SDP.

The protocols we consider achieve zero knowledge thanks to the following fundamental property: there must be a set X and a set of maps $\mathscr{T}$ that act transitively on X, with the property that

$$\forall x \in X, \sigma(x) \text{ is uniformly distributed over } X \text{ when } \sigma \xleftarrow{\$} \mathscr{T}. \tag{3}$$

Consequently, when $x \in X$ is the secret key, revealing $y = \sigma(x)$ without revealing σ leaks no information about x.

For schemes based on the SDP, Property (3) is satisfied by choosing X as the Hamming sphere with some radius w and $\mathscr{T}$ as the set of linear isometries, i.e., the set of monomial transformations. A monomial transformation can be described as $(\pi, \mathbf{v})$ with $\pi \in S_n$ a permutation and $\mathbf{v} \in (\mathbb{F}_q^*)^n$. The action of $\sigma = (\pi, \mathbf{v})$ on a vector $\mathbf{a} = (a_1, \ldots, a_n) \in \mathbb{F}_q^n$ corresponds to

$$\sigma(\mathbf{a}) = \left(v_1 a_{\pi^{-1}(1)}, \ldots, v_n a_{\pi^{-1}(n)}\right) = \pi(\mathbf{a}) \star \mathbf{v},$$

where $\star$ denotes component-wise multiplication.

4.1 Zero Knowledge Masking of Restricted Vectors

To use R-SDP, we will make use of the following choices. First, we set

$$\mathbb{E} = \left\{g^j \mid j \in \{0, 1, \dots, z-1\}\right\},$$

where $g \in \mathbb{F}_q^*$ has multiplicative order $z < q-1$. In other words, we choose $\mathbb{E}$ as the cyclic subgroup of $\mathbb{F}_q^*$ which is generated by g and, to have $\mathbb{E} \neq \mathbb{F}_q^*$, we require that g is not primitive. Then, we set $X := \mathscr{S}_w^{\mathbb{E}}$, i.e., choose the secret key as an element of the restricted Hamming sphere with radius w. Also, we set $\mathscr{T} := S_n \times \mathbb{E}^n$, which contains only the monomial transformations having restricted scaling coefficients. It is easy to see that, with these choices, Property (3) holds. Notice that the action of any $\sigma := (\pi, \mathbf{v}) \in \mathscr{T}$ is given by

$$\sigma(\mathbf{a}) = \pi(\mathbf{a}) \star \mathbf{v} = \pi(\mathbf{a}) \star \left(g^{i_1}, \dots, g^{i_n}\right), \tag{4}$$

with $(i_1, \dots, i_n) \in \{0, 1, \cdots, z-1\}^n$. We refer to $\mathbb{E}^n$ as *restricted group* and to $\mathscr{T}$ as the group of *restricted maps*. Notice that $(\mathbb{E}^n, \star)$ is an abelian group: we investigate its properties in Sect. 5.

We observe that, when $w = n$, i.e., we have full weight, we can choose a simpler description for $\mathscr{T}$. Indeed, we have $\mathscr{S}_w^{\mathbb{E}} = \mathbb{E}^n$ and $\mathscr{T} := \mathbb{E}^n$, that is, the restricted maps can be represented by restricted full-weight vectors. In fact, for any $\mathbf{e}, \mathbf{e}' \in \mathbb{E}^n$, there exists a unique $\sigma \in \mathscr{T}$ such that $\mathbf{e}' = \sigma(\mathbf{e})$. Moreover, $\sigma := \mathbf{v}$ for some $\mathbf{v} \in \mathbb{E}^n$ and $\sigma(\mathbf{e}) = \mathbf{e} \star \mathbf{v}$. More interesting properties of this setting can be found in Sect. 5. For the moment, it is sufficient to anticipate that this choice is the one that will yield the best performances for ZK protocols.

4.2 The Case Study of CVE with R-SDP

The CVE protocol [17] has been, historically, the first ZK protocol based on non-binary SDP with low Hamming weight. It has been derived from the famous protocol by Stern [36] and Shamir's permuted kernel protocol [33]. Modern solutions, such as [26], are built on CVE. Hence, it makes sense to start by adapting this protocol to the R-SDP setting as a preparatory step. This shows that the most common techniques to build a ZK protocol in the SDP setting also hold for the R-SDP setting. The CVE based on R-SDP is depicted in Fig. 2.

It is easy to see that, as the original CVE scheme, also the R-CVE protocol achieves ZK. Indeed, $\mathbf{u}$ is chosen uniformly at random in $\mathbb{F}_q^n$ and the same holds for $\mathbf{e}' = \sigma(\mathbf{e})$, thanks to Property (3). Also, the soundness error remains the same as in CVE, that is, $\varepsilon = \frac{q}{2(q-1)}$, and an adversary achieving a larger success probability is either able to solve R-SDP or find hash collisions. A rigorous proof of this fact would be identical to the one in [17] and is hence omitted. Finally, using the Fiat-Shamir transform on this $q2$-identification scheme, due to [27] we get EUF-CMA security.

We consider two possible choices for R-SDP.

Private Key $\mathbf{e} \in \mathcal{S}_w^{\mathbb{E}}$
Public Key $\mathbb{E}, w, \mathbf{H} \in \mathbb{F}_q^{r \times n}, \mathbf{s} = \mathbf{e}\mathbf{H}^\top \in \mathbb{F}_q^r$

PROVER		VERIFIER
Choose $\mathbf{u} \xleftarrow{\$} \mathbb{F}_q^n$, $\sigma \xleftarrow{\$} \mathcal{T}$		
Set $c_0 = \mathsf{Hash}(\sigma, \mathbf{u}\mathbf{H}^\top)$		
Set $c_1 = \mathsf{Hash}(\sigma(\mathbf{u}), \sigma(\mathbf{e}))$	$\xrightarrow{\mathsf{Com}=(c_0, c_1)}$	
	$\xleftarrow{\beta}$	Choose $\beta \xleftarrow{\$} \mathbb{F}_q^*$
Set $\mathbf{y} = \sigma(\mathbf{u} + \beta\mathbf{e})$		
	$\xrightarrow{\mathbf{y}}$	
	$\xleftarrow{b}$	Choose $b \xleftarrow{\$} \{0, 1\}$
If $b = 0$, set $\mathsf{Rsp} := \sigma$		
If $b = 1$, set $\mathsf{Rsp} := \mathbf{e}' = \sigma(\mathbf{e})$	$\xrightarrow{\mathsf{Rsp}}$	If $b = 0$, accept if: $c_0 = \mathsf{Hash}(\sigma, \sigma^{-1}(\mathbf{y})\mathbf{H}^\top - \beta\mathbf{s})$ If $b = 1$, accept if: $\mathbf{e}' \in \mathcal{S}_w^{\mathbb{E}}$ and $c_1 = \mathsf{Hash}(\mathbf{y} - \beta\mathbf{e}', \mathbf{e}')$

Fig. 2. R-CVE: CVE scheme based on R-SDP

Choice I Values of z such that $W^* < 1$. We set $w = W^*n < n$ and $\mathcal{T} := S_n \times \mathbb{E}^n$. Representing σ and $\mathbf{e}'$ requires

$$\begin{cases} \mathrm{Size}(\sigma) = \lceil \log_2(n!) + n\log_2(z) \rceil, \\ \mathrm{Size}(\mathbf{e}') = \lceil \log_2\left(\binom{n}{w}\right) + w\log_2(z) \rceil. \end{cases} \qquad \text{(Choice I)}$$

The sizes are derived considering that σ and $\mathbf{e}'$ are uniformly distributed in two sets with sizes $|\mathcal{T}| = |S_n| \cdot |\mathbb{E}^n| = n! \cdot z^n$ and $|\mathcal{S}_w^{\mathbb{E}}| = \binom{n}{w} z^w$.

Choice II Values of z for which (2) returns $W^* = 1$. Remember that, asymptotically, this is guaranteed when $z \leq q^{1-R}$. In this case, we can choose $\mathcal{T} := \mathbb{E}^n$, and consequently have

$$\mathrm{Size}(\sigma) = \mathrm{Size}(\mathbf{e}') = \lceil n\log_2(z) \rceil. \qquad \text{(Choice II)}$$

When SDP is used, we instead have

$$\begin{cases} \mathrm{Size}(\sigma) = \lceil \log_2(n!) + n\log_2(q-1) \rceil, \\ \mathrm{Size}(\mathbf{e}') = \lceil \log_2\left(\binom{n}{w}\right) + w\log_2(q-1) \rceil. \end{cases} \qquad \text{(SDP)}$$

In Table 1, we have compared how the above sizes behave when targeting a security level of $\lambda = 128$ bits. For SDP, we have used the parameters which are recommended in [26], while for R-SDP we have designed some instances taking into account the cost of ISD attacks on R-SDP. Table 1 shows that R-SDP yields much smaller sizes than SDP for the same security level. In particular, Choice II seems to be better suited for ZK protocols. Indeed, we are able to completely avoid the use of permutations and thus reduce the original cost of sending a map to $\lceil n\log_2(z) \rceil$.

Table 1. Comparison between communication costs for SDP and R-SDP, for the case of $\lambda = 128$ and $R \approx 0.5$; all sizes are expressed in bytes.

	q	z	n	k	w	Size(σ)	Size($\mathbf{e}'$)	Size($\mathbf{y}$)
	512	511	196	92	84	372.4	118.1	220.0
SDP	256	255	207	93	90	369.3	115.0	207.0
	128	127	220	101	90	367.3	105.0	192.5
	677	26	84	42	73	102.0	48.5	105.0
R-SDP I	379	21	103	52	82	124.8	54.0	108.1
	197	14	103	51	91	117.1	49.6	103.0
	2017	63	70	32	70	52.5	52.5	96.3
R-SDP II	1021	30	79	40	79	49.4	49.4	98.8
	197	14	102	51	102	51.0	51.0	102.0

We would like to point out that, in modern protocols, several techniques can be applied to reduce the communication cost, the simplest one being sending generating seeds instead of random objects. However, almost every scheme makes use, at some point, of messages containing the objects we have considered in Table 1. As the sizes of these objects are significantly smaller for R-SDP, the problem is very promising.

For the remainder of the paper we will only focus on R-SDP Choice II, i.e., we will consider R-SDP with maximum Hamming weight $w = n$, since this allows for greater reductions.

Remark 2. For SDP and R-SDP Case I, we have considered optimal (i.e., as small as possible) sizes for σ and $\mathbf{e}'$. Notice that, to achieve such sizes, one should use encoding/decoding schemes (e.g., the Lehmer code) which require rather involved operations. In certain applications, these techniques may not be applicable as the resulting protocol would become too slow: in such cases, the sizes for SDP and R-SDP Case I would get larger than those in Table 1. For instance, the standard encoding for permutations is through a list of n integers in the range $[0; n-1]$, thus taking $n \log_2(n)$ bits (instead of the optimal $\log_2(n!) \approx n \log_2(n/e)$ bits).

5 R-SDP(G): Using Subgroups of the Restricted Group

In this section, we present a generalization of R-SDP, which allows to represent objects in an even more compact way. The idea consists of identifying a set of restricted maps that i) has small cardinality (but not too small, since this may facilitate attacks), and ii) admits a compact and easy-to-compute representation. We extend this reasoning to restricted vectors and in the end obtain that, for a security level of λ bits, we can represent any restricted object with $(1+\alpha)\lambda$ bits, with α being a small positive constant. Since we are reducing the space from which secret keys and ephemeral objects are sampled, security issues may arise. Yet, with coding theory arguments, we argue that incorporating this information into existing attacks does not lead to significant speed-ups.

5.1 Properties of the Restricted Group

Let us make some observations on the properties of $\mathbb{E}^n$, seen as a group.

Recall that $\mathbb{E} = \{g^i \mid i \in \{0, \dots, z-1\}\}$ is the cyclic subgroup of $\mathbb{F}_q^*$ generated by g, with order z. We focus on the case $n = w$, so that restricted vectors are given by $\mathbf{e} = (g^{i_1}, \dots, g^{i_n}) \in \mathbb{E}^n$, for $i_j \in \{0, \dots, z-1\}$.

As we have already shown in the previous section, in such a setting also the restricted maps can be represented by restricted vectors. In fact, any map sending $\mathbf{e} = (g^{i_1}, \dots, g^{i_n})$ to $\mathbf{e}' = (g^{j_1}, \dots, g^{j_n})$ is simply given by component-wise multiplication with $(g^{j_1-i_1}, \dots, g^{j_n-i_n})$. Indeed, one can simply check that

$$\sigma(\mathbf{e}) = (g^{j_1-i_1}, \dots, g^{j_n-i_n}) \star (g^{i_1}, \dots, g^{i_n}) = (g^{j_1}, \dots, g^{j_n}) = \mathbf{e}'.$$

We thus use restricted maps σ in $\mathbb{E}^n$ and write $\sigma(\mathbf{e})$ to mean $\sigma \star \mathbf{e}$. Notice that $\mathbb{E}^n$ acts transitively and freely on itself: for any pair $\mathbf{e}, \mathbf{e}' \in \mathbb{E}^n$, there is a unique map $\sigma \in \mathbb{E}^n$ such that $\mathbf{e}' = \sigma(\mathbf{e})$.

There exists a natural bijection $\ell : \mathbb{E}^n \to \mathbb{Z}_z^n$, which allows for a compact representation of the restricted vectors in $\mathbb{E}^n$, as

$$\ell((g^{i_1}, \dots, g^{i_n})) = (i_1, \dots, i_n).$$

It is easy to see that $(\mathbb{E}^n, \star)$ is isomorphic to $(\mathbb{Z}_z^n, +)$, and that both groups are abelian. This also allows for a more efficient computation of $\sigma(\mathbf{e})$. Indeed, if $\sigma = (g^{s_1}, \dots, g^{s_n}) \in \mathbb{E}^n$ and $\mathbf{e} = (g^{i_1}, \dots, g^{i_n}) \in \mathbb{E}^n$, instead of computing

$$\sigma(\mathbf{e}) = (g^{s_1}, \dots, g^{s_n}) \star (g^{i_1}, \dots, g^{i_n}) = (g^{s_1+i_1}, \dots, g^{s_n+i_n}),$$

one can simply add the two exponents over $\mathbb{Z}_z$ as

$$\ell(\sigma) + \ell(\mathbf{e}) = (s_1, \dots, s_n) + (i_1, \dots, i_n) = \ell(\sigma(\mathbf{e})).$$

Any restricted vector $\mathbf{e} = (e_1, \cdots, e_n) \in \mathbb{E}^n$ generates a cyclic subgroup

$$\{\mathbf{e}^i = (e_1^i, \cdots, e_n^i) \mid i \in \mathbb{N}\} < \mathbb{E}^n.$$

Due to the isomorphism to $\mathbb{Z}_z^n$, the order of $\mathbf{e}$ is the same as the order of $\ell(\mathbf{e})$ in $(\mathbb{Z}_z^n, +)$. Recall that $x \in \mathbb{Z}_z$ has order $\frac{z}{\gcd(x,z)}$. Thus, $\mathbf{e} = (g^{i_1}, \dots, g^{i_n})$, has order

$$\operatorname{ord}(\mathbf{e}) = \operatorname{lcm}(\operatorname{ord}(i_1), \dots, \operatorname{ord}(i_n)) = \operatorname{lcm}\left(\frac{z}{\gcd(i_1,z)}, \dots, \frac{z}{\gcd(i_n,z)}\right),$$

where lcm denotes the least common multiple. One can easily construct $\mathbf{e}$ with maximum order z, e.g., by taking one of the i_j coprime to z.

5.2 Cyclic Subgroups of the Restricted Group

We now consider the subgroup G of $(\mathbb{E}^n, \star)$ which is generated by m many restricted vectors $\mathbf{x}_1, \ldots, \mathbf{x}_m \in \mathbb{E}^n$. In other words,

$$G = \langle \mathbf{x}_1, \ldots, \mathbf{x}_m \rangle = \left\{ \mathbf{x}_1^{u_1} \star \cdots \star \mathbf{x}_m^{u_m} \,|\, u_j \in \{0, \ldots, z-1\} \right\}.$$

In the following, we will call G the *restricted subgroup.* To any $\mathbf{a} \in G$, we can associate a vector representation through $\ell_G : G \to \mathbb{Z}_z^m$, as follows

$$\ell_G \left(\mathbf{x}_1^{u_1} \star \cdots \star \mathbf{x}_m^{u_m} \right) = (u_1, \ldots, u_m). \tag{5}$$

Clearly, $(G, \star)$ is a subgroup of $(\mathbb{E}^n, \star)$ and ℓ_G is a group homomorphism. Note that a priori the elements of G do not have a unique representation in $\mathbb{Z}_z^m$ (we later give a condition to have a unique $\ell_G(\mathbf{a}) \in \mathbb{Z}_z^m$).

Thus, for any $\mathbf{a}, \mathbf{b} \in G$, we have

$$\ell_G(\mathbf{a} \star \mathbf{b}) = \ell_G(\mathbf{a}) + \ell_G(\mathbf{b}) \mod z.$$

In the following proposition we show the connection between ℓ and ℓ_G.

Proposition 1. *Let $\mathbf{M}_G \in \mathbb{Z}_z^{m \times n}$ be the matrix whose j-th row is $\ell(\mathbf{x}_j)$, and $\mathscr{B} = \{\mathbf{u}\mathbf{M}_G \mid \mathbf{u} \in \mathbb{Z}_z^m\}$. We have that $\ell(\mathbf{a}) = \ell_G(\mathbf{a})\mathbf{M}_G \mod z$, for any $\mathbf{a} \in G$ and $|\mathscr{B}| = |G|$.*

Proof. Let $\mathbf{x}_j = \left(g^{i_1^{(j)}}, \ldots, g^{i_n^{(j)}} \right)$, hence $\ell(\mathbf{x}_j) = \left(i_1^{(j)}, \ldots, i_n^{(j)} \right)$, and $\mathbf{a} \in G$. Then, it holds that

$$\mathbf{a} = \star_{j=1}^{m} \left(g^{u_j i_1^{(j)}}, \ldots, g^{u_j i_n^{(j)}} \right) = \left(g^{\sum_{j=1}^m u_j i_1^{(j)}}, \ldots, g^{\sum_{j=1}^m u_j i_n^{(j)}} \right).$$

By construction, the element in the j-th row and v-th column of $\mathbf{M}_G$ is $i_v^{(j)}$. Hence, for $\mathbf{u} = \ell_G(\mathbf{a}) = (u_1, \ldots, u_m) \in \mathbb{Z}_z^m$ we get

$$\ell(\mathbf{a}) = \left(\sum_{j=1}^{m} u_j i_1^{(j)}, \ldots, \sum_{j=1}^{m} u_j i_n^{(j)} \right) = \mathbf{u}\mathbf{M}_G \in \mathbb{Z}_z^n.$$

The second claim follows, since $\ell : \mathbb{E}^n \mapsto \mathbb{Z}_z^n$ is a bijection. □

Remark 3. When z is a prime number, we can easily construct a G of maximal order z^m, by taking $\mathbf{x}_1, \ldots, \mathbf{x}_m \in \mathbb{E}^n$ such that $\{\ell(\mathbf{x}_1), \ldots, \ell(\mathbf{x}_m)\}$ are linearly independent. This is equivalent to asking for a full-rank matrix $\mathbf{M}_G$.

Note that $\mathbf{M}_G$ acts like the generator matrix of G and for $\ell(\mathbf{a}) = \mathbf{u}\mathbf{M}_G$ we have that $\mathbf{u} = \ell_G(\mathbf{a})$ is the information vector. Thus, if we require z to be prime and $\mathbf{M}_G \in \mathbb{F}_z^{m \times n}$ to have full rank m, then for any $\mathbf{a} \in G$ we have a unique $\ell_G(\mathbf{a}) = \mathbf{u}$, which is such that $\mathbf{u}\mathbf{M}_G = \ell(\mathbf{a}) \in \mathbb{F}_z^n$. We thus from now on focus on prime order z.

To summarize, in order to represent a vector $\mathbf{e} \in G$, respectively a transformation $\sigma \in G$, it is enough to use $\ell_G(\mathbf{e})$, respectively $\ell_G(\sigma)$. Given the matrix $\mathbf{M}_G$, containing all the $\ell(\mathbf{x}_i)$ of the generators, the $\ell_G(\mathbf{e})$ is the length-m vector of coefficients in $\mathbb{F}_z$ required to generate $\ell(\mathbf{e}) \in \mathbb{F}_z^n$.

This will also have an impact on the sizes of restricted vectors and restricted transformations, as now elements of G are represented with an element of $\mathbb{Z}_z^m$, of size $m\lceil \log_2(z) \rceil$.

5.3 Solving R-SDP with Restricted Subgroup

In this section, we focus only on restrictions $\mathbb{E} = \{g^i \mid i \in \{0, \dots, z-1\}\}$ such that z is prime, $w = n$ and restricted subgroups with $|G| = z^m$. We now introduce R-SDP with the additional constraint that the solution is an element of G.

Problem 3 R-SDP(G): SDP with Restricted Diagonal Subgroup G *Let $G = \langle \mathbf{x}_1, \dots, \mathbf{x}_m \rangle$, $\mathbf{H} \in \mathbb{F}_q^{r \times n}$ and $\mathbf{s} \in \mathbb{F}_q^r$. Does there exist a vector $\mathbf{e} \in G$ with $\mathbf{e}\mathbf{H}^\top = \mathbf{s}$?*

Since $|G| = z^m$, the criterion to have (on average) a unique solution gets modified as follows

$$m \log_2(z) \leq (1 - R) n \log_2(q).$$

Since the subgroup G possesses some additional structure and introduces a smaller solution space, we argue in the remainder of this section on how to choose parameters, such that attacks exploiting this structure can be ruled out.

First, it is obvious that G must have a sufficiently large order, i.e., $|G| \geq 2^\lambda$. Indeed, if $|G|$ is too small, then R-SDP(G) can be solved with a trivial brute-force attack over G, taking time $O(|G|)$.

On the other hand, one can also disregard G, find all solutions $\mathbf{e} \in \mathbb{E}^n$ using for example the restricted Stern/Dumer algorithm, and check their validity, i.e., whether $\mathbf{e} \in G$, afterwards. Such attacks can be thwarted by choosing instances which have more than 2^λ solutions in $\mathbb{E}^n$. In this case, checking for all candidate solutions whether $\mathbf{e} \in G$ guarantees the security level. Notice that this choice is rather conservative: we are neglecting the cost of actually finding these solutions in $\mathbb{E}^n$, using the exponential cost algorithms. It follows that any efficient solver for R-SDP(G) has to directly take G into account. Since this is not possible for a representation-based ISD, we only consider a solver based on restricted Stern/Dumer in the following.

ISD attacks for R-SDP(G). An improved collision search requires a method to enumerate a part of solution vector $\mathbf{e}_T$ of length $t \geq k/2$ in time smaller than z^t (since else one could just enumerate all $\mathbf{e}_T \in \mathbb{E}^t$). This can be done with the following procedure, which starts from a set $T \subseteq \{1, \dots, n\}$ of size t and returns all candidates for $\mathbf{e}_T$:

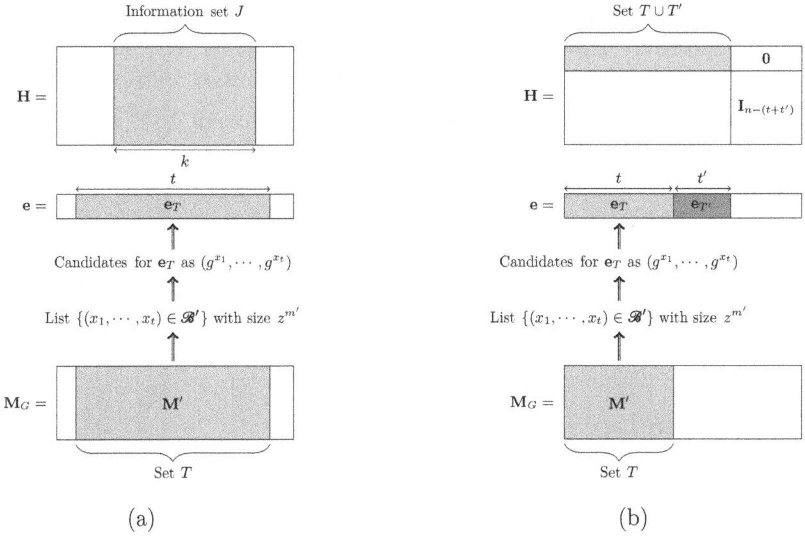

Fig. 3. Strategies to speed-up ISD with the knowledge about G.

1) set $\mathbf{M}' \in \mathbb{F}_z^{m \times t}$ consisting of the columns of $\mathbf{M}_G$ indexed by T;
2) enumerate all length-t vectors which can be obtained as linear combinations of the rows of $\mathbf{M}'$;
3) use any such vector as exponents for a candidate $\mathbf{e}_T$. To do this, one first enumerates $\mathscr{B}' = \{\mathbf{u}\mathbf{M}' \mid \mathbf{u} \in \mathbb{F}_z^m\} \subseteq \mathbb{F}_z^t$. Then, to each $\mathbf{x} \in \mathscr{B}'$, associates a candidate $\mathbf{e}_T = \ell^{-1}(\mathbf{x})$.

With the above approach, one can enumerate all candidates for $\mathbf{e}_T$ in time $O(|\mathscr{B}'|) = O\big(z^{m'}\big)$, where $m' = \text{rank}(\mathbf{M}') \leq \min\{m, t\}$. If $m' = t$, we have that enumeration takes time $O(|\mathscr{B}'|) = O(z^t)$, and by choosing $z^t > 2^\lambda$, we can ignore this case. Thus, an attacker can only hope for a speed-up if $m' < t$.

The problem of finding a set T with the desired properties can be stated as follows.

Problem 4 (Submatrix Rank Problem). *Let $\mathbf{M}_G \in \mathbb{F}_z^{m \times n}$, with $m < n$ and $m' \leq m$. Is there a set $T \subset \{1, \ldots, n\}$ of size t, such that rk$((\mathbf{M}_G)_T) = m'$?*

Assuming that one is able to find a set T such that $\mathbf{M}' := (\mathbf{M}_G)_T$ has rank $m' < t$, one can possibly speed-up ISD algorithms:

- if $t > k$, then T contains[3] an information set $J \subseteq T$. So, we can enumerate all candidates for $\mathbf{e}_J$ in time $z^{m'}$. If m' is particularly low (say, lower than $\lambda \log_z(2)$) the attack can use a single list of size $z^{m'}$ in which we put candidates for $\mathbf{e}_J$. See Fig. 3a for a representation of this strategy;

[3] Unless all $k \times t$ matrices are singular, however, a random $k \times t$ matrix has probability $\prod_{i=0}^{k-1}(1 - q^{i-t}) \geq (1 - q^{-(t-k+1)})^k$ to be invertible.

- if $t < k$, then we can use the $z^{m'}$ candidates for $\mathbf{e}_T$ to build one of the lists for Stern's algorithm. However, we also require an enumeration of all $\mathbf{e}_{T'}$, with T' disjoint from T, of size t', such that $t+t' \geq k$. Thus, a collision search leads to a cost of $\max\left\{z^{m'}, z^{t'}, z^{m+m'}q^{k-(t+t')}\right\}$. So, this approach is convenient only if $t \geq k/2$. See Fig. 3b for a representation of this strategy;
- assume that one is able to find several sets T of size t such that $m' < t$. Then, we can enumerate several portions of the solution $\mathbf{e}$, of size t, in time $z^{m'}$. We can use them to build several lists, which we can combine with a collision search approach with more than one level. Again, there is no guarantee that this yields an attack with overall cost $z^{m'}$ since we also need to consider how list sizes grow after merging.

5.4 Criteria to Design R-SDP(G)

We will adopt the following very conservative criterion to completely cut out all the above possibilities.

Requirement 1. *Let $rk((\mathbf{M}_G)_T) = m'$. For any $t \in \{1, \dots, n\}$ and any set $T \subseteq \{1, \dots, n\}$ of size t, we want that $m' \geq \min\left\{t, \frac{\lambda}{\log_2(z)}\right\}$.*

In the case of full rank, one cannot improve over enumerating all errors in the space. Regarding rank deficiency, Requirement 1 ensures that the enumeration of possible error vectors exceeds the security level.

This implies that any strategy that exploits the structure of G to speed up ISD attacks will not be more efficient than generic ISD attacks and we choose our instances such that these have a cost of at least 2^λ.

We now provide strong evidence that Requirement 1 is rather conservative. First, we show that Problem 4 is NP-hard. This implies that, even if some set T with the desired properties exists, finding it is hard. The NP-hardness proof will make use of the following result.

Theorem 1. Relation between m' and subcodes of $\mathscr{B}$
Let $\mathbf{M}_G \in \mathbb{F}_z^{m\times n}$ and $\mathscr{B} = \langle \mathbf{M}_G \rangle \subseteq \mathbb{F}_z^n$ be a linear code of dimension m. Then, there exists $T \subseteq \{1, \dots, n\}$ of size t, such that $m' = rk((\mathbf{M}_G)_T)$, if and only if

i) $m' \leq t \leq m$, then $\mathscr{B}^\perp$ contains a subcode with dimension $t - m'$ and support size $\leq t$;
ii) $m' \leq m \leq t$, then $\mathscr{B}$ contains a subcode with dimension $m - m'$ and support size $\leq n - t$.

Proof. We start with the case $m' \leq t \leq m$. Since $\mathbf{M}' = (\mathbf{M}_G)_T$ has m rows and $t \leq m$ columns, if its rank is lower than t this implies that there exist $k' = t - m'$ linearly independent vectors $\mathbf{x}_1, \dots, \mathbf{x}_{k'} \in \mathbb{F}_z^t$ such that $\mathbf{M}'\mathbf{x}_i^\top = \mathbf{0}$. We can use such vectors to define a generator matrix $\mathbf{X} \in \mathbb{F}_z^{k'\times t}$ for the right kernel of $\mathbf{M}'$. Now, let $\mathbf{C} \in \mathbb{F}_q^{k'\times n}$ be a matrix such that $\mathbf{C}_T = \mathbf{X}$ and $\mathbf{C}_{T^C} = \mathbf{0} \in \mathbb{F}_z^{k'\times(n-t)}$. By construction, it holds that $\mathbf{C}$ has rank k' and is such that $\mathbf{M}_G\mathbf{C}^\top = \mathbf{0}$, so

$\mathbf{C}$ is a generator matrix for a k'-dimensional subcode of $\mathscr{B}^\perp$. Since $\mathbf{C}$ has at least $n-t$ null columns (the ones indexed by T^C), we know that $\mathbf{C}$ generates a code with dimension k' and support size not greater than t. For the proof of the other direction, one can proceed in the same way. If there is a subcode of $\mathscr{B}^\perp$ of dimension $t-m'$ and support size $\leq t$, we can find a generator matrix $\mathbf{C}$, which has (at least) $n-t$ zero columns and denote these indices by T^C.

The case of $m' \leq m \leq t$ is treated analogously, with the only difference that we need to focus on the left kernel of $\mathbf{M}'$. □

Theorem 2. *The Submatrix Rank Problem is NP-complete.*

Proof. We present a reduction from the low weight codeword finding problem, which is NP-complete [13]: given $d \in \mathbb{N}$ and $\mathbf{G} \in \mathbb{F}_z^{k\times n}$, are there codewords in $\mathscr{C} = \langle \mathbf{G} \rangle$ with weight $\leq d$? Due to the Singleton bound [34], we know that $d < n-k+1$. We show that any instance $\{\mathbf{G}, d\}$ can be transformed, in polynomial time, into an instance of the Submatrix Rank Problem. We will denote by Solve an algorithm that, on input a matrix $\mathbf{M}_G \in \mathbb{F}_z^{m\times n}$ and two integers $t, m' \in \mathbb{N}$, returns "YES" if $T \subseteq \{1, \ldots, n\}$ of size t and $m' = \mathrm{rk}((\mathbf{M}_G)_T)$ exists, and "NO" otherwise. We can set $\mathbf{M}_G := \mathbf{G}$ and $t := n-d$. Notice that $m := k$ and $t > n-(n-k+1) = m-1$. We run Solve for all $m' \leq m-1$.

- Assume that the call for $m^\star$ on Solve returns a "YES". Since $t \geq m$, we apply ii) of Theorem 1 and learn that $\mathscr{C} = \langle \mathbf{G} \rangle$ has a subcode $\mathscr{C}'$ of dimension $m-m^\star$ with support size $s \leq n-t = d$. Since $d(\mathscr{C}) \leq d(\mathscr{C}') \leq s \leq d$, we return "YES" for the original problem.
- Assume that none of the calls on Solve return a "YES", then all subcodes have a support size greater than $t-n = d$. Notice that we also tried $m' = m-1$, so Solve has also considered existence of subcodes of dimension $m-m' = 1$, that is, codewords. So, we return "NO" for the original problem.

□

Notice that, as a consequence of Theorem 1, finding sets T with the desired properties implies finding subcodes with small supports. This can be done using ISD, with a time complexity that (more or less) grows exponentially with the desired support size. Thus, finding a set T is also inefficient. However, we describe how to choose the value of m so that such useful subcodes are not expected to exist. For a random code with length n and dimension k, over $\mathbb{F}_z$, the average number of subcodes with dimension k' and support size w is well estimated by [32, Theorem 1]

$$N_k(k', w) = \binom{n}{w}(z^{k'}-1)^{w-k'} \begin{bmatrix} k \\ k' \end{bmatrix}_z \begin{bmatrix} n \\ k' \end{bmatrix}_z^{-1}. \tag{6}$$

Since for $\mathbf{M}_G$ we do not impose any structure, apart from the full rank property, we can safely study its row space $\mathscr{B}$ as a random code with dimension m. Analogously, we can treat its dual $\mathscr{B}^\perp$ as a random code, with dimension $n-m$. So, we can update Requirement 1 as follows.

Requirement 2. *We set $m > \lambda \log_z(2)$ as the minimum integer such that*

- *for any $m' \le t \le m$ with $\sum_{i=1}^{t} N_{n-m}(t-m', i) < 1$, we have $m' > \lambda \log_z(2)$;*
- *for any $m' \le m < t$ with $\sum_{i=1}^{n-t} N_m(m-m', i) < 1$, we have $m' > \lambda \log_z(2)$.*

Thus, even if such subcodes exist, the enumeration cost $z^{m'}$ exceeds the security level.

5.5 R-SDP(G) in Practice: Easy to Implement and Tight Parameters

Let us first briefly comment on some implementation aspects for R-SDP(G).

When R-SDP(G) is used, the generators $\mathbf{x}_1, \ldots, \mathbf{x}_m$ must be publicly known. To do so, one can use a matrix $\mathbf{M}_G$ in systematic form, i.e., $\mathbf{M}_G = (\mathbf{I}_m, \mathbf{U})$ with $\mathbf{U} \in \mathbb{F}_z^{m \times (n-m)}$ sampled at random from the seed. Since $\mathbf{M}_G$ is guaranteed to have full rank, we can then take its rows $\mathbf{m}_i$ and define the generators $\mathbf{x}_1, \ldots, \mathbf{x}_m$ as the vectors with exponents $\mathbf{m}_1, \ldots, \mathbf{m}_m$ respectively. The seed can also be used to sample $\mathbf{H} \in \mathbb{F}_q^{r \times n}$ (again, one can conveniently use the systematic form). This way, the public key is $\{\mathbf{s}, \mathsf{Seed}_{\mathsf{pk}}\}$ and has size $(n-k)\log_2(q) + |\mathsf{Seed}_{\mathsf{pk}}|$; we will use $\mathsf{Seed}_{\mathsf{pk}}$ with λ bits. We consider that both restricted maps and vectors are always sampled from G. Property (3), which guarantees ZK, holds since G acts transitively and freely on itself. In other words, for any $\mathbf{e} \in G$, $\sigma(\mathbf{e})$ is uniformly random over G when $\sigma \xleftarrow{\$} G$. When $\mathbf{e}$ and $\widetilde{\mathbf{e}}$ are two restricted vectors, the map σ that maps $\widetilde{\mathbf{e}}$ into $\mathbf{e}$ is $\ell_G(\mathbf{e}) - \ell_G(\widetilde{\mathbf{e}})$ and it can be represented using only $m \log_2(z)$ bits. To sample uniformly at random some $\mathbf{a} \in G$, a convenient procedure is:

1. sample $\mathbf{u} \xleftarrow{\$} \mathbb{F}_z^m$,
2. obtain the exponents $\mathbf{x} = \mathbf{u}\mathbf{M}_G \in \mathbb{F}_z^n$,
3. set $\mathbf{a} = \left(g^{x_1}, \ldots, g^{x_n}\right) \in \mathbb{F}_q^n$.

Using $\mathbf{M}_G$ in systematic form, we have some computational advantages since $\mathbf{x} = (\mathbf{u}, \mathbf{u}\mathbf{U})$ and computing $\mathbf{u}\mathbf{U}$ requires only $O\big(m(n-m)\big)$ operations over $\mathbb{F}_z$. To verify that some $\mathbf{a} \in \mathbb{F}_q^n$ is indeed in G, it is enough to check that $\ell(\mathbf{a})$ is a linear combination of the rows of $\mathbf{M}_G$. This can be done using a parity-check matrix $\mathbf{C} \in \mathbb{F}_z^{(n-m) \times n}$ for $\langle \mathbf{M}_G \rangle$: $\mathbf{a} \in G$, if and only if $\ell(\mathbf{a})\mathbf{C}^\top = \mathbf{0}$. We can set $\mathbf{C} = (-\mathbf{U}^\top, \mathbf{I}_{n-m})$, which speeds up the computation of $\ell(\mathbf{a})\mathbf{C}^\top$.

We show that even with the conservative Requirement 2, R-SDP(G) allows us to use much more aggressive parameters than those for R-SDP. From now on, we will write $|G| = z^m = 2^{(1+\alpha)\lambda}$, as we required $z^m > 2^\lambda$ for some $\alpha \in \mathbb{R}$: the value of α gives an idea of how tight we can be, when representing elements of G. We clearly require $\alpha > 0$ to thwart brute-force attacks, yet, by choosing $0 < \alpha < 1$, we can have restricted objects with sizes that are not greater than 2λ, that is, the binary size of a digest. In other words, we are making restricted objects smaller than some of the objects that the parties cannot avoid exchanging (e.g., the initial commitments). As we show in the following, we can use α in the

Table 2. Instances of R-SDP(G) for $\lambda = 128$ and corresponding sizes for objects expressed in bytes.

Range for q	$\frac{z}{q-1}$	q	z	n	k	m	α	Size(σ)	Size($\mathbf{y}$)
$2^8 < q < 2^{10}$	1/2	1019	509	40	16	18	0.2644	20.2	49.9
		347	173	41	20	23	0.3359	21.4	43.2
		719	359	49	17	20	0.3262	21.2	58.1
	< 1/2	971	97	44	26	26	0.3406	21.4	54.8
		643	107	60	25	26	0.3604	21.9	70.0
		269	67	52	27	29	0.3743	21.9	52.5
$2^6 < q < 2^8$	1/2	227	113	43	22	24	0.2789	20.5	42.1
		107	53	53	26	31	0.3872	22.2	44.7
		83	41	73	28	35	0.4650	23.4	58.2
	< 1/2	223	37	56	33	34	0.3838	22.1	54.6
		103	17	76	44	48	0.5328	24.5	63.5
		79	13	82	49	54	0.5611	25.0	64.6
$2^4 < q < 2^6$	1/2	59	29	63	31	38	0.4422	23.1	46.3
		47	23	69	34	42	0.4843	23.7	47.9
		23	11	93	46	61	0.6486	26.4	52.6
	< 1/2	53	13	82	47	54	0.5611	25.0	58.7

range $0.2 \div 0.6$: which means we are very close to achieving security with the minimum amount of required bits, i.e., λ bits.

Some example instances for R-SDP(G) used in CVE are shown in Table 2. The parameters are chosen according to the cost of the ISD algorithm presented in Sect. 5.3 and Requirement 2. Recall from Fig. 2 that $\mathbf{y}$ and σ have size $n\log_2(q)$, respectively, $m\log_2(z)$ and that the parameters m, z are chosen such that $z^m > 2^\lambda$.

We see that there are several trade-offs in how parameters can be chosen. For instance, large values of q lead to slightly smaller sizes for $\mathbf{y}$, while the arithmetic over $\mathbb{F}_q$ becomes slower. Another degree of freedom is in the choice of z: setting $z = \frac{q-1}{2}$ leads to smaller sizes, but choosing large z might make the arithmetic over $\mathbb{F}_z$ slower.

Comparing these numbers with those in Table 1, we see that using R-SDP(G) allows for a significant reduction of the communication cost. In the next sections, we apply the problem to existing ZK schemes and derive their performances in terms of signature size.

6 ZK Protocols from the R-SDP: Modern Protocols

This section presents concrete ZK protocols based on R-SDP and R-SDP(G). Note that one can replace the SDP with R-SDP or R-SDP(G) in any ZK protocol, however, in the following, we only present the two schemes which result in the smallest signature sizes, namely the GPS [26] and BG protocol [15].

Note that several signature schemes make use of MPCitH paradigm to reduce their signature sizes. We refer to the extended version [9] of this manuscript for a brief discussion on how existing MPCitH schemes may be adapted to use R-SDP.

6.1 R-GPS: The GPS Scheme with R-SDP

The GPS scheme [26] applies the protocol-with-helper paradigm to the CVE scheme. In a nutshell, the idea is to simulate a trusted third entity (the helper), which generates some of the messages which would be exchanged between the prover and the verifier. The helper is asked to generate the commitments and the first public response (that is, c_0, c_1 and $\mathbf{y}$ for the scheme in Fig. 2). The *cut&choose* technique is used to remove the helper. The helper is first simulated by the prover for N rounds, generating random objects from seeds and committing to the obtained quantities. The verifier will ask to *open* only $M < N$ rounds: she will receive the verifying maps for the chosen rounds and the seeds for the other $N - M$ rounds.

Since GPS is based on SDP, converting it to R-SDP is rather straightforward; for the sake of completeness, the resulting protocol is presented in Fig. 4. As applying the Fiat-Shamir transform on a ZK protocol is straightforward and a well-known procedure, we omit to write out the resulting signature scheme.

The ZK property, as well as soundness and EUF-CMA security, are obtained in the exact same way as for the original GPS scheme. Also, the security analysis and signature size easily follow from [26]. To prevent the attack in [30], N and M must be such that

$$\max_{x\in\{0,\ldots,M\}} \binom{N-x}{M-x}\binom{N}{M}^{-1}(q-1)^{x-M} \geq 2^{\lambda}. \tag{7}$$

When R-SDP(G) is used, the communication cost of an opened round is

$$L = \underbrace{n\log_2(q)}_{\mathbf{y}\in\mathbb{F}_q^n} + \underbrace{2\lambda}_{\text{Randomness}} + \underbrace{m\lceil\log_2(z)\rceil}_{\sigma\in G}. \tag{8}$$

When relying on R-SDP, the resulting communication cost is obtained by replacing $m\lceil\log_2(z)\rceil$ with $n\lceil\log_2(z)\rceil$. The size of a signature in the resulting R-GPS signature scheme is

$$|\texttt{Signature}| = \underbrace{2\lambda\left(2 + M\log_2\left(\frac{N(q-1)}{M}\right)\right)}_{\text{Merkle proofs and commitments}} + \underbrace{\lambda M\log_2\left(\frac{N}{M}\right)}_{\text{Seeds}} + M\cdot L.$$

In Table 3, we report examples for the signature sizes we can achieve and compare them with the ones of GPS [26, Table 1]. We have chosen the parameters according to the cost of the generic decoders (Sect. 5.3 and the extended version

Private Key $\mathbf{e} \in G$

Public Key $G = \langle \mathbf{x}_1, \ldots, \mathbf{x}_m \rangle$, $\mathbf{H} \in \mathbb{F}_q^{r \times n}$, $\mathbf{s} = \mathbf{e}\mathbf{H}^\top \in \mathbb{F}_q^r$

PROVER		VERIFIER
For $i = 1, \ldots, N$:		
Sample $\{\mathsf{Seed}_i\}_{1 \le i \le N} \xleftarrow{\$} \{0;1\}^\lambda$		
Compute $\mathbf{u}_i \xleftarrow{\mathsf{Seed}_i} \mathbb{F}_q^n$		
Compute $\tilde{\mathbf{e}}_i \xleftarrow{\mathsf{Seed}_i} G$		
For all $v \in \mathbb{F}_q$:		
Compute $r_v \xleftarrow{\mathsf{Seed}_i} \{0;1\}^\lambda$		
Compute $c_v = (r_v, \mathbf{u}_i + v\tilde{\mathbf{e}}_i)$		
Set $a_i = (c_v)_{v \in \mathbb{F}_q}$		
Compute $\sigma_i \in G$, s.t. $\sigma_i(\tilde{\mathbf{e}}_i) = \mathbf{e}$		
Sample $r_i \xleftarrow{\$} \{0;1\}^\lambda$		
Set $c_i = (r_i, \sigma_i, \sigma_i(\mathbf{u}_i)\mathbf{H}^\top)$		
Set $\mathsf{Com} = ((a_i)_{1 \le i \le N}, (c_i)_{1 \le i \le N})$	$\xrightarrow{\mathsf{Com}}$	
		Sample $i \xleftarrow{\$} \{1, \ldots, N\}$
		Sample $\beta \xleftarrow{\$} \mathbb{F}_q$
Compute $r_\beta \xleftarrow{\mathsf{Seed}_i} \{0;1\}^\lambda$	$\xleftarrow{i, \beta}$	
Compute $\mathbf{y}_i = \mathbf{u}_i + \beta\tilde{\mathbf{e}}_i$		
Set $\mathsf{Rsp}_i = (r_i, r_\beta, \sigma_i, \mathbf{y}_i)$	$\xrightarrow{\mathsf{Rsp}_i, \mathsf{Seed}_{\ell \ne i}}$	
		For all $j \in \{1, \ldots, N\} \setminus \{i\}$:
		For all $v \in \mathbb{F}_q$:
		Compute $r_v \xleftarrow{\mathsf{Seed}_j} \{0;1\}^\lambda$
		Compute $c_v = (r_v, \mathbf{u}_j + v\tilde{\mathbf{e}}_j)$
		Set $a'_j = (c_v)_{v \in \mathbb{F}_q}$
		Check $a'_j = a_j$
		Check $\sigma_i \in G$
		Compute $\mathbf{t} = \sigma_i(\mathbf{y}_i)\mathbf{H}^\top - \beta\mathbf{s}$.
		Check $c_i = (r_i, \sigma_i, \mathbf{t})$.
		Check $c_\beta = (r_\beta, \mathbf{y}_i)$.

Fig. 4. One round of the R-GPS protocol

of this manuscript [9]) and the soundness error. Employing R-SDP, we can reduce the signature sizes by a factor of approximately 0.6. Considering R-SDP(G), the gain becomes more significant, and, with respect to the instances based on R-SDP, we save approximately 1 to 2 kB.

6.2 R-BG: The BG-PKP Scheme with R-SDP

As another protocol-with-helper, one may consider the FJR scheme [24]. To reduce the soundness error, FJR uses the idea of shared permutations: the random masking is obtained by combining the actions of N random permutations, so that a cheating prover cannot cheat for more than one permutation. This reduces the soundness error of a single round to $1/N$. The idea of shared permutations has been applied also to PKP, for a protocol that we will refer to as BG-PKP [15]. Notice that BG-PKP is the PKP-based scheme with the smallest signatures. We show that, with minor modifications, the scheme can be adapted to the R-SDP setting and derive the resulting signature sizes.

For PKP, the prover first samples a vector $\mathbf{e} \in \mathbb{F}_q^n$, a full rank $\mathbf{H} \in \mathbb{F}_q^{r \times n}$, a permutation $\pi \in S_n$ and computes $\mathbf{s} = \pi(\mathbf{e})\mathbf{H}^\top$. The secret key is the permutation π and the public key is $\{\mathbf{H}, \mathbf{e}, \mathbf{s}\}$. For R-SDP, we can do the same, with the

Table 3. Performances of the GPS scheme [26] based on different problems.

	q	z	n	k	w	m	N	M	Sign. Size (kB)
SDP	128		220	101	90		512	23	24.6
	256		207	93	90		1024	19	22.4
	512		196	92	84		2024	16	20.6
	1024		187	90	80		4096	14	19.5
R-SDP	67	11	147	63	147		512	24	14.8
	197	14	105	53	105		1024	19	13.4
	991	33	77	48	77		2048	16	12.9
	991	33	77	38	77		4096	14	12.5
R-SDP(G)	53	13	82	47	82	54	512	25	12.7
	103	17	76	44	76	48	1024	21	12.7
	223	37	56	33	56	34	2048	19	11.8
	1019	509	40	16	40	18	4096	14	11.5

only difference that $\mathbf{e}$ and the map σ are sampled from the restricted subgroup G; namely, once $\mathbf{H}$ and G have been defined, we sample $\mathbf{e}, \sigma \xleftarrow{\$} G$, set the secret key as σ and the public key as $\{G,\ \mathbf{H},\ \mathbf{e},\ \mathbf{s} = \sigma(\mathbf{e})\mathbf{H}^\top\}$. To compress the public key size, everything but $\mathbf{s}$ can be generated from a seed $\mathsf{Seed}^{(pk)}$.

The resulting protocol is shown in Fig. 5. We have implicitly introduced some additional notation: SeedTree, SeedPath are the functions to operate with the seed tree (respectively, generate the tree from a master seed, compute a path and regenerate all seeds but one), while $\xleftarrow{\mathsf{Seed}}$ means sampling with randomness source Seed. It can be seen that the protocol structure is the same as BG, so it inherits all of its features, in particular, the soundness error is as in [15, Thm. 2]

$$\varepsilon(N, q) = \frac{1}{N} + \frac{N-1}{N(q-1)}.$$

Also, the completeness and ZK property follow in a straightforward manner. Nevertheless, we give the proof for soundness, completeness, and the ZK property in the extended version [9] of this manuscript.

Signature Scheme. To obtain a signature scheme, we consider t parallel executions and then apply the Fiat-Shamir transform. The corresponding algorithms for signature generation and verification are given in Figs. 6 and 7. In the algorithms, we have indicated by `Msg` the message to be signed and by t the number of executed rounds. The round index has been indicated with u, and the quantities referred to each round are specified by the superscript (u). For instance, $\sigma_1^{(u)}, \ldots, \sigma_N^{(u)}$ are the transformations used in the u-th round. The resulting scheme is essentially the repetition of t rounds of the R-BG protocol, plus some minor modifications which we list below.

Private Key $\sigma \in G$
Public Key $G = \langle \mathbf{x}_1, \ldots, \mathbf{x}_m \rangle$, $\mathbf{e} \in G$, $\mathbf{H} \in \mathbb{F}_q^{r \times n}$, $\mathbf{s} = \sigma(\mathbf{e})\mathbf{H}^\top \in \mathbb{F}_q^r$

PROVER | **VERIFIER**

Sample $\mathtt{MSeed} \xleftarrow{\$} \{0;1\}^\lambda$
Compute $\{\mathtt{Seed}_i\}_{1 \le i \le N} = \mathsf{SeedTree}(\mathtt{MSeed})$
For $i = 2, \ldots, N$:
  Sample $\mathtt{Seed}_i^*, \mathtt{Salt}_i \xleftarrow{\mathtt{Seed}_i} \{0;1\}^\lambda$
  Sample $\sigma_i \xleftarrow{\mathtt{Seed}_i^*} G$, $\mathbf{v}_i \xleftarrow{\mathtt{Seed}_i^*} \mathbb{F}_q^n$
  Set $c_i = \mathsf{Hash}(\mathtt{Salt}_i, \mathtt{Seed}_i^*)$
Set $\sigma_1 = \sigma_2^{-1} \circ \cdots \circ \sigma_N^{-1} \circ \sigma$
Sample $\mathtt{Seed}_1^*, \mathtt{Salt}_1 \xleftarrow{\mathtt{Seed}_1} \{0;1\}^\lambda$
Sample $\mathbf{v}_1 \xleftarrow{\mathtt{Seed}_1^*} \mathbb{F}_q^n$
Set $c_1 = \mathsf{Hash}(\mathtt{Salt}_1, \mathtt{Seed}_1^*, \sigma_1)$
Compute $\mathbf{v} = \mathbf{v}_N + \sum_{i=1}^{N-1} \sigma_N \circ \cdots \circ \sigma_{i+1}(\mathbf{v}_i)$
Set $c = \mathsf{Hash}(\mathbf{v}\mathbf{H}^\top, \{c_i\}_{1 \le i \le N})$ $\xrightarrow{c}$

  Sample $\beta \xleftarrow{\$} \mathbb{F}_q^*$

$\xleftarrow{\beta}$ Set $\widetilde{\mathbf{e}}_0 = \beta \mathbf{e}$
For $i = 1, \ldots, N$:
  Set $\widetilde{\mathbf{e}}_i = \sigma_i(\widetilde{\mathbf{e}}_{i-1}) + \mathbf{v}_i$
Set $h = \mathsf{Hash}(\{\widetilde{\mathbf{e}}_i\}_{1 \le i \le N})$ $\xrightarrow{h}$

  Sample $i \xleftarrow{\$} \{1, \ldots, N\}$

$\xleftarrow{i}$ Compute $\mathtt{Seeds} = \mathsf{SeedPath}(\mathtt{MSeed}, i)$
If $i \neq 1$:
  Set $\mathtt{Resp} = \{c_i, \widetilde{\mathbf{e}}_i, \sigma_1, \mathtt{Seeds}\}$
Else:
  Set $\mathtt{Resp} = \{c_1, \widetilde{\mathbf{e}}_1, \mathtt{Seeds}\}$ $\xrightarrow{\mathtt{Resp}}$

  Generate $\{\mathtt{Seed}_j\}_{j \neq i} = \mathsf{GenSeeds}(\mathtt{Seeds})$
  For $j \neq i$:
    Sample $\mathtt{Seed}_j^*, \mathtt{Salt}_j \xleftarrow{\mathtt{Seed}_j} \{0;1\}^\lambda$
    Sample $\sigma_j \xleftarrow{\mathtt{Seed}_j^*} G$, $\mathbf{v}_j \xleftarrow{\mathtt{Seed}_j^*} \mathbb{F}_q^n$
    Set $c_j = \mathsf{Hash}(\mathtt{Salt}_j, \mathtt{Seed}_j^*)$
  If $i \neq 1$:
    Compute $c_1 = \mathsf{Hash}(\mathtt{Salt}_1, \mathtt{Seed}_1^*, \sigma_1)$
  Set $\widetilde{\mathbf{e}}_0 = \beta \mathbf{e}$
  For $j \neq i$:
    $\widetilde{\mathbf{e}}_j = \sigma_j(\widetilde{\mathbf{e}}_{j-1}) + \mathbf{v}_j$
  Compute $\widetilde{\mathbf{s}} = \widetilde{\mathbf{e}}_N \mathbf{H}^\top - \beta \mathbf{s}$
  Verify $c = \mathsf{Hash}(\widetilde{\mathbf{s}}, \{c_j\}_{1 \le j \le N})$
  Verify $h = \mathsf{Hash}(\{\widetilde{\mathbf{e}}_j\}_{1 \le j \le N})$
  If $i \neq 1$: verify also $\sigma_1 \in G$

Fig. 5. One round of the R-BG protocol

- A length-2λ salt is employed for the commitments (namely, in the computation of each $c_i^{(u)}$ and $c^{(u)}$), as well as to generate the challenges. This is necessary to prevent certain types of attacks (see e.g., [18]).
- As recommended in [18], to compute seeds and commitments, the salt is concatenated also with the round index u.
- To reduce the signature the signature size, the t commitments $c^{(1)}, \ldots, c^{(t)}$ are hashed into a single commitment c. The validity of c is checked at the end of the verification algorithm. The same optimization is employed for the t first responses $h^{(1)}, \ldots, h^{(t)}$.

Private Key $\sigma \in G$
Public Key $G = \langle \mathbf{x}_1, \dots, \mathbf{x}_m \rangle$, $\mathbf{e} \in G$, $\mathbf{H} \in \mathbb{F}_q^{r\times n}$, $\mathbf{s} = \sigma(\mathbf{e})\mathbf{H}^\top \in \mathbb{F}_q^r$

PROVER **VERIFIER**

Sample $\texttt{Salt} \xleftarrow{\$} \{0;1\}^{2\lambda}$
For $u = 1, \dots, t$:
  Sample $\texttt{MSeed}^{(u)} \xleftarrow{\$} \{0;1\}^{\lambda}$
  Set $\overline{\texttt{MSeed}}^{(u)} = (\texttt{MSeed}^{(u)}, \texttt{Msg}, \texttt{Salt}, u)$ **\\Concatenate salt and round index to master seed**
  Compute $\{\texttt{Seed}_i^{(u)}\}_{1\le i\le N} = \mathsf{SeedTree}(\overline{\texttt{MSeed}}^{(u)})$ **\\Generate seeds for u-th round**
  For $i = 2, \dots, N$:
    Sample $\texttt{Seed}_i^{*(u)}, \texttt{Salt}_i^{(u)} \xleftarrow{\texttt{Seed}_i^{(u)}} \{0;1\}^{\lambda}$
    Sample $\sigma_i^{(u)} \xleftarrow{\texttt{Seed}_i^{*(u)}} G$, $\mathbf{v}_i^{(u)} \xleftarrow{\texttt{Seed}_i^{*(u)}} \mathbb{F}_q^n$
    Set $c_i^{(u)} = \mathsf{Hash}(\texttt{Salt}_i^{(u)}, \texttt{Seed}_i^{*(u)}, \texttt{Msg}, \texttt{Salt}, u)$ **\\Hash also message, salt and round index**
  Set $\sigma_1^{(u)} = \sigma_2^{(u)-1} \circ \cdots \sigma_N^{(u)-1} \circ \sigma^{(u)}$
  Sample $\texttt{Seed}_1^{*(u)}, \texttt{Salt}_1^{(u)} \xleftarrow{\texttt{Seed}_1^{(u)}} \{0;1\}^{\lambda}$
  Sample $\mathbf{v}_1^{(u)} \xleftarrow{\texttt{Seed}_1^{*(u)}} \mathbb{F}_q^n$
  Set $c_1^{(u)} = \mathsf{Hash}(\texttt{Salt}_1^{(u)}, \texttt{Seed}_1^{*(u)}, \sigma_1^{(u)}, \texttt{Msg}, \texttt{Salt}, u)$
  Compute $\mathbf{v}^{(u)} = \mathbf{v}_N^{(u)} + \sum_{i=1}^{N-1} \sigma_N^{(u)} \circ \cdots \circ \sigma_{i+1}^{(u)}(\mathbf{v}_i^{(u)})$
  Set $c^{(u)} = \mathsf{Hash}(\mathbf{v}^{(u)}\mathbf{H}^\top, \{c_i^{(u)}\}_{1\le i\le N}, \texttt{Msg}, \texttt{Salt}, u)$
Set $c = \mathsf{Hash}(\{c^{(u)}\}_{1\le u\le t})$ **\\Single commitment of size 2λ**

Set $(\beta^{(1)}, \dots, \beta^{(t)}) = \mathsf{Hash}(\texttt{Msg}, \texttt{Salt}, c)$ **\\Generate first challenge**

For $u = 1, \dots, t$:
  Set $\widetilde{\mathbf{e}}_0^{(u)} = \beta^{(u)}\mathbf{e}$
  For $i = 1, \dots, N$:
    Set $\widetilde{\mathbf{e}}_i^{(u)} = \sigma_i^{(u)}(\widetilde{\mathbf{e}}_{i-1}^{(u)}) + \mathbf{v}_i^{(u)}$
  Set $h^{(u)} = \mathsf{Hash}(\{\widetilde{\mathbf{e}}_i^{(u)}\}_{1\le i\le N})$
Set $h = \mathsf{Hash}(\{h^{(u)}\}_{1\le u\le t})$
\\Single first response of size 2λ
Set $(i^{(1)}, \dots, i^{(t)}) = \mathsf{Hash}(\texttt{Msg}, \texttt{Salt}, c, h)$ **\\Generate second challenge**

For $u = 1, \dots, t$:
  Compute $\texttt{Seeds}^{(u)} = \mathsf{SeedPath}(\overline{\texttt{MSeed}}^{(u)}, i^{(u)})$ **\\Compute seeds path for u-th round**
  If $i^{(u)} \neq 1$:
    Set $\texttt{Resp}^{(u)} = \{c_i^{(u)}, \widetilde{\mathbf{e}}_i^{(u)}, \sigma_1^{(u)}, \texttt{Seeds}^{(u)}\}$
  Else:
    Set $\texttt{Resp}^{(u)} = \{c_1^{(u)}, \widetilde{\mathbf{e}}_1^{(u)}, \texttt{Seeds}^{(u)}\}$
Set $\texttt{Signature} = \left\{\texttt{Salt}, c, h, \{\texttt{Rsp}^{(u)}\}_{1\le u\le t}\right\}$

$\xrightarrow{\texttt{Signature}}$

Fig. 6. The R-BG signature scheme: signature generation

To set the value of t such that the attack in [30] is mitigated, we rely on the analysis in [15, Sect. 4.2]. To this end, let

$$P(t', t, N) = \sum_{j=t'}^{t} \binom{t}{j} \left(\frac{1}{q-1}\right)^j \left(\frac{N-1}{N}\right)^{t-j},$$

$$t^* = \arg\min_{0\le x\le t} \left\{ \frac{1}{P(x,t,N)} + N^{t-x} \right\}. \tag{9}$$

Then, we choose t so that $P(t^*, t, N)^{-1} + N^{t-t^*} > 2^{\lambda}$.

The signature size is given by

$$|\texttt{Signature}| = 6\lambda + t\big(\underbrace{n\lceil\log_2(q)\rceil}_{\widetilde{\mathbf{e}}_i} + \underbrace{m\lceil\log_2(z)\rceil}_{\sigma_1} + \underbrace{\lambda\lceil\log_2(N)\rceil}_{\text{Seeds}} + \underbrace{2\lambda}_{c_i}\big).$$

Private Key $\sigma \in G$
Public Key $G = \langle \mathbf{x}_1, \dots, \mathbf{x}_m \rangle$, $\mathbf{e} \in G$, $\mathbf{H} \in \mathbb{F}_q^{r \times n}$, $\mathbf{s} = \sigma(\mathbf{e})\mathbf{H}^\top \in \mathbb{F}_q^r$

PROVER	VERIFIER
$\xrightarrow{\texttt{Signature}}$	
Generate first challenge\\	Set $(\beta^{(1)}, \dots, \beta^{(t)}) = \mathsf{Hash}(\texttt{Msg}, \texttt{Salt}, c)$
Generate second challenge\\	Set $(i^{(1)}, \dots, i^{(t)}) = \mathsf{Hash}(\texttt{Msg}, \texttt{Salt}, c, h)$
	For $u = 1, \dots, t$:
Generate seeds for u-th round \\	Generate $\{\mathsf{Seed}_j^{(u)}\}_{j \neq i} = \mathsf{GenSeeds}(\mathsf{Seeds}^{(u)})$
	For $j \neq i^{(u)}$:
	Sample $\texttt{Seed}_j^{*(u)}, \texttt{Salt}_j^{(u)} \xleftarrow{\texttt{Seed}_j^{(u)}} \{0;1\}^\lambda$
	Sample $\sigma_j^{(u)} \xleftarrow{\texttt{Seed}_j^{*(u)}} G$, $\mathbf{v}_j^{(u)} \xleftarrow{\texttt{Seed}_j^{*(u)}} \mathbb{F}_q^n$
	Set $c_j^{(u)} = \mathsf{Hash}(\texttt{Salt}_j, \texttt{Seed}_j^*, \texttt{Msg}, \texttt{Salt}, u)$
	If $i^{(u)} \neq 1$:
	Compute $c_1^{(u)} = \mathsf{Hash}(\texttt{Salt}_1^{(u)}, \texttt{Seed}_1^{*(u)}, \sigma_1^{(u)}, \texttt{Msg}, \texttt{Salt}, u)$
	Set $\widetilde{\mathbf{e}}_0^{(u)} = \beta^{(u)}\mathbf{e}$
	For $j \neq i^{(u)}$:
	$\widetilde{\mathbf{e}}_j^{(u)} = \sigma_j^{(u)}(\widetilde{\mathbf{e}}_{j-1}^{(u)}) + \mathbf{v}_j^{(u)}$
	Compute $\widetilde{\mathbf{s}}^{(u)} = \widetilde{\mathbf{e}}_N^{(u)}\mathbf{H}^\top - \beta^{(u)}\mathbf{s}$
	Compute $c^{(u)} = \mathsf{Hash}(\widetilde{\mathbf{s}}, \{c_j\}_{1 \leq j \leq N}, \texttt{Msg}, \texttt{Salt}, u)$
	Compute $h^{(u)} = \mathsf{Hash}(\{\widetilde{\mathbf{e}}_j^{(u)}\}_{1 \leq j \leq N})$
Reject the signature if $\sigma_1^{(u)}$ is badly formed\\	If $(i^{(u)} = 1) \wedge (\sigma_1^{(u)} \notin G)$:
	Output Reject
Verify single commitment\\	If $c \neq \mathsf{Hash}(\{c_{1 \leq u \leq t}^{(u)}\})$:
	Output Reject
Verify single first response\\	If $h \neq \mathsf{Hash}(\{h_{1 \leq u \leq t}^{(u)}\})$:
	Output Reject
Signature is valid\\	Output Accept

Fig. 7. The R-BG signature scheme: signature verification

When R-SDP is used, $m\lceil \log_2(z) \rceil$ gets replaced by $n\lceil \log_2(z) \rceil$.

Some instances of the resulting signature scheme are reported in Table 4, where the parameters are chosen in accordance with the above formula for the number of executions and the respective generic decoders. Signatures obtained from R-SDP are slightly larger than those based on PKP; instead, when using R-SDP(G), we achieve significant reductions with respect to R-SDP and, ultimately, beat PKP. We have considered the case of $z = (q-1)/2$ and $z \ll q$; the latter has slightly larger signatures but, when implemented, should lead to a faster scheme due to the arithmetics over $\mathbb{F}_z$.

Timings. We have developed a Proof of Concept implementation for the R-BG protocol based on R-SDP(G)[4,5]. The measured timings are reported in Table 5. Even though the implementation is very basic and does not use any advanced optimization (e.g., no AVX2 instructions nor parallelism), the obtained timings are already very promising. This was expected, as all the required operations are essentially symmetric primitives and linear algebra (multiplications and sums) with small vectors and matrices. As expected, choosing small values for z leads to

[4] https://github.com/secomms/RBG.

[5] The provided code considers only one round of the protocol. Multiplying the timings by t (the number of parallel executions), we obtain a very reliable estimate of the overall required time.

some speed-ups since operations over $\mathbb{F}_z$ (e.g., sampling from G and combining restricted objects) get easier.

Table 4. Performances of the BG scheme [15] based on different problems

	q	z	n	k	m	N	t	Sign. Size (kB)
PKP	997		61	33		32	42	10.0
						256	31	8.9
R-SDP	991	33	77	38		32	42	10.0
						256	31	8.9
R-SDP(G)	971	97	44	26	26	32	42	8.1
						256	31	7.5
	1019	509	40	16	18	32	42	7.8
						256	31	7.2

Table 5. Benchmarks for the R-BG protocol based on R-SDP(G), taken on a 3.4 GHz Intel i7-6700 CPU. The reported timings are the average values, measured with 10 000 tests.

Parameters (q, z, n, k, m)	Variant	Sign. Size (kB)	**KeyGen**		**Sign**		**Verify**	
			MCycles	ms	MCycles	ms	MCycles	ms
971, 97, 44, 26, 26	fast	8.1	0.06	< 0.1	18.7	5.46	12.2	3.57
	small	7.5	0.06	< 0.1	108.4	31.08	72.5	21.3
1019, 509, 40, 16, 18	fast	7.8	0.05	< 0.1	20.4	6.0	12.8	3.8
	small	7.2	0.05	< 0.1	117.7	34.5	75.8	22.2

7 Comparison with NIST Candidates

In this section, we compare the schemes discussed in this paper with signature schemes submitted to the NIST additional call. We first consider code-based schemes and then widen the comparison to other relevant schemes.

Comparison with Code-Based Signatures. In Table 6, we compare the two schemes R-GPS and R-BG with the code-based signature schemes submitted to NIST. Data about these schemes are also visualized in Fig. 8; Fig. 8a reports signature sizes and public key size, while Fig. 8b shows signatures size and verification times[6]. All schemes in the category use the ZK/MPCitH approach and have a signing time that is more or less equal to the verification time. The only remarkable exception is WAVE, which is a hash&sign scheme and for which signing is approximately 5 times slower than verifying. Note that some of the

[6] Which we have collected from https://pqshield.github.io/nist-sigs-zoo/. Data are referred to October 15, 2023.

Table 6. Comparison between NIST submissions and R-BG, R-GPS for Level I; all sizes are expressed in kB.

Problem	Scheme	Pk size	Sign. size	Pk+Sign. size	Variant
SDP	SDitH [3]	0.12	8.24	8.36	small
		0.12	10.12	10.24	fast
Rank SDP	RYDE [4]	0.09	5.96	6.04	small
		0.09	7.45	7.53	fast
Matrix rank SDP	MIRA [5]	0.08	5.64	5.72	small
		0.08	7.38	7.46	fast
	MiRitH [2]	0.13	4.54	4.67	small
		0.14	9.11	9.25	fast
PKP	PERK [1]	0.24	6.10	6.30	small
		0.15	8.35	8.50	fast
large weight $(U, U+V)-$ code	WAVE [10]	3677	0.82	3678	-
Code Equivalence	LESS [6]	14.03	8.60	22.63	small
		98.20	5.33	103.53	fast
Matrix code equivalence	MEDS [20]	9.92	9.90	19.82	small
		13.22	12.98	26.20	fast
R-SDP	CROSS [7]	0.06	10.30	10.36	small
		0.06	12.94	13.01	fast
	R-BG	0.1	8.9	9.0	small
		0.1	10.0	10.1	fast
	R-GPS	0.1	12.5	12.6	small
		0.1	14.8	14.9	fast
R-SDP(G)	CROSS [7]	0.04	7.63	7.66	small
		0.04	8.67	8.7	fast
	R-BG	0.1	7.2	7.3	small
		0.1	7.8	7.9	fast
	R-GPS	0.1	11.5	11.6	small
		0.1	12.7	12.8	fast

proposed schemes have more than just the usual two "fast" and "small" parameter sets, however, in order for all the schemes to fit into one table, we chose to show for each scheme the smallest and largest total sizes, i.e., signature size plus public key size. This is a common measure, as for example certificates would require to download both. We did not include the two broken schemes FuLeeca [31] and Enhanced pqsigRM [19]. We only compare the schemes for Level 1, which corresponds to 128 AES gates.

For R-GPS, the fast instances are those with $N = 512$ and the short ones have $N = 4096$; for R-BG, fast instances have $N = 32$ and $t = 42$ and short variants have $N = 256$ and $t = 31$. As we see from Table 6, the presented protocols are very competitive towards the submitted schemes. In particular, comparing R-BG

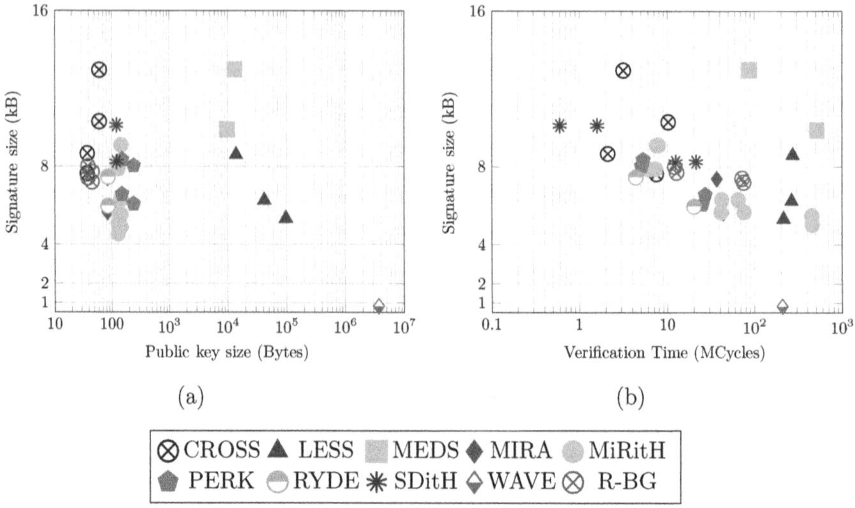

Fig. 8. Comparison between R-BG and code-based signature schemes from the NIST competition.

using R-SDP(G), we are able to achieve signatures that are smaller than those of SDitH [3], which is based on SDP.

Among the considered schemes, there is also CROSS [7], a NIST candidate that originated from the work presented in this paper. CROSS uses a very simple ZK protocol, with soundness error $\approx \frac{1}{2}$, which can be thought of as an optimized version of the CVE protocol [17]. It has been designed for algorithmic efficiency and simplicity, while R-BG aims to reduce signature sizes at the cost of some computational overhead. The trade-offs achieved by the two schemes are different, as it is visible in Fig. 8. Observe that the only scheme with faster verification is SDitH. Notice that timings for SDitH are already referred to those of an optimized implementation; instead, the timings for CROSS are referred to the reference implementation. Likely, an optimized implementation can significantly boost timings and make CROSS much faster.

More generally, we see that solutions based on R-SDP and R-SDP(G) compare favorably with the other code-based schemes. Again, a remarkable exception is WAVE which has much shorter signatures but has much larger public keys and is slower. LESS and MEDS, instead, have a somewhat similar profile analysis. They have large public keys and are generically slower than the other schemes. Signature sizes are in the same ballpark as those of the other schemes, even though LESS instances with larger public keys have shorter signatures (using more equivalent codes in the public key reduces linearly the soundness error).

Finally, we remark that we have not explored optimizations for the implementation of R-BG. We expect that a more careful implementation can receive a significant boost.

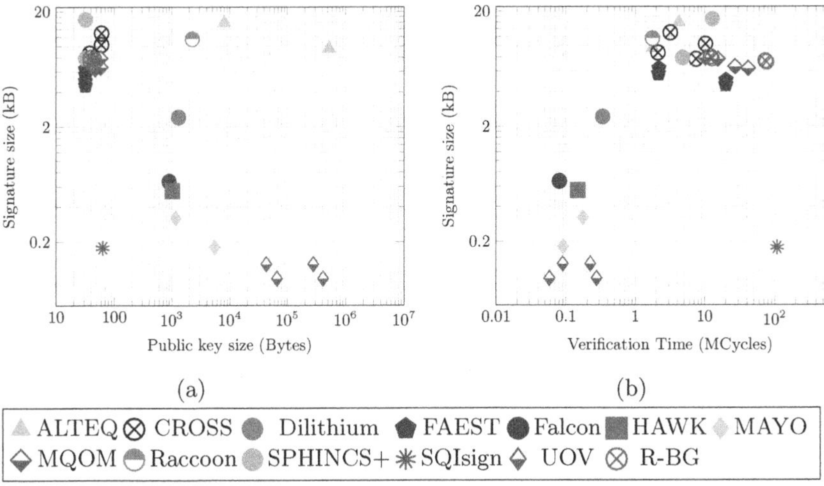

Fig. 9. Comparison between CROSS, R-BG, and other signature schemes from the NIST competition

Comparison with Signatures Based on Other Problems. To see more comparisons, in Fig. 9 we consider other relevant signature schemes from the NIST competition. The comparison shows that both CROSS and R-BG have performances which are, essentially, analogous to those of FAEST and MQOM (even though the latter scheme appears to be slower); this was somehow expected, since also these two schemes are based on ZK/MPCitH paradigms. SQIsign has signatures which are among the shortest in the competition and very compact public keys, but pays a significant price in terms of efficiency (it is the slowest scheme among those in Fig. 9b).

The figures show that there is still a significant gap between schemes based on restricted errors and lattice-based schemes such as HAWK, Falcon and Dilithium (for both signature sizes and timings). An exception is Raccoon, whose signatures and timings are in the same range as those of CROSS and R-BG, hence, are larger than those of typical lattice-based schemes: this is not surprising since, differently from the other lattice-based schemes, Raccoon has been designed aiming for inherent protection against side-channel attacks.

Multivariate hash&sign schemes (MAYO and UOV) have shorter signatures and are faster, but require larger public keys, in particular, UOV. The public keys of MAYO are significantly shorter but the scheme is based on somewhat very new security assumptions. MQOM is, instead, a multivariate-based MPCitH scheme: its performances are essentially analogous to those of CROSS and R-BG.

Finally, we consider SPHINCS+, which comes with two versions. The short version has signatures which are essentially as large as those of R-BG (≈ 8 kB), while the fast version has much larger signatures (≈ 17 kB). Verification for SPHINCS+ takes time in the same ballpark as both CROSS and R-BG, while signing is, for both the fast and short versions, much slower.

After these comparisons, we can conclude that using R-SDP and R-SDP(G) leads to competitive solutions. The performances for what concerns all the relevant figures (public keys, signatures and computational complexity) are analogous to those of other ZK/MPCitH schemes, even though schemes based on restricted errors are very promising in terms of timings.

8 Conclusion

We studied the Restricted Syndrome Decoding Problem (R-SDP) and introduced a new version of the problem, called R-SDP(G). Both problems are NP-complete, however, as for most code-based problems it is unknown whether an average case reduction exists - we leave this as an interesting open problem. These two problems allow us to represent data to be exchanged in ZK protocols very compactly. We analyzed the security of these problems and gave conservative criteria for parameter choices. We adapted some existing ZK protocols to these new problems and considered the resulting signature schemes, called R-GPS and R-BG. The resulting schemes are able to achieve signatures in the order of 7 kB, which are highly competitive and compare well with other signature schemes submitted to NIST. The theory developed in this paper has been used as a basis for CROSS, a signature scheme submitted to the NIST call for additional signatures.

Acknowledgements. The authors would like to thank the anonymous reviewers for their helpful comments.

Violetta Weger is supported by the European Union's Horizon 2020 research and innovation programme under the Marie Skłodowska-Curie grant agreement no. 899987.

Marco Baldi is supported by the Italian Ministry of University's PRIN 2022 program under the "Mathematical Primitives for Post Quantum Digital Signatures" (P2022J4HRR) and "POst quantum Identification and eNcryption primiTives: dEsign and Realization (POINTER)" (2022M2JLF2) projects funded by the European Union - Next Generation EU.

Sebastian Bitzer and Antonia Wachter-Zeh acknowledge the financial support by the Federal Ministry of Education and Research of Germany in the program of "Souverän. Digital. Vernetzt.". Joint project 6G-life, project identification number: 16KISK002.

Declarations. The authors have no competing interests to declare that are relevant to the content of this article.

References

1. Aaraj, N., et al.: PERK: PERmuted Kernels. Submission to the NIST Post-Quantum Standardization project (2023)
2. Adj, G., et al.: MiRitH: MinRank in-the-Head. Submission to the NIST Post-Quantum Standardization project (2023)
3. Aguilar Melchor, C., et al.: SDitH: Syndrome Decoding in-the-Head. Submission to the NIST Post-Quantum Standardization project (2023)

4. Aragon, N., et al.: RYDE: Rank Decoding in-the-Head. Submission to the NIST Post-Quantum Standardization project (2023)
5. Aragon, N., et al.: MIRA: MinRank in-the-Head. Submission to the NIST Post-Quantum Standardization project (2023)
6. Baldi, M., et al.: LESS: Linear Equivalence Signature Scheme. Submission to the NIST Post-Quantum Standardization project (2023)
7. Baldi, M., et al.: CROSS: codes and restricted objects signature scheme. Submission to the NIST Post-Quantum Standardization project (2023)
8. Baldi, M., et al.: A new path to code-based signatures via identification schemes with restricted errors. arXiv preprint arXiv:2008.06403 (2020)
9. Baldi, M., Bitzer, S., Pavoni, A., Santini, P., Wachter-Zeh, A., Weger, V.: Zero knowledge protocols and signatures from the restricted syndrome decoding problem. Cryptology ePrint Archive (2023)
10. Banegas, G., et al.: WAVE. Submission to the NIST Post-Quantum Standardization project (2023)
11. Barg, S.: Some new NP-complete coding problems. Problemy Peredachi Informatsii **30**(3), 23–28 (1994)
12. Becker, A., Coron, J.-S., Joux, A.: Improved generic algorithms for hard knapsacks. In: Paterson, K.G. (ed.) EUROCRYPT 2011. LNCS, vol. 6632, pp. 364–385. Springer, Heidelberg (2011). https://doi.org/10.1007/978-3-642-20465-4_21
13. Berlekamp, E., McEliece, R., Van Tilborg, H.: On the inherent intractability of certain coding problems. IEEE Trans. Inf. Theory **24**(3), 384–386 (1978)
14. Beullens, W.: Sigma protocols for MQ, PKP and SIS, and fishy signature schemes. In: Canteaut, A., Ishai, Y. (eds.) Advances in Cryptology – EUROCRYPT 2020: 39th Annual International Conference on the Theory and Applications of Cryptographic Techniques, Zagreb, Croatia, May 10–14, 2020, Proceedings, Part III, pp. 183–211. Springer International Publishing, Cham (2020). https://doi.org/10.1007/978-3-030-45727-3_7
15. Bidoux, L., Gaborit, P.: Shorter signatures from proofs of knowledge for the SD, MQ, PKP and RSD Problems. arXiv preprint arXiv:2204.02915 (2022)
16. Carrier, K., Debris-Alazard, T., Meyer-Hilfiger, C., Tillich, J.-P.: Statistical decoding 2.0: reducing decoding to LPN. In: Agrawal, S., Lin, D. (eds.) Advances in Cryptology – ASIACRYPT 2022: 28th International Conference on the Theory and Application of Cryptology and Information Security, Taipei, Taiwan, December 5–9, 2022, Proceedings, Part IV, pp. 477–507. Springer Nature Switzerland, Cham (2022). https://doi.org/10.1007/978-3-031-22972-5_17
17. Cayrel, P.-L., Véron, P., El Yousfi Alaoui, S.M.: A zero-knowledge identification scheme based on the q-ary syndrome decoding problem. In: Biryukov, A., Gong, G., Stinson, D.R. (eds.) Selected Areas in Cryptography, pp. 171–186. Springer Berlin Heidelberg, Berlin, Heidelberg (2011). https://doi.org/10.1007/978-3-642-19574-7_12
18. Chailloux, A., Etinski, S.: On the (in) security of optimized stern-like signature schemes. Designs, Codes and Cryptography (2023)
19. Cho, J., No, J.S., Lee, Y., Kim, Y.S., Koo, Z.: Enhanced pqsigRM. Submission to the NIST Post-Quantum Standardization project (2023)
20. Chou, T., et al.: MEDS: Matrix equivalence digital signature. Submission to the NIST Post-Quantum Standardization project (2023)
21. Debris-Alazard, T., Sendrier, N., Tillich, J.P.: Wave: A new code-based signature scheme. In: Asiacrypt 2019 (2019)
22. Debris-Alazard, T., Tillich, J.P.: Statistical decoding. In: 2017 IEEE International Symposium on Information Theory (ISIT), pp. 1798–1802. IEEE (2017)

23. Dumer, I.I.: Two decoding algorithms for linear codes. Problemy Peredachi Informatsii **25**(1), 24–32 (1989)
24. Feneuil, T., Joux, A., Rivain, M.: Shared permutation for syndrome decoding: New zero-knowledge protocol and code-based signature, pp. 1–46. Designs, Codes and Cryptography pp (2022)
25. Fiat, A., Shamir, A.: How to prove yourself: practical solutions to identification and signature problems. In: Odlyzko, A.M. (ed.) CRYPTO 1986. LNCS, vol. 263, pp. 186–194. Springer, Heidelberg (1987). https://doi.org/10.1007/3-540-47721-7_12
26. Gueron, S., Persichetti, E., Santini, P.: Designing a practical code-based signature scheme from zero-knowledge proofs with trusted setup. Cryptography **6**(1), 5 (2022)
27. Hülsing, A., Rijneveld, J., Samardjiska, S., Schwabe, P.: From 5-pass MQ-based identification to MQ-based signatures. IACR Cryptol. ePrint Arch. **2016**, 708 (2016)
28. Ishai, Y., Kushilevitz, E., Ostrovsky, R., Sahai, A.: Zero-knowledge from secure multiparty computation. In: Proceedings of the Thirty-ninth Annual ACM Symposium on Theory Of Computing, pp. 21–30 (2007)
29. Jabri, A.A.: A statistical decoding algorithm for general linear block codes. In: Honary, B. (ed.) Cryptography and Coding 2001. LNCS, vol. 2260, pp. 1–8. Springer, Heidelberg (2001). https://doi.org/10.1007/3-540-45325-3_1
30. Kales, D., Zaverucha, G.: An attack on some signature schemes constructed from five-pass identification schemes. In: Krenn, S., Shulman, H., Vaudenay, S. (eds.) CANS 2020. LNCS, vol. 12579, pp. 3–22. Springer, Cham (2020). https://doi.org/10.1007/978-3-030-65411-5_1
31. Ritterhoff, S., et al.: FuLeeca: A Lee-based Signature Scheme. Submission to the NIST Post-Quantum Standardization project (2023)
32. Santini, P., Baldi, M., Chiaraluce, F.: Computational hardness of the permuted kernel and subcode equivalence problems. Cryptology ePrint Archive (2022)
33. Shamir, A.: An efficient identification scheme based on permuted kernels (extended abstract). In: Brassard, G. (ed.) CRYPTO 1989. LNCS, vol. 435, pp. 606–609. Springer, New York (1990). https://doi.org/10.1007/0-387-34805-0_54
34. Singleton, R.: Maximum distance q-nary codes. IEEE Trans. Inf. Theory **10**(2), 116–118 (1964)
35. Stern, J.: A method for finding codewords of small weight. In: Cohen, G., Wolfmann, J. (eds.) Coding Theory 1988. LNCS, vol. 388, pp. 106–113. Springer, Heidelberg (1989). https://doi.org/10.1007/BFb0019850
36. Stern, J.: A new identification scheme based on syndrome decoding. In: Stinson, D.R. (ed.) CRYPTO 1993. LNCS, vol. 773, pp. 13–21. Springer, Heidelberg (1994). https://doi.org/10.1007/3-540-48329-2_2
37. Stern, J.: Designing identification schemes with keys of short size. In: Desmedt, Y.G. (ed.) CRYPTO 1994. LNCS, vol. 839, pp. 164–173. Springer, Heidelberg (1994). https://doi.org/10.1007/3-540-48658-5_18
38. Weger, V., Khathuria, K., Horlemann, A.L., Battaglioni, M., Santini, P., Persichetti, E.: On the hardness of the Lee syndrome decoding problem. In: Advances in Mathematics of Communications (2022)

Ring/Module Learning with Errors Under Linear Leakage – Hardness and Applications

Zhedong Wang[1,2], Qiqi Lai[2,3(✉)], and Feng-Hao Liu[4]

[1] School of Cyber Science and Engineering, Shanghai Jiao Tong University, Shanghai, China
wzdstill@sjtu.edu.cn

[2] State Key Laboratory of Cryptology, P. O. Box 5159, Beijing 100878, China
laiqq@snnu.edu.cn

[3] School of Computer Science, Shaanxi Normal University, Xi'an, China

[4] Washington State University, Pullman, WA, USA
feng-hao.liu@wsu.edu

Abstract. This paper studies the hardness of decision Module Learning with Errors (MLWE) under linear leakage, which has been used as a foundation to derive more efficient lattice-based zero-knowledge proofs in a recent paradigm of Lyubashevsky, Nguyen, and Seiler (PKC 21). Unlike in the plain LWE setting, it was unknown whether this problem remains provably hard in the module/ring setting.

This work shows a reduction from the standard search MLWE to decision MLWE with linear leakage. Thus, the main problem remains hard asymptotically as long as the non-leakage version of MLWE is hard. Additionally, we also refine the paradigm of Lyubashevsky, Nguyen, and Seiler (PKC 21) by showing a more fine-grained tradeoff between efficiency and leakage. This can lead to further optimizations of lattice proofs under the paradigm.

1 Introduction

Ring/Module Learning with Errors (RLWE/MLWE) is an important foundation in the category of lattice-based cryptography, which is a plausible direction for post-quantum cryptography. RLWE/MLWE facilities more efficient constructions of public-key encryption, e.g., several candidates in the NIST PQC call, as well as advanced crypto systems including identity-based encryption [1,27,45,46] and fully homomorphic encryption [16], in comparison to those based on the plain LWE [2,3,14]. Due to the efficiency advantage, this problem has drawn a lot of attentions since its proposal [29,37,38,44].

Zero-knowledge proof (ZKP) is a key technical tool in many applications with strong privacy requirements. Towards quantum-safe solutions, researchers have put a lot of efforts in the direction of lattice-based ZKP [7,9,11,19,20,23, 32,35,36,39]. Despite feasibility results (though not practical) in the standard common reference string (CRS) model [43], many new highly efficient solutions

Q. Tang and V. Teague (Eds.): PKC 2024, LNCS 14602, pp. 275–304, 2024.
https://doi.org/10.1007/978-3-031-57722-2_9

are constructed in the random oracle model in recent years, using the technique of *Fiat-Shamir with aborts* [32]. In recent years, tremendous progress has been made to optimize the concrete efficiency, e.g., improving the proof sizes for showing knowledge of an $\boldsymbol{s}$ with small coefficients satisfying $\mathbf{A}\boldsymbol{s} = \boldsymbol{t}$, from 384 KB [11] to 47 KB [23]. Additionally, research in this line has deep impacts on the design of efficient lattice-based signatures [19,20,34] and as well other privacy-preserving protocols [24,25,30].

Recently, Lyubashevsky, Nguyen, and Seiler [36] identified a new paradigm that can improve the proof size by roughly 30% over the prior best constructions [23,35], by using *leakage* to trade efficiency. More specifically, they derive a novel modified rejection sampling strategy, called *subset rejection sampling*, that leaks one bit of the randomness of a one-time commitment, which is used in the commit-and-prove paradigm. This key technique to the efficiency improvements, is allowing smaller proofs. For security, as long as the one-time commitment is leakage resilient against this class of leakage, then the overall scheme is secure.

Now, the question turns to whether we can prove that the one-time commitment is leakage resilient to one bit. To do this, the work [36] showed that this task can be reduced to a leakage version of the *decisional* MLWE problem against linear functions,[1] i.e., as long as the decisional MLWE problem is leakage resilient for linear functions (over the coefficients of the secret and the error), then so is the one-time commitment against the same class, implying security against the bit leakage applied to any linear function.

Despite the fact that there are reduction results showing positive results in the plain-LWE settings [4,36,41], it was identified as an important open question in [36] whether the same results carry to the ring setting. On the other hand, the work [36] speculated that one-bit leakage will not hurt security, at least under the currently best known attacks. However, it is not clear whether the leakage version of RLWE/MLWE is inherently hard or we just have not found an attack yet by exploiting the ring structure with the leakage. This motivates the main research goal of the work:

> (**Main Research Goal**) Determine whether the leakage version of decisional RLWE/MLWE against linear functions (as required in [36]) is inherently hard (as RLWE/MLWE).

The new rejection sampling paradigm [36] provides a promising opportunity for achieving more practical lattice proofs, with numerous identified applications. Therefore, it is crucial to thoroughly investigate the underlying hardness foundations, to ensure that using leakage to trade efficiency does not hurt security in a provable manner. This would enhance the confidence in the practical adoption of this emerging paradigm. Our main goal is the key to achieve this.

1.1 Our Results

This work provides an affirmative answer to the main task. Particularly, our main result is to prove the following informal theorem.

[1] In fact, the work [36] only needs a slightly weaker version known as extended (R)LWE.

Theorem 1.1 (Main Result, Informally Stated). *Under the hardness of search* RLWE *(for appropriate parameters), the decisional* RLWE *under leakage of linear functions (required as [36]) is hard.*

In summary, our result provides stronger theoretical justification, increasing confidence in the foundation of the design paradigm [36]. This result has practical implications, as it can be applied to enhance the efficiency of Zero-Knowledge Proofs (ZKP) and other lattice-based cryptographic systems. Additionally, our reduction can be generalized to the module setting, i.e., MLWE, offering more flexibility in terms of design choices.

An important aspect of our contribution is that our reduction works in the full-splitting setting, where $q\mathcal{R}$ completely splits into linear factors. Before this paper, as far as we know, there is limited knowledge regarding MLWE/RLWE with leakage in the full-splitting setting, as compared to the low-splitting setting [31]. Given that the full-splitting structure plays a crucial role in various efficient lattice proofs, including some recent works of [7,23,33] for establishing more general relations and improving efficiency, our advances in this setting are significant.[2] We present further details in the technical overview (Sect. 1.2) and Sect. 4.

Our second contribution is to refine the subset rejection sampling strategy of [36], showing a more fine-grained tradeoff between efficiency and leakage, in the case of full-splitting underlying ring. Particularly, as listed in Table 1, if we allow $\log_2 6$ bits of leakage, the rejection sampling parameter α can be slightly improved from 175.67 to 171.42, which slightly reduces the proof size from 16.56 KB to 16.48 KB. This can be further stretched – using $\log q$ bits of leakage to improve the parameters by a factor of 52% (83.138 versus 175.67), which reduces the proof size by a factor of 10% (14.96 KB versus 16.56 KB). Here, q is the underlying modulus. By Theorem 1.1, the problem remains hard in these leakage settings, at least asymptotically. An interesting open problem is to determine concrete security of ℓ-bit leakage and the efficiency tradeoff, finding the optimal parameters for the best efficiency. We present more details later in the technical overview and Sect. 4.3.

1.2 Technical Overview

In this section, we present an overview of our techniques. First we describe the computational problem of the main focus – decisional Module Learning with Errors (MLWE) with linear leakage, and then the hardness results and applications.

Problem Statement. Let $\mathcal{R}_q$ denote some (polynomial) residual ring of degree d and modulus q, e.g., $\mathcal{R}_q = \mathbb{Z}_q[X]/(X^d+1)$, and later on $\mathcal{R}$ refers the underlying ring and q is the modulus. We notice that the MLWE problem can be stated as the

[2] In the very recent work [33], while the full-splitting structure is not required to prove the ℓ_2 norm, it is still necessary to prove the ℓ_∞ norm or the knowledge of the component-wise product of two vectors.

Table 1. Rough comparison of efficiency under different rejection sampling algorithms for the opening protocol with full-splitting underlying ring in Fig. 2. Here rep. denotes prover's expected repetition times, $\mathfrak{l}$ the number of leakage bits, α the derivation of the discrete Gaussian, which will influences the proof size of $\boldsymbol{z}_i$. The concrete parameters are listed using the following example setting: the dimension η of $\boldsymbol{z}_i$ is 3, the ring dimension d is 1024, the modulus q is roughly 2^{32}, and the boosting parameter $\hat{k}$ is 4.

	rep.	α	Size of $\boldsymbol{z}_i$: $\hat{k}\eta d \log_2(12 \cdot \alpha)$	$\mathfrak{l}$
Rej_1	≈ 6	175.67	16.56 KB	1
Rej_2	≈ 6	171.42	16.48 KB	$\log_2 6$
Rej_3	≈ 6	83.138	14.96 KB	≈ 32

following: given a ring matrix/vector $\mathbf{A} \in \mathcal{R}_q^{m \times n}$ and a ring vector $\boldsymbol{b} = \mathbf{A} \cdot \boldsymbol{s} + \boldsymbol{e}$ where $\boldsymbol{s} \in \mathcal{R}_q^n$ is some secret ring vector and $\boldsymbol{e} \in \mathcal{R}_q^m$ is some small error ring vector, the search problem asks to find the secret $\boldsymbol{s}$ and the decision version asks to distinguish $\boldsymbol{b}$ from a uniformly random vector. The module setting captures both the RLWE and plain LWE as special cases – if the module rank is one, i.e., $n = 1$, then the problem is RLWE. On the other hand, if the underlying ring has degree $d = 1$, then this is the plain LWE. All these variants have been extensively studied [29,37,42] and we have strong confidence in their hardness.

To study the leakage version of the MLWE, we first define the leakage function of our interests, which is the class required in [36]. Let $L_{\boldsymbol{a},\boldsymbol{a}'}(\boldsymbol{s}, \boldsymbol{e})$ be defined as $\langle \phi(\boldsymbol{a}), \phi(\boldsymbol{s}) \rangle + \langle \phi(\boldsymbol{a}'), \phi(\boldsymbol{e}) \rangle \in \mathbb{Z}_q$, where ϕ is the coefficient embedding function, i.e., it maps a ring element into a vector of $\mathbb{Z}_q^d$ that represents the coefficient vector with respect to the power basis $(1, X, X^2, \ldots, X^{d-1})$, and maps ring vectors $\mathcal{R}_q^n$ to $\mathbb{Z}_q^{nd}$, analogously. In this work, we consider the class that contains all such functions regarding the inner product of the coefficient embeddings over both the secret $\boldsymbol{s}$ and the error $\boldsymbol{e}$.[3] Again, we would emphasize that leakage over *both* the secret and error is a critical requirement in the paradigm of [36].

Given the above context, MLWE with linear leakage can be defined in a simple way – the adversary/solver is given $L_{\boldsymbol{a},\boldsymbol{a}'}(\boldsymbol{s}, \boldsymbol{e})$ in addition to the regular MLWE samples. The task of the problem then becomes to find the secret $\boldsymbol{s}$ or distinguish $\boldsymbol{b}$ from the uniform vector, given the leakage. We notice that this problem is very related to another notion called extended MLWE [12] with the following difference: the extended MLWE chooses $\boldsymbol{a}, \boldsymbol{a}'$ from a small discrete Gaussian distribution, yet our leakage version of MLWE allows the adversary to specify $\boldsymbol{a}, \boldsymbol{a}'$ in the beginning of the experiment. Thus, our leakage version of MLWE is stronger than the extended MLWE.

[3] In fact, our leakage class in the main body is slightly more general, i.e., the leakage function can include slight multiplicative shifts. Nevertheless, this simplified version is sufficient to demonstrate our core ideas in the introduction.

For the application need, we consider the case where the secret $\boldsymbol{s}$ is sampled according to the discrete Gaussian distribution, the same as the error $\boldsymbol{e}$.

Some Prior Results. We first review previous works and then discuss their limitations, particularly the obstacles they face in analyzing the foundation of [36].

- In the context of plain LWE, it was demonstrated that the extended LWE is provably as hard as LWE [4,41]. However, as highlighted in [36], this technique does not extend to the ring/module setting due to either a loss of exponential reduction or a dimension mismatch during the reduction transformation.
- The work [12] (and the later journal version [13]) studied a version of extended MLWE. Their leakage function takes the form $\langle \boldsymbol{z}, \boldsymbol{e} \rangle$, where the inner product is defined according to the ring vectors. It should be noted that there exists a gap between the reduction in [13] and the application of ZKP in [36], as the latter requires the leakage is over both the secret and error, and the inner product is defined according to the vectors over $\mathbb{Z}_q$ (under the coefficient embeddings). Besides, their reduction limits to the MLWE (i.e. module rank $k \geq 2$), and is unable to capture the case of RLWE.
- Two recent and concurrent works [22,28] considered the case of MLWE with leakages. Among them, [22] examined a scenario where the leakage is applied to the error but not the secret, and [28] examined the scenario where the leakage is applied to both the secrete and error. However, these two works both have several limitations. Specifically, the leakage function in [22] takes the form $\boldsymbol{e} \cdot \mathbf{Z} + \boldsymbol{e}'$, where $\mathbf{Z}$ is a low-norm ring matrix specified by the adversary and $\boldsymbol{e}'$ is an independent Gaussian error hidden to the adversary. As their analysis relies on the inclusion of $\boldsymbol{e}'$, their results are not expected to be applicable to our setting and are therefore insufficient for analyzing the framework of [36]. [28] specified the leakage function with the form $c \cdot \begin{pmatrix} \boldsymbol{s} \\ \boldsymbol{e} \end{pmatrix} + \boldsymbol{y}$, where $\boldsymbol{y}$ is a gaussian vector hidden to adversary. The analysis of [28] is also unable to be directly applied for the framework of [36], as the latter requires to analyze the leakage function with the form $\left\langle \phi \begin{pmatrix} \boldsymbol{s} \\ \boldsymbol{e} \end{pmatrix}, \phi(\boldsymbol{z}) \right\rangle$, which can not be simulated by the function in [28].
  We note that it is unknown whether our results can be inferred from those of [22,28] or vice versa, so we consider them as incomparable results.
- Another approach to analyze leakage is by employing the lossy-matrix technique [5,15,31], yet the current developments have several limitations. For instance, the work [5] is only applicable to the plain LWE setting due to the absence of the leftover hash lemma in the ring setting at that time. The work [15] is limited to the search version, and it was unclear how to extend their techniques to the decision version. The work [31] derived a ring-leftover hash lemma (LHL), and generalized the analysis of [5] to the module setting, i.e., MLWE. Nonetheless, there are subtleties where their analytical techniques [31] cannot be applied, as elaborated below.
  Particularly, let n be the module rank, d be the ring dimension, and $q\mathcal{R}$ splits into c factors for $1 \leq c \leq d$. Their result (particularly the ring LHL) requires

that $n = \omega(c)$ in order to guarantee the required entropy lower bound. Thus, in the low-splitting setting (e.g., $c = 2$), the techniques [31] can be used to analyze for $n = O(1)$, e.g., $n = 2$. However, for the high-splitting (e.g., $c = d$), then their technique requires $n > d$. To choose more competitive parameters in many practical works, n is set to be $O(1)$ (even 1 for the RLWE), e.g., [23]. Thus, the technique of [31] is not sufficient to analyze these practical parameter choices in the full/high splitting setting.

- Besides the reductions of several versions of MLWEwith leakages, the work [18] also considers the concrete security estimation of (M)LWE with side information. We note that the reduction and concrete security estimation are two different perspectives for studying the hardness of (M)LWE with leakages. Combining the two ways provides us more comprehensive understanding about the hardness of this problem.

To summarize, we observe that the setting involving low module rank and high-splitting is not well understood compared to other settings. As many efficient lattice proofs rely on specific algebraic advantages in this setting, e.g., [7,23], and [33] for more general relationships, there is a strong motivation to address the challenges and develop new analytical techniques for the foundation and applications.

Our New Analysis. To achieve this, we prove a new reduction from search MLWE (without leakage) to decisional MLWE with linear leakage, meaning that the linear leakage does not decrease the hardness up to a polynomial factor. Our proof structure is similar to that of [29,31,37], consisting of six steps as Fig. 1. Below we briefly elaborate on the intermediate problems and the technical advances over the prior work, i.e., why prior analyses do not go through directly and how our new techniques solve the challenges.

Our reduction works in the case where $q\mathcal{R}$ splits completely into d ideals with linear degree, i.e., $q\mathcal{R} = \mathfrak{q}_1 \dots \mathfrak{q}_d$. Next we describe the notations in the diagram – S and D to denote search and decision version. LE denotes leakage of linear error and LS denotes leakage of linear secret (and error), and (A)/(W) denotes average-case/worst-case over the secret distribution. The $\mathfrak{q}_i$-MLWE problem asks the solver to find $\boldsymbol{s} \mod \mathfrak{q}_i$. The decisional MLWELE^i is to distinguish $\boldsymbol{b} + \boldsymbol{h}$ where $\boldsymbol{h}$ is either from A^i or A^{i-1} defined as follow. A^i is uniformly random mod $\mathfrak{q}_j\mathcal{R}$ for all $j \le i$, and 0 mod all the other ideals, i.e., $\mathfrak{q}_j\mathcal{R}$'s for $j > i$.

In our reduction route, we introduce an intermediate problem denoted as MLWELE, for which the leakage function is only applied to the error. We first establish the one-way hardness of MLWELE on the hardness of search MLWE. The idea of this step is directly from a random guess of leakage, resulting $1/q$ reduction loss. Then we further show a search-to-decision reduction of MLWELE, which follows the framework from [31,37], but makes several important changes. Finally, we show a reduction from the intermediate problem MLWELE to our target MLWE-LS problem.

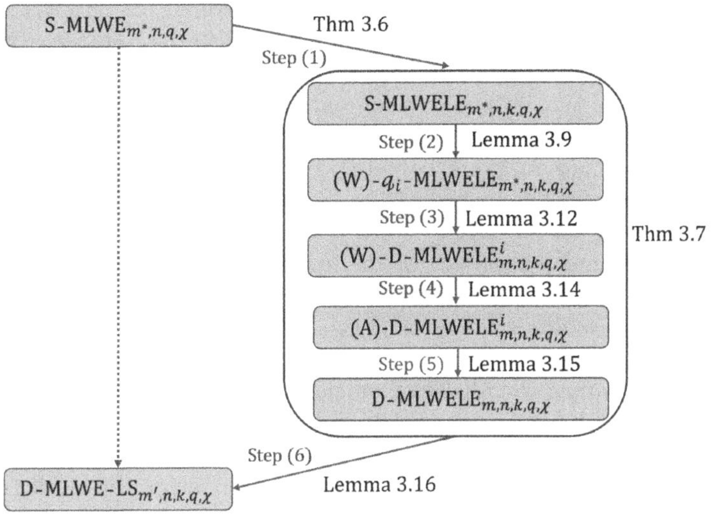

Fig. 1. Our reduction route

Now we briefly discuss each step in the figure. As Steps (1), (3), (4) and (5) follow essentially the same idea from the prior work [31,37], we do not repeat the ideas. So next we focus on Steps (2) and (6).

For Step (2), we would like to prove the following – if we can find $\boldsymbol{s} \mod \mathfrak{q}_i$ for some i, then we can find $\boldsymbol{s}$ (given leakage of error). To achieve this, we first try to apply the automorphism argument of [31,37] – finding $\sigma(\boldsymbol{s}) \mod \mathfrak{q}_i$ implies finding $\boldsymbol{s} \mod \mathfrak{q}_j$ for another j. By going through all the automorphisms, we would recover $\boldsymbol{s}$ modulo every ideal, and thus by the Chinese Remainder Theorem recover $\boldsymbol{s}$. This idea faces a subtlety in the presence of leakage – the reduction needs to simulate $L_{\sigma(\boldsymbol{a})}(\sigma(\boldsymbol{e}))$ faithfully in order to call the underlying solver that finds $\sigma(\boldsymbol{s}) \mod \mathfrak{q}_i$. For general leakage functions, this task is unclear. Fortunately for the linear leakage in our case, we can prove $\langle \phi(\boldsymbol{a}), \phi(\boldsymbol{e}) \rangle = \langle \phi(\sigma(\boldsymbol{a})), \phi(\sigma(\boldsymbol{e})) \rangle$ under the coefficient embedding in the cyclotomic rings of two's powers. This implies that the linear leakage is invariant under automorphism, and thus our reduction can faithfully simulate the leakage and complete the process as in the prior work.

We remark that this invariance of linear leakage under automorphism is non-trivial. Particularly, it requires that the bases corresponding to the coefficient embeddings are invariant (up to some re-ordering and sign) under automorphisms. This requirement however, does not always hold, and even for some rings such a basis does not exist. Currently, we only know that the Normal Integral Basis (NIB) mentioned in [31] and the power basis of cyclotomic rings with 2's powers considered in this paper meet this requirement.

For Step (6), our target is to show a reduction from MLWE with linear leakage of error to MLWE with linear leakage of both secret and error – if we can transform an instance of MLWELE to a valid instance of MLWE-LS or a random sample to another random sample, then we can distinguish the instance of MLWELE from random sample by invoking the distinguisher of MLWE-LS. Our idea is somehow similar to the hardness reduction of HNF-MLWE in prior works [6,29], but needs very subtle analysis due to the introduced hints and leakage. Briefly, let $(\boldsymbol{a}, b, \boldsymbol{z}, (c_1, \cdots, c_k), \langle\phi(\boldsymbol{z}), \phi(c_1 e, \cdots, c_k e)\rangle$ be the instance of MLWELE, where $\boldsymbol{z}$ and $(c_1, \cdots, c_k)$ are the hints of leakage. The goal is to simulate an instance of MLWE-LS with the form: $(\boldsymbol{a}', b', \boldsymbol{z}', (c_1', \cdots, c_k'), \langle\phi(\boldsymbol{z}'), \phi(c_1'(s,e), \cdots, c_k'(s,e))\rangle$. We can use the similar approach of the hardness reduction of HNF-MLWE to transform b to $b' = \langle\boldsymbol{a}', \bar{\boldsymbol{e}}\rangle + e$, where $\bar{\boldsymbol{e}}$ is the error vector corresponding to the invoked instances, and e is the error of the initial instance. Thus the leakage in MLWE-LS can be simulated by the linear combination of the leakages of error obtained during calling the MLWELE oracle.

We would like to point out a subtle issue involved in this transformation where the hints $\boldsymbol{z}', (c_1', \cdots, c_k')$ should be consistent with the leakage. As described above, our reduction is similar to the approach of the hardness reduction of HNF-MLWE, and thus requires to sample $n+1$ instances of MLWELE. Therefore, we need to determine the hint vectors $(\boldsymbol{z}', c_1', \cdots, c_k')$ of MLWE-LS from $n+1$ tuples of hints of MLWELE. We tackle this barrier by a precise design of hints $\boldsymbol{z}'$ and $(c_1', \cdots, c_k')$, which makes use of the linearity of our leakage function and the ability of the adversary of MLWELE. The details can be referred to the proof of Lemma 3.16 in the full version of our paper.

Our Second Contribution. Under the hardness of MLWE with linear leakage, our second contribution shows how to further improve the generalized rejection sampling paradigm of [36], deriving a more fine-grained tradeoff between efficiency and leakage. We elaborate on the high level ideas below.

Briefly speaking, the rejection sampling-style lattice proofs have the following structure: $\boldsymbol{z} = \boldsymbol{y} + c\boldsymbol{s}$, where c is some small ring element, $\boldsymbol{s}$ is some small secret, $\boldsymbol{y}$ is some Gaussian mask, and $\boldsymbol{z}$ is the proof message sent to the verifier. To achieve zero-knowledge, $\boldsymbol{y}$ must wipe out the information of $\boldsymbol{s}$. If $\boldsymbol{y}$ is super-polynomially larger than $c\boldsymbol{s}$, then this is the well-known smudging noise technique [41]. However, this would require a very large proof $\boldsymbol{z}$. To reduce the size, Lyubashevsky [32] introduced the rejection sampling technique where $\boldsymbol{z}$ might be set to $\perp$ with a certain probability. In this way, the dependency on $\boldsymbol{s}$ can be removed with a much smaller $\boldsymbol{y}$. To further improve the size, [36] identified a new way – by imposing an additional condition on $\langle\phi(\boldsymbol{z}), c\phi(\boldsymbol{s})\rangle \geq 0$ (or rejecting the case when the inner product is negative), one can further reduce the size of $\boldsymbol{y}$. This comes at the price of leaking one bit, i.e., the sign bit. If MLWE under linear leakage is hard, then leaking this bit would not hurt security of the protocol.

To further improve the size of $\boldsymbol{y}$, we observe that we can use a stronger condition $\langle\phi(\boldsymbol{z}), c\phi(\boldsymbol{s})\rangle \geq T$ for some parameter $T > 0$. Intuitively, a larger T can result in smaller proof, yet at the cost of more leakage. If we completely leak $\langle\phi(\boldsymbol{z}), c\phi(\boldsymbol{s})\rangle$, the size of $\boldsymbol{y}$ can be minimized. However, if the whole $\mathbb{Z}_q$ element is leaked, then the concrete hardness might be affected by the attack of [18].

Even though [18] does not solve the MLWE asymptotically, leaking $\log q$-bits (i.e., one element in $\mathbb{Z}_q$) might decrease the concrete security by a noticeable amount, whereas leaking one or two bits might not (as the framework of [18] does not apply). Therefore, stretching the leakage too much might be worse in practice. We leave it as an interesting open problem to determine the best tradeoff between leakage and concrete security.

A recent work [28] developed new ideas to improve the proof of knowledge protocols in [36]. Specifically, their approach can remove the computational overhead from repetition (abort) in the framework of [36]. We clarify that same as [36], our framework also requires more computational overhead compared with [28]. However, our framework can achieve better communication overhead than [28]. Concretely, the output size of our improved algorithm is smaller than [28]. As a fair comparison, we calculate the parameters under the same benchmark defined in [28]. By accurate calculation, we can achieve output size that is approximately 3.6x smaller than their output size. More details of comparison can be referred to the end part of Sect. 4.3.

2 Preliminaries

Notations. In this paper, $\mathbb{Z}$ and $\mathbb{R}$ denote the sets of integers and real numbers. We use λ to denote the security parameter, which is the implicit input for all algorithms presented in this paper. A function $f(\lambda) > 0$ is negligible and denoted by $\mathsf{negl}(\lambda)$ if for any $c > 0$ and sufficiently large λ, $f(\lambda) < 1/\lambda^c$. A probability is called to be overwhelming if it is $1-\mathsf{negl}(\lambda)$. A column vector is denoted by a bold lower case letter (e.g., $\boldsymbol{x}$). A matrix is denoted by a bold upper case letter (e.g., $\mathbf{A}$). For a vector $\boldsymbol{x}$, its Euclidean norm (also known as the ℓ_2 norm) is defined to be $\|\boldsymbol{x}\| = (\sum_i x_i^2)^{1/2}$. For a matrix $\mathbf{A}$, its ith column vector is denoted by $\boldsymbol{a}_i$ and its transposition is denoted by $\mathbf{A}^\top$. And the norm of an element in $\mathcal{R}_q$ will be the norm of its unique representative with coefficients in $[-(q-1)/2, (q-1)/2]$. For positive $\beta \in \mathbb{R}$, we use S_β to denote the set of all polynomials of infinity norm less than β, i.e., $S_\beta = \{a \in \mathcal{R} \mid \|a\|_\infty \leq \beta\}$.

For positive integers n, q, let $[n]$ denote the set $\{1, ..., n\}$ and $\mathbb{Z}_q$ denote the ring of integers modulo q. For a distribution or a set X, we write $x \xleftarrow{\$} X$ to denote the operation of sampling an uniformly random x according to X. We denote as $\mathsf{Supp}(X)$ the support of a distribution X. For two distributions X, Y, we let $\mathsf{SD}(X, Y)$ denote their statistical distance. We write $X \overset{s}{\approx} Y$ to mean that they are statistically close, and $X \overset{c}{\approx} Y$ to say that they are computationally indistinguishable.

2.1 Cyclotomic Rings

Throughout this paper, we use $\mathcal{R}$ to denote a polynomial ring of the form $\mathbb{Z}[X]/(\Phi_m(X))$, where $\Phi_m(X)$ is the mth cyclotomic polynomial. For an integer $q \in \mathbb{Z}$, we also consider the quotient ring $\mathcal{R}_q = \mathcal{R}/q\mathcal{R}$. We recall that for d

being a power of 2, the $2d$-th cyclotomic polynomial is given as $\Phi_{2d}(x) = x^d + 1$. Then the ring of integers of the $2d$-th cyclotomic field $\mathcal{R} = \mathbb{Z}[x]/(x^d + 1)$. Thus, we can use the coefficients of an integer polynomial modulo $(x^n + 1)$ to represent a ring element.

Embedding and Rotation. In this work, we view elements of $\mathcal{R}$ as $\mathbb{Z}^d$ through certain embeddings. For example, for $\mathcal{R} = \mathbb{Z}[x]/(x^d + 1)$ with d a power of 2, we view any $a = a_0 + a_1 x + \cdots + a_{d-1}x^{d-1} \in \mathcal{R}$ for $a_i \in \mathbb{Z}$ as the coefficient vector $(a_0, \cdots, a_{d-1})$, and denote $\phi(a) = (a_0, \cdots, a_{d-1})$; and for $\mathcal{R} = \mathbb{Z}[x]/\Phi_m(X)$ with m a prime, we view any $b = b_0 + b_1\zeta + \cdots + b_{m-1}\zeta^{m-1} \in \mathcal{R}$ for $b_i \in \mathbb{Z}$ as $(b_0, \cdots, b_{d-1})$, where ζ is the m-th root of unity. Similarly, we denote $\mathsf{Rot}(a)$ as rotation matrix of a, i.e.,

$$\mathsf{Rot}(a) = \begin{bmatrix} \phi(a \bmod q\mathcal{R})^\top \\ \phi(a \cdot x \bmod q\mathcal{R})^\top \\ \vdots \\ \phi(a \cdot x^{d-1} \bmod q\mathcal{R})^\top \end{bmatrix}.$$

It's easy to verify $\phi(sr) = \phi(s) \cdot \mathsf{Rot}(r) = \phi(rs) = \phi(r) \cdot \mathsf{Rot}(s)$ for any $s, r \in \mathcal{R}_q$.

Ideal Factorization. An ideal $I \subset \mathcal{R}$ is an additive subgroup that is closed under multiplication by $\mathcal{R}$. For an integer prime $q \in \mathbb{Z}$, $q\mathcal{R}$ is an ideal of $\mathcal{R}$, and the factorization of $q\mathcal{R}$ is as $q\mathcal{R} = \Pi_i \mathfrak{q}_i^e$, where $\mathfrak{q}_i$ are distinct prime ideals, each of norm $q^{\frac{d}{te}}$ with t the number of distinct ideals.

The number field $\mathbb{Q}[X]/(\Phi_m(X))$ has $\varphi(m)$ automorphisms σ_k, which are defined by $\sigma_k(\zeta) = \zeta^k$ for $k \in \mathbb{Z}_m^*$. Particularly, for $\mathbb{Q}[X]/(X^d + 1)$, σ_k are defined by $\sigma_k(X) = X^k$. The following lemma says that the automorphisms σ_k "act transitively" on the prime ideals $\mathfrak{q}_i$, i.e., each $\mathfrak{q}_i$ is sent to each $\mathfrak{q}_j$ by some automorphism σ_k.

Lemma 2.1 ([37], **Lemma 2.16**). *For any $i, j \in \mathbb{Z}_m^*$, we have $\sigma_j(\mathfrak{q}_i) = \mathfrak{q}_{i/j}$.*

Next we recall the Chinese Remainder Theorem (CRT) for $\mathcal{R}$.

Lemma 2.2 (Chinese Remainder Theorem). *Let $\mathfrak{q}_i$ be pairwise coprime ($\mathfrak{q}_i + \mathfrak{q}_j = \mathcal{R}$ for any $i \neq j$) ideals in $\mathcal{R} = \mathbb{Z}[X]/(\Phi_m(X))$, then natural ring homomorphism is an isomorphism: $\mathcal{R}/\left(\prod_i \mathfrak{q}_i\right)\mathcal{R} \to \bigoplus_i(\mathcal{R}/\mathfrak{q}_i\mathcal{R})$.*

2.2 Discrete Gaussian Distribution

For a ring $\mathcal{R}$ of degree d, we can define the discrete Gaussian distribution over it in the following way.

Definition 2.3. *For any positive integer ℓ, the discrete Gaussian distribution over $\mathcal{R}^\ell$ centered around $\boldsymbol{v} \in \mathcal{R}^\ell$ with standard deviation $\sigma > 0$ is given by*

$$D_{\boldsymbol{v},\sigma}^{\ell \cdot d}(\boldsymbol{z}) = \frac{e^{-\|\boldsymbol{z}-\boldsymbol{v}\|^2/2\sigma^2}}{\sum_{\boldsymbol{z}' \in \mathcal{R}^\ell} e^{-\|\boldsymbol{z}'\|^2/2\sigma^2}}.$$

When $\boldsymbol{v} = 0$, we just write $D_\sigma^{\ell \cdot d}$ for simplicity.

We also need to use the following facts about the discrete Gaussian distribution.

Lemma 2.4 (Generalize of [8]). *For any positive integer ℓ and any real $\sigma > 0$, a sample sampled from $D_\sigma^{\ell \cdot d}$ defined as above has norm at most $\sigma\sqrt{\ell d}$ except with probability at most $2^{-2\ell d}$.*

Lemma 2.5 (Lemma 4.3 in [32]). *For any vector $\boldsymbol{v} \in \mathbb{R}^m$ and any $\sigma, r > 0$,*

$$\Pr[|\langle \boldsymbol{z}, \boldsymbol{v} \rangle| > r : \boldsymbol{z} \xleftarrow{\$} D_\sigma^m] \leq 2e^{-\frac{r^2}{2\|\boldsymbol{v}\|^2\sigma^2}}.$$

2.3 MLWE

Now we introduce the hard problems discussed in this paper, which are denoted as S-MLWE and D-MLWE, and we consider the "*non-dual*" version problems.

Definition 2.6 (S-MLWE [29]). *The search* MLWE *problem with parameters n, m, q, and an error distribution χ such that* $\mathsf{Supp}(\chi) \in \mathcal{R}$ *denoted as S-*$\mathsf{MLWE}_{n,m,q,\chi}$ *is defined as follows. For $\boldsymbol{s} \xleftarrow{\$} \mathcal{R}^n$, use $A_{q,\boldsymbol{s}}$ to denote the distribution of $(\boldsymbol{a}, \langle \boldsymbol{a}, \boldsymbol{s} \rangle + e) \in \mathcal{R}_q^n \times \mathcal{R}_q$, where $\boldsymbol{a} \xleftarrow{\$} \mathcal{R}_q^n$ and $e \xleftarrow{\$} \chi$. The goal is to find secret $\boldsymbol{s}$ from m samples.*

Definition 2.7 (S-MLWE in HNF [29]). *The search* MLWE *problem with parameters n, m, q, and an error distribution χ such that* $\mathsf{Supp}(\chi) \in \mathcal{R}$ *denoted as S-*$\mathsf{MLWE}_{n,m,q,\chi}$ *is defined as follows. For $\boldsymbol{s} \xleftarrow{\$} \chi^n$, use $A_{q,\boldsymbol{s}}$ to denote the distribution of $(\boldsymbol{a}, \langle \boldsymbol{a}, \boldsymbol{s} \rangle + e) \in \mathcal{R}_q^n \times \mathcal{R}_q$, where $\boldsymbol{a} \xleftarrow{\$} \mathcal{R}_q^n$ and $e \xleftarrow{\$} \chi$. The goal is to find secret $\boldsymbol{s}$ from m samples.*

Definition 2.8 (D-MLWE in HNF [29]). *The decision* MLWE *problem with parameters n, m, q, and an error distribution χ such that* $\mathsf{Supp}(\chi) \in \mathcal{R}$ *denoted as D-*$\mathsf{MLWE}_{n,m,q,\chi}$ *is defined as follows. For $\boldsymbol{s} \xleftarrow{\$} \chi^n$, use $A_{q,\boldsymbol{s}}$ to denote the distribution of $(\boldsymbol{a}, \langle \boldsymbol{a}, \boldsymbol{s} \rangle + e) \in \mathcal{R}_q^n \times \mathcal{R}_q$, where $\boldsymbol{a} \xleftarrow{\$} \mathcal{R}_q^n$ and $e \xleftarrow{\$} \chi$. The goal is to distinguish m samples from either $A_{q,\boldsymbol{s}}$ or $\mathcal{U}(\mathcal{R}_q^n, \mathcal{R}_q)$.*

We notice that the latter two types MLWE problems defined above are the so-called "Hermite Normal Form" version, which can be easily reduced to the standard MLWE via the approach in [6]. For standard MLWE, it is known to be at least as hard as certain standard lattice problems over ideal lattice in the worst case [29]. It should be pointed out that RLWE is the special case of $n = 1$.

3 Hardness: MLWE with Linear Leakage

In this section, we present our main result for the MLWE under linear leakage. First we describe a table of parameters used in this section. Then we define the class of *linear leakage* in the ring/module setting, and Module Learning with Errors, i.e., MLWE in the leakage setting of this class. Finally we present the reduction result.

Table 2. Notation of parameters in this section

Parameters	Description
n	MLWE rank
m	number of MLWE samples
q	modulus of MLWE
d	ring dimension
ℓ	number of prime ideal factors of $q\mathcal{R}$
k	number of computing inner product times

Definition 3.1. *Let $l, q, d, k > 0$ be integers, $\mathcal{R} = \mathbb{Z}[X]/(X^d + 1)$. For $\boldsymbol{z} = (\boldsymbol{z}_i)_{i\in[k]} \in \mathcal{R}_q^{kl}, \boldsymbol{c} = (c_1, \ldots, c_k)^\top \in \mathcal{R}_q^k$, we define the function $L_{\boldsymbol{z},\boldsymbol{c}} : \mathcal{R}_q^l \to \mathbb{Z}_q$ as $L_{\boldsymbol{z},\boldsymbol{c}}(\boldsymbol{x}) = \sum_{i=1}^k \langle \phi(\boldsymbol{z}_i), \phi(c_i\boldsymbol{x})\rangle$, where ϕ is a "coefficient embedding" map from $\mathcal{R}_q^l$ to $\mathbb{Z}_q^{dl}$, i.e., embeds each ring element in $\mathcal{R}_q$ as a vector in $\mathbb{Z}_q^d$.*

Here we can think of $\boldsymbol{x}$ as the secret, and the linear leakage is regarding the inner product of the coefficients as specified above. Additionally, the parameter l is the dimension of the secret key that can be set as m or n, or $m + n$, the parameter k is a dynamic parameter that is related to the latter applications (boosting soundness of ZKP protocol in Sect. 4), the leakage can also multiplicatively shift the secret to $\phi(c_i\boldsymbol{x})$ specified by the parameters c_i's.

Next we define the search and decision versions of MLWE, with linear leakage. We note that, the hard problems we focus on in this work are with the "Hermite Normal Form". Particularly, the leakage function is defined over both secret and noise. Besides, in our hard problems, the leakage hints ($\boldsymbol{z}$ and c) can be specified by the solver (adversary). The adversary in our definition is less restricted than prior "*Extended LWE*" assumptions for which the hints need to be designated by the challenger, and thus makes our hardness result stronger.

Definition 3.2 (MLWE with Linear Secret Leakage, HNF, Search). *Let $m, n, q, k, d > 0$ be integers, $\mathcal{R} = \mathbb{Z}[X]/(X^d + 1)$, χ be error distribution over $\mathcal{R}$. We define the search problem S-MLWE-$\mathsf{LS}_{m,n,k,q,\chi}$ by the experiment between the adversary $\mathcal{A}$ and the challenger $\mathcal{C}$ as:*

- *$\mathcal{A}$ specifies k pairs $\{(\boldsymbol{z}_i, c_i)\}_{i\in\{1,\cdots,k\}}$, where $\boldsymbol{z}_i \in \mathcal{R}_q^{m+n}, c_i \in \mathcal{R}_q$, and sends $\{(\boldsymbol{z}_i, c_i)\}_{i\in\{1,\cdots,k\}}$ to $\mathcal{C}$.*
- *$\mathcal{C}$ first samples $\boldsymbol{x} \leftarrow \chi^{n+m}$, $\mathbf{A} \xleftarrow{\$} \mathcal{R}_q^{m\times n}$, and computes $\boldsymbol{b} = [\mathbf{A}|\mathbf{I}_m] \cdot \boldsymbol{x} \in \mathcal{R}_q^m$. Then, for $\boldsymbol{z} = (\boldsymbol{z}_i)_{i\in[k]}, \boldsymbol{c} = (c_1, \cdots, c_k)^\top$, $\mathcal{C}$ computes $y = L_{\boldsymbol{z},\boldsymbol{c}}(\boldsymbol{x})$. Finally, $\mathcal{C}$ returns $(\mathbf{A}, \boldsymbol{b}, y)$ to $\mathcal{A}$.*
- *$\mathcal{A}$ finally attempts to find $\boldsymbol{s}$.*

The search problem S-MLWE-$\mathsf{LS}_{m,n,k,q,\chi}$ is hard, if it holds: for any $\boldsymbol{z} = (\boldsymbol{z}_1^\top, \ldots, \boldsymbol{z}_k^\top)^\top \in \mathcal{R}_q^{k(n+m)}, (c_1, \cdots, c_k)^\top \in \mathcal{R}_q^k$ and every PPT adversary $\mathcal{A}$ that

$$\Pr\big[\mathcal{A}(\mathbf{A}, \boldsymbol{b}, \boldsymbol{z}, (c_1, \cdots, c_k), y) = \boldsymbol{s}\big] \leq \mathsf{negl}(\lambda).$$

Definition 3.3 (MLWE with Linear Secret Leakage, HNF, Decision). *Let $m, n, q, k, d > 0$ be integers, $\mathcal{R} = \mathbb{Z}[X]/(X^d + 1)$, χ be error distribution over $\mathcal{R}$. We define the decision problem $D\text{-MLWE-LS}_{m,n,k,q,\chi}$ by the experiment between adversary $\mathcal{A}$ and challenger $\mathcal{C}$ as:*

- *$\mathcal{A}$ specifies k pairs $\{(\boldsymbol{z}_i, c_i)\}_{i\in\{1,\cdots,k\}}$, where $\boldsymbol{z}_i \in \mathcal{R}_q^{m+n}, c_i \in \mathcal{R}_q$, and sends $\{(\boldsymbol{z}_i, c_i)\}_{i\in\{1,\cdots,k\}}$ to $\mathcal{C}$.*
- *$\mathcal{C}$ first samples $\boldsymbol{x} \leftarrow \chi^{n+m}$, $\mathbf{A} \xleftarrow{\$} \mathcal{R}_q^{m\times n}$, and computes $\boldsymbol{b} = [\mathbf{A}|\mathbf{I}_m] \cdot \boldsymbol{x} \in \mathcal{R}_q^m$, and also samples $\boldsymbol{u} \xleftarrow{\$} \mathcal{R}_q^m$. Then, for $\boldsymbol{z} = (\boldsymbol{z}_i)_{i\in[k]}, \boldsymbol{c} = (c_1, \cdots, c_k)^\top$, $\mathcal{C}$ computes $y = L_{\boldsymbol{z},\boldsymbol{c}}(\boldsymbol{x})$. Finally, $\mathcal{C}$ samples a random bit $b \in \{0, 1\}$, and sends $(\mathbf{A}, \boldsymbol{b}, y)$ to $\mathcal{A}$ if $b = 1$, or sends $(\mathbf{A}, \boldsymbol{u}, y)$ to $\mathcal{A}$ if $b = 0$.*
- *$\mathcal{A}$ finally outputs a bit b' as the guess of b.*

The advantage of $\mathcal{A}$ in the game is defined as $\mathsf{Adv}^{D\text{-MLWE-LS}}_{\mathcal{A},m,n,q,k,d,\chi} = |\Pr[b' = b] - \frac{1}{2}|$.

The decision problem $D\text{-MLWE-LS}_{m,n,k,q,\chi}$ is hard, if it holds: for any $\boldsymbol{z} \in \mathcal{R}_q^{k(n+m)}, (c_1, \cdots, c_k)^\top \in \mathcal{R}_q^k$ and every PPT adversary $\mathcal{A}$ that

$$\mathsf{Adv}^{D\text{-MLWE-LS}}_{\mathcal{A},m,n,q,k,d,\chi} \leq \mathsf{negl}(\lambda).$$

In addition, we present two intermediate hard problems, denoted as S-MLWELE and D-MLWELE, which will be used in the hardness reduction of $D\text{-MLWE-LS}_{m,n,k,q,\chi}$.

Definition 3.4 (MLWE with Linear Error Leakage, Search). *Let $m, n, q, k, d > 0$ be integers, $\mathcal{R} = \mathbb{Z}[X]/(X^d + 1)$, χ be error distribution over $\mathcal{R}$. We define the search problem $S\text{-MLWE-LS}_{m,n,k,q,\chi}$ by the experiment between adversary $\mathcal{A}$ and challenger $\mathcal{C}$ as:*

- *$\mathcal{A}$ specifies k pairs $\{(\boldsymbol{z}_i, c_i)\}_{i\in\{1,\cdots,k\}}$, where $\boldsymbol{z}_i \in \mathcal{R}_q^m, c_i \in \mathcal{R}_q$, and sends $\{(\boldsymbol{z}_i, c_i)\}_{i\in\{1,\cdots,k\}}$ to $\mathcal{C}$.*
- *$\mathcal{C}$ first samples $\boldsymbol{s} \xleftarrow{\$} \mathcal{R}^n$, $\boldsymbol{e} \leftarrow \chi^m$, $\mathbf{A} \xleftarrow{\$} \mathcal{R}_q^{m\times n}$, and computes $\boldsymbol{b} = \mathbf{A} \cdot \boldsymbol{s} + \boldsymbol{e} \in \mathcal{R}_q^m$. Then, for $\boldsymbol{z} = (\boldsymbol{z}_i)_{i\in[k]}, \boldsymbol{c} = (c_1, \cdots, c_k)^\top$, $\mathcal{C}$ computes $y = L_{\boldsymbol{z},\boldsymbol{c}}(\boldsymbol{e})$. Finally, $\mathcal{C}$ returns $(\mathbf{A}, \boldsymbol{b}, y)$ to $\mathcal{A}$.*
- *$\mathcal{A}$ finally attempts to find $\boldsymbol{s}$.*

The search problem $S\text{-MLWELE}_{m,n,k,q,\chi}$ is hard, if it holds: for any $\boldsymbol{z} = (\boldsymbol{z}_1^\top, \ldots, \boldsymbol{z}_k^\top)^\top \in \mathcal{R}_q^{km}, (c_1, \cdots, c_k)^\top \in \mathcal{R}_q^k$ and every PPT adversary $\mathcal{A}$ that

$$\Pr\left[\mathcal{A}(\mathbf{A}, \mathbf{A}\boldsymbol{s} + \boldsymbol{e}, \boldsymbol{z}, (c_1, \cdots, c_k), y) = \boldsymbol{s}\right] \leq \mathsf{negl}(\lambda).$$

Definition 3.5 (MLWE with Linear Error Leakage, Decision). *Let $m, n, q, k, d > 0$ be integers, $\mathcal{R} = \mathbb{Z}[X]/(X^d + 1)$, χ be error distribution over $\mathcal{R}$. We define the decision problem $D\text{-MLWELE}_{m,n,k,q,\chi}$ by the experiment between adversary $\mathcal{A}$ and challenger $\mathcal{C}$ as:*

– $\mathcal{A}$ *specifies* k *pairs* $\{(\boldsymbol{z}_i, c_i)\}_{i\in\{1,\cdots,k\}}$, *where* $\boldsymbol{z}_i \in \mathcal{R}_q^m, c_i \in \mathcal{R}_q$, *and sends* $\{(\boldsymbol{z}_i, c_i)\}_{i\in\{1,\cdots,k\}}$ *to* $\mathcal{C}$.
– $\mathcal{C}$ *first samples* $\boldsymbol{s} \xleftarrow{\$} \mathcal{R}^n$, $\boldsymbol{e} \leftarrow \chi^m$, $\mathbf{A} \xleftarrow{\$} \mathcal{R}_q^{m\times n}$, *and computes* $\boldsymbol{b} = \mathbf{A}\cdot\boldsymbol{s} + \boldsymbol{e} \in \mathcal{R}_q^m$, *and also samples* $\boldsymbol{u} \xleftarrow{\$} \mathcal{R}_q^m$. *Then, for* $\boldsymbol{z} = (\boldsymbol{z}_i)_{i\in[k]}, \mathbf{c} = (c_1, \cdots, c_k)^\top$, $\mathcal{C}$ *computes* $y = L_{\boldsymbol{z},\mathbf{c}}(\boldsymbol{x})$. *Finally,* $\mathcal{C}$ *samples a random bit* $b \in \{0,1\}$, *and sends* $(\mathbf{A}, \boldsymbol{b}, y)$ *to* $\mathcal{A}$ *if* $b = 1$, *or sends* $(\mathbf{A}, \boldsymbol{u}, y)$ *to* $\mathcal{A}$ *if* $b = 0$.
– $\mathcal{A}$ *finally outputs a bit* b' *as the guess of* b.

The advantage of $\mathcal{A}$ *in the game is defined as* $\mathsf{Adv}^{D\text{-}\mathsf{MLWELE}}_{\mathcal{A},m,n,q,k,d,\chi} = |\Pr[b' = b] - \frac{1}{2}|$.

The decision problem D-$\mathsf{MLWELE}_{m,n,k,q,\chi}$ *is hard, if it holds: for any* $\boldsymbol{z} \in \mathcal{R}_q^{km}, (c_1, \cdots, c_k)^\top \in \mathcal{R}_q^k$ *and every PPT adversary* $\mathcal{A}$ *that*

$$\mathsf{Adv}^{D\text{-}\mathsf{MLWELE}}_{\mathcal{A},m,n,q,k,d,\chi} \leq \mathsf{negl}(\lambda).$$

Now we will give our concrete reductions. To start, we first show a reduction from S-$\mathsf{MLWE}_{m,n,q,\chi}$ to S-$\mathsf{MLWELE}_{m,n,k,q,\chi}$. Generally, a search problem with $\log q$ bits of leakage can only decrease security by a factor of q. Therefore, if $q = \mathsf{poly}(\lambda)$, then the leakage version can be reduced from the non-leakage version of the problem.

Theorem 3.6. *Let* $m, n, k, d, q > 0$ *be integers, and* q *is a polynomial of the security parameter* λ, $\mathcal{R} = \mathbb{Z}[X]/(X^d+1)$, χ *be error distribution over* $\mathcal{R}$. *There exists a* PPT *reduction from* S-$\mathsf{MLWE}_{m,n,q,\chi}$ *to* S-$\mathsf{MLWELE}_{m,n,k,q,\chi}$, *such that if* ε *is the advantage of* S-$\mathsf{MLWELE}_{m,n,k,q,\chi}$ *solver, then* $\varepsilon' = \frac{1}{q}\varepsilon$ *is the advantage of* S-$\mathsf{MLWE}_{m,n,q,\chi}$ *solver.*

The theorem can be proved by a simple idea to randomly guess the value of the inner product. We put the proof in full version of this paper.

The hardness result of D-MLWELE as an important intermediate reduction of our main result can be summarized as the following Theorem.

Theorem 3.7. *Let* $m, n, k, d > 0$ *be integers,* $\mathcal{R} = \mathbb{Z}[X]/(X^d+1)$, q *be the prime modulus such that* $q\mathcal{R}$ *splits as* $q\mathcal{R} = \mathfrak{q}_1 \cdots \mathfrak{q}_\ell$, *where* $\ell = d/c$ *for a constant* $c \in \mathbb{Z}$ *and* $q \geq \ell^2$, χ *be an error distribution that is invariant under all the automorphisms of* $K = \mathbb{Q}[X]\backslash(X^d+1)$. *There exists a reduction from S-*$\mathsf{MLWELE}_{\bar{m}^*,n,k,q,\chi}$ *to* D-$\mathsf{MLWELE}_{m,n,k,q,\chi}$, *such that if* ε *is the advantage of D-*MLWE-$\mathsf{LS}_{m,n,k,q,\chi}$ *solver, then* $\varepsilon' \geq 1 - \frac{\varepsilon}{8}$ *is the advantage of* S-$\mathsf{MLWELE}_{\bar{m}^*,n,k,q,\chi}$ *solver, and* $\bar{m}^* = \ell q^c mn \cdot \lceil 1/\varepsilon^2 \rceil$.

Proof. We first summarize the reduction route as follows, and then explain the concrete steps later:

$$S\text{-}\mathsf{MLWELE}_{\bar{m}^*,n,k,q,\chi} \xrightarrow{(1)} (W)\text{-}\mathfrak{q}_i\text{-}\mathsf{MLWELE}_{m^*,n,k,q,\chi} \xrightarrow{(2)} (W)\text{-}D\text{-}\mathsf{MLWELE}^i_{m,n,k,q,\chi}$$
$$\xrightarrow{(3)} (A)\text{-}D\text{-}\mathsf{MLWELE}^i_{m,n,k,q,\chi} \xrightarrow{(4)} D\text{-}\mathsf{MLWELE}_{m,n,k,q,\chi}.$$

To start, we define the first intermediate assumption (W)-$\mathfrak{q}_i$-$\mathsf{MLWELE}_{m^*,n,k,q,\chi}$ as follows.

Definition 3.8 ((W)-$\mathfrak{q}_i$-MLWELE$_{m^*,n,k,q,\chi}$). *Let $m^*, n, k, d > 0$ be integers, $\mathcal{R} = \mathbb{Z}[X]/(X^d+1)$, q be the modulus such that $q\mathcal{R}$ splits as $q\mathcal{R} = \mathfrak{q}_1 \cdots \mathfrak{q}_\ell$, where $\ell = d/c$ for a constant $c \in \mathbb{Z}$, χ be error distribution over $\mathcal{R}$. For any $\mathfrak{q}_i, i \in [\ell]$, the worst-case search problem $\mathfrak{q}_i$-MLWELE$_{m^*,n,k,q,\chi}$ is defined as: given access to $(\mathbf{A}, \mathbf{A}\boldsymbol{s} + \boldsymbol{e}, \boldsymbol{z}, (c_1, \cdots, c_k), \langle \phi(\boldsymbol{z}), \phi(c_1\boldsymbol{e}, \cdots, c_k\boldsymbol{e})\rangle)$ for some arbitrary $\boldsymbol{s} \in \mathcal{R}_q^n$, where $\mathbf{A} \xleftarrow{\$} \mathcal{R}_q^{m^* \times n}, \boldsymbol{e} \leftarrow \chi^{m^*}$, $\boldsymbol{z} \in \mathcal{R}_q^{k \cdot m^*}$ and $(c_1, \cdots, c_k) \in \mathcal{R}_q^k$ as defined in Definition 3.2, find $\boldsymbol{s}$* mod $\mathfrak{q}_i$.

Then, we have the following reduction.

Lemma 3.9 (S-MLWELE$_{\bar{m}^*,n,k,q,\chi}$ to (W)-$\mathfrak{q}_i$-MLWELE$_{m^*,n,k,q,\chi}$). *Let $m^*, n, k, d > 0$ be integers, $\mathcal{R} = \mathbb{Z}[X]/(X^d + 1)$, q be the modulus such that $q\mathcal{R}$ splits completely as $q\mathcal{R} = \mathfrak{q}_1 \cdots \mathfrak{q}_\ell$, where $\ell = d/c$ for a constant $c \in \mathbb{Z}$, χ be error distribution over $\mathcal{R}$ and invariant under all the automorphisms of $K = \mathbb{Q}[X] \backslash (X^d + 1)$. Then for every $i \in \{1, \cdots, \ell\}$, there exists a deterministic poly-time reduction from S-MLWELE$_{\bar{m}^*,n,k,q,\chi}$ to (W)-$\mathfrak{q}_i$-MLWELE$_{m^*,n,k,q,\chi}$, such that if $1-\varepsilon$ is the advantage of (W)-$\mathfrak{q}_i$-MLWELE$_{m^*,n,k,q,\chi}$ solver, then $1-\ell\varepsilon$ is the advantage of S-MLWELE$_{\bar{m}^*,n,k,q,\chi}$ solver, where $\varepsilon < \frac{1}{\ell}$, and $\bar{m}^* = \ell m^*$.*

The reduction can be proved by a similar approach to that of Lemma 4.16 in [29] combining with a subtle simulation of inner product leakage under automorphisms. Due to the space limit, we put the proof in full version of this paper.

In order to describe the second intermediate assumption, the following definition is needed.

Definition 3.10 (Hybrid MLWELE distribution). *For $i \in \{1, \cdots, \ell\}$, a distribution χ over $\mathcal{R}_q$ and $\boldsymbol{s} \xleftarrow{\$} \mathcal{R}^n$, we define the distribution $A^i_{m^*,k,\boldsymbol{s},\chi}$ over $\mathcal{R}_q^{m^* \times n} \times \mathcal{R}_q^{m^*} \times \mathcal{R}_q^{km^*} \times \mathcal{R}_q^k \times \mathbb{Z}_q$ as: sample $(\mathbf{A}, \boldsymbol{b}, \boldsymbol{z}, (c_1, \cdots, c_k), \langle \phi(\boldsymbol{z}), \phi(c_1\boldsymbol{e}, \cdots, c_k\boldsymbol{e})\rangle)$ as Definition 3.8 and output $(\mathbf{A}, \boldsymbol{b} + \boldsymbol{h}, \boldsymbol{z}, (c_1, \cdots, c_k), \langle \phi(\boldsymbol{z}), \phi(c_1\boldsymbol{e}, \cdots, c_k\boldsymbol{e})\rangle)$ where $\boldsymbol{h} \in \mathcal{R}_q^{m^*}$ are uniformly random mod $\mathfrak{q}_j\mathcal{R}$ for all $j \leq i$, and 0 over mod all the other ideals, i.e., $\mathfrak{q}_j\mathcal{R}$'s for $j > i$.*

We note that $A^0_{m^*,k,\boldsymbol{s},\chi}$ is the original distribution as Definition 3.8, $A^\ell_{m^*,k,\boldsymbol{s},\chi}$ is the distribution as the random case defined in Definition 3.3, and the other $A^i_{m^*,k,\boldsymbol{s},\chi}$'s are intermediate hybrids, which will be used via a hybrid argument later.

Now, the second intermediate assumption is as follows.

Definition 3.11 ((W)-D-MLWELE$^i_{m,n,k,q,\chi}$). *The worst-case D-MLWELE$^i_{m,n,k,q,\chi}$ problem is defined as follows: given access to an oracle sampling from $A^i_{m,k,\boldsymbol{s},\chi}$ for arbitrary $\boldsymbol{s} \in \mathsf{Supp}(\chi^n)$ and $j \in \{i-1, i\}$, find j.*

The following lemma states a reduction from (W)-$\mathfrak{q}_i$-MLWELE$_{m^*,n,k,q,\chi}$ to (W)-D-MLWELE$^i_{m,n,k,q,\chi}$.

Lemma 3.12 ((W)-$\mathfrak{q}_i$-$\mathsf{MLWELE}_{m^*,n,k,q,\chi}$ to (W)-D-$\mathsf{MLWELE}^i_{m,n,k,q,\chi}$). *For any $i \in \{1, \cdots, \ell\}$, and ideal $\mathfrak{q}_i$ with $N(\mathfrak{q}_i) = q^{d/\ell} = q^c$ where $c \geq 1$ is a constant integer, there exists a probabilistic polynomial time reduction from $\mathfrak{q}_i$-$\mathsf{MLWELE}_{m^*,n,k,q,\chi}$ to (W)-D-$\mathsf{MLWELE}^i_{m,n,k,q,\chi}$, such that if ε is the advantage of (W)-D-$\mathsf{MLWELE}^i_{m,n,k,q,\chi}$ solver, then $\varepsilon' \geq 1 - \frac{\varepsilon}{8}$ is the advantage of $\mathfrak{q}_i$-$\mathsf{MLWELE}_{m^*,n,k,q,\chi}$ solver, where $m^* = q^c mn \cdot \lceil \frac{1}{\varepsilon^2} \rceil$.*

The proof of this lemma is similar to that of Lemma 5.9 in [37]. Due to the space limit, we put it in full version of this paper.

The third intermediate assumption in the reduction route is as follows.

Definition 3.13 (Average-case Decision LWE relative to $\mathfrak{q}_i$). *For $i \in \{1, \cdots, \ell\}$ and a distribution χ over error $\mathcal{R}_q$, we say that an algorithm solves the D-$\mathsf{MLWELE}^i_{m,n,k,q,\chi}$ problem if with a non-negligible probability over the choice of a random $\boldsymbol{s} \leftarrow U(\mathcal{R}_q^n)$, it has a non-negligible difference in acceptance probability on inputs from $A^{i-1}_{m,k,\boldsymbol{s},\chi}$ versus inputs from $A^i_{m,k,\boldsymbol{s},\chi}$.*

We have the worst-case to average-case reduction as follows.

Lemma 3.14 (Worst-case to Average-case). *There exists a randomized poly-time reduction from worst-case (W)-D-$\mathsf{MLWELE}^i_{m,n,k,q,\chi}$ to average-case D-$\mathsf{MLWELE}^i_{m,n,k,q,\chi}$, such that if ε is the advantage of D-$\mathsf{MLWELE}^i_{m,n,k,q,\chi}$ distinguisher, then ε is the advantage of (W)-D-$\mathsf{MLWELE}^i_{m,n,k,q,\chi}$ distinguisher.*

The reduction performs a re-randomization of the secret, which is a standard approach to prove a worst-case to average-case reduction. We omit here, and provide the rigorous proof in the full version.

The following lemma states the step (4) of the reduction route.

Lemma 3.15 (D-$\mathsf{MLWELE}^i_{m,n,k,q,\chi}$ to D-$\mathsf{MLWELE}_{m,n,k,q,\chi}$). *For any oracle solving the D-$\mathsf{MLWELE}_{m,n,k,q,\chi}$ problem with advantage ε, there exists an $i \in \{1, \cdots, \ell\}$ and an efficient algorithm that solves D-$\mathsf{MLWELE}^i_{m,n,k,q,\chi}$ with advantage ε/ℓ using this oracle.*

The lemma can be proved by a simple hybrid argument. We put the proof in full version of this paper.

The proof of Theorem 3.7 follows from Lemmas 3.9, 3.12, 3.14 and 3.15. □

Finally, we show a reduction from D-$\mathsf{MLWELE}_{m,n,k,q,\chi}$ to D-MLWE-$\mathsf{LS}_{m,n,k,q,\chi}$ as follows.

Lemma 3.16 (D-$\mathsf{MLWELE}_{m(nd)^2,n,k,q,\chi}$ to D-MLWE-$\mathsf{LS}_{m,n,k,q,\chi}$). *There exists a probabilistic poly-time reduction from D-$\mathsf{MLWELE}_{m(nd)^2,n,k,q,\chi}$ to D-MLWE-$\mathsf{LS}_{m,n,k,q,\chi}$, such that if ε is the advantage of D-MLWE-$\mathsf{LS}_{m,n,k,q,\chi}$ distinguisher, then ε is the advantage of D-$\mathsf{MLWELE}_{m(nd)^2,n,k,q,\chi}$ distinguisher.*

The main idea of this reduction is similar to the reduction from MLWE to the HNF-MLWE in the work [29]. Due to space limit, we put the proof in full version of this paper.

Combine Theorem 3.7 ,Theorem 3.6 and Lemma 3.16, the hardness of D-MLWE-LS can be reduced to the hardness of the fundamental problem S-MLWE by the following Corollary.

Corollary 3.17. *Let $m, n, k, d > 0$ be integers, $\mathcal{R} = \mathbb{Z}[X]/(X^d + 1)$, q be the modulus such that $q\mathcal{R}$ splits as $q\mathcal{R} = \mathfrak{q}_1 \cdots \mathfrak{q}_\ell$, where $\ell = d/c$ for a constant $c \in \mathbb{Z}$, χ be an error distributions over $\mathcal{R}$ that is invariant under all the automorphisms of $K = \mathbb{Q}[X]/(X^d + 1)$. There exists a reduction from S-$\mathsf{MLWE}_{m^*,n,q,\chi}$ to D-$\mathsf{MLWE\text{-}LS}_{m,n,k,q,\chi}$, such that if ε is the advantage of D-$\mathsf{MLWE\text{-}LS}_{m,n,k,q,\chi}$ solver, then $\varepsilon' \geq \frac{1}{q} \cdot (1 - \frac{\varepsilon}{8})$ is the advantage of S-$\mathsf{MLWE}_{m^*,n,q,\chi}$ solver, and $m^* = \ell q^c m n^3 d^2 \cdot \lceil 1/\varepsilon^2 \rceil$.*

Remark 3.18. In our reduction, we consider the ring $\mathbb{Z}[X]/(X^d + 1)$ which is frequently used in many applications. It should be noted that we can generalize the ring to the more general cyclotomic setting by representing a ring element as integer linear combinations of a certain $\mathbb{Z}$-basis of the ring. Then, the map ϕ and the automorphism are defined according to the $\mathbb{Z}$-basis.

4 Application: More Efficient Opening Proof for One-Time BDLOP Commitment

In this section, we present an important application of MLWE with linear leakage, leading to more efficient opening proofs for one-time BDLOP commitments under the paradigm [36]. Our particular contribution is to derive a more fine-grained tradeoff between efficiency and leakage of the paradigm [36], which can potentially lead to even more efficient proofs.

The section is organized as follow. We first recall the classical opening proof for BDLOP commitment in [9], together with two rejection sampling algorithms [32,36] in Sect. 4.1. Then in Sect. 4.2, we further generalize the *subset rejection sampling* algorithm proposed by [36] in two ways: (1) we use a smaller subset S_v for the accepting condition; (2) we extends the constant value M to a real-valued function $\mathcal{M}$ of (v, z), whose output can vary based on the input. These two ideas can improve efficiency of the opening proof for the setting of one-time BDLOP commitment. Finally, in Sect. 4.3, we compare in detail the efficiency differences of the opening protocol under four different rejection sampling algorithms in Figs. 3 and 4. Below we first present the parameters used in this section in Table 3.

4.1 Classical Opening Proof of BDLOPCommitment and Rejection Sampling Algorithms

Let us first recall the standard opening proof for BDLOP commitment scheme in [9]. Particularly, for a BDLOP commitment scheme with public parameters $\mathbf{A}_1 \in \mathcal{R}_q^{n\times\eta}, \mathbf{A}_2 \in \mathcal{R}_q^{l\times\eta}$, a message vector $\boldsymbol{m} \in \mathcal{R}_q^l$ is committed as $\mathsf{comm} := \begin{bmatrix} \boldsymbol{t}_1 \\ \boldsymbol{t}_2 \end{bmatrix} = \begin{bmatrix} \mathbf{A}_1 \\ \mathbf{A}_2 \end{bmatrix} \boldsymbol{r} + \begin{bmatrix} \mathbf{0} \\ \boldsymbol{m} \end{bmatrix}$, where $\boldsymbol{r} \xleftarrow{\$} S_\beta^\eta$. Without loss of generality, we assume that $q\mathcal{R}$ splits as $q\mathcal{R} = \mathfrak{q}_1 \cdots \mathfrak{q}_\ell$, where $\ell = d/c$ for a constant $c \in \mathbb{Z}$, and $q - 1 = 2\ell (\bmod 4\ell)$. Clearly, if $\ell = d$, we say the ring $\mathcal{R}$ is full-splitting.

Table 3. Notation of parameters in this section

Parameters	Description
$\mathcal{R}$	Cyclotomic Ring $\mathcal{R} = \mathbb{Z}[X]/(X^d + 1)$ used in this section
d	ring dimension of $\mathcal{R}$
S_β	Set of all elements in $\mathcal{R}$ with ℓ_∞ norm at most β
q	modulus of BDLOP commitment
n, l, η	dimension parameters of BDLOP commitment
$\mathcal{C}$	Challenge set of the opening ZKP system for BDLOP commitment
κ	$\mathcal{C} = \{c \in \mathcal{R} : \|c\|_1 = \kappa, \|c\|_\infty = 1\}$
m	dimension parameters of rejection sampling
$\hat{k}$	the parameter with respect to boosting soundness
$\mathcal{M}$	function from $(V, \mathbb{Z}^m)$ to $\mathbb{R}$
α	derivation of discrete Gaussian distribution for rejection sampling
$\hat{S}_v$	The subset of $\mathbb{Z}^m$ used for subset rejection sampling
$M, \mathfrak{c}$	constant parameters for subset rejection sampling
rep.	prover's expected repetition times for one non-abort
ℓ	the number of irreducible ideal modulo q, i.e., $q\mathcal{R} = \mathfrak{q}_1 \cdots \mathfrak{q}_\ell$
$\mathfrak{l}$	the bit-length of randomness leakage during the opening proof

According to [7,9], in order to prove knowledge of an opening to comm, one just needs to give an approximate proof for the first equation $\boldsymbol{t}_1 = \mathbf{A}_1 \cdot \boldsymbol{r}$ in the form of a three-round Schnorr-type Σ-protocol. Particularly in the first step, the prover first chooses a random vector $\boldsymbol{y}$, and then sends $\boldsymbol{w} = \mathbf{A}_1\boldsymbol{y}$ to the verifier. Then, the verifier sends a short polynomial $c \in \mathcal{C} \subset R$ as a challenge. Finally, the prover replies with the vector $\boldsymbol{z} = \boldsymbol{y} + c\boldsymbol{r}$. To achieve zero-knowledge, intuitively the masking vector $\boldsymbol{y}$ is used to hide the private randomness $\boldsymbol{r}$ of the commitment comm. Trivially one can set $\boldsymbol{y}$ to be super-polynomially larger than $c\boldsymbol{r}$ as some smudging noise, yet this would incur a large overhead in the proof size. To improve efficiency, [32] introduced the technique of *rejection sampling* that outputs $\perp$ instead of $\boldsymbol{z}$ with an appropriate probability, effectively wiping out the dependency of $c\boldsymbol{r}$ in $\boldsymbol{z}$.

Furthermore, in some settings such as proving the infinity norm of a vector as in [7,23,36], we need to set the underlying ring $\mathcal{R}$ to be full-splitting. In this case, the above mentioned initial Σ-protocol can only provide $1/q$ soundness, which is far away from negligible. In order to boost soundness, the work [7] applys Galois automorphisms. At a high level, given $\boldsymbol{r}, \boldsymbol{t}_1, \boldsymbol{t}_2$ as before, the prover $\mathcal{P}$ first generates $\boldsymbol{y}_1, \cdots, \boldsymbol{y}_{\hat{k}} \leftarrow \mathcal{D}_\alpha^\eta$. Then it outputs $(\boldsymbol{w}_1, \cdots, \boldsymbol{w}_{\hat{k}})$, where $\boldsymbol{w}_i = \mathbf{A}_1 \cdot \boldsymbol{y}_i$. After receiving a challenge $c \leftarrow \mathcal{C}$ from the verifier, $\mathcal{P}$ computes

$$\boldsymbol{z}_i = \boldsymbol{y}_i + \sigma^{i-1}(c) \cdot \boldsymbol{r} \text{ for } i = 1, \cdots, \hat{k}$$

where $\sigma := \sigma_{2d/\hat{k}+1} \in \mathrm{Aut}(\mathcal{R}_q)$ is the automorphism of order $\hat{k}d/\ell$ and $\hat{k}$ is a divisor of d. After this, the prover applies rejection sampling $\mathsf{Rej}(\boldsymbol{z}, \boldsymbol{v}, \sigma)$ where $\boldsymbol{z} = \boldsymbol{z}_1 \| \cdots \| \boldsymbol{z}_{\hat{k}}$ and $\boldsymbol{v} = \sigma^0(c) \cdot \boldsymbol{r} \| \cdots \| \sigma^{\hat{k}-1}(c) \cdot \boldsymbol{r}$. If it does not abort, then $\mathcal{P}$ outputs $\boldsymbol{z}$. Finally, the verifier checks that $\boldsymbol{z}$ is small and

$$\mathbf{A}_1 \boldsymbol{z}_i = \boldsymbol{w}_i + \sigma^{i-1}(c) \cdot \boldsymbol{t}_1$$

for $i = 1, \cdots, \hat{k}$. As argued by [7], this protocol has soundness around $q^{-\hat{k}}$.

More formally, the protocol is described in Fig. 2, and the used rejection sampling algorithm is described as Rej_0 in Fig. 3.

Prover $\mathcal{P}$		Verifier $\mathcal{V}$
Inputs:		
$\mathbf{A}_1 \in R_q^{n \times \eta}$		$\mathbf{A}_1, \mathbf{A}_2$
$\mathbf{A}_2 \in R_q^{\ell \times \eta}$		$B \geq \alpha \cdot \sqrt{d \cdot \eta}$
$\boldsymbol{m} \in R_q^{\ell}$, $\boldsymbol{r} \leftarrow S_\beta^\eta$		
$\boldsymbol{t}_1 = \mathbf{A}_1 \cdot \boldsymbol{r}$		$\boldsymbol{t}_1, \boldsymbol{t}_2$
$\boldsymbol{t}_2 = \mathbf{A}_2 \cdot \boldsymbol{r} + \boldsymbol{m}$		
For $i = 1, \ldots, \hat{k}$:		
$\boldsymbol{y}_i \leftarrow \mathcal{D}_\alpha^i$		
$\boldsymbol{w}_i = \mathbf{A}_1 \cdot \boldsymbol{y}_i$		
	$\xrightarrow{\boldsymbol{w}_i}$	
		$c \xleftarrow{\$} \mathcal{C}$
	$\xleftarrow{c}$	
For $i = 1, \ldots, \hat{k}$:		
$\boldsymbol{z}_i = \boldsymbol{y}_i + \sigma^{i-1}(c) \cdot \boldsymbol{r}$		
$\mathsf{Rej}_j((\boldsymbol{z}_i), (\sigma^{i-1}(c) \cdot \boldsymbol{r}), \sigma) = 1$, abort	$\xrightarrow{\boldsymbol{z}_i}$	
		For $i = 1, \ldots, \hat{k}$, check:
		$\|\boldsymbol{z}_i\| \leq B$
		$\mathbf{A}_1 \cdot \boldsymbol{z}_i = \boldsymbol{w}_i + \sigma^{i-1}(c) \cdot \boldsymbol{t}_1$

Fig. 2. Opening proof of BDLOP commitment through using our generalized rejection sampling, where $j = 0, \ldots, 3$.

Particularly, if we sample $\boldsymbol{y}_i$ from the discrete Gaussian distribution with derivation α, i.e., $\boldsymbol{y}_i \leftarrow D_\alpha^\eta$, then the vector $\boldsymbol{z}_i = \boldsymbol{y}_i + \sigma^{i-1}(c)\boldsymbol{r}$ follows the shifted discrete Gaussian distribution $D_{\boldsymbol{v},\alpha}^\eta$ centered at $\boldsymbol{v} = \sigma^0(c) \cdot \boldsymbol{r} \| \cdots \| \sigma^{\hat{k}-1}(c) \cdot \boldsymbol{r}$. According to [32], we can "transform" the distribution $D_{\boldsymbol{v},\alpha}^\eta$ into the distribution D_α^η, by outputting $\boldsymbol{z} = \boldsymbol{z}_1 \| \cdots \| \boldsymbol{z}_{\hat{k}}$ with probability $\frac{D_\alpha^\eta}{M \cdot D_{\boldsymbol{v},\alpha}^\eta}$ (or otherwise $\perp$), where M is some positive integer so that this ratio is always smaller than 1. To further determine the concrete value for M, we need to compute an upper bound of $\frac{D_\alpha^\eta}{D_{\boldsymbol{v},\alpha}^\eta}$ as

$$\frac{D_\alpha^m}{D_{\boldsymbol{v},\alpha}^m} = \exp\left(\frac{-2\langle \boldsymbol{z}, \boldsymbol{v}\rangle + \|\boldsymbol{v}\|^2}{2\alpha^2}\right) \leq \exp\left(\frac{24\alpha\|\boldsymbol{v}\| + \|\boldsymbol{v}\|^2}{2\alpha^2}\right) = M, \quad (1)$$

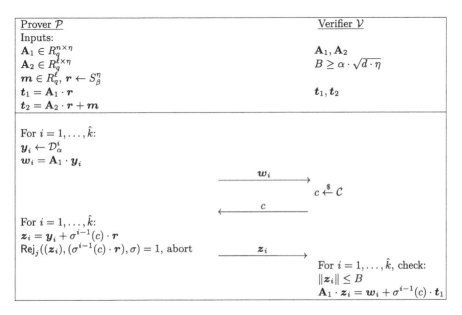

$\mathsf{Rej}_0(\boldsymbol{z}, \boldsymbol{v}, \alpha)$	$\mathsf{Rej}_1(\boldsymbol{z}, \boldsymbol{v}, \alpha)$
01 $u \xleftarrow{\$} [0,1)$	01 If $\langle \boldsymbol{z}, \boldsymbol{v} \rangle < 0$
02 If $u > \frac{1}{M} \cdot \exp(\frac{-2\langle \boldsymbol{z},\boldsymbol{v}\rangle + \|\boldsymbol{v}\|^2}{2\alpha^2})$	02 $\quad$ return 1
03 $\quad$ return 1	03 $u \xleftarrow{\$} [0,1)$
04 Else	04 If $u > \frac{1}{M} \cdot \exp(\frac{-2\langle \boldsymbol{z},\boldsymbol{v}\rangle + \|\boldsymbol{v}\|^2}{2\alpha^2})$
05 $\quad$ return 0	05 $\quad$ return 1
	06 Else
	07 $\quad$ return 0

Fig. 3. Rejection Sampling. Here, implicitly, the outcome 1 implies abort, and 0 implies non-abort.

where the above inequality is obtained through using a standard one-dimensional tail bound for the inner product of a discrete Gaussian with arbitrary vector. Clearly, if we want to set $M = \exp(1)$, then we need to set $\alpha = 12\|\boldsymbol{v}\|$. In this case, the size of $\boldsymbol{z}$ is about $\hat{k}\eta d \log(12\alpha) = \hat{k}\eta d \log(144\|\boldsymbol{v}\|)$, which depends on the value of α. This is essentially the intuition of [32].

In a recent work, Lyubashevsky et al. [36] observed that a much tighter upper bound for the ratio $D_\alpha^\eta / D_{\boldsymbol{v},\alpha}^\eta$ would imply a much smaller α, further lowering the size of $\boldsymbol{z}$. Particularly, if we assume that $\langle \boldsymbol{z}, \boldsymbol{v} \rangle \geq 0$, then we have

$$\frac{D_\alpha^\eta}{D_{\boldsymbol{v},\alpha}^\eta} = \exp\left(\frac{-2\langle \boldsymbol{z}, \boldsymbol{v} \rangle + \|\boldsymbol{v}\|^2}{2\alpha^2}\right) \leq \exp\left(\frac{\|\boldsymbol{v}\|^2}{2\alpha^2}\right) = M. \tag{2}$$

In this case, if we want to set $M = \exp(1)$ in the following rejection sampling procedure again, we can set $\alpha = \|\boldsymbol{v}\|/\sqrt{2}$, which results in a decrease of around a factor of 17. This will clearly reduce the size of $\boldsymbol{z}$ to $\hat{k}\eta d \log(12\alpha) = \hat{k}\eta d \log(8.487\|\boldsymbol{v}\|)$. More formally, Lyubashevsky et al. [36] call such more efficient rejection sampling as *subset rejection sampling*, which is described as Rej_1 in Fig. 3. Clearly, Rej_1 can improve the size of the proof protocol in Fig. 2.

Additional Costs of [36]. It is not for free however for the improvement [36]. All the above analyses have a precondition – $\langle \boldsymbol{z}, \boldsymbol{v} \rangle \geq 0$. For randomly chosen $\boldsymbol{y}, \boldsymbol{r}$, this precondition happens with a probability $\approx 1/2$. This means that if we want to leverage the above subset rejection sampling, the prover will first abort the protocol with a probability $\approx 1/2$ to ensure $\langle \boldsymbol{z}, \boldsymbol{v} \rangle \geq 0$, and then conduct the regular rejection sampling. So, for the same constant value M, even the output size of $\boldsymbol{z}$ is reduced, the running time of the prover inherently becomes almost 2 times longer than that of [9].

Of course, one can easily balance the prover's running time and the size of his output $\boldsymbol{z}$. Particularly, we can set the upper bound of probability ratio to be $M/2$, which will derive that the finally expected abort time is about M. But, this will result in a slightly larger α', i.e., $\alpha' = \alpha\sqrt{\frac{\ln M}{\ln M/2}}$.

Besides and more importantly, there is a security concern. After the prover outputting $\boldsymbol{z}$ successfully, it imposes the precondition $\langle \boldsymbol{z}, \boldsymbol{v} \rangle \geq 0$, which leaks almost one bit information of r to the adversary. In this case, we need to consider whether this would affect the security of the opening proof of the BDLOP commitment, and even the whole privacy-preserving protocols.

To analyze this, Lyubashevsky et al. [36] identified a new variant of extended MLWE, and prove security of the protocol based on the variant of extended MLWE. As noticed in the introduction, this extended MLWE can be captured by MLWE with linear leakage analyzed in Sect. 3 of this work, using a formal reduction argument. This strengthens the foundation of the paradigm, as the leakage variant is no easier than the standard MLWE asymptotically. Thus, we would be more confident in the practical parameters of [36] obtained by cryptanalysis arguments.

4.2 More Efficient One-Time Opening Proof Through Using Generalized Subset Rejection Sampling Algorithms

Now we define our new *generalized subset rejection sampling algorithms* Rej_2 and Rej_3 as in Fig. 4. Then we show that the algorithms themselves can be simulated, and the opening protocol with Rej_2 or Rej_3 satisfies correctness, knowledge soundness and simulatability. This means we can replace Rej_0 or Rej_1 for the protocol in Fig. 2 in a black-box way, by using our generalized algorithms (Fig. 4).

$\mathsf{Rej}_2(\boldsymbol{z}, \boldsymbol{v}, \alpha)$	$\mathsf{Rej}_3(\boldsymbol{z}, \boldsymbol{v}, \alpha)$
01 If $\langle \boldsymbol{z}, \boldsymbol{v} \rangle < \mathfrak{c} \cdot \alpha \|\boldsymbol{v}\|$	01 If $\langle \boldsymbol{z}, \boldsymbol{v} \rangle \notin [0, (\alpha^2 * \ln M)/3]$
02 return 1	02 return 1
03 $u \xleftarrow{\$} [0,1)$	03 $u \xleftarrow{\$} [0,1)$
04 If $u > \exp(\frac{-2\langle \boldsymbol{z}, \boldsymbol{v} \rangle + \|\boldsymbol{v}\|^2}{2\alpha^2})$	04 If $u > \frac{1}{\exp(\frac{3\langle \boldsymbol{v}, \boldsymbol{z} \rangle}{\alpha^2})} \cdot \exp(\frac{-2\langle \boldsymbol{z}, \boldsymbol{v} \rangle + \|\boldsymbol{v}\|^2}{2\alpha^2})$
05 return 1	05 return 1
06 Else	06 Else
07 return 0	07 return 0

Fig. 4. Generalized Rejection Sampling.

Simulation of Generalized Subset Rejection Sampling

To argue that the algorithms Rej_2 and Rej_3 themselves can be simulated successfully, we first define a more general version of subset rejection sampling algorithm $\mathcal{A}$, i.e., Rej_2 and Rej_3 can be viewed as two special cases of $\mathcal{A}$. Then we show that $\mathcal{A}$ can be simulated successfully by another algorithm $\mathcal{F}$ in Theorem 4.1. Furthermore, by setting parameters appropriately, we can obtain two Theorems 4.3 and 4.4, which correspond to Rej_2 and Rej_3, respectively.

Theorem 4.1 (Generalized Subset Rejection Sampling). *Let V be an arbitrary set, and $h : V \to \mathbb{R}$ and $f : \mathbb{Z}^m \to \mathbb{R}$ be probability distributions.*

Define a family of set $\hat{S}_v \subset \mathbb{Z}^m$ *for* $v \in V$. *Suppose* $g_v : \mathbb{Z}^m \to \mathbb{R}$ *is a family of probability distributions indexed by all* $v \in V$ *and there exist two constants* $M \geq 1$, $1 \geq \gamma \geq 0$, *and a function* $\mathcal{M} : V \times \mathbb{Z}^m \to \mathbb{R}$, *which satisfy:*

$$\forall\ v \in V, z \in \hat{S}_v : \mathcal{M}(v,z) \cdot g_v(z) \geq f(z)$$
$$\forall\ v \in V, z \in \hat{S}_v : 1 \leq \mathcal{M}(v,z) \leq M$$
$$\forall\ v \in V : \sum_{z \in \hat{S}_v} f(z) \geq \gamma.$$

then the output distribution of the following algorithm $\mathcal{A}$*:*

1. $v \xleftarrow{\$} h$
2. $z \xleftarrow{\$} g_v$
3. *if* $z \notin \hat{S}_v$ *then abort*
4. *output* (z, v) *with probability* $\frac{f(z)}{\mathcal{M}(v,z) \cdot g_v(z)}$

is identical to the distribution of the following algorithm $\mathcal{F}$*:*

1. $v \xleftarrow{\$} h$
2. $z \xleftarrow{\$} f$
3. *if* $z \notin \hat{S}_v$ *then abort*
4. *output* (z, v) *with probability* $1/\mathcal{M}(v, z)$.

Moreover, the probability of $\mathcal{A}$ *and* $\mathcal{F}$ *outputting something is at least* γ/M.

Proof. Given $v \in V$, if $z \in \hat{S}_v$, the probability of $\mathcal{A}$ outputting $z \in \mathbb{Z}^m$ is $g_v(z) \cdot \frac{f(z)}{\mathcal{M}(v,z) \cdot g_v(z)} = \frac{f(z)}{\mathcal{M}(v,z)}$. Otherwise, the probability that $\mathcal{A}$ outputs $z \notin \hat{S}_v$ is 0. As a result, it holds

$$\Pr[\mathcal{A} \text{ outputs something}] = \sum_{v \in V} h(v) \sum_{z \in \hat{S}_v} \frac{f(z)}{\mathcal{M}(v,z)} \geq \frac{\gamma}{M}.$$

Notice also that the probability of $\mathcal{F}$ outputting something is $\sum_{(v,z) \in V \times \hat{S}_v} \frac{h(v) f(z)}{\mathcal{M}(v,z)} \geq \frac{\gamma}{M}$. Besides, it holds

$$\begin{aligned}
\Delta(\mathcal{A}, \mathcal{F}) &= \frac{1}{2} \left(\sum_{(v,z) \in V \times \hat{S}_v} |\mathcal{A}(v,z) - \mathcal{F}(v,z)| \right) \\
&= \frac{1}{2} \sum_{v \in V} h(v) \left(\sum_{z \in \hat{S}_v} \left| g_v(z) \cdot \frac{f(z)}{\mathcal{M}(v,z) \cdot g_v(z)} - \frac{f(z)}{\mathcal{M}(v,z)} \right| \right) \\
&= \frac{1}{2} \sum_{v \in V} h(v) \left(\sum_{z \in \hat{S}_v} \left| \frac{f(z)}{\mathcal{M}(v,z)} - \frac{f(z)}{\mathcal{M}(v,z)} \right| \right) \\
&= 0.
\end{aligned}$$

□

Remark 4.2. We note that compared with the original rejection sampling of Lemma 3.2 in [36], this generalized version just extends the constant value M to a real-valued function $\mathcal{M}(v, z)$, whose output may vary based on (v, z).

Next, we consider the special case where $\boldsymbol{v} \in V \subseteq \mathbb{Z}^m$, $f := D_\alpha^m$, $g_{\boldsymbol{v}} := D_{\boldsymbol{v},\alpha}^m$, constant $M = 1$ and the constant function $\mathcal{M}(\boldsymbol{v}, \boldsymbol{z}) = 1$. Thus, we have the following theorem for the rejection sampling algorithm Rej_2.

Theorem 4.3. *Let V be an arbitrary subset of $\mathbb{Z}^m$, and $h : V \to \mathbb{R}$ be probability distribution. Let $M = 1$. Given any $\boldsymbol{v} \in V$ and any constant $\mathfrak{c}$, define $\hat{S}_{\boldsymbol{v},\mathfrak{c}} = \{\boldsymbol{z} : \langle \boldsymbol{z}, \boldsymbol{v}\rangle \geq \mathfrak{c} \cdot \sigma\|\boldsymbol{v}\|\}$. Then it holds that the output distribution of $\mathcal{A}_2$:*

1. $\boldsymbol{v} \overset{\$}{\leftarrow} h$
2. $\boldsymbol{z} \overset{\$}{\leftarrow} D_{\boldsymbol{v},\alpha}^m$
3. *if* $\boldsymbol{z} \notin \hat{S}_{\boldsymbol{v},\mathfrak{c}}$ *then abort*
4. *output* $(\boldsymbol{z}, \boldsymbol{v})$ *with probability* $\frac{D_\alpha^m(\boldsymbol{z})}{D_{\boldsymbol{v},\alpha}^m(\boldsymbol{z})}$.

is identical to the distribution of the following algorithm $\mathcal{F}_2$:

1. $\boldsymbol{v} \overset{\$}{\leftarrow} h$
2. $\boldsymbol{z} \overset{\$}{\leftarrow} D_\alpha^m$
3. *if* $\boldsymbol{z} \notin \hat{S}_{\boldsymbol{v},\mathfrak{c}}$ *then abort*
4. *output* $(\boldsymbol{z}, \boldsymbol{v})$ *with probability* 1.

Moreover, the probability of $\mathcal{A}_2$ and $\mathcal{F}_2$ outputting something is at least α, where α is the probability of a randomly chosen vector from $D_{\boldsymbol{v},\alpha}^m$ belonging to $\hat{S}_{\boldsymbol{v},\mathfrak{c}}$.

Next, we consider the special case where $\boldsymbol{v} \in V \subseteq \mathbb{Z}^m$, $f := D_\alpha^m$, $g_{\boldsymbol{v}} := D_{\boldsymbol{v},\alpha}^m$, and $\mathcal{M}(\boldsymbol{v}, \boldsymbol{z}) = \exp\left(\frac{3\langle \boldsymbol{v},\boldsymbol{z}\rangle}{\alpha^2}\right)$. Thus, we have the following theorem for the rejection sampling algorithm Rej_3.

Theorem 4.4. *Let M be a constant and V be an arbitrary subset of $\mathbb{Z}^m$, and $h : V \to \mathbb{R}$ be probability distribution. Given any $\boldsymbol{v} \in V$, define $\hat{S}_{\boldsymbol{v},\mathfrak{c}} = \{\boldsymbol{z} : \langle \boldsymbol{z}, \boldsymbol{v}\rangle \geq \mathfrak{c} \cdot \alpha\|\boldsymbol{v}\|\}$. Then there exists a function $\mathcal{M}(\boldsymbol{v}, \boldsymbol{z}) = \exp\left(\frac{3\langle \boldsymbol{v},\boldsymbol{z}\rangle}{\alpha^2}\right)$ with $1 \leq \mathcal{M}(\boldsymbol{v}, \boldsymbol{z}) \leq M$ and $\mathcal{M}(\boldsymbol{v}, \boldsymbol{z}) \cdot D_{\boldsymbol{v},\alpha}^m(\boldsymbol{z}) \geq D_\alpha^m(\boldsymbol{z})$, such that the output distribution of $\mathcal{A}_3$:*[4]

1. $\boldsymbol{v} \overset{\$}{\leftarrow} h$
2. $\boldsymbol{z} \overset{\$}{\leftarrow} D_{\boldsymbol{v},\alpha}^m$
3. *if* $\boldsymbol{z} \notin \hat{S}_{\boldsymbol{v},\mathfrak{c}}$ *then abort*
4. *output* $(\boldsymbol{z}, \boldsymbol{v})$ *with probability* $\frac{D_\alpha^m(\boldsymbol{z})}{\exp\left(\frac{3\langle \boldsymbol{v},\boldsymbol{z}\rangle}{\alpha^2}\right) \cdot D_{\boldsymbol{v},\alpha}^m(\boldsymbol{z})} = \exp\left(\frac{-8\langle \boldsymbol{z},\boldsymbol{v}\rangle + \|\boldsymbol{v}\|^2}{2\alpha^2}\right)$.

[4] For such function $\mathcal{M}(\boldsymbol{v}, \boldsymbol{z}) = \exp\left(\frac{3\langle \boldsymbol{v},\boldsymbol{z}\rangle}{\alpha^2}\right)$, the condition $\mathcal{M}(\boldsymbol{v}, \boldsymbol{z}) \in [1, M]$ implies $\langle \boldsymbol{z}, \boldsymbol{v}\rangle \in [0, (\alpha^2 \cdot \ln M)/3]$.

is identical to the distribution of the following algorithm $\mathcal{F}_3$:

1. $\boldsymbol{v} \xleftarrow{\$} h$
2. $\boldsymbol{z} \xleftarrow{\$} D_{\alpha}^{m}$
3. *if* $\boldsymbol{z} \notin \hat{S}_{\boldsymbol{v},c}$ *then abort*
4. *output* $(\boldsymbol{z}, \boldsymbol{v})$ *with probability* $\frac{1}{\exp(\frac{3\langle \boldsymbol{v}, \boldsymbol{z} \rangle}{\alpha^2})}$.

Moreover, the probability of $\mathcal{A}_3$ and $\mathcal{F}_3$ outputting something is at least $\frac{\gamma}{M}$, where γ is the probability of a randomly chosen vector from $D_{\boldsymbol{v},\alpha}^{m}$ belonging to $\hat{S}_{\boldsymbol{v},c}$.

Security of Opening Proof Protocol with Rej_2 and Rej_3

Here, we need to prove that the opening proof protocol with Rej_2 or Rej_3 satisfies correctness, knowledge soundness and simulatability, whose formal definitions are deferred to the full version of this paper. Similar to [36], we first represent the opening proof of BDLOP commitment as the commit-and-prove functionality $CP = (\mathsf{Gen}, \mathsf{Com}, \mathsf{Prove}, \mathsf{Verify})$, and then show that CP satisfies simulatability, since the properties of correctness and knowledge soundness can be proven almost identically as in [7].

More formally, with random oracle $H : \{0,1\}^* \to \mathcal{C}$, the commit-and-prove functionality $CP = (\mathsf{Gen}, \mathsf{Com}, \mathsf{Prove}, \mathsf{Verify})$ with respect to the language R_L is described as follows, where R_L is defined as $(\mathsf{params}, x, \boldsymbol{m}) \in R_L \Leftrightarrow \boldsymbol{m} \in \mathcal{R}_q$ for certain statement x.

- $\mathsf{Gen}(1^\lambda)$: Given a security parameter λ, the algorithm generates a commitment public parameter params, which specifies $\mathcal{R}_q^l$ as message space, $S_1^\eta \subset \mathcal{R}^\eta$ as randomness space, and $\mathcal{R}^{n+l}$ as the commitment space. Besides, it also generates $\mathbf{A}_1 \in \mathcal{R}_q^{n\times\eta}, \mathbf{A}_2 \in \mathcal{R}_q^{l\times\eta}$. Without loss of generality, for the underlying ring $\mathcal{R} = \mathbb{Z}[X]/\langle X^d + 1\rangle$ and modulus q, we assume that $q\mathcal{R}$ splits as $q\mathcal{R} = \mathfrak{q}_1 \cdots \mathfrak{q}_\ell$, where $\ell = d/c$ for a constant $c \in \mathbb{Z}$, and $q - 1 = 2\ell (\mathrm{mod} 4\ell)$. Clearly, if $\ell = d$, we say the ring $\mathcal{R}$ is full-splitting.
  Besides, the algorithm further chooses k as the public boosting parameter,[5] such that $\hat{k}|d$ and $q^{-1/\hat{k}}$ is negligible in λ, and set $\sigma := \sigma_{2d/\hat{k}+1} \in \mathrm{Aut}(\mathcal{R}_q)$ is the automorphism of order $\hat{k}d/\ell$.
- $\mathsf{Com}(\mathsf{params}, x, \boldsymbol{m}; \boldsymbol{r})$: Given params, $\boldsymbol{m} \in \mathcal{R}_q^l$, and randomness $\boldsymbol{r} \in S_1^\eta$, the algorithm generates a commitment $\mathsf{comm} := \begin{bmatrix} \boldsymbol{t}_1 \\ \boldsymbol{t}_2 \end{bmatrix} = \begin{bmatrix} \mathbf{A}_1 \\ \mathbf{A}_2 \end{bmatrix} \boldsymbol{r} + \begin{bmatrix} \mathbf{0} \\ \boldsymbol{m} \end{bmatrix}$.
- $\mathsf{Prove}(\mathsf{params}, x, \mathsf{comm}, \boldsymbol{m}, \boldsymbol{r})$: Given params, $\mathsf{comm} \in \mathcal{R}_q^{n+l}$, and randomness $\boldsymbol{r} \in S_1^\eta$, the algorithm first samples $\boldsymbol{y}_i \leftarrow D_\alpha^\eta$ and computes $c = H(\{\mathbf{A}_1 \cdot \boldsymbol{y}_i\})$ for $i \in [\hat{k}]$. Then, it computes $\boldsymbol{z}_i = \boldsymbol{y}_i + \sigma^{i-1}(c) \cdot \boldsymbol{r}$ and gets $b \leftarrow \mathsf{Rej}_j((\boldsymbol{z}_i), (c \cdot \boldsymbol{r}), \alpha)$ for $j = 2$ or 3. If $b = 0$, it outputs $\pi = (c, \boldsymbol{z})$ with $\boldsymbol{z} := (\boldsymbol{z}_i)$. Otherwise abort.

[5] Of course, the number of $\hat{k}$ will affect the proof size of opening proof. Thus, we try to set it as small as possible.

– $\mathsf{Verify}(\mathsf{params}, x, \mathsf{comm}, \pi)$: given $\mathsf{params}, \mathsf{comm}, \pi$, the algorithm parse comm as $\boldsymbol{t}_1 \in \mathcal{R}^n, \boldsymbol{t}_2 \in \mathcal{R}^l$, and parse π as $(c, \boldsymbol{z})$ with $\boldsymbol{z} := (\boldsymbol{z}_i)$. If $\|\boldsymbol{z}_i\| \leq \alpha \cdot \sqrt{d \cdot \eta}$ and $c = H(\{\mathbf{A}_1 \cdot \boldsymbol{z}_i - \sigma^{i-1}(c)\boldsymbol{t}_1\})$, accept. Otherwise, reject.

Furthermore, we have the following theorem.

Theorem 4.5. *In the random oracle model, if* D-MLWE-$\mathsf{LS}_{n+l,\eta,\hat{k},q,\chi}$ *assumption holds, then the CP with* Rej_2 *or* Rej_3 *is simulatable.*

We prove this theorem by a standard hybrid argument. Due to the limitation of space, we defer the proof to full version of this paper.

Further Decreasing Standard Deviation. It should be noted that the boosting procedure in Fig. 2 enlarges the norm of the vector $\boldsymbol{z}$ by a factor of $\hat{k}$, compared with the original proof with non-splitting underlying ring $\mathcal{R}$ in [9]. To deal with this issue, the work [35] proposed a simple modification of the protocol. As a result, one can decrease the standard deviation possibly by a factor of $\hat{k}$. Due to the limitation of space, we defer the details to full version of this paper.

4.3 Comparison of Efficiency

Intuitively, by using Rej_2 or Rej_3, we can get much better upper bounds for $\frac{D^\eta_\alpha}{D^\eta_{\boldsymbol{v},\alpha}}$ than Eqs. (1) and (2), allowing us to derive much smaller values for α. Particularly, for Rej_2 and the corresponding Theorem 4.3, if we use the condition that $\langle \boldsymbol{z}, \boldsymbol{v} \rangle \geq \mathfrak{c} \cdot \alpha \|\boldsymbol{v}\|$, then we have

$$\frac{D^\eta_\alpha(\boldsymbol{z})}{D^\eta_{\boldsymbol{v},\alpha}(\boldsymbol{z})} = \exp\left(\frac{-2\langle \boldsymbol{z}, \boldsymbol{v} \rangle + \|\boldsymbol{v}\|^2}{2\alpha^2}\right) \leq \exp\left(\frac{-2\mathfrak{c} \cdot \alpha \|\boldsymbol{v}\| + \|\boldsymbol{v}\|^2}{2\alpha^2}\right) = 1. \tag{3}$$

Here, we set $-2\mathfrak{c} \cdot \alpha \|\boldsymbol{v}\| + \|\boldsymbol{v}\|^2 = (-2\mathfrak{c} \cdot \alpha + \|\boldsymbol{v}\|) \cdot \|\boldsymbol{v}\| = 0$. Thus, we just need to set $\alpha = \frac{\|\boldsymbol{v}\|}{2\mathfrak{c}}$. Besides, we notice that the event of Rej_2's abort only depends on whether the random vector $\boldsymbol{z}$ is in the subset $\hat{S}_{\boldsymbol{v},\mathfrak{c}}$, for any fixed $\boldsymbol{v}$ and $\mathfrak{c}$. Clearly, by careful balancing the parameter $\mathfrak{c}$, we can get a much smaller α, for the same expected repetition times. The detailed example data are listed in Table 4.

Then, for Rej_3 and the related Theorem 4.4, if we assume that $\mathcal{M}(\boldsymbol{v}, \boldsymbol{z}) = \exp\left(\frac{3\langle \boldsymbol{v}, \boldsymbol{z} \rangle}{\alpha^2}\right)$, then we have

$$\frac{D^\eta_\alpha(\boldsymbol{z})}{\mathcal{M}(\boldsymbol{v}, \boldsymbol{z}) \cdot D^\eta_{\boldsymbol{v},\alpha}(\boldsymbol{z})} = \frac{\exp\left(\frac{-2\langle \boldsymbol{z}, \boldsymbol{v} \rangle + \|\boldsymbol{v}\|^2}{2\alpha^2}\right)}{\exp\left(\frac{3\langle \boldsymbol{v}, \boldsymbol{z} \rangle}{\alpha^2}\right)} = \exp\left(\frac{-8\langle \boldsymbol{z}, \boldsymbol{v} \rangle + \|\boldsymbol{v}\|^2}{2\alpha^2}\right) \leq 1. \tag{4}$$

Here, we set $-8\mathfrak{c} \cdot \alpha \|\boldsymbol{v}\| + \|\boldsymbol{v}\|^2 = (-8\mathfrak{c} \cdot \alpha + \|\boldsymbol{v}\|) \cdot \|\boldsymbol{v}\| = 0$. Thus, we just need to set $\alpha = \frac{\|\boldsymbol{v}\|}{8\mathfrak{c}}$. Besides, we notice that the probability of Rej_3's abort depends on $\hat{S}_{\boldsymbol{v},\mathfrak{c}}$ and function $\mathcal{M}(\boldsymbol{v}, \boldsymbol{z})$, i.e., the probability of Rej_3's non-abort is $\Pr[\boldsymbol{z} \in \hat{S}_{\boldsymbol{v},\mathfrak{c}}] \cdot \frac{1}{\exp(\frac{3\langle \boldsymbol{v}, \boldsymbol{z} \rangle}{\alpha^2})}$, for $\boldsymbol{z} \xleftarrow{\$} D^m_\alpha$. Clearly, for any fixed $\boldsymbol{v}, \alpha$, $\boldsymbol{z} \xleftarrow{\$} D^m_\alpha$, $\Pr[\boldsymbol{z} \in \hat{S}_{\boldsymbol{v},\mathfrak{c}}]$ depends on the choice of $\mathfrak{c}$. Notice also that, the condition $\mathcal{M}(\boldsymbol{v}, \boldsymbol{z}) \in [1, M]$

implies $\langle \boldsymbol{z}, \boldsymbol{v} \rangle \in [0, (\alpha^2 \cdot \ln M)/3]$. Thus, through setting different M, we can compute the prover's expected repetition numbers for one time non-abort, and the detailed data are listed in Table 4.

According to the above principles, we can determine the concrete proof sizes under various sets of parameters. The detailed numbers are presented in Tables 1 and 4.

Table 4. Comparison with the usage of different rejection sampling algorithms for the protocol in Figs. 2 and 4, where M and $\mathfrak{c}$ denote the parameters for each of four algorithms, rep. denotes prover's expected repetition times for one non-abort, η denotes the dimension of $\boldsymbol{z}$, d denotes the ring dimension of the underlying ring $\mathcal{R}$, $\hat{k}$ denotes the parameter for boosting the soundness. And $\mathfrak{l}$ denotes the number of leakage bits on random during the security proof. Moreover, $\boldsymbol{v} = (\sigma^0(c)\boldsymbol{r} \| \ldots \| \sigma^{\hat{k}-1}(c)\boldsymbol{r})$, where $\boldsymbol{r}$ is the randomness vector for BDLOP commitment, and c is the challenge from the verifier in the opening proof protocol.

	M	$\mathfrak{c}$	rep.	α	Size of $\boldsymbol{z}$	$\mathfrak{l}$
Rej_0	3	-	≈ 3	$11 \cdot \lVert \boldsymbol{v} \rVert$	$\hat{k}\eta d \log_2(12 \cdot 11 \cdot \lVert \boldsymbol{v} \rVert)$	0
	6		≈ 6	$6.74 \cdot \lVert \boldsymbol{v} \rVert$	$\hat{k}\eta d \log_2(12 \cdot 6.74 \cdot \lVert \boldsymbol{v} \rVert)$	
Rej_1	3	0	≈ 3	$1.11 \cdot \lVert \boldsymbol{v} \rVert$	$\hat{k}\eta d \log(12 \cdot 1.11 \cdot \lVert \boldsymbol{v} \rVert)$	1
	4		≈ 4	$0.85 \cdot \lVert \boldsymbol{v} \rVert$	$\hat{k}\eta d \log_2(12 \cdot 0.85 \cdot \lVert \boldsymbol{v} \rVert)$	
	6		≈ 6	$0.675 \cdot \lVert \boldsymbol{v} \rVert$	$\hat{k}\eta d \log_2(12 \cdot 0.675 \cdot \lVert \boldsymbol{v} \rVert)$	
Rej_2	1	0.438	≈ 3	$1.142 \cdot \lVert \boldsymbol{v} \rVert$	$\hat{k}\eta d \log_2(12 \cdot 1.155 \cdot \lVert \boldsymbol{v} \rVert)$	$\log_2 3$
		0.672	≈ 4	$0.744 \cdot \lVert \boldsymbol{v} \rVert$	$\hat{k}\eta d \log_2(12 \cdot 0.744 \cdot \lVert \boldsymbol{v} \rVert)$	2
		0.97	≈ 6	$0.515 \cdot \lVert \boldsymbol{v} \rVert$	$\hat{k}\eta d \log_2(12 \cdot 0.515 \cdot \lVert \boldsymbol{v} \rVert)$	$\log_2 6$
		1.149	≈ 8	$0.435 \cdot \lVert \boldsymbol{v} \rVert$	$\hat{k}\eta d \log_2(12 \cdot 0.435 \cdot \lVert \boldsymbol{v} \rVert)$	3
Rej_3	1.8	0.5	≈ 5.8	$0.25 \cdot \lVert \boldsymbol{v} \rVert$	$\hat{k}\eta d \log_2(12 \cdot 0.25 \cdot \lVert \boldsymbol{v} \rVert)$	$\log_2 q$
	2	0.5	≈ 6.48	$0.25 \cdot \lVert \boldsymbol{v} \rVert$	$\hat{k}\eta d \log_2(12 \cdot 0.25 \cdot \lVert \boldsymbol{v} \rVert)$	
	2.5	0.5	≈ 8.1	$0.25 \cdot \lVert \boldsymbol{v} \rVert$	$\hat{k}\eta d \log_2(12 \cdot 0.25 \cdot \lVert \boldsymbol{v} \rVert)$	

Comparison with [28]. As mentioned in the introduction, a concurrent work [28] also improves the state-of-the-art proof of knowledge protocols for BDLOP commitment schemes. Particularly, they remove the additional computational overheads produced by the rejections in the framework of [36], and provide a comparison of the output size under their framework with that under [36]'s framework. We clarify that as a framework similar to [36], our framework also needs more computational overheads than [28]. For the output size, we can provide a fair comparison between our framework and theirs by utilize the benchmark introduced in Sect. 5.1 of [28].

Concretely, same to [28], we measure the hardness of MSIS and MLWE in terms of the root Hermite factor δ, targeting for $\delta \approx 1.0043$ which gives 128-bit security. In this case, the parameters can be set as: $q \approx 2^{32}, d = 128, \kappa =$

$32, \ell = 1$. As claimed in [28], one should set $n = 6, \eta = 10$ to achieve the 128-bit security in the framework of [36], and they can set $n = 5, \eta = 9$ to achieve the same security level. On the other hand, their output size is bounded by $(\kappa\alpha_1 + \alpha_2)\sqrt{(n+\eta+\ell)d/\pi}$, where $\alpha_1 \geq 2\sqrt{\frac{2\log(2d(1+1/\varepsilon))}{\pi}}, \alpha_2 \geq 2\sqrt{2}\kappa \cdot \sqrt{\frac{2\log(2d(1+1/\varepsilon))}{\pi}}$, and ε is a security parameter that should be set at most 2^{-128} to be consistent with the 128-bit security. Under these parameters, the output size of [28] is approximately 35490 (ℓ_2-norm of the output vector $\boldsymbol{z}$, following from the presentation of [28]). In our case, we set $n = 6, \eta = 10$, albeit our improvement of [36]'s framework. Meanwhile, the output size in our framework is bounded by $\tau \cdot \frac{\kappa(n+\ell+\eta)d}{\sqrt{\pi}}$, where $\tau = 0.25$ in Rej_3. Therefore, output size of our framework is approximately 9824.

To sum up, the output size in our framework is smaller than that in [28] (approximate 3.6x). Consequently, our framework and [28]'s framework provide a trade-off between computational overhead and communication overhead.

Acknowledgement. We would like to thank the reviewers of PKC 2024 for their insightful advices. Zhedong Wang is supported by National Natural Science Foundation of China (Grant No. 62202305), Young Elite Scientists Sponsorship Program by China Association for Science and Technology (YESS20220150), Shanghai Pujiang Program under Grant 22PJ1407700, and Shanghai Science and Technology Innovation Action Plan (No. 23511100300). Qiqi Lai is supported by the National Natural Science Foundation of China (Grant No. 62172266). Feng-Hao Liu is supported by the NSF Career Award CNS-2402031.

References

1. Abla, P., Liu, F.-H., Wang, H., Wang, Z.: Ring-based identity based encryption – asymptotically shorter MPK and tighter security. In: Nissim, K., Waters, B. (eds.) TCC 2021, Part III. LNCS, vol. 13044, pp. 157–187. Springer, Cham (2021). https://doi.org/10.1007/978-3-030-90456-2_6
2. Agrawal, S., Boneh, D., Boyen, X.: Efficient lattice (H)IBE in the standard model. In: Gilbert, H. (ed.) EUROCRYPT 2010. LNCS, vol. 6110, pp. 553–572. Springer, Heidelberg (2010). https://doi.org/10.1007/978-3-642-13190-5_28
3. Agrawal, S., Boneh, D., Boyen, X.: Lattice basis delegation in fixed dimension and shorter-ciphertext hierarchical IBE. In: Rabin, T. (ed.) CRYPTO 2010. LNCS, vol. 6223, pp. 98–115. Springer, Heidelberg (2010). https://doi.org/10.1007/978-3-642-14623-7_6
4. Alperin-Sheriff, J., Peikert, C.: Circular and KDM security for identity-based encryption. In: Fischlin, M., Buchmann, J., Manulis, M. (eds.) PKC 2012. LNCS, vol. 7293, pp. 334–352. Springer, Heidelberg (2012). https://doi.org/10.1007/978-3-642-30057-8_20
5. Alwen, J., Krenn, S., Pietrzak, K., Wichs, D.: Learning with rounding, revisited - new reduction, properties and applications. In: Canetti, R., Garay, J.A. (eds.) CRYPTO 2013, Part I. LNCS, vol. 8042, pp. 57–74. Springer, Heidelberg (2013). https://doi.org/10.1007/978-3-642-40041-4_4

6. Applebaum, B., Cash, D., Peikert, C., Sahai, A.: Fast cryptographic primitives and circular-secure encryption based on hard learning problems. In: Halevi, S. (ed.) CRYPTO 2009. LNCS, vol. 5677, pp. 595–618. Springer, Heidelberg (2009). https://doi.org/10.1007/978-3-642-03356-8_35
7. Attema, T., Lyubashevsky, V., Seiler, G.: Practical product proofs for lattice commitments. In: Micciancio and Ristenpart [40], pp. 470–499 (2020). https://doi.org/10.1007/978-3-030-56880-1_17
8. Banaszczyk, W.: New bounds in some transference theorems in the geometry of numbers. Math. Ann. **296**(1), 625–635 (1993)
9. Baum, C., Damgård, I., Lyubashevsky, V., Oechsner, S., Peikert, C.: More efficient commitments from structured lattice assumptions. In: Catalano, D., De Prisco, R. (eds.) SCN 2018. LNCS, vol. 11035, pp. 368–385. Springer, Cham (2018). https://doi.org/10.1007/978-3-319-98113-0_20
10. Boldyreva, A., Micciancio, D. (eds.): CRYPTO 2019, Part I. LNCS, vol. 11692. Springer, Heidelberg (2019). https://doi.org/10.1007/978-3-030-26948-7
11. Bootle, J., Lyubashevsky, V., Seiler, G.: Algebraic techniques for short(er) exact lattice-based zero-knowledge proofs. In: Boldyreva and Micciancio [10], pp. 176–202 (2019). https://doi.org/10.1007/978-3-030-26948-7_7
12. Boudgoust, K., Jeudy, C., Roux-Langlois, A., Wen, W.: On the hardness of module-LWE with binary secret. In: Paterson, K.G. (ed.) CT-RSA 2021. LNCS, vol. 12704, pp. 503–526. Springer, Cham (2021). https://doi.org/10.1007/978-3-030-75539-3_21
13. Boudgoust, K., Jeudy, C., Roux-Langlois, A., Wen, W.: On the hardness of module learning with errors with short distributions. Cryptology ePrint Archive, Paper 2022/472 (2022). https://eprint.iacr.org/2022/472
14. Brakerski, Z.: Fully homomorphic encryption without modulus switching from classical GapSVP. In: Safavi-Naini, R., Canetti, R. (eds.) CRYPTO 2012. LNCS, vol. 7417, pp. 868–886. Springer, Heidelberg (2012). https://doi.org/10.1007/978-3-642-32009-5_50
15. Brakerski, Z., Döttling, N.: Lossiness and entropic hardness for ring-LWE. In: Pass, R., Pietrzak, K. (eds.) TCC 2020, Part I. LNCS, vol. 12550, pp. 1–27. Springer, Cham (2020). https://doi.org/10.1007/978-3-030-64375-1_1
16. Brakerski, Z., Gentry, C., Vaikuntanathan, V.: (Leveled) fully homomorphic encryption without bootstrapping. In: Goldwasser, S. (ed.) ITCS 2012, pp. 309–325. ACM (2012)
17. Cheon, J.H., Takagi, T. (eds.): ASIACRYPT 2016, Part II. LNCS, vol. 10032. Springer, Heidelberg (2016). https://doi.org/10.1007/978-3-662-53890-6
18. Dachman-Soled, D., Ducas, L., Gong, H., Rossi, M.: LWE with side information: attacks and concrete security estimation. In: Micciancio and Ristenpart [40], pp. 329–358 (2020). https://doi.org/10.1007/978-3-030-56880-1_12
19. del Pino, R., Katsumata, S.: A new framework for more efficient round-optimal lattice-based (partially) blind signature via trapdoor sampling. In: Dodis and Shrimpton [21], pp. 306–336 (2022). https://doi.org/10.1007/978-3-031-15979-4_11
20. del Pino, R., Lyubashevsky, V., Seiler, G.: Lattice-based group signatures and zero-knowledge proofs of automorphism stability. In: Lie, D., Mannan, M., Backes, M., Wang, X. (eds.) ACM CCS 2018, pp. 574–591. ACM Press (2018)
21. Dodis, Y., Shrimpton, T. (eds.): CRYPTO 2022, Part II. LNCS, vol. 13508. Springer, Heidelberg (2022). https://doi.org/10.1007/978-3-031-15979-4

22. Döttling, N., Kolonelos, D., Lai, R.W.F., Lin, C., Malavolta, G., Rahimi, A.: Efficient laconic cryptography from learning with errors. Cryptology ePrint Archive, Paper 2023/404 (2023). https://eprint.iacr.org/2023/404
23. Esgin, M.F., Nguyen, N.K., Seiler, G.: Practical exact proofs from lattices: new techniques to exploit fully-splitting rings. In: Moriai, S., Wang, H. (eds.) ASIACRYPT 2020, Part II. LNCS, vol. 12492, pp. 259–288. Springer, Cham (2020). https://doi.org/10.1007/978-3-030-64834-3_9
24. Esgin, M.F., Steinfeld, R., Liu, J.K., Liu, D.: Lattice-based zero-knowledge proofs: new techniques for shorter and faster constructions and applications. In: Boldyreva, A., Micciancio, D. (eds.) CRYPTO 2019. LNCS, vol. 11692, pp. 115–146. Springer, Cham (2019). https://doi.org/10.1007/978-3-030-26948-7_5
25. Esgin, M.F., Zhao, R.K., Steinfeld, R., Liu, J.K., Liu, D.: MatRiCT: efficient, scalable and post-quantum blockchain confidential transactions protocol. In: Cavallaro, L., Kinder, J., Wang, X., Katz, J. (eds.) ACM CCS 2019, pp. 567–584. ACM Press (2019)
26. Gilbert, H. (ed.): EUROCRYPT 2010. LNCS, vol. 6110. Springer, Heidelberg (2010). https://doi.org/10.1007/978-3-642-13190-5
27. Katsumata, S., Yamada, S.: Partitioning via non-linear polynomial functions: more compact IBEs from ideal lattices and bilinear maps. In: Cheon and Takagi [17], pp. 682–712 (2016). https://doi.org/10.1007/978-3-662-53890-6_23
28. Kim, D., Lee, D., Seo, J., Song, Y.: Toward practical lattice-based proof of knowledge from hint-mlwe. Cryptology ePrint Archive, Paper 2023/623 (2023). https://eprint.iacr.org/2023/623
29. Langlois, A., Stehle, D.: Worst-case to average-case reductions for module lattices. Des. Codes Cryptogr. (2015)
30. Libert, B., Ling, S., Mouhartem, F., Nguyen, K., Wang, H.: Signature schemes with efficient protocols and dynamic group signatures from lattice assumptions. In: Cheon and Takagi [17], pp. 373–403 (2016). https://doi.org/10.1007/978-3-662-53890-6_13
31. Liu, F.-H., Wang, Z.: Rounding in the rings. In: Micciancio and Ristenpart [40], pp. 296–326 (2020). https://doi.org/10.1007/978-3-030-56880-1_11
32. Lyubashevsky, V.: Lattice signatures without trapdoors. In: Pointcheval, D., Johansson, T. (eds.) EUROCRYPT 2012. LNCS, vol. 7237, pp. 738–755. Springer, Heidelberg (2012). https://doi.org/10.1007/978-3-642-29011-4_43
33. Lyubashevsky, V., Nguyen, N.K., Plançon, M.: Lattice-based zero-knowledge proofs and applications: shorter, simpler, and more general. In: Dodis and Shrimpton [21], pp. 71–101 (2022). https://doi.org/10.1007/978-3-031-15979-4_3
34. Lyubashevsky, V., Nguyen, N.K., Plancon, M., Seiler, G.: Shorter lattice-based group signatures via "Almost Free" encryption and other optimizations. In: Tibouchi, M., Wang, H. (eds.) ASIACRYPT 2021, Part IV. LNCS, vol. 13093, pp. 218–248. Springer, Cham (2021). https://doi.org/10.1007/978-3-030-92068-5_8
35. Lyubashevsky, V., Nguyen, N.K., Seiler, G.: Practical lattice-based zero-knowledge proofs for integer relations. In: Ligatti, J., Ou, X., Katz, J., Vigna, G. (eds.) ACM CCS 2020, pp. 1051–1070. ACM Press (2020)
36. Lyubashevsky, V., Nguyen, N.K., Seiler, G.: Shorter lattice-based zero-knowledge proofs via one-time commitments. In: Garay, J.A. (ed.) PKC 2021, Part I. LNCS, vol. 12710, pp. 215–241. Springer, Cham (2021). https://doi.org/10.1007/978-3-030-75245-3_9
37. Lyubashevsky, V., Peikert, C., Regev, O.: On ideal lattices and learning with errors over rings. In: Gilbert [26], pp. 1–23 (2010). https://doi.org/10.1007/978-3-642-13190-5_1

38. Lyubashevsky, V., Peikert, C., Regev, O.: A toolkit for ring-LWE cryptography. In: Johansson, T., Nguyen, P.Q. (eds.) EUROCRYPT 2013. LNCS, vol. 7881, pp. 35–54. Springer, Heidelberg (2013). https://doi.org/10.1007/978-3-642-38348-9_3
39. Lyubashevsky, V., Seiler, G.: Short, invertible elements in partially splitting cyclotomic rings and applications to lattice-based zero-knowledge proofs. In: Nielsen, J.B., Rijmen, V. (eds.) EUROCRYPT 2018, Part I. LNCS, vol. 10820, pp. 204–224. Springer, Cham (2018). https://doi.org/10.1007/978-3-319-78381-9_8
40. Micciancio, D., Ristenpart, T. (eds.): CRYPTO 2020, Part II. LNCS, vol. 12171. Springer, Heidelberg (2020). https://doi.org/10.1007/978-3-030-56880-1
41. O'Neill, A., Peikert, C., Waters, B.: Bi-deniable public-key encryption. In: Rogaway, P. (ed.) CRYPTO 2011. LNCS, vol. 6841, pp. 525–542. Springer, Heidelberg (2011). https://doi.org/10.1007/978-3-642-22792-9_30
42. Peikert, C.: A decade of lattice cryptography. Cryptology ePrint Archive, Report 2015/939 (2015). https://eprint.iacr.org/2015/939
43. Peikert, C., Shiehian, S.: Noninteractive zero knowledge for NP from (plain) learning with errors. In: Boldyreva and Micciancio [10], pp. 89–114 (2019). https://doi.org/10.1007/978-3-030-26948-7_4
44. Stehlé, D., Steinfeld, R., Tanaka, K., Xagawa, K.: Efficient public key encryption based on ideal lattices. In: Matsui, M. (ed.) ASIACRYPT 2009. LNCS, vol. 5912, pp. 617–635. Springer, Heidelberg (2009). https://doi.org/10.1007/978-3-642-10366-7_36
45. Yamada, S.: Adaptively secure identity-based encryption from lattices with asymptotically shorter public parameters. In: Fischlin, M., Coron, J.-S. (eds.) EUROCRYPT 2016, Part II. LNCS, vol. 9666, pp. 32–62. Springer, Heidelberg (2016). https://doi.org/10.1007/978-3-662-49896-5_2
46. Yamada, S.: Asymptotically compact adaptively secure lattice IBEs and verifiable random functions via generalized partitioning techniques. In: Katz, J., Shacham, H. (eds.) CRYPTO 2017, Part III. LNCS, vol. 10403, pp. 161–193. Springer, Cham (2017). https://doi.org/10.1007/978-3-319-63697-9_6

Succinct Verification of Compressed Sigma Protocols in the Updatable SRS Setting

Moumita Dutta(✉), Chaya Ganesh, and Neha Jawalkar

Indian Institute of Science, Bangalore, India
{moumitadutta,chaya,jawalkarp}@iisc.ac.in

Abstract. We propose protocols in the Compressed Sigma Protocol framework that achieve a succinct verifier. Towards this, we construct a new inner product argument and cast it in the Compressed Sigma Protocol (CSP) framework as a protocol for opening a committed linear form, achieving logarithmic verification.

We then use our succinct-verifier CSP to construct a zero-knowledge argument for circuit satisfiability (under the discrete logarithm assumption in bilinear groups) in the updatable Structured Reference String (SRS) setting that achieves $O(\log n)$ proof size and $O(\log n)$ verification complexity. Our circuit zero-knowledge protocol has concretely better proof/prover/verifier complexity compared to the state-of-the-art protocol in the updatable setting under the same assumption. Our techniques of achieving verifier-succinctness in the compression framework is of independent interest.

We then show a commitment scheme for committing to group elements using a structured commitment key. We construct protocols to open a committed homomorphism on a committed vector with verifier succinctness in the designated verifier setting. This has applications in making the verifier in compressed sigma protocols for bilinear group arithmetic circuits, succinct.

1 Introduction

Zero-knowledge proof systems [20] are an important primitive in theory of computation and a fundamental building block in various cryptographic constructions. In real-world applications, the proof size and efficiency of verification are crucial efficiency parameters. *Succinct* arguments, where the proof size is logarithmic in the size of the statement were first constructed by Kilian [25] based on probabilistically checkable proofs (PCP). Micali's construction [32] made this non-interactive in the random oracle model (ROM). Non-interactivity in the plain model is achieved by assuming a Common Reference String (CRS) generated during a setup phase. There has been a series of works on constructing (zero-knowledge) Succinct Non-interactive ARguments of Knowledge (zk-SNARKs) [9,10,19,22,23,28,29,33], which have very short proofs and admit efficient verification. The constructions with concretely better proof sizes are in the Structured Reference String (SRS) model and require a one-time setup or

Q. Tang and V. Teague (Eds.): PKC 2024, LNCS 14602, pp. 305–336, 2024.
https://doi.org/10.1007/978-3-031-57722-2_10

preprocessing that needs to be *trusted.* A line of work attempts to reduce the degree of trust in the setup phase by constructing SNARKS in an updatable setting [14,18,24,31] where the SRS is *updatable*, meaning parties can continuously contribute to the randomness of the SRS, and the assumption is that at least one of the updates was honest. SNARKs that do not need a trusted setup and the verifier randomness consists of only public coins are called transparent.

Bulletproofs [12], building on the work of [11] introduced techniques that achieve logarithmic communication complexity in discrete logarithm (DL) based zero-knowledge proofs. The beautiful work of Attema and Cramer [5] introduced *compressed sigma protocol* theory by using a blackbox compression technique, which also places Bulletproofs in the framework of Sigma protocol theory. The idea of employing a compression mechanism on a pivot protocol has become a versatile tool leading to compressed sigma protocol theory for lattices [6], and compressed sigma protocols for bilinear group arithmetic circuits [7].

Compressed Sigma Protocols (CSP) are attractive in applications due to their reliance on weaker assumptions (DL), conceptual simplicity, logarithmic proof size and transparent setup. One downside of this class of protocols is that they are only proof-succinct but not verifier-succinct – the verification is linear. In this paper we study succinct verification of compressed sigma protocols while retaining most of their advantages.

1.1 Our Contributions

In this work, we present compressed sigma protocols that are both proof and verifier-succinct in the updatable SRS model. CSP compresses a pivot Sigma protocol for proving knowledge of a long vector $\mathbf{x}$ while revealing a public linear form $L(\mathbf{x})$, given a Pedersen commitment, resulting in a protocol for opening linear forms on committed vectors with proof size $O(\log n)$ and verification complexity $O(n)$ where n is the size of the witness $\mathbf{x}$.

Protocol for Opening a Committed Linear Form. A core building block of our succinct verifier constructions is a protocol to open a committed linear form on a committed vector. It is an inner product argument, but in the spirit of CSP, one of the vectors – the linear form, is public and not a witness. This vector is committed to only for the sake of succinctness, and looking ahead, this commitment encodes the structure of the circuit and is computed during preprocessing. We use a commitment scheme with a structured key introduced by [15]. This protocol with logarithmic proof size and logarithmic verification complexity is secure under the DL assumption (same as CSP), albeit in a bilinear group and at the cost of moving to an updatable SRS setting. We compare our inner product protocol with [15] and [27] in Table 1.

Succinct Verifier Protocol for Circuit Satisfiability. We construct a succinct argument of knowledge for circuit satisfiability in the universal updatable SRS model. The proof size and verifier is logarithmic in the size of the circuit. This is secure under DL and can be made non-interactive in the ROM using the Fiat-Shamir transform. We compare the concrete costs of our protocol, with that of [15] in Table 2[1]. Since we use the same structure of SRS, the complexity of updating the SRS and verifying the updates remain the same as in [15]. Dory's [27] polynomial commitment can be used to obtain a protocol for circuit-satisfiability. The exact costs will depend on the underlying information-theoretic object (Polynomial interactive oracle proof) that is compiled using Dory. For univariate polynomials of degree n, and opening one evaluation, Dory's costs are: proof size of $(4 \log n + 10)\mathbb{G} + (\log n + 8)\mathbb{Z}_q$, prover's computation of $(n + \log n)E + n^{1/2}P$, verifier's computation of $4 \log nE + O(1)P$. Note that Dory's prover requires pairing operations and the security relies on a decisional assumption.

Table 1. Comparison of our Linear Form opening (or equivalently inner product arguments) protocols for vectors of length n. We compare in terms of most expensive operations, i.e. multi-exponentiations E, pairings P and exponentiations E^* (to provide aggregate values for non-constant multi-exponentiations).

Protocol	Setup	Assumption	Proof size	$\mathcal{P}$ complexity	$\mathcal{V}$ complexity
[15]	Updatable	DL	$8 \log n\ \mathbb{G}$ $2 \log n\ \mathbb{Z}_q$	$(8n - 4)\ E^*$	$2 \log n\ P$ $4 \log n\ E$
[27]	Transparent	SXDH	$12 \log n\ \mathbb{G}$ $\log n\ \mathbb{Z}_q$	$O(n^{1/2})$ P	$9 \log n\ E$ $1\ P$
This work ($\Pi_{1\text{-}\mathcal{R}}$)	Updatable	DL	$4 \log n\ \mathbb{G}$ $3 \log n\ \mathbb{Z}_q$	$(8n - 4)\ E^*$ $2 \log n\ E$	$2 \log n\ P$ $2 \log n\ E$
This work ($\Pi_{2\text{-}\mathcal{R}}$)	Updatable	DL	$2 \log n\ \mathbb{G}$ $\log n\ \mathbb{Z}_q$	$(4n - 2)\ E^*$ $\log n\ E$	$\log n\ P$ $\log n\ E$

Table 2. Circuit SAT protocol for a preprocessed circuit of size n (which is roughly $3m$ for m multiplication gates). Both protocols are updatable zkSNARKs that rely on the DL assumption. As in [15], we only compare in terms of the most expensive operations (exponentiations E and pairings P), and omit constant terms. M is a parameter that determines the processed circuit's fan-in and fan-out upper bound, and can be fine-tuned to balance the prover/verifier computations.

Protocol	Proof size	$\mathcal{P}$ complexity	$\mathcal{V}$ complexity
[15]	$12 \log n\,\mathbb{G} + 4 \log n\,\mathbb{Z}_q$	$(22 + 10M)n\ E^*$	$12 \log n\ E^* + 8 \log n\ P$
[27]	$(27/2) \log n\,\mathbb{G} + 3 \log n\,\mathbb{Z}_q$	$O(n^{1/2})$ P	$((27/2) \log n + O(1))\ E + O(1)\ P$
This work (Π_{csat})	$2 \log n\,\mathbb{G} + \log n\,\mathbb{Z}_q$	$(13 + 4M)n\ E^*$	$\log n\ E + \log n\ P$

[1] We note that other SNARKs in the universal, updatable setting that have better communication and/verifier complexity ($O_\lambda(1)$) rely on the Algebraic Group Model or Knowledge Type assumptions *in addition* to the Random Oracle Model. In this work, we are interested in constructions in the Random Oracle Model, and relying on standard assumptions.

Protocol for Opening a Committed Homomorphism. We then construct a protocol for opening a homomorphism, where both the vector and the homomorphism are committed to. A homomorphism is given by a vector of group elements. We extend commitment schemes to group elements from [7,26] to one that uses a structured key and show binding based on SXDH. Succinct verifier protocols for opening homomorphisms are useful in constructing proofs of partial knowledge with succinct verifier. We then extend our protocol to general homomorphisms (on commitments to $\mathbb{Z}_q, \mathbb{G}_1, \mathbb{G}_2, \mathbb{G}_T$ elements simultaneously) motivated by applications to bilinear group arithmetic circuit zero-knowledge protocols. Our constructions for opening homomorphisms are in the *designated-verifier* setting. In applications like verification of structure preserving signatures and attribute-based authentication, public verifiability might not be necessary since there is a designated credential verifier, and indeed the homomorphism itself is given by the statement to prove (signature verification algorithm) that can be committed to in a preprocessing phase. Therefore, our protocols can be used in similar applications as in [26], like proving knowledge of signature for complex access structures. While [26] has proof that scales logarithmically with the size of the statement, our protocol additionally yields logarithmic verification (albeit for designated verifier, which we believe is not a limitation for credential verification).

1.2 Related Work

Daza et al [15] construct inner product arguments with logarithmic verifier by replacing the unstructured CRS or commitment key with a structured one. This also yields a protocol for circuit satisfiability with logarithmic verification in the updatable setting. Our construction and the protocols of [15] achieve the same result asymptotically. However, while we crucially rely on a structured commitment key to make the verifier logarithmic like in [15], our techniques are different. The work of [15] extend the protocols of [11,12], while we take the approach of CSP. This has the advantage of applying *compression mechanism* on standard protocols for linear relations (or non-linear relations after linearization). The CSP approach also allows us to extend our techniques to other applications where compression applies in a black-box way. Second, our protocols are concretely better than [15] with smaller constants (See Table 2).

Dory [27] presents a transparent protocol for inner products between committed vectors with logarithmic proof size and logarithmic verification. Dory relies on a decisional assumption (SXDH) whereas our inner product protocol relies on DL. Additionally, our prover work is only group operations as opposed to $(O(n^{1/2}))$ pairing operations required by the prover in Dory, and our constants in the proof size are better.

Other SNARKs in the updatable setting [14,18,30,31] rely on knowledge-type assumptions or Algebraic Group Model (AGM), and constructions in the transparent setting with similar and better asymptotics [4,13] require unknown order groups with concretely expensive operations.

Lai et al [26], show a generalization of Bulletproof's circuit zero-knowledge protocol to work for bilinear group arithmetic circuits directly, without requiring these circuits to be translated into arithmetic circuits. Attema et al [7] generalize compressed sigma protocols for bilinear group arithmetic circuits. Both these constructions rely on a protocol for opening a group homomorphism where the verifier is linear. Using our protocol for opening a committed homomorphism will yield a succinct verifier at the expense of making it a designated verifier system. We provide the comparison in Table 4. Note that for application like Threshold Signature Schemes (following Algorithm 4 of [7]), we retain the logarithmic size of the signature similar to prior works, however we improve the verification complexity from linear to logarithmic.

Performance Comparison for MiMC and Poseidon Hash. We report the timing using a third party implementation calculator https://zka.lc, where we estimate using BLS12-381 curve implemented in arkworks-rs provided using Amazon Linux 2 8-core Intel(R) Xeon(R) Platinum 8259CL CPU @ 2.50 GHz, 32 GB. In Table 3, we use the reported number of gates for MiMC in [3], having 1293 multiplication gates and 646 addition gates. We achieve 1.77× improvement in prover time and more than 7× improvement in verification time as compared to Daza et al [15]. Similarly, we achieve 1.79× improvement in prover time and more than 7× improvement in verification time compared to Daza et al. for Poseidon (assuming number of R1CS constraints is equal to the number of multiplication gates, with 276 R1CS constraints [1]).

Similarly, we obtain 1.42× improvement in prover time as compared to Dory [27] for MiMC hash instantiation and 2.69× improvement in prover time for Poseidon hash instantiation, at a slight cost of verifier time. Note that for circuits of smaller sizes, we do fairly better than Dory in prover time complexity, while not losing much in verifier time complexity. Also, for both comparisons we assume that Dory has atleast $6n^{1/2}$ pairings computation by prover, and 3 pairing checks performed by the verifier. For statements that show up in practice, like proving knowledge of opening of a Merkle tree leaf using MiMC/Poseidon Hash functions, the reported number for the prover increases by a factor of depth d of the tree.

Table 3. Performance of MiMC and Poseidon Hash Instantiation using https://zka.lc and in μs.

Hash	Protocol	Prover Time	Verifier Time
MiMC	[15]	729,272	151,831
	[27]	586,381	7,054
	This work	411,809	19,319
Poseidon	[15]	181,058	123,610
	[27]	270,912	6,769
	This work	100,636	15,780

Table 4. Comparison of protocols for opening homomorphism for vectors of length n. We compare in terms of most expensive operations, i.e. pairings P and exponentiations E and dominant communication cost with respect to elements of the field $\mathbb{Z}_q$ and groups $\mathbb{G}_1$, $\mathbb{G}_2$ and $\mathbb{G}_T$. Note that our verifier complexity is $2\log n\ E\ +\ \log n\ P$.

Protocol	Proof size	$\mathcal{P}$ complexity	$\mathcal{V}$ complexity
[26]	$O(n)\ \mathbb{G}_T$ $+ O(\log n)\ \mathbb{G}_1$ $+ O(\log n)\ \mathbb{G}_2$ $+ O(\log n)\ \mathbb{Z}_q$	$O(n)\ E$	$O(n)\ E$
[7]	$O(\log n)\ \mathbb{G}_T$ $+ O(\log n)\ \mathbb{Z}_q$	$O(n)\ E$	$O(n)\ E$
This work	$O(\log n)\ \mathbb{G}_T$ $+ O(\log n)\ \mathbb{G}_1$ $+ O(\log n)\ \mathbb{G}_2$ $+ O(\log n)\ \mathbb{Z}_q$	$O(n)\ E$	$O(\log n)\ E$ $+ O(\log n)\ P$

1.3 Technical Overview

The high level idea behind the inner product argument of [11] and the compressed sigma protocol of [5] is to compress a vector using a Pedersen commitment, and then in each round reduce the instance and the commitment key to another one of half the size by using the verifier's challenge. At a high level, the source of the verifier's linear complexity is in having to compute the new keys at every step.

We use a structured commitment key proposed in [15] that consists of encodings of multilinear monomials of a secret vector of logarithmic length, i.e., $\dot{\mathbf{a}} = (\dot{a}_1, \ldots, \dot{a}_\ell), \overline{\mathbf{a}} = \left(\prod_{i=1}^{\ell} \dot{a}_i^{b_i}\right)_{b_i \in \{0,1\}}$, for $n = 2^\ell$, the commitment key is $g^{\overline{\mathbf{a}}}$ where $g^{\mathbf{x}} = (g^{x_1}, \ldots, g^{x_n})$ for a vector $\mathbf{x} = (x_1, \ldots, x_n)$. The commitment to a vector $\mathbf{x}$ under key $g^{\overline{\mathbf{a}}}$ is $g^{\langle \overline{\mathbf{a}}, \mathbf{x} \rangle}$. This key is updatable, a party can sample new ℓ secrets and update the encoding in a verifiable way. A compressed version of this key, $g^{\dot{\mathbf{a}}} \in \mathbb{G}_1^\ell$ allows the verifier to be logarithmic.

Linear Form Opening with Succinct Verifier. We build on the inner product arguments of [11] and [15]. The verifier's work in [11] involves computing an updated key in each round, and in [15], the verifier is only given a compressed key (logarithmic) and the prover convinces the verifier that the reduced statement in each round is with respect to a new key that is correctly updated. New commitment keys with size half of the original one are created by splitting them in half and then combining them based on the verifier's challenge. A logarithmic verifier can check that a structured key has been updated correctly using a pairing operation.

While our protocol uses the same structured key, we take a slightly different approach: we exploit the fact that we can go from a commitment to a vector with respect to the second half of the original basis to a commitment to the same vector with respect to the first half of the original basis. Now, if a prover produces commitment to both halves of a vector with respect to the first half of the basis, the verifier can perform one multiplication in the exponent to check the consistency. Consider, $\dot{\mathbf{a}} = (\dot{a}_1, \ldots, \dot{a}_\ell), \overline{\mathbf{a}} = \left(\prod_{i=1}^{\ell} \dot{a}_i^{b_i}\right)_{b_i \in \{0,1\}}$, for $n = 2^\ell$, the commitment key is $g^{\overline{\mathbf{a}}} = \left(g^{\overline{\mathbf{a}}_L} \| g^{\dot{a}_\ell \overline{\mathbf{a}}_L}\right)$, the verification key is $H^{\dot{\mathbf{a}}}$, and $P = \mathrm{COM}_{\overline{\mathbf{a}}}(\mathbf{x})$. In each step, for $\mathbf{x} = (\mathbf{x}_L \| \mathbf{x}_R)$, if the prover produces $A_1 = \mathrm{COM}_{\overline{\mathbf{a}}_L}(\mathbf{x}_L), A_2 = \mathrm{COM}_{\overline{\mathbf{a}}_L}(\mathbf{x}_R)$, the verifier can perform the check $e(\frac{P}{A_1}, H) = e(A_2, H^{\dot{a}_\ell})$. Thus, the commitment key updates are done implicitly by simply dropping off the last element $\dot{a}_\ell$, and using the challenge only to fold the instance vectors $\mathbf{x}' = \mathbf{x}_L + c\mathbf{x}_R$. This observation allows us to shave off about 4 group elements in each round from the Daza et al inner product argument. Our protocol also has the advantage of allowing efficient batching, i.e., for vectors of length n, the prover can prove, for distinct $L_1, \ldots, L_m$ and $\mathbf{x}_1, \ldots, \mathbf{x}_m$ that $L_1(\mathbf{x}_1) = y_1, \ldots, L_m(\mathbf{x}_m) = y_m$ while incurring a cost that is $\mathcal{O}(m + \log n)$ as opposed to $\mathcal{O}(m \log n)$.

Succinct ZK Argument for Circuit Satisfiability. We construct an improved protocol for arithmetic circuit satisfiability in the universal updatable SRS setting. The CSP approach to handle multiplication gates by linearizing them renders the verifier linear. We propose a protocol for computing a commitment to the linear form that captures the multiplication gates in the circuit in a verifiable way while keeping the verifier succinct. We use the ideas from [15] to preprocess a circuit, and obtain a commitment to the linear constraints. Now, all relations are linearized, we have commitments to all linear forms, and we show how to batch all linear form openings into one protocol for opening a committed linear form on a committed vector.

The following are two key new ideas to make a CSP-like proof have succinct verification. (i) The first relates to how we handle multiplication gates. For linearizing multiplication constraints, CSP uses a linear combination of polynomial evaluations at $1, \ldots, m$ to evaluate a polynomial at a new value z rendering the verifier linear. We handle multiplication in the same way as CSP, but instead of computing the public linear form for multiplication, the verifier instead *succinctly* verifies a commitment to it. We construct a succinct-verifier protocol for obtaining a *commitment* to the linear form used for verifying multiplication constraints. In order to do this, impose some structure; specifically, we use a linear combination of polynomial evaluations at $2, 2^2, \ldots, 2^m$. This choice allows us to compute the value of a polynomial at any point z while keeping the verifier succinct. This idea gives a protocol where the prover computes a commitment to the linear form that the verifier can efficiently check. The linearization is now via a committed linear form. (ii) The second idea relates to how we handle linear gates. Here, we employ the ideas of Daza et al., by reducing the problem of verifying linear gates to checking that two committed vectors are permutations of each other; and a Hadamard product argument. We deviate from [15] by first reducing the permutation argument to the CSP pivot of opening linear forms on committed vectors. We then use our techniques from (i) to obtain commitments to these linear forms. Finally, we take advantage of our ability to batch the openings of linear forms, which allows us to prove circuit constraints while paying the cost of essentially a single invocation of our linear form protocol.

Homomorphism Opening with Succinct Verifier. Our ideas for succinct verifier in linear form openings do not extend to opening homomorphism. First, we need to commit to a homomorphism, and we extend the commitment scheme for group elements used in [7,26] to a commitment scheme with a structured key in order to make the verifier logarithmic. We show that binding is implied by SXDH (same assumption as the scheme with uniform key). Since we rely on SXDH, we cannot encode the commitment key randomness in the second group as the verification key. Thus a pairing check to verify correct key updates is not possible anymore, making our constructions designated verifier. A second hurdle is that the commitment itself lives in the target group. This means that our idea to check correct updation of the key in each round of split-and-fold (which involved a pairing operation) does not work anymore. We tackle this by having the commitment key in both $\mathbb{G}_1$ and $\mathbb{G}_T$. Now, the prover updates the commitment key in $\mathbb{G}_1$ and proves that this has been done correctly. The verifier can check this using a pairing, move this updated commitment key in $\mathbb{G}_1$ to $\mathbb{G}_T$, and then finally at the end of the recursion verify the commitment with respect to the updated key in $\mathbb{G}_T$.

2 Preliminaries

Notation. A finite field is denoted by $\mathbb{F}$. Let $\mathbb{G}$ be a group of order q. We denote by λ a security parameter, by negl a negligible function. For any integer $c > 0$, there exists $n \in \mathbb{N}$, such that $\forall\ x > n$, $\mathsf{negl}(x) \leq 1/n^c$. We denote vectors by boldface letters, and inner product between $\mathbf{a}$ and $\mathbf{b}$ by $\langle \mathbf{a}, \mathbf{b} \rangle$. We define $\mathcal{L}(\mathbb{Z}_q^n) = \{L : L \text{ is a linear map from } \mathbb{Z}_q^n \text{ to } \mathbb{Z}_q\}$. A linear map $L \in \mathcal{L}(\mathbb{Z}_q^n)$ is given by a vector $(a_1, \dots, a_n)$ where $a_1, \dots, a_n \in \mathbb{Z}_q$ and $L(x_1, \dots, x_n) = a_1x_1 + \dots + a_nx_n$ for $(x_1, \dots, x_n) \in \mathbb{Z}_q^n$. For $x = (x_1, \dots, x_n) \in \mathbb{Z}_q^n$, its reversal is defined as $\mathsf{rev}(x) = (x_n, \dots, x_1)$. A vector $\mathbf{a} = (a_1, \dots, a_n)$ naturally defines a $(n-1)$-degree polynomial by considering the vector $\mathbf{a}$ as the vector of coefficients, which gives us the polynomial $\mathbf{a}(X) = a_1 + a_2X + a_3X^2 + \dots + a_nX^{n-1}$. Also, a commitment to a polynomial $\mathbf{a}(X) = a_1 + a_2X + a_3X^2 + \dots + a_nX^{n-1}$ is provided by a commitment to the vector of coefficients also denoted by $\mathbf{a} = (a_1, \dots, a_n)$. Hence, for ease of notation, we use the vector and polynomial notation interchangeably throughout the paper.

Let $[n]$ denote the set $\{1, \dots, n\}$. For $\mathbf{g} = (g_1, \dots, g_n) \in \mathbb{G}^n$ and $\mathbf{x} = (x_1, \dots, x_n) \in \mathbb{Z}_q^n$, the multi-exponentiation $\mathbf{g}^{\mathbf{x}}$ is defined by $\mathbf{g}^{\mathbf{x}} = g_1^{x_1} \cdots g_n^{x_n}$. Also, for $g \in \mathbb{G}$ and $\mathbf{x} = (x_1, \dots, x_n) \in \mathbb{Z}_q^n$, $g^{\mathbf{x}}$ is defined by $g^{\mathbf{x}} = (g^{x_1}, \cdots, g^{x_n})$. The inner product between elements of $\mathbb{Z}_q^n$, $\mathbf{a} = (a_1, \dots, a_n)$ and $\mathbf{b} = (b_1, \dots, b_n)$, is denoted by $\langle \mathbf{a}, \mathbf{b} \rangle = a_1b_1 + \dots + a_nb_n$. For $a \in \mathbb{Z}_q^m, b \in \mathbb{Z}_q^n$, $a \| b \in \mathbb{Z}_q^{m+n}$ denotes the concatenation of a and b in that order, similarly, the notation is used for the vectors in a group $\mathbb{G}$ to denote concatenation of two vectors. For $\mathbf{a} = (a_1, \dots, a_n) \in \mathbb{Z}_q^n$ and $\mathbf{b} = (b_1, \dots, b_n) \in \mathbb{Z}_q^n$, the hadamard product $\mathbf{a} \circ \mathbf{b}$

is defined by $\mathbf{a} \circ \mathbf{b} = (a_1b_1, \ldots, a_nb_n)$. Also, for $v, n \in \mathbb{Z}_q$, $\mathbf{v^n}$ denotes the vector $\mathbf{v^n} = (1, \ldots, v^n)$.

A bilinear group is denoted by the tuple $(q, \mathbb{G}_1, \mathbb{G}_2, \mathbb{G}_T, e, G, H) \leftarrow_R \mathcal{G}(1^\lambda)$, where $\mathbb{G}_1$, $\mathbb{G}_2$ and $\mathbb{G}_T$ are groups of prime order q, G and H are generators of $\mathbb{G}_1$ and $\mathbb{G}_2$, and $e : \mathbb{G}_1 \times \mathbb{G}_2 \to \mathbb{G}_T$ is efficiently computable bilinear map.

We define $\mathcal{ML}_{2^\ell} \in \mathbb{Z}_q^n$ to be the set of all n-length multilinear vectors of the form $(1, \dot{a}_1, \dot{a}_2, \ldots, \dot{a}_1 \cdots \dot{a}_\ell)$, determined by ℓ-mutually independent scalars $\dot{a}_1, \ldots, \dot{a}_\ell$. We denote the set of ℓ scalars by $\dot{\mathbf{a}} = (\dot{a}_1, \ldots, \dot{a}_\ell)$ and the n-length vector by $\bar{\mathbf{a}} = (1, \dot{a}_1, \dot{a}_2, \ldots, \dot{a}_1 \cdots \dot{a}_\ell)$. More formally, $\mathcal{ML}_n = \{\bar{\mathbf{a}} : \dot{\mathbf{a}} = (\dot{a}_1, \ldots, \dot{a}_\ell) \leftarrow_R \mathbb{Z}_q^\ell,\ \bar{\mathbf{a}} = (\prod_{i=1}^{\ell} \dot{a}_i^{x_i})_{x_i \in \{0,1\}}\}$.

2.1 Interactive Arguments

We consider interactive arguments for relations, where a prover P convinces the verifier that it knows a witness w such that for a public statement x, $(x, w) \in \mathcal{R}$. For a pair of PPT interactive algorithms P, V, we denote by $\langle P(w), V \rangle(x)$, the output of V on its interaction with P where w is P's private input and x is a common input. Let $\mathcal{R} = \{(x, w)\}$ be a relation and $\mathcal{L}$ be the corresponding NP language.

Definition 1 (Argument of knowledge). *An interactive argument of knowledge(AoK) for a relation $\mathcal{R}$ consists of a PPT algorithm* $\mathsf{setup}(1^\lambda)$ *that takes a security parameter λ and outputs public parameters* srs, *and a pair of PPT interactive algorithms $\langle \mathcal{P}, \mathcal{V} \rangle$. The triple* $(\mathsf{setup}, \mathcal{P}, \mathcal{V})$ *satisfy the following properties.*

1. *Completeness. For all $\lambda \in \mathbb{N}$, $(x, w) \in \mathcal{R}$,*

$$\Pr\left(\langle \mathcal{P}(w) \mathcal{V} \rangle(\mathsf{srs}, x) = 1 \,:\, \mathsf{srs} \leftarrow \mathsf{setup}(1^\lambda)\right) = 1.$$

2. *Knowledge Soundness. An argument system $(\mathcal{P}, \mathcal{V})$ for a relation $\mathcal{R}$ is knowledge sound with error κ if there exists an expected polynomial time extractor* Ext *such that for every efficient adversary $\tilde{\mathcal{P}}$, for every $x \in \{0,1\}^*$, whenever $\tilde{\mathcal{P}}$ makes $\mathcal{V}$ accept with probability $\epsilon > \kappa$, $\mathsf{Ext}^{\tilde{\mathcal{P}}}(x)$ outputs w^* such that $(x, w^*) \in \mathcal{R}$ with probability at least $\frac{\epsilon - \kappa}{q}$ for some polynomial q.*

Definition 2 (Honest verifier zero-knowledge (HVZK)). *An argument system $(\mathcal{P}, \mathcal{V})$ for a relation $\mathcal{R}$ is HVZK if there exists an efficient simulator $\mathcal{S}$ such that for every $(x, w) \in \mathcal{R}$, the distribution $\mathcal{S}(x)$ is identical to* $\mathsf{View}_{\langle \mathcal{P}(x,w), \mathcal{V}(x) \rangle}$, *where* $\mathsf{View}_{\langle \mathcal{P}(x,w), \mathcal{V}(x) \rangle}$ *is the distribution of the view of the verifier in the protocol on common input x and prover's witness w.*

We now recall the special soundness property which is typically simpler than knowledge soundness.

Definition 3 (Tree of transcripts). *A set of* $k = \prod_{i=1}^{\ell} k_i$ *accepting transcripts for an argument system* $(\mathcal{P}, \mathcal{V})$ *is a* $(k_1, \ldots, k_\ell)$*-tree of accepting transcripts if they are in the following tree structure: The nodes of the tree are formed by* $\mathcal{P}$*'s messages, and the edges correspond to* $\mathcal{V}$*'s messages. Each node at depth* i *has exactly* k_i *children corresponding to* k_i *distinct messages from the verifier. Each transcript is given by a path from a leaf node to the root.*

Definition 4 (Special Soundness). *A* $(2\ell + 1)$ *move protocol is said to be* $(k_1, \ldots, k_\ell)$ *special sound if there exists an extractor* Ext *that given a* $(k_1, \ldots, k_\ell)$*-tree of accepting transcripts for an instance* x*, outputs* w *such that* $(x, w) \in \mathcal{R}$*.*

Definition 5 (Succinct Argument of knowledge). *An argument system is* proof-succinct *if the communication complexity between prover and verifier is bounded by* $\mathsf{poly}(\lambda)$*, and* verifier-succinct *if the running time of* $\mathcal{V}$ *is bounded by* $\mathsf{poly}(\lambda + |x|)$ *and independent of the size of the circuit computing* $\mathcal{R}$*.*

Fiat-Shamir and Non-interactive AoK. An argument system is said to be *public coin* if the verifier's messages are uniformly random strings. Public coin interactive protocols can be heuristically compiled into non-interactive arguments by applying the Fiat-Shamir [17] transform (FS) in the Random Oracle Model (ROM). Since our protocols are all public coin, we show special soundness of the interactive version and then rely on FS.

Updatable SRS SNARK. Introduced by Groth at al. [24], the updatable universal structured reference string (SRS) enables parties to update the parameters, while retaining computational soundness against any probabilistic-polynomial time adversary, as long as at least one honest update is made. We follow the model used in Daza et al. [15] based on [24], where anyone can deterministically compute the circuit-specific preprocessing material given the (updated) universal SRS, which ensures that the circuit-specific preprocessing is performed publicly without any involvement of secrets.

2.2 Assumptions

Definition 6 (DLOG Assumption). *The discrete logarithm (DLOG) assumption for a group* $\mathbb{G}$ *states that, given a generator* g *of the group* $\mathbb{G}$*, for all PPT adversaries* $\mathcal{A}$ *we have*

$$\Pr\left(r = r' \mid r \leftarrow_R \mathbb{Z}_q \wedge r' \leftarrow \mathcal{A}(g^r)\right) \leq \mathsf{negl}(\lambda)$$

When the commitment key is structured, we need the following Find-rep assumption to hold in bilinear groups, which is known to follow from DLOG, as shown in [15].

Definition 7 (Find-rep Assumption). *The Find-rep assumption holds with respect to a bilinear group generator $\mathcal{G}$ if for all PPT adversaries $\mathcal{A}$ we have*

$$\Pr\left(\begin{array}{c} g^{\langle \mathbf{a},\mathbf{x}\rangle} = 1_{\mathbb{G}} \wedge \mathbf{x} \neq 0 \\ (q, \mathbb{G}_1, \mathbb{G}_2, \mathbb{G}_T, e, g, h) \leftarrow_R \mathcal{G}(1^\lambda) \\ \mathbf{a} \leftarrow_R \mathcal{ML}_n, \mathbf{x} \leftarrow \mathcal{A}(g^{\mathbf{a}}, h^{\mathbf{a}}) \end{array}\right) \leq \mathsf{negl}(\lambda)$$

Definition 8 (DDH Assumption). *For a group $\mathbb{G}$, decisional Diffie-Hellman (DDH) problem is to determine, when given a tuple (g, g^a, g^b, g^c) for some $g \in \mathbb{G}$, whether $c = ab$. Decisional Diffie-Hellman (DDH) assumption in a group $\mathbb{G}$ states that DDH problem is hard in that group.*

Definition 9 (SXDH Assumption). *For $(q, \mathbb{G}_1, \mathbb{G}_2, \mathbb{G}_T, e, G, H) \leftarrow_R \mathcal{G}(1^\lambda)$, the Symmetric External Diffie-Hellman (SXDH) assumption states that the decisional Diffie-Hellman (DDH) assumption holds for both $\mathbb{G}_1$ and $\mathbb{G}_2$.*

3 CSP for Committed Linear Forms

We construct a protocol to reveal $L(x)$ for a committed vector x, and committed linear form L. The idea is to honestly generate a commitment to the linear form in a preprocesing phase. Once generated, a commitment to a linear form L can be used to open L on any committed vector. When used as a subprotocol for arithmetic circuit SAT, we generate these commitments during a one-time circuit-specific setup phase.

Definition 1
(Commitment to $\mathbb{Z}_q$-vectors ([15])). *Let $(q, \mathbb{G}_1, \mathbb{G}_2, \mathbb{G}_T, e, g, H)$ be a bilinear group and let $n \geq 0$. We define a commitment scheme for vectors in $\mathbb{Z}_q^n$ with the following setup and commitment phase:*

- *Setup: Let* $\dot{\mathbf{a}} := (\dot{a}_1, \ldots, \dot{a}_\ell) \leftarrow \mathbb{Z}_q^\ell$ *where* $\ell = \log(n+1)$. *Let* $\overline{\mathbf{a}} = (a_1, \ldots, a_n) \in \mathbb{Z}_q^{n+1}$ *be defined as* $a_j = \prod_{i=1}^{\ell} \dot{a}_i^{b_{ji}}$, *where* $(b_{j1}, \ldots, b_{j\ell})$ *is the binary representation of* j. *Output* $(g^{\overline{\mathbf{a}}}, H^{\dot{\mathbf{a}}})$, *where* $g^{\overline{\mathbf{a}}} \in \mathbb{G}_1^{n+1}$ *is the commitment key, and* $H^{\dot{\mathbf{a}}} \in \mathbb{G}_2^\ell$ *is the verification key.*
- *Commit:* COM $: \mathbb{Z}_q^{n+1} \rightarrow \mathbb{G}_1$, $\gamma \leftarrow_R \mathbb{Z}_q$ *and define*
  - $\mathrm{COM}_{\overline{\mathbf{a}}}(\mathbf{x}; \gamma) \rightarrow g^{\langle \overline{\mathbf{a}}, (\mathbf{x} \| \gamma)\rangle}$

Lemma 1. *The above scheme is perfectly hiding and computationally binding under the DLOG assumption [15].*

The proof is provided in Appendix A.1 of the full version of the paper [16].

We start with a Σ-Protocol for opening a linear form which is similar to the initial protocol in [5] but using structured keys instead of uniformly random keys for the commitments. We consider the following relation

$$\mathcal{R} = \{(P \in \mathbb{G}, L \in \mathcal{L}(\mathbb{Z}_q^n), y \in \mathbb{Z}_q; \mathbf{x} \in \mathbb{Z}_q^n, \gamma \in \mathbb{Z}_q) : P = \mathrm{COM}_{\overline{\mathbf{a}}}(\mathbf{x}; \gamma) \ \wedge\ L(\mathbf{x}) = y\}$$

Parameters

- Common parameters : $(P \in \mathbb{G}, L \in \mathcal{L}(\mathbb{Z}_q^n), y \in \mathbb{Z}_q)$, $P = \mathrm{COM}_{\overline{\mathbf{a}}}(\mathbf{x}; \gamma), y = L(\mathbf{x})$
- $\mathcal{P}$'s input : $(\mathbf{x} \in \mathbb{Z}_q^n, \gamma \in \mathbb{Z}_q)$

Protocol

1. $\mathcal{P}$ samples $\mathbf{r} \leftarrow_R \mathbb{Z}_q^n, \rho \leftarrow_R \mathbb{Z}_q$, computes $A = \mathrm{COM}_{\overline{\mathbf{a}}}(\mathbf{r}; \rho)$, $t = L(\mathbf{r})$ and sends A, t to $\mathcal{V}$
2. $\mathcal{V}$ samples $c \leftarrow_R \mathbb{Z}_q$ and sends c to $\mathcal{P}$
3. $\mathcal{P}$ computes $\mathbf{z} = c\mathbf{x} + \mathbf{r}$ and $\phi = c\gamma + \rho$ and sends $\mathbf{z}, \phi$ to $\mathcal{V}$
4. $\mathcal{V}$ checks if $\mathrm{COM}_{\overline{\mathbf{a}}}(\mathbf{z}; \phi) = AP^c$ and $L(\mathbf{z}) = cy + t$, outputs 1 if it holds, outputs 0 otherwise.

Fig. 1. Protocol Π_0 for relation $\mathcal{R}$

which corresponds to showing opening of a public commitment P and a public value y, obtained by operating a linear form L on a secret $\mathbb{Z}_q^n$ vector $\mathbf{x}$. This is the same relation as in [5] but using the commitment COM with a structured commitment key $(g^{\overline{\mathbf{a}}}, H^{\dot{\mathbf{a}}})$ (Definition 1). We rely on the SXDH assumption for providing the structured key $(g^{\overline{\mathbf{a}}}, H^{\dot{\mathbf{a}}})$ while maintaining security.

Theorem 1. *Π_0 is a 3-move protocol for relation $\mathcal{R}$. It is perfectly complete, special honest-verifier zero-knowledge and computationally special sound.*

Proof. **Completeness.** If the protocol is executed correctly by the prover, then we have $\mathbf{z} = c\mathbf{x} + \mathbf{r}$, and it satisfies the final two checks by the verifier

$$\begin{aligned} \mathrm{COM}_{\overline{\mathbf{a}}}(\mathbf{z}; \phi) &= g^{\langle \overline{\mathbf{a}}, (\mathbf{z} \| \phi) \rangle}, \\ &= g^{\langle \overline{\mathbf{a}}, (c\mathbf{x} + \mathbf{r} \| c\gamma + \rho) \rangle} \\ &= g^{c\langle \overline{\mathbf{a}}, (\mathbf{x} \| \gamma) \rangle} g^{\langle \overline{\mathbf{a}}, (\mathbf{r} \| \rho) \rangle} \\ &= P^c A \end{aligned} \qquad \begin{aligned} L(\mathbf{z}) &= L(c\mathbf{x} + \mathbf{r}) \\ &= cL(\mathbf{x}) + L(\mathbf{r}) \\ &= cy + t \end{aligned}$$

Special Honest-Verifier Zero-Knowledge. We construct a simulator $\mathcal{S}$, which produces a transcript indistinguishable from the transcript of the real execution of the protocol, provided a challenge $c \in \mathbb{Z}_q$. (i) $\mathcal{S}$ samples $\mathbf{z}, \phi$, (ii) $\mathcal{S}$ computes $\mathrm{COM}_{\overline{\mathbf{a}}}(\mathbf{z}; \phi)$ and sets $A = \frac{\mathrm{COM}_{\overline{\mathbf{a}}}(\mathbf{z}; \phi)}{P^c}$ and $t = L(\mathbf{z}) - cy$.

The transcript produced by the simulator $\mathcal{S}$ is indistinguishable from the transcript of the real execution of the protocol due to the hiding property of the commitment scheme $\mathrm{COM}_{(.)}(.)$, which ensures that a commitment sampled uniformly at random from the set of all possible commitments is indistinguishable from a commitment computed from a message chosen uniformly at random.

Special Soundness. We consider 2 accepting transcripts $(A, t, c_1, \mathbf{z}_1, \phi_1)$ and $(A, t, c_2, \mathbf{z}_2, \phi_2)$, such that $c_1 \neq c_2$. Then we have,

$$\begin{aligned} &\mathrm{COM}_{\bar{\mathbf{a}}}\,(\mathbf{z}_1; \phi_1) = AP^{c_1}, L(\mathbf{z}_1) = c_1 y + t, && \text{and} \\ &\mathrm{COM}_{\bar{\mathbf{a}}}\,(\mathbf{z}_2; \phi_2) = AP^{c_2}, L(\mathbf{z}_2) = c_2 y + t && \\ \Longrightarrow\ &g^{\langle \bar{\mathbf{a}}, (\mathbf{z}_1 \| \phi_1) \rangle} = AP^{c_1}, L(\mathbf{z}_1) = c_1 y + t, && \text{and} \\ &g^{\langle \bar{\mathbf{a}}, (\mathbf{z}_2 \| \phi_2) \rangle} = AP^{c_2}, L(\mathbf{z}_2) = c_2 y + t && \end{aligned}$$

Dividing the first two equations, and subtracting the second equations, we get

$$g^{\langle \bar{\mathbf{a}}, (\mathbf{z}_1 - \mathbf{z}_2 \| \phi_1 - \phi_2) \rangle} = P^{c_1 - c_2}, L(\mathbf{z}_1 - \mathbf{z}_2) = (c_1 - c_2) y$$

We define $\mathbf{x} = (\mathbf{z}_1 - \mathbf{z}_2)/(c_1 - c_2)$ and $\gamma = (\phi_1 - \phi_2)/(c_1 - c_2)$, and this gives us $g^{\langle \bar{\mathbf{a}}, (\mathbf{x}, \gamma) \rangle} = \mathrm{COM}_{\bar{\mathbf{a}}}\,(\mathbf{x}, \gamma) = P$, and $L(\mathbf{x}) = y$.

3.1 Opening a Committed Linear Form

In Π_0, the communication complexity as well as the verifier complexity is linear due to the last message sent by the prover and the last check performed by the verifier. To improve both complexities, we replace the message sent in the last step of Π_0 with a proof of knowledge. We define a relation that captures this and reduce the verifier's work by committing to the linear form and compressing the check using the split-and-fold technique used in [5]. The protocol Π_1 is in Fig. 2. We compress recursively until the size of instance is constant and can be sent in the clear.

We now consider the new relation $\mathcal{R}_{\mathrm{CLF}}$ with respect to an updated linear form, where the new linear form L is defined as $L(\mathbf{z}, \phi) := L(\mathbf{z})$, and hence, the check performed by the verifier in step 5 of Π_0 (Fig. 1) corresponds to the new relation, where the message sent by the prover $\mathcal{P}$ to the verifier $\mathcal{V}$ in step 4 corresponds to a witness in the new relation.

$$\begin{aligned} \mathcal{R}_{\mathrm{CLF}} = \{(P \in \mathbb{G}, Q \in \mathbb{G}, y \in \mathbb{Z}_q; \mathbf{x} \in \mathbb{Z}_q^n, L \in \mathcal{L}(\mathbb{Z}_q^n)) : \\ P = \mathrm{COM}_{\bar{\mathbf{a}}}\,(\mathbf{x}) \ \wedge\ Q = \mathrm{COM}_{\bar{\mathbf{a}}}\,(L) \ \wedge\ L(\mathbf{x}) = y\}\} \end{aligned}$$

This corresponds to showing opening of a public commitment P and a public value y, which is the output of a linear form L on a secret $\mathbb{Z}_q^n$ vector $\mathbf{x}$, given a commitment to the linear form L. We present the Σ-Protocol Π_1 for $\mathcal{R}_{\mathrm{CLF}}$ in Fig. 2, and use this protocol instead of step 5 of Π_0 to improve the communication and verifier complexity.

Finally, we define $\Pi_{1\text{-}\mathcal{R}}$ as $\Pi_{1\text{-}\mathcal{R}} = \Pi_1 \circ \Pi_0$ for relation $\mathcal{R}$, whose communication and computational complexity are dominated by that of Π_1. The concatenation of the protocols Π_1 and Π_0 proceeds by replacing the last message sent in clear by the prover in Π_0 with a proof of knowledge using Π_1.

Parameters

- **Common parameters** : $(P \in \mathbb{G}, Q \in \mathbb{G}, y \in \mathbb{Z}_q, H^{\dot{\mathbf{a}}} \in \mathbb{G}_2^{\ell})$,
  - $P = \text{COM}_{\bar{\mathbf{a}}}(\mathbf{x}), Q = \text{COM}_{\bar{\mathbf{a}}}(L), y = L(\mathbf{x})$,
  - $n = 2^{\ell}, \dot{\mathbf{a}} = (\dot{a}_1, \ldots, \dot{a}_{\ell}), \bar{\mathbf{a}} = \left(\prod_{i=1}^{\ell} \dot{a}_i^{b_i}\right)_{b_i \in \{0,1\}}$
  - A bilinear group description $(q, \mathbb{G}, \mathbb{G}_2, \mathbb{G}_T, e, g, H)$, where $e : \mathbb{G} \times \mathbb{G}_2 \mapsto \mathbb{G}_T$ is an efficient bilinear map and g, H and $e(g, H)$ are generators of groups $\mathbb{G}, \mathbb{G}_2$ and $\mathbb{G}_T$, respectively, each of order q.
- **$\mathcal{P}$'s input** : $(g^{\bar{\mathbf{a}}} \in \mathbb{G}^n, \mathbf{x} \in \mathbb{Z}_q^n, L \in \mathcal{L}(\mathbb{Z}_q^n))$

Protocol

1. $\mathcal{P}$ parses $\mathbf{x} = (\mathbf{x}_L \| \mathbf{x}_R), L = (L_L \| L_R)$ and $g^{\bar{\mathbf{a}}} = \left(g^{\bar{\mathbf{a}}_L} \| g^{\dot{a}_{\ell}\bar{\mathbf{a}}_L}\right)$, and computes and sends the following to $\mathcal{V}$:
   (a) $A_1 = \text{COM}_{\bar{\mathbf{a}}_L}(\mathbf{x}_L), A_2 = \text{COM}_{\bar{\mathbf{a}}_L}(\mathbf{x}_R)$
   (b) $B_1 = \text{COM}_{\bar{\mathbf{a}}_L}(L_L), B_2 = \text{COM}_{\bar{\mathbf{a}}_L}(L_R)$
   (c) $y_1 = \langle L_R, \mathbf{x}_L \rangle, y_2 = \langle L_L, \mathbf{x}_R \rangle$
2. $\mathcal{V}$ checks the following, proceeds to step 3 if it holds, and aborts otherwise
$$e\left(\frac{P}{A_1}, H\right) = e\left(A_2, H^{\dot{a}_{\ell}}\right) \wedge e\left(\frac{Q}{B_1}, H\right) = e\left(B_2, H^{\dot{a}_{\ell}}\right)$$
3. $\mathcal{V}$ samples $c \leftarrow_R \mathbb{Z}_q$ and sends c to $\mathcal{P}$
4. $\mathcal{P}$ sets $\mathbf{x}' = \mathbf{x}_L + c\mathbf{x}_R$, $L' = cL_L + L_R$ and implicitly sets $\dot{\mathbf{a}}' = (\dot{a}_1, \ldots, \dot{a}_{\ell-1})$ and $\bar{\mathbf{a}}' = \bar{\mathbf{a}}_L$.
5. $\mathcal{P}$ and $\mathcal{V}$ both compute the following :
$$P' = A_1 A_2^c, \; Q' = B_1^c B_2, \; y' = y_1 + cy + c^2 y_2$$
6. If $\mathbf{x}' \notin \mathbb{Z}_q^2$: $\mathcal{P}$ runs PoK Π_1 to prove knowledge of $\mathbf{x}', L'$ such that $\text{COM}_{\bar{\mathbf{a}}'}(\mathbf{x}') = P'$, $\text{COM}_{\bar{\mathbf{a}}'}(L') = Q'$ and $\langle L', \mathbf{x}' \rangle = y'$.
   Hence, $\mathcal{P}$ and $\mathcal{V}$ runs the protocol Π_1 with updated common parameters $(P', Q', y', g^{\dot{\mathbf{a}}'})$ and prover's input $(g^{\bar{\mathbf{a}}'}, \mathbf{x}', L')$, for $(P', Q', y'; \mathbf{x}') \in \mathcal{R}_{\text{CLF}}$
7. If $\mathbf{x}' \in \mathbb{Z}_q^2$:
   (a) $\mathcal{P}$ sends $\mathbf{x}', L'$ to $\mathcal{V}$
   (b) $\mathcal{V}$ outputs 1 if the following checks hold, and 0 otherwise:
$$\text{COM}_{\bar{\mathbf{a}}'}(\mathbf{x}') = P' \wedge \text{COM}_{\bar{\mathbf{a}}'}(L') = Q' \wedge \langle L', \mathbf{x}' \rangle = y'$$

Fig. 2. Protocol Π_1 for relation $\mathcal{R}_{\text{CLF}}$

Theorem 2. *Π_1 is a $(k_1, \ldots, k_{\ell})$-move protocol for relation $\mathcal{R}_{CLF}$, where $k_i = 3, \forall i \in [\ell], \ell = \log n$. It is perfectly complete and computationally special sound. It incurs total communication of $4 \log n$ group elements and $4 + 3 \log n$ field elements.*

Proof Sketch. Here we present the proof sketch for the special soundness of Π_1. Given 3 accepting transcripts $(A_1, A_2, B_1, B_2, y_1, y_2, c_i, \mathbf{x}'_i, L'_i)$ for one iteration of Π_1 (where one iteration consists of steps 1–5, and step 6 follows by sending $\mathbf{x}', L'$ instead of providing a PoK) for three distinct challenges c_1, c_2 and c_3, extractor proceeds as follows. It computes a_1, a_2, a_3 as $(a_1, a_2, a_3)^T = V^{-1}(0, 1, 0)^T$, where V is the Vandermonde matrix defined by the challenges, and sets $\mathbf{w} = \sum_i a_i(c_i\mathbf{x}_i' \| \mathbf{x}_i')$ to be the extracted value. We show that $\mathrm{COM}_{\bar{\mathbf{a}}}(\mathbf{w}) = P$; and similarly we extract a valid opening $\mathbf{m}$ of the commitment Q.

We then show that the extracted $\mathbf{w}, \mathbf{m}$ satisfy $\mathbf{x}_i' = \mathbf{w}_L + c_i\mathbf{w}_R$ and $L_i' = \mathbf{m}_L + c_i\mathbf{m}_R$ for all $i = 1, 2, 3$, which when substituted in the verification equation $\langle L_i', \mathbf{x}_i' \rangle = y_i'$ (Step 7(b)) gives us $\langle \mathbf{m}_R, \mathbf{w}_L \rangle + c_i\langle \mathbf{m}, \mathbf{w} \rangle + c_i^2\langle \mathbf{m}_L, \mathbf{w}_R \rangle = y_1 + c_i y + c_i^2 y_2$, for the distinct challenges c_1, c_2 and c_3. Hence, $\langle \mathbf{m}, \mathbf{w} \rangle = y$ holds, which shows that $(\mathbf{w}, \mathbf{m})$ is a valid witness for $(P, Q, y) \in \mathcal{R}_{\mathrm{CLF}}$. We defer the full proof to Appendix B.1 of the full version [16].

3.2 Improved Protocol for Opening a Committed Linear Form

We recall that for $x = (x_1, \ldots, x_n) \in \mathbb{Z}_q^n$, $\mathsf{rev}(x)$ is defined as $\mathsf{rev}(x) = (x_n, \ldots, x_1)$. We present an alternative protocol that achieves better communication complexity at the cost of degrading soundness; it needs $2n$ transcripts to extract. Consider a modified version of the relation $\mathcal{R}_{\mathrm{CLF}}$ defined earlier, where instead of committing to the linear form we now commit to the reverse of the linear form, and define the new relation $\mathcal{R}_{\mathrm{CLF\text{-}rev}}$ as follows:

$$\mathcal{R}_{\mathrm{CLF\text{-}rev}} = \{(P \in \mathbb{G}, Q \in \mathbb{G}, y \in \mathbb{Z}_q; \mathbf{x} \in \mathbb{Z}_q^n, L \in \mathcal{L}(\mathbb{Z}_q^n)) : \\ P = \mathrm{COM}_{\bar{\mathbf{a}}}(\mathbf{x}) \land Q = \mathrm{COM}_{\bar{\mathbf{a}}}(\mathsf{rev}(L)) \land L(\mathbf{x}) = y\}\}$$

where the relation $\mathcal{R}_{\mathrm{CLF\text{-}rev}}$ corresponds to showing opening of a public commitment P and a public value y, obtained by operating a linear form L on a secret $\mathbb{Z}_q^n$ vector $\mathbf{x}$, where we also have a commitment to the reverse of linear form L which is represented as a vector. We note that the randomness used for the commitments are implicitly assumed from here onwards.

We have the following protocol for the relation $\mathcal{R}_{\mathrm{CLF\text{-}rev}}$ (Fig. 3).

The protocol aims to reduce the verification of the statement $(P, Q, y; \mathbf{x}) \in \mathcal{R}_{\mathrm{CLF\text{-}rev}}$ by prover $\mathcal{P}$ and verifier $\mathcal{V}$, to a polynomial check where we have the equation

$$\mathbf{x}(U) \cdot \mathsf{rev}(L)(U) = p_L(U) \cdot U^{-1} + y \cdot U^{n-1} + p_R(U) \cdot U^n$$

and we have a commitment to each polynomial. The polynomials are then evaluated at a random challenge sent by the verifier $\mathcal{V}$, and the consistency of the evaluations with respect to the equation satisfied by the polynomials is checked. Sometimes, when $\mathbf{x}$ or $\mathsf{rev}(L)$ is public and highly structured (e.g. $\mathbf{t}^{\mathbf{n}-1}$ for some $t \in \mathbb{Z}_q$), we avoid committing to it and instead have the verifier compute $\mathbf{x}(U)$ locally while retaining succinctness. We abuse notation to write $(\mathbf{x}, Q, y; L)$ or $(P, L, y; \mathbf{x}) \in \mathcal{R}_{\mathrm{CLF\text{-}rev}}$ whenever this happens.

Parameters

- **Common parameters** : $(P \in \mathbb{G}, Q \in \mathbb{G}, y \in \mathbb{Z}_q, H^{\dot{\mathbf{a}}} \in \mathbb{G}^{\ell})$,
  - $P = \mathrm{COM}_{\bar{\mathbf{a}}}(\mathbf{x}), Q = \mathrm{COM}_{\bar{\mathbf{a}}}(\mathsf{rev}(L)), y = L(\mathbf{x})$,
  - $n = 2^{\ell}, \dot{\mathbf{a}} = (\dot{a}_1, \dots, \dot{a}_n), \bar{\mathbf{a}} = \left(\prod_{i=1}^{\ell} \dot{a}_i^{b_i}\right)_{b_i \in \{0,1\}}$
- **$\mathcal{P}$'s input** : $(g^{\bar{\mathbf{a}}} \in \mathbb{G}^n, \mathbf{x} \in \mathbb{Z}_q^n, L \in \mathcal{L}(\mathbb{Z}_q^n))$

Protocol

1. Let us define $\mathbf{B} \in \mathbb{Z}_q^n$ as $\mathbf{B} = \mathsf{rev}(L)$. Let $\mathbf{x}(U)$ be a polynomial of degree $(n-1)$ defined with coefficient vector $\mathbf{x} = (x_1, \dots, x_n)$, such that $\mathbf{x}(U) = \sum_{i=0}^{n-1} x_{i+1} U^i$. Similarly, we define the polynomial $\mathbf{B}(U)$ of degree $(n-1)$ for the vector $\mathbf{B}$.
2. $\mathcal{P}$ defines a $(2n-2)$ degree polynomial $\boldsymbol{p}$ by
$$\boldsymbol{p}(U) = \mathbf{x}(U) \cdot \mathbf{B}(U) = \sum_{i,j} x_{i+1} B_{j+1} U^{i+j},$$
and parses the computed polynomial as
$$\boldsymbol{p}(U) = \boldsymbol{p}_L(U) \cdot U^{-1} + y \cdot U^{n-1} + \boldsymbol{p}_R(U) \cdot U^n,$$
where p_L is a polynomial of degree $(n-1)$ and p_L is a polynomial of degree $(n-2)$ (which is trivially extended to a vector of length n by appending 0 appropriately).
3. $\mathcal{P}$ computes $A_1 = \mathrm{COM}_{\bar{\mathbf{a}}}(\boldsymbol{p}_L)$ and $A_2 = \mathrm{COM}_{\bar{\mathbf{a}}}(\boldsymbol{p}_R)$, and sends A_1, A_2 to $\mathcal{V}$
4. $\mathcal{V}$ samples $c \leftarrow_R \mathbb{Z}_q$ and sends c to $\mathcal{P}$
5. $\mathcal{P}$ computes the evaluations of the polynomials on the random challenge c as follows, and then sends z_1, z_2, z_3 and z_4 to $\mathcal{V}$: $z_1 = \mathbf{x}(c)$, $z_2 = \mathbf{B}(c)$, $z_3 = p_L(c)$, $z_4 = p_R(c)$.
6. $\mathcal{V}$ checks if the following relation holds, aborts if the check fails and continues to the next step otherwise.
$$z_3 \cdot c^{-1} + y \cdot c^{n-1} + z_4 \cdot c^n = z_1 \cdot z_2$$
7. $\mathcal{V}$ samples $t \leftarrow_R \mathbb{Z}_q$ and sends t to $\mathcal{P}$
8. $\mathcal{P}$ sets $\mathbf{w} = \mathbf{x} + t \cdot \mathbf{B} + t^2 \cdot \boldsymbol{p}_L + t^3 \cdot \boldsymbol{p}_R$ and sends $\mathbf{w}$ to $\mathcal{V}$
9. $\mathcal{P}$ and $\mathcal{V}$ both compute the following :
$$R = P \cdot Q^t \cdot A_1^{t^2} \cdot A_2^{t^3} \quad \text{and} \quad z = z_1 + t \cdot z_2 + t^2 \cdot z_3 + t^3 \cdot z_4$$
10. $\mathcal{V}$ outputs 1 if for $\mathbf{c}^{\mathbf{n-1}} = (1, \dots, c^{n-1})$ the following relation holds, and outputs 0 otherwise:
$$\mathrm{COM}_{\bar{\mathbf{a}}}(\mathbf{w}) = R \quad \wedge \quad \langle \mathbf{w}, \mathbf{c}^{\mathbf{n-1}} \rangle = z$$

Fig. 3. Protocol Π_2 for relation $\mathcal{R}_{\text{CLF-rev}}$

Theorem 3. *Π_2 is a protocol for relation $\mathcal{R}_{CLF\text{-}rev}$. It is perfectly complete and computationally special sound.*

The proof is deferred to Appendix B.2 of the full version [16].

Now we note that the last message $\mathbf{w}$ sent by the prover to the verifier in Π_2 (Fig. 3) is a witness for the relation $\mathcal{R}$, where $\mathcal{R} = \{(P \in \mathbb{G}, L \in \mathcal{L}(\mathbb{Z}_q^n), y \in \mathbb{Z}_q; \mathbf{x} \in \mathbb{Z}_q^n) : P = \mathrm{COM}_{\bar{\mathbf{a}}}(\mathbf{x}) \ \wedge \ L(\mathbf{x}) = y\}\}$, and the check computed by the verifier in step 10 of Π_2 corresponds to ensuring that $(R, \mathbf{c^{n-1}}, z; \mathbf{w}) \in \mathcal{R}$.

We state the following protocol for relation $\mathcal{R}$ which is the compressed proof of knowledge protocol stated in [5] with the following key differences: the linear form evaluation is checked in the clear, the commitment uses a structured commitment key, and the commitments to the left and right halves of the witness are being used to establish consistency with the original commitment which is only possible due to the structure in the commitment key.

We note that even with the same protocol technique as [5] which inherently incurs linear computational complexity for the verifier, we manage to retain logarithmic computational complexity. This is because of our structured commitment key, which does not require the verifier to compute a challenge dependent commitment key for the next iteration, and a nicely-structured linear form, which ensures that the verifier can compute the challenge dependent linear form required for the next iteration efficiently. This suffices for our cause as we aim to use this protocol for providing proof of knowledge of the last message sent in step 8 of Π_2 such that it satisfies the verifier check in the step 10, which provides us with a witness for the relation $\mathcal{R}$ (Fig. 4).

We note that the last message vector (polynomial) sent by the prover to the verifier of Π_2 is aimed to convince the verifier that the vector is consistent with opening of a group element computed by the verifier and evaluation of the polynomial at a random field element is consistent with a public field element computed by the verifier. We provide protocol Π_2' for this.

We treat the evaluation of the polynomial $\mathbf{w}$ at a fixed point, denoted by $\mathbf{w}(c)$ as an inner-product relation with a univariate polynomial, denoted by $\langle \mathbf{w}, \mathbf{c^{n-1}} \rangle$, where $\mathbf{c^{n-1}} = (1, c, \ldots, c^{n-1})$. Now, provided that the evaluation point is fixed at $c \in \mathbb{Z}_q$, this inner product relation can be thought of as a linear form evaluation, where the public linear form $\mathbf{c^{n-1}}$ evaluation at a secret vector $\mathbf{w}$ is equal to the public value $z \in \mathbb{Z}_q$. Now, we note that, the claim in step 10 is equivalent to providing a Proof of Knowledge of witness $\mathbf{w}$ in the following relation:

$$\mathcal{R} = \{(P \in \mathbb{G}, L \in \mathcal{L}(\mathbb{Z}_q^n), y \in \mathbb{Z}_q; \mathbf{x} \in \mathbb{Z}_q^n) : P = \mathrm{COM}_{\bar{\mathbf{a}}}(\mathbf{x}) \ \wedge \ L(\mathbf{x}) = y\}\}$$

where we have that $(R, \mathbf{c^{n-1}}, z; \mathbf{w}) \in \mathcal{R}$.

Theorem 4. *Π_2' is a $(k_1, \ldots, k_\ell)$-move protocol for relation $(R, \mathbf{c^{n-1}}, z; \boldsymbol{w}) \in \mathcal{R}$, where $k_i = 3$, $\forall i \in [\ell]$. It is perfectly complete and computationally special sound.*

The proof is presented in Appendix B.3 of the full version [16].

Theorem 5. *$(\Pi_2)_c = \Pi_2' \circ \Pi_2$ is a $(2n, 4, k_1, \ldots, k_\ell)$-move protocol for relation $\mathcal{R}_{CLF\text{-}rev}$, where $k_i = 3$, $\forall i \in [\ell]$. It is perfectly complete and computationally special sound. It incurs total communication of $(2 + 2\log n)$ group elements and $6 + 2\log n$ field elements.*

Parameters

- **Common parameters** : $(R \in \mathbb{G}, L_c \in \mathbb{Z}_q^n, z \in \mathbb{Z}_q, H^{\dot{\mathbf{a}}} \in \mathbb{G}^\ell)$
  - $R = \mathrm{COM}_{\overline{\mathbf{a}}}(\mathbf{w}), L_c = \mathbf{c}^{\mathbf{n-1}} = (1, c, \ldots, c^{n-1}), z = L_c(\mathbf{w})$,
  - $n = 2^\ell, \dot{\mathbf{a}} = (\dot{a}_1, \ldots, \dot{a}_n), \overline{\mathbf{a}} = \left(\prod_{i=1}^{\ell} \dot{a}_i^{b_i}\right)_{b_i \in \{0,1\}}$
- **$\mathcal{P}$'s input** : $(g^{\overline{\mathbf{a}}} \in \mathbb{G}^n, \mathbf{w} \in \mathbb{Z}_q^n, L_c = \mathbf{c}^{\mathbf{n-1}} \in \mathbb{Z}_q^n)$

Protocol

1. $\mathcal{P}$ computes and sends A_1, A_2, z' to $\mathcal{V}$
   (a) $A_1 = \mathrm{COM}_{\overline{\mathbf{a}}_L}(\mathbf{w}_L)$
   (b) $A_2 = \mathrm{COM}_{\overline{\mathbf{a}}_L}(\mathbf{w}_R)$
   (c) $z' = \langle \mathbf{w}_L, (L_c)_L \rangle = \langle \mathbf{w}_L, \mathbf{c}^{\frac{\mathbf{n-1}}{\mathbf{2}}} \rangle$
2. $\mathcal{V}$ checks if
$$e\left(\frac{R}{A_1}, g\right) = e\left(A_2, g^{\dot{a}_\ell}\right)$$
   If the check fails, $\mathcal{V}$ aborts, otherwise $\mathcal{V}$ continues.
3. $\mathcal{V}$ samples $s \leftarrow_R \mathbb{Z}_q$ and sends s to $\mathcal{P}$
4. $\mathcal{P}$ sets $\mathbf{w}' = \mathbf{w}_L + s \cdot \mathbf{w}_R, L_c' = s(L_c)_L + (L_c)_R = (s + c^{n/2})\mathbf{c}^{\mathbf{n/2-1}}$ and implicitly sets $\dot{\mathbf{a}}' = (\dot{a}_1, \ldots, \dot{a}_{\ell-1})$ and $\overline{\mathbf{a}}' = \overline{\mathbf{a}}_L$
5. $\mathcal{P}$ and $\mathcal{V}$ both compute the following :
$$R' = A_1 A_2^s \ \text{ and } \ d = c^{n/2} \cdot z' + s \cdot z + s^2 \cdot c^{-n/2} \cdot (z - z')$$
6. If $\mathbf{w}' \notin \mathbb{Z}_q^2$: $\mathcal{P}$ runs PoK Π_2' to prove knowledge of $\mathbf{w}', L_c'$ such that $\mathrm{COM}_{\overline{\mathbf{a}}'}(\mathbf{w}') = P'$ and $\langle L_c', \mathbf{x}' \rangle = d$.
   Hence, $\mathcal{P}$ and $\mathcal{V}$ runs the protocol Π_2' with updated common parameters $(P', L_c', d, g^{\dot{\mathbf{a}}'})$ and prover's input $(g^{\overline{\mathbf{a}}'}, \mathbf{w}')$, for $(P', L_c', d; \mathbf{w}') \in \mathcal{R}$
7. If $\mathbf{w}' \in \mathbb{Z}_q^2$:
   (a) $\mathcal{P}$ sends $\mathbf{w}', L_c'$ to $\mathcal{V}$
   (b) $\mathcal{V}$ outputs 1 if the following holds, and outputs 0 otherwise:
$$\mathrm{COM}_{\overline{\mathbf{a}}'}(\mathbf{w}') = R' \ \wedge \ \langle L_c', \mathbf{w}' \rangle = d$$

Fig. 4. Protocol Π_2' for $(R, L_c, z; \mathbf{w}) \in \mathcal{R}$

We note that $(\Pi_2)_c$ performs better than Π_1 for the relation $\mathcal{R}_{\text{CLF-rev}}$, however the pre-processing step needs a commitment to reverse of the linear forms. This is fine in our application to construct proofs for circuit satisfiability, since the commitments to the reverse of these linear forms is computed in the preprocessing phase. In case we only have a commitment to the linear form, we can still use our protocol by having the prover send the commitment to the reversed linear form, together with a proof that it is indeed correct. This can be achieved by the observation that for $L \in \mathcal{L}(\mathbb{Z}_q^n)$ considered as a polynomial, being evaluated at c has equal value as that of its reverse being evaluated at c^{-1} and the result being multiplied with c^{n-1}.

$$L(c) = c^{n-1} \cdot (\mathsf{rev}(L))\left(c^{-1}\right) \quad \Longleftrightarrow \quad \langle L, \mathbf{c}^{\mathbf{n-1}} \rangle = c^{n-1} \cdot \langle \mathsf{rev}(L), (\mathbf{c}^{-1})^{\mathbf{n-1}} \rangle$$

Hence, if $P = \mathrm{COM}_{\overline{\mathbf{a}}}(L)$ is computed in the pre-processing phase, then the prover can compute $Q = \mathrm{COM}_{\overline{\mathbf{a}}}(\mathsf{rev}(L))$ and send Q along with the proof that opening of P evaluated at a random challenge c is c^{n-1} times Q evaluated at c^{-1}, at the onset of the protocol and proceed with $(\Pi_2)_c$. This gives us an overhead of 1 group element and 2 field elements. Finally, we define $\Pi_{2\text{-}\mathcal{R}} = (\Pi_2)_c \circ \Pi_0$ for relation $\mathcal{R}$, whose communication and computational complexity are dominated by that of $(\Pi_2)_c$.

4 Updatable SRS zkSNARK for Circuit Satisfiability

In this section we construct a zkSNARK with updatable SRS for circuit satisfiability by reducing a statement about a circuit with respect to a public input to opening a linear form.

We take the approach of Attema et al. [5] to handle multiplication gates by linearizing them, but we need to employ some new ideas to keep the verifier succinct. We recall the technique for handling multiplication gates in Attema et al. [5], where we have the left input wire values $\mathbf{w}_a$, the right input wire values $\mathbf{w}_b$ and the output wire values $\mathbf{w}_o$, secret shared via packed secret sharing, with the randomness embedded in the constant term. Let f, g and h be the polynomials with the packed secret sharing of $\mathbf{w}_a$, $\mathbf{w}_b$ and $\mathbf{w}_o$ respectively, such that $f(X) \cdot g(X) = h(X)$. Attema et al. [5] handles multiplication by sending a commitment to the wire values in a long vector, opening them at a random point c, and then using the Schwartz-Zippel lemma to argue that the polynomials are identical if $f(c) \cdot g(c) = h(c)$ holds. However, the protocol to check if $f(c) \cdot g(c) = h(c)$ renders the verifier linear, since the linear form for opening the polynomials at the random value is linear in the size of the witness and needs to be computed by the verifier. We circumvent this drawback of linear verification complexity from having to compute the linear form by obtaining *commitments* to the linear form. The goal is to commit to linear forms required for openings of f, g and h, and then invoke our succinct-verifier linear form protocol. We then proceed to prove that, given A, B and C as commitment to some secret vectors $\mathbf{a}, \mathbf{b}$ and $\mathbf{c}$ respectively from $\mathbb{Z}_q^n$, the committed vectors satisfies the hadamard relation $\mathbf{a} \circ \mathbf{b} = \mathbf{c}$, i.e. $a_i b_i = c_i$ for all $i \in [n]$.

Following that, we show how to prove that given commitments A, B to two vectors $\mathbf{s}, \mathbf{r} \in \mathbb{Z}_q^n$, they are some committed permutation of each other. Concretely, $\mathbf{s}, \mathbf{r} \in \mathbb{Z}_q^n$ are such that $\mathbf{s} = \sigma(\mathbf{r})$ for some known permutation σ. Finally, we show how to put together these building blocks to construct a protocol for circuit satisfiability with logarithmic proof size and verification complexity.

Parameters

- Common input:
  - V is the Vandermonde matrix defined in equation 1.

Protocol

1. $\mathcal{V}$ samples $c \leftarrow_R \mathbb{Z}_q$ and sends it to $\mathcal{P}$.
2. $\mathcal{P}$ sets ρ_c, where $\rho_c = (\rho_{c_1}, \cdots, \rho_{c_n}) = V^{-1}(1\ c\ c^2 \cdots c^{n-1})^T$ and $\rho_c' = (0, \rho_{c_1}, \cdots, \rho_{c_n})$, and computes $A = \text{COM}_{\bar{\mathbf{a}}}\ (\mathsf{rev}(\rho_c)), A' = \text{COM}_{\bar{\mathbf{a}}}\ (\mathsf{rev}(\rho_c'))$.
3. $\mathcal{P}$ sends A, A' to $\mathcal{V}$.
4. $\mathcal{V}$ samples $t \leftarrow_R \mathbb{Z}_q \setminus \{2^{-1}, \cdots, 2^{-i}, \cdots, 2^{-n}\}$ and sends t to $\mathcal{P}$.
5. $\mathcal{P}$ sets the jth row of V as $V_j := (2^{j-1},\ 2^{2(j-1)}, \cdots, 2^{i(j-1)}, \cdots, 2^{n(j-1)})\ \forall j \in \{1, \cdots, n\}$, and computes $B := \text{COM}_{\bar{\mathbf{a}}}\ (V(t))$, where $V(t) := \mathbf{t^{n-1}}V = \sum_{j=0}^{n} t^{n-1} V_j$.
6. $\mathcal{P}$ sends B to $\mathcal{V}$.
7. The verifier samples $y \leftarrow_R \mathbb{Z}_q \setminus \{1, 2^{-1}\}, d \leftarrow_R \mathbb{Z}_q$ and sends y, d to $\mathcal{P}$.
8. $\mathcal{P}$ sets $\mathbf{z} = (2^i t - 1)_{i \in [n]}$, $\gamma = \langle \rho_c, \mathbf{d^{n-1}} \rangle$ and sends γ to $\mathcal{V}$.
9. $\mathcal{P}$ and $\mathcal{V}$ independently compute $\alpha = 2^n t^n \frac{(2^n y)^n - 1}{2^n y - 1} - \frac{y^n - 1}{y - 1}$ and $\beta = \frac{(ct)^n - 1}{ct - 1}$.
10. $\mathcal{P}$ and $\mathcal{V}$ interact to prove the following relations:
    (a) runs $(\Pi_2)_c$ for $(B, A, \beta; (V(t))^T, \rho_c) \in \mathcal{R}_{\textsf{CLF-rev}}$
    (b) runs $(\Pi_2)_c$ for $(\mathbf{d^{n-1}}, A, \gamma; \rho_c), (\mathbf{d^{n-1}}, A', d\gamma; \rho_c') \in \mathcal{R}_{\textsf{CLF-rev}}$
    (c) runs $(\Pi_2)_c$ for $(B, \mathbf{y^{n-1}} \circ \mathbf{z}, \alpha; V(t)) \in \mathcal{R}_{\textsf{CLF-rev}}$

Fig. 5. Protocol $\Pi_{\textsf{com-mult}}$ for obtaining commitment to linear form for multiplication gates.

4.1 Committing to a Linear Form for Multiplication Gates

Let $\rho_c = V^{-1}(1\ c\ c^2\ \cdots\ c^{n-1})^T$ for a random challenge c chosen by the verifier, where V is the Vandermonde matrix of some public evaluation points $\alpha_i, i \in [n]$. This allows us to compute $f(c) = f \cdot V \cdot \rho_c = (f(\alpha_1) \ldots f(\alpha_n)) \cdot \rho_c$ for a polynomial $f \in \mathbb{Z}_q{}^{\leq n}[X]$. Now, instead of having the verifier compute a commitment to ρ_c (which would render it linear), we instead offload the computation of ρ_c to the prover and have the verifier *check* this computation in logarithmic time.

To check if a group element is indeed a commitment to ρ_c, our key idea is to instantiate V as

$$V = \begin{pmatrix} 1 & \cdots & 1 & \cdots & 1 \\ 2 & \cdots & 2^i & \cdots & 2^n \\ 2^2 & \cdots & 2^{2i} & \cdots & 2^{2n} \\ \vdots & & \vdots & & \vdots \\ 2^{(n-1)} & \cdots & 2^{(n-1)i} & \cdots & 2^{(n-1)n} \end{pmatrix} \quad (1)$$

This allows us to reduce the verification of ρ_c to n linear form openings, where the linear forms are the rows of V. The structure of V allows us to express a random linear combination of its rows in a way that a commitment produced to it by the prover can be easily verified.

Looking ahead, we need a commitment to $\mathsf{rev}(\rho_c)$ and not ρ_c in our protocol for circuit satisfiability. Let us define the relation $\mathcal{R}_{\mathsf{com\text{-}mult}}$ as follows:

$$\begin{aligned}\mathcal{R}_{\mathsf{com\text{-}mult}} = \{ \quad & (A_1 \in \mathbb{G}, A_2 \in \mathbb{G}, V \in \mathbb{Z}_q^{n\times n}, \mathbf{c^{n-1}} \in \mathbb{Z}_q^n; \rho_c, \rho_c{}') : \\ & \mathbf{c^{n-1}} = (1\ c\ \ldots\ c^{n-1}), \rho_c = V^{-1}\mathbf{c^{n-1}}, \rho_c{}' = 0\|\rho_c, \\ & A_1 = \mathrm{COM}_{\bar{\mathbf{a}}}\ (\mathsf{rev}(\rho_c)), A_2 = \mathrm{COM}_{\bar{\mathbf{a}}}\ (\mathsf{rev}(\rho_c{}'))\} \end{aligned} \quad (2)$$

This relation captures obtaining a commitment to the reverse of a linear form of public linear combination coefficients to obtain the evaluation of an $n-1$-degree polynomial at a point c. We note that $\rho_c{}'$ here denotes the vector (linear form) ρ_c shifted to the right by one, which is used in the protocols in the subsequent sections. We use it to open 'adjacent' polynomials at the same point, i.e., given a $\mathbb{Z}_q^{n+1}$-vector $(1, v_1, \ldots, v_n)$ of polynomial evaluations, we use ρ_c and $\rho_c{}'$ to open the $(n-1)$-degree polynomials whose evaluations are given by $(1, \cdots, v_{n-1})$ and $(v_1, \cdots, v_n)$ at the same point c. Figure 5 presents the protocol $\Pi_{\mathsf{com\text{-}mult}}$ for the relation $\mathcal{R}_{\mathsf{com\text{-}mult}}$. We do not need commitments to $\mathbf{d^{n-1}}$ or $\mathsf{rev}(\mathbf{y^{n-1}} \circ \mathbf{z})$ in Steps 10a and 10b to execute $(\Pi_2)_c$ as the verifier can compute $\langle \mathbf{d^{n-1}}, \mathbf{c'^{n-1}} \rangle$ and $\langle \mathsf{rev}(\mathbf{y^{n-1}} \circ \mathbf{z}), \mathbf{c'^{n-1}} \rangle$ for a random challenge c' locally by computing $\frac{(dc')^n - 1}{dc' - 1}$ and $\frac{2t(2^n y^n - c'^n)}{2y - c'} - \frac{y^n - c'^n}{y - c'}$.

Note that it is easy to add zero checks to the protocol in Fig. 5 to get a commitment to $\mathsf{rev}(\rho_{\mathsf{n}}\|\mathbf{0}) \in \mathbb{Z}_q^{n'}$, which we need in our protocol for circuit satisfiability. Let $n' > n$ be the length of the commitment key. The verifier samples a challenge $t \leftarrow_R \mathbb{Z}_q$ and checks that the commitment P_n claimed to be to $\mathsf{rev}(\rho_{\mathsf{n}}) \in \mathbb{Z}_q^n$ satisfies $(\mathbf{0}^n \| \mathbf{t}^{n'-n}, P_n, 0; \rho_{\mathsf{n}}\|\mathbf{0}) \in \mathcal{R}_{\text{CLF-rev}}$.

Theorem 6. *$\Pi_{\mathsf{com\text{-}mult}}$ is a $(7, 4, k_1, \ldots, k_\ell)$-move protocol for relation $\mathcal{R}_{\mathsf{com\text{-}mult}}$ (Eq. 2). It is perfectly complete and computationally special sound.*

The proof is deferred to Sect. 4.1 of the full version [16].

4.2 Hadamard Product Argument

Let $\mathbf{a}, \mathbf{b} \in \mathbb{Z}_q^n$, recall that the Hadamard product is defined as $\mathbf{a} \circ \mathbf{b} = (a_1 b_1, \ldots, a_n b_n) \in \mathbb{Z}_q^n$. Our goal is to prove knowledge of three vectors that satisfy the hadamard product relation, given succinct commitments to the vectors.

Concretely, given three vectors $\mathbf{a}, \mathbf{b}, \mathbf{c} \in \mathbb{Z}_q^n$ such that $\mathbf{a} \circ \mathbf{b} = \mathbf{c}$, we define $p_{\boldsymbol{a}}(X), p_{\boldsymbol{b}}(X), p_{\boldsymbol{c}}(X) \in \mathbb{Z}_q^n[X]$ such that $p_{\boldsymbol{a}}(2^i) = a_i, p_{\boldsymbol{b}}(2^i) = b_i$ for all $i \in [n]$ and $p_{\boldsymbol{c}}(X) := p_{\boldsymbol{a}}(X) \cdot p_{\boldsymbol{b}}(X)$. We define $h_{(\mathbf{c})} = (p_{\boldsymbol{c}}(2^{n+1}), \ldots, p_{\boldsymbol{c}}(2^{2n-1}))$. The protocol proceeds as follows. The prover computes commitments A, B, C to the vectors $\mathbf{a}, \mathbf{b}$ and $\mathbf{c}' := \mathbf{c}\|h_{(\mathbf{c})}$ respectively. The verifier then samples a challenge z, and the prover responds with commitments P_n, P_{2n} to the reverse of ρ_{n} and ρ_{2n}, where ρ_{n} and ρ_{2n} are defined as $\rho_{\mathsf{n}} = V^{-1}(1\ z\ z^2\ \cdots\ z^{n-1})^T$, $\rho_{\mathsf{2n}} = V^{-1}(1\ z\ z^2\ \cdots\ z^{2n-2})^T$. Then the prover opens the polynomial evaluations of $p_{\boldsymbol{a}}(X), p_{\boldsymbol{b}}(X), p_{\boldsymbol{c}}(X)$ at a random point chosen by the verifier, using the commitments to the vectors and the linear forms.

The hadamard relation $\mathcal{R}_{\mathsf{had}}$ with suitable modification to incorporate the commitments to the vectors is defined below, and the protocol Π_{had} presents the protocol for relation $\mathcal{R}_{\mathsf{had}}$. Note that to ensure zero-knowledge property of the protocol Π_{had}, to prove $\mathbf{a} \circ \mathbf{b} = \mathbf{c}$, we invoke the protocol for $(A, B, C; \mathbf{a}\|d, \mathbf{b}\|e, \mathbf{c}\|de) \in \mathcal{R}_{\mathsf{had}}$ where $d, e \leftarrow_R \mathbb{Z}_q$ (Fig. 6).

$$\mathcal{R}_{\mathsf{had}} = \{(A \in \mathbb{G}, B \in \mathbb{G}, C \in \mathbb{G}; \mathbf{a} \in \mathbb{Z}_q^n, \mathbf{b} \in \mathbb{Z}_q^n, \mathbf{c} \in \mathbb{Z}_q^n) : \\ A = \mathrm{COM}_{\overline{\mathbf{a}}}(\mathbf{a}), B = \mathrm{COM}_{\overline{\mathbf{a}}}(\mathbf{b}), \mathbf{c}' = \mathbf{c}\|h_{(\mathbf{c})}, C = \mathrm{COM}_{\overline{\mathbf{a}}}(\mathbf{c}')\}$$

Parameters

- Common input:
  - V is the Vandermonde matrix defined in equation 1.
  - $A = \mathrm{COM}_{\overline{\mathbf{a}}}(\mathbf{a}), B = \mathrm{COM}_{\overline{\mathbf{a}}}(\mathbf{b}), C = \mathrm{COM}_{\overline{\mathbf{a}}}(\mathbf{c}')$, such that $\mathbf{c}' = \mathbf{c}\|h_{(\mathbf{a}\circ\mathbf{b})}$
- $\mathcal{P}$'s input: $\mathbf{a} = \mathbf{a}^*\|d, \mathbf{b} = \mathbf{b}^*\|e, \mathbf{c} = \mathbf{c}^*\|de$ such that $\mathbf{a}^* \circ \mathbf{b}^* = \mathbf{c}^*$ and $d, e \leftarrow_R \mathbb{Z}_q$

Protocol

1. $\mathcal{P}$ computes the polynomials $p_{\mathbf{a}}, p_{\mathbf{b}} \in \mathbb{Z}_q^n[X]$ as $p_{\mathbf{a}}(2^i) := a_i, p_{\mathbf{b}}(2^i) := b_i \ \forall i \in [n]$. It defines $p_{\mathbf{c}}(X) := p_{\mathbf{a}}(X) \cdot p_{\mathbf{b}}(X)$.
2. $\mathcal{P}$ samples $\mathbf{u} \leftarrow_R \mathbb{Z}_q^n, \mathbf{u}' \leftarrow_R \mathbb{Z}_q^{2n-1}$ and defines $p_{\mathbf{u}} \in \mathbb{Z}_q^n[X], p_{\mathbf{u}'} \in \mathbb{Z}_q^{2n-1}[X]$ as $p_{\mathbf{u}}(2^i) := u_i \ \forall i \in [n], p_{\mathbf{u}'}(2^i) := u'_i \ \forall i \in [2n-1]$. $\mathcal{P}$ computes $U = \mathrm{COM}_{\overline{\mathbf{a}}}(\mathbf{u}), U' = \mathrm{COM}_{\overline{\mathbf{a}}}(\mathbf{u}')$ and sends U, U' to $\mathcal{V}$.
3. $\mathcal{V}$ samples $z \leftarrow_R \mathbb{Z}_q$ and sends z to $\mathcal{P}$.
4. Define $\rho_{\mathsf{n}} = V^{-1}(1 \ z \ z^2 \ \cdots \ z^{n-1})^T$ and $\rho_{2\mathsf{n}} = V^{-1}(1 \ z \ z^2 \ \cdots \ z^{2n-2})^T$. $\mathcal{P}$ and $\mathcal{V}$ run $\Pi_{\mathsf{com\text{-}mult}}$ to obtain commitments P_n, P_{2n} to the reverse of $\rho_{\mathsf{n}}, \rho_{2\mathsf{n}}$.
5. $\mathcal{P}$ sets w_1, w_2 as $w_1 = p_{\mathbf{a}}(z)$, and $w_2 = p_{\mathbf{b}}(z)$. $\mathcal{P}$ also sets v_1, v_2 as $v_1 = p_{\mathbf{u}}(z), v_2 = p_{\mathbf{u}'}(z)$.
6. $\mathcal{P}$ sends w_1, w_2, v_1, v_2 to $\mathcal{V}$.
7. $\mathcal{V}$ samples $r \leftarrow_R \mathbb{Z}_q$ and sends r to $\mathcal{P}$.
8. $\mathcal{P}$ and $\mathcal{V}$ independently compute $Y = UA^r B^{r^2}$, $Y' = U'C^r$, $\mathbf{y} = \mathbf{u} + r\mathbf{a} + r^2\mathbf{b}$, $\mathbf{y}' = \mathbf{u}' + r\mathbf{c}$, $q = v_1 + rw_1 + r^2 w_2$ and $q' = v_2 + rw_1w_2$.
9. $\mathcal{P}$ and $\mathcal{V}$ runs $(\Pi_2)_c$ for
   (a) $(Y, P_n, q; \ \mathbf{y}, \rho_{\mathsf{n}}) \in \mathcal{R}_{\mathrm{CLF\text{-}rev}}$.
   (b) $(Y', P_{2n}, q'; \ \mathbf{y}', \rho_{2\mathsf{n}}) \in \mathcal{R}_{\mathrm{CLF\text{-}rev}}$.

Fig. 6. Protocol Π_{had} for $\mathcal{R}_{\mathsf{had}}$

Theorem 7. *Π_{had} is a protocol for $\mathcal{R}_{\mathsf{had}}$. It is perfectly complete, special honest-verifier zero-knowledge and computationally special sound.*

The proof is deferred to Appendix C.1 of the full version [16].

4.3 Permutation Argument

Our starting point is the Bayer-Groth protocol [8]. Let $\mathsf{PERM}_n = \{f : f : [n] \rightarrow [n]$ such that f is a permutation$\}$ and $\sigma \in \mathsf{PERM}_n$. For two vectors

$\mathbf{r} = (r_1, \ldots, r_n) \in \mathbb{Z}_q^n$ and $\mathbf{s} = (s_1, \ldots, s_n) \in \mathbb{Z}_q^n$, we aim to prove that $\sigma(\mathbf{r}) = \mathbf{s}$ for some publicly known σ. To prove this, we use the technique of Bayer and Groth of proving $\prod_{i=1}^n (r_i + i\beta + \gamma) = \prod_{i=1}^n (s_i + \sigma(i)\beta + \gamma)$ for the verifier's choice of $\beta, \gamma \in \mathbb{Z}_q$ sampled uniformly at random.

The proof is instantiated by having the verifier choose two challenges $\beta, \gamma \in \mathbb{Z}_q$ and the prover constructing two vectors $\mathbf{a} = (a_1, \ldots, a_n)$ and $\mathbf{b} = (b_1, \ldots, b_n)$ defined as $a_i = r_i + i\beta + \gamma$ and $b_i = s_i + \sigma(i)\beta + \gamma$ for all $i = 1, \ldots, n$, and providing a proof that $\prod_{i=1}^n a_i = \prod_{i=1}^n b_i$. The proof for $\prod_{i=1}^n a_i = \prod_{i=1}^n b_i$ proceeds by constructing two vectors $\mathbf{c}', \mathbf{d}' \in \mathbb{Z}_q^{n+1}$ such that $c_0' = 1, d_0' = 1$ and $c_j' := \prod_{i=1}^j (r_i + i\beta + \gamma), d_j' := \prod_{i=1}^j (s_i + \sigma(i)\beta + \gamma)$, for all $j \in [n]$. We consider two circuits with n multiplication gates. The circuits are fully defined by the left inputs, right inputs and output of each multiplication gate. The first circuit has a vector of left inputs $\mathbf{a} = (a_1, \ldots, a_n)$, vector of right inputs $\mathbf{e} = (e_1, \ldots, e_n) = (1, c_1, \ldots, c_{n-1})$ and vector of outputs $\mathbf{c} = (c_1, \ldots, c_n)$. The second circuit has left inputs $\mathbf{b} = (b_1, \ldots, b_n)$, right inputs $\mathbf{f} = (f_1, \ldots, f_n) = (1, d_1, \ldots, d_{n-1})$ and outputs $\mathbf{d} = (d_1, \ldots, d_n)$. Our idea is to check the hadamard product relations $\mathbf{a} \circ \mathbf{e} = \mathbf{c}$ and $\mathbf{b} \circ \mathbf{f} = \mathbf{d}$ by using the shifted structure of the vectors in the hadamard products; and using protocol $\Pi_{\mathsf{com\text{-}mult}}$ yielding a succinct verifier permutation argument.

We consider the following relation $\mathcal{R}_{\mathsf{perm}}$ for the permutation argument.

$$\begin{aligned}\mathcal{R}_{\mathsf{perm}} = \{\ (R, S, P; \mathbf{r}, \mathbf{s}, \sigma) : R = \mathrm{COM}_{\bar{\mathbf{a}}}\ (\mathbf{r}), S = \mathrm{COM}_{\bar{\mathbf{a}}}\ (\mathbf{s}), P = \mathrm{COM}_{\bar{\mathbf{a}}}\ (\sigma(I)),\\ I = (1, \ldots, n), \mathbf{s} = \sigma(\mathbf{r})\}\end{aligned}$$

We present the protocol Π_{perm} for the same in Fig. 7. We define ρ_{n}, ρ_{2n}, δ_{n} and δ_{2n} as $\rho_{\mathsf{n}} = V^{-1}(1\ z\ z^2 \ldots z^{n-1})$, $\rho_{\mathsf{2n}} = V^{-1}(1\ z\ z^2 \ldots z^{2n-1})$, $\delta_{\mathsf{n}} = V^{-1}(1\ w\ w^2 \ldots w^{n-1})$ and $\delta_{\mathsf{2n}} = V^{-1}(1\ w\ w^2 \ldots w^{2n-1})$ where V is a Vandermonde matrix defined by the public evaluation points. We recall that the linear forms $\rho_{\mathsf{n}}, \rho_{\mathsf{2n}}$ are for computing evaluation at a random point z, and the linear forms $\delta_{\mathsf{n}}, \delta_{\mathsf{2n}}$ are for computing evaluation at a random point w. We note that we can batch the invocations of $(\Pi_2)_{\mathsf{c}}$ for $\mathcal{R}_{\mathrm{CLF\text{-}rev}}$ in each of the steps (a),(b) and (c) in Step 11 of Π_{perm} using the techniques of Attema et al. [5].

Theorem 8. *Π_{perm} is a protocol for $\mathcal{R}_{\mathsf{perm}}$. It is perfectly complete and computationally special sound.*

The proof is deferred to Appendix C.2 of the full version [16].

4.4 Putting Things Together – zkSNARK for Circuit SAT

Given an upper bound on the circuit size m, the universal updatable SRS is generated by running COM $.Setup$ to commit to $2m+2$-length vectors to obtain the commitment key $(g^{\bar{\mathbf{a}}}, H^{\dot{\mathbf{a}}})$. Here $g^{\bar{\mathbf{a}}}$ is the proving key and $H^{\dot{\mathbf{a}}}$ is the verification key. Since the SRS is universal, we need a circuit dependent setup phase so the verifier will read the circuit only once. We omit the description of algorithms for updating and verifying the SRS since this corresponds to updating and verifying

Parameters

- Parameters from preprocessing:
  - $P = \mathsf{COM}_{\bar{\mathbf{a}}}\ (\sigma(I))$, $P' = \mathsf{COM}_{\bar{\mathbf{a}}}\ (I)$ for $I = (1, \dots, n)$
  - $\mathsf{left} = \mathsf{COM}_{\bar{\mathbf{a}}}\ (\mathsf{rev}(1\|\mathbf{0}\|\mathbf{0}))$ and $\mathsf{right} = \mathsf{COM}_{\bar{\mathbf{a}}}\ (\mathsf{rev}(\mathbf{0}\|1\|\mathbf{0}))$ for linear forms $(1\|\mathbf{0}\|\mathbf{0})$ and $(\mathbf{0}\|1\|\mathbf{0})$, where $\mathbf{0} = (0, \dots, 0) \in \mathbb{Z}_q^n$
  - $T = \mathsf{COM}_{\bar{\mathbf{a}}}\ (\mathbf{1})$, $\mathbf{1} = (1, \dots, 1) \in \mathbb{Z}_q^n$
- Common Input:
  - $R = \mathsf{COM}_{\bar{\mathbf{a}}}\ (\mathbf{r}), S = \mathsf{COM}_{\bar{\mathbf{a}}}\ (\mathbf{s})$
- $\mathcal{P}$'s input : $(\mathbf{r}, \mathbf{s}, \sigma, g^{\bar{\mathbf{a}}})$

Protocol

1. $\mathcal{V}$ samples $\beta, \gamma \leftarrow_R \mathbb{Z}_q$ and sends β, γ to $\mathcal{P}$.
2. $\mathcal{P}$ computes $x := \prod_{i=1}^{n}(r_i + i\beta + \gamma)$ and sends x to $\mathcal{V}$.
3. $\mathcal{P}$ computes the vectors $\mathbf{a}, \mathbf{b} \in \mathbb{Z}_q^n$ such that $a_i = r_i + i\beta + \gamma$ and $b_i = s_i + \sigma(i)\beta + \gamma$ for all $i \in [n]$. $\mathcal{P}$ additionally computes $\mathbf{c}', \mathbf{d}' \in \mathbb{Z}_q^{n+1}$ such that $c_1' = 1, d_1' = 1$ and $c_j' := \prod_{i=1}^{j-1} a_i, d_j' := \prod_{i=1}^{j-1} b_i$, for all $j \in [n+1] \setminus \{1\}$, and defines $\mathbf{c}, \mathbf{d}, \mathbf{e}, \mathbf{f} \in \mathbb{Z}_q^n$ such that $c_i = c_{i+1}', d_i = d_{i+1}', e_i = c_i', f_i = d_i'$ for all $i \in [n]$, i.e. $c_j := \prod_{i=1}^{j} a_i, d_j := \prod_{i=1}^{j} b_i$, for all $j \in [n]$, and $e_1 = 1, f_1 = 1$ and $e_j := \prod_{i=1}^{j-1} a_i, d_j := \prod_{i=1}^{j-1} b_i$, for all $j \in [n]$.
4. $\mathcal{P}$ computes the polynomials $p_{\mathbf{a}}, p_{\mathbf{e}}$ and $p_{\mathbf{c}}$ as $p_{\mathbf{a}}(2^i) := a_i, p_{\mathbf{e}}(2^i) := e_i$ and $p_{\mathbf{c}} := p_{\mathbf{a}} \cdot p_{\mathbf{e}}$, and similarly computes $p_{\mathbf{b}}, p_{\mathbf{f}}$ and $p_{\mathbf{d}}$ as $p_{\mathbf{b}}(2^i) := b_i, p_{\mathbf{f}}(2^i) := f_i$ and $p_{\mathbf{d}} := p_{\mathbf{b}} \cdot p_{\mathbf{f}}$.
5. $\mathcal{P}$ and $\mathcal{V}$ independently compute $A = R(P')^{\beta} T^{\gamma}$ and $B = SP^{\beta} T^{\gamma}$.
6. $\mathcal{P}$ computes $\mathbf{c}'' = \mathbf{c}'\|(p_{\mathbf{c}}(2^{n+1}), \dots, p_{\mathbf{c}}(2^{2n-1}))$ and $\mathbf{d}'' = \mathbf{d}'\|(p_{\mathbf{d}}(2^{n+1}), \dots, p_{\mathbf{d}}(2^{2n-1}))$, $C = \mathsf{COM}_{\bar{\mathbf{a}}}\ (\mathbf{c}'')$ and $D = \mathsf{COM}_{\bar{\mathbf{a}}}\ (\mathbf{d}'')$ and sends C, D to $\mathcal{V}$.
7. $\mathcal{V}$ samples $z, w \leftarrow_R \mathbb{Z}_q$ and sends z, w to $\mathcal{P}$.
8. $\mathcal{P}$ computes $\rho_{\mathsf{n}} = V^{-1}(1\ z\ z^2 \dots z^{n-1})$, $\rho_{\mathsf{2n}} = V^{-1}(1\ z\ z^2 \dots z^{2n-2})$, $\delta_{\mathsf{n}} = V^{-1}(1\ w\ w^2 \dots w^{n-1})$ and $\delta_{\mathsf{2n}} = V^{-1}(1\ w\ w^2 \dots w^{2n-2})$.
9. $\mathcal{P}$ and $\mathcal{V}$ runs $\Pi_{\mathsf{com\text{-}mult}}$ to obtain commitments P_n, P_{2n}, Q_n and Q_{2n} to the reverse of $\rho_{\mathsf{n}}, \rho_{\mathsf{2n}}', \delta_{\mathsf{n}}$ and δ_{2n}' where $\rho_{\mathsf{2n}}' = 0\|\rho_{\mathsf{2n}}$ and $\delta_{\mathsf{2n}}' = 0\|\delta_{\mathsf{2n}}$.
10. $\mathcal{P}$ sets z_1, z_2, w_1, and w_2 as $z_1 = p_{\mathbf{a}}(z)$, $z_2 = p_{\mathbf{e}}(z)$, $w_1 = p_{\mathbf{b}}(w)$, and $w_2 = p_{\mathbf{f}}(w)$.
11. $\mathcal{P}$ and $\mathcal{V}$ run $(\Pi_2)_c$ to prove the following:
    (a) $(C, \mathsf{left}, 1; \mathbf{c}'', (1\|\mathbf{0}\|\mathbf{0}))$, $(C, \mathsf{right}, x; \mathbf{c}'', (\mathbf{0}\|1\|\mathbf{0}))$, $(D, \mathsf{left}, 1; \mathbf{d}'', (1\|\mathbf{0}\|\mathbf{0}))$, $(D, \mathsf{right}, x; \mathbf{d}'', (\mathbf{0}\|1\|\mathbf{0})) \in \mathcal{R}_{\mathbf{CLF\text{-}rev}}$
    (b) $(A, P_n, z_1; \mathbf{a}, \rho_{\mathsf{n}})$,$(C, P_n, z_2; \mathbf{c}'', \rho_{\mathsf{n}}) \in \mathcal{R}_{\mathbf{CLF\text{-}rev}}$
    (c) $(B, Q_n, w_1; \mathbf{b}, \delta_{\mathsf{n}})$, $(D, Q_n, w_2; \mathbf{d}'', \delta_{\mathsf{n}}) \in \mathcal{R}_{\mathbf{CLF\text{-}rev}}$
    (d) $(C, P_{2n}, z_1 z_2; \mathbf{c}'', \rho_{\mathsf{2n}}')$, $(D, Q_{2n}, w_1 w_2; \mathbf{d}'', \delta_{\mathsf{2n}}') \in \mathcal{R}_{\mathbf{CLF\text{-}rev}}$.

Fig. 7. Protocol Π_{perm} for Permutation Argument

the commitment key, and are the same as in Daza et al [15]. We note that the circuit-specific preprocessing material can be deterministically computed from the universal SRS and the circuit description, without any secrets.

We describe the protocol as an interactive public coin argument. The final zkSNARK construction is in the Random Oracle model using the Fiat-Shamir heuristic.

Preprocessing. We use the preprocessing phase used by Daza et al. [15] to obtain a commitment to the linear gates. They establish a circuit preprocessing methodology that constrains the fan-in and fan-out of each gate in the circuit to at most M, while only incurring a linear expansion in the size of the circuit.

Let $\chi_1, \dots, \chi_\nu$ be the public inputs of the circuit. Let m be the number of multiplication gates in the circuit. We then require a commitment key of size $n = 2m + 2$. Let x_i^L, x_i^R, x_i^O denote the left input, right input and output of the ith multiplication gate. Let $\mathbf{x}^L = (x_i^L)_{i \in [m]}, \mathbf{x}^R = (x_i^R)_{i \in [m]}, \mathbf{x}^O = (x_i^O)_{i \in [m]}$. Then $\mathbf{x}^L \circ \mathbf{x}^R = \mathbf{x}^O$. Additionally, there exist vectors $\mathbf{w}_i^L, \mathbf{w}_i^R \in \mathbb{Z}_q^m$ with at most M non-zero entries such that $\langle \mathbf{w}_i^L, \mathbf{x}^O \rangle + \mathbf{x}_i^L = \chi_i, \forall i \in [\nu]$, $\langle \mathbf{w}_i^L, \mathbf{x}^O \rangle = x_i^L, \forall i \in \{\nu + 1, \dots, m\}$ and $\langle \mathbf{w}_i^R, \mathbf{x}^O \rangle = x_i^R \; \forall i \in [m]$. Let $W^L, W^R \in \mathbb{Z}_q^{m \times m}$ be matrices with their i^{th} rows equal to $\mathbf{w}_i^L$ and $\mathbf{w}_i^R$ respectively. Then W^L and W^R have $\leq M$ entries in each row and each column. The following applies to W^k for $k \in \{L, R\}$. W^k can be written as the sum of M permutation matrices, i.e. $W^k = \sum_{i=1}^M W_i^k$, where each W_i^k is a permutation matrix.

In addition to the preprocessing of [15], additional preprocessing material is generated that is required by our sub-protocols, $\Pi_{\mathsf{com\text{-}mult}}$ Π_{had}, and Π_{perm}. The verifier obtains commitments to W_i^k, I and $\sigma(I)$, where $I = (1, \dots, n)$, W_i^k and $\sigma_i^k : [n] \to [n]$ are as defined above. The verifier also obtains commitments to $\mathbf{1}$, $(\mathbf{0}\|1\|\mathbf{0})$, $(\mathbf{0}\|\mathbf{0}\|1)$ where $\mathbf{0} = (0, \dots, 0) \in \mathbb{Z}_q^n$, $\mathbf{1} = (1, \dots, 1) \in \mathbb{Z}_q^n$.

Protocol Overview. Post circuit preprocessing, our circuit is now fully defined by $\tilde{\mathbf{w}}_i^k, \sigma_i^k$, where $\tilde{\mathbf{w}}_i^k$ is the vector containing the non-zero entry (if there is one) in each column of W_i^k and $\sigma_i^k : [n] \to [n]$ is the permutation that takes as input a column number j and outputs the row to which the jth entry of $\mathbf{w}_i$ belongs. Our goal is to get a commitment to a random linear combination of the rows of W^k, i.e. a commitment to $W^k(c) = \sum_{i=1}^M \tilde{\mathbf{w}}_i^k \circ \sigma_i^k(\mathbf{c^m})$. To do this, we first demand commitments to $\sigma_i^k(\mathbf{c^m})$ from the prover, for a random challenge c chosen by the verifier. We can check that these commitments are honestly generated using Π_{perm}. We additionally ask the prover to provide us with commitments to $\tilde{\mathbf{w}}_i^k \circ \sigma_i^k(\mathbf{c^m})$ and a proof $h_{(\tilde{\mathbf{w}}_i^k \circ \sigma_i(\mathbf{c^m}))}$ that attests to the correct computation of a Hadamard product. To check this Hadamard product, we deploy our Π_{had} protocol. Since $\tilde{\mathbf{w}}_i^k, \sigma_i^k$ are public, Π_{had} can be invoked without requiring zero knowledge.

The above protocol allows us to get commitments to $W^L(c)$ and $W^R(c)$, but to show that the constraints of the circuit are satisfied, we need to prove that $\langle W^L(c) + uW^R(c), \mathbf{x}^O \rangle = \langle \mathbf{c^m}, \mathbf{x}^L \rangle - \sum_{i=1}^\nu c^{i-1}\chi_i + u\langle \mathbf{c^m}, \mathbf{x}^R \rangle = \langle \mathbf{c^m}, \mathbf{x}^L + u\mathbf{x}^R \rangle - \sum_{i=1}^\nu c^{i-1}\chi_i$ for $u \leftarrow_R \mathbb{Z}_q$. We cannot test for equality directly since that would require the prover to send out linear combinations of $\mathbf{x}^L, \mathbf{x}^R$ and $\mathbf{x}^O$, violating zero knowledge. Set $K = \sum_{i=1}^\nu c^{i-1}\chi_i, L_1 = W^L(c) + uW^R(c), L_2 = \mathbf{c^m}, \mathbf{y}_1 = \mathbf{x}^O$ and $\mathbf{y}_2 = \mathbf{x}^L + u\mathbf{x}^R$. Let $\tilde{L}_2$ be the $m-1$ vector comprising of the first $m-1$ elements of L_2. Let $(L_2)_m$ be the last element of L_2. The above constraint can then be written as $\langle L_1, \mathbf{y}_1\rangle = \langle L_2, \mathbf{y}_2\rangle - K$. To prove this in zero knowledge, we have the prover sample $\mathbf{r}_1 \leftarrow \mathbb{Z}_q^m, \tilde{\mathbf{r}}_2 \leftarrow \mathbb{Z}_q^{m-1}$ and set $\mathbf{r}_2 = \tilde{\mathbf{r}}_2 || (\langle L_1, \mathbf{r}_1\rangle - \langle \tilde{L}_2, \tilde{\mathbf{r}}_2\rangle)(L_2)_m^{-1}$. This ensures that $\langle L_1, \mathbf{r}_1\rangle = \langle L_2, \mathbf{r}_2\rangle$. The protocol now proceeds as follows: the verifier samples a challenge z and the prover proves that $\langle L_1, z\mathbf{y}_1 + \mathbf{r}_1\rangle = \langle L_2, z\mathbf{y}_2 + \mathbf{r}_2\rangle - zK$. We can directly test for equality here since the prover now needs to reveal $\langle L_1, z\mathbf{y}_1 + \mathbf{r}_1\rangle$, which is a random value that reveals nothing about the input.

This allows us to conclude that the commitments to $\mathbf{x}^L$, $\mathbf{x}^R$ and $\mathbf{x}^O$ satisfy the linear combination constraints imposed by the circuit. Testing for multiplication, i.e. checking if $\mathbf{x}^L \circ \mathbf{x}^R = \mathbf{x}^O$ can be done by invoking our protocol Π_{had} by adding randomness to the input vectors in order to preserve zero-knowledge.

Since we reduce circuit satisfiability to opening a series of committed linear forms on committed vectors, we can optimize by batching the opening of several linear forms together. Consider two instances (P_1, Q_1, y_1) and (P_2, Q_2, y_2) claimed by the prover to belong to $\mathcal{R}_{\mathsf{CLF\text{-}rev}}$. To prove this, we modify the protocol in Fig. 3 as follows: let $\mathbf{x}_1, \mathbf{x}_2$ be the vectors to which P_1 and P_2 are commitments. Let B_1, B_2 be the linear forms to which Q_1 and Q_2 are commitments. We first demand that the prover send us commitments to $p_{L,1}, p_{R,1}, p_{L,2}$ and $p_{R,2}$ as it would in the original protocol. We then ask the prover to make claims about $\mathbf{x}_1(c), \mathbf{B}_1(c), \mathbf{p}_{L,1}(c), \mathbf{p}_{R,1}(c)$ and $\mathbf{x}_2(c), \mathbf{B}_2(c), \mathbf{p}_{L,2}(c), \mathbf{p}_{R,2}(c)$ with respect to the *same* challenge c. This allows us to combine the prover's claims to open $\mathbf{c}^{\mathbf{n}\text{-}\mathbf{1}}$ on a *single* vector given by $\mathbf{x}_1 + t\mathbf{B}_1 + t^2\mathbf{p}_{L,1} + t^3\mathbf{p}_{R,1} + t^4\mathbf{x}_2 + t^5\mathbf{B}_2 + t^6\mathbf{p}_{L,2} + t^7\mathbf{p}_{R,2}$ for a random challenge t. Thus, we can open $\mathcal{O}(M)$ linear forms while incurring the communication overhead of opening a single linear form. The complete protocol Π_{csat} is presented in the full version [16] in Fig 8 (Sect. 4.4), along with the proof of security in Appendix C.3.

Theorem 9. *Π_{csat} is a Public Coin, Honest Verifier Zero Knowledge Argument of Knowledge for CSAT with $\mathcal{O}(\log m)$ round complexity, $\mathcal{O}_\lambda(m)$ prover complexity, and $\mathcal{O}_\lambda(\log m)$ communication and verification complexity, where m is the number of multiplication gates in the preprocessed circuit.*

5 CSP for Committed Homomorphism

A bilinear group arithmetic circuit is a circuit in which the wire values are from $\mathbb{G}_1, \mathbb{G}_2, \mathbb{G}_T$ or $\mathbb{Z}_q$, and the gates are group operations, $\mathbb{Z}_q$-scalar multiplication, or bilinear pairings. Bilinear circuits are of interest since they directly capture relations arising in identity-based and attribute-based encryption [21,34], structure preserving signatures [2] etc. Handling bilinear circuits directly in a ZK system avoids expensive NP reductions or arithmetizations to represent group operations as an arithmetic circuit. The work of Attema et al. [7], building on the work of Lai et al. [26], gives a succinct argument system for bilinear group arithmetic circuits, by generalizing the compressed sigma protocol framework. A key building block is a protocol for opening a homomorphism on a committed vector. However, as in the case of arithmetic circuits, the verifier remains linear.

We construct a *designated-verifier* succinct argument for opening a committed homomorphism on a committed vector, where the verifier is *logarithmic*.

5.1 Commitment Scheme

In this section, we use additive notation for groups in line with prior works for bilinear circuits. We begin by generalizing the homomorphic commitment scheme of [26], to work with logarithmic amount of randomness. We note that $\dot{\mathbf{a}}$ denotes $\dot{\mathbf{a}} = (a_1, \ldots, a_\ell)$ and for $g \in \mathbb{G}$ and $\mathbf{x} = (x_1, \ldots, x_n) \in \mathbb{Z}_q^n$, $g\mathbf{x}$ denotes $g\mathbf{x} = (gx_1, \ldots, gx_n)$, for $\mathbf{g} = (g_1, \ldots, g_n) \in \mathbb{G}^n$ and $\mathbf{x} = (x_1, \ldots, x_n) \in \mathbb{Z}_q^n$, inner product with scalar $\langle \mathbf{g}, \mathbf{x} \rangle$ denotes $\langle \mathbf{g}, \mathbf{x} \rangle = g_1 x_1 + \ldots g_n x_n$; for $\mathbf{g} = (g_1, \ldots, g_n) \in \mathbb{G}_1^n$ and $\mathbf{h} = (h_1, \ldots, h_n) \in \mathbb{G}_2^n$, inner product $e(\mathbf{g}, \mathbf{h})$ denotes $e(\mathbf{g}, \mathbf{h}) = e(g_1, h_1) + e(g_2, h_2) + \ldots + e(g_n, h_n)$. We recall the key distribution $\mathcal{ML}_n$, for $n = 2^\ell$, and subsequently consider a similar distribution over group elements,

$$\mathcal{ML}_n = \{\overline{\mathbf{a}} : \dot{\mathbf{a}} = (\dot{a}_1, \ldots, \dot{a}_\ell) \leftarrow_R \mathbb{Z}_q^\ell, \overline{\mathbf{a}} = (\prod_{i=1}^{\ell} \dot{a}_i^{x_i})_{x_i \in \{0,1\}}\}$$

$$\mathcal{ML}_n(\mathbb{G}) = \mathcal{ML}_{2^\ell}(\mathbb{G}) := \{g\overline{\mathbf{a}} : g \leftarrow_R \mathbb{G}, \dot{\mathbf{a}} = (\dot{a}_1, \ldots, \dot{a}_\ell) \leftarrow_R \mathbb{Z}_q^\ell, \overline{\mathbf{a}} = (\prod_{i=1}^{\ell} \dot{a}_i^{x_i})_{x_i \in \{0,1\}}\}$$

We define a new commitment scheme which differs from the one proposed in [26] (and subsequently used in [7]) only in that we sample the commitment key from $\mathcal{ML}_n(\mathbb{G})$.

Definition 2 (Commitment to $(\mathbb{Z}_q, \mathbb{G}_1, \mathbb{G}_2)$-vectors). *Let $(q, \mathbb{G}_1, \mathbb{G}_2, \mathbb{G}_T, e, G, H)$ be a bilinear group and $n_0, n_1, n_2 \geq 0$. We define a commitment scheme $\mathrm{COM}^{\mathbb{G}}$ for vectors in $\mathbb{Z}_q^{n_0} \times \mathbb{G}_1^{n_1} \times \mathbb{G}_2^{n_2}$, given by the following setup and commitment phase:*

- *Setup :* $(\mathbf{h}, \mathbf{g}) \leftarrow_R \mathcal{ML}^2_{n_0+1}(\mathbb{G}_T), \mathbf{H} \leftarrow_R \mathcal{ML}^2_{n_1}(\mathbb{G}_2), \mathbf{G} \leftarrow_R \mathcal{ML}^2_{n_2}(\mathbb{G}_1)$
  Here, $(\mathbf{h}, \mathbf{g}, \mathbf{H}, \mathbf{G}) = (\overline{\mathbf{a}}h, \overline{\mathbf{b}}g, \overline{\mathbf{c}}H, \overline{\mathbf{d}}G)$ *for some structured $\mathbb{Z}_q$ vectors $\overline{\mathbf{a}}, \overline{\mathbf{b}}, \overline{\mathbf{c}}, \overline{\mathbf{d}}$, where h, g is sampled to be $h = e(h_1, H), g = e(g_1, H)$ for some $h_1, g_1 \leftarrow_R \mathbb{G}_1$.*[2] *Then,* $(\mathsf{ck}_0 = ((\overline{\mathbf{a}}h_1, \overline{\mathbf{a}}h), (\overline{\mathbf{b}}g_1, \overline{\mathbf{b}}g)), \mathsf{ck}_1 = \overline{\mathbf{c}}H, \mathsf{ck}_2 = \overline{\mathbf{d}}G)$ *are the commitment keys and* $(\dot{\mathsf{ck}}_0 = (\overline{\mathbf{a}}H, \overline{\mathbf{b}}H), \dot{\mathsf{ck}}_1 = \overline{\mathbf{c}}G, \dot{\mathsf{ck}}_2 = \overline{\mathbf{d}}H)$ *is the verification key.*
- *Commit :* $\mathrm{COM}^{\mathbb{G}} : \mathbb{Z}_q^{n_0} \times \mathbb{G}_1^{n_1} \times \mathbb{G}_2^{n_2} \times \mathbb{Z}_q \to \mathbb{G}_T^2$,
  - $(\mathbf{x}, \mathbf{y}, \mathbf{z}; \gamma) \to \mathbf{h}\gamma + \langle \mathbf{g}, \mathbf{x} \rangle + e(\mathbf{y}, \mathbf{H}) + e(\mathbf{G}, \mathbf{z})$,
  - *where* $\mathbf{h}\gamma + \langle \mathbf{g}, \mathbf{x} \rangle + e(\mathbf{y}, \mathbf{H}) + e(\mathbf{G}, \mathbf{z}) = \begin{pmatrix} h_1\gamma + \langle \mathbf{g}_1, \mathbf{x} \rangle + e(\mathbf{y}, \mathbf{H}_1) + e(\mathbf{G}_1, \mathbf{z}) \\ h_2\gamma + \langle \mathbf{g}_2, \mathbf{x} \rangle + e(\mathbf{y}, \mathbf{H}_2) + e(\mathbf{G}_2, \mathbf{z}) \end{pmatrix}$

---

[2] We note that the distribution remains the same even when $\overline{\mathbf{a}}g_1$ is sampled from $\mathcal{ML}_{n_0}(\mathbb{G}_1)$ and g is then set to $g = e(g_1, H)$, making the final commitment key for $\mathbb{Z}_q$-vector to be $\mathbf{g} = \overline{\mathbf{a}}g$, as opposed to when $\mathbf{g}$ is directly sampled from $\mathcal{ML}_{n_0}(\mathbb{G}_T)$.

The verification key is used to check that the commitment key has been updated by the prover, by having the prover send the first element of the commitment key ck to the verifier, and the verifier using the pairing check to ensure that the split-and-fold technique has been used correctly to update the commitment key and check that the updated commitment (sent by the prover) with respect to the updated commitment key is consistent.

We define an assumption called eGDLR assumption along the lines of GDLR assumption in [26], show that it is implied by SXDH (Lemma 6 of the full version [16]) and prove binding of $\mathrm{COM}^{\mathbb{G}}$ under eGDLR.

Lemma 2. $\mathrm{COM}^{\mathbb{G}}$ *is computationally hiding under DDH in* $\mathbb{G}_T$*, and computationally binding under SXDH.*

The proof is presented in Lemma 4 and 5 in Appendix A.1 of the full version [16].

5.2 Succinct Verifier Σ-Protocol for Opening Committed Homomorphism

Notation. Let $(q, \mathbb{G}_1, \mathbb{G}_2, \mathbb{G}_T, e, G, H)$ be a bilinear group. Let $g^{\overline{\mathbf{a}}} \in \mathbb{G}_1$ be the commitment key used to commit to a vector of $\mathbb{Z}_q$ elements in $\mathrm{COM}_{\overline{\mathbf{a}}}(\mathbf{x}) = \langle \overline{\mathbf{a}}, \mathbf{x} \rangle g \in \mathbb{G}_1$, where $\mathbf{x} \in \mathbb{Z}_q^n, \overline{\mathbf{a}} \in \mathbb{Z}_q^n$. We consider the group homomorphism $f : \mathbb{Z}_q^n \to \mathbb{G}_2$, and define $\mathrm{HOM}(\mathbb{Z}_q^n, \mathbb{G}_2) = \{f : f \text{ is a homomorphism from } \mathbb{Z}_q^n \text{ to } \mathbb{G}_2\}$. We use $\mathrm{COM}^{\mathbb{G}}$ given in Definition 2 and use a modified version to commit to element of only one source group of bilinear pairing as follows : $\mathrm{COM}^{\mathbb{G}} : \mathbb{G}_2^n \to \mathbb{G}_T$, where $\mathrm{COM}^{\mathbb{G}}(\mathbf{x}) = e(\mathbf{G}, \mathbf{x})$, for $n = 2^\ell, h \leftarrow_R \mathbb{G}_T, \dot{\mathbf{a}} = (\dot{a}_1, \ldots, \dot{a}_\ell) \leftarrow_R \mathbb{Z}_q^\ell, \overline{\mathbf{a}} = \left(\prod_{i=1}^{\ell} \dot{a}_i^{b_i}\right)_{b_i \in \{0,1\}}, \mathbf{G} = \overline{\mathbf{a}} G$, and we use the notation to $\mathrm{COM}_{\overline{\mathbf{a}}}^{\mathbb{G}}$ to explicitly specify the commitment key for ease of exposition, and define it as $\mathrm{COM}_{\overline{\mathbf{a}}}^{\mathbb{G}}(\mathbf{x}) = \mathrm{COM}^{\mathbb{G}}(\mathbf{x}) = e(\mathbf{G}, \mathbf{x})$, where $\mathbf{G} = \overline{\mathbf{a}} G$.

Opening Group Homomorphism. We aim to prove that a committed vector $\mathbf{x} \in \mathbb{Z}_q^n$ is opening of an element $y \in \mathbb{G}$ with respect to group homomorphism defined by $f : \mathbb{Z}_q^n \to \mathbb{G}_2$, i.e. the opening of a given commitment $\mathrm{COM}_{\overline{\mathbf{a}}}(\mathbf{x}), \mathbf{x} \in \mathbb{Z}_q^n$ is such that $f(\mathbf{x}) = y$ for some $y \in \mathbb{G}_2$. We note that the homomorphism $f : \mathbb{Z}_q^n \to \mathbb{G}$ can be defined as $f \in \mathbb{G}_2^n$, and we extend the techniques discussed in Sect. 3. We use the commitment scheme from Definition 2 $\mathrm{COM}^{\mathbb{G}} : \mathbb{Z}_q \times \mathbb{G}_1^{n_1} \times \mathbb{G}_2^{n_2} \to \mathbb{G}_T^2$ to succinctly commit to $f = (f_1, \ldots, f_n) \in \mathbb{G}_2^n$ and $\mathsf{rev}(f) = (f_n, \ldots, f_1) \in \mathbb{G}_2^n$ using the structured commitment key $g^{\overline{\mathbf{a}}} \in \mathbb{G}_1$ used to commit to the vector.

We note that while techniques of Sect. 3.2 for committed linear forms can extend to a committed homomorphism, there are some differences that we need to handle. First, the representation of a group homomorphism is given by group elements as opposed to field elements in linear forms, and this requires a commitment to group elements. Since the commitment scheme relies on SXDH, we cannot encode the commitment randomness in the second group anymore. This is however crucial to verify that the commitment key is updated correctly in each step of split-and-fold. This makes our protocol designated verifier since the encoding of the randomness is available only to the verifier and binding still holds under SXDH. We define the relation $\mathcal{R}$ for opening a group homomorphism f below, and then present the protocol $\Pi_{0\text{-hom}}$ for relation $\mathcal{R}$.

$$\mathcal{R} = \{(P \in \mathbb{G}_1, f \in \mathrm{HOM}(\mathbb{Z}_q^n, \mathbb{G}_2), y \in \mathbb{G}_2; \mathbf{x} \in \mathbb{Z}_q^n, \gamma \in \mathbb{Z}_q) : P = \mathrm{COM}_{\overline{\mathbf{a}}}(\mathbf{x};\gamma) \ \wedge \ f(\mathbf{x}) = y\}\}$$

Parameters

- Common parameters : $(P \in \mathbb{G}_1, f \in \mathrm{HOM}(\mathbb{Z}_q^n, \mathbb{G}_2), y \in \mathbb{G}_2)$, $P = \mathrm{COM}_{\overline{\mathbf{a}}}(\mathbf{x};\gamma), y = f(\mathbf{x})$
- $\mathcal{P}$'s input : $(\mathbf{x} \in \mathbb{Z}_q^n, \gamma \in \mathbb{Z}_q)$

Protocol

1. $\mathcal{P}$ samples $\mathbf{r} \leftarrow_R \mathbb{G}, \rho \leftarrow_R \mathbb{Z}_q$, computes $A = \mathrm{COM}_{\overline{\mathbf{a}}}(\mathbf{r};\rho)$, $t = f(\mathbf{r})$ and sends A, t to $\mathcal{V}$.
2. $\mathcal{V}$ samples $c \leftarrow_R \mathbb{Z}_q$ and sends c to $\mathcal{P}$
3. $\mathcal{P}$ computes $\mathbf{z} = c\mathbf{x} + \mathbf{r}$ and $\phi = c\gamma + \rho$ and sends $\mathbf{z}, \phi$ to $\mathcal{V}$
4. $\mathcal{V}$ checks if $\mathrm{COM}_{\overline{\mathbf{a}}}(\mathbf{z};\phi) = A + cP$ and $f(\mathbf{z}) = cy + t$, outputs 1 if it holds, outputs 0 otherwise.

Fig. 8. Protocol $\Pi_{0\text{-hom}}$ for relation $\mathcal{R}$

Theorem 10. *$\Pi_{0\text{-hom}}$ (Fig. 8) is a 3-move protocol for relation $\mathcal{R}$. It is perfectly complete, special honest-verifier zero-knowledge and computationally special sound.*

This theorem follows from the fact that this protocol is identical to the one introduced in [7], and the properties of the protocol relies on the hiding and binding of the commitment scheme which are satisfied by our commitment scheme 2 used here.

Here we use similar techniques used to handle protocols for opening of linear forms efficiently, by introducing commitment to the homomorphism (which is equivalently defined by a vector of group elements). We elaborate the same in Sect. 5 of full version of the paper [16] with constructions and its proofs. First we provide Protocol $\Pi_{1\text{-hom}}$ (Fig 10 of the full version [16]) which uses commitment to the reverse (mirror image of the homomorphism), similar to the technique used in Π_2, and use the split-and-fold technique to get the updated witness and generators for the same relation with halved dimensions, while using the commitments to prove consistency of the witness update and pairing check to prove consistency of the underlying generator update.

Compressed Σ-Protocol for Opening General Homomorphisms. We also extend our protocol to opening homomorphisms on committed vectors with coefficients in multiple groups. We believe that using our protocols in applications of CSP to Threshold Signature Schemes and circuit zero-knowledge protocols with bilinear gates [7] will result in analogs with succinct verifier after an appropriate preprocessing phase. We present the protocol for opening general homomorphisms, state and prove the theorem in Sect. 5.3 of the full version [16].

Acknowledgement. The research of the second author was supported by Core Research Grant CRG/2020/004488, SERB, Department of Science and Technology, India.

References

1. https://www.zellic.io/blog/zk-friendly-hash-functions
2. Abe, M., Fuchsbauer, G., Groth, J., Haralambiev, K., Ohkubo, M.: Structure-preserving signatures and commitments to group elements. In: Rabin, T. (ed.) CRYPTO 2010. LNCS, vol. 6223, pp. 209–236. Springer, Heidelberg (2010). https://doi.org/10.1007/978-3-642-14623-7_12
3. Albrecht, M., Grassi, L., Rechberger, C., Roy, A., Tiessen, T.: MiMC: efficient encryption and cryptographic hashing with minimal multiplicative complexity. In: Cheon, J.H., Takagi, T. (eds.) ASIACRYPT 2016, Part I. LNCS, vol. 10031, pp. 191–219. Springer, Heidelberg (2016). https://doi.org/10.1007/978-3-662-53887-6_7
4. Arun, A., Ganesh, C., Lokam, S., Mopuri, T., Sridhar, S.: Dew: a transparent constant-sized polynomial commitment scheme. In: Boldyreva, A., Kolesnikov, V. (eds.) PKC 2023, Part II. LNCS, vol. 13941, pp. 542–571. Springer, Cham (2023). https://doi.org/10.1007/978-3-031-31371-4_19
5. Attema, T., Cramer, R.: Compressed Σ-protocol theory and practical application to plug & play secure algorithmics. In: Micciancio, D., Ristenpart, T. (eds.) CRYPTO 2020, Part III. LNCS, vol. 12172, pp. 513–543. Springer, Cham (2020). https://doi.org/10.1007/978-3-030-56877-1_18
6. Attema, T., Cramer, R., Kohl, L.: A Compressed Σ-protocol theory for lattices. In: Malkin, T., Peikert, C. (eds.) CRYPTO 2021, Part II. LNCS, vol. 12826, pp. 549–579. Springer, Cham (2021). https://doi.org/10.1007/978-3-030-84245-1_19
7. Attema, T., Cramer, R., Rambaud, M.: Compressed Σ-protocols for bilinear group arithmetic circuits and application to logarithmic transparent threshold signatures. In: Tibouchi, M., Wang, H. (eds.) ASIACRYPT 2021, Part IV. LNCS, vol. 13093, pp. 526–556. Springer, Cham (2021). https://doi.org/10.1007/978-3-030-92068-5_18
8. Bayer, S., Groth, J.: Efficient zero-knowledge argument for correctness of a shuffle. In: Pointcheval, D., Johansson, T. (eds.) EUROCRYPT 2012. LNCS, vol. 7237, pp. 263–280. Springer, Heidelberg (2012). https://doi.org/10.1007/978-3-642-29011-4_17
9. Ben-Sasson, E., Chiesa, A., Tromer, E., Virza, M.: Succinct non-interactive zero knowledge for a von neumann architecture. In: Fu, K., Jung, J. (eds.) USENIX Security 2014, pp. 781–796. USENIX Association, August 2014
10. Bitansky, N., Chiesa, A., Ishai, Y., Paneth, O., Ostrovsky, R.: Succinct non-interactive arguments via linear interactive proofs. In: Sahai, A. (ed.) TCC 2013. LNCS, vol. 7785, pp. 315–333. Springer, Heidelberg (2013). https://doi.org/10.1007/978-3-642-36594-2_18

11. Bootle, J., Cerulli, A., Chaidos, P., Groth, J., Petit, C.: Efficient zero-knowledge arguments for arithmetic circuits in the discrete log setting. In: Fischlin, M., Coron, J.-S. (eds.) EUROCRYPT 2016, Part II. LNCS, vol. 9666, pp. 327–357. Springer, Heidelberg (2016). https://doi.org/10.1007/978-3-662-49896-5_12
12. Bünz, B., Bootle, J., Boneh, D., Poelstra, A., Wuille, P., Maxwell, G.: Bulletproofs: short proofs for confidential transactions and more. In: 2018 IEEE symposium on security and privacy (SP), pp. 315–334. IEEE (2018)
13. Bünz, B., Fisch, B., Szepieniec, A.: Transparent SNARKs from DARK compilers. In: Canteaut, A., Ishai, Y. (eds.) EUROCRYPT 2020, Part I. LNCS, vol. 12105, pp. 677–706. Springer, Cham (2020). https://doi.org/10.1007/978-3-030-45721-1_24
14. Chiesa, A., Hu, Y., Maller, M., Mishra, P., Vesely, N., Ward, N.: Marlin: preprocessing zkSNARKs with universal and updatable SRS. In: Canteaut, A., Ishai, Y. (eds.) EUROCRYPT 2020, Part I. LNCS, vol. 12105, pp. 738–768. Springer, Cham (2020). https://doi.org/10.1007/978-3-030-45721-1_26
15. Daza, V., Ràfols, C., Zacharakis, A.: Updateable inner product argument with logarithmic verifier and applications. In: Kiayias, A., Kohlweiss, M., Wallden, P., Zikas, V. (eds.) PKC 2020, Part I. LNCS, vol. 12110, pp. 527–557. Springer, Cham (2020). https://doi.org/10.1007/978-3-030-45374-9_18
16. Dutta, M., Ganesh, C., Jawalkar, N.: Succinct verification of compressed sigma protocols in the updatable SRS setting. Cryptology ePrint Archive, Paper 2024/075 (2024). https://eprint.iacr.org/2024/075
17. Fiat, A., Shamir, A.: How To prove yourself: practical solutions to identification and signature problems. In: Odlyzko, A.M. (ed.) CRYPTO 1986. LNCS, vol. 263, pp. 186–194. Springer, Heidelberg (1987). https://doi.org/10.1007/3-540-47721-7_12
18. Gabizon, A., Williamson, Z.J., Ciobotaru, O.: Plonk: permutations over lagrange-bases for oecumenical noninteractive arguments of knowledge. Cryptology ePrint Archive, Report 2019/953 (2019). https://ia.cr/2019/953
19. Gennaro, R., Gentry, C., Parno, B., Raykova, M.: Quadratic span programs and succinct NIZKs without PCPs. In: Johansson, T., Nguyen, P.Q. (eds.) EUROCRYPT 2013. LNCS, vol. 7881, pp. 626–645. Springer, Heidelberg (2013). https://doi.org/10.1007/978-3-642-38348-9_37
20. Goldwasser, S., Micali, S., Rackoff, C.: The knowledge complexity of interactive proof systems. SIAM J. Comput. **18**(1), 186–208 (1989)
21. Goyal, V., Pandey, O., Sahai, A., Waters, B.: Attribute-based encryption for fine-grained access control of encrypted data. In: Juels, A., Wright, R.N., De Capitani di Vimercati, S. (eds.) ACM CCS 2006, pp. 89–98. ACM Press, October/November 2006. Available as Cryptology ePrint Archive Report 2006/309
22. Groth, J.: Short pairing-based non-interactive zero-knowledge arguments. In: Abe, M. (ed.) ASIACRYPT 2010. LNCS, vol. 6477, pp. 321–340. Springer, Heidelberg (2010). https://doi.org/10.1007/978-3-642-17373-8_19
23. Groth, J.: On the size of pairing-based non-interactive arguments. In: Fischlin, M., Coron, J.-S. (eds.) EUROCRYPT 2016, Part II. LNCS, vol. 9666, pp. 305–326. Springer, Heidelberg (2016). https://doi.org/10.1007/978-3-662-49896-5_11
24. Groth, J., Kohlweiss, M., Maller, M., Meiklejohn, S., Miers, I.: Updatable and universal common reference strings with applications to zk-SNARKs. In: Shacham, H., Boldyreva, A. (eds.) CRYPTO 2018, Part III. LNCS, vol. 10993, pp. 698–728. Springer, Cham (2018). https://doi.org/10.1007/978-3-319-96878-0_24
25. Kilian, J.: A note on efficient zero-knowledge proofs and arguments. In: Proceedings of the Twenty-Fourth Annual ACM Symposium on Theory of Computing, pp. 723–732 (1992)

26. Lai, R.W.F., Malavolta, G., Ronge, V.: Succinct arguments for bilinear group arithmetic: practical structure-preserving cryptography. In: Cavallaro, L., Kinder, J., Wang, X.F., Katz, J. (eds.) ACM CCS 2019, pp. 2057–2074. ACM Press, November 2019
27. Lee, J.: Dory: efficient, transparent arguments for generalised inner products and polynomial commitments. In: Nissim, K., Waters, B. (eds.) TCC 2021. LNCS, vol. 13043, pp. 1–34. Springer, Cham (2021). https://doi.org/10.1007/978-3-030-90453-1_1
28. Lipmaa, H.: Progression-free sets and sublinear pairing-based non-interactive zero-knowledge arguments. In: Cramer, R. (ed.) TCC 2012. LNCS, vol. 7194, pp. 169–189. Springer, Heidelberg (2012). https://doi.org/10.1007/978-3-642-28914-9_10
29. Lipmaa, H.: Succinct non-interactive zero knowledge arguments from span programs and linear error-correcting codes. In: Sako, K., Sarkar, P. (eds.) ASIACRYPT 2013, Part I. LNCS, vol. 8269, pp. 41–60. Springer, Heidelberg (2013). https://doi.org/10.1007/978-3-642-42033-7_3
30. Lipmaa, H., Siim, J., Zajac, M.: Counting vampires: from univariate sumcheck to updatable ZK-SNARK. In: Agrawal, S., Lin, D. (eds.) ASIACRYPT 2022, Part II. LNCS, vol. 13792, pp. 249–278. Springer, Cham (2022). https://doi.org/10.1007/978-3-031-22966-4_9
31. Maller, M., Bowe, S., Kohlweiss, M., Meiklejohn, S.: Sonic: zero-knowledge SNARKs from linear-size universal and updatable structured reference strings. In: Cavallaro, L., Kinder, J., Wang, X.F., Katz, J. (eds.) ACM CCS 2019, pp. 2111–2128. ACM Press, November 2019
32. Micali, S.: CS proofs. In: Proceedings 35th Annual Symposium on Foundations of Computer Science, pp. 436–453. IEEE (1994)
33. Parno, B., Howell, J., Gentry, C., Raykova, M.: Pinocchio: nearly practical verifiable computation. In: 2013 IEEE Symposium on Security and Privacy, pp. 238–252. IEEE Computer Society Press, May 2013
34. Sahai, A., Waters, B.: Fuzzy identity-based encryption. In: Cramer, R. (ed.) EUROCRYPT 2005. LNCS, vol. 3494, pp. 457–473. Springer, Heidelberg (2005). https://doi.org/10.1007/11426639_27

Lookup Arguments: Improvements, Extensions and Applications to Zero-Knowledge Decision Trees

Matteo Campanelli[1], Antonio Faonio[2(✉)], Dario Fiore[3], Tianyu Li[4(✉)], and Helger Lipmaa[5]

[1] Protocol Labs, Aarhus, Denmark
matteo.campanelli@gmail.com
[2] EURECOM, Sophia Antipolis, France
faonio@eurecom.fr
[3] IMDEA Software Institute, Madrid, Spain
dario.fiore@imdea.org
[4] Delft University of Technology, Delft, Netherlands
tianyu.li@tudelft.nl
[5] University of Tartu, Tartu, Estonia

Abstract. Lookup arguments allow to prove that the elements of a committed vector come from a (bigger) committed table. They enable novel approaches to reduce the prover complexity of general-purpose zkSNARKs, implementing "non-arithmetic operations" such as range checks, XOR and AND more efficiently. We extend the notion of lookup arguments along two directions and improve their efficiency: (1) we extend vector lookups to matrix lookups (where we can prove that a committed matrix is a submatrix of a committed table). (2) We consider the notion of zero-knowledge lookup argument that keeps the privacy of both the sub-vector/sub-matrix and the table. (3) We present new zero-knowledge lookup arguments, dubbed cq+, zkcq+ and cq++, more efficient than the state of the art, namely the recent work by Eagen, Fiore and Gabizon named cq. Finally, we give a novel application of zero-knowledge matrix lookup argument to the domain of zero-knowledge decision tree where the model provider releases a commitment to a decision tree and can prove zero-knowledge statistics over the committed data structure. Our scheme based on lookup arguments has succinct verification, prover's time complexity asymptotically better than the state of the art, and is secure in a strong security model where the commitment to the decision tree can be malicious.

1 Introduction

General-purpose zero-knowledge succinct arguments of knowledge (zkSNARKs) promise to efficiently and succinctly prove any kind of NP-statement while keeping privacy, integrity and verifiability guarantees. Thanks to their generality, a great number of real-world applications can be performed with built-in security. The two-step recipe for building a brand new zero-knowledge application typically consists of first describing the application in a low-level constraint system

Q. Tang and V. Teague (Eds.): PKC 2024, LNCS 14602, pp. 337–369, 2024.
https://doi.org/10.1007/978-3-031-57722-2_11

(for example, Rank-1 Constraint System [4] or Plonk arithemization [19]) and then use the latest fully-developed zkSNARK as *backend*. Unfortunately, most often, the *unfolded circuit* of the applications at hand becomes huge and, thus, the proving time could become unfeasible for real-world applications.

Lookup arguments [6,14,32,38,39] are a novel approach to reducing the size of unfolded circuits, bringing back to the real world many interesting applications. Briefly and informally, a lookup argument allows to trade *sub-circuits* evaluations for lookup into their truth tables. For example, instead of having n different sub-circuits describing the computation of a hash function in the final unfolded circuit, the protocol designer could define n different *custom gates* that perform efficient lookup operations in the truth table of such a hash function. More concretely, lookup arguments are used in current zkSNARKs for representing "non-arithmetic operations" that cannot be expressed efficiently through the finite field operations supported by the zkSNARK, such as range checks, XOR and AND (see for example [6,18]). Very recently, the work of Arun, Setty and Thaler [3] shows how to use lookup arguments to create SNARKs for virtual-machine executions, namely a new SNARK scheme, called Jolt, that allows verification of the correct execution of a computer program specified with an assembly language. Informally, in Jolt, the truth table of each assembly instruction is encoded in a (predefined and highly structured) table. Then, lookup arguments enforce the correct instructions execution, namely checking the inputs and outputs described by their truth tables.

In this work, we advance on lookup arguments in multiple ways. We propose new lookup arguments that improve over the state of the art [14]. One of our schemes enjoys, almost for free, an extended notion of zero-knowledge, which we call fully zero-knowledge, which protects the privacy of arbitrary commitments to the tables. Orthogonally, we consider two natural extensions from vectors to matrices and give constructions for such extensions. Finally, we motivate the extensions to matrix and to fully zero-knowledge by giving a new application to privacy-preserving machine learning that crucially relies on them.

New Lookup Arguments Based on cq. In a lookup argument, the prover aims to show that each coefficient of a (short) committed vector $\mathbf{f}$ of size n belongs to the (large) table $\mathbf{t}$ of size $N \gg n$. Since $N \gg n$, one of the desiderata of lookup arguments is that the prover's computation does not depend on N. Following a fast-pace line of recent works, Eagen, Fiore, and Gabizon [14] proposed an efficient lookup argument called cq (cq for *cached quotients*). Notably, cq's prover's computation is quasi-linear in n, while the proof size and verifier's computation are constant (e.g., proofs are 3840 bits, when using the standard BLS12-381 elliptic curve). In spite of appearing nearly optimal in efficiency, cq comes with two shortcomings. The first one is that it is not designed to have zero knowledge in mind. The second, more technical, one is that its use in larger protocols likely requires additional proof elements and pairing computations.[1] In this

[1] This is due to the fact that cq assumes an SRS of the same size as the table $\mathbf{t}$, and this allows avoiding a degree check. This condition, though, is often not guaranteed (e.g., in a SNARK for constraint systems larger than such a table).

work, we propose a new lookup argument, dubbed cq^+, that addresses all these shortcomings of cq and even achieves better efficiency. Namely, cq^+ achieves (standard) zero-knowledge at no overhead: it has the same prover's computation of cq and shorter proofs (3328 bits, and 2944 bits without ZK). Additionally, we consider two variations of cq^+: the first, dubbed zkcq^+, is fully zero-knowledge, while the second, dubbed cq^{++}, has shorter proofs. Both schemes require in verification only one pairing computation more than cq^+.

Lookup Arguments for Matrices. A lookup argument could be used to show that a database $\mathbf{f}$ is a selection of the rows of a database $\mathbf{t}$. However, to naively use lookup arguments for such an application, each row of the database must be efficiently encoded in one single field element (supported by the lookup argument). We consider two natural extensions to matrices. We focus on Kate *et al.* [25] polynomial commitment (also known as KZG commitment scheme) adapted to matrices. We give two lookup arguments for matrices that internally call a lookup argument for KZG commitments. The first scheme allows proving that a committed database $\mathbf{f}$ is a selection of the rows of a committed database $\mathbf{t}$, the second one allows proving that $\mathbf{f}$ is a selection of a projection of a database $\mathbf{t}$.

A New Approach to Zero-Knowledge for Decision Trees. We show an application of fully zero-knowledge matrix lookup arguments to zero-knowledge for decision trees (zkDT). We improve over the framework of Zhang *et al.* [40], which showed zkSNARKs for evaluations of committed decision trees and zkSNARKs for accuracy of committed decision trees. The former kind of zero-knowledge protocols can prove that a committed decision tree T, on input a vector $\mathbf{x}$, outputs a label v, while the latter schemes enable to validate the accuracy (namely, the ratio of true positives) of a decision tree on a given dataset.

Our framework can instantiate different kinds of statistics over committed decision trees, including evaluation and accuracy. Our design decouples the computation of the committed decision tree and the performed statistics. This allows for a plug-and-play approach. For security, we extend the notion of security from [40] considering possibly maliciously generated commitments to decision trees.

1.1 Technical Overview

Our Zero-Knowledge Lookup Arguments. Similarly to cq, cq^+ uses the technique of logarithmic derivates of Haböck [23]. However, we diverge from cq early, introducing several novel ideas that allow us to improve on cq's efficiency. One of the differences is that, while cq uses Aurora's sumcheck [5] twice, our cq^+ only runs it once. Nicely, this technique allows us to kill two birds with one stone, in fact, cq^+ does not require any additional low-degree tests. We give a more detailed technical overview in Sect. 4.1.

Matrix Lookup from Vector Lookup. To commit to a matrix, we can commit the concatenation of the rows of the matrix. Our matrix lookup arguments label all the entries of such a vectorization with the coordinates of each cell of the sub-matrix $\mathbf{F}$ into the bigger table $\mathbf{T}$. Similarly, in the precomputation phase, they label each cell in the big table $\mathbf{T}$ with its coordinate. To prove that the k-th row of $\mathbf{F}$ appears in $\mathbf{T}$, we show that the *labelled* matrix $\mathbf{F}^* = (i_j, j, \mathbf{F}_{k,j})_{j\in[d]}$ is a sub-matrix of labeled table $\mathbf{T}^* = (i, j, \mathbf{T}_{i,j})_{i,j}$ and that $i_1 = i_2 = \cdots = i_d$ (in particular $i_j = k$), where d is the number of columns of the matrices. Notice that the first claim can be proved efficiently with a (non-succinct) matrix commitment for matrices with $N \cdot d$ rows and 3 columns following techniques from [6], while the second claim can be efficiently expressed through polynomial equations following techniques from [10]. In particular, for the first part, given a challenge $\rho \leftarrow \mathbb{F}$, the prover hashes $h(\mathbf{F}^*) = \sum_{i=1}^{3} \rho^{i-1} \cdot \mathbf{F}_i^*$ to a single column (where $\mathbf{F}_i^*$ are the columns of $\mathbf{F}^*$). Since $h(\cdot)$ is a universal hash function, if $h(\mathbf{F}^*)$ is a subvector of $h(\mathbf{T}^*)$, then with overwhelming probability, $\mathbf{F}^*$ is a submatrix of $\mathbf{T}^*$, thus reducing matrix lookup argument to vector lookup. For the second part, we notice that the first column $\mathbf{F}_1^*$ of $\mathbf{F}^*$ is a *step* function, thus we first commit to the shift of $\mathbf{F}_1^*$ and then show that the difference between the shifted column and the column $\mathbf{F}_1^*$ is a function that has zeros in well-defined positions. More details in Sect. 5.2. The second scheme goes even further and proves that a matrix $\mathbf{F}$ with d' columns and $d' < d$ is a submatrix of $\mathbf{T}$. As before, we set $\mathbf{F}^* = (i, j, \mathbf{F}_{i,j})_{i\in R, j\in D}$ for subset $R = \{r_1, \ldots, r_{d'}\} \subset [N]$ and $D \subset [d]$. Additionally, using the technique of shifted polynomials, $\mathbf{F}^*_{2,id'+j} = \mathbf{F}^*_{2,(i+1)d'+j} = r_j$ for any i, j. More details in in our full version [7, Appendix D].

Our Approach to ZK for Decision Trees. A decision tree is an algorithm that performs a sequence of adaptive queries reading from its input and outputs a value. At each query, the algorithm moves from a node in the tree to one of its children, and the output is defined by the label of the reached leaf. Two important parameters are the total number of nodes N_{tot} and the number of features d of the inputs. Following the work of Chen *et al.* [11], we can efficiently (although redundantly) encode a decision tree as a matrix with N_{tot} rows and $2d + 1$ columns. An evaluation of a decision tree under this alternative representation consists of locating the row corresponding to the correct leaf and then showing that the input vector matches all the constraints described by such a row. Thus, we can commit to a decision tree by committing to its matrix encoding, and to prove correct evaluation, we can commit to the single row corresponding to the correct leaf and prove with a matrix lookup argument that the committed row is indeed a leaf of the committed decision tree. Once isolated such a row, we can then prove that the input vector matches all the constraints described by the row. Notice that our strategy scales well with the number of different evaluations. In fact, to prove statements which involve multiple input vectors for the decision tree, we can commit at proving time to a matrix whose rows correspond to the entries of the leaves reached by the evaluations (instead of committing to a single row). Thanks to the efficiency property of the matrix lookup argument, the prover time complexity is independent of the size of decision trees.

Beyond a Trusted Commitment to the Tree. A malicious committer could commit to a matrix that contains a row that matches a leaf with a label, let's say, 0, and another row that matches the same leaf but where it maliciously assigns the label 1. Now, such a bogus commitment to a decision tree could allow the malicious prover to show both $\mathsf{T}(\mathbf{x}) = 0$ and $\mathsf{T}(\mathbf{x}) = 1$. The problem is that the committed matrix does not *encode* a decision tree. To solve this problem, we show a set of sufficient algebraic conditions (cf. Sect. 6.2) for a matrix to *encode* a decision tree. We can check efficiently these algebraic conditions through a general-purpose zkSNARKs for R1CS (see for example [5,8,21,29,31,33,34]). However, the number of constraints is $O(dN_{\mathsf{tot}}^2)$, and thus the prover time complexity is quadratic in the number of nodes. The algebraic constraints we propose are essentially linear equations between matrices and Hadamard-product equations, which are the kind of equation checks performed in R1CS-based zkSNARKs. In fact, if we gave up on the privacy of the decision tree[2], we could define an R1CS circuit that depends on the tree-structure of the decision tree, and we would go down to $O(dN_{\mathsf{tot}})$ number of constraints. We can restore zero-knowledge using this approach, by privately committing to such an R1CS-like circuit and prove in zero-knowledge that the circuit belongs to a well-defined family of circuits (defined in Sect. 6.2). We use the techniques from Zapico *et al.* [38] for committing to a *basic* matrix, whose rows are elementary vectors, and to prove its basic-matrix structure and the permutation argument from Plonk [19] to prove the rows of the matrix are all different.

1.2 Related Work

Lookup Arguments. Lookup arguments were introduced by Bootle, Cerulli, Groth, Jakobsen and Maller [6]. The state-of-art for lookup arguments for arbitrary tables[3] is the recent work of Eagen, Fiore, Gabizon [14] named cq and based on the technique of logarithmic derivates of Haböck [23]. cq has prover complexity proportional only to the size of the smaller vector and independent of the bigger table assuming pre-processing for table. To our knowledge, all lookup arguments with similar efficiency properties are based on the Kate *et al.* (commonly known as KZG) polynomial commitment scheme [25]. Among these, we mention Caulk+ by Posen and Kattis [32] (based on Caulk [38] by Zapico *et al.*) and Baloo [39] by Zapico *et al.*. The latter work introduces the notion of Commit-and-Prove Checkable Subspace Argument (extending over [33]) that we use for our (extractable) commitment scheme (cf. Sect. 6.3).

Comparison with [14]**.** As previously mentioned, we diverge from cq, introducing several novel ideas that allow us to improve on cq's efficiency. As the end result, cq^+'s communication is about 14% (or even 23% in a variant without the ZK) better than cq's. All other efficiency parameters of cq^+ are similar to cq's. Moreover, we propose cq^{++}, a batched variant of cq^+. cq^{++} saves 23% (or 33%,

2 Specifically, giving up only to the privacy of the *structure of* the decision tree while keeping private the values of the thresholds and labels.

3 Recently, Setty, Thaler and Wahby [35] introduced a new lookup argument for a restricted subclass of tables. Their work is extremely efficient, and in particular more efficient than cq, for such a restricted class of tables. On the other hand, cq can handle arbitrary tables. For this reason, we refer to cq as the state-of-art for arbitrary tables.

in a variant without ZK) communication compared to cq. A slight drawback of cq^{++} is that the verifier has to execute one more pairing. We emphasize that cq is already almost optimally efficient, and thus improving on it is non-trivial.

Concurrent Work. Choudhuri *et al.* [13] very recently introduced the notion of *segment lookup arguments* which, besides some syntactical differences, matches the simpler of our notions of matrix lookup arguments. Additionally, in [13], they show, in our lingo, a matrix lookup argument based on cq. Their matrix lookup argument is less efficient than ours; we defer to Table 1 for more details. Interestingly, in the same paper, the authors build a general-purpose zkSNARK based on Plonk and matrix lookup, which they call Sublonk, showing another application for matrix lookup arguments. The main feature of Sublonk is that the prover's running time grows with the size of the *active part* of the circuit, namely the part of the circuit activated by its execution on a given instance. Sublonk makes black-box use of the underlying matrix lookup argument. Thus, we can plug in our scheme to obtain a more efficient version of Sublonk.

Privacy-Preserving Machine Learning. We focus on the related work on zero-knowledge proofs for decision trees and, more in general, for machine learning algorithms. The main related work for decision trees is the paper of Zhang *et al.* [40], where they introduce the notions of zero-knowledge proofs for decision tree predictions and accuracy. Besides decision trees, zero-knowledge proofs and verifiable computation for machine learning is a vibrant area of research (see for example [1,16,24,26,30,36,37]).

Comparison with [40]**.** Briefly, the main techniques of [40] consist of an authenticated data structure for committing to decision trees and highly-tuned R1CS circuits to evaluate the authenticated data structure in zero-knowledge. More in detail, they commit to a decision tree with a *labelled Merkle Tree* whose labelled nodes are the nodes of the decision tree. This commitment scheme is binding and hiding and allows for path openings (with proof size proportional to the length of the path). On top of this authenticated data structure, they use general-purpose zkSNARKs for R1CS to prove, for example, the knowledge of a valid opening for a path and the labelling of the leaf. While the basic ideas are simple, the paper needs to solve many technical details and presents many optimizations which are necessary to obtain a practical scheme. The *backend* general-purpose zero-knowledge scheme they use is Aurora [5]. Thanks to this choice and because of the Merkle-Tree approach, their zero-knowledge scheme has a transparent setup and is presumably post-quantum secure.

Their security model stipulates that the decision tree is adversarially chosen, but the commitment to a decision tree is honestly generated. On the other hand, in our security model, we require the commitment scheme to be extractable, thus allowing for maliciously generated commitments. Notice that, besides improving security, our definitional choices allow for more efficient design. In fact, the (proof for the) extractable commitment is generated only once, let's say in an offline phase, while the (multiple) proofs of evaluation, in the online phase, can leverage extra security properties offered by the extractable commitment and thus faster.

For comparison with our work, we consider the extractability of their scheme for decision tree evaluation. This is not immediate: the main reason is that the witness for the zkSNARK is a single path from the root to the evaluated leaf (which could be extracted) while, to obtain our notion of extractability, it would be required to extract the full decision tree. Additionally, their authenticated data structure could allow to commit (and prove statements) to 2-fan-in direct-acyclic graphs (DAGs), which are more general than trees[4]. We believe their second scheme for the accuracy of decision trees can be proved secure in our model. In fact, proposed as an efficiency optimization, their second scheme computes a consistency check over the full decision tree. Thanks to this, we could extract the full tree from the zkSNARK. We also believe that our techniques could be integrated into theirs. Our approach separating the extractable commitment from the "online-stage" of the zero-knowledge proof could be adapted to their scheme for accuracy (thus improving its efficiency). Interestingly, by using our approach, their scheme could be interpreted as an application of a lookup argument based on [5,6] to decision trees. The main difference is this: our scheme runs lookup arguments over the leaves associated with the evaluation vectors, while the scheme in [40] requires lookups for paths from the root to the leaves associated with the evaluation vectors.

For other points of comparison efficiency-wise (we refer the reader to Sect. 6.5 for more details), we mention that their commitments require hashing only, while ours requires multiexponentations in a group. Therefore, their commitment stage is faster than ours. Our proof size is concretely smaller (few kilobytes vs hundreds of kilobytes). To compare proving time, we start from observing the asymptotic advantages of our solutions: their prover is linear in the size of the tree and in the complexity of a hash function; ours is sublinear in all these dimensions. This results in *concretely* faster proving times *despite* the fact that our prover requires group operations and theirs only field operations. This is a consequence of removing the constants deriving from the hash function size, the sublinearity in the tree and of the efficient lookup argument instantiations[5]. Our improvements also translate to a better verification time. Our estimates show improvements of almost one order of magnitude for proving time (regardless of the underlying backend proof systems for [40]; see [7, Appendix A]) and two orders of magnitude for verification time.

2 Preliminaries

We denote matrices with capital and bold, for example, $\mathbf{M}$, and vectors with lowercase and bold, for example, $\mathbf{v}$. We denote with $\circ$ the Hadamard product

[4] We believe that this does not pose any problems neither for correctness nor for soundness, as indeed, one could argue this is a feature rather than a bug.

[5] As a bottleneck, the dependency [40] has on the hash function is one that is hard to remove. Applying a hash function optimized for SNARK constraints, e.g. the one we used to experimentally run [40]—SWIFFT—*nonetheless* yields high constants in practice *regardless* of the proof system used as a backend.

between two matrices/vectors of the same size, while $\cdot$ is reserved for the matrix-vector/vector-vector multiplication. Given two vectors $\mathbf{a}, \mathbf{b}$ we define $\mathbf{a} < \mathbf{b}$ if and only if $\forall i : \mathbf{a}_i < \mathbf{b}_i$ (and similarly for $\leq$). We denote $\|$ the concatenation by columns of two matrices. We denote by $\mathbb{F}$ a finite field, by $\mathbb{F}[X]$ the ring of univariate polynomials, and by $\mathbb{F}_{<d}[X]$ (resp. $\mathbb{F}_{\leq d}[X]$) the set of polynomials in $\mathbb{F}[X]$ of degree $< d$ (resp. $\leq d$). For any subset $S \subseteq \mathbb{F}$, we denote by $\nu_S(X) \stackrel{\text{def}}{=} \prod_{s \in S}(X - s)$ the *vanishing polynomial* of S, and by $\lambda_s^S(X)$ the *s-th Lagrange basis polynomial*, which is the unique polynomial of degree at most $|S| - 1$ such that for any $s' \in S$, it evaluates to 1 if $s = s'$ and to 0 otherwise. Any multiplicative subgroup of a finite field is cyclic. Thus, given a group $\mathbb{H}$, we can find an element ω that generates the subgroup $\mathbb{H}$. For convenience, given a subgroup $\mathbb{H}$ of order n we denote with ω_n a fixed generator of $\mathbb{H}$. If $\mathbb{H} \subseteq \mathbb{F}$ is a multiplicative subgroup of order n, then its vanishing polynomial has a compact representation $\nu_{\mathbb{H}}(X) = (X^n - 1)$ and $\lambda_i^{\mathbb{H}}(X) = \nu_{\mathbb{H}}(X)\omega_n^{i-1}/(n(X - \omega_n^{i-1}))$. Both $\nu_{\mathbb{H}}(X)$ and $\lambda_i^{\mathbb{H}}(X)$ can be evaluated in $O(\log n)$ field operations. For any vector $\mathbf{v} \in \mathbb{F}^n$, we denote by $v_{\mathbb{H}}(X)$ the *low degree encoding* (LDE) in $\mathbb{H}$ of $\mathbf{v}$, i.e., the unique degree-($|\mathbb{H}| - 1$) polynomial such that, $v_{\mathbb{H}}(\omega_n^{i-1}) = v_i$, when the subgroup $\mathbb{H}$ is clear from the context, we simply write $v(X)$. Similarly, we consider the k-degree *randomized low-degree encoding* (RLDE) in $\mathbb{H}$ of a vector $\mathbf{v} \in \mathbb{F}^n$ to be a randomized polynomial of the form $\hat{v}_{\mathbb{H}}(X) = v_{\mathbb{H}}(X) + \nu_{\mathbb{H}}(X)\rho_v(X)$ for a random polynomial ρ_v of degree k. Sometimes, we will not explicitly mention the degree of the randomizer. In this case, the reader should assume that the degree is set to be the minimum degree necessary to keep zero-knowledge of v in the presence of evaluations (on points outside of $\mathbb{H}$) of the polynomial $\hat{v}$.

A type-3 bilinear group $\mathbb{G}$ is a tuple $(q, \mathbb{G}_1, \mathbb{G}_2, \mathbb{G}_T, e, P_1, P_2)$. $\mathbb{G}_1, \mathbb{G}_2$ and $\mathbb{G}_T$ are groups of prime order q. P_1, P_2 are generators of $\mathbb{G}_1, \mathbb{G}_2$. $e \colon \mathbb{G}_1 \times \mathbb{G}_2 \to \mathbb{G}_T$ is an efficiently-computable non-degenerate bilinear map, and there is no efficiently computable isomorphism between $\mathbb{G}_1$ and $\mathbb{G}_2$. We use the implicit notation $[a]_i := aP_i$, for elements in $\mathbb{G}_i, i \in \{1, 2, T\}$ and set $P_T := e(P_1, P_2)$.

Definition 1 (Power Discrete Logarithm [27]**).** *Let* $d_1(\lambda), d_2(\lambda) \in \mathsf{poly}(\lambda)$. *A bilinear group generator* $\mathsf{GroupGen}$ *is* (d_1, d_2)-PDL (Power Discrete Logarithm) secure *if for any non-uniform PPT* $\mathcal{A}$, $\mathsf{Adv}^{\mathsf{pdl}}_{d_1,d_2,\mathsf{GroupGen},\mathcal{A}}(\lambda) :=$

$$\Pr\left[\mathsf{pp} \leftarrow \mathsf{GroupGen}(1^\lambda); s \leftarrow\!\!\$\ \mathbb{F}^* : \mathcal{A}\left(\mathsf{pp}, \left[(s^i)_{i=0}^{d_1}\right]_1, \left[(s^i)_{i=0}^{d_2}\right]_2\right) = s\right] = \mathsf{negl}(\lambda).$$

2.1 Commit-and-Prove SNARKs

A commitment scheme is a tuple of algorithm $\mathsf{CS} = (\mathsf{KGen}, \mathsf{Com})$ where the first algorithm samples a commitment key ck and the second algorithm, upon input of the commitment key, a message p and opening material ρ, outputs a commitment c. The basic notions of security for the commitment scheme are (perfect) *hiding* and (computational) *binding*.

Following Groth *et al.* [22], we define a relation $\mathcal{R}$ verifying triple $(\mathsf{pp}; x; w)$. We say that w is a witness to the instance x being in the relation defined by the parameters pp when $(\mathsf{pp}; x; w) \in \mathcal{R}$ (equivalently, we sometimes write $\mathcal{R}(\mathsf{pp}; x; w) = 1$). For example, the parameters pp could be the description of a bilinear group, or additionally contain a commitment key for a commitment scheme or a common reference string. Whenever it is clear of the context, we will write $\mathcal{R}(x; w)$ as a shortcut for $\mathcal{R}(\mathsf{pp}; x; w)$.

Briefly speaking, Commit-and-Prove SNARKs (CP-SNARKs) are zkSNARKs whose relations verify predicates over commitments [9]. Given a commitment scheme CS, we consider relations $\mathcal{R}$ whose instances are of the form $x = ((\mathsf{c}_j)_{j\in[\ell]}, \hat{x})$, where we can un-ambiguously parse the witness $w = ((p_j)_{j\in[\ell]}, (\rho_j)_{j\in[\ell]})$ for some $\ell \in \mathbb{N}$ with $\forall j : p_j$ is in the domain of a commitment scheme CS, and such that there exists a PT relation $\hat{\mathcal{R}}$ such that let $\hat{w} = (p_j)_{j\in[\ell]}$:

$$\mathcal{R}(\mathsf{pp}; x; w) = 1 \iff \hat{\mathcal{R}}(\mathsf{pp}; \hat{x}; \hat{w}) = 1 \wedge \forall j \in [\ell] : \mathsf{c}_j = \mathsf{Com}(\mathsf{ck}, p_j, \rho_j).$$

We refer to a relation $\hat{\mathcal{R}}$ as derived above as a *Commit-and-Prove* (CP) relation. Given a CP-relation $\hat{\mathcal{R}}$ and a commitment scheme CS, we can easily derive the *associated* NP-relation $\mathcal{R}$. Instances of NP-relations may contain only commitments. Therefore, using the notation above, the instances of the associated CP-relation are empty strings ε, namely, $\hat{\mathcal{R}}$ is a predicate over the committed witness. To avoid cluttering the notation, in these cases, we may omit the (empty) instance and simply write $\hat{\mathcal{R}}(\mathsf{pp}, \hat{w})$.

A CP-SNARK for $\hat{\mathcal{R}}$ and commitment scheme CS is a zkSNARK for the associated relation $\mathcal{R}$ as described above. More in detail, we consider a tuple of algorithms $\mathsf{CP} = (\mathsf{KGen}, \mathsf{Prove}, \mathsf{Verify})$ where:

- $\mathsf{KGen}(\mathsf{ck}) \to \mathsf{srs}$ is a probabilistic algorithm that takes as input a commitment key ck for CS and it outputs $\mathsf{srs} := (\mathsf{ek}, \mathsf{vk}, \mathsf{pp})$, where ek is the evaluation key, vk is the verification key, and pp are the parameters for the relation $\mathcal{R}$ (which include the commitment key ck).
- $\mathsf{Prove}(\mathsf{ek}, x, w) \to \pi$ takes an evaluation key ek, a statement x, and a witness w such that $\mathcal{R}(\mathsf{pp}, x, w)$ holds, and returns a proof π.
- $\mathsf{Verify}(\mathsf{vk}, x, \pi) \to b$ takes a verification key, a statement x, and either accepts $(b = 1)$ or rejects $(b = 0)$ the proof π.

In some cases, the KGen algorithm would simply (and deterministically) re-parse the commitment key ck information. In these cases, we might omit KGen and refer to the CP-SNARK as a tuple of two algorithms.

Zero-Knowledge in the SRS (and RO) Model. The zero-knowledge simulator $\mathcal{S}$ of a CP-SNARK is a stateful PPT algorithm that can operate in three modes. $(\mathsf{srs}, \mathsf{st}_\mathcal{S}) \leftarrow \mathcal{S}(0, 1^\lambda, d)$ takes care of generating the parameters and the simulation trapdoor (if necessary). $(\pi, \mathsf{st}_\mathcal{S}) \leftarrow \mathcal{S}(1, \mathsf{st}_\mathcal{S}, x)$ simulates the proof for a statement x. $(a, \mathsf{st}_\mathcal{S}) \leftarrow \mathcal{S}(2, \mathsf{st}_\mathcal{S}, s)$ takes care of answering random oracle queries. The state $\mathsf{st}_\mathcal{S}$ is shared and updated after each operation. We define zero-knowledge similarly to [15,20]:

Definition 2 (Zero-Knowledge). *We say that a CP-SNARK* CP *for a CP-relation* $\hat{\mathcal{R}}$ *and commitment scheme* CS *is (perfect) zero-knowledge if there exists a PPT simulator* $\mathcal{S}$ *such that for all adversaries* $\mathcal{A}$ *and for all* $d \in \mathbb{N}$*:*

$$\Pr\left[\begin{array}{l}\mathsf{ck} \leftarrow \mathsf{CS.KGen}(1^\lambda, d)\\ \mathsf{srs} \leftarrow \mathsf{CP.KGen}(\mathsf{ck})\\ \mathcal{A}^{\mathsf{Prove}(\mathsf{srs},\cdot,\cdot),\mathsf{RO}(\cdot)}(\mathsf{srs}) = 1\end{array}\right] \approx \Pr\left[\begin{array}{l}(\mathsf{srs}, \mathsf{st}_\mathcal{S}) \leftarrow \mathcal{S}(0, \mathsf{pp}_\mathbb{G})\\ \mathcal{A}^{\mathcal{S}_1(\cdot,\cdot),\mathcal{S}_2(\cdot)}(\mathsf{srs}) = 1\end{array}\right]$$

where $\mathcal{S}_1, \mathcal{S}_2$ *are stateful (wrapper) algorithms that share their state* $\mathsf{st} = (\mathsf{st}_\mathcal{S}, \mathcal{Q}_{\mathsf{RO}})$ *where* $\mathsf{st}_\mathcal{S}$ *is initially set to be the empty string, and* $\mathcal{Q}_{\mathsf{RO}}$ *is initially set to be the empty set, such that:*

- $\mathcal{S}_1(x, w)$ *denotes an oracle that first checks* $(\mathsf{pp}, x, w) \in \mathcal{R}$ *where* pp *is part of* srs *and then runs the first output of* $\mathcal{S}(1, \mathsf{st}_\mathcal{S}, x)$*.*
- $\mathcal{S}_2(s)$ *denotes an oracle that first checks if the query* s *is already present in* $\mathcal{Q}_{\mathsf{RO}}$ *and in case answers accordingly, otherwise it returns the first output* a *of* $\mathcal{S}(2, \mathsf{st}_\mathcal{S}, s)$*. The oracle updates* $\mathcal{Q}_{\mathsf{RO}}$ *by adding the tuple* (s, a) *to the set.*

Knowledge Soundness. Our definition of knowledge soundness is in the algebraic group model [17]. An algorithm $\mathcal{A}$ is called *algebraic* if for all group elements that $\mathcal{A}$ outputs, it additionally provides the representation relative to all previously received group elements. That is, if elems is the list of group elements that $\mathcal{A}$ has received, then for any group element z in output, the adversary must also provide a vector $\mathbf{r}$ such that $\mathsf{z} = \langle \mathbf{r}, \mathsf{elems}\rangle$. We define the notion of knowledge soundness in the algebraic model.

Definition 3 (Knowledge Soundness in the AGM). *A CP-SNARK is knowledge extractable in the Algebraic Group Model if for any PT algebraic adversary, there exists a PT extractor* $\mathcal{E}$ *that receives in input the algebraic representations* $\mathbf{r}_1, \ldots, \mathbf{r}_l$ *of* $\mathcal{A}$ *and such that:*

$$\Pr\left[\begin{array}{l}\mathsf{ck} \leftarrow \mathsf{CS.KGen}(1^\lambda, d); \mathsf{srs} \leftarrow \mathsf{CP.KGen}(\mathsf{ck});\\ (x, \pi, \mathbf{r}_1, \ldots, \mathbf{r}_l) \leftarrow \mathcal{A}(\mathsf{srs}); w \leftarrow \mathcal{E}(\mathsf{srs}, \mathbf{r}_1, \ldots, \mathbf{r}_l)\\ \mathsf{Verify}(\mathsf{srs}, x, \pi) \wedge \neg\mathcal{R}(\mathsf{pp}, x, w)\end{array}\right] \leq \mathsf{negl}(\lambda)$$

Indexed Relations and Universal CP-SNARKs. We extend the notion of relations to indexed relations [12]. We define a PT indexed relation $\mathcal{R}$ verifying tuple (pp, ind, x, w). We say that w is a witness to the instance x being in the relation defined by the pp and index ind when $(\mathsf{pp}, ind, x, w) \in \mathcal{R}$ (equivalently, we sometimes write $\mathcal{R}(\mathsf{pp}, ind, x, w) = 1$).

Briefly, we say that a CP-SNARK is *universal* if there exists a deterministic algorithm Der that takes as input an srs and an index ind, and outputs a specialized reference string $\mathsf{srs}_{ind} = (\mathsf{vk}_{ind}, \mathsf{ek}_{ind})$ where vk_{ind} is a succinct verification key and ek_{ind} is a proving key for such an index. Moreover, we require that the verifier Verify (resp. the P) of a Universal CP-SNARK takes as additional input the specialized verification key vk_{ind} (resp. the specialized ek_{ind}). We refer to [7, Appendix B] for more details.

2.2 Extractable Commitment Schemes

An extractable commitment scheme for a domain $\mathcal{D} = \{\mathcal{D}_\lambda\}_\lambda$ is a commitment scheme equipped with a CP-SNARK that proves the knowledge of an opening of the commitments.

Definition 4. *Given a domain* $\mathcal{D}$, $\mathsf{CS} = (\mathsf{KGen}, \mathsf{Com}, \mathsf{VerCom})$ *is an extractable commitment scheme for the domain* $\mathcal{D}$ *if there exist two algorithms* $\mathsf{Com}', \mathsf{Prove}'$ *such that* $\mathsf{Com}(\mathsf{ck}, p, \rho)$ *executes (1)* $\mathsf{c} \leftarrow \mathsf{Com}'(\mathsf{ck}, p, \rho)$ *and (2)* $\pi \leftarrow \mathsf{Prove}'(\mathsf{ck}, \mathsf{c}, (p, \rho))$ *and outputs* (c, π)*, and* $(\mathsf{Prove}', \mathsf{VerCom})$ *is a CP-SNARK for the commitment scheme* $(\mathsf{KGen}, \mathsf{Com}')$ *and for the CP-Relation* $\hat{\mathcal{R}}_{\mathsf{open}}$ *defined below:*

$$\hat{\mathcal{R}}_{\mathsf{open}} = \{\mathsf{pp}; \varepsilon; p : p \in \mathcal{D}_\lambda\}.$$

2.3 Polynomial, Vector and Matrix Commitment Schemes

We use the KZG polynomial commitment scheme of [25] described below:

$\mathsf{KGen}(1^\lambda, d_1, d_2)$ samples a type-3 pairing group with security level λ and outputs commitment key $\mathsf{ck} := (([s^i]_1)_{i\in[d_1]}, ([s^i]_2)_{i\in[d_2]},)$ for random secrets $s \in \mathbb{Z}_q$.
$\mathsf{Com}(\mathsf{ck}, p)$ outputs $[p(s)]_1$.

We notice that the above commitment scheme is not hiding and it is extractable[6] for the domain of polynomial of degree d_1 in the algebraic group model of [17] under the power discrete logarithm assumption (PDL), which informally states that find s is hard given a freshly sampled commitment key, see Definition 1 for details. The commitment scheme allows for a very efficient CP-SNARK $\Pi_{\mathsf{eval}} = (\mathsf{Prove}_{\mathsf{eval}}, \mathsf{Verify}_{\mathsf{eval}})$ for the CP-relation $\hat{\mathcal{R}}_{\mathsf{eval}} = \{(x, y; p) \colon p(x) = y\}$. In particular, the prover $\mathsf{Prove}_{\mathsf{eval}}$ upon input the SRS ck, an instance $([p(s)]_1, x, y)$ and the witness p, computes the unique polynomial $w(X) = (p(X) - y)/(X - x)$ and outputs $[w(s)]_1$ as its proof. On the other hand, the verifier $\mathsf{Verify}_{\mathsf{eval}}$ upon input the SRS ck, an instance (c, x, y) and a proof π, checks $e(\mathsf{c} - [y]_1, [1]_2) = e(\pi, [s - x]_2)$.

Vector and Matrix Commitment Schemes. From a polynomial commitment scheme, we can define a *vector* commitment. Specifically, let $\mathbb{H}$ be multiplicative subgroup of $\mathbb{F}$ with order N, and let ω_N be a fixed generator of $\mathbb{H}$. We can commit to vector $\mathbf{v}$ by committing to the low degree encoding of v over $\mathbb{H}$. Namely, $[v_{\mathbb{H}}(s)]_1$ is a commitment to $\mathbf{v}$. The commitment key should additionally contain the description of the subgroup $\mathbb{H}$ to allow for verification. Notice that

[6] As argued in [8], we can define a *vacuous* CP-SNARK for opening in the AGM where the prover does nothing and the verifier checks that the commitment is a valid group element. However, Lipmaa et al. [28] recently defined AGMOS, a more realistic variant of the AGM where the algebraic adversary can obliviously sample group elements. They pointed out that KZG is only extractable after the prover has successfully opened the commitment at some point. In this case, such a vacuous CP-SNARK is not sufficient. We leave it to further work to prove the security of our protocols in AGMOS.

such a commitment scheme is not hiding. We can make it hiding by committing to a RLDE of v over $\mathbb{H}$ instead of its LDE.

We define the *vectorization* of a matrix $\mathbf{M} \in \mathbb{F}^{n \times d}$ to be the vector $\bar{\mathbf{m}} \in \mathbb{F}^{n \cdot d}$ which is the concatenation of the rows of $\mathbf{M}$. Namely, for any $i \in [n], j \in [d]$, we define $\bar{\mathbf{m}}_{d \cdot i+j} = \mathbf{M}_{i,j}$. To commit to a matrix $\mathbf{M}$, we commit to its vectorization $\bar{\mathbf{m}}$. Notice that, additionally, the commitment key should contain the values n and d, and the subgroup $\mathbb{H}$ should be of cardinality $n \cdot d$.

3 Zero-Knowledge Matrix Lookup Arguments

Given two vectors $\mathbf{f}, \mathbf{t}$, we say that $\mathbf{f}$ is a *sub-vector* of $\mathbf{t}$ if there exits a (multi) set $K = \{k_1, \ldots, k_n\}$ such that $\mathbf{f}_j = \mathbf{t}_{k_j}$ for any j. We write $\mathbf{f} \prec \mathbf{t}$ to denote that $\mathbf{f}$ is a sub-vector of $\mathbf{t}$. Notice we diverge from the usual notion of sub-vector. Namely, we assume that a sub-vector $\mathbf{f}$ may contain multiple copies of an element in $\mathbf{t}$ and, moreover, any permutation of $\mathbf{f}$ is a sub-vector of $\mathbf{t}$. We extend the notion of sub-vectors to matrices. We say that a matrix $\mathbf{F} \in \mathbb{F}^{n \times d}$ is a (rows) sub-matrix of a matrix $\mathbf{T} \in \mathbb{F}^{N \times d}$ if $\mathbf{F}$ parsed as a $\mathbb{F}^d$-vector of length n is a sub-vector of $\mathbf{T}$ parsed as a $\mathbb{F}^d$-vector of length N. In other words, $\mathbf{F}$ is a matrix whose rows are also rows in $\mathbf{T}$. Similarly, given a multi set $K = \{k_1, \ldots, k_l\}$ we can define the sub-matrix $\mathbf{F}_{|K}$ as the sub-matrix of $\mathbf{F}$ which j-th row is the row $\mathbf{F}_{k_j}$. Notice that our notion of sub-matrix is not standard. Besides the differences mentioned for the notion of sub-vector, we consider the special case where the number of columns of $\mathbf{F}$ and $\mathbf{T}$ are the same. This is sufficient for our application. However, for completeness, in [7, Appendix D.1], we consider the more general case where $\mathbf{F}$ may be a selection of a projection of $\mathbf{T}$. We call the latter the rows-columns sub-matrix relationship. We consider the following indexed CP-relation, where we will refer to $\mathbf{T}$ as the table and to $\mathbf{F}$ as the sub-vector (or sub-matrix):

$$\hat{\mathcal{R}}_{\mathsf{zklkp}} := \{\mathsf{pp}; (N, d, n); \varepsilon; (\mathbf{T}, \mathbf{F}) : \mathbf{F} \prec \mathbf{T}, |\mathbf{T}| = N \times d, |\mathbf{F}| = n \times d\}, \quad (1)$$

Previous work focuses on $d = 1$, namely the lookup argument for vector commitments, where the table $\mathbf{T}$ is public. Moreover, some of the previous work did not focus on zero-knowledge. Namely, previous work focused on (ZK or not) CP-SNARKs for the following CP-relation:

$$\hat{\mathcal{R}}_{\mathsf{lkp}} := \{\mathsf{pp}; (\mathbf{t}, n); \varepsilon; \mathbf{f} : \mathbf{f} \prec \mathbf{t}, |\mathbf{f}| = n\}. \quad (2)$$

A *fully* zero-knowledge lookup argument for a commitment scheme CS is a CP-SNARK for the CP-relation $\hat{\mathcal{R}}_{\mathsf{zklkp}}$ and for the commitment scheme CS. We use the adjective fully zero-knowledge to distinguish our definition from the definition from previous work. State-of-the-art lookup arguments have prover time complexity independent of the length of the table and quasi-linear (or even linear) on the length of the sub-vector. To obtain such a property, all the lookup arguments for arbitrary tables in previous work precompute the table $\mathbf{T}$, producing auxiliary material that is then used during the proving phase. Thus, using the notational framework of Universal SNARK, the precomputation is handled by the Der algorithm (since $\mathbf{t}$ is in the index).

Definition 5. *A tuple of algorithm* $\mathsf{CP} = (\mathsf{KGen}, \mathsf{Der}, \mathsf{Prove}, \mathsf{Verify})$ *is a lookup argument for a commitment scheme* CS *if (1)* CP *forms a CP-SNARK for* $\hat{\mathcal{R}}_{\mathsf{lkp}}$ *and* CS*, (2)* Der *is a* $\mathbb{F}$*-linear function (with respect to the proving key in its output) and the commitment scheme is linearly homomorphic and (3)* Prove *has running time* $\mathsf{poly}(n, \lambda)$.

We define an additional algorithm $\mathsf{Preproc}$ to handle our stronger privacy requirement. Similarly to Der, the algorithm $\mathsf{Preproc}$ performs an offline preprocessing — both algorithms are necessary *only* for speeding up the proving and verification algorithms. The difference is that Der works over *public* information, meanwhile $\mathsf{Preproc}$ works over *private* information[7].

Definition 6. *A tuple of algorithm* $\mathsf{CP} = (\mathsf{KGen}, \mathsf{Der}, \mathsf{Preproc}, \mathsf{Prove}, \mathsf{Verify})$ *is a fully zero-knowledge lookup argument for a matrix commitment scheme* CS *if (1)* $(\mathsf{KGen}, \mathsf{Der}, \mathsf{Prove}', \mathsf{Verify})$ *forms a CP-SNARK for* $\hat{\mathcal{R}}_{\mathsf{zklkp}}$ *and* CS *where* Prove' *is the algorithm that upon witness* $(\mathbf{T}, \mathbf{F}, \rho_T, \rho_M)$ *such that* $\mathbf{T}_{|K} = \mathbf{F}$ *first runs* $(\mathsf{aux}_j)_{j\in[N]} \leftarrow \mathsf{Preproc}(\mathsf{srs}, \mathbf{T}, \rho_T)$ *and then runs* Prove *with witness* $(\mathbf{F}, \rho_M, (\mathsf{aux}_j)_{j\in K}))$*; (2)* $\mathsf{Preproc}$ *is a* $\mathbb{F}$*-linear function and the commitment scheme is linearly homomorphic and (3)* Prove *has running time* $\mathsf{poly}(nd, \lambda)$.

4 Our New Zero-Knowledge Lookup Arguments

In this section, we present our new lookup arguments for KZG-based vector commitments. Let the commitment $\mathsf{c_t}$ and $\mathsf{c_f}$, to the vectors $\mathbf{t}$ and $\mathbf{f}$ respectively, be KZG commitments to randomized low-degree encodings of $\mathbf{t}$ and $\mathbf{f}$. We denote these polynomials $\mathsf{T}(X)$ and $\mathsf{F}(X)$, respectively. Since $\mathbf{t}$ and $\mathbf{f}$ have different sizes, we interpolate them over two multiplicative subgroups of $\mathbb{F}$: $\mathbb{K}$ of order N and $\mathbb{H}$ of order $n \le N$. In our construction, we need $n \mid N$; however, this usually holds in practice where both n and N are powers of two. Hence, we have

$$\mathsf{T}(X) := \sum_{j=1}^{N} \mathsf{t}_j \lambda_j^{\mathbb{K}}(X) + \rho_{\mathsf{T}} \cdot \nu_{\mathbb{K}}(X), \quad \mathsf{F}(X) := \sum_{i=1}^{n} \mathbf{f}_i \lambda_i^{\mathbb{H}}(X) + \rho_{\mathsf{F}}(X) \cdot \nu_{\mathbb{H}}(X)$$

Above, $\rho_{\mathsf{F}}(X)$ is a random polynomial of degree $< \mathsf{b}_F$ so that $\mathsf{c_f} = [\mathsf{F}(s)]_1$ is perfectly hiding. Furthermore, our lookup arguments work (and are zero-knowledge) for any choice of $\mathsf{b}_F \ge 0$; this property matters whenever the commitment $\mathsf{c_f}$ is generated by other protocols with their own zero-knowledge requirements (e.g., $\mathsf{c_f}$ may come from a SNARK construction where b_F is carefully set to meet the number of leaked evaluations of $\mathsf{F}(X)$ in that protocol). Our lookup arguments achieve zero knowledge without leaking additional evaluations of $\mathsf{F}(X)$.

On the other hand, if $\rho_{\mathsf{T}} \leftarrow\$ \mathbb{F}$ is a random field element, then $\mathsf{c_t} = [\mathsf{T}(s)]_1$ is a perfectly hiding commitment to $\mathbf{t}$. Otherwise, if $\rho_{\mathsf{T}} = 0$, we capture the case of public tables (that is the common use case of lookup arguments).

---

[7] Alternatively, one could define one single algorithm Der that handles both public and private data. In this case, one needs to redefine the Universal SNARK's framework to handle zero knowledge correctly. Our definition instead is only functional as we require that $\mathsf{Preproc}$, Prove form a two-step prover algorithm for a Universal SNARK.

Lemma 1 (Set inclusion, [23]). *Let $\mathbb{F}$ be a field of characteristic $p > N$, and suppose that $(a_i)_{i=1}^N$, $(b_i)_{i=1}^N$ are arbitrary sequences of field elements. Then $\{a_i\} \subseteq \{b_i\}$ as sets (with multiples of values removed), if and only if there exists a sequence $(m_i)_{i=1}$ of field elements from $\mathbb{F}_p \subseteq \mathbb{F}$ such that*

$$\sum_{i=1}^N \frac{1}{X-a_i} = \sum_{i=1}^N \frac{m_i}{X-b_i} \tag{3}$$

in the function field $\mathbb{F}(X)$. Moreover, we have equality of the sets $\{a_i\} = \{b_i\}$, if and only if $m_i \neq 0$, for every $i = 1, \ldots, N$.

Roadmap. For the sake of presentation, we first describe our main lookup argument cq^+, which works for a public table $\mathbf{t}$, thus meeting Definition 5. This protocol is fully described in Fig. 1 and explained in the next section. Next, we discuss an optimized variant, cq^{++}. Finally, in Sect. 4.2 we show how to obtain the protocol meeting the fully zero-knowledge notion of Definition 6.

4.1 cq^+ Lookup Argument

For ease of exposition, we present our protocol as a public coin interactive argument. We can compile it into a CP-SNARK using the Fiat-Shamir heuristic.

Setup. We assume a universal $\mathsf{srs} = (([s^j]_1)_{j=0}^{N_1}, ([s^j]_2)_{j=0}^{N_2}))$ for any $N_1 \geq N + \max(\mathsf{b}_F, 1) - 1$ and $N_2 \geq N + \max(\mathsf{b}_F, 1) + 1$, where b_F is the degree of the randomization polynomial $\rho_{\mathsf{F}}(X)$ explained earlier.

Round 1. Our interactive lookup protocol cq^+ starts the same as cq [14]. Namely, based on Lemma 1, the prover computes the multiplicities vector $\mathbf{m}$ such that $\sum_{j=1}^N \frac{m_j}{\mathsf{t}_j+X} = \sum_{i=1}^n \frac{1}{\mathsf{f}_i+X}$, and sends to the verifier a commitment $[m(s)]_1$ to a randomized low-degree encoding $m(X)$ of $\mathbf{m}$ over $\mathbb{K}$.

Round 2. The verifier sends a random challenge β. At this point, the goal of the prover is to convince the verifier that

$$\sum_{j=1}^N \frac{m_j}{\mathsf{t}_j+\beta} = \sum_{i=1}^n \frac{1}{\mathsf{f}_i+\beta} \tag{4}$$

which, by Schwartz-Zippel, implies the polynomial identity over $\mathbb{F}[X]$ and thus $\mathbf{f} \prec \mathbf{t}$ by Lemma 1. To this end, the prover commits to randomized low-degree encodings of the two vectors containing the terms of the two sums, i.e.,

$$A(X), B(X) \text{ s.t. } A_j = A(\omega_N^{j-1}) = \frac{m_j}{\mathsf{t}_j+\beta} \quad \text{and} \quad B_i = B(\omega_n^{i-1}) = \frac{1}{\mathsf{f}_i+\beta}\ . \tag{5}$$

In order to prove the well-formedness of $A(X)$ and $B(X)$, as in cq, the prover commits to the polynomials $Q_A(X) = (A(X)(\mathsf{T}(X) + \beta) - m(X))/\nu_{\mathbb{K}}(X)$ and $Q_B(X) = (B(X)(\mathsf{F}(X) + \beta) - 1)/\nu_{\mathbb{H}}(X)$. As we discuss later, we compute a commitment to $Q_A(X)$ using the cached quotients technique of [14] to meet the efficiency requirement (3) of Definition 5.

From this Point, Our Protocol Diverges from cq. At this point of the protocol, cq would proceed by applying Aurora's univariate sumcheck on both $A(X)$ and

$B(X)$ to prove the correctness of results $A(0) = \sum_j A(\omega_N^{j-1})/N$ and $B(0) = \sum_i B(\omega_n^{i-1})/n$ and then the verifier would check that the results are equal.

In cq^+, we instead apply Aurora's univariate sumcheck on a scaled sum of $A(X)$ and $B(X)$ and prove that the result is zero. More precisely, we define $C(X) := A(X) - \vartheta^{-1}B(X)\mathsf{z}(X)$ where we denote $\vartheta := N/n$ and $\mathsf{z}(X) := \nu_{\mathbb{K}\setminus\mathbb{H}}(X)$ and use the following lemma (see [7, Appendix C] for its proof).

Lemma 2. *$\sum_{j=0}^{N} A(\omega_N^{j-1}) = \sum_{i=0}^{n} B(\omega_n^{i-1})$ iff $\sum_{j=0}^{N} C(\omega_N^{j-1}) = 0$.*

The lemma relies on the observation that the polynomial $\Delta(X) := \vartheta^{-1}B(X)\mathsf{z}(X)$ encodes over $\mathbb{K}$ the same vector encoded by $B(X)$ over $\mathbb{H}$, i.e., $\left(\frac{1}{\mathsf{f}_i+\beta}\right)_i$, but in different positions; while in the rest of positions it encodes zeros. Thus, $\sum_{j=0}^{N} \Delta(\omega_N^{j-1}) = \sum_{i=0}^{n} B(\omega_n^{i-1})$. Moreover, multiplying $B(X)$ by $\mathsf{z}(X)$ gives us for free a low-degree test on $B(X)$.

Thus, towards proving (4), we use Aurora's sumcheck on $C(X)$ to show

$$\exists R_C(X) \in \mathbb{F}_{\leq N-2}[X],\ Q_C(X) \text{ s.t. } C(X) = R_C(X)X + Q_C(X)\nu_{\mathbb{K}}(X)\ . \quad (6)$$

However, we do not send commitments to these two polynomials but use alternative techniques that allow us to obtain both zero knowledge and an efficient degree check on $R_C(X)$. More precisely, to obtain zero-knowledge, we use the sparse ZK sumcheck technique from Lunar [8]: the prover commits to a polynomial $S(X) := R_S X + \rho_S \nu_{\mathbb{K}}(X)$, with the idea that in the next round we perform a sumcheck on $C(X) + \eta^2 S(X)$, for a random challenge η to be chosen by the verifier in the following round. Actually, although for ease of expositions we introduced the use of $S(X)$ here; this polynomial is computed and committed as $[S(s)]_1$ in round 1. In summary, in round 2, the prover sends $[A(s), B(s), Q_B(s)]_1$.

Round 3. The verifier sends random challenges γ, η. In this round, the prover's goal is to show that

$$A(X)(\mathsf{T}(X) + \beta) - m(X) = Q_A(X)\nu_{\mathbb{K}}(X), \quad (7)$$

$$B(X)(\mathsf{F}(X) + \beta) - 1 = Q_B(X)\nu_{\mathbb{H}}(X), \quad (8)$$

$$A(X) - \vartheta^{-1}B(X)\mathsf{z}(X) + \eta^2 S(X) - (R_C(X) + \eta^2 R_S)X = Q_{C,S}(X)\nu_{\mathbb{K}}(X) \quad (9)$$

where $Q_{C,S}(X) = Q_C(X) + \eta^2\rho_S$ in (9). To prove Eq. (7), we use the cached quotient technique of [14] to compute a commitment $[Q_A(s)]_1$ using n scalar group multiplications (see below).

To prove Eq. (8), notice that we already sent $Q_B(X)$; thus, using a linearization trick and random point evaluations, we set $B_\gamma = B(\gamma)$ and we show $B(X)$ evaluates to B_γ on γ, $D(X) := B_\gamma(\mathsf{F}(X) + \beta) - 1 - Q_B(X)\nu_{\mathbb{H}}(\gamma)$ evaluates at 0 on γ. We batch these claims using the verifier's challenge η. Namely, we send the KZG-evaluation proof $P(X) := ((B(X) - B_\gamma) + \eta D(X))/(X - \gamma)$.

To prove Eq. (9), we apply a novel idea that allows obtaining, for free, a degree check on $R_C(X)$. We set the polynomial $U(X) = (X^\mu - 1)$ where $\mu = N_1 - N + 2$

and ask the prover to send $R^*_C(X) = (R_C(X) + \eta^2 R_S)U(X)$. To balance this, we multiply the rest of Eq. (9) by $U(X)$, obtaining

$$(A(X) - \vartheta^{-1}B(X)\mathsf{z}(X) + \eta^2 S(X))U(X) - R^*_C(X)X = Q_{C,S}(X)\nu_{\mathbb{K}}(X)U(X) \quad (10)$$

To further optimize this, we batch Eqs. (7) and (10) by using the verifier's random challenge η (and multiplying (7) by $U(X)$), finally obtaining:

$$\begin{aligned} A(X) \cdot \mathsf{T}(X)U(X) + ((\beta + \eta)A(X) - m(X) + \eta^2 S(X)) \cdot U(X) \\ - \frac{\eta}{\vartheta}B(X) \cdot \mathsf{z}(X)U(X) - Q(X)\nu_{\mathbb{K}}(X)U(X) = \eta R^*_C(X) \cdot X \quad (11) \end{aligned}$$

The idea of this batching is that after multiplying (7) by $U(X)$, both equations aim to prove that the left-hand side is divisible by $\nu_{\mathbb{K}}(X)$ and thus we can send a single quotient polynomial $Q(X) = Q_A(X) + \eta Q_C(X) + \eta^2 \rho_S$.

To summarize, in round 3, the prover sends $[P(s), R^*_C(s), Q(s)]_1$ and B_γ.

Verification. The verifier proceeds as described in Verify of Fig. 1. The verification Item (ii) is a standard technique to check the batched evaluation proof $[P(s)]_1$. The verification Item (i) instead implements the check of Eq. (11) using pairings. Doing this requires the verifier to have in the verification key the $\mathbb{G}_2$ elements $[\mathsf{T}(s)U(s)]_2$ as well as $[U(s), \mathsf{z}(s)U(s), \nu_{\mathbb{K}}(s)U(s)]_2$. Therefore, we let Der compute all these elements and include them in the verification key.

Prover Efficiency. We discuss how the prover algorithm can be implemented with $O(n)$ scalar multiplications in $\mathbb{G}_1$ and $O(n \log n)$ $\mathbb{F}$ operations. First, one can easily see that by preprocessing the computation of the elements $[\lambda^{\mathbb{K}}_j(s)]_1$ and $[\nu_{\mathbb{K}}(s)]_1$ and by using the n-sparsity of $\mathbf{m}$, it is possible to compute $[m(s), A(s)]_1$ using $2(n+1)$ scalar multiplications. Computing $Q_B(X)$ is the only step that requires time $O(n \log n)$ (in field operations). Computing $[B(s), Q_B(s), P(s)]_1$ requires $\approx 3n$ scalar multiplications.

Computing the commitments $[R^*_C(s)]_1$ and $[Q_A(s)]_1$ with $\approx 2n$ and n scalar multiplications, respectively, can be achieved thanks to the cached quotients and, again, the sparseness of $\mathbf{m}$. Following [14], in Der for $\mathbf{t}$, we compute and store

$$[Q_j(s)]_1 \text{ where } Q_j(X) := \frac{(\mathsf{T}(X) - \mathbf{t}_j)\lambda^{\mathbb{K}}_j(X)}{\nu_{\mathbb{K}}(X)} .$$

Then, we use this auxiliary input to compute, with $n+1$ scalar multiplications,

$$[Q_A(s)]_1 \leftarrow \sum_{m_j \neq 0} A_j \, [Q_j(s)]_1 + [\rho_A(T(s) + \beta) - \rho_m]_1 \ . \quad (12)$$

The correctness of $Q_A(s)$ is due to

$$\begin{aligned} \sum_{j=1}^N A_j Q_j(X) &= \sum_{j=1}^N \frac{A_j(\mathsf{T}(X) - \mathbf{t}_j)\lambda^{\mathbb{K}}_j(X)}{\nu_{\mathbb{K}}(X)} \\ &= \sum_{j=1}^N \frac{A_j(\mathsf{T}(X) + \beta)\lambda^{\mathbb{K}}_j(X)}{\nu_{\mathbb{K}}(X)} - \sum_{j=1}^N \frac{A_j(\mathbf{t}_j + \beta)\lambda^{\mathbb{K}}_j(X)}{\nu_{\mathbb{K}}(X)} \\ &\overset{(5)}{=} (\mathsf{T}(X) + \beta)\sum_{j=1}^N \frac{A_j\lambda^{\mathbb{K}}_j(X)}{\nu_{\mathbb{K}}(X)} - \sum_{j=1}^N \frac{m_j\lambda^{\mathbb{K}}_j(X)}{\nu_{\mathbb{K}}(X)} \\ &= \frac{(A(X) - \rho_A\nu_{\mathbb{K}}(X))(\mathsf{T}(X) + \beta) - m(X) + \rho_m\nu_{\mathbb{K}}(X)}{\nu_{\mathbb{K}}(X)} \\ &= Q_A(X) - \rho_A(T(X) + \beta) + \rho_m \ . \end{aligned}$$

Using a similar technique, in Der we can precompute $\left[(r_j^{\mathbb{K}}(s))_{j=1}^N, (r_i^{\mathbb{H}}(s))_{i=1}^n\right]_1$ where $\left\{r_j^{\mathbb{K}}(X) = \frac{\lambda_j^{\mathbb{K}}(X)-\lambda_j^{\mathbb{K}}(0)}{X} U(X)\right\}_{j\in[N]}$, and $\left\{r_i^{\mathbb{H}}(X) = \frac{\lambda_i^{\mathbb{H}}(X)\mathsf{z}(X)-\lambda_i^{\mathbb{H}}(0)}{X} U(X)\right\}_{i\in[n]}$, and use them to compute $[R_C^*(s)]_1$ in $2n$ scalar multiplications.

Thus, the prover's computation is dominated by $8n$ scalar multiplications, which was also the case in cq that did not achieve zero-knowledge and assumed $A(X)$ to be of degree $< N$.

cq^{++}**: A Variant with a Shorter Proof.** We can further optimize cq^+ by applying one more batching technique that consists of sending a single group element $[P^*(s)]_1 = [P(s) + R_C^*(s)]_1$ and in merging the two verification equations ((i)) and ((ii)) as follows:

$$\begin{aligned}&e\left([A(s)]_1, [\mathsf{T}(s)U(s)(s-\gamma)]_2\right)\cdot e\left(\left[(\beta+\eta)A(s) - m(s) + \eta^2 S(s)\right]_1, [U(s)(s-\gamma)]_2\right)\cdot\\&\quad e\left(\tfrac{\eta}{\vartheta}[B(s)]_1, [\mathsf{z}(s)U(s)(s-\gamma)]_2\right)^{-1}\cdot e\left([Q(s)]_1, [\nu_{\mathbb{K}}(s)U(s)(s-\gamma)]_2\right)^{-1}\cdot\\&\quad e\left(\eta\,[B(s)+\eta D(s) - B_\gamma]_1, [s]_2\right) = e\left(\eta\,[P^*(s)]_1, [s(s-\gamma)]_2\right)\ .\end{aligned}$$

This change also requires some small changes. First, we require in the srs to have $N_2 \geq N + \max(\mathsf{b}_F, 1) + 2$. Second, the verification key $\mathsf{vk}_{N,n}$ computed by Der must include $\left[(s^k U(s), s^k \mathsf{z}(s)U(s), s^k \nu_{\mathbb{K}}(s)U(s))_{k=0}^1\right]_2$. Third, the table-dependent verification key for $\mathbf{t}$ should include $\left[(s^k \mathsf{T}(s)U(s))_{k=0}^1\right]_2$.

Overall Efficiency. Assume that we use a standard curve like BLS12-381, where elements of $\mathbb{G}_1$ (resp., $\mathbb{F}$) are $\mathfrak{g}_1 = 384$ (resp., $\mathfrak{f} = 256$) bits long. Then, in cq^+, the communication is $8\mathfrak{g}_1 + 1\mathfrak{f}$ (3328 bits) and in cq^{++}, $7\mathfrak{g}_1 + 1\mathfrak{f}$ (2944 bits). The prover executes $\approx 8n$ scalar multiplications. Verifier has to execute 5 pairings in cq^+ or 6 in cq^{++}. Importantly, two or three of the pairings are with the standard $\mathbb{G}_2$ element (depending on the variant, $[1, x]_2$ or $\left[1, x, x^2\right]_2$). Hence they can be batched with other pairings in the master protocol and essentially come for free.

If one does not wish ZK, we can remove $[S(s)]_1$ from the argument, and proof size is $7\mathfrak{g}_1 + 1\mathfrak{f}$ (2944 bits) in cq^+, and $6\mathfrak{g}_1 + 1\mathfrak{f}$ (2560 bits) in cq^{++}.

To compare, in cq [14] (that is not ZK), the communication is $8\mathfrak{g}_1 + 3\mathfrak{f}$ (3840 bits), the prover's computation is $\approx 8n$ scalar multiplications, and the verifier has to execute 5 pairings. Hence, even cq^+ (*with* ZK) has better communication than cq (*without* ZK) while having the same cost in the rest of the parameters.

Security. In the following theorem, we argue the security of cq^+ (see [7, Appendix C] for the proof and the definition of the Power Discrete Logarithm (PDL) assumption); the proof of cq^{++} is very similar.

Theorem 1. *The protocol cq^+ from Fig. 1 is a lookup argument according to Definition 5. Specifically, cq^+ is knowledge-sound in the AGM and ROM under the (N_1, N_2)-PDL assumption (see Definition 1), and, furthermore, the protocol is zero-knowledge.*

4.2 Our Fully Zero-Knowledge Lookup Argument

In this setting we have $\mathsf{T}(X) = \sum_{j=1}^{N} = \mathbf{t}_j \lambda_j^{\mathbb{K}}(X) + \rho_{\mathsf{T}} \cdot \nu_{\mathbb{K}}(X)$ where $\rho_{\mathsf{T}} \leftarrow\$ \mathbb{F}$ and $\mathsf{c_t} = [\mathsf{T}(s)]_1$. We need only slight modifications to turn cq^+ to a fully zero-knowledge lookup argument. We refer to the modified lookup argument as zkcq^+. First, we defer, from Der to $\mathsf{Preproc}$, the computation of all the *table-dependent* group elements. Namely, $\mathsf{Preproc}(\mathsf{srs}, \mathbf{t}, \rho_{\mathsf{T}})$ computes $([Q_j(s))]_1)_{j=1}^{N}$ and $\tilde{\mathsf{c}}_{\mathsf{t}} \leftarrow [\mathsf{T}(s)U(s)]_2$. The latter group element is included as part of the proof at proving time by the algorithm Prove. As consequence, Verify needs to additionally run the pairing check $e([1]_1, \tilde{\mathsf{c}}_{\mathsf{t}}) = e(\mathsf{c_t}, [U(s)]_2)$ to verify the well-formedness of the commitment $\mathsf{c_t}$. In the proof of knowledge soundness, this check allows us to

---

$\mathsf{Der}(\mathsf{srs}, \mathbf{t}, n)$: // Assume that $|\mathbf{t}| = N = |\mathbb{K}|$, $n = |\mathbb{H}|$ and $n \mid N$, $\mathsf{srs} = ([(s^j)_{j \in [N_1]}]_1, [(s^j)_{j \in [N_2]}]_2)$ for any $N_1, N_2 \geq N + \max(\mathsf{b}_F, 1) - 1$.

Set $\mu = N_1 - N + 2$; define $U(X) := (X^{\mu} - 1)$, $\vartheta = N/n$, and $\mathsf{z}(X) = \nu_{\mathbb{K} \setminus \mathbb{H}}(X)$;

Define $\mathsf{T}(X) := \sum_{j=1}^{N} = \mathbf{t}_j \lambda_j^{\mathbb{K}}(X)$;

Let $\left\{ r_j^{\mathbb{K}}(X) = \frac{\lambda_j^{\mathbb{K}}(X) - \lambda_j^{\mathbb{K}}(0)}{X} U(X) \right\}_{j \in [N]}$, $\left\{ r_i^{\mathbb{H}}(X) = \frac{\lambda_i^{\mathbb{H}}(X)\mathsf{z}(X) - \lambda_i^{\mathbb{H}}(0)}{X} U(X) \right\}_{i \in [n]}$,

and $\left\{ Q_j(X) = \frac{(\mathsf{T}(X) - \mathbf{t}_j)\lambda_j^{\mathbb{K}}(X)}{\nu_{\mathbb{K}}(X)} \right\}_{j \in [N]}$.

Compute $\mathsf{ek}_{\mathbf{t},n} := \left[(r_j^{\mathbb{K}}(s))_{j=1}^{N}, (r_i^{\mathbb{H}}(s))_{i=1}^{n}, U(s), \nu_{\mathbb{K}}(s), s\nu_{\mathbb{K}}(s), (Q_j(s))_{j=1}^{N}, \mathsf{T}(s) \right]_1$;

Compute $\mathsf{vk}_{\mathbf{t},n} := [1, U(s), \mathsf{z}(s)U(s), \nu_{\mathbb{K}}(s)U(s), \mathsf{T}(s)U(s)]_2$;

Return $(\mathsf{ek}_{\mathbf{t},n}, \mathsf{vk}_{\mathbf{t},n})$.

$\mathsf{Prove}(\mathsf{ek}_{N,n}, \mathsf{c_f}, (\mathbf{f}, \rho_{\mathsf{F}}(X)))$: $// \mathsf{c_f} = \left[\sum_i \mathsf{f}_i \lambda_i^{\mathbb{H}}(s) + \rho_{\mathsf{F}}(s) \nu_{\mathbb{H}}(s) \right]_1$, $deg(\rho_{\mathsf{F}}) = \mathsf{b}_F$.

Compute $\mathbf{m} = (m_1, \ldots, m_N)$ s.t. $\forall j : \mathbf{t}_j$ appears m_j times in $\mathbf{f}$; samples $\rho_m \leftarrow\$ \mathbb{F}$;

Compute $[m(s)]_1 \leftarrow \sum_{j=1}^{N} m_j \cdot \left[\lambda_j^{\mathbb{K}}(s) \right]_1 + \rho_m \cdot [\nu_{\mathbb{K}}(s)]_1$; // n scalar mults

Sample $R_S, \rho_S \leftarrow\$ \mathbb{F}$ and compute $[S(s)]_1 \leftarrow R_S \cdot s + \rho_S \cdot \nu_{\mathbb{K}}(s)$;

$\beta \leftarrow \mathsf{RO}(\mathsf{vk}_{N,n} \| (\mathsf{c_t}, \mathsf{c_f}) \| [m(s)]_1)$ //Fiat-Shamir challenge.

Sample $\rho_A \leftarrow\$ \mathbb{F}$, $\rho_B(X) \leftarrow\$ \mathbb{F}_{\leq 1}[X]$;

Let $A_j \leftarrow m_j / (\mathbf{t}_j + \beta)$ $\forall j = 1, \ldots, N$ and $B_i \leftarrow 1/(\mathbf{f}_i + \beta)$ $\forall i = 1, \ldots, n$;

Compute $[A(s)]_1 \leftarrow \sum_{j=1}^{N} A_j \left[\lambda_j^{\mathbb{K}}(s) \right]_1 + \rho_A \cdot [\nu_{\mathbb{K}}(s)]_1$;

Compute $[B(s)]_1 \leftarrow \sum_{i=1}^{n} B_i \left[\lambda_i^{\mathbb{H}}(s) \right]_1 + \rho_B(s) \cdot [\nu_{\mathbb{H}}(s)]_1$;

Compute $Q_B(X) \leftarrow (B(X)(\mathsf{F}(X) + \beta) - 1)/\nu_{\mathbb{H}}(X)$ and $[Q_B(s)]_1$;

$(\gamma, \eta) \leftarrow \mathsf{RO}(\beta \| [A(s), B(s), Q_B(s), S(s)]_1)$;//Fiat-Shamir challenge.

Compute $B_\gamma \leftarrow B(\gamma)$, $D(X) \leftarrow B_\gamma \cdot (\mathsf{F}(X) + \beta) - 1 - Q_B(X)\nu_{\mathbb{H}}(\gamma)$;

Compute $P(X) \leftarrow ((B(X) - B(\gamma)) + \eta D(X))/(X - \gamma)$ and $[P(s)]_1$; // KZG-proof for (8).

Compute $[R_C^*(s)]_1 \leftarrow \sum_{m_j \neq 0} A_j \cdot \left[r_j^{\mathbb{K}}(s) \right]_1 - \vartheta^{-1} \sum_{i=1}^{n} B_i \cdot \left[r_i^{\mathbb{H}}(s) \right]_1 + \eta^2 R_S \cdot [U(s)]_1$

Compute $[Q_A(s)]_1 \leftarrow \sum_{m_j \neq 0} A_j \cdot [Q_j(s)]_1 + [\rho_A(T(s) + \beta) - \rho_m]_1$;

Compute $[Q_C(s)]_1 \leftarrow \left[\rho_A + \vartheta^{-1} \rho_B(s) \right]_1$;

Compute $[Q(s)]_1 \leftarrow [Q_A(s)]_1 + \eta [Q_C(s)]_1 + \eta^2 [\rho_S]_1$;

Return $\pi = ([m(s), S(s), A(s), B(s), Q_B(s), P(s), R_C^*(s), Q(s)]_1, B_\gamma)$.

$\mathsf{Verify}(\mathsf{vk}_{\mathbf{t},n}, \mathsf{c_f}, \pi)$:

Compute $[D(s)]_1 \leftarrow B_\gamma(\mathsf{c_f} + [\beta]_1) - [1]_1 - \nu_{\mathbb{H}}(\gamma) [Q_B(s)]_1$.

Return 1 if and only if the following holds:

(i) $e([A(s)]_1, \mathsf{c_t}) \cdot e((\beta + \eta) \cdot [A(s)]_1 - [m(s)]_1 + \eta^2 [S(s)]_1, [U(s)]_2) \cdot e(\eta/\vartheta \cdot [B(s)]_1, [\mathsf{z}(s)U(s)]_2)^{-1} \cdot e([Q(s)]_1, [\nu_{\mathbb{K}}(s)U(s)]_2)^{-1} = e(\eta \cdot [R_C^*(s)]_1, [x]_2)$,

(ii) $e([B(s)]_1 + \eta [D(s)]_1 - [B_\gamma]_1, [1]_2) = e([P(s)]_1, [s - \gamma]_2)$

Fig. 1. Our zero-knowledge lookup argument cq^+.

ensure that the polynomials extracted from $\mathsf{c_t}$ and $\tilde{\mathsf{c}}_\mathsf{t}$ are of the form $\mathsf{T}^*(X)$ and $\mathsf{T}^*(X)U(X)$ for some $\mathsf{T}^*(X)$; thus, after verifying this we can apply virtually the same proof of Theorem 1.

5 Our Matrix Lookup Argument

We show a compiler from a fully zero-knowledge vector lookup argument for KZG-based vector commitment to a fully zero-knowledge matrix lookup for the (succinct) KZG-based matrix commitment from Sect. 2.3. The same construction applies for lookup argument as in Definition 5.

5.1 The Straw Man Solution

An alternative approach to commit to a matrix is to one-by-one vector commit to its columns. The obvious shortcoming is that the commitment scheme is not succinct in the number of columns. Nonetheless, this approach already results in a matrix lookup argument (under the assumption that the vector commitment is linearly homomorphic). In particular, consider the lookup argument that hashes together the columns $\mathbf{t}_j$ of the table $\mathbf{T}$ and the columns $\mathbf{f}_j$ of the sub-matrix $\mathbf{F}$ using a random challenge ρ computing vectors

$$\mathbf{t}^* = \sum_j \mathbf{t}_j \rho^{j-1} \qquad\qquad \mathbf{f}^* = \sum_j \mathbf{f}_j \rho^{j-1}.$$

Notice that by Schwartz-Zippel lemma we that $\mathbf{f}^* \prec \mathbf{t}^*$ implies $\mathbf{F} \prec \mathbf{T}$ with overwhelming probability. Thus, we could run a vector lookup argument over $(\mathbf{f}^*, \mathbf{t}^*)$, thanks to the linear homomorphic property of the commitment scheme the verifier can compute commitments to $\mathbf{f}^*$ and $\mathbf{t}^*$ and verify the proof. Notice the prover time complexity is $\mathsf{poly}(n, d, \lambda)$ thanks to the $\mathbb{F}$-linearity of the pre-computation algorithm. However, the verification time is linear in in the number of columns. We show in the next section how to restore succinct verification time and commitment size.

5.2 Our Scheme

In Fig. 2 we describe our scheme $\mathsf{mtx}[\mathsf{CP}]$ that runs internally a lookup argument CP for KZG-based vector commitment scheme. The proof of the following theorem is in [7, Appendix D]. In the description of the scheme, we let $\mathbb{K}$ (resp. $\mathbb{H}$) be a multiplicative subgroup of $\mathbb{F}$ of order $N \cdot d$ (resp. of order $n \cdot d$), we let $\omega := \omega_{n \cdot d}$ be the fixed generator for $\mathbb{H}$ and we consider the following matrices and polynomial:

1. the matrix $\mathbf{R} \in \mathbb{F}^{N \times d}$ where $R_{i,j} = i$,
2. for any k the matrix $\mathbf{C}^{(k)} \in \mathbb{F}^{k \times d}$ where $C_{i,j} = j$.
3. Let $\nu_{\bar{\mathbb{H}}}(X)$ be the vanishing polynomial of $\bar{\mathbb{H}} = \{\omega^{d \cdot i + j} : j \in [1, d-1], i \in [n]\}$.

Theorem 2. *The lookup argument* mtx[CP] *defined in Fig. 2 is knowledge-sound in the AGM and ROM under the* $(N\cdot d, N\cdot d)$*-PDL assumption and assuming that* CP *is knowledge-sound. Furthermore, the protocol is zero-knowledge assuming* CP *is zero-knowledge.*

A Row-Column Matrix Lookup Argument. In [7, Appendix D.1] we consider the rows-columns sub-matrix relation where $\mathbf{F} \prec \mathbf{T}$ if and only if there exist (multi)sets $R = \{r_1, \ldots, r_n\}$ and $C = \{c_1, \ldots, c_d\}$ with $\mathbf{F}_{i,j} = \mathbf{T}_{r_i, c_j}$, and give an *rows-columns* matrix-lookup argument system mtx*[CP] for such a relation. Briefly, the main difference with the scheme in this section is that we commit to an additional vector $\bar{\boldsymbol{\sigma}}^C$ which is the concatenation of the vector $(c_1, \ldots, c_d)$ for n times, prove in zero-knowledge its tensor structure, and show that $\bar{\mathbf{f}}^* = \bar{\mathbf{f}} + \rho \cdot \bar{\boldsymbol{\sigma}}^C + \rho^2 \cdot \bar{\boldsymbol{\sigma}}$ is a sub-vector of $\bar{\mathbf{t}}^*$.

$\underline{\mathsf{Der}(\mathsf{srs}, N, d, n)}$:

Let $\bar{\mathbf{f}}, \bar{\mathbf{r}}_N, \bar{\mathbf{c}}_N$ and $\bar{\mathbf{c}}_n$ be vectorizations of the matrices $\mathbf{F}, \mathbf{R}, \mathbf{C}^{(N)}$ and $\mathbf{C}^{(n)}$.
Compute $\mathsf{c}_{r,N} \leftarrow \mathsf{Com}(\mathsf{ck}, \bar{\mathbf{r}}_N)$, $\mathsf{c}_{c,N} \leftarrow \mathsf{Com}(\mathsf{ck}, \bar{\mathbf{c}}_N)$ and $\mathsf{c}_{c,n} \leftarrow \mathsf{Com}(\bar{\mathbf{c}}_n)$.
Compute $(\mathsf{ek}', \mathsf{vk}') \leftarrow \mathsf{CP.Der}(\mathsf{srs}, Nd, nd)$.
Return $(\mathsf{ek}', \mathsf{vk}_n)$ where $\mathsf{vk}_n = (\mathsf{c}_{r,N}, \mathsf{c}_{c,N}, \mathsf{c}_{c,n}, [\nu_{\hat{\mathbb{H}}}(s)]_2, \mathsf{vk}')$.

$\underline{\mathsf{Preproc}(\mathsf{srs}, \mathbf{T}, \rho_T)}$:

Let $\bar{\mathbf{t}}$ be vectorization of the matrix $\mathbf{T}$.
Compute $(\mathsf{aux}_{T,j})_{j\in[Nd]} \leftarrow \mathsf{CP.Preproc}(\mathsf{srs}, \bar{\mathbf{t}}, \rho_T)$,
$(\mathsf{aux}_{R,j})_{j\in[Nd]} \leftarrow \mathsf{CP.Preproc}(\mathsf{srs}, \bar{\mathbf{r}}_N)$,
$(\mathsf{aux}_{C,j})_{j\in[Nd]} \leftarrow \mathsf{CP.Preproc}(\mathsf{srs}, \bar{\mathbf{c}}_N)$.
Let $\mathsf{aux}_i = (\mathsf{aux}_{T,di+j}, \mathsf{aux}_{R,di+j}, \mathsf{aux}_{C,di+j})_{j\in[d]}$.
Return $(\mathsf{aux}_i)_{i\in[N]}$.

$\underline{\mathsf{Prove}(\mathsf{ek}, (\mathsf{c}_\mathbf{T}, \mathsf{c}_\mathbf{F}), \mathbf{F}, (\mathsf{aux}_j)_{j\in K})}$: $//\mathbf{T}_{|K} = \mathbf{F}$, $K = \{k_1, \ldots, k_n\}$.

Let $\mathbf{S}$ be s.t. $\mathbf{S}_{i,j} = k_i$ for $i \in [n], j \in [d]$.
Let $\sigma(X)$ be the randomized low-degree encoding over $\mathbb{H} = \langle\omega\rangle$ of the vectorization of $\mathbf{S}$.
Compute $w(X)$ such that $\sigma(\omega \cdot X) - \sigma(X) = w(X) \cdot \nu_{\hat{\mathbb{H}}}(X)$.
$(\rho, \zeta) \leftarrow \mathsf{RO}(\mathsf{vk}_n \| (\mathsf{c}_\mathbf{T}, \mathsf{c}_\mathbf{F}) \| (\mathsf{c}_{R,n}, \mathsf{c}_{R',n}, \mathsf{c}_w))$. //Fiat-Shamir challenge.
Compute $z \leftarrow \sigma(\omega \cdot \zeta)$.
Compute proofs π_R and $\pi_{R'}$ for $\hat{\mathcal{R}}_{\mathsf{eval}}(\omega \cdot \zeta, z; \sigma(X)) = 1$ and $\hat{\mathcal{R}}_{\mathsf{eval}}(\zeta, z; \sigma(\omega \cdot X)) = 1$;
Let π^* proof for $\hat{\mathcal{R}}_{\mathsf{zklkp}}((N \cdot d, n \cdot d); \varepsilon; (\bar{\mathbf{t}}^*, \bar{\mathbf{f}}^*)) = 1$ where

$$\bar{\mathbf{t}}^* = \bar{\mathbf{t}} + \rho \cdot \bar{\mathbf{c}}_N + \rho^2 \cdot \bar{\mathbf{r}}_N \qquad \bar{\mathbf{f}}^* = \bar{\mathbf{f}} + \rho \cdot \bar{\mathbf{c}}_n + \rho^2 \cdot \bar{\boldsymbol{\sigma}} \tag{13}$$

Return $\pi = ([\sigma(s)]_1, [\sigma(\omega \cdot s)]_1, [w(s)]_1, \pi_R, \pi_{R'}, \pi^*, z)$.

$\underline{\mathsf{Verify}(\mathsf{vk}_n, (\mathsf{c}_\mathbf{T}, \mathsf{c}_\mathbf{F}), \pi)}$:

Parse the proof $\pi = (\mathsf{c}_{R,n}, \mathsf{c}_{R',n}, \mathsf{c}_w, \pi_R, \pi_{R'}, \pi^*, z)$.
$(\rho, \zeta) \leftarrow \mathsf{RO}(\mathsf{vk}_n \| (\mathsf{c}_\mathbf{T}, \mathsf{c}_\mathbf{F}) \| (\mathsf{c}_{R,n}, \mathsf{c}_{R',n}, \mathsf{c}_w))$. //Fiat-Shamir challenge.
Compute $\mathsf{c}^*_\mathbf{T} \leftarrow \mathsf{c}_\mathbf{T} + \rho \mathsf{c}_{c,N} + \rho^2 \mathsf{c}_{r,N}$ and $\mathsf{c}^*_\mathbf{F} \leftarrow \mathsf{c}_\mathbf{F} + \rho \mathsf{c}_{c,n} + \rho^2 \mathsf{c}_{R,n}$.
Return 1 if the following checks hold (else 0):
(i) $\mathsf{Verify}_{\mathsf{eval}}(\mathsf{ck}, (\mathsf{c}_{R,n}, \omega \cdot \zeta, z)) = 1$,
(ii) $\mathsf{Verify}_{\mathsf{eval}}(\mathsf{ck}, (\mathsf{c}_{R',n}, \zeta, z)) = 1$,
(iii) $e(\mathsf{c}_{R',n} - \mathsf{c}_{R,n}, [1]_2) = e(\mathsf{c}_w, [\nu_{\hat{\mathbb{K}}}(s)]_2)$,
(iv) $\mathsf{CP.Verify}(\mathsf{srs}, \mathsf{vk}', (\mathsf{c}^*_\mathbf{T}, \mathsf{c}^*_\mathbf{F}), \pi^*) = 1$.

Fig. 2. Our Matrix Lookup Argument mtx[CP].

5.3 Concrete Efficiency

In Table 1, we describe the complexity of proving a matrix lookup in a table T described by a matrix of size $N \times d$. The size of the submatrix we are looking up in the larger table is $n \times d$. In [7, Appendix F], we describe a breakdown of efficiency measurements for our fully zero-knowledge construction ($\mathsf{mtx}[\mathsf{zkcq}^+]$). The values for [13] are taken directly from the paper, the number of pairings in verification is computed by simple inspection of the protocol, the extra $O(\log nd)$ factor in the number of exponentiations in $\mathbb{G}_1$ for the prover arises from their sub-protocol adapted from [38].

Table 1. Summary of efficiency of our constructions for matrix lookups. The relation considered is parametrized with table size of size $N \times d$ and looked-up submatrix of size $n \times d$. $\mathbb{P}$ is the cost of one pairing. Proof size includes commitment to the witness.

Scheme	Preprocessing	Proof size	Time (P)	Time (V)
$\mathsf{mtx}^{\mathsf{longprf}}[\mathsf{zkcq}^+]$ (Sect. 5.1)	$O(dN \log N)\mathbb{F}, \mathbb{G}$	$(d+9)\mathfrak{g}_1 + 1\mathfrak{f}$	$O(nd)\mathbb{G}_1 + O(nd \log n)\mathbb{F}$	$d\mathbb{G}_1 + 7\mathbb{P}$
$\mathsf{mtx}[\mathsf{zkcq}^+]$ (Fig. 2)	$O(dN \log dN)\mathbb{F}, \mathbb{G}$	$16\mathfrak{g}_1 + 2\mathfrak{f}$	$O(nd)\mathbb{G}_1 + O(nd \log(nd))\mathbb{F}$	$13\mathbb{P}$
[13]	$O(dN \log dN)\mathbb{F}, \mathbb{G}$	$20\mathfrak{g}_1 + 6\mathfrak{f}$	$O(nd \log nd)\mathbb{G}_1 + O(nd \log(nd))\mathbb{F}$	$23\mathbb{P}$

6 Zero-Knowledge Decision Tree Statistics

A decision tree is an algorithm that, upon an input, performs a finite sequence of adaptive queries on the input and eventually outputs a value. Concretely, we consider binary decision trees where the inputs are vectors in $[B]^d$ for natural numbers d and B, where the queries are comparisons and the outputs (often called the labels) are in $[B]$. We let N_{tot} be the number of nodes in a decision tree T, and we index the root node with 1. A binary tree with N_{tot} nodes and where each node has either zero children or exactly two children, has $N_{\mathsf{leaf}} := (N_{\mathsf{tot}} + 1)/2$ leaf nodes, and the remaining $N_{\mathsf{int}} = N_{\mathsf{tot}} - N_{\mathsf{leaf}}$ nodes are called internal nodes (including the root node). We index the internal nodes of the decision tree with numbers in $[N_{\mathsf{int}}]$. The computation of a decision tree T upon input $\mathbf{x}$, denoted as $\mathsf{T}(\mathbf{x})$, consists of a traversal of the tree from the root node to a leaf. During the traversal, the computation fetches, from each internal node i, a threshold t_i and a feature index $e_i \in [d]$. If $x_{e_i} < t_i$, the computation continues recurring on the left child of node i, and otherwise, to the right child. Once reaches a leaf, the computation outputs the label v_i assigned to the leaf i as the final output.

Therefore, seen as a data structure, a decision tree T is made by a binary tree (namely, the *structure* of the tree), by the values d_i, t_i for each internal node i, and by the label v_i for each leaf node i. We refer to this encoding of a tree as the *standard encoding*. We define $\mathcal{T}_{N_{\mathsf{tot}},B,d}$ to be the set of decision trees with N_{tot} nodes that maps vector in $[B]^d$ to the co-domain $\mathbb{F}$.

Quasi-Complete Decision Tree. We define the notion of *quasi-complete* decision tree. The difference with a standard tree is that during the traversal, the computation fetches from each internal node i two vectors $\mathbf{E}_i$ and $\mathbf{T}_i$, we call the vector $\mathbf{E}_i \in \{0,1\}^d$ the feature vector associated to the node i and vector $\mathbf{T}_i \in [B]^d$ the threshold vector associated to the node i. The computation continues recurring on the left child of node i if $\forall j \in [d] : \mathbf{E}_{i,j} = 1 \Rightarrow x_j < \mathbf{T}_{i,j}$, on to the right child of the node i if $\forall j \in [d] : \mathbf{E}_{i,j} = 1 \Rightarrow x_j \geq \mathbf{T}_{i,j}$, or outputs $\perp$ if neither of the two conditions holds.

Similarly to decision trees, we define $\mathcal{T}^*_{N_{\text{tot}},B,d}$ to be the set of quasi-complete decision trees with N_{tot} nodes that maps feature vector in $[B]^d$ to the co-domain $\mathbb{F}$. Notice that when for any node j the (row) vector $\mathbf{E}_j$ is an elementary vector (namely with only one position set to 1) then the quasi-complete decision tree is indeed a standard decision tree thus $\mathcal{T}_{N_{\text{tot}},B,d} \subset \mathcal{T}^*_{N_{\text{tot}},B,d}$.

The class of quasi-complete decision trees defines a correct but not complete computational model. In fact, every input is either correctly labelled to one label or to the error message $\perp$. Being a more general class of computation than standard decision trees, it is easier to decide whether a data structure is a quasi-complete decision tree than to decide if it is a standard decision tree. This allows for faster prover time. On the other hand, an adversary that commits to (strictly) quasi-complete decision tree (namely, a decision tree in $\mathcal{T}^*_{N_{\text{tot}},B,d} \setminus \mathcal{T}_{N_{\text{tot}},B,d}$) cannot prove contradicting statements, in particular, we require that it cannot prove any statistics on an input $\mathbf{x}$ whenever $\mathsf{T}(\mathbf{x}) = \perp$.

6.1 Security Model

We consider the scenario where a *model producer* commits to a decision tree T, the model producer can delegate the computation of statistics on a set of data points and predictions over T to a server, a user can obtain such statistics. Informally, we require integrity of the computation, namely the statistics are correctly computed over the set of data points and predictions over the committed decision tree T, and privacy, namely the user does not learn anything more than the validity of such statistics.

We consider an adversarial model where either the model producer and the server can be corrupted, or the user is corrupted. Previous work considered only the case where the model producer is honest [40] (and either the server or user are corrupted). Notice that a corrupted model producer could commit to a *useless/bogus* decision tree. Unfortunately, we cannot do anything to prevent that. On the other hand, we would like to prevent the corrupted model producer and corrupted server can convince the user of the validity of *incoherent* statistics. For example, an attacker should not be able to convince the user that simultaneously $\mathsf{T}(\mathbf{x}) = 1$ and $\mathsf{T}(\mathbf{x}) = 0$ for a data point $\mathbf{x}$.

To formalize such property, we use the notion of knowledge soundness for argument systems. In particular, we require that whenever the verifier is convinced (w.r.t. a commitment c) of the statistic over a set of data points, there must exist an extractor that outputs an opening of the commitment to a decision tree T where such a statistic over such data is correct. Notice the commitment to the decision tree is binding. Thus we must obtain coherent statistics over many queries on the same committed decision tree. To optimize the efficiency of the statistic evaluations, we split in two parts the generation of a valid commitment from the evaluation of a proof for a given tuple statistic/data points.

Definition 7. *Let $\mathcal{S}$ be an arbitrary set of tuples (S, m) such that $S : [B]^m \rightarrow \{0,1\}^*$ and $m \in \mathbb{N}$ where S is an efficiently computable function (a statistic). A (commit-and-prove)* decision-tree-statistic argument *for a set of statistics $\mathcal{S}$ is a tuple* $\mathsf{zkDT} = (\mathsf{KGen}, \mathsf{Com}, \mathsf{VerCom}, \mathsf{Der}, \mathsf{Prove}, \mathsf{Verify})$ *where:*

(i) $\mathsf{CS}_{DT} = (\mathsf{KGen}, \mathsf{Com}, \mathsf{VerCom})$ *define an extractable commitment scheme for the domain $\mathcal{T}^*$ of (quasi-complete) decision tree. In particular,* KGen *takes in input a natural number N_{tot} the maximum number of nodes, and the natural numbers B and d, besides the security parameter and generates a commitment key for the set $\mathcal{T}^*_{B,d,N_{\mathsf{tot}}}$.*
(ii) $\mathsf{CP}_{DT} = (\mathsf{Der}, \mathsf{Prove}, \mathsf{Verify})$ *define a Universal CP-SNARK for the indexed CP-relation $\hat{\mathcal{R}}_{\mathsf{DTstat}}$ defined below.*

$$\hat{\mathcal{R}}_{\mathsf{DTstat}} = \left\{ \mathsf{pp}; (S, m); y, (\mathbf{x}_j)_{j \in [m]}); \mathsf{T} : \begin{array}{c} y = S(\mathsf{T}(\mathbf{x}_1), \ldots, \mathsf{T}(\mathbf{x}_m)), \\ \forall i : \mathsf{T}(\mathbf{x}_i) \neq \bot, \quad (S, m) \in \mathcal{S} \end{array} \right\}.$$

6.2 The Extended Encoding of Decision Trees

We introduce an alternative encoding of a decision tree as a data structure before presenting our zero-knowledge decision-tree statistics argument. We follow the work of Chen *et al.* [11]. In particular, we define a d-dimensional *box* as a tuple of vectors in $[B+1]^d$, where the first vector defines the *left bounds* and the second vector defines the *right bounds*. We say that a vector $\mathbf{x} \in [B]^d$ *is contained* in a box $(\mathbf{b}^{\leftarrow}, \mathbf{b}^{\rightarrow})$ if $\mathbf{b}^{\leftarrow} \leq \mathbf{x} < \mathbf{b}^{\rightarrow}$. We can assign to each node of a decision tree a $d-$dimensional box. In particular, we denote with $(\mathbf{N}^{\leftarrow}_i, \mathbf{N}^{\rightarrow}_i)$ the box assigned to the i-th node in the tree and with $\mathbf{N}^{\leftarrow}, \mathbf{N}^{\rightarrow}$ the tuple of matrices of all the boxes of a decision tree (mapping the i-th row to the box of i-th node).

We can associate a (quasi-complete) decision tree to a tuple of matrices, below we define such a relation:

Definition 8. *Given a quasi-complete decision tree* T *with N_{tot} nodes and given matrices $\mathbf{N}^{\leftarrow}, \mathbf{N}^{\rightarrow}$, we say that $(\mathbf{N}^{\leftarrow}, \mathbf{N}^{\rightarrow})$ is a* boxes-encoding *of* T *if*

1. *$\mathbf{N}^{\leftarrow}_1 = \mathbf{0}$ and $\mathbf{N}^{\rightarrow}_1 = \mathbf{B} + \mathbf{1}$, where $\mathbf{0}$ (resp. $\mathbf{1}$ and $\mathbf{B}$) is the vector of all 0 (resp. of all 1 and of all B).*
2. *Let $p \in [N_{\mathsf{int}}]$ be the index of a node and let l and r respectively be the indexes of the left child and right child of the node with index p.*

$$\mathbf{N}^{\leftarrow}_l - \mathbf{N}^{\leftarrow}_p = \mathbf{0} \qquad \mathbf{N}^{\rightarrow}_r - \mathbf{N}^{\rightarrow}_p = \mathbf{0} \tag{14}$$

$$\mathbf{E}_p \circ (\mathbf{N}^{\rightarrow}_l - \mathbf{T}_p) = \mathbf{0} \qquad \mathbf{E}_p \circ (\mathbf{N}^{\leftarrow}_r - \mathbf{T}_p) = \mathbf{0} \tag{15}$$

$$(\mathbf{1} - \mathbf{E}_p) \circ (\mathbf{N}^{\rightarrow}_l - \mathbf{N}^{\rightarrow}_p) = \mathbf{0} \qquad (\mathbf{1} - \mathbf{E}_p) \circ (\mathbf{N}^{\leftarrow}_r - \mathbf{N}^{\leftarrow}_p) = \mathbf{0} \tag{16}$$

The computation, through a boxes-encoding, of a decision tree $\mathsf{T}(\mathbf{x})$ consists in finding the index k of the leaf whose box contains $\mathbf{x}$ and outputs the label associated with such a leaf. For a quasi-complete decision tree, such an index k might not exist. We formalize this in the next definition and prove such a computational equivalence in the next lemma whose proof is in [7, Appendix E].

Definition 9. *Let* T *be a quasi-complete decision tree with* N_{tot} *nodes (with domain* $[B]^d$*) and* $(\mathbf{N}^{\leftarrow}, \mathbf{N}^{\rightarrow})$ *be a boxes-encoding of* T*. For any* $\mathbf{x} \in [B]^d$*, if* $\mathbf{x}$ *is contained in the box of a leaf of* T *define the index of the leaf as* $k_{\mathsf{T}}(\mathbf{x})$ *such that* $\mathbf{x}$ *is contained in* $(\mathbf{N}^{\leftarrow}_{k_{\mathsf{T}}(\mathbf{x})}, \mathbf{N}^{\rightarrow}_{k_{\mathsf{T}}(\mathbf{x})})$ *else* $k_{\mathsf{T}}(\mathbf{x})$ *is set to* $\perp$.

Whenever it is clear from the context, we will omit the subscript T and write $k(\mathbf{x})$ to refer to such an index.

Lemma 3. *Let* T *be a quasi-complete decision tree with* N_{tot} *nodes and* $(\mathbf{N}^{\leftarrow}, \mathbf{N}^{\rightarrow})$ *be a boxes-encoding of* T*. Let* $\mathbf{v}$ *be the vector of the labels assigned to the leaf nodes of* T*, namely for any* $i \in [N_{\mathsf{int}} + 1, N_{\mathsf{tot}}]$*, we have* v_i *as the label assigned to the i-th leaf. For any* $\mathbf{x} \in [B]^d$*,* $\mathsf{T}(\mathbf{x}) = v_{k(\mathbf{x})}$ *or* $\mathsf{T}(\mathbf{x}) = \perp$.

As corollary of the above lemma, we have that the boxes of leaf do not overlap because no vector $\mathbf{x}$ can be contained in more than one of the boxes of the leaves.

Before giving the next definition, we set some notation: given a decision tree, we say that node p splits at coordinate $i^* \in [d]$ if i^* is a coordinate where p's left and right child boundaries are different, namely, $\mathbf{N}^{\rightarrow}_{p,i} \neq \mathbf{N}^{\rightarrow}_{\ell,i}$ and $\mathbf{N}^{\leftarrow}_{p,i} \neq \mathbf{N}^{\leftarrow}_{r,i}$ where ℓ and r are the left and right child of p. We are ready to describe our (more redundant but ZKP-friendly) encoding of a quasi-complete decision tree.

Definition 10. *Let* T *be a quasi-complete decision tree with* N_{tot} *nodes. Let* $\mathcal{T} = (\mathbf{N}^{\leftarrow}, \mathbf{N}^{\rightarrow}, \mathbf{v}, \mathbf{L}, \mathbf{R}, \mathbf{E})$ *be a tuple of matrices (described below). We say that* $\mathcal{T}$ *is an extended encoding of* T *if the following conditions hold:*

(i) $(\mathbf{N}^{\leftarrow}, \mathbf{N}^{\rightarrow})$ *is a boxes-encoding of* T*;*
(ii) $\mathbf{v}$ *is the vector of the labels assigned to the leaf nodes of* T*;*
(iii) $\mathbf{L}$ *(resp.* $\mathbf{R}$*) is the* $N_{\mathsf{int}} \times N_{\mathsf{tot}}$ *bit matrix whose p-th row is the elementary vector* $\mathbf{e}_\ell^\mathsf{T}$ *(resp.* $\mathbf{e}_r^\mathsf{T}$*) if* ℓ *is the left (resp. r is the right) child of node p's in* T*,*
(iv) $\mathbf{E} \in \{0,1\}^{N_{\mathsf{int}} \times d}$ *is the bit matrix such that its p-th row and i column is* 1 *iff the node p splits at coordinate i.*

Let Encode *be the algorithm that, given a quasi-complete decision tree* T*, computes the extended encoding of* T.

Let the matrices $\mathbf{P}^{\leftarrow}, \mathbf{P}^{\rightarrow} \in \mathbb{F}^{N_{\mathsf{int}} \times d}$ describe the boxing encodings of the internal nodes, and $\mathbf{F}^{\leftarrow}, \mathbf{F}^{\rightarrow} \in \mathbb{F}^{N_{\mathsf{leaf}} \times d}$ describe the boxing encodings of the leaves. Thus:

$$\mathbf{N}^{\leftarrow} = \begin{pmatrix} \mathbf{P}^{\leftarrow} \\ = \\ \mathbf{F}^{\leftarrow} \end{pmatrix} \text{ and } \mathbf{N}^{\rightarrow} = \begin{pmatrix} \mathbf{P}^{\rightarrow} \\ = \\ \mathbf{F}^{\rightarrow} \end{pmatrix}.$$

The function Encode in Definition 10 is injective but not surjective. In the next lemma (whose proof is in [7, Appendix E]), we give sufficient conditions for belonging in the image of Encode.

Lemma 4. *Consider a tuple* $(\mathbf{N}^{\leftarrow}, \mathbf{N}^{\rightarrow}, \mathbf{L}, \mathbf{R}, \mathbf{E}, \mathbf{v})$ *such that the following constraints hold:*

a) The following equations hold:

$$\mathbf{N}^{\leftarrow}_1 = \mathbf{0}, \mathbf{N}^{\rightarrow}_1 = \mathbf{B} + \mathbf{1}, \tag{17}$$

$$\mathbf{L} \cdot \mathbf{N}^{\leftarrow} = \mathbf{P}^{\leftarrow}, \mathbf{R} \cdot \mathbf{N}^{\rightarrow} = \mathbf{P}^{\rightarrow}, \tag{18}$$

$$\mathbf{E} \circ (\mathbf{L} \cdot \mathbf{N}^{\rightarrow} - \mathbf{R} \cdot \mathbf{N}^{\leftarrow}) = \mathbf{0} \tag{19}$$

$$(\mathbf{1} - \mathbf{E}) \circ (\mathbf{P}^{\leftarrow} - \mathbf{R} \cdot \mathbf{N}^{\leftarrow}) = \mathbf{0}, \qquad (\mathbf{1} - \mathbf{E}) \circ (\mathbf{P}^{\rightarrow} - \mathbf{L} \cdot \mathbf{N}^{\rightarrow}) = \mathbf{0} \tag{20}$$

b) All the boxes are not empty. Namely, for all i, j *we have* $\mathbf{N}^{\leftarrow}_{i,j} < \mathbf{N}^{\rightarrow}_{i,j}$.

c) The matrix $\left(\frac{\mathbf{L}}{\mathbf{R}}\right)$ *is a (row) permutation of the (squared) matrix* $(\mathbf{0} \| \mathbf{I}_{N_{\mathsf{tot}}-1})$ *(the matrix whose rows are the row vectors* $(\mathbf{e}_i)_{i \in [2, N_{\mathsf{tot}}]}$ *of length* N_{tot}*).*

Then there exists a quasi-complete decision tree T *with* N_{tot} *nodes such that* $\mathsf{Encode}(\mathsf{T}) = (\mathbf{N}^{\leftarrow}, \mathbf{N}^{\rightarrow}, \mathbf{L}, \mathbf{R}, \mathbf{E}, \mathbf{v})$.

6.3 Extractable Commitment to Decision Trees

In a nutshell our commitment procedure on input a decision tree computes the encoding described in Sect. 6.2, then it commits to the matrices $\mathbf{F}^{\leftarrow}, \mathbf{F}^{\rightarrow}$ and $\mathbf{v}$ and prove in zero-knowledge the constraints from Lemma 4. We can implement the latter zero-knowledge proof using a general-purpose R1CS circuit describing the constraints of the lemma, however, the size of the circuit would be $O(dN^2_{\mathsf{tot}})$, in fact, we would need to commit to the remaining matrices $\mathbf{P}^{\leftarrow}, \mathbf{P}^{\rightarrow}, \mathbf{L}, \mathbf{R}$ and $\mathbf{E}$ and we would need already $O(dN^2_{\mathsf{tot}})$ multiplication gates for Eq. (18). We show how to remove the quadratic dependency from the number of total nodes. The main idea is to notice that $\mathbf{L}$ and $\mathbf{R}$ have sparsity linear in N_{tot}, thus we can use techniques from [39] to commit to such sparse matrices and then prove in zero-knowledge that the constraints in Item c) of Lemma 4 hold for the committed matrices. The remaining constraints can be proved in $O(dN_{\mathsf{tot}} \log(dN_{\mathsf{tot}}))$.

The Building Blocks. Consider the following (indexed) CP-relations:

$$\hat{\mathcal{R}}_{\mathsf{lin}} = \{\mathsf{pp}; \varepsilon; (\mathbf{M}, \mathbf{N}, \mathbf{R}) : \mathbf{M} \cdot \mathbf{N} = \mathbf{R}\} \tag{21}$$

$$\hat{\mathcal{R}}_{\mathsf{had}} = \{\mathsf{pp}; \varepsilon; (\mathbf{M}, \mathbf{N}) : \mathbf{M} \circ \mathbf{N} = \mathbf{0}\} \tag{22}$$

$$\hat{\mathcal{R}}_{\mathsf{perm}} = \left\{\mathsf{pp}; (N, i(X)); \varepsilon; p(X) : \exists \pi, \forall j \in [N] : i(\pi(\omega^j)) = p(\omega^j)\right\} \tag{23}$$

$$\hat{\mathcal{R}}_{\mathsf{shift}} = \left\{\mathsf{pp}; S; \varepsilon; (\mathbf{v}, \mathbf{u}) : \mathbf{v}_i = \mathbf{u}_{(i+S \pmod{|\mathbf{u}|})}\right\} \tag{24}$$

$$\hat{\mathcal{R}}_{\mathsf{rng}} = \left\{\mathsf{pp}; (B, n, d); \varepsilon; \mathbf{X} : \mathbf{X} \in [B]^{n \times d}\right\} \tag{25}$$

$$\hat{\mathcal{R}}_{\mathsf{sm}} = \left\{\mathsf{pp} : K; \varepsilon; \mathbf{M} : \mathbf{M}_{|K} = \mathbf{0}\right\} \tag{26}$$

Our scheme uses CP-SNARKs for all the relations above as building blocks. The first three relations are standard, and CP-SNARKs for them can be found in the related work. Given a CP-SNARK for $\hat{\mathcal{R}}_{\mathsf{lin}}$, we can define a CP-SNARK for

$\hat{\mathcal{R}}_{\mathsf{shift}}$ in fact that the shifting operator can be described through a linear transformation. The latter linear transformation can be public, thus the underlying CP-SNARK (for $\hat{\mathcal{R}}_{\mathsf{lin}}$) does not need to be zero-knowledge w.r.t. the first matrix $\mathbf{M}$, in particular, a commitment to such a matrix could be part of the index polynomials. A CP-SNARK for $\hat{\mathcal{R}}_{\mathsf{rng}}$ can be realized using our lookup argument and considering the table $\mathbf{b} = (j)_{j\in[B]}$ and proving that the vectorization $\bar{\mathbf{x}}$ of $\mathbf{X}$ is such that $\bar{\mathbf{x}} \prec \mathbf{b}$. Finally, a CP-SNARK for $\hat{\mathcal{R}}_{\mathsf{sm}}$ can be easily realized by committing to a matrix $\bar{\mathbf{T}}$ such that $\bar{\mathbf{T}}_K = \mathbf{T}$ and 0 everywhere else and to the vanishing polynomial in ν_K in $\mathbb{G}_2$ as part of the index. At proving time, the prover returns as proof a commitment to the quotient polynomial q such that $f'(X) = q(X) \cdot \nu_K(X)$ where $f'(X)$ is the polynomial associated to the matrix $\mathbf{M} - \bar{T}$. At verification time the verifier checks $e(\mathsf{c}_{\mathbf{M}} - \mathsf{c}_{\bar{\mathbf{T}}}, [1]_2) = e(\pi, [\nu_K]_2)$.

For the CP-SNARK for $\hat{\mathcal{R}}_{\mathsf{lin}}$, we require two different commitment schemes, one for the first matrix and one for the other two. In particular, we consider an alternative way to commit to matrices following the work of [33,39]. Let $\mathbf{M}$ be a *basic matrix*, namely a matrix whose rows are elementary vectors. Let $\mathbb{H}$ be any fixed subgroup with $|\mathbb{H}| \geq N_{\mathsf{tot}}$[8] of $\mathbb{F}$ with generator ω. For any basic matrix $\mathbf{M} \in \{0,1\}^{n\times k}$ and $n, k \in \mathbb{N}$, let $col_{\mathbf{M}}(X)$ be the (low-degree) polynomial such that $col_{\mathbf{M}}(\omega^i) = \omega^j$ where the i-th row of $\mathbf{M}$ is the vector $\mathbf{e}_j^\top$ (notice that $col_{\mathbf{M}}$ is the LDE of the vector whose i-th element is the value ω^j). We define the sparse (hiding) commitment of a matrix $\mathbf{M}$ as a (hiding) polynomial commitment of $col_{\mathbf{M}}$. Namely, we define:

$$\mathsf{sparseCom}(\mathsf{ck}, \mathbf{M}, \rho) := \mathsf{Com}(\mathsf{ck}, col_{\mathbf{M}}, \rho).$$

Notice that, by the above definition, a sparse commitment to a basic matrix $\mathbf{M}$ has a dual interpretation (as a sparse matrix or as a vector *col*).

Let $\mathsf{CP}_{\mathsf{lin}}$ be a CP-SNARK for the $\hat{\mathcal{R}}_{\mathsf{lin}}$ relation where the first matrix is committed using $\mathsf{sparseCom}$ while the other matrices are committed with the matrix commitment scheme from Sect. 2.3. An instantiation of such a scheme can be found for the matrix-times-vector case (namely, $\mathbf{N} \in \mathbb{F}^{n\times 1}$) in Baloo by [39] (see Sects. 5.2, 5.3 and 5.4 of the paper). We show a generalization to matrix-times-matrix case in [7, Appendix E.4]. We write $\boxed{\mathbf{M}}$ to underline that the matrix $\mathbf{M}$ is committed with a sparse matrix commitment. For example, we can write $(\mathsf{pp}, \varepsilon; \boxed{\mathbf{M}}, \mathbf{N}, \mathbf{R}) \in \hat{\mathcal{R}}_{\mathsf{lin}}$ to identify the statement that there are commitments $\mathsf{c}_M, \mathsf{c}_N, \mathsf{c}_R$ where the first is a sparse matrix commitment and that open to $\mathbf{M}, \mathbf{N}$ and $\mathbf{R}$ with $\mathbf{M} \cdot \mathbf{N} = \mathbf{R}$.

Let $\mathsf{CP}_{\mathsf{had}}$ be a CP-SNARK for the $\hat{\mathcal{R}}_{\mathsf{had}}$ relation where all the matrices are committed using the commitment scheme from Sect. 2.3. Notice that a CP-SNARK for our matrix commitment scheme for such a CP-relation derives directly from CP-SNARK for vector commitment. Finally, let $\mathsf{CP}_{\mathsf{perm}}$ be a CP-SNARK for the CP-relation $\hat{\mathcal{R}}_{\mathsf{perm}}$. The permutation argument of Plonk [19] is a CP-SNARK for such a relation.

[8] Alternatively, we can consider the same subgroup used for the matrix commitment and thus $|\mathbb{H}| = N_{\mathsf{tot}} \cdot d$.

The Extractable Commitment to Decision Tree. We define our extractable commitment scheme for the domain of quasi-complete decision trees. The main idea is, as part of the proof of opening, to commit to the matrices $\mathbf{L}$ and $\mathbf{R}$ through sparse commitments to basic matrices and then prove the linear relations from Lemma 4 in zero-knowledge with a complexity that is linear in the sparsity of the matrices and the dimension d. The additional constraints on the two matrices $\mathbf{L}$ and $\mathbf{R}$ are proved using the permutation argument. To improve readability, we list below shortcuts used in the protocol's description.

$$\bar{\mathbf{F}}_{\leftarrow} := \begin{pmatrix} \mathbf{0} \\ \hline \mathbf{F}^{\leftarrow} \end{pmatrix},\ \bar{\mathbf{F}}_{\rightarrow} := \begin{pmatrix} \mathbf{0} \\ \hline \mathbf{F}^{\rightarrow} \end{pmatrix},\ \bar{\mathbf{P}}_{\leftarrow} := \begin{pmatrix} \mathbf{P}^{\leftarrow} \\ \hline \mathbf{0} \end{pmatrix},\ \bar{\mathbf{P}}_{\rightarrow} := \begin{pmatrix} \mathbf{P}^{\rightarrow} \\ \hline \mathbf{0} \end{pmatrix},$$

$$\bar{\mathbf{L}} := \begin{pmatrix} \mathbf{L} \\ \hline \mathbf{0} \end{pmatrix},\ \bar{\mathbf{R}} := \begin{pmatrix} \mathbf{R} \\ \hline \mathbf{0} \end{pmatrix},\ \underline{\mathbf{R}} := \begin{pmatrix} \mathbf{0} \\ \hline \mathbf{R} \end{pmatrix},\ \bar{\mathbf{E}} := \begin{pmatrix} \mathbf{E} \\ \hline \mathbf{0} \end{pmatrix}$$

The padding for the matrices make them all to have N_{tot} rows. Moreover, we let $\mathbf{B}$ be the matrix whose first row is the vector $(B+1, \ldots, B+1)$ and the remaining rows are set to $\mathbf{0}$, and we let $b(X)$ be the LDE of the vectorization of such a

$\underline{\mathsf{KGen}(1^\lambda, (N_{\mathsf{tot}}, B, d))}$:

Sample a type-3 pairing group pp_G with security level λ.
Set $\mathsf{ck}' \leftarrow (\mathsf{pp}_G, ([s^i]_1)_{i \in [N_1]}, ([s^i]_2)_{i \in [N_2]}$ for random secrets $s \leftarrow\!\$\ \mathbb{Z}_q$.
Let $\mathcal{N}_1 := [N_{\mathsf{int}}], \mathcal{N}_2 := (N_{\mathsf{int}}, N_{\mathsf{tot}}], \mathcal{N}_3 := \{1\}$, for $i \in [3]$ compute $\mathsf{srs}_{\mathsf{sm},1} \leftarrow \mathsf{CP}_{\mathsf{sm}}.\mathsf{Der}(\mathsf{ck}', \mathcal{N}_i)$.
Compute $\mathsf{srs}_{\mathsf{perm}} \leftarrow \mathsf{CP}_{\mathsf{perm}}.\mathsf{Der}(\mathsf{ck}', (N_{\mathsf{tot}} - 1, id))$.
Compute $\mathsf{srs}_{\mathsf{rng}} \leftarrow \mathsf{CP}_{\mathsf{rng}}.\mathsf{Der}(\mathsf{ck}', (B, N_{\mathsf{tot}}, d))$.
Compute $\mathsf{srs}_{\mathsf{shift}} \leftarrow \mathsf{CP}_{\mathsf{shift}}.\mathsf{Der}(\mathsf{ck}', N_{\mathsf{int}})$.
Return $\mathsf{ck} := (\mathsf{ck}', [b(s)]_1, \mathsf{srs}_{\mathsf{perm}}, \mathsf{srs}_{\mathsf{rng}}, \mathsf{srs}_{\mathsf{shift}}, (\mathsf{srs}_{\mathsf{sm},j})_{j \in [3]})$.

$\underline{\mathsf{Com}(\mathsf{ck}, \mathsf{T}, \rho_{\mathsf{T}})}$:

Compute $(\mathbf{L}, \mathbf{R}, \mathbf{E}, \mathbf{N}^{\leftarrow}, \mathbf{N}^{\rightarrow}, \mathbf{v}) \leftarrow \mathsf{Encode}(\mathsf{T})$, parses ρ_{T} as $(\rho_v, \rho_{\leftarrow}, \rho_{\rightarrow})$.
$\mathsf{c}_v \leftarrow \mathsf{Com}(\mathsf{ck}, \mathbf{v}, \rho_v)$. // Parse $\mathbf{v}$ as a $N_{\mathsf{tot}} \times d$ matrix whose last $d-1$ columns are empty.
$\mathsf{c}_{\leftarrow} \leftarrow \mathsf{Com}(\mathsf{ck}, \bar{\mathbf{F}}_{\leftarrow}, \rho_{\leftarrow}), \mathsf{c}_{\rightarrow} \leftarrow \mathsf{Com}(\mathsf{ck}, \bar{\mathbf{F}}_{\rightarrow}, \rho_{\rightarrow}), \mathsf{c}'_{\leftarrow} \leftarrow \mathsf{Com}(\mathsf{ck}, \bar{\mathbf{P}}_{\leftarrow}, \rho_{\leftarrow}), \mathsf{c}'_{\rightarrow} \leftarrow \mathsf{Com}(\mathsf{ck}, \bar{\mathbf{P}}_{\rightarrow}, \rho_{\rightarrow})$.
$\mathsf{c}_{ln} \leftarrow \mathsf{Com}(\mathsf{ck}, \bar{\mathbf{L}} \cdot \mathbf{N}^{\rightarrow},), \mathsf{c}_{rn} \leftarrow \mathsf{Com}(\mathsf{ck}, \bar{\mathbf{R}} \cdot \mathbf{N}^{\leftarrow})$ and $\mathsf{c}_E \leftarrow \mathsf{Com}(\mathsf{ck}, \mathbf{E})$.
$\mathsf{c}_L \leftarrow \mathsf{sparseCom}(\mathsf{ck}, \bar{\mathbf{L}}), \mathsf{c}_R \leftarrow \mathsf{sparseCom}(\mathsf{ck}, \bar{\mathbf{R}})$ and $\mathsf{c}'_R \leftarrow \mathsf{sparseCom}(\underline{\mathbf{R}})$.
Let $col_{\bar{\mathbf{L}}}, col_{\bar{\mathbf{R}}}$ and $col_{\underline{\mathbf{R}}}$ be the underlying polynomials.
Prove the following statements, let $\boldsymbol{\pi} = (\pi_1, \ldots, \pi_{16})$ be the proofs.

$$\begin{aligned}
\pi_1, \ldots, \pi_4 :&\quad (\boxed{\bar{\mathbf{L}}}, \mathbf{N}^{\leftarrow}, \bar{\mathbf{P}}_{\leftarrow}),\ (\boxed{\bar{\mathbf{L}}}, \mathbf{N}^{\rightarrow}, \bar{\mathbf{L}} \cdot \mathbf{N}^{\rightarrow}),\ (\boxed{\bar{\mathbf{R}}}, \mathbf{N}^{\rightarrow}, \bar{\mathbf{P}}_{\rightarrow}),\ (\boxed{\bar{\mathbf{R}}}, \mathbf{N}^{\leftarrow}, \bar{\mathbf{R}} \cdot \mathbf{N}^{\leftarrow}) \in \hat{\mathcal{R}}_{\mathsf{lin}},\\
\pi_5, \pi_6, \pi_7 :&\quad (\bar{\mathbf{E}}, \bar{\mathbf{L}} \cdot \mathbf{N}^{\rightarrow} - \bar{\mathbf{R}} \cdot \mathbf{N}^{\leftarrow}),\ (\mathbf{1} - \bar{\mathbf{E}}, \mathbf{P}^{\leftarrow} - \bar{\mathbf{R}} \cdot \mathbf{N}^{\leftarrow}),\ (\mathbf{1} - \bar{\mathbf{E}}, \mathbf{P}^{\rightarrow} - \bar{\mathbf{L}} \cdot \mathbf{N}^{\rightarrow}) \in \hat{\mathcal{R}}_{\mathsf{had}},\\
\pi_8, \pi_9 :&\quad ((B, N_{\mathsf{tot}}, d); \mathbf{N}^{\rightarrow} - \mathbf{N}^{\leftarrow} - \mathbf{1}) \in \hat{\mathcal{R}}_{\mathsf{rng}},\quad (N_{\mathsf{tot}} - 1, id; col_{\bar{\mathbf{L}}}(X) + col_{\underline{\mathbf{R}}}(X)) \in \hat{\mathcal{R}}_{\mathsf{perm}},\\
\pi_{10} :&\quad (N_{\mathsf{int}}, col_{\bar{\mathbf{R}}}, col_{\underline{\mathbf{R}}}) \in \hat{\mathcal{R}}_{\mathsf{shift}},\\
\pi_{11}, \ldots, \pi_{16} :&\quad (\mathcal{N}_1; \bar{\mathbf{F}}_{\leftarrow}), (\mathcal{N}_1; \bar{\mathbf{F}}_{\rightarrow}), (\mathcal{N}_2; \bar{\mathbf{P}}_{\leftarrow}), (\mathcal{N}_2; \bar{\mathbf{P}}_{\rightarrow}), (\mathcal{N}_3; \bar{\mathbf{P}}_{\leftarrow}), (\mathcal{N}_3; \bar{\mathbf{P}}_{\rightarrow} - \mathbf{B}) \in \hat{\mathcal{R}}_{\mathsf{sm}}.
\end{aligned}$$

Return $(\mathsf{c}_{\leftarrow}, \mathsf{c}_{\rightarrow}, \mathsf{c}_v), \pi$ where $\pi = (\mathsf{c}'_{\leftarrow}, \mathsf{c}'_{\rightarrow}, \mathsf{c}_{ln}, \mathsf{c}_{rn}, \mathsf{c}_E, \mathsf{c}_L, \mathsf{c}_R, \mathsf{c}'_R, \boldsymbol{\pi})$.

$\underline{\mathsf{Verify}(\mathsf{ck}, \mathsf{c}_{\mathsf{T}})}$:

Let $\mathsf{c}_{\mathsf{T}} = (\mathsf{c}_{\leftarrow}, \mathsf{c}_{\rightarrow}, \mathsf{c}_v, \pi)$ and parse π. Let $\mathsf{c}_{N,\leftarrow} \leftarrow \mathsf{c}_{\leftarrow} + \mathsf{c}'_{\leftarrow}$ and $\mathsf{c}_{N,\rightarrow} \leftarrow \mathsf{c}_{\rightarrow} + \mathsf{c}'_{\rightarrow}$.

1. Verify $\pi_1, \pi_2, \pi_3, \pi_4$ w.r.t. $(\mathsf{c}_L, \mathsf{c}_{N,\leftarrow}, \mathsf{c}'_{\leftarrow}), (\mathsf{c}_L, \mathsf{c}_{N,\rightarrow}, \mathsf{c}_{ln}), (\mathsf{c}_R, \mathsf{c}_{N,\rightarrow}, \mathsf{c}'_{\rightarrow}), (\mathsf{c}_R, \mathsf{c}_{N,\leftarrow}, \mathsf{c}_{rn})$.
2. Verify π_5, π_6, π_7 w.r.t. $(\mathsf{c}_E, \mathsf{c}_{ln} - \mathsf{c}_{rn}), ([1]_1 - \mathsf{c}_E, \mathsf{c}'_{\leftarrow} - \mathsf{c}_{rn}), ([1]_1 - \mathsf{c}_E, \mathsf{c}'_{\rightarrow} - \mathsf{c}_{ln})$.
3. Verify π_8, π_9 w.r.t. $((B, N_{\mathsf{tot}}, d); \mathsf{c}_{N,\rightarrow} - \mathsf{c}_{N,\leftarrow} - [1]_1)$ and $(N_{\mathsf{tot}} - 1, id; \mathsf{c}_L + \mathsf{c}'_R)$.
4. Verify π_{10} w.r.t. $(N_{\mathsf{int}}; (\mathsf{c}_R, \mathsf{c}'_R))$.
5. Verify $\pi_{11}, \ldots, \pi_{16}$ w.r.t. $(\mathcal{N}_1, \mathsf{c}_{\leftarrow}),(\mathcal{N}_1, \mathsf{c}_{\rightarrow}),(\mathcal{N}_2, \mathsf{c}'_{\leftarrow}),(\mathcal{N}_2, \mathsf{c}'_{\rightarrow}),(\mathcal{N}_3, \mathsf{c}'_{\leftarrow}), (\mathcal{N}_3, \mathsf{c}'_{\rightarrow} - [b(s)]_1)$.

Fig. 3. Our extractable commitment CS_{DT}. The value $N_1 \geq N_{\text{tot}} \cdot d$, N_1 and N_2 are big enough to support all the building-block.

matrix. This polynomial can be computed in $O(d \log d)$ operations, however, for simplicity, we commit to the polynomial at key-generation phase. We let id be the low-degree polynomial that evaluates $id(\omega^i) = \omega^{i+1}$ for $i \in [N_{\mathsf{tot}} - 1]$ (equivalently, the commitment $[id(s)]_1$ is a sparse-matrix commitment to the matrix $(\mathbf{0} \| \mathbf{I}_{N_{\mathsf{tot}}-1})$).

Theorem 3. *The commitment scheme* CS_{DT} *defined in Fig. 3 is hiding and it is an extractable commitment scheme for the domain* $\{\mathcal{T}^*_{N_{\mathsf{tot}},B,d}\}_{N_{\mathsf{tot}},d,B}$ *in the AGM and assuming the building blocks are knowledge-sound and zero-knowledge.*

Efficiency. The extractable commitment in this section has constant proof size when the CP-SNARK for $\hat{\mathcal{R}}_{\mathsf{lin}}$ is instantiated with the building block described in [7, Appendix E.4]. Its proving time is $O(dN_{\mathsf{tot}} \log(dN_{\mathsf{tot}}))$ when applied to a decision tree with d features and N_{tot} nodes. Notice that N_{tot} is usually at least one order of magnitude larger than d.

6.4 CP-SNARK for Statistics on Decision Trees

Consider the scheme CP_{DT} in Fig. 4 based on the following building blocks:

1. Let $\mathsf{CP}_{\mathsf{lkp*}}$ be a CP-SNARK for the indexed CP-relation:

$$\hat{\mathcal{R}}_{\mathsf{lkp*}} = \left\{ \mathsf{pp}; (N, d, n); \varepsilon; (\mathbf{T}_j)_{j \in [m]}, (\mathbf{F}_j)_{j \in [m]} : \begin{array}{c} (\mathbf{F}_1 \| \dots \| \mathbf{F}_m) \prec (\mathbf{T}_1 \| \dots \| \mathbf{T}_m) \\ \forall j : |\mathbf{T}_j| = N \times d, |\mathbf{F}_j| = n \times d \end{array} \right\}$$

2. Let $\mathsf{CP}_{\mathsf{rng}}$ be a CP-SNARK for $\hat{\mathcal{R}}_{\mathsf{rng}}$ in Eq. (25).
3. Let $\mathsf{CP}_{\mathsf{stat}}$ be a CP-SNARK for the following indexed CP-relation:

$$\hat{\mathcal{R}}_{\mathsf{stat}} = \{\mathsf{pp}, (S, m); y; \mathbf{v} : S(\mathbf{v}) = y \wedge |\mathbf{v}| = m\}$$

Notice, we can easily define a CP-SNARK for $\hat{\mathcal{R}}_{\mathsf{lkp*}}$ on top of our compiler from Sect. 5. Namely, we batch together the matrices $\mathbf{T}_j$ and the matrices $\mathbf{F}_j$ using a random challenge, as described in Sect. 5.1, and then we run our matrix lookup argument. As corollary of Theorem 3 and the theorem below, we have that the CP_{DT} and the commitment scheme CS_{DT} from the previous section define a decision-tree statistic argument.

Theorem 4. $\mathsf{CP}_{DT} = (\mathsf{Der}, \mathsf{Prove}, \mathsf{Verify})$ *in Fig. 4 defines an Universal CP-SNARK for the indexed CP-relation* $\hat{\mathcal{R}}_{\mathsf{DTstat}}$.

6.5 Efficiency and Concrete Instantiations

We discuss how to instantiate our scheme above, the resulting system has a universal trusted setup.

- $\mathsf{CP}_{\mathsf{lkp*}}$ can be instantiated with our construction $\mathsf{mtx}[\mathsf{zkcq}^+]$ from Sect. 3;

<u>$\mathsf{Der}(\mathsf{srs}, (S, m))$:</u>

Compute $\mathsf{srs}_{(S,m)} \leftarrow \mathsf{CP}_{\mathsf{stat}}.\mathsf{Der}(\mathsf{ck}, (S, m))$, $\mathsf{srs}_m \leftarrow \mathsf{CP}_{\mathsf{lkp*}}.\mathsf{Der}(\mathsf{ck}, N_{\mathsf{tot}}, d, m)$.
Compute $\mathsf{srs}_{(B,m,d)} \leftarrow \mathsf{CP}_{\mathsf{rng}}.\mathsf{Der}(\mathsf{ck}, (B, m, d))$ with values B, d contained in srs.
Return the specialized SRSs.

<u>$\mathsf{Prove}(\mathsf{srs}, (\mathsf{c}_\mathsf{T}, y, (\mathbf{x}_j)_{j\in[m]}), (\mathsf{T}, \rho_\mathsf{T}))$:</u>

Parse $\mathsf{c}_\mathsf{T} = (\mathsf{c}_{\leftarrow}, \mathsf{c}_{\rightarrow}, \mathsf{c}_v)$ and $\rho_\mathsf{T} = (\rho_{\leftarrow}, \rho_{\rightarrow}, \rho_v)$.
Let $k_i = k_\mathsf{T}(\mathbf{x}_i)$ and $K = \{k_1, \ldots, k_m\}$, where $k_\mathsf{T}(\cdot)$ as defined in Definition 9.
Compute matrix commitments $\mathsf{c}_1, \mathsf{c}_2, \mathsf{c}_3$ to the matrices $(\bar{\mathbf{F}}_{\leftarrow})_{|K}, (\bar{\mathbf{F}}_{\rightarrow})_{|K}, \mathbf{v}_{|K}$.
Compute a proof π_{zklkp} that

$$(m; \varepsilon; ((\bar{\mathbf{F}}_{\leftarrow}, \bar{\mathbf{F}}_{\rightarrow}, \mathbf{v}), (\bar{\mathbf{F}}_{\leftarrow})_{|K}, (\bar{\mathbf{F}}_{\rightarrow})_{|K}, \mathbf{v}_{|K})) \in \hat{\mathcal{R}}_{\mathsf{lkp*}}.$$

Compute a (not hiding) commitment to the matrix $\mathbf{X}$ whose rows are the vectors $(\mathbf{x}_j)_{j\in[m]}$.
Compute proofs $\pi_{\mathsf{rng}}^{\leftarrow}$ and $\pi_{\mathsf{rng}}^{\rightarrow}$ for the following two statements:

$$((B, m, d); \mathbf{X} - (\bar{\mathbf{F}}_{\leftarrow})_{|K}) \in \hat{\mathcal{R}}_{\mathsf{rng}}, \qquad ((B, m, d); (\bar{\mathbf{F}}_{\rightarrow})_{|K} - \mathbf{X} - \mathbf{1}) \in \hat{\mathcal{R}}_{\mathsf{rng}}.$$

Compute a proof π_{stat} that $((S, m); y; \mathbf{v}_{|K})) \in \hat{\mathcal{R}}_{\mathsf{stat}}$.
Return $(\mathsf{c}_1, \mathsf{c}_2, \mathsf{c}_3, \pi_{\mathsf{zklkp}}, \pi_{\mathsf{rng}}^{\leftarrow}, \pi_{\mathsf{rng}}^{\rightarrow}, \pi_{\mathsf{stat}})$.

<u>$\mathsf{Verify}(\mathsf{srs}, \mathsf{vk}_{(S,m)}, (\mathsf{c}_\mathsf{T}, y, (\mathbf{x}_j)_{j\in[m]}), \pi_\mathsf{T})$:</u>

Parse the proof $\pi_\mathsf{T} = (\mathsf{c}_1, \mathsf{c}_2, \mathsf{c}_3, \pi_{\mathsf{zklkp}}, \pi_{\mathsf{rng}}^{\leftarrow}, \pi_{\mathsf{rng}}^{\rightarrow}, \pi_{\mathsf{stat}})$.
Compute $\mathsf{c}_\mathbf{X} \leftarrow \mathsf{Com}(\mathsf{ck}, \mathbf{X})$ ($\mathbf{X}$ computed from $(\mathbf{x}_j)_{j\in[m]}$) . Return 1 if the following statements hold (else 0):

1. $\mathsf{CP}_{\mathsf{lkp*}}.\mathsf{Verify}(\mathsf{srs}, \mathsf{vk}_m, (\mathsf{c}_1, \mathsf{c}_2, \mathsf{c}_3, \mathsf{c}_{\leftarrow}, \mathsf{c}_{\rightarrow}, \mathsf{c}_v), \pi_{\mathsf{zklkp}}) = 1$
2. $\mathsf{CP}_{\mathsf{rng}}.\mathsf{Verify}(\mathsf{srs}, \mathsf{vk}_{(B,m,d)}, (\mathsf{c}_\mathbf{X} - \mathsf{c}_1), \pi_{\mathsf{rng}}^{\leftarrow}) = 1$ and
   $\mathsf{CP}_{\mathsf{rng}}.\mathsf{Verify}(\mathsf{srs}, \mathsf{vk}_{(B,m,d)}, (\mathsf{c}_2 - \mathsf{c}_\mathbf{X} - [1]_1), \pi_{\mathsf{rng}}^{\rightarrow}) = 1$
3. $\mathsf{CP}_{\mathsf{stat}}.\mathsf{Verify}(\mathsf{srs}, \mathsf{vk}_{(S,m)}, (\mathsf{c}_3, y), \pi_{\mathsf{stat}}) = 1$
4. $\mathsf{VerCom}(\mathsf{ck}, \mathsf{c}_\mathsf{T}) = 1$.

Fig. 4. Our CP-SNARK CP_{DT}. The pre-processing algorithm runs the preprocessing of the matrix lookup argument on $\bar{\mathbf{F}}_{\leftarrow}, \bar{\mathbf{F}}_{\rightarrow}, \mathbf{v}$ and openings $\rho_T = (\rho_{\leftarrow}, \rho_{\rightarrow}, \rho_v)$.

- $\mathsf{CP}_{\mathsf{rng}}$ can be implemented through a (vector) lookup in a table of size B where the subvector being looked up is of size m[9];
- $\mathsf{CP}_{\mathsf{stat}}$ can be implemented through a general-purpose commit-and-prove SNARK, such as [2,8]. For concreteness, and to minimize proof size, in the remainder of this document, we consider the proof scheme CP-LunarLite from [8] (Sect. 9.4).

We can provide an upper bound on the total proof size for the instantiations above to $20\mathbb{G}_1$ elements[10] per each of the proof above (this is a loose upper bound)—see Table 1 in this work, Table 1 and Sect. 9.4 in [8]. On a concrete curve like BLS12-381 this yields a total proof size of *at most* approximately 3.84 KB (this is a generous lower bound). For comparison, the proof size in [40] is of the order of hundreds of kilobytes.

[9] The idea is to consider the table $\mathbf{b} = (j)_{j\in[B]}$ and prove, through a lookup argument, that that $\bar{\mathbf{x}} \prec \mathbf{b}$ where $\bar{\mathbf{x}}$ is the vectorization of $\mathbf{X}$.

[10] We approximate the size of field elements with that of $\mathbb{G}_1$ elements.

Decision Tree Accuracy. In the specific case of proving decision tree accuracy we prove that a decision tree is able to correctly estimate a specific fraction of a given data sample. Namely we consider the statistic that upon input $(v_j)_{j\in[m]}, (y_j)_{j\in[m]}$ computes $\sum_j \mathsf{eq}_k (v_j, y_j) / m$, $v_j = \mathsf{T}(\mathbf{x}_j)$ for $j \in [m]$ where $k \in \mathbb{N}$ is a small constant and eq_k is the function returning 1 when its two arguments, of size k, are equal[11]; otherwise it returns 0. Thanks to Theorem 4 this can be reduced to a CP-SNARK for the following relation[12]:

$$\mathcal{R}_{\mathsf{acc}} = \left\{ (m, k); \left((y_j)_{j\in[m]}, n^*\right); (v_j)_{j\in[m]} : n^* = \sum_j \mathsf{eq}_k (v_j, y_j) \right\} \tag{27}$$

Even with an R1CS-based (Rank-1 Constraint System) general purpose SNARK, the relation above can be implemented very efficiently.

Our estimates show improvements of almost one order of magnitude for proving time and two orders of magnitude for verification time for representative choices of parameters (see full version for details). Our prover runs in the order of a few seconds; our verifier in the order of 100 ms. The construction in [40] in contrast has a prover running in the order of minutes (2–5 m) and a verifier running in the order of 10 s[13].

Table 2. Comparison between our solution and [40] for zero-knowledge decision tree accuracy. Parameters are d (number of attributes), m (size of sample), $|\mathcal{H}|$ is the cost of hash function invocation (such as SHA256); $|\mathcal{H}_{\mathrm{circ}}|$ is the cost of a hash function invocation as a circuit; $\mathbb{P}$ is the cost of one pairing. Notation $\tilde{O}(f)$ refers to $O(f \log f)$. This table does not include the one-time cost of preprocessing for the prover (see Table 1 for concrete costs). Notice that the asymptotics in the row for our construction account for just the commitment algorithm and the *extractability* proof. The asymptotics reported for [40] are actually a lower bound and do not include some additional factors in their complexity, such as tree height. Dominated factors, such as B and k (input and output size of decision tree respectively), are also not included in the asymptotics.

Scheme	Commit Time	Prover Time	Verifier Time	Proof Size
[40]	$O(N_{\mathrm{tot}})\|\mathcal{H}\|$	$\tilde{O}(md + N_{\mathrm{tot}} \log m + N_{\mathrm{tot}}\|\mathcal{H}_{\mathrm{circ}}\|)\mathbb{F}$	$O(md)\mathbb{F}$	$O(\log^2(md))\mathfrak{f}$
Our solution	$\tilde{O}(dN_{\mathrm{tot}})(\mathbb{G} + \mathbb{F})$	$\tilde{O}(md)(\mathbb{G} + \mathbb{F})$	$O(m)\mathbb{G} + O(1)\mathbb{P}$	$O(1)(\mathfrak{g}_1 + \mathfrak{f})$

Acknowledgements. This work has received funding from the MESRI-BMBF French-German joint project named PROPOLIS (ANR-20-CYAL-0004-01), the Dutch Research Council (NWO) under Project Spark! Living Lab (439.18.453B), the European Research Council (ERC) under the European Union's Horizon 2020 research and innovation programme under project PICOCRYPT (grant agreement No. 101001283),

[11] In typical applications of decision trees the labels are integer values belonging to a small domains, for example, either booleans or bytes.

[12] Here expressed as a sum instead of a fraction. Since the size of the sample is public this is equivalent.

[13] These estimates refer to running times on an AWS EC2 c5.9xlarge. This architecture is comparable to the one used in [40].

and from the Spanish Government MCIN/AEI/ 10.13039/501100011033/ under projects PRODIGY (TED2021-132464B-I00) and ESPADA (PID2022-142290OB-I00). The last two projects are co-funded by European Union FEDER and NextGenerationEU/PRTR funds.

We thank Melek Onën for her contributions during the early stages of this project.

References

1. Ali, R.E., So, J., Avestimehr, A.S.: On polynomial approximations for privacy-preserving and verifiable RELU networks. arXiv preprint arXiv:2011.05530 (2021)
2. Aranha, D.F., Bennedsen, E.M., Campanelli, M., Ganesh, C., Orlandi, C., Takahashi, A.: ECLIPSE: enhanced compiling method for Pedersen-committed zkSNARK engines. In: Hanaoka, G., Shikata, J., Watanabe, Y. (eds.) PKC 2022, Part I. LNCS, vol. 13177, pp. 584–614. Springer, Heidelberg (2022). https://doi.org/10.1007/978-3-030-97121-2_21
3. Arun, A., Setty, S., Thaler, J.: Jolt: Snarks for virtual machines via lookups. Cryptology ePrint Archive, Paper 2023/1217 (2023). https://eprint.iacr.org/2023/1217
4. Ben-Sasson, E., Chiesa, A., Genkin, D., Tromer, E., Virza, M.: SNARKs for C: verifying program executions succinctly and in zero knowledge. In: Canetti, R., Garay, J.A. (eds.) CRYPTO 2013, Part II. LNCS, vol. 8043, pp. 90–108. Springer, Heidelberg (2013). https://doi.org/10.1007/978-3-642-40084-1_6
5. Ben-Sasson, E., Chiesa, A., Riabzev, M., Spooner, N., Virza, M., Ward, N.P.: Aurora: transparent succinct arguments for R1CS. In: Ishai, Y., Rijmen, V. (eds.) EUROCRYPT 2019, Part I. LNCS, vol. 11476, pp. 103–128. Springer, Heidelberg (2019). https://doi.org/10.1007/978-3-030-17653-2_4
6. Bootle, J., Cerulli, A., Groth, J., Jakobsen, S.K., Maller, M.: Arya: nearly linear-time zero-knowledge proofs for correct program execution. In: Peyrin, T., Galbraith, S. (eds.) ASIACRYPT 2018, Part I. LNCS, vol. 11272, pp. 595–626. Springer, Heidelberg (2018). https://doi.org/10.1007/978-3-030-03326-2_20
7. Campanelli, M., Faonio, A., Fiore, D., Li, T., Lipmaa, H.: Lookup arguments: improvements, extensions and applications to zero-knowledge decision trees. Cryptology ePrint Archive, Paper 2023/1518 (2023). https://eprint.iacr.org/2023/1518
8. Campanelli, M., Faonio, A., Fiore, D., Querol, A., Rodríguez, H.: Lunar: a toolbox for more efficient universal and updatable zkSNARKs and commit-and-prove extensions. In: Tibouchi, M., Wang, H. (eds.) ASIACRYPT 2021, Part III. LNCS, vol. 13092, pp. 3–33. Springer, Heidelberg (2021). https://doi.org/10.1007/978-3-030-92078-4_1
9. Campanelli, M., Fiore, D., Querol, A.: LegoSNARK: modular design and composition of succinct zero-knowledge proofs. In: Cavallaro, L., Kinder, J., Wang, X., Katz, J. (eds.) ACM CCS 2019, pp. 2075–2092. ACM Press (2019). https://doi.org/10.1145/3319535.3339820
10. Chen, B., Bünz, B., Boneh, D., Zhang, Z.: HyperPlonk: Plonk with linear-time prover and high-degree custom gates. In: EUROCRYPT 2023, Part II. LNCS, vol. 14005, pp. 499–530. Springer, Heidelberg (2023). https://doi.org/10.1007/978-3-031-30617-4_17
11. Chen, H., Zhang, H., Si, S., Li, Y., Boning, D.S., Hsieh, C.: Robustness verification of tree-based models. In: Wallach, H.M., Larochelle, H., Beygelzimer, A., d'Alché-Buc, F., Fox, E.B., Garnett, R. (eds.) NeurIPS 2019, pp. 12317–12328. Curran Associates, Inc., Red Hook (2019). https://proceedings.neurips.cc/paper/2019/hash/cd9508fdaa5c1390e9cc329001cf1459-Abstract.html

12. Chiesa, A., Hu, Y., Maller, M., Mishra, P., Vesely, P., Ward, N.P.: Marlin: preprocessing zkSNARKs with universal and updatable SRS. In: Canteaut, A., Ishai, Y. (eds.) EUROCRYPT 2020, Part I. LNCS, vol. 12105, pp. 738–768. Springer, Heidelberg (2020). https://doi.org/10.1007/978-3-030-45721-1_26
13. Choudhuri, A.R., Garg, S., Goel, A., Sekar, S., Sinha, R.: Sublonk: sublinear prover plonk. Cryptology ePrint Archive, Paper 2023/902 (2023). https://eprint.iacr.org/2023/902
14. Eagen, L., Fiore, D., Gabizon, A.: cq: Cached quotients for fast lookups. Cryptology ePrint Archive, Report 2022/1763 (2022). https://eprint.iacr.org/2022/1763
15. Faust, S., Kohlweiss, M., Marson, G.A., Venturi, D.: On the non-malleability of the Fiat-Shamir transform. In: Galbraith, S.D., Nandi, M. (eds.) INDOCRYPT 2012. LNCS, vol. 7668, pp. 60–79. Springer, Heidelberg (2012). https://doi.org/10.1007/978-3-642-34931-7_5
16. Feng, B., Qin, L., Zhang, Z., Ding, Y., Chu, S.: ZEN: an optimizing compiler for verifiable, zero-knowledge neural network inferences. Cryptology ePrint Archive, Report 2021/087 (2021). https://eprint.iacr.org/2021/087
17. Fuchsbauer, G., Kiltz, E., Loss, J.: The algebraic group model and its applications. In: Shacham, H., Boldyreva, A. (eds.) CRYPTO 2018, Part II. LNCS, vol. 10992, pp. 33–62. Springer, Heidelberg (2018). https://doi.org/10.1007/978-3-319-96881-0_2
18. Gabizon, A., Williamson, Z.J.: plookup: a simplified polynomial protocol for lookup tables. Cryptology ePrint Archive, Report 2020/315 (2020). https://eprint.iacr.org/2020/315
19. Gabizon, A., Williamson, Z.J., Ciobotaru, O.: PLONK: permutations over lagrange-bases for oecumenical noninteractive arguments of knowledge. Cryptology ePrint Archive, Report 2019/953 (2019). https://eprint.iacr.org/2019/953
20. Ganesh, C., Orlandi, C., Pancholi, M., Takahashi, A., Tschudi, D.: Fiat-Shamir bulletproofs are non-malleable (in the algebraic group model). In: Dunkelman, O., Dziembowski, S. (eds.) EUROCRYPT 2022, Part II. LNCS, vol. 13276, pp. 397–426. Springer, Heidelberg (2022). https://doi.org/10.1007/978-3-031-07085-3_14
21. Groth, J.: On the size of pairing-based non-interactive arguments. In: Fischlin, M., Coron, J.S. (eds.) EUROCRYPT 2016, Part II. LNCS, vol. 9666, pp. 305–326. Springer, Heidelberg (2016). https://doi.org/10.1007/978-3-662-49896-5_11
22. Groth, J., Kohlweiss, M., Maller, M., Meiklejohn, S., Miers, I.: Updatable and universal common reference strings with applications to zk-SNARKs. In: Shacham, H., Boldyreva, A. (eds.) CRYPTO 2018, Part III. LNCS, vol. 10993, pp. 698–728. Springer, Heidelberg (2018). https://doi.org/10.1007/978-3-319-96878-0_24
23. Haböck, U.: Multivariate lookups based on logarithmic derivatives. Cryptology ePrint Archive, Report 2022/1530 (2022). https://eprint.iacr.org/2022/1530
24. Kang, D., Hashimoto, T., Stoica, I., Sun, Y.: Scaling up trustless DNN inference with zero-knowledge proofs. arXiv preprint arXiv:2210.08674 (2022)
25. Kate, A., Zaverucha, G.M., Goldberg, I.: Constant-size commitments to polynomials and their applications. In: Abe, M. (ed.) ASIACRYPT 2010. LNCS, vol. 6477, pp. 177–194. Springer, Heidelberg (2010). https://doi.org/10.1007/978-3-642-17373-8_11
26. Lee, S., Ko, H., Kim, J., Oh, H.: vcnn: Verifiable convolutional neural network based on zk-snarks. IEEE Trans. Depend. Secur. Comput. 1–17 (2023). https://doi.org/10.1109/TDSC.2023.3348760
27. Lipmaa, H.: Progression-free sets and sublinear pairing-based non-interactive zero-knowledge arguments. In: Cramer, R. (ed.) TCC 2012. LNCS, vol. 7194, pp. 169–189. Springer, Heidelberg (2012). https://doi.org/10.1007/978-3-642-28914-9_10

28. Lipmaa, H., Parisella, R., Siim, J.: Algebraic group model with oblivious sampling. In: Rothblum, G., Wee, H. (eds.) TCC 2023 (4). LNCS, vol. 14372, pp. 363–392. Springer, Cham (2023). https://doi.org/10.1007/978-3-031-48624-1_14
29. Lipmaa, H., Siim, J., Zajac, M.: Counting vampires: from univariate sumcheck to updatable ZK-SNARK. In: Agrawal, S., Lin, D. (eds.) ASIACRYPT 2022, Part II. LNCS, vol. 13792, pp. 249–278. Springer, Heidelberg (2022). https://doi.org/10.1007/978-3-031-22966-4_9
30. Liu, T., Xie, X., Zhang, Y.: zkCNN: zero knowledge proofs for convolutional neural network predictions and accuracy. In: Vigna, G., Shi, E. (eds.) ACM CCS 2021, pp. 2968–2985. ACM Press (2021). https://doi.org/10.1145/3460120.3485379
31. Maller, M., Bowe, S., Kohlweiss, M., Meiklejohn, S.: Sonic: zero-knowledge SNARKs from linear-size universal and updatable structured reference strings. In: Cavallaro, L., Kinder, J., Wang, X., Katz, J. (eds.) ACM CCS 2019, pp. 2111–2128. ACM Press (2019). https://doi.org/10.1145/3319535.3339817
32. Posen, J., Kattis, A.A.: Caulk+: table-independent lookup arguments. Cryptology ePrint Archive, Report 2022/957 (2022). https://eprint.iacr.org/2022/957
33. Ràfols, C., Zapico, A.: An algebraic framework for universal and updatable SNARKs. In: Malkin, T., Peikert, C. (eds.) CRYPTO 2021, Part I. LNCS, vol. 12825, pp. 774–804. Springer, Heidelberg, Virtual Event (2021). https://doi.org/10.1007/978-3-030-84242-0_27
34. Setty, S.: Spartan: efficient and general-purpose zkSNARKs without trusted setup. In: Micciancio, D., Ristenpart, T. (eds.) CRYPTO 2020, Part III. LNCS, vol. 12172, pp. 704–737. Springer, Heidelberg (2020). https://doi.org/10.1007/978-3-030-56877-1_25
35. Setty, S., Thaler, J., Wahby, R.: Unlocking the lookup singularity with lasso. Cryptology ePrint Archive, Paper 2023/1216 (2023). https://eprint.iacr.org/2023/1216
36. Wang, H., Hoang, T.: ezdps: an efficient and zero-knowledge machine learning inference pipeline. PoPETs **2023**(2), 430–448 (2023). https://doi.org/10.56553/popets-2023-0061
37. Weng, J., Weng, J., Tang, G., Yang, A., Li, M., Liu, J.: PVCNN: privacy-preserving and verifiable convolutional neural network testing. IEEE Trans. Inf. Forens. Secur. **18**, 2218–2233 (2023). https://doi.org/10.1109/TIFS.2023.3262932
38. Zapico, A., Buterin, V., Khovratovich, D., Maller, M., Nitulescu, A., Simkin, M.: Caulk: lookup arguments in sublinear time. In: Yin, H., Stavrou, A., Cremers, C., Shi, E. (eds.) ACM CCS 2022, pp. 3121–3134. ACM Press (2022). https://doi.org/10.1145/3548606.3560646
39. Zapico, A., Gabizon, A., Khovratovich, D., Maller, M., Ràfols, C.: Baloo: nearly optimal lookup arguments. Cryptology ePrint Archive, Report 2022/1565 (2022). https://eprint.iacr.org/2022/1565
40. Zhang, J., Fang, Z., Zhang, Y., Song, D.: Zero knowledge proofs for decision tree predictions and accuracy. In: Ligatti, J., Ou, X., Katz, J., Vigna, G. (eds.) ACM CCS 2020, pp. 2039–2053. ACM Press (2020). https://doi.org/10.1145/3372297.3417278

Short Code-Based One-out-of-Many Proofs and Applications

Xindong Liu[1,2] and Li-Ping Wang[1,2](✉)

[1] Key Laboratory of Cyberspace Security Defense, Institute of Information Engineering, CAS, Beijing, China
{liuxindong,wangliping}@iie.ac.cn
[2] School of Cyber Security, University of Chinese Academy of Sciences, Beijing, China

Abstract. In this work, we propose two novel succinct one-out-of-many proofs from coding theory, which can be seen as extensions of the Stern's framework and Veron's framework from proving knowledge of a preimage to proving knowledge of a preimage for one element in a set, respectively. The size of each proof is short and scales better with the size of the public set than the code-based accumulator in [35]. Based on our new constructions, we further present a logarithmic-size ring signature scheme and a logarithmic-size group signature scheme. Our schemes feature short signature sizes, especially our group signature. To our best knowledge, it is the most compact code-based group signature scheme so far. At 128-bit security level, our group signature size is about 144 KB for a group with 2^{20} members while the group signature size of the previously most compact code-based group signature constructed by the above accumulator exceeds 3200 KB.

Keywords: code-based cryptography · one-out-of-many proofs · set-membership proofs · ring signatures · group signatures

1 Introduction

Code-based cryptography is the study of cryptosystems based on error-correcting codes that originated from the pioneering work of McEliece [29]. It is able to resist quantum attacks and is widely regarded as an important research branch in post-quantum cryptography. In particular, NIST's recent call for post-quantum standardization has propelled advancements in this area.

Zero-knowledge proofs are a fundamental primitive in cryptography. In 1993, Stern proposed the first code-based zero-knowledge argument of knowledge (ZKA oK) based on the hardness of the syndrome decoding (SD) problem [38]. This proof enables one to demonstrate knowledge of a low-weight preimage for a syndrome. Later, Veron introduced a ZKAoK for the general syndrome decoding (GSD) problem, which is the "dual" problem of the SD problem [39]. Subsequently, several optimization schemes have been proposed within this framework [5,7,11,31,39], as well as applied to other hard problem settings [20,24,26].

Q. Tang and V. Teague (Eds.): PKC 2024, LNCS 14602, pp. 370–399, 2024.
https://doi.org/10.1007/978-3-031-57722-2_12

Moreover, variants of the Stern protocol or the Veron protocol have been utilized to construct numerous advanced cryptographic schemes, such as proofs of valid opening for code-based commitment schemes [35], verifiable encryption [34], ring signatures [9,10,30], group signatures [1,8,17] and accumulators [3,35].

An important tool in zero-knowledge proofs is one-out-of-many proofs, which enable one to demonstrate knowledge of an opening to a commitment within a list of commitments. This concept is closely related to some primitives such as set-membership proofs and ring signatures. Groth and Kohlweiss initially provided an efficient one-out-of-many proof based on discrete logarithms and applied it in ring signatures [21]. Subsequently, Esgin et al. constructed a lattice-based one-out-of-many proof [16]. In 2022, Lyubashevsky et al. further constructed a more efficient lattice-based one-out-of-many proof and based on this proof, they proposed a logarithmic ring signature and a logarithmic group signature [28].

However, similar constructions in code-based cryptography are not practical. In 2015, Ezerman et al. proposed a construction for proving knowledge of a secret for one syndrome in a public set, and applied it to build a code-based group signature scheme [17]. The group signature size is linear to the number N of group members. While it has a short signature size with a small N, as N grows to 2^{20}, its signature size increases to 19 MB under the 128-bit security level. The similar construction can be found in [2,8]. In 2019, Nguyen et al. put forward a code-based Merkle-tree accumulator, which is a logarithmic-size set-membership proof [35]. Based on this building block, the authors constructed logarithmic-size ring signature and group signature schemes. In 2020, Beullers et al. developed a general group-action based ring signature framework [6]. Subsequently, Barenghi et al. and Chou et al. instantiated the group action using the code equivalence problem [4] and the matrix code equivalence problem [13], respectively, and proposed efficient ring signature schemes. However, no group signature scheme has been constructed based on these two problems so far.

1.1 Our Contributions

Our main cryptographic results are summarized as follows (we describe them in more detail in our technique overview):

- We propose a novel short code-based one-out-of-many proof. Our construction can be seen as an extension of Stern's framework from proving knowledge of a preimage to proving knowledge of a preimage for one element in a public set. The main advantage of our framework is that the growth rate of the proof size relative to the public set size N is very low even compared to the code-based accumulator (Asiacrypt 2019). This is because the term related to N in the expression of the signature size of our schemes is simply determined by the path of a $\log N$-deep Merkle tree, that is $2\lambda \log N$, where λ is the security level, and so is independent of the parameters of the hard problem. The code-based accumulator achieves membership proof by proving knowledge of a hash chain that is linearly related to the parameters of the regular SD problem. This makes the coefficient of $\log N$ much larger than ours.

- To further reduce the proof size, we propose a more efficient GSD-based one-out-of-many proof based on Veron's framework and optimization techniques proposed in [23,31]. Then, we apply this one-out-of-many proof to the construction of a logarithm-size ring signature. Next, we compare our ring signature with other code-based ring signatures in Table 1.
- We construct a new set membership proof by transforming the framework of building one-out-of-many proofs into the framework of building set membership proofs. This transformation is similar to the ideas in [21]. Moreover, this set membership proof serves as a building block in our group signature.
- Combining our GSD-based one-out-of-many proof and the set-membership proof, we present a logarithm-size group signature, which is the most compact code-based group signature scheme to date. We also make the comparison with other code-based group signatures in Table 2. For convenience, we use the parameter sets for SD problem in [18], and the parameter sets for the McEliece encryption scheme in [12]. The above comparison indicates that the signature sizes of both our ring signature and group signature schemes are significantly shorter than previous schemes except the BBNPS in [4], whose security relies on the code equivalence problem.

Table 1. Comparison of ring signature size (KB) under the 128-bit security level.

	N			asymptotic sig.size	hardness assumption
	2^8	2^{12}	2^{20}		
ELLNW [17]	55	124	19273	$\mathcal{O}(N)$	SD
BGM [8]	134	205	19354	$\mathcal{O}(N)$	rank SD
NTWZ [35]	1189	1741	2847	$\mathcal{O}(\log N)$	regular SD
BBNPS [4]	16	20	28	$\mathcal{O}(\log N)$	code equivalence
Our work	55	65	83	$\mathcal{O}(\log N)$	GSD

Table 2. Comparison of group signature size (KB) under the 128-bit security level.

	N			asymptotic sig.size	Anonymity
	2^8	2^{12}	2^{20}		
ELLNW [17]	171	241	19391	$\mathcal{O}(N)$	CPA
BGM [8]	1322	1392	20542	$\mathcal{O}(N)$	CPA
NTWZ [35]	1570	2122	3228	$\mathcal{O}(\log N)$	CCA
Our work	116	126	144	$\mathcal{O}(\log N)$	CPA

1.2 Technical Overview

SD-Based One-out-of-Many Proofs. Our novel SD-based one-out-of-many proof is an extension to Stern's framework. To construct the protocol, we begin by making a modification to the original Stern protocol. Let $\mathbf{H} \in \mathbb{F}_2^{(n-k)\times n}$ and $\mathbf{s} \in \mathbb{F}_2^{n-k}$ denote a matrix and a syndrome, respectively. To prove the possession of a small-weight vector $\mathbf{e} \in \mathbb{F}_2^n$ such that $\mathbf{He}^\top = \mathbf{s}^\top$, a prover samples a random vector $\mathbf{r} \in \mathbb{F}_2^n$ and a random permutation ϕ, and then sends commitments $c_1 = \mathrm{Com}(\phi, \mathbf{Hr}^\top + \mathbf{s}^\top; \rho_1)$, $c_2 = \mathrm{Com}(\phi(\mathbf{r}); \rho_2)$ and $c_3 = \mathrm{Com}(\phi(\mathbf{r}+\mathbf{e}); \rho_3)$ to a verifier. If the challenge ch is 1, the prover opens c_2 and c_3. If $ch = 2$, it opens c_1 and c_3. If $ch = 3$, it opens c_1 and c_2. The modified Stern protocol is depicted in Fig. 1. The only difference between our protocol in Fig. 1 and the original Stern protocol is that in the former $c_1 = \mathrm{Com}(\phi, \mathbf{Hr}^\top + \mathbf{s}^\top; \rho_1)$ while in the latter $c_1 = \mathrm{Com}(\phi, \mathbf{Hr}^\top; \rho_1)$. Clearly, this modification does not affect the completeness, soundness, and zero-knowledge property of the modified protocol.

Observe two key facts: (1) The modified protocol's c_1 is related to the public key $\mathbf{s}$, while c_2 and c_3 are not related to $\mathbf{s}$. (2) During the verification phase, only when $ch = 3$, the verifier needs to use the public key $\mathbf{s}$ to check the value of c_1. These two observations inspire us to construct a one-out-of-many proof based on our modified protocol.

For a statement composing of a matrix $\mathbf{H}$ and N syndromes $(\mathbf{s}_1, \cdots, \mathbf{s}_N)$, a prover claims that it knows the small-weight preimage $\mathbf{e}$ of one of the syndromes satisfying $\mathbf{He}^\top = \mathbf{s}_I^\top$ for some $I \in [N]$, $[N] := \{1, \cdots, N\}$. To demonstrate this, the prover begins by sampling a random mask vector $\mathbf{r}$, a random permutation ϕ and N random coins $\{b_i\}_{i=1}^N$ to simulate $c_1^i = \mathrm{Com}(\phi, \mathbf{He}^\top + \mathbf{s}_i^\top; b_i)$ for all $i \in [N]$. Subsequently, it samples two random coins ρ_2 and ρ_3 to generate $c_2 = \mathrm{Com}(\phi(\mathbf{r}); \rho_2)$ and $c_3 = \mathrm{Com}(\phi(\mathbf{r}+\mathbf{e}); \rho_3)$. The prover then permutes $(c_1^1, \cdots, c_1^N)$ in random order and sends them along with c_2 and c_3 to a verifier. If the verifier returns 1, the prover will open c_2 and c_3 by revealing $(\phi(\mathbf{r}), \phi(\mathbf{r}+\mathbf{e}), \rho_2, \rho_3)$. This does not leak any information about the witness $\mathbf{e}$ and the index I. If the verifier returns 2, the prover will open c_1^I and c_3 by revealing $(\phi, \mathbf{r}+\mathbf{e}, \rho_1, b_I, \rho_3)$. Since the verifier receives a random permutation of $(c_1^1, \cdots, c_1^N)$ and only verifies whether c_1^I is in it, this also does not leak any information about the index I and witness $\mathbf{e}$. If the verifier returns 3, the prover will open all $\{c_1^i\}_{i=1}^N$ and c_2 by outputting ϕ, $\mathbf{r}$ and all random coins $\{b_i\}_{i=1}^N$. Therefore, no information about the witness $\mathbf{e}$ and the index I is leaked.

In the above process, the prover sends $N+2$ commitments $(\{c_1^i\}_{i=1}^N, c_2, c_3)$ during the commitment phase. In the response phase, when the received challenge is 3, the prover needs to open these $N+2$ commitments by outputting $N+2$ random coins. Therefore, the proof size grows linearly with N. To reduce the proof size, we use a seedtree to generate N random coins required for these N commitments $\{c_1^i\}_{i=1}^N$, and compress these commitments into a root using a Merkle tree. Specifically, the prover first samples a random seed, and then uses a pseudo-random number generator (PRNG) to iteratively generate N random coins required for the N commitments $\{c_1^i\}_{i=1}^N$. Subsequently, the prover arranges these N commitments in lexicographical order and compresses the sorted list into a root using a Merkle tree. This trick is inspired by [6]. Next, the prover sends $(\mathrm{root}, c_2, c_3)$ to the verifier. If the verifier returns 1, the prover's output remains unchanged. If the verifier returns 2, the prover opens c_I and c_3 by outputting

Round 1: $\mathcal{P}((\mathbf{H},\mathbf{s}),\mathbf{e})$ chooses the following random objects:

$$\mathbf{r} \xleftarrow{\$} \mathbb{F}_2^n, \phi \xleftarrow{\$} \mathcal{S}_n, \rho_1, \rho_2, \rho_3 \xleftarrow{\$} \{0,1\}^\lambda.$$

and sends CMT $:= (c_1, c_2, c_3)$ to $\mathcal{V}$, where

$$c_1 = \text{Com}(\phi, \mathbf{Hr}^\top + \mathbf{s}^\top; \rho_1), c_2 = \text{Com}(\phi(\mathbf{r}); \rho_2), c_3 = \text{Com}(\phi(\mathbf{r}+\mathbf{e}); \rho_3).$$

Round 2: $\mathcal{V}(\text{CMT})$ sends a $ch \leftarrow \{1,2,3\}$ to $\mathcal{P}$.
Round 3: $\mathcal{P}((\mathbf{H},\mathbf{s}),\mathbf{e},ch)$:
- $ch = 1$: Set $\mathbf{v}_1 = \phi(\mathbf{r}), \mathbf{v}_2 = \phi(\mathbf{e})$ and send RSP $= (\mathbf{v}_1, \mathbf{v}_2, \rho_2, \rho_3)$ to $\mathcal{V}$.
- $ch = 2$: Set $\mathbf{u}_1 = \mathbf{r}+\mathbf{e}, \pi_1 = \phi$ and send RSP $= (\mathbf{u}_1, \pi_1, \rho_1, \rho_3)$ to $\mathcal{V}$.
- $ch = 3$: Set $\mathbf{u}_2 = \mathbf{r}, \pi_2 = \phi$ and send RSP $= (\mathbf{u}_2, \pi_2, \rho_1, \rho_2)$ to $\mathcal{V}$.

Verification: $\mathcal{V}(\text{CMT}, ch, \text{RSP})$:
- $ch = 1$: Check if $c_2 = \text{Com}(\mathbf{v}_1; \rho_2), c_3 = \text{Com}(\mathbf{v}_1 + \mathbf{v}_2; \rho_3)$ and $\mathbf{v}_2 \in B(n,t)$.
- $ch = 2$: Check if $c_1 = \text{Com}(\pi_1, \mathbf{Hu}_1^\top; \rho_1)$ and $c_3 = \text{Com}(\pi_1(\mathbf{u}_1); \rho_3)$.
- $ch = 3$: Check if $c_1 = \text{Com}(\pi_2, \mathbf{Hu}_2^\top + \mathbf{s}^\top; \rho_1)$ and $c_2 = \text{Com}(\pi_2(\mathbf{u}_2); \rho_2)$.

Fig. 1. The modified Stern protocol. Let $B(n,t)$ denote the set of vectors $\mathbf{v} \in \mathbb{F}_2^n$ such that its Hamming weight $w(\mathbf{v}) = t$, $\mathcal{S}_n$ denote the symmetric group of all permutations of n elements and Com denote a commitment scheme with the binding and hiding property.

$(\phi, \mathbf{r}+\mathbf{e}, \rho_1, b_I, \rho_3)$ and the path of c_I in the Merkle tree. So the length of the path is $\log N$. If the verifier returns 3, the verifier opens all $\{c_1^i\}_{i=1}^N$ and c_2 by outputting $(\phi, \mathbf{r})$ and seed.

GSD-Based One-out-of-Many Proofs. In 1997, Veron pointed that the GSD-based protocol with a ternary challenge space has lower communication cost than the Stern protocol [39]. The GSD problem is to find two vectors $\mathbf{x} \in \mathbb{F}_2^k$ and $\mathbf{e} \in B(n,t)$ such that $\mathbf{y} = \mathbf{xG} + \mathbf{e}$ given a matrix $\mathbf{G} \in \mathbb{F}_2^{k\times n}$ and a vector $\mathbf{y} \in \mathbb{F}_2^n$. Although the security proof of this construction [39] has been pointed out to have an issue [22], it has been fixed by Gaborit et al. [5]. The fixed protocol still maintains low communication cost. This improvement is due to the use of the GSD problem instead of the SD problem. In fact, the hardness of two problems is equivalent, while the only difference lies in the use of a generator matrix in the former and a parity-check matrix in the latter. Inspired by this, we construct a GSD-based one-out-of-many proof. Additionally, we use three techniques, namely small-weight vector compression functions [31], seedtrees and Merkle trees [23] to reduce the communication cost of multi-iteration protocols. Seedtrees are used to generate random objects required while Merkle trees are employed to compress commitments in multi-iteration protocols.

Our GSD-based one-out-of-many proof naturally lead to a ring signature scheme by the Fiat-Shamir transform [19]. Specifically, each user i has a public-private key pair $(\mathbf{y}_i, (\mathbf{x}_i, \mathbf{e}_i))$, where $\mathbf{y}_i = \mathbf{x}_i\mathbf{G} + \mathbf{e}_i$. The signature of user i for a message μ is a zero-knowledge proof using our GSD-based one-out-of-many proof for the pair $(\mathbf{x}_i, \mathbf{e}_i)$ satisfying the above equation, where μ is the input in the random oracle in the Fiat-Shamir heuristic.

Set-Membership Proofs. First we briefly introduce the code-based commitment scheme [33]. For a message $\mathbf{m} \in \{0,1\}^{k_2}$, one initially chooses two random vectors $\mathbf{v} \in \mathbb{F}_2^{k_1}$, $\mathbf{e} \in B(n,t)$, and obtains a McEliece-type commitment

$$\mathrm{Com}_{\mathrm{McE}}(\mathbf{m};(\mathbf{v},\mathbf{e})) = (\mathbf{v}||\mathbf{m})\mathbf{G} + \mathbf{e},$$

where $\mathbf{G} = \begin{pmatrix} \mathbf{G}_1 \\ \mathbf{G}_2 \end{pmatrix} \in \mathbb{F}_2^{k\times n}$ is randomly generated, $\mathbf{G}_1 \in \mathbb{F}_2^{k_1\times n}, \mathbf{G}_2 \in \mathbb{F}_2^{k_2\times n}, k = k_1 + k_2$. To open a commitment $\mathbf{c}$, one reveals $\mathbf{m}, \mathbf{v}, \mathbf{e}$ and a receiver verifies if $\mathbf{c} = (\mathbf{v}||\mathbf{m})\mathbf{G} + \mathbf{e}$.

In our set-membership proof, the public information includes a public set $\mathcal{I} = \{\alpha_1, \cdots, \alpha_N\}$ and a commitment $\mathbf{c}$ for some α_i. A prover's goal is to demonstrate that $\mathbf{c}$ is a commitment to an element in the set $\mathcal{I}$. To achieve this, the prover first generates $[\mathbf{c}_1 = \mathbf{c} + \mathrm{Com}_{\mathrm{McE}}(\alpha_1, (\mathbf{0},\mathbf{0})), \cdots, \mathbf{c}_N = \mathbf{c} + \mathrm{Com}_{\mathrm{McE}}(\alpha_N, (\mathbf{0},\mathbf{0}))]$, and then proves that one of $(\{\mathbf{c}_i\}_{i=1}^N)$ is a commitment to $\mathbf{0}$. This is equivalent to proving that a prover knows a certain $\mathbf{c}_i$ having the form of $\mathbf{v}\mathbf{G}_1 + \mathbf{e}$, where $\mathbf{e} \in B(n,t)$ and $i \in [N]$.

Group Signatures. We use the enc-then-prove framework to construct our group signature scheme. This framework typically requires three cryptographic layers: a secure signature scheme, a semantically secure encryption scheme and a zero-knowledge protocol connecting the first two layers. Let's now explain the construction of the three components used in our group signature scheme.

Consider a group of size N, with each user being denoted by an integer $i \in [N]$. For each i, the public key of the User i is $(\mathbf{G}, \mathbf{y}_i = \mathbf{x}_i\mathbf{G} + \mathbf{e}_i) \in \mathbb{F}_2^{k\times n} \times \mathbb{F}_2^n$, and the private key is $(\mathbf{x}_i, \mathbf{e}_i) \in \mathbb{F}_2^k \times B(n,t)$.

The Signature Layer. The construction in this layer is similar to our ring signature. User i uses our GSD-based one-out-of-many proof to prove that it has a pair $(\mathbf{x}_i, \mathbf{e}_i) \in \mathbb{F}_2^k \times B(n,t)$ satisfying $\mathbf{x}_i\mathbf{G} + \mathbf{e}_i = \mathbf{y}_i$.

The Encryption Layer. To achieve the traceability of group signatures, User i encrypts its index i using the randomized McEliece encryption scheme [36] as follows:

$$\mathbf{ct} = \mathrm{Enc}_{\mathrm{McE}}(\mathrm{bin}(i), (\mathbf{z},\mathbf{s})) = (\mathbf{z}||\mathrm{bin}(i))\mathbf{G}_{\mathrm{McE}} + \mathbf{s},$$

where $\mathbf{G}_{\mathrm{McE}} \in \mathbb{F}_2^{\ell\times m}$ is the public key of McEliece encryption scheme, $\mathrm{bin}(i)$ is the binary representation of i with length ℓ_2, $\mathbf{z} \in \mathbb{F}_2^{\ell_1}$, $\ell = \ell_1 + \ell_2$ and $\mathbf{s} \in B(m,w)$. Then, User i needs to prove that $\mathbf{ct}$ is an encryption to an index in the set $\{1, \cdots, N\}$. This is similar to our set-membership proof. Specifically, User i first generates the set

$$[\mathbf{ct}_1 = \mathbf{ct} + \mathrm{Enc}_{\mathrm{McE}}(1, (\mathbf{0},\mathbf{0})), \cdots, \mathbf{ct}_N + \mathrm{Enc}_{\mathrm{McE}}(N, (\mathbf{0},\mathbf{0}))],$$

and proves that $\mathbf{ct}_i$ is the encryption of 0, which means that $\mathbf{ct}_i$ has the form of $(\mathbf{z}||0)\mathbf{G}_{\mathrm{McE}} + \mathbf{s}$, where $\mathbf{z} \in \mathbb{F}_2^{\ell_1}$ and $\mathbf{s} \in B(m,w)$.

The Third Layer. User i must prove that it encrypts its own index i honestly, which requires combining the former one-out-of-many proof with the latter set-memberships proof. The overarching concept is to pair the $N + 2$ commitments from the former proof with the $N+2$ commitments from the latter proof respectively, forming $N+2$ pairs sequentially from 1 to $N+2$. Then shuffle the last N commitment pairs related to $\{\mathbf{y}_i\}_{i=1}^N$ and $\{\mathbf{ct}_i\}_{i=1}^N$, and send them along with another two pairs to a verifier. The remaining steps are similar to our GSD-based one-out-of-many proof, with the difference being what needs to be revealed and verified is the commitment pair.

Finally, we obtain a logarithmic-size group signature through the Fiat-Shamir transform, and we also prove its correctness, traceability, and CPA-anonymity.

1.3 Roadmap

The rest of the article is organized as follows. Section 2 provides some required preliminaries for our study. In Sect. 3, we present our novel SD-based and GSD-based one-out-of-many protocols. Our logarithmic-size ring signature scheme and its security proof is provided in Sect. 4. In Sect. 5, we give our logarithmic-size group signature scheme. Finally, we choose our parameter sets for our ring signature scheme and group signature scheme in Sect. 6.

2 Preliminaries

2.1 Hard Problems

For integers a, b and $a \leq b$, the notation $[a; b]$ denotes the set $\{a, \cdots, b\}$. If $a = 1$, then it simplifies to $[b]$. Bold lowercase and uppercase letters denote row vectors and matrices respectively. The transpose of a vector $\mathbf{x}$ is represented by $\mathbf{x}^\top$. Let $B(n,t)$ be a set of vectors $\mathbf{v} \in \mathbb{F}_2^n$ such that the Hamming weight $w(\mathbf{v}) = t$. For a set X, $x \xleftarrow{\$} X$ means that x is sampled from X randomly and $\mathbf{x} \xleftarrow{\$, \zeta} X$ denotes $\mathbf{x}$ is sampled from X using the seed ζ. Let $\mathcal{O}(\cdot)$ denote a random oracle and $\mathcal{A}^{\mathcal{O}(\cdot)}$ denote that an algorithm $\mathcal{A}$ has access to $\mathcal{O}(\cdot)$.

Problem 1 (SD Problem). On input a matrix $\mathbf{H} \xleftarrow{\$} \mathbb{F}_2^{(n-k)\times n}$ and a syndrome $\mathbf{s} \in \mathbb{F}_2^{n-k}$, the syndrome decoding problem $\mathrm{SD}(n,k,t)$ asks to find a vector $\mathbf{e} \in \mathbb{F}_2^n$ such that $\mathbf{s}^\top = \mathbf{He}^\top$ and $\mathbf{e} \xleftarrow{\$} B(n,t)$.

We only present search version of SD problem. In [32], a reduction from the search version to the decision version is provided. Its dual problem is as follows.

Problem 2 (GSD Problem). On input a matrix $\mathbf{G} \xleftarrow{\$} \mathbb{F}_2^{k\times n}$ and a vector $\mathbf{y} \in \mathbb{F}_2^n$, the general syndrome decoding problem $\mathrm{GSD}(n,k,t)$ asks to find a vector $\mathbf{x} \in \mathbb{F}_2^k$ and a vector $\mathbf{e} \in \mathbb{F}_2^n$ such that $\mathbf{y} = \mathbf{xG} + \mathbf{e}$, $\mathbf{x} \xleftarrow{\$} \mathbb{F}_2^k$ and $\mathbf{e} \xleftarrow{\$} B(n,t)$.

The hardness of the GSD problem is equivalent to that of the SD problem [39].

Problem 3 (DOOM Problem). On input a matrix $\mathbf{H} \xleftarrow{\$} \mathbb{F}_2^{k\times n}$ and a set of N syndromes $\{\mathbf{s}_i\}_{i=1}^N$, the decoding one-out-of-many problem $\mathrm{DOOM}(n,k,t,N)$ asks to find a vector $\mathbf{e}_i \in \mathbb{F}_2^n$ for some $i \in [N]$ such that $\mathbf{s}_i^\top = \mathbf{He}_i^\top$ and $\mathbf{e}_i \xleftarrow{\$} B(n,t)$.

As [37] stated, a variant of information set decoding algorithms can be adapted to the DOOM(n, k, t, N) problem, resulting in a speedup factor of approximately $\sqrt{N}$. We give the dual version of the DOOM problem.

Problem 4 (GDOOM Problem). On input a matrix $\mathbf{G} \xleftarrow{\$} \mathbb{F}_2^{k\times n}$ and a set of N vectors $\{\mathbf{y}_i\}_{i=1}^N$, the general decoding one-out-of-many problem GDOOM(n, k, t, N) asks to find a vector $\mathbf{x}_i \in \mathbb{F}_2^k$ and a vector $\mathbf{e}_i \in \mathbb{F}_2^n$ for some $i \in [N]$ such that $\mathbf{y}_i = \mathbf{x}_i\mathbf{G} + \mathbf{e}_i, \mathbf{x}_i \xleftarrow{\$} \mathbb{F}_2^k$ and $\mathbf{e}_i \xleftarrow{\$} B(n, t)$.

2.2 Merkle Trees

A Merkle tree is a binary tree that compresses a list of data into a value. It is constructed layer by layer from bottom to top using a collision-resistant hash function. Each node in each layer is a hash value of the concatenation of its associated child nodes. In [6] a special type of Merkle trees called index-hiding Merkle trees was introduced. This tree has the characteristic of sorting the leaf nodes in lexicographical order, rather than based on their indices. Let $\mathcal{H} : \{0, 1\}^* \to \{0, 1\}^{2\lambda}$ denote a collision-resistant hash function, and $D = (d_0, \cdots, d_{2^\ell-1})$ denote a data list. A Merkle tree includes the following algorithms.

1. Mtree$(D) \to$ (root, tree): With a data list D as input, set $M_{\ell,j} = \mathcal{H}(d_j)$ for $j \in [0, 2^\ell - 1]$, and iteratively calculate
$$M_{i,j} = \mathcal{H}(M_{i+1,2j-1}, M_{i+1,2j}), i \in [0, \ell - 1], j \in [0, 2^i - 1].$$
Output $M_{0,0}$ as the root.
2. IH-Mtree$(D) \to$ (root, tree): With a data list D as input, set $M_{\ell,j} = \mathcal{H}(d_j)$ for $j \in [0, 2^\ell - 1]$, and iteratively calculate
$$M_{i,j} = \mathcal{H}((M_{i+1,2j-1}, M_{i+1,2j})_{lex}), i \in [0, \ell - 1], j \in [0, 2^i - 1].$$
Output $M_{0,0}$ as the root.
3. Gpath(tree, B) $\to$ path: With the structure of a tree and a subset B of D as input, output a list of intermediate nodes that cover all $D \setminus B$. Here, one says that a node set U covers a leaf set L if the union of the leaves in a subtree rooted at each node $u \in U$ is exactly the set L.
4. Rebuild(path, B) $\to$ root$'$: With a subset B and a path as input, output a rebuilt root$'$.

There are two important properties about Merkle trees: the binding property and the index-hiding property of the index-hiding Merkle trees. The binding property means that for any subset S that does not belong to the set D, finding a path such that Rebuild(S, path) = Mtree(D) is the same as discovering a collision in $\mathcal{H}$. The index-hiding property means that for any subset B belonging to the set D, the path of index-hiding Merkle trees will not reveal any information about the set B.

Lemma 1. *[6] For a Merkle tree generated by a data list D, there exists an algorithm $\mathcal{F}$ that uses the tree and a pair $(S, path)$ satisfying $S \not\subset D$ and $Rebuild(S, path) = root$ to generate a collision in $\mathcal{H}$.*

Lemma 2. *[6] Given an integer $N = 2^\ell$ and two distributions $\mathcal{X}_1$ and $\mathcal{X}_2$ over $\{0,1\}^*$, the distribution $\mathcal{L}_I$, for any $I \in [N]$, is defined as*

$$\mathcal{L}_I = \left[(a_I, \text{path}, \text{root}) \;\middle|\; \begin{array}{c} d_I \xleftarrow{\$} \mathcal{X}_1, \\ d_i \xleftarrow{\$} \mathcal{X}_2, \forall 1 \le i \le N, i \ne I, \\ (\text{tree}, \text{root}) \leftarrow \text{IH-Mtree}(D), \\ \text{path} \leftarrow \text{Gpath}(\text{tree}, I). \end{array} \right],$$

where $D = (d_1, \cdots, d_N)$. Then $\mathcal{L}_I = \mathcal{L}_J$ for $\forall I, J \in [N]$.

2.3 Seedtrees

A seedtree is also a completely balanced binary tree, but its construction differs from that of a Merkle tree. In this case, a sender starts by selecting a seed as the root of a tree. Then, a pseudo-random number generator is used to create intermediate nodes from top to bottom. By sending some intermediate nodes, the sender reveals specific leaf nodes without disclosing any information about the remaining leaves. Let PRNG : $\{0,1\}^\lambda \to \{0,1\}^{2\lambda}$ represent a pseudo-random number generator. A seedtree includes the following algorithms.

1. Stree(root, N) $\to (l_0, \cdots, l_{2^\ell-1})$: With a seed root and an integer N as input, set $M_{0,0}$ = root and iteratively compute
$$(M_{i+1,2j-1}, M_{i+1,2j}) = \text{PRNG}(M_{i,j}), i \in [0, \ell-1], j \in [0, 2^i - 1].$$
Define $(M_{\ell,0}, \cdots, M_{\ell,2^\ell-1})$ as leaf nodes $(l_0, \cdots, l_{2^\ell-1})$ and then output them.
2. Oseeds(root, **ch**) $\to$ seed$_{\text{inter}}$: With a root and a challenge **ch** as input, return a set seed$_{\text{inter}}$ that covers all the leaves with index i such that $ch_i = 1$.
3. Recover(seed$_{\text{inter}}$, **ch**) $\to \{l_i\}_{i,s.t.ch_i=1}$: With a set seed$_{\text{inter}}$ and a challenge **ch** as input, return all leaf nodes rooted at the nodes in seed$_{\text{inter}}$.
4. Simseeds(**ch**) $\to$ seed$_{\text{inter}}$: With a challenge **ch** as input, return a set seed$_{\text{inter}}$ via random sampling, enabling seed$_{\text{inter}}$ to cover all leaves with index i satisfying $ch_i = 0$.

Lemma 3. *[6] Given an integer N and a challenge* **ch**, *the distributions $\mathcal{X}_1$ and $\mathcal{X}_2$ are defined by*

$$\mathcal{X}_1 = \left[seed_{inter}, \{\text{leaf}_i\}_{ch_i=0} \;\middle|\; \begin{array}{c} \text{seed} \leftarrow \{0,1\}^\lambda, \\ \{\text{leaf}_i\}_{i=1}^N \leftarrow \text{Stree}(\text{root}, N), \\ seed_{inter} \leftarrow Oseeds(seed_{root}, \mathbf{ch}). \end{array} \right] \text{ and}$$

$$\mathcal{X}_2 = \left[seed_{inter}, \{\text{leaf}_i\}_{ch_i=0} \;\middle|\; \begin{array}{c} \{\text{leaf}_i\}_{ch_i=0} \leftarrow \{0,1\}^\lambda, \\ seed_{inter} \leftarrow \text{Simseeds}(\mathbf{ch}). \end{array} \right].$$

For any adversary who queries an oracle $\mathcal{Q}$ times, the advantage of distinguishing the two distributions $\mathcal{X}_1$ and $\mathcal{X}_2$ is at most $\mathcal{Q}/2^\lambda$.

3 Short One-out-of-Many Proofs from Coding Theory

We first propose an SD-based one-out-of-many proof along with the security proof. To achieve a lower communication cost, we introduce a GSD-based one-out-of-many proof, in which we decrease the communication cost by employing optimization techniques [23,31].

3.1 The SD-Based One-out-of-Many Proof

In this subsection, we put forward our SD-based one-out-of-many proof in Fig. 2 for proving knowledge of the preimage for one syndrome in a public set $(\mathbf{s}_1, \cdots, \mathbf{s}_N)$. More specifically, the proof is a ZKAoK for the following relation:

$$R = \{(\mathbf{H}, \mathbf{s}_1, \cdots, \mathbf{s}_N), (\mathbf{e}_I, I) | \text{ for some } I \in [N], \mathbf{s}_I^\top = \mathbf{H}\mathbf{e}_I^\top, \mathbf{e}_I \in B(n,t)\}, \quad (1)$$

where $\mathbf{H} \in \mathbb{F}_2^{(n-k)\times n}$ and $\mathbf{s}_i \in \mathbb{F}_2^{n-k}$ for all $i \in [N]$.

Our idea stems from a key observation that in the modified Stern protocol in Fig. 1, the commitment $c_1 = \text{Com}(\delta, \mathbf{H}\mathbf{r}^\top + \mathbf{s}^\top; \rho_1)$ needs to be verified in two different ways, in which one is related to the syndrome $\mathbf{s}$ while the other is unrelated to $\mathbf{s}$. Based on this, we replace c_1 with the following set

$$(\text{Com}(\delta, \mathbf{H}\mathbf{r}^\top + \mathbf{s}_1^\top; b_1), \cdots, \text{Com}(\delta, \mathbf{H}\mathbf{r}^\top + \mathbf{s}_N^\top; b_N)),$$

while keeping c_2 and c_3 unchanged, and compress it into a root using an index-hiding Merkle tree. Then, the root, c_2 and c_3 are sent to a verifier.

When the challenge is 1, the verifier checks c_2 and c_3 as the original Stern protocol. When the challenge is 2, the verifier checks the root and c_3 by using the path of the index-hiding Merkle tree, $\mathbf{r} + \mathbf{e}_I$ and δ. When the challenge is 3, the verifier calculates all leaf nodes using $\mathbf{r}$ and checks the root and c_2 by leaf nodes and δ.

In the following we first show that our protocol in Fig. 2 satisfies perfect completeness. That is, if $\mathcal{P}$, which possesses the witness $(\mathbf{e}_I, I)$, faithfully executes the protocol, $\mathcal{V}$ will output "accept" with a probability of 1. If $ch = 1$, $\mathcal{V}$ only needs to repeat the calculation process of c_2 and c_3, and so it always outputs "accept". If $ch = 2$, $\mathcal{V}$ needs to reconstruct the root using the I-th leaf node and repeat the calculation process of c_3. The reconstructed root is the same as the one constructed using all leaves, and hence it always outputs "accept". If $ch = 3$, $\mathcal{V}$ only needs to repeat the calculation process of the root and c_2, and also it always outputs "accept".

Next, the following Theorems 1 and 2 state that our protocol in Fig. 2 is sound and zero-knowledge.

Theorem 1. *Assuming that Com is a computational binding commitment scheme and the hash function $\mathcal{H}$ used in the Merkle tree is collision-resistant, the protocol in Fig. 2 is an argument of knowledge with soundness error 2/3.*

Proof. Assuming there is an adversary $\mathcal{A}$ who is accepted with a probability greater than 2/3, i.e., $\mathcal{A}$ can effectively respond all three challenges. Then, we can construct an extractor $\mathcal{E}$ which either breaks the binding property of Com, or outputs a collision in $\mathcal{H}$, or $\mathbf{e} \in B(n,t)$ such that $\mathbf{H}\mathbf{e}^\top = \mathbf{s}_I^\top$ for a certain $I \in [N]$. Formally, given a CMT(c_1, c_2, c_3) and its three valid responses

$$\mathrm{RSP}_1 = (\mathbf{w}_1, \mathbf{w}_2, \rho_2, \rho_3), \mathrm{RSP}_2 = (\mathbf{w}_3, \xi_\delta, b, \mathrm{path}, \rho_3), \mathrm{RSP}_3 = (\xi_s, \xi_r, \xi_\delta', \rho_2),$$

each of them corresponds to distinct challenges $ch = 1$, $ch = 2$ and $ch = 3$ respectively. $\mathcal{E}$ first calculates

$$\begin{cases} \pi_1 \xleftarrow{\$,\xi_\delta} \mathcal{S}_n, \mathbf{p}_1 \xleftarrow{\$,\xi_r} \mathbb{F}_2^n, \pi_2 \xleftarrow{\$,\xi_\delta'} \mathcal{S}_n; \\ (b_1', \cdots, b_N') = \mathrm{Stree}(\xi_s, N); \\ \mathrm{leaf}' = (\mathrm{Com}(\pi_2, \mathbf{H}\mathbf{p}_1^\top + \mathbf{s}_1^\top; b_1'), \cdots, \mathrm{Com}(\pi_2, \mathbf{H}\mathbf{p}_1^\top + \mathbf{s}_N^\top; b_N')); \\ \mathrm{R}_1' = \text{IH-Mtree}(\mathrm{leaf}'); \\ \mathrm{R}_2' = \mathrm{Rebuild}(\mathrm{path}, \mathrm{Com}(\pi_1, \mathbf{H}\mathbf{w}_3^\top; b)). \end{cases}$$

Due to the validity of these responses, we have

$$\begin{cases} c_1 = \mathrm{R}_1' = \mathrm{R}_2', \mathbf{w}_2 \in B(n,t); \\ c_2 = \mathrm{Com}(\mathbf{w}_1; \rho_2) = \mathrm{Com}(\pi_2(\mathbf{p}_1); \rho_2); \\ c_3 = \mathrm{Com}(\mathbf{w}_1 + \mathbf{w}_2; \rho_3) = \mathrm{Com}(\pi_1(\mathbf{w}_3); \rho_3). \end{cases}$$

Then, $\mathcal{E}$ checks if $(\mathbf{w}_1, \rho_2) \neq (\pi_2(\mathbf{p}_1), \rho_2)$. If so, $\mathcal{E}$ breaks the binding property of Com. Similarly, $\mathcal{E}$ checks if $(\mathbf{w}_1 + \mathbf{w}_2, \rho_3) \neq (\pi_1(\mathbf{w}_3), \rho_3)$. If neither of these two inequalities holds true, we have

$$\mathbf{w}_1 = \pi_2(\mathbf{p}_1), \mathbf{w}_1 + \mathbf{w}_2 = \pi_1(\mathbf{w}_3). \tag{2}$$

Next, $\mathcal{E}$ checks if $\mathrm{Com}(\pi_1, \mathbf{H}\mathbf{w}_3^\top; b) \neq \mathrm{leaf}_i'$ for $\forall i \in [N]$. If so, it finds a collision in $\mathcal{H}$ by employing the Merkle tree extractor in Lemma 1 with the input $(\mathrm{tree}, \mathrm{Com}(\pi_1, \mathbf{H}\mathbf{w}_3^\top; b), \mathrm{path})$. Otherwise, there exists an index $I \in [N]$ satisfying $\mathrm{Com}(\pi_1, \mathbf{H}\mathbf{w}_3^\top; b) = \mathrm{leaf}_I'$. Furthermore, $\mathcal{E}$ checks if $(\pi_1, \mathbf{H}\mathbf{w}_3^\top, b) \neq (\pi_2, \mathbf{H}\mathbf{p}_1^\top + \mathbf{s}_I^\top, b_I)$. If so, $\mathcal{E}$ breaks the binding property of Com. Otherwise, $\mathcal{E}$ gets $\pi_1 = \pi_2$, $\mathbf{H}\mathbf{w}_3^\top = \mathbf{H}\mathbf{p}_1^\top + \mathbf{s}_I^\top$ and $b = b_I$. From this and Eq. (2), we deduce that $\mathbf{H}\pi_1^{-1}(\mathbf{w}_2^\top) = \mathbf{s}_I^\top$, where $\pi_1^{-1}(\mathbf{w}_2) \in B(n,t)$. This means that $\mathcal{E}$ outputs the witness $\mathbf{e} = \pi_1^{-1}(\mathbf{w}_2) \in B(n,t)$ such that $\mathbf{He} = \mathbf{s}_I$, $I \in [N]$. □

Theorem 2. *The protocol in Fig. 2 is honest-verifier zero-knowledge, that is, there exists a simulator Sim, such that for any statement-witness pair (s, w) belonging to the relation* (1), *any $ch \in \{1, 2, 3\}$ and any adversary $\mathcal{A}$ that accesses the oracle $\mathcal{Q}$ times, the following holds*

$$\left|\Pr[\mathcal{A}^{\mathcal{O}}(\mathcal{P}(s, w, ch)) \to 1] - \Pr[\mathcal{A}^{\mathcal{O}}(Sim(s, ch)) \to 1]\right| \leq \frac{2\mathcal{Q}}{2^\lambda}.$$

Round 1: $\mathcal{P}_1^h((\mathbf{H}, \mathbf{s}_1, \cdots, \mathbf{s}_N), (\mathbf{e}_I, I))$:

$$\{\zeta_s, \zeta_r, \zeta_\delta, \rho_1, \rho_2\} \xleftarrow{\$} \{0,1\}^\lambda, \mathbf{r} \xleftarrow{\$,\zeta_r} \mathbb{F}_2^n, \delta \xleftarrow{\$,\zeta_\delta} \mathcal{S}_n.$$

- $(b_1, \cdots, b_N) = \text{Stree}(\zeta_s, N)$.
- leaf $= (\text{Com}(\delta, \mathbf{H}\mathbf{r}^\top + \mathbf{s}_1^\top; b_1), \cdots, \text{Com}(\delta, \mathbf{H}\mathbf{r}^\top + \mathbf{s}_N^\top; b_N))$.
- (root, tree) = IH-Mtree(leaf).
- Send CMT $:= (c_1, c_2, c_3)$ to $\mathcal{V}$, where

$$c_1 = \text{root}, c_2 = \text{Com}(\delta(\mathbf{r}); \rho_2), c_3 = \text{Com}(\delta(\mathbf{r} + \mathbf{e}_I); \rho_3).$$

Round 2: $\mathcal{V}_1^h(\text{CMT})$ sends a $ch \xleftarrow{\$} \{1,2,3\}$ to $\mathcal{P}$.

Round 3: $\mathcal{P}_2^h((\mathbf{H}, \mathbf{s}_1, \cdots, \mathbf{s}_N), (\mathbf{e}_I, I), ch)$:

- Case $ch = 1$: Set $\mathbf{w}_1 = \delta(\mathbf{r}), \mathbf{w}_2 = \delta(\mathbf{e}_I)$.
  Send RSP $= (\mathbf{w}_1, \mathbf{w}_2, \rho_2, \rho_3)$ to $\mathcal{V}$.
- Case $ch = 2$: Set $\mathbf{w}_3 = \mathbf{r} + \mathbf{e}_I, \xi_\delta = \zeta_\delta, b = b_I, \text{path} = \text{Gpath}(\text{tree}, I)$.
  Send RSP $= (\mathbf{w}_3, \xi_\delta, b, \text{path}, \rho_3)$ to $\mathcal{V}$.
- Case $ch = 3$: Set $\xi_s = \zeta_s, \xi_r = \zeta_r, \xi'_\delta = \zeta_\delta$.
  Send RSP $= (\xi_s, \xi_r, \xi'_\delta, \rho_2)$ to $\mathcal{V}$.

Verification: $\mathcal{V}_2^h((\mathbf{H}, \mathbf{s}_1, \cdots, \mathbf{s}_N), \text{CMT}, ch, \text{RSP})$:

- Case $ch = 1$: Check if $\mathbf{w}_2 \in B(n,t)$ and

$$c_2 = \text{Com}(\mathbf{w}_1; \rho_2), c_3 = \text{Com}(\mathbf{w}_1 + \mathbf{w}_2; \rho_3).$$

- Case $ch = 2$: Set $\pi_1 \xleftarrow{\$,\xi_\delta} \mathcal{S}_n$, $\text{R}_1 = \text{Rebuild}(\text{path}, \text{Com}(\pi_1, \mathbf{H}\mathbf{w}_3^\top; b))$, and check if

$$c_1 = \text{R}_1, c_3 = \text{Com}(\pi_1(\mathbf{w}_3); \rho_3).$$

- Case $ch = 3$: Set $(b_1, \cdots, b_N) = \text{Stree}(\xi_s, N)$, $\mathbf{p}_1 \xleftarrow{\$,\xi_r} \mathbb{F}_2^n$, $\pi_2 \xleftarrow{\$,\xi'_\delta} \mathcal{S}_n$ and leaf $= (\text{Com}(\pi_2, \mathbf{H}\mathbf{p}_1^\top + \mathbf{s}_1^\top; b_1), \cdots, \text{Com}(\pi_2, \mathbf{H}\mathbf{p}_1^\top + \mathbf{s}_N^\top; b_N))$.
  Compute R_2 as IH-Mtree(leaf) and check if

$$c_1 = \text{R}_2, c_2 = \text{Com}(\pi_2(\mathbf{p}_1); \rho_2).$$

$\mathcal{V}$ outputs 1 when all conditions are met, else it outputs 0.

Fig. 2. The SD-based one-out-of-many proof $\Pi^h = (\mathcal{P}^h = (\mathcal{P}_1^h, \mathcal{P}_2^h), \mathcal{V}^h = (\mathcal{V}_1^h, \mathcal{V}_2^h))$.

Proof. To simplify the proof, we use the random oracle $\mathcal{O}^*(\cdot)$ to instantiate the hash function, the algorithm Stree, and Com, where $*$ denotes the instantiated object. The simulator Sim is constructed as follows:

Case $ch = 1$:

1. Sim selects the following random objects:

$$\mathbf{w}_1 \xleftarrow{\$} \mathbb{F}_2^n, \mathbf{w}_2 \xleftarrow{\$} B(n,t), \{\rho_2, \rho_3\} \xleftarrow{\$} \{0,1\}^\lambda, c_1 \xleftarrow{\$} \{0,1\}^{2\lambda}.$$

2. Sim lets CMT $= (c'_1, c'_2, c'_3)$, where

$$c'_1 = c_1, c'_2 = \text{Com}(\mathbf{w}_1; \rho_2), c'_3 = \text{Com}(\mathbf{w}_1 + \mathbf{w}_2; \rho_3).$$

3. Sim lets RSP $= (\mathbf{w}_1, \mathbf{w}_2, \rho_2, \rho_3)$ and returns (CMT, 1, RSP).

Case $ch = 2$:

1. Sim selects the following random objects:

$$\mathbf{w}_3 \xleftarrow{\$} \mathbb{F}_2^n, \{b, \xi_\delta, \rho_3, \{\text{leaf}_i\}_{i=2}^N\} \xleftarrow{\$} \{0,1\}^\lambda, c_2 \xleftarrow{\$} \{0,1\}^{2\lambda}, \pi_1 \xleftarrow{\$,\xi_\delta} \mathcal{S}_n.$$

2. Sim sets $\text{leaf}_1 = \text{Com}(\pi_1, \mathbf{H}\mathbf{w}_3^\top; b)$ and obtains (tree, root) = IH-Mtree(leaf).
3. Sim lets CMT $= (c_1', c_2', c_3')$, where

$$c_1' = \text{root}, c_2' = c_2, c_3' = \text{Com}(\pi_1(\mathbf{w}_3); \rho_3).$$

4. Sim runs the algorithm GPath(tree, 1) to retrieve the path.
5. Sim lets RSP $= (\mathbf{w}_3, \xi_\delta, b, \text{path}, \rho_3)$ and returns (CMT, 2, RSP).

Case $ch = 3$:

1. Sim selects the following random objects:

$$\{\xi_s, \xi_r, \xi_\delta, \rho_2\} \xleftarrow{\$} \{0,1\}^\lambda, c_3 \xleftarrow{\$} \{0,1\}^{2\lambda}, \mathbf{v}_2 \xleftarrow{\$,\xi_r} \mathbb{F}_2^n, \pi_2 \xleftarrow{\$,\xi_\delta} \mathcal{S}_n.$$

2. Sim sets leaf $= (\text{Com}(\mathbf{H}\mathbf{p}_1^\top + \mathbf{s}_1^\top; b_1), \cdots, \text{Com}(\mathbf{H}\mathbf{p}_1^\top + \mathbf{s}_N^\top; b_N))$ and calculates its root, where $(b_1, \cdots, b_N) = \text{Stree}(\xi_s, N)$.
3. Sim lets CMT $= (c_1', c_2', c_3')$, where

$$c_1' = \text{root}, c_2' = \text{Com}(\pi_2(\mathbf{v}_2); \rho_2), c_3' = c_3.$$

4. Sim lets RSP $= (\xi_s, \xi_r, \xi_\delta, \rho_2)$ and returns (CMT, 3, RSP).

If Com is statistically hiding, then two CMTs generated by Sim and a honest prover, respectively, are statistically indistinguishable. Therefore, we only need to check the case of RSP.

$ch = 1$: Since Sim draws $(\mathbf{w}_1, \mathbf{w}_2)$ at random from $\mathbb{F}_2^n \times B(n,t)$, both RSPs generated by a honest prover and Sim respectively, follow the random distribution on $\mathbb{F}_2^n \times B(n,t)$.

$ch = 2$: Set five simulators $\{Sim_i\}_{i=1}^5$ to prove that Sim and a honest prover are indistinguishable. Sim_1 and Sim_5 represent a honest prover and Sim, respectively. Let E_i denote $\mathcal{A}^{\mathcal{O}}(Sim_i(s, ch)) = 1$, for $i \in [5]$.

Sim_2: The only difference between Sim_2 and Sim_1 is that $\{b_i\}_{i=1}^N$ are randomly sampled from $\{0,1\}^\lambda$ instead of being generated by the $\mathcal{O}^{\text{Stree}}(\cdot)$ algorithm Stree with an input ζ_s. If ζ_s has not been queried by $\mathcal{A}$ to the oracle $\mathcal{O}^{\text{Stree}}(\cdot)$, Sim_2 and Sim_1 are indistinguishable. Thus, if $\mathcal{O}^{\text{Stree}}(\cdot)$ is accessed $\mathcal{Q}$ times and the probability of colliding with ζ_s is 2^λ for each query, the probability of colliding with ζ_s after $\mathcal{Q}$ queries is $\mathcal{Q}/2^\lambda$. Thus, we have $|\Pr[E_2] - \Pr[E_1]| \leq \mathcal{Q}/2^\lambda$.

Sim_3: The only difference between Sim_3 and Sim_2 is that $\{\text{leaf}_i\}_{i=1, i\neq I}^N$ are randomly sampled from $\{0,1\}^{2\lambda}$ instead of being generated by $\mathcal{O}^{\text{Com}}(\cdot)$ with the tuple $(\pi_1, \mathbf{H}\mathbf{r}^\top + \mathbf{s}_i^\top; b_i)$ for $i \neq I$. If all tuples have not been queried by $\mathcal{A}$ to the oracle $\mathcal{O}^{\text{Com}}(\cdot)$, Sim_3 and Sim_2 are indistinguishable. We use $\mathcal{Q}_{\text{com}_i}$ to represent the number of times $\mathcal{O}^{\text{Com}_i}(\cdot)$ is accessed. Since the minimum entropy of b_i is $1/2^\lambda$, the minimum entropy of tuple $(\pi_1, \mathbf{H}\mathbf{r}^\top + \mathbf{s}_i^\top; b_i)$ is at most $1/2^\lambda$. Therefore, the probability of collision with the tuple in each query is at most $1/2^\lambda$. Furthermore, since $\sum_{i=1}^N \mathcal{Q}_{\text{leaf}_i} \leq \mathcal{Q}$, we have $|\Pr[E_3] - \Pr[E_2]| \leq Q/2^\lambda$.

Sim_4: There are two differences between Sim_4 and Sim_3. Firstly, c_3 is randomly sampled from $\{0,1\}^{2\lambda}$. Secondly, $\text{leaf}_I = \text{Com}(\pi_1, \mathbf{H}\mathbf{w}_3^\top; b_I)$, where $\mathbf{w}_3$ is randomly sampled from $\mathbb{F}_2^n$. Since $\mathbf{w}_3$ and c_3 follows the random distribution as the real transcript, we have $\Pr[E_4] = \Pr[E_3]$.

Sim_5: The only difference between Sim_5 and Sim_4 is that 1 is used instead of I in witness. Lemma 2 states that regardless of whether the selected index is 1 or I, the root and path follow the same distribution. Therefore, we have $\Pr[E_5] = \Pr[E_4]$.

Thus, we have $\left|\Pr[\mathcal{A}^{\mathcal{O}}(\mathcal{P}(s,w,2)) \to 1] - \Pr[\mathcal{A}^{\mathcal{O}}(Sim(s,2)) \to 1]\right| \leq \frac{2\mathcal{Q}}{2^\lambda}$.

$ch = 3$: Since a honest prover does not use the witness, Sim can perfectly simulate RSP.

In summary, we obtain the required result. □

3.2 The GSD-Based One-out-of-Many Proof

We first propose a GSD-based one-out-of-many proof in one-iteration in Fig. 3. This protocol is for the following relation:

$$R = \{(\mathbf{G}, \{\mathbf{y}_i\}_{i=1}^N), (\mathbf{x}, \mathbf{e}, I)| \text{ for some } I \in [N], \mathbf{y}_I = \mathbf{x}\mathbf{G} + \mathbf{e}, \mathbf{x} \in \mathbb{F}_2^k, \mathbf{e} \in B(n,t)\}, \tag{3}$$

where $\mathbf{G} \in \mathbb{F}_2^{k\times n}$ and $\mathbf{y}_i \in \mathbb{F}_2^n$ for all $i \in [N]$. Next, we present its multi-iteration version in Fig. 4 by using additional optimization techniques such as commitments compression [23,31], seedtrees [6,23] and small-weight vector compression functions [31]. In the following we first explain how to use them to obtain the multi-iteration version, which is called the GSD-based one-out-of-many proof.

Commitments Compression: The soundness error of the GSD-based one-out-of-many proof in one-iteration in Fig. 3 is $2/3$, and so this protocol needs to be repeated κ times to reduce the soundness error. Since three commitments $(c_1^j, c_2^j, c_3^j), j \in [\kappa]$ need to be output in each iteration, the total cost of commitments is $3\kappa|\text{Com}|$. To reduce the total cost of commitments, we optimize the above protocol by using three Merkle trees Tree_1, Tree_2 and Tree_3 to compress $(c_1^1, \cdots, c_1^\kappa)$, $(c_2^1, \cdots, c_2^\kappa)$ and $(c_3^1, \cdots, c_3^\kappa)$ as root_1, root_2 and root_3 respectively, where (c_1^j, c_2^j, c_3^j) denotes the commitment of the j-th iteration. The prover sends $\text{CMT} = \mathcal{H}(\text{root}_1, \text{root}_2, \text{root}_3)$. Since the verifier can reconstruct two out of the three commitments (c_1^j, c_2^j, c_3^j) in each iteration, the prover transmits those commitments that cannot be computed by the verifier through certain intermediate nodes of the tree. In summary, this will reduce the cost of commitments from $3\kappa|\text{Com}|$ to $|\mathcal{H}| + \frac{5\kappa|\text{Com}|}{6}$.

Seedtrees: In one-iteration protocol, a set of seeds needs to be generated for sampling random objects and so certain seeds are revealed based on the challenge. To reduce the communication cost of seeds, we use a set of master seeds along with a set of seedtrees to generate κ sets of seeds in κ iterations. During the response phase, we provide those revealed seeds by outputting certain intermediate nodes in the seedtree. If the probability of a seed being transmitted in one iteration is $1/p$, then using a seedtree reduces the transmission cost of this seed by about $1/2p$.

Small-Weight Vector Compression: Since the protocol in Fig. 3 may transmit a small weight vector, we employ a small vector compression function in multi-iteration version to reduce the cost of transmitting small weight vectors from n to approximately $n/2$.

By using the above optimization techniques, a multi-iteration version is proposed in Fig. 4. As mentioned in [6], to ensure a tighter security proof and avoid multi-target attacks [14], we use a "salt", a 2λ-bit prefix string, in these seedtrees to distinguish the random oracles used in the seedtrees of different iterations. The "salt" has a negligible impact on practice.

The following theorem provides the security of the protocol in Fig. 4.

Theorem 3. *The protocol described in Fig. 4 is an argument of knowledge with the perfect completeness and honest-verifier zero-knowledge.*

Proof. **Completeness:** This protocol has perfect completeness, which is immediately obtained by the correctness of the seedtrees, Merkle trees, and index-hiding Merkle trees.

Soundness: Assume there is an adversary $\mathcal{A}$ who is accepted with a probability $> (2/3)^\kappa$, i.e., $\mathcal{A}$ is able to successfully answer all three challenges in some iteration j where $j \in [\kappa]$. We build an extractor $\mathcal{E}$ which either breaks the binding property of Com, or outputs a collision in $\mathcal{H}$, or outputs $\mathbf{x} \in \mathbb{F}_2^k, \mathbf{e} \in B(n,t)$ such that $\mathbf{xG}+\mathbf{e} = \mathbf{y}_I$ for some $I \in [N]$. First, $\mathcal{E}$ obtains the seeds, random coins and the commitment of the j-th iteration by $\mathrm{RSP}_1, \mathrm{RSP}_2, \mathrm{RSP}_3$ and the algorithms of seedtrees and Merkle trees.

$$\{\xi_s^j, \xi_u^j, \xi_\delta^j, \xi_{\delta'}^j, \rho_1^j, \rho_2^j, c_1^j, c_2^j, c_3^j\} \longleftarrow (\mathrm{RSP}_1, \mathrm{RSP}_2, \mathrm{RSP}_3).$$

Then, $\mathcal{E}$ performs the following steps:

$$\begin{cases} (b_1^j, \cdots, b_N^j) = \mathrm{Stree}(\xi_s^j, N); \\ \mathbf{p}_1^j \xleftarrow{\$,\xi_{\delta'}^j} \mathbb{F}_2^n, \pi_1^j \xleftarrow{\$,\xi_{\delta'}^j} \mathcal{S}_n, \mathbf{p}_2^j \xleftarrow{\$,\xi_u^j} \mathbb{F}_2^{k_1}, \mathbf{p}_2^3 \xleftarrow{\$,\xi_\delta^j} \mathbb{F}_2^n, \pi_2^j \xleftarrow{\$,\xi_\delta^j} \mathcal{S}_n; \\ \mathrm{leaf}^j = (\mathrm{Com}(\pi_2^j(\mathbf{p}_2^j\mathbf{G}_1 + \mathbf{y}_1) + \mathbf{p}_3^j; b_1^j), \cdots, \mathrm{Com}(\pi_2^j(\mathbf{p}_2^j\mathbf{G}_1 + \mathbf{y}_N) + \mathbf{p}_3^j; b_N^j)); \\ \mathrm{R}_1^j = \mathrm{IH\text{-}Mtree}(\mathrm{leaf}^j); \\ \mathrm{R}_2^j = \mathrm{Rebuild}(\mathrm{path}^j, \mathrm{Com}(\mathbf{w}_2^j + \mathbf{w}_3^j; b^j)). \end{cases}$$

Due to the validity of these responses, we have

$$\begin{cases} c_1^j = \mathrm{R}_1^j = \mathrm{R}_2^j, \mathbf{w}_3^j \in B(n,t); \\ c_2^j = \mathrm{Com}(\pi_1^j, \mathbf{p}_1^j; \rho_2^j) = \mathrm{Com}(\pi_2^j, \mathbf{p}_3^j; \rho_2^j); \\ c_3^j = \mathrm{Com}(\mathbf{w}_2^j, \rho_3^j) = \mathrm{Com}(\pi_1^j(\mathbf{w}_1^j\mathbf{G}_1) + \mathbf{p}_1^j; \rho_3^j). \end{cases}$$

Round 1: $\mathcal{P}_1^g((\mathbf{G}, \mathbf{y}_1, \cdots, \mathbf{y}_N), (I, \mathbf{x}, \mathbf{e}))$ chooses the following random objects:

$$\{\zeta_s, \zeta_u, \zeta_\delta, \rho_1, \rho_2\} \xleftarrow{\$} \{0,1\}^\lambda; \mathbf{u} \xleftarrow{\$,\zeta_u} \mathbb{F}_2^k, \mathbf{v} \xleftarrow{\$,\zeta_\delta} \mathbb{F}_2^n, \delta \xleftarrow{\$,\zeta_\delta} \mathcal{S}_n.$$

- $(b_1, \cdots, b_N) = \text{Stree}(\zeta_s, N)$.
- $\text{leaf} = (\text{Com}(\delta(\mathbf{uG} + \mathbf{y}_1) + \mathbf{v}; b_1), \cdots, \text{Com}(\delta(\mathbf{uG} + \mathbf{y}_N) + \mathbf{v}; b_N))$.
- $(\text{root}, \text{tree}) = \text{IH-Mtree}(\text{leaf})$.
- Send $\text{CMT} := (c_1, c_2, c_3)$ to $\mathcal{V}$, where

$$c_1 = \text{root}, c_2 = \text{Com}(\delta, \mathbf{v}; \rho_2), c_3 = \text{Com}(\delta((\mathbf{u} + \mathbf{x})\mathbf{G}) + \mathbf{v}; \rho_3).$$

Round 2: $\mathcal{V}_1^g(\text{CMT})$ sends a challenge $ch \xleftarrow{\$} \{1,2,3\}$ to $\mathcal{P}$.
Round 3: $\mathcal{P}_2^g((\mathbf{G}, \mathbf{y}_1, \cdots, \mathbf{y}_N), (I, \mathbf{x}, \mathbf{e}), ch)$ responds as follows:
- Case $ch = 1$: Set $\xi'_\delta = \zeta_\delta, \mathbf{w}_1 = \mathbf{u} + \mathbf{x}$.
  Send $\text{RSP} = (\xi'_\delta, \mathbf{w}_1, \rho_2, \rho_3)$ to $\mathcal{V}$.
- Case $ch = 2$: Set

$$\mathbf{w}_2 = \delta((\mathbf{u} + \mathbf{x})\mathbf{G}) + \mathbf{v}, \mathbf{w}_3 = \delta(\mathbf{e});\ b = b_I, \text{path} = \text{Gpath}(\text{tree}, I).$$

  Send $\text{RSP} = (\mathbf{w}_2, \mathbf{w}_3, b, \text{path}, \rho_3)$ to $\mathcal{V}$.
- Case $ch = 3$: Set $\xi_s = \zeta_s, \xi_u = \zeta_u, \xi_\delta = \zeta_\delta$.
  Send $\text{RSP} = (\xi_s, \xi_u, \xi_\delta, \rho_2)$ to $\mathcal{V}$.

Verification: $\mathcal{V}_2^g((\mathbf{G}, \mathbf{y}_1, \cdots, \mathbf{y}_N), \text{CMT}, ch, \text{RSP})$ proceeds as follows:
- Case $ch = 1$: Set $\mathbf{p}_1 \xleftarrow{\$,\xi'_\delta} \mathbb{F}_2^n, \pi_1 \xleftarrow{\$,\xi'_\delta} \mathcal{S}_n$ and check if

$$c_2 = \text{Com}(\pi_1, \mathbf{p}_1; \rho_2), c_3 = \text{Com}(\pi_1(\mathbf{w}_1\mathbf{G}_1) + \mathbf{p}_1; \rho_3).$$

- Case $ch = 2$: Compute R_1 as $\text{Rebuild}(\text{path}, \text{Com}(\mathbf{w}_2 + \mathbf{w}_3; b))$,
  Check if $\mathbf{w}_3 \in B(n, t)$ and

$$c_1 = \text{R}_1, c_3 = \text{Com}(\mathbf{w}_2; \rho_3).$$

- Case $ch = 3$: Set $\mathbf{p}_2 \xleftarrow{\$,\xi_u} \mathbb{F}_2^k, \mathbf{p}_3 \xleftarrow{\$,\xi_\delta} \mathbb{F}_2^n, \pi_2 \xleftarrow{\$,\xi_\delta} \mathcal{S}_n$.
  $(b_1, \cdots, b_N) = \text{Stree}(\xi_s, N)$.
  $\text{leaf} = (\text{Com}(\pi_2(\mathbf{p}_2\mathbf{G}_1 + \mathbf{y}_1) + \mathbf{p}_3; b_1), \cdots, \text{Com}(\pi_2(\mathbf{p}_2\mathbf{G}_1 + \mathbf{y}_N) + \mathbf{p}_3; b_N))$.
  Obtain R_2 as $\text{IH-Mtree}(\text{leaf})$ and check if

$$c_1 = \text{R}_2, c_2 = \text{Com}(\pi_2, \mathbf{p}_3; \rho_2).$$

$\mathcal{V}$ outputs 1 when all conditions are met, else it outputs 0.

Fig. 3. The one-iteration GSD-based one-out-of-many proof $\Pi^g = (\mathcal{P}^g = (\mathcal{P}_1^g, \mathcal{P}_2^g), \mathcal{V}^g = (\mathcal{V}_1^g, \mathcal{V}_2^g))$.

$\mathcal{E}$ first checks if $(\pi_1^j, \mathbf{p}_1^j, \rho_2^j) \neq (\pi_2^j, \mathbf{p}_3^j, \rho_2^j)$. If so, $\mathcal{E}$ breaks the binding property of Com. Similarly, $\mathcal{E}$ checks if $(\mathbf{w}_2^j, \rho_3^j) \neq (\pi_1^j(\mathbf{w}_1^j\mathbf{G}_1) + \mathbf{p}_1^j, \rho_3^j)$. If neither of these two inequalities holds true, we have

$$\pi_1^j = \pi_2^j, \mathbf{p}_1^j = \mathbf{p}_3^j, \mathbf{w}_2^j = \pi_1^j(\mathbf{w}_1^j\mathbf{G}_1) + \mathbf{p}_1^j. \tag{4}$$

Round 1: $\mathcal{P}_1^{oom}((\mathbf{G}, \{\mathbf{y}_i\}_{i=1}^N), (I, \mathbf{x}, \mathbf{e}))$ chooses the following random objects:

$$\{\zeta_s^{\text{root}}, \zeta_u^{\text{root}}, \zeta_\delta^{\text{root}}, \rho_1^{\text{root}}, \rho_2^{\text{root}}\} \xleftarrow{\$} \{0,1\}^\lambda, \theta \xleftarrow{\$} \{0,1\}^{2\lambda}.$$

- $(\{\zeta_s^i\}_{i=1}^\kappa) = \text{Stree}(\zeta_s^{\text{root}}, \kappa)$, $(\{\zeta_u^i\}_{i=1}^\kappa) = \text{Stree}(\zeta_u^{\text{root}}, \kappa)$, $(\{\zeta_\delta^i\}_{i=1}^\kappa) = \text{Stree}(\zeta_\delta^{\text{root}}, \kappa)$.
- $(\{\rho_1^i\}_{i=1}^\kappa) = \text{Stree}(\rho_1^{\text{root}}, \kappa)$, $(\{\rho_2^i\}_{i=1}^\kappa) = \text{Stree}(\rho_2^{\text{root}}, \kappa)$.
- **For** j from 1 to κ **do**
  - $(c_1^j, c_2^j, c_3^j) \leftarrow \mathcal{P}_1^g((\mathbf{G}, \{\mathbf{y}_i\}_{i=1}^N), (I, \mathbf{x}, \mathbf{e}), (\zeta_s^j, \zeta_u^j, \zeta_\delta^j, \rho_1^j, \rho_2^j), \theta)$.
  - $(\text{Mtree}_1, C_1) = \text{Mtree}(c_1^1, \cdots, c_1^\kappa)$, $(\text{Mtree}_2, C_2) = \text{Mtree}(c_2^1, \cdots, c_2^\kappa)$,
  - $(\text{Mtree}_3, C_3) = \text{Mtree}(c_3^1, \cdots, c_3^\kappa)$.
- Send CMT $:= (\mathcal{H}(C_1, C_2, C_3), \theta)$ to $\mathcal{V}$.

Round 2: $\mathcal{V}_1^{oom}(\text{CMT})$ sends a challenge $\mathbf{ch} = (ch_1, \cdots, ch_\kappa) \xleftarrow{\$} \{1,2,3\}^\kappa$ to $\mathcal{P}$.

Round 3: $\mathcal{P}_2^{oom}((\mathbf{G}, \{\mathbf{y}_i\}_{i=1}^N), (I, \mathbf{x}, \mathbf{e}), \mathbf{ch})$ responds as follows:
- $\text{path}_1 = \text{Gpath}(\text{Mtree}_1, \{j\}_{ch^j=1})$.
- $\text{path}_2 = \text{Gpath}(\text{Mtree}_2, \{j\}_{ch^j=2})$, $\text{path}_3 = \text{Gpath}(\text{Mtree}_3, \{j\}_{ch^j=3})$.
- $\zeta_s^{\text{inter}} \leftarrow \text{Oseeds}(\zeta_s^{\text{root}}, \{j\}_{ch^j=2})$.
- $\zeta_\delta^{\text{inter}} \leftarrow \text{Oseeds}(\zeta_\delta^{\text{root}}, \{j\}_{ch^j\neq 1})$, $\zeta_u^{\text{inter}} \leftarrow \text{Oseeds}(\zeta_u^{\text{root}}, \{j\}_{ch^j=2})$.
- $\zeta_{\rho_1}^{\text{inter}} \leftarrow \text{Oseeds}(\zeta_{\rho_1}^{\text{root}}, \{j\}_{ch^j\neq 1})$, $\zeta_{\rho_2}^{\text{inter}} \leftarrow \text{Oseeds}(\zeta_{\rho_2}^{\text{root}}, \{j\}_{ch^j\neq 2})$.
- **For** j from 1 to κ **do**
  - **If** $ch^j = 1$ **Then**
    - Set $\mathbf{w}_1^j = \mathbf{u}^j + \mathbf{x}$.
    - $\text{rsp}^j = \mathbf{w}_1^j$.
  - **If** $ch^j = 2$ **Then**
    - Set $\mathbf{w}_2^j = \delta^j((\mathbf{u}^j + \mathbf{x})\mathbf{G}_1) + \mathbf{v}^j$, $\mathbf{w}_3^j = \text{compress}(\delta^j(\mathbf{e}))$.
    - $b^j = b_I^j$, $\text{path}^j = \text{Gpath}(\text{tree}^j, I)$.
    - $\text{rsp}^j = (\mathbf{w}_2^j, \mathbf{w}_3^j, b^j, \text{path}^j)$.
- Send RSP $= (\{\text{rsp}^i\}_{i=1}^\kappa, \text{path}_1, \text{path}_2, \text{path}_3, \zeta_*^{\text{inter}})$.

Verification: $\mathcal{V}_2^{oom}((\mathbf{G}, \{\mathbf{y}_i\}_{i=1}^N), \text{CMT}, \mathbf{ch}, \text{RSP}, \theta)$:
- $\{\zeta_s^j\}_{ch^j=2} \leftarrow \text{Recover}(\zeta_s^{\text{inter}}, \{j\}_{ch^j=2})$.
- $\{\zeta_\delta^j\}_{ch^j\neq 1} \leftarrow \text{Recover}(\zeta_\delta^{\text{inter}}, \{j\}_{ch^j\neq 1})$, $\{\zeta_u^j\}_{ch^j=2} \leftarrow \text{Recover}(\zeta_u^{\text{inter}}, \{j\}_{ch^j=2})$.
- $\{\zeta_{\rho_1}^j\}_{ch^j\neq 1} \leftarrow \text{Recover}(\zeta_{\rho_1}^{\text{inter}}, \{j\}_{ch^j\neq 1})$, $\{\zeta_{\rho_2}^j\}_{ch^j\neq 2} \leftarrow \text{Recover}(\zeta_{\rho_2}^{\text{inter}}, \{j\}_{ch^j\neq 2})$.
- **For** j from 1 to κ **do**
  - **If** $ch^j = 1$ **Then**
    - Set $(c_2^j, c_3^j) \leftarrow \mathcal{V}_2^g(ch^j, rsp_j, \zeta_{\delta'}^j, \rho_2^j, \rho_3^j, \theta)$.
  - **If** $ch^j = 2$ **Then**
    - Set $(c_1^j, c_3^j) \leftarrow \mathcal{V}_2^g(ch^j, \text{rsp}^j, \rho_3^j, \theta)$.
  - **If** $ch^j = 3$ **Then**
    - Set $(c_1^j, c_2^j) \leftarrow \mathcal{V}_2^g(ch^j, \text{rsp}^j, \zeta_s^j, \zeta_r^j, \zeta_\delta^j, \rho_2^j, \theta)$.
- $C_1 = \text{Rebuild}(\{c_1^j\}_{ch^j\neq 1}, \text{path}_1)$, $C_2 = \text{Rebuild}(\{c_2^j\}_{ch^j\neq 2}, \text{path}_2)$,
- $C_3 = \text{Rebuild}(\{c_3^j\}_{ch^j\neq 3}, \text{path}_3)$.
- Check if CMT $= \mathcal{H}(C_1, C_2, C_3)$. If the above are met, output 1; otherwise, output 0.

Fig. 4. The GSD-based one-out-of-many proof $\Pi^{\text{oom}} = (\mathcal{P}^{\text{oom}} = (\mathcal{P}_1^{\text{oom}}, \mathcal{P}_2^{\text{oom}}), \mathcal{V}^{\text{oom}} = (\mathcal{V}_1^{\text{oom}}, \mathcal{V}_2^{\text{oom}}))$. Let $\zeta_*^{\text{inter}} = (\zeta_s^{\text{inter}}, \zeta_u^{\text{inter}}, \zeta_\delta^{\text{inter}}, \zeta_{\rho_1}^{\text{inter}}, \zeta_{\rho_2}^{\text{inter}})$.

For convenience, in later proof we let $\pi^j = \pi_1^j, \mathbf{p}^j = \mathbf{p}_1^j$. $\mathcal{E}$ then checks if $\text{Com}(\mathbf{w}_2^j + \mathbf{w}_3^j; b^j)) \neq \text{leaf}_i^j$ for $\forall i \in [N]$. If indeed, by employing the Merkle tree extractor in Lemma 1 with input $(\text{tree}^j, \text{Com}(\mathbf{w}_2^j + \mathbf{w}_3^j; b^j)), \text{path})$, it outputs a collision in $\mathcal{H}$. Otherwise, there exists an index $I \in [N]$ satisfying $\text{Com}(\mathbf{w}_2^j + \mathbf{w}_3^j; b^j) = \text{leaf}_I^j$ and $\mathcal{E}$ further checks if $(\mathbf{w}_2^j + \mathbf{w}_3^j, b^j) \neq$

$(\pi^j(\mathbf{p}_2^j\mathbf{G}_1^j + \mathbf{y}_I^j) + \mathbf{p}^j, b_I^j)$. If so, $\mathcal{E}$ breaks the binding property of Com. Otherwise, $\mathcal{E}$ gets $\mathbf{w}_2^j + \mathbf{w}_3^j = \pi^j(\mathbf{p}_2^j\mathbf{G}_1 + \mathbf{y}_I^j) + \mathbf{p}^j$ and $b^j = b_I^j$ and so it deduces that $(\mathbf{w}_1^j - \mathbf{p}_2^j)\mathbf{G}_1 + (\pi^j)^{-1}(\mathbf{w}_3^j) = \mathbf{y}_I$ by Eq. (4), where $(\pi^j)^{-1}(\mathbf{w}_3^j) \in B(n,t)$. This means that for some $I \in [N]$, $\mathcal{E}$ outputs the witness $(\mathbf{w}_1^j - \mathbf{p}_2^j, (\pi^j)^{-1}(\mathbf{w}_3^j))$.

Honest-Verifier Zero-Knowledge: Assume that $\mathcal{A}$ has accessed the oracle $\mathcal{O}^*(\cdot)$ a total of $\mathcal{Q}$ times, where $\mathcal{O}^*(\cdot)$ instantiates the hash function, algorithm Stree, and Com. Let E_i denote the $\mathcal{A}^{\mathcal{O}}(Sim_i(s, \mathbf{ch})) = 1$, for $i = 1, \cdots, 6$. Sim is built as follows:

Sim first runs

$$\begin{cases} \theta \leftarrow \{0,1\}^{2\lambda}, \zeta_\delta^{\text{inter}} \leftarrow \text{Simseeds}(\{j\}_{ch^j \neq 1}, \theta); \\ \zeta_{\rho_1}^{\text{inter}} \leftarrow \text{Simseeds}(\{j\}_{ch^j \neq 1}, \theta), \zeta_{\rho_2}^{\text{inter}} \leftarrow \text{Simseeds}(\{j\}_{ch^j \neq 2}, \theta); \\ \zeta_s^{\text{inter}} \leftarrow \text{Simseeds}(\{j\}_{ch^j = 2}, \theta), \zeta_u^{\text{inter}} \leftarrow \text{Simseeds}(\{j\}_{ch^j = 2}, \theta). \end{cases}$$

Then, Sim obtains random coins by

$$\begin{cases} \{\zeta_{\rho_1}^j\}_{ch^j \neq 1} \leftarrow \text{Recover}(\zeta_{\rho_1}^{\text{inter}}, \{j\}_{ch^j \neq 1});\ \{\zeta_{\rho_2}^j\}_{ch^j \neq 2} \leftarrow \text{Recover}(\zeta_{\rho_2}^{\text{inter}}, \{j\}_{ch^j \neq 2}); \\ \{\zeta_s^j\}_{ch^j = 2} \leftarrow \text{Recover}(\zeta_s^{\text{inter}}, \{j\}_{ch^j = 2});\ \{\zeta_u^j\}_{ch^j = 2} \leftarrow \text{Recover}(\zeta_u^{\text{inter}}, \{j\}_{ch^j = 2}); \\ \{\zeta_\delta^j\}_{ch^j \neq 1} \leftarrow \text{Recover}(\zeta_\delta^{\text{inter}}, \{j\}_{ch^j \neq 1}). \end{cases}$$

For $j = 1$ to κ : Sim performs
Case $ch^j = 1$:

1. Sim samples $\mathbf{w}_1^j \xleftarrow{\$} \mathbb{F}_q^k, c_1^j \xleftarrow{\$} \{0,1\}^{2\lambda}$ and sets $\mathbf{p}_1^j \xleftarrow{\$, \xi_\delta^j} \mathbb{F}_2^n, \pi_1^j \xleftarrow{\$, \xi_\delta^j} \mathcal{S}_n$.
2. Sim sets $c_2^j = \text{Com}(\pi_1^j, \mathbf{p}_1^j; \rho_2^j)$ and $c_3^j = \text{Com}(\pi_1^j(\mathbf{w}_1^j\mathbf{G}_1) + \mathbf{p}_1^j; \rho_3^j)$.
3. Sim sets $\text{rsp}^j = \mathbf{w}_1^j$.

Sim computes CMT $:= \mathcal{H}(C_1, C_2, C_3)$, where

$$C_1 \leftarrow \text{Mtree}(c_1^1, \cdots, c_1^\kappa), C_2 \leftarrow \text{Mtree}(c_2^1, \cdots, c_2^\kappa), C_3 \leftarrow \text{Mtree}(c_3^1, \cdots, c_3^\kappa).$$

and obtains $\text{path}_i = \text{Gpath}(\text{Mtree}_i, \{j\}_{ch^j = i})$ for $i = 1, 2, 3$. It sets

$$\text{RSP} = (\{\text{rsp}^i\}_{i=1}^\kappa, \text{path}_1, \text{path}_2, \text{path}_3, \zeta_*^{\text{inter}})$$

and returns $(\text{CMT}, \mathbf{ch}, \text{RSP}, \theta)$.
Case $ch^j = 2$:

1. Sim chooses the following random objects:

$$\mathbf{w}_2^j \xleftarrow{\$} \mathbb{F}_2^n, \mathbf{w}_3^j \xleftarrow{\$} B(n,t), b^j \xleftarrow{\$} \{0,1\}^\lambda; \text{leaf}_i^j \xleftarrow{\$} \{0,1\}^{2\lambda}, \forall i \in [2; N], c_2^j \xleftarrow{\$} \{0,1\}^{2\lambda}.$$

2. Sim sets $\text{leaf}_1^j = \text{Com}(\mathbf{w}_2^j + \mathbf{w}_3^j; b^j)$ and $(\text{tree}^j, \text{root}^j) = \text{IH-Mtree}(\text{leaf}^j)$.
3. Sim sets $c_1^j = \text{root}^j$ and $c_3^j = \text{Com}(\mathbf{w}_2^j; \rho_3^j)$.
4. Sim runs $\text{Gpath}(\text{tree}^j, 1)$ to retrieve the path and sets $\text{rsp}^j = (\mathbf{w}_2^j, \mathbf{w}_3^j, b^j, \text{path}^j)$.

Case $ch^j = 3$:

1. *Sim* samples the following random objects:

$$\mathbf{p}_2^j \xleftarrow{\$,\xi_u^j} \mathbb{F}_2^{k_1}; \mathbf{p}_3^j \xleftarrow{\$,\xi_\delta^j} \mathbb{F}_2^n; \pi_2^j \xleftarrow{\$,\xi_\delta^j} \mathcal{S}_n, c_3^j \xleftarrow{\$} \{0,1\}^{2\lambda}.$$

2. *Sim* sets $\text{leaf}^j = (\text{Com}(\pi_2^j(\mathbf{p}_2^j\mathbf{G}_1 + \mathbf{y}_1) + \mathbf{p}_3^j; b_1^j), \cdots, \text{Com}(\pi_2^j(\mathbf{p}_2^j\mathbf{G}_1 + \mathbf{y}_N) + \mathbf{p}_3^j; b_N^j))$ and calculates its root^j, where $(b_1^j, \cdots, b_N^j) = \text{Stree}(\xi_s^j, N)$.
3. *Sim* sets $c_1^j = \text{root}^j$ and $c_2^j = \text{Com}(\pi_2^j, \mathbf{p}_3^j; \rho_2^j)$.

Similar to the proof of Theorem 2, we only need to check the case of RSP. We use a sequence of simulators $\{Sim_i\}_{i=1}^6$ to prove that *Sim* and an honest prover are indistinguishable, in which Sim_1 and Sim_6 represent the honest prover and *Sim*, respectively.

Sim_2: The only difference between Sim_2 and the honest prover is that the tuple internal seeds ζ_*^{inter} are generated by the algorithm Simseeds with the input **ch** intead of being generated by the algorithms Stree and Oseeds with inputs ζ_*^{root} and **ch**. According to Lemma 3, the advantage of distinguishing between these two tuples internal seeds is $\mathcal{Q}/2^\lambda$ when the oracle $\mathcal{O}^{\text{Stree}}(\cdot)$ is accessed $\mathcal{Q}$ times. Therefore, we have $|\Pr[E_2] - \Pr[E_1]| \leq \mathcal{Q}/2^\lambda$.

Observe that, if ζ_*^{inter} has not been queried, when $ch^j = 1$ and $ch^j = 3$, Sim_2 can perfectly simulate. We only prove the case of $ch^j = 2$.

Sim_3: The only difference between Sim_3 and Sim_2 is that $\{b_i^j\}_{i=1}^N$ are randomly sampled from $\{0,1\}^\lambda$ instead of being generated by $\mathcal{O}^{\text{Stree}}(\cdot)$ with the input ζ_s^j, where ζ_s^j is generated by $\mathcal{O}^{\text{Oseeds}}(\zeta_*^{\text{inter}})$. If ζ_s^j has not been queried by $\mathcal{A}$ to the oracle $\mathcal{O}^{\text{Stree}}(\cdot)$, Sim_3 and Sim_2 are indistinguishable. Thus, if $\mathcal{O}^{\text{Stree}}(\cdot)$ is accessed $\mathcal{Q}$ times and the probability of colliding with ζ_s^j each query is 2^λ, the probability of colliding with ζ_s^j after $\mathcal{Q}$ queries is $\mathcal{Q}/2^\lambda$. Thus, we have $|\Pr[E_3] - \Pr[E_2]| \leq \mathcal{Q}/2^\lambda$.

Sim_4: The only difference between Sim_3 and Sim_2 is that $\{\text{leaf}_i^j\}_{i=1, i\neq I}^N$ are randomly sampled from $\{0,1\}^{2\lambda}$ instead of being generated by $\mathcal{O}^{\text{Com}}(\cdot)$ with the tuple $(\delta^j(\mathbf{p}_2^j\mathbf{G} + \mathbf{y}_i) + \mathbf{p}_3^j; b_i^j)$ for $i \neq I$. If all tuples have not been queried by $\mathcal{A}$ to $\mathcal{O}^{\text{Com}}(\cdot)$, Sim_3 and Sim_2 are indistinguishable. Let $\mathcal{Q}_{\text{com}_i}$ represent the number of times $\mathcal{O}^{\text{Com}_i}(\cdot)$ is accessed. Since the minimum entropy of b_i^j is $1/2^\lambda$, the minimum entropy of tuple $(\delta^j(\mathbf{p}_2^j\mathbf{G} + \mathbf{y}_i) + \mathbf{p}_3^j; b_i^j)$ is at most $1/2^\lambda$. Hence, the probability of collision with the tuple in each query is at most $1/2^\lambda$. Furthermore, since $\sum_{i=1}^N \mathcal{Q}_{\text{com}_i} \leq \mathcal{Q}$, we have $|\Pr[E_4] - \Pr[E_3]| \leq \mathcal{Q}/2^\lambda$.

Sim_5: There are two differences between Sim_5 and Sim_4. Firstly, c_3^j is randomly sampled from $\{0,1\}^{2\lambda}$. Secondly, $\text{leaf}_I^j = \text{Com}(\mathbf{w}_2^j + \mathbf{w}_3^j; b_I^j)$, where $\mathbf{w}_2^j$ and $\mathbf{w}_3^j$ are randomly sampled from $\mathbb{F}_2^n$ and $B(n,t)$ respectively. Since $\mathbf{w}_2^j$ and $\mathbf{w}_3^j$ follows the random distribution as the real transcript, we have $\Pr[E_5] = \Pr[E_4]$.

Sim_6: The only difference between Sim_6 and Sim_5 is that 1 is used instead of I in witness. Lemma 2 states that regardless of whether the selected index is 1 or I, the root and path follow the same distribution. Therefore, we have $\Pr[E_6] = \Pr[E_5]$.

Thus, we have $\left|\Pr[\mathcal{A}^{\mathcal{O}}(\mathcal{P}(s,w,\mathbf{ch})) \rightarrow 1] - \Pr[\mathcal{A}^{\mathcal{O}}(Sim(s,\mathbf{ch})) \rightarrow 1]\right| \leq \frac{3Q}{2^\lambda}$.

□

Communication Cost: *(1)* The cost of commitments is $2\lambda(5\kappa/6+1)$. *(2)* The cost of seeds is about $(\kappa/3)(20\lambda/3) + 2\lambda$. *(3)* The cost of vectors and the path of the Merkle tree is about $(\kappa/3)(\frac{3n}{2} + k + 2\lambda \log N)$.

3.3 Our Set-Membership Proof

A set-membership proof is a concept similar to an one-out-of-many proof. It allows one to prove that an element in a public set satisfies a given property, i.e. given a publicly set $\mathcal{I}$ and a property G, one proves the existence of an element α_i such that $\alpha_i \in \mathcal{I}$ and $G(\alpha_i)$ holds. Consider an example where a commitment $\mathbf{c} = \text{Com}_{\text{McE}}$ and a public set $\mathcal{I} = \{\alpha_1, \cdots, \alpha_N\}$ are given. The goal is to demonstrate that $\mathbf{c}$ is a commitment to an element in $\mathcal{I}$ and so our set-membership proof can be achieved by the protocol in Fig. 4 with the input of the set $[\mathbf{c}_1 = \mathbf{c} + \text{Com}_{\text{McE}}(\alpha_1; (\mathbf{0},\mathbf{0})), \cdots, \mathbf{c}_N = \mathbf{c} + \text{Com}_{\text{McE}}(\alpha_N; (\mathbf{0},\mathbf{0}))]$ and public commitment key $\mathbf{G}$.

4 Our Code-Based Logarithmic-Size Ring Signature Scheme

A ring signature enables a ring member to sign a message on behalf of the ring anonymously. Our GSD-based one-out-of-many proof can be transformed into a ring signature scheme through Fiat-Shamir transform. Specifically, each user has a public-private key pair $(\mathbf{y}_i, (\mathbf{x}_i, \mathbf{e}_i))$, where $\mathbf{y}_i = \mathbf{x}_i\mathbf{G} + \mathbf{e}_i$ and $\mathbf{e}_i$ is small. The signature for a message μ is our GSD-based one-out-of-many proof for $(\mathbf{x}_i, \mathbf{e}_i)$ satisfying Eq. (3), where μ is the input of the random oracle in Fiat-Shamir heuristic. Our ring signature scheme is presented in Fig. 5.

RS.Setup(1^λ):
- $\mathbf{G} \xleftarrow{\$} \mathbb{F}_2^{k\times n}$, where $n = \mathcal{O}(\lambda)$ and $k = \mathcal{O}(\lambda)$.
- $\mathcal{H}_{com} \xleftarrow{\$} \mathcal{H}(1^\lambda)$, $\mathcal{H}_{FS} \xleftarrow{\$} \mathcal{H}(1^\lambda, \kappa)$, $\mathcal{H}_{Merkle} \xleftarrow{\$} \mathcal{H}(1^\lambda, N)$, where $\kappa = \omega(\log(\lambda))$.
- Return $pp = (\mathbf{G}, \mathcal{H}_{FS}, \mathcal{H}_{com})$.

RS.KeGen(pp, N):
- $\mathbf{x} \xleftarrow{\$} \mathbb{F}_2^k, \mathbf{e} \xleftarrow{\$} B(n,t)$, $\mathbf{y} = \mathbf{x}\mathbf{G} + \mathbf{e}$.
- Return $(pk, sk) = (\mathbf{y}, (\mathbf{x}, \mathbf{e}))$.

RS.Sign(sk_j, M, R):
- $\text{CMT} \leftarrow \mathcal{P}_1^{oom}(\mathbf{G}, R, sk_j)$.
- $\mathbf{ch} \leftarrow \mathcal{H}_{FS}(M, R, \text{CMT})$.
- $\text{RSP} \leftarrow \mathcal{P}_2^{oom}(\mathbf{G}, R, \mathbf{ch}, sk_j)$.
- Return $\sigma = (\text{CMT}, \text{RSP})$.

RS.Verify(M, σ):
- $(\text{CMT}, \text{RSP}) \leftarrow \sigma$.
- $\mathbf{ch} \leftarrow \mathcal{H}_{FS}(M, R, \text{CMT})$.
- Return $\mathcal{V}_2^{oom}(\mathbf{G}, R, (\text{CMT}, \mathbf{ch}, \text{RSP}))$.

Fig. 5. Our ring signature scheme. Set $R := (pk_1, \cdots, pk_N)$.

First, we introduce the definition and security requirements of a ring signature scheme.

Definition 1. *A ring signature scheme contains four polynomial-time algorithms* $\mathcal{RS} = (\mathbf{RS.Setup}, \mathbf{RS.KeyGen}, \mathbf{RS.Sign}, \mathbf{RS.Verify})$,

- $pp \leftarrow \mathbf{RS.Setup}(1^\lambda)$: *Taking a security parameter* 1^λ *as input, output the public parameters* pp.
- $(pk, sk) \leftarrow \mathbf{RS.KeyGen}(pp, N)$: *Taking the public parameter* pp *and the number* N *of ring users as input, publish a pair of public-private keys* (pk_i, sk_i) *for each user* $i \in [N]$.
- $\sigma \leftarrow \mathbf{RS.Sign}(R, M, sk)$: *Taking the list of public keys* $R = (pk_1, \cdots, pk_N)$, *a private key* sk *and a message* M *as input, generate a signature* σ.
- $b \leftarrow \mathbf{RS.Verify}(R, M, \sigma)$: *Taking the list of public keys* R, *a message* M, *and a signature* σ *as input, output* b *either* 1 *(accept) or* 0 *(reject).*

A ring signature needs to satisfy three properties: correctness, unforgeability, and anonymity. Correctness ensures that a valid signature can always be verified. Unforgeability guarantees that only users in the ring can generate valid signatures. Anonymity ensures that the output signature does not leak the identity of the signer.

Definition 2 (Correctness). *A ring signature scheme achieves correctness if for any* $\lambda \in \mathbb{N}$, $N = poly(\lambda)$, $j \in [N]$ *and every message* M, *the following holds:*

$$\Pr\left[\mathbf{RS.Verify}(R, M, \sigma) = 1 \;\middle|\; \begin{array}{c} pp \leftarrow \mathbf{RS.Setup}(1^\lambda), \\ (pk_i, sk_i) \leftarrow \mathbf{RS.KeyGen}(pp), \forall i \in [N], \\ R = (pk_1, \cdots, pk_N), \\ \sigma \leftarrow \mathbf{RS.Sign}(R, M, sk_j). \end{array}\right] = 1.$$

Definition 3 (Unforgeability w.r.t. insider corruption). *A ring signature scheme* $\mathcal{RS} = (\mathbf{RS.Setup}, \mathbf{RS.KeyGen}, \mathbf{RS.Sign}, \mathbf{RS.Verify})$ *is unforgeable if the advantage of* $\mathcal{A}$ *is negligible in the following game:*

1. $pp \leftarrow \mathbf{RS.Setup}(1^\lambda)$, $(pk_i, sk_i) \leftarrow \mathbf{RS.KeyGen}(pp, N), \forall i \in [N]$;
2. $\mathcal{A}$ *can have access to the corrupted oracle* $\mathbf{Co}(\cdot)$ *with any* $pk_j \in R$ *and* $\mathbf{Co}(\cdot)$ *returns the* sk_j *to* $\mathcal{A}$ *and adds* pk_j *to the set* CU;
3. $\mathcal{A}$ *can have access to the* $\mathbf{RS.Sign}(\cdot)$ *with* (pk_j, M) *and then* $\mathbf{RS.Sign}(\cdot)$ *returns a signature* σ *using the secret key* sk_j;
4. $\mathcal{A}$ *outputs* (R^*, M^*, σ^*) *such that* $\mathbf{RS.Verify}(R^*, M^*, \sigma^*) = 1$, *where* (R^*, M^*) *has never been asked and* $R^* \cap CU = \emptyset$.

The advantage of breaking unforgeability is

$$\mathrm{Adv}_{\mathcal{A}}^{Unf}(\lambda) = \Pr[\mathbf{RS.Verify}(R, M, \sigma) = 1].$$

Definition 4 (Anonymity). *A ring signature scheme* $\mathcal{RS} = (\mathbf{RS.Setup}, \mathbf{RS.KeyGen}, \mathbf{RS.Sign}, \mathbf{RS.Verify})$ *is anonymous if the advantage of* $\mathcal{A}$ *is negligible in the following game:*

1. $pp \leftarrow \mathbf{RS.Setup}(1^\lambda), (pk_i, sk_i) \leftarrow \mathbf{RS.KeyGen}(pp, N), \forall i \in [N]$;
2. $\mathcal{A}$ *selects a tuple* $(M, pk_{i_0}, pk_{i_1}), i_0, i_1 \in [N]$;
3. $\sigma \leftarrow \mathbf{RS.Sign}(M, sk_{i_b}), b \xleftarrow{\$} \{0, 1\}$;
4. $\mathcal{A}$ *returns a* b'.

The advantage of breaking anonymity is

$$\mathrm{Adv}_{\mathcal{A}}^{Anon}(\lambda) = |\Pr[b = b'] - 1/2|. \tag{5}$$

Theorem 4. *Our ring signature scheme in Fig. 5 achieves correctness, anonymity and unforgeability with respect to insider corruptions in the random oracle model.*

Proof. **Correctness:** The correctness in Fig. 5 can be directly inferred from the completeness in Fig. 4.

Anonymity: Since our GSD-based one-out-of-many proof is zero-knowledge, it implies that the protocol is witness-indistinguishable. As a result, the anonymity in Fig. 5 can be obtained immediately.

Unforgeability: Without providing specific details we only provide the proof framework as follows. The challenger first selects an index j^* and set the pk_{j^*} as the challenge instance. The rest pk_j are generated as the same as the real **RS.KeGen**. If $\mathcal{A}$ queries $\mathbf{RS.Sign}(\cdot)$ with pk_{j^*}, the challenger uses the simulator of Fig. 4 to output the signature. Otherwise, the challenger honestly generates the signature. Under the condition that j^* has not been queried with $\mathbf{Co}(\cdot)$ and $\mathcal{A}$ outputs a forged signature about pk_{j^*}, the challenger is able to extract the solution to the challenge problem via rewind techniques. □

5 Code-Based Group Signatures

Our GSD-based one-out-of-many proof can be applied in the construction of a group signature. However, unlike ring signatures, a group signature scheme cannot be obtained by directly applying the Fiat-Shamir transform to our one-out-of-many proofs. Therefore, we first construct a ZKAoK that allows a signer to prove both its membership in the group and the honest encryption of its own identity using the public key of the openers. Then, we utilize the Fiat-Shamir transform on the ZKAoK to get our group signature scheme. The overarching concept of this ZKAoK is to combine our GSD-based one-out-of-many proof and our set-memberships proof. We first give the definition and security requirements of a group signature.

Definition 5. *A group signature scheme contains five polynomial-time algorithms* (**GS.Setup**, **GS.KeyGen**, **GS.Sign**, **GS.Verify**, **GS.Open**) *in which:*

- $(pp, mpk, msk) \leftarrow \mathbf{GS.Setup}(1^\lambda)$: *Taking a security parameter* λ *as input, output the public parameters* pp *and the group manager's public-secret key pair* (mpk, msk).

- $(pk, sk) \leftarrow$ **GS.KeyGen**(pp, N) : *Taking the public parameter pp and the number N of group members as input, publish a pair of public and private keys* (pk_i, sk_i) *for each user i,* $i \in [N]$.
- $\sigma \leftarrow$ **GS.Sign**(R, mpk, M, sk) : *Taking the list of public keys* $R = (pk_1, \cdots, pk_N)$*, the manager's public key mpk, a private key sk and a message M as input, generate a signature* σ.
- $b \leftarrow$ **GS.Verify**(R, M, σ) : *Taking the public key R, a message M, and a signature* σ *as input, output b either* 1 *(accept) or* 0 *(reject).*
- $i \leftarrow$ **GS.Open**(R, msk, M, σ) : *Taking the public key R, the group manager's secret key msk, a message M and a group signature* σ *as input, output an index* $i \in [N]$ *or* $\perp$*, indicating failure.*

A group signature scheme needs to achieve three requirements: correctness, anonymity and traceability. We give the relaxed anonymity requirement, namely CPA-anonymity.

Definition 6 (Correctness). *A group signature scheme is correct if for* $\forall \lambda \in \mathbb{N}$, $N = poly(\lambda)$, $j \in [N]$ *and any message M, the following is true:*

$$\Pr\left[\begin{array}{c|c} \mathbf{GS.Verify}(R, M, \sigma) = 1 & (pp, mpk, msk) \leftarrow \mathbf{GS.Setup}(1^\lambda), \\ \mathbf{GS.Open}(msk, R, M, \sigma) = j. & (pk_i, sk_i) \leftarrow \mathbf{GS.KeyGen}(pp), \forall i \in [N], \\ & R = (pk_1, \cdots, pk_N), \\ & \sigma \leftarrow \mathbf{GS.Sign}(R, mpk, M, sk_j). \end{array}\right] = 1.$$

Definition 7 (CPA-anonymity). *A group signature scheme* $\mathcal{GS}$ = (**GS.Setup**, **GS.KeyGen**, **GS.Sign**, **GS.Verify**, **GS.Open**) *is CPA-anonymous if the advantage of any PPT adversary* $\mathcal{A}$ *is negligible in the following game:*

1. $(pp, mpk, msk) \leftarrow$ **GS.Setup**$1^\lambda)$;
2. $(pk_i, sk_i) \leftarrow$ **GS.KeyGen**$(pp, N), \forall i \in [N]$;
3. $\mathcal{A}$ *selects a tuple* $(M, pk_{i_0}, pk_{i_1}), i_0, i_1 \in [N]$;
4. $\sigma \leftarrow$ **GS.Sign**$(R, mpk, M, sk_{i_b}), b \xleftarrow{\$} \{0, 1\}$;
5. $\mathcal{A}$ *outputs a guess* b'.

The advantage of $\mathcal{A}$ *in breaking CPA-anonymity is denoted by*

$$\mathrm{Adv}_{\mathcal{A}}^{Anon}(\lambda) = |\Pr[b = b'] - 1/2|.$$

Definition 8 (Traceability). *A group scheme* $\mathcal{GS}$ = (**GS.Setup**, **GS.**, **KeyGen**, **GS.Sign**, **GS.Verify**, **GS.Open**) *is traceable if the advantage of any PPT* $\mathcal{A}$ *is negligible in the following game:*

1. $(pp, mpk, msk) \leftarrow$ **GS.Setup**(1^λ);
2. $(pk_i, sk_i) \leftarrow$ **GS.KeyGen**$(pp, N), \forall i \in [N]$;
3. $\mathcal{A}$ *can have access to the corrupted oracle* **Co**$(\cdot)$ *with any* $pk_j \in R$*, and* **Co**$(\cdot)$ *returns the* sk_j *to* $\mathcal{A}$ *and adds* pk_j *to the set CU;*

4. *$\mathcal{A}$ can have access to the* **GS.Sign**$(\cdot)$ *with* (pk_j, M) *and* **GS.Sign**$(\cdot)$ *returns a signature* σ *using the secert key* sk_j;
5. *$\mathcal{A}$ outputs* (R^*, M^*, σ^*) *such that* **GS.Verify**$(R^*, M^*, \sigma^*) = 1$, *where* (R^*, M^*) *have never been asked and* $R^* \cap CU = \emptyset$.

The advantage of breaking traceability is denoted by

$$\mathrm{Adv}_{\mathcal{A}}^{Trac}(\lambda) = \Pr\begin{bmatrix} \mathbf{GS.Verify}(R, mpk, M^*, \sigma^*) = 1, \\ \mathbf{GS.Open}(R, msk, M^*, \sigma^*) \notin CU. \end{bmatrix}.$$

CPA-McEliece: We review the randomized McEliece encryption scheme [36]. It includes the following three algorithms: $\mathrm{KeyGen}_{\mathrm{McE}}$, $\mathrm{Enc}_{\mathrm{McE}}$, and $\mathrm{Dec}_{\mathrm{McE}}$.

- $(pk = \mathbf{G}_{\mathrm{McE}}, sk = (\mathbf{S}, \mathbf{G}', \mathbf{P})) \leftarrow \mathrm{KeyGen}_{\mathrm{McE}}(1^\lambda)$: With an integer λ as input, select a generator matrix $\mathbf{G}'$ of a random w-error-correcting (m, ℓ) code, and sample a random matrix $\mathbf{S} \in \mathbb{F}_2^{\ell\times\ell}$ and a random m-dimension permutation matrix $\mathbf{P}$, where $m = \mathcal{O}(\lambda), \ell = \mathcal{O}(\lambda), w = \mathcal{O}(\lambda)$. Output the encryption key as $\mathbf{G}_{\mathrm{McE}} = \mathbf{S}\mathbf{G}'\mathbf{P}$ and the decryption key as $(\mathbf{S}, \mathbf{G}', \mathbf{P})$.
- $\mathbf{ct} \leftarrow \mathrm{Enc}_{\mathrm{McE}}(\mathbf{G}_{\mathrm{McE}}, \mathbf{m})$: With a plaintext $\mathbf{m} \in \{0,1\}^{\ell_2}$ and the $\mathbf{G}_{\mathrm{McE}}$ as input, sample two random vectors $\mathbf{z} \in \mathbb{F}_2^{\ell_1}$ and $\mathbf{s} \in B(m, w)$, where $\ell = \ell_1 + \ell_2$. Output the ciphertext $\mathbf{ct} = (\mathbf{z}||\mathbf{m})\mathbf{G} + \mathbf{s}$.
- $\mathbf{m} \leftarrow \mathrm{Dec}_{\mathrm{McE}}(\mathbf{ct}, sk)$: With the ciphertext $\mathbf{ct}$ and sk as input, compute $\mathbf{m}' = \mathbf{S}^{-1}\mathcal{D}_{\mathbf{G}'}(\mathbf{ct}\mathbf{P}^{-1})$, where $\mathcal{D}_{\mathbf{G}'}$ is the error-correcting algorithm. Parse the $\mathbf{m}' = (\mathbf{z}, \mathbf{m}) \in \mathbb{F}_2^{\ell_1} \times \mathbb{F}_2^{\ell_2}$ and outputs $\mathbf{m}$.

The above scheme's CPA-security is based on the following two problems.

Problem 5 (Decisional McEliece problem [36]*).* Given a matrix $\mathbf{G} \in \mathbb{F}_2^{k\times n}$, determine whether it is randomly sampled or generated by the $\mathrm{KeyGen}_{\mathrm{McE}}$.

Problem 6 (Decisional Learning Parity with (fixed-weight) Noise problem [15]*).* Given a matrix $\mathbf{G} \in \mathbb{F}_2^{k\times n}$ and a vector $\mathbf{y} \in \mathbb{F}_2^n$, determine whether $\mathbf{y}$ is randomly generated or generated by $\mathbf{x}\mathbf{G} + \mathbf{e}$, where $\mathbf{x} \in \mathbb{F}_2^k$ and $\mathbf{e} \in B(n, t)$.

5.1 The Underlying Protocol of Our Group Signature

In this subsection, we construct a ZKAoK in Fig. 6 to act as the foundational component of our group signature scheme. We first give an overview of our construction. Let $k, n, \ell = \ell_1 + \ell_2$, m denote integers, and $\mathrm{bin}(j)$ denote the binary representation of j with length ℓ_2. The public input includes two matrices $\mathbf{G} \in \mathbb{F}_2^{k\times n}, \mathbf{G}_{\mathrm{McE}} = \begin{pmatrix} \mathbf{G}_{\mathrm{McE}}^1 \\ \mathbf{G}_{\mathrm{McE}}^2 \end{pmatrix} \in \mathbb{F}_2^{\ell\times m}$, any vector $\mathbf{y}_i \in \mathbb{F}_2^n, i \in [N]$ and a ciphertext $\mathbf{ct} \in \mathbb{F}_2^m$. The protocol allows one to prove the following relation in zero-knowledge

$$-\, \mathbf{x}\mathbf{G} + \mathbf{e} = \mathbf{y}_I \wedge \mathbf{x} \in \mathbb{F}_2^k, \mathbf{e} \in B(n, t), \tag{6}$$

$$-\, (\mathbf{z}||\,\mathrm{bin}(I))\mathbf{G}_{\mathrm{McE}} + \mathbf{s} = \mathbf{ct} \wedge \mathbf{z} \in \mathbb{F}_2^{\ell_1}, \mathbf{s} \in B(m, w), \tag{7}$$

$$-\, I \in [N]. \tag{8}$$

Round 1: $\mathcal{P}_1^{\mathrm{GS}}(\triangle, (I, \mathbf{x}, \mathbf{e}, \mathbf{z}, \mathbf{s}))$:

$$\begin{cases} \{\zeta_s, \zeta_{u,r}, \zeta_{\delta,\phi}, \rho_1, \rho_2\} \xleftarrow{\$} \{0,1\}^\lambda; \\ \mathbf{u} \xleftarrow{\$;\zeta_{u,r}} \mathbb{F}_2^k, \mathbf{v} \xleftarrow{\$;\zeta_{\delta,\phi}} \mathbb{F}_2^n, \delta \xleftarrow{\$;\zeta_{\delta,\phi}} \mathcal{S}_n; \\ \mathbf{r} \xleftarrow{\$;\zeta_{u,r}} \mathbb{F}_2^{\ell_1}, \mathbf{f} \xleftarrow{\$;\zeta_{\delta,\phi}} \mathbb{F}_2^m, \phi \xleftarrow{\$;\zeta_{\delta,\phi}} \mathcal{S}_m. \end{cases}$$

- $(b_1, \cdots, b_N) = \mathrm{Stree}(\zeta_s, N)$.
- $\{\mathrm{leaf}_i\}_{i=1}^N = \{\mathrm{Com}(\delta(\mathbf{uG} + \mathbf{y}_i) + \mathbf{v}, \phi((\mathbf{r}\|\,\mathrm{bin}(i))\mathbf{G}_{\mathrm{McE}} + \mathbf{ct}) + \mathbf{f}; b_i)\}_{i=1}^N$.
- $(\mathrm{root}, \mathrm{tree}) = \text{IH-Mtree}(\mathrm{tree})$.
- Send CMT := (c_1, c_2, c_3) to $\mathcal{V}$, where

$$\begin{cases} c_1 = \mathrm{root}; \\ c_2 = \mathrm{Com}(\delta, \phi, \mathbf{v}, \mathbf{f}; \rho_2); \\ c_3 = \mathrm{Com}(\delta((\mathbf{u}+\mathbf{x})\mathbf{G}) + \mathbf{v}, \phi((\mathbf{r}+\mathbf{z}\|\mathbf{0})\mathbf{G}_{\mathrm{McE}}) + \mathbf{f}; \rho_3). \end{cases}$$

Round 2: $\mathcal{V}_1^{\mathrm{GS}}(\mathrm{CMT})$ sends a challenge $ch \xleftarrow{\$} \{1,2,3\}$ to $\mathcal{P}$.
Round 3: $\mathcal{P}_2^{\mathrm{GS}}(\triangle, (I, \mathbf{x}, \mathbf{e}, \mathbf{z}, \mathbf{s}), ch)$:
- Case $ch = 1$: Set $\xi'_{\delta,\phi} = \zeta_{\delta,\phi}, \mathbf{w}_1 = \mathbf{u} + \mathbf{x}, \mathbf{w}_2 = \mathbf{r} + \mathbf{z}$.
  Send RSP $= (\xi'_{\delta,\phi}, \mathbf{w}_1, \mathbf{w}_2, \rho_2, \rho_3)$ to $\mathcal{V}$.
- Case $ch = 2$: Set

$$\begin{cases} \mathbf{w}_3 = \delta((\mathbf{u}+\mathbf{x})\mathbf{G}) + \mathbf{v}, \mathbf{w}_4 = \delta(\mathbf{e}), \mathbf{w}_5 = \phi((\mathbf{r}+\mathbf{z}\|\mathbf{0})\mathbf{G}_{\mathrm{McE}}) + \mathbf{f}; \\ \mathbf{w}_6 = \phi(\mathbf{s}), b = b_I, \mathrm{path} = \mathrm{Gpath}(\mathrm{tree}, I). \end{cases}$$

  Send RSP $= (\mathbf{w}_3, \mathbf{w}_4, \mathbf{w}_5, \mathbf{w}_6, b, \mathrm{path}, \rho_3)$ to $\mathcal{V}$.
- Case $ch = 3$: Set $\xi_s = \zeta_s, \xi_{u,r} = \zeta_{u,r}, \xi_{\delta,\phi} = \zeta_{\delta,\phi}$.
  Send RSP $= (\xi_s, \xi_{u,r}, \xi_{\delta,\phi}, \rho_2)$ to $\mathcal{V}$.

Verification: $\mathcal{V}_2^{\mathrm{GS}}(\triangle, \mathrm{CMT}, ch, \mathrm{RSP})$:
- Case $ch = 1$: Set $\mathbf{p}_1 \xleftarrow{\$;\xi_{\delta,\phi}} \mathbb{F}_2^n, \pi_1 \xleftarrow{\$;\xi_{\delta,\phi}} \mathcal{S}_n, \mathbf{p}_2 \xleftarrow{\$;\xi_{\delta,\phi}} \mathbb{F}_2^m, \pi_2 \xleftarrow{\$;\xi_{\delta,\phi}} \mathcal{S}_m$
  and check if

$$c_2 = \mathrm{Com}(\pi_1, \pi_2, \mathbf{p}_1, \mathbf{p}_2; \rho_2), c_3 = \mathrm{Com}(\pi_1(\mathbf{w}_1\mathbf{G}) + \mathbf{p}_1, \pi_2(\mathbf{w}_2\mathbf{G}_{\mathrm{McE}}^1) + \mathbf{p}_2; \rho_2).$$

- Case $ch = 2$: Compute R_1 as Rebuild(path,Com($\mathbf{w}_3 + \mathbf{w}_4, \mathbf{w}_5 + \mathbf{w}_6; b$)),
  and check if $\mathbf{w}_4 \in B(n,t)$, $\mathbf{w}_6 \in B(m,w)$ and

$$c_1 = \mathrm{R}_1, c_3 = \mathrm{Com}(\mathbf{w}_3, \mathbf{w}_5; \rho_3).$$

- Case $ch = 3$: Set $\mathbf{p}_3 \xleftarrow{\$;\xi_{u,r}} \mathbb{F}_2^k, \mathbf{p}_4 \xleftarrow{\$;\xi_{\delta,\phi}} \mathbb{F}_2^n, \mathbf{p}_5 \xleftarrow{\$;\xi_{u,r}} \mathbb{F}_2^{\ell_1}, \mathbf{p}_6 \xleftarrow{\$;\xi_{\delta,\phi}} \mathbb{F}_2^m, \pi_3 \xleftarrow{\$;\xi_{\delta,\phi}} \mathcal{S}_n,$
  $\pi_4 \xleftarrow{\$;\xi_{\delta,\phi}} \mathcal{S}_m$. $(b_1, \cdots, b_N) = \mathrm{Stree}(\xi_s, N)$.
  $\{\mathrm{leaf}_i\}_{i=1}^N = \{\mathrm{Com}(\pi_3(\mathbf{p}_3\mathbf{G} + \mathbf{y}_i) + \mathbf{p}_4, \pi_4((\mathbf{p}_5\|\,\mathrm{bin}(i))\mathbf{G}_{\mathrm{McE}} + \mathbf{ct}) + \mathbf{p}_6; b_i)\}_{i=1}^N$.
  Obtain R_2 as IH-Mtree(leaf) and check if

$$c_1 = \mathrm{R}_2, c_2 = \mathrm{Com}(\pi_3, \pi_4, \mathbf{p}_4, \mathbf{p}_6; \rho_2).$$

$\mathcal{V}$ outputs 1 when all conditions are met, else it outputs 0.

Fig. 6. The underlying ZKAoK $\Pi^{\mathrm{GS}} = (\mathcal{P}^{\mathrm{GS}} = (\mathcal{P}_1^{\mathrm{GS}}, \mathcal{P}_2^{\mathrm{GS}}), \mathcal{V}^{\mathrm{GS}} = (\mathcal{V}_1^{\mathrm{GS}}, \mathcal{V}_2^{\mathrm{GS}}))$ of our group signature scheme. Use $\triangle$ to denote $(\mathbf{G}, \mathbf{G}_{\mathrm{McE}}, \mathbf{y}_1, \cdots, \mathbf{y}_N, \mathbf{ct})$.

To prove Eqs. (6) and (8), we can utilize our GSD-based one-out-of-many proof with the public input $(\mathbf{G}, \{\mathbf{y}\}_{i=1}^{N})$. Likewise, to prove Eqs. (7) and (8), we can employ our set-membership proof with the public input $(\mathbf{G}_{\mathrm{McE}}, \mathbf{ct})$. To prove Eqs. (6), (7), and (8) simultaneously, we need to merge these two proofs. The overarching concept is to pair the $N+2$ corresponding commitments from the former proof with the $N+2$ commitments from the latter proof in sequential order, and then compress the last N pairs of commitments related to $(\{\mathbf{y}_i\}_{i=1}^{N}, \mathbf{ct})$ into a single root using the IH-Mtree. Next, the prover sends the root along with the remaining two pairs to the verifier. The rest steps are similar to the Fig. 4, with the difference being that what needs to be revealed and verified is the commitment pair. The protocol for this relation (6)(7)(8) is in Fig. 6.

Theorem 5. *The protocol in Fig. 6 is an argument of knowledge with the perfect completeness and zero-knowledge.*

Proof. We only provide the framework of the proof. Completeness: This can be obtained from the correctness of the Merkle tree and seedtree. Soundness: If a adversary can be accepted with a probability greater than 2/3, then we proceed as in Theorem 3. Namely, we construct an extractor to extract $(I, \mathbf{x}, \mathbf{e}, \mathbf{z}, \mathbf{s})$ from three valid responses. Zero-knowledge: Using the similar steps in Theorem 3, we can build a simulator for this protocol. □

Communication cost: *(1)* The cost of commitments is about $2\lambda(5\kappa/6 + 1)$. *(2)* The cost of seeds is about $(\kappa/3)(20\lambda/3) + 2\lambda$. *(3)* The cost of vectors and the path of Merkle tree is about $(\kappa/3)(\frac{3n}{2} + \frac{3m}{2} + k + \ell + 2\lambda \log N)$.

5.2 Our Code-Base Logarithmic-Size Group Signature Scheme

Our group signature scheme is described in Fig. 7, and its correctness can be directly inferred from the completeness in Fig. 6.

The security of our group signature is guaranteed by Theorems 6 and 7. The proofs for these theorems can be found in [27, Section 5.2].

Theorem 6. *Our group signature scheme in Fig. 7 is CPA-anonymous based on the hardness of* $\mathrm{DMcE}(m, \ell, w)$ *and* $\mathrm{DLPN}(m, \ell_1, w)$ *problems, and the zero-knowledge property of protocol in Fig. 6.*

Theorem 7. *Our group scheme satisfies full traceability based on the hardness of GSD problem in the random oracle model.*

6 Concrete Instantiation

We choose parameter sets for our ring signature and group signature schemes under the 128-bit security level. The parameters are set as follows:

1. The parameters (n, k, t) for GSD problem and the parameters (m, ℓ, w) for McEliece encryption scheme are set to achieve the 128-bit security level.

GS.Setup(1^λ):
- $\mathbf{G} \leftarrow \mathbb{F}_2^{k\times n}$, where $n = \mathcal{O}(\lambda)$ and $k = \mathcal{O}(\lambda)$.
- $(\mathbf{G}_{\text{McE}}, sk_{\text{McE}}) \leftarrow \text{KeyGen}_{\text{McE}}(1^\lambda)$, where $\mathbf{G}_{\text{McE}} \in \mathbb{F}_2^{\ell\times m}$.
- $\mathcal{H}_{com} \xleftarrow{\$} \mathcal{H}(1^\lambda)$, $\mathcal{H}_{FS} \xleftarrow{\$} \mathcal{H}(1^\lambda, \kappa)$, $\mathcal{H}_{Merkle} \xleftarrow{\$} \mathcal{H}(1^\lambda, N)$ where $\kappa = \omega(\log(\lambda))$.
- Return $pp = (\mathbf{G}, \mathbf{G}_{\text{McE}}, \mathcal{H}_{FS}, \mathcal{H}_{com})$.

GS.KeGen(pp):
- $\mathbf{x} \xleftarrow{\$} \mathbb{F}_2^k, \mathbf{e} \xleftarrow{\$} \mathrm{B}(n,t)$, $\mathbf{y} = \mathbf{xG} + \mathbf{e}$.
- Return $(pk, sk) = (\mathbf{y}, (\mathbf{x}, \mathbf{e}))$.

GS.Sign$(sk_j, M, R = (pk_1, \cdots, pk_N))$:
- $\mathbf{z} \xleftarrow{\$} \mathbb{F}_2^\ell, \mathbf{s} \xleftarrow{\$} B(m, w)$.
- $\mathbf{ct} = \text{Enc}_{\text{McE}}(M, (\mathbf{z}, \mathbf{s}))$
  $= (\mathbf{z} \| \operatorname{bin}(j))\mathbf{G}_{\text{McE}} + \mathbf{s}$.
- for $i = 1$ to κ:
  $\text{CMT}_i \leftarrow \mathcal{P}_1^{\text{GS}}(\mathbf{G}, \mathbf{G}_{\text{McE}}, \mathbf{ct}, R, sk_j)$.
- $\text{CMT} \leftarrow (\text{CMT}_1, \cdots, \text{CMT}_\kappa)$.
- $\mathbf{ch} \leftarrow \mathcal{H}_{FS}(M, R, \text{CMT})$.
- for $i = 1$ to κ:
  $\text{RSP}_i \leftarrow \mathcal{P}_2^{\text{GS}}(\mathbf{G}, \mathbf{G}_{\text{McE}}, \mathbf{ct}, R, \mathbf{ch}_i, sk_j)$.
- $\text{RSP} \leftarrow (\text{RSP}_1, \cdots, \text{RSP}_\kappa)$.
- Return $\sigma = (\mathbf{ct}, \text{CMT}, \text{RSP})$.

GS.Verify(R, M, σ):
- $(\mathbf{ct}, \text{CMT}, \text{RSP}) \leftarrow \sigma$.
- $\mathbf{ch} = \mathcal{H}_{FS}(M, R, \text{CMT}, \mathbf{ct})$.
- Return $\mathcal{V}_2^{\text{GS}}(\mathbf{G}, \mathbf{G}_{\text{McE}}, R, (\text{CMT}, \mathbf{ch}, \text{RSP}), \mathbf{ct})$.

GS.Open$(sk_{\text{McE}}, M, \sigma)$:
- $(\mathbf{ct}, \text{CMT}, \text{RSP}) \leftarrow \sigma$.
- If $\text{Dec}_{\text{McE}}(sk_{\text{McE}}, \mathbf{ct})$ fails, return $\perp$, else return $j \leftarrow \text{Dec}_{\text{McE}}(sk_{\text{McE}}, \mathbf{ct})$.

Fig. 7. Our group signature scheme.

2. To ensure the one-wayness of the public and private keys, the parameters (n, k, t, N) for GDOOM problem 4 are set to achieve the 128-bit security level.
3. The repetition number κ of the protocols in Fig. 4 and Fig. 6 is set to 220 in order to achieve soundness error 2^{-128}.
4. We use cSHAKE to instantiate the hash functions in our scheme and the Merkle tree, as well as the pseudorandom number generator in the seedtree [25].
5. The signature size of our ring signature scheme is equal to the proof size in Fig. 4, i.e. $2\lambda(\frac{5\kappa}{6} + 2) + \frac{\kappa}{3}(\frac{20\lambda}{3} + \frac{3n}{2} + k + 2\lambda \log N)$.
6. The signature size of our group signature scheme is equal to the proof size in Fig. 6 plus the size of $\mathbf{ct}$, i.e. $2\lambda(\frac{5\kappa}{6}+2)+\frac{\kappa}{3}(\frac{20\lambda}{3}+\frac{3n}{2}+k+\frac{3m}{2}+\ell+2\lambda\log N)+m$.

We set $(n, k, t) = (1280, 640, 132), (1300, 650, 135), (1360, 680, 141)$ for $N = 2^6, 2^{12}, 2^{21}$, respectively, and $(m, \ell, w) = (3488, 2720, 64)$ as in [12]. Then, we present the signature sizes of our ring signature scheme and group signature scheme under different N in Table 3 and Table 4.

Table 3. Ring signature sizes for N.

N	(user) PK size	Signature Size
2^6	0.240 KB	51 KB
2^{12}	0.247 KB	65 KB
2^{21}	0.255 KB	87 KB

Table 4. Group signature sizes for N.

N	(user) PK size	Signature Size
2^6	0.240 KB	112 KB
2^{12}	0.247 KB	126 KB
2^{21}	0.255 KB	148 KB

Acknowledgment. The authors would like to thank the anonymous reviewers for their valuable comments and suggestions that substantially improved the quality of this paper. This research was supported by the National Natural Science Foundation of China under Grant No. 62372446, the National Key Research and Development Program of China under Grant No. 2018YFA0704703 and the Key Research Program of the Chinese Academy of Sciences, Grant No. ZDRW-XX-2022-1.

References

1. Alamélou, Q., Blazy, O., Cauchie, S., Gaborit, P.: A code-based group signature scheme. Des. Codes Crypt. **82**, 469–493 (2017)
2. Assidi, H., Ayebie, E.B., Souidi, E.M.: An efficient code-based threshold ring signature scheme. J. Inf. Secur. Appl. **45**, 52–60 (2019)
3. Ayebie, E.B., Souidi, E.M.: New code-based cryptographic accumulator and fully dynamic group signature. Des. Codes Crypt. **90**(12), 2861–2891 (2022)
4. Barenghi, A., Biasse, J.F., Ngo, T., Persichetti, E., Santini, P.: Advanced signature functionalities from the code equivalence problem. Int. J. Comput. Math. Comput. Syst. Theory **7**(2), 112–128 (2022)
5. Bettaieb, S., Bidoux, L., Blazy, O., Gaborit, P.: Zero-knowledge reparation of the véron and AGS code-based identification schemes. In: ISIT 2021, pp. 55–60. IEEE (2021). https://doi.org/10.1109/ISIT45174.2021.9517937
6. Beullens, W., Katsumata, S., Pintore, F.: Calamari and falafl: Logarithmic (linkable) ring signatures from isogenies and lattices. In: Moriai, S., Wang, H. (eds.) ASIACRYPT 2020. LNCS, vol. 12492, pp. 464–492. Springer, Cham (2020). https://doi.org/10.1007/978-3-030-64834-3_16
7. Bidoux, L., Gaborit, P., Kulkarni, M., Sendrier, N.: Quasi-cyclic stern proof of knowledge. In: ISIT 2022, pp. 1459–1464. IEEE (2022). https://doi.org/10.1109/ISIT50566.2022.9834642
8. Blazy, O., Gaborit, P., Mac, D.T.: A rank metric code-based group signature scheme. In: Wachter-Zeh, A., Bartz, H., Liva, G. (eds.) CBCrypto 2021. LNCS, vol. 13150, pp. 1–21. Springer, Cham (2021). https://doi.org/10.1007/978-3-030-98365-9_1
9. Branco, P., Mateus, P.: A code-based linkable ring signature scheme. In: Baek, J., Susilo, W., Kim, J. (eds.) ProvSec 2018. LNCS, vol. 11192, pp. 203–219. Springer, Cham (2018). https://doi.org/10.1007/978-3-030-01446-9_12
10. Branco, P., Mateus, P.: A traceable ring signature scheme based on coding theory. In: Ding, J., Steinwandt, R. (eds.) PQCrypto 2019. LNCS, vol. 11505, pp. 387–403. Springer, Cham (2019). https://doi.org/10.1007/978-3-030-25510-7_21

11. Cayrel, P.-L., Véron, P., El Yousfi Alaoui, S.M.: A zero-knowledge identification scheme based on the q-ary syndrome decoding problem. In: Biryukov, A., Gong, G., Stinson, D.R. (eds.) SAC 2010. LNCS, vol. 6544, pp. 171–186. Springer, Heidelberg (2011). https://doi.org/10.1007/978-3-642-19574-7_12
12. Chen, L., Moody, D., Liu, Y.K.: Post-quantum cryptography round 4 submissions. NIST (2022). https://csrc.nist.gov/Projects/post-quantum-cryptography/round-4-submissions
13. Chou, T., et al.: Take your MEDS: digital signatures from matrix code equivalence. In: Mrabet, N.E., Feo, L.D., Duquesne, S. (eds.) AFRICACRYPT 2023. LNCS, vol. 14064, pp. 28–52. Springer, Cham (2023). https://doi.org/10.1007/978-3-031-37679-5_2
14. Dinur, I., Nadler, N.: Multi-target attacks on the picnic signature scheme and related protocols. In: Ishai, Y., Rijmen, V. (eds.) EUROCRYPT 2019. LNCS, vol. 11478, pp. 699–727. Springer, Cham (2019). https://doi.org/10.1007/978-3-030-17659-4_24
15. Döttling, N.: Cryptography based on the Hardness of Decoding. Ph.D. thesis, Karlsruhe, Karlsruher Institut für Technologie (KIT), Diss., 2014 (2014)
16. Esgin, M.F., Steinfeld, R., Sakzad, A., Liu, J.K., Liu, D.: Short lattice-based one-out-of-many proofs and applications to ring signatures. In: Deng, R.H., Gauthier-Umaña, V., Ochoa, M., Yung, M. (eds.) ACNS 2019. LNCS, vol. 11464, pp. 67–88. Springer, Cham (2019). https://doi.org/10.1007/978-3-030-21568-2_4
17. Ezerman, M.F., Lee, H.T., Ling, S., Nguyen, K., Wang, H.: A provably secure group signature scheme from code-based assumptions. In: Iwata, T., Cheon, J.H. (eds.) ASIACRYPT 2015. LNCS, vol. 9452, pp. 260–285. Springer, Heidelberg (2015). https://doi.org/10.1007/978-3-662-48797-6_12
18. Feneuil, T., Joux, A., Rivain, M.: Syndrome decoding in the head: Shorter signatures from zero-knowledge proofs. In: Dodis, Y., Shrimpton, T. (eds.) CRYPTO 2022. LNCS, vol. 13508, pp. 541–572. Springer, Cham (2022). https://doi.org/10.1007/978-3-031-15979-4_19
19. Fiat, A., Shamir, A.: How to prove yourself: practical solutions to identification and signature problems. In: Odlyzko, A.M. (ed.) CRYPTO 1986. LNCS, vol. 263, pp. 186–194. Springer, Heidelberg (1986). https://doi.org/10.1007/3-540-47721-7_12
20. Gaborit, P., Schrek, J., Zémor, G.: Full cryptanalysis of the chen identification protocol. In: Yang, B.-Y. (ed.) PQCrypto 2011. LNCS, vol. 7071, pp. 35–50. Springer, Heidelberg (2011). https://doi.org/10.1007/978-3-642-25405-5_3
21. Groth, J., Kohlweiss, M.: One-out-of-many proofs: or how to leak a secret and spend a coin. In: Oswald, E., Fischlin, M. (eds.) EUROCRYPT 2015. LNCS, vol. 9057, pp. 253–280. Springer, Heidelberg (2015). https://doi.org/10.1007/978-3-662-46803-6_9
22. Jain, A., Krenn, S., Pietrzak, K., Tentes, A.: Commitments and efficient zero-knowledge proofs from learning parity with noise. In: Wang, X., Sako, K. (eds.) ASIACRYPT 2012. LNCS, vol. 7658, pp. 663–680. Springer, Heidelberg (2012). https://doi.org/10.1007/978-3-642-34961-4_40
23. Katz, J., Kolesnikov, V., Wang, X.: Improved non-interactive zero knowledge with applications to post-quantum signatures. In: Lie, D., Mannan, M., Backes, M., Wang, X. (eds.) CCS 2018, pp. 525–537. ACM (2018). https://doi.org/10.1145/3243734.3243805

24. Kawachi, A., Tanaka, K., Xagawa, K.: Concurrently secure identification schemes based on the worst-case hardness of lattice problems. In: Pieprzyk, J. (ed.) ASIACRYPT 2008. LNCS, vol. 5350, pp. 372–389. Springer, Heidelberg (2008). https://doi.org/10.1007/978-3-540-89255-7_23
25. Kelsey, J., Chang, S.J., Perlner, R.: Sha-3 derived functions: cshake, kmac, tuplehash, and parallelhash. NIST special publication **800**, 185 (2016)
26. Ling, S., Nguyen, K., Stehlé, D., Wang, H.: Improved zero-knowledge proofs of knowledge for the ISIS problem, and applications. In: Kurosawa, K., Hanaoka, G. (eds.) PKC 2013. LNCS, vol. 7778, pp. 107–124. Springer, Heidelberg (2013), https://doi.org/10.1007/978-3-642-36362-7_8
27. Liu, X., Wang, L.P.: Short code-based one-out-of-many proofs and applications. Cryptology ePrint Archive, Paper 2024/093 (2024), https://eprint.iacr.org/2024/093, https://eprint.iacr.org/2024/093
28. Lyubashevsky, V., Nguyen, N.K.: BLOOM: bimodal lattice one-out-of-many proofs and applications. In: Agrawal, S., Lin, D. (eds.) ASIACRYPT 2022. LNCS, vol. 13794, pp. 95–125. Springer, Cham (2022), https://doi.org/10.1007/978-3-031-22972-5_4
29. McEliece, R.J.: A public-key cryptosystem based on algebraic. Coding Thv **4244**, 114–116 (1978)
30. Melchor, C.A., Cayrel, P.L., Gaborit, P., Laguillaumie, F.: A new efficient threshold ring signature scheme based on coding theory. IEEE Trans. Inf. Theory **57**(7), 4833–4842 (2011)
31. Melchor, C.A., Gaborit, P., Schrek, J.: A new zero-knowledge code based identification scheme with reduced communication. In: ITW 2011. pp. 648–652. IEEE (2011), https://doi.org/10.1109/ITW.2011.6089577
32. Meurer, A.: A coding-theoretic approach to cryptanalysis. Ph.D. thesis, Verlag nicht ermittelbar (2013)
33. Morozov, K., Roy, P.S., Sakurai, K.: On unconditionally binding code-based commitment schemes. In: IMCOM, p. 101. ACM (2017). https://doi.org/10.1145/3022227.3022327
34. Morozov, K., Takagi, T.: Zero-knowledge protocols for the McEliece encryption. In: Susilo, W., Mu, Y., Seberry, J. (eds.) ACISP 2012. LNCS, vol. 7372, pp. 180–193. Springer, Heidelberg (2012). https://doi.org/10.1007/978-3-642-31448-3_14
35. Nguyen, K., Tang, H., Wang, H., Zeng, N.: New code-based privacy-preserving cryptographic constructions. In: Galbraith, S.D., Moriai, S. (eds.) ASIACRYPT 2019. LNCS, vol. 11922, pp. 25–55. Springer, Cham (2019). https://doi.org/10.1007/978-3-030-34621-8_2
36. Nojima, R., Imai, H., Kobara, K., Morozov, K.: Semantic security for the mceliece cryptosystem without random oracles. Des. Codes Crypt. **49**, 289–305 (2008)
37. Sendrier, N.: Decoding one out of many. In: Yang, B.-Y. (ed.) PQCrypto 2011. LNCS, vol. 7071, pp. 51–67. Springer, Heidelberg (2011). https://doi.org/10.1007/978-3-642-25405-5_4
38. Stern, J.: A new paradigm for public key identification. IEEE Trans. Inf. Theory **42**(6), 1757–1768 (1996)
39. Véron, P.: Improved identification schemes based on error-correcting codes. Appl. Algebra Eng. Commun. Comput. **8**, 57–69 (1997)

Efficient KZG-Based Univariate Sum-Check and Lookup Argument

Yuncong Zhang[1], Shi-Feng Sun[1(✉)], and Dawu Gu[1,2(✉)]

[1] Shanghai Jiao Tong University, Shanghai, China
{shjdzhangyuncong,shifeng.sun,dwgu}@sjtu.edu.cn

[2] Shanghai Jiao Tong University (Wuxi) Blockchain Advanced Research Center, Wuxi, China

Abstract. We propose a novel KZG-based sum-check scheme, dubbed Losum, with *optimal* efficiency. Particularly, its proving cost is *one* multi-scalar-multiplication of size k—the number of non-zero entries in the vector, its verification cost is *one* pairing plus one group scalar multiplication, and the proof consists of only *one* group element.

Using Losum as a component, we then construct a new lookup argument, named Locq, which enjoys a smaller proof size and a lower verification cost compared to the state of the arts cq, cq+ and cq++. Specifically, the proving cost of Locq is comparable to cq, keeping the advantage that the proving cost is independent of the table size after preprocessing. For verification, Locq costs four pairings, while cq, cq+ and cq++ require five, five and six pairings, respectively. For proof size, a Locq proof consists of four $\mathbb{G}_1$ elements and one $\mathbb{G}_2$ element; when instantiated with the BLS12-381 curve, the proof size of Locq is 2304 bits, while cq, cq+ and cq++ have 3840, 3328 and 2944 bits, respectively. Moreover, Locq is zero-knowledge as cq+ and cq++, whereas cq is not. Locq is more efficient even compared to the non-zero-knowledge (and more efficient) versions of cq+ and cq++.

Keywords: Sum-check Scheme · Lookup Argument · zkSNARK

1 Introduction

Lookup arguments [GW20,EFG22] are protocols that allow a prover to convince a verifier that all the elements in a *lookup vector* $\boldsymbol{v}$ appear in another vector $\boldsymbol{t}$ called the *table*, where the verifier holds only the commitments to these vectors. Lookup arguments are usually *succinct*, i.e., the running time of the verifier is sublinear to the vector sizes.

Lookup argument has been widely used to improve SNARKs [PFM+22, CBBZ22] and is one of the key reasons for the recent rapid development of Zero-Knowledge Virtual Machines (ZKVMs) [Ris22,VM22,Mid22]. Before the introduction of lookup arguments, it is very expensive to prove 32- to 256-bit boolean operations using SNARKs [Gro16,CHM+20,COS,Set20] as it is costly to simulate them in arithmetic circuits; thus they are considered *SNARK-unfriendly*.

Q. Tang and V. Teague (Eds.): PKC 2024, LNCS 14602, pp. 400–425, 2024.
https://doi.org/10.1007/978-3-031-57722-2_13

Lookup arguments mitigate this issue by transforming the SNARK-unfriendly operations into lookups in tables. For example, the expensive-to-verify statement "a op $b = c$" is replaced by "(a, b, c) is a row of T_{op}" that is efficiently handled by lookup arguments, where T_{op} is a table whose rows range over of all possible values of (a, b, c) that are valid input-output combinations, and "op" can be arbitrary operation.

However, the table sizes for the lookup arguments can be huge for operations with even small input sizes. For example, the 16-bit XOR operation has a lookup table whose number of rows is as large as 2^{32}. Therefore, recent works have focused on constructing lookup arguments whose proving cost is sublinear or even independent of the table size [ZBK+22, PK22, GK22, ZGK+22, EFG22]. All these works use KZG [KZG10] as the underlying polynomial commitment scheme, thus enjoying constant proof size (constant number of group and field elements) and verification costs (constant number of pairing checks). As the state of the art in this line of works, Eagen et al. [EFG22] proposed cq, which, for the first time, reduces the proving cost to $O(m)$ group operations plus $O(m \log m)$ field operations where m is the size of the lookup vector. Meanwhile, compared to the previous works, the verification cost of cq is comparable (five pairings), and the proof size is the smallest. As its core technique, cq uses the *logarithmic derivative* [Hab22] method to reduce the lookup argument to the *univariate sum-check* [BCR+19]. To eliminate the dependence of the proving cost on the table size, cq proposes the *cached quotient* method that shifts the majority of the prover work to the preprocessing phase. Despite the performance improvements, cq does not consider zero-knowledge.

Very recently[1], following the framework of cq, Companelli et al. [CFF+23] propose cq+ and cq++ that improve the proof size of cq. More specifically, these schemes use the univariate sum-check [BCR+19] and the cached quotient technique as cq does, and come with the zero-knowledge property with small overheads—the zero-knowledge versions have one more group element in proof sizes compared to the non-zero-knowledge version. In addition, they propose zkcq+ that achieves *full zero-knowledge*, which further conceals the table content from the verifier[2], at the cost of two more group elements in the proof.

Because of the wide applications of lookup arguments in building SNARKs deployed in blockchain-based cryptocurrencies [zkS22, GPR21], any small efficiency improvements to lookup arguments may bring significant financial benefits in practice. In this work, we make further progress in this line of work on table-size independent lookup arguments. Our contributions are summarized in Sect 1.1.

[1] Concurrent to this work.

[2] This requires the table has been randomized by a mask when computing its commitment, before putting it into the lookup argument.

Table 1. Locq has a comparable proving cost, a smaller proof size, and a lower verification cost, compared to the state of the arts in the line of KZG-based lookup arguments with sublinear-or-zero independence on table size. Here m is the lookup vector size, N is the table size, P stands for "pairing check". **Prep.** stands for "Preprocessing Cost". **Vrf.** stands for "Verification Cost". The $\mathbb{F}, \mathbb{G}_1, \mathbb{G}_2$ in "Proof Size" refer to field/group elements, and in "Preprocessing" and "Proving Cost" they refer to field/group operations. "#Bits" is the bit size of the proof when instantiated with BLS12-381, for which a $\mathbb{G}_1$ element takes 384 bits, a $\mathbb{G}_2$ element takes 768 bits, and a $\mathbb{F}$ element takes 256 bits. **Hom.** means this lookup argument supports multi-column table lookups by homomorphically combining the columns using random linear combination. **ZK.** stands for zero-knowledge, where ✓ means it is zero-knowledge only if the table polynomial $t(X)$ is not considered secret, while ✓✓ means the protocol is *full zero-knowledge*, i.e., it also works when $t(X)$ is masked by a random $\rho \cdot Z_{\mathbb{H}}(X)$, in which case the verifier learns no information of $t(X)$, either. The "*" stands for the zero-knowledge versions of cq+ or cq++.

Scheme	Prep.	Proof Size				Proving Cost	Vrf.	Hom.	ZK.
	$\mathbb{F}+\mathbb{G}_1$	$\mathbb{G}_1$	$\mathbb{G}_2$	$\mathbb{F}$	#Bits				
Caulk [ZBK+22]	$O(N \log N)$	14	1	4	7168	$O(m^2 + m\log(N))(\mathbb{F}+\mathbb{G}_1)$	$4P$	✓	✓✓
Caulk+ [PK22]	$O(N \log N)$	7	1	2	3968	$O(m^2)(\mathbb{F}+\mathbb{G}_1)$	$3P$	✓	✓✓
Flookup [GK22]	$O(N \log^2 N)$	6	1	4	4096	$6m\mathbb{G}_1 + m\mathbb{G}_2 + O(m\log^2 m)\mathbb{F}$	$3P$	×	×
Baloo [ZGK+22]	$O(N \log N)$	12	1	4	6400	$13m\mathbb{G}_1 + m\mathbb{G}_2 + O(m\log^2 m)\mathbb{F}$	$5P$	✓	×
cq [EFG22]	$O(N \log N)$	8	–	3	3840	$8m\mathbb{G}_1 + O(m\log m)\mathbb{F}$	$5P$	✓	×
cq+ [CFF+23]	$O(N \log N)$	7	–	1	2944	$8m\mathbb{G}_1 + O(m\log m)\mathbb{F}$	$5P$	✓	×
cq++ [CFF+23]	$O(N \log N)$	6	–	1	2560	$8m\mathbb{G}_1 + O(m\log m)\mathbb{F}$	$6P$	✓	×
cq+* [CFF+23]	$O(N \log N)$	8	–	1	3328	$8m\mathbb{G}_1 + O(m\log m)\mathbb{F}$	$5P$	✓	✓
cq++* [CFF+23]	$O(N \log N)$	7	–	1	2944	$8m\mathbb{G}_1 + O(m\log m)\mathbb{F}$	$6P$	✓	✓
zkcq+ [CFF+23]	$O(N \log N)$	9	–	1	3712	$8m\mathbb{G}_1 + O(m\log m)\mathbb{F}$	$6P$	✓	✓✓
Locq (This work)	$O(N \log N)$	4	1	–	2304	$6m\mathbb{G}_1 + m\mathbb{G}_2 + O(m\log m)\mathbb{F}$	$4P$	✓	✓✓

1.1 Contributions

We put forward a novel KZG-based zero-knowledge lookup argument, Locq, with the proving cost independent of the table size and with smaller proof size and verification cost, compared to the state of the arts cq and even the non-zero-knowledge versions of cq+ and cq++. As a core component of Locq, we introduce a new KZG-based univariate sum-check, Losum, with optimal proving cost, verification cost and proof size. Our main contributions are summarized as follows.

- We propose a more efficient univariate sum-check scheme called Losum, which improves the existing univariate sum-check protocol [BCR+19] in the KZG setting. The cost of Losum is (arguably) optimal for KZG-based sum-checks: (1) the proving cost is a single multi-scalar-multiplication (MSM) of size k in $\mathbb{G}_1$—the first group of the pairing scheme, where k is the number of non-zero entries in the input vector; (2) the verification cost is one pairing and one scalar multiplication[3] in $\mathbb{G}_1$; and (3) the proof size is a single $\mathbb{G}_1$ element.

[3] The cost of one scalar multiplication can be ignored compared to the pairing.

- We then use Losum as a building block to construct a new lookup argument, named Locq. Our new lookup argument keeps the property that the proving cost is independent of the table size. Moreover, it has a smaller proof size ($4\mathbb{G}_1 + 1\mathbb{G}_2$, compared to $8\mathbb{G}_1 + 3\mathbb{F}$ for cq and $6\mathbb{G}_1 + \mathbb{F}$ for the non-zero-knowledge version of cq++) and a smaller verification cost (four pairings checks compared to five in cq and cq+ and six in cq++). Moreover, our scheme enjoys full zero-knowledge as zkcq+. The zero-knowledge property in our scheme is achieved with almost no additional cost, because Locq (a) does not contain any field element in the proof, so adding zero-knowledge is as simple as adding random masks to the committed polynomials; and (b) does not involve any degree check as in cq, cq+ or cq++, thanks to using Losum instead of the traditional univariate sum-check [BCR+19]. More detailed comparisons of this work with existing works on KZG-based table-size-independent lookup arguments are shown in Table 1.

In addition, both Losum and Locq enjoy the property that they can work for *arbitrary* field $\mathbb{F}$.[4] In practice, this allows Losum and Locq to choose from much wider candidates for $\mathbb{F}$ that may enjoy better optimization techniques. Particularly, Losum and Locq work even when $|\mathbb{F}| - 1$ is not *smooth*—has a large power-of-two factor, which is required by all prior schemes because they only work for $\mathbb{F}$ with large smooth multiplicative subgroups. More precisely, the smooth multiplicative subgroups still benefit Losum and Locq, but only in (prover-side) efficiency. Specifically, without such subgroups, the complexity of the preprocessing cost of both Losum and Locq would increase from $O(N \log N)$ to $O(N \log^2 N)$; the number of field operations in the proving cost of Locq would increase from $O(m \log m)$ to $O(m \log^2 m)$; and everything else is not affected. In comparison, all prior schemes completely stop working *unless* $\mathbb{F}$ has large smooth multiplicative subgroups.

We remark that our Losum and Locq require additional trusted setups besides that of KZG. This slight disadvantage is acceptable in real-world scenarios, as the setup is only executed once for each different *vector size*. This reliance on the trusted party is much weaker than the application-specific trusted setup of Groth16, which is still widely used in practice. Moreover, the setup for Locq is only executed *once* for each different *table size* and can be reused for all sizes of lookup vectors. Therefore, in practice, the setups of Losum and Locq can be accomplished together with that of KZG to avoid additional invocation of the trusted third party.

1.2 Technical Overview

For a quick understanding of our work, we give a high-level explanation about how we achieve the smaller proof size and verification cost in both Losum and Locq.

[4] As long as $\mathbb{F}$ is sufficiently large, as required by all succinct arguments.

Univariate Sum-Check. Let $\mathbb{F}$ be a finite field whose size is a large prime. Given a commitment to a polynomial $f(X)$ and a domain $\mathbb{H} \subset \mathbb{F}$, the goal of the univariate sum-check protocol is to prove to a succinct verifier that the sum of the evaluations of $f(X)$ over $\mathbb{H}$ is $s \in \mathbb{F}$, i.e., $\sum_{h\in\mathbb{H}} f(h) = s$. Our new sum-check method is based on the following observation: for the special case where $s = 0$, which we refer to as the *zero sum-check*, the set of all the polynomials that satisfy the requirement forms a linear space, and thus can be represented as the linear combination of a set of basis polynomials, denoted by $c_1(X), \cdots, c_d(X)$, where d is the dimension of this linear space and is determined by the degree bound on $f(X)$. Therefore, the zero sum-check on $f(X)$ is equivalent to proving that there exist coefficients $b_1, \cdots, b_d \in \mathbb{F}$ such that $f(X) = \sum_{i=1}^{d} b_i c_i(X)$. For a concrete choice of basis polynomials, please refer to Sect. 3.

When $f(X)$ is committed using the KZG scheme, this relation of linear combination is easy to prove using the following technique, which is heavily used in Groth16 [Gro16]. In the setup phase, we sample a secret random α, and precompute the commitments to $\alpha \cdot c_i(X)$ for every i. In the online phase, the prover computes the commitment to $f'(X) := \alpha \cdot f(X)$ by linearly combining the precomputed commitments to $\alpha \cdot c_i(X)$, which is only possible when $f(X)$ is a linear combination of $c_i(X)$ since the prover does not know α. The proof thus contains a single group element, which is the commitment to $f'(X)$. The verification costs a single pairing that checks the relation $f(X) \cdot \alpha = f'(X) \cdot 1$, and no additional group scalar multiplication is needed. By properly choosing the basis polynomials $c_i(X)$, computing the coefficients b_i brings no cost at all, so the total prover cost is a single multi-scalar multiplication (MSM) for computing the commitment to $f'(X)$.

For the case where $s \neq 0$, we pick a polynomial $\ell(X)$ that trivially satisfies $\sum_{h\in\mathbb{H}} \ell(h) = 1$, and apply the above technique to $f(X) - s \cdot \ell(X)$ instead. The prover cost is still a single MSM, the proof size is still one group element, and the only additional verification cost besides the pairing is one group scalar multiplication for computing the commitment to $f(X) - s \cdot \ell(X)$.

Table-Size Independent Lookup Argument. We then use this sum-check scheme to construct a lookup argument. Given the commitments to two polynomials $f(X)$ and $t(X)$ and two domains $\mathbb{D}, \mathbb{H} \subset \mathbb{F}$, where $\mathbb{D}$ is a subset of $\mathbb{H}$ and $|\mathbb{D}|$ is far smaller than $|\mathbb{H}|$, the goal of the lookup argument is to prove that for every $u \in \mathbb{D}$, there exists $h \in \mathbb{H}$ such that $f(u) = t(h)$.

Our work follows the framework of cq by exploiting the following statement equivalent to the one to prove by the lookup argument: there exists a polynomial $m(X)$, such that $\sum_{u\in\mathbb{D}} \frac{1}{X-f(u)} = \sum_{h\in\mathbb{H}} \frac{m(h)}{X-t(h)}$. Intuitively, this equality implies that every hole (position where the equation evaluates to infinity) in the left function is also a hole in the right function, so $f(u)$ must equal some $t(h)$.

Using the Schwartz-Zippel Lemma, this equation is checked at a random β sampled by the verifier, and the equality between two fractional functions is transformed to a sum-check for the polynomials $g(X) - w(X)$, where $g(X), w(X)$ are prover-committed polynomials that satisfy $g(u) = \frac{1}{\beta - f(u)}$ for $h \in \mathbb{D}$ and

$g(h) = 0$ for $h \in \mathbb{H}\backslash\mathbb{D}$, and $w(h) = \frac{m(h)}{\beta - t(h)}$ for every $h \in \mathbb{H}$. Note that here Locq differs from cq, as cq does not require $g(h) = 0$ for $h \in \mathbb{H}\backslash\mathbb{D}$, so cq executes two sum-checks for $g(X)$ and $w(X)$ respectively over $\mathbb{D}$ and $\mathbb{H}$, whereas Locq only uses one sum-check.

We use Losum for the zero sum-check on $g(X) - w(X)$. It remains to prove the correctness of $g(X)$ and $w(X)$. We accomplish this by exploiting their definitions—it suffices for the prover show that both $g(X) \cdot (\beta - f(X)) - U(X)$ and $w(X) \cdot (\beta - t(X)) - m(X)$ are divided by $Z_{\mathbb{H}}(X)$, where $U(X)$ is the polynomial that evaluates to 1 over $\mathbb{D}$ and 0 over $\mathbb{H}\backslash\mathbb{D}$, and $Z_{\mathbb{H}}(X) := \prod_{h \in \mathbb{H}}(X - h)$ is the *vanishing polynomial* over $\mathbb{H}$.

To prove this divisibility, the prover computes $q_1(X)$ and $q_2(X)$ by dividing the two polynomials with $Z_{\mathbb{H}}(X)$, respectively. By random linear combination, the two divisibility checks can be merged into one, and the prover only needs to commit to a single quotient polynomial $q(X)$.

Note that all the polynomials involved in computing $q(X)$ are of degree $O(|\mathbb{H}|)$. To reduce the prover cost from $O(|\mathbb{H}|)$ to $O(|\mathbb{D}|)$, making the lookup argument table-size independent, we note that $g(X)$, $U(X)$ and $Z_{\mathbb{H}}(X)$ are all divided by $Z_{\mathbb{H}}(X)/Z_{\mathbb{D}}(X)$, so $q_1(X)$ can be computed by dividing two polynomials of degree $O(|\mathbb{D}|)$ instead. Then we apply the *cached quotient* technique that is the same as in cq to compute the commitment to $q_2(X)$. The details will be explained in Sect. 4.

Applying all the techniques above, our lookup argument proof consists of only five group elements, i.e., the polynomial commitments for $m(X), g(X), w(X), q(X)$, and the proof of Losum.

1.3 Related Works

The concept of lookup argument is initially introduced by Gabizon et al. in Plookup [GW20], though the related ideas have been demonstrated in some earlier works [BEG+91, BCG+18]. Since lookup arguments are particularly useful for proving SNARK-unfriendly relations, i.e., relations that are expensive to express as arithmetic computations, they have been extensively used to boost the performance of SNARKs [PFM+22, CBBZ22]. Moreover, they work as an indispensable component in the recent popular ZKVM projects [Mid22, VM22, Ris22, zkS22, Scr22]. Lookup argument has been extensively studied since its introduction and researchers have focused on improving its efficiency.

Starting from Caulk [ZBK+22], whose proving cost relies on the table size logarithmically, there is a line of follow-up works that assume the table is much larger than the lookup vector, and focus on achieving table-size-independent proving cost, including Caulk+ [PK22], Flookup [GK22], Baloo [ZGK+22], cq [EFG22], and cq+, cq++, zkcq+ by Campanelli et al. [CFF+23]. These schemes can be used to prove lookups for large tables such as the 32-bit range check and 16-bit boolean operations, where the tables are fixed and can be preprocessed offline. Among these schemes, Flookup, Baloo and cq are not zero-knowledge. The latest cq, cq+ and cq++ are the state of the arts in this line as they have the smallest asymptotic proving cost. Meanwhile, their verifications cost 2 or 3 more pairings compared to Caulk+ and Flookup. Our work follows this line of research to further reduce the proof size and verification cost, and achieves zero-knowledge.

The recently proposed Lasso [STW23] works with huge tables with exponential sizes, but requires that the table is structured, i.e., is a generalized tensor product of smaller (size close to the lookup vector) tables.

Other lookup arguments assume the table size is close to that of the lookup vector, just as Plookup, so these works can be used in cases where the table is dynamically generated and committed by the prover online. These schemes include mvlookup [Hab22], Tip5 [SLST23], and the lookup argument inside the HyperPlonk SNARK [CBBZ22]. The mvlookup scheme proposes a powerful technique called *logarithmic derivative*, which reduces the lookup argument into a sum-check [LFKN90] statement. This technique is then adapted to the univariate case by cq and Tip5, whereas cq uses the *univariate sum-check* [BCR+19] and Tip5 uses the running sum vector for doing the sum-check. Both the multivariate and univariate sum-checks are widely used in constructing succinct argument systems [GKR08,BCR+19,CHM+20,COS,ZXZS20,XZZ+19].

2 Preliminaries

Let λ denote the security parameter. Let p be a prime of λ bits. Let $\mathbb{F} = \mathbb{F}_p$ be the prime field of size p. Let $\boldsymbol{v} \in \mathbb{F}^N$ be a vector of size N. Let $\langle \boldsymbol{u}, \boldsymbol{v} \rangle$ be the inner product between the two vectors. We say a probabilistic algorithm is *PPT* if it runs in polynomial time.

2.1 Bilinear Pairing

A bilinear pairing is a tuple $\mathsf{bp} = (p, e, g, h, \mathbb{G}_1, \mathbb{G}_2, \mathbb{G}_T)$ where p is a prime, $|\mathbb{G}_1| = |\mathbb{G}_2| = |\mathbb{G}_T| = p$, g is a generator of $\mathbb{G}_1$ and h is a generator of $\mathbb{G}_2$. The function $e : \mathbb{G}_1 \times \mathbb{G}_2 \to \mathbb{G}_T$ is a bilinear map that satisfies:

- $e(g, h)$ is a generator of $\mathbb{G}_T$.
- $e(g^a, h^b) = e(g, h)^{ab}$ for every $a, b \in \mathbb{Z}_p$.

For any $x \in \mathbb{F}_p$, let $[x]_1$ denote g^x, $[x]_2$ denote h^x and $[x]_T$ denote $e(g, h)^x$. Based on this notation, we use the addition notation for group operations, i.e., $[x]_1 + [y]_1 = [x + y]_1$ and $c \cdot [x]_1 = [c \cdot x]_1$.

This work assumes that q-DLOG problem is hard for the bilinear pairing groups, i.e., no PPT adversaries can solve this problem with more than negligible probability.

Definition 1 (q-DLOG Problem). *Let x be uniformly randomly sampled from $\mathbb{F}$. On input the bilinear pairing parameters* bp *and group elements* $[1]_1$, $[x]_1$, $[x^2]_1, \cdots, [x^q]_1$, $[1]_2$, $[x]_2, \cdots, [x^q]_2$, *find* x.

Assuming q-DLOG is hard on the given bilinear pairing groups, it is easy to see that the following problem is also hard: given $[x^{-1}]_1$, $[1]_1$, $[x]_1$, $[x^{-1}]_2$, $[1]_2$, $[x]_2$, to find x. To see why this is hard, assume we have an algorithm that solves this problem efficiently, we show that we can solve q-DLOG for $q = 2$, i.e., given any $[1]_1, [x]_1, [x^2]_1, [1]_2, [x]_2, [x^2]_2$, find x. To accomplish this, we choose new generators $g' = [x]_1$ and $h' = [x]_2$, and let $\mathsf{bp}' := (p, e, g', h', \mathbb{G}_1, \mathbb{G}_2, \mathbb{G}_T)$. Using this new set of parameters, the inputs are written as $[x^{-1}]_1$, $[1]_1$, $[x]_1$, $[x^{-1}]_2$, $[1]_2$ and $[x]_2$, which can be solved efficiently by our assumption, leading to contradiction.

2.2 The KZG Polynomial Commitment

The KZG-polynomial commitment [KZG10] is constructed based on bilinear pairings. This work only involves the setup and committing algorithms of KZG and does not use the opening or verification algorithms, because all the polynomial equations in our scheme are checked by the *ideal check* introduced later in Sect. 2.4, without evaluating any polynomials. Therefore, we recall the setup and committing algorithms of KZG as follows.

- $\mathsf{Setup}(D_1, D_2) \to \sigma_{KZG}$: Given the bilinear pairing parameters bp and the degree bounds D_1, D_2, uniformly sample $x \in \mathbb{F}$ and output $\sigma_{KZG} = ([1]_1, [x]_1, \cdots, [x^{D_1}]_1, [1]_2, [x]_2, \cdots, [x^{D_2}]_2)$.
- $\mathsf{Commit}(\sigma_{KZG}, f(X), b) \to \mathsf{cm}$: Given the setup parameters σ_{KZG}, polynomial $f(X) = f_0 + f_1 X + \cdots + f_d X^d$, and $b \in \{1, 2\}$ indicating which group this polynomial is committed in, check that $d \le D_b$, and output $\mathsf{cm} = [f(x)]_b = f_0 \cdot [1]_b + \cdots + f_d \cdot [x^d]_b$.

2.3 Polynomials and Lagrange Basis

Let $\mathbb{H}$ be a subset of $\mathbb{F}$ with $|\mathbb{H}| = N$. The Lagrange basis polynomials over $\mathbb{H}$ are the set of polynomials $\{L_h(X)\}_{h \in \mathbb{H}}$ where $L_h(h) = 1$ and $L_h(h') = 0$ for any $h' \in \mathbb{H} \backslash \{h\}$. For any polynomial $f(X)$ of degree less than N, $f(X)$ can be uniquely represented as a linear combination of the Lagrange basis, i.e., $f(X) = \sum_{h \in \mathbb{H}} f(h) L_h(X)$. We call $Z_{\mathbb{H}}(X) := \prod_{h \in \mathbb{H}} (X - h)$ the *vanishing polynomial* over $\mathbb{H}$. Assuming an implicit ordering over the elements in $\mathbb{H}$, we let $f(\mathbb{H})$ denote either the vector $(f(h))_{h \in \mathbb{H}}$ or the set $\{f(h)\}_{h \in \mathbb{H}}$, depending on the context. For any two polynomials $f(X)$ and $g(X)$, the vectors $f(\mathbb{H}) = g(\mathbb{H})$ if and only if $f(X) - g(X)$ can be divided by $Z_{\mathbb{H}}(X)$.

We will use the univariate version of the Schwartz-Zippel Lemma about polynomials.

Lemma 1 (Schwartz-Zippel). *Let $f(X)$ be a univariate polynomial of degree d over $\mathbb{F}$, S be a finite subset of $\mathbb{F}$, and z be selected randomly and uniformly from S. Then*

$$\Pr[f(z) = 0] \le \frac{d}{|S|}.$$

Schwartz-Zippel Lemma can be extended to rational functions of the form $f(X)/g(X)$, in which case the probability is bounded by $\frac{d}{|S|}$ where $d := \max\{\deg(f(X)), \deg(g(X))\}$.

2.4 Algebraic Group Model

The algebraic group model (AGM) [FKL17], introduced by Fuchsbauer et al., is widely used to prove the security of protocols and schemes that involve elliptic curve groups. In this model, it is required that whenever the adversary A outputs an element a in $\mathbb{G}_i$ for $i \in \{1, 2\}$, A must simultaneously output a vector $\boldsymbol{s} \in \mathbb{F}_p^\ell$ such that $\langle \boldsymbol{s}, \boldsymbol{t} \rangle = a$, where $\boldsymbol{t} \in \mathbb{G}_i^\ell$ is the collection of all $\mathbb{G}_i$ elements that A has received. We say such an adversary is *algebraic*.

Assuming q-DLOG is hard, the bilinear pairing check becomes computationally equivalent to checking quadratic relations on polynomials, explained as follows.

Suppose the adversary is given inputs $[1]_1, [x]_1, \cdots, [x^q]_1$ and $[1]_2, [x]_2, \cdots, [x^q]_2$, where x is secretly uniformly chosen from $\mathbb{F}$, and outputs $a, b \in \mathbb{G}_1$ and $c, d \in \mathbb{G}_2$ such that $e(a, c) = e(b, d)$. Being algebraic, the adversary simultaneously outputs the coefficients $a_0, \cdots, a_q \in \mathbb{F}$, such that $a = \sum_{i=0}^{q} a_i [x^i]_1$ (similar for b, c, d).

Let $f_a(X) = a_0 + a_1 X + \cdots + a_q X^q$, then by definition $a = [f_a(x)]_1$ (similar for $f_b(X), f_c(X)$ and $f_d(X)$). For convenience, we say whenever the adversary outputs $a \in \mathbb{G}_1$, it *simultaneously outputs the polynomial* $f_a(X)$ such that $a = [f_a(x)]_1$.

Since $e(a, c) = e(b, d)$, we have $f_a(x)f_c(x) = f_b(x)f_d(x)$. Now we claim that the polynomial equation $f_a(X)f_c(X) = f_b(X)f_d(X)$ also holds. Otherwise, the polynomial $f_a(X)f_c(X) - f_b(X)f_d(X)$ would be a non-zero polynomial that has a root at x. Then by computing the at most $2q$ roots of this polynomial, we restrict x to $2q$ candidates and then solve the q-DLOG problem by brute force. Therefore, the hardness of q-DLOG problem implies the polynomial equation $f_a(X)f_c(X) = f_b(X)f_d(X)$.

The same argument can be extended to any quadratic relations on the polynomials. This technique is heavily exploited by the line of works from Caulk to cq, where the pairing check on the group elements is referred to as the *real pairing check*, and the implied polynomial equation is referred to as the *ideal check*.

2.5 Argument of Knowledge

An argument of knowledge Π is a protocol involving two parties, a prover and a verifier. In general, it consists of three algorithms, namely Setup, Prove and Verify, and allows the prover to convince the verifier that given a string x it knows a witness w such that (x, w) is in an NP relation.

Definition 2. *An argument of knowledge for an indexed family of NP relations* $\{\mathcal{R}_{ind}\}_{ind \in \mathcal{I}}$ *is a triple of algorithms* $\Pi = (\mathsf{Setup}, \mathsf{Prove}, \mathsf{Verify})$ *with the following syntax:*

- $\mathsf{Setup}(ind, 1^\lambda) \rightarrow (\sigma, \sigma_V, \tau)$: *in the offline phase,* Setup *is given the index ind and* 1^λ *outputs a common reference string (SRS) denoted by* σ*, a verifier SRS* σ_V*, and a trapdoor* τ *that is optional for zero-knowledge.*
- $\langle \mathsf{Prove}(\sigma, x, w), \mathsf{Verify}(\sigma_V, x)\rangle \rightarrow b$: *in the online phase,* Prove *receives input* σ, σ_V *and a pair of* $(x, w) \in \mathcal{R}_{ind}$*, and* Verify *receives input* σ_V *and* x*. The parties interact with each other. Finally,* Verify *outputs* 0 *or* 1.

The algorithms should satisfy the following security requirements.

- Completeness. *For any* $ind \in \mathcal{I}$ *and* $(x, w) \in \mathcal{R}_{ind}$,

$$\Pr\left[b = 1 \,\middle|\, \begin{array}{l} \mathsf{Setup}(ind, 1^\lambda) \rightarrow (\sigma, \sigma_V, \tau) \\ \langle \mathsf{Prove}(\sigma, x, w), \mathsf{Verify}(\sigma_V, x)\rangle \rightarrow b \end{array}\right] = 1.$$

- Argument-of-Knowledge. *For any PPT algorithm* Prove^**, there exists a PPT extractor* E *such that for any* $ind \in \mathcal{I}$ *and auxiliary inputs* $z \in \{0,1\}^*$

$$\Pr\left[b = 1 \wedge (x, w) \notin \mathcal{R}_{ind} \,\middle|\, \begin{array}{l} \mathsf{Setup}(ind, 1^\lambda) \rightarrow (\sigma, \sigma_V, \tau) \\ \mathsf{Prove}^*(\sigma, z, \perp; r) \rightarrow (x, \mathsf{st}) \\ \langle \mathsf{Prove}^*(\sigma, z, \mathsf{st}; r), \mathsf{Verify}(\sigma_V, x)\rangle \rightarrow b \\ \mathsf{E}(\sigma, z; r) \rightarrow w \end{array}\right] = \mathsf{negl}.$$

An argument of knowledge may optionally be:

- *Non-interactive*: The entire interaction consists of a single message π from the prover to the verifier.
- *Public-coin*: All the messages sent from the verifier are fresh random coins. In this case, the argument of knowledge can be transformed into a non-interactive protocol by the Fiat-Shamir transformation [FS86].
- *Succinct*: The communication cost is sublinear to the witness size, and the verification cost is sublinear to the cost of verifying $(x, w) \in \mathcal{R}_{ind}$ using its standard NP verification.
- *Zero-Knowledge*: Let $tr\langle \mathsf{Prove}(\sigma, x, w), \mathsf{Verify}(\sigma_V, x)\rangle$ denote the *transcript* of an execution, i.e., all the messages exchanged during the interaction. There exists a PPT simulator S such that for any $ind \in \mathcal{I}$, $(x, w) \in \mathcal{R}_{ind}$, the following two distributions have negligible statistical distance

$$\left\{\begin{array}{l} tr\langle \mathsf{Prove}(\sigma, x, w), \mathsf{Verify}(\sigma_V, x)\rangle : \\ \mathsf{Setup}(ind, 1^\lambda) \rightarrow (\sigma, \sigma_V, \tau) \end{array}\right\} \approx_s \left\{\begin{array}{l} \mathsf{S}(\sigma_V, x, \tau) : \\ \mathsf{Setup}(ind, 1^\lambda) \rightarrow (\sigma, \sigma_V, \tau) \end{array}\right\}.$$

Univariate sum-checks (in the KZG-setting) are a class of arguments of knowledge for the following relation, indexed by the bilinear pairing parameters, the domain $\mathbb{H} \subset \mathbb{F}$ and the KZG setup parameters $\sigma_{KZG} := (\{[x^i]_1\}_{i=0}^{D}, \{[1]_2, [x]_2\})$.

$$\mathcal{R}_{\mathsf{Sum}} := \left\{((c, s), f(X)) : c = [f(x)]_1, \sum_{h \in \mathbb{H}} f(h) = s\right\}_{\mathsf{bp}, \mathbb{H}, \sigma_{KZG}}. \quad (1)$$

Lookup arguments are a class of arguments of knowledge for the following relation, indexed by the bilinear pairing parameters, the domains $\mathbb{D}, \mathbb{H} \subset \mathbb{F}$ and the KZG setup parameters $\sigma_{KZG} := (\{[x^i]_1\}_{i=0}^D, \{[x^i]_2\}_{i=0}^D)$:

$$\mathcal{R}_{\mathsf{Lookup}} := \left\{ \left(\begin{matrix} (c_f, c_t), \\ (f(X), t(X)) \end{matrix} \right) \middle| \begin{matrix} c_f = [f(x)]_1, c_t = [t(x)]_2, \\ \deg(f(X)) < |\mathbb{D}|, \deg(t(X)) < |\mathbb{H}|, \\ f(\mathbb{D}) \subseteq t(\mathbb{H}) \end{matrix} \right\}_{\mathsf{bp}, \mathbb{D}, \mathbb{H}, \sigma_{KZG}} . \quad (2)$$

3 Losum: Optimal Sum-Check for KZG

We introduce Losum, a new univariate non-interactive sum-check scheme whose communication cost is a single group element, proving cost is a single MSM, and verification cost is dominated by one pairing. Moreover, unlike the existing univariate sum-check [BCR+19], Losum does not require the interpolation domain $\mathbb{H}$ to have any special structure, so it works for any field $\mathbb{F}$ as long as the field is sufficiently large.

3.1 Overview

Our method is based on the following observation: for a polynomial $f(X)$ of degree at most D, where $D \geq |\mathbb{H}|$, proving the equality $\sum_{h \in \mathbb{H}} f(h) = 0$ is equivalent to proving that $f(X)$ is a linear combination of a given set of basis polynomials. In more detail:

- The set $\mathcal{Z} := \{f(X) \in \mathbb{F}^{\leq D}[X] : \sum_{h \in \mathbb{H}} f(h) = 0\}$ forms a linear space of dimension D.
- For all $h \in \mathbb{H} \backslash \{h^*\}$, $L_h(X) - L_{h^*}(X) \in \mathcal{Z}$ for a fixed h^* in $\mathbb{H}$.
- For all $i \leq D - |\mathbb{H}|$, $X^i Z_{\mathbb{H}}(X) \in \mathcal{Z}$.
- The set $B := \{L_h(X) - L_{h^*}(X)\}_{h \in \mathbb{H} \backslash \{h^*\}} \cup \{X^i Z_{\mathbb{H}}(X)\}_{i=0}^{D-|\mathbb{H}|}$ is a linearly independent subset of $\mathcal{Z}$. Since $|B| = D$, B is a basis of $\mathcal{Z}$.

Therefore, proving that a committed $f(X)$ satisfies $\sum_{h \in \mathbb{H}} f(h) = 0$ is equivalent to proving that $f(X)$ is a linear combination of B. For a more general sum-check, i.e., $\sum_{h \in \mathbb{H}} f(h) = s$ for any $s \in \mathbb{F}$, we choose a representative polynomial $\ell_s(X)$ whose sum is trivially s, and prove that $f(X) - \ell_s(X) \in \mathcal{Z}$. One obvious choice of $\ell_s(X)$ is $s \cdot L_{h^*}(X)$.

Formally, the sum-check problem is reduced to the following statement: there exist $\{b_h\}_{h \in \mathbb{H} \backslash \{h^*\}}$ and $\{q_i\}_{i=0}^{D-|\mathbb{H}|}$ such that

$$f(X) - s \cdot L_{h^*}(X) = \sum_{h \in \mathbb{H} \backslash \{h^*\}} b_h \cdot (L_h(X) - L_{h^*}(X)) + \sum_{i=0}^{D-|\mathbb{H}|} q_i \cdot X^i Z_{\mathbb{H}}(X).$$

Note that q_i are exactly the coefficients of the quotient polynomial from dividing $f(X)$ by $Z_{\mathbb{H}}(X)$. To compute b_h, we evaluate both sides of this equation at every

$h \in \mathbb{H}\backslash\{h^*\}$, and get that b_h is just $f(h)$. Therefore, if the prover starts the protocol from the evaluation representation of $f(X)$, the prover does not need any additional computation to compute the linear combination coefficients. This is the reason why we choose this basis. Depending on the scenario in which the protocol is used, a different basis may be more appropriate. For example, if the prover stores $f(X)$ by its coefficients, then a better basis would be the set of polynomials of the form $a_k X^k - b_k$.

Using the same technique as in Pinocchio [PHGR13], Groth16 [Gro16] and Marlin [CHM+20], we can force the prover to output a linear combination of a given polynomial set $\{c_i(X)\}$ as follows. The idea is to let the trusted third party select a random secret $\alpha \in \mathbb{F}$ and produce a set of $\mathbb{G}_1$ elements $\{[\alpha c_i(x)]_1\}$. These elements are included in the SRS. Moreover, the verifier SRS should include $[\alpha]_2$. The prover simply produces the proof $\pi := [\alpha f(x)]_1$ computed by linearly combining the elements $\{[\alpha c_i(x)]_1\}$, and the verifier checks that $e(\pi, [1]_2) = e([f(x)]_1, [\alpha]_2)$. Intuitively, without learning the secret α, the only way for the prover to generate $[\alpha f(x)]_1$ is linearly combing $\{[\alpha c_i(x)]_1\}$, which would be impossible if $f(X)$ is not a linear combination of $\{c_i(X)\}$.

3.2 Protocol Description

Exploiting the above techniques, we propose Losum for proving that the sum of $f(X)$ over $\mathbb{H}$ is s, presented as follows.

Setup. On input the pairing $\mathsf{bp} = (p, e, g, h, \mathbb{G}_1, \mathbb{G}_2, \mathbb{G}_T)$, the domain $\mathbb{H}$ of size N, and the SRS $\sigma_{KZG} := (\{[x^i]_1\}_{i=0}^{D}, \{[1]_2, [x]_2\})$ previously generated by the KZG setup where $D \geq N$, the trusted third party samples $\alpha \in \mathbb{F}$, and outputs the SRS that include:

- $\{[\alpha \cdot (L_h(x) - L_{h^*}(x))]_1\}_{h \in \mathbb{H}\backslash\{h^*\}}$, and $\{[\alpha \cdot x^i Z_{\mathbb{H}}(x)]_1\}_{i=0}^{D-N}$ where h^* is picked from $\mathbb{H}$ arbitrarily;
- Verifier SRS: $[1]_2$, $[L_{h^*}(x)]_1$, and $[\alpha]_2$.

Prove. On input $f(X)$ and $\mathbb{H}$:

1. Divide $f(X)$ by $Z_{\mathbb{H}}(X)$ and let the quotient be $q(X) = \sum_{i=0}^{d} q_i X^i$.
2. Output the proof π computed as below

$$\pi := \sum_{h \in \mathbb{H}\backslash\{h^*\}} f(h) \cdot [\alpha \cdot (L_h(x) - L_{h^*}(x))]_1 + \sum_{i=0}^{d} q_i \cdot [\alpha x^i \cdot Z_{\mathbb{H}}(x)]_1.$$

Verify. On input $\pi, s, [f(x)]_1$, check

$$e([f(x)]_1 - s \cdot [L_{h^*}(x)]_1, [\alpha]_2) = e(\pi, [1]_2).$$

3.3 Security and Efficiency Analysis

We prove that Losum is an argument of knowledge.

Theorem 1. *The three algorithms in Sect. 3.2 form an argument of knowledge for the relation $\mathcal{R}_{\mathsf{Sum}}$ defined in Eq. (1), in the algebraic group model.*

Proof. Completeness. Let $\tilde{f}(X)$ denote $f(X)$ mod $Z_{\mathbb{H}}(X)$, then the right side, after divided by α, has exponent

$$\begin{aligned}
&\sum_{h\in\mathbb{H}\setminus\{h^*\}} f(h)\cdot(L_h(x)-L_{h^*}(x))+q(x)\mathbb{Z}_{\mathbb{H}}(x)\\
&=\sum_{h\in\mathbb{H}\setminus\{h^*\}} f(h)L_h(x)-\sum_{h\in\mathbb{H}\setminus\{h^*\}} f(h)L_{h^*}(x)+q(x)Z_{\mathbb{H}}(x)\\
&=(\tilde{f}(x)-f(h^*)L_{h^*}(x))-(s-f(h^*))L_{h^*}(x)+q(x)Z_{\mathbb{H}}(x)\\
&=\tilde{f}(x)-sL_{h^*}(x)+q(x)Z_{\mathbb{H}}(x)\\
&=f(x)-sL_{h^*}(x),
\end{aligned}$$

which is the same as the exponent of the left side.

Knowledge Soundness. Let $\mathcal{A}$ be any PPT adversary. Since $\mathcal{A}$ is algebraic, whenever $\mathcal{A}$ outputs $c,\pi\in\mathbb{G}_1$, $\mathcal{A}$ simultaneously outputs the linear coefficients corresponding to $\sigma_{KZG},[L_{h^*}(x)]_1,[\alpha\cdot(L_h(x)-L_{h^*}(x))]_1$ and $\alpha x^i Z_{\mathbb{H}}(x)$. We can then build the extractor E that executes whatever $\mathcal{A}$ executes, obtains the linear coefficients, and computes the polynomials $f_1(X),f_2(X),p_1(X)$ and $p_2(X)$ satisfying $c=[f_1(x)]_1+\alpha\cdot[f_2(x)]_1$ and $\pi=[p_1(x)]_1+\alpha\cdot[p_2(x)]_2$ by linearly combining the polynomials corresponding to the $\mathbb{G}_1$ elements in the SRS. Then our extractor outputs $f(X)=f_1(X)$. Now we prove that $[f(x)]_1=c$, i.e. $f_2(X)$ must be the zero polynomial, and $\sum_{h\in\mathbb{H}} f(h)=s$.

If the verification passes, i.e.,

$$e([f_1(x)]_1+\alpha\cdot[f_2(x)]_1-s\cdot[L_{h^*}(x)]_1,[\alpha]_2)=e(\pi,[1]_2),$$

we have

$$\alpha\cdot(f_1(x)-sL_{h^*}(x))+\alpha^2\cdot f_2(x)=p_1(x)+\alpha\cdot p_2(x)$$

which can be rewritten into

$$-p_1(x)+\alpha\cdot(f_1(x)-p_2(x)-sL_{h^*}(x))+\alpha^2\cdot f_2(x)=0.$$

Then by q-DLOG assumption, $p_1(x)=0$, $f_1(x)-p_2(x)-sL_{h^*}(x)=0$ and $f_2(x)=0$, except with negligible probability. Otherwise, we will get a non-trivial equation of α. We can then build an adversary that solves α with non-negligible probability from $[\alpha]_1$ and $[\alpha]_2$, by preparing the SRS using the target $[\alpha]_1$ and $[\alpha]_2$, breaking the q-DLOG assumption.

By q-DLOG assumption again, $p_1(X)=0$, $f_1(X)-p_2(X)-sL_{h^*}(X)=0$ and $f_2(X)=0$, except with negligible probability. Otherwise, we would obtain non-trivial equations for x and construct an adversary that solves x given the KZG parameters.

Therefore, $f(X) = f_1(X) = p_2(X) + sL_{h^*}(X)$, where $p_2(X)$ is the linear combination of $L_h(X) - L_{h^*}(X)$ and $X^i Z_{\mathbb{H}}(X)$, thus sums to 0 over $\mathbb{H}$. We then have $\sum_{h \in \mathbb{H}} f(h) = s$ and $[f(x)]_1 = [f_1(x)]_1 = c$. □

Efficiency. The setup algorithm is dominated by computing $\{\alpha \cdot (L_h(x) - L_{h^*}(x))\}$ and $\{[\alpha x^i Z_{\mathbb{H}}(x)]_1\}$. So the cost is $O(D \log D)$ scalar multiplications in $\mathbb{G}_1$ if $\mathbb{H}$ is a multiplicative group, in which case we use FFT on $\mathbb{G}_1$ elements. Otherwise, these can be computed with $O(D \log^2 D)$ scalar multiplications using the multi-point evaluation algorithm [Kun73].

The prover is dominated by computing π and $q(X)$. Computing π requires an MSM of size $k+\deg(f(X))-N$ or simply k if $\deg(f(X)) < N$, where k is the number of non-zero entries in $f(\mathbb{H})$. Computing $q(X)$ costs only $O(\deg(f(X)) - N)$ additions in $\mathbb{F}$ if $\mathbb{H}$ is a multiplicative group, since $Z_{\mathbb{H}}(X)$ would have the simple form $X^N - 1$. For general $\mathbb{H}$, this takes $O(\deg(f(X)) - N) \log^2(\deg(f(X)) - N)$ field operations. Note that computing $q(X)$ can be ignored if $\deg(f(X)) < N$. In practice, $f(X)$ is usually computed by adding a masking polynomial $\rho \cdot Z_{\mathbb{H}}(X)$ to a polynomial of degree less than N in the first place, as in our lookup argument described in the next section. In this case, $q(X)$ is simply ρ.

The verifier is dominated by a pairing, plus a scalar multiplication for computing $s \cdot [L_{h^*}(x)]_1$. Note that this scalar multiplication is omitted if $s = 0$, which is a common situation in the use cases of sum checks.

4 Locq: Improved Lookup Argument

We construct a new zero-knowledge lookup argument Locq that has a smaller proof size and a smaller verification cost than cq and its subsequent works cq+, cq++, the state-of-the-art lookup arguments.

4.1 Overview

The design of Locq essentially follows the framework of cq. To explain our idea more clearly, we briefly recall the cq scheme. The goal of lookup argument is to make the prover convince the verifier that, given two committed polynomials $f(X)$ and $t(X)$, the set $f(\mathbb{D}) := \{f(u) : u \in \mathbb{D}\}$ is a subset of $t(\mathbb{H}) := \{t(h) : h \in \mathbb{H}\}$, where $\mathbb{D}$ and $\mathbb{H}$ are two different domains inside $\mathbb{F}$. We will refer to $f(X)$ or $f(\mathbb{D})$ as the lookup vector and $t(X)$ or $t(\mathbb{H})$ as the table. Let $m := |\mathbb{D}|$ and $N := |\mathbb{H}|$. We assume m is much smaller than N and $\mathbb{D}$ is a subset of $\mathbb{H}$. Note that, like in Losum, we do not require any algebraic structure on $\mathbb{D}$ or $\mathbb{H}$. However, we will mention where the running time can be reduced from $O(m \log^2 m)$ to $O(m \log m)$ when $\mathbb{D}$ or $\mathbb{H}$ are multiplicative subgroups.

To prove $f(\mathbb{D}) \subseteq t(\mathbb{H})$, cq leverages a technique called *logarithmic derivative*, first proposed by Habock et al. [Hab22], which is based on the observation that $f(\mathbb{D}) \subseteq t(\mathbb{H})$ if and only if there exist m_h for every $h \in \mathbb{H}$ such that

$\sum_{u\in\mathbb{D}} \frac{1}{X-f(u)} = \sum_{h\in\mathbb{H}} \frac{m_h}{X-t(h)}$. Intuitively, this equality is possible only if both sides have the same set of holes, implying that every $f(u)$ is a hole on the right side, which is possible only if $f(u) \in t(\mathbb{H})$. Note that when $f(\mathbb{D}) \subseteq t(\mathbb{H})$, the unique choice of m_h is the number that $t(h)$ appears in $f(\mathbb{D})$.

To prove this equality between two rational functions, the prover commits the polynomial $m(X)$ such that $m(h) = m_h$ for $h \in \mathbb{H}$. Note that committing $m(X)$ only requires $O(m)$ scalar multiplications because $\{m_h\}_{h\in\mathbb{H}}$ contain at most m non-zero elements. Then the verifier samples a random β and asks the prover to show that $\sum_{u\in\mathbb{D}} \frac{1}{\beta-f(u)} = \sum_{h\in\mathbb{H}} \frac{m(h)}{\beta-t(h)}$. Intuitively, by Schwartz-Zippel Lemma (for rational functions), the unpredictability of β guarantees that the original equality holds with overwhelming probability. Now it remains for the prover to convince the verifier of the equality between these two sums.

To show this equality, the prover commits two polynomials $g(X)$ and $w(X)$ of degree less than $|\mathbb{D}|$ and $|\mathbb{H}|$, respectively, such that $g(u) = \frac{1}{\beta-f(u)}$ for $u \in \mathbb{D}$ and $w(h) = \frac{m(h)}{\beta-t(h)}$ for $h \in \mathbb{H}$. To prove that it has committed to the correct $g(X)$ and $w(X)$, the prover shows the committed polynomials satisfy that $g(X)(\beta - f(X)) - 1$ is divided by $Z_{\mathbb{D}}(X)$ and $w(X)(\beta - t(X)) - m(X)$ is divided by $Z_{\mathbb{H}}(X)$. These are achieved by committing the quotient polynomials $q_1(X)$ and $q_2(X)$, where the commitment to $q_2(X)$ is computed by the *cached quotient* technique to make the prover complexity independent of N. Finally, the prover shows that $\sum_{u\in\mathbb{D}} g(u) = \sum_{h\in\mathbb{H}} w(h)$, which is equivalent to the original equality. This step is accomplished using univariate sum-check [BCR+19].

We explain the cached quotient technique in more detail as it is also used in Locq to compute $[q_2(x)]_1$. Note that $q_2(X) = \lfloor \frac{w(X)t(X)}{Z_{\mathbb{H}}(X)} \rfloor$ since $w(X)t(X)$ is the only item that has degree at least N. To compute the commitment $[q_2(x)]_1$ with $O(m)$ group operations online, the prover preprocesses, in the offline phase, $[q_h(x)]_1$ for $h \in \mathbb{H}$ where $q_h(X) := \lfloor \frac{L_h(X)t(X)}{Z_{\mathbb{H}}(X)} \rfloor$. These pre-computed $[q_h(x)]_1$ are called the cached quotients for the table $t(X)$. In the online phase, $[q_2(x)]_1$ is computed by $[q_2(x)]_1 = \sum_{h\in\mathbb{H}} w(h)[q_h(x)]_1$, which involves at most m group scalar multiplications because there are at most m nonzero $w(h)$.

Locq improves over cq exploiting the following techniques.

Interpolate $g(X)$ *over* $\mathbb{H}$ *instead of over* $\mathbb{D}$. Instead of defining $g(X)$ by interpolating $\frac{1}{\beta-f(u)}$ over $\mathbb{D}$, we additionally require that $g(h) = 0$ for $h \in \mathbb{H}\backslash\mathbb{D}$. In this way, the sum of $g(X)$ over $\mathbb{H}$ is still the desired sum $\sum_{u\in\mathbb{H}} \frac{1}{\beta-f(u)}$, we thus merge the two sum-checks: the prover only needs to show that the sum of $g(X) - w(X)$ over $\mathbb{H}$ is zero. This optimization is also adopted by cq+, although presented in a different form.

This redefinition of $g(X)$ brings several challenges, which we address as follows.

1. The degree of $g(X)$ increases from m to N, so the prover should avoid computing its coefficients explicitly, and instead compute its commitment using precomputed commitments for $L_h(X)$.

2. To prove the correctness of $g(X)$, in addition to checking that $g(X)(\beta - f(X))$ evaluates to 1 over $\mathbb{D}$, the verifier should also check that it evaluates to zero over $\mathbb{H}\backslash\mathbb{D}$. Therefore, we redefine $q_1(X)$ to be the quotient between $g(X)(\beta - f(X)) - U(X)$ and $Z_{\mathbb{H}}(X)$, where $U(X)$ is the polynomial that evaluates to 1 over $\mathbb{D}$ and 0 over $\mathbb{H}\backslash\mathbb{D}$. In general, $U(X)$ has degree $N-1$. However, when $\mathbb{H}$ and $\mathbb{D}$ are multiplicative subgroups, $U(X)$ is $\frac{m}{N} \cdot \frac{Z_{\mathbb{H}}(X)}{Z_{\mathbb{D}}(X)} = \frac{m \cdot (X^N - 1)}{N \cdot (X^m - 1)}$ and has degree $N - m$.
3. Although the degree of $q_1(X)$ is still $O(m)$, computing $q_1(X)$ naïvely would bring $O(N \log^2 N)$ cost to the prover. To address this, note that all of $Z_{\mathbb{H}}(X)$, $g(X)$ and $U(X)$ are divided by the polynomial $\frac{Z_{\mathbb{H}}(X)}{Z_{\mathbb{D}}(X)}$, so $q_1(X)$ can be alternatively computed by dividing $g'(X)(\beta - f(X)) - U'(X)$ with $Z_{\mathbb{D}}(X)$, where $g'(X)$ and $U'(X)$ are defined by dividing $g(X), U(X)$ with $\frac{Z_{\mathbb{H}}(X)}{Z_{\mathbb{D}}(X)}$, respectively. Note that $U'(X)$ can be precomputed offline, and $g'(X)$ can be computed by interpolating $g(u) \cdot c_u^{-1}$ over $\mathbb{D}$, where c_u is the evaluation of $\frac{Z_{\mathbb{H}}(X)}{Z_{\mathbb{D}}(X)}$ at $u \in \mathbb{D}$. Both can be accomplished with $O(m \log^2 m)$ complexity. When $\mathbb{H}$ and $\mathbb{D}$ are multiplicative subgroups, both $U'(X)$ and c_u^{-1} become the constant $\frac{m}{N}$, and the total cost of computing $q_1(X)$ can be reduced to $O(m \log m)$.

Merge the Two Quotient Polynomials. Since the correctness of both $g(X)$ and $w(X)$ are reduced to divisibility by $Z_{\mathbb{H}}(X)$, the two divisibility checks can be merged into one by random linear combination. Specifically, the verifier samples ζ, and the prover shows that the polynomial

$$(\beta - f(X)) \cdot g(X) - U(X) + \zeta \cdot ((\beta - t(X) \cdot w(X)) - m(X))$$

is divided by $Z_{\mathbb{H}}(X)$ by sending one quotient polynomial $q(X)$, instead of $q_1(X)$ and $q_2(X)$ separately.

Use Losum *Instead of Univariate Sum-Check.* We apply a slightly modified Losum to prove that the sum of $g(X) - w(X)$ over $\mathbb{H}$ is zero, rather than the univariate sum-check [BCR+19] used by cq. The modification to Losum is because $g(X)$ and $w(X)$ are committed in different groups, so instead of multiplying α to $g(X) - w(X)$, the verifier multiplies α^{-1} to the proof π in the pairing check. Moreover, because the degree of $g(X) - w(X)$ is smaller than N, there is no need to include $\alpha X^i Z_{\mathbb{H}}(X)$ in the SRS (unless for $i = 0$, if zero-knowledge is needed, as explained later). Losum reduces the overall cost of Locq because it costs a single $\mathbb{G}_1$ element in the proof and a single pairing in the verification. Moreover, it does not require any degree check as the original univariate sum-check, nor introduce any additional divisibility check.

Add Zero-Knowledge. Finally, we make the protocol zero-knowledge with almost zero overhead. The idea is to add random multiples of $Z_{\mathbb{H}}(X)$ to $m(X), g(X)$ and $w(X)$, respectively. This will make the degree of $g(X) - w(X)$ achieve N, so we additionally add $\alpha Z_{\mathbb{H}}(X)$ to the SRS of Losum. Because our protocol does not involve any degree check and the proof does not contain any polynomial evaluations, these randomizations suffice to guarantee zero-knowledge without affecting the performance.

4.2 Protocol Description

The complete protocol is presented as follows, where we split the setup algorithm into a universal setup and a preprocessing procedure. The universal setup is executed once for all tables of the specific size, while the preprocessing is executed for each table without a trusted third party.

Setup. On input $\mathbb{D}, \mathbb{H}$ of size m, N, respectively, where $\mathbb{D} \subset \mathbb{H}$, the bilinear pairing parameter $\mathsf{bp} = (p, e, g, h, \mathbb{G}_1, \mathbb{G}_2, \mathbb{G}_T)$, and the SRS for KZG $\sigma_{KZG} = (\{[x^i]_1\}_{i=0}^{D}, \{[x^i]_2\}_{i=0}^{D})$, the setup procedure outputs the SRS computed as follows:

1. Let $\{L_h(X)\}_{h\in\mathbb{H}}$ be the Lagrange basis polynomials over $\mathbb{H}$, $U(X) = \sum_{u\in\mathbb{D}} L_u(X)$, $U'(X) = \frac{U(X)\cdot Z_{\mathbb{D}}(X)}{Z_{\mathbb{H}}(X)}$, and c_u be the evaluation of $\frac{Z_{\mathbb{H}}(X)}{Z_{\mathbb{D}}(X)}$ at u for $u \in \mathbb{D}$.
2. Execute the modified setup algorithm of Losum to generate $\sigma_{losum} = ([\alpha^{-1}]_2, [\alpha \cdot Z_{\mathbb{H}}(x)]_1, \{[\alpha \cdot (L_h(x) - L_{h^*}(x))]_1\}_{h\in\mathbb{H}\setminus\{h^*\}})$, where h^* is picked from $\mathbb{D}$ arbitrarily.
3. Output srs that includes
   - σ_{KZG}, σ_{losum}, $\{[L_h(x)]_1, [L_h(x)]_2\}_{h\in\mathbb{H}}$, $[Z_{\mathbb{H}}(x)]_1$, $U'(X)$, and $\{c_u\}_{u\in\mathbb{D}}$.
   - Verifier SRS: $[U(X)]_1$, $[Z_{\mathbb{H}}(x)]_2$, $[\alpha^{-1}]_2$, $[1]_1$, and $[1]_2$.

Preprocess. On input $t(X)$ and srs, the preprocessor outputs $\mathsf{srs}_{t(X)}$ as follows:

1. For $h \in \mathbb{H}$, divide $L_h(X)t(X)$ by $Z_{\mathbb{H}}(X)$ and get the quotient $q_h(X)$.
2. Output $\{[q_h(x)]_1\}_{h\in\mathbb{H}}$ and $[t(x)]_1$.

Prover. On input $f(X), t(X), [f(x)]_1, [t(x)]_2$, srs and $\mathsf{srs}_{t(X)}$, the prover interacts with the verifier as follows:

Round 1. For $h \in \mathbb{H}$, let m_h be the number of times that $t(h)$ appears in $f(\mathbb{D})$. Sample $\delta_1 \xleftarrow{\$} \mathbb{F}$. Send $[m(x)]_1 := \sum_{h\in\mathbb{H}} m_h[L_h(x)]_1 + \delta_1 \cdot [Z_{\mathbb{H}}(x)]_1$ to the verifier.

Round 2. Receive β from the verifier.

Round 3

1. Sample $\delta_2, \delta_3 \xleftarrow{\$} \mathbb{F}$ and let

$$g(X) := \sum_{u\in\mathbb{D}} \frac{1}{\beta - f(u)} \cdot L_u(X) + \delta_2 \cdot Z_{\mathbb{H}}(X),$$

$$w(X) := \sum_{h\in\mathbb{H}} \frac{m_h}{\beta - t(h)} \cdot L_h(X) + \delta_3 \cdot Z_{\mathbb{H}}(X).$$

2. Compute the commitments $[g(x)]_2$ and $[w(x)]_1$ by

$$[g(x)]_2 := \sum_{u \in \mathbb{D}} \frac{1}{\beta - f(u)} \cdot [L_u(x)]_2 + \delta_2 \cdot [Z_{\mathbb{H}}(x)]_2$$

$$[w(x)]_1 := \sum_{h \in \mathbb{H}} \frac{m_h}{\beta - t(h)} \cdot [L_h(x)]_1 + \delta_3 \cdot [Z_{\mathbb{H}}(x)]_1.$$

3. Invoke the proving algorithm of Losum to compute π_{sum} for $g(X) - w(X)$. In detail,

$$\pi_{sum} = \sum_{u \in \mathbb{D} \backslash \{h^*\}} \frac{1}{\beta - f(u)} \cdot [\alpha \cdot (L_u(x) - L_{h^*}(x))]_1 - \sum_{h \in \mathbb{H} \backslash \{h^*\}} \frac{m_h}{\beta - t(h)} \cdot [\alpha \cdot (L_h(x) - L_{h^*}(x))]_1 + (\delta_2 - \delta_3) \cdot [\alpha \cdot Z_{\mathbb{H}}(x)]_1.$$

4. Send $[g(x)]_2, [w(x)]_1, \pi_{sum}$ to the verifier.

Round 4. Receive ζ from the verifier.

Round 5

1. Interpolate $\frac{c_u^{-1}}{\beta - f(u)}$ over $\mathbb{D}$ to get $g'(X) := \sum_{u \in \mathbb{D}} \frac{c_u^{-1}}{\beta - f(u)} \cdot K_u(X)$ where $K_u(X)$ is the Lagrange basis polynomial over $\mathbb{D}$. Divide $g'(X) \cdot f(X)$ by $Z_{\mathbb{D}}(X)$, take the quotient, then add $\delta_2 \cdot (\beta - f(X))$ to get $q_1(X)$.
2. Compute $[q_1(x)]_1$ using its coefficients and σ_{KZG}, and compute $[q_2(x)]_1$ by

$$[q_2(x)]_1 := \sum_{h \in \mathbb{H}} \frac{m_h}{\beta - t(h)} \cdot [q_h(x)]_1 + \delta_3 \cdot (\beta \cdot [1]_1 - [t(x)]_1).$$

3. If $t(X)$ has been masked by a random $\rho \cdot Z_{\mathbb{H}}(X)$, then $[q_2(x)]_1$ should additionally add $\rho \cdot [w(x)]_1$.
4. Send $[q(x)]_1 := [q_1(x)]_1 + \zeta \cdot [q_2(x)]_1$ to the verifier.

Verifier. On input $[f(x)]_1, [t(x)]_2$ and the verifier SRS, the verifier interacts with the prover as follows.

Round 1. Receive $[m(x)]_1$ from the prover.

Round 2. Sample a uniformly random $\beta \in \mathbb{F}$ and send β to the prover.

Round 3. Receive $[g(x)]_2, [w(x)]_1, \pi_{sum}$ from the prover.

Round 4. Sample a uniformly random $\zeta \in \mathbb{F} \backslash \{0\}$ and send ζ to the prover.

Round 5. Receive $[q(x)]_1$ from the prover, then

1. Invoke the verification algorithm of Losum to check π_{sum}. In detail

$$e(\pi_{sum}, [\alpha^{-1}]_2) = e(-[w(x)]_1, [1]_2) \cdot e([1]_1, [g(x)]_2).$$

2. Check the correctness of $[g(x)]_2$ and $[w(x)]_1$ in batch

$$e(\beta \cdot [1]_1 - [f(x)]_1, [g(x)]_2) \cdot e(\zeta \cdot [w(x)]_1, \beta \cdot [1]_2 - [t(x)]_2) \\ = e([U(x)]_1 + \zeta \cdot [m(x)]_1, [1]_2) \cdot e([q(x)]_1, [Z_{\mathbb{H}}(x)]_2).$$

Note that in the two pairing checks, $[w(x)]_1$ and $[g(x)]_2$ are repeatedly multiplied to different polynomials, so the two checks can be merged into one using random linear combination to save one pairing. Specifically, they are statistically equivalent to: sample $\delta \in \mathbb{F}$, then check

$$e((\beta + \delta) \cdot [1]_1 - [f(x)]_1, [g(x)]_2) \cdot e([w(x)]_1, (\zeta\beta - \delta) \cdot [1]_2 - \zeta \cdot [t(x)]_2) \\ = e(\delta \cdot \pi_{sum}, [\alpha^{-1}]_2) \cdot e([U(x)]_1 + \zeta \cdot [m(x)]_1, [1]_2) \cdot e([q(x)]_1, [Z_{\mathbb{H}}(x)]_2).$$

4.3 Security and Efficiency Analysis

We prove that Locq is a zero-knowledge argument of knowledge.

Theorem 2. *Viewing the preprocessing algorithm as part of the setup algorithm, the four algorithms in Sect. 4.2 form a zero-knowledge argument of knowledge for the relation $\mathcal{R}_{\mathsf{Lookup}}$ defined in Eq. (2), in the algebraic group model.*

Proof. For simplicity, we prove the completeness and soundness of the protocol without the final merge of two pairing checks. The equivalence between the original two pairing checks and the merged check holds for any pairing checks of this form.

Completeness. The second pairing equation is satisfied by definition if $g(X)$, $w(X)$, $q(X)$ are computed as expected. Then, by definition, the sums $\sum_{h \in \mathbb{H}} g(u)$ and $\sum_{h \in \mathbb{H}} w(h)$ are equal. Then the first pairing equation follows from the fact that, after divided by α, π_{sum} is a commitment to the polynomial

$$\sum_{u \in \mathbb{D} \setminus \{h^*\}} \frac{1}{\beta - f(u)} (L_u(X) - L_{h^*}(X)) + \sum_{h \in \mathbb{H} \setminus \{h^*\}} \frac{1}{\beta - t(h)} (L_h(X) - L_{h^*}(X)) \\ + (\delta_2 - \delta_3) \cdot Z_{\mathbb{H}}(X) = g(X) - w(X).$$

This equality of polynomials holds because, by definition of $g(X)$ and $w(X)$, the two sides (a) have the same leading coefficient for X^N, i.e., $\delta_2 - \delta_3$; (b) evaluate to the same value at every $h \in \mathbb{H} \setminus \{h^*\}$; and (c) both sides sum to zero over $\mathbb{H}$, so their evaluations must also match at 1.

Knowledge Soundness. Note that all the group elements in srs allow the adversary to compute $\mathbb{G}_1$ elements as commitments to polynomials of the form $a_0(X) + \alpha \cdot a_\alpha(X)$ where the degree of $a_0(X)$ is at most D and the degree of $a_\alpha(X)$ is at most N, and the sum of $a_\alpha(X)$ over $\mathbb{H}$ is zero. For $\mathbb{G}_2$ elements, the adversary can only output commitments to polynomials of the form $a_0(X) + a_{\alpha^{-1}} \cdot \alpha^{-1}$. Being algebraic, whenever the adversary outputs a $\mathbb{G}_1$ (resp.

$\mathbb{G}_2$) group element, it simultaneously outputs the linear coefficients that allow us to recover $a_0(X)$ and $a_\alpha(X)$ (resp. $a_{\alpha^{-1}}$).

Specifically, when the adversary outputs c_q, c_m, c_p, c_w, c_f that are supposed to be $[q(x)]_1, [m(x)]_1, \pi_{sum}$, $[w(x)]_1$ in the proof and $[f(x)]_1$ in the instance, respectively, the adversary also outputs $q_0(X), q_\alpha(X)$ where $q_\alpha(X)$ sums to 0 over $\mathbb{H}$, such that $c_q = [q_0(x)]_1 + \alpha \cdot [q_\alpha(X)]_1$, and similarly outputs $m_0(X), m_\alpha(X)$, $p_0(X), p_\alpha(X)$, $f_0(X), f_\alpha(X)$, $w_0(X), w_\alpha(X)$.

Likewise, when the adversary outputs c_g and c_t that are supposed to be $[g(x)]_2$ in the proof and $[t(x)]_2$ in the instance, it simultaneously outputs $g_0(X), g_{\alpha^{-1}}$, $t_0(X), t_{\alpha^{-1}}$, such that $c_g = [g_0(x)]_2 + g_{\alpha^{-1}} \cdot [\alpha^{-1}]_2$ and $c_t = [t_0(x)]_2 + t_{\alpha^{-1}} \cdot [\alpha^{-1}]_2$.

By the first pairing check, we have

$$\begin{aligned}(g_0(x) + \alpha^{-1} \cdot g_{\alpha^{-1}}) - (w_0(x) + \alpha \cdot w_\alpha(x)) \\ = \alpha^{-1} \cdot (p_0(x) + \alpha \cdot p_\alpha(x)) \quad (3)\end{aligned}$$

which can be reformulated into

$$g_{\alpha^{-1}} - p_0(x) + \alpha \cdot (g_0(x) - w_0(x) - p_\alpha(x)) - \alpha^2 \cdot w_\alpha(x) = 0 \quad (4)$$

We then have that

1. $p_0(x) = g_{\alpha^{-1}}$,
2. $g_0(x) - w_0(x) = p_\alpha(x)$,
3. $w_\alpha(x) = 0$.

Otherwise, the adversary would get a non-zero equation of α that allows the adversary to solve for α. We can then build an adversary that computes α from $[\alpha^{-1}]_2$ and $[\alpha]_1$ by breaking the q-DLOG assumption. Then we claim that the corresponding polynomials output from the adversary also satisfy

1. $p_0(X) = g_{\alpha^{-1}}$,
2. $g_0(X) - w_0(X) = p_\alpha(X)$,
3. $w_\alpha(X) = 0$.

Otherwise, we can build an adversary that uses these non-zero polynomials to solve for x, breaking the q-DLOG assumption. Therefore, we have $w(X) = w_0(X)$ and that $g_0(X) - w(X)$ is a polynomial that sums to zero over $\mathbb{H}$ since $p_\alpha(X)$ is guaranteed to have this property.

By the second pairing check (and applying q-DLOG assumption again),

$$\begin{aligned}(\beta - (f_0(X) + \alpha \cdot f_\alpha(X))) \cdot (g_0(X) + \alpha^{-1} \cdot g_{\alpha^{-1}}) + \zeta \cdot w(X) \cdot (\beta - (t_0(X) + t_{\alpha^{-1}} \cdot \alpha^{-1})) \\ = U(X) + \zeta \cdot (m_0(X) + \alpha \cdot m_\alpha(X)) + (q_0(X) + \alpha \cdot q_\alpha(X)) \cdot Z_{\mathbb{H}}(X), \quad (5)\end{aligned}$$

where we have already applied the conclusion that $w_0(X) = w(X)$. Therefore, $Z_{\mathbb{H}}(X)$ divides the polynomial

$$\begin{aligned}(\beta - (f_0(X) + \alpha \cdot f_\alpha(X))) \cdot (g_0(X) + \alpha^{-1} \cdot g_{\alpha^{-1}}) - U(X) \\ + \zeta \cdot (w(X) \cdot (\beta - (t_0(X) + t_{\alpha^{-1}} \cdot \alpha^{-1})) + (m_0(X) + \alpha \cdot m_\alpha(X))).\end{aligned}$$

Because ζ is sampled after all these polynomials are output from the adversary, and this division with non-negligible probability over ζ, we conclude that both

$$(\beta - (f_0(X) + \alpha \cdot f_\alpha(X))) \cdot (g_0(X) + \alpha^{-1} \cdot g_{\alpha^{-1}}) - U(X) \tag{6}$$

and

$$w(X) \cdot (\beta - (t_0(X) + t_{\alpha^{-1}} \cdot \alpha^{-1})) + (m_0(X) + \alpha \cdot m_\alpha(X)) \tag{7}$$

are divided by $Z_{\mathbb{H}}(X)$ with overwhelming probability, i.e., evaluates to zero over $\mathbb{H}$.

For polynomial (6), because β is sampled after $f(X)$ is output from the adversary, so the part $(\beta - (f_0(X) + \alpha \cdot f_\alpha(X)))$ evaluates to nonzero values over $\mathbb{H}$ except with negligible probability. Therefore, $g_0(X) + \alpha^{-1} \cdot g_{\alpha^{-1}}$ must be zero over $\mathbb{H}\backslash\mathbb{D}$. However, if $g_\alpha^{-1} \neq 0$, the adversary would be able to solve for α, breaking the q-DLOG assumption. So $g_\alpha^{-1} = 0$ and $g_0(X) = g(X)$. Then if $f_\alpha(u) \neq 0$ for any $u \in \mathbb{D}$, the adversary can solve α by substituting h in this equation. So $f_\alpha(u) = 0$ for every $u \in \mathbb{D}$. By definition of $U(X)$, we have $g(u) = \frac{1}{\beta - f_0(u)}$ for $u \in \mathbb{D}$.

From polynomial (7), we conclude that for every h, $m_\alpha(h) = 0$, otherwise, we would get a non-trivial equation of α and the adversary solves for α. So $m_\alpha(X)$ is a constant multiple of $Z_{\mathbb{H}}(X)$. We also have $t_{\alpha^{-1}} = 0$, because otherwise, $w(h)$ must be zero for all $h \in \mathbb{H}$ to prevent the adversary from getting a non-trivial equation of α. However, since we have already proved that $g(X) - w(X)$ sums to zero over $\mathbb{H}$, so $w(h) = 0$ over $\mathbb{H}$ would imply that the sum of $g(X)$ over $\mathbb{H}$ is zero. By the conclusion we obtained from polynomial (6), this means $\sum_{u \in \mathbb{D}} \frac{1}{\beta - f_0(u)} = 0$. However, since β is sampled after $f_0(u)$ is fixed, this equality holds with negligible probability. This justifies the claim that $t_{\alpha^{-1}} = 0$, so $t(X) = t_0(X)$. Then we have $w(h) = \frac{m_0(h)}{\beta - t(h)}$ for every $h \in \mathbb{H}$.

Finally, we show that $f(X) = f_0(X)$, i.e., $f_\alpha(X) = 0$. To achieve this, we revisit Eq. (5), which can now be simplified to

$$\begin{aligned}(\beta - (f_0(X) + \alpha \cdot f_\alpha(X))) \cdot g(X) + \zeta \cdot (w(X) \cdot (\beta - t(X)) \\ - (m_0(X) + \alpha \cdot m_\alpha(X))) = U(X) + (q_0(X) + \alpha \cdot q_\alpha(X)) \cdot Z_{\mathbb{H}}(X).\end{aligned}$$

We have already proved that $w(X) \cdot (\beta - t(X)) - m_0(X)$ is divided by $Z_{\mathbb{H}}(X)$. Define $m'_\alpha = m_\alpha(X)/Z_{\mathbb{H}}(X)$, which is a constant as we have already proved. So we subtract it from both sides by appropriately redefining $q_0(X)$. Then we have

$$(\beta - (f_0(X) + \alpha \cdot f_\alpha(X))) \cdot g(X) - U(X) = (q_0(X) + \alpha \cdot (q_\alpha(X) + \zeta m'_\alpha)) \cdot Z_{\mathbb{H}}(X),$$

which can be reformulated into

$$(\beta - f_0(X)) \cdot g(X) - U(X) - q_0(X) \cdot Z_{\mathbb{H}}(X) = \alpha \cdot (f_\alpha(X) g(X) + (q_\alpha(X) + \zeta m'_\alpha) \cdot Z_{\mathbb{H}}(X)).$$

Then both sides must be zero. Otherwise, the adversary would solve for α. The right side being zero implies $m'_\alpha = 0$, because $f_\alpha(X)$ and $g(X)$ are both selected before ζ is sampled. If m'_α is nonzero then the prover must select $q_\alpha(X) =$

$-\frac{f_\alpha(X)g(X)}{Z_{\mathbb{H}}(X)} - \zeta m'_\alpha$. However, this is unlikely to be a polynomial whose sum over $\mathbb{H}$ is zero. So m'_α must be zero, and $q_\alpha(X) = -\frac{f_\alpha(X)g(X)}{Z_{\mathbb{H}}(X)}$ sums to zero over $\mathbb{H}$. Since $f_\alpha(X)$ is selected before β is sampled, and we have proved that $g(u) = \frac{1}{\beta - f_0(u)}$, we must have $\frac{f_\alpha(X)L_u(X)}{Z_{\mathbb{H}}(X)}$ sums to zero over $\mathbb{H}$ for every $u \in \mathbb{H}$. Moreover, $f_\alpha(X)$ itself also has a zero sum. Together we have $|\mathbb{H}| + 1$ linearly independent constraints over the coefficient vector of $f_\alpha(X)$, whose size is also at most $|\mathbb{H}| + 1$. We thus conclude that $f_\alpha(X)$ must be zero, so is $q_\alpha(X)$.

Combining all the conclusions we have so far, we finally obtain the equality $\sum_{u\in\mathbb{D}} \frac{1}{\beta - f(u)} = \sum_{h\in\mathbb{H}} \frac{m(h)}{\beta - t(h)}$ that holds with overwhelming probability for a non-negligible fraction of β. We then conclude that the rational function $\sum_{u\in\mathbb{D}} \frac{1}{X - f(u)} - \sum_{h\in\mathbb{H}} \frac{m(h)}{X - t(h)}$ must be zero, otherwise this function does not evaluate to 0 except for negligible fraction of β. Therefore, this rational function does not contain any poles, which means that for every $f(u)$, there must exist some $t(h) = f(u)$. We then define the extractor by invoking the adversary and outputting $t(X), f(X)$.

Zero-Knowledge. Given σ_{KZG}, c_f, c_t and the trapdoor α, the simulator outputs the transcript $c_m, \beta, c_g, c_w, \pi_{sum}, \zeta, c_q$ as follows. First, uniformly sample $\beta, w, g, q \in \mathbb{F}$ and $\zeta \in \mathbb{F}\backslash\{0\}$ and let $c_w = [w]_1$, $c_g = [g]_2$, $c_q = [q]_1$. Then compute $c_m = \zeta^{-1} \cdot (g \cdot ([\beta]_1 - c_f) - [U(x)]_1 - q \cdot [Z_{\mathbb{H}}(x)]_1) + w \cdot ([\beta]_2 - c_t)$. Finally, compute $\pi_{sum} = [\alpha \cdot (g - w)]_1$. This transcript passes the verification by design. We then argue that its distribution is statistically close to an honest transcript.

We accomplish this by introducing an intermediate distribution of c_m, β, c_g, c_w, π_{sum}, ζ, c_q and argue that this distribution is close to both the aforementioned distribution and the honest distribution. This distribution is defined as follows. Sample m, β, g, w, ζ uniformly independently, then define $\pi_{sum} = [\alpha \cdot (g - w)]_1$ and $q = \frac{g\cdot(\beta - f(x)) + \zeta \cdot w \cdot (\beta - t(x)) - U(x) - \zeta \cdot m}{Z_{\mathbb{H}}(x)}$. Finally, let $c_w = [w]_1$, $c_g = [g]_2$, $c_q = [q]_1$, $c_m = [m]_1$. Note that the simulator cannot directly sample following the definition of this intermediate distribution because it does not learn $f(x)$ and $t(x)$.

First, we argue that the distribution is statistically close to the simulated distribution. Because in both distributions, β, g, w, ζ are sampled uniformly independently, we only need to show that the conditional distributions of π_{sum}, c_q, c_m given β, g, w, ζ are close. In both distributions, π_{sum} is deterministically decided by g, w, so its distributions in both cases are the same. Then we note that in both distributions, q and m satisfy the same equation of the form $A \cdot q + B \cdot m = C$, where A, B, C are decided by $\beta, g, w, \zeta, f(x), t(x), U(x), Z_{\mathbb{H}}(x)$. For the simulator, the distribution of q, m is first sampling q uniformly and then solving for m, whereas the intermediate distribution is first sampling m and then solving for q. Both strategies are uniformly sampling the solution space of this equation, thus producing the same distribution.

Next, we show that the intermediate distribution is close to the distribution of an honest transcript. In the honest execution, $\delta_1, \delta_2, \delta_3$ and β, ζ are uniformly and independently sampled, so the distributions of $c_m, \beta, c_g, c_w, \zeta$ are the same as in the intermediate distribution. Then in both distributions, π_{sum} and c_q are the unique elements that satisfy the pairing checks and are decided deterministically by $c_m, \beta, c_g, c_w, \zeta$. We thus conclude that the simulated transcript is statistically indistinguishable from an honest transcript. □

Efficiency. The verifier cost, after the optimization by the final random linear combination, is dominated by four pairings (one pairing check plus three additional pairings). The proof consists of 4 $\mathbb{G}_1$ elements and 1 $\mathbb{G}_2$ elements. The prover cost consists of:

- Computing $[m(x)]_1$ and $[w(x)]_1$ each costs one MSM of size m in $\mathbb{G}_1$.
- Computing $[g(x)]_2$ costs one MSM of size m in $\mathbb{G}_2$.
- Computing $q_1(X)$ can be accomplished as follows:
  1. Interpolate $\frac{c_u^{-1}}{\beta - f(u)}$ over $\mathbb{D}$ into $g'(X)$.
  2. Evaluate $f(X)$ over $\mathbb{D}' \subset \mathbb{F}$ of size m that is disjoint from $\mathbb{D}$ by one interpolation followed by one multi-point evaluation (assuming we only have the evaluation representation of $f(X)$).
  3. Evaluate $g'(X)$ over $\mathbb{D}'$ by one multi-point evaluation of size m.
  4. Evaluate $r(X) := f(X) \cdot g'(X) \bmod Z_{\mathbb{D}}(X)$ over $\mathbb{D}'$, by interpolating $\frac{c_u^{-1} \cdot f(u)}{\beta - f(u)}$ over $\mathbb{D}$ followed by multi-point evaluation over $\mathbb{D}'$.
  5. Divide the evaluation of $f(X) \cdot g'(X) - r(X)$ over $\mathbb{D}'$ by the evaluations of $Z_{\mathbb{D}}(X)$.
  6. Get the coefficients of $q_1(X)$ by one interpolation.

  This costs seven interpolation/multi-point evaluations of size m. Then computing $[q(x)]_1$ costs one MSM of size $2m$ in $\mathbb{G}_1$.
- Computing π_{sum} costs one MSM of size $2m$ in $\mathbb{G}_1$.

In conclusion, the prover cost is dominated by two $\mathbb{G}_1$-MSM of size m, two $\mathbb{G}_1$-MSM of size $2m$, one $\mathbb{G}_2$-MSM of size m, and seven size-m interpolation or multi-point evaluations that have cost $O(m \log^2 m)$. When $\mathbb{H}$ and $\mathbb{D}$ are multiplicative subgroups, the interpolation or multi-point evaluations are replaced with IFFT and FFTs that have cost $O(m \log m)$.

Compared to cq, the proving cost of Locq is almost the same: we exchange $2m$ scalar multiplications in $\mathbb{G}_1$ with m scalar multiplications in $\mathbb{G}_2$. According to the data provided in `zkalc`[5], multiplications in $\mathbb{G}_2$ is roughly three times slower than multiplications in $\mathbb{G}_1$ for the BLS12-381 curve implemented by `ark-works`, so the overall proving efficiency of Locq is slightly worse than cq. However, the concrete impact varies significantly by the concrete implementations.

5 Conclusion

We proposed new schemes respectively for the univariate sum-check and the lookup argument that are essential tools in SNARK and ZKVM constructions.

[5] https://zka.lc.

Both schemes advance the state of the art by reducing the proving costs, verification costs, and/or proof sizes. Our schemes can be directly deployed as drop-in replacements for the existing schemes. Meanwhile, our prover complexity is still $O(m \log m)$, and it is still an open question to reduce the number of field operations in the prover to $O(m)$.

Acknowledgement. This work is partially supported by Shanghai Science and Technology Innovation Action Plan (Grant No. 23511101100), the National Key Research and Development Project (Grant No. 2020YFA0712300) and the National Natural Science Foundation of China (Grant No. 62272294). We thank Ren Zhang and Alan Szepieniec for their valuable comments and feedback. We thank the anonymous reviewers for their careful examination of our work and their insightful comments and constructive suggestions.

References

BCG+18. Bootle, J., Cerulli, A., Groth, J., Jakobsen, S., Maller, M.: Arya: nearly linear-time zero-knowledge proofs for correct program execution. In: Peyrin, T., Galbraith, S. (eds.) ASIACRYPT 2018. LNCS, vol. 11272, pp. 595–626. Springer, Cham (2018). https://doi.org/10.1007/978-3-030-03326-2_20

BCR+19. Ben-Sasson, E., Chiesa, A., Riabzev, M., Spooner, N., Virza, M., Ward, N.P.: Aurora: transparent succinct arguments for R1CS. In: Ishai, Y., Rijmen, V. (eds.) Advances in Cryptology – EUROCRYPT 2019, vol. 11476, pp. 103–128. Springer, Cham (2019). https://doi.org/10.1007/978-3-030-17653-2_4, http://link.springer.com/10.1007/978-3-030-17653-2_4

BEG+91. Blum, M., Evans, W.S., Gemmell, P., Kannan, S., Naor, M.: Checking the correctness of memories. In: 32nd Annual Symposium on Foundations of Computer Science, San Juan, Puerto Rico, 1–4 October 1991, pp. 90–99. IEEE Computer Society (1991)

CBBZ22. Chen, B., Bünz, B., Boneh, D., Zhang, Z.: HyperPlonk: plonk with linear-time prover and high-degree custom gates (2022). https://eprint.iacr.org/2022/1355

CFF+23. Campanelli, M., Faonio, A., Fiore, D., Li, T., Lipmaa, H.: Lookup arguments: improvements, extensions and applications to zero-knowledge decision trees (2023)

CHM+20. Chiesa, A., Hu, Y., Maller, M., Mishra, P., Vesely, N., Ward, N.: Marlin: preprocessing zkSNARKs with universal and updatable SRS. In: Canteaut, A., Ishai, Y. (eds.) EUROCRYPT 2020. LNCS, vol. 12105, pp. 738–768. Springer, Cham (2020). https://doi.org/10.1007/978-3-030-45721-1_26

COS. Chiesa, A., Ojha, D., Spooner, N.: Fractal: post-quantum and transparent recursive proofs from holography. In: Canteaut, A., Ishai, Y. (eds.) EUROCRYPT 2020. LNCS, vol. 12105, pp. 769–793. Springer, Cham (2020). https://doi.org/10.1007/978-3-030-45721-1_27

EFG22. Eagen, L., Fiore, D., Gabizon, A.: CQ: cached quotients for fast lookups (2022). https://eprint.iacr.org/2022/1763

FKL17. Fuchsbauer, G., Kiltz, E., Loss, J.: The algebraic group model and its applications. Technical report 620 (2017). http://eprint.iacr.org/2017/620

FS86. Fiat, A., Shamir, A.: How to prove yourself: practical solutions to identification and signature problems. In: Odlyzko, A.M. (ed.) CRYPTO 1986. LNCS, vol. 263, pp. 186–194. Springer, Heidelberg (1987). https://doi.org/10.1007/3-540-47721-7_12

GK22. Gabizon, A., Khovratovich, D.: Flookup: fractional decomposition-based lookups in quasi-linear time independent of table size (2022). https://eprint.iacr.org/2022/1447

GKR08. Goldwasser, S., Kalai, Y.T., Rothblum, G.N.: Delegating computation: interactive proofs for muggles. In: Proceedings of the Fourtieth Annual ACM Symposium on Theory of Computing - STOC 2008, p. 113. ACM Press (2008). http://dl.acm.org/citation.cfm?doid=1374376.1374396

GPR21. Goldberg, L., Papini, S., Riabzev, M.: Cairo – a Turing-complete STARK-friendly CPU architecture. Technical report 1063 (2021). http://eprint.iacr.org/2021/1063

Gro16. Groth, Jens: On the size of pairing-based non-interactive arguments. In: Fischlin, Marc, Coron, Jean-Sébastien. (eds.) EUROCRYPT 2016. LNCS, vol. 9666, pp. 305–326. Springer, Heidelberg (2016). https://doi.org/10.1007/978-3-662-49896-5_11, http://link.springer.com/10.1007/978-3-662-49896-5_11

GW20. Gabizon, A., Williamson, Z.J.: Plookup: a simplified polynomial protocol for lookup tables. Technical report 315 (2020). http://eprint.iacr.org/2020/315

Hab22. Haböck, U.: Multivariate lookups based on logarithmic derivatives (2022)

Kun73. Kung, H.-T.: Fast evaluation and interpolation. Carnegie-Mellon University, Department of Computer Science (1973)

KZG10. Kate, A., Zaverucha, G.M., Goldberg, I.: Constant-size commitments to polynomials and their applications. In: Abe, M. (eds.) Advances in Cryptology – ASIACRYPT 2010. ASIACRYPT 2010. LNCS, vol. 6477, pp. 177–194. Springer, Heidelberg (2010). https://doi.org/10.1007/978-3-642-17373-8_11, http://link.springer.com/10.1007/978-3-642-17373-8_11

LFKN90. Lund, C., Fortnow, L., Karloff, H.J., Nisan, N.: Algebraic methods for interactive proof systems. In: 31st Annual Symposium on Foundations of Computer Science, vol. 1, pp. 2–10. IEEE Computer Society (1990)

Mid22. Team Miden. Miden VM Documentation (2022). https://maticnetwork.github.io/miden/

PFM+22. Pearson, L., Fitzgerald, J., Masip, H., Bellés-Munoz, M., Munoz-Tapia, J.L.: PlonKup: reconciling PlonK with Plookup. Technical report 086 (2022). https://eprint.iacr.org/2022/086

PHGR13. Parno, B., Howell, J., Gentry, C., Raykova, M.: Pinocchio: nearly practical verifiable computation. In: 2013 IEEE Symposium on Security and Privacy, pp. 238–252. IEEE, May 2013. http://ieeexplore.ieee.org/document/6547113/

PK22. Posen, J., Kattis, A.A.: Caulk+: table-independent lookup arguments. Cryptology ePrint Archive (2022). https://eprint.iacr.org/2022/957

Ris22. Team RiscZero. RISC Zero: General-Purpose Verifiable Computing (2022). https://risczero.com/

Scr22. Team Scroll. Scroll (2022). https://scroll.io/

Set20. Setty, S.: Spartan: efficient and general-purpose zkSNARKs without trusted setup. In: Micciancio, D., Ristenpart, T. (eds.) CRYPTO 2020. LNCS, vol. 12172, pp. 704–737. Springer, Cham (2020). https://doi.org/10.1007/978-3-030-56877-1_25

SLST23. Szepieniec, A., Lemmens, A., Sauer, J.F., Threadbare, B.: The Tip5 Hash Function for Recursive STARKs (2023)
STW23. Setty, S., Thaler, J., Wahby, R.: Unlocking the lookup singularity with Lasso (2023)
VM22. Triton VM. Triton VM, September 2022
XZZ+19. Xie, T., Zhang, J., Zhang, Y., Papamanthou, C., Song, D.: Libra: succinct zero-knowledge proofs with optimal prover computation. In: Boldyreva, A., Micciancio, D. (eds.) CRYPTO 2019. LNCS, vol. 11694, pp. 733–764. Springer, Cham (2019). https://doi.org/10.1007/978-3-030-26954-8_24
ZBK+22. Zapico, A., Buterin, V., Khovratovich, D., Maller, M., Nitulescu, A., Simkin, M.: Caulk: lookup arguments in sublinear time. Technical report 621 (2022)
ZGK+22. Zapico, A., Gabizon, A., Khovratovich, D., Maller, M., Ràfols, C.: Baloo: nearly optimal lookup arguments (2022). https://eprint.iacr.org/2022/1565
zkS22. zkSync Team. zkSync (2022). https://zksync.io/
ZXZS20. Zhang, J., Xie, T., Zhang, Y., Song, D.: Transparent polynomial delegation and its applications to zero knowledge proof. In: 2020 IEEE Symposium on Security and Privacy, SP 2020, pp. 859–876. IEEE (2020)

On Sigma-Protocols and (Packed) Black-Box Secret Sharing Schemes

Claudia Bartoli[1,2(✉)] and Ignacio Cascudo[1]

[1] IMDEA Software Institute, Madrid, Spain
{claudia.bartoli,ignacio.cascudo}@imdea.org
[2] Universidad Politécnica de Madrid, Madrid, Spain

Abstract. Σ-protocols are a widely utilized, relatively simple and well understood type of zero-knowledge proofs. However, the well known Schnorr Σ-protocol for proving knowledge of discrete logarithm in a cyclic group of known prime order, and similar protocols working over this type of groups, are hard to generalize to dealing with other groups, in particular those of hidden order, due to the inability of the knowledge extractor to invert elements modulo the order.

In this paper, we introduce a universal construction of Σ-protocols designed to prove knowledge of preimages of group homomorphisms for any abelian finite group. In order to do this, we first establish a general construction of a Σ-protocol for $\mathfrak{R}$-module homomorphism given only a linear secret sharing scheme over the ring $\mathfrak{R}$, where zero knowledge and special soundness can be related to the privacy and reconstruction properties of the secret sharing scheme. Then, we introduce a new construction of 2-out-of-n packed black-box secret sharing scheme capable of sharing k elements of an arbitrary (abelian, finite) group where each share consists of $k+\log n-3$ group elements. From these two elements we obtain a generic "batch" Σ-protocol for proving knowledge of k preimages of elements via the same group homomorphism, which communicates $k+\lambda-3$ elements of the group to achieve $2^{-\lambda}$ knowledge error. For the case of class groups, we show that our Σ-protocol improves in several aspects on existing proofs for knowledge of discrete logarithm and other related statements that have been used in a number of works.

Finally, we extend our constructions from group homomorphisms to the case of ZK-ready functions, introduced by Cramer and Damgård in Crypto 09, which in particular include the case of proofs of knowledge of plaintext (and randomness) for some linearly homomorphic encryption

This work has been partially supported by the grant PIPF-2022/COM-25517, funded by the Madrid Regional Government, and by the projects SecuRing (PID2019-110873RJ-I00/MCIN/AEI/10.13039/501100011033), PRODIGY (TED2021-132464B-I00) funded by MCIN/AEI/10.13039/501100011033/ and the European Union NextGenerationEU/PRTR, and CONFIDENTIAL-6G funded by the European Union (GA 101096435). Views and opinions expressed are however those of the author(s) only and do not necessarily reflect those of the European Union or the European Commission. Neither the European Union nor the European Commission can be held responsible for them.

Q. Tang and V. Teague (Eds.): PKC 2024, LNCS 14602, pp. 426–457, 2024.
https://doi.org/10.1007/978-3-031-57722-2_14

schemes such as Joye-Libert encryption. However, in the case of Joye-Libert, we show a better alternative, using Shamir secret sharing over Galois rings, which achieves 2^{-k} knowledge soundness by communicating k ciphertexts to prove k statements.

Keywords: Sigma Protocol · Black-Box Secret Sharing Schemes · Batch Proofs

1 Introduction

Σ-protocols are one of the most well known and understood types of zero-knowledge proofs. Their simplicity and concrete efficiency makes them widely used in various cryptographic applications and protocols, such as digital signatures, group signatures or anonymous credential systems, as well as secure multiparty computation protocols.

One of the best examples of Σ-protocols is Schnorr's proof of knowledge of discrete logarithm [32]. Given a cyclic group $\mathbb{G} = \langle G \rangle$ of (large) *known* prime order p, and $X \in \mathbb{G}$, the prover claims to a verifier that she knows $w \in \mathbb{Z}_p$ with $X = wG$. To prove it, she samples $r \in \mathbb{Z}_p$ at random and sends $A = rG$, the verifier replies with a uniformly random challenge $c \in \mathbb{Z}_p$, and the prover "opens" the linear combination $z = r + cw$; the verifier accepts if $zG = A + cX$.

This Σ protocol is a zero-knowledge proof of knowledge (ZKPoK) of w with knowledge error $1/p$. However this relies on the ability of inverting the difference $c - c'$ of any two different challenges, which is possible because the group order is known and prime. Namely, from conversations (A, c, z) and (A, c', z') the witness can be extracted as $w = (c - c')^{-1}(z - z')$.

This makes it hard to adapt Schnorr's protocol to other groups and in particular *hidden order groups*, where inverting $c - c'$ modulo the order of the group may not be feasible or even possible. For example, consider the task of proving knowledge of a discrete logarithm in a *class group*, which has an order assumed to be hard to compute. In this scenario existing Σ-protocols either: *i)* resort to using Schnorr's proof with binary challenges and repeating it many times to reduce the soundness error, which is somewhat inefficient [9]; *ii)* rely on hardness assumptions which in particular need the basis G to be uniformly random, which makes them harder to use in protocols [10]; or *iii)* are only sound proofs and not proofs of knowledge, in addition to relying on somewhat less studied assumptions [7].

A similar problem arises when proving plaintext knowledge in the Joye-Libert encryption scheme [26], which operates on RSA groups where the plaintext is encoded in a subgroup of $\mathbb{Z}_N^*$ of order 2^l. Mon$\mathbb{Z}_{2^k}$a [14], a protocol for MPC for arithmetic circuits over $\mathbb{Z}_{2^l}$, resorts to extracting only part of the witness, which leads to overheads in the protocol; and a recent threshold ECDSA protocol from [33], facing this same problem, circumvents it constructing a more involved protocol that uses a modified Joye-Libert scheme instead.

The motivation for this work is to generalize Schnorr's protocol, in a manner that it can be extended to a larger family of groups, starting from the observation that Schnorr's protocol can be interpreted in terms of *Shamir secret sharing* in the following sense: with her first message, the prover is committing to randomness r for a degree-1 Shamir sharing of the witness w; the challenge implicitly specifies a share-index; the share z corresponding to that index is sent in the last message by the prover. The secret sharing scheme is a variant of Shamir secret sharing where shares are evaluations of $f(T) = w \cdot T + r \in \mathbb{Z}_p[T]$ at points of $\mathbb{Z}_p$, and the secret is the evaluation at "the point at infinity". The usual security properties of special-soundness and honest-verifier zero knowledge can be interpreted in terms of 2-reconstruction and 1-privacy of the scheme, respectively.

The observation about this connection between Schnorr's protocol and (1-private, 2-reconstruction)-secret sharing schemes was made in the introduction of [15] (and its journal version [16]). More loosely, it can be related to the MPC-in-the-head paradigm for zero knowledge introduced in [25], in the sense that the prover is implicitly creating views of an MPC protocol (in this case a secret sharing) for virtual parties, committing to them, and then revealing one of them on demand.

Very recently and independently to us, [34] developed a similar connection between secret sharing and Σ-protocols, providing a general construction of Σ-protocols from *verifiable* secret sharing. They subsequently use it to build commit-and-proof arguments for general, non necessarily algebraic, statements using an MPC-in-the-head based approach.

Our work, while starting with the same observation as [34], focuses on improving the *concrete* complexity of Σ-protocols for *algebraic* statements, more concretely proofs of knowledge of preimages of elements via group homomorphisms, later extending this to ZK-ready functions, a notion introduced in [15]. We present a general construction of Σ-protocols for these types of relations from *linear* secret sharing schemes (LSSS), where the properties of special honest-verifier zero knowledge and (ν-)special soundness are based on the linearity, privacy and reconstruction of the linear secret sharing scheme.

In the case of proofs of knowledge of homomorphism-preimage involving groups of known prime order, using degree-1 Shamir secret sharing scheme (1-privacy, 2-reconstruction) leads to Schnorr's protocol in the case of discrete logarithm (and the generalization in [29] for other group homomorphisms); using the Franklin-Yung [22] "packed" (also called "ramp") version of Shamir with 1-privacy, $k+1$-reconstruction and k secrets leads to the batched Schnorr protocol from [23].

However, in the case of hidden groups, our construction can be instantiated to yield new results of batched ZKPoKs with improved complexity. By instantiating our construction with a new family of *black-box secret sharing* (BBSS) schemes that we introduce, we obtain Σ-protocols that can be used over any finite abelian group (regardless of its order or structure). In this case, we obtain improved amortized communication complexity with respect to the Σ-protocols in [15,16].

When applied to algebraic statements on *class groups* (e.g. ZKPoK of discrete logarithm), our protocol improves on previous alternatives [7,9,10] in either amortized complexity (in the case of [9]), or lack of reliance on additional assumptions while still matching their amortized complexity, in the case of [7,10].

While this black-box secret sharing approach also yields batch ZKPoKs of plaintext knowledge of Joye-Libert ciphertexts, in that case we show a better alternative using Shamir secret sharing over Galois rings. This approach is essentially the one used in [2] to prove knowledge of opening of a vector commitment that was introduced there, but we have not seen it being mentioned explicitly for the case of Joye-Libert and moreover, we provide a more generalized construction that allows more tradeoffs between communication complexity and soundness. We detail these contributions below.

1.1 Contributions

Σ-Protocols for Knowledge of Homomorphism Preimage from Monotone Span Programs. Given a ring $\mathfrak{R}$, modules $\mathfrak{M}_1$, $\mathfrak{M}_2$ over $\mathfrak{R}$, and a $\mathfrak{R}$-module homomorphism $F : \mathfrak{M}_1 \to \mathfrak{M}_2$, our first goal is to describe a $\Sigma-$protocol for the language $\{(\boldsymbol{w}, \boldsymbol{x}) \in \mathfrak{M}_1^k \times \mathfrak{M}_2^k : F(w_i) = x_i \ \forall i \in [k]\}$ using $\mathfrak{R}$-linear secret sharing schemes, see Theorem 1. This includes the case of group homomorphisms, where $\mathfrak{M}_1$ and $\mathfrak{M}_2$ are two finite abelian groups: we can always see these as modules over $\mathfrak{R} = \mathbb{Z}$, and in cases such as cyclic groups of known order m, they are furthermore modules over $\mathfrak{R} = \mathbb{Z}_m$.

Our construction uses the language of monotone span programs [28] because it allows us to capture simultaneously linear secret sharing schemes over different domains (namely $\mathfrak{M}_1$ and $\mathfrak{M}_2$) as long as they are modules over the same ring. In Sect. 2 we introduce a definition of k-monotone span programs over a ring $\mathfrak{R}$ for a monotone access structure (Δ, Γ) which yields, for every $\mathfrak{R}$-module $\mathfrak{M}$, $\mathfrak{R}$-LSSS where secrets are vectors of k elements in $\mathfrak{M}$, each share may be one or more elements in $\mathfrak{M}$, and such that there is respectively privacy and reconstruction for (at least) all sets in Δ and Γ.

Our construction of the Σ-protocol mimics the idea described above for Schnorr's protocol: namely, the prover chooses randomness in $\mathfrak{M}_1$, sends the images of the randomness via F, receives a challenge specifying one or more share-indices and replies with the corresponding shares of the witness using the randomness committed to in the first message.

In Sect. 3 we prove that the protocol has zero knowledge as long as the set $\mathcal{C}$ of possible challenges is contained in Δ. For special soundness, we introduce the notion of *extraction number* $\nu(\mathcal{C}, \Gamma)$ of the challenge set $\mathcal{C}$ with respect to Γ, which is the minimum ν for which the union of any ν challenges is in Γ. We show that the Σ-protocol has $\nu(\mathcal{C}, \Gamma)$-special soundness, leading to a knowledge error upper bounded by $(\nu - 1)/|\mathcal{C}|$. This bound cannot be improved in general.

New "Packed" Black-Box Secret Sharing Schemes with Small Shares. In the case of homomorphisms involving groups of large prime order p (exponential in the security parameter), which are modules over $\mathbb{Z}_p$, using 1-private Shamir's scheme for $k = 1$ and their packed variant for larger k is optimal: in that case, one has a scheme with an exponential number of shares, so $\mathcal{C}$ is of exponential size and we obtain negligible soundness error already for challenges of size 1.

However, the situation is more interesting in the case of groups of unknown order. In this case, we can instantiate our protocol using the notion of black-box secret sharing [21]. A black-box secret sharing scheme can be applied to *any* abelian finite group $\mathbb{G}$ obliviously to its order and structure: sharing and reconstruction only use black-box access to the group operation, inversion and random sampling of elements. The notion is equivalent to that of a monotone span program over $\mathbb{Z}$. Note that Shamir secret sharing "over the integers" is not a threshold black-box secret sharing scheme since it only allows to reconstruct a *multiple* of the secret instead of the secret itself.

It is known [17] that threshold black-box secret sharing schemes require shares of average size $\log n$ group elements, where n is the number of parties. A line of work [17–19] has led to the construction of general-threshold (t-privacy, $t+1$-reconstruction) black-box secret sharing schemes essentially matching the bound. However, in those constructions the secret is just one element of $\mathbb{G}$. Furthermore the aforementioned constructions have one important caveat for its use in our Σ-protocols: in all these constructions the computation *of just one share* has complexity linear in n. This means that, unlike in the prime order groups case, we cannot set n to be exponential in the security parameter.

The situation is better in the specific case of 1-privacy and 2-reconstruction, which we denote $(1, 2, n)$-BBSSS. A family of $(1, 2, n)$-BBSSS with $n = 2^k$, secrets in $\mathbb{G}^k$ and shares in $\mathbb{G}^{2k-1}$ appears implicit in [15], where they use it exactly in the same way as in our Σ-protocol.

In Sect. 4 we show that this construction can be generalized and improved. First, we show that for general $k, n > 0$ (i.e. not necessarily $n = 2^k$) the construction above can be generalized to obtain $(1, 2, n)$-BBSSS with secrets in $\mathbb{G}^k$ and every share in $\mathbb{G}^{h_*}$ where $h_* = k + \lceil \log n \rceil - 1$. Next we show that this can be improved to $h_* = k + \log n - 2$ if $k = 0 \mod 2$ and $n = 4^m$ for some $m > 0$, and to $h_* = k + \log n - 3$ if $k = 0 \mod 3$ and $n = 8^m$ for some $m > 0$. Moreover, in both [15] and our construction, the shares are computed efficiently using a matrix with entries in $\{-1, 0, 1\}$ making them suitable for our Σ-protocols.

Batched Proofs of Knowledge for Statements on Class Groups for Statements over Class Groups. In Sect. 5 we apply our Σ-protocol construction from Sect. 3 together with the black-box secret sharing scheme from Sect. 4 to obtain new protocols for proving batches of statements on class groups. We illustrate these with the examples of ZKPoK of discrete logarithm and ZKPoK of plaintext and randomness corresponding to ciphertexts under the CL-HSM encryption [11], but our results can easily be extended to other types of statements: discrete logarithm equality, correct multiplication of ciphertexts etc.

With this we obtain ZKPoK for those relations that compare positively (in an amortized way) with the ones we know of in the literature. They are more efficient in communication and computation than the proofs using binary challenges from [9], and have similar complexity to the proofs in [7,10] but *do not require additional assumptions* (in particular they can be applied in protocols where the prover might have chosen the basis of the discrete logarithm, unlike [10]), *and they are proofs of knowledge*, as opposed to just sound proofs like [7]. We remark that [7] also contain proofs of plaintext knowledge for a CL-HSM encryption, where the prover shows knowledge of only the plaintext and not the randomness. However, this proof (and also the one in [10]) only works for the version of CL-HSM where the plaintext space $\mathbb{Z}_m$ is such that m is a large prime (or a product of large primes) and would not work directly for more general m, in particular, for the case considered in [13] where $m = 2^u$. Since our PoK work regardless of the factorization of m, as far as we know our proofs are the most efficient proofs of plaintext knowledge (again in an amortized sense) for the more general version of CL-HSM.

Extension for ZK-Ready Functions and Batched PoKs for Joye-Libert. We can also extend our construction to deal with proving knowledge of preimage of group elements via *ZK-ready functions*, see Theorem 8. These capture "almost-group homomorphisms" that arise in particular as encryption functions of schemes such as Paillier [31] or Joye-Libert [26]. Considered as maps that take as argument a plaintext message in an additive group U and a random element in a multiplicative group S, and output a ciphertext in a third multiplicative group X, these encryption functions are homomorphic only "up to a correction factor in the S-argument", meaning that $f(u, s) \cdot f(u', s') = f(u + u', s \cdot s' \cdot \delta(u, u'))$ for some δ depending only on u and u'. We extend our Σ-protocols to deal with this case in a similar way as is done in [15]. In the third message the prover needs to adjust the "S-part of the share" to account for the above phenomenon, since she is opening a linear combination of shares. The one technical difference that we find with the homomorphism case is that because of this correction factor, proving zero knowledge seems to require additional properties of "share uniformity" and "randomness-uniqueness", see Theorem 8, but these are satisfied by all our BBSSS.

However, in the case of Joye-Libert encryption scheme we can obtain improved packed ZKPoK by using the fact that $(\mathbb{Z}_{2^l})^d$ is isomorphic to the Galois ring $GR(2^l, d)$. A Shamir secret sharing scheme over that Galois ring can then allocate up to 2^d participants, and using this as a LSSS over $\mathbb{Z}_{2^l}$ we obtain batched Σ-protocols for proving knowledge of plaintext for k ciphertexts with 2^{-k} soundness error, which communicate only k elements in $\mathbb{Z}_{2^l}$ and $\mathbb{Z}_N$. Moreover, tradeoffs are possible if we use packed versions of Shamir instead.

1.2 Related Work and Open Questions

As we mentioned earlier, [34] independently observed that Schnorr's protocol, as well as other Σ-protocols such as "batched Schnorr" [23], Okamoto [30] and Guillou-Quisqater [24], can be interpreted in terms of secret sharing as described above. Nevertheless, the direction of their work from there on is then different than ours, as they go to investigate proofs of statements containing a non-algebraic component from verifiable secret sharing, using an MPC-in-the-head-like technique. In their work, the protocol is applied to validate statements containing a non-algebraic component, for which they employ MPC-in-the-head. On the other hand we use this connection between secret sharing and Σ-protocols to improve their concrete complexity for some classes of algebraic statements, as we have discussed. Another difference is that the general construction of their work uses Verifiable Secret Sharing (VSS) and the Σ-protocol check is done through the share correctness verification algorithm. Our Σ-protocols can be seen as a special case: cast in their framework, we implicitly define a VSS using the fact that MSPs induce linear secret sharing schemes in both the domain $\mathfrak{M}_1$, and the range $\mathfrak{M}_2$ of the homomorphism F; the verifier checks the validity of a share from $\mathfrak{M}_1$ by comparing it with the share in $\mathfrak{M}_2$, which can be computed by the verifier himself, since he has received the randomness in the first message.

The best comparison point for our results is the work [15] and its journal version [16]. As mentioned before, they implicitly provide a $(1,2,n)$-BBSSS for $n = 2^k$, with secrets in $\mathbb{G}^k$ and each share in $\mathbb{G}^{2k-1}$, which leads to Σ-protocols to simultaneously prove k instances of statements at $2k-1$ group elements communication cost and soundness error 2^{-k}. For other values of n this share size can be generalized to $k + \lceil \log n \rceil - 1$. Our results imply that, if there exists a family of 2^s square matrices in $\mathbb{Z}^{s \times s}$ such that any difference of two of them is invertible over the integers, this share size can be improved to $k + \log n - s$ group elements when n is of the form $n = 2^{sm}$ for some m and we show this is the case for $s = 2$ and 3. This leaves a natural question open: can we find families of 2^s matrices in $\mathbb{Z}^{s \times s}$ with the property above for larger values of s? This would provide packed BBSSS with smaller share size and Σ-protocols with smaller communication complexity.

Another interesting question is whether one can obtain (t, r, n)-black-box secret sharing schemes that lead to better parameters in the corresponding secret sharing schemes. Works such as [17–19] construct threshold $(t, t+1, n)$-BBSSS with quasioptimal (in n) share size $\log n + c$ group elements for small constants c. However, their constructions only consider secrets which are a single group element and furthermore, constructing a single share requires $O(n)$ computation. Nevertheless, an appropriate packed generalization of these schemes could potentially make them useful for our construction if the setting where $t = \text{poly}(\lambda)$ and $n = \text{poly}(\lambda)$ for security parameter λ, leading to negligible soundness error.

With respect to our applications to batched PoK in hidden order groups, we have already discussed the improvements we obtained in the case of class groups, and more details are given in Sect. 5.

Our construction of batched proofs of plaintext and randomness knowledge for Joye-Libert ciphertexts follows the steps of the proof of knowledge of opening of certain homomorphic vector commitments over rings in [2]. In that work they use that Σ-protocol as basis for a *compressed* Σ-protocol [3] for proving knowledge of a committed vector satisfying a certain linear constraint. We note that compressed Σ-protocols (and bulletproofs [8], on which this abstraction is based) provide an amortization which is different than ours, where the statements consists on proving knowledge of a vector of the form $\mathbf{w}$ such that $L(\mathbf{w}) = x$, $Com(\mathbf{w}) = C$ for a linear form L and homomorphic commitment Com, and the proofs become logarithmic in the length of the vector. In contrast we prove knowledge of $\mathbf{w}$ satisfying $F(w_i) = x_i$ for a group homomorphism (or ZK ready function F). We do not rule out that our results can be combined with the compressed Σ-protocol technique to obtain amortized proofs of knowledge of several openings of commitments constrained to a linear form, as in [2].

As mentioned above, the problem of batching proofs of knowledge for Joye-Libert ciphertexts has arisen in applications such as multiparty computation [14] and threshold ECDSA [33]. These works have found different ways of circumventing the fact that extraction with a straightforward Schnorr protocol would fail due to the fact that the challenges differences are not invertible. In the former work, the authors resort to a proof of knowledge where only part of the witness can be extracted, which creates overhead in the protocol, as it requires to embed the actual data in a larger ring $\mathbb{Z}_{2^l}$. In the latter, the authors also acknowledge that they need to construct a more involved protocol due to this obstacle. Therefore we expect that our results can lead to improvements in these and other applications.

Lastly, the Black Box Secret Sharing Scheme introduced in this paper is formulated through a matrix with coefficients in $\{-1, 0, 1\}$, as detailed in Sect. 4.3. Hence, it would be worthwhile to explore its potential applications in lattice-based cryptography, where such properties are useful, see e.g. [4].

2 Preliminaries

2.1 General Notation

Throughout this work, we denote vectors with bold font (e.g. $\boldsymbol{v}$). A bold font of a function is used to represent the vector resulting from applying the function to each element of another vector, e.g. if $\boldsymbol{v} = (v_1, \ldots, v_n)$, then $\boldsymbol{f}(\boldsymbol{v}) := (f(v_1), \ldots, f(v_n))$. $V^\top$ denotes the transpose of a matrix V. $|\mathcal{C}|$ denotes the cardinality of a set $\mathcal{C}$ and $\log n$ denotes the logarithm in base 2 of n. For $m \leq n$, $[m, n]$ represents the set of integers $\{m, \ldots, n\}$ and for $n \geq 1$ we denote by $[n]$ the set $[1, n] = \{1, \ldots, n\}$. For any $T \subset [n]$ and matrix $M \in \mathfrak{R}^{h \times e}$, for a ring $\mathfrak{R}$ and $h \geq n$, M_T denotes the submatrix of M obtained from the i−rows, $i \in T$ and h_T is the number of rows of M_T.

2.2 Σ−protocols

Let $\mathcal{W}$, $\mathcal{X}$ be two finite sets, and let $R \subseteq \mathcal{W} \times \mathcal{X}$ be a relation. A zero-knowledge proof of knowledge is a protocol between a prover P and a verifier V, both of whom have a common input x and where P wants to convince V she knows a witness $w \in \mathcal{W}$ for x with respect to R, i.e. $(w, x) \in R$, without revealing any additional information about w. Σ-protocols are zero-knowledge proofs that follow the template in Fig. 1, where $\mathcal{C}$ is a finite set, called challenge set.

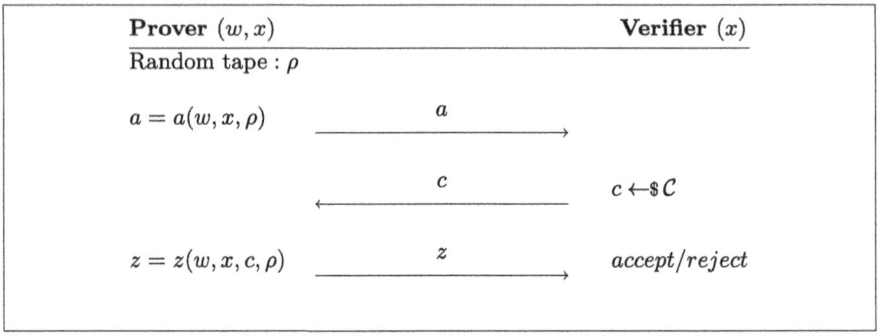

Fig. 1. Σ-protocol template

Definition 1. ***Σ-protocol:*** *A Σ-protocol for relation R is one that follows the template in Fig. 1 and satisfies the properties below:*

- ***Completeness:*** *if P and V follow the protocol, then V always accepts;*
- ***κ-Special Soundness:*** *There exists an p.p.t extractor that, given x and κ accepting conversations (a, c_1, z_1),..., (a, c_κ, z_κ), where $c_i \neq c_j$ for all $i, j \in [\kappa]$, efficiently computes w with $(w, x) \in R$;*
- ***Honest-verifier zero knowledge(HVZK):*** *There exists a p.p.t simulator $\mathcal{S}$, which on input $x \in \mathcal{X}$ and $c \in \mathcal{C}$, outputs a "conversation" (a, c, z) with the same distribution as a real conversation between the honest P and V on input x and where V chooses c as a challenge.*

Most definitions in the literature require $\kappa = 2$. However, it is worth to admit larger κ, since in [3] the following result is provided.

Proposition 1 ([3]). *A Σ-protocol with κ-special soundness is a HVZK proof of knowledge with knowledge error at most $(\kappa - 1)/|\mathcal{C}|$.*

2.3 Secret Sharing

Definition 2 (Access structure). *Let $n \geq 1$ be an integer, $2^{[n]}$ be the family of all subsets of $[n]$ and let $\Delta, \Gamma \subset 2^{[n]}$. The pair (Δ, Γ) is a* access structure (for $[n]$) *if $\emptyset \in \Delta$, $[n] \in \Gamma$, and $\Delta \cap \Gamma = \emptyset$.*

In addition, (Δ, Γ) *is* monotone *if the following holds: (i) if* $T_1 \in \Delta$ *and* $T_2 \subset T_1$ *then* $T_2 \in \Delta$*; (ii) if* $S_1 \in \Gamma$ *and* $S_1 \subset S_2$ *then* $S_2 \in \Gamma$*.*

For $0 \le \mathfrak{t} < \mathfrak{r} \le n$*, the* threshold *access structure* $(\Delta, \Gamma)_{\mathfrak{t},\mathfrak{r},n}$ *is defined by* $\Delta = \{T \subseteq [n] : |T| \le \mathfrak{t}\}$*, and* $\Gamma = \{S \subseteq [n] : |S| \ge \mathfrak{r}\}$*.*

All access structures considered in this work will be monotone.

Definition 3 (Secret sharing). *For the purpose of this paper, a* secret sharing scheme*(SSS) for a monotone access structure* (Δ, Γ) *consists of a space of secrets* $\mathcal{S}_0$*, a space of randomness* $\mathcal{R}$*, spaces of shares* $\mathcal{S}_1, \cdots, \mathcal{S}_n$ *and a map* $\mathsf{Sh} : \mathcal{S}_0 \times \mathcal{R} \longrightarrow \mathcal{S}_1 \times \cdots \times \mathcal{S}_n$*, such that, if* Sh_A *denotes the projection of* Sh *to* $\times_{i \in A} \mathcal{S}_i$*:*

- *Every set* $S \in \Gamma$ *is a* reconstructing set*: for any* $a_S \in \times_{i \in S} \mathcal{S}_i$*, there exists* at most *one* $s \in \mathcal{S}_0$ *with* $\mathsf{Sh}_S(s, r) = a_S$ *for some (possibly non-unique)* $r \in \mathcal{R}$*;*
- *Every set* $T \in \Delta$ *is a* privacy set*: for any* $a_T \in \times_{i \in T} \mathcal{S}_i$*, and any* s*,* s' *in* $\mathcal{S}_0$ *we have* $|\{r \in \mathcal{R} : \mathsf{Sh}_T(s, r) = a_T\}| = |\{r' \in \mathcal{R} : \mathsf{Sh}_T(s', r') = a_T\}|$*. In other words, conditioned to the shares for* T *being* a_T*, every element in* $\mathcal{S}_0$ *has the same probability of being the secret.*

Definition 4. *A* $(\mathfrak{t}, \mathfrak{r}, n)$*−secret sharing scheme is an SSS for* $(\Delta, \Gamma)_{\mathfrak{t},\mathfrak{r},n}$*.*

In this work we will be considering secret sharing schemes which are linear over certain ring, as defined next.

Definition 5. *Let* $\mathfrak{R}$ *be a commutative ring with an identity, and* $\mathfrak{M}$ *a finite module over* $\mathfrak{R}$*. A linear secret sharing scheme (LSSS) over* $\mathfrak{R}$ *is a SSS with* $\mathcal{S}_0 = \mathfrak{M}^k$*,* $\mathcal{R} = \mathfrak{M}^e$*,* $\mathcal{S}_i = \mathfrak{M}^{h_i}$ *for* $i \in [n]$ *where* k*,* e*,* h_i *are positive integers, and* $\mathsf{Sh} : \mathfrak{M}^k \times \mathfrak{M}^e \to \times_{i=1}^n \mathfrak{M}^{h_i}$ *is given by a* sharing matrix $M \in \mathfrak{R}^{h \times (k+e)}$ *(where* $h = \sum_{i=1}^n h_i$*). Namely* $(\boldsymbol{\sigma}_1, \ldots, \boldsymbol{\sigma}_n)^\top = \mathsf{Sh}(\boldsymbol{s}, \boldsymbol{r}) = M(\boldsymbol{s}, \boldsymbol{r})^\top$*.*

The same matrix $M \in \mathfrak{R}^{h \times (k+e)}$ can define secret sharing schemes for different instances of $\mathfrak{M}$. Seeing M through the lens of *Monotone Span Programs*, which we detailed next, we can capture properties of reconstruction and privacy that apply to every secret sharing scheme defined by M, regardless of the module $\mathfrak{M}$.

2.4 Monotone Span Programs

Monotone Span Programs (MSP) were introduced in [27] and are closely related to LSSS. We provide a slight generalization that endows MSPs with k linearly independent target vectors (rather than just one as in [27]) and detail its relation to LSSS with secrets of size k.

Definition 6 (k-Monotone Span Program). *Let* $k, n \ge 1$ *be integers, and let* (Δ, Γ) *be a monotone access structure for* $[n]$*. A* k-Monotone Span Program (k-MSP) $\mathcal{M}$ over a ring $\mathfrak{R}$ computing (Δ, Γ) *is a quadruple* $(\mathfrak{R}, M, \Psi, k)$ *with* $M \in \mathfrak{R}^{h \times (k+e)}$*,* $e \ge 0$*,* $h \ge n$ *and* $\Psi : [h] \to [n]$ *surjective, that satisfies the two properties* (P_1) *and* (P_2) *below.*

- *(P_1) for every $T \in \Delta$, there exist vectors $\boldsymbol{\lambda}_T^{(1)}, ..., \boldsymbol{\lambda}_T^{(k)} \in \mathfrak{R}^{k+e}$ with:*
  - $\boldsymbol{\lambda}_T^{(i)} = (\overbrace{0, \ldots, 0}^{i-1}, 1, \overbrace{0, \ldots, 0}^{k-i}, *, \ldots, *)$, *i.e. the projection of $\boldsymbol{\lambda}^{(i)}$ to the first k components is the i-th unit vector.*
  - $\boldsymbol{\lambda}_T^{(i)} \in Ker\ M_T$, *i.e.,* $M_T \cdot \boldsymbol{\lambda}^{(i)\top} = \mathbf{0}_{h_T}{}^\top$.
- *(P_2) for any $S \in \Gamma$, for all $i \in [k]$,* $\boldsymbol{\mu}^{(i)} := (\overbrace{0, \ldots, 0}^{i-1}, 1, \overbrace{0, \ldots, 0}^{k+e-i}) \in \mathrm{Im}(M_S^\top)$. *I.e., there exist vectors $\boldsymbol{\rho}_S^{(i)} \in \mathfrak{R}^{h_S}$, $i = 1, \ldots, k$ (called "reconstruction vectors") that satisfy the equations $\boldsymbol{\rho}_S^{(i)} \cdot M_S = \boldsymbol{\mu}^{(i)}$.*

Notation: In some cases we will define a MSP from a collection $M_i \in \mathfrak{R}^{h_i \times (k+e)}$, $i \in [n]$, hence we write $\mathcal{M} = (\mathfrak{R}, \{M_i\}_{i \in [n]}, k)$ meaning M is defined by stacking the blocks M_i in the rows $\Psi^{-1}(\{i\})$.

Monotone Span Programs and Secret Sharing. The following is a direct generalization of a result in [28], see the full version of this paper [5] for a proof.

Proposition 2. *Let $\mathcal{M}$ be a k-MSP over a ring $\mathfrak{R}$. If $\mathcal{M}$ computes (Δ, Γ) then every $T \in \Delta$ is a privacy set, and every $S \in \Gamma$ is a reconstructing set of every LSSS over $\mathfrak{R}$ with sharing matrix M.*

3 Σ-Protocols from Secret Sharing Schemes

In this section we present a general construction of Σ−protocols from $\mathfrak{R}$-linear secret sharing schemes (k-MSPs over $\mathfrak{R}$). The Σ-protocols apply to relations of the form $R = \{(\boldsymbol{w}, \boldsymbol{x}) \in \mathfrak{M}_1^k \times \mathfrak{M}_2^k : F(w_i) = x_i\ \forall\ i \in [k]\}$, where $\mathfrak{M}_1, \mathfrak{M}_2$ are modules over $\mathfrak{R}$, and $F : \mathfrak{M}_1 \to \mathfrak{M}_2$ is an (efficiently-computable) $\mathfrak{R}$-linear map.

Recalling our notation that $\boldsymbol{F}(\boldsymbol{w}) := (F(w_1), \ldots, F(w_k))$, the relation is abbreviated as $\boldsymbol{F}(\boldsymbol{w}) = \boldsymbol{x}$.

Definition 7. *A* challenge set $\mathcal{C}$ compatible with *the access structure (Δ, Γ) is a non-empty subfamily $\emptyset \neq \mathcal{C} \subseteq \Delta$ (i.e. a family of $E \subseteq [n]$ such that all $E \in \Delta$). The* extraction number *of $\mathcal{C}$ with respect to (Δ, Γ) is*

$$\nu(\mathcal{C}, \Gamma) := min\{\nu > 0 : \bigcup_{i=1}^{\nu} E_i \in \Gamma\ \forall\ pairwise\ distinct\ E_1, \ldots, E_\nu \in \mathcal{C}\}.$$

The following theorem showcases our Σ−protocol construction.

Theorem 1. *Let $\mathfrak{R}$ be a ring and $\mathfrak{M}_1, \mathfrak{M}_2$ be finite $\mathfrak{R}$−modules. We assume we can compute the action of $\mathfrak{R}$ on $\mathfrak{M}_1$, $\mathfrak{M}_2$ efficiently. Let $F : \mathfrak{M}_1 \to \mathfrak{M}_2$ be an $\mathfrak{R}$−module homomorphism. Let $\mathcal{M} = (\mathfrak{R}, M, \Psi, k)$ be a k−MSP over $\mathfrak{R}$ computing (Δ, Γ), where $M \in \mathfrak{R}^{h \times (k+e)}$.*

Let $\mathcal{C}$ be a compatible challenge set with respect to (Δ, Γ) and $\nu = \nu(\mathcal{C}, \Gamma)$ its extraction number. Assume it is possible to sample efficiently uniformly from $\mathcal{C}$ and $\mathfrak{M}_1$, that for every $E \in \mathcal{C}$, M_E can be computed efficiently, and that for *any pairwise distinct* $E_1, \ldots, E_\nu \in \mathcal{C}$ *it is efficient to compute the reconstruction vectors* $\boldsymbol{\rho}_{\mathcal{E}}^{(i)}$, *where* $\mathcal{E} = \bigcup_{i=1}^{\nu} E_i$, *promised by Definition 6.*

Then Fig. 2 provides a Σ*-protocol with* ν*-special soundness and perfect honest verifier zero knowledge for* $R = \{(\boldsymbol{w}; \boldsymbol{x}) \in \mathfrak{M}_1^k \times \mathfrak{M}_2^k : F(w_i) = x_i \ \forall i \in [k]\}$.

Prover		**Verifier**
$\boldsymbol{r} \leftarrow\!\!\$\ \mathfrak{M}_1^e$	$\boldsymbol{a} = \boldsymbol{F}(\boldsymbol{r})$ $\longrightarrow$	
	E $\longleftarrow$	$E \leftarrow\!\!\$\ \mathcal{C}$
$\boldsymbol{z}_E = M_E \cdot \begin{pmatrix} \boldsymbol{w}^\top \\ \boldsymbol{r}^\top \end{pmatrix}$	$\boldsymbol{z}_E = (z_j)_{j \in E}$ $\longrightarrow$	$\boldsymbol{F}(\boldsymbol{z}_E) \stackrel{?}{=} M_E \cdot \begin{pmatrix} \boldsymbol{x}^\top \\ \boldsymbol{a}^\top \end{pmatrix}$

Fig. 2. Σ-protocol from k-MSP

Proof. – **Completeness:** Since F is a $\mathfrak{R}$-linear map, it satisfies $F(a \cdot m) = a \cdot F(m)$ and $F(m+n) = F(m) + F(n)$ for $a \in \mathfrak{R}$, $m, n \in \mathfrak{M}_1$, and hence, $\boldsymbol{F}(A \cdot \boldsymbol{m}^\top) = A \cdot \boldsymbol{F}(\boldsymbol{m})^\top$ for any matrix A over $\mathfrak{R}$ and vector $\boldsymbol{m}$ over $\mathfrak{M}_1$ of matching dimensions. Therefore, for the challenge E and $\boldsymbol{z}_E = M_E \cdot \boldsymbol{v}^\top$ we have the equality $\boldsymbol{F}(\boldsymbol{z}_E) = \boldsymbol{F}(M_E \cdot \boldsymbol{v}^\top) = M_E \cdot \boldsymbol{F}(\boldsymbol{v})^\top$ where $\boldsymbol{F}(\boldsymbol{v}) = (\boldsymbol{F}(\boldsymbol{w}), \boldsymbol{F}(\boldsymbol{r})) = (\boldsymbol{x}, \boldsymbol{a})$.

- **ν-Special Soundness**: We want to prove that there is an extractor that, given ν accepted conversations of the form $(\boldsymbol{a}, E_i, \boldsymbol{z}_{E_i})$ for $i \in [\nu]$ with same vector $\boldsymbol{a} \in \mathfrak{M}_2^e$ and different challenges E_i, reconstructs the secrets $w_1, \ldots, w_k$. Let $\mathcal{E} = \cup_{j=1}^{\nu} E_j$, we define a vector $\boldsymbol{z}_{\mathcal{E}}$ with coordinates indexed by $\mathcal{E}$ as follows: for each $c \in \mathcal{E}$, c is in some E_j. The extractor chooses one such E_j, and defines the c-th coordinate z_c of $\boldsymbol{z}_{\mathcal{E}}$ to be the corresponding coordinate of $\boldsymbol{z}_{E_j}$ (the extractor will work even if different $\boldsymbol{z}_{E_j}$ disagree in a common c-th coordinate). Since the conversations above are accepted, we have $F(z_c) = M_c \cdot (\boldsymbol{x}, \boldsymbol{a})^\top$ for all $c \in \mathcal{E}$ and therefore $\boldsymbol{F}(\boldsymbol{z}_{\mathcal{E}}) = M_{\mathcal{E}} \cdot (\boldsymbol{x}, \boldsymbol{a})^\top$. By assumption, $\mathcal{E}$ is a reconstruction set for the MSP, consequently, for each $j \in [k]$, there is a reconstruction vector $\boldsymbol{\rho}_{\mathcal{E}}^j \in \mathfrak{R}^{|\mathcal{E}|}$ such that $x_j = \boldsymbol{\rho}_{\mathcal{E}}^j \cdot \boldsymbol{F}(\boldsymbol{z}_{\mathcal{E}})^\top$. Set $w_j = \boldsymbol{\rho}_{\mathcal{E}}^j \cdot \boldsymbol{z}_{\mathcal{E}}^\top$, then $F(w_j) = \boldsymbol{F}(\boldsymbol{\rho}_{\mathcal{E}}^j \cdot \boldsymbol{z}_{\mathcal{E}}^\top) = \boldsymbol{\rho}_{\mathcal{E}}^j \cdot \boldsymbol{F}(\boldsymbol{z}_{\mathcal{E}})^\top = x_j$, for all $j \in [k]$.
- **Honest-verifier zero knowledge:** We prove the existence of a simulator that, given $\boldsymbol{x}$ in the language and a challenge $E \in \mathcal{C}$, produces conversations whose distribution is the same to that of an honest conversation using a witness $\boldsymbol{w}$ for $\boldsymbol{x}$. Here, intuitively, we will use the fact that in the real protocol the shares $\boldsymbol{z}_E$ do not give any information about $\boldsymbol{w}$ because of the privacy of the secret sharing scheme for the set E, so these can be simulated by a sharing of an arbitrary element, for example $\boldsymbol{0}_k := (0, \ldots, 0) \in \mathfrak{M}_1^k$.

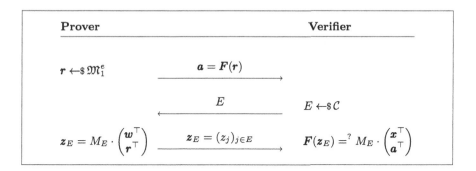

Concretely the simulator:

1. Samples $\widehat{\boldsymbol{r}}$ uniformly at random in $\mathfrak{M}_1^e$ and sets $\widehat{\boldsymbol{z}}_E = M_E(\mathbf{0}_k, \widehat{\boldsymbol{r}})^\top$.
2. For $i \in [k]$ let $\boldsymbol{\lambda}^{(i)}$ be an (arbitrary) element from the space

$$\Lambda_{E,i} = \{\boldsymbol{\lambda}^{(i)} \in \mathfrak{R}^{k+e} : (\boldsymbol{\lambda}^{(i)})_i = 1, (\boldsymbol{\lambda}^{(i)})_j = 0\, \forall j \in [k]\backslash\{i\}, M_E {\boldsymbol{\lambda}^{(i)}}^\top = \mathbf{0}_E\}$$

which is non-empty by definition of k-MSP (Definition 6,(P2)). Define $\overline{\boldsymbol{\lambda}}^{(i)}$ to be the projection of $\boldsymbol{\lambda}^{(i)}$ to the last e coordinates.
3. Define $\widehat{\boldsymbol{a}} = \boldsymbol{F}(\widehat{\boldsymbol{r}}) + \overline{\boldsymbol{\lambda}}^{(1)} \cdot x_1 + \cdots + \overline{\boldsymbol{\lambda}}^{(k)} \cdot x_k$[1]
4. Output $(\widehat{\boldsymbol{a}}, E, \widehat{\boldsymbol{z}}_E)$.

We show that $(\hat{\boldsymbol{a}}, E, \hat{\boldsymbol{z}}_E)$ has the same distribution as a real honest transcript with witness $\boldsymbol{w}$. In fact, $(\hat{\boldsymbol{a}}, E, \hat{\boldsymbol{z}}_E)$ is exactly the real conversation that arises when the prover chooses $\boldsymbol{r} = \widehat{\boldsymbol{r}} + \sum_{i=1}^k \overline{\boldsymbol{\lambda}}^{(i)} w_i$ as randomness at the beginning of the protocol. Since in the simulation $\widehat{\boldsymbol{r}}$ is chosen uniformly at random, $\boldsymbol{r}$ is also uniformly random.

Indeed, if the prover uses this randomness, the first message of the real conversation is $\boldsymbol{F}(\boldsymbol{r}) = \boldsymbol{F}(\widehat{\boldsymbol{r}} + \sum_{i=1}^k \overline{\boldsymbol{\lambda}}^{(i)} w_i) = \boldsymbol{F}(\widehat{\boldsymbol{r}}) + \sum_{i=1}^k \overline{\boldsymbol{\lambda}}^{(i)} x_i = \widehat{\boldsymbol{a}}$, while the third message is $M_E(\boldsymbol{w}, \boldsymbol{r})^\top = M_E(\boldsymbol{w}, \widehat{\boldsymbol{r}} + \sum_{i=1}^k \overline{\boldsymbol{\lambda}}^{(i)} w_i)^\top = M_E(\mathbf{0}, \widehat{\boldsymbol{r}})^\top + M_E(\boldsymbol{w}, \sum_{i=1}^k \overline{\boldsymbol{\lambda}}^{(i)} w_i)^\top$.

Recall that $\boldsymbol{\lambda}^{(i)} = (0, \ldots, 1, \ldots, 0, \overline{\boldsymbol{\lambda}}^{(i)})$, so $(\boldsymbol{w}, \sum_{i=1}^k \overline{\boldsymbol{\lambda}}^{(i)} w_i) = \sum_{i=1}^k \boldsymbol{\lambda}^{(i)} w_i$. Since $M_E {\boldsymbol{\lambda}^{(i)}}^\top = 0\ \forall i \in [k]$, we conclude $M_E(\boldsymbol{w}, \boldsymbol{r})^\top = M_E(\mathbf{0}, \widehat{\boldsymbol{r}})^\top = \widehat{\boldsymbol{z}}_E$. □

Corollary 1. *The protocol in Fig. 2 is a Σ-protocol with knowledge error $\leq (\nu - 1)/|\mathcal{C}|$ (from Proposition 1). Its average communication complexity is e elements in $\mathfrak{M}_2$ (first message), $\sum_{E_i \in \mathcal{C}} \log |E_i|/|\mathcal{C}|$ bits (second message), $\sum_{E_i \in \mathcal{C}} h_{E_i}/|\mathcal{C}|$ elements in $\mathfrak{M}_1$ (third message).*

Example 1. Protocols from Shamir secret sharing and variants As mentioned in the introduction, if $\mathfrak{M}_1 = \mathbb{Z}_p$ and $\mathfrak{M}_2 = \langle g \rangle$ is a group of large prime order p, and $F(w) = g^w$, for the case $k = 1$ (the usual proof of knowledge of DL of one element) we can use $(1, 2, n)$-Shamir's secret sharing scheme with $n \leq p$ and recover Schnorr's protocol. Similarly we can capture known protocols for other languages like discrete log equality. This type of protocols for group homomorphisms of large order have been for example unified under a common framework in [29]. In the case $k > 1$, we obtain the generalization of Schnorr's protocol, we can use a k-MSP for $(\Delta, \Gamma)_{1,k+1,n}$ (again $n \leq p$) where to share $(s_1, \ldots, s_k) \in \mathbb{Z}_p^k$ we sample a random coefficient $r \in \mathbb{Z}_p$ and define the shares as evaluations of $s_1 + s_2 X \cdots + s_k X^{k-1} + r X^k$ in nonzero points of $\mathbb{Z}_p$ (we can include r, the "evaluation at infinity" as an additional share), this is the same construction as in [23]. We obtain a Σ-protocol with $k+1$-special soundness and knowledge soundness k/p. In this case, it does not make much sense to use other privacy thresholds, on account of the fact that 1-privacy protocols already lead to negligible soundness if we take p exponential in the security parameter.

[1] Note $\overline{\boldsymbol{\lambda}}^{(i)} \cdot x_i$ denotes the coordinate-wise action of vector $\overline{\boldsymbol{\lambda}}^{(i)} \in \mathfrak{R}^{k+e}$ on the element $x_i \in \mathfrak{M}_2$, that is, if $\overline{\boldsymbol{\lambda}}^{(i)} = (\overline{\lambda}_1^{(i)}, \ldots, \overline{\lambda}_{k+e}^{(i)})$, then $\overline{\lambda}^{(i)} \cdot x_i = (\overline{\lambda}_1^{(i)} \cdot x_i, \ldots, \overline{\lambda}_{k+e}^{(i)} \cdot x_i)$.

Remark 1.
- *On exponential number of shares:* Note only M_E, the submatrix of the rows of M corresponding to the challenge E, needs to be computed. Therefore, even if n is exponential in security parameter λ, the protocol can be efficient, as long as M_E can be computed in polynomial time.
- *Threshold access structure:* In the full version [5] we consider the following question: if we fix Δ and Γ to respectively be the sets of at most $\mathfrak{t}$ elements and at least $\mathfrak{r}$ elements, what is the choice of $\mathcal{C}$ that minimizes the knowledge error bound $(\nu - 1)/|\mathcal{C}|$? We find out that an optimal choice in that sense is to select $\mathcal{C}$ to be the family of all sets of size exactly $\mathfrak{t}$. However, surprisingly in some cases this is not *the only* choice minimizing this bound and choosing a smaller $\mathcal{C}$ can achieve the same knowledge error, which makes it preferable from the point of view of communication complexity. We prove that optimal choices are characterized by *combinatorial designs.*
- *Optimality of knowledge error bound:* In general the knowledge error bound in Fig. 2 is optimal for our protocol: we show in the full version [5] that for the discrete logarithm equality relation a malicious prover breaks soundness with probability $(\nu - 1)/|\mathcal{C}|$.

3.1 Non-interactive Σ-Protocols

The well known Fiat-Shamir heuristic allows to turn the $\Sigma-$protocols from Theorem 1 into a non-interactive argument in the random oracle model. Let $\mathcal{H} : \{0,1\}^* \rightarrow \mathcal{C}$ be a random oracle mapping strings into elements of the challenge space. The honest prover constructs $\boldsymbol{a}$ as in the protocol, computes $E = \mathcal{H}(\boldsymbol{x}, \boldsymbol{a})$ with the random oracle and $\boldsymbol{z}_E$ as in the protocol and outputs the proof $(\boldsymbol{a}, E, \boldsymbol{z}_E)$. The verifier performs the same check as in the protocol, and verifies that $E = \mathcal{H}(\boldsymbol{x}, \boldsymbol{a})$, accepting iff both checks pass. This protocol requires the same average communication as in the above corollary, only that now is sent by the prover in one go.

A more interesting question is whether we can perform a commonly used optimization available in Schnorr's protocol and similar ones, consisting on only sending the second and third messages (in our case $(E, \boldsymbol{z}_E)$) in the protocol from Theorem 1. The verifier then reconstructs the first message $(\boldsymbol{a})$ from those messages and the statement $\boldsymbol{x}$ using the verification equation from the Σ-protocol, and finally the verifier checks the random oracle equation $E = \mathcal{H}(\boldsymbol{x}, \boldsymbol{a})$.

In our case this works if, given any possible $\boldsymbol{x}, E, \boldsymbol{z}_E$, there is a unique $\boldsymbol{a}$ such that $F(\boldsymbol{z}_E) = M_E \cdot (\boldsymbol{x}, \boldsymbol{a})^\top$ and this can be efficiently obtained by the verifier. It may be convenient to rephrase the uniqueness condition as follows (which is a consequence of linearity of M): for any $E \in \mathcal{C}$, $\boldsymbol{d} = \boldsymbol{0}$ is the only solution to $\boldsymbol{0} = M_E \cdot (\boldsymbol{0}, \boldsymbol{d})^\top$. In summary, we have:

Theorem 2. *In the conditions of Theorem 1, let in addition M satisfy that for any $E \in \mathcal{C}$,*

- *$\boldsymbol{d} = \boldsymbol{0} \in \mathfrak{M}_2^{\mathfrak{e}}$ is the only solution to $\boldsymbol{0} = M_E \cdot (\boldsymbol{0}, \boldsymbol{d})^\top$;*
- *Given $\boldsymbol{x} \in \mathfrak{M}_2^k$, $\boldsymbol{y} \in \mathfrak{M}_2^{h_E}$, computing the unique $\boldsymbol{a} \in \mathfrak{M}_2^{\mathfrak{e}}$ with $M_E \cdot (\boldsymbol{x}, \boldsymbol{a})^\top = \boldsymbol{y}$ is efficient.*

Prover		**Verifier**
$\boldsymbol{r} \leftarrow\$ \mathfrak{M}_1^e, \boldsymbol{a} = \boldsymbol{F}(\boldsymbol{r})$		
$E = \mathcal{H}(\boldsymbol{x}, \boldsymbol{a})$		
$\boldsymbol{z}_E = M_E \cdot \begin{pmatrix} \boldsymbol{w}^\top \\ \boldsymbol{r}^\top \end{pmatrix}$	$\xrightarrow{(E, \boldsymbol{z}_E)}$	Finds $\boldsymbol{a}$ s.t. $\boldsymbol{F}(\boldsymbol{z}_E) = M_E \cdot \begin{pmatrix} \boldsymbol{x}^\top \\ \boldsymbol{a}^\top \end{pmatrix}$
		$E =^? \mathcal{H}(\boldsymbol{x}, \boldsymbol{a})$

Fig. 3. Optimized NI-Σ-protocol from k-MSP

Then assuming the Fiat-Shamir heuristic, the protocol in Fig. 3 is a non-interactive zero-knowledge proof of knowledge for R, with the same security properties as in Theorem 1, in the random oracle model.

Remark 2. In Sect. 4 below, we introduce (black-box) secret sharing schemes with 1-privacy (hence $\mathcal{C}$ contains only sets of size 1) where each share is of the form $\boldsymbol{\sigma}_i = N_i\boldsymbol{w} + \boldsymbol{a}$, for a public matrix N_i. In this case, given the index i, the share $\boldsymbol{\sigma}_i$ and the secret $\boldsymbol{w}$, the randomness can be determined uniquely as $\boldsymbol{a} = \sigma_i - N_i\boldsymbol{w}$, and clearly this is an efficient computation as it requires the same operations as constructing a share. Therefore those secret sharing schemes fulfil the additional properties in the theorem above.

4 Packed Black-Box Secret Sharing Schemes

In this section we present constructions of packed black-box secret sharing schemes with 1-privacy and 2-reconstruction, where our main goal is to optimize the secret-to-share size ratio. We introduce constructions derived from a secret sharing scheme outlined in [15] and make improvements to reduce its share size. The BBSS scheme will be utilized in later applications involving class groups, Sect. 5. Finally, we will discuss the outcomes when applied on Σ-protocols.

4.1 Background on Black-Box Secret Sharing

First introduced by Desmedt and Frankel [21] and further studied in works such as [17–19], a black-box secret sharing scheme (BBSSS) is a SSS that can be applied to every finite abelian group, *obliviously to its structure*, i.e., sharing and reconstruction only use black-box access to the group operation and group inverse, as well as random sampling of group elements. As argued in [17], since every abelian group $\mathbb{G}$ is a $\mathbb{Z}$-module, a MSP over $\mathbb{Z}$ computing the access structure (Δ, Γ) yields a black-box secret sharing scheme for that structure, so we can reduce the problem to finding MSPs over $\mathbb{Z}$ for the desired structure.

To the best of our knowledge, previous works have focused on sharing a *single* secret of a group $\mathbb{G}$. [18] provides BBSSS for threshold structures $(\Delta, \Gamma)_{t,t+1,n}$ where $h_i = \lceil \log n \rceil$ for $i \in [n]$, i.e., every share is $\lceil \log n \rceil$ elements of $\mathbb{G}$. This is known to be very close to optimal, as the average share size must be at least $\lfloor \log n \rfloor - 1$ [17]. However, this bound does not rule out that one can share a larger secret "at roughly the same price" (even in the threshold case).

Apart from the fact that these schemes share a single secret, a greater obstacle in using the constructions from the line of work [17–19] as a basis for our Σ-protocols is that the computational complexity of *even computing one share* in all those schemes is $\Omega(n)$. That means that Remark 1 does not apply: setting $n = \exp(\lambda)$ would make the computation time be exponential in λ too. Setting $n = \text{poly}(\lambda)$ means that a soundness error of $2^{-\lambda}$ requires to either use a privacy threshold and challenges of size $\Omega(\lambda)$ or (if we want smaller privacy threshold and challenges) to use repetition to amplify soundness, both options incurring still in considerable (although polynomial in λ) communication overhead.

These two issues motivate us to search for (threshold) packed BBSS where the size of the shares does not grow too much in comparison to the secret, and where we can compute each share in time polylog n.

4.2 General Framework

For the next constructions, we use the following blueprint: each share will consist of the same number $h_i = h_*$ of group elements, and the corresponding block in the MSP will be of the form $M_i = (N_i | I_{h_* \times h_*}) \in \mathbb{Z}^{h_* \times (k+h_*)}$, where $I_{h_* \times h_*}$ represents the identity matrix of size $h_* \times h_*$. Therefore, the shares of $\boldsymbol{s} \in \mathbb{G}^k$ are $N_i \boldsymbol{s}^\top + \boldsymbol{r}$, $i \in [n]$ (for a uniformly random common $\boldsymbol{r} \in \mathbb{G}^{h_*}$).

First we will set the relation between a family of matrices and the existence of a black-box secret sharing scheme in the following theorem.

Theorem 3. *Let $\{N_i\}_{i \in [n]}$ be a collection of matrices with $N_i \in \mathbb{Z}^{h_* \times k}$. Let $M_i := (N_i | I_{h_* \times h_*})$, $i = 1, \ldots, n$, M be the stacking of all these matrices, and let $\mathcal{M} = (\mathbb{Z}, \{M_i\}_{i \in [n]}, k)$.*

If, for all $i \neq j$, $N_i - N_j$ has a left pseudoinverse $R_{ij} \in \mathbb{Z}^{k \times h_*}$ (i.e. $R_{ij}(N_i - N_j) = I_{k \times k}$), then $\mathcal{M}$ is a k-MSP over $\mathbb{Z}$ computing $(\Delta, \Gamma)_{1,2,n}$ and hence a $(1, 2, n)$-BBSSS with $\mathcal{S}_0 = \mathbb{G}^k$ and $\mathcal{S}_i = \mathbb{G}^{h_*}$ for $i \in [n]$.

Proof. We argue the properties directly in terms of secret sharing. Each share is $\boldsymbol{\sigma}_i = N_i \boldsymbol{s}^\top + \boldsymbol{r}$ where $\boldsymbol{r}$ is uniformly random in $\mathbb{G}^{h_*}$. Hence, each individual share is independent from $\boldsymbol{s}$, and we have 1-privacy. The scheme has 2-reconstruction because for every set $\{i, j\} \subseteq [n]$, there exists R_{ij} such that $R_{ij}(\boldsymbol{\sigma}_i - \boldsymbol{\sigma}_j)^\top = \boldsymbol{s}^\top$. Here it is crucial that R_{ij} has coordinates in $\mathbb{Z}$, so that $R_{ij}(\boldsymbol{\sigma}_i - \boldsymbol{\sigma}_j)^\top$ can be computed with black-box access to the group operation and inversion. □

Remark 3. The conditions imply $h_* \geq k$. In the case $h_* = k$, $N_i - N_j$ has an inverse defined over $\mathbb{Z}$ iff $\det(N_i - N_j) = \pm 1$. For the more general case $h_* > k$, if $N_i - N_j$ has a $(k \times k)$-submatrix with determinant ± 1 then it has a left pseudoinverse, but the converse is not necessarily true.

4.3 Constructions of Packed $(1, 2, n)-$BBSSS

We recall and generalize a black-box secret sharing scheme implicit in a Σ-protocol in [15] and its journal version [16]. The construction originally fixed $n = 2^k$ and obtained $h_* = 2k - 1$, but we can easily "decouple" both parameters. We present directly this generalization. We define $\ell = \lceil \log n \rceil$. We identify elements of $[n]$ with pairwise different vectors $i = (i_0, \ldots, i_{\ell-1}) \in \{0,1\}^\ell$. Let the k columns of N_i be shifts of the vector i padded with $k-1$ zeros, as follows:

$$N_i := \begin{pmatrix} i_0 & & \mathbf{0} \\ \vdots & \ddots & \\ i_{\ell-1} & & i_0 \\ & \ddots & \vdots \\ \mathbf{0} & & i_{\ell-1} \end{pmatrix} \in \mathbb{Z}^{(k+\ell-1)\times k}$$

Lemma 1. *For every $i \neq j$, $N_i - N_j$ has an integer left pseudoinverse.*

Proof. Let m be the smallest index in $[0, \ell - 1]$ where $i_m \neq j_m$. Then the $k \times k$ submatrix of $N_i - N_j$ containing rows m to $m + k - 1$ (where we start indexing rows at 0) is a lower triangular square matrix with its diagonal containing all 1's or -1's, hence with determinant ± 1. □

Combining Lemma 1 with Theorem 3 we have:

Theorem 4. *Let $1 \leq k, n$ be integers. There exists a k-MSP over $\mathbb{Z}$ for $(\Delta, \Gamma)_{1,2,n}$ with $h_i = h_* := k + \lceil \log n \rceil - 1$ for all $i \in [n]$. Consequently there is a packed black-box secret sharing scheme with secrets in $\mathbb{G}^k$, and every share in $\mathbb{G}^{h_*}$. In particular for $n = 2^k$, every share is in $\mathbb{G}^{2k-1}$.*

Next we show that this scheme is *not* always optimal, in terms of share size h_* for given k and n. First, for $k = 2$ and $k = 3$, $n = 2^k$, there are optimal $(1, 2, n)$-BBSSS with $h_* = k = \log n$, given by the N_i below.[2]

$k = 2$

$$N_1 = \begin{pmatrix} 0 & 0 \\ 0 & 0 \end{pmatrix},\ N_2 = \begin{pmatrix} 1 & 0 \\ 0 & 1 \end{pmatrix},\ N_3 = \begin{pmatrix} 0 & 1 \\ 1 & 1 \end{pmatrix},\ N_4 = \begin{pmatrix} 1 & 1 \\ 1 & 0 \end{pmatrix}. \tag{1}$$

$k = 3$

$$N_1 = \begin{pmatrix} 0&0&0 \\ 0&0&0 \\ 0&0&0 \end{pmatrix},\ N_2 = \begin{pmatrix} 1&0&0 \\ 0&1&0 \\ 0&0&1 \end{pmatrix},\ N_3 = \begin{pmatrix} 0&1&0 \\ 0&0&1 \\ 1&1&0 \end{pmatrix},\ N_4 = \begin{pmatrix} 0&0&1 \\ 1&1&0 \\ 0&1&1 \end{pmatrix}$$

$$N_5 = \begin{pmatrix} 1&1&0 \\ 0&1&1 \\ 1&1&1 \end{pmatrix},\ N_6 = \begin{pmatrix} 0&1&1 \\ 1&1&1 \\ 1&0&1 \end{pmatrix},\ N_7 = \begin{pmatrix} 1&1&1 \\ -1&0&1 \\ 1&0&0 \end{pmatrix},\ N_8 = \begin{pmatrix} 1&0&1 \\ -1&0&0 \\ 0&-1&0 \end{pmatrix}. \tag{2}$$

[2] The matrices have been found by first taking matrices N'_i representing multiplication by different elements of the fields $\mathbb{F}_{2^k}$, which leads to $\det(N'_i - N'_j) = 1 \mod 2$, and then (for $k = 3$) using brute force to fix the cases where $\det(N'_i - N'_j) \neq \pm 1$.

Lemma 2. *The matrices above define, respectively for $k = 2$ and $k = 3$, $(1, 2, n)$-BBSS schemes with $n = 2^k$, secrets in $\mathbb{G}^k$, and each share in $\mathbb{G}^k$.*

The lemma can be verified directly by computing the determinant of every $N_i - N_j$. Next, we use these as a basis for improving on Theorem 4. We need the following generalization of the construction in that theorem, where we replace the entries i_j by square blocks A_j: i.e., given a vector $A = (A_0, \ldots, A_{\ell'-1})$ of ℓ' square matrices where each $A_i \in \mathbb{Z}^{s\times s}$, consider the matrix

$$\tilde{N}_A = \begin{pmatrix} A_0 & & & \mathbf{0} \\ \vdots & A_0 & & \\ A_{\ell'-1} & \vdots & \ddots & \\ & A_{\ell'-1} & & A_0 \\ & & \ddots & \vdots \\ \mathbf{0} & & & A_{\ell'-1} \end{pmatrix} \in \mathbb{Z}^{s\cdot(\ell'+k'-1)\times s\cdot k'}$$

Lemma 3. *Let $\mathcal{N} = \{N_i\}$ be a collection of matrices in $\mathbb{Z}^{s\times s}$ such that for each $i \neq j$, $N_i - N_j$ has an inverse in $\mathbb{Z}^{s\times s}$. Then for every $k' \leq \ell'$ and $A, B \in \mathcal{N}^{\ell'}$ with $A \neq B$, the matrix $\tilde{N}_A - \tilde{N}_B$ has a left pseudoinverse. Therefore, in these conditions there exists a $(1, 2, |\mathcal{N}|^{\ell'})$-BBSSS with secrets in $\mathbb{G}^{k' s}$ and each share in $\mathbb{G}^{(\ell'+k'-1)s}$.*

Proof. This is proved similarly to Lemma 1, by considering the first index i in $[0, \ell' - 1]$ where $A_i \neq B_i$ differ, and noticing that the $(sk' \times sk')$ square submatrix of $\tilde{N}_A - \tilde{N}_B$ containing row-blocks i to $i + k' - 1$ is "block-lower triangular" and hence must have determinant $\det(A_i - B_i)^{k'} = (\pm 1)^{k'} = \pm 1$. This proves $\tilde{N}_A - \tilde{N}_B$ has a left pseudoinverse. The last part is a consequence of Theorem 3. □

Lemma 2 gives us, for $s = 2$ and 3, families $\mathcal{N}_s$ of matrices in $\mathbb{Z}^{s\times s}$ with $|\mathcal{N}_s| = 2^s$. Plugging each of this constructions into Lemma 3 we have:

Theorem 5. *For $s = 2$ and 3, and any $k', \ell' > 0$, there exists a $(1, 2, 2^{s\ell'})$-BBSSS with secrets in $\mathbb{G}^k$ and each share in $\mathbb{G}^{h_*}$ where $k = s \cdot k'$ and $h_* = s \cdot (\ell' + k' - 1)$. This implies that for any n there exists:*

- *If $k \equiv 0 \mod 2$, a $(1, 2, n) - BBSSS$ with $h_* = 2\lceil \log n/2 \rceil + k - 2$; in particular, if $n = 4^m$ for $m \in \mathbb{N}$, then $h_* = \log n + k - 2$.*
- *If $k \equiv 0 \mod 3$, a $(1, 2, n) - BBSSS$ with $h_* = 3\lceil \log n/3 \rceil + k - 3$; in particular, if $n = 8^m$ for $m \in \mathbb{N}$, then $h_* = \log n + k - 3$.*

Remark 4. Note that the secret sharing schemes from Theorem 5 are indeed of the form of Theorem 3, i.e. the i-th share is computed from the secret $\boldsymbol{s}$ as $\tilde{N}_i \boldsymbol{s}^\top + \boldsymbol{r}$ for some matrix $\tilde{N}_i \in \mathbb{Z}_{h_* \times k}$ and some randomness $\boldsymbol{r}$ common to all shares. Moreover, all entries in $\tilde{N}_i$ are from $\{-1, 0, 1\}$, since they are constructed with the matrices in Eqs. 4.3 as blocks. Each row of every $\tilde{N}_i$ has at most $\log n$ entries which are non-zero. These facts will be important in the application to Σ-protocols for class groups in Sect. 5.

4.4 Implications for Σ-Protocols

Let $\mathbb{G}_1$ be any abelian group. Applying Theorem 1, a packed $(1,2,n)$-BBSSS with secret in $\mathbb{G}_1^k$ and each share in $\mathbb{G}_1^{h_*}$ induces a $\Sigma-$protocol for *any* relation of the form $R = \{(w_i, x_i)|F(w_i) = x_i, i \in [k]\}$, where $F : \mathbb{G}_1 \longrightarrow \mathbb{G}_2$ is a group homomorphism. The resulting Σ-protocol has 2−special soundness, a knowledge error of $\frac{1}{n}$, and communicates h_* elements in $\mathbb{G}_1$ and $\mathbb{G}_2$, and $\log n$ bits to communicate the challenge. In particular, if we consider the packed $(1,2,n)-$black-box secret sharing scheme in Theorem 5, for $n = 2^\lambda$ and $k \equiv 0 \bmod 3$ we get the following $\Sigma-$protocol:

Theorem 6. *Let $\mathfrak{R}$ be a ring, $\mathfrak{M}_1$,$\mathfrak{M}_2$ be $\mathfrak{R}-$modules and let $F : \mathfrak{M}_1 \longrightarrow \mathfrak{M}_2$ be a $\mathfrak{R}-$module homomorphism. Then there exists a $\Sigma-$protocol for the relation $R = \{(\boldsymbol{w}, \boldsymbol{x}) \in \mathfrak{M}_1^k \times \mathfrak{M}_2^k : F(w_i) = x_i, \forall i \in [k]\}$, with 2−special soundness, error soundness $2^{-\lambda}$ and communication complexity $k + \lambda - 3$ elements of $\mathfrak{M}_1$ and $\mathfrak{M}_2$ (and λ bits for the challenge).*

The proof is almost equivalent to the one provided in Theorem 1. Note that in case $k \not\equiv 0 \bmod 3$ we can include additional "superfluous" secrets so that we get an appropriate k. In any case the resulting communication complexity would be no more than $k+\lambda-1$ elements of $\mathfrak{M}_1$ and $\mathfrak{M}_2$ (and λ bits for the challenge).

5 Proofs of Knowledge for Statements on Class Groups

The results presented in Theorem 6 provide assurance that an efficient $\Sigma-$protocol can be constructed to prove knowledge of preimages of group homomorphisms. This capability extends to groups of unknown order because of the usage of a black-box secret sharing scheme and in particular class groups, with some slight tweaks due to the fact that the space of witnesses will be an infinite $\mathbb{Z}$-module in this case, as we will see in this section.

Background. We consider the framework proposed by Castagnos and Laguillaumie. Given a large integer ℓ, the framework defines a finite commutative group $\hat{G}$ and a cyclic subgroup $G \subset \hat{G}$ both of unknown order. G is in turn a direct product $G \cong F \times G^\ell$, where F is of order ℓ, while the order of G^ℓ is computationally hard to determine. Moreover, F is endowed with an algorithm to compute discrete logarithms easily. While in earlier works [11] ℓ was taken to be prime, subsequent works [6,13,20] have considered other cases, such as ℓ being a power of a prime or a product of primes. In particular, ℓ can be of the form 2^u [13] which is useful for secure computation.

There are several variants of the Castagnos-Laguiallumie encryption, but all consist on essentially applying an El-Gamal-like encryption principle where the encryption of $m \in \mathbb{Z}_\ell$ is of the form $(c_1, c_2) = (g^r, \mathsf{pk}^r f^m)$ with f being a generator of F and the public key pk being of the form $\mathsf{pk} = g^{\mathsf{sk}}$ for a secret key sk. In perhaps the most used form of the scheme, CL-HSM [12], g is a generator of G^ℓ. The owner of sk can obtain m since it can first retrieve $f^m = c_2 c_1^{-\mathsf{sk}}$ (as in El Gamal) and then solve the discrete logarithm in F.

Proofs in the CL Framework. Proofs of knowledge for statements involving discrete logarithms are not too easy to construct in class groups due to the fact that the order of the group is unknown. Let us consider first the case of proving knowledge of $w \in \mathbb{Z}$ such that $g^w = x$, for some $g, x \in G$, which can be used for proving knowledge of secret keys, proving correct decryption or VSS and distributed key generation [7]. To achieve zero knowledge the proof is defined with respect to some $[-S, S]$ interval in which an honest witness is supposed to be (typically in protocols it does not help the malicious prover to have a witness in a larger interval instead).

In these conditions, [9] defines a proof of knowledge, similar to Schnorr, where the challenge is binary and achieves soundness error $1/2$, reduced to $1/2^\lambda$ by repetition. In short the proof, parametrized by $A, \lambda \in \mathbb{N}$ is as follows.

Repeat λ times:

- Prover sends $a = g^u$ where $u \leftarrow\$ [0, A]$;
- Verifier sends $b \leftarrow\$ \{0, 1\}$;
- Prover replies with $z = u + wb$;
- Verifier checks $z \in [-S, S + A]$ and $g^z = a \cdot x^b$.

Zero-knowledge is achieved as long as $\ell S/A$ is negligible (and ℓ is polynomial).

To increase efficiency, [10] avoids the repetition above by replacing $\{0, 1\}$ by a larger interval $[0, C]$ and increasing A. This achieves $1/C$ error-soundness and zero knowledge as long as CS/A is negligible. *However*, one needs to rely on two hardness assumptions, called low order and strong root assumption, and perhaps more crucially for applications, the latter in addition requires g to be uniformly random, which may prevent its use in protocols where the adversary chooses g (see [7] for such a situation and more information). Finally, based on a different assumption, called rough order assumption, [7] defines a sound argument that allows to prove the existence of x and allow for adversarially chosen g, but this is *not* a proof of knowledge, achieving only standard soundness.

We also consider the scenario in which the witness has some coordinates in $\mathbb{Z}$ and others in $\mathbb{Z}_\ell$, which occurs for example in proving knowledge of plaintext and randomness (r, m) for a given CL-HSM ciphertext $(c_1, c_2) = (g_\ell^r, \mathsf{pk}^r f^m)$. The proof from [9] can still be used for this relation. The proof of [10] can be used if ℓ is a large enough prime (or has large enough prime factors) but cannot be used (at least as a proof of knowledge) e.g. in the case $\ell = 2^u$, because in this case the difference of two challenges may not be invertible as soon as $C \geq 2$. For the case ℓ prime, [7] defines a proof of plaintext knowledge, where the extractor can extract m but not r; however, again this will not work if $\ell = 2^u$.

Proofs of Knowledge from Our Framework. For simplicity, we directly use the BBSSS derived from Theorem 5, defined by $N_1, \ldots, N_n \in \mathbb{Z}^{h_* \times k}$ so that each difference $N_i - N_j$ has a left pseudoinverse. Recall that given a **finite** abelian group $\mathbb{G}$, the shares for $\boldsymbol{w} \in \mathbb{G}^k$ are $\boldsymbol{\sigma}_i = N_i \boldsymbol{w} + \boldsymbol{r}$ for uniformly random $\boldsymbol{r} \leftarrow\$ \mathbb{G}^{h_*}$.

In the case of the **infinite** group $\mathbb{G} = \mathbb{Z}$, we cannot sample $\boldsymbol{r}$ uniformly in $\mathbb{Z}^{h_*}$ any more. Instead we achieve statistical 1-privacy by sampling $\boldsymbol{r}$ uniformly from an interval $[0, A]^{h_*}$, for some $A \in \mathbb{Z}_{>0}$ large enough so that $\boldsymbol{w} \in [-S, S]^k$ is statistically hidden by each individual share $N_i\boldsymbol{w} + \boldsymbol{r}$. Here it is helpful, that the N_i from Theorem 5 have coefficients in $\{-1, 0, 1\}$, as this prevents A from growing too much. On the other hand, 2-reconstruction holds without change.

Proof of Discrete Logarithm. Given $G = \langle g \rangle$ the aforementioned cyclic group of unknown order we first consider the relation $R_{DLCG,k} := \{(\boldsymbol{w}, \boldsymbol{x}) \in \mathbb{Z}^k \times G^k \mid g^{w_i} = x_i \ \forall i = 1, \dots k\}$. Let $\psi : \mathbb{Z} \to G$ be given by $\psi(w) = g^w$ and as usual let $\boldsymbol{\psi}(\boldsymbol{w}) := (\psi(w_1), \dots, \psi(w_k))$. We assume the honest witness $\boldsymbol{w}$ will be in an interval $[-S, S]^k$. Then, consider the protocol in Fig. 4 for the relation $R_{DLCG,k}$, parametrized by the integer A. $\boldsymbol{x}^{N_i}$ is defined as the vector in G^{h_*} whose j-th coordinate is $\prod_{l=1}^k x_l^{(N_i)_{j,l}}$ where $(N_i)_{j,l}$ is the entry in row j, column l of N_i, and $*$ represents coordinate-wise product.

Prover		**Verifier**
$\boldsymbol{r} \leftarrow\$ [0, A]^{h_*}$	$\boldsymbol{a} = \boldsymbol{\psi}(\boldsymbol{r}) = (g^{r_1}, \dots, g^{r_{h_*}})$ $\longrightarrow$	
	i $\longleftarrow$	$i \leftarrow\$ C = [n]$
$\boldsymbol{z}_i = N_i \cdot \boldsymbol{w}^\top + \boldsymbol{r}$	$\boldsymbol{z}_i$ $\longrightarrow$	$\boldsymbol{\psi}(\boldsymbol{z}_i) \stackrel{?}{=} \boldsymbol{x}^{N_i} * \boldsymbol{a}$, i.e.
		$g^{(\boldsymbol{z}_i)_j} \stackrel{?}{=} (\prod_{l=1}^{k} x_l^{(N_i)_{j,l}}) \cdot a_j \ \forall j \in [h_*]$

Fig. 4. Σ-protocol over Class Groups

Theorem 7. *Assume $N_1, \dots, N_n \in \mathbb{Z}^{h_* \times k}$ are such that $N_i - N_j$ has a left pseudoinverse for all $i \neq j$. Moreover let $D \in \mathbb{Z}^+$ such that it is an upper bound for the sum of absolute values of the entries of every row in every matrix (namely, $\forall i \in [n], j \in [h_*]$, we have $\sum_{l=1}^k |(N_i)_{j,l}| \leq D$).*

Then the protocol in Fig. 4 is a Σ-protocol with 2-special soundness and, as long as $\epsilon = SDh_*/A$ is negligible and h_* is polynomial, it is statistical honest-verifiable zero knowledge. For the specific case of N_i as in Theorem 5, the result above holds with $D = \min\{k, \log n\}$.

Proof. Completeness and 2-special soundness follow from Theorem 1 and the fact that the secret sharing scheme has 2-reconstruction, see the full version [5]. As for statistical zero knowledge, given $\boldsymbol{x}$ and a challenge $i \in [n]$, the simulator chooses $\boldsymbol{z}_i$ uniformly at random in the set $[-SD, SD + A]^{h_*}$ and then selects the unique $\boldsymbol{a}$ that makes the proof accept, namely $\boldsymbol{a} = \boldsymbol{\psi}(\boldsymbol{z}_i) * \boldsymbol{x}^{-N_i}$.

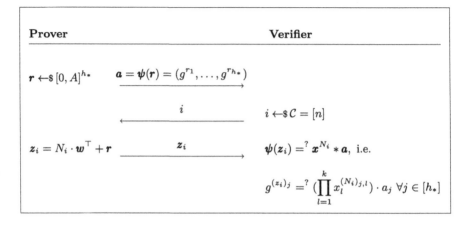

In the real protocol, each component of $\boldsymbol{z}_i = N_i\boldsymbol{w} + \boldsymbol{r}$ is uniform in some subinterval of $[-SD, SD + A]$ of length A, because $N_i\boldsymbol{w}$ is some fixed vector in $[-SD, SD]^{h_*}$ by assumptions on $\boldsymbol{w}$ and D. As long as $\epsilon = SDh_*/A$ is negligible and h_* is polynomial this is statistically close to the uniform distribution in $[-SD, SD + A]^{h_*}$, with statistical distance given by $1 - (\frac{1}{1+2\epsilon})^{h_*}$. □

Remark 5. The proof from [9], described above, can be cast as the instance of that in Fig. 4, with $k = 1$, $n = 2^\ell$ and with N_i being the matrices of dimensions $\ell \times 1$ given by vectors in $\{0,1\}^\ell$. Note in that case $h_* = \log n = \ell$, $D = 1$.

Corollary 2. *Let* $k = 0 \mod 3$. *When using the matrices* N_i *given by the BBSSS from Theorem 5 the protocol in Fig. 4 is a* Σ*-Protocol for* $R_{DLCG,k}$ *with the following properties where* $D = \min\{k, \log n\}$

- *Knowledge error at most* $1/n$;
- *Statistical honest verifier zero knowledge with assuming the witness is in* $[-S, S]^k$ *and* $A > 2^\kappa(k + \log n - 3)D \cdot S$ *for statistical security parameter* κ;
- *Communication complexity:* $k + \log n - 3$ *elements of* G *and* $k + \log n - 3$ *integers in* $[-SD, SD + A]$, *as well as* $\log n$ *bits for the challenge.*

Its Fiat-Shamir non-interactive version therefore communicates $k + \log n - 3$ *integers in* $[-SD, SD + A]$ *(and* $\log n$ *bits).*

Proofs of plaintext and randomness knowledge (and other 'hybrid' statements) The same template applies to situations where part of the witness will be in $\mathbb{Z}$ (because we do not know the order of the cyclic subgroup it acts on) and part in $\mathbb{Z}_q$. The most clear example is that of proofs of knowledge of plaintext, which we will use to illustrate this case. The encryption function of CL-HSM is $\psi : \mathbb{Z}_\ell \times \mathbb{Z} \to G^\ell \times G$ given by $\psi(m, r) = (g_\ell^r, \mathsf{pk}^r \cdot f^m)$ for generators g_ℓ, f respectively of G^ℓ and F, and public key pk in G^ℓ. Let then

$$R_{CL,k} := \{(\boldsymbol{m}, \boldsymbol{r}); (\boldsymbol{c}, \boldsymbol{d}) \in (\mathbb{Z}\times\mathbb{Z}_\ell)^k \times (G^\ell \times G)^k \mid \psi(m_i, r_i) = (c_i, d_i)\ \forall i = 1, \dots k\}.$$

The Σ-protocol for $R_{CL,k}$ is then very similar to that in Fig. 4, with the difference that now the space of witnesses is $\mathbb{Z}_\ell \times \mathbb{Z}$, rather than $\mathbb{Z}$. But this is easy to deal with, because our BBSSS can of course be applied to the former space. We present the proof in Fig. 5.

The analysis of the security properties of this protocol works exactly as in Theorem 7. For the communication complexity, we observe that, in addition to the h_* integers in $[-DS, A+DS]$, the prover sends h_* elements of $\mathbb{Z}_\ell$ but the size of these are independent of D. We also emphasize that this proof has witness extraction regardless of whether ℓ is prime or not.

Remark 6 (Comparisons). In Table 1 we compare the communication cost of the non-interactive version of our proof for the relation $R_{DLCG,k}$ with the protocols we would get by adapting [7,9,10] to this case. For this comparison, we take a statistical security parameter λ, and we aim at having soundness error $2^{-\lambda}$.

Prover		**Verifier**
$\boldsymbol{m}' \leftarrow\$\, \mathbb{Z}_\ell^{h_*}$		
$\boldsymbol{r}' \leftarrow\$\, [0, A]^{h_*}$		
$(\boldsymbol{a_c}, \boldsymbol{a_d}) = (g_\ell^{r'_j}, \mathsf{pk}^{r'_j} \cdot f^{m'_j})_{j\in[h_*]}$	$\xrightarrow{(\boldsymbol{a_c}, \boldsymbol{a_d})}$	
	$\xleftarrow{i}$	$i \leftarrow\$\, \mathcal{C} = [n]$
$\boldsymbol{z}_i = N_i \cdot \boldsymbol{m}^\top + \boldsymbol{m}' (\mathrm{mod}\ \ell)$		
$\boldsymbol{v}_i = N_i \cdot \boldsymbol{r}^\top + \boldsymbol{r}'$	$\xrightarrow{(\boldsymbol{z}_i, \boldsymbol{v}_i)}$	$\psi(\boldsymbol{z}_i, \boldsymbol{v}_i) =^? (\boldsymbol{c}^{N_i} * \boldsymbol{a_c}, \boldsymbol{d}^{N_i} * \boldsymbol{a_d})$, i.e.
		$g_l^{(v_i)_j} =^? (\prod_{l=1}^{k} c_l^{(N_i)_{j,l}}) \cdot (a_c)_j$
		$\mathsf{pk}^{(v_i)_j} \cdot f^{(z_i)_j} =^? (\prod_{l=1}^{k} d_l^{(N_i)_{j,l}}) \cdot (a_d)_j$
		$\forall j \in [h_*]$

Fig. 5. Σ-protocol over Class Groups for R_{CL}

Moreover, we select $A > 2^\lambda h_* S$ in our case, and similarly $A > 2^\lambda \ell S$ in [9] and $A > 2^\lambda CS$ in [7,10]. We ignore the cost of the challenge, since it is λ bits in all cases, and much smaller than the rest of the proof.

For k larger enough than λ (but still much smaller than 2^λ) the protocol from Fig. 4 saves a multiplicative factor around λ with respect to the proof in [9]. On the other hand, as the dominant factor is $k \log S$ the complexity is quite comparable to the protocols in [10]. However, we emphasize that the advantage we get with our proofs is that we do not require any hardness assumption for the proof, that the basis g does not need to be uniformly random and can be a value that was chosen by the adversary in a protocol and that ours is a proof of knowledge (as opposed to [7,10]).

The case of R_{CL} (Fig. 5) is similar, but now in our case the communication includes in addition h_* elements of $\mathbb{Z}_\ell$, while the other protocols we compare with would add k elements instead. We remark that in this case, for ℓ a large prime, the proof in [10] has an extractor for the plaintext. However, this is not the case if ℓ has a divisor smaller than the challenge bound C, e.g. in $\ell = 2^u$.[3] In contrast, in our case we can extract the witness regardless of the modulus.

[3] We do point out that it may be worthwhile to investigate whether the techniques from Sect. 6.1 using Galois rings can be used to construct proofs of plaintext knowledge in that case.

Table 1. Communication complexity of ZK proofs for $R_{DLCG,k}$

Proof	Communication (bits)	Knowledge	Assumptions
[9]	$\lambda k(\log S + \lambda + \log \lambda)$	Yes	None
[10]	$k(\log S + 2\lambda)$	Yes	Low order, Strong Root, uniform random h
[7]	$k(\log S + 2\lambda)$	No	Rough Order
Fig. 4	$(k+\lambda-3)(\log S+\lambda+\log(k+\lambda)$ $+\log\min(\lambda, k))$	Yes	None

Regarding computational complexity, the number of operations of our proof is comparable to the one in [7,10]. When counting the left side of the verification we obtain the same relation as with the last message communication shown in the table, since there is one exponentiation per group element sent. The right side of the verification has a computational complexity of $k \cdot \log n$ group operations, equivalent to [7,10]. Indeed the number of group operations equals the maximum number of non-zero entries in the matrix N_i which is $7/9 \cdot k \cdot \log n$. The exponentiations required in [7,10] lead to $k \cdot \log n$ operations when counting an exponentiation (with exponent in $[0, A]$) as $\log A$ operations.

Remark 7. While we have stated the results above for proofs of discrete logarithm knowledge, they can be easily extended to other statements on the class group, e.g. discrete logarithm equality or more generally linear relations as defined in [7] (namely statements of the form $\bigwedge_{i=1}^{n} Y_i = X_{i,1}^{w_1} \cdot \dots \cdot X_{i,s}^{w_s}$).

6 Extension to ZK-Ready Functions

So far we have considered $\Sigma-$protocols for relations of the form $(w, x = F(w))$ where F is a module homomorphism, e.g. a group homomorphism. We now extend our result to the case of ZK-ready functions, defined in [16]. These are maps $f : U \times S \longrightarrow X$ where $(U, +)$, $(S, \cdot)$, $(X, \cdot)$ are groups i.e. and are homomorphic "up to a correction factor in their second argument"; namely, we have $f(u, s) \cdot f(u', s') = f(u + u', s \cdot s' \cdot \delta(u, u'))$ for some function δ. This notion is relevant because it e.g. captures encryption functions from several cryptosystems with homomorphic properties (Joye-Libert, Paillier), where U and S are the plaintext and randomness spaces.

Definition 8. *[16] Let $(U, +), (S, \cdot), (X, \cdot)$ be abelian groups, $\mathfrak{R}$ a commutative ring with 1 and $f : U \times S \longrightarrow X$ a function. The function f is said to be ZK-ready with respect to $\mathfrak{R}$ if:*

- *There exist $g : U \longrightarrow X$ and a group homomorphism $h : S \longrightarrow X$ such that $g(0) = 1$, $f(u, s) = g(u)h(s)$ and $(\pi \circ g)(u + u') = (\pi \circ g)(u) \cdot (\pi \circ g)(u')$ for all $u, u' \in U$, $s \in S$, where $\pi : X \longrightarrow X/Im(h)$ is the canonical projection.*

- *Every $a \in \mathfrak{R}$ acts as an endomorphism of X, i.e. $(xy)^a = x^a y^a$, $x^0 = 1, x^1 = x$ for all $x, y \in X$.*
- *U and $Im(\pi)$ are $\mathfrak{R}$−modules, $Im(\pi \circ g)$ is a submodule, $\pi \circ g$ is a $\mathfrak{R}$−module homomorphism and $\pi(x^a) = \pi(x)^a$ for all $a \in \mathfrak{R}$, $x \in X$.*

The next lemma from [16] ensures that this functions satisfy the almost homomorphic property we referred to before.

Lemma 4 **([16]).** *Let f be ZK-ready with respect to $\mathfrak{R}$. Then there exist $\delta : U \times U \longrightarrow S$ and $\gamma : \mathfrak{R} \times U \times S \longrightarrow S$ such that for all $a \in \mathfrak{R}$, $u, u' \in U$ and $s, s' \in S$, $f(u,s)f(u',s') = f(u+u', ss'\delta(u,u'))$ and $f(u,s)^a = f(au, \gamma(a,u,s))$.*

From now on we will consider only the case of functions ZK-ready with respect to $\mathbb{Z}$ or $\mathbb{Z}_\ell$. In this scenario, the function $\gamma(a,u,s)$ the second equation can be reduced to a simpler form using the lemma below.

Lemma 5. *If $\mathfrak{R} = \mathbb{Z}$ or $\mathfrak{R} = \mathbb{Z}_\ell$ and f is ZK-ready with respect to $\mathfrak{R}$, then there exists an efficiently computable $\xi : \mathfrak{R} \times U \to S$ such that for $a \in \mathfrak{R}, u \in U, s \in S$, $f(u,s)^a = f(au, s^a \cdot \xi(a,u))$ (where if $\mathfrak{R} = \mathbb{Z}_\ell$, s^a is computed by embedding a in $[0, \ell-1] \subseteq \mathbb{Z}$).*

Proof. For $\mathfrak{R} = \mathbb{Z}$, the proof follows the same as for Theorem 1 in [16], where $\xi(a,u) = \prod_{i=2}^{|a-1|} \delta(i \cdot u, u)^{sign(a)}$. The same holds when $\mathfrak{R} = \mathbb{Z}_\ell$, but then we interpret a as an integer in $[0, \ell-1]$. □

When a matrix $M \in \mathfrak{R}^{n \times m}$ acts over a vector $\boldsymbol{z} = (z_1, \ldots, z_m)$ in either S^m or X^m, we assume it acts as a matrix of integers, even when $\mathfrak{R} = \mathbb{Z}_\ell$ (we just embed $\mathbb{Z}_\ell$ in $[0, \ell-1] \subseteq \mathbb{Z}$ as above). Since the notation of these groups is multiplicative, we will write $\boldsymbol{z}^M := (\prod_{i=1}^m z_i^{M_{1i}}, \ldots, \prod_{i=1}^m z_i^{M_{ni}})^\top \in S^n$ or (X^n), with M_{ij} being the (i,j)-th entry of M). If $N \in \mathfrak{R}^{p \times n}$ is another matrix, we have that $(\boldsymbol{z}^M)^N = \boldsymbol{z}^{N \cdot M}$. The next lemma is a generalization of Lemma 5.

Lemma 6. *If $\mathfrak{R} = \mathbb{Z}$ or $\mathfrak{R} = \mathbb{Z}_\ell$, and f is ZK-ready with respect to $\mathfrak{R}$, then given $m, n > 0$, there exists efficiently computable $\Xi : \mathfrak{R}^{n \times m} \times U^m \to S^n$ such that for all $M \in \mathfrak{R}^{n \times m}, \boldsymbol{u} \in U^m, \boldsymbol{s} \in S^m$, $\boldsymbol{f}(\boldsymbol{u}, \boldsymbol{s})^M = \boldsymbol{f}(M \cdot \boldsymbol{u}, \boldsymbol{s}^M * \Xi(M, \boldsymbol{u}))$ where $*$ denotes coordinate-wise product in S^n.*

We extend our protocol of Theorem 1 so that it can be used to prove knowledge of preimages of elements via a ZK-ready function. However, in this case we need additional assumptions. In the case $\mathfrak{R} = \mathbb{Z}$, we need that the induced SSS on U and S by the MSP M over $\mathbb{Z}$ satisfy "share-uniformity" for the shares corresponding to E, for every challenge set E. Moreover we need "randomness-uniqueness" on the one induced on X, meaning that for a given secret x and given shares for set E, there is at most one choice of randomness that gives those shares for that secret. When $\mathfrak{R} = \mathbb{Z}_\ell$ we can no longer assume M generates a linear secret sharing scheme on S and X, since only U is guaranteed to be a $\mathfrak{R}$-module. However we still state the assumptions above in algebraic terms, and we will see these can be achieved for some constructions of MSPs. We also need an additional assumption that given $y \in X$, it is easy to find $t \in S$ with $f(0,t) = y^\ell$. This is the case when f is the encryption function for Joye-Libert ($\ell = 2^l$).

Theorem 8. *Let $\mathfrak{R}$ be $\mathbb{Z}$ or $\mathbb{Z}_\ell$, $(U,+),(S,\cdot),(X,\cdot)$ finite abelian groups. Let $f : U \times S \to X$ be ZK-ready with respect to $\mathfrak{R}$. Let $\mathcal{M} = (\mathfrak{R}, M, \Psi, k)$ be a $k-$MSP over $\mathfrak{R}$ computing (Δ, Γ), where $M \in \mathfrak{R}^{h\times(k+e)}$. Let $\mathcal{C}$ be a compatible challenge set with respect to (Δ, Γ) and $\nu = \nu(\mathcal{C}, \Gamma)$ its extraction number. Assume it is possible to sample efficiently uniform from $\mathcal{C}$, U and S, that for every $E \in \mathcal{C}$, M_E can be computed efficiently, and that for any pairwise distinct $E_1, \ldots, E_\nu \in \mathcal{C}$ it is efficient to compute the reconstruction vectors $\boldsymbol{\rho}_{\mathcal{E}}^{(i)}$, where $\mathcal{E} = \bigcup_{i=1}^{\nu} E_i$, promised by Definition 6. Assume in addition:*

- *For any $E \in \mathcal{C}$ the distributions of $M_E(\mathbf{0}, \boldsymbol{u}')^\top$ and $(\mathbf{1}, \boldsymbol{s}')^{M_E}$ when $\boldsymbol{u}' \leftarrow_\$ U^e$, $\boldsymbol{s}' \leftarrow_\$ S^e$, are uniformly random in U^{h_E}, S^{h_E} respectively.*
- *For any $E \in \mathcal{C}$, any $\boldsymbol{y} \in X^{h_E}$, and any $\boldsymbol{x} \in X^k$ there is at most one $\boldsymbol{a} \in X^e$ such that $(\boldsymbol{x}, \boldsymbol{a})^{M_E} = \boldsymbol{y}$.*
- *For the case $\mathfrak{R} = \mathbb{Z}_\ell$ we also assume that f is such that given $y \in X$ it is easy to find $t \in S$ with $f(0,t) = y^\ell$.*

Let Ξ as in Lemma 6. Then Fig. 6 provides a Σ-protocol with ν-special soundness for the relation $R = \{(\boldsymbol{u}, \boldsymbol{s}; \boldsymbol{x}) \in (U^k \times S^k) \times X^k : f(u_i, s_i) = x_i \ \forall i \in [k]\}$.

Prover		**Verifier**
$\boldsymbol{u}' = (u'_1, \ldots, u'_e) \leftarrow_\$ U^e$		
$\boldsymbol{s}' = (s'_1, \ldots, s'_e) \leftarrow_\$ S^e$	$\boldsymbol{a} = \boldsymbol{f}(\boldsymbol{u}', \boldsymbol{s}') \in X^e$ $\longrightarrow$	
	E $\longleftarrow$	$E \leftarrow_\$ \mathcal{C}$
$\boldsymbol{z}_E = M_E \cdot (\boldsymbol{u}, \boldsymbol{u}')^\top$		
$\boldsymbol{v}_E = (\boldsymbol{s}, \boldsymbol{s}')^{M_E} * \Xi(M_E, (\boldsymbol{u}, \boldsymbol{u}'))$	$\boldsymbol{z}_E, \boldsymbol{v}_E$ $\longrightarrow$	$\boldsymbol{f}(\boldsymbol{z}_E, \boldsymbol{v}_E) \stackrel{?}{=} (\boldsymbol{x}, \boldsymbol{a})^{M_E}$

Fig. 6. Σ-Protocol for preimages of ZK-ready functions

A detailed proof can be found in the full version [5].

Remark 8 (achieving additional assumptions). When the challenge space consists of sets $E = \{i\}$ of size 1, and the M_i are of the form $M_i = (N_i | I_{e\times e})$ (in this case $h_E = e$), the assumptions of Theorem 8 are achieved. Indeed in that case, $(\boldsymbol{s}, \boldsymbol{s}')^{M_i} = \boldsymbol{s}^{N_i} * \boldsymbol{s}'$, so if $\boldsymbol{s}'$ is uniform $(\boldsymbol{s}, \boldsymbol{s}')^{M_i}$ is uniform too. This holds even if

S is not a $\mathfrak{R}$-module, because we are embedding $I_{e\times e} \in \mathbb{Z}_\ell^{e\times e}$ into $I_{e\times e} \in \mathbb{Z}^{e\times e}$. By the same token $(\boldsymbol{x}, \boldsymbol{a})^{M_i} = \boldsymbol{x}_i^N * \boldsymbol{a}$ so there is exactly one $\boldsymbol{a} = (\boldsymbol{x}^{N_i})^{-1} * \boldsymbol{y}$ satisfying $(\boldsymbol{x}, \boldsymbol{a})^{M_i} = \boldsymbol{y}$. In particular, this holds for the $(1, 2, n)-$ BBSS schemes described in Theorem 3 and in particular the ones in Theorem 5.

If in addition to the uniqueness of $\boldsymbol{a}$ we assume that $\boldsymbol{a}$ can be computed efficiently, as for example in the case of the schemes mentioned in Remark 8, we can define the optimized non-interactive version of the proof as in Fig. 7. Finally, plugging the BBSS scheme from Theorem 5 into Theorem 8 we get the following general result for ZK-ready functions with respect to $\mathfrak{R} = \mathbb{Z}$.

Prover		**Verifier**
$\boldsymbol{u}' \leftarrow\$\, U^e, \boldsymbol{s}' \leftarrow\$\, S^e$,		
$\boldsymbol{a} = \boldsymbol{f}(\boldsymbol{u}', \boldsymbol{s}'), E = \mathcal{H}(\boldsymbol{x}, \boldsymbol{a})$,		
$\boldsymbol{z}_E = M_E \cdot (\boldsymbol{u}, \boldsymbol{u}')^\top$,		
$\boldsymbol{v}_E = (\boldsymbol{s}, \boldsymbol{s}')^{M_E} * \Xi(M_E, (\boldsymbol{u}, \boldsymbol{u}'))$	$\xrightarrow{E, (\boldsymbol{z}_E, \boldsymbol{v}_E)}$	Finds $\boldsymbol{a}$ s.t.
		$\boldsymbol{f}(\boldsymbol{z}_E, \boldsymbol{v}_E) = (\boldsymbol{x}, \boldsymbol{a})^{M_E}$
		$E =^? \mathcal{H}(\boldsymbol{x}, \boldsymbol{a})$

Fig. 7. Optimized NI-Σ-protocol from ZK-ready functions

Corollary 3. *Let $(U, +), (S, \cdot), (X, \cdot)$ finite abelian groups. Let $f : U \times S \to X$ be ZK-ready with respect to $\mathbb{Z}$ and let $\lambda \geq 0$ be a security parameter. Then there exist a $\Sigma-$protocol for the relation $R = \{(\boldsymbol{u}, \boldsymbol{s}; \boldsymbol{x}) \in (U^k \times S^k) \times X^k : f(u_i, s_i) = x_i\ \forall i \in [k]\}$, for $k \geq \lambda$, with $2-$special soundness, knowledge error at most $2^{-\lambda}$ and communication complexity $k + \lambda - 3$ elements of U, S and X (and λ bits for the challenge). Its non-interactive version communicates $k + \lambda - 3$ elements of U, S and λ bits.*

6.1 Improvement for Joye-Libert Encryption

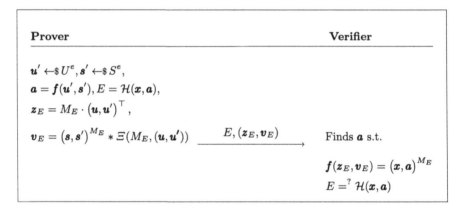

We show that Joye-Libert encryption for $\mathbb{Z}_{2^l}$ is a ZK-ready function with respect to both the rings $\mathbb{Z}$ and $\mathbb{Z}_{2^l}$. The former implies that we can apply Corollary 3 to obtain a batch protocol to show knowledge of plaintext and randomness in k Joye-Libert ciphertexts. However, in this case we can do better by considering the encryption function as ZK-ready with respect to $\mathbb{Z}_{2^l}$ and using as secret sharing scheme a version of Shamir over an extension ring, namely a Galois ring. The idea of this construction, at least when we use standard (non-packed) Shamir secret sharing, is exactly the one in [2] where it was applied to a certain vector commitment scheme construction over $\mathbb{Z}_{2^l}$ instead of Joye-Libert. Moreover, it is a quite direct generalization of Sect. 4.2 to the setting of fields. However, we have not seen this Σ-protocol applied to Joye-Libert encryption and, given its applications, we think it is important to point it out. We also generalize it by using the packed version of Shamir secret sharing, so that we can trade communication complexity by soundness.

Joye-Libert encryption. Let (public) $k \in \mathbb{N}$, and two (private) primes with $p \equiv 1 \mod 2^l$, $q \equiv 3 \mod 4$ and set $N = pq$. Let $g \in \mathbb{Z}_N^*$ of order $\phi(N)/2$. Then let $U = \mathbb{Z}_{2^l}$, $S = \mathbb{Z}_N^*$, $X = \mathbb{Z}_N^*$, $\mathfrak{R} = \mathbb{Z}$; and $f : \mathbb{Z}_{2^l} \times \mathbb{Z}_N^* \longrightarrow \mathbb{Z}_N^*$ given by $f(u, s) := g^u \cdot s^{2^l}$ where we see u embedded as an integer in $[0, 2^l - 1]$.

f is *not* an homomorphism since the argument u lives in $\mathbb{Z}_{2^l}$ but $g^{2^l} \neq 1$ in $\mathbb{Z}_N^*$, and therefore there will be cases for which the operations over $\mathbb{Z}_{2^l}$ "do not match" the operations over $\mathbb{Z}_N^*$[4].

Lemma 7. *f is ZK-ready with respect to both $\mathfrak{R} = \mathbb{Z}$ and $\mathfrak{R} = \mathbb{Z}_{2^l}$.*

Proof (Sketch). Indeed, let $U = \mathbb{Z}_{2^l}$, $S = X = \mathbb{Z}_N^*$. Consider $g : \mathbb{Z}_{2^l} \longrightarrow \mathbb{Z}_N^*$ such that $g(u) = g^u$ and $h : \mathbb{Z}_N^* \longrightarrow \mathbb{Z}_N^*$ with $h(s) = s^{2^l}$. Then it is easy to see f satisfies the conditions of Definition 8 for $\mathfrak{R} = \mathbb{Z}$. In the case of $\mathfrak{R} = \mathbb{Z}_{2^l}$, note that x^a for $x \in X$ is computed by embedding a in $[0, 2^l - 1] \subseteq \mathbb{Z}$ and then computing $x^a \in \mathbb{Z}_N^*$. Clearly the action of a defines an endomorphism on $\mathbb{Z}_N^*$. Moreover since $Im\ h = (\mathbb{Z}_N^*)^{2^l}$, $\pi : \mathbb{Z}_N^* \to \mathbb{Z}_N^*/(\mathbb{Z}_N^*)^{2^l}$ where $\pi(x) = x \cdot (\mathbb{Z}_N^*)^{2^l}$. Then $\mathbb{Z}_N^*/(\mathbb{Z}_N^*)^{2^l}$ is a $\mathbb{Z}_{2^l}$-module with the action of $a \in \mathbb{Z}_{2^l}$ on $x \cdot (\mathbb{Z}_N^*)^{2^l}$ being $x^a \cdot (\mathbb{Z}_N^*)^{2^l}$, since $a + b = c \mod 2^l$ implies $x^a \cdot x^b = x^c \cdot y$ with y in $(\mathbb{Z}_N^*)^{2^l}$. From here the rest of the properties can be easily verified.

Next, we compute the function Ξ from Lemma 6. For $u, u' \in \mathbb{Z}_{2^l}$ denote $(u+u')_{\mathbb{Z}}$ the sum in $\mathbb{Z}$ of the representatives of u and u' in $[0, 2^l-1]$, while $u+u'$ is their sum in $\mathbb{Z}_{2^l}$ (i.e. modulo 2^l). Define $\delta : \mathbb{Z}_{2^l} \times \mathbb{Z}_{2^l} \longrightarrow \mathbb{Z}_N^*$ by $\delta(u, u') = g^{q(u,u')}$ where $q(u, u') = \lfloor \frac{(u+u')_{\mathbb{Z}}}{2^l} \rfloor$. Then we get $f(u, s)f(u', s') = f(u + u', ss'\delta(u, u'))$.[5] For $M \in \mathbb{Z}^{n\times m}$, we get $f(\boldsymbol{u}, \boldsymbol{s})^M = f(M \cdot \boldsymbol{u}, \boldsymbol{s}^M * \Xi(M, \boldsymbol{u}))$, where

$$\Xi(M, \boldsymbol{u}) = \begin{pmatrix} \prod_{i=1}^m \xi(M_{1i}, u_i) \\ \vdots \\ \prod_{i=1}^m \xi(M_{ni}, u_i) \end{pmatrix} = \begin{pmatrix} g^{\lfloor \frac{(M_1 \boldsymbol{u})_{\mathbb{Z}}}{2^l} \rfloor} \\ \vdots \\ g^{\lfloor \frac{(M_n \boldsymbol{u})_{\mathbb{Z}}}{2^l} \rfloor} \end{pmatrix}.$$

Note that here for $i = 1, \dots n$, M_i denote the rows of the matrix M and $(M_i\boldsymbol{u})_{\mathbb{Z}}$ represent the multiplication of the row M_i and the vector $\boldsymbol{u}$ as elements

[4] e.g. $(2^l - 1) + 1 = 0$ in $\mathbb{Z}_{2^l}$, but $f(2^l - 1, 1) \cdot f(1, 1) = g^{2^l} \neq f(0, 1)$.

[5] In the example of the previous footnote if $u = 2^l - 1$, $u' = 1$, we would have $(u + u')_{\mathbb{Z}} = 2^l$, so $q(u, u') = 1$ and $\delta(u, u') = g$. Indeed $f(2^l - 1, 1) \cdot f(1, 1) = g^{2^l} = f(0, g) = f(0, 1 \cdot g)$.

with coordinates in $\mathbb{Z}$ (again embedding the coordinates of $\boldsymbol{u}$ in $[0, 2^l - 1]$). On the other hand $M \cdot \boldsymbol{u}$ denotes a matrix-vector product on $\mathbb{Z}_{2^l}$, computed using of actions of elements of $\mathbb{Z}$ on elements on $\mathbb{Z}_{2^l}$ and sums in $\mathbb{Z}_{2^l}$. Now we define our secret sharing scheme for secrets in $(\mathbb{Z}_{2^l})^k$.

Definition 9. *A Galois ring is a ring of the form $\mathbb{Z}_{p^l}[Y]/(F(Y))$ where $F(Y)$ is a polynomial in $\mathbb{Z}_{p^l}[Y]$ such that its reduction modulo p is irreducible in $\mathbb{Z}_p[Y]$. Any two Galois rings $\mathbb{Z}_{p^l}[Y]/(F(Y))$, $\mathbb{Z}_{p^l}[Y]/(F'(Y))$ where F, F' are of the same degree d are isomorphic, and hence we denote by $GR(p^l, d)$ any of them.*

Lemma 8 ([1]). *Given a Galois ring $GR(p^l, d)$ the subset $S = \{a_0 + a_1Y + \cdots + a_{d-1}Y^{d-1} : a_i \in [0, p-1]\}$ is an exceptional set, meaning that for any x, x' in S, $x - x'$ is invertible, and it has p^d elements.*

Lemma 9. *Let $S' = \{\alpha_1, \ldots, \alpha_n\} \subseteq \mathfrak{R}' = GR(p^l, d)$ be an exceptional set of size $n \leq |S| = p^d$. Let $0 < t < n$. We define the Shamir secret sharing scheme with space of secrets $\mathcal{S}_0 = (\mathfrak{R}')^{k'}$, randomness space $\mathcal{R} = (\mathfrak{R}')^t$ and spaces of shares $\mathcal{S}_i = \mathfrak{R}'$ for all $i \in [n]$ given by $\mathsf{Sh}(\boldsymbol{s}, \boldsymbol{r}) = (m(\alpha_1), \ldots, m(\alpha_n))$ where $m(X) = r_1 + \cdots + r_tX^{t-1} + s_1X^t + \cdots + s_{k'}X^{t+k'-1} \in \mathfrak{R}'[X]$. Then this a linear (over $\mathfrak{R}'$) secret sharing scheme with t-privacy and $(t + k')$-reconstruction.*

A proof of Lemma 9 can be found in the full version of this article [5]. Now we want to recast the SSS in Lemma 9 as a SSS with $\mathcal{S}_0 = (\mathbb{Z}_{p^l}^d)^{k'}, \mathcal{S}_i = \mathbb{Z}_{p^l}^d$, $\mathcal{R} = (\mathbb{Z}_{p^l}^d)^t$. Let $\phi : \mathbb{Z}_{p^l}^d \to \mathfrak{R}' = GR(2^l, d)$, be a module isomorphism, where $\phi(a_1, \ldots, a_d) = a_1 + a_2Y + \cdots + a_dY^{d-1}$.

Then we define $\mathsf{Sh}(\boldsymbol{s}_1, \ldots, \boldsymbol{s}_{k'}, \boldsymbol{r}_1, \ldots, \boldsymbol{r}_t) = (\phi^{-1}(m(\alpha_1)), \ldots, \phi^{-1}(m(\alpha_n)))$ where $m(X) = \phi(\boldsymbol{r}_1) + \cdots + \phi(\boldsymbol{r}_t)X^{t-1} + \phi(\boldsymbol{s}_1)X^t + \cdots + \phi(\boldsymbol{s}_{k'})X^{t+k'-1}$.

The scheme is clearly linear over $\mathbb{Z}_{p^l}$ because ϕ is a isomorphism of modules. Therefore, it defines a dk'-MSP $(\mathbb{Z}_{p^l}, \{M_i\}_{i\in[n]}, dk')$ where each $M_i \in \mathbb{Z}_{p^l}^{d\times(d+dt)}$.

Note that for $t = 1$, calling $\boldsymbol{r} = \boldsymbol{r}_1$ each share is of the form $N_i \cdot (\boldsymbol{s}_1, \ldots, \boldsymbol{s}_{k'})^\top + \boldsymbol{r}$ for some matrix N_i, so $M_i = (N_i | I_{d\times d})$. By Remark 8, the scheme in this case, $t = 1$, satisfies the conditions of Theorem 8. So we can obtain the following result by setting $p = 2$, $t = 1$, $k = dk'$, $n = 2^d$ above:

Corollary 4. *Let $k > 0$. For every $d > 0$ with $d \mid k$, there exists a Σ-protocol which is a Zero Knowledge Proof of Knowledge for the relation*

$$R_{JL,k} = \{(\boldsymbol{u}, \boldsymbol{s}; \boldsymbol{x}) \in \mathbb{Z}_{2^l}^k \times (\mathbb{Z}_N^*)^k \times (\mathbb{Z}_N^*)^k : x_i = g^{u_i} s_i^{2^l} \forall i \in [k]\}$$

with $(\frac{k}{d} + 1)$-special soundness, knowledge error $\frac{k}{d2^d}$, and whose non-interactive version has size d elements of both $\mathbb{Z}_{2^l}$ and $\mathbb{Z}_N^*$, and d bits.

In particular when $k = d$, this proof has error soundness $1/2^k$ and communicates k elements of both $\mathbb{Z}_{2^l}$ and $\mathbb{Z}_N^*$, and k bits.

References

1. Abspoel, M., Cramer, R., Damgård, I., Escudero, D., Yuan, C.: Efficient information-theoretic secure multiparty computation over $\mathbb{Z}/p^k\mathbb{Z}$ via galois rings. In: Hofheinz, D., Rosen, A. (eds.) TCC 2019, Part I. LNCS, vol. 11891, pp. 471–501. Springer, Heidelberg (2019). https://doi.org/10.1007/978-3-030-36030-6_19
2. Attema, T., Cascudo, I., Cramer, R., Damgård, I., Escudero, D.: Vector commitments over rings and compressed Σ-protocols. In: Kiltz, E., Vaikuntanathan, V. (eds.) TCC 2022, Part I. LNCS, vol. 13747, pp. 173–202. Springer, Heidelberg (2022). https://doi.org/10.1007/978-3-031-22318-1_7
3. Attema, T., Cramer, R.: Compressed Σ-protocol theory and practical application to plug & play secure algorithmics. In: Micciancio, D., Ristenpart, T. (eds.) CRYPTO 2020. Part III, volume 12172 of LNCS, pp. 513–543. Springer, Heidelberg (2020)
4. Ball, M., Çakan, A., Malkin, T.: Linear threshold secret-sharing with binary reconstruction. In: Tessaro, S. (ed.) 2nd Conference on Information-Theoretic Cryptography, ITC 2021, July 23-26, 2021, Virtual Conference, LIPIcs, vol. 199, pp. 12:1–12:22. Schloss Dagstuhl - Leibniz-Zentrum für Informatik (2021)
5. Bartoli, C., Cascudo, I.: On sigma-protocols and (packed) black-box secret sharing schemes. Cryptology ePrint Archive, Paper 2023/1652 (2023). https://eprint.iacr.org/2023/1652
6. Bouvier, C., Castagnos, G., Imbert, L., Laguillaumie, F.: I want to ride my BICYCL?: BICYCL implements cryptography in class groups. J. Cryptol. **36**(3), 17 (2023)
7. Braun, L., Damgård, I., Orlandi, C.: Secure multiparty computation from threshold encryption based on class groups. In: Handschuh, H., Lysyanskaya, A. (eds.) CRYPTO 2023. LNCS, vol. 14081, pp. 613–645. Springer, Cham (2023). https://doi.org/10.1007/978-3-031-38557-5_20
8. Bünz, B., Bootle, J., Boneh, D., Poelstra, A., Wuille, P., Maxwell, G.: Bulletproofs: short proofs for confidential transactions and more. In: 2018 IEEE Symposium on Security and Privacy, pp. 315–334. IEEE Computer Society Press (2018)
9. Castagnos, G., Catalano, D., Laguillaumie, F., Savasta, F., Tucker, I.: Two-party ECDSA from hash proof systems and efficient instantiations. In: Boldyreva, A., Micciancio, D. (eds.) CRYPTO 2019, Part III. LNCS, vol. 11694, pp. 191–221. Springer, Heidelberg (2019). https://doi.org/10.1007/978-3-030-26954-8_7
10. Castagnos, G., Catalano, D., Laguillaumie, F., Savasta, F., Tucker, I.: Bandwidth-efficient threshold EC-DSA. In: Kiayias, A., Kohlweiss, M., Wallden, P., Zikas, V. (eds.) PKC 2020, Part II. LNCS, vol. 12111, pp. 266–296. Springer, Heidelberg (2020). https://doi.org/10.1007/978-3-030-45388-6_10
11. Castagnos, G., Laguillaumie, F.: Linearly homomorphic encryption from DDH. In: Nyberg, K. (ed.) CT-RSA 2015. LNCS, vol. 9048, pp. 487–505. Springer, Cham (2015). https://doi.org/10.1007/978-3-319-16715-2_26
12. Castagnos, G., Laguillaumie, F., Tucker, I.: Practical fully secure unrestricted inner product functional encryption modulo p. In: Peyrin, T., Galbraith, S. (eds.) ASIACRYPT 2018. LNCS, vol. 11273, pp. 733–764. Springer, Cham (2018). https://doi.org/10.1007/978-3-030-03329-3_25
13. Castagnos, G., Laguillaumie, F., Tucker, I.: Threshold linearly homomorphic encryption on $\mathbf{Z}/2^k\mathbf{Z}$. In: Agrawal, S., Lin, D. (eds.) ASIACRYPT 2022, Part II. LNCS, vol. 13792, pp. 99–129. Springer, Heidelberg (2022). https://doi.org/10.1007/978-3-031-22966-4_4

14. Catalano, D., Di Raimondo, M., Fiore, D., Giacomelli, I.: Mon$\mathbb{Z}_{2^k}$a: fast maliciously secure two party computation on $\mathbb{Z}_{2^k}$. In: Kiayias, A., Kohlweiss, M., Wallden, P., Zikas, V. (eds.) PKC 2020, Part II. LNCS, vol. 12111, pp. 357–386. Springer, Heidelberg (2020). https://doi.org/10.1007/978-3-030-45388-6_13
15. Cramer, R., Damgård, I.: On the amortized complexity of zero-knowledge protocols. In: Halevi, S. (ed.) CRYPTO 2009. LNCS, vol. 5677, pp. 177–191. Springer, Heidelberg (2009). https://doi.org/10.1007/978-3-642-03356-8_11
16. Cramer, R., Damgård, I., Keller, M.: On the amortized complexity of zero-knowledge protocols. J. Cryptol. **27**(2), 284–316 (2014)
17. Cramer, R., Fehr, S.: Optimal black-box secret sharing over arbitrary Abelian groups. In: Yung, M. (ed.) CRYPTO 2002. LNCS, vol. 2442, pp. 272–287. Springer, Heidelberg (2002). https://doi.org/10.1007/3-540-45708-9_18
18. Cramer, R., Fehr, S., Stam, M.: Black-box secret sharing from primitive sets in algebraic number fields. In: Shoup, V. (ed.) CRYPTO 2005. LNCS, vol. 3621, pp. 344–360. Springer, Heidelberg (2005). https://doi.org/10.1007/11535218_21
19. Cramer, R., Xing, C.: Blackbox secret sharing revisited: a coding-theoretic approach with application to expansionless near-threshold schemes. In: Canteaut, A., Ishai, Y. (eds.) EUROCRYPT 2020. LNCS, vol. 12105, pp. 499–528. Springer, Cham (2020). https://doi.org/10.1007/978-3-030-45721-1_18
20. Das, P., Jacobson, M.J., Scheidler, R.: Improved efficiency of a linearly homomorphic cryptosystem. In: Carlet, C., Guilley, S., Nitaj, A., Souidi, E.M. (eds.) C2SI 2019. LNCS, vol. 11445, pp. 349–368. Springer, Cham (2019). https://doi.org/10.1007/978-3-030-16458-4_20
21. Desmedt, Y., Frankel, Y.: Threshold cryptosystems. In: Brassard, G. (ed.) CRYPTO 1989. LNCS, vol. 435, pp. 307–315. Springer, New York (1990). https://doi.org/10.1007/0-387-34805-0_28
22. Franklin, M.K., Yung, M.: Communication complexity of secure computation (extended abstract). In: 24th ACM STOC, pp. 699–710. ACM Press (1992)
23. Gennaro, R., Leigh, D., Sundaram, R., Yerazunis, W.: Batching schnorr identification scheme with applications to privacy-preserving authorization and low-bandwidth communication devices. In: Lee, P.J. (ed.) ASIACRYPT 2004. LNCS, vol. 3329, pp. 276–292. Springer, Heidelberg (2004). https://doi.org/10.1007/978-3-540-30539-2_20
24. Guillou, L.C., Quisquater, J.-J.: A "Paradoxical" Indentity-based signature scheme resulting from zero-knowledge. In: Goldwasser, S. (ed.) CRYPTO 1988. LNCS, vol. 403, pp. 216–231. Springer, New York (1990). https://doi.org/10.1007/0-387-34799-2_16
25. Ishai, Y., Kushilevitz, E., Ostrovsky, R., Sahai, A.: Zero-knowledge proofs from secure multiparty computation. SIAM J. Comput. **39**(3), 1121–1152 (2009)
26. Joye, M., Libert, B.: Efficient cryptosystems from 2^k-th power residue symbols. In: Johansson, T., Nguyen, P.Q. (eds.) EUROCRYPT 2013. LNCS, vol. 7881, pp. 76–92. Springer, Heidelberg (2013). https://doi.org/10.1007/s00145-016-9229-5
27. Karchmer, M., Wigderson, A.: Characterizing non-deterministic circuit size. In: 25th ACM STOC, pp. 532–540. ACM Press (1993)
28. Karchmer, M., Wigderson, A.: On span programs. In: Proceedings of the Eight Annual Structure in Complexity Theory Conference, San Diego, CA, USA, May 18-21, 1993, pp. 102–111. IEEE Computer Society (1993)
29. Maurer, U.M.: Unifying zero-knowledge proofs of knowledge. In: Preneel, B. (ed.) AFRICACRYPT 2009. LNCS, vol. 5580, pp. 272–286. Springer, Heidelberg (2009). https://doi.org/10.1007/978-3-642-02384-2_17

30. Okamoto, T., Uchiyama, S.: A new public-key cryptosystem as secure as factoring. In: Nyberg, K. (ed.) EUROCRYPT 1998. LNCS, vol. 1403, pp. 308–318. Springer, Heidelberg (1998). https://doi.org/10.1007/BFb0054135
31. Paillier, P.: Public-key cryptosystems based on composite degree residuosity classes. In: Stern, J. (ed.) EUROCRYPT 1999. LNCS, vol. 1592, pp. 223–238. Springer, Heidelberg (1999). https://doi.org/10.1007/3-540-48910-X_16
32. Schnorr, C.P.: Efficient identification and signatures for smart cards. In: Brassard, G. (ed.) CRYPTO 1989. LNCS, vol. 435, pp. 239–252. Springer, New York (1990). https://doi.org/10.1007/0-387-34805-0_22
33. Xue, H.,et al.: Efficient multiplicative-to-additive function from Joye-Libert cryptosystem and its application to threshold ECDSA. Cryptology ePrint Archive, Paper 2023/1312 (2023). https://eprint.iacr.org/2023/1312. *To appear in ACM CCS 23*
34. Zhang, M., Chen, Y., Yao, C., Wang, Z.: Sigma protocols from verifiable secret sharing and their applications. In: Guo, J., Steinfeld, R. (eds.) ASIACRYPT 2023. LNCS, pp. 208–242. Springer, Singapore (2023). https://doi.org/10.1007/978-981-99-8724-5_7

Correction to: Zero Knowledge Protocols and Signatures from the Restricted Syndrome Decoding Problem

Marco Baldi, Sebastian Bitzer, Alessio Pavoni, Paolo Santini, Antonia Wachter-Zeh, and Violetta Weger

Correction to:
Chapter 8 in: Q. Tang and V. Teague (Eds.):
***Public-Key Cryptography – PKC 2024*, LNCS 14602,**
https://doi.org/10.1007/978-3-031-57722-2_8

In the originally published version of chapter 8, the acknowledgment section had been rendered incorrectly. This has been corrected.

The updated version of this chapter can be found at
https://doi.org/10.1007/978-3-031-57722-2_8

Q. Tang (Ed.): PKC 2024, LNCS 14602, p. C1, 2024.
https://doi.org/10.1007/978-3-031-57722-2_15

Author Index

Q. Tang and V. Teague (Eds.): PKC 2024, LNCS 14602, p. 459, 2024.
https://doi.org/10.1007/978-3-031-57722-2

Printed in the United States
by Baker & Taylor Publisher Services